The Collected Papers of J. L. Moles

*PHOTO*: RUTH CHAMBERS

# The Collected Papers of J. L. Moles

*Volume 1: Studies in Dio Chrysostom, Cynic Philosophy, and the New Testament*

Edited by

John Marincola

BRILL

LEIDEN | BOSTON

Cover illustration: Diogenes (1882) by John William Waterhouse. Art Gallery of NSW. With permission

Library of Congress Cataloging-in-Publication Data

Names: Moles, J. L. (John L.), author. | Marincola, John, editor.
Title: The collected papers of J.L. Moles / edited by John Marincola.
Description: Leiden ; Boston : Brill, [2023]- | Includes bibliographical
   references and index. | Contents: Volume 1. Studies in Dio Chrysostom,
   Cynic philosophy, and the New Testament —
Identifiers: LCCN 2023001839 (print) | LCCN 2023001840 (ebook) |
   ISBN 9789004537101 (v. 1 ; hardback) | ISBN 9789004538047 (v. 2 ; hardback) |
   ISBN 9789004541283 (hardback) | ISBN 9789004538719 (v. 1 ; ebook) |
   ISBN 9789004538726 (v. 2 ; ebook)
Subjects: LCSH: Rome—Historiography. | Greece—Historiography. |
   Dio, Chrysostom. | Cynics (Greek philosophy) | Latin poetry—History and
   criticism. | Bible. New Testament—Criticism, interpretation, etc.
Classification: LCC D56 .M65 2023  (print) | LCC D56  (ebook) |
   DDC 937.007202—dc23/eng/20230131
LC record available at https://lccn.loc.gov/2023001839
LC ebook record available at https://lccn.loc.gov/2023001840

Typeface for the Latin, Greek, and Cyrillic scripts: "Brill". See and download: brill.com/brill-typeface.

ISBN 978-90-04-53710-1 (hardback, vol. 1)
ISBN 978-90-04-53871-9 (e-book, vol. 1)
ISBN 978-90-04-53804-7 (hardback, vol. 2)
ISBN 978-90-04-53872-6 (e-book, vol. 2)
ISBN 978-90-04-54128-3 (hardback, set)

Copyright 2023 by the Estate of J. L. Moles. Published by Koninklijke Brill NV, Leiden, The Netherlands.
Koninklijke Brill NV incorporates the imprints Brill, Brill Nijhoff, Brill Hotei, Brill Schöningh, Brill Fink, Brill mentis, Vandenhoeck & Ruprecht, Böhlau, V&R unipress and Wageningen Academic.
Koninklijke Brill NV reserves the right to protect this publication against unauthorized use. Requests for re-use and/or translations must be addressed to Koninklijke Brill NV via brill.com or copyright.com.

This book is printed on acid-free paper and produced in a sustainable manner.

*For Rachel and Thomas*

# Contents

Preface    XI
   *John Marincola*
Appreciation    XIV
   *Ruth Chambers*
Publications of J. L. Moles    XV
Abbreviations    XXII
Permissions    XXIV

Professor J. L. Moles    1
   *A. J. Woodman*

Introduction to Parts 1 and 2    8
   *Aldo Brancacci*

**PART 1**
*Studies in Dio Chrysostom*

1   The Career and Conversion of Dio Chrysostom (1978) [1]*    23

2   Dio Chrysostom: Exile, Tarsus, Nero, and Domitian (1983) [13]    63

3   The Date and Purpose of the Fourth Kingship Oration of Dio Chrysostom (1983) [11]    73

4   The Addressee of the Third Kingship Oration of Dio Chrysostom (1984) [19]    105

5   The Kingship Orations of Dio Chrysostom (1990) [37]    111

6   Review of D. A. Russell, ed., *Dio Chrysostom: Orations VII, XII, XXXVI* (1993) [57]    185

7   Dio Chrysostom, Greece, and Rome (1995) [66]    188

---

\*  Numbers in square brackets refer to the section 'Publications of J. L. Moles'.

8   The Dionian *Charidemus* (2000) [74]   205

9   Dio and Trajan (2003) [80]   228

10  The Thirteenth Oration of Dio Chrysostom: Complexity and Simplicity, Rhetoric and Moralism, Literature and Life (2005) [81]   250

11  Defacing the Currency: Cynicism in Dio Chrysostom (previously unpublished) [86]   293

## PART 2
## *Studies in Cynic Philosophy*

12  '*Honestius quam Ambitiosius*'? An Exploration of the Cynic's Attitude to Moral Corruption in His Fellow Men (1983) [12]   317

13  The Woman and the River: Diogenes' Apophthegm from Herculaneum and Some Popular Misconceptions about Cynicism (1983) [16]   353

14  Cynicism in Horace *Epistles* 1 (1985) [26]   361

15  The Cynics and Politics (1995) [65]   389

16  Cynic Cosmopolitanism (1996) [70]   421

17  The Political Thought of the Cynics (2000) [75]   440

18  Philosophy and Ethics in Horace (2007) [84]   462

19  *Romane, Memento*: Antisthenes, Dio, and Virgil on the Education of the Strong (2017) [99]   480

Introduction to Part 3   511
   *Jane Heath*

## PART 3
## *Studies in the New Testament*

20  Cynic Influence upon First-Century Judaism and
    Early Christianity? (2006) [82]   523

21  Jesus and Dionysus in the Acts of the Apostles and Early Christianity
    (2006) [83]   553

22  Luke's Preface: The Greek Decree, Classical Historiography, and
    Christian Redefinitions (2011) [88]   587

23  Jesus the Healer in the Gospel, the Acts of the Apostles, and
    Early Christianity (2011) [89]   612

24  Time and Space Travel in Luke-Acts (2013) [93]   678

25  Accommodation, Opposition, or Other? Luke-Acts' Stance
    Towards Rome (2014) [96]   707

26  Matthew the Mathete: Sphragis, Authority, Mathesis, Succession, and
    Gospel Truth (previously unpublished) [94]   735

27  Luke and Acts: Prefaces and Consequences
    (previously unpublished) [91]   786

28  Greek, Roman, Jewish, and Christian Philosophy in
    Luke-Acts (previously unpublished) [95]   846

29  What's in a Name? Χριστός/χρηστός and χριστιανοί/χρηστιανοί in the
    First Century AD (previously unpublished) [92]   937

30  Selling Christian Happiness to Pagans: The Case of
    Luke-Acts (previously unpublished) [98]   980

    Index Locorum   1003

# Preface

At his untimely death in October 2015, John Moles was already recognised as one of the great classical scholars of his time. His expertise ranged widely over Greek and Latin literature, philosophy, biography, historiography, and the New Testament, especially the books of Luke and Acts. His work, which was and continues to be extremely influential, is distinguished by its close reading of texts, its careful attention to language (examining both what is said and what is unsaid), and a consistent interdisciplinary approach.

This two-volume collection brings together fifty-nine of John's previously published notes, articles, and book chapters, eight reviews, and seven previously unpublished papers. The papers appear in chronological order by section, the one exception being the final chapter, which seemed to me a fitting envoi to the entire collection.

John's work appeared in a variety of publications in different countries over nearly forty years. Methods of citation varied greatly in the original publications, and so in editing these papers I have tried to bring uniformity by doing the following: (1) standardising spelling, punctuation, abbreviations, and manner of citation throughout; (2) correcting obvious minor misprints and slips; (3) reformatting a very few of the earliest pieces to make them easier to read and follow; (4) updating references to standard works of ancient authors or collections that have appeared since the publication of the papers; (5) inserting references to reprints (and occasionally updated editions) of scholarly articles and books; and (6) providing a bibliography for each chapter. My editorial intrusions are marked with curly brackets, thus: { }. The page numbers of the original publication are placed within the text in white square brackets, thus: ⟦ ⟧.

Although I have checked each item in the bibliography for accuracy, it was not possible to check the many thousands of references in these volumes. (In a few cases, where I became aware of a mis-citation or the like, I have corrected it without indication.) Nor have I tried to update the articles either by listing bibliography subsequent to their publication or by reference to those scholars who have engaged with the articles (either in agreement or disagreement). It would have required a scholar of John's calibre to do so, and as with all scholarship, these pieces are of their time. In any case, specialists will know where John's influence has been felt.

His unpublished papers, as one would expect, were in various stages of completeness. Those appearing here were in sufficiently good shape to make clear the lines of thought and interpretation that John intended to pursue. Where it was possible and I felt myself competent to do so, I filled in references. At the same time, the reader will understand that these papers did not receive John's *ultima manus*. There is a certain amount of repetition in them (which I have let stand), and there is little doubt that John would have added more references throughout.

There are, however, two exceptions. First, Professor Justin Reid Allison expended a truly impressive effort in editing 'Matthew the Mathete' (ch. 26) so as to bring it up to the standards John himself would have maintained, and I am very grateful to him for his efforts, as all readers of the article will be. Second, Professor Damien Nelis was of enormous help in clarifying and updating a number of references in 'Vergil's Loss of Virginity' (ch. 73), immensely improving the article while retaining John's signature voice. To both of these scholars I am greatly indebted.

It has been nearly seven years since John's death, and I regret that it has taken so long to bring this project to light. I have been sustained over the years by the kindness of colleagues and friends. Ruth Chambers, John's widow, has supported the project from the very beginning, offering every assistance and displaying a patience in awaiting the final product that was exemplary. Federico Santangelo tracked down much of John's unpublished material. Aldo Brancacci, Jane Heath, and Chris Pelling were very helpful in providing feedback at various stages, and I am grateful to them not least for their illuminating introductions. For offering assistance in a variety of matters, and/or for providing material in hard copy or electronically, I thank Justin Reid Allison, Alexander Hardie, Stephen Harrison, Adam Kemezis, Christina Kraus, Manfred Lang, Damien Nelis, Chris Pelling, Fran Titchener, Tony Woodman, and Harvey Yunis. At Brill I am very grateful to Mirjam Elbers, the Classics editor, who agreed to take on the publication, and to Giulia Moriconi, who has assisted in all aspects of getting the materials ready for publication. I thank also Theo Joppe who has been indispensable in the production of these volumes. I am indebted as always to the Interlibrary Loan department at Florida State University's Strozier Library for help in procuring a large number of items. Towards the final stages of this project St Hugh's College, Oxford provided generous hospitality.

Two people deserve special thanks. My wife, Laurel Fulkerson, has lived with this project every step of the way, and has offered support and assistance throughout. And Tony Woodman's advice and generosity at all stages of the project was invaluable. Without his assistance and support, this collection would have never come to fruition.

This project has been both a joy and a challenge. A joy, because I got to spend it in John's intellectual company, but a challenge because I wanted to do justice to his rich output and to do my best to make it more accessible to others, since I believe it is of value not only for the numerous brilliant insights it offers, but also because of the methodology employed, which is of a value independent of the content of any individual chapter.

As a young scholar, I, like many, benefitted from John's astonishing generosity in reading and commenting on my work. I hope that this collection may represent not just my own gratitude to John but also that of all the young scholars and colleagues whose work over the years he cultivated, nurtured, and improved. We owe him more thanks than we can ever express.

The collection is dedicated to John's children.

*J. M.*
Oxford, May 2022

# Appreciation

*Ruth Chambers*

This collection of John's papers brings to the classical world a definitive view of the breadth and brilliance of his scholarly output. That this has been accomplished is due to an act of selfless dedication for which John would be deeply grateful. I speak for him, and his family, friends, and colleagues, in expressing profound thanks to John Marincola for his painstaking editorial work and his unwavering devotion to ensuring that all John's papers are gathered and presented under one imprint. Bringing John's lifetime writings to publication in this way is an outstanding achievement and a lasting tribute to a friend.

# Publications of J. L. Moles

Note: The dates for unpublished articles are approximations and based on indications in the manuscripts.

### 1978
1. 'The Career and Conversion of Dio Chrysostom', *JHS* 98: 79–100.

### 1979
2. *A Commentary on Plutarch's* Brutus (diss. Oxford; unpublished; see below, no. 100).
3. 'Notes on Aristotle, *Poetics* 13 and 14', *CQ* n.s. 29: 77–94.
4. 'A Neglected Aspect of *Agamemnon* 1389–92', *LCM* 4: 179–89.

### 1980
5. 'A Note on *Antigone* 1238f.', *LCM* 5: 193–6.

### 1982
6. 'A Note on Cicero, *ad Quintum fratrem* 2.10(9).3', *LCM* 7: 63–5.
7. 'The Ides of March and Anna Perenna', *LCM* 7: 89–90.
8. 'Plutarch, Crassus 13.4–5, and Cicero's *de consiliis suis*', *LCM* 7: 136–7.
9. Review of M. L. Clarke, *The Noblest Roman* (London and New York, 1981), *LCM* 7: 137–9.
10. Review of P. A. Stadter, *Arrian of Nicomedia* (Chapel Hill and London, 1980), *JHS* 102: 254–5.

### 1983
11. 'Dio Chrysostom: Exile, Tarsus, Nero, and Domitian', *LCM* 8: 130–4.
12. '"*Honestius quam Ambitiosius*"? An Exploration of the Cynic's Attitude to Moral Corruption in his Fellow Men', *JHS* 103: 103–23.
13. 'The Date and Purpose of the Fourth Kingship Oration of Dio Chrysostom', *ClAnt* 2: 251–78.
14. 'Some "Last Words" of M. Iunius Brutus', *Latomus* 42: 763–79.
15. 'Virgil, Pompey and the *Histories* of Asinius Pollio', *CW* 76: 287–8.
16. 'The Woman and the River: Diogenes' Apophthegm from Herculaneum and Some Popular Misconceptions about Cynicism', *Apeiron* 17: 125–30.
17. 'Fate, Apollo and M. Iunius Brutus', *AJPh* 104: 249–56.

## 1984

18. 'Aristotle and Dido's *Hamartia*', *G&R* 31: 48–54.
19. 'The Addressee of the Third Kingship Oration of Dio Chrysostom', *Prometheus* 10: 65–69.
20. 'Aeschylus: *Agamemnon* 36–37 Again', *LCM* 9: 5–6.
21. 'Brutus and Dido Revisited', *LCM* 9: 156.
22. '*Philanthropia* in the *Poetics*', *Phoenix* 38: 325–35.
23. Review of J. L. Strachan-Davidson, *Appian: Civil Wars I*' (Chicago reprint, 1983), *JACT Bulletin Review* 64: viii.
24. Review of N. G. L. Hammond, *Three Historians of Alexander the Great* (Cambridge, 1983), *JACT Review* 1: 32–33.
25. Review of A. J. Woodman, *Velleius Paterculus: The Caesarian and Augustan Narrative* (Cambridge, 1983), *JRS* 74: 242–4.

## 1985

26. 'Cynicism in Horace *Epistles* I', *PLLS* 5: 33–60.
27. 'Plutarch, Brutus and the Ghost of Caesar', *PACA* 82: 19–20.
28. 'The Interpretation of the "Second Preface" in Arrian's *Anabasis*', *JHS* 105: 162–8.
29. Review of C. Carena, M. Manfredini, and L. Piccirilli, edd., *Plutarco: Le vite di Temistocle e Camillo* (Milan, 1983), *CR* 35: 260–1.

## 1986

30. Review of S. Goldhill, *Language, Sexuality, Narrative: The Oresteia* (Cambridge, 1984), *LCM* 11: 55–64.

## 1987

31. 'Politics, Philosophy and Friendship in Horace *Odes* 2.7', *QUCC* 25: 59–72.
32. 'The Attacks on L. Cornelius Cinna, Praetor in 44 B.C.', *RhMus* 130: 124–8.
33. 'The Tragedy and Guilt of Dido', in M. Whitby, M. Whitby, and P. R. Hardie, edd., *Homo Viator: Classical Essays for John Bramble* (Bristol and Chicago, 1987), 153–61.

## 1988

34. *Plutarch: The Life of Cicero* (Warminster).

## 1989

35. Review of J. Geiger, *Cornelius Nepos and Ancient Political Biography* (Wiesbaden, 1985), *CR* 39: 229–33.

36. Review of P. McGushin, *Sallust: the Conspiracy of Catiline* (Bristol, 1987), *CR* 39: 393–4.

1990
37. 'The Kingship Orations of Dio Chrysostom', *PLLS* 6: 297–375.
38. Review of A. J. Woodman, *Rhetoric in Classical Historiography: Four Studies* (London, Sydney, and Portland, 1988)', *History of the Human Sciences* 3.2: 317–21.
39. Review of L. Pearson, *The Greek Historians of the West: Timaeus and his Predecessors* (Atlanta, 1987), *JHS* 110: 231–2.
40. Review of P. J. Rhodes, ed., *Thucydides: History II* (Warminster, 1988) and J. S. Rusten, ed., *Thucydides: The Peloponnesian War II* (Cambridge, 1989), *JACT Review* 7: 28–9.
41. Review of A. B. Bosworth, *From Arrian to Alexander* (Oxford, 1988), *JACT Review* 7: 29–30.

1991
42. 'The Dramatic Coherence of Ovid, *Amores* 1.1 and 1.2', *CQ* 41: 551–4.

1992
43. 'The Text and Interpretation of Plutarch, *Vit. Cic.* 45.1', *Hermes* 120: 240–44.
44. 'Plutarch, *Vit. Ant.* 31.3 and Suetonius, *Aug.* 69.2', *Hermes* 120: 245–7.
45. Review of V. J. Gray, *The Character of Xenophon's* Hellenica (London and Baltimore, 1989)', *CR* 13: 281–4.
46. Review of N. Horsfall, *Cornelius Nepos: a selection, including the lives of Cato and Atticus* (Oxford, 1989), *CR* 42: 314–6.
47. Review of J. R. Bradley, *The Sources of Cornelius Nepos* (New York, 1991), *Ploutarchos* 8: 30–2.
48. Review of C. Habicht, *Cicero* (Baltimore 1990), *Ploutarchos* 9: 28–31.
49. Review of P. A. Stadter, *A Commentary on Plutarch's* Pericles (Chapel Hill, 1989), *CR* 42: 289–94.

1993
50. 'Le cosmopolitisme cynique', in M.-O. Goulet-Cazé and R Goulet, edd., *Le Cynisme et ses prolonguements* (Paris) 259–80. [English version no. 70, below.]
51. 'Livy's Preface', *PCPhS* 39: 141–68.
52. 'On Reading Cornelius Nepos with Nicholas Horsfall', *LCM* 18: 76–80.

53. 'Truth and Untruth in Greek and Roman Historiography', in C. Gill and T. P. Wiseman, edd., *Lies and Fiction in the Ancient World* (Exeter and Austin) 88–121.
54. 'Textual and Interpretative Notes on Plutarch's *Cicero*', in H. D. Jocelyn and H. Hurt, edd., *Tria Lustra: Essays Presented to John Pinsent* (Liverpool) 151–6.
55. 'Thucydides', *JACT Review* 14: 14–18.
56. Review of P. A. Stadter, ed., *Plutarch and the Historical Tradition* (London and New York, 1992), *CR* 43: 29–32.
57. Review of D. A. Russell, *Dio Chrysostom: Orations VII, XII, XXXVI* (Cambridge, 1992), *CR* 43: 256–8.
58. Review of J. M. Alonso-Núñez, *La historia universal de Pompeyo Trogo* (Madrid, 1992), *CR* 43: 285–6.
59. Review of A. J. Pomeroy, *The Appropriate Comment: Death Notices in the Ancient Historians* (Frankfurt am Main, 1991), *CR* 43: 295–6
60. Review of *Oxford Studies in Ancient Philosophy: Supplementary Volume 1991: Aristotle and the Later Tradition* (Oxford, 1991), *Ploutarchos* 9: 32–4.

1994
61. 'Xenophon and Callicratidas', *JHS* 114: 70–84.
62. Review of N. G. L. Hammond, *Sources for Alexander the Great: an Analysis of Plutarch's* Life *and Arrian's* Anabasis Alexandrou (Cambridge, 1993), *CR* 44: 344–5.
63. Review of T. J. Figueira, *Excursions in Epichoric History: Aiginetan Essays* (Lanham, Md., 1993), *CR* 44: 331–3.
64. Review of F. Chamoux, P. Bertrac, and Y. Vernière, edd., *Diodore de Sicile: Bibliotheque Historique I* (Paris, 1993), *CR* 44: 272–4.

1995
65. 'The Cynics and Politics', in A. Laks and M. Schofield, edd., *Justice and Generosity: Studies in Hellenistic Social and Political Philosophy* (Cambridge) 129–58.
66. 'Dio Chrysostom, Greece, and Rome', in H. Hine, D. C. Innes, and C. Pelling, edd., *Ethics and Rhetoric: Studies Presented to Donald Russell* (Oxford) 177–92.
67. Review of E. Badian, *From Plataea to Potidaea: Studies in the History and Historiography of the Pentekontaetia* (Baltimore and London, 1993), *JHS* 115: 213–5.
68. Review of R. Mayer, ed., *Horace: Epistles I* (Cambridge, 1994), *BMCR* 6.2: 160–70 (= *BMCR* 1995.02.37).

## 1996

69. 'Herodotus Warns the Athenians', *PLLS* 9: 259–84.
70. 'Cynic Cosmopolitanism', in M.-O. Goulet-Cazé and R. B. Branham, edd., *The Cynics: the Cynic Movement in Antiquity and its Legacy* (Berkeley, Los Angeles and London) 105–20.

## 1997

71. 'Plutarch, Brutus, and Brutus' Greek and Latin Letters', in J. Mossman, ed., *Plutarch and his Intellectual World* (London) 141–68.

## 1998

72. 'Cry Freedom: Tacitus *Annals* 4.32–35', *Histos* 2: 95–184.

## 1999

73. 'ΑΝΑΘΗΜΑ ΚΑΙ ΚΤΗΜΑ: the Inscriptional Inheritance of Ancient Historiography', *Histos* 3: 27–69.

## 2000

74. 'The Dionian *Charidemus*', in S. Swain, ed., *Dio Chrysostom: Politics, Letters, and Philosophy* (Oxford) 187–210.
75. 'The Cynics', in C. J. Rowe and M. Schofield, edd., *The Cambridge History of Greek and Roman Political Thought* (Cambridge) 415–34. (Entitled 'The Political Thought of the Cynics' in this collection.)

## 2001

76. 'A False Dilemma: Thucydides' *History* and Historicism', in S. J. Harrison, ed., *Texts, Ideas, and the Classics: Scholarship, Theory, and Classical Literature* (Oxford) 195–219.

## 2002

77. 'Reconstructing Plancus: Horace, *C.* 1.7', *JRS* 92: 86–109.
78. 'Poetry, Philosophy, Politics and Play: *Epistles* 1', in T. Woodman and D. Feeney, edd., *Traditions and Contexts in the Poetry of Horace* (Cambridge) 141–57, 235–7.
79. 'Herodotus and Athens', in E. J. Bakker, I. J. F. de Jong, and H. van Wees, edd., *Brill's Companion to Herodotus* (Leiden) 33–52.

## 2003

80. 'Dio und Trajan', in K. Piepenbrink, ed., *Philosophie und Lebenswelt in der Antike* (Darmstadt) 186–207. (English edition, previously unpublished, is entitled 'Dio and Trajan' in this collection.)

## 2005

81. 'The Thirteenth Oration of Dio Chrysostom: Complexity and Simplicity, Rhetoric and Moralism, Literature and Life', *JHS* 125: 112–38.

## 2006

82. 'Cynic Influence upon First-Century Judaism and Early Christianity?', in B. McGing and J. Mossman, edd., *The Limits of Biography* (London and Swansea) 89–116.
83. 'Jesus and Dionysus in The Acts of the Apostles and Early Christianity', *Hermathena* 180: 65–104.

## 2007

84. 'Philosophy and Ethics', in S. Harrison, ed., *Cambridge Companion to Horace* (Cambridge) 165–80. (Entitled 'Philosophy and Ethics in Horace' in this collection.)
85. '"Saving" Greece from the "Ignominy" of Tyranny? The "Famous" and "Wonderful" Speech of Socles (5.92)', in E. Irwin and E. Greenwood, edd., *Reading Herodotus: A Study of the Logoi in Book 5 of Herodotus' Histories* (Cambridge) 245–68.

## 2008

86. 'Defacing the Currency: Cynicism in Dio Chrysostom' (unpublished)

## 2010

87. 'Narrative and Speech Problems in Thucydides Book I', in C. S. Kraus, J. Marincola, and C. Pelling, edd., *Ancient Historiography and its Contexts: Studies in Honour of A. J. Woodman* (Oxford) 15–39.

## 2011

88. 'Luke's Preface: the Greek Decree, Classical Historiography, and Christian Redefinitions', *NTS* 57: 461–82.
89. 'Jesus the Healer in the Gospels, the Acts of the Apostles, and Early Christianity', *Histos* 5: 117–82.

## 2012

90. 'Horace: Life, Death, Friendship and Philosophy', in *The Horatian Society Addresses* (Horatian Society, London) 5–18.
91. 'Luke and Acts: Prefaces and Consequences' (previously unpublished)
92. 'What's in a Name? Χριστός/χρηστός and χριστιανοί/χρηστιανοί in the First Century AD' (previously unpublished).

2013

93. 'Time and Space Travel in Luke-Acts', in R. Dupertuis and T. Penner, edd., *Engaging Early Christian History: Reading Acts in the Second Century* (Durham) 101–22.
94. 'Matthew the Mathete: Sphragis, Authority, Mathesis, Succession, and Gospel Truth' (previously unpublished)
95. 'Greek, Roman, Jewish, and Christian Philosophy in Luke-Acts' (previously unpublished)

2014

96. 'Accommodation, Opposition or Other: Luke–Acts' Stance Towards Rome', in J. M. Madsen and R. Rees, edd., *Roman Rule in Greek and Latin Writing: Double Vision* (Leiden) 79–104.
97. 'Vergil's Loss of Virginity: Reading the Life' (previously unpublished)
98. 'Selling Christian Happiness to Pagans: the Case of Luke-Acts' (previously unpublished)

2017

99. 'Romane, Memento: Antisthenes, Dio and Virgil on the Education of the Strong', in A. J. Woodman and J. Wisse, edd., *Word and Context in Latin Poetry: Studies in Memory of David West* (Cambridge) 105–30.
100. *A Commentary on Plutarch's* Brutus, edited with updated bibliography by C. B. R. Pelling (*Histos* Supplement 7; Newcastle).

Moles also wrote the entry 'Demonax' in D. J. Zeyl, ed., *Encyclopedia of Classical Philosophy* (Westport, 1997) 172–3, and various entries on Cynicism in OCD³: 'Bion of Borysthenes' (243); 'Diatribe' (463–4); 'Diogenes the Cynic' (473–4); 'Cynics' (418–19); 'Crates of Thebes' (406); and 'Oenomaos' (562).

# Abbreviations

**Ancient Authors.** Abbreviations for ancient authors generally follow H. G. Liddell and R. Scott, edd., *Greek–English Lexicon*, and P. G. W. Glare, ed., *Oxford Latin Dictionary*.

Note, however, that Dio Chrysostom is always and everywhere cited simply as 'Dio'.

**Modern Works.** Abbreviations for journals follow those of *L'Année Philologique*, with the usual English-language modifications. For frequently cited modern works, the following are used.

| | |
|---|---|
| *ABD* | D. N. Freedman, ed., *Anchor Bible Dictionary*, 6 vols (New York, 1992). |
| *ANRW* | H. Temporini, et al., edd., *Aufstieg und Niedergang der römischen Welt* (Berlin and New York, 1972–). |
| *CAH*$^2$ | *Cambridge Ancient History*, 2nd ed. (Cambridge, 1961–2005). |
| *CIG* | A. Boeckh, et al., edd., *Corpus Inscriptionum Graecarum* (Berlin, 1828–77). |
| *CIL* | *Corpus Inscriptionum Latinarum* (Berlin, 1863–). |
| Cohoon / Crosby | J. W. Cohoon and H. L. Crosby, *Dio Chrysostom* (London and Cambridge, Mass. 1932–51), 5 vols. Cohoon edited and translated Orations 1–31, Crosby Orations 32–80; cited by author's name, followed by volume and page number. |
| D–K | H. Diels and W. Kranz, edd., *Die Fragmente der Vorsokratiker* (Berlin, $^6$1951). |
| *FGrHist* | F. Jacoby, et al., *Die Fragmente der griechischen Historiker* (Berlin and Leiden, 1923–56; Leiden, 1994–). Texts are cited by the number of the historian, and T(estimonium) or F(ragment). |
| *FRHist* | T. J. Cornell, ed., *Fragments of the Roman Historians* (Oxford, 2017). Texts are cited by the number of the historian, and T(estimonium) or F(ragment). |
| *HRR* | H. Peter, *Historicorum Romanorum Fragmenta* (Leipzig, 1906; vol. 1$^2$, 1914). |
| *IEG*$^2$ | M. L. West, *Iambi et Elegi Graeci*, 2nd ed. (Oxford, 1989–92). |
| *IGR* | R. Cagnat, ed., *Inscriptiones Graecae ad Res Romanas Pertinentes* (Paris, 1906–27). |
| *ILLRP* | A. Degrassi, ed., *Inscriptiones Latinae Liberae Rei Publicae* (Florence, 1963; vol. 1$^2$, 1965). |

| | |
|---|---|
| *ILS* | H. Dessau, *Inscriptiones Latinae Selectae* (Berlin, 1892–1916). |
| L–M | A. Laks and G. Most, edd., *Early Greek Philosophy*, 9 vols. (Cambridge, Mass. and London, 2016). |
| Long–Sedley | A. A. Long and D. N. Sedley, edd., *The Hellenistic Philosophers*, 2 vols. (Cambridge, 1987). |
| LSJ⁹ | H. G. Liddell, R. Scott, and H. S. Jones, *A Greek–English Lexicon*, 9th ed. (Oxford, 1968; repr. with new supplement, ed. P. G. W. Glare, 1996). |
| L&S | C. T. Lewis and C. Short, *A Latin Dictionary* (Oxford, 1880). |
| *OCD*² | N. G. L. Hammond and H. H. Scullard, edd., *The Oxford Classical Dictionary*, 2nd ed. (Oxford, 1970). |
| *OCD*³ | S. Hornblower and A. J. Spawforth, edd., *The Oxford Classical Dictionary*, 3rd ed. (Oxford, 1996). |
| *OCD*⁴ | S. Hornblower, A. J. Spawforth, and E. Eidinow, edd., *The Oxford Classical Dictionary*, 4th ed. (Oxford, 2012). |
| *OGIS* | W. Dittenberger, *Orientis Graecae Inscriptiones Selectae* (Leipzig, 1915–24). |
| *OLD* | P. G. W. Glare, ed., *Oxford Latin Dictionary* (Oxford, 1982). |
| *PCG* | R. Kassell and C. Austin, eds., *Poetae Comici Graeci* (Berlin, 1983–). Cited by fragment number with volume and page number in parentheses. |
| *PIR*¹ | E. Klebs and H. Dessau, edd., *Prosopographia Imperii Romani* (Berlin, 1897–8). |
| *PIR*² | E. Groag, A. Stein, et al., edd., *Prosopographia Imperii Romani*, 2nd ed. (Berlin, 1933–). |
| *PSI* | *Papiri Greci e Latini: Pubblicazioni della Società italiana per la ricerca dei papiri greci e latini in Egitto* (Florence, 1912–) |
| *RE* | A. von Pauly, G. Wissowa, and W. Kroll, edd., *Real-Encyclopädie der klassischen Altertumswissenschaft* (Stuttgart, 1894–1978). |
| *SIG*³ | W. Dittenberger, *Sylloge Inscriptionum Graecarum*, 3rd ed. (Leipzig, 1915–24). |
| *SR* | G. Giannantoni, *Socraticorum Reliquiae*, 4 vols. (Naples, 1983–5). |
| *SSR* | G. Giannantoni, *Socratis et Socraticorum Reliquiae*, 4 vols. (Naples, 1990). |
| *SVF* | H. von Arnim, ed., *Stoicorum Veterum Fragmenta*, 4 vols. (1903–24). |
| *TrGF* | B. Snell et al., edd., *Tragicorum Graecorum Fragmenta* (Göttingen, 1971–2004). |
| *TLL* | *Thesaurus Linguae Latinae* (Munich, 1900–). |

# Permissions

We gratefully acknowledge the following publishers and individuals for permission to reprint the papers for which they hold the copyright. Numbers in parentheses refer to the chapters in this volume.

**E. J. Brill, Leiden**
  (Introduction to Part 1) Aldo Brancacci, 'John Moles, Historian of Ancient Philosophy', *Méthexis* 29 (2017) 141–69.
  (25) 'Accommodation, Opposition or Other: Luke–Acts' Stance Towards Rome', in J. M. Madsen and R. Rees, edd., *Roman Rule in Greek and Latin Writing: Double Vision* (Leiden, 2014) 79–104.

**University of California Press, Berkeley, California:**
  (2) 'The Date and Purpose of the Fourth Kingship Oration of Dio Chrysostom', *Classical Antiquity* 2 (1983) 251–78.
  (16) 'Cynic Cosmopolitanism', in M.-O. Goulet-Cazé and R. B. Branham, edd., *The Cynics: the Cynic Movement in Antiquity and its Legacy* (Berkeley, Los Angeles, and London, 1996) 105–20.

**Cambridge Philological Society, Cambridge:**
  (19) 'Romane, Memento: Antisthenes, Dio and Virgil on the Education of the Strong', in A. J. Woodman and J. Wisse, edd., *Word and Context in Latin Poetry: Studies in Memory of David West* (Cambridge, 2017) 105–30.

**Cambridge University Press, Cambridge and New York:**
  (1) 'The Career and Conversion of Dio Chrysostom', *Journal of Hellenic Studies* 98 (1978) 79–100.
  (6) Review of D. A. Russell, *Dio Chrysostom: Orations VII, XII, XXXVI* (Cambridge, 1992), *Classical Review* 43 (1993) 256–8.
  (10) 'The Thirteenth Oration of Dio Chrysostom: Complexity and Simplicity, Rhetoric and Moralism, Literature and Life', *Journal of Hellenic Studies* 125 (2005) 112–38.
  (12) '"Honestius quam Ambitiosius"? An Exploration of the Cynic's Attitude to Moral Corruption in his Fellow Men', *Journal of Hellenic Studies* 103 (1983) 103–23.

(15) 'The Cynics and Politics', in A. Laks and M. Schofield, edd., *Justice and Generosity: Studies in Hellenistic Social and Political Philosophy* (Cambridge, 1995) 129–58.

(17) 'The Cynics', in C. J. Rowe and M. Schofield, edd., *The Cambridge History of Greek and Roman Political Thought* (Cambridge, 2000) 415–34.

(18) 'Philosophy and Ethics', in S. Harrison, ed., *Cambridge Companion to Horace* (Cambridge, 2007) 165–80.

(22) 'Luke's Preface: the Greek Decree, Classical Historiography, and Christian Redefinitions', *New Testament Studies* 57 (2011) 461–82.

**Classical Press of Wales, Swansea and London**

(20) 'Cynic Influence upon First-Century Judaism and Early Christianity?', in B. McGing and J. Mossman, edd., *The Limits of Biography* (London and Swansea, 2006) 89–116.

**Walter de Gruyter, Berlin**

(13) 'The Woman and the River: Diogenes' Apophthegm from Herculaneum and Some Popular Misconceptions about Cynicism', *Apeiron* 17 (1983) 125–30.

**Firenze University Press, Florence**

(4) 'The Addressee of the Third Kingship Oration of Dio Chrysostom', *Prometheus* 10 (1984) 65–69.

**Francis Cairns Publications, Prenton, UK**

(14) 'Cynicism in Horace *Epistles* 1', *Papers of the Liverpool Latin Seminar* 5 (1985) 33–60.

(5) 'The Kingship Orations of Dio Chrysostom', *Papers of the Leeds Latin Seminar* 6 (1990) 297–375.

**Ruth Moles and the Estate of John L. Moles**

(3) 'Dio Chrysostom: Exile, Tarsus, Nero and Domitian', *Liverpool Classical Monthly* 8 (1983)

(9) 'Dio and Trajan' (English version previously unpublished) 130–4.

(11) 'Defacing the Currency: Cynicism in Dio Chrysostom' (previously unpublished)

(23) 'Jesus the Healer in the Gospels, the Acts of the Apostles, and Early Christianity', *Histos* 5 (2011) 117–82.

(26) 'Matthew the Mathete' (previously unpublished)

(27) 'Luke and Acts: Prefaces and Consequences' (previously unpublished)

(28) 'Greek, Roman, Jewish, and Christian Philosophy in Luke-Acts' (previously unpublished)

(29) 'What's in a Name? Χριστός/χρηστός and χριστιανοί/χρηστιανοί' (previously unpublished)

(30) 'Selling Christian Happiness to Pagans: the Case of Luke-Acts' (previously unpublished)

**Oxford University Press, Oxford and New York**

(7) 'Dio Chrysostom, Greece, and Rome', in H. Hine, D. C. Innes, and C. Pelling, edd., *Ethics and Rhetoric: Studies Presented to Donald Russell* (Oxford, 1995) 177–92.

(8) 'The Dionian Charidemus', in S. Swain, ed., *Dio Chrysostom: Politics, Letters, and Philosophy* (Oxford, 2000) 187–210.

**Routledge, London and New York**

(24) 'Time and Space Travel in Luke-Acts', in R. Dupertuis and T. Penner, edd., *Engaging Early Christian History: Reading Acts in the Second Century* (Durham, 2013) 101–22.

**Trinity College Dublin, Department of Classics**

(21) 'Jesus and Dionysus in The Acts of the Apostles and Early Christianity', *Hermathena* 180 (2006) 65–104.

**Professor A. J. Woodman**

(Introductory Material) 'Professor J. L. Moles', *Histos* 9 (2015) 312–18.

# Professor J. L. Moles

*A. J. Woodman*

John Moles, born in Belfast in 1949, came from a linguistically gifted family.*
His father was a headmaster whose hobby was learning new languages; his mother was a modern linguist; his uncle taught Classics at John's school; and his sister taught French at the University of Glasgow. He attended the Royal Belfast Academical Institution, which was also the *alma mater* of E. Courtney, J. C. McKeown and R. K. Gibson; while there, he twice became Ulster Chess Champion; he was also Irish Champion in 1966 and 1971, and twice a member of the Olympiad Team. He would go on to write *The French Defence Main Line Winawer* (1975), described by Wolfgang Heidenfeld as 'perhaps the best of all chess opening monographs', and *French Winawer: Modern and Auxiliary Lines* (1979, with K. Wicker). He invested the royalties in wine, of which he was a connoisseur. In later years he resisted all attempts at persuading him to return to chess.

After an outstanding school career, John followed his brother to Oxford, winning a scholarship to Corpus Christi College, where he was in the first cohort to be allowed to offer literature for 'Greats' (previously there had been no alternative to philosophy and ancient history). At Corpus he was taught by Ewen Bowie, John Bramble, Frank Lepper and Robin Nisbet; after Firsts in 'Mods' and 'Greats' he wrote *A Commentary on Plutarch's 'Brutus'* for his D.Phil., supervised by both Bowie and Donald Russell. One of his later regrets was that he never seemed to have the time or opportunity to revise his thesis for publication.[1] For a year (1974–5) he held a temporary lectureship at Reading, which was followed by permanent positions at Queen's University, Belfast, and University College of North Wales, Bangor (respectively 1975–9 and 1979–87), where there was a small Department of Classics headed by M. F. Smith.

I first met John more than thirty years ago, in 1983, when he turned up at the 'Past Perspectives' conference on historiography which I had helped to organise in Leeds. He made an immediate impression because of his hair, which in those days stuck out rather wildly on each side of his head; but this was not the reason that we came to be colleagues in Durham, to which I had moved from

---

\* This remembrance appeared originally in *Histos* 9 (2015) 312–18; the updated version is printed here by kind permission of the author.
1 His thesis has now been published as *Histos* Supplement 7 (2017), with updated bibliography by Christopher Pelling.

Leeds in 1984. In the second half of the 80s the Classics Department at Durham, which at the time attracted more students than anywhere else in the country apart from Oxford and Cambridge, found itself in a developing crisis: several colleagues in quick succession departed either through retirement or resignation, but the university refused to replace any of them, with the result that our staff:student ratio was becoming almost insupportable. Since this was a period when the University Grants Committee was encouraging departmental mergers, I suggested to our Vice-Chancellor that, if vacant positions were not to be filled, we should perhaps try to tempt some other Department of Classics to transfer itself to Durham. When he agreed to this in principle, I made the further suggestion that perhaps we should open negotiations with the small Department in Bangor. I reckoned that its members would be attracted by the prospect of teaching Greek and Latin literature in the original languages to large numbers of students, while we for our part would acquire the desired new colleagues, amongst whom was a brilliant young historiographer.

The transfer of Bangor Classics to Durham, strongly supported by Professor J. A. Cannon of the UGC, was the first merger of Classics Departments in the country. John arrived in 1987 and immediately made his mark: occupying a large room in the Department, he covered every surface with mounds of files, papers and books, which he then proceeded to impregnate with cigar smoke. The cleaners were forbidden to touch anything, and indeed couldn't have done any cleaning even if they had wanted to. (Nor did they have to face Boris, the legendarily neurotic dog, as had often been the case with their counterparts in Bangor. John was always very fond of dogs.) Although he lived out of town and refused ever to learn to drive a car, he would get the bus back into town in the evening and would spend several hours working in the Department until it was time for the last bus home again. Very often he would come along to my room, slump into the ancient armchair, and test out his latest ideas in collegial conversation, delighted to be in the company of someone who at that time smoked even more cigars than he did. Many of my pleasantest hours in Durham were passed with John in this way, discussing the issues and problems raised by Latin or life.

Before coming to Durham John had already published over twenty articles or book chapters on a wide range of major Greek and Latin authors; the year after he arrived in Durham, there appeared the only classical book to be published in his lifetime, a translation of, and commentary on, Plutarch's *Life of Cicero* in the Aris & Phillips series. It is unusually good at providing material at all levels: an excellent introduction to Plutarch for beginners, it is also much more quoted than most other volumes in the series because of its contributions to scholarship (his discussion of the concept of 'truth' is especially noteworthy).

In his translation he sought to reproduce in English the verbal patterns which articulated the author's meaning: he regarded this as an extremely important function of translation, and his method became a feature of much of his later scholarship, proving especially fruitful in his various analyses of Thucydides. His sensitivity to verbal patterns was also part of what became a larger project, namely his attempt at persuading readers of Greek and Latin literature that many classical texts were filled with puns, plays, and verbal wit of all kinds, especially those relating to proper names. This became one of his particular concerns when, at a later stage, he turned his attention to New Testament texts.

John's move to Durham did nothing to interrupt his productivity, with the result that by the end of the 1990s he had published (often more than once) on Aeschylus, Sophocles, Herodotus, Thucydides, Xenophon, Arrian, Aristotle, Livy, Cornelius Nepos, Horace, Virgil, Ovid, Tacitus, Plutarch, and Dio Chrysostom, as well as several studies of Cynicism (on which he would later be interviewed by Melvyn Bragg on the radio). He regarded the interdisciplinary nature of classical scholarship as one of its great glories, and he endeavoured to put it into practice, gratified that his own work crossed the boundaries of literature, history, and philosophy. This substantial and remarkably diverse range of scholarship has as its defining and unifying feature John's consistent attempt at arriving at original positions on the texts and authors he discussed. The outstanding quality of his work was such that he was promoted to Reader in 1993 and was awarded a personal Chair in 1996.

The late 1990s saw Durham Classics experience a second crisis a decade after the first. The University was using a financial model which projected that the Department of Classics would be in debt to the tune of £1 million by the year 2000. This was regarded as unsustainable, and the administration in its wisdom proposed to close down the Department. Colleagues were sent a letter by the relevant Pro-Vice-Chancellor (formerly a medieval historian of considerable distinction), suggesting that they take early retirement and threatening redundancy if not. The immediate response to this intimidation was panic, and we naturally looked to our leader to see what should be done. Our leader at the time happened to be John, who was now paying the price for his personal Chair and, rather improbably, was serving his term of office as Head of Department. Over the critical period that followed, John almost single-handedly devised a rescue plan, which, though to some of us it seemed to contain elements of pure fantasy, nevertheless was sufficient to persuade the administration of the viability of our continued existence. Any success that the Department has enjoyed during the past decades is due significantly to John; without his inventive genius there might not now be a Department at all.

It is absolutely characteristic that, while this crisis consumed an enormous amount of John's time and energy, he nevertheless thought it vital to fulfil his more personal responsibilities as Head of Department. He was, for example, painstakingly supportive of his short-term colleagues and junior researchers, for whom he would make time to check if they were happy in his Department, to advise them on all academic matters, and even to organise social events at his own expense. It was also thanks to the trust he inspired and to the confidence in themselves which he helped them develop that they proceeded to their future careers at a time when such a prospect seemed almost impossible. His tenure of the headship is remembered with affection as well as gratitude; and his concern for junior colleagues remained unchanged throughout his career.

John's promotion to Professor coincided also with the birth of *Histos*, whose first issue, under his editorship, came out in 1997. Since John had been an early user of word-processors and computers, in retrospect it was perhaps less surprising that he conceived the striking notion of combining a modern method of communication with what was then, and remains, a hot topic in classical scholarship. At the time, however, an online journal devoted to classical historiography seemed—and indeed was—revolutionary; and, when one looks back at that issue of 1997, one cannot fail to be amazed at the glittering names of the contributors. Each of these scholars—scholars of the distinction of F. W. Walbank and T. P. Wiseman, to give two examples—had contributed either as the result of a direct invitation from John or because of his reputation. As founder and editor, John did everything himself, apart from the technical business of putting the papers and reviews on screen, which was done by our colleague and fellow historiographer David Levene.

*Histos* brought immense prestige and welcome publicity to the Durham department at a difficult period, but, when the Chair of Latin at Newcastle was advertised in 2000, John felt it was the moment for a new challenge and submitted an application. As it happened, there were several professorial vacancies at the time, and highly eligible applicants for them; but it seemed to me then, as it still does now, that Newcastle were interested only in capturing John, who thus became their fourth Professor of Latin in succession to Jonathan Powell (1992–2001), David West (1969–92) and G. B. A. Fletcher (1946–69, having first joined the Department as Professor of Classics in 1937): a more distinguished line-up is difficult to imagine. When he took up his Chair, John went out of his way to encourage the participation of David West, who was still living locally, in seminars and the like; in just the same way he would make a point each week of socialising with another long-retired Newcastle Latinist, Donald Hill. Although he had a decidedly contrary streak (which came out especially in his wicked sense of humour and love of provocative statements), John always displayed a highly developed sense of responsibility.

John's departure for Newcastle meant a break in the publication of *Histos*, partly because the journal's website remained at Durham; but, thanks to the persistent enthusiasm and effort of John Marincola, there was a new start in 2011 under the joint banners of Florida State and Newcastle universities and under the joint editorship of Professors Marincola and Moles. The new start included a complete re-formatting and up-dating of the earlier issues, all of them utterly professional in appearance, accessibility, and navigability. Some of the papers published in *Histos* have become classics, and beginning in 2014 a supplementary series of monographs was begun. *Histos*, in other words, goes from strength to strength, all due to John Moles' foresight more than two decades ago. It was his pride and joy, and rightly so.

For someone who relied so much on computers, John was a strangely reluctant user of email; he much preferred the telephone as a means of communication, and thought nothing of extended long-distance phone-calls to colleagues—sometimes across the Atlantic, and sometimes to scholars scarcely known to him—to satisfy his curiosity about some point in a Latin or Greek text. His phone-calling probably reached its height during his last years in Durham, when he was trying to increase the number of submissions to *Histos*, and it was *Histos* which also accounted for much of his scholarly energy. He was repeatedly dismayed by the standard of submissions in terms of argument or stylistic presentation. He loved the making of a case and would often spend many days trying to improve a single submission, writing comments and corrections or re-writing entire sections. Exactly the same treatment was given to the work of postgraduate students, some of whose first publications owe far more to Moles than to the authors themselves. His role as creative reader and critic of draft papers was not confined to his own department. Not long after I first met him, I sent him the draft of what would eventually become a book-chapter on Thucydides, an author in whom John had an intense interest (at one point he planned to co-author a commentary on Book 1). A substantial interval elapsed, as usually happened where John was concerned; but in due course I received many closely typed pages of detailed notes and comments, which were so helpful that I singled him out for special mention in the preface to my book. In the years that followed I would very often take advantage of his generosity and acumen in this way; and I was not alone in so doing, as Christopher Pelling amongst others will testify.

Although one would scarcely describe John as one of Nature's administrators, his research achievements meant that he was a natural choice to chair the departmental Research Committee in Durham for three years in the mid-90s.

He was a most effective chairman, encouraging colleagues to write and publish and, as always, offering help where necessary. He also oversaw the departmental research seminar, and, after he had moved to Newcastle, undertook similar roles there. In particular he was responsible for co-ordinating the Newcastle Classics submission for the 2014 'Research Excellence Framework', a task not to be wished on anyone.

The move from Durham to Newcastle saw a dramatic new development in John's scholarly interests, although he saw it more as a natural extension of work on which he had been engaged for many years. While he continued to publish on his favourite classical authors, from the mid-2000s he began research on the New Testament, especially Luke-Acts, on which he became an expert and published extensively. If this latest interest typified his intellectual curiosity and need for challenge, it should not lead us to forget another manifestation of them: for many years he was also a prolific reviewer. In the 80s and 90s he had reviewed for various journals on a wide variety of topics. His review-discussion of Simon Goldhill's first book created almost as much stir as the book itself, while his review of Joseph Geiger is rightly seen as a classic contribution to the study of political biography. Although he eventually abandoned reviewing as too time-consuming, it was a task which he took extremely seriously, regarding himself as a fearless critic.

John's love of argument meant that he was always on top form in seminars or at conferences, for which he was correspondingly in great demand; and the fertility of his brain allowed him to accept invitations to speak on widely different subjects at many different venues in the United Kingdom and across Europe and the United States. What turned out to be his last conference was in Heidelberg in the summer of 2015, where he delivered the key-note address on the subject of Seneca and Horace. He 'contributed massively to the discussions', wrote one of the organisers in tribute. 'He was an example of insight, openness, and modesty' (John, though a scholar of firm views, was famously self-deprecating).[2] In advance of the conference, as was usual, he had tested out on me his ideas and insights during the course of numerous weekly meetings over coffee; we held these meetings without fail during my periods at home in England, and they were always extremely enjoyable occasions: it seems impossible to believe that tomorrow, or perhaps the next day, I shall not get one of his phone calls demanding my immediate presence at our regular rendezvous.

---

[2] The volume, *Horace and Seneca: Interactions, Intertexts, Interpretations*, edited by Martin Stöckinger, Kathrin Winter, and Andreas T. Zanker has now been published (Berlin and Boston, 2017), and is dedicated to John's memory.

Sociability was very important to him. He loved company, especially if there was good food and drink. He believed that scholarly visitors, whether lecturing or examining, should not only be treated with the respect due to their function but also given a good time, often resorting to his own pocket when limited departmental resources failed. Many visitors to Durham and Newcastle will have pleasure in remembering—or, in some cases, trying to remember—the hospitality to which they were treated when John was master of ceremonies. He had been greatly looking forward to welcoming to Newcastle the new co-editor of *Histos*, Christopher Krebs, whose visit was scheduled for the week after he died: it is beyond sad that he was denied the opportunity of offering the hospitality for which he had made such elaborate and far-sighted arrangements.

John died suddenly in the afternoon of Sunday, 4 October, from heart failure. Although he produced so much brilliant scholarship, he always felt that he could have done more. The fact is that he devoted so much of his time, almost all of it unheralded and unrewarded, to the work of others; in all the tributes that have been paid to him since his death, the most consistent reference has been to his kindness. Although it is perhaps only natural that scholars will never feel satisfied with their work, John leaves as a legacy of his genius a body of scholarship which in its range and quantity, imagination, and acuity, one finds hard to parallel.[3]

---

3  For comments and memories I am most grateful to members of John's family, as well as to Ewen Bowie, Anna Chahoud, John Marincola, Damien Nelis, Christopher Pelling, Elizabeth Pender, Martin Smith, and Rowland Smith.

# Introduction to Parts 1 and 2

*Aldo Brancacci*

In his treatment of John Moles' career that opens this volume, A. J. Woodman touches on the wide range of Moles' studies, which encompass a huge variety of authors: Aeschylus, Sophocles, Herodotus, Thucydides, Xenophon, Arrian, Livy, Cornelius Nepos, Horace, Virgil, Ovid, Tacitus, and Plutarch—to which we must add Dio Chrysostom, Cynicism, and Aristotle.* His account is rich in observations which will profit anyone in the future who engages with Moles' studies—and, above all, with the interdisciplinary commitment that underlay all his scholarly activity. This commitment, I believe, did not derive from an abstract cultural programme, but rather from the soul of the genuine classicist, who in all ages, and on different levels, has always perceived, and sometimes theorised, the unity and indivisibility of the various disciplines within Classics, as well as the immense textual, intellectual, and spiritual scope of classical studies. Moles was generous, restless, open-minded, curious, and resistant to the fragmentation of Classics into separate fields, a fragmentation which sometimes comes from a kind of reductionism that he strongly rejected. And, if I am not mistaken, he also rejected the idea that personal motivation should be absent from the intellectual rigour necessary to classical studies; nor did he appreciate the tendency to follow the easiest positions or the most commonly accepted solutions. Rigour entails neither a limited perspective nor a relentlessly austere treatment, given the difficulty of grounding serious scholarship through the effort required from passion informed by methodological rigour.

My task in this Preface is to deal with Moles' studies on Dio Chrysostom and Cynicism. Both series of articles are arranged in chronological order in this volume. These complex fields of research, to which Moles devoted a number of extremely significant articles, delineate the specifically philosophical character of his contribution to classical studies.

1

The scholarly tradition on Dio is situated at the intersection of different disciplines, including philosophy, Roman history, intellectual history, political

---

\* This essay is derived from Brancacci (2017), where fuller references and more detailed discussion of specific philosophical issues can be found.

history, literary criticism, rhetoric, and the history of ideas. A proper evaluation and understanding of Dio's work requires a synthesis of these different approaches, something which, however, has hardly ever been achieved, especially in earlier scholarship. At the very least, it requires the awareness that Dio's work comprehends all these various areas. Such an awareness clearly emerges from the articles which Moles devoted to Dio.

Moles' first article (Ch. 1) focuses on the well-known idea that Dio 'converted' from Sophistic to philosophy, an idea first suggested by Synesius of Cyrene,[1] one of Dio's most informed and skilled readers. This theory was taken up by Hans von Arnim, who, in his famous, influential, and in many respects still fundamental, monograph on Dio,[2] further developed and refined it by turning Dio's conversion into a three-stage process. Through an attentive and acute analysis of numerous texts of the *corpus Dioneum*, Moles argues that the conversion is an invention to be explained partly by Synesius' naïveté and love for Dio, but partly also by Dio himself, who skilfully weaves into his works a complex web of relations between philosophy, Sophistic, and imperial power between the first and second centuries AD. Despite the appearance of spontaneity or immediacy, Dio's works hide a complex structure, which is needed to convey and adapt different messages to different audiences and different types of readers. I think that Moles' deconstruction of Dio's famous conversion starts from this intuition, which is also a premise further developed and expounded in his later works on Dio.

In rereading Moles' article today, the reader is struck by a contrast, which is, in fact, very significant: despite the clarity of the answers and the confidence of the tone, what stands out is the actual problem of the questions and issues raised by the article itself. The very enquiry into the conversion motif stems from a sense of dissatisfaction and questioning. Moles' articles show the need to read Dio's work as testimony to the relationship between the Greeks of the early imperial age and their literary past, and then to use the results that might derive from this approach to get important information about the politics, ethics, and culture of that period. This programme is highly original and sophisticated: it does not limit Dio to just one dimension, not even the political dimension, so important to modern scholarship. This is central to Moles' works too, but only as part of a richer and more densely aware interpretative framework, a framework that is unique to Moles and exerted a fruitful influence on later scholarship on Dio, especially in Britain.

---

1   On this reading and, in general, on Synesius' interpretation of Dio, see Brancacci (1986) 137–97.
2   Cf. von Arnim (1898).

In the following years, Moles devoted extensive studies to the four *Kingship Orations*, which culminated in two long and important articles which, taken together, constitute a sort of monograph on this important group of speeches. The first article (Ch. 3) is devoted to the fourth oration, while the second (Ch. 5), particularly broad, discusses all the orations together, with special attention devoted, as might be expected, to the first three; the two articles are completed by a note (Ch. 4). At first glance, the articles strike the reader for methodically addressing all the issues commonly faced by scholars working on the *Kingship Orations*. Most significantly, all these issues are treated as equally important: chronology, study of the sources, philosophical and political interpretation, literary evaluation, and historical investigation are all dimensions with which Moles deals tirelessly. But if he makes a preliminary distinction between them, he never makes the mistake of preferring one at the expense of the others. Instead, he synthesises them, and then justifies his interpretation through this very plurality of perspectives.

In 'Dio Chrysostom, Greece and Rome' (Ch. 7), Moles deals with a broad and crucial issue by examining the *Euboicus*, *Olympicus*, and *Borystheniticus*, three speeches which must be numbered among Dio's greatest works. The article completes Moles' work on the four *Kingship Orations* by situating Dio's conception in a wider cultural and philosophical framework in order to provide a deeper understanding of Dio's ideas and political activity. It is rich in detailed and precise observations, but also in more general ones concerning philosophy, literature, and politics, and expands Moles' point of view on Dio, with respect both to Greece and his being Greek, and to Rome and the Empire. At the same time, the article shows a distinctive and perhaps unique theme in Moles' interpretation of Dio: Dio's capacity to face in two directions at the same time, with language that is now direct, now dissimulated, to effect compromises and denouncements, and achieve moral and political, but also religious, aims which draw upon Stoicism, but to which even Cynicism and, to some extent, Platonic themes make their contribution.

At the end of the 1990s, Moles devoted his efforts to the analysis and interpretation of one of Dio's most demanding, and perhaps most complex and dense, orations: the *Charidemus* (Ch. 8). Besides a few notable and isolated exceptions, this oration has not been much studied by scholars, owing to doubts concerning its authenticity (even though the suspicion was not based on any solid evidence), which lasted, I would say, until the appearance of Moles' article. Moles' analysis is masterful for two reasons. On the one hand, he starts from the hypothesis of inauthenticity and progressively destroys it, through a detailed analysis of the text's content, language, and philosophical ideas, as well as of its narrative structure, whose complexity he reveals. On the other hand, the analysis progressively lists a series of elements which show that the *Charidemus* is characterised by an intention of self-representation on the part of Dio, both in the details of its composition (probably related to the death of one of his children) and in its deeper philosophical theme, namely, life and death, and the destiny of human beings after death. All this is clearly the best proof for the authenticity of the text, which, we may add, was considered spurious for a long time—just as Gorgias' rhetorical works and Antisthenes' speeches were still considered inauthentic at the end of the 19th century—simply because it had not been properly studied or understood. According to Moles, with whom I agree, the *Charidemus* is Dio's masterpiece, even superior to Plutarch's *Consolation to his Wife*.

Moles' interpretation of Dio differs from that of other important scholars, who in many cases do not even take into account the philosophical dimension (mainly ethical, but also theological and, as shown by the *Charidemus*, also eschatological) present in the texts. Even worse, some keep their analysis at a para-philosophical level. In the light of these considerations, it is no surprise that, in the full maturity of his studies, Moles devoted a rich and detailed article to Dio's speech 13, *In Athens, about his Exile* (Ch. 10). This is the speech that Hans von Arnim considered Dio's finest work, as it sums up the entire sense of his cultural activity. Moles, who agrees with von Arnim, thinks that the text is also one of Dio's most demanding. Moles' analysis is dense and compact: every aspect of the oration is examined in order to provide a thorough account of it. Moles' intention is to re-examine, through the reading of this important text, the main characteristics of Dio's literary, philosophical, and political commitments. Furthermore, Moles is explicit in clarifying his overall interpretation of Dio, by addressing debated and controversial issues which are, in fact, essential to understanding Dio's work thoroughly. According to Moles, the entire content of *Oration* 13—from Dio's self-representation to his attitude towards the audience, both internal (the Romans) and external (the Greeks), as well as his use of classical Greek sources and his treatment of spatial and temporal relations—clearly shows that the work has a precise and serious philosophical aim, namely to defend, promote, and propose an Antisthenic or Cynic *paideia* as the only serious alternative to the actual *paideia* of the Romans—but also to that of the Greeks.[3] Through attentive analysis of the speech, Moles notes the 'cosmopolitan' character of exile, the motif of philosophical autobiography, the protreptic dimension, the many literary allusions (for example, to Aristophanes), and also the epic tropes and the references to tragedy, and most importantly, the allusions to Herodotus and Thucydides—all conveying the

---

3  See below, pp. 278–9.

idea of a truthful exposition, characterised by sober seriousness and elevated moral aims. Particular attention is devoted to the issue of the philosophical material used by Dio, especially in the central part of the oration, but also in the conclusion. Moreover, Dio's use of Antisthenes and of his conception of the right *paideia* is compatible with the Cynic character of the text, since, even if Antisthenes was not the founder of Cynicism, there can be no doubt that he greatly influenced it, as Dio himself knew.[4] Moles concludes his article by noticing that it is this *paideia* that Dio proposes to his audience, aware of the fact that the apparent simplicity of the Antisthenic-Cynic message, after careful scrutiny, reveals itself as the only true, serious message capable of grasping, and thereby solving, the problem facing both Romans and Greeks: that of how to reform human conduct and achieve the moral life.

Moles' work on Dio Chrysostom over almost forty years culminated in two unpublished articles, the first entitled 'Defacing the Currency: Cynicism in Dio Chrysostom' (originally a paper given in Liverpool on 30 June 2001) and the second 'Dio and Cynicism'. Both pieces are now unified and published here (Ch. 11).[5] It draws important conclusions about a central issue in Dio's scholarship, namely that of his relation to Cynicism, and it sums up, with notable clarity and firmness, the conclusions reached by Moles after long and careful consideration. First of all, Moles deals with the problem of Antisthenes' influence on Dio, by referring to many works which I devoted to this topic. In particular, Moles considers the following two theses of mine: first, that the doctrine of the 'double paideia', expounded by Diogenes in the fourth *Kingship Oration*, and other doctrines contained in *Orations* 2 and 13 are Antisthenic; second, that the *diadochē* Socrates–Antisthenes–Diogenes was very important to Dio.[6]

Furthermore, Moles tackles a 'global' issue on which we worked in parallel for many decades, that of Dio's Cynicism, especially in the so-called Diogenic orations. At the outset, it must be noted, Moles dates these orations too to Trajan's age, against a long-standing opinion according to which they were written during the reign of Domitian. He advances his dating in a careful and prudent way, eventually concluding that 'the "ideal reader" of the Diogenics is Trajan'. As to Dio's Antisthenic and Cynic sources, in particular as regards the construction of the figure of the ideal king, Moles states that they play a central role in Dio.[7]

---

4   Here Moles refers to and approves my interpretation of Dio 8.1 (*SSR* V A 1 = *SSR* V B 584) in Brancacci (2000) 256–7.
5   The editor recognised that the shorter paper, 'Dio and Cynicism', was an earlier version of the longer one, 'Defacing the Currency'.
6   Moles agrees with my arguments: below, p. 301.
7   Below, pp. 299–300 and 301.

## 2

At the beginning of the 1980s, Moles wrote his first article on Cynicism, '"*Honestius quam ambitiosius*"? An Exploration of the Cynic's Attitude to Moral Corruption in His Fellow Men' (Ch. 12). The article is very rich and acute, and Moles demonstrates his thesis with virtuosity. He also adds a long appendix on the continuity of Cynicism from its origins to the imperial age, showing the extent of his investigation into Cynicism, which he considered absolutely essential to the study of Dio. Moles manages to master completely the very philosophical tradition which, on other occasions, he himself defines as almost impossible to master due to its long history. For Cynicism remained influential until the end of antiquity (6th c. AD), and it also had an impact on literature, both Greek (e.g., Menippus and Cercidas) and Latin (e.g., Horace and Varro). Furthermore, even though he relies on his personal and original interpretative approach, Moles demonstrates that he possesses a deep and extensive knowledge of the scholarship on Cynicism, including the oldest and most erudite, which is indispensable for navigating the long and complex history of this philosophical tradition. But when we consider the scholarly trend which began in the 1970s, we can observe that Moles' position is successfully unconventional. It is not by chance that in the introduction to the article Moles explicitly reacts against the scholars of that time, who candidly and straightforwardly, but nonetheless dogmatically, maintained (and still maintain) that it is impossible to establish the evidential value of the texts which constitute the Cynic tradition. Moreover, the article, which focuses on the great and complex figure of Demetrius, the Cynic warmly admired by Seneca, thematises an interpretative issue regarding Demetrius which had been passed unnoticed by scholars. Lastly, it must be noticed that the set of events which Moles examines entails a thorough knowledge of the history of the Roman Empire in the first century AD. Indeed, the article is interdisciplinary not only in the way in which it is presented, but also in its principal theme, which is: why did Demetrius, a philosopher whose profession of Cynicism cannot be questioned, and who was renowned for his honesty and sincerity, and deeply admired by Seneca, defend in the Senate P. Egnatius Celer, rightly accused of being a *delator* and of having been decisive in securing the death sentence for Barea Soranus and his sister, both accused of treason, even though Egnatius was a friend of Barea (the brother of the heroic Thrasea Paetus) and also his teacher in philosophy? The case of Demetrius and his defence of Egnatius Celer provide Moles with the opportunity to reconstruct a series of themes and concepts central to Cynic philosophy. On top of this, an ambitious Appendix, which I mentioned above, completes exhaustively and with geometrical precision, a line of argument based on various theoretical assumptions about the interpretation of Cynicism which Moles carefully makes explicit, explains, and justifies, instead of asserting them dogmatically.

Moles' article on 'Cynic Cosmopolitanism' (Ch. 16) is on the same level as the previous one in its significance and skilfulness, but is probably even more important and profound, as it deals with one of the most central philosophical themes of Cynicism, perhaps the decisive one for a correct interpretation of Cynicism as philosophy. The theme is vast, and its implications great. Moles deals with this wide-ranging topic in a sober and, I would say, simple style, which, it must be stressed, derives from logical, coherent, and carefully-weighed reasoning, always based on the analysis and study of the texts (this is characteristic of all Moles' scholarship). The article encompasses the entire range of Cynic material, but in order to demonstrate his thesis, Moles also considers both its literary and philosophical antecedents. His treatment of Antisthenes provides another example of his exegetical acuity (founded on his excellent and detailed knowledge of the texts). For, even though he agrees with the thesis, now almost unanimously accepted, that quite rightly does not consider Antisthenes the founder of the Cynic school, Moles is equally correct in not separating him from Cynicism, regarding him an important theoretical influence on the school.[8] As usual, Moles is attentive to the methodological problems related to the particular nature of the evidence about the Cynic school. However, this does not prevent him from asserting with frankness—another of his characteristics—how limited and lazy those modern interpretations are according to which Cynic cosmopolitanism is only negative, i.e., which claim that Cynics are 'cosmopolitan' only because they do not fare well in any part of the world or any historical city: or, in other words, that they are cosmopolitan because they are stateless. Moles rightly observes that such interpretations do not take into account a series of secondary testimonies which, on the one hand, refute the alleged equation *apolis* = *kosmopolitēs* (these two things are, in fact, quite distinct concepts); and, on the other hand, help us grasp the broader and more precise meaning of the theme of cosmopolitanism.

Two additional studies on Cynicism are very important, since they broaden the perspective of his investigation, while still devoting special attention to political issues. They have an ambitious aim—namely, to outline a coherent history of Cynicism (or, at least, of its principal trends), valid on the theoretical level, but also historically defined by the very textual bases which it presupposes. In the first of these (Ch. 15), Moles elaborates a distinction between 'hard'

---

8   See below, p. 319 n. 8; p. 389 n. 2; and p. 424 n. 17.

and 'soft' Cynicism. Hard Cynicism is that of Diogenes or that derived from him, and thereby the most authentic. It is defined by the rejection of power and *nomos* in all its forms, and, consequently, of any kind of compromise with political power. It aims at the complete self-sufficiency of the individual and repudiates socially accepted values and norms of behaviour. Soft Cynicism, which dates back to Onesicritus, retains the fundamental dogmas of Cynicism, which, as Moles makes clear, is an actual philosophy, with its own restricted, but precise and infallible, set of principles. However, soft and hard Cynicism differ on a crucial point: the former admits collaboration with kings or rulers, in the attempt to redefine the notion of the good king, i.e., the Cynic king endowed with the fundamental Cynic virtues. In this way, soft Cynicism brings about a break within the history of Cynicism which alters the sense of the doctrine as a whole: for the hard Cynic, the Cynic king ought also to be poor, and thereby abandon wealth and not yield to the constraints imposed by royal status. The article is thus solidly based on the succession Diogenes–Crates (who is an intermediary figure between Diogenes and Onesicritus)–Onesicritus–Bion of Borysthenes–Cercidas–Dio Chrysostom.

But Moles also elucidates with extreme clarity an essential distinction which has not always been appreciated: 'political "freedom" is not the same as Cynic "freedom", and political "freedom" entails political obligations: anathema to Cynics'.[9] Moles' subtle distinction between 'Cynic freedom' and 'political freedom' is not the same as the trite, banal, and much repeated distinction between 'freedom from' (purely negative freedom) and 'freedom to' (positive, or active, freedom). According to a commonly shared opinion, only the first type of freedom is characteristic of Cynicism. Rather, Cynic freedom is a freedom rooted in ethics, whose aims are realised on three different levels: the level of one's way of life, the psychological/behavioural level, and the moral level. And Moles is right in observing that, after all, Cynic 'politics' was nothing but Cynicism itself, that is, the realisation and fulfilment of the Cynic way of life and of what it means to be Cynic truly, and not in words only.

In 'The Political Thought of the Cynics' (Ch. 17), Moles reaffirms his most important views on the history and theoretical system of Cynicism, but also calibrates and refines them further. Along with cosmopolitanism and the importance of 'soft' Cynicism—from Onesicritus to Dio Chrysostom, but also its influence on Diogenes via Antisthenes—and of Cynic political doctrines, Moles deals with more general issues: he examines and problematises the entire Cynic ethico-political project, especially as regards the conditions for its

---

9  Below, p. 412.

realisation, but he also offers a serious, competent, and rational discussion of the problem of sources and the related problem of the historical reconstruction of Cynicism. The final paragraph focuses on the other characteristic trait of Cynicism, namely its wide-ranging influence on Greek and Roman thought, literature, and poetry.

As a classicist, and a scholar of historiography and of Greek and Latin literature, Moles could not ignore the particular influence which Cynicism had on Horace. Indeed, he devotes two very erudite and acute articles to the topic. The first, entitled 'Cynicism in Horace Epistles 1' (Ch. 14), is an extremely perceptive treatment, in which Moles deals with this theme by consideration of a broader and more general framework. The main problem consists not only in determining the extent of the influence of specific philosophical schools on Horace, especially Cynicism, or in documenting the Cynic sources in Horace, but also in understanding the function which philosophical language has in Horace's poetry. In order to tackle this complex issue, Moles isolates Cynic themes in Horace by distinguishing them from Stoic or Epicurean ones, and then, through a detailed and acute analysis, he shows the different ways in which Horace appropriated them, depending on the particular philosophical interpretation which he adopted. Moles concludes that Horace's use of Cynicism is not only justified per se, but also that it effectively contributes to the elaboration of moral ideas essential to poetry itself, which in some rare cases might even entail a resolute stance on specific philosophical schools.

Moles' second article on Horace, 'Philosophy and Ethics in Horace' (Ch. 18), complements but also extends the previous study. Here Moles deals again with the problem regarding the philosophical influences present in Horace's works, by examining it work by work and, I would say, line by line. He considers the well-known influence of Bion of Borysthenes on Horace, the traces of which he assembles and identifies, and then devotes his attention to Cynicism and other philosophical schools, in order to reconstruct the various strands and tendencies of Cynicism present in Horace's works, as well as the different aims which they served. The study is especially noteworthy because it skilfully documents not only the poetical use of philosophy, but also that 'poetry of philology' in which philology itself—understood as a repertoire of images, linguistic patterns, single terms, allusions, and citations—becomes the matter of literary or poetic creation.

In the last decade of his life, Moles undertook intensive studies on the New Testament, partly because, as a classicist, he had always been open to new trends in research, and partly because, as became clearer and clearer during the twentieth century, and has done so even more recently, the study of the New Testament is connected to that of Cynicism. Although they form part of the next section, a few words here are useful in connecting them to the themes of Moles' scholarship on cynicism. In 'Cynic Influence upon First Century Judaism and Early Christianity?' (Ch. 20), Moles deals with the issue with admirable intellectual honesty and impartiality. He offers a long and cautious methodological prologue, after which he evaluates various topics in modern scholarship, such as the influence of Cynicism (and Antisthenes) on Paul, the Church Fathers, and the Gospels. He also critically examines the conclusions drawn by numerous scholars (especially Downing) working on the subject. His discussion is preceded by a detailed articulation of the Cynic interface. One could say that this article represents the victory of Moles' empirical approach—always illuminated by a vivid moral light—over the confusion and approximation which, hidden beneath fine words, can sometimes sneak into scholarship. Moles' conclusion is important: 'the Cynic material seems sufficiently strong to challenge, even to undermine, the contention that Jesus is to be understood solely within Jewish traditions'.[10]

I mention finally the article '*Romane, Memento*: Antisthenes, Dio, and Virgil on the Education of the Strong' (Ch. 19), which brilliantly summarises many constituent aspects of John Moles' scholarship: history and philosophy, Greek literature and Latin literature, and the various authors he favoured. The aim of Moles' paper is to demonstrate that Antisthenes' double education doctrine, expressed especially by a fragment from the *On Virtue* by Themistius (4.29–33 = *SSR* V A 96), underlies Virg. *Aen.* 6.847–53. After having analysed Themistius' testimony and having compared it with Dio's Fourth Kingship, Moles deals with the parallels between *Aen.* 6.847–53 and the educational theory of Antisthenes. Through a thorough and acute analysis, Moles agrees with Francis Cairns' thesis that Virgil's general representation of kingship and heroism is Cynic. According to Moles, Virg. *Aen.* 6.847–53, is clearly influenced by Antisthenes' philosophy, particularly by the thesis of the 'double paideia'.[11] At the end of the paper, Moles also shows that Dio in *Oration* 13 knows that Virgil, in this *locus*, reworks Antisthenes' philosophy for the celebration of the Roman Empire; and that Dio offers a different interpretation of Antisthenic education and 're-establish[es] some distance between Antisthenes and Roman power'.[12]

---

10   Below, p. 543.
11   Below, p. 501.
12   Below, p. 502.

An accurate appendix concludes this important paper, showing clearly how Virgil and Dio use and depend on Antisthenic reflection on education.

### 3

In these papers, then, we can see how Moles gives a unique portrait of Dio Chrysostom, deep and characterised by a personal and original perspective. He does not overlook any one of the many traits of Dio's intellectual personality: the political dimension, but also the literary and philosophical dimension, as well as the ethical value of Dio's rhetoric, are equally taken into account and highlighted. Moles' studies on Cynicism have the same, great value. Indeed, among modern scholars of Cynicism, Moles was the most original, and certainly one of the most erudite, fair-minded, and convincing. He was always open to the ideas and arguments of others, but equally was robust in his own positions, and rigorous in demonstrating and asserting them. Moles was moved—at least as a normative ideal—by an attempt to understand texts in an unconventional and impartial way, which aimed, as far as possible, at truth. To have at our disposal Moles' studies on this philosophical tradition, so important and influential in antiquity, and now brought back to the limelight of contemporary philosophy by studies such as those of Michel Foucault and Peter Sloterdijk, and to the attention of classical studies, due to the interest raised by the vast and complex relationship between Cynicism and the New Testament, will be of great benefit to the progress of research. Like his work on Dio Chrysostom, his work on the Cynics is a tribute to the excellence of British scholarship.

Ultimately, these studies highlight the fundamental characteristics of Moles' approach to the history of ancient philosophy, which is grounded in a firm historical basis and in detailed, acute, and always rigorously demonstrative analyses of texts. Moles' analytical method hinges on a thorough knowledge of scholarship in all languages (not only English, but also French, German, and Italian) combined with the capacity to find creative, original, and innovative solutions; a scrupulous semantic and conceptual analysis of philosophical *termini technici*, and a close attention to the different contexts in which the same term appears; a firm grasp of the general framework in which specific issues are situated; and a clear theoretical interest in textual analysis. Lastly, I would like to point out that Moles' contribution to the history of ancient philosophy is marked by strong ethical motivations and a commitment to trace in classical texts not just mere data, but rather values and ideas to be preserved and reflected upon.

## Bibliography

Arnim, H. von (1898) *Leben und Werke des Dio von Prusa. Mit einer Einleitung: Sophistik, Rhetorik, Philosophie in ihrem Kampf um die Jugendbildung* (Berlin; repr. Hildesheim, 2004).

Brancacci, A. (1986) *Rhetorike philosophousa: Dione Crisostomo nella cultura antica e bizantina*, ('Elenchos', 11; Naples).

Brancacci, A. (2000) 'Dio, Socrates, and Cynicism', in S. Swain, ed., *Dio Chrysostom: Politics, Letters, and Philosophy* (Oxford, 2000) 240–60.

Brancacci, A. (2017) 'John Moles, Historian of Ancient Philosophy', *Méthexis* 29: 141–69.

# PART 1

## *Studies in Dio Chrysostom*

∴

CHAPTER 1

# The Career and Conversion of Dio Chrysostom

Dio of Prusa (Dio Chrysostom) is nowadays mostly read only as a historical source for the Graeco-Roman world of the late first and early second centuries AD.[1] But he is of course one of the relatively few Greek writers of the early Imperial era who are worth reading at all[2] and his career raises important questions of a more general kind: how valid is it to analyse a writer's or philosopher's life in terms of conversion and how firm a line can be drawn between the activities of the philosopher and those of the sophist?

In this paper I shall argue that the theory of Dio's conversion is not borne out by the facts of his career, and that the originator of the theory was not Synesius of Cyrene but Dio himself, who found it a convenient way both of suppressing the memory of his early time-serving attacks on philosophy under Vespasian and of gratifying his personal taste for self-dramatisation. The discussion falls into five parts. Part 1 consists of some general remarks on the methodology of conversion-analysis intended to emphasise some of the dangers of the approach. In Part 2 I consider the evidence of Synesius and of the facts, as far as they can be established, of Dio's early career. In Part 3 I set out and analyse Dio's editorial attitude to sophists and rhetoric and try to show that there is good evidence for sophistic activity late in life. In Part 4 I consider to what extent there is change or development in Dio's career. In Part 5 I argue that Dio's account of his conversion in the *De Exilio* has to be seen in the light of his general use of *exempla* or *personae* from the past and interpreted accordingly.

## 1       The Methodology of Conversion-Analysis

As a concept 'conversion' is naturally most often applied to major religious or philosophical experiences like the great conversions of St Paul, Constantine,

---

1   The classic work remains von Arnim (1898). Sympathetic general studies include Martha (1865) 292–312, Dill (1905) 367–83, Dudley (1937) 148–58, Phillips (1957) 107–13. Momigliano (1950) offers a notably uncharitable view. There is much authoritative analysis of Dio's cynicism in Höistad (1948), esp. 50–63, 87–91, 150–222. No doubt the publication of C. P. Jones' forthcoming book {Jones (1978)} will do much to stimulate wider interest in Dio.
2   For a still more jaundiced view of the contemporary literature see van Groningen (1965), and for a much more sympathetic approach Reardon (1971). Bowie (1970) discusses the extreme literary archaism of the period and offers a political explanation for it.

and St Augustine. But it is important to recognise that conversion does not necessarily involve complete spiritual upheaval or radical change of life-style. It would for example be perfectly reasonable to say that when C. Cassius Longinus became an Epicurean towards the end of 48 BC,[3] he underwent an intellectual 'conversion', though Epicureanism, a humane quietist philosophy, had little discernible influence upon Cassius, who remained a man of inhumanity, restless activity, and fervent political conviction. Philosophical conversion *may* of course have a dramatic effect upon political attitude, especially in the case of such serious-minded philosophers as the Stoics and Cynics of the first century AD. The sharp divergence of behaviour by Helvidius Priscus between 70 and 71 AD can be analysed in terms of conversion from Stoic reformism to Cynic radicalism.[4] A conversion-type [[80]] concept can also sometimes be usefully applied to the careers of men of letters, like the orator Isocrates,[5] who achieved fame first as a logographer but later repudiated his past with such fervour that his adopted son was able to claim that he had never written any forensic speeches at all, even though, as Aristotle pointed out, the bookshops were still full of them (D. Hal. 1.85.13–86.8 U–R {= *Isoc.* 18.2–4}; Arist. F 140 Rose). All these categories have to be taken into consideration in assessing the role of conversion in the career of Dio Chrysostom.

The obvious danger of *any* conversion-analysis is oversimplification. For example it was once maintained that the career of Lysias fell into two rigidly defined parts: pre-403 Gorgias-inspired sophistic rhetoric, post-403 logographic work written in the chastest of Attic prose.[6] But speech 20 in the *Corpus Lysiacum*, against whose authenticity there are no arguments of substance and which was perhaps written as early as 409,[7] is the work of a logographer; the

---

3 For the date see Shackleton Bailey (1977) on Cic. *Ad Fam.* 15.16.3 and 15.17.3; an important corrective of the dates given by Momigliano (1941) 151 {= (1984) 379}, Rostagni (1956) 160, and Flacelière–Chambry (1972) 194. Cassius' conversion may have been triggered by the Republican defeat at Pharsalia but that his Epicureanism had little lasting effect upon his behaviour is patent. Naturally the statement in the unreliable life of Lucretius by Girolamo Borgia that Lucretius was a friend of Atticus, Cicero, Brutus, and Cassius proves nothing: Cicero and Brutus were not Epicureans.
4 Thus Toynbee (1944). The position of Momigliano (1951) 148–9 = (1975) 964–5 is not fundamentally different. See also n. 41 below.
5 Cf. Kennedy (1963) 177–8.
6 Müller (1858) II.139ff.; cf. Adams (1905) 21–2. *Contra*, Jebb (1893) I.162.
7 Dover (1968) 9, 19, 44 (date), 56, 122, 133, 138, 143, 147. For Dover absence of evidence against does not amount to a positive argument in favour of authenticity but I would agree with the more optimistic attitude of Usher (1971). But the abusive use of the term λογογράφος at Plat. *Phaedr.* 257d (dramatic date perhaps pre-415: Dover (1968) 32–3) does not in itself prove logographic activity: the context is much more general.

*Epitaphios*, whose authenticity also it is unreasonable to deny,[8] dating from c.392 or later, is evidently nothing more than a rhetorical display-piece, replete with Gorgianic purple patches; and in c.340 Apollodorus can refer to Lysias as 'the sophist' (in Dem. 59.21).[9] At that time Lysias had been dead for about forty years and it seems unlikely that Apollodorus has in mind his literary activities of over sixty years before, rather than those of the last twenty years of his life. The rigid schematisation of Lysias' career, then, does not work, though of course it does reflect a certain *general* truth.

Sometimes, too, the conversion-schema is simply a disguise for an elaborately circular system of argument: Plutarch was 'converted' from rhetoric to philosophy in c.65 AD, therefore all his overtly rhetorical works can be classed as *juvenilia*, while anything of a more philosophical character becomes automatically a work of his maturity.[10] This admittedly is an attractive schema, because it enables scholars to put an approximate date on works for which there are no reliable dating criteria, and because it produces a morally uplifting picture of Plutarch putting behind him the rhetorical frivolities of his youth and advancing resolutely in maturity of style and thought until death. But some of its implications are awkward. For instance *De Fortuna Romanorum*, a work of definitely sophistic cast, shows an extremely detailed knowledge of Roman history, with precise references to Valerius Antias (323C) and Livy (326A), and it is simply perverse to assert on the strength of a general assumption—rhetorical works are pre-'conversion'—against all the obvious indications, that Plutarch wrote it when he was less than twenty.[11]

Conversion-analysis clearly needs to be handled with especial care in the fields of rhetoric and philosophy. It is obviously unsafe to assume that what is sophistic is necessarily lightweight: λόγοι ἐπιδεικτικοί can be divided into πανηγυρικοί and παίγνια[12] and πανηγυρικοί—at least in theory—are serious works, designed for solemn public occasions. The outstanding public services

---

8   For a sensible though unenthusiastic defence see Bizos (1955) I.42–5.
9   For the identification see Dover (1968) 36–7. Usher (1971) 148 is unnecessarily sceptical. σοφιστής can of course be applied derisively to political orators but here must denote professional status.
10  Thus, e.g., Ziegler (1951) 716–17 {= (1964) 80–1}, Hamilton (1969) xxiii; Jones (1966) 70 {= Scardigli (1995) 115} and (1971) 14–16, 67–71, 135. *Contra*, Russell (1972) 226–7, less trenchant in (1970) 849 and (1973) 3.
11  The dilemma is spelled out but not fully resolved by Barrow (1967) 128. Cf. Russell (1972).
    Of course explanations in terms of the conversion from rhetoric to philosophy were also often canvassed in antiquity, sometimes with just as little justification as now. Cf., e.g., Plut. *Mor.* 791A–B on Carneades (given the lie by Carneades' eminently sophistic behaviour in Rome in 155 BC) and Dio 19.3 in the light of the discussion below.
12  For this classification cf. D.Hal. {*Lys.* 1.5, 3.7, 16.2, 3.7 =} I.9.1, 11.15, 26.22–27.1, 11.16f. U–R.

of leading sophists of both the fifth and fourth centuries BC and of the so-called Second Sophistic movement are abundantly documented,[13] and the use of exaggerated rhetorical technique does ⟦81⟧ not necessarily mean that such writings must always lack serious content. Gorgias' *Epitaphios*, perhaps the ultimate in sophistic overkill, concealed a fundamentally worthwhile political message (Philostr. *VS* 493).[14] Furthermore, certain individuals, like the unfortunate 'Stoic sophist'[15] who was the butt of Plutarch's dinner guests (*Quaest. Conv.* 710B), or the ambiguous Favorinus, pupil of Dio and friend and perhaps pupil of Plutarch, obviously found little difficulty in operating as sophists and philosophers simultaneously.[16] And the attitude of the most fanatical champions of philosophy to sophistic rhetoric might be secretly rather ambivalent: some of Plato's dialogues—the *Phaedrus* and *Menexenus*, for example—seem partly devoted to establishing the proposition that while in theory Socrates despised the skills of conventional rhetoric, in practice he was really rather good at it.[17]

These are all obvious *caveats*, designed not to deny outright the possibility of a genuine conversion from rhetoric to philosophy but simply to highlight some of the dangers inherent in such conversion-analyses, if they are pursued without regard to the general cultural background against which both sophists and philosophers worked and the rhetorical education system in which both, by the first century AD, were brought up, or the definite chronological checks that can sometimes be made upon them.

So much by way of introduction.

---

13  See, e.g., Guthrie (1969/1971) 40, 44; Bowersock (1969).
14  The weight of the tradition is decisively against the contention of Dodds (1959) 7, that Gorgias was not a sophist in some accepted sense of the term. Cf. Harrison (1964); Guthrie (1969) 36. For attempts to define the term 'sophist' see, e.g., Guthrie (1969) 27–34, Harrison (1964) 190–1, Bowersock (1969) 12–14 (the imperial period). Dio refers to Gorgias as a sophist at 12.14 and 54.1 (cf. 37.28, Favorinus).
15  For this type of formulation cf. Cass. Dio 66.15 σοφισταὶ κύνειοι.
16  For other examples of this dual role see Bowersock (1969) 11–12 and for an excellent discussion of the fusion of philosophy and rhetoric in the Second Sophistic and later, Barnes (1971) 211–32.
17  Cf. Kennedy (1963) 158–64. It is of interest to note that Synesius (*Dion* 37d) considers Socrates' speech in the *Menexenus* purely rhetorical. In Dio 4.79–81 Diogenes' behaviour has a Socratic flavour about it.

## 2  The Evidence of Synesius and Dio's Early Career

The most explicit[18] source for Dio's conversion from rhetoric to philosophy is Synesius of Cyrene. In his essay on Dio he takes issue with Philostratus, who had categorised Dio among the philosophers who were *reputed* to be sophists because of their eloquence (*vs* 484, 492) though in fact they were not. Synesius maintains that Dio was first an ἀγνώμων σοφιστής but ended up an unadulterated φιλόσοφος (36a), the change taking place during his exile (38a–b). This view was accepted by H. von Arnim[19] and also—as one would expect—by A. D. Nock,[20] though von Arnim introduced the refinement of a tripartite division of Dio's career: a sophistic period ending with his exile under Domitian, a Cynic period during his exile, and a period after his recall from exile when he achieved a successful synthesis between philosophy and rhetoric without actually engaging in separate sophistic activity. But it has often been questioned,[21] though not in much detail, most trenchantly by A. D. Momigliano.[22]

The problem cannot be settled simply by a consideration of Synesius' possible motivation. It is true, as Momigliano points out, quoting his letter to Hypatia (no. 154 in Hercher, *Epistol. Graeci*, ed. Didot, p. 735), that he had a personal interest in showing that Dio was ultimately able to combine good philosophy with good Greek. And a man who shared the characteristic [[82]] Neoplatonic concern with the occult might be thought to be intrinsically susceptible to explanation in terms of conversion. It is also true that he wrote the *Dio* with polemical intent and that he himself indulges in a fair amount of rhetorical point-scoring over Philostratus. But on the other hand he is obviously well informed about Dio:[23] he is able to cite works which are not in the extant *corpus* and some of which certainly are typically sophistic;[24] and his discussion of Dio's style and the way Dio manipulates it according as his subject matter is sophistic or philosophical shows some insight. He also believes

---

18  It can hardly be regarded as the *primary* source for reasons that will appear below. Cf. also n. 147.
19  Von Arnim (1898) 223.
20  His brief discussion in Nock (1933) 173–4 is wholly uncritical.
21  E.g., Hirzel (1895) II.85 n. 3, 88; Valdenberg (1926) 946; Browning (1970); Russell (1972); Jones (1973) 303. There are signs that scepticism about conversion-analysis in the context of the Second Sophistic is spreading—see, e.g., Bompaire (1977) and Tatum (1977). Nevertheless, acceptance of Dio's conversion remains common, e.g., Parke–Wormell (1956) 1.409, Grube (1965) 327, Lesky (1966) 834, MacMullen (1966) 65–6.
22  Momigliano (1951) 149–53 = (1975) 966–74.
23  Cf. Terzaghi (1944) 238.
24  *Viz.* the Ψιττακοῦ ἔπαινος, Κατὰ τῶν φιλοσόφων, Πρὸς Μουσώνιον, his work on the Essenes, Τέμπη, Μέμνων, Κώνωπος ἔπαινος.

that he has Dio's own authority for his schema.²⁵ It would then be quite unfair to Synesius to dismiss his views out of hand as being (for example) the pious wishful thinking of a Christian bishop.²⁶ They can only be adequately tested by a detailed examination of the evidence for Dio's relations with philosophers and sophists.

It will rapidly become apparent that there are many holes in the Synesian schema followed by von Arnim but it is still worth trying to assess whether there is any truth in it at all and attempting to answer the question: exactly why did Synesius believe in it?

Dio was born in Prusa, perhaps *c*. AD 40,²⁷ of a rich and distinguished family, which played a prominent part in local politics but which also had loyalties to the imperial house in Rome. His maternal grandfather²⁸ had been friends with a Roman emperor (46.3–4, 44.5, 41.6), perhaps Claudius,²⁹ and both he and his daughter, Dio's mother, were granted Roman citizenship (41.6). Dio does not record his *father* as having Roman citizenship and in context this strongly suggests that he did not have it.³⁰ If so, Dio's own Roman citizenship was not inherited but earned: precisely when is an intriguing question possibly of some relevance to the problem of Dio's early relations with philosophers in Rome.³¹

According to Fronto (133 van den Hout = II.50 Haines) Dio, along with Euphrates, Timocrates, and Athenodotus, was a pupil of the Roman Stoic philosopher Musonius Rufus. The only serious piece of evidence, as opposed to the Synesius–von Arnim schematisation, that can be advanced against this tradition is the existence of Dio's Πρὸς Μουσώνιον, attested by Synesius (37b), which undoubtedly contained some sort of attack on Musonius.³² But it is not unusual for pupils to quarrel with their teachers. And since Musonius himself

---

25  This important point is discussed further below.
26  This would be out of character anyway. For discussion of Synesius' career see Marrou (1963).
27  Dio's date of birth can only be conjectured. Von Arnim (1898) 147 gives by implication 44/45, but this is based on a probable misdating of the *Melancomas Orations* (see n. 65 below). The criterion of earliest recorded activity would tend to favour the later dating but would make Dio refer to his old age in 97 (12.12) when only just over 50. On balance AD 40, as argued for by Schmid (1903) 850, seems preferable.
28  He owed his second fortune to his παιδεία (46.3) but it is impossible to infer from this that he was a ῥήτωρ (as tentatively Momigliano (1950) 257) rather than just a highly cultured man.
29  Von Arnim (1898) 123. At 46.3 τῶν αὐτοκρατόρων might suggest more than one emperor but it is probably just a rhetorical plural: cf. the specific τὴν τοῦ αὐτοκράτορος προθυμίαν immediately below.
30  Von Arnim (1898) 124.
31  See further below.
32  See further below.

probably wrote little or nothing[33] the Πρὸς Μουσώνιον cannot have been the kind of address which could be made to an established literary figure even if he was personally quite unknown to the author or perhaps even dead hundreds of years before (like Dio's own Ὑπὲρ Ὁμήρου πρὸς Πλάτονα, attested by the *Suda*), and its existence is, therefore, if anything positive evidence of some sort of association between the two men. A Musonius–Dio link is also comfortably supported by the two letters attributed to Dio addressed Ῥούφῳ (Hercher 259)[34] and more substantially by the reference in section 122 of the *Rhodian Oration* to a philosopher 'inferior in birth to no Roman', who reproved the Athenians for taking pleasure in gladiatorial shows. The piety displayed by the philosopher, his high birth (Musonius was an *eques* of Etruscan origin), his great reputation for virtue and his ⟦83⟧ insistence on practising what he preached all fit 'the Roman Socrates' very well.[35] Lucian, too (*Peregr.* 18), seems to associate Dio with Musonius and Epictetus. The most direct evidence for links between Dio and the leading philosophers of the day is of course provided by Philostratus' *Life of Apollonius*, a work whose historical value is notoriously difficult to assess.[36]

In a famous scene (5.27–38), apparently also referred to in the *Lives of the Sophists* (vs 488), Apollonius, Euphrates, and Dio discuss the respective merits of democracy and monarchy in the presence of Vespasian in his camp at Alexandria in AD 69/70. Naturally this scene is quite fictitious.[37] It is simply an agreeable reworking of two standard historiographical τόποι: the discussion of the ideal constitution (Otanes, Megabyzus, and Darius in Herodotus; Agrippa, Maecenas, and Octavian in Cassius Dio) and the encounter of the great king and the great philosopher (Croesus–Solon, Alexander–Diogenes). On the other hand, Philostratus' portrayal of the relations between these philosophers is at least internally consistent, with Apollonius and Dio, despite some disagreements, constant friends and Apollonius and Euphrates—after this

---

33  For discussion with some qualification see Lutz (1947) 5 n. 8 and 9 n. 22.
34  Attribution and identification are both of course speculative but it would be rash to dismiss them just because Dio takes a positive attitude to rhetoric in the second and expects his friend's oratorical skills to benefit from association with 'Rufus': in practice philosophers' attitude to rhetoric was not generally as intolerant as it was in theory. Cf. below.
35  The accepted identification. Another suggested candidate is Apollonius of Tyana, of whom a very similar story is told in Philostratus, *VA* 4.22, but the phraseology 'inferior in birth to no Roman' rules this out completely. In fact the Apollonius passage is probably modelled on the *Rhodian*: thus Bowie (1978). Cf. *VA* 5.26 for another Dionian doublet.
36  See, e.g., Grosso (1954); Bowersock (1970) 16; Bowie (1978). On the novelistic aspects of the work, which naturally detract from its historical reliability, see also Anderson (1977) 37.
37  Bowersock (1970) 19 is, surprisingly, not wholly convinced of this.

incident—equally constant enemies.³⁸ Is it any more than that? Can any firm inferences be made from this passage about Dio's early philosophical career?

It is of little use to try to estimate its reliability by appealing to the general validity or otherwise of Philostratus' information about Dio, some of which is convincing, some considerably less so.³⁹ The passage has to be tested on its own merits.

A case can be made for regarding Philostratus' evidence as in some measure authoritative and the analysis would go something like this.⁴⁰

When after his accession it became clear that Vespasian would never fulfil the lofty expectations of leading Stoic philosophers, many were disillusioned, and some, including Helvidius Priscus, actually seem to have been prepared to argue for a restoration of the Republic instead of campaigning as in the past simply for reform of the Principate.⁴¹ Thus when Philostratus attributes such sentiments to Euphrates and Dio in 70 in the presence of a friendly Vespasian he is being slightly anachronistic (and rather inaccurate since Dio took quite the opposite stance in 71) but the mere fact that he does so shows some knowledge of the philosophical crisis of 71 and what to some extent it was about.⁴²

---

38  Apollonius/Dio: *VA* 5.27–8, 31–2, 37–8; 8.7.2; *Epp.* 10, 90. Disagreements: *VA* 5.40; *Ep.* 9. Apollonius/Euphrates: *VA* 1.13; 2.26; 5.28, 33, 37, 39; 6.7, 9, 13, 28; 7.9, 36; 8.3, 7.11, 7.12, 7.16; *Epp.* 1–8, 15–18, 50–2, 60.

39  For a full discussion see von Arnim (1898) 142, 224ff. For example, Philostratus' statement that Dio had Plato's *Phaedo* and Demosthenes' *De falsa legatione* with him during the exile (*VS* 488) presumably derives from a lost work of Dio's (so Momigliano (1950) 261) or a reliable oral tradition, and his observation that Dio was exceptionally good at extemporisation (*VA* 5.37) can be substantiated from Dio's extant writings—cf. von Arnim (1898) 181ff. and Dio 5.24; 7.102; 12.38, 43; 34.53; 48.15; 65.7, 8, 10, 13 for practical examples. On the other hand his characterisation of Dio as a man who avoided quarrels is plainly ludicrous (*VA* 5.37). On the question of the reliability of Philostratus' description of Dio digging etc. during the exile see n. 135.

40  This analysis is a paraphrase and expansion of Momigliano (1951) 148–9, 152–3 = (1975) 964–5, 972–4. Expansions are noted below.

41  Cf. (besides Momigliano) Toynbee (1944) 51–6; MacMullen (1966) 55; Sandbach (1975) 146 (a more cautious formulation). Cass. Dio 66.12.2 and Philost. *VA* 5.33ff., can be argued to be mutually corroborative—but see below. For Republican ideals under the empire cf. Tac. *Ann.* 1.4.2, 33.3; 2.82.3; Gell. *NA* 13.13.2; Hor. *Sat.* 1.3.81 with Porphyrio *ad loc.*; Joseph. *A.J.* 19.162ff.; Suet. *Claud.* 10.3ff.; Cass. Dio 60.15.3; Tac. *Ann.* 15.52.4 (as late as 65, which surely makes the idea of a thoroughly disillusioned Helvidius turning to Republicanism not difficult). If this unfashionable view of Helvidius Priscus is rejected, Philostratus' account of the discussions between Vespasian and the philosophers could still be considered valuable as reflecting something of the flavour of the debate about the nature of kingship then in progress—but see below.

42  This would not exclude more normal explanations such as Vespasian's refusal to take action against the *delatores* or surround himself with *boni amici* or even the much

His association of Euphrates and Dio is supported by Fronto and [[84]] there is nothing intrinsically implausible about an attempt by two pupils of Musonius, a friend of the Flavians and a fervent advocate of the need for the philosopher to engage in political action, to exert influence upon a Flavian emperor. Apollonius, an acquaintance of Musonius, had other links with the Flavians according to Philostratus,[43] and Dio's Flavian connections can be substantiated by independent evidence: his two obituaries of the athlete Melancomas (*Orr.* 28, 29), who according to Themistius (*Or.* 10.139a = 211.11 Downey), perhaps drawing on a lost work of Dio,[44] was reputedly a lover of Titus;[45] his probable friendship with Flavius Sabinus, the son or grandson of Vespasian's elder brother;[46] his probable role as an apologist for Vespasian's purge of the philosophers in 71;[47] and his *possible* role—he compares himself to Hermes sent by Zeus (32.21)—as an imperial envoy of Vespasian in Alexandria in the early 70s.[48] Thus on this interpretation Philostratus' evidence is extremely valuable

---

maligned 'Rostovsteff hypothesis' that Helvidius objected to the entire principle of hereditary monarchy. The argument is that failure on all normal fronts drove Helvidius into Republicanism as a last resort.

43  Apollonius/Musonius: *VA* 4.46; 5.19; 7.16. Apollonius/Vespasian: 5.27–38, 41; 8.7.2, 7.3. Apollonius/Titus: 6.28–33. Apollonius/Domitian: *Epp.* 20–21. Momigliano does not use this argument.

44  Scharold (1912). Cf. Dio 28.5–7/29.4–8/Themist. 10.139.

45  Lemarchand (1926) 30ff. argued that Melancomas was a purely imaginary character because Themistius' evidence has no independent value (cf. n. 44 above), there is no other reference in ancient literature to the great Melancomas, and he is described by Dio in thoroughly idealised terms. Even if this were correct it would not completely destroy the link with Titus (which is of course extremely likely on *a priori* grounds) but it seems clear that Lemarchand is wrong. Athenodorus, an athlete friend of Melancomas' ἀπὸ παιδός (28.10), can probably be identified with the Athenodorus who appears in the list of winners at Olympia in AD 49, 53, and 61 (Eusebius, *Chron.* p. 101 Karst; cf. Schmid (1903) 849). The fact that Dio makes Athenodorus a παγκρατιάστης whereas Eusebius registers him as a winner in the stadion is trivial (*pace* Momigliano (1951) 152 {= (1975) 972–3} and Moretti (1957) no. 775 [Melankomas])—discrepancies of that kind between Eusebius and other sources are very common. And granted that Themistius was working from Dio, the information that Titus was a lover of Melancomas, even if reported as hearsay (φασίν), seems a bit bold to be pure invention. As to the idealisation of Melancomas, there was nothing to prevent Dio from using a real-life athlete as a peg upon which to hang his ethical ideals, a technique familiar from many Greek funerary writings. Finally, the lack of other attestation is always a dangerous argument for non-existence, especially in the light of the Athenodorus identification.

46  For the friendship see Dio 13.1, the identification, von Arnim (1898) 228–31, and the relationship to Vespasian, Townend (1961) 54–6.

47  See below.

48  Jones (1973) makes a good circumstantial case for dating the *Alexandrian Oration* to the early 70s, which I accept. Arguments against this dating (some not mentioned by Jones)

for the general information it provides about Dio's philosophical acquaintances, however suspect the precise dramatic setting.

Such an analysis, taken as a whole, is of course very controversial, though some of its constituent elements—the association of Dio, Euphrates, and Musonius, the links between Musonius and the Flavians and between Dio and the Flavians—are incontrovertible. The *general* chronological setting of Philostratus' narrative is about right, since at that stage philosophers in Rome clearly still did have high hopes of Vespasian. Against that, the analysis partly depends upon a view of the development of the political thought of Helvidius Priscus and others like him which is today rather out of favour, though it is one which, arguably, still has much to be said for it. More important is the question whether Philostratus' evidence can really be regarded as independent.⁴⁹ If—for the sake of argument—he had decided to reproduce a standard philosophical debate about the best form of government he could easily have done so out of his own [[85]] head: Dio's *Kingship Orations* would be an obvious source among many. The apparent tie-up therefore between Philostratus and the (arguable) political Republicanism of Helvidius Priscus could simply be a happy accident. Equally, the impressive-looking cross-network of relationships between Apollonius and Musonius, Dio, Euphrates, Demetrius,⁵⁰ Vespasian, Titus, and Domitian could just be skilful embroidery upon secure historical data—the links between Musonius, Dio, and Euphrates, between Musonius

---

are: (i) the phraseology of 32.9, where Dio makes a distinction between Cynic behaviour and the excellence of their philosophical tenets, might be thought appropriate to a man who was embarrassed about his own past Cynic career but unwilling to repudiate it utterly. Yet equally it could have been used by Dio before his exile. (ii) The difference in tone between the Κατὰ τῶν φιλοσόφων of 71 (below) and the *Alexandrian Oration* in Dio's attitude to the Cynics (see n. 58 below—not a problem for Jones as he does not recognise that there is a difference). But such an argument from consistency is always dangerous, especially if the Κατὰ τῶν φιλοσόφων was a work of expediency written at a time of crisis (below). (iii) Would Dio have emphasised that he was an envoy of Vespasian, an unpopular figure in the Alexandria of the 70s? This is a difficult question to assess but after all the point is made attractively and amusingly and the explicit references to the emperor (32.60, 95, 96, cf. perhaps 29) are skilfully prepared for. It is clear that Dio's brief was invidious whichever emperor he was representing. (iv) The parallels with the Trajanic *Kingship Orations* (e.g. 32.26 ~ 1.23–4, 32.95 ~ 1.7, 4.19). But these are simply τόποι. (v) The parallels with *Or.* 33 (e.g. 32.88 ~ 33.22, 32.35–7 ~ 33.24, 32.67 ~ 33.57, 32.47 ~ 33.41). The first three of these are just τόποι and the resemblance between 32.47 and 33.41 is not striking. In any case the dating of *Or.* 33 is not certain. Cf. n. 73 below. (vi) The parallels with securely dated Trajanic orations (e.g. 32.29 ~ 39.5, 32.29 ~ 39.3, 32.2 ~ 48.7). But these are also τόποι. (vii) The parallels with *Or.* 34 (von Arnim (1898) 461–2) hardly amount to much, nor is *Or.* 34 securely dated. Cf. n. 73 below.

49  I owe much to Mr E. L. Bowie for the sceptical discussion that follows. Cf. also n. 35 above.
50  Apollonius/ Demetrius: *VA* 4.25, 42; 5.19; 6.31, 33; 7.10; 8.10, 12, 13.

and the Flavians, between Musonius and Demetrius, between Dio and the Flavians—designed to secure Apollonius a respectable place in the world of contemporary philosophers. The *minimum* inference from Philostratus' account of the meeting of Apollonius, Vespasian, Dio, and Euphrates is that he was fairly sure that his readers would regard the conjunction of Dio, Euphrates, and Vespasian as historically plausible. But in view of the strong possibility that his main interest was to establish the proposition that Apollonius had an international reputation as a philosopher during his own lifetime this may also be the *maximum* inference: hence Philostratus' evidence may be regarded as consistent with the testimony of Fronto and with the attested relationship between Musonius, Dio, and the Flavians but in all probability not an advance upon them.

However that may be, it is quite beyond dispute that the young Dio had a philosophical education in the company of some of the leading philosophers of the day. How then to explain his Κατὰ τῶν φιλοσόφων and Πρὸς Μουσώνιον, the works which Synesius took as proof that Dio started his career as an out-and-out sophist?

The very use of κατά in the title implies that the Κατὰ τῶν φιλοσόφων was a sharp attack on philosophers.[51] It is possible to gauge something of its content from Synesius' remark that in his sophistic works 'Dio hurled at Socrates and Zeno the coarse jests of the Dionysiac festival and demanded that their disciples be expelled from every land and sea in the belief that they are Messengers of Death to states and civic organisation alike' (38b, trans. H. Lamar Crosby). Despite the reference to Dio's Aristophanic abuse, Synesius was convinced that the work was a genuine attack 'utterly unabashed and shrinking from no rhetorical device'. The specific attack on Socrates and Zeno corresponds to nothing in Dio's extant works[52] and it is natural to suppose that he ridiculed Socrates and Zeno[53] in the same work as that in which he demanded the expulsion of their followers from land and sea, i.e.—plausibly—the Κατὰ τῶν φιλοσόφων.

---

51  The distinction between κατά and πρός is made very clear by Treu (1958) *ad loc.* 'Der Titel der ersten Rede mit κατά c. gen. deutet auf eine gerichtliche Anklage, während für die an den geachteten Philosophen Musonius gerichtete Rede eine mildere Art der Polemik anzunehmen ist, die von persönlicher Animosität frei war'. Πρός does not *necessarily* denote opposition but it is quite clear from Synesius that it does so here.

52  Though 47.7 and 54 do provide a context for στεφανοῦντι ... αὐτοὺς καὶ παράδειγμα τιθεμένῳ γενναίου βίου καὶ σώφρονος.

53  Treu (1958) takes Σωκράτη καὶ Ζήνωνα as imprecise, suggesting that it is just Synesius' way of saying 'philosophers in general', with which he compares Διογένας τε καὶ Σωκράτας (39a). But there the plural makes a difference (= 'people like Diogenes and Socrates') though even so the names are chosen because these two philosophers loom so large in Dio's writings—Synesius makes this quite plain.

Presumably the point of the attack was that Socrates, teacher of Antisthenes, was often regarded as a Cynic champion,[54] while Zeno of course was the founder of Stoicism. The Κατὰ τῶν φιλοσόφων therefore, besides being directed against philosophers in general, contained specific abuse of Cynics and Stoics. This consideration, taken in conjunction with Dio's recommendation that their followers be expelled from every land and sea, establishes beyond reasonable doubt the correctness of von Arnim's suggestion[55] that the work is to be connected with Vespasian's expulsion of the philosophers in 71.[56] In this purge, persecution of philosophers transcended the Stoic–Cynic opposition but was particularly concerned to curb the political independence of these two sects.[57] The melancholy but inevitable inference is that Dio, sycophantically outdoing Vespasian, who was content to exclude philosophers merely from Rome and Italy, lost his nerve [[86]] and denounced his former friends with the most lurid of invective.[58] And it is tempting to surmise that the reward offered to and accepted by Cocceianus Dio for this service was a grant of Roman citizenship obtained for him by M. Cocceius Nerva, the saintly friend of philosophers who yet managed to emerge unscathed and even enhanced from every major

---

54  For Diogenes represented in Socratic terms cf. his 'conversion' to philosophy after visiting the Delphic Oracle (discussed below) and in Dio, e.g., 8.12 (Socratic personal mannerism) and 4.79–81 (see n. 17 above).

55  Von Arnim (1898) 150–1.

56  The conventional dating, consistent with Cass. Dio 66.13. For the purposes of the attempted reconstruction of the chronology of Dio's early career which follows it is of considerable importance that it should be right. Bowie's conjecture (n. 59 below) adds useful support.

57  Cass. Dio 66.13.

58  Thus Momigliano (1951) 152 = (1975) 973. Jones (1973) 305 links the Κατὰ τῶν φιλοσόφων with the *Alexandrian Oration*. In that case Dio's behaviour in 71 could be seen as responsible and statesmanlike rather than panicky and opportunist. It is true that both speeches show him acting in the interests of Vespasian but there are considerable differences both in tone—the Κατὰ τῶν φιλοσόφων extremely shrill and overstated (contrast 32.9)—and content: the Κατὰ τῶν φιλοσόφων attacked Stoics, Cynics, and philosophers in general, the *Alexandrian* only certain Cynics and philosophers who did not do their job properly. Hence Momigliano's analysis is right. It would of course be methodologically unsound to argue back from Dio's celebrated παρρησία under Domitian (Lucian, *Peregr.* 18; cf. Dio 3.13; 45.1ff.; 50.8), which is in any case largely unverifiable (the veiled attacks in the Diogenes exile discourses or at 66.6 need not have been very perilous), or from his ἐλευθερία (3.12; cf. 6.34, 58; 7.66; 13.13), and reject the possibility that Dio could have sold out in 71.

That Dio had already in 71 contracted philosophical friendships was naturally denied by von Arnim, who thought that the K. τ. φ. proved complete ignorance of philosophy, but this view, apart from being naïve and schema-based, cannot be reconciled with the chronological evidence for Dio's association with Musonius and the Flavians. See below.

philosophical crisis from Nero to Domitian and who as it happened was *consul ordinarius* in 71 with Vespasian.[59]

The significance of the Πρὸς Μουσώνιον is more difficult to assess. Synesius makes it quite clear that it was an attack on the same general lines as the Κατὰ τῶν φιλοσόφων. On the other hand the use of πρός instead of κατά suggests that it was of a milder character and contained a strong element of intellectual debate free from personal abuse.[60] Its content may perhaps be inferred from Synesius' statement that at the time of his attacks on philosophy Dio was convinced that it was better to live in accord with 'common notions' (κοιναὶ ὑπολείψεις) than in accord with philosophy. This Isocratean doctrine would have been anathema to Musonius, who tried to apply his philosophy not only to such down-to-earth questions as 'What is the best viaticum for old age?' or 'Should daughters be educated in the same way as sons?' but also—notoriously—to problems of political life. The Πρὸς Μουσώνιον, therefore, could easily have had a political application: if philosophy is irrelevant to practical living Stoics have no business meddling in high politics. A final point of considerable interest arising from Synesius' discussion of Dio's chequered early career is that in these works Dio seems actually to have accepted the title 'sophist' and to have gloried in it.[61]

If the general outlines of Dio's early relations with philosophers are clear the exact chronology is not. The period when Musonius was his teacher is especially hard to pin down. Musonius followed Rubellius Plautus into exile in Asia Minor in *c.*60 and on Rubellius' death in 62 returned to Rome only to be banished to Gyaros in 65/66. He got back, probably, under Galba.[62] If the Κατὰ

---

59   I owe this suggestion to E. L. Bowie. Dio's acquisition of citizenship is usually dated to Nerva's principate: von Arnim (1898) 125. If Nerva, like Petronius, was a member of Nero's literary coterie it might be conjectured that he was peculiarly well qualified to secure the services of a young Greek from Bithynia.

60   See n. 51 above.

61   This seems to be clearly implied by Synesius' remarks (*Dion* 36b–c): 'For no matter what treatise of theirs [i.e., of Carneades and Eudoxus] you may take, it is philosophic in nature, though handled in sophistic fashion, that is, phrased brilliantly and cleverly and provided with charm in abundance. In this way, too, they were deemed worthy of the title sophist by the persons whom they beguiled in their speeches by the beauty of their language. And yet they themselves would have rejected that title, methinks, and would not have accepted it when offered, philosophy having lately made it a term of reproach, since Plato had rebelled against the name. Dio, on the contrary, not only championed in brilliant fashion each of the two types of career separately, but he is also at variance with his own principles, having published treatises based upon the opposite foundations.' The point is important since it was perfectly possible to engage (in effect) in sophistic activity while at the same time denying that you were doing so, and Synesius here seems to be aware of the fact. See below.

62   For biographical details see Lutz (1947) 14–24.

τῶν φιλοσόφων can be taken as a *terminus ante* the choice lies between 69/71, 62–65/66, or even earlier.[63] The evidence of Philostratus, unreliable though it is chronologically,[64] taken together with *Orr.* 28 and 29, which show Dio in Naples shortly after the death of [[87]] Melancomas, which probably occurred before 70,[65] tips the scales in favour of the early or middle 60s or possibly even slightly earlier, when Dio could have been 20–25.[66] When, therefore, was the Πρὸς Μουσώνιον written? That in turn depends on the correct dating of the *Rhodian Oration* with its complimentary reference to Musonius. On the basis of the historical evidence Momigliano dates the *Rhodian Oration* within the limits 69–c.75,[67] and in the light of Jones' dating of the *Alexandrian Oration*, a closely related speech,[68] a dating of about post-72 seems right.[69] Perhaps therefore the most likely sequence of events is this: pupillage under Musonius early/middle 60s; pragmatic attack upon philosophy 71; elegant recantation (at least with regard to Musonius) in the *Rhodian Oration* post-72. The Πρὸς Μουσώνιον could have been written either in 71, with Dio safeguarding himself further against his former philosophical connections (though in the event Musonius was exempted from the expulsions of that year), or slightly later, but in any case *before* the *Rhodian Oration*.[70]

So far, then, Dio's career shows both a philosophical and sophistic side. The complexity of the relationship between the two is well illustrated by the

63  It is natural to assume that Dio would have got his philosophical education in Rome even though he clearly travelled around a lot even at this stage of his career and even though Musonius did run a sort of school on Gyaros (MacMullen (1966) 65 and 310 n. 22). Dio *could* also presumably have met Musonius in Asia Minor.

64  Philostratus' words at *VA* 5.31 (Apollonius to Vespasian) Εὐφράτης καὶ Δίων πάλαι σοι γνώριμοι ὄντες are suggestive of superior knowledge but they naturally would be, whether based on it or not.

65  Schmid (1903) 849. Von Arnim's dating of *Orr.* 28 and 29 to 74 (1898: 145), when Titus was involved in the *Ludi Augustales* in Naples, is therefore probably too late. Cf. n. 45—for the purposes of chronology it is the identification of Athenodorus, not the historicity of Melancomas, that is important.

66  Cf. Momigliano (1950) 258: 'The philosopher Musonius Rufus was his master, evidently before being exiled by Nero'. For possible ages for a philosophical education see Rohde (1901) II.51, paraphrased by Butler and Owen (1914) ix n. 5.

67  Momigliano (1951) 150–1 = (1975) 971–3. 31.110 gives further support.

68  Lemarchand (1926) 103–4, 107; Jones (1973) 304. Most important is 32.52/31.162–3.

69  The parallel between 32.52 and 31.162–3 certainly suggests *close* proximity of date, with the *Rhodian* almost certainly composed first.

70  This sequence differs from Momigliano (1951) 153 = (1975) 973–4, who offers two possibilities:

(i) If the Κατὰ τῶν φιλοσόφων *either* was written some years after 71 *or* made an emphatic exception of Musonius, the *Rhodian Oration* with its complimentary reference to Musonius would fit satisfactorily into the period 70–5.

*Rhodian* and *Alexandrian Orations*. The fact that both have a serious political purpose—the *Rhodian* making the point that the status of a *civitas libera*, as Rhodes then was, was worth nothing if it could only be maintained by constant use of *adulatio*, the *Alexandrian* appealing to the Alexandrians to give up their practice of rioting at public spectacles—does not of itself qualify them as 'philosophical'.[71] The *Rhodian*, in particular, bristles with sophistry[72] and both speeches put a very high premium on the need to entertain their audiences with a fulsome display of rhetoric. In fact the style of the speeches corresponds rather well to the picture drawn by Philostratus in his *Life of Apollonius* 5.40 (cf. *Ep.* 9): 'Dio's philosophy [[88]] struck Apollonius as being too rhetorical and overmuch adapted to please and flatter, and that is why he addressed to him

---

(ii) If the Κατὰ τῶν φιλοσόφων was written in 71 and if its sentiments were irreconcilable with those of the *Rhodian Oration*, the latter has to be dated to the early years of Domitian.

Momigliano himself prefers a version of (i), giving the sequence: *Rhodian Oration* (c.70), Κατὰ τῶν φιλοσόφων, Πρὸς Μουσώνιον, composed after Musonius had lost Vespasian's favour.

Both are difficult. (i) can be rejected in the light of the practically secure dating of the Κατὰ τῶν φιλοσόφων to 71 and the extreme unlikelihood that it made an exception of Musonius: Synesius' evidence does not remotely suggest this, and he would surely have been surprised by, and have mentioned, the fact if it had been so. Momigliano's version of it is also open to the objection that his proposed dating for the *Rhodian Oration* does not sit happily with a closely-related *Alexandrian Oration* composed post-72. (ii) does not follow and is also hard to square with the probable dating of the *Alexandrian*.

It is not known when Musonius was exiled under Vespasian—exempted from the purge of 71 he must have fallen out of favour later for he was *recalled* under Titus (Hieron. *Chron.* p. 189 Helm). Under the scheme argued for in the text, therefore, the *Rhodian Oration* might (but there is no way of checking) have been delivered *before* Musonius was exiled. But it would not have been impossible for it to have been delivered *after* his exile—the reference to him was very allusive and in context praise of a *Roman* philosopher was compliment enough to the Roman authorities. Besides, on any view the *Alexandrian Oration*, where Dio poses as a philosopher (see n. 74 below), and the *Rhodian*, where he *commends* a philosopher, are not strictly reconcilable with the Κατὰ τῶν φιλοσόφων or (probably) the Πρὸς Μουσώνιον (if it had political application).

The argument is not substantially affected by Lemarchand's theory that the extant *Rhodian Oration* is a conflation of two speeches, delivered at an interval of nearly ten years. In any case this theory rests partly upon a misinterpretation of sections 45–6, which do not *necessarily* imply that Rhodes was not a *civitas libera*, partly upon a mistaken acceptance of von Arnim's contention that Rhodes recovered her freedom under Titus, but perhaps mostly upon a mistaken desire to impose artistic respectability upon a speech which is diffuse, rambling, and self-contradictory—characteristics which regrettably are not always alien to Dio's style.

71   Cf. above, pp. 24–6.
72   Note that Synesius (*Dion* 41c) classes the *Rhodian* with the *Trojan* and the Κώνωνος ἔπαινος, i.e., as a sophistic work.

by way of correction the words: "You should use a pipe and a lyre if you want to tickle men's senses, and not speech". And in many passages of his letters to Dio he censures his use of words to captivate the crowd' (trans. F. C. Conybeare; dramatic date appropriately post-70—appropriately, although perhaps accidentally). The two speeches would be sufficient in themselves to prove that Dio was heavily influenced by his rhetorical education and put it to sophistic use at an early stage of his career: he did not just suddenly affect a sophistic pose out of nowhere in the crisis of 71. It is easy to see how the writer of the *Rhodian* and *Alexandrian Orations* could have composed a Κόμης ἐγκώμιον, Κώνωνος ἐγκώμιον, or Ψιττακοῦ ἔπαινος.[73] Nevertheless, in the *Alexandrian* Dio seems also to be taking a consciously philosophical stance: though he doesn't *call* himself a philosopher in so many words the implication is clear when Dio draws attention to the τριβώνιον he is wearing (32.22):[74] obsession with his humble philosopher's garb was to become a characteristic of the later Dio, as of so many other philosophers.[75] And he launches several broadsides against sophists (32.11, 39, 68). Does this *necessarily* mean that Dio has finally renounced separate sophistic activity while remaining for a time stylistically under the influence of sophistic technique?

---

73   On grounds of style and general approach there would be a case for dating the two Tarsic Orations (*Orr.* 33, 34)—or at any rate the first—and the *Celaenae Oration* (*Or.* 35) to the same general period (a possibility hinted at by Jones (1973) 304: 'a humour that is absent from the demonstrably late speeches'?). Von Arnim's dating of all three speeches ((1898) 460ff.) is essentially schema-based and the attempt of Kienast (1971), building on von Arnim's Trajanic dating, to connect the second *Tarsic Oration* with Trajan's Parthian war is highly speculative, though in other respects the speech can be made to fit a Trajanic context. {Moles subsequently withdrew this suggestion: see below, p. 67 n. 9.}

74   Thus von Arnim (1898) 435–6, rightly; cf. also 32.18–19, where Dio is clearly contrasting himself with philosophers who funk their duty. Jones' remarks on this ((1973) 303 and n. 9) are extremely weak, though of course it is not difficult to pick holes in von Arnim's rigid chronological schema. No reliance can be placed on Dio's statement (13.11) that he only began to be known as a philosopher during his exile (cf. further below). Momigliano (1950) 259 maintains that Dio at this stage of his career took care not to be regarded as a philosopher in the strict sense but after all this was a claim that could be made lightly enough and—the evidence of the *Alexandrian Oration* apart—it is *a priori* unlikely that Dio, a man not noted for his modesty and a pupil of the great Musonius, would have missed the opportunity to make it. This need not have been dangerous for a philosopher who had sold out. Cf. also 33.8, 14–16; 34.2–3, 11; 35.2, 4 in the light of n. 73 above.

75   E.g., 12.1–13 (owl v. peacock-like sophists, 12.9 particularly), 12.85; 33.14, 15; 34.2; 47.25; 66.25; 70.8; 72; cf. 1.50; 7.8, 117; 8.30–1; 9.9; 12.2; 13.10. Naturally the τόπος can be treated satirically: 34.3; 35.3, 11–12; 49.11–12; 66.2; 72.15–16. Photius, followed by the *Suda*, reports that Dio reputedly wore a lion-skin in public, perhaps a mistaken inference from the *figurative* use of a lion-skin to denote political activity (as, e.g., in Plut. *An sen.* 785F–786A).

The question is best approached by an examination of what Dio himself says about sophists, sophistry, and rhetoric throughout the body of his work.

## 3    Dio on Sophists and Rhetoric

Dio represents himself as being on consistently bad terms with sophists[76] and he runs through the whole gamut of traditional philosophical attacks.

Sophists are characterised as conceited,[77] obsessed with love of glory and reputation,[78] quarrelsome and contentious,[79] noisy,[80] ignorant,[81] and surrounded by crowds of pupils as foolish and misguided as their masters.[82] They are attacked for being clever-clever and interested [[89]] not in the truth but in variety and paradox for its own sake,[83] for falsely laying claim to wisdom and omniscience,[84] for taking pay[85] and being ready to say whatever their audiences want,[86] and for the total practical uselessness of their

---

[76] E.g., 11.6, 14; 12.13; 47.16. Reardon (1971) 80 n. 63 cites 18.12 as evidence that Dio moved freely in the world of the sophists. That he did so is clear (see below) but 18.12 is not evidence for it since the men under discussion flourished before Dio's time and cannot in any case automatically be classified as σοφισταί.

[77] E.g., 6.21; 8.33; 12.2–3, 5, 14 (of Hippias, Polus, and Gorgias); 55.7; 77/78.27.

[78] E.g., 4.132; 6.21; 8.33; 12.11; 35.1, 8; cf. 32.10 (attack on philosophers motivated by δόξα), 11 (rarity of man not so motivated).

[79] E.g., 8.9; 11.6, 14.

[80] E.g., 4.33–8; 8.36.

[81] E.g., 4.28, 33–8; 10.32; 32.10; 35.9; 54; 55.7.

[82] E.g., 4.14, 33–8; 8.9; 11.14; 12.5, 10, 13; 35.8–10; 66.12, 77/78.27; cf. 12.15 (*Dio* has no pupils); 33.14 (the philosopher walks alone); 35.10 (pupils to be rejected at all costs). Rejection of pupils whether categorical or partial (to avoid crowds of hangers-on), was a position that could be taken by philosophers of any school anxious to make a clear distinction between themselves and meretricious sophists. Cf., e.g., D.L. 6.21 (Antisthenes), 69 (Diogenes); 7.182 (Chrysippus); 10.120 (Epicurus). Dio's statements about himself in this regard are not trustworthy. He himself had been a 'pupil' and he had pupils during his exile and later.

[83] E.g., 3.27; 4.32; 33.14; 38.10; cf. 58.2.

[84] E.g., 4.33–8; 6.21; 10.32; 33.4; 35.9.

[85] E.g., 4.132 (sophists linked with demagogues as mercenary leaders, cf. 66.12; 77/78.27); 12.10ff., 13; 54; 56.12; 77/78.27; cf. 3.15; 12.13; 32.11; 35.1; 43.6, where Dio emphasises that *he* does not take money; cf. 54.3 (Socrates though poor never accepted anything). Cf. also 7.123 (corrupting effects of μισθός on lawyers and advocates); 22.1 and 5 (attack on ῥήτορες who work only for money); 32.10 (attack on philosophers motivated by κέρδος), 11 (rarity of man not motivated by ἀργύριον).

[86] E.g., 12.13; 33.2ff.; 35.8ff.; cf. 38.1 (flattery of the masses, apparently with reference to sophists).

accomplishments.[87] Nearly all the references Dio makes to sophists are pejorative. The word σοφιστής in itself frequently conveys a sneer: Hippias of Elis is described ἅτε σοφιστής as laughing at Socrates for always saying the same thing and ἅτε σοφιστής means 'that's the sort of frivolous reaction you expect from a sophist'.[88] On the whole, Dio refers to 'the sophists' in general and he makes no distinction between sophists of the fifth and fourth centuries BC and those of his own day, voicing the same criticisms and using the same terminology of both.[89] The dating of many of these references is of course problematic. A large proportion are certainly *post*-exile but some are *exile* and those of the *Alexandrian Oration* arguably *pre*-exile.[90] It is difficult, therefore, to posit any real change in Dio's attitudes over the years.

Dio's general *editorial* position in relation to rhetoric is also impeccably correct. He himself uses it 'only for the encouragement of myself and such others as I meet from time to time' (1.9) and frequently disclaims any competence in the art through assumed modesty or irony as circumstances dictate.[91] But he asserts the usefulness of rhetoric to those in any position of authority, such as

---

87  E.g., 12.43; 32.10, 39; 33.1–5, 23; 34.29; 54.1 and *passim*. Cf. 4.78 (inadequacy of sophists' rhetorical powers in comparison with man truly δεινὸς λέγειν); 7.124 (Dio's contempt for mere γλωσσοτέχναι in general).

  Other attacks on the sophists include 7.98 (apparent dig at sophists' misuse of citations from the poets); 12.17 (scorn for congratulatory embassies); and 32.68 (attack on the affectation of the 'ode').

  Of general relevance to Dio's views on sophists are his attitudes to δόξα (wholly conventional: δόξα *per se* is of no value and pursuit of it for its own sake is to be avoided)—because sophists are so concerned with acquiring it—and to the opinions of οἱ πολλοί (again wholly conventional: οἱ πολλοί are nearly always mistaken about everything)—because it is from them that sophists get their δόξα. Cf. also 12.13: *Dio* has nothing to gain from attracting the interests of οἱ πολλοί; *contra*, 12.84: his speech as suitable τῷ πλήθει as for philosophers (the point being that Dio can beat the sophists at their own game [securing the attention of the masses] without descending to their level).

88  3.27; cf. [37].28; 58.2. σοφός can also be used in the same contemptuous way, e.g., 7.123; 12.10, 36, 37; 18.7; 21.11; 27.6; 31.10; 33.5; 35.2. For the pejorative use of the term σόφισμα cf. 1.57, 61; 4.38.

89  E.g., 4.38 = 8.9 = 11.6; cf. 1.61.

90  *Post*-exile, e.g., 3.27; 4.14, 28, 32, 35, 36, 132; 12.2ff., 5, 10 f., 13, 14, 15; 47.16. Exile, e.g., 6.21; 8.9, 33, 36; 10.32; 55.7. I accept von Arnim's arguments for dating the Diogenes discourses to the exile period, despite the reservations of Momigliano (1950) 261–2. The arguments are circumstantial but persuasive and it is precisely in relation to these discourses that Momigliano's remark (262) 'The tension and the bitterness we should expect in a persecuted man appear only too rarely in Dio's extant compositions' appears most inappropriate. Even if the evidence of the *Alexandrian Oration* is excluded it must be regarded as *a priori* extremely likely that when posing as a philosopher (cf. n. 74 above) the pre-exile Dio indulged in attacks on sophists *despite* his pro-sophistic stance in 71. Cf. further below.

91  E.g., 19.4; 32.39; 33.1–3; 35.1–2; 42; 47.1, 8. *Contra*, e.g., 36.8; 46.7; cf. *Ep.* 5 (attributed to Dio).

rulers or teachers:[92] 'a king might find that even rhetoric was useful to him' (2.18), subject of course to the all-important proviso that it is ῥητορικῆς τῆς ἀληθοῦς (2.24; cf. 22.2).[93] It is the use to which rhetoric is put that is important: the correct rhetorical approach is to control one's discourse like an obedient and tractable horse (4.79)—it is not through the pursuit of eloquence alone but also from the pursuit of wisdom that good men are produced in Prusa (44.10). He appears to have little time for σχολικὰ πλάσματα (18.18–19). The attitude is a familiar one: for Dio, as for Plutarch, rhetoric has its uses but it is not an end in itself, merely the tool by which something that is worth saying may be said well.

All this seems very impressive at first sight but it is important not to accept it in too reverential ⟦90⟧ a spirit. Many of Dio's speeches are occasional and there is always the possibility that he is simply using whatever arguments or pandering to whatever prejudices will best meet the needs of the particular situation.[94] And Dio frequently poses as a philosopher.[95] In that capacity it is virtually unthinkable[96] that he could speak well of σοφισταί or adopt an attitude other than that of traditional philosophical hostility. The context of the attack, therefore, is very important. When Philostratus, himself a sophist and a pupil of several of the sophists whom he eulogises in his *Lives of the Sophists*, wrote

---

92   E.g., 1.10 (Πειθώ); 2.18–24; 4.124; 18 (underpinned by this whole theme); 24.3–4; 57 *passim*, esp. 8.

93   For the distinction between rhetoric and 'true rhetoric' cf. Dio's concept of the διττὴ παιδεία (4.29). Most of his references to ῥήτορες and rhetoric are naturally pejorative, the reality falling so far short of the ideal: e.g., 7.49; 13.22–3; 18.14; 22; 32.19, 39, 68; 34.31; 35.15; 43.6; 54.3; 69.3, 5; 76.4. *Contra*, e.g., 12.5, 15 (ῥητορική one of the nobler arts); 19.4 (indulgent); 32.10 (harmless if without pretensions); 43.6; 56.12; 63.3; 80.1. Cf. further below.

94   In some cases this is immediately verifiable: e.g., the honorific tone of the first and third speeches on Kingship, delivered before Trajan, contrasts sharply with the pessimism and disillusionment of the fourth, perhaps delivered before a Greek audience (so Momigliano (1950) 265 persuasively); the characterisation of the *demos* in his speech to the *boule* at Apameia (41.12) is markedly different from that of his speech to the *ekklesia* at Rhodes (31.6); the sentiments of *Orr.* 75 and 76, sophistic *tours de force*, are flatly contradictory.

95   Sometimes he contents himself with a modest implication of his philosophical character as in the *Alexandrian Oration* (n. 74 above) or in *Or.* 49, in which after a lengthy discussion about the duty of the philosopher to take part in public affairs it finally becomes clear (49.14) that all along he has in fact been talking about himself. Sometimes he is more direct: e.g., 12.9, 38, 48; 13.12; 23.9; 33.8, 14, 16; 34.2–3; 48.14; 50.8; 60.9; etc. *Contra, Or.* 42 (a pleasant piece of humorous self-deprecation, denying all philosophical or rhetorical competence). Naturally the assumption of a philosophical character does not preclude attacks on 'bad' philosophers, e.g., 32.8, 9 (Cynics), 20; 34.3; 45.12; 49.11–13; 70.8–10.

96   One exception is 35.10. The circumstances are slightly special—the whole tone of the speech is humorous and good-natured and it was directed at an audience which was extremely devoted to rhetoric (35.1). Cf. also n. 16 above.

his *Life of Apollonius*, he regularly characterised Apollonius as a φιλόσοφος.[97] The inevitable consequence is that several times in the course of the biography he is flatteringly contrasted with σοφισταί,[98] even though he himself engages in some typical sophistic activities and on occasion Philostratus' real, as opposed to his assumed, attitude to sophists and rhetoric peeps through and they are referred to with approval.[99]

Denial of sophistic activity is also often mere intellectual affectation.[100] In the proem of his *Olympic Oration*, delivered c.389 BC, Lysias speaks contemptuously of the trivialities of the sophists (33.3). Yet at that date he himself was still engaged in sophistic activity;[101] the style of the speech is very similar to his *Epitaphios*,[102] arguably a rhetorical exercise pure and simple, and furthermore its content is not necessarily unsophistic: witness the earlier efforts of Gorgias along the same lines.[103] And it is not even particularly unusual for denial or criticism of sophistic activity to occur within what by any normal criteria is a sophistic work. Thus Plutarch's *De Gloria Atheniensium* contains a regulation swipe at the foolishness of the sophists (351A), while in Aelius Aristides, much of whose work may be classed as sophistic and who frequently adopts a traditional sophistic stance (e.g., 46, p. 404 Dindorf), σοφιστής is nearly always a term of abuse,[104] as of course it very often is in Plutarch.[105] Dio's own *Trojan Oration* is another example of this general phenomenon. Dio sets out to demonstrate that Troy was never captured, and the obvious interpretation of the speech is

---

97  E.g., 1.2, 7, 16; 2.20, 26, 40; etc.
98  E.g., 5.27; 7.16; 8.21.
99  E.g., 6.36; 8.7.3.
100 There are obvious parallels in many of the arts today, e.g., the refusal of many Black American jazz musicians to admit that they in fact play jazz at all or the reluctance of many science fiction writers to accept that title.
101 Cf. above.
102 For a detailed stylistic comparison see Dover (1968) 59–69.
103 Examples of such literary posturing could easily be multiplied, e.g., Apuleius and Themistius, both clearly products of the rhetorical climate of their times, like to be known as 'philosophers' and normally refer to sophists abusively (e.g., Themist. 245d, 260c, 336c, 345c; Apul. *Florid.* 18.18; *De Plat.* 2.9.14; *Asclep.* 14.1). From the Classical period Xenophon's *Cynegeticus*, which opens in the most sophistic of styles and ends with a savage attack upon the sophists, would be another good example were the arguments for disunity in this case not rather more securely based than usual (see Lesky (1966) 621–2).
104 So Mensching (1965) 62 n. 3; Behr (1968) 106 n. 39. Bowersock (1969) 13 n. 3 points to Aristid. 50.100 Keil, an example of a neutral usage which Behr unwisely emends. The fact that Aristides uses the word neutrally here does not invalidate the general principle—cf. Dio.
105 E.g., *Dem.* 9.1; *Brut.* 33.5; *De prof. virt.* 80A; *Quaest. Conv.* 613A, 613C, 615B, 621B, 659F; *Max. cum princ. diss.* 776C, 778B; but the term can be neutral, e.g., *Quaest. Conv.* 618E, 667D; *An seni* 785A, 790F, 791E, though the pejorative use is more common.

that it belongs to a familiar sophistic genre—the rhetorical exercise on a mythical theme, designed to show that with skill even the most unpromising case could be defended. Well-known examples of this type are Gorgias' *Helen* and *Palamedes* and Philostratus' *Heroicus*, while Dio's *Or*. 60, a reconstruction from the myth of Nessus and Deianeira, is clearly a member of the same genre. But because Dio makes a few disparaging remarks about miserable ⟦91⟧ sophists (11.6) and their wretched disciples (11.14)[106] and because he handles the theme with such panache some scholars have felt that there must be some 'message', for example that the Roman people stemmed from a respectable state with strong cultural links with Greece, and one which—contrary to tradition—was never conquered.[107] This view might appear to gain some slight support from passages like 11.137, 138, and 141–2, but it is hard to see them as the *raison d'être* of the discourse: they are directly appropriate to their context and to the general argument as well as being elegantly complimentary to the Trojans, before whom in the first instance Dio was making his speech (11.4). It is much better to recognise the speech for what it self-evidently is: a sophistic παίγνιον of considerable accomplishment. The abuse of the sophists contained in it is just intellectual affectation[108] or—who can say?—in such a light-hearted context it might just be playful irony.

There are, then, sound reasons for caution before taking Dio's *professed* attitude to sophists and rhetoric at face value.

The case can be strengthened by a re-examination of the primary evidence. Contrary to first impressions Dio's apparently blanket condemnation of 'the sophists' (the generalisation is his) *is* qualified on certain occasions. Such a remark as 'The most ignorant of the sophists are boastful and brazen' (55.7; cf. 4.28) leaves open the theoretical possibility that *some* sophists are not and indeed in his speech to the people of Celaenae, the general tone of which is relaxed and friendly, Dio hastens to assure his audience (35.10) that he is not attacking all sophists, 'for there are some who follow that calling honourably and for the good of others'. Nor is the word σοφιστής in itself necessarily pejorative: Diogenes can refer to τοὺς καλουμένους σοφιστάς (4.35) and the point

---

106   Von Arnim (1898) 168–9 maintains that the words μάλιστα δὲ οἶμαι τοὺς κακοδαίμονας σοφιστάς (11.6) are an interpolation but the phraseology is Dionian (cf. n. 89) and the 'unparenthetical' use of οἶμαι unobjectionable (cf. 11.7), while the gratuitous attack on sophists is typical. He also argues that the point of 11.14 is that Dio has no school; but, I think, Dio is attacking sophists, who (it is assumed) will have pupils, not the particular category of sophists who have pupils.
107   Thus, e.g., Palm (1959) 22–3.
108   'A pretence to make his auditors forget that he is a sophist himself, though he is at that very time performing one of the sophists' most characteristic acts', Cohoon I.445.

in context seems to be that the term is inapplicable to the people who use it, not that to be a σοφιστής is automatically a bad thing. Still more striking is Diogenes' reference (10.26) to Croesus having met Solon καὶ ἄλλοις παμπόλλοις σοφισταῖς. The use of the word here is partly conditioned by the mention of Solon, one of the Seven Sages, who were regularly characterised as σοφισταί in the tradition.[109] Even so, it is relevant to Dio's attitudes to sophists since Solon could be regarded as a precursor of the whole sophistic movement.[110] Naturally, therefore, philosophers sometimes baulked at describing the Seven Sages as σοφισταί (cf., e.g., Plut. *De E* 385E), whereas Dio does not seem to. Of course the context shows that σοφιστής is also being used in an etymological sense (cf. φρονιμώτερος ... Κροίσου) but even that is still of significance as it indicates that Dio does not register automatic hostility at the term. *Or.* 71 is built around an elaborate σύγκρισις between Hippias and Odysseus on the one hand and the philosopher on the other. The conclusion naturally is that the philosopher is their superior in versatility, but their claim to excellence in their particular spheres is not denied, and this in a context where virulent abuse of Hippias might be expected.

At unguarded moments, too, Dio does express simple admiration for oratory and rhetoric, as for example in the enthusiastic praise of λόγος, somewhat reminiscent of the famous passage in Gorgias' *Helen* 8–14, in *Or.* 18.2ff., or in such casual remarks as 'I say this not to criticise the art of rhetoric or the good rhetorician' (22.5) or 'I was amazed at their gift of eloquence' (44.6). Similarly it is a point in favour of Callistratus of Borysthenes that he was enthusiastic both about oratory and philosophy, to such an extent that he wished to sail with Dio to receive instruction (36.8), or of Euripides' sagacity that it is ῥητορικωτάτη (52.11). And Dio himself does from ⟦92⟧ time to time admit his own competence in oratory and rhetoric.[111] Perhaps most revealing is an entertaining passage in *Or.* 19 (3ff.), which was written after his exile:

> For even now [= now when I'm old and wiser and ought to know better] I am often affected as they were ['they' being the animals who followed

---

109 E.g., Hdt. 1.29; Isocr. *Antid.* 251; Arist. F 5 Rose; etc.
110 Cf. the much quoted passage from Plutarch's *Themistocles* (2.4): 'Mnesiphilus ... was neither a rhetorician nor one of the so-called physical philosophers, but a cultivator of what was then called wisdom although it was really nothing more than cleverness in politics and practical sagacity. Mnesiphilus received this wisdom and handed it down as though it were the doctrine of a sect, in unbroken tradition from Solon. His successors blended it with forensic arts and shifted its application from public affairs to language and were dubbed sophists'.
111 Cf. n. 91 above.

Orpheus] whenever I attend a sophist's lecture, on account of the uncontrolled craving which possesses me for the spoken word; and so I herd with the sort of creatures I have mentioned, graceful and beautiful to be sure, but yet noisy and eager for a chance to kick up their heels. And this is the way I have nearly always been affected when listening to sophists and orators. Just as beggars on account of their own destitution envy the moderately well-to-do, so I admire and applaud those who are in any way at all proficient in speech, because I myself am lacking in such proficiency.

The tone of course is ironic but not savagely so—this is very different from the attitude of Dio the aggressive philosopher and scourge of the sophists. In fact the rather indulgent flavour of the description brings to mind the mixture of respect, affection, and irony with which Plato represents Socrates as regarding sophists like Prodicus. It is, therefore, still a consciously philosophical stance but when allowance is made for this the fact remains that the passage is secure evidence for Dio having attended sophists' lectures for most of his life.

In the light of all this, then, it would be wrong to exclude utterly the possibility that Dio engaged in separate sophistic activity even after he had finally established himself as a philosopher. Though it is naturally difficult to prove such activity there are a few pointers. The suggestion[112] that the *Trojan Oration* shows such maturity of style and grasp of the techniques of argument that it must be a work of Dio's 'maturity', i.e., of the *post*-exile period,[113] does not impress: Dio could easily have achieved maturity in the sophistic style before his exile. Discourses, however, such as 74 (strongly illustrated from mythology), 77/78 (starting off from interpretation of Hesiod), 55 (on Socrates and Homer), and 60 (obviously of the same genre as the *Trojan Oration*) all share strong sophistic elements and are all plausibly dated by von Arnim to the exile period.[114] The Κόμης ἐγκώμιον poses particularly severe problems for the conversion theory since it seems to be a straightforward sophistic παίγνιον written *after* Dio's return from exile. Possible let-outs for conversion-enthusiasts are to question the authenticity of the work or to dispute the dating, but the case for doing either is weak.[115] In more general terms, Philostratus characterises

---

112   Cf. Palm (1959) 23 n. 1 for references.
113   This view is of course often a corollary of the idea that the speech is 'serious' but need not necessarily be so. A case could be made for an *exile* dating in the light of the rather Cynic-like posturing of 11.37 and 150 and the close parallel between 11.22–3 and 10.23.
114   Von Arnim (1898) 289–90; 254, 288, 299; 290; 299–300. *Orr.* 75 and 76, which are wholly sophistic, are simply undatable.
115   For discussion of the problems posed by the speech see von Arnim (1898) 154–5. Its sophistic character is self-evident and on the face of it the close parallel between its

Dio's use of similes as 'most sophistic' (*vs* 488) though it does not appear to vary much throughout the *corpus*. In AD 95 Callistratus of Borysthenes could apparently expect to receive instruction from Dio in oratory (36.8). Finally, both Favorinus (*vs* 490, 492) and Polemo (*vs* 539), sophists[116] of differing hue, were Dio's pupils, and Polemo actually travelled to Bithynia to hear him. It has generally[117] been assumed that this must refer to philosophical training but the only reason for doing so is the conversion-schema and while the context of *vs* 490 could fit either interpretation, those of *vs* 492 (Δίωνος ... ἀκοῦσαι λέγεται) and 539 (ἠκροᾶσθαι καὶ Δίωνα) rather suggest that the reference is to *rhetorical* training. This inference gains support from the presence in the Dionian *corpus* of two speeches, *Orr.* 37 and 64, which are almost certainly the work of Favorinus and both of which appear to be influenced by Dio himself, *Or.* 37 by the *Rhodian* and 64 by 65. These models are among the most sophistic of Dio's whole production. The case is practically clinched by the opening of *Or.* 47, where Dio as good as admits he has gained a considerable reputation among the public and in all the cities for λόγων ... θαυμαστῶν [καὶ] ἐπισήμων· λέγω δὲ οἷον πρὸς ἡδονήν τινα ἢ κάλλος ἢ σοφίαν εἰργασμένων. Perhaps this goes some way to explaining the virulence of some of Dio's attacks on 'the sophists'—he may have had the nasty suspicion that he was one himself. From some of his remarks it would appear that other people certainly thought ⟦93⟧ so.[118] A similar 'psychological' approach might help in understanding the jaundiced editorial attitudes of Plutarch, who perhaps tried to jump on the sophistic bandwagon but certainly did not succeed,[119] and Aelius Aristides, pupil of Herodes Atticus,

---

opening sentence and the proem of *Or.* 52, arguably a post-exile discourse (Crosby IV.337; *contra*, von Arnim (1898) 162), taken in conjunction with the reference to Dio's ill-health, points to a post-exile date.

116  For Favorinus as sophist cf. Philostratus, *vs* 491, 576, both in contradiction with Philostratus' editorial position.

117  For a typical view see MacMullen (1966) 66.

118  This may be inferred from three facts: (i) Dio was often accused by his enemies of vices which can be regarded as typical of sophists, such as ἀδολεσχία (cf. 1.56; 7.81; 47.8: for ἀδολεσχία as a typically sophistic vice see, e.g., Ar. fr. 490 {= F 506 *PCG* (III.2.267)}; Pl. *Polit.* 299b7), δοξοκοπία (32.24—cf. n. 78 above), pretensions to superior oratorical ability and knowledge above the average (42.2), ἀλαζονεία (43.2—cf. 4.33 and 55.7), and γλωσσαργία (47.16, though the accuser is himself a sophist!). (ii) He is constantly on the defensive about his own μακρολογία (7.127–32; 31.161; 32.33) and ἀδολεσχία (12.16, 38, 43), which he often represents as the proverbial ἀδολεσχία of old age (7.1), wanderers (7.1; 12.16), or victims of misfortune in general (cf. also 52.9). (iii) The note of special pleading in the *De Exilio* (cf. especially 13.11–12, 14–15) suggests that Dio's claim to being a φιλόσοφος had evoked a sceptical response in certain quarters. Cf. further below.

119  See the suggestive comments of Russell (1973) 7 and (1970) 849 (less persuasively dependent on the rhetoric/*juvenilia* equation).

whose chances of a great public career were cut short at an early age by a succession of illnesses. It might also explain why without stretching the evidence much Philostratus was able, perhaps even obliged, to include 'philosophers' like Dio and Favorinus in his *Lives of the Sophists* and refer to them himself as 'sophists' (*VS* 487, 491) in contradiction of his editorial categorisation.

If it is certain then that Dio's *pre*-exile career had both a sophistic and philosophical side and very likely indeed that his *post*-exile career was similarly ambiguous, is it possible to trace any 'change' or 'development' in Dio's career at all?

## 4 Change and Development in Dio's Career

Real change either in political activity or political attitude is hard to substantiate. The *Rhodian* and *Alexandrian Orations* of the early 70s clearly foreshadow the later philosopho-political symbouleutics, with the typical figure of the external adviser intervening from a higher plane. Their central concern—the need for a right relationship with the Roman government—is characteristic of the later Dio. The sentiments of *Or.* 46, dating from perhaps as early as 75,[120] are also extremely familiar in post-exile works: the strength of a πόλις consists not in violent internal political protest but in wisdom and justice (46.2) and it is folly to antagonise the Roman proconsuls (46.14). In the 70s Dio seems also to have acted in the role of philosophical σύμβουλος to Flavius Sabinus[121] and the unknown (probably Greek) recipient of *Or.* 18.[122] Political and perhaps also

---

120  Von Arnim (1898) 205–7 dates this speech only shortly before the exile but two factors favour an earlier dating: (i) if Dio's son became an ἄρχων in c.102, as he almost certainly did (48.17; 50.5–6, 10), the statement καὶ τὸ παιδίον λαβόντα (46.13) fits a dating of c.75 or earlier better than one of c.80; (ii) if Dio did engage in important political activity in the 70s or earlier, as is virtually proven, his failure to claim respect because of his own merits suggests a dating a good bit earlier than von Arnim's.

121  On the identification see n. 46 above. That Dio acted as philosophical σύμβουλος to Flavius Sabinus cannot be proved but is extremely likely. The wording ὡς δὴ τἀνδρὶ φίλον ὄντι καὶ σύμβουλον (13.1) reproduces the terms of the charge brought against him and σύμβουλος is of course a key word for such a role. Dio's friendship with Musonius, his association with Vespasian, and Musonius' friendship with Titus are also relevant. Cf. also n. 122 below.

122  The identity and nationality of the recipient and the question whether he is a real or imaginary character have been much discussed, but von Arnim (1898) 139–40 is right to point to 18.16ff. as being strongly suggestive that Dio has in mind a local Greek official occupying a high rank in some large Greek city of Asia Minor. Palm's objections to this view ((1959) 21–2) are pedestrian.

The dating of the speech is necessarily imprecise. The fact that Dio does not recommend the reading of any philosophical works to this would-be orator proves nothing

philosophical links with Vespasian and Titus are assured and must date from at least the late 60s. Further evidence for Dio's early association with the imperial house is provided by his claim (7.66) to have known 'the houses and tables of satraps and kings', which must refer to the period before his exile. Hence the case for a sharp change of political attitude can only be advanced [[94]] in the context of the exile period and largely depends on the question to what extent it can be regarded as a time of Cynical iconoclasm.

Dio must have known the celebrated Cynic Demetrius in Rome through his connections with Musonius[123] and his early work suggests that he was not out of sympathy with Cynic tenets. In the *Rhodian Oration*, for example (31.16), Dio is already using Heracles in accepted Cynic style as the pattern of one who pursues virtue for its own sake and in the *Alexandrian*, which contains an attack on the irresponsibility of certain Cynics (32.9), he is careful to emphasise that their doctrines 'contain practically nothing spurious or ignoble'. And if the second *Tarsic Oration* can be accepted as another product of the 70s,[124] Dio seems already before his exile to have been prepared to rank himself as a Cynic: he is ready to admit that when people are dressed as he is they are popularly called Cynics and he does not appear to disclaim the title (34.2). As against this the evidence of the Κατὰ τῶν φιλοσόφων is unimportant, for the anti-Cynicism expressed in it was only part of a general attack on philosophy which was a pose of expediency adopted at a moment of crisis.

But his Cynicism becomes much more pronounced during the exile period (and later) and is heavily implicit throughout the Diogenes discourses. Von Arnim saw this Cynicism as rebellious and anti-monarchic, drawing attention to the fact that Dio apparently dropped the use of the word μόναρχος after his return from exile, when he was clearly reconciled to the whole concept of kingship.[125] But it is a question how much this alleged hostility to monarchy as such is simply hostility to Domitian. A remark like 'the desires and hopes of

---

about what stage of his career he himself was at—the reading of philosophy would hardly be relevant to Dio's purpose here. On the other hand the enthusiastic praise of λόγος at 18.2–3 might be held to be inappropriate to Dio's role as a φιλόσοφος but need not necessarily be so (cf. the casual approval of φιλοσοφία at 18.7). The fact that Dio seems to represent himself as considerably younger than his addressee, who is at the height of his powers, is, however, a fairly strong argument for a pre-exile date. Dio's role in *Or*. 18 cannot be dismissed as purely literary—it is literary with a political purpose (18.2, etc.).

123  Demetrius was mentioned in Favorinus' writings (*VA* 4.25) and was the friend of Thrasea Paetus (*Ann.* 16.34).
124  See n. 73 above.
125  Von Arnim (1898) 267. In what follows I accept von Arnim's datings for the *Orations* mentioned so that they can at least be used as an *argumentum ad hominem*. But they are all plausible enough—cf. n. 90 above.

monarchs quite often reach a fulfilment that is grievous and terrible' (20.24) could be agreed to by any Stoic enthusiast for kingship. Nor is it inconsistent with the attitudes of the later Dio, whose *Kingship Orations* show him very alive to the fact that the justice or injustice of one-man rule depends very largely on the character of the particular ruler.[126] Such sarcastic quips as 'Do you not know how great the might of the giver is? For example, wherever and whenever it is necessary to appoint an emperor, they choose the wealthiest man' (21.8) are counter-balanced by the enthusiasm for kingship obvious in *Or.* 36 (32), which records a discussion which took place in Borysthenes during his exile. And, despite von Arnim, it is impossible to restrict Dio's interest in the philosophy of kingship to the post-exile period. In *Or.* 56, dated by von Arnim to the exile, the central proposition—a favourite of kingship literature—is that the ruler ought to make use of σύμβουλοι, and in 25 the analogy between δαίμονες and rulers is the main theme: the topic 'the wise man alone is happy', stated at the beginning of the discourse, is only a lead-in and Dio's promise to explain it is never kept.[127] And of course the Trajanic *Kingship Orations* are shot through with Cynic doctrine.[128]

It is likewise difficult to trace any real progression in Dio's Stoicism. As he was a pupil of Musonius the slight Stoic flavour of parts of the *Rhodian Oration*[129] comes as no surprise, while Stoic doctrine is prominent in some of the exile discourses: 14 and 15, the wise man alone is free; 16, there being so many hurtful things in life we should fortify our spirits to be insensible to them; 23 and 25, the wise man alone is happy. Dio represents himself explicitly as a Stoic during his exile in *Or.* 36 (30 τῶν ἡμετέρων in an obviously Stoic context). His subsequent Stoicism hardly requires documentation.[130]

It is true that the writings of the exile period exude a general air of pessimism and iconoclasm. The Diogenes discourses show a morbid preoccupation with exile and tyranny and a strong element of autobiographical allegory, especially in *Orr.* 6, 8, 9, and 10, is not to be denied.[131] *Or.* 73 is almost entirely devoted to an exposition of the dangers of taking up office or assuming ⟦95⟧ responsibility, and the net implication seems to be that Dio's anonymous

---

126  E.g., 3.10; 62.3 and 7.
127  So, rightly, Cohoon II.323.
128  Toynbee (1944) 56 n. 9 denies this but quite wrongly. Dudley (1937) 154–6 is still adequate. Cf. Höistad (1948) 150ff.
129  31.15, 37, 58, 75.
130  Von Arnim (1898) 476ff., Brunt (1973) (largely restricted to the *Euboicus*). Stoic doctrine is prominent in, e.g., the *Euboicus*, the *Olympic* and *Kingship Orations*, the *Borysthenitic Oration*, and *Or.* 40.35–41.
131  Von Arnim (1898) 260ff.

acquaintance should remain true to philosophy, which in this instance apparently means opting out of political life—a total reversal of Dio's usual view.[132] *Or.* 74 is equally bitter and argues the case that it is well-nigh impossible to trust anyone. It is tempting to suppose that Dio is here presenting the fruits of his own bitter experience. The iconoclastic approach is illustrated by Diogenes' ridicule of athletes (9.14ff.), his scorn for such sacred cows as the prizes at the Greek games (8.15, cf. 9.10–11), and his contemptuous rejection of the conventional Hellenic view of Oedipus (10.30). And there are many appropriately Cynic attacks on materialism, most of which Dio himself later ignored on his return to prosperity.[133] Dio's spiritual journey during and after his exile is apparently reflected in the enigmatic dialogue, the *Charidemus*, where Charidemus, despite Dio's own presence in the scene, seems to be used as a mouth-piece for Dio's own opinions (30.20, 23, and 25 all look autobiographical).[134] If this is correct then it would appear that during his exile Dio believed that the world was a prison in which men were punished by the gods, who hated them because of the blood of the Titans (30.10–24), afterwards that the gods were merely indifferent (30.25–7), and finally that the world was a beautiful place (30.28–45). Naturally not too much should be read into all this—liberal allowance must be made for mythological embellishment and allegorical intent. Nevertheless it is evidence of a kind, at any rate for the sort of impression Dio intended to create of the philosophical heart-searching he had been through.

One of the difficulties of assessing the reliability of all this evidence is that it is all provided by Dio himself. At first sight, Philostratus (*VS* 488) seems to provide an independent check on his colourful description of the manner in which Dio spent his exile: 'occupying himself in various ways in various lands ... he planted and dug, drew water for baths and gardens, and performed many such

---

132  E.g., 20.2; 22 *passim*; 26.8; 32.8, 20; 34.34; 40.12; 47.2–3, 49.3; and *passim*.

133  E.g., *Or.* 10 argues that not only is it better to be without a slave or any kind of property if you do not know how to use it, but it is better still to have no property at all. Not surprisingly, when Dio returned from exile he clearly felt exactly the same way about the loss of his slaves as Diogenes' unfortunate victim in *Or.* 10 (45.10).

134  The authenticity of this dialogue has been disputed by Nilsson (1961) 401 n. 2, but its general structural resemblance to the *Phaedo*, Dio's favourite book of philosophy (Philostr. *VS* 488), the precise correspondences between Charidemus' speech and other of Dio's discourses (Wilhelm (1918) 364–5), and its links in style and conception with the *Melancomas Orations* still argue strongly in its favour. The question whether Charidemus is a real or imaginary person is irrelevant in this context.

For the interpretation of the dialogue accepted in the text see the useful brief discussion by Cohoon II.395–8. If it is right, then even if the dialogue is not by Dio it is still of some importance as preserving a view of Dio's development substantially in agreement with the evidence of Dio himself. {Fuller treatment of the *Charidemus* below, Ch. 8.}

menial tasks for a living ...' But even this could well go back to Dio in the final analysis.[135] It is clear that the exile was not unmitigated hardship: Dio became a figure of considerable renown among his friends and fellow-citizens (19.1) and evidently remained in communication with Prusa (ibid.); he was able to indulge on occasion in philosophical lectures before large audiences,[136] and he had sufficient leisure and sufficient enthusiasm to be able to plan his *History of the Getae* while in residence in Borysthenes.[137] On the other hand he could not have made so much of his wanderings,[138] his long hair,[139] his poor attire,[140] and the ruination of his health brought about by his exile,[141] if his audience could not verify these things for ⟦96⟧ themselves.[142] Dio did not need to occupy his exile as he did: banished from Rome and Italy and Bithynia he did not lose his property nor was he confined to any one place, and he could have sold his possessions and moved elsewhere in relative comfort.[143] That he did not do so must be explained at least partly in terms of a deliberate decision to enlarge his experience of life at a humble level, like the typical Cynic sage or indeed like George Orwell (*Down and Out in Paris and London*).[144] Yet he had already—in

---

135 Brunt (1973) 10 regards it as independent but suspect. Suspect it probably is, but a man who could describe himself as a 'mere wanderer and self-taught philosopher, who find what happiness I can in toil and labour' (1.9) might surely have provided such details of his way of life in his exile. Those of a suspicious turn of mind may recall that Cleanthes is said to have made his living by watering gardens and digging earth (D.L. 7.168, 169, 171). Another Dionian *persona*? Cf. below. For Dio's knowledge of Cleanthes' personal life as preserved in the tradition cf. 33.53–4.
136 36.17; cf. 12.1, which presumably can be back-dated to the exile period: 13.12.
137 Cf. Von Arnim (1898) 303–4. For the decision to make the actual journey Delphic influence may have been responsible.
138 E.g., 1.9, 50, 55, 56; 7.1, 3, 9, 81; 12.16; 13.10–11; 19.1 (self-deprecatory irony); 45.2, 12; cf. 8.29; 30.20 and perhaps 53.9.
139 E.g., 12.15; 33.14; 35.2; 36.17; 47.25; 72.2; 77/78.37; Κόμης ἐγκώμιον, *passim*; *contra*, 2.12; 7.4 (peculiarity of Euboean hair-style in Homer). Cf. his enthusiasm for beards (7.4) and long hair (36.17) and his dislike of elaborate hairdos (7.117). Naturally, long hair is not an instant guarantee of philosophical probity (35.2–3; 72.15–16).
140 See n. 75 above.
141 E.g., 7.8; 12.12, 15, 19, 85; 19.1; 39.7; 40.2; 45.1–2; 47.23; 48.8; cf. 52.1, 3, the Κόμης ἐγκώμιον, and perhaps 52.6.
142 Equally Dio could hardly have produced such a work as *Or.* 10 if he himself had not manifestly been without property when he wrote it. Of course the credibility gap between philosophical theory and practice is depressingly familiar (for an exhaustive treatment of the problem see Griffin (1976)) but in this case the argument for consistency is a strong one in the light both of the Diogenes/Dio allegory and of Dio's verifiable physical state.
143 Von Arnim (1898) 223ff. Cf. 44.6. Of course Dio would have incurred *some* financial loss, e.g., of revenue from his estates.
144 I owe this parallel to Phillips (1957) 109 n. 24.

all probability—at least on some occasions donned the poor clothing and assumed the appearance of the philosopher. Exile, then, *perhaps* led to a greater degree of seriousness both in his writings and his style of life, reflected in the loftier tone of the later political speeches (the *Rhodian* and *Alexandrian Orations* are quite humorous in parts), in an increased emphasis on his philosophical character, and *perhaps* in a developing sense of divine mission,[145] though this is already heralded in the *Alexandrian Oration* (32.12) and is not in any case to be accepted uncritically.[146] Yet all this only adds up to a change of emphasis, by no means a radical change of direction, and it is impossible to discern any substantial difference between Dio's pre- and post-exile careers.

## 5  The *De Exilio* and Dio's Use of *Personae*

To return to Synesius. Where did he get his conversion theory from? First, he had read overtly sophistic works of Dio, two of which, the Κατὰ τῶν φιλοσόφων and Πρὸς Μουσώνιον, were definitely products of Dio's youth and could be recognised by Synesius as such. Secondly, he had Dio's own authority: 'Dio, after having been a headstrong sophist, ended by becoming a philosopher; yet this was the result of chance rather than of set purpose as he himself has narrated' (*Dion* 36b).[147] The reference is to the *De Exilio* (13.11), where Dio gives a wholly disingenuous account of his philosophical career. Dio implies that during his exile he was compelled to think about good and evil and about the duties of man and the things that were likely to profit him, simply because people started to call him 'philosopher' and ask him such questions. He does not say outright that he thought about them 'for the first time', but that is the clear implication, and what is quite obvious is that he is not admitting to his earlier philosophical training under Musonius, when he must certainly have thought about good and evil and the duties of man, and saying nothing of his earlier career as philosophical σύμβουλος. Similar implications can be detected in the first

---

145  1.55 (in an obviously fictitious context); 12.5–8; 32.12–13, 21; 34.4–5; 45.1; cf. 36.25; 37.27 (Favorinus); 38.51; 45.1.

146  See further below.

147  One might reasonably infer from the facts that *Or.* 46 has the title Πρὸ τοῦ φιλοσοφεῖν and that Synesius (*Dion* 38a) found that the speeches in which the exile was referred to had already by this time been entitled μετὰ τὴν φυγήν by 'certain persons' that research on the chronology of Dio's speeches (cf. also 39a) and perhaps therefore investigation of the whole question of the development of Dio's career predates the fourth century. But Synesius is the first to articulate the conversion theory (so far as we know) and clearly has thought the matter out for himself, whether influenced by previous research or not.

*Kingship Oration*, where Dio describes himself as a 'wanderer and self-taught philosopher' (1.9), in the *Olympic Oration*, where he is a 'layman fond of talking' (12.16), and in the *Charidemus*, with its reference to a 'wandering philosopher' (30.20) and to 'a certain morose man who had suffered a great deal in his life and only late had gained true education' (30.25). In rather similar style Dio suppresses all mention of his career as political σύμβουλος *before* his exile in *Or.* 44 (6). Dio's statement that he did not seek or even want the title φιλόσοφος rings quite false both in the light of his apprenticeship with Musonius and his implied claim in the *Alexandrian* and perhaps other pre-exile orations. What then is the explanation of this whole elaborate charade?

Dio, like most Greeks of his time, was excessively fond of interpreting his own experience in the light of the experience of the great men of old. And he exploits the possibilities of this widespread tendency to a quite remarkable degree. He operates several distinct *personae*, the most [[97]] striking being those of 'the wanderer', whether the wandering philosopher, a type which goes back at least as far as Solon (Hdt. 1.29)—one thinks also of Xenophanes—or the long-suffering Odysseus, Socrates, and Diogenes. It is worth exploring briefly the manner in which he makes use of these illustrious exemplars.[148]

Dio's general emphasis on himself as 'a wanderer' does not require detailed discussion. He clearly did 'wander'[149] but on the other hand the pathetic associations of such a characterisation will not always have been very apposite even in the exile period, still less after his recall. And the *persona* of the wandering philosopher conveniently serves to distract attention from Dio the successful sophist. The more particular manifestation of the wanderer-*persona*, that of Odysseus, is more interesting and rather more subtly presented. Dio makes

---

148 Another possible *persona* is that of Cleanthes (see n. 135 above). And the loaded description of Heracles (8.29–35) clearly has some application to Dio (von Arnim (1898) 265). Dio's manipulation of *personae*, which often involves a certain duplicity, should be carefully distinguished from his skill at creating fictitious situations for his acquisition of knowledge. Examples include his meeting with the Arcadian prophetess (1.52ff., πλασάμενός τι μεταξὺ τῶν λόγων says Arethas; cf. Crosby v.410); his adventures in Euboea (*Or.* 7), based on themes drawn from New Comedy (Highet (1973)) or the novel (Jouan (1977)); his interview with the aged Egyptian priest (11.37ff.); the alleged dying words of Charidemus (30.8ff.)—clearly modelled on the last words of Socrates in the *Phaedo*; the alleged authority of the Phrygian kinsman of Aesop for the story of Orpheus in the *Alexandrian Oration* (32.63–6); the alleged authority of the Magi for the myth of the *Borysthenitic Oration* (36.39–40). No educated Greek or Roman reader would have taken any of these very seriously, nor would Dio have intended them to do so. Nevertheless, skill at creating fictitious dramatic settings is an analogous skill to the adroit manipulation of dramatic *personae* and requires the same sort of imagination.

149 For details see von Arnim (1898) 223–308.

several *direct* comparisons between himself and Odysseus. He reflects that at the beginning of his exile he was dismayed by the example of Odysseus, who found his separation from his native land so hard to bear (13.4). He decides to continue his wanderings in obedience to the command of the Delphic Oracle because Odysseus had resumed his wanderings too (13.10). He finds a parallel between his position when he addresses the decadent Tarsians in philosophical (i.e., humble) attire and Odysseus' when he entered the town of the debauched in the guise of a slave (33.15). He compares the financial losses he incurred because of his exile with those suffered by the absent Odysseus (45.11). The most revealing example of Dio's theatrical prowess in the *explicit* Odysseus-*persona* is preserved by Philostratus (*vs* 488, presumably from Dio himself). Its full flavour can only be appreciated by direct quotation:

> He often visited the military camps in the rags he was wont to wear, and after the assassination of Domitian, when he saw that the troops were beginning to mutiny, he could not contain himself at the sight of the disorder that had broken out, but stripped off his rags, leaped on to a high altar, and began his harangue with the verse: 'Then Odysseus of many counsels stripped himself of his rags.' [*Od.* 22.1]

There are also cases where an Odysseus parallel, while not explicit, is nevertheless very strongly implied. Dio portrays himself (1.50) as a vagabond beggar 'demanding crusts, not cauldrons fine nor swords' (*Od.* 17.222, Melanthius to Odysseus). He compares Diogenes, poor and reviled by many of his contemporaries, to Odysseus, reviled by the suitors: Diogenes in the guise of a beggar was really like a king (9.9). Because of the Diogenes/Dio allegorical equation the comparison with Odysseus applies to Dio as well as Diogenes. And there are occasions where the implication is considerably more oblique. The opening of the *Euboicus* (7.2–3), with Dio shipwrecked and left alone by his crew, has an Odyssean quality about it. The opening of *Or.* 19 has too:[150] Dio describes how his friends and fellow-citizens wanted to meet him to hear his story, believing that he had a certain advantage over most men because of his wanderings and the reversal of his fortune and the bodily hardships which he was supposed to have experienced. The tone here is humorous but the point is made and the passage fits well enough into the general scheme. Finally, Dio's description of his own physical decrepitude, his hardships, and the ruinous state of his domestic affairs because of his long absence from home (40.2) is again Odyssean in flavour (cf. 45.11).

---

150  Noted by Cohoon II.236 n. 1.

The Diogenes *persona* is mostly confined to the Diogenes exile discourses except in so far as ⟦98⟧ poor philosophical garb may be regarded as characteristically, though not exclusively, Cynic, and the *De Exilio* and Dio's sense of divine mission can be analysed in Diogenic as well as Socratic terms.[151] Both are discussed below. The important point to make here is that the Diogenes-*persona*, like that of the wanderer (philosophical or Odyssean), is at best a half-truth.

Before discussing the Socratic *persona*, it is important to emphasise what has always been recognised: the tremendous importance of Socrates as an exemplar for the philosophers of the first century and later. Cato Uticensis, a cult figure for later Stoics, had clearly had Socrates' death in mind on the night of his suicide[152] and Thrasea Paetus[153] and Seneca[154] both followed his lead by modelling their own death scenes on Socrates'. Socrates was by far the most important philosopher for Epictetus,[155] and Philostratus represents Apollonius in strongly Socratic terms.[156] Musonius was linked with Socrates by Origen and Julian.[157] Apuleius bases his *Apology* upon Socrates'.[158]

Dio naturally makes no secret of his indebtedness to Socrates. In the third *Kingship Oration* he draws a parallel of situation between Socrates in relation to the Persian king and himself in relation to Trajan (3.1–2), notes that he always says the same things, as Socrates did, and reproduces Socrates' teaching on kingship in dialogue form (3.30–41). In the *De Exilio* he makes it clear that he based his teaching on Socrates' and again gives a résumé of Socrates' views on the need for right education (13.14–37). In the *Olympic Oration* he remarks that his own claim to know nothing was also used as a defence by Socrates (12.13–14). He compares the political difficulties he himself is experiencing in Prusa to Socrates' in Athens (43.8–12); one of his pupils comments that he is an admirer of Socrates (55.1), another that Dio's treatment of the myth of Nessus and Deianeira is in line with Socratic technique (60.10). But Dio's defensive assertion in the *De Exilio* (13.15), 'By no means ... did I pretend that the appeal was mine but gave the credit where it was due', suggests that he had been accused of playing a Socratic role without acknowledging that he was doing so, and the truth of this accusation is clear enough from his extant writings. His

---

151  Cf. also 4.1–3: there is a similarity of situation between Dio in relation to his audience (a Greek one? See n. 94 above) and Diogenes in relation to *his* (i.e., Alexander).
152  Plut. *Cat. Min.* 67–70.
153  Tac. *Ann.* 16.34–5; Wirszubski (1950) 142; Questa (1963) 248–9.
154  Tac. *Ann.* 15.62–4; Questa (1963) 248–9, Griffin (1976) 369–72.
155  MacMullen (1966) 312 n. 29.
156  Ibid.
157  Lutz (1947) 3.
158  See Tatum (1977).

question-and-answer method is thoroughly Socratic (*Or.* 70 is a good example). The claim to keep conveying the same message can be made without reference to Socrates (e.g., 17.2, 5), as can the claim to know nothing (e.g., 12.5, 9, 15). His modesty or irony about his powers of oratory and rhetoric[159] is also fundamentally Socratic. And his claims to a sense of divine mission[160] will hardly stand up to scrutiny. Behind, for example, the lofty sentiment 'In my own case, for instance, I feel that I have chosen that role not of my own volition, but by the will of some δαιμόνιον' (32.12) lurks the most famous δαιμόνιον of them all.[161]

Dio's operation of *personae* therefore is remarkably detailed and sustained. The *explicit* comparisons between himself and his eminent forerunners are used to suggest that he is in the great tradition and to some extent can be mentioned in the same breath as the great Greeks of the past.[162] The *implicit* or *suppressed* comparisons help to invest Dio with something of the aura of these men while at the same time avoiding the admission that he himself is not a great original. It is true that he can use a *persona* humorously (19.1) or disclaim any direct comparison between himself and the men of old (47.6) but these are exceptional examples, made in the one case because there are occasions when Dio can relax sufficiently to stop projecting an image,[163] in the other because the constant use of *exempla* from the past must sometimes have irritated contemporary Greeks as much as it does the modern reader.[164]

⟦99⟧ The way is now cleared for a return to the *De Exilio*, which responds extremely well to a 'Socrates-analysis'.[165] It cannot of course be doubted that Dio did go to Delphi to consult the oracle for whatever motives,[166] but in

---

159   References in n. 91 above.
160   References in n. 145 above.
161   This seems to have been appreciated by Crosby III.182 n. 2. It is also perhaps relevant that Diogenes too seems to have had a δαιμόνιον according to Julian 7.212d. This need not be dismissed as a late tradition since the process of Socratising Diogenes was evidently well established by the first century. Cf. n. 54 above.
162   Cf. Arethas' shrewd observations on this point (most accessible in Crosby V.410–15).
163   Cf. his attitude to sophists and rhetoric, discussed above.
164   That Dio was aware of this is also clear from 43.3; 50.2; cf. 18.12.
165   Cohoon II.96 n. 1 seems to hint at this. The point has certainly not escaped C. P. Jones (private letter to me, Feb. 1976) but had occurred to me independently. Von Arnim (1898) 227–8 notes the Socratic colouring but makes nothing of it. The comments of Hirzel (1895) I.88 are still very perceptive.
166   Parke–Wormell (1956) 1.409 stress the unusualness of the step of consulting the oracle and accept Dio's own explanation that he was influenced by the ancient custom of the Greeks when men had consulted Apollo about childlessness or famine. Dio himself also suggests a precise Croesus parallel (13.6–8). Momigliano (1950) 261 hints at the influence of Xenophon's example. In the light of Dio's previous philosophical career and the strong

several important respects Dio's account of his experiences bears suspicious resemblances to the account Socrates gives of himself in the *Apology*.[167]

In both works the Delphic oracle plays a central role. The parallel is not factually exact in all details: it is Chaerephon not Socrates who consults the oracle and the mere fact that he does so and receives so favourable a response pre-supposes that Socrates already had a considerable reputation for wisdom, whereas Dio does it himself at a time when (by his own account) he had had no previous philosophical yearnings, though he had already embarked upon his wanderings (13.10). Yet the resemblances are striking. Both men stress the reliability of the evidence of the oracle (13.9/*Apol.* 20e), the strangeness of the oracular response, the perplexity of its recipient, and the impossibility that the god could be lying (13.9–10/*Apol.* 20e). The oracle given to Dio impels him to continue his wanderings (13.10ff.); that given to Chaerephon gives rise to the 'wanderings' of Socrates in pursuit of wiser men than himself (*Apol.* 21cff., esp. 22b). In more general terms, Dio's reflections on the foolishness of mankind in general (13.13) are reminiscent of Socrates' discovery that all the allegedly wise people he visits are fools in reality. And the picture Dio paints of greatness thrust upon him (13.11) recalls the manner in which a reputation for wisdom is conferred upon an essentially passive Socrates.

The Diogenes *persona* is also relevant, for Diogenes too owed his 'conversion' to philosophy to the Delphic oracle and its famous exhortation to him to 'falsify the currency'.[168] So did Zeno.[169] The links between Delphi and the Seven Sages and such sage-like figures as Lycurgus, Aesop, and Croesus are well known, if in many cases of rather dubious historicity, and the association of philosophers with the Delphic oracle is heavily emphasised in the tradition.[170] Dio's account of his conversion must be seen against this general background, but the prototypes of Diogenes, Zeno, and above all Socrates are directly relevant. Diogenes and Zeno were both Stoic sages and the Stoics (Panaetius was something of an exception) accepted the truth of oracles. Dio also could be

---

association between the Delphic oracle and great philosophers of the past, philosophical influence seems most likely.

167 *Prima facie* a further argument for scepticism over the reliability of Dio's evidence in the *De Exilio* might be that the theme, though clearly of great relevance in a period of philosophical persecution, had already become something of a literary genre by Dio's day. But while the *De Exilio* does employ some standard τόποι (e.g., 13.2, 3, 5, 8) it clearly does not conform to the general pattern, and the real arguments for scepticism are *sui generis*.

168 D.L. 6.20–1, 49 esp.; Julian 6.188a–b; cf. 7.208d, 211b–d, 238b–d; Parke–Wormell (1956) I.406–7; II. no. 180. Dio's familiarity with this tradition, likely on *a priori* grounds, is supported by 31.24.

169 D.L. 7.2; Parke–Wormell (1956) I.406–7; II. no. 421.

170 Parke–Wormell (1956) I.400ff. Cf. Galen's 'conversion' to medicine, ibid. I.409; II. no. 463.

classed as a Stoic, among other things. The accounts of Diogenes' and Zeno's conversions to philosophy were almost certainly modelled upon Socrates' and Dio puts himself in the great tradition by representing his own visit to the Delphic oracle and its repercussions in highly Socratic terms. This process necessarily involved a certain falsification of the facts but Dio was not the man to worry about that.

That Dio in the *De Exilio* is in fact assuming a composite Socrates/Diogenes/Zeno *persona* may be regarded as proven. The question arises, however, as to what reaction he would expect to evoke from his audience: were they supposed to recognise the implicit comparison between Dio and his illustrious predecessors while at the same time accepting the essential truth of the factual core of the conversion story? That they were meant to accept the truth of the story is certain and explains the defensive or apologetic tone of much of the speech. That they were meant to recognise the *persona* is less likely. Dio is not using the *persona* to enrich by illustrious association facts which were in themselves largely incontrovertible: he is using it to misrepresent the circumstances in which he became interested in philosophy. And his characterisation of himself [[100]] elsewhere as a 'wanderer', a 'wandering philosopher', and 'self-taught philosopher' depends for its validity on the sort of misleading reconstruction of his life that he gives in the *De Exilio*. It is significant that it is when Dio has *completed* his account of his conversion that he defends himself (implicitly) against the charge of plagiarising Socrates' teaching. The effect of this is to distract attention from the fact that he has actually been plagiarising Socrates' biography earlier in the speech. This is of course a well-known rhetorical technique, which can be paralleled several times in Dio's other works.[171] It seems clear enough that Dio is going as far as he reasonably can in not revealing the source of the story of his conversion.

## Conclusion

Synesius, then, was simply misled by Dio, who was not called 'Golden-mouthed' for nothing.[172] As to Dio's motives in laboriously constructing a timely 'con-

---

171  E.g., 11.6 and 14 (abuse of sophists in a sophistic speech), 145 (use of a Thucydidean motif followed by a reference to Thucydides in 146); 12.5, 9, 15 (use of a Socratic claim with a casual reference to the fact that Socrates did the same thing in 12.14).

172  It is true, however, that Synesius has gone a little further than Dio, by suggesting that the 'conversion' was *sudden* (*Dion* 37c, rather at odds with 36a). This is perhaps to be explained by the fact that Synesius naturally regards Dio as a Stoic (37d) and Stoics necessarily (in theory) viewed conversion as an *instantaneous* process.

version' to philosophy two possibilities, not mutually exclusive, suggest themselves:

(i) Dio's behaviour in the early part of his career, especially in 71, required a good bit of explaining and the best way to solve the problem was—as far as possible—to blot out his murky past.
(ii) The accident of his exile and the peripatetic life which he then chose to lead provided Dio with a splendid opportunity for sustained self-dramatisation as the wanderer, the self-taught philosopher, who owed his conversion to the inspiration of the Delphic oracle.

In any event the 'conversion' of Dio Chrysostom is a fraud.

It remains to spell out the consequences of this analysis of Dio's career, if it is accepted. On a general level it may be thought to shed some light on the methodological problems of assessing conversion-analyses; on the complex question of the real attitudes of self-styled philosophers to their traditional rivals, the sophists; and on the extreme difficulty of precise interpretation of the practice of Greek authors of using *exempla* or *personae* drawn from the remote past, a difficulty that is central to the understanding of practically all ancient literature. More specifically, it may help in unravelling the complications of Dio's career and the ambiguity of the man himself, as well, incidentally, as suggesting some of the uses to which he put his not inconsiderable literary skills.[173]

## Bibliography

Adams, C. D., ed. (1905) *Lysias: Selected Speeches* (New York).
Anderson, G. (1977) '*Apollonius of Tyana* as a Novel', in Reardon (1977) 37.
von Arnim, H. (1898) *Leben und Werke des Dio von Prusa* (Berlin).
Barnes, T. D. (1971) *Tertullian: a Historical and Literary Study* (Oxford; reissued with corrections and postscript, 1985).
Barrow, R. H. (1967) *Plutarch and his Times* (London and New York).
Behr, C. A. (1968) *Aelius Aristides and the Sacred Tales* (Amsterdam).
Bizos, M., ed. (1955) *Lysias: Discours I* (Paris).
Bompaire, J. (1977) 'Le décor sicilien dans le roman et dans la littérature contemporaine (II$^e$ siècle)', *REG* 90: 55–68; résumé in Reardon (1977) 87–90.

---

[173] This paper was originally delivered at a meeting of the Hibernian Hellenists, 27 February 1976. I am grateful to all those who made helpful comments on that occasion. Mr E. L. Bowie and Professor G. L. Huxley kindly read a later draft and made many constructive criticisms.

Bowersock, G. W. (1969) *Greek Sophists in the Roman Empire* (Oxford).
Bowersock, G. W. (1970) 'Introduction', in Jones (1970) 9–22.
Bowie, E. L. (1970) 'Greeks and their Past in the Second Sophistic', *P&P* 46: 3–41.
Bowie, E. L. (1978) 'Apollonius of Tyana: Tradition and Reality', *ANRW* II.16.2: 1652–99.
Browning, R. (1970) 'Dio (1) Cocceianus', *OCD*²: 345.
Brunt, P. A. (1973) 'Aspects of the Social Thought of Dio Chrysostom and the Stoics', *PCPhS* 199: 9–33; repr. in id., *Studies in Stoicism*, edd. M. Griffin and A. Samuels (Oxford, 2013) 151–79.
Butler, H. S. and A. S. Owen, edd. (1914) *Apulei Apologia, sive pro se de magia liber* (Oxford).
Dill, S. (1905) *Roman Society from Nero to Marcus Aurelius* (London).
Dodds, E. R., ed. (1959) *Plato:* Gorgias (Oxford).
Dover, K. J. (1968) *Lysias and the Corpus Lysiacum* (Berkeley and Los Angeles).
Dudley, D. R. (1937) *A History of Cynicism from Diogenes to the 6th century A.D.* (London).
Farrington, B. (1939) *Science and Politics in the Ancient World* (London).
Flacelière, R. and E. Chambry, edd. (1972) *Plutarque: Vies VII: Cimon–Lucullus, Nicias–Crassus* (Paris).
Griffin, M. T. (1976) *Seneca: a Philosopher in Politics* (Oxford; repr. with addenda, 1992).
van Groningen, B. A. (1965) 'General Literary Tendencies in the Second Century', *Mnemosyne* 18: 41–56.
Grosso, F. (1954) 'La vita di Apollonio di Tiana come fonte storico', *Acme* 7: 333–532.
Grube, G. M. A. (1965) *The Greek and Roman Critics* (London).
Guthrie, W. K. C. (1969) 'The World of the Sophists', in *A History of Greek Philosophy III: The Fifth-Century Enlightenment* (Cambridge) 3–319 = *The Sophists* (Cambridge, 1971).
Hamilton, J. R. (1969) *Plutarch, Alexander: A Commentary* (Oxford).
Harrison, E. L. (1964) 'Was Gorgias a Sophist?', *Phoenix* 18: 183–92.
Highet, G. (1973) 'The Huntsman and the Castaway', *GRBS* 14: 35–40.
Hirzel, R. (1895) *Der Dialog*, 2 vols. (Leipzig).
Höistad, R. (1948) *Cynic Hero and Cynic King: Studies in the Cynic Conception of Man* (Uppsala).
Jebb, R. C. (1893) *The Attic Orators*, 2 vols. (London).
Jones, C. P. (1966) 'Towards a Chronology of Plutarch's Works', *JRS* 56: 61–74; repr. in B. Scardigli, ed., *Essays on Plutarch's* Lives (Oxford, 1995) 95–123.
Jones, C. P., ed. and trans. (1970) *Philostratus: Life of Apollonius* (Harmondsworth).
Jones, C. P. (1971) *Plutarch and Rome* (Oxford).
Jones, C. P. (1973) 'The Date of Dio of Prusa's Alexandrian Oration', *Historia* 22: 302–9.
Jones, C. P. (1978) *The Roman World of Dio Chrysostom* (Cambridge, Mass. and London).
Jouan, F. (1977) 'Les thèmes romanesques dans l'*Euboïcos* de Dion Chrysostome', *REG* 90: 38–46.

Kennedy, G. (1963) *The Art of Persuasion in Greece* (Princeton).

Kienast, D. (1971) 'Ein vernachlässigtes Zeugnis für die Reichspolitik Trajans: die zweite tarsische Rede des Dion von Prusa', *Historia* 20: 62–83.

Lemarchand, L. (1926) *Dion de Pruse: Les oeuvres d'avant l'exil* (Paris).

Lesky, A. (1966) *A History of Greek Literature* (London and New York); trans. by J. Willis and C. de Heer of *Geschichte der griechischen Literatur*² (Bern, 1963).

Lutz, C. E. (1947) 'Musonius Rufus, "The Roman Socrates"', *YCS* 10: 3–147.

MacMullen, R. (1966) *Enemies of the Roman Order: Treason, Alienation and Unrest in the Roman Empire* (Cambridge, Mass.).

Marrou, H. I. (1963) 'Synesius of Cyrene and Alexandrian Neoplatonism', in A. D. Momigliano, ed., *The Conflict between Paganism and Christianity in the Fourth Century* (Oxford) 126–50.

Martha, C. (1865) *Les Moralistes sous l'empire romaine* (Paris).

Mensching, E. (1965) 'Zu Aelius Aristides' 33. Rede', *Mnemosyne* 18: 57–63.

Momigliano, A. D. (1941) 'Review of Farrington (1939)', *JRS* 31: 149–57; repr. in id., *Secondo contributo alla storia degli studi classici* (Rome, 1984) 375–88.

Momigliano, A. D. (1950) 'Dio Chrysostomos' (Unpublished Lecture, 1950), in id., *Quarto Contributo alla Storia degli studi classici e del mondo antico* (Rome, 1969) 257–69.

Momigliano, A. D. (1951) 'Review of Wirszubski (1950)', *JRS* 41: 146–53; repr. in id., *Quinto Contributo alla Storia degli studi classici e del mondo antico*, 2 vols. (Rome, 1975) II.958–75.

Moretti, L. (1957) *Olympionikai: i vincitori negli antichi agoni olimpici* (MAL VIII.8.2) (Rome).

Müller, K. O. (1858) *A History of the Literature of Ancient Greece*, 3 vols. (London).

Nilsson, M. P. (1961) *Geschichte der griechischen Religion*, II² (Munich).

Nock, A. D. (1933) *Conversion: the Old and the New in Religion from Alexander the Great to Augustine of Hippo* (Oxford).

Palm, J. (1959) *Rom, Römertum und Imperium in der griechischen Literatur der Kaiserzeit* (Lund).

Parke, H. W. and D. E. W. Wormell (1956) *The Delphic Oracle*, 2 vols. (Oxford).

Phillips, E. D. (1957) 'Three Greek Writers on the Roman Empire', *C&M* 18: 102–19.

Questa, C. (1963) *Studi sulle fonti degli Annales di Tacito*² (Rome).

Reardon, B. P. (1971) *Courants littéraires grecs de II$^e$ et III$^e$ siècles après J.-C.* (Paris).

Reardon, B. P., ed. (1977) *Erotica Antiqua: ICAN 1976* (Acta of the First International Conference on the Ancient Novel 1976) (Bangor).

Rohde, E. (1901) *Kleine Schriften*, 2 vols. (Tübingen and Leipzig).

Rostagni, A. (1956) *Scritti minori* II.2 (Turin).

Russell, D. A. (1970) 'Plutarch', *OCD*²: 848–50.

Russell, D. A. (1972) 'Review of Jones (1971)', *JRS* 62: 226–7.

Russell, D. A. (1973) *Plutarch* (London and New York).

Sandbach, F. H. (1975) *The Stoics* (London and New York).
Scharold, J. (1912) *Dio Chrysostom und Themistius* (Burghausen).
Schmid, W. (1903) 'Dion (18)', *RE* V: 848–77.
Shackleton Bailey, D. R., ed. (1977) *Cicero: Epistulae ad Familiares*, 2 vols. (Cambridge).
Tatum, J. (1977) 'The Two Lives of the Sophist Apuleius', in Reardon (1977) 140–1.
Terzaghi, N. (1944) *Synesii Cyrenensis Opuscula II* (Rome).
Townend, G. (1961) 'Some Flavian Connections', *JRS* 51: 54–62.
Toynbee, J. M. C. (1944) 'Dictators and Philosophers in the First Century A.D.', *G&R* 13: 43–58.
Treu, K. (1958) *Synesios von Kyrene: Dion Chrysostomos oder vom Leben nach seinem Vorbild* (Berlin).
Usher, S. (1971) 'Review of Dover (1968)', *JHS* 91: 147–50.
Valdenberg, V. (1926) 'The Political Philosophy of Dio Chrysostom', *Izvestija Akad. Nauk SSSR* 6, ser. 20: 943–74, 1281–1302, 1533–54; 21: 287–306 (in Russian).
Wilhelm, F. (1918) 'Zu Dion Chrys. Or. 30 (Charidemos)', *Philologus* 75: 364–83.
Wirszubski, Ch. (1950) *Libertas as a Political Idea at Rome during the Late Republic and Early Principate* (Cambridge).
Ziegler, K. (1951) 'Plutarchos (2)', *RE* XXI: 636–962.
Ziegler, K. (1964) *Plutarchos von Chaeroneia*, rev. ed. of 1951 with addenda (Stuttgart).

CHAPTER 2

# Dio Chrysostom: Exile, Tarsus, Nero, and Domitian

In *LCM* 7.10, A. A. R. Sheppard offered some interesting speculations about the career of Dio Chrysostom: *Orationes* 33, 66, 79, and 80 were all delivered in Tarsus during Dio's exile, and show him, to some extent, in the role of political 'dissident'.[1]

The veracity of Dio's claim (3.13; 45.1; 50.8; cf. Lucian, *Peregr.* 18) to have exercised unfettered παρρησία under Domitian has been doubted. Some have supposed either that the claim is greatly exaggerated or that the relevant works have perished.[2] Sheppard's reconstruction seems to provide an attractive answer to the problem: Dio did practise παρρησία, but of a veiled kind. One may well sympathise in general with this view of Dio[3] (especially if one dates the Diogenes discourses to the exile period[4]). Nevertheless, while any detailed reconstruction of this period of Dio's career must be speculative, Sheppard's seems suspect in several respects.

His case goes as follows (for convenience I have rearranged the various steps, without, I hope, misrepresenting the argument):

1. At 40.1 (in a speech datable to 101) Dio refers to the ambitions of the Tarsians and Antiochenes in such a way as (possibly) to suggest a prior visit to the Levant, which would have to be dated to the exile period (*c.*83–96/7).
2. *Orr.* 79 and 80 were delivered in Tarsus and should be dated to the exile period.
3. *Or.* 33, explicitly delivered in Tarsus, is also exilic.
4. *Or.* 66 is exilic, and *may* have been delivered in Tarsus in 89.

I consider these arguments in turn. If the following analysis seems rather finicky, I hope that it will at least bring out one fundamental point: the \*\*\*ical[4a] approach to so multi-faceted a writer as Dio.

---

1 {Sheppard (1982).} Dr Sheppard and I have discussed some of these points in conversation without reaching agreement.
2 So Jones (1978) 50.
3 Well expounded by Dudley (1937) 152f.
4 This traditional dating is challenged by Momigliano (1950) 261f., and Jones (1978) 49f. with (in my view) unconvincing arguments. I have not seen Brancacci (1980), and do not know what his position is.
4a {There is a lacuna in the original printed text at the end of the line, and the next begins 'ical'; presumably Moles wrote something on the order of 'need for a careful philosophical and philological' approach, etc.}

1. This inference is nowhere near 'convincing' (Dio might easily have known of these rivalries without visiting Tarsus); on the other hand, it is of course *possible*. In any event, this is only a small part of Sheppard's case.

2. The inference that *Orr.* 79 and 80 were delivered in Tarsus depends solely on the manuscript titles Περὶ Πλούτου τῶν ἐν Κιλικίᾳ (Parisinus 2985) and Τῶν ἐν Κιλικίᾳ Περὶ Ἐλευθερίας (all manuscripts except Parisinus 2985) respectively.

In both speeches the internal indications of place of delivery require discussion.

(a) *Or.* 79. The speech begins: Φέρε πρὸς θεῶν, ἐπὶ τίνι μάλιστα θαυμάζειν καὶ ἐπὶ τῷ μέγα φρονεῖν καὶ μακαρίζειν ἄξιον πόλιν ἁπασῶν μεγίστην καὶ δυνατωτάτην; Two questions arise: (i) what πόλις is referred to here? (ii) is this the πόλις in which the speech was made?

H. L. Crosby (v.303), assuming that the πόλις here referred to must be the place of delivery, argues that it cannot be Rome, on the ground that 'were that the case, one may question whether he would have identified himself with his hearers as he does on 5' (79.5: ἆρα ἐνθυμεῖσθε ὅτι πάντες οὗτοι ... φόρους παρ' ἡμῶν λαμβάνουσιν, οὐ τῆς χώρας οὐδὲ τῶν βοσκημάτων, ἀλλὰ τῆς ἀνοίας τῆς ἡμετέρας;). He suggests that, given the manuscript title of Parisinus 2985, the πόλις should be Tarsus, and he cites as a parallel the description of Tarsus in 34.7: μεγίστην ... τὴν πόλιν τῶν ἐν τῇ Κιλικίᾳ καὶ μητρόπολιν ἐξ ἀρχῆς.

But there the qualification τῶν ἐν τῇ Κιλικίᾳ makes a vital difference, as is shown by comparison with the descriptions of Rhodes in 31.62 (τὸ χωρὶς μιᾶς [sc. Rome] πασῶν τῶν ἄλλων ὑπερέχειν), Alexandria in 32.35 (ἡ ... πόλις ὑμῶν τῷ μεγέθει καὶ τῷ τόπῳ πλεῖστον ὅσον διαφέρει καὶ περιφανῶς ἀποδέδεικται δευτέρα τῶν ὑπὸ τὸν ἥλιον [i.e., second to Rome]), and Rome itself in 11.138 (πόλιν ... τὴν μεγίστην πασῶν). That the bare superlatives of 79.1 denote Rome is confirmed by the sequel. Dio describes the city as adorned with paintings and statues whose former owners are now 'slaves, of low estate, and poor', and then pointedly observes that the Corinthians' art and commerce failed to preserve their political independence, clearly alluding to the sack of Corinth in 146 BC. Crosby's other argument, from 79.5, is equally unconvincing (*pace* Sheppard (1982) 149). Philosophers in 'diatribes' (like the clergymen in sermons) often include themselves in the category 'we foolish people' in order to bridge the gap between them and their audience. From that point of view, Dio could have counted himself among the ἡμεῖς of practically any prosperous πόλις (especially after the very general ἡμῖν and ἡμῶν references in 79.4).

Sheppard and Desideri[5] believe that, while 79.1 alludes to Rome, the speech was delivered elsewhere. There are difficulties with such a reading of the

---

5 Desideri (1978) 232ff. Since in what follows I disagree with Desideri on nearly every point, and since his book has not, on the whole, had the reception it deserves, I take this opportunity

speech. For it seems only natural to assume (*à la* Crosby and Jones (1978) 128) that the first and only πόλις explicitly mentioned is the place of delivery. Moreover, just as Rome is enriched by the wealth of the Babylonians, by amber produced by the Celts [[131]] (79.4), and by ivory produced by the Indians (79.4), so the ἡμεῖς of 79.5 import wealth from the Celts, Indians, and Babylonians, and just as Rome teems with silver and gold imported from the ends of the earth, so silver and gold in ἡ ἡμετέρα γῆ (79.5) are used to acquire amber and gold from far-off lands (79.6). Dio's organisation of his material in this speech is a little loose[6] (*suo more*), but *prima facie* Rome, the πόλις of 79.1, and the ἡμεῖς of 79.5 are equated. Again, the development of thought from 79.1 *seems* to fall into a pattern repeatedly used by Dio in his major public addresses in large cities when he wishes to disconcert his audience: the emphatic rejection of the conventional sophistic ἐγκώμιον of the physical attributes of the city in question, followed by the insistence that these things are worthless and what matters is the moral wellbeing of the citizens (cf., e.g., 32.35ff.; 33.2ff., 17ff.; 34.7ff.; 39.2ff.; 48.9). In sum, the *natural* reading of the speech is that it was delivered in Rome. Nevertheless, the speech would make some sort of sense (though it would be less well written) if we suppose that it was delivered in a Greek city, and that Dio's purpose was to hold up the decadence of Rome as a particularly striking example of the decadence to which all so-called civilised states are subject. Thus the natural reading would have to be set aside *if* other considerations seemed to make that necessary. I shall consider the possible 'other considerations' below.

(b) *Or.* 80. Dio alludes casually to Numa in a list of law-givers in 80.3 (the others are Solon, Dracon, and Zaleucus). This need not imply delivery in Rome—educated Greeks would have heard of Numa, and in fact the characterisation of Homer at 80.7 as τοῦ καθ' ὑμᾶς σοφωτάτου indicates a Greek audience. But Sheppard's suggestion (149) that 'the comments on vain strife in 80.4 may recall those of 34.45' (from the Second Tarsic Oration) is unhappy: not only are the contexts rather different but also, on Sheppard's own view, *Or.* 80 is exilic and *Or.* 34 Trajanic.

So much for the internal indications of place of delivery in *Orr.* 79 and 80. One must also consider arguments from dating: the two questions are naturally interrelated (if *Or.* 79 were provably exilic, it could not have been made in Rome).

Sheppard (1982) 150 seems to accept the arguments of Desideri (1978) 209f. and 232ff. for dating both speeches to the exile period. But these arguments,

---

of registering my view that it is a formidable and impressive work which makes most recent research on Dio look superficial.

6 Cf. Crosby v.309 n. 2.

though not unreasonable, fall very short of proof. In general Desideri regards the thought of the speeches—in 79 the strong attack on material riches and the specific criticism of Rome, in 80 the emphasis on the true freedom possessed by the philosopher—as characteristic of Dio's exile. Characteristic it may very well be, but that is hardly enough to exclude the possibility that Dio could well have expressed such views, commonplace as they are, either earlier or later. One could argue that the rather Cynic tone of both speeches favours an exile, or possibly a post-exile, dating, but this leads one into other areas of controversy.[7] The most solid indication of dating seems to be provided by Dio's description of the philosopher in 80.1, which has obvious self-reference. The philosopher is seen not so much as a 'wanderer' (the discussion of Jones (1978) 135 is a little inaccurate) but as completely disengaged from public life. This suggests an exilic or post-exile context, the former being more plausible since the description would be less appropriate when Dio had returned to political prominence both in Rome and in Prusa. Certainty is unattainable, but I think it likely that *Or.* 80 is exilic and that it *may* have been delivered in Tarsus, as the manuscript titles would seem to imply.

But this need not mean that *Or.* 79 belongs to the same period. Sheppard seems just to assume that the two speeches are a pair. In reality (if we exclude insubstantial arguments based on 'similarity of thought'), the only reasons for linking the speeches are: (a) their proximity in the extant corpus of Dio's works and (b) the manuscript titles. But (a) cannot be pressed: some of the works in the corpus are grouped in chronological groups, but some are not. As for (b), while all manuscripts except Parisinus 2985 title *Or.* 80 Τῶν ἐν Κιλικίᾳ Περὶ Ἐλευθερίας, *only* Parisinus 2985 titles *Or.* 79 Περὶ Πλούτου ἐν Κιλικίᾳ. In this confused state of affairs, it seems arbitrary to rely on the supposed authority of 'early scholia': one must rather weigh that supposed authority against the natural reading of *Or.* 79, which is (as I have argued) that it was delivered in Rome. At best, the conclusion must be *non liquet*, though in my opinion it is more probable that the speech was delivered in Rome, and if so, after, rather than before, the exile.

3. Sheppard (1982) 150 shows that *if Or.* 33, the First Tarsic Oration, is pre-Trajanic, it must at least be post-72. He disputes Desideri's Vespasianic dating because of Dio's clear philosophical claims, which would, he thinks, be out of place in 'a speech to a public meeting in a provincial capital after Vespasian's quarrel with the philosophers and Dio's own ignominious recantation in the

---

7  It is disputed whether, or how far, or in what sense, Dio 'went Cynic' during his exile. For my view see Moles (1978) 94 {above, p. 48}; other views: Jones (1978) 49f.; Desideri (1978) 200f., 537ff.; and presumably Brancacci (1980).

speech *Against the Philosophers*'. It is hard to know what formal weight to attach to such an argument. After all, on Sheppard's own reconstruction, Dio said provocative things in a provincial capital during his exile under Domitian. Could he not similarly have claimed to be a philosopher and praised philosophy in speeches to provincial audiences in the 70s, despite the unhappy events of 71? It is, indeed, possible, perhaps even probable, that the Rhodian Oration, in which Dio pays a warm, though veiled, tribute to Musonius Rufus (31.122), and the Alexandrian Oration (*Or.* 32), in which Dio certainly makes philosophical claims, should both be dated to the early 70s *after* 71.[8]

⟦132⟧ But the real question is whether *Or.* 33 is pre-Trajanic at all.[9] Desideri again relies heavily on the criteria of 'similarity of thought' as an argument for contemporaneity and, conversely, dissimilarity of thought as an argument for chronological separation. Thus on his view *Or.* 33 belongs in the 70s because it has 'numerosi punti di contatto' with the Alexandrian and Rhodian Orations (Desideri (1978) 122ff.) and because there are great differences, of various kinds (Desideri (1978) 423), between it and *Or.* 34, the Second Tarsic Oration, which is probably Trajanic.[10] Again, one suspects that Desideri takes Dio's thought a little too seriously—not because Dio's thoughts are trivial (they are admittedly mostly simple, but often worthwhile, particularly in context) but because on the whole they are of such an unremarkable character that it is difficult to trace (and perhaps implausible to suppose) real change or development in them.[11]

Here one wonders also whether Desideri and Sheppard (who follows Desideri in this respect) do not overstate the differences in tone and content between *Orr.* 33 and 34. As for tone, *Or.* 33, a moral address which concentrates on the manners, tastes, and deportment of the Tarsians, is written in the σπουδαιογέλοιον tradition; *Or.* 34, which is a formal political speech, is not. These differences prove nothing whatsoever about dating. As for content, Desideri's claim that the speeches differ *radically* depends largely on the correctness of 'identifying the orientalizing troublemakers of 33.38 and 48 with the linen workers of 34.21; Dio ridicules the former, but urges that the latter should

---

8   Date of the Rhodian: Momigliano (1951) 150f. = (1975) 11.971ff.; Jones (1978) 133; Musonius at 31.122: Moles (1978) 82f. {above, pp. 27f.}; Rhodian post-71?: see my attempted reconstruction in Moles (1978) 86f. {above, pp. 35f.}; Vespasianic dating of the Alexandrian (?): Jones (1973) and (1978) 134; though there are difficulties with this dating (see Moles (1978) 84 {above, p. 31} n. 48; Sheppard also raises doubts in an as yet unpublished paper {= Sheppard (1984)}), it still seems to me plausible (the arguments against it of Kindstrand [1978] depend on an uncritical reading of *Or.* 13).
9   I here retract my own suggestion in Moles (1978) 88 {above, p. 38} n. 73.
10  Cf. Jones (1978) 136f.; Desideri (1978) 423ff.
11  Cf. in general Moles (1978) 93ff. {above, pp. 47ff.}

be given citizenship. If the two speeches were made during the same visit, the change of viewpoint on a matter of serious and immediate political importance would be surprising' (Sheppard (1982) 150). This argument seems to me very unconvincing. In the first place, the 'identification' is forced. In 33.37ff. Dio does not seem to singling out any *particular* group for condemnation: his argument rather is that practically the whole population of Tarsus behaves in an unseemly and un-Hellenic way (33.41), and for most of the speech he uses second-person plurals in talking about the objects of his disapproval. In the second place, *even if* the 'identification' is conceded, there seems no great inconsistency in (a) making a speech criticising the decadent, un-Hellenic, oriental habits of some of the populace and (b) urging in another speech that—in the interests of civic harmony—these people should be brought within the political system. The first is a plea for the maintenance of Greek cultural integrity, the second a practical recognition of the fact that immigrant groups, especially those of long standing, are best assimilated into the political life of the city. So today a British politician of conservative, but not entirely blinkered, views might, if he were being frank (and Dio is being frank in *Or.* 33), argue that the integrity of the British way of life was threatened by immigrant cultural influences but at the same time maintain that it would be foolish to exclude such immigrants from the British political system.[12]

Sheppard also suggests that the allusion in *Or.* 34 (34.10–11) to the quarrel between Tarsus and Aegaeae as 'belonging to the former time' supports an earlier dating for *Or.* 33 (since 33.51 attests contemporary hostility between Tarsus and Aegaeae). But nothing can be made of this; there seems to have been continuous hostility between Tarsus and Aegaeae (33.51 // 34.47; Jones (1978) 137 even takes 33.51 // 34.14, 47, as indicating a *single* visit to Tarsus). More substantially, Crosby (v.335) points out that in *Or.* 33 Dio appears as an invited guest (33.1ff.), whereas in 34 he comes as a messenger from God in a time of need (34.4—i.e., presumably, as a messenger from Trajan: cf. Desideri [1978] 118). But even this need not entail two separate visits: Dio could have delivered *Or.* 34 as an imperial agent and then been asked to deliver 33. On the other side, Jones (1978) 136 correctly observes that in 33.14 Dio implies that he is not young. Dio's claims to philosophical status (33.8 and 13–16) are also interesting. The way in which the description of the philosopher is couched rather strongly suggests an exile or post-exile dating, when Dio's *persona* as a philosopher who

---

12   A 'liberal' might welcome the cultural diversity introduced by different racial groups, a 'fascist' might argue for their repatriation or disfranchisement; Dio falls somewhere in between—he is a conservative cultural nationalist capable of relatively enlightened attitudes to outsiders.

had been through hard times was firmly established: 33.14: 'do not expect from such a man any flattery or deception, or that clever and seductive language which is most in use in dealing with democracies and satraps and tyrants' (is court life under Domitian alluded to here?); 33.15: '... a man, having seen how much there is that is dreadful and hateful in the world, and that everywhere are countless enemies, both public and private, with whom luxury and deceit hold sway, "subdues his body with injurious blows, | casts round his shoulders sorry rags, in guise | a slave, steals into the wide-wayed town of those | who hold debauch" [*Od.* 4.244–6, 'reinterpreted' by Dio], meaning no harm to his neighbours ... but on the contrary seeking if perchance he may unobtrusively do them some good ...' (this is clearly autobiographical).[13]

To sum up. To put it at its lowest, the case that *Or.* 33 is much earlier than 34 has not been made out. It seems to me much more likely that the speech is late and that it belongs to the same general period as *Or.* 34, both speeches being Trajanic. The two speeches may even have been made in ⟦133⟧ the same visit.

4. The critical passage in *Or.* 66 is a sentence in 66.6:

ἔτι δὲ ἰδεῖν ἔστιν ἑτέραν οἰκίαν συντριβεῖσαν πλουσιωτέραν ἐκείνης [sc. the house of Pelops] διὰ γλῶτταν καὶ νὴ Δία ἑτέραν κινδυνεύουσαν.
    γλῶτταν MSS: δόξαν Herwerden

The traditional interpretation, following von Arnim, is that the house ruined because of a tongue is Nero's and the house in jeopardy is Domitian's.

Sheppard (1982) 149 suggests to the contrary that (a) better candidates for the first οἰκία are the families of L. Aelius Plautius Lamia Aelianus, the historian Hermogenes of Tarsus, and the rhetor Maternus, of whom Plautius had a reputation for great wealth and Hermogenes may have been very wealthy (the possible allusion to Hermogenes seems in fact to be Sheppard's only argument for placing *Or.* 66 in Tarsus); (b) if the second house is Domitian's (Sheppard is agnostic over this), 89—the time of the open rebellion of Saturninus—would be a better context than 95/6 (von Arnim's dating). (One notes that, if so, the family of Maternus, executed in 91, is excluded as a candidate for the first οἰκία reference).

Sheppard's arguments against von Arnim's interpretation are as follows:

---

13   Cf. in general Moles (1978) 94ff. {above, pp. 48ff.} The picture of the philosopher in 33.14–15 fuses Dio's Odysseus *persona* (Moles (1978) 97 {above, p. 54}) with the Cynic conception of the philosopher, which was of course itself heavily influenced by the figure of Odysseus. Cf. especially Antisthenes' *Ajax* and *Odysseus* (FF 15 and 16 DC {= 54 and 62 Prince}) with the excellent discussion of Höistad (1948) 94ff.

(1) von Arnim associated Dio's remarks with the reports of prophecies of Domitian's death being circulated in 95/6, but these prophecies must in many cases have been either *post eventum* or clandestine;

(2) γλῶττα 'is not used of singing, but of speech, especially of a tactless or licentious kind, like the English "lip"'. This objection seems to have been anticipated by Jones (1978) 50, who sees indeed an allusion to Nero, but of a different kind from von Arnim's: 'The house ... could well be the line of the Julii and Claudii, for Dio elsewhere ascribes Nero's ruin to his garrulity (*Or.* 21.9)'. It is presumably to counter Jones' suggestion that Sheppard remarks: 'It is true that Dio himself at one time apparently believed that Nero owed his downfall to tales told by Sporus, but he implies that this story was not generally current (Dio 21.9)'. In fact, both these statements are inaccurate. In 21.9 Dio does not imply that the story was not generally current—he merely says: 'the truth about this has not come out even yet'. On the other hand, he does not attribute Nero's downfall to his garrulity: he attributes it to his ὕβρις, i.e., his revolting treatment of Sporus. But these are details. How to assess Sheppard's main arguments?

We may agree that von Arnim was perhaps a little naïve in taking stories about prophecies in 95/6 at face value (nobody, I hope, will believe Philostratus, *VA* 8.26, Apollonius' blow-by-blow vision of Domitian's assassination). Nevertheless, prophecies and omens may be genuine in the sense that events occur in which superstitious people may see prophetic significance at the time, or which may be exploited (also at the time) for propaganda purposes. And, quite apart from alleged prophecies and omens, it seems perfectly rational to believe that the very last years of Domitian's reign had a sort of 'end of dynasty' air about them, and still more so that those who hated Domitian, like Dio, might reasonably have hoped for his imminent downfall.

Sheppard's argument that Dio could not have used γλῶττα with reference to Nero's singing (or acting) seems to me misconceived. It is irrelevant that, when applied to an utterance, γλῶττα usually refers to speech. The word *means* 'tongue', and the tongue is the organ which produces vocal sound of any kind. Of course, to say that Nero's house perished because of his *tongue* is very striking, but the literary context requires precisely that Dio should express himself in an arresting manner. For he is developing a prolonged *reductio ad absurdam* (in Cynic style) of the careers of those who come to grief through ambition. Men beggar themselves to win crowns at athletic games—crowns such as cattle wear (66.2); their names are proclaimed in public—like those of runaway slaves (66.2). Men 'buy' at vast expense in political life the marks of distinction which can be bought for a few drachmas in the market-place (66.4). The prizes at the games are useless; the diadems of kings are rags (66.5). The house of Pelops was destroyed because of a golden lamb! It would be perfectly fitting, after all this, if Dio attributed the collapse of the Julio-Claudian dynasty to Nero's tongue. This would simply be a normal view of the relationship between Nero 'artifex' and his fall (cf. Dio 3.134; Plut. *Mor.* 56F = *Quom. adul. ab amic. intern.* 12; Tac. *Ann.* 15.67; Cass. Dio 62(63).9), expressed in suitably striking form. An allusion to Nero would also come naturally after the preceding λέγεται ... ἐν μέσοις τοῖς θεάτροις (of stories about the house of Pelops), the more so as Dio may have found piquancy in the thought that Nero, a king, used to impersonate kings on stage (Dio 3.134; cf. Cass. Dio 62(63).9). The use of γλῶττα may be further appropriate for two reasons:

(1) Dio seems deliberately to be enumerating all possible media of communication (τούτοις δὲ οὐκ ἄξιον ἀπιστεῖν, ἃ γέγραπται μὲν οὐχ ὑπὸ τῶν τυχόντων ἀνδρῶν, Εὐριπίδου καὶ Σοφοκλέους, λέγεται δὲ ἐν μέσοις τοῖς θεάτροις· ἔτι δὲ ἰδεῖν ἔστιν ἑτέραν οἰκίαν συντριβεῖσαν πλουσιωτέρου ἐκείνης διὰ γλῶτταν ...), as if to emphasise the overwhelming evidence for the folly of ambition;

(2) διὰ γλῶτταν may follow through to the second οἰκία (i.e., Dio may be implying that the other οἰκία *also* is in danger διὰ γλῶτταν, and not just observing *obiter* 'and by the way another great house is in danger'). If so, the expression can refer to Domitian's boastfulness, which was certainly a factor in the hatred he aroused, as well as to Nero's singing. All this seems sufficient to justify the use of γλῶττα *if* the allusion is to Nero's singing (and acting).

There are indeed good reasons for supposing that this is the required allusion. After the discussion of the fall of the house of Pelops a reference to a kingly house seems appropriate. The Julio-Claudian house, extinct with Nero's death, could well be described as συντριβεῖσα. The context demands an illustration not just of 'the perils of fame' (Sheppard) but of the *folly* of ambition (which hardly applies to any of the candidates suggested by Sheppard): Nero fits the bill excellently. Finally, the first οἰκία is πλουσιωτέρα than the house of Pelops: the richest and most illustrious house in Greek mythology. Again, the Roman imperial house seems indicated.

Thus an allusion to Nero and the Julio-Claudians seems virtually certain. If so, an allusion to Domitian and the Flavians will follow almost inevitably, especially as Domitian's γλῶττα could ⟦134⟧ reasonably (at least from the point of view of the case argued by *Or.* 66) be regarded as a cause of the insecurity of his reign.

Finally, if the second οἰκία is the Flavian house, which dating is better, 89 or 95/6?[14] 89 is of course possible, but 95/6, as I have argued above, is equally possible, and perhaps rather more likely, because there are some quite close

---

14 Mr E. L. Bowie has suggested to me, mischievously enough, that the whole ἔτι δέ ... sentence is a later insertion by Dio, as proof of both his παρρησία and prescience. But the

thematic correspondences between *Or.* 66 and the Fourth Kingship Oration (*Or.* 4), a speech which I believe to have been delivered early in Trajan's reign.[15] But such an argument cannot be pressed. What does seem certain is that there is nothing at all to connect *Or.* 66 with Tarsus.

## Bibliography

Brancacci, A. (1980) 'Tradizione cinica e problemi di datazione nelle orazioni diogeniane di Dione di Prusa', *Elenchos* 1: 92–122.

Desideri, P. (1978) *Dione di Prusa: un intelletuale greco nell'impero romano* (Messina/Florence).

Dudley, D. R. (1937) *A History of Cynicism from Diogenes to the 6th century A.D.* (London).

Höistad, R. (1948) *Cynic Hero and Cynic King: Studies in the Cynic Conception of Man* (Uppsala).

Jones, C. P. (1973) 'The Date of Dio of Prusa's Alexandrian Oration', *Historia* 22: 302–9.

Jones, C. P. (1978) *The Roman World of Dio Chrysostom* (Cambridge, Mass. and London).

Kindstrand, J. F. (1978) 'The Date of Dio of Prusa's Alexandrian Oration—A Reply', *Historia* 27: 378–83.

Moles, J. L. (1978) 'The Career and Conversion of Dio Chrysostom', *JHS* 98: 79–100 [above, Ch. 1].

Moles, J. L. (1983) 'The Date and Purpose of the Fourth Kingship Oration of Dio Chrysostom', *ClAnt* 2: 251–78 [below, Ch. 3].

Momigliano, A. D. (1950) 'Dio Chrysostomos' (Unpublished Lecture, 1950), in id., *Quarto Contributo alla Storia degli studi classici e del mondo antico* (Rome, 1969) 257–69.

Momigliano, A. D. (1951) 'Review of Wirszubski (1950)', *JRS* 41: 146–53; repr. in id., *Quinto Contributo alla Storia degli studi classici e del mondo antico*, 2 vols. (Rome, 1975) II.958–75.

Sheppard, A. A. R. (1982) 'A Dissident in Tarsus? (Dio Chrysostom, Or. 66)', *LCM* 7: 149–50.

Sheppard, A. A. R. (1984) 'Dio Chrysostom: the Bithynian Years', *L'Antiquité Classique* 53: 157–73.

Wirszubski, Ch. (1950) *Libertas as a Political Idea at Rome during the Late Republic and Early Principate* (Cambridge).

---

sentence looks integral (for reasons implicit in the above analysis), and, if such sceptical solutions are accepted, we may as well abandon the interpretative task.

15  Correspondences: for the most important see Desideri (1978) 343 n. 49; date of the Fourth Kingship Oration: see my forthcoming study in *Classical Antiquity* {= Moles (1983)} (admittedly controversial).

CHAPTER 3

# The Date and Purpose of the Fourth Kingship Oration of Dio Chrysostom

The fourth Kingship Oration of Dio Chrysostom is not usually considered one of his finest works. Scholars have generally found it the least interesting of all four Kingship Orations. This adverse judgement seems unjustified. *Or.* 4 has obvious literary merit: it is couched largely in an attractive and racy style, similar to that of the Diogenes discourses (*Orr.* 6, 8, 9, 10), and the elaborate, sophistic second half (4.75–139) is in its way impressive. The speech also raises fascinating and difficult questions which must be answered before we can make a proper literary assessment.[1] Was it written under Domitian, [[252]] Nerva, or Trajan? If under Trajan, early or late in his reign? Was it delivered before Trajan or to a Greek audience? Is it an artistic unity or an uneasy amalgam of disparate strands written at different times? Is its philosophy radically Cynic or merely a hodgepodge of commonplaces drawn from different schools? How should the speech be interpreted? Is it seriously critical of Roman imperial values generally, or of the aspirations of a particular emperor? Does it even have a real political purpose, or is it simply a piece of empty court ceremonial? Or is it, rather, concerned with individual ethics, without political reference at all? Each of these propositions has been advocated by one scholar or another. Firm answers to these questions would enable us not only to make a better literary assessment of the speech but also to document the political attitudes and philosophical position assumed by Dio at a particular juncture in his career, and to gain a fuller understanding both of Dio's attitude to Roman power and of the degree of freedom of speech enjoyed by a Greek philosopher at the imperial court.

In this paper I shall argue that the speech is Trajanic, that it was delivered before Trajan himself early in his reign, and that it is fundamentally a criticism of, or a warning against, certain aspects of Trajan's character and his policy, though this criticism is masked by the tact with which it is made, by the use of allegory, by the exploitation of the type of humour allowed by the literary

---

1 I thank Mr E. L. Bowie, Dr A. R. R. Sheppard, Professor B. P. Reardon, and two anonymous referees for criticism of an earlier draft of this paper. I am particularly grateful to Professor Reardon and Mr Bowie for practical advice on the reduction and presentation of a script that had expanded to ridiculous lengths.

and philosophical tradition within which Dio is working (a tradition that is basically Cynic), and by a number of graceful implicit compliments whose function is to alleviate the otherwise astringent analysis of Trajan's character and imperial policy. This case is not completely new but has never been argued with sufficient rigour.[2] Nor is it susceptible of final proof: there are no external dating criteria. But it makes by far the best sense of the complexities and ambiguities of the speech and, if accepted, it will demonstrate that the Fourth Kingship Oration is a very skilfully executed piece whose moral and philosophical content, whatever its intrinsic interest or value, is well adapted to the circumstances of its delivery.

Space forbids a detailed critique of earlier discussions, but the key areas of disagreement are as follows.

Some[3] argue for an exile dating on the ground that *Or.* 4 is radically critical of worldly kingship and imperial ideals, whereas the other three kingship speeches, all of which are certainly Trajanic and were almost certainly delivered before Trajan,[4] take a positive view of kingship and are complimentary to Trajan. Others argue on the same ground that *Or.* 4, while of Trajanic date, ⟦253⟧ could not have been delivered before Trajan.[5] The speech is indeed radically critical of worldly kingship and imperial ideals. But this does not validate the conclusions reached. We should not expect total doctrinal consistency from a man like Dio, who was an orator and sophist as well as a philosopher, and who could change his position (not necessarily frivolously) as circumstances dictated.[6] It is, anyway, perilous to infer difference of date from difference of doctrine. Moreover, on my view the differences between *Or.* 4 and *Orr.* 1–3 have been exaggerated: *Orr.* 1–3 are not simply honorific speeches—they combine compliment with serious philosophical instruction[7]—and even *Or.* 4 contains some complimentary allusions to Trajan, as we shall see.

Dio's critical portrayal of Alexander in *Or.* 4 (especially when contrasted with the mainly laudatory portrayal in *Or.* 2) has similarly been used as an

---

2   Phillips (1957) 111, and Szarmach (1976) 174f. offer interpretations similar to mine, but neither develops his case.
3   Notably Höistad (1948) 219f., followed by Fears (1977) 157.
4   Dio 57.11 attests λόγοι τινὲς ῥηθέντες πρὸς τὸν αὐτοκράτορα. Desideri's Nervan dating of *Or.* 3 ([1978] 297) is untenable.
5   Momigliano (1950) 265, followed by Moles (1978) 90 n. 94, 98 n. 151 {above, pp. 41, 55}; Levick (1980) 193.
6   Cf. Brunt (1977) 39 {= (2013) 350}; Moles (1978) 90 {above, p. 91}; Jones (1978) 32f., 126ff.
7   For this general view cf. Dudley (1937) 155f.; Phillips (1957) 111f.; Rostovtzeff (1957) I.119–21; Szarmach (1976) 163ff.; Desideri (1978) 304ff. The same technique appears in Seneca's *De Clementia*: cf. Griffin (1976) 136ff. Jones (1978) 115ff. stresses the complimentary and honorific elements in *Orr.* 1–3 to the exclusion of all else.

argument either for an exile dating or for non-delivery before Trajan,[8] since Trajan was an admirer of Alexander.[9] But in my view Dio uses Alexander in his address to Trajan in *Or.* 4 precisely because of Trajan's known admiration for Alexander. Nor is the portrayal of Alexander wholly critical:[10] it is so designed as to encourage Trajan to reject Alexander's bad qualities while emulating his good.

Some scholars likewise have seen the philosophy of the speech as fundamentally Cynic and have inferred an exile dating on the ground that it was during the exile that Dio held (or expounded) Cynic views.[11] On my view, the core of the speech is indeed Cynic, and Dio's exile may well have been marked to some extent by a radical form of Cynicism.[12] But it does not necessarily follow that every work of Dio's in which there are Cynic elements must be exilic.[13] Furthermore, ⟦254⟧ as we shall see, the philosophy of the speech is not completely Cynic—there are Platonist and perhaps Stoic elements as well, the Cynic model itself is presented with a certain degree of irony, and Dio cleverly moves away from it in the second half of the speech in order to end on a more positive note. The philosophy of the speech is mainly Cynic not because this reflected Dio's philosophical convictions at the time but because it suited Dio's didactic purpose on this occasion.

A few passages have been thought to yield precise pointers to date and circumstances of delivery.

According to von Arnim the wording of 4.3—'since it happens that I/we have leisure from all other business'—must have been spoken when Dio was part of Trajan's entourage and the plural (τυγχάνομεν) shows that Dio was speaking for the whole court on some festal occasion.[14] These inferences are

---

8   Exile dating: Höistad (1948) 219f.; Fears (1977) 157; non-delivery before Trajan: Momigliano (1950) 265; Lepper (1948) 194ff., 203f. (hypothesising two stages of composition, one Trajanic, the other Hadrianic).
9   Cass. Dio 68.29–30; Julian, *Caes.* 333a, 335d; SHA, *Hadr.* 4.9; cf. also Lepper (1948) 198; Syme (1958) II.770f.; Millar (1969) 13; Fears (1977) 249f. and (1974) 127; Jones (1975) 406; Wirth (1975) 197ff.; Stadter (1980) 139f. These discussions convince me that the historical tradition is solid, though, as I shall show, the link between Alexander and Trajan in *Or.* 4 can be made on purely internal grounds.
10  Against Höistad, Fears, Momigliano, and Lepper, one may note that the portrayal of Alexander in 1.7 is also critical, despite delivery before Trajan.
11  So Höistad, Fears, and Professor Brunt (in conversation).
12  This is controversial. For my view see Moles (1978) 94 {above, p. 000} and (1983a). For other views: Jones (1978) 49f.; Desideri (1978) 200f., 537ff.; Brancacci (1980).
13  It is possible to expound Cynic views without living a Cynic life (*pace* Jones (1978) 49), just as it is possible to profess Christianity without practising it.
14  Von Arnim (1898) 400, followed by Szarmach (1976) 174.

uncompelling: the 'leisure' referred to may just be the proverbial 'leisure' of the philosopher, and in Greek such first-person plurals can have singular force.[15] This reading, indeed, would create a neat parallelism between Diogenes 'who had much leisure' conversing with Alexander 'who had not much leisure', and Dio 'at leisure' discoursing before an audience 'which had not much leisure', a type of parallelism also used in the other kingship speeches (below). Far more interesting is von Arnim's interpretation of 4.139, but I discuss this difficult passage below.

Höistad reaches the opposite conclusion from 4.3. His argument involves the relationship between *Or.* 4 and *Or.* 5 (the Libyan Myth). He follows Hirzel in supposing that Dio would have inserted the Libyan Myth at 4.73 during his recitation of *Or.* 4, against von Arnim's view that the Libyan Myth formed an alternative ending to the long 'spirits' exposition which now stands in 4.75–139. He then links the wording of 4.3 with that of 5.18 ('a garrulous man who perhaps has more leisure than he should'), arguing that 5.18 cross-refers to 4.3 and that they are an ironical self-description during the exile.[16] This is unconvincing. If 4.3 and 5.18 are taken together they complement each other nicely, but they also make good sense separately. Dio could, anyway, have described himself in such terms after returning from exile.[17]

Most of these arguments, then, are rather unsubtle, simply because scholars generally have failed to come to terms with Dio's literary artistry. On the whole, provided that the portrayal of Alexander can be explained satisfactorily, a stronger cumulative case can be made for a Trajanic date and delivery before Trajan than for other interpretations. This case rests on several factors: the general consideration that Dio's main works on kingship were written after his [[255]] return from exile, when he could hope for a receptive audience;[18] Trajan's interest in Alexander; the fact that, as in the Diogenes discourses, Diogenes is obviously Dio's mouthpiece, and the parallelism Diogenes–Alexander/Dio–Trajan would be highly appropriate and would mirror closely Dio's technique in 1.1–10 (Dio performs before Trajan as Timotheus did before Alexander), 2.79 (Aristotle was honoured by Philip and Alexander, Dio by Nerva and Trajan),[19] and 3.1–3 (Socrates expresses his views on the Persian king, Dio on Trajan); the implicit attacks on Domitian, which seem

---

15   So Cohoon 1.169.
16   Höistad (1948) 220, followed by Desideri (1978) 338 n. 12; Hirzel (1895) II.108 n. 3; von Arnim (1898) 412ff. (whose arguments are in fact superior).
17   He actually does so in 1.56; 7.81; 12.16; 47.8 (all post-exile).
18   Though—unsurprisingly—Dio's interest in kingship is not *restricted* to the exile period: Moles (1978) 94 {above, p. 48}.
19   The implication is clear: cf. Jones (1978) 119 and n. 40; Desideri (1978) 286, 290.

to focus on areas where Trajan's behaviour conspicuously differed (another technique found in the other kingship speeches):[20] certain parallels between *Or.* 4 and *Orr.* 1–3;[21] and certain points where the dramatic illusion seems to be broken in a way that would be odd if Dio did not have a reason and where an allusion to Trajan seems to provide a satisfying explanation for the dislocation. But cumulative arguments, however good, fall short of proof. We must therefore consider what I believe to be the key passage, 4.139.

At 4.75 Diogenes tells Alexander that he will never be a true king until he has propitiated his own spirit. Alexander, misunderstanding Diogenes, asks the name of this 'spirit' and what sacrifices and purifications are necessary to propitiate it (4.76). Diogenes then gives an elaborate discourse about 'spirits' (δαίμονες). The good and evil spirits that bring happiness and misery to men are not external beings but each man's character (4.79–80). The defective lives of the majority are of three kinds, each with its corresponding spirit: the luxurious, the avaricious, and the vainglorious (4.83–4). The miseries of each are described in detail (4.91–132). Those possessed by more than one spirit are still worse off (4.133–8). Then come the final words of the speech: 'But come, taking in exchange a harmony pure and better than our former harmony, let us hymn the good and prudent spirit and god—us to whom the Good Fates spun that we should one day receive [or, fall in with] him, when we had obtained a share of sound education and reason.'[22]

There are two difficulties here. (1) What does the passage mean? (2) Why [[256]] does the speech just stop—why does Dio not fulfil his promise to 'hymn the good and prudent spirit and god'?

In an attempt to resolve the second difficulty Synesius suggested that Dio would have proceeded immediately with a recitation of the *Euboicus* (*Or.* 7).[23] This will hardly do—the themes of the two speeches are different, and the

---

20   Cf. especially Jones (1978) 118ff.
21   E.g., 4.4 // 1.14, 17 // 3.1.
22   4.139: ἀλλὰ δὴ μεταλαβόντες καθαράν τε καὶ κρείττω τῆς πρότερον ἁρμονίας τὸν ἀγαθὸν καὶ σώφρονα ὑμνῶμεν δαίμονα καὶ θεόν, οἷς ποτε ἐκείνου τυχεῖν ἐπέκλωσαν ἀγαθαὶ Μοῖραι παιδείας ὑγιοῦς καὶ λόγου μεταλαβοῦσι.

I have not tried to translate this intricate Greek elegantly. The μετα- in μεταλαβόντες denotes, I think, the idea of 'exchange', the μετα- in μεταλαβοῦσι the idea 'a share of'. Τυχεῖν denotes both 'attain, acquire' and 'meet' (as I shall show below). Von Arnim suggested that instead of οἷς ποτε, οἷς τε should be read, giving the meaning 'let us hymn the good and prudent spirit and god *and* those to whom ... etc.' This seems wrong. μεταλαβοῦσι clearly picks up μεταλαβόντες, so those who 'hymn' are the same as those 'to whom the Good Fates spun': Dio is hardly saying 'Let us [the good] praise the good [ourselves]'!
23   Synes. *Dion* 39a (where μετά clearly = 'after', not 'next in order of excellence').

combination would be intolerably long.[24] Wilamowitz held that the end of the speech was missing and that Dio would have recited a hymn to Zeus—a suggestion first endorsed, but later rejected, by von Arnim. After the first three spirits the transition to a totally different kind of spirit would be very harsh, and the terminology of 4.139 does not suit a reference to Zeus. Jones suggests that the speech ends suddenly because that is often Dio's way.[25] But this ending, in a formal kingship speech, seems abnormally abrupt. If the ending is not lost, we must find an explanation for Diogenes' words that will somehow invest them with a significance and completeness beyond their surface meaning. This brings us back to the first difficulty.

On one level, 4.139 is straightforward Platonic psychology.[26] Acquisition of the good and prudent character, with the right 'harmony', depends on 'education and reason'. The idea of the spirit maintains the spirit/character equivalence begun at 4.79. 'Hymning' fits the religious imagery (cf. also 4.75–6). But two problems remain. (1) How can this 'spirit' also be a 'god'? (2) What is the precise implication of the relative clause ('us to whom ...'), apart from the general emphasis on the need for 'education and reason'?

Treatment of these problems involves considering the philosophical basis of the whole 'spirits' section (4.75–139). The spirit/character equivalence (spirits not external deities but something within the individual) follows the rationalising attitude to 'spirits' of Heraclitus and others.[27] But there is also a general Platonic influence. The detailed description of inferior types of life is a Platonic technique (cf., e.g., *Rep.* 360eff., 367bff., 420cff., 445cff., 491aff., 544aff., 618a, etc.). As for content, the main elements of 4.75–139 can all be found in the *Republic*. 'Prudence', the characteristic of the fourth spirit, appears as a signal political virtue in *Rep.* 389e, 399b–c, 402e, 442c, 485e, 490c, 555c, etc. The vainglorious is one of the five individual types of character (*Rep.* 545aff.), as is the avaricious (*Rep.* 551aff.; cf. 548a). In the ⟦257⟧ threefold division of the soul, avarice marks the third element (581a) and vaingloriousness the passionate element (581a–b). Love of strife and love of profit characterise two of the

---

24 Cf. also von Arnim (1898) 400f.; Treu (1958) 40f.
25 Jones (1978) 121 and 194 n. 44.
26 Cf., e.g., *Rep.* 580d–581d, 401a–402a, 443d.
27 4.80: ὁ δὲ ἴδιος ἑκάστου νοῦς, οὗτός ἐστι δαίμων τοῦ ἔχοντος ἀνδρός. Heraclitus F 119 D–K = 121B {= D111 L–M}: ἦθος ἀνθρώπῳ δαίμων. [Epicharmus] 17D: ὁ τρόπος ἀνθρώποισι δαίμων ἀγαθός, οἷς δὲ καὶ κακός. The implications of Anaxagoras' ὁ νοῦς ἡμῶν ἐστιν ἐν ἑκάστῳ θεός (Eur. F 1018 N {= *TrGF* F 1018 (v.2.988)}), which is verbally closer to Dio, are quite different. In 4.80 I have translated νοῦς as 'character', because that is what the context requires, though in fact Dio deliberately uses νοῦς instead of ἦθος to facilitate the 'slide' to the 'god within' doctrine of 4.139—cf. below.

three types of men (581c). Avarice is constantly seen as a civic and political vice (373d–e, 390d–e, 391c, 485e; cf. 347b), as is, if to a lesser extent, love of honour (cf., e.g., 545aff., 347b, 475a–b). Luxury distinguishes decadent societies and individuals (372eff., 399e, 422a, 556b, etc.). After all this, Platonic psychology comes very naturally in 4.139.

The Platonism of the *Republic* also goes some way towards explaining the 'god' reference. If all the characters are personified as spirits, the fourth character—a pure 'harmony' produced by 'culture and reason'—can be regarded as a 'god', since in Platonism virtue is divine. Later Platonism offers formulations even closer to 4.139.[28] However, the most economical explanation for Dio's wording lies in the Stoic doctrine of 'the god within' as popularised by Posidonius, which is often expressed in terms identical to those of 4.139.[29] Thus the idea of the fourth spirit as a god is philosophically easy.

What, then, of the following relative clause? The philosophical source should be one which (a) equates 'spirit' and men's essential characters, (b) emphasises the need for improvement of character by moral struggle, and (c) contains an eschatology in which the prophetic Fates are instrumental in allocating 'spirits'. Given the Platonic influence, especially from the *Republic*, on the whole 'spirits' section, that source must be the Myth of Er.[30]

The philosophical argument of 4.75–139 therefore goes:
1. 'Spirit' is 'each man's character' (4.75ff.). This rationalising vindication of free will against external 'spirit' follows the Heraclitan tradition.
2. Three defective 'spirits' hold sway over the majority of mankind (4.83–138). Both the content and style of this section are Platonic.
3. The right 'spirit' comes from the 'harmony' attained from 'education and reason', as the Fates have prophesied. This doctrine is Platonic, with specific reference to the Myth of Er.

The spirit is also a god, as in the Stoic doctrine of 'the god within'. In other words, it is open to the individual to acquire as his spirit or character the spirit or god that is within all men: virtue consists in fostering this divine element until it becomes one's personal character or spirit. At first sight, section (3) is inconsistent with section (1): the latter dismisses the idea of external spirit in favour [[258]] of free will, while the former credits God with the presence of

---

28   E.g., *Tim.* 90a: (αὐτὸ [τὸ λογιστικὸν] δαίμονα θεὸς ἑκάστῳ δέδωκεν), and *Laws* 713e (quoted below).
29   E.g., Posidonius, F 187 E–K, 6–8; Sen. *Ep.* 41.1–2; Epict. 1.14.12–14, 2.7.3, 2.8.11ff., 2.16.33; M. Aurel. 2.13, 2.17, 3.3.2, 3.4.3, 3.5.1, 3.6.2, 3.7 (τὸν ἑαυτοῦ νοῦν καὶ δαίμονα), 3.12, 3.16.2, 5.10.2, 5.27 (ὁ δαίμων ... οὗτος ... ἐστὶν ὁ ἑκάστου νοῦς καὶ λόγος), 7.17, 8.45, 10.13, 12.3, 12.26; cf. also Cic. *Off.* 3.44; *Rep.* 6.26; general discussion in Farquharson (1944) II.527ff.
30   Cf. especially *Rep.* 617d–e, 618a–b, 620d–e.

spirit within man. But the inconsistency is only apparent. Both sections assert human free will and reject vulgar theories of external spirits. The combination of the rationalising Heraclitan attitude to spirits with the belief that it is God who is responsible for spirit in man is found both in Platonism—as in the Myth of Er—and in Stoicism.[31]

It is thus clear that the philosophical content of the 'spirit' section of *Or.* 4, though somewhat syncretist, is essentially coherent, and that 4.139, though trickily expressed, forms the logical culmination of the whole argument. Indeed, the tricky conjunction 'spirit' and 'god', after the weak use of 'spirit' to mean 'character', positively reinforces the philosophical message. Is 4.139, therefore, totally explained?

Von Arnim, who admittedly failed to analyse the philosophical import of the passage, produced a very clever interpretation of Dio's words. Assuming that *Or.* 4 was delivered before Trajan, he argues that ever since 4.75, and throughout the descriptions of the false spirits that afflict mankind, Trajan's spirit would, as it were, be suspended in view, in implicit and striking contrast with the degenerate kinds. The audience would thus expect a description of Trajan's spirit and would readily see an allusion to it in 4.139. Further, von Arnim, having inferred from the wording of 4.3 that *Or.* 4 was made on a festal occasion, conjectures that 'the good and prudent spirit and god' denotes Trajan's 'genius'. The occasion might have been Trajan's birthday, when his 'genius' would be celebrated, and the abrupt conclusion of the speech could be explained by the hypothesis that at Dio's exhortation the audience immediately struck up a hymn to honour that 'genius'.[32]

As formulated, von Arnim's interpretation contains weaknesses—his failure to investigate the philosophy of 4.139, his assumption (it is no more than that) that the speech was delivered before Trajan, his unconvincing reading of 4.3. Nevertheless, the suggested context is attractive.[33] Moreover, von Arnim's

---

31  Cf. Farquharson (1944) 11.529: 'the doctrine of M., however obscure, affords a kind of compromise between reliance upon the higher or idealised self ... and the assurance of divine grace and protection'.
    Note how Dio has paved the way for the transition from 1 to 3 by using (a) νοῦς in 4.80 (cf. above, n. 27) and (b) religious imagery in 4.83ff. The use of δαιμόνιος and θεία as synonyms in 4.29, with reference to the 'divine' education, may also anticipate the apparently paradoxical association of δαίμων and θεός in 4.139 (though some may refuse to credit Dio with such subtleties).
32  Von Arnim (1898) 402, followed by Lepper (1948) 195, Phillips (1957) 110, Ferrante (1975) 15f., Szarmach (1976) 174, and Jones (1978) 121 (a modified view).
33  For speeches and hymns in the imperial cult cf., e.g., Robert (1960) 321f. = (1969) 837f.; Pleket (1965); on the celebration of imperial birthdays generally cf., e.g., Weinstock (1971) 206ff.

instinct that there is some ambiguity in Dio's words finds, I believe, support not only in the unheralded introduction of the fourth spirit but also in the emphatic phraseology 'let us hymn the good and prudent spirit and god', the elaborate verbal juggling, and the abruptness with which the speech ends. An ⟦259⟧ allusion to Trajan would also cohere with Dio's practice in the other Kingship Orations, all of which finish with a reference to the emperor.[34]

Without excluding von Arnim's interpretation, I wish to propose an alternative—one which would automatically suggest itself to an audience at Trajan's court, but which also constitutes a positive argument that *Or.* 4 was delivered under such circumstances.

Trajan himself could be described both as a 'spirit' and a 'god'. In *Or.* 25 Dio explores the proposition that a spirit is not something within a man, but some other man who controls him and determines his destiny. Such a man may rule many men, in a city, race, or empire, and may fittingly be described as their spirit.[35] Trajan could thus be regarded as the spirit of the Roman Empire. (On this reading, the 'spirit' of 4.139 is *both* something within the individual and an external ruler. This, as we shall see, poses no difficulty.) In the light of imperial cult, Trajan could equally well be referred to as a god. The fuller description 'good spirit' could also apply to Trajan: Roman emperors could be associated, sometimes even assimilated, with the 'good spirit' of Greek religion.[36] If so, we might detect an implicit contrast with Domitian, whom Dio labels a 'bad spirit' in *Or.* 45.1: Trajan would be the Good Spirit, Domitian the Evil Spirit.[37] If we further regard Trajan as the embodiment of the philosophical ruler, we may recall that the Cynic sage was sometimes connected with the Good Spirit.[38] For this

---

34   1.84; 2.79 (with n. 19 above); 3.135ff. (with Jones [1978] 120).
35   Desideri (1978) 324ff. usefully discusses *Or.* 25. He suggests (370 n. 53) Plat. *Laws* 713d as the ultimate philosophical source, whereas Cohoon II.323 suggests *Rep.* 540b. For reasons that will become clear later, the former is more likely.
36   The most famous case is Nero, who was Νέος Ἀγαθὸς Δαίμων and Ἀγαθὸς Δαίμων τῆς οἰκουμένης (*CIG* III.4699; *OGIS* 666.3), but there is documentation also for Claudius, Nerva, Hadrian, and Antinous: see Harrison (1927) 277ff.; Nock (1928) 34 {= (1972) I.148}. Various ideas both in emperor cult and imperial ideology make the association/identification easy. Cf. also Dio 25.7.
37   The usual view that the Greeks lacked this concept requires modification: cf. Epict. 4.4.38 with the interesting remarks of Oldfather (1925–8) II.327). The concept is often implicit in demonological systems, particularly those influenced by Zoroastrianism (as, e.g., in Plutarch's *De Iside et Osiride*).
38   D.L. 6.74 (Diogenes); Apul. *Flor.* 22; Julian, 6.200b (Crates); Lucian, *Demonax* 63. Of course, in the general Platonic, Cynic, and Stoic tradition the wise man is θεῖος, and, in Stoicism, virtually θεός.

general approach to 4.139 to work, we must find an explanation for the relative clause that will make sense on the level of reference to Trajan.

Since Diogenes in *Or.* 4 is a mask for Dio himself, there is nothing against an interpretation that draws on Dio's own experience, real or alleged. The most famous event in Dio's whole career is his 'conversion' to philosophy. This he describes at length in *Or.* 13 and alludes to on several other occasions.[39] For present purposes the most interesting allusion is in the First Kingship Oration, ⟦260⟧ delivered before Trajan (1.52 ff.). There Dio records a meeting (no doubt fictitious) which he allegedly had with an Arcadian prophetess during his exile. She told him that the period of his wandering and suffering would not be long, nor would the wandering and suffering of the world at large (1.55—'wandering' has both literal and metaphorical application).[40] One day in the future he would meet 'a mighty man, the ruler of very many lands and peoples' (1.56), who in context must be Trajan. Dio clearly implies that his 'wandering', both physical and spiritual, came to an end when he met Trajan, as did the sufferings of the whole world on Trajan's accession. The wording of 4.139 conveys the same implication. Trajan is referred to in the words 'the good and prudent spirit and god', the prophecy of the Arcadian woman in the words 'the Good Fates spun',[41] 'one day' corresponds to 'one day' in 1.56, while 'when we had obtained a share of sound education and reason' alludes to Dio's own celebrated 'conversion' to philosophy. On this reading, the first person plural refers both to 'me, Dio', and to 'us', the suffering world in general, and τυχεῖν both to Dio's first 'meeting' with Trajan after his return from exile and to the fortunate 'acquisition' by the Roman world at large of Trajan as a Saviour God.[42] Thus 'the good and prudent spirit and god' denotes simultaneously the 'good fortune' (εὐδαιμονία) which men may acquire if they make the right choice in their way of life, and Trajan, the 'good spirit' of the Roman empire and Saviour God (θεός), whose accession

---

39  See Moles (1978) *passim*, especially 96ff. {above, pp. 51ff.}—an analysis to which I adhere, despite the reservations of several scholars, and which I now believe to be strengthened by the allusions at 1.52ff. and 4.139.

40  A referee disputes this, yet how can mankind at large be said to 'wander' *literally*? 'Wandering' is of course a very common philosophical metaphor for moral ignorance.

41  The Fates usually 'spin' at birth, but not always (cf., e.g., Callin. 1.8–9). But in any case the sense 'spin at birth' is *also* relevant because of the reference to the Myth of Er.

42  For the ideas 'saviour', 'golden/new age', etc. in imperial ideology see Weinstock (1971) 163ff., 188ff.; Wallace-Hadrill (1982); for Trajan and *salus* cf. Weinstock (1971) 173 n. 11; note also the claim that Trajan's reign inaugurated a 'new age' (Florus, *praef.* 7) and Trajan's championship of Heracles, one of the great saviour deities (below, n. 71).

I presume that 1.52ff., like 4.139, is Dio's version of a tradition like Plin. *Pan.* 5.2–9—cf. *Ep.* 10.1, 10.102—transmuted by (a) a Greek philosophical flavouring (cf. Diotima) and (b) synthesis with the story of Dio's own alleged conversion.

has allowed—or, indeed, is synonymous with—the spiritual regeneration of the suffering world in general and Dio Chrysostom in particular. The idea of Trajan as Saviour may be reinforced by further philosophical considerations. Both the Cynic sage, with whom Trajan *ex hypothesi* is here equated, and the 'divine part within man' can be credited with the role of saviour.[43]

Finally, we need a philosophical parallel for the identification 'spirit' = 'external ruler' and 'spirit' = 'divine part within'. Plato *Laws* 713d has been suggested as the ultimate source of the doctrine of Dio's *Or.* 25 (where 'spirit' = 'external ruler'). According to Plato, human happiness in the age of Kronos was guaranteed by the spirits (δαίμονες) which Kronos appointed to ⟦261⟧ rule over men. The meaning of the myth is explained in the multiple puns of the final sentence. Men must imitate Kronos' dispensation as far as possible, by obeying 'what little spark of immortality lies in us'. Law consists in 'distribution of reason'. The Greek contains numerous puns: νοῦ ... νόμον, ἐπονομάζοντας νόμον, διανομήν ... νόμον, νοῦ διανομήν, and, above all διανομήν/δαίμονες. In place of the external spirits appointed by Kronos, men must employ as their governor the spirit within them.[44] Moreover, this spirit is associated, or identified, with νοῦς. Given the link between δαίμων and νοῦς, the pun on the two references of 'spirit', and the probable relationship of this passage to Dio's *Or.* 25, whose doctrine appears relevant to 4.139, we may conclude that Dio has forged a double reference of 'spirit' in 4.139 from *Laws* 713c–d.[45] The associations of the reign of Kronos are very apposite to a context honorific of Trajan.

Interpreted as I have suggested, 4.139 is a brilliant piece of writing. We can also see why the speech stops immediately: Dio would have ended with a remarkable rhetorical flourish in Trajan's honour, and anything more would have been jejune and indeed undignified. The convoluted allusiveness of Dio's wording also makes best sense on the assumption that the speech was actually delivered before Trajan. In what follows I shall work from that assumption. For those who find my reading of 4.139 unconvincing, I hope that my analysis of the rest of the speech, taken in conjunction with the cumulative case already sketched, will establish at least an a priori likelihood that it was delivered before Trajan and that this will in turn reinforce the suggested interpretation of 4.139.

---

43  Cf., e.g., Antisthenes F 15.8, 10 DC {= 54.8, 10 Prince}; Dio 1.84 (Heracles and—by extension—Trajan); 32.3 (with Höistad [1948] 160); Plat. *Laws* 775e; Men. *Epit.* 1096 (OCT).
44  For these word-plays see England (1921) I.441f.
45  There may have been something similar to 4.139 in Posidonius, but Dio's use of Plato elsewhere in *Or.* 4 shows that he need not be following an intermediary source.

The fundamental problem is: to what extent, if any, does Alexander represent Trajan?

That Trajan hoped to emulate Alexander, especially in war, seems certain.[46] Dio's own First and Second Kingship Orations support this tradition. In the introduction to the first (1.1–8) Dio draws a delicate parallel between the effect of Timotheus' playing on Alexander and the effect of his own philosophy on Trajan. The Second Oration takes the form of a dialogue between Alexander and Philip of Macedon, in which Alexander expounds the correct doctrines on kingship. The implicit Alexander/Trajan parallel is brought out by the laborious concluding remarks about the benefits Philip and Alexander have conferred on Aristotle: an allusion to Dio himself is unmistakeable.[47] The start of *Or.* 4 creates the same general impression. It is immediately obvious that Diogenes (as in the Diogenes discourses) is a mask of Dio himself—a point made all but explicit when Dio points out (4.3) that he, like Diogenes, has much 'leisure'. The natural inference, therefore, both from the immediate context and from Dio's ⟦262⟧ use of Alexander in the First and Second Orations, is that Alexander represents Trajan, at least to some extent. (This inference does not depend on the reliability of the historical tradition linking Alexander and Trajan, though it is, naturally, strengthened if that tradition is correct.)

But from the very beginning of the speech Dio strikes a rather ambiguous note. He says that the encounter of Alexander and Diogenes has been recorded by many, in admiration of Alexander just as much as Diogenes,[48] 'because, although he was ruler over so many people and had greater power than any other man of his day, he did not disdain to converse with a poor man who had intelligence and the power of endurance' (4.1). This picture of Alexander seems wholly favourable. It looks as if Trajan is being complimented for the fact that, although as great a ruler as Alexander with as little 'leisure' to spare, he too has found time to listen to the philosophical advice of his own Diogenes. But Dio also observes that, in their enthusiasm, men introduce into their accounts of such meetings exaggeration and distortion, departing from historical accuracy, whereas 'I shall tell what in all likelihood was the nature of their association' (4.3). The implication clearly is that Dio's account of the meeting of Alexander and Diogenes will be truer to historical fact.[49] Höistad comments: 'Dio is at

---

46  Cf. above, n. 9.

47  Cf. above, n. 19.

48  Reiske's ἥκιστα (accepted by Desideri [1978] 337 n. 10) is actually less subtle than the MSS ἧττον. Von Arnim's (τὸν Διογένη ἀγάμενοι τῆς παρρησίας καὶ) is also redundant—cf. Cohoon *ad loc.* But on any reading, οἱ ἐπαινοῦντες praise *both* Alexander *and* Diogenes.

49  The vocabulary—τἀληθῆ διηγοῦνται, πλάττουσιν ὑπερβάλλοντες, εἰκός—is consciously historiographical. Note that δέ (4.3) is adversative (*pace* Cohoon).

pains to proclaim that he intends to oppose the panegyric representation of Alexander.'[50] But this is too simple. The 'admirers' of 4.1 who recount the story of Alexander and Diogenes are panegyrists of Alexander—but they are also panegyrists of Diogenes. And their apparently dubious behaviour is characteristic of human nature, but human nature seen as a benevolent force: 'for all men are naturally delighted when they see wisdom honoured by the greatest power and might' (4.2). These last words are extremely significant. They convey a clear allusion to the (pseudo-)Platonic Second Letter, 310eff.: 'It is *natural* for *wisdom and great power* to *associate* together and they are forever pursuing and seeking each other and *consorting* together. Moreover, these are things which people *delight* in discussing themselves in private conversations and hearing discussed in poems.' Dio's association with Trajan is in the same great tradition as Plato's with Dionysius the Younger.[51] Thus, while on the one hand Dio does indeed suggest that previous accounts of the meeting of Alexander and Diogenes have erred on the side of exaggeration and invention, on the other he blurs the obvious contrast between panegyrists of Alexander acting from unworthy motives and sober historians recording the unvarnished truth. The exaggerations and inventions appear as pardonable errors, which spring from ⟦263⟧ the best of intentions and from a true recognition that there is indeed something praiseworthy in the association of great kings and philosophers.

Dio's description of the form taken by the usual exaggerations also requires careful analysis: men 'strip their wise men of all else, such as wealth, honours, and physical strength, so that the high regard in which they are held may seem to be due to their intelligence alone.' Again, we must recognise the literary and philosophical model if we are fully to appreciate Dio's meaning. The model is the *Republic* 361b–c, where Glaucon defines the essentials of the just man:

> Beside our picture of the unjust man let us set one of the just man .... We must, indeed, not allow him to *seem* good, for if he does he will have the *rewards and honours* paid to the man who has a reputation for justice, and we shall not be able to tell whether his motive is love of justice or love of the rewards and honours. No, we must *strip him of everything* except his justice ... for our just man must have the *worst of reputations* even though he has done no wrong.

---

50  Höistad (1948) 213.
51  A question arises: was Trajan sufficiently well-educated to detect such allusions? Some would say not. But even if they are right (I am not convinced of this), what matters is *Dio's* intention.

The obvious difference between the two passages is that Diogenes, unlike Glaucon's just man, enjoys a favourable reputation, but this is of course a datum of the Alexander–Diogenes tradition, explaining why Alexander became interested in Diogenes in the first place (cf. section 7 of our speech). The really significant difference is that Glaucon 'strips' the just man in order to isolate his very essence, but in the accounts of the meeting of Alexander and Diogenes such stripping exemplifies how men 'add extravagant embellishments of their own.' In short, conventional accounts are just as exaggerated and unhistorical in their treatment of Diogenes as of Alexander. Yet Dio himself in the rest of *Or.* 4 will 'strip' Diogenes of 'wealth and honours' and will even expound the Cynic philosophical doctrine of 'the strip' (4.66—a passage to which I shall return).

How should we understand this seeming contradiction? Dio, I suggest, is being ironical and rather subtle here: his account of the meeting of Alexander and Diogenes will have serious content—it will be historical, yet it should not be taken wholly literally, for it will repeat some of the exaggerations characteristic of those who 'add extravagant embellishments of their own'. The detail that in the exaggerated accounts the wise are stripped of their *physical strength* also challenges our preconceptions. Of course, a contrast is implied with the worldly strength of kings, yet one of the most notable characteristics of men like Socrates and Diogenes in the philosophical tradition was precisely their remarkable physical toughness—which, indeed, is the impression Dio gives of Diogenes in *Or.* 4. Perhaps the explanation partly is that Dio is gently mocking one of his own self-stereotypes: the image of the physically broken man, exhausted by wandering and illness, but philosophically still indomitable.[52] In any event, it seems significant that whereas Glaucon's conception of the perfectly ⟦264⟧ just man entails willingness to undergo the extremes of physical humiliation and torture (*Rep.* 361d–e), to Dio lack of physical strength is one of the *exaggerated* attributes of the wise man. This seems another indication that Dio's portrait of Diogenes should not be taken at face value.

The introduction, then, contains several ambiguities, and these ambiguities seem consciously employed by Dio to minimise the offense that his speech may cause Trajan. Three different effects are achieved: (1) Trajan is compared to Alexander and complimented for listening to Dio, the latter-day Diogenes;

---

52    For this self-stereotype see Moles (1978) 95 {above, p. 51} and n. 141. *Or.* 19.1 (with Moles [1978] 98 {above, p. 54}) shows that Dio can sometimes operate such stereotypes with irony. If 4.2 does allude to Dio's own experience one might compare Epictetus' apparent references to his lameness in 1.1.23, 18.17, 19.8; 3.10.5, 26.27; 4.1.151; *Ench.* 9 (with Oldfather [1925–8] I.ix and n. 1).

(2) the point is made that Dio's account of the meeting of Alexander and Diogenes will not be the usual panegyric representation of Alexander but will be more sternly realistic; (3) there is, however, also a clever implication that even Dio's account should not be interpreted too literally, for it contains some exaggeration and idealisation of Diogenes. In this way a certain parallel is drawn between Alexander and Trajan but Dio skilfully manages to avoid the exact equivalence, which would be too close for comfort.

I turn now to the main body of the speech, trying as far as possible not simply to paraphrase the content but, rather, to highlight those elements relevant to Dio's education of Trajan and to indicate the techniques by which Dio strives to make his advice palatable.

In 4.4–10 Dio describes the contrasting characters of Alexander and Diogenes. A serious interpretative problem immediately arises with the insistent and critical emphasis on Alexander's ambition—an emphasis maintained throughout the speech. Now, Trajan was not only an admirer of Alexander: he was also known to be highly ambitious.[53] Is Dio here therefore implicitly criticising, or warning Trajan against, his ambition? The inference seems inescapable. But in the immediate context Dio has framed his criticism in a rather clever way. Alexander, absurdly, would like to be honoured, if possible, by the birds and beasts (4.4). This remark may remind us of a similar passage in *Or.* 1.14. There Dio maintains that the bad king can never be king 'even though all the world, both Greeks and barbarians, men and women, affirm the contrary, yea, though not only men admire and obey him, but the birds of the air and the beasts on the mountains no less than men submit to him and do his bidding.' This alludes to Domitian, for whom his flatterers had claimed that the birds and beasts obeyed him, and it illustrates Dio's general technique in *Or.* 1 of complimenting Trajan by implicitly contrasting his character with the evil character of Domitian.[54] Thus, at 4.4, Alexander possesses almost Domitianic characteristics, and the effect is to distance Trajan from comparison with Alexander. Dio, in short, has it both ways: he can hint at criticism of Trajan's ambition by attacking the ludicrous ambition of Trajan's exemplar, Alexander, but by giving Alexander 〖265〗 a Domitianic, or tyrannical, attribute he manages to avoid making the criticism too explicit. If the touch is in fact recognisably Domitianic, Dio may even be regarded as paying Trajan a compliment at

---

53   Plin. *Ep.* 10.41.1 and 5; Cass. Dio 68.17.1; Fronto II.213 Haines = 198 van den Hout; Trajan's imitation of Alexander is, naturally, also relevant.
54   Cf. also Jones (1978) 118 and n. 29, citing Martial 14.73; Desideri (1978) 338 n. 13; *Or.* 4.25 (below) and 3.38.

the very moment when he criticises him, the characters of the two emperors being in general (according to Dio) so completely different.

The rest of this initial character-sketch takes the form almost of a reciprocal catalogue of the differences between Alexander and Diogenes as seen by the envious Alexander. Thus:[55]

*Portrait of Diogenes* (4.6–10)

| | |
|---|---|
| 1. Poverty and simplicity of life | (4.6; cf. 4.10) |
| 2. Manliness | (4.7) |
| 3. Endurance | (4.7; cf. 4.1) |
| 4. Reputation | (4.7) |
| 5. 'He went forth alone in perfect safety' | (4.8) |
| 6. 'He cajoled no man by flattery' | (4.10) |
| 7. 'He told everybody the truth' | (4.10) |
| 8. 'He possessed not a single drachma' | (4.10) |
| 9. 'He did as he pleased' | (4.10; cf. 4.8) |
| 10. 'He failed in nothing he set before himself' | (4.10) |
| 11. 'He was the only man who lived the life he considered the best and happiest' | (4.10) |
| 12. 'He would not have accepted Alexander's throne or the wealth of the Medes and the Persians in exchange for his own poverty' | (4.10) |

Alexander is filled with astonishment and envy, largely because of the great reputation Diogenes enjoys despite his poverty (4.7; cf. 4.11).

*Portrait of Alexander* (4.6–10)

| | |
|---|---|
| 1. 'He had been brought up in regal vanity' | (4.7; cf. 4.10) |
| 5. 'He himself needed his Macedonian phalanx, his Thessalian cavalry, Thracians, Paeonians, and many others' | (4.8) |
| 9. 'so as to fulfil any of his wishes' | (4.9) |
| (cf. 'wherever he cared to go') | (4.8) |
| 10. 'to attain what he desired' | (4.8) |
| 8. 'he himself required huge sums of gold and silver' | (4.9) |
| 6. 'If he expected to keep the Macedonians and Greeks submissive, he had often to curry the favour of their rulers and the general populace by words and gifts.' | (4.9) |

---

55   This analysis slightly modifies that of Höistad (1948) 213f.

⟦266⟧ In this last catalogue nothing corresponds explicitly to the idea 'manliness' (no. 2), but it is implicitly conceded to Alexander by the mere statement that he admired the manliness of Diogenes (4.7) and, at 4.15, Alexander is explicitly 'courageous' in a good sense. Similarly, a degree of endurance is conceded to Alexander by the statement that he admired Diogenes' endurance (4.7) and by the description of his contempt for those corrupted by luxury (4.6). On the other hand, Alexander, himself 'brought up in royal vanity', 'despises' Diogenes' 'poverty and simplicity of life' (4.6). The remaining elements are, as Höistad emphasises, framed around stock Cynic antitheses:

| | |
|---|---|
| frankness–flattery | (6/7) |
| poverty–wealth | (1/8) |
| freedom–slavery | (5) |
| safety–fear | (implicit in [5] and developed later in the speech: 4.63–4) |

Another important question arises here: why, if Diogenes' life is one of complete happiness (4.10), while Alexander's falls short in so many respects, does Dio imply that Alexander's reasons for being interested in Diogenes are not all dishonourable (cf. 4.6–7)?

This is a question we must face at all the points in the speech where Alexander appears to be conceded a measure of virtue. For Höistad the explanation simply is that 'Dio has chosen the method of granting Alexander certain meritorious characteristics in order to give still greater prominence to Diogenes' superiority'. Of course, there is truth in this. Even in those areas of life where he can offer Diogenes some competition, Alexander is clearly inferior: he himself has reputation, but that of Diogenes is superior; he can go where he likes, but Diogenes can go where he likes without the physical protection Alexander needs; and so on. But even in the present context, and still more so later in the speech, Höistad's explanation seems insufficient. For all his erroneous values, Alexander appears to possess certain stimuli to a life of true virtue. The explanation suggested for Alexander's behaviour in 4.6 ('he himself was young and had been brought up in regal vanity') is important.[56] Alexander's misconceptions are a function of his youth and upbringing, and in Greek ethics both these things are often felt to be mitigating factors of poor behaviour, which may allow for the possibility of development and improvement of

---

56  For a similar emphasis on 4.6 see Hoffmann (1907) 77; Fears (1974) 123 n. 62; Jones (1978) 121 (implicitly).

character as a man gets older and as he changes his company for the better,[57] which Alexander of course may [[267]] do if he associates with Diogenes. Dio also skilfully suggests Alexander's latent capacity for moral improvement in two other ways. First, in describing Alexander's (entirely justified) contempt for everybody except Diogenes (4.5) he uses the sort of terminology a Cynic might use: 'he *despised* all other men and thought that no one was a *match for him* (ἀξιόμαχον αὐτῷ) in this matter—neither the *Persian king* nor the Scythian nor the Indian nor any man or city among the Greeks.'[58] Alexander has faint stirrings towards the Cynic view of life. Second, the elaborate catalogue of the differences between the two men (4.4–10) is presented through the eyes of Alexander. Alexander already has some glimmerings of the moral gulf between himself and Diogenes.

The emphasis on ambition aside, has this section any further reference to Trajan? There is certainly no implication that Trajan lacked endurance: Alexander seems to be conceded it (above) and it undoubtedly was a quality possessed by the historical Trajan.[59] Nor is there likely to be any implication that Trajan, like Alexander (4.9), had to curry favour with his subjects to keep them malleable.[60] In fact, the emphasis on Alexander's needing his Macedonian phalanx, Thessalian cavalry, Thracians, Paeonians, and many others if he wished to travel in safety (4.8) should probably be seen as another distancing device to obscure the general comparison between Trajan and Alexander, for Trajan, in emphatic contrast to Domitian, was famous for the carefree way in which he dispensed with bodyguards.[61]

Alexander is now described as going to see Diogenes (4.11–15). When Diogenes tells him not to obstruct the sun (4.14), Alexander is absolutely delighted. As a courageous man dealing with a courageous man, he admires

---

57  For the ethical implications of youth and environment see in general Dover (1974) 83ff., 102ff. Some deny that the Greeks had the concept of character development. They are wrong! In *Or.* 4 we are told that Alexander has natural nobility, he is young and has been badly brought up, his present attitudes are faulty, and Diogenes seeks to influence him towards the good. We infer that in Diogenes' opinion Alexander has the potential for the development of a good character, and we need not insult Dio (or any intelligent ancient Greek) by asserting that this simple analysis was beyond his intellectual capacity.

58  Contempt for the world's values is a Cynic attitude: cf., e.g., D.L. 6.71, 104; Stob. 4.29.19; Lucian, *Pro. imag.* 17; Cynics were also fond of military imagery: cf. Kindstrand (1976) 32 n. 47. Comparison of the Cynic way of life with that of the Persian king was a Cynic commonplace: cf., e.g., Cic. *Tusc.* 5.92; Dio 6.1ff., 35; Epict. 3.22.60.

59  E.g., Plin. *Pan.* 13.1ff.

60  This was an available contemporary view (cf. Fronto II.216 Haines = 199f. van den Hout), but the context excludes it here (below).

61  E.g., Cass. Dio 68.15.4–6; 68.7.3; Dio 1.25.

Diogenes' 'boldness' and 'composure' and finds his 'truth' and 'frankness' naturally congenial—unlike cowards, who suspect and hate frankness but welcome flattery and deceit (4.15). This very favourable description of Alexander's response to Diogenes, which develops into a general statement of the contrasting attitudes towards plain speaking of the courageous and the cowardly, cannot just be dismissed as one of 'the panegyric vestiges which remain in Dio's portrayal of Alexander' (Höistad). It must be taken as a further indication that Alexander has some good in him. But the passage remains curiously emphatic for this to be ⟦268⟧ the whole explanation, and we should surely detect contemporary resonances: Dio is alluding to Trajan's much-vaunted encouragement of freedom of speech, in contrast to the cowardice and suspicion of Domitian, under whom flattery and deceit were rife.[62] This veiled compliment might also have helped to mollify Trajan as he sat listening to Dio's own frank observations.

There follows some preliminary badinage by Diogenes (4.16–19), in which Alexander is effectively cut down to size. As usual in Cynic diatribe,[63] the tone is satirical and humorous, although serious points are certainly being made. Alexander consistently misunderstands Diogenes' cryptic remarks and is revealed as an absolute beginner in the quest for virtue (4.16, 18), whereas Diogenes, it is hinted, embodies true kingship (4.18).[64] But it is noticeable that Diogenes' response to Alexander is far from totally hostile. After upsetting Alexander with the jibe that he is a 'bastard', Diogenes (4.19) 'seeing his embarrassment, decided to change his throw, just like men playing at dice.' Diogenes is ready to change his approach as necessary. He is willing to instruct Alexander if Alexander is willing to learn, and, like a good teacher, will vary his techniques to suit his pupil. Thus Dio builds on the emphasis of 4.6: *Or.* 4 will describe the beginnings of the true education of Alexander under the skilful instruction of Diogenes. There is nothing un-Cynic about this conception of Diogenes' role: the Cynic philosopher traditionally feels a sense of missionary duty towards his fellow men—he tries to help them, he is possessed by 'love of mankind' (φιλανθρωπία), etc. But in Cynicism the emphasis could often appear less positive, and in playing up this aspect of the Cynic's role Dio is

---

62   E.g., Plin. *Pan.* 66.4; Dio 1.26 (a very similar passage); 3.2.
63   I use the term *diatribe* for convenience, without claiming for it a precision it does not in fact possess. On Cynic literary style see Kindstrand (1976) 43ff., and below, n. 84.
64   This alludes to the idea that only true kings can stand the brightness of true kingship; cf. 1.71 and 1.74 with Höistad (1948) 215f. with n. 9; Fears (1977) 156 with n. 42. For Cynic 'kingship' cf. e.g., Crates F 5.4 Diels = 7.4 Diehl; Epict. 3.22.18; Julian 6.195b; Dio 9.9; and—more generally—D.L. 6.29, 30, 74.

emphasising the element in Cynicism most suited to this purpose.⁶⁵ He could

---

65   I discuss the philanthropic aspects of Cynicism in Moles (1983b).
I believe (with von Arnim and Höistad) that the philosophy of the whole section 4.4–74 is basically Cynic. I cannot substantiate the case in detail here, but as a referee expresses strong disagreement, I briefly summarise the main points:
1. The style is Cynic—cf. above, n. 63 and below, nn. 81 and 84.
2. The piece falls firmly within the main Cynic tradition concerning the meetings of Alexander with Diogenes and the Gymnosophists. There are many parallels in literary style, philosophical content, and attitude towards Alexander between *Or.* 4 and (e.g.) the Berlin papyrus of *c.*100 BC (P. 13044; cf. Wilcken (1923), 161ff.), the Geneva papyrus of *c.*150 AD (*Pap. génèv. inv.* 271; cf. Martin (1959)), and [Diog.] *Ep.* 33, as the interested reader may verify for himself.
3. The philosophical doctrine is expounded by Diogenes the Cynic.
4. Virtually all the doctrine is characteristically Cynic. Typically Cynic are the virtues/ attributes/states 'intelligence', 'endurance', 'poverty', 'simplicity of life', 'manliness', 'safety', 'aloneness', 'freedom', 'truth', 'happiness', 'ease of life', [[269]] 'boldness', 'composure', and 'frankness'; equally typical are the attacks on 'ambition', 'glory', 'luxury', 'idleness', 'money and pleasure', 'vanity' (τῦφος), 'flattery', 'deceit', 'education' (of the conventional kind), 'folly', and 'external fripperies'. There are many conventional Cynic motifs: e.g., the contrasts between the outer and inner man, between the worldly king and the Cynic philosopher-king, between the armed and wealthy ruler and the unarmed and poor philosopher; the statement that Diogenes had no home but the public buildings and shrines; the paradoxical idea that the Cynic philosopher has 'property'; the general emphasis on the need for self-knowledge; the advice to 'strip off' (4.66 with below, n. 85).
Objections may be raised:
1. Non-Cynics can use 'Cynic style' (the influence of the 'diatribe' being widespread), and much of the doctrine of 4.4–74 would be acceptable to other philosophers, especially Stoics. True enough, but it is a question of emphasis and of relative density. All can agree (e.g.) that 'simplicity of life' is a good thing, but it was the Cynics who made it the key to 'freedom' and 'happiness'. Again, 'luxury', to most ancient thinkers, is by definition a bad thing, but the threshold of luxury is much lower for Cynics than for others. Thus in *Or.* 4.6 everybody is corrupted by luxury except Diogenes! Further, in 4.4–74 doctrine after doctrine can be categorised as Cynic, even if nearly everything individually can be paralleled in other schools, and the whole is spoken by Diogenes. And some of the doctrine seems more exclusively Cynic (e.g., the 'Cynic Strip' of 4.66).
2. According to Bernays and Zeller, Cynicism in the first century AD was no longer an independent phenomenon but merely an available option within Stoicism. I have refuted this contention in Moles (1978).
3. Section 4.33 uses the Platonic doctrine of 'recollection'. True, but this can be given significant point (below).
4. Insofar as 4.4–74 implies acceptance of the institution of kingship, it is un-Cynic, since Cynicism rejected all conventional social and political institutions. But:
a. It is not clear that 4.4–74 does accept kingship as an institution (*Or.* 4 as a whole obviously does, but that is a different point).
b. Even if 4.4–74 does imply acceptance of worldly kingship, this need not destroy its generally Cynic character. Strictly speaking, Cynicism did involve rejection of kingship as an institution (the only true πόλις is the κόσμος, which of course is not a πόλις in the usual

simply have ⟦269⟧ confined himself to castigation of Alexander's folly, but he does not do so, and again we may sense a veiled parallel between the fruitful 'association' (συνουσία)[66] of Diogenes and Alexander and the equally productive meeting between Trajan and Dio himself.

The conversation now turns to discussion of true kingship (4.19ff.), with Alexander consistently failing to grasp Diogenes' deeper meanings until they are spelled out to him (4.20, 23, 24). The content (the divine origin of kingship, the ⟦270⟧ 'sign' of kingship) is conventional in kingship literature.[67] Then at 4.24f., in reply to Alexander's question 'How could one be the best king?', Diogenes explains that it is impossible for the (true) king to be other than kingly. Although the content is commonplace (it is acceptably, but of course not exclusively, Cynic), the mode of expression is more interesting: 'It is impossible, even if all the Greeks and barbarians acclaim him as such and load him with many diadems and sceptres and tiaras.' If we compare this with the similar passages at 1.14 and 4.4, where, as we have seen, there is an implicit allusion to Domitian, and at 45.1, 'he who was called by all Greeks and barbarians both master and god', where the allusion to Domitian is explicit, we may fairly conclude that this too contains a hit at Domitian, and hence—by implication—a compliment to Trajan, who did not demand such sycophantic behaviour from his subjects. This, then, seems to be another example of the distancing technique employed by Dio to placate Trajan.

Alexander now, fearful lest he be thought ignorant of the science of kingship, asks where one must go to learn it (4.26), and this leads to Diogenes' exposition of the 'twofold education' (4.29), one human, the other divine. By now our feeling that true kingship is represented by Diogenes should be acute: kings are 'sprung from Zeus' (διογενεῖς) and no ancient listener or reader would

---

sense at all), but, obviously enough, Cynicism, like other systems, could be modified and adapted to worldly circumstances (thus both Onesicritus and Bion are usually and rightly placed within the Cynic tradition, even though in their political attitudes they had turned their backs on proper Cynic teaching). The result, certainly, is a dilution of Cynicism, but something much closer to Cynicism than to anything else.

4.4–74, then is Cynic, and recognition of this fact enables us to take the measure both of the tone of the section and of the level of literalness with which it should be understood (below). I reemphasise here that I am not claiming that Dio expounds all this as a sincere and dedicated Cynic himself; his relationship to his material is more subtle.

66  Συνουσία (4.3) may of course be used of philosophical conversation and of the association between teacher and pupil (LSJ, s.v. 1 and 3). Similarly, [Plat.] *Ep.* 2.310d refers to the συνουσία between Plato and Dionysius.

67  Cf. Fears (1977) 157f.; Dio 1.33; 4.61ff.; Valdenberg (1927) 151. In 4.61ff. note the very close parallels in Sen. *De clem.* 1.19.2f. and Epict. 3.22.99.

overlook the meaning of Diogenes' own name.⁶⁸ According to the doctrine of the twofold education, divine education, which is illustrated by the pattern of Heracles, confers moral qualities such as courage and high-mindedness and is much the more important of the two. The human is insignificant in itself, but to be completely educated one needs it as well. Since this doctrine derives from Antisthenes,⁶⁹ it fits well enough into a generally Cynic context. But the choice of doctrine is also well suited to delivery before Trajan. Cohoon⁷⁰ reasonably sees a 'compliment to Trajan, who had little interest in letters', at 4.31: 'Whoever, then, being noble by nature, possesses that higher education, readily acquires this other also, having only to learn a few things in a few lessons, merely the greatest and most important things, and is already initiated and treasures them in his soul.' The appeals to the precedent of Heracles (4.32, 72) may also be regarded as complimentary to Trajan, for Heracles was not only one of the great exemplars of the Cynics, he was also the favourite hero of the emperor.⁷¹

⟦271⟧ Another interesting point emerges from 4.31. At this juncture Diogenes is engaging in continuous exposition, not in biting Cynic cross-examination, and simply because of this change in style, just as in Socratic dialogue, one gains the impression that Alexander is quietly listening to the words of the master with greater comprehension than he has previously displayed. Thus Diogenes' remark, 'Whoever, then, being noble by nature, possesses that higher education, readily acquires this other also', seems to suggest some natural nobility in Alexander, his listener. This impression is confirmed by 4.38, where Diogenes explicitly concedes natural nobility in Alexander. The emphasis, as already argued, is important, because it allows for the possibility of development in Alexander's character, and thus helps to render the criticisms made of him, serious and weighty though they are, less severe than they would have been, had Alexander been painted as naturally depraved. Again, this is a sop to Trajan, for Dio's attacks on the character of Alexander are not irrevocable. Trajan could even have inferred that in Dio's opinion there was nothing wrong with the Alexander pose per se, just with imitation of Alexander as he actually turned out rather than imitation of Alexander as (according to Dio) he might have been if he had been able under wise instruction to develop the nobility of soul that he undoubtedly possessed.

---

68  Cercidas had already emphasised the significance of Diogenes' name: Διογένης Ζανὸς γόνος (D.L. 6.77).
69  Antisthenes F 27 DC {= 96 Prince}; Höistad (1948) 56ff.
70  Cohoon I.183 n. 1.
71  For Trajan and Heracles see Jones (1978) 117f. I do not imply that compliment of Trajan is the *sole* function of 4.31f. See above, n. 7.

These sections (4.27–39) are laden with abuse of the sophists, to such an extent (despite the fact that the historical Diogenes must also have abused sophists) that one is bound to conclude that at the very least Dio is indulging in one of his favourite intellectual pastimes—sophist-bashing.[72] But the emphasis is so heavy that one may well suspect some more specific point. Perhaps Dio felt under pressure from the competition of other advisers of Trajan, who were proffering what in Dio's view was worthless and possibly dangerous advice.[73] One's general feeling that Dio is really talking about himself, Trajan, and others is reinforced by 4.33, where Diogenes argues against the need for lengthy instruction by invoking the Platonic doctrine of 'recollection'—a doctrine ridiculed by Cynics.[74] The dramatic illusion is shattered, and we hear the voice, not of Diogenes the Cynic, but of Dio the (*inter alia*) Platonist. The remark at 4.38—'and you, since you have been born with the right nature, if you come upon a man of understanding, will find a single day sufficient to get a grasp of his subject ⟦272⟧ and art, and you will no longer have any need of subtle claptrap and discussions'—has not only, as already indicated, significance for Dio's portrayal of Alexander, but surely also must be complimentary to Trajan, both for his natural potential and for his choice of Dio as his philosophical mentor to enable him to fulfil that potential. The image from hunting (4.34–5) may be a graceful allusion to Trajan's devotion to that sport[75] (perhaps with the punning point that the sophists are false 'dogs', unlike the true 'dog', Dio/Diogenes).

At the end of his attack upon sophists as purveyors of ignorance and intellectual confusion Diogenes reintroduces, with an obliquity typical of Cynic argument, the idea that Homer is the source of the doctrine that true kings are disciples of Zeus (4.39f.). Then comes the most important passage in the speech. From this definition of kingship the discussion builds up to the assertion that the true king is 'shepherd of peoples' (4.43) and that 'the shepherd's business is simply to oversee, guard, and protect flocks, not ... to slaughter,

---

72  Discussion and references in Moles (1978) 88ff. {above, pp. 39ff.}
73  For such rivalry see 3.12–25 and 1.56. Little is known about Trajan's relations with 'sophists', but his treatment of Dio, honouring of Plutarch (cf. Jones [1971] 28–31), and friendship with Polemon, to whom he granted the privilege of free travel (Philostr. *VS* 532), show the feasibility of such a background. 'Sophist' can also be a derogatory description of practically any kind of intellectual. That Dio has in mind a corrupt court context may also be suggested by the comparison of sophists to eunuchs (4.35).
74  Von Arnim, followed by Desideri (1978) 341 n. 29, deletes the reference to the doctrine of 'recollection', presumably as being un-Cynic and unexampled elsewhere in Dio. This seems irresponsible, especially as the allusion can be given artistic point.
75  Dio may also be thinking hereabouts of Domitian, who was highly πεπαιδευμένος in 'human education' and who had honoured 'sophists' such as Quintilian. Trajan and hunting: Plin. *Pan.* 81; Cass. Dio 68.7.3.

butcher, and skin them' (4.44); hence the aggressive campaigns of Xerxes and Darius against Greece, which resulted in the deaths of a whole host of their subjects, were the actions of butchers rather than true kings (4.45). Questioned by Alexander, Diogenes maintains that neither is the Great King a true king, nor will Alexander become one by the mere fact that he will defeat the Great King. The quarrels and struggles between kings are as trivial and unimportant as games played by boys (4.46–9). Alexander, grieved at this because of his yearning to conquer the whole world and always to rule over somebody else (4.50–1), is driven to the conclusion that Diogenes must be joking, and he continues to believe that if he conquers Persia and India he will be the greatest king who ever lived. Diogenes perceives that Alexander is aflame with ambition and tells him that he will never be a king so long as he maintains his present state of mind, even if he performs the most startling military feats.

When Alexander asks what enemy will be left when he has defeated all the people mentioned, two exchanges take place that demonstrate that Alexander's mind is still concerned almost exclusively with military achievement, not the attainment of moral virtue, and then Diogenes finally reveals, to Alexander's rage (4.59), that his greatest enemy is himself, so long as he remains bad and foolish. Diogenes even invites Alexander to run him through with his spear, secure in the knowledge that Alexander would never jeopardise his reputation (4.59–60). There follows a series of exchanges in which Alexander's ignorance is again exposed. The thought that he does not even possess the 'sign' of kingship gives rise to the assertion that kingship is not marked by tiaras or purple, but by the absence of weapons—in complete contrast to Alexander, who even sleeps under arms (4.61–4). Alexander at this very nearly does run Diogenes through, but the latter is unflinching (cf. 4.51) in his efforts to direct Alexander ⟦273⟧ towards justice and away from reliance on arms (4.65). Unlike the king bee, the perfect exemplar of kingship, which has no sting, Alexander has within himself the sharp sting of ambition. Diogenes advises Alexander to throw off his armour and ridiculous diadem, don the vest worn by slaves and working men, and serve his betters (4.65–6). The Sacian feast held by the Persians (in which Alexander, for military reasons eager to learn about all things Persian, is greatly interested) illustrates the fact that royal power is often acquired by the foolish and wicked, and that wisdom is an absolute prerequisite for the attainment of kingship (4.66–70). Consequently Alexander would do better to live in solitude, clad in a sheepskin (4.70). Alexander, descendant of Heracles, is aghast at this, but Diogenes points out that another of his ancestors, Archelaus, was a goatherd (4.72).

I have paraphrased this part of the speech at length because it is so important for the interpretation of the whole. What should we make of it?

For Höistad,[76] 'This portrait of the basileus is wholly non-political: basileus is an allegorical term and coincides with the introductory comparison between Alexander and Diogenes with its antithetic structure.' Similarly, Höistad thinks that in the introductory comparison 'Dio is here not theorizing about the basileus as such. Alexander is not so much the tyrant in the ordinary sense of the term as an unfree and unhappy man full of erroneous ideas about the true values of life.' This approach presupposes that an absolute distinction can sometimes be made between 'political' analysis of kingship and the discussion of ethical ideals of 'true kingship'. But this distinction is sometimes invalid. Discussion of ethical ideals of true kingship can take place without direct political implication, but the converse rarely applies. In Greek philosophical thought ever since Socrates, and indeed earlier, political analysis of kingship very often involved the discussion of ethical ideals of true kingship (no man can be a good ruler unless he can rule himself first—and good ruling implies the need for a good moral character, etc.). Consequently, while some of *Or.* 4 is indeed concerned with 'basileus as an allegorical term', it does not necessarily follow that there is no political application. On the face of it, the present section of the speech contains a swinging attack upon mindless militarism, and this can reasonably be described as a political statement.

For Jones there is no particular point: 'the subject of Alexander inevitably evoked that of his most notable campaign'.[77] This seems inadequate. First, the statement is not even literally true: though mention of Alexander's most notable campaign is natural, it is certainly not inevitable—cf. *Or.* 1.1–8 and the whole of *Or.* 2! Second, and more important, Jones' observation does nothing to explain the thoroughly critical emphasis on Alexander's megalomaniac lust for conquest. The section 4.43–72 is not only heavily emphatic in itself: the preceding sections are designed to build up to 43–72 as a climactic statement. ⟦274⟧ We have seen that Alexander, for all the falsity of his value system, is depicted as possessing innate nobility and as having the potential for moral growth under wise tutorship, and that his encounter with Diogenes takes on something of the character of a meeting of master and pupil, with Alexander, despite his tremendous ignorance, showing glimmerings of response to Diogenes' message. Then at the start of this section, when Diogenes compares the struggles of kings, and in particular the forthcoming struggles between Alexander and Darius, to games played by children, Alexander is described as being 'hurt' and 'vexed' and driven to suppose that Diogenes is joking (4.46–51). Why, we may ask, does he not yet lose his temper? It is only when Diogenes makes a still more forceful

---

76  Höistad (1948) 218.
77  Jones (1978) 121.

attack upon useless conquest, and finally reveals that Alexander's greatest enemy is himself, that Alexander loses control. It does not seem fanciful to suppose that Dio has chosen to trace Alexander's reactions with some care.[78] If so, the statement that he was (only) 'grieved' by Diogenes' initial attack upon his imperial ambitions seems significant. Alexander is grieved because he has begun to understand that Diogenes' views deserve respect, and he is therefore upset when they do not coincide with his own on a subject so dear to his heart. But when Diogenes launches a full-scale assault upon his imperial ambitions and his very self, he can no longer contain his feelings, and we are made to feel that now at last the ultimate disagreement between the two men has been exposed. The section is also the logical culmination of several hints already dropped about Alexander's insane desire for conquest.[79]

Here, if anywhere in the speech, the characters of Alexander and Trajan most nearly coincide—both men were highly ambitious and eager for military glory. The conclusion seems inescapable that Dio is attacking Trajan's imperialist dreams. Yet some scholars have denied that Dio could have said such things to an autocrat, however benevolent. This is to underestimate Dio's literary art.

The general ethos of *Or.* 4 is Cynic,[80] and Cynic philosophers often strove to impart serious instruction by means of humour, paradox, and exaggeration. Not everything they said was to be taken as literally true.[81] The comparison of the foolish behaviour of kings to games played by children (4.47–9), which is appropriately insulting to the vain and impetuous Alexander, need not amount to a considered statement that kingship is an intrinsically worthless human institution. The tone of 4.50–1, where it is said that Alexander would have no interest in becoming a god unless he became king of the gods, and that the only reason he would not have despised Zeus, along with the rest of the gods, was ⟦275⟧ that Zeus was a king, is humorous—a serious point is being made, but in an amusing way. Amusing also are the descriptions of Alexander about to rage and prance about (4.58) or to impale Diogenes with his spear (4.59, 64)—there is no reason why Trajan too should not have found this an agreeable picture: he had a sense of humour.[82] Particularly entertaining is

---

78  They are described at each stage of the philosophical lesson: 4.15, 18, 20, 23, 26, 36, 39, 49, 52, 55, 58, 61, 64, 71, 77–8.
79  E.g., 4.4–5, 10–12, 16, 30.
80  See above, n. 65. Szarmach (1976) 175 also sees the Cynic ethos as important for the interpretation of the speech.
81  Cf. D.L. 6.35: 'Diogenes used to say that he followed the example of the trainers of choruses; for they too set the note a little high, to ensure that the rest should hit the right note.'
82  Cass. Dio 68.7.3.

the passage 4.60–4—characteristically Cynic in its method of argument, and quite absurd if taken literally. Nor is Diogenes' statement that the true king has no need of tiaras or purple in real contradiction with *Or.* 2.49, where such trappings are allowed the king, provided that they do not extend to luxury. In context Alexander's tiara and purple robe symbolise his love of empty show, but on hearing Diogenes' exhortation to Alexander, Trajan would hardly feel obliged to lay aside the purple! Similarly, the jibe at Alexander's boast to be descended from Heracles (4.62) must be seen in context. There is no contrast with *Or.* 1.62ff., where Dio invokes the example of Heracles: the point simply is that Diogenes is ridiculing the pretensions of the Heraclids by pungent comparison with the king bee, and that Alexander does not imitate Heracles (who, after all, is the great Cynic exemplar, approved by Diogenes at 4.32) in the proper way.[83] The admonitions to Alexander to get rid of his armour and don the workman's vest, or even a sheepskin *à la* Archelaus, can also be understood as Cynic exaggeration. They do not mean that it is wrong for an emperor to wear armour, they simply emphasise Alexander's obsession with arms and the pomp of royal power. Such an interpretation of these swipes at Alexander is truer to the spirit of the characteristically Cynic mixture of jesting with seriousness (σπουδαιογέλοιον) than any merely literal reading.[84] But we have also seen that in his carefully ambiguous introduction Dio ensures in advance against prosaic interpretation of the bolder flights of his Cynic sage. He has pointed out that those who exaggerate in order that their wise men should be honoured for their wisdom alone 'strip them of all else, such as wealth, honours, and physical strength'—which is exactly what he himself is doing by making Diogenes demand that Alexander don a sheepskin if he is to become truly wise.[85] In short, this section of the speech has a very serious purpose, but the message is put across entertainingly: Trajan could smile at the more outrageous elements in Diogenes' prescription and at the discomfiture of the hapless Alexander, but he might still realise that Dio was trying to say something of great importance. At the same time Dio again skilfully obfuscates the analogy [[276]] between the ambitions of Trajan and Alexander, real as it is, by a

---

83  These alleged contradictions between *Or.* 4 and *Orr.* 1 and 2 are one of Lepper's arguments (1948: 194ff.) for non-delivery before Trajan.

84  On Cynic σπουδαιογέλοιον see Kindstrand (1976) 47f. Epictetus understood this aspect of Cynic exposition: Epict. 3.22.90: 'the Cynic must possess great natural charm and wit—otherwise he becomes mere snot.'

85  In 4.70; 4.66 alludes to the Cynic doctrine of the 'strip'—the change of garment symbolising philosophical conversion. For the general motif see Kindstrand (1976) 164; for its more dramatic Cynic form see, e.g., Strab. 15.1.64, 65 = Onesicr. *FGrHist* 134 F 17; [Diog.] *Ep.* 24; 29.2; *Pap. génèv. inv.* 271, col. IV, 53ff.

number of implied contrasts: Alexander is quick-tempered—Trajan was not;[86] Alexander has a weakness for luxury—Trajan was the reverse; Alexander is utterly dependent on arms (4.63)—Trajan was not.[87] We may admire Dio's courage, but we should also recognise that he has deployed all the resources of his literary skill to sugar the pill.

In section 75 Diogenes begins the long 'spirits' exposition that lasts to the end of the speech. The theme, as before, is that true kingliness resides in a man's inner character, but it is now developed at length. Diogenes introduces the section with a devastating attack upon Alexander's 'spirit'. Alexander is amazed at Diogenes' courage in describing his 'spirit' in such unflattering terms, 'yet, deeming him to have greater knowledge than other men, he urgently besought him not to refuse him but to explain what his "spirit" was.' Such is the attitude Trajan should take to Dio's equally pungent criticism. After all Diogenes' ridicule of his imperial ambitions and savage attacks upon his personality, Alexander still wants to listen to Diogenes. Even now a few more criticisms are made of Alexander—of his emotional volatility and lack of steadiness, his ambition and failure to appreciate Diogenes' style of discourse (4.77–8)—but these form a kind of summing-up before the final exposition, and for the rest of the speech we may imagine Alexander placidly absorbing the words of the master, who in turn adjusts his teaching methods to the taste of his difficult pupil by stretching out on a ripe piece of sophistic rhetoric (4.78ff.).

It remains to consider (briefly, for by its very nature the final section of the speech contains less meat than the rest) the political content of the 'spirits' exposition. Of the three spirits that dominate the lives of most men, the first two, the avaricious and luxurious, have little or no reference to either Alexander or Trajan.[88] The third, the vainglorious, has direct application to both. Some of the imagery in the description of the vainglorious spirit seems to recall earlier descriptions of Alexander (4.117–21 // 4.52, 77). But since Dio intends to end the speech on a placatory note, the criticism is progressively muted. This effect is achieved in various ways. Alexander at last appears as a docile pupil, willing to learn. The vivid and lengthy descriptions of the avaricious and luxurious spirits, which have nothing to do with Trajan, provide a lull in the sequence of criticism. Again, while the basic content of the section is acceptably Cynic, the style of exposition becomes less challenging. It is both sophistic, and hence less overtly 'serious'; and also Platonic, and hence relatively more lenient in its

---

86  Cass. Dio 68.7.3; cf. 68.6.4 (though Trajan's temper may have deteriorated at the end).
87  Cf. above, nn. 59 and 61.
88  Alexander is rather prone to 'luxury' (4.6). Trajan's life-style may be implicitly contrasted with that of the 'luxurious spirit' in 4.101. Sections 4.103 and 110 hardly allude to Alexander's and Trajan's heavy drinking.

attitude to worldly kingship. Dio also, within the 'vainglorious' section itself, continues to use various distancing devices: the graceful allusion to hunting (4.127), the rather clumsy exclusion of generals, educators, and statesmen from the [[277]] list of those conquered by ambition (4.132), and the equally uncomfortable concession that rhetoric can be useful (4.124). All represent a further softening of the rigours of true Cynicism. There may also be another factor at work, if Jones[89] is right in suggesting that 'several aspects of Domitian appear to be embodied in the three "spirits"'. The combination of all three vices in such a way as to recall Domitian will further help to distance Trajan even from that error, ambition, for which he is still on one level implicitly criticised.

Finally, what will be the effect of 4.139? On the simple level, that of the encounter between Alexander and Diogenes, the passage maintains the idea that Alexander has it within himself to attain the true spirit (δαίμων) of happiness (εὐδαιμονία), and thus again suggests to Trajan that if Alexander is to be emulated at all, it can only be as the Alexander led by Diogenes along the path of virtue. But on another level the dramatic illusion is broken, both by the fact that the Cynic Diogenes expounds Platonic (and Stoic) doctrine (analogously to his exposition of the Platonic doctrine of 'recollection' in 4.33) and (as we have seen) by the precise wording. Thus the reference to Dio and Trajan implicit in the whole dialogue is finally made virtually explicit. But simultaneously, by recalling his meeting with the Arcadian prophetess and the prophecy she allegedly made to him, Dio blurs the parallel between Trajan and Alexander and finishes his speech with an ingenious flourish to Trajan as the symbol of his own 'conversion' to philosophy and as the Saviour of the Roman world. The ambiguity and complexity of the effect in 4.139 make an appropriate end to an elusive and complicated work.

To sum up: the argument of this paper has been that the Fourth Kingship Oration is fundamentally a criticism of, or a warning against, Trajan's ambition and hopes of imperialist expansion, but that Dio couches this message with great skill to avoid, as far as possible, giving direct offense. If this general interpretation is accepted, can we be more precise about the date of delivery?

Lepper and Momigliano have argued for a late dating (c.115 or even after Trajan's death) because they believe that the speech attacks Trajan's Parthian war policy. The equation Parthia/Persia is indeed tempting, especially in view of the historical tradition that Trajan embarked on his Eastern campaigns from personal ambition.[90] Certainly, if we knew for a fact that the speech was

---

89   Jones (1978) 121.
90   Lepper (1948) 194ff. (the speech partly Hadrianic); Momigliano (1950) 265 (contemporary with the Parthian War but delivered to a Greek audience); the historical tradition: Cass. Dio 68.17.1; Fronto II.213 Haines = 198 van den Hout. Cf. also Trajan's 'Alexandri imitatio'.

delivered c.115, Lepper's and Momigliano's interpretation would be compelling. But the possible equation between Parthia and Persia cannot itself provide a dating criterion. Great ambition may well have been discernible in Trajan long before it manifested (or was thought to manifest) itself so disastrously in the Parthian wars. Indeed, if Trajan assumed an Alexander pose early in his reign (as Dio's First and Second Kingship Orations, among other evidence, suggest), Dio's use [[278]] of the Alexander–Persia model is already sufficiently explained. Besides, on any reasonable view, Trajan projected himself as a martial emperor from the outset, and his ambitions were plain for all to see.[91] From the very beginning of the reign, thinking men could have been apprehensive about the dangers to come. Further, the whole tenor of the speech, as I have tried to show, presupposes actual delivery before Trajan, which tells strongly against Lepper's and Momigliano's interpretation, for we do not know if Dio was with Trajan shortly before the Parthian campaign and it is hardly likely that Dio would have delivered such a speech before Trajan once the campaign was under way. *Or.* 4 is a warning while there is still time, not a contemporary attack on a policy already being pursued, still less a retrospective justification of Hadrian's retrenchment.

In my opinion, an early dating makes the best sense of the implicit complimentary contrasts between Trajan and Domitian; the marked Dio/Diogenes allegory, which is a product of Dio's struggle against Domitian; the broad similarity of the speech to the Diogenes discourses, which are exilic;[92] the characterisation of Alexander, which seems to show Dio attempting to mould Trajan's Alexander pretensions at their inception and, more generally, making what looks like an early and emphatic bid for the role of philosophical counsellor; and the oblique reference at 4.139, which should be as close as possible in time to the start of the reign. If pressed, I would date *Or.* 4 to 100, perhaps to September 18 (Trajan's birthday).

The problem of precise dating apart, this interpretation of the speech makes it (it seems to me) a thoroughly impressive work, impressive not only for the control and skill with which Dio oscillates between praise and reproof of Trajan, and between the nominal framework of the speech—the encounter of Alexander and Diogenes—and the contemporary situation that it illustrates, but impressive also for its integrity. On any fair interpretation, this is a good speech, worthy in content, well written and, in its way, entertaining, but if the interpretation I have argued for is correct, it is much more: it is a

---

91  Cf. Plin. *Ep.* 10.41.1 and 5; Syme (1958) I.49 and 41 (a very suggestive portrait).
92  So, rightly (I believe), von Arnim (1898) 245; Dudley (1937) 151; Moles (1978) 89 {above, p. 40} n. 90; Desideri (1978) 200ff.

magnificent speech by a man who, despite all the vicissitudes of a rather spotty career, his posturings, and his unamiable personal character, nevertheless did say some things worth saying, and said some of them very well. For a Greek court philosopher, dependent to some extent on the patronage and goodwill of the emperor, yet far from indifferent to his responsibilities as imperial counsellor, *Or.* 4 could almost be a textbook example of how 'to steer a way between perilous insubordination and degrading servility'. Trajan, of course, failed to take its message to heart, but that does nothing to detract from the exemplary seriousness with which Dio fulfilled his role and the sheer subtlety and tact with which he expressed himself.

## Bibliography

von Arnim, H. (1898) *Leben und Werke des Dio von Prusa* (Berlin).

Brancacci, A. (1980) 'Tradizione cinica e problemi di datazione nelle orazioni diogeniane di Dione di Prusa', *Elenchos* 1: 92–122.

Brunt, P. A. (1977) 'From Epictetus to Arrian', *Athenaeum* n.s. 55: 19–48; repr. in id., *Studies in Stoicism*, edd. M. Griffin and A. Samuels (Oxford, 2013) 331–59.

Desideri, P. (1978) *Dione di Prusa: un intelletuale greco nell'impero romano* (Messina/Florence).

Dover, K. J. (1974) *Greek Popular Morality in the Time of Plato and Aristotle* (Oxford and Berkeley).

Dudley, D. R. (1937) *A History of Cynicism from Diogenes to the 6th century A.D.* (London).

England, E. B. (1921) *The Laws of Plato*, 2 vols. (Manchester).

Farquharson, A. S. L., ed. (1944) *The Meditations of the Emperor Marcus Antoninus*, 2 vols. (Oxford).

Fears, J. R. (1974) 'The Stoic View of the Career and Character of Alexander the Great', *Philologus* 118: 113–30.

Fears, J. R. (1977) *Princeps a diis electus: The Divine Election of the Emperor as a Political Concept at Rome* (Rome).

Ferrante, D. (1975) *Περὶ Βασιλείας (Or. IV): introduzione, testo, traduzione e commentario* (Naples).

Griffin, M. T. (1976) *Seneca: a Philosopher in Politics* (Oxford; repr. with addenda, 1992).

Harrison, J. E. (1927) *Themis: a Study of the Social Origins of Greek Religion*[2] (Cambridge).

Hirzel, R. (1895) *Der Dialog*, 2 vols. (Leipzig).

Hoffmann, W. (1907) *Das literarische Porträt Alexanders des Grossen im griechischen und römischen Altertum* (Leipzig).

Höistad, R. (1948) *Cynic Hero and Cynic King: Studies in the Cynic Conception of Man* (Uppsala).

Jones, C. P. (1971) *Plutarch and Rome* (Oxford).
Jones, C. P. (1975) 'An Oracle Given to Trajan', *Chiron* 5: 403–6.
Jones, C. P. (1978) *The Roman World of Dio Chrysostom* (Cambridge, Mass. and London).
Kindstrand, J. F. (1976) *Bion of Borysthenes: a Collection of the Fragments with Introduction and Commentary* (Uppsala).
Lepper, F. A. (1948) *Trajan's Parthian War* (Oxford).
Levick, B. M. (1980) 'Review of Jones (1978) and Desideri (1978)', *CR* n.s. 30: 192–4.
Martin, V. (1959) 'Un recueil de diatribes cyniques: Pap. Genev. inv. 271', *MH* 16: 77–115.
Millar, F. (1969) 'P. Herennius Dexippus: the Greek World and the Third-Century Invasions', *JRS* 59: 12–29.
Moles, J. L. (1978) 'The Career and Conversion of Dio Chrysostom', *JHS* 98: 79–100 [above, Ch. 1].
Moles, J. L. (1983a) 'Dio Chrysostom: Exile, Tarsus, Nero and Domitian', *LCM* 8: 130–4 [above, Ch. 2].
Moles, J. L. (1983b) '"*Honestius quam Ambitiosius*"? An Exploration of the Cynic's Attitude to Moral Corruption in his Fellow Men', *JHS* 103: 103–23 [below, Ch. 12].
Momigliano, A. D. (1950) 'Dio Chrysostomos' (Unpublished Lecture, 1950), in id., *Quarto Contributo alla Storia degli studi classici e del mondo antico* (Rome, 1969) 257–69.
Nock, A. D. (1928) 'Notes on Ruler Cult, I–IV', *JHS* 48: 21–43; repr. in id., *Essays on Religion and the Ancient World*, ed. Z. Stewart, 2 vols. (Oxford) 1.134–59.
Oldfather, W. A. (1925–8) *Epictetus: Discourses*, 2 vols. (London and Cambridge, Mass.).
Phillips, E. D. (1957) 'Three Greek Writers on the Roman Empire', *C&M* 18: 102–19.
Pleket, H. (1965) 'An Aspect of Emperor Cult: Imperial Mysteries', *HThR* 58: 331–47.
Robert, L. (1960) 'Récherches Epigraphiques IV–IX', *REA* 62: 276–361; repr. in id., *Opera Minora Selecta* II (Amsterdam, 1969) 792–877.
Rostovtzeff, M. (1957) *The Social and Economic History of the Roman Empire*$^2$, rev. by P. M. Fraser, 2 vols. (Oxford).
Stadter, P. A. (1980) *Arrian of Nicomedia* (Chapel Hill and London).
Syme, R. (1958) *Tacitus*, 2 vols. (Oxford).
Szarmach, M. (1976) 'Les discours περὶ βασιλείας de Dion de Pruse', *Eos* 64: 163–76.
Treu, K. (1958) *Synesios von Kyrene: Dion Chrysostomos oder vom Leben nach seinem Vorbild* (Berlin).
Valdenberg, V. (1927) 'La théorie monarchique de Dion Chrysostome', *REG* 40: 142–62.
Wallace-Hadrill, A. W. (1982) 'The Golden Age and Sin in Augustan Ideology', *P&P* 95: 19–36.
Weinstock, S. (1971) *Divus Julius* (Oxford).
Wilcken, U. (1923) 'Alexander der Grosse und die indischen Gymnosophisten', *SB Berlin* 23: 150–83.
Wirth, G. (1975) 'Alexander und Rom', in *Alexandre le Grand: image et réalité* (Vandoeuvres-Genève) 181–221.

CHAPTER 4

# The Addressee of the Third Kingship Oration of Dio Chrysostom

In his important recent book on Dio Chrysostom P. Desideri argues, against the traditional view, that the Third Kingship Oration was addressed to Nerva, not Trajan.[1] C. P. Jones includes this among several new hypotheses of Desideri 'which, if not necessarily mistaken, will at least raise eyebrows'.[2] In this article I shall show that this particular hypothesis is indeed 'necessarily mistaken', even though Desideri's original arguments often elsewhere command our admiration and nearly always stimulate us to look at old problems in a fresh way.

The nub of Desideri's case is as follows (1):

> il fatto che Dione dichiari di conoscere bene l'imperatore in carica, e il tono confidenziale di cui è pervaso tutto il discorso, sembrano concordare perfettamente con quanto Dione dice altrove dei suoi rapporti con Nerva, accennando alla sua morte: 'mi fu tolto un imperatore benevolo e che mi amava e da tempo era mio amico'.

He also maintains, however, that (2) the wording of 3.2 would apply less well to Trajan with whom 'Dione appare assai più riservato, anche a distanza di anni dal loro primo incontro: συνηθείας οὔσης μοι πρὸς τὸν αὐτοκράτορα, ἴσως δὲ καὶ φιλίας (47.22; cf. 45.3)'; (3) a Nervan dating better fits the fact that 'Dione allude al periodo dell'esilio come a cosa molto recente (13), specialmente per la contrapposizione πρότερον μέν ... νῦν δέ'; and (4) the Trajanic dating depends solely on the hypothesis that Dio did not return to Rome immediately on the assassination of Domitian—a hypothesis Desideri himself necessarily contests.[3]

Arguments (1), (2), and (3) need not detain us long. We cannot really ⟦66⟧ know how friendly Dio's relations with Trajan were: we can only consider how

---

1 Desideri (1978) 279; the traditional view: von Arnim (1898) 399; Jones (1978) 119; and many others.
2 Jones (1980) 172 (reviewing Desideri).
3 Desideri (1978) 297, 344 nn. 2 and 3. *Or.* 3.2 runs, ἐγὼ δέ, ὦ γενναῖε αὐτοκράτορ, παραγέγονά σοι, καὶ τυχὸν οὐδενὸς ἧττον ἔμπειρός εἰμι τῆς σῆς φύσεως .... 3.13 runs: εἰ δὲ ἐγὼ πρότερον μέν ὅτε πᾶσιν ἀναγκαῖον ἐδόκει ψεύδεσθαι διὰ φόβον, μόνος ἀληθεύειν ἐτόλμων, καὶ ταῦτα κινδυνεύων ὑπὲρ τῆς ψυχῆς, νῦν δέ, ὅτε πᾶσιν ἔξεστι τἀληθῆ λέγειν, ψεύδομαι, μηδενὸς κινδύνου παρεστῶτος, οὐκ ἂν εἰδείην οὔτε παρρησίας οὔτε κολακείας καιρόν.

Dio represents them. From that point of view 3.2 makes just as good sense on the hypothesis of delivery to Trajan: after the First Kingship Oration Dio has moved (*ex hypothesi*) to a position of greater intimacy with Trajan[4] (or at least can claim to have done so); 47.22 and 45.3 *do* attest φιλία with Trajan; and if in 47.22 Dio does not stress this too much, we can see why (he wishes to avoid the charge of excessive cultivation of the emperor and prominent Romans, to the neglect of local interests). There could be equally good reasons for great emphasis on his φιλία with Trajan in the Third Kingship Oration: one of the main concerns of the beginning of the speech is to defend Dio against accusations of flattery and it is important that he should stress his knowledge of the emperor's character in order to demonstrate both that he knows what he is talking about and that Trajan is by nature opposed to sycophancy. As for the implication that the exile was recent, if there really is such an implication,[5] the exile could still be 'recent' under Trajan three or four years later, and the broad contrast between life under Domitian and life under Trajan, without allusion to the intervening rule of Nerva, is common elsewhere both in Dio himself and in Pliny's *Panegyricus*.[6] These three arguments, then, do not support Desideri's case, though equally they do not count against it.

But it is in argument (4) that we find the first major difficulty for Desideri's hypothesis. Desideri ignores the fact that there are positive arguments for a Trajanic dating. More important, against the usual view that Dio did not return to Rome on Domitian's assassination, Desideri refers us to his earlier discussion of this period of Dio's career, but when we consult this discussion we are simply told that, 'In realtà a Dione non devono essere mancate occasioni di incontrarsi con Nerva a Roma dopo la sua ascesa al trono, come dimostra lo stesso terzo discorso *Sullà regalità*, che è stato pronunciato secondo me di fronte a Nerva'.[7] Thus a difficulty in the hypothesised dating of *Or.* 3 is resolved by reference to … the hypothesised dating of *Or.* 3! This methodologically dubious procedure could only be justified if other arguments for the hypothesised dating were very strong. As we have seen, they are not.

⟦67⟧ Moreover, the usual hypothesis that Dio did not return to Rome immediately on Domitian's assassination seems soundly based. The critical passage is Dio's own account of his movements in *Or.* 45.2–3:

---

4  So von Arnim (1898) 399; Cohoon I.103; Jones (1978) 119.
5  This is the sort of inference historians often make. It is not unreasonable, but neither is it compelling.
6  Cf. Jones (1978) 118 for examples from Dio's First Kingship Oration and Moles (1983) for examples from *Or.* 4; Plin. *Paneg.* 47–9.
7  Desideri (1978) 263.

Τελευτήσαντος δὲ ἐκείνου καὶ τῆς μεταβολῆς γενομένης ἀνῄειν μὲν πρὸς τὸν βέλτιστον Νέρβαν. ὑπὸ δὲ νόσου χαλεπῆς κατασχεθεὶς ὅλον ἐκεῖνον ἐζημιώθην τὸν καιρόν, ἀφαιρεθεὶς αὐτοκράτορος φιλανθρώπου κἀμὲ ἀγαπῶντος καὶ πάλαι φίλου. καὶ ὀμνύω τοὺς θεοὺς ὑμῖν ἅπαντας, οὐκ ἐφ' οἷς ἂν εἰς ἐμαυτὸν ἢ τῶν ἐμῶν τινα ἔλαβον, οὐκ ἐπὶ τούτοις ἄχθομαι διαμαρτών, ἀλλ' ἐφ' οἷς ὑμῖν καὶ δημοσίᾳ τῇ πόλει παρασχεῖν ἐδυνάμην, ταύτην ἐγὼ μεγάλην ἀριθμῷ βλάβην καὶ ζημίαν. ὧν γὰρ νῦν ἐτύχομεν, τότε ἐξῆν ταῦτα ἔχειν καὶ τῷ παρόντι καιρῷ πρὸς ἑτέρας κεχρῆσθαι δωρεάς. ἐπεὶ δ' οὖν ὑπῆρξε παρὰ τούτου φιλανθρωπία καὶ σπουδὴ τοσαύτη περὶ ἡμᾶς ὅσην ἐπίστανται μὲν οἱ παρατυχόντες, ἐγὼ δὲ ἂν λέγω νῦν, σφόδρα λυπήσω τινάς—ἴσως δὲ οὐδὲ φανεῖται πιστὸς ὁ λόγος τὸ τηλικαύτης τιμῆς τυγχάνοντα καὶ συνηθείας καὶ φιλίας ἅπαντα ταῦτα ἐᾶσαι καὶ παριδεῖν, ἐπιθυμήσαντα τῆς ἐνταῦθα ταραχῆς καὶ τῆς ἀσχολίας, ἵνα μηδὲν εἴπω πλέον—ὅμως δ' εἰς οὐδὲν τῶν ἰδίων κατεθέμην τὸν καιρὸν ἐκεῖνον οὐδὲ τὴν τοῦ κρατοῦντος εὔνοιαν οὐδὲ ἀπὸ μέρους, οἷον τὰ τῆς οὐσίας ἐπανορθώσας διεφθαρμένης ἢ προσλαβών τινα ἀρχὴν ἢ δύναμιν, ἀλλ' ἅπαν ὅσον ποτὲ ἦν εἰς ὑμᾶς ἔτρεψα καὶ μόνον εἶδον τὸ τῆς πόλεως.

On the usual interpretation the imperfect ἀνῄειν is inceptive or conative and implies that Dio did not *succeed* in reaching Nerva.[8] This reading is supported by (i) the μέν ... δέ contrast ('I *was going* to Nerva, *but* I was κατασχεθείς by a serious illness') and (ii) the verbal contrast between 'movement' and 'stopping' and ἀνα- and κατα-. Although κατέχω can be used of a disease in the sense 'seize, come upon',[9] I do not believe that a skilful stylist like Dio could have written ἀνῄειν μέν ... ὑπὸ δὲ νόσου ... κατασχεθείς without being aware of the implication 'I made a movement which was *stopped*'. Dio surely cannot be interpreted as meaning 'I went to Nerva but *when I reached him* a severe illness prevented me from soliciting him on behalf of Prusa (though I did deliver a kingship oration before him)'. The sequel demonstrates this still more plainly. By his illness Dio lost ὅλον ἐκεῖνον τὸν καιρόν and the καιρός he missed under Nerva and the lost opportunities of that period are implicitly contrasted with the καιρός he did obtain with Trajan and the successful solicitations he then made (ὅλον ἐκεῖνον τὸν καιρόν ~ τῷ παρόντι καιρῷ ~ τὸν καιρὸν ἐκεῖνον, αὐτοκράτορος ... φίλου [[68]] ~ παρὰ τούτου ... συνηθείας καὶ φιλίας, οὐκ ἐφ' οἷς ... ἀλλ' ἐφ' οἷς ... ~ ὅμως δ' ... ἀλλ' ... πόλεως). Dio had no opportunity to speak with Nerva at all. This reading finds further confirmation from two other passages in Dio's works. In *Or.* 44.12 (a speech delivered in Prusa after Dio's return from exile) Dio writes: ἵνα δὲ

---

8 So Crosby IV.209: 'I was on the point of going to visit Nerva; but, having been prevented by a serious illness ...'; von Arnim (1898) 335; Jones (1978) 52.
9 Cf. LSJ s.v., II.6, 10.

καὶ ἀλλαχόθεν εἰδῆτε τὴν ἐμὴν γνώμην, ἀναγνώσομαι ὑμῖν ἐπιστολὴν ἥν τε αὐτὸς ἐπέστειλα τῷ αὐτοκράτορι ὅτε ἐκλήθην, ὅτι ἐν ἐκείνῃ παρεκάλουν ἀφεθῆναι πρὸς ὑμᾶς, καὶ ἣν ἐκεῖνος ἀντέγραψεν. Since the emperor here in question must be Nerva,[10] this passage confirms that Dio did not succeed in reaching Rome in the period 96–98. Similarly, in *Or.* 40.5 Dio describes his activities since his return from exile:

πρότερον γὰρ οὐδ' ἐπ' ὀλίγον σχολὴν ἤγαγον ἴσως διὰ τὴν ἐμαυτοῦ πολυπραγμοσύνην, ὃς δέον ἐντυχεῖν ὑμῖν καὶ φιλοφρονήσασθαι τοσοῦτο μόνον καὶ θῦσαι τοῖς θεοῖς καὶ νὴ Δία ἀναγνῶναι τὰ γράμματα τὰ τοῦ αὐτοκράτορος, ὅτι ἀναγκαῖον ἦν, ἔπειτα εὐθὺς ἀναχωρῆσαι καὶ τρέπεσθαι καθ' αὑτόν, λόγον τινὰ εἶπον ὑπὲρ ἔργου τινός, οὐκ αὐτὸς μόνον, ἀλλὰ καὶ τῶν ἡγεμόνων ἐσπουδακότων, ἴσως μὲν ὑμῖν, ἴσως δὲ κἀμοὶ χαρίζεσθαι βουλομένων καὶ τὴν πόλιν ἄμεινον κατασκευάζειν καὶ σεμνοτέραν ποιεῖν ἅπασαν.

There is no mention here of any meeting with Nerva, as there surely would have been had such a meeting taken place, but there is a reference to a letter from 'the emperor', and this letter must be the same one as at that referred to in 44.12.[11]

In my opinion, therefore, the evidence is absolutely decisive that Dio did not manage to visit Nerva after his accession.

However, even if this conclusion is not accepted, there are several internal indications within *Or.* 3 which rule out delivery before Nerva, unless indeed we are prepared to attribute to Dio a quite incredible degree of stupidity and tactlessness.

(i) The addressee of the speech is 'a general more courageous than the soldiers in the ranks' (3.5), whose 'courage is able, not only to save the less valiant, but even to fire them with greater courage' (3.7), and 'with whom victory is certain' (3.8). All this is much too specific to be dismissed as merely an allusion to conventional imperial 'virtus': it [[69]] would be highly inappropriate to Nerva, who was not a soldier and who was indeed

---

10   So, rightly, von Arnim (1898) 315; Jones' dating of *Or.* 44 to after Dio's return from the embassy to Trajan is demonstrably incorrect (44.11 does *not* imply that Prusa has already gained the various privileges mentioned—cf. 44.10); Desideri's dating of Dio's return to Prusa to 100 or later (Desideri (1978) 264), which entails that the emperor of 44.12 be Trajan, seems too late; on both these points see a forthcoming article, Sheppard (1984).

11   So von Arnim (1898) 345; Desideri (1978) 277 n. 20 (though for Desideri the emperor is Trajan); Jones' belief that two different letters are referred to (Jones (1978) 176 n. 65) depends on an erroneous reconstruction—cf. n. 10 above.

threatened by military revolt, but highly appropriate to Trajan, the great soldier-emperor.

(ii) At 3.12ff. Dio defends himself at length against the charge of flattering the addressee. Later he also defends his practice of 'always saying the same things' about kingship (3.26). It is natural to infer (a) that he has already in the past spoken to the addressee about βασιλεία and (b) that this material has provided his enemies with ammunition for the charge of flattery. This picture coheres badly with delivery before Nerva (why should Dio defend himself against flattering Nerva? what other speeches about kingship is he supposed to have made to Nerva?) but excellently with delivery before Trajan (before whom, on the normal view, he had already spoken at least *Or.* 1, some of which could indeed be represented by hostile critics as 'flattery').

(iii) The addressee is devoted to πόνος and in some cases this implies actual *physical* toil (e.g., 3.3, 56, 83–4, 123, 127). He is also distinguished by καρτερία and is physically extremely fit (3.123ff.). This is appropriate to Trajan, a tough man who took strenuous physical exercise, but not at all to Nerva, whose physical frailty during his brief reign was notorious.[12]

(iv) In 3.133ff. Dio considers the various recreations open to kings. One former king (clearly Nero) wasted his time in singing and acting; another (clearly Ptolemy Auletes) filled his leisure by playing the αὐλός; but the good king 'considers hunting his best recreation'. Dio then describes the pleasures of hunting in some detail (3.135ff.). Not only is Nerva not known ever to have hunted, but in his physical state in 96–98 any suggestion that he should do so would have been grotesque. But hunting was Trajan's favourite sport.[13]

Thus Desideri's hypothesis that *Or.* 3 was delivered before Nerva is refuted by (1) the evidence of *Or.* 45.2, which clearly shows that Dio never met Nerva after he had become emperor, and (2) the internal indications of *Or.* 3, which contains several ideas incompatible with delivery before Nerva and extremely suitable to delivery before Trajan. The traditional view is right.

---

12 It is well understood that, although from 3.25 Dio is explicitly describing the ideal king, there are numerous points of contact between this ideal and the addressee: cf. especially Jones (1978) 116ff. Trajan's toughness: cf., e.g., Plin. *Paneg.* 81–2; Nerva's frailty: cf., e.g., Cass. Dio 68.1.3.

13 Plin. *Paneg.* 81; Cass. Dio 68.7.3. Indeed, there is a certain generic resemblance between 3.133ff. and *Paneg.* 81f.

## Bibliography

von Arnim, H. (1898) *Leben und Werke des Dio von Prusa* (Berlin).

Desideri, P. (1978) *Dione di Prusa: un intelletuale greco nell'impero romano* (Messina/Florence).

Jones, C. P. (1978) *The Roman World of Dio Chrysostom* (Cambridge, Mass. and London).

Jones, C. P. (1980) 'Review of Desideri (1978)', *Phoenix* 34: 170–3.

Moles, J. L. (1983) 'The Date and Purpose of the Fourth Kingship Oration of Dio Chrysostom', *ClAnt* 2: 251–78 [above, Ch. 3].

Sheppard, A. R. R. (1984) 'Dio Chrysostom: the Bithynian Years', *L'Antiquité Classique* 53: 157–73.

CHAPTER 5

# The Kingship Orations of Dio Chrysostom

### The Main Problem[1]

The key question about Dio Chrysostom's Kingship Orations has always been whether they aim to praise Trajan or to improve him; or, to be more precise (since on Dio's own admission the speeches contain much praise of Trajan), whether praise is their main, if not sole, aim, or the vehicle of moral instruction. In this instance modern attempts to erase questions of intent from literary texts will not do.[2] That question is explicit in the speeches themselves and exercised persons at the time and later. Dio's detractors at court accused him of gross flattery, an accusation he found necessary to combat in public (3.12–25; cf. 57.10); he himself maintained that the speeches were 'helpful and useful' (57.11) and his admirer Arethas was mightily impressed by their wisdom and practical helpfulness.[3] Both positive and negative views of the speeches have found distinguished advocates to this day, the former group including von Arnim, Dudley, Momigliano, Wirszubski, Rostovtzeff, and Desideri, the latter Lepper, Syme, K. H. Waters, Fears, and C. P. Jones.[4] In a previous paper I considered the question with reference only to the Fourth Oration;[5] here I consider all four speeches.

---

1   [[364]] This paper was given in June 1987 to the Oxford 'Roman Philosophy and Politics' seminar organised by Miriam Griffin and Jonathan Barnes. I thank all who made helpful comments. The present version has benefited enormously from the acute criticisms and suggestions of Professors Tony Woodman and Donald Russell and Dr Malcolm Heath, though I have of course resisted on some points.
2   [[365]] A typical formulation: Wallace-Hadrill (1987) 223: 'Let us not ask what Ovid's purpose was, and whether he meant it (for this drags us into the whole theoretical quagmire of authorial intention), but how Augustus and other Romans would have received the *Fasti*'. Note Wallace-Hadrill's inability, in the face of the challenges posed by the text, to maintain his position (228f.).
3   Most accessible in Crosby v.409; cf. Brancacci (1986) 235ff.
4   [[366]] Von Arnim (1898) 399–435; Dudley (1937) 154–6; Momigliano (1950) 262–5; Wirszubski (1950) 135, 145; Rostovtzeff (1957) 120f.; Desideri (1978) 283–375; Lepper (1948) 193–7; Syme (1958) 40; Waters (1975) 393, 429; Fears (1977) 154–8; C. P. Jones (1978) 115–23.
5   Moles (1983a).

## 1 Preliminary Principles and Problems

### 1.1 *The Kingship Orations as Texts*

So controversial a question cannot be resolved by appeal to Dio's 〚298〛 general moral character. For one thing, that arouses equal controversy, as it did already in Dio's own lifetime and later;[6] the Kingship Orations themselves are an important element in the moral equation. For another, a text is not a person: to some extent it must be judged as a self-contained thing, independent to some degree, once it is written, of the person who wrote it. Of course text and writer ultimately cannot be separated, especially when the writer himself appears in the text, as he does explicitly in Dio's First and Third Kingship Orations and implicitly in the other two speeches, and when all four orations raise the problem of intent, but at least the text's meaning should not be prejudged by the facts—or presumed facts—of the writer's life, still less by any moral assessment based on them. In-depth analysis of the speeches' internal logic is a prerequisite of balanced interpretation, yet has often been conspicuously lacking; many discussions see the speeches as little more than lists of propositions about the good king, which can be wrenched from their context and deployed as evidence for general 'imperial ideology'.

The requisite analysis must be multidisciplinary: it must address the speeches as literature (with regard to internal logic, resourcefulness in use of traditional material, skill of exposition, aesthetic claims, etc.), as philosophy (in the broad sense of moral instruction, in the more restricted sense of the traditions of philosophical writings about kingship and philosophers' addresses to kings, in the still narrower sense of specific philosophical doctrine), as history (with regard to the truthfulness of their portrayal of Domitian, Nerva, and Trajan, to date and political context) and as philosophy and history combined (as one item in the history of the relations of emperors and philosophers in the early Empire).

### 1.2 *External Problems—Historical and Other*

Thus the multidisciplinary approach itself raises problems which are in a sense external but which may greatly affect the texts' interpretation. Some of these problems are historical. If, for example, modern attempts to rehabilitate Domitian's moral character or undermine Nerva's were correct,[7] Dio's Kingship Orations would immediately be condemned as lying and hypocritical

---

6 See in general Desideri (1978) 1–60; Brancacci (1986).
7 Domitian: e.g., Waters (1964) and (1975) 386; B. W. Jones (1973) and (1979); Nerva: e.g., Waters (1975) 386f.

(as would Pliny's *Panegyricus*, Tacitus' *Agricola*, and several passages in the *Histories*). This paper assumes that the traditional pictures of Domitian and Nerva are substantially justified. Again, assessment of the speeches' integrity and of their appositeness must be affected by our view of Trajan—of his general worth, interests, and intellectual ⟦299⟧ capacity. Two problems are especially important:

(1) Trajan and Alexander the Great. The tradition found in Cassius Dio (68.29f.), Julian (*Caes.* 333a, 335d), and the *Historia Augusta* (SHA *Hadr.* 4.9), that at least at the end of his reign Trajan wished to imitate Alexander, seems solid; it does not necessarily entail that Trajan's Parthian war was misconceived and misconducted, though I personally agree with both those propositions.[8]

Alexander appears prominently in the Kingship Orations: in 1.1–8 (a key appearance, I shall argue), throughout 2 (the dialogue between Alexander and Philip), and for most of 4 (the dialogue between Alexander and Diogenes). In all cases a link between Alexander and Trajan can be made internally with significant implications; but these implications would be still more significant if Trajan was already an imitator of Alexander: Dio would be working from a known predilection of Trajan's and skilfully adapting his material to his addressee. It would follow that the emperor was already regarded as ambitious for military glory, so that if Dio registers doubts about its value, these cannot be dismissed as conventional moralising.

The problem is whether Trajan's interest in Alexander can be backdated to the beginning of his reign, when (as we shall see) all Dio's Kingship Orations were delivered. There is nothing difficult about the hypothesis that any Roman general and, still more, any emperor might be interested in Alexander, and there is an ancient tradition that Trajan was ambitious for military glory (Plin. *Ep.* 10.41.1 and 5; Cass. Dio 68.17.1; Fronto II.213 Haines = van den Hout 198). This tradition, though sometimes doubted, is supported by the extent of Trajan's military activity, by imperial propaganda in the first years of the reign,[9] by the

---

8  Trajan–Alexander: Moles (1983a) 253 n. 9, 261ff. {above, pp. 75, 83ff.} (with bibliography). Since Lepper (1948), modern scholarship has tended to give Trajan the benefit of the doubt over the Parthian war (Syme [1958] 41, 235, and Sutherland–Hammond (1970) are exceptions): typical formulations in Garzetti (1974) 363–73; Luttwak (1976) 108–11; in my view such revisionism takes insufficient account of (a) the Alexander imitation; (b) Trajan's rejection of diplomacy; (c) geography: Trajan's deep penetration of Parthian territory is incompatible with 'frontier rectification'.
9  Syme (1958) 41, 45–9.

strong military emphasis in Pliny's *Panegyricus*,[10] and by the immediacy of the Dacian campaign.

There are also positive arguments. First, C. P. Jones has shown that in 45.4 ('a city possessing so great a claim upon the emperor, inasmuch as the god they worship had prophesied and foretold his leadership to him and had been the first of all openly to proclaim him master of the world') Dio alludes to the oracle of Apollo at Didyma, and Jones surmises that as early as 79/80 Trajan had consulted that oracle in imitation of Alexander.[11] Second, Parthia was always 'unfinished business' for the Romans in the first century and for no one more so than Trajan, who in his youth had fought against the Parthians under his father (*Paneg.* 14.1). Third, imitation of Alexander need not be restricted to eastern expansionism: Trajan's first campaigns as emperor were against Dacia, as were Alexander's.[12] [[300]] Finally, can the emphasis on Alexander in the Kingship Orations themselves be fortuitous?

The only difficulty is the silence of the *Panegyricus*, but this could be explained by several factors: the work's pointedly Roman orientation (a reaction to Domitian's philhellenism);[13] the need to suppress a precise parallel with Domitian;[14] general anxiety to avoid the politically controversial. This paper, then, works from the premise that from the beginning of his reign Trajan was a known admirer of Alexander.

(2) Trajan's intellectual capacity. This involves two separate things:

(a) Trajan's education: Trajan knew Greek, read Homer, attempted to write Greek poetry but perpetrated a false quantity, produced military commentaries on the Dacian wars, and (even excluding his relationship with Dio) honoured philosophers, sophists, and literary men, some of whom visited the palace in Rome. (The Epicurean sympathies and literary interests of his wife Plotina are also relevant.)[15]

---

10    *Paneg.* 6.7, 8.2, 9.2f., 10.3, 12.1–15.5, 16.3–19.4; the note of 16.1f., however interpreted (below, n. 60), is much less prominent.
11    C. P. Jones (1975).
12    Wirth (1976) 199; C. P. Jones (1978) 116. Wirth and Fergus Millar see a further parallel in Trajan's numerous colonial foundations in honour of himself and his family after the Dacian wars.
13    Note especially *Paneg.* 13.5 (particularly striking given Pliny's Greek contacts).
14    Domitian's imitation of Alexander: cf., e.g., Fears (1974) 127 n. 90; (1977) 249f.; Coleman (1988) 79; in *Paneg.* 88.5 Pliny dismisses *magnus* as a possible cognomen for Trajan.
15    Cf. in general Syme (1958) 40; Jones (1978) 115f.; Rawson (1989) 249–56 (citing Aelian's *Tactica* as well as Pliny and Julian); Greek: Plin. *Ep.* 6.31.12; Cass. Dio 68.3.4 (Homer); *AP* 11.418 (Greek poetry); there are also the Kingship Orations themselves, since the suggestion of extreme sceptics (e.g., Waters [1974] 235, 237) that they may not have been delivered to Trajan at all ignores (a) Dio's presence in Rome at the right time; (b) both the

It might be said that it was one thing to understand and speak *koine*, another to comprehend elaborate, archaic, and classicising productions like the Kingship Orations. Philostratus classes Trajan among οἱ μὴ τὰ Ἑλλήνων ἀκριβοῦντες.¹⁶ Against this, one may make the following points: the enormous popularity of sophists indicates some comprehension of classical Greek among numerous 'modern' Greeks; Trajan seems to have had the opportunity to read the speeches as well (as we shall see); he did read classical works besides Homer (3.2f.); although the Kingship Orations are rich in content, they contain sections whose 'entertainment-quotient' is quite high and employ a fair amount of repetition, both of which lighten the listener's task; it is easy to underrate an audience's concentration in performance.

So much for linguistic difficulty—what of content? The usual assumption that Trajan's education was limited is consistent with the Kingship Orations themselves, with their stress on a simple education (1.8, 61; 2.26; 4.29ff.), their relatively sparing literary allusion, and the undemanding manner in which explicit allusions are introduced,¹⁷ with Plutarch's *To an Uneducated Prince*,¹⁸ and with Cassius Dio's judgement (68.7.4). This assumption receives positive support from the Second Kingship Oration.

Nevertheless, the speeches contain implicit literary allusions which Trajan would have been unlikely to recognise but which have ⟦301⟧ interpretative consequences. Such allusions can be given value as reflecting Dio's intentions, and failure to recognise them need not affect general interpretation. It is also possible that they would have been explained to Trajan later. On the whole, then, the speeches seem well adapted to Trajan's education but there must have been occasions when Dio was talking over his head.

---

explicit statements and the detailed implications of the Kingship Orations; (c) Dio's statements outside the Kingship Orations (57.10f.; cf. 56 *passim*, especially 8–16; 62 *passim*; 7.66); (d) his claim to have been Trajan's 'friend' (45.3; 47.22); (e) the subsequent literary tradition (not all deriving from Dio); Philostr. *VS* 488 (n. 16) does not imply Trajan did not know Greek; Greek poetry: *AP* 11.418 with Weinreich (1941); military commentaries: Priscian 2.205.6 Keil; philosophers, sophists, and literary men: Plin. *Paneg.* 47.1–3, cf. 49.8; Julian *Caes.* 328b; C. P. Jones (1971) 28–31; Moles (1983a) 271 {above, p. 95} and n. 73; Fuhrmann (1988) v–x (arguing genuineness of the *Regum et imperatorum apophthegmata* and dedicatory letter to Trajan); Plotina: *SIG*³ 834.21; *ILS* 7784; Oliver (1938).

16   Philost. *VS* 488. Scholars generally allow this anecdote some historicity; sharp discussion in Bowie (1982) 44 n. 49.
17   ⟦367⟧ Cf., e.g., 1.12, 13, 47, 58, 59; 3.1; 4.1.
18   The suggestion that this work addresses Trajan (Goodenough [1928] 94ff.; Scott [1929] 126ff.) is unpopular (and rejected by Rawson [1989] 250f.) but convinces me: the ruler is a world-ruler and there are suggestive parallels with Dio.

(b) Trajan's intelligence: Do relatively subtle interpretations of the Kingship Orations, detecting implication and innuendo, founder on Trajan's intellectual limitations? To this there are several replies. First, we do not know how intelligent Trajan was: intelligence is not necessarily stunted by limited formal education. Second, even granted that Trajan's intelligence was limited, we might again posit some gap between Dio's orations and the capacities of their addressee (though at some point we would have to say either that the gap was too great to be plausible, or that Dio had miscalculated, or that he was not interested in communication with Trajan and wanted simply to impress him). Third, we must allow for the ease with which in the classical world contemporary allusion was incorporated into, and detected in, works formally concerned with the historical or mythical past or with abstract generalisation; also for the fact that under authoritarian systems political debate is characteristically conducted through analogy or allegory and people's antennae become sensitised to hidden meanings. If the performance by the younger Helvidius Priscus of a mime about Paris and Oenone could be taken as a satire on Domitian's marital problems (Suet. *Domit.* 10.4), then any intelligent person would consider the possibility that in Dio's Fourth Kingship Oration Alexander and Diogenes stand for Trajan and Dio. Techniques for conveying veiled political opinions were recognised by ancient rhetorical theory, a point to which I shall return.

### 1.3 The Kingship Orations and the Panegyricus

Another problem is both historical and literary: the speeches' relationship to Pliny's *Panegyricus*. As is generally recognised, there are many parallels between the two,[19] a circumstance which bears both on their origin and on their interpretation. The closeness of the parallels indicates not merely shared reliance by Dio and Pliny upon kingship *topoi* but some direct relationship; is that relationship a case of Pliny imitating Dio or vice versa, or of a common source? The *Panegyricus* was delivered on September 1, 100 and Dio's First Oration is undoubtedly closely contemporary. But there is no ⟦302⟧ consensus on priority, and given Dio and Pliny's different status and nationality, most scholars find direct imitation in either direction implausible.[20]

Who is the common source? Trajan himself or his advisers (there are parallels for writers accepting detailed directions from patrons, including emperors)[21] or leading senators? If the former, the works might seem unlikely

---

19  Trisoglio (1972).
20  Exceptions are Trisoglio (1972) 43, arguing Pliny's influence on Dio, and Morr (1915) [*non vidi*], arguing the reverse.
21  See, e.g., Vessey (1973) 28; Hardie (1983) 53f., 70f.; Coleman (1988) 60.

to have didactic content, if the latter, the chances would be at least theoretically increased. In the absence of external evidence, the question can only be answered from the works themselves. How then to break the circle? If one or other tendency, 'imperial' or 'senatorial', is demonstrably predominant in the *Panegyricus*, must the same be true of the Kingship Orations?

On one view, while praise of Trajan is obviously the *Panegyricus*' main tendency, Pliny sounds some cautionary notes. That was Pliny's claim, which has been accepted by modern scholars such as Durry, Radice, and Griffin.[22] If so, presumably Dio may be allowed to take a similar line, especially as the works are of different genres; encomium is built into the *Panegyricus* as an *actio gratiarum*, but not, or not to the same degree, into Dio's works; although as speeches addressed to an emperor they have points of contact with βασιλικοὶ λόγοι, they are formally λόγοι περὶ βασιλείας. If on the other hand the *Panegyricus* is solely 'imperial' in inspiration, it is more difficult to regard the Kingship Orations as independent, but presumably Dio might be allowed to take imperial prescriptions and modify them, so that Trajan or his advisers might be the common source but differently interpreted by Dio and Pliny.

Scholars such as Lepper, Trisoglio, Fears, and C. P. Jones have seen little real difference between the two in their approach to Trajan,[23] whereas for others the difference is fundamental; thus Rostovtzeff:

> no doubt, in this programme as specified by Dio, there are many points which are not theoretical but correspond to the character and activity of Trajan. But a mere glance at Pliny's consular speech in praise of Trajan, and a comparison of it with Dio's first and third speeches on kingship, show to what extent these latter were not only a registration of existing facts but, first and foremost, a registration of eternal norms which must be accepted or rejected by Trajan.

Similarly, Desideri approves Münscher's judgement, 'che passando dal *Panegirico* al discorso dioneo "ci si sente trasportati dalle bassure del torbido fumo della cortigianeria nella pura luce della corte"'.[24] We must surely acknowledge a considerable difference of tone:[25] Dio's speeches seem much

---

22  Durry (1938) 23f. (cf. also [1947] 87f.); Radice (1968); M. T. Griffin (1976) 137; Garzetti (1974) 318 and 662 writes very ambiguously; Pliny's own claims: below, n. 33 (the claim that the *Panegyricus* will guide future emperors has no Dionian parallel).
23  Lepper (1948) 193; Trisoglio (1972) *passim*; Fears (1977) 154, 156, 158; (1981) 91f.; C. P. Jones (1978) 117–20.
24  Rostovtzeff (1957) 120; Desideri (1978) 350 n. 1; Münscher (1920) 147 n. 1.
25  Trisoglio (1972) 36, 41–3 and Kennedy (1972) 579 have good comments on this.

less directly complimentary, much more ⟦303⟧ abstract and elevated; Dio is never as oleaginous as Pliny so frequently is. This difference we may explain by such factors as generic difference and differences between Dio and Pliny of personality and political and cultural status. Pliny was not a man of independent thought or behaviour, and as a leading Roman politician who had survived Domitian's dark and dangerous reign, and as consul in 100, he was much more directly, and (in one sense) much more seriously, involved than Dio in Roman politics. Interpretation of the *Panegyricus* is beyond the present paper. But some of the parallels between Dio and Pliny will be discussed in the following analysis and it will become clear that although I think that the *Panegyricus* does sound some cautionary notes, I basically agree with Rostovtzeff. That is, though Pliny's purpose is laudable enough, he is not the man to carry it off. We should also acknowledge a considerable difference in literary quality: in the words of George Kennedy, the *Panegyricus* is 'tiresome in the extreme'.[26]

### 1.4  Cynicism

There are also problems concerning Cynicism (a major influence upon the First and Fourth Orations) and Dio's relationship to it. Could Cynicism accept the institution of kingship? Could a Cynic philosopher legitimately become a philosophical counsellor of a worldly king? Was Dio himself ever a Cynic? These are difficult problems upon which I shall comment briefly as and when they arise in the speeches, for, though they must affect interpretation, they need not do so fundamentally.[27]

### 1.5  Exhortation, Criticism, and Praise

There are also theoretical problems about the possibility of serious moral exhortation or criticism in works addressed to politicians, kings, tyrants, or emperors, or anyone classifiable as the writer's social superior, and about the role of praise in such works. For scholars such as Cairns it is inconceivable that a work 'addressed to a patron-cum-dedicatee should be uncomplimentary';[28] apparent exhortations are only apparent—the writer tells the addressee to do what he is doing already[29]—and the assumption is that dedication is a form of compliment, hence the work's basic orientation must be encomiastic, and

---

26   Kennedy (1972) 546.
27   Moles (1978), (1983a), (1983b), (1985). The fundamental work on Cynic ideas of kingship remains Höistad (1948), which includes valuable discussion of Cynicism in Dio; important now is Cairns (1989) 33–8.
28   Cairns (1972) 4.
29   E.g., Nisbet–Hubbard (1978) 52 (but cf. below, n. 31).

encomium admits no criticism.[30] As a general proposition this may be acceptable: the question is whether it is always true. At the least it need not be: an addressee is not necessarily a *laudandus*[31] and even when he is, it may be laudable to be receptive [[304]] to honest criticism (Plutarch's *De cohibenda ira* is a typical case). Both the theoretical possibility and the practical occurrence of genuinely paraenetic works addressed to the writer's social superior must be conceded.

But is this possibility excluded in the particular case of works addressed to potentates or emperors? In theory, no. Pliny recognises the existence of such works (*Ep.* 3.18.2f.), Seneca's *De Clementia* essays to be one, Dio can claim not only to have advised Trajan but to have had his advice accepted (57.10), Quintilian (3.8.70) sees a role for deliberative oratory in advising emperors. Ancient rhetoricians such as Demetrius (*Eloc.* 287–98), Pseudo-Dionysius (II.295ff. U–R), Quintilian (9.2.64–99) and Hermogenes (*De inventione* 204ff. Rabe) discussed how to criticise or admonish tyrants, kings, or powerful people generally without giving offence or the opportunity to take offence (criticism could be softened or veiled by various techniques or so conveyed that the taking of offence would look ridiculous and be avoided). These techniques come under the general heading of 'figured speech' (λόγος ἐσχηματισμένος), which is a mean between flattery, which is disgraceful, and direct criticism, which is perilous (Demetr. *Eloc.* 294). A related technique is ἔμφασις: *cum ex aliquo dicto latens aliquid eruitur* (Quint. 9.2.64; cf. 65). Recently, these ancient discussions have been extensively analysed, and their prescriptions applied in the criticism of Roman imperial literature, by Frederick Ahl. Whatever one thinks of his practical interpretations, in demonstrating that criticism of emperors is not per se excluded in works addressed to them, he has at least established an important theoretical principle.[32]

---

30   Thus the rhetoricians (e.g., Menander 368.3–8) but practice can be looser (e.g., Xen. *Ages.* 2.12 criticises Agesilaus).

31   Cf., e.g., Moles (1985) 36, 46f., 59f. n. 77 {below, pp. 365, 378–80 with n. 77}; (1987); J. Griffin (1981) 44 = (1985) 56; Nisbet–Hubbard are inconsistent on this question (cf., e.g., [1978] 157); Giancotti (1954); M. T. Griffin (1976) 133–71; Mortureux (1989); in any case, 'social superiority' is a less relevant criterion when the writers are philosophers, who to some extent represent a different scale of values (the same may be true of poets); also relevant is the friend who dispenses salutary criticism: Moles (1985) 41, 57 nn. 46f. {below, pp. 372–3}.

32   Ahl (1984a) and (1984b); anticipated in Ahl (1976), esp. 25–35. Some scholars may find Ahl's theoretical conclusions quite unacceptable; I do not, though one may have reservations about some of his claims and greater reservations about his practical criticism. Ahl mentions the Kingship Orations at (1984a) 200 and (1984b) 84f., but his meaning eludes me (? that they are flattery).

How can praise be integrated into this picture? Ancient discussions of praise recognise several different types: base flattery; honest praise for things well done; praise as a form of moral encouragement; praise as a way of obtaining something, not necessarily dishonourably, from a superior; praise as a way of softening criticism, or even, if carried to absurd lengths or patently inapposite, of conveying it.[33] Obviously several of these could have a role in works addressed to kings which offer serious moral instruction, and praise can also be part of 'figured speech' (cf., e.g., Demetr. *Eloc.* 292, 295). Obviously also, some of these types overlap or may operate simultaneously. Thus the occurrence of praise of Trajan in Dio's speeches is insufficient to prove that praise is their sole intent.[34] And again obviously, it is possible to conceive of allusions which, even as they convey praise, fulfil other functions as well.

⟦305⟧ The relationship between rhetorical theory and practice is always debatable and my discussions of the Kingship Orations will not correlate the two systematically, but Dio's familiarity with such theories may be assumed, and the apparent convergence of these interpretations with the rhetorical theory has some interest and some corroborative force.[35]

### 1.6   *The First Kingship Oration*

Dio's initial approach is disarming and somewhat oblique. The speech opens in casual, conversational, style, with a λεγόμενον, a 'once-upon-a-time' story (φασί ποτε), that of the first performance of the celebrated aulos-player Timotheus before Alexander the Great (1–3). Since χρείαι such as this were regarded by ancient rhetoricians as useful propaedeutic material for children or beginners,[36] the style should appeal to Trajan.

But the story clearly suggests an analogy with the situation of the speech itself (the technique is found in 'figured speech': cf., e.g., Demetr. *Eloc.* 292). On one level, the analogy compliments both Trajan, imitator of Alexander, and Dio, orator extraordinary, embarking upon his own first performance before

---

33   A few examples: praise for things well done: Arist. *EN* 1101b; Dio 1.15; 3.18; Plin. *Ep.* 3.18.2; as a form of moral encouragement: Demetr. *Eloc.* 295; Sen. *Ep.* 94.39; Plin. *Ep.* 3.18.2; *Paneg.* 4.1 (justification of the *Panegyricus*); Dio 1.15; Plut. *Quom. adul.* ⟦368⟧ *ab amic. internosc.* 55B, 59B; to soften criticism: Demetr. *Eloc.* 292, 294; to convey it: ibid. 291; Plin. *Paneg.* 3.4.
34   Cf. Levick (1980) 193.
35   I put matters circumspectly because I am unsure how far I accept 'generic analysis' of ancient literature and Ahl's theoretical model (a form of generic analysis), and I do not want my case to depend on them. But there is truth in both—even though Ahl's views will be repudiated by many orthodox genericists, and one of Dio's attractions is that he generally seems to write much more loosely than the theorists prescribe.
36   χρεία: Kindstrand (1981) 99f. (with bibliography); useful: Kindstrand (1976) 150; propaedeutic: e.g., Quint. 1.9.1–5.

the great king. The complimentary note continues: Timotheus' performance was no mere ἐπίδειξις; it had moral effect. Timotheus blew a mode appropriate to Alexander's character, not soft or slow, but the war-like mode of Athene, which brought Alexander bounding to his feet and off to fetch his weapons (1f.): on the face of it an admirable response. Yet Alexander's response was determined less by the skill of the performer than by his own character (2f.): Sardanapallus would not have been roused from his harem by Timotheus or any of the moderns nor even by the legendary Marsyas or Olympus; and even if Athene herself had played her own mode he would not have grasped his weapons but either danced (a vigorous reaction, but inappropriate), or run away (the reaction of a coward).

By comparison with Sardanapallus' moral depravity, Alexander's energetic and warlike nature is commendable. The warlike Trajan, imitator of Alexander, could take this as a further compliment, especially as Sardanapallus recalls Domitian, who was lazy, a womaniser, a devotee of Minerva/Athene, an enthusiast of weird dances, and a military failure (so his enemies alleged, not without justification).[37] This is Dio's ingenious and witty variation on the [[306]] conventional contrast between Trajanic dynamism and Domitianic torpor. It is also the first of many comparisons in the Kingship Orations between Trajan and Domitian to the former's advantage; such comparisons, found also in Tacitus (*Agr.* 3.1; 44.5; *Hist.* 1.1), Martial (10.72), and Pliny (e.g., *Ep.* 1.10.1, 13.1; 3.18.5), were an important element of Trajanic propaganda, but in Dio's Kingship Orations and the *Panegyricus* also reflect the influence of the βασιλικὸς λόγος (cf. Men. Rhet. 372.21–5, 377.2–9).[38]

The analogy between Timotheus and Alexander on the one hand and Dio and Trajan on the other, and the contrast between Alexander and Sardanapallus, suggest two further thoughts: first, that a teacher can only do so much by way of exhortation—his pupil must have the right disposition and a desire to learn (this implication is spelled out in 4f. and 9); second, that the older and more divinely-inspired the moral teaching, the more efficacious (the progression Timotheus–Marsyas–Athene anticipates the explicit stress in 9f. on ancient

---

37   Lazy: Suet. *Dom.* 19.1; womaniser: Suet. *Dom.* 22; Minerva: Suet. *Dom.* 4.4; Fears (1981) 78; Coleman (1988) 74, 164–5; dances: e.g., *Paneg.* 54.1; military failure: e.g., Tac. *Agr.* 39.1; 41.1–3; Plin. *Paneg.* 16.3; Cass. Dio 67.4.1; while on this last the dominant literary tradition is badly prejudiced, one should not gloss over (as many do) Domitian's military setbacks.

38   Although the *Panegyricus* is in its way original and well adapted to its circumstances, Russell–Wilson (1981) xviii n. 40 are hardly right to regard the βασιλικός as irrelevant; Durry (1938) 27f. has a better emphasis; admittedly Menander stigmatises criticism of previous emperors as ἄτεχνον (377.1), but this indicates that the practice occurred.

wisdom). Thus Dio's performance before Trajan must have real moral content and the emperor must respond appropriately to it.

In his ἔργον Dio must equal Timotheus' skill (4). What is this ἔργον? Obviously, the task of performing before Trajan, but this simple conception soon acquires depth. Dio must find λόγοι as ἀνδρεῖοι and μεγαλόφρονες as Timotheus' notes (4); indeed, even more is demanded of him than of Timotheus—he must find λόγους ... μὴ ἕνα τρόπον ἡρμοσμένους ἀλλὰ τοὺς αὐτοὺς σφοδρούς τε καὶ πράους καὶ πολεμικοὺς ἅμα καὶ εἰρηνικοὺς καὶ νομίμους καὶ τῷ ὄντι βασιλικούς, ἅτε οἶμαι πρὸς ἀνδρεῖον βουλόμενον εἶναι καὶ νόμιμον ἡγεμόνα, πολλοῦ μὲν δεόμενον θάρσους, πολλῆς δὲ καὶ ἐπιεικείας (5). 'Finding' may seem simply to be the process that leads to literary creation;[39] but it too will acquire a deeper meaning as the speech progresses.

Why must Dio's theme be more complex than Timotheus'? The skilful performer adapts his performance to his listener's character and Alexander's is (merely) ἀνδρεῖος καὶ μεγαλόφρων. That seems to imply a further compliment to Trajan, though this time based on difference from Alexander rather than similarity. But Dio does not quite say that Trajan's character is superior to Alexander's: τρόπον here refers to the musical 'mode' (as it were) that Dio must adopt, not directly to the τρόπον of the addressee; it is a matter rather of Trajan's superior βούλησις—and even that implication is formally qualified by οἶμαι. And there may be a gap between βούλησις and fulfilment. This suggestion is underlined by Dio's responsibility to [[307]] find words 'truly kingly' for Trajan, who 'desires to be both a brave and law-abiding ruler': it is because Trajan is not yet a king in the truest sense that Dio's words to him must be truly kingly.

So this section conveys conflicting messages. In so far as he is an imitator of Alexander the war-like Trajan risks stressing the martial virtues at the expense of other, more important, requirements. On one level a compliment, at another level the Alexander–Trajan analogy is a criticism of, or a warning to, the new emperor. Dio's technique coheres with rhetorical theory concerning 'figured speech': the criticism is not direct (cf. Demetr. *Eloc.* 288, 292; Quint. 9.2.66, 75), but latent (cf. Quint. 9.2.64f., 75), inasmuch as it is conveyed by analogy (Demetr. *Eloc.* 292), and to avoid offence it is tempered by praise (Demetr. *Eloc.* 295).

Further, although in Dio's opinion Trajan has the right βούλησις and in this surpasses Alexander, he still needs Dio to teach him. This reservation might seem without substance, for surely the military Trajan does not lack courage (a point reinforced by the contrast between Alexander and Sardanapallus–Domitian), but throughout the speech Dio works from the qualities Trajan possesses to

---

39  Cf., e.g., Macleod (1973) 304 = (1983) 181.

delineation of the ideal, a technique with many parallels in rhetorical theory (e.g., Demetr. *Eloc.* 295). And in the present passage, the stress falls less on martial 'courage' than on general 'moderation' of rule. Thus the implication that Trajan is, or may be, lacking in certain areas is softened by allusion to an area in which he is not actually deficient—softened, but not removed. Moreover, at the end of the speech (71, 73) 'courage' will be redefined into something much more general than military courage. The word δεόμενος is also adroitly ambiguous, covering both 'requiring' and 'lacking' and nicely obscuring the degree of Trajan's shortcoming.

Had Timotheus, besides his skill in performing the war-like mode, possessed the knowledge of aulos-music which could inculcate all the various virtues required by a king, he would have been an invaluable companion for Alexander, not only when he sacrificed but also when he needed moral correction (6f.); this observation spells out what the teaching of the required 'moderation' entails, and suggests concrete aspects to the role that Dio seeks: he should be Trajan's court philosopher, not only performing on public occasions such as weddings (as Timotheus did) or sacrifices (occasions like the delivery of the First Kingship Speech), but also dispensing private advice to enable Trajan to overcome his various faults. But even as it is made, this implication is softened by the fact that Alexander's faults are in 〖308〗 one respect the opposite of the virtues which Dio has already attributed to Trajan—or at least portrayed Trajan as aspiring to: πικρότερον τοῦ νομίμου καὶ ἐπιεικοῦς (7) contrasts with βουλόμενον εἶναι ... νόμιμον ἡγεμόνα ... πολλῆς ... ἐπιεικείας [δεόμενον] (5). Indeed, Alexander's faults (like Sardanapallus') are reminiscent of Domitian's: excessive passions and punishments; violence towards φίλοι; contempt for his father; arrogation of divinity. Thus Dio attempts further to moderate Trajan's enthusiasm for Alexander by stressing his negative, un-Trajanic, even tyrannical, qualities—a technique which he deploys more extensively in the Fourth Oration. And the final picture of Alexander is critical (7). The opening section of the speech sees Alexander's status as a role model progressively undermined.

Dio has used the Timotheus–Alexander analogy with great skill to move from initial complimenting of Trajan to the suggestion that he still needs philosophical instruction, and then to implied criticism or warning. Further, at the end of the speech he will put forward Heracles as the right model; the speech is framed by Trajan's two great models: the one to be avoided at the beginning, the one to be emulated at the end. Even this simple framework indicates a developing argument. Moreover, two of Alexander's faults contrast with two characteristics of the ideal king—his right attitude to friends (20, 30–2) and correct relationship with his parents (59, 64, 73, 84).

In fact, Dio continues, music cannot achieve the comprehensive moral healing or help required (8). Trajan might think of the moral status of such fervent music-lovers among his predecessors as Domitian and Nero. Only the λόγος of the φρόνιμοι and σοφοί, such as were the majority of those of former times,[40] can provide complete help and guidance for the 'persuadable and virtuous nature'. (This λόγος is 'the true music'—cf. ἐμμελῶς.) Implicit compliment to Trajan—who presumably has such a nature and thus a sure foundation for his meritorious βούλησις—combines with implicit moral exhortation: he needs 'help', though less than Alexander, Domitian, or Nero, and while his being 'persuadable' is commendable, it concedes the need for improvement. The true λόγος will not be harsh or hypercritical but 'encouraging' and 'leading' Trajan 'to complete virtue', as on a moral or spiritual journey. The stress on the self-sufficiency of the λόγος anticipates a Cynic programme.

Thus Dio must produce two things: a discourse that is 'suitable' for Trajan (as aspiring king), 'worthy' of his 'willingness' (προθυμία), and worth his while (διατριβή)—emperors do not have time to waste ⟦309⟧ (cf. 48 below; 2.26; 4.1; Hor. *Ep.* 2.1.1ff., Vitr. *praef.* 1, Martial 12.4, [Plut.] *Reg. et imp. apophth.* 172E); and a τέλειος οὕτω λόγος, i.e., one 'completely sufficient' to lead Trajan's 'persuadable and virtuous nature to all virtue' (οὕτω looks back through τῆς σῆς προθυμίας to 8). The two things are of course simply different aspects of the 'word' or 'words' Dio seeks, the διατριβή relating more to theme, the λόγος to moral function.

The importance and difficulty of Dio's task is emphasised by a pair of rhetorical questions. How can Dio find (ἂν εὕροιμεν)

> τέλειον οὕτω λόγον, ἄνδρες ἀλῆται καὶ αὐτουργοὶ τῆς σοφίας, πόνοις τε καὶ ἔργοις ὅσον δυνάμεθα χαίροντες τὰ πολλά, τοὺς δὲ αὖ λόγους παρακλήσεως ἕνεκεν φθεγγόμενοι πρὸς αὐτοὺς καὶ τῶν ἄλλων ἀεὶ τὸν ἐντυγχάνοντα; ὥσπερ οἱ κινοῦντες καὶ μεταφέροντες οὐκ εὔφορον βάρος φθέγγονταί τε καὶ ᾄδουσιν ἡσυχῇ τὸ ἔργον παραμυθούμενοι, ἐργάται ὄντες, οὐκ ᾠδοί τινες οὐδὲ ποιηταὶ μελῶν (9).

This subtle and complex passage is shot through with ambiguities. On one level Dio's self-characterisation is self-disparaging. An ἀλήτης can be just a vagrant (cf. 56 πλάνητος) and Dio is a self-taught philosopher, a mere amateur, not on

---

40  Alexander at start, Heracles at end: Heuss (1954) 93f.; Nero and Domitian: Desideri (1978) 305; τῶν προτέρων of men (Cohoon 1.7) or λόγοι (Russell)? Passages such as Cic. *De Inv.* 1.2, 3; D.Hal. *Praef. De ant. orat.* 1 might seem to favour the latter, but the former is much more natural, a plurality of λόγοι (before 10) is intrusive, and Dio may be imitating Homeric phraseology (*Il.* 12.383, etc.). Of course the important thing is the link between true λόγος and the past (cf. Dio 3.3; 12.12; 13.14f.; 72.16).

a par with 'the prudent and wise men' whose λόγος can provide complete salvation. On another, this self-disparagement can suggest very strong claims; in being an ἀλήτης, Dio may be like one of the famous 'wandering' philosophers of old:[41] in the narrative enclosing the myth his 'wanderings' do acquire philosophical and spiritual significance, and it is on such 'wanderings' that one 'finds' things; again, αὐτουργὸς τῆς σοφίας is the self-description used by Socrates in Xenophon, *Memorablilia* 1.5, so that while formally self-depreciatory, as in Xenophon, it may link Dio with the greatest philosopher of the past.

The stress on 'self-help' and 'do-it-yourself philosophy' also suits the whole argument from 2ff.: while for moral improvement one needs a guide, one must do the 'work' oneself, a point driven home by emphatic verbal repetition—ἔργον (4), αὐτουργοί, ἔργοις, ἔργον, ἐργάται (9), μὴ παρέργως (10). As Socratic αὐτουργὸς τῆς σοφίας, therefore, Dio is not only qualified to be Trajan's philosophical teacher; he is himself a suitable role model. The self-characterisation also alludes to a famous historical king–philosopher relationship: between the great king Antigonus Gonatas and his court philosopher Bion of Borysthenes; one of Bion's fragments (F 16A Kindstrand) contrasts the roles of the βασιλεύς and the ἀλήτης and of the ἄρχων and the ἀρχόμενος, with a similar blend of self-disparagement and [[310]] self-assertiveness (a blend characteristically Cynic).[42] The attitude towards λόγοι is correspondingly ambiguous: on the one hand Dio is absorbed in 'labours and works', a Cynic concern with struggle and activity above all else, so that λόγοι merely have the peripheral function of exhortation of Dio himself or chance passers-by; on the other, as one of the category of 'workers', not singers or poets (like Timotheus), he seems capable only of 'work-songs, to encourage' the work, not the lofty λόγοι required by the present situation (performance before a Roman emperor, the need to find a λόγος that will be τέλειος in the sense of 8).[43] This ambiguity in the conception of λόγοι is further paralleled by an ambiguity in the conception of ἔργα, which are at once the only things that matter and things of lowly status (another Cynic ambiguity).

Three questions arise. First, would Trajan have detected the literary allusions? The answer is surely no, but it is possible that the allusions would have been explained to Trajan, if he thought about the speech later, as at 49 Dio assumes that he will. Second, is Dio really representing himself as Cynic? This

---

41  Cf., e.g., Hdt. 1.30.2; Plat. *Apol.* 22a (with implicit Heracles parallel; cf. n. 90); Kindstrand (1976) 208; Dio's wanderings: Moles (1978) 95 (and n. 138), 100 {above, pp. 51, 58}.
42  Kindstrand (1976) 183; Höistad (1948) 60f., 97, 101, 196f.; Demetr. *Eloc.* 261.
43  The ambiguous attitude to λόγοι is anticipated in 4 ἀνδρὸς αὐλητοῦ: on the one hand, Timotheus' professional skills are beyond Dio; on the other, aulos-music is generally condemned by moralists (e.g., by Dio himself in 2.55f.).

question goes together with the third, what is the point of these multiple ambiguities concerning the status of Dio himself, of λόγοι and of ἔργα?

How far, if at all, Dio ever practised the Cynic way of life and whether, if he did, he would have accepted the often invidious name 'Cynic', remain controversial questions. Certainly, the manner in which he spent his exile could be described in Cynic terms.[44] And with his long hair, beard, and τρίβων, he would have looked typically Cynic, as he elsewhere admits (34.2; cf. 33.14; 72.2). Adopting a broadly Cynic stance has numerous advantages. It suits his recent celebrated biography (19.1), as that of a wanderer, an exile, a sufferer from the tyranny of Domitian. Moreover, while in real life Cynics were sometimes regarded as, and no doubt often were, repulsive eccentrics, in popular thought the great Cynic figures like Diogenes (precisely Dio's *alter ego* in the Diogenes discourses) and Crates enjoyed the reputation of philosophers *par excellence*, an appropriate aura for Dio to adopt in his efforts to impress Trajan. And the simplicities of Cynic thought suit a first approach to a philosophical tyro.[45] Further, though strict Cynicism can have nothing to say to worldly kings,[46] from Dio's point of view a modified Cynic stance connects neatly with Trajan's imitation of Alexander, who was traditionally associated with Diogenes and his oriental counterparts, the Gymnosophists, and invested with Cynic features by one of his historians, Onesicritus.[47] The stance also creates fruitful ambiguities: ⟦311⟧ at one and the same time, Dio himself is both a great philosopher in the mould of Socrates and the Cynics (this to impress Trajan) and a mere nothing (this to disarm him), both a teacher (expounding wisdom) and a pattern (exemplifying it); Dio's λόγοι are both insignificant (by comparison with ἔργα) and the vehicle of a λόγος which holds the key to everything; Dio's ἔργα are both trifling (this to disarm Trajan) and somehow illustrative both of correct philosophical and correct kingly behaviour. The Cynic is of course himself a 'king', whose true kingliness consists in poverty and suffering.[48]

---

44   Cf. von Arnim (1898) 245; Höistad (1948) 50–61, 86–94, 150–220; Moles (1978) 94–6 {above, pp. 48–51}; (1983a) 268f. {above, pp. 92f.} and n. 65; (1983b) 108 {below, p. 326} n. 41; Desideri (1978) 200f., 537–47; C. P. Jones (1978) vi, 49f.; exile in Cynic terms: *Orations* 6 and 8 (Diogenes/Dio's exile); Brancacci (1980).
45   Cf. Hor. *Epist.* 1.2 with Moles (1985) 36 {below, p. 365}.
46   So I believe: Moles (1983a) 269 n. 65 (from 268) {above, p. 92}; (1983b) 106 {below, p. 322} n. 26; (1985) 43f. {below, pp. 374f.} and n. 59; some do not: e.g., Kindstrand (1976) 14f. (confused).
47   Cf. Fisch (1937); Brown (1949) 24–53; Höistad (1948) 89f., 135–8; Pearson (1960) 83–111 (with reservations); Hamilton (1969) xxxi, lvii; Moles (1983b) 116 {below, p. 337} n. 98; cf. also Dio's *On the Virtues of Alexander*.
48   ⟦369⟧ Höistad (1948) is fundamental.

Two final points. First, though all these implications are present, it is difficult to disentangle them; one of the functions of 9 is to create an ambiguous impression: Dio appears as a man of mystery, whose true nature is not fully revealed until the final myth. Second, the stress on the difficulty of Dio's task creates the impression that, while he is the teacher and Trajan the pupil, the two are united in the moral quest.

10 goes some way to resolving the multiple ambiguities. 'There are many philosophical λόγοι, and all worth hearing and possessing wonderful helpfulness for those who work at listening'. Among all these λόγοι Dio must 'find the one that is near and that will touch (Trajan) most closely'.[49] Dio now makes explicit the claim that only philosophical λόγοι can effect the necessary moral improvement (a substantial point, given the chequered relations of philosophers and emperors), and he re-emphasises the precondition that listeners have to respond appropriately. Such people contrast with the 'chance persons' for whose benefit Dio has hitherto used λόγοι: they are people for whom the act of listening is itself a 'work': the gap between ἔργα and λόγοι can be bridged. So can the gap between Dio, the philosophical teacher, and his pupil Trajan: just as it is Trajan's 'work' to listen to Dio, it is Dio's 'work' to address Trajan (4). There must also be some connection between Trajan's 'work' in listening to Dio and Dio's 'labours and works', though its significance is not yet revealed. The description of the λόγος as 'near' sounds another Cynic note, reflecting the doctrine 'use what lies to hand'.[50]

Two interconnected questions arise: first, what is the λόγος in 10? second, what is the 'logical' relationship between 10 and 8f.? On the first point, the answer is given by 11: the λόγος is about kingship, 'near' and 'likely to touch most closely' in that Dio is addressing Trajan, who wants to be both a brave and law-abiding ruler' (5) (and 10 μάλιστα ἁψάμενον [λόγον] makes a ring with πρέπουσα ... διατριβή). On the second, the λόγος of the prudent and wise in 8f. is ⟦312⟧ the general σοφία or φιλοσοφία of the past, while the λόγοι of 10 are the many separate philosophical λόγοι of which this consists (8 ὠφέλειαν ~ 10 ὠφέλειαν, 8 ὁ ... σοφῶν λόγος ~ 10 πολλοὶ ... κατὰ φιλοσοφίαν λόγοι, 9 ἀξία ~ 10 ἄξιοι). Of the many philosophical λόγοι, the 'near and most closely touching λόγος' about kingship is the one most relevant to Trajan's moral needs. And since the First Kingship Oration is a 'speech about kingship' and a 'worthy discourse', it is itself one of these 'worthy and wonderfully helpful philosophical λόγοι and representative of the λόγος of the prudent and wise men of the past.

---

49  Thus Professor Russell; Cohoon 1.7 mistranslates as 'we have found as our hearer one who is near at hand and readily eager to grasp our words'.

50  Cf. Kindstrand (1976) 66.

To compensate for his inadequacies, as described in 9, Dio must invoke Persuasion, the Muses, and Apollo, the first to 'persuade' the 'persuadable' Trajan, the second as goddesses of literature and the arts; why Apollo? as god of the arts or prophecy? Only the sequel will show. Dio must give his speech προθύμως: speaker and addressee must be united in 'willingness'. Dio's speech therefore will somehow unite both λόγοι and ἔργα and Dio and Trajan. Finally, Dio must do the best he can (ὡς δυνατόν): so, later, must the good king (13): both philosophical teacher and kingly pupil must strive for perfection, knowing its impossibility (cf. also 50).

Dio begins with a summary treatment of the good king (11). This section, which in one sense ends at 14, already poses most of the main interpretative problems of the speech. Is the appeal to Homer complimentary (or merely complimentary), Homer apparently being Trajan's favourite poet?[51] Again, the insistence that the good king derives his authority from Zeus (12) is found, *mutatis mutandis*, throughout the Kingship Orations (e.g. 1.37–41, 45, 59, 64–7, 73, 83f.; 2.72; 3.50–4; 4.21–3, 27, 31, 38–43) and throughout the *Panegyricus* (e.g., 1.3–6, 5.1f., 7.5, 8.1–3, 10.4, 65.2, 80.4f., 88.8); is it merely graceful allusion to Trajan's cultivation of, and in certain contexts, virtual identification with, Jupiter Optimus Maximus?[52] Should Trajan see in the brevity of the good king's sleep (cf. 3.65) his own laudable *parcus et brevis somnus* (*Paneg.* 49.8)? Is Trajan expected to congratulate himself on being free of the manifold faults of the bad king? In particular, does the implicit (but clear) attack on Domitian in 14 (the bad king can never be a king even though he is acclaimed and obeyed as such by all Greeks and barbarians, men and women, birds and beasts) praise Trajan by contrast?[53]

For scholars such as Lepper and C. P. Jones the answer to these questions is self-evident: Dio's sole interest is compliment. It is better to acknowledge the existence of the compliment but insist on two [[313]] points already mentioned. First, compliment may itself be a form of moral encouragement. The λόγος of the 'prudent and wise' is explicitly 'encouraging' (8). There is also an important extra-textual consideration: date. In 99 or 100 no one could know that Trajan would turn out differently from Domitian (under whom he, unlike Dio, had

---

51   This is only an inference from Cass. Dio 68.3.4 and the Kingship Orations but virtually certain (cf. esp. *Or.* 2).

52   Trajan and Jupiter: cf., e.g., Garzetti (1974) 354, 674f.; Waters (1975) 399f.; Fears (1977) 227–36, 193–6; (1981) 80–5; C. P. Jones (1978) 117f.

53   On 1.14 and the parallel 1.79, 4.4, 4.25, 3.38 and 3.41 see C. P. Jones (1978) 118, 193 n. 29; Desideri (1978) 338 n. 13; Moles (1983a) 264 {above, p. 87} and n. 54; Domitian's general claims to power over nature: Coleman (1988) 88, 90, 123f.; implicit attacks on Domitian and compliments of Trajan in 11–14: e.g., Trisoglio (1972) 6, 8f., 10f., 13; C. P. Jones (1978) 118.

prospered): most emperors started well; one must allow the possibility that praise of emperors at the beginning of their reigns may be intended as a way of setting them on the right road, emphasising those aspects of their character which can be fruitfully developed: that surely applies to Seneca's *De clementia* or Helvidius Priscus' speech in 69/70 concerning Vespasian (Tac. *Hist.* 4.7), it was the claim Pliny made for the *Panegyricus*,[54] and Dio himself alludes to this function of praise (15).

Secondly, compliment may be only one of several functions. Appeal to Homer is almost inevitable in any Greek discussion of kingship and so ancient, divine, and wise a source (12, 14) belongs in the category of the prudent and wise men of the past (8). Again, the tremendous emphasis on the faults of the bad king—the good king is almost exclusively defined in terms of the vices he lacks and these vices recall Sardanapallus, the negative side of Alexander, and Domitian—seems to convey warning as well as compliment. Finally, the whole section, but especially 12, insists on the conditionality of kingship: a king is only a king if he behaves properly, winning the approval of Zeus and labouring for the welfare of his subjects; by this standard, while Trajan has indeed the requisite 'desire' (5) and 'willingness' (9), he is not yet actually a king. Similarly, Zeus' delegation of authority to good kings is an incentive to virtuous behaviour, not a guarantee of the virtue of any king (cf. 12 and 16). This general emphasis on conditionality is maintained throughout the speech. Dio reserves full approval of Trajan until he has shown that he merits it.

It is true that Pliny also emphasises the conditionality of his subjects' approval of Trajan and that Trajan himself propounded this emphasis (cf., e.g., *Paneg.* 67.4–8, 68.1, 94.5), but this need not detract from Dio's seriousness on this point: the emphasis is far more sustained in Dio than in Pliny; it is anyway one of the best pieces of evidence for interpreting the *Panegyricus* as genuinely paraenetic; further, this is a case where 'imperial' claims and 'senatorial' prescriptions may be allowed to coincide—when an emperor proclaims some lofty ideal and his subjects reiterate it, they are not necessarily parroting their master's voice: they may again be ⟦314⟧ trying to build on his virtuous beginnings (once more the *De Clementia* furnishes apt parallels); and the point itself is valid and important.

15–36 can be regarded either as a new section concerning the 'Homeric and true king' (36 makes a ring with 15) or (better) as a more detailed treatment of the material summarised in 11–14. Thus 15f. (the king's relations with the gods) ~ 12; 17ff. (the king's relations with his fellow men and subjects, his role as herdsman and shepherd) ~ 12f. Again, the description of the bad king contains

---

54  Cf. above, n. 33.

more implicit attacks on Domitian (e.g., impiety [16], alienation of φίλοι, who plot against him [20], though they are his best defence [31f.], assumption of the title 'master' [22], terror inspired by his presence [25], deceit [26], excessive love of honour [27], and military cowardice [28]); correspondingly, the description of the good king contains more implicit compliments of Trajan (e.g., concern for φίλοι [20, 30–2], devotion to πόνοι [21], address of soldiers as 'fellow soldiers' [22], title 'Father of his Country' [22], delight in conferring benefits [23], the fact that he inspires not fear but respect [25], sincerity and truthfulness [26]). The *Panegyricus* shows many parallels.[55] And there are again parallels, whose full significance remains unclear, between Trajan (or those aspects of the good king which recall Trajan) and Dio: both are devoted to simplicity (15, 26, 36), truthfulness (15, 26, 36), and πόνοι (21, 9). By 37 Dio has already completed one λόγος; the First Kingship Oration, an example of the many worthy and helpful philosophical λόγοι and representative of the general λόγος of the prudent and wise, is itself subdivided into various λόγοι of different lengths and levels of intensity.

The multiplying allusions to Trajan and Domitian and the parallels with the *Panegyricus* further sharpen the main interpretative problem: is the speech mere compliment or serious moral exhortation? Hence Dio himself confronts the problem at the beginning (15)[56] and end (36) of the section. In the latter passage the double μακαρισμός presumably alludes to the senate's acclamations of Trajan and itself, recorded by Pliny *Paneg.* 74.1 and 4.[57] But in Dio the εἰ-clause is adroitly ambiguous, and there is a further ambiguity in προσήκειν, which can mean both 'belong to' ('if you really possess any of the attributes of the good king') and 'befit' ('if you think fit to adopt any of these prescriptions'), so that on one level Dio presents Trajan with a choice (anticipating the Choice of Heracles in the myth); on the other hand Dio has already implicitly conceded Trajan a virtuous nature (8). But the main point is that ⟦315⟧ Dio's allusions expose him to the charge of flattering Trajan (a charge made by his detractors: 3.12–25); his defence is that praise is justifiable in so far as it is related to the ideal to which Trajan is, or should be, aspiring; in short it has both a diagnostic and a protreptic function (for the former cf. also 69; 3.25, 43;

---

55   E.g.: title 'master': *Paneg.* 2.3; terror: *Paneg.* 4.5, 47.6, 48.3; πόνοι: *Paneg.* 7.3, 77.5, 79.5, 86.3; 'fellow-soldiers': *Paneg.* 13.3, 15.5, 19.3; Syme (1958) 38; cf. in general Lepper (1948) 194 n. 3; Rostovtzeff (1957) 588 n. 27; Trisoglio (1972) *passim*; C. P. Jones (1978) 117, 193; Desideri (1978) 306f., 352f.

56   The formula of 1.15 closely parallels 3.25.

57   For imperial acclamations see Talbert (1984) 297–302. Dio re-uses the motif in 1.83 and 3.3-3-5.

*Paneg.* 2.6); his attacks on Domitian (in so far as the bad king has Domitianic features) have a diagnostic and deterrent function.

Dio's profession of sincerity and disclaimer of flattery and abuse prove nothing in themselves: flatterers do not admit to flattery and the formulation of 1.15 is sufficiently close to *Paneg.* 4.1 to suggest direct Trajanic input on this point. Nevertheless, several factors tell in Dio's favour.

First, beyond attributing a virtuous nature and 'willingness' to Trajan, Dio (unlike Pliny) does not yet praise the emperor directly, and even his implicit praises are constantly related to an ideal, which is described at great length and in detail, so that it must be given some weight, and which Trajan has explicitly not yet attained. This concern with the ideal, and the diagnostic aspect, remind us that a λόγος περὶ βασιλείας is formally a general statement, some elements of which will be there for that reason, rather than because they reflect well or badly upon the particular addressee.

Second, the full significance of some of the implicit praises (e.g., those making a parallel between Trajan and Dio) is not yet clear.

Third, there is the question of emphasis: the fact that Trajan advertised his excellent relations with his 'friends'[58] cannot fully explain the lengthy treatment of 'friendship' (from its widest to its narrowest sense) in 20, 25, and 30–3. An emperor's treatment of 'friends' matters. Nero had neglected the armies, flattered the urban masses, allowed his flock to be attacked both by wild beasts and his own dogs (28); Domitian had demoralised and terrorised the senate and his *amici*, and lost his best defences (25, 30–2). 27, 30, and 33 also touch on the king's choice of friends, a topic again raised in 64 and at length in the Third Oration. An emperor's choice of friends also matters, and never more than at the beginning of his reign, the time of this speech. Would the influence of Domitian's more pernicious 'friends' continue under Trajan, just as it was Eprius Marcellus, Nero's friend, and not Helvidius Priscus, who captured Vespasian's ear in 70? One recalls also the famous story told by Pliny (*Ep.* 4.22.4–6), showing how even the saintly Nerva kept on some of Domitian's most vicious associates. True, as an earnest of intent, Trajan expelled a number of minor *delatores* (*Paneg.* 34f.), but ⟦316⟧ he also said that though Domitian was the worst of emperors he had good friends (SHA *Alex.* 65.5)—an indication of what was anyway likely: that he took over many of Domitian's friends himself. If the story (*ibid.*) that Homullus remarked to Trajan that it was perhaps better to have a bad emperor like Domitian surrounded by good friends than a good emperor like Trajan who gave power to bad men points in the

---

58   Cf. Trisoglio (1972) 15–19; C. P. Jones (1978) 117, 193.

other direction, it at least confirms the importance of the question at the start of Trajan's reign.⁵⁹

Fourth, when all compliments have been discounted, substance remains. While the statement about the good king's 'war policy' at 27 parallels *Paneg.* 16.2 *nec times bella nec prouocas* and may or may not reflect Trajan's official line,⁶⁰ it gains force from the contrast with the picture in 2 and 5 of Trajan's hero, the excessively warlike Alexander. Again, the climactic statement of this section—that the 'clearest sign' of the good king is when good men feel no shame in praising him either in the present or in time to come—stresses that Trajan must earn praise throughout his life, not just in the honeymoon period of AD 99/100. Dio's approval is again conditional upon Trajan's continued good behaviour.⁶¹ The emphasis on the good king's need for the praise not of vulgar layabouts but of 'the free and noble, for whom a life of lies is not worth living' (35) is also pointed, for at the beginning of his reign Trajan had already given signs of becoming the 'populist' emperor, overgenerous in largesse, of his later years.⁶² And who are the superior people whose good opinion Trajan must win? Surely pre-eminently Dio himself, the living embodiment of simplicity and truthfulness, who 'formerly when mendacity seemed to everybody else through fear a necessity, alone dared to tell the truth, and that at the peril of his life' (3.13). The narrative enclosing the myth will reinforce this point.

The next section (37–47), clearly marked off (37, 48), is double, treating first the supreme king Zeus (37–41), the model of worldly kings, then the administration of the universe and the position of the worldly king within that whole (42–7); the doctrine is characteristically Stoic, and while not necessarily in contradiction with the Cynic character of the preface⁶³ nevertheless suggests a more elevated philosophical conception. The section is another λόγος (48), in the form of an extended *praeteritio*.

The main thrust is that the good king, the ruler of others, is himself under the higher authority of Zeus. Is Dio warning Trajan that although an emperor is

---

59   Nero in 28: Rostovtzeff (1957) 588 n. 27; Domitian's and Trajan's 'friends': Crook (1955) 54f.; Syme (1958) 50f., 649–51. The Homullus story is branded an invention by Syme (1968) 170 (and later works), but see Chilver (1985) 29 (the existence of the suffect consul Homullus in 102 helps the case).
60   Depending on how far the *Panegyricus* is Trajan-inspired or whether this emphasis indicates senatorial disapproval of the Dacian war (cf., e.g., Garzetti [1974] 318, 662). A further complication is the traditional formulation: cf. Thuc. 1.124.2; Otto (1890) 54.
61   For a similar stress in Pliny cf. *Paneg.* 28.6, 43.3, 45.6, 62.9, 85.7 with Durry (1938) 23; Kennedy (1972) 544.
62   Cf. *Paneg.* 33.1–4; Fronto 2.216 Haines = van den Hout 199f.; Syme (1958) 41; Garzetti (1974) 313.
63   Cynic theology is controversial (cf., e.g., Kindstrand [1976] 224–40).

above human law,[64] he is not omnipotent? [[317]] The renewed compliments to Trajan and attacks on Domitian seem to tell against this interpretation, especially as the compliments are now, and uniquely, explicit. Trajan's own character provides a moral pattern for his generals, magistrates, and governors, so that if they opposed him he would be justified in reproving or even deposing them and replacing them with better men (44). But the same principle applies to kings. The king who looks to Zeus and rules accordingly obtains a happy lot and fortunate end (45), unlike the king who dishonours Zeus, whose wickedness is recognised both by contemporaries and later generations, and who suffers Phaethon's fate (46f.). After a lengthy Homeric quotation to illustrate the point, Dio says that though he himself would be delighted to expatiate on the λόγος concerning Zeus and the universe, there is not sufficient time but there may be on some other occasion, and he then offers a μῦθος instead (49).

It is adroitly done: the move from the real Roman world of Trajan's relations with his governors and generals to seemingly abstract generalisations about the relations of 'kings' with Zeus, the lofty appeals to Greek myth and Homeric poetry, the fleeting return to the philosophical λόγος with the promise of further philosophical delights to come, and the rapid change of subject to the myth. Nevertheless, the implication is plain: if Trajan acknowledges and obeys the higher authority of the gods, he will enjoy a happy lot and a fortunate end, unlike Domitian, who was hated in his lifetime and is still hated and mocked, who hybristically tried, like Phaethon,[65] to behave like a god and was justly killed; just as Trajan can depose generals and governors who fail in their duty, he himself can be deposed from office and come to as violent an end as did Phaethon and Domitian. Thus the function of the explicit compliment at 44 is to alleviate a message of stark and uncompromising import.

Account must again be taken of the facts that the same point is made by Pliny and that Pliny is here again to some extent following the lead of Trajan himself, who in a famous incident alluded to in the *Paneg.* (67.8), handed to his prefect of the guard his sword of office with the words 'Take this sword, in order that, if I rule well, you may use it for me, but if ill, against me' (Cass. Dio 68.16.1; Aur. Vict. *Caes.* 13.9). But, for the same sort of reasons as before, these facts do not undermine the seriousness of Dio's message here, seriousness implicit in the very obliquity of expression. *Si duo idem faciunt, non est idem*: it was one thing for Caesar to bare his neck and shout his readiness to be stabbed to death, another for Cicero [[318]] surreptitiously to urge this course upon Brutus,

---

64 A common theme in Imperial writings on kingship: cf., e.g., Wirszubski (1950) 130–6; M. T. Griffin (1976) 148; Brunt (1977), esp. 108ff.; Plin. *Paneg.* 65.1; Dio 3.4f., 10, 88f.
65 On Phaethon see below, nn. 114 and 98.

yet another for Brutus and his friends to do the deed (when Caesar put up considerable resistance).[66]

There is a further parallel in that Pliny rejects the notion of the emperor as *praesens deus* (*Paneg.* 2.3, 11.3, 33.4, 49.1, 52.2f.), which Domitian claimed to be (Stat. *Silu.* 4.3.128f.; Sil. Ital. 3.625f.; Suet. *Dom.* 13.2; Dio 45.1; etc.); similar considerations again apply, and it is worth noting that in this area Pliny seems rather more equivocal than Dio and rather embarrassed—a reflection no doubt of Trajan's own equivocation over his divine status.[67]

So far, the speech has consisted of a series of λόγοι, which have become progressively more serious and elevated, the last combining a warning of the penalty that awaits Trajan should he abuse his high office and an exposition of the position of the Roman emperor within the ordered hierarchy of the universe.

In Platonic fashion, the speech closes with a myth. On one level this comes appropriately after the overt and lofty philosophising of 42–8 and is another illustration of the general movement within the speech from Cynicism into more elevated philosophical regions. On another level it seems to mark a change of direction; yet this latter impression is to some extent illusory, since the myth will recapitulate and amplify much of the material of 42–8 and earlier parts of the speech. The myth is introduced as something Trajan might like to hear (49)—an entertaining 'story': 'would you like to hear a story?', as one might speak to a child (cf. the opening χρεία).[68] The conception of both myth and audience—playful, indulgent, almost patronising—is a common philosophical stance: after the rigorous philosophical exposition the philosopher undertakes to entertain his pupil with less demanding fare. But such a stance is usually doubly ironic, since the myth itself may be deeply serious.

Dio himself immediately remarks on the underlying seriousness: (49) μῦθον ... μᾶλλον δὲ ἱερὸν καὶ ὑγιῆ λόγον σχήματι μύθου λεγόμενον. The description is paradoxical, since μῦθος and λόγος are generally distinguished; the effect is to force the listener or reader to probe the myth's true meaning (hence Dio envisages Trajan later pondering it by himself). There are Platonic parallels for this effect.[69] As ὑγιής, this μῦθος/λόγος reflects the λόγος of the prudent and wise which will bring complete salvation and healing (~ 8f. ~ 8 ἴασιν), but its full meaning will only gradually be revealed and will require later thought. As ἱερός, the μῦθος/λόγος evokes the ἱερὸς 〚319〛 λόγος connected with religious

---

66  〚370〛 Plut. *Caes.* 60.6; Cic. *Brut.* 331 with Balsdon (1958) 91 and Douglas (1966) 233.
67  Cf., e.g., *Paneg.* 1.3–5, 52.2–4, 80.3.
68  Cf., e.g., Pl. *Protag.* 320c; *Polit.* 268e; *Rep.* 2.376d, 377a; *Phaedr.* 276e; Dio 4.74; 5.24; 55.11; 72.13; Max. Tyr. 4.3c; Ael. Arist. 36.96 K.
69  E.g., *Gorg.* 523a; *Laws* 865d, 927a, 872d; cf. also Dio 5.3; Burkert (1979) 3, 145 n. 14; Vernant (1980) 186–204; Hunter (1983) 47, 114 n. 99.

rites:⁷⁰ Trajan seems to be in the position of initiand into the holy office of true kingship.

Dio claims to have been told the μῦθος/λόγος by a woman of Elis or Arcadia: ὃν ἐγώ ποτε ἤκουσα γυναικὸς Ἠλείας ἢ Ἀρκαδίας ὑπὲρ Ἡρακλέους διηγουμένης. Authenticity is formally guaranteed by Dio's own testimony. The uncertainty over the woman's background seems a nice (pseudo-) realistic touch, but perhaps also echoes the teasing Platonic equivocation of *Gorgias* 493a concerning the author of the myth of the Watercarriers: Σικελός τις ἢ Ἰταλικός.⁷¹ Moreover, Dio's words recall Socrates' introduction to Diotima's account of Love in Plato's *Symposium*: 201d: τὸν δὲ λόγον τὸν περὶ τοῦ Ἔρωτος, ὅν ποτ' ἤκουσα γυναικὸς Μαντινικῆς Διοτίμας. Dio is beginning to upgrade his own philosophical credentials after the ambiguous self-description and the latent Socratic parallelism of 9. Indeed, the *Symposium* provides the myth's whole framework; to quote Trapp: 'The priestess herself—a *mantis* with a message for the man who is now relaying it to his present audience—is a grandchild of Diotima, the γυνὴ Μαντινική, whose teachings are reported by Socrates in the *Symposium*'.⁷²

Aspects of Dio's description (50f.) of his exile further increase the sense of his being in reality a formidable philosophical figure of Socratic or Cynic hue—he is a 'wanderer', an 'observer' engaged in 'research' into peoples of all kinds, and (the quotation of *Od.* 17.222 implies) a latter-day Odysseus (himself one of the great Cynic exemplars):⁷³ again the ambiguity of 9 is brought nearer clarification. If Dio's stance here also seems Herodotean (Odysseus being the common element: Hdt. 1.5.3 ~ *Od.* 1.3), that colouring helps to reinforce our sense both of Dio's moral odyssey and of the narrative's truth. Given the philosophical implications, the initial stress on the role of 'chance' in Dio's wanderings (50) already seems deceptive. Dio, too, traversed 'as much land as I could': again the emphasis on performing to the best of one's ability (cf. 10, 13). Further, the verbal parallel between ἐν ἀγύρτου σχήματι and σχήματι μύθου suggests a parallel between the deceptiveness of Dio's own appearance (the poor Cynic exterior which conceals inner kingliness) and the deceptiveness of the μῦθος (the mere 'story' which is in fact the τέλειος λόγος).

When he reached the Peloponnese on his travels he avoided the cities (51): true wisdom will be found in the country, true nobility among the humble,

---

70   E.g., Hdt. 2.81.2; Plat. *Ep.* 7.335a; Vernant (1980) 186f.; cf. also Aristides' Ἱεροὶ Λόγοι.
71   So Professor Russell.
72   Trapp (whom I thank for this advance reference) (1990) 143.
73   Wanderer: above, n. 41; Cynic scout/observer: Moles (1983b) 112 {below, p. 331} and n. 112; Dio's adoption of the Odysseus-persona: Moles (1978) 97 {above, p. 54}; C. P. Jones (1978) 46–50; Desideri (1978) 174f. n. 2; Cynic Odysseus: Höistad (1948) 94–102, 196f.; Moles (1985) 34–7 {below, pp. 362–7}; Cairns (1989) 35f.

simplicity, a kingly attribute (26) and the characteristic of Dio himself as he speaks to Trajan (36), is a cardinal [[320]] virtue. The narrative seems to illustrate the emphasis of 33, and the rejection of city life (with all it implies) is the more pointed because Dio's narrative contrasts with *Od.* 1.3 and Hdt. 1.5.3 in this respect alone. The humble folk consist of herdsmen (paradigms of the good king, cf. 17, 19) and huntsmen (paradigms both of the good king [19] and Cynic toughness).[74] (Trajan the huntsman[75] might take the commendation of hunters as a compliment, but this is utterly incidental.) We are now in the world of Cynic primitivism.[76]

Dio was walking from Heraea to Pisa along the Alpheus. The geographical precision creates a pleasant illusion of authenticity, sets the scene in Heracles and Hermes country, and provides the first of several echoes of Plato's *Phaedrus*, for if the framework of the myth is inspired by the *Symposium*, 'the circumstances of the *mantis*' encounter with Dio are modelled on the encounter between Socrates and Phaedrus in the *Phaedrus*', as Trapp argues,[77] instancing *inter alia* the common elements of the river, the sacred grove decorated with offerings, the noon meeting, the divine inspiration of the main speaker, the discussion of inspiration and the superior value of its products. The main function of these echoes is still further to strengthen Dio's Socratic credentials; the pointed divergences from his model give even greater emphasis to the ruggedness of Dio's specific philosophical prescription. More generally, Dio's story conforms to a standard pattern whereby a solitary traveller meets on the road a god or his representative, who promises the help needed to overcome a crisis.[78]

Dio 'hit upon the road (ἐπετύγχανον τῆς ὁδοῦ) up to a certain point but then fell into rough country (δυσχωρίαν)' and 'missed' (διαμαρτάνω) his way and 'began to wander' (ἐπλανώμην). It is already difficult not to sense allegory: 'the right road', 'wandering', which can be positive (philosophical wandering in pursuit of wisdom) or negative (a metaphor for moral ignorance), 'rough country' (true wisdom resides in the country but it is easy to become lost in pursuit of it).

---

74   D.L. 6.31; Höistad (1948) 78, 175; Cairns (1989) 36.
75   *Paneg.* 81.1–3; Cass. Dio 68.7.3; Dio 4.34f. (with Moles [1983a] 272 {above, pp. 95f.}); 2.1f.; 3.135–8.
76   Goulet-Cazé (1986) 57–66; Moles (1983b) 116f. {below, pp. 338f.} and nn. 103, 105; (1985) 40 {below, p. 371} and n. 40; in Dio, e.g., 7.65f., 81f.
77   Trapp (1990) 143f.
78   Pointed divergences: the interpretation of Trapp (1990) 144 ('a piquant transposition ... trading on the familiar antithesis of Attic and Ionian elegance with the harsher ethos of the Dorians') is a little too 'literary'; the general pattern: Williams (1993).

Dio then made his way to an oak grove on a hill. The detailed description of this grove increases realism, emphasises the holiness of the location and its link with Zeus as god of prophecy, and (through the offerings) anticipates the introduction of Heracles. The rough simplicity of shrine and offerings contrasts with the pomp and magnificence of state cult. A little further on he met a woman tall, old, rustic, long-haired, and Doric-speaking—in all respects a suitable mouthpiece for the 'ancient wisdom' enshrined in the λόγος [[321]] of the prudent and wise (8), the more so as the inhabitants of that part of Greece did not actually speak Doric; the Dorian ethos also suits the ruggedness of Cynic thought. Here as elsewhere, Dio exhibits enviable skill at creating fictitious settings for the exposition of knowledge. 'Oldness' is often a guarantee of wisdom and Dio's own appearance at this stage of his career should be borne in mind.[79] (Trajan's reign championed a return to 'ancient values',[80] but this is a bonus for Dio, not an explanation of his emphasis.) The woman spoke gently and kindly to Dio, informing him that the place was sacred to Heracles, that she had a son who was a shepherd, whose sheep she herself often pastured, and that she had the gift of prophecy from the Mother of the Gods, and was often consulted by neighbouring herdsmen and farmers on the raising and preservation (or salvation) of their crops and cattle.

The significance of several of these items—the introduction of Heracles, the woman's prophetic powers, her status as an authority figure, the hierarchy linking humans to the greatest of the gods through prophecy—is apparent, that of others will become clear later. The prophetess then directed her powers to Dio himself (55). The self-control and moderation of her delivery further guarantee her credentials. The contemptuous dismissal of the conventional stereotype of prophets (56) seems to reflect a Cynic rejection of oracles.[81] Dio has come to this place through divine, not mere, chance (56 ~ 50). The linkage of Dio's wanderings and tribulations with those of mankind in general makes explicit the allegorical or spiritual significance of the wanderings.[82] Dio's

---

79   Oldness and reliable testimony: Dio 11.37 with Fehling (1989) 167f.; rustic wisdom: Hor. *Sat.* 2.2 (Ofellus); Dio 30.25; above, n. 76; etc.; woman's Doric speech: Williams (1993); Trapp (1990) 144 and n. 3 (citing Hermogenes 491 Sp. for the σεμνότης of the Dorian accent); cf. also Cynic admiration for Spartan austerity (e.g., D.L. 6.27); philosophical long hair: Moles (1978) 95 {above, p. 51} and n. 139.
80   Cf., e.g., Plin. *Paneg.* 11.4, 12.1, 13.4f., 18.1, 61.1, 76.1.
81   Cf. Kindstrand (1976) 237f.; Attridge (1978) 56–60; Hammerstaedt (1988).
82   For this interpretation see Desideri (1978) 355 n. 60; Moles (1983a) 260 {above, p. 82} and n. 40; Professor Russell wonders if τοῖς ἄλλοις ἀνθρώποις might mean, not 'mankind at large' (Desideri; Moles; Cohoon 1.29), but simply 'the other people' (the other exiles under Domitian, who suffered literal ἄλη). But (a) Dio's ἄλη links back to 52, which reinforces its allegorical quality; (b) the implication 'men' (as opposed to gods or 'real men') seems

exile, wanderings, and tribulations were directly caused by Domitian's tyranny (alluded to at the start of the narrative enclosing the myth [50]), a tyranny also responsible for the wanderings and tribulations of mankind at large. They will end when he 'one day meets a mighty man, ruler over very many lands and peoples', who in context must be Trajan.

So during his exile in the dark days of Domitian Dio allegedly received from an impeccable source a prophecy of his present meeting with Trajan,[83] a meeting which marks the end of all his sufferings and indeed of his moral error. (The unhistoricity of the prophecy needs no emphasis.) This is the truly significant meeting, in contrast to Dio's earlier random encounters during his wanderings (9). His moral error? Dio is here surely alluding to the story of his own (alleged) philosophical conversion, a story which originated with Dio himself.[84] It also looks as if he is paying Trajan an extreme compliment. For it is as if Trajan has not merely a virtuous nature [[322]] and some of the attributes of the good king: within the exile-narrative he almost seems to be the Saviour of both Dio in particular and mankind in general, and not merely Dio's Saviour in the sense that he will end Dio's sufferings; since those sufferings have involved moral 'wandering' as well as physical, he also seems to be Dio's moral or spiritual Saviour.

How can this conception be reconciled with the earlier portrayal of Trajan as a man of good parts but having much to learn under Dio's tutelage, with the conditionality of Dio's approval, with the pointed warning that if Trajan turns out like Domitian he will suffer the same penalty, with Dio's own status as great Cynic and Socratic philosopher? There is a major interpretative problem here, but for the moment it is enough to note that Dio does not pay this compliment to Trajan outright: he does not say 'Trajan will end all your sufferings', but rather 'your sufferings will not last much longer; one day you will meet a mighty man', and the listener has to supply the implicit logical connection between the two statements. An ambiguous effect is created whereby a compliment is both paid and not paid and Trajan is both the Saviour and not the Saviour.

The prophetess (56) instructs Dio to tell Trajan the myth which she herself will now recite, even though some may despise him as a 'babbler and

---

important: cf. 55 θείας τύχης; 56 ἀνδρὶ καρτερῷ ... ἀνθρώπων; 57 οἱ γὰρ ἀνθρώπων λόγοι ... τὴν παρὰ τῶν θεῶν ἐπίνοιαν καὶ φήμην; (c) 55 τοῖς ἄλλοις ἀνθρώποις ~ 56 πλείστης ἄρχοντι χώρας καὶ ἀνθρώπων.

83   [[371]] Prophecies of Trajan's rule: e.g., Dio 45.4; Tac. *Agr.* 44.5; Plin. *Paneg.* 5.2–9; *Ep.* 10.1, 10.102; Cass. Dio 67.12.1.

84   Synesius, *Dio* 36a–38b; the analysis in Moles (1978), cf. (1983a) 259f. {above, pp. 81f.} and nn. 39, 42, has found both acceptance (e.g., Levick [1980] 193; Berry [1983] 80 n. 2; Bowie (1985) 669) and rejection (e.g., Desideri (1978) vi; Reardon [1983] 291 and [1980]; D'Espèrey [1986] 3061). I adhere to it.

vagrant' (that is, choosing the negative of the two possible interpretations of Dio-ἀλήτης in 9). He should not hesitate to do so, for the λόγοι of men and all their σοφίσματα are worthless: the wise and true λόγοι among men concerning the gods and the universe were sown in men's souls by divine will and by the first prophets and θεῖοι ἄνδρες. By contrast those who have purveyed λόγοι as true without this divine inspiration are aberrant (ἄτοποι) and wicked.

The myth comes into the right category and the emphasis on its divine origin corresponds both to Dio's earlier insistence on the divine overlordship over worldly kings (37–47) and to his initial description of the λόγος of the prudent and wise in 8f. Similarly, the examples in 58 of men inspired by the Muses recall Dio's own invocation to the Muses in 10.[85] And in being ἄτοποι the corrupt teachers contrast with Dio, whose initiation into his prophetic role began with his arrival εἰς τόνδε τὸν τόπον (55). Further, in suggesting that Trajan might reflect on the myth, Dio had opined τυχὸν οὐκ ἄτοπός σοι φανήσεται (49). Both when he received the message and delivered it Dio was in the right place at the right time: truly divine providence had brought him and Trajan together.

[[323]] It now appears that Dio's role before Trajan has three aspects: the indomitable Cynic-Socratic philosopher, Trajan's teacher; the wretched wanderer, whose tribulations and errors have been ended by the accession of Trajan as Saviour; and the divine messenger. This last role above all qualifies Dio to 'find' and retail to Trajan the μῦθος/λόγος which encapsulates the divine wisdom of old (8f.). The divine sanction of his role is underlined by the phrase οὐκ ἄνευ θείας τε βουλήσεως καὶ τύχης (of the divine origin of the true λόγοι), which picks up the prophetess' words in 55 (καὶ σὺ δὲ ἐλήλυθας ... οὐκ ἄνευ θείας τύχης) and Dio's own deceptive wording in 50 (ὡς γὰρ ἔτυχον).

In themselves, the figures of the Cynic philosopher, the wretched wanderer, and the θεῖος ἀνήρ are not incompatible, but there is a difficulty in that Dio's wretched wandering here spells not philosophical indomitableness but moral error, and there still seems to be a sharp contradiction in the two conceptions of Trajan. Nevertheless, it is at least clear that the prophecy of Domitian's replacement by Trajan has itself two aspects—as compliment, and as an essential link in the transmission of true knowledge from the gods—and that these two aspects correspond to the two conceptions of Trajan.

The myth concerns Heracles, son of Zeus, and a great king. In both respects, he stands for the good, or true, king whom Dio has described in his earlier λόγοι. But it must also be relevant that, along with Alexander, Heracles was

---

85   The reference of 58 is not to Linus (Cohoon I.31 n. 2; Kindstrand [1973] 117) but Hesiod (so also Desideri [1978] 508 n. 41), who will be important in the Second Kingship Oration (the allusion is deliberately undemanding—cf. n. 17).

Trajan's special hero.⁸⁶ Yet the relationship works both ways, for Heracles is rapidly endowed with Trajanic characteristics: the description in 60 must allude to Trajan not only as admirer of Heracles, who had a famous temple at Gades in Trajan's native land, but also as himself a world-ruler with marked Heraclean characteristics. It is hard also not to sense an ulterior meaning to the radical recasting of the myth in 59: Trajan was always the 'true king' even during the ostensible reign of Domitian/Eurystheus; there may also be an allusion to Trajan's role in the suppression of Saturninus' revolt (cf. *Paneg.* 14.5).⁸⁷ So Dio is to report to Trajan a myth about Heracles, which on another level is about Trajan himself.

Then follows a description of Heracles' education (61), which on one level can be regarded as complimentary to Trajan, with his apparently limited education; yet with its evocation of the Cynic Heracles and its attack on sophistic education and its purveyors, it must also have reference to Dio himself, Cynic philosopher and scourge of sophists.⁸⁸ Here, as at 56 and in the Third and Fourth [[324]] Orations (3.12–25; 4.27–39), one becomes acutely aware that Dio is only one of a number of people competing for the ear of the new emperor. 'Simplicity' also is something that Dio shares with Heracles and the good king, and—by extension—with Trajan himself.

The following description (61–3) combines aspects of the Cynic Heracles (γυμνός except for lionskin and club, αὐτουργός, and a supreme exponent of πόνος) with a much more worldly ruler who needed an army to sack cities, overthrow tyrants, and give orders to everyone everywhere. This awkward combination reflects the multiplicity of Dio's purpose—compliment to Trajan (who, unlike Domitian, disdained armed guards about his person),⁸⁹ the attempt to accommodate the Cynic Heracles to imperial realities (emperors did need armies to deal with 'tyrants' such as Decebalus, hence Dio's rejection of the extreme Cynic concept of the completely free and self-sufficient 'loner'), the application of Cynic values to personal morality (as opposed to imperial role). There are other interesting details in 63. Heracles is αὐτουργός and an

---

86  Cf., e.g., Durry (1938) 108 (on *Paneg.* 14.5); C. P. Jones (1978) 117f. and notes on 193; Desideri (1978) 356 n. 61; Jaczynowska (1981) 636f.; Moles (1983a) 270 {above, p. 94} and n. 71.

87  The text here is corrupt, its meaning clear (Cohoon I.32f. outlines the problems); the same thought in more philosophical form in Dio 8.29 and Epict. 3.26.31f.

88  Cynic Heracles: Höistad (1948) 33–63; Goulet-Cazé (1986) 208–10; Dio and sophists: Moles (1978) 88f. {above, pp. 39ff.}; Desideri (1978) 152 n. 25, 242f. n. 65a, 356 n. 67.

89  Cf., e.g., *Paneg.* 49.2f.; Cass. Dio 68.15.4–6, 68.7.3; Dio 4.8 with Moles (1983a) 267 {above, p. 90}.

international traveller/wanderer—like Dio himself (9, 50):[90] there is some parallel between the two and again some sense that Dio is a suitable model for Trajan. Heracles is also 'willing' and devoted to πόνος, as are Dio, the good king, and Trajan himself (9, 10, 21).

64 describes at length the care of Heracles' father Zeus for his son, with whom he communicates by divination. The relationship symbolises the good king's relationship to Zeus and mirrors the relationship between the prophetess and her shepherd son, whose flocks she often tended; she was also consulted by herdsmen and farmers nearby on the raising and salvation of their crops and cattle: the prophetess is a paradigm both of the good king and of his philosophical counsellor. She also addressed Dio gently and kindly—the same deportment of superior to inferior as is required of the good king (20).

There is a further layer of meaning: in so far as Heracles represents Trajan, Zeus recalls Nerva, who will be prominent as Trajan's solicitous father in Oration 2 (the equivalence is helped by Nerva's deification). Hence the myth also reflects Nerva's adoption of Trajan.[91] In both speeches Dio seems concerned to stress the Nerva–Trajan link, far more than Pliny or Trajan's imperial propaganda.[92] Most significant is the characterisation of Heracles. He has the 'desire' to rule and his motives are honourable—like Trajan; his nature is noble—like Trajan's, and nobility is defined by opposition to riches and material aggrandisement, like the nobility of the ⟦325⟧ humble folk among whom Dio spent his exile; Zeus' anxiety that Heracles should not be led astray by bad examples but have the benefit of association with virtuous men (64) again (cf. 33, 56, 61) reflects Dio's anxiety that in the competition for influence over the new emperor the counsels of worthless men should not prevail and Trajan's

---

90    Heracles as wanderer: Plat. *Apol.* 22a (n. 41 above), Eur. *HF* 1197; Hor. *C.* 3.3.9; Epict. 3.24.13; Dio 8.29; Cairns (1989) 35f.; cf. also the strange notice in Photius (*Bibl.* cod. 209) that Dio reportedly appeared in public in a lion-skin; however interpreted (cf. Moles [1978] 88 {above, p. 38} n. 75; Desideri [1978] 246 n. 18), it reinforces the parallel between the Cynic Heracles and the Cynicising Dio.

91    Cf. Desideri (1978) 312f. and n. 71 on 357f. Whether Desideri is right to suppose further (a) that a coherent theory of 'adoption' existed and that some took it seriously, and (b) that the allusion in Dio also has future reference (to Trajan's choice of successor) are important questions, the second more directly relevant here. As to (a) I think there was at least a theory: cf. the balanced observations of Sherwin-White (1966) 241 and Desideri's spirited self-defence ([1978] 357 n. 71); as to (b) I see no future reference (contrast Plin. *Paneg.* 94.5); in this concentration on Trajan and neglect of the future (cf. also above, n. 22) the Kingship Orations are actually more 'practical' than the *Panegyricus*.

92    Pliny also emphasises the link (how could he not?) but unlike Dio does not disguise, indeed stresses, Nerva's parlous position (*Paneg.* 6.1–7.3, 8.4–6, 10.1, etc.); Trajan's cool commemoration of Nerva: Syme (1958) 12; Waters (1975) 387, 395; Fears (1977) 227.

excellent nature not be corrupted. Great stress is laid on the dangers arising from the large mortal element in Heracles; Heracles' double nature is one of many reasons why he provides so apt a paradigm for any Roman emperor, human by birth, divine by virtue of the imperial cult and the prospect of deification or heroisation[93] as posthumous reward. But Dio here uses the paradigm for cautionary, not encomiastic, purposes.

Now Hermes enters the story (65ff.), acting as messenger from Zeus to Heracles at the start of his kingly apprenticeship, when he is still young and malleable; in effect the message he brings is the Choice of Heracles; he says who he is and who sent him; similarly, Dio is a messenger (58) from the prophetess and hence from the gods to Trajan at the beginning of his reign, bringing as his message the divine myth of that choice, the myth whose meaning Trajan is to ponder; he says who he is (9) and who sent him (56, 58). To some extent Hermes represents Dio. (Dio compares himself to Hermes as messenger of Zeus in the Alexandrian Oration, 32.21.) Dio reports to Trajan the role assumed by Hermes/Dio in relation to Heracles/Trajan (and Dio was the friend of Nerva/Zeus, 45.2): reality and myth, past, present, and future are all interfused.

The figure of Hermes helps to unify other details within the narrative enclosing the myth, the myth, and the speech generally: he is a god of Arcadia, the scene of Dio's meeting with the prophetess, of herdsmen, of the heap of stones (ἕρμα) as described in 53, of boundaries and crossing of boundaries and of youths, all relevant aspects to Heracles/Trajan as they begin their reigns, god also of prophecy, of 'finding' (cf. 4, 9, 10), of initiation (49 ἱερὸς λόγος), of λόγος itself (cf. 8f., 49).[94] These aspects matter far more than Hermes in his role in imperial cult[95] (especially since he represents not the emperor but his philosophical counsellor).

Hermes leads Heracles off the main road to a remote area where there is a conspicuous and lofty mountain (66), just as Dio in his wanderings got off the main road and ended up on a lofty spot, where he met the priestess (52–4). Again we sense an implicit parallel between the spiritual journey Dio has already made and the one Trajan has yet to make. And Hermes 'leads' Heracles (66, 69): this [[326]] action of Hermes–λόγος, at once literal and metaphorical, reflects the role of the μῦθος/λόγος itself, the 'guide of life' which will 'lead' the virtuous nature to all virtue (~ 8). In its conspicuousness, height, precipitousness, and perilousness (there is a dangerous river below) the mountain represents the position of Roman emperor. It has two peaks, that of kingship and

---

93 Cf. Dio 3.54.
94 Cf. in general Burkert (1985) 156–9.
95 Cf., e.g., Combet Farnoux (1981).

that of tyranny, though to anyone looking up from the bottom there appears to be only one, a point re-emphasised in 68: Dio is anxious to dismiss a view favoured by certain modern scholars, that it made little practical difference whether a Roman emperor was 'good' or 'bad'.

This fundamental contrast between Kingship and Tyranny makes another parallel with the *Panegyricus*: in the words of Trisoglio 'Il contrasto tra questi due sistemi di governo costituisce il motivo genetico principale del Panegirico e forma la parte più ampia del mito di Eracle che occupa quasi per intero la seconda metà della prima orazione *De regno*.'[96] The description of Peak Royalty as 'holy to Zeus the King' (67) reinforces the analogy between Zeus and the good king but also conveys compliment of Trajan, who was adopted under the auspices of Jupiter (cf. *Paneg.* 1.5, 5.3f., 8.1). There are two paths: that to the peak of kingship is broad and safe, that to the peak of tyranny narrow and hazardous—most of those who take it fall off and drown. By contrast, in Xenophon's version of Prodicus' Choice of Heracles (*Mem.* 2.1.23, 29), the road to virtue is hard and long, that to vice easy and short.[97] By transposing the physical characteristics of the roads, Dio again (cf. 45–7) gives a pointed reminder of the fate of tyrannical emperors.

Hermes then 'demonstrated' (ἐπέδειξε) the nature of the place (69). This is a philosophical 'demonstration' superior to the musical ἐπίδειξις given by Timotheus before Alexander (1). Heracles wants more—he wants to see 'the things inside', inasmuch as he is 'young' and 'ambitious' (like Trajan) and 'willing' (like Trajan and Dio). The parallel between Hermes' philosophical 'demonstration' before Heracles and Dio's before the 'willing' Trajan is obvious. The stress on 'the things inside', on Heracles' 'clear sight' as opposed to the blindness of the foolish and the weak sight of the evil man, and on the radiant light of Royalty suggests the language of religious initiation (cf. 49). Heracles can look at Royalty's radiant countenance, as the good can look at the sun, because he, unlike Phaethon (~ 46), is a true king.[98]

Other parallels come to mind. The appearance of Royalty is much more impressive than that of the prophetess, yet cannot fail to recall 〚327〛 her (70 ~ 53): there is again a parallel between Dio's spiritual quest and Heracles/Trajan's. Yet Royalty also has the look of Trajan himself: Royalty's πρόσωπον is φαιδρὸν ὁμοῦ καὶ σεμνόν, ὡς τοὺς μὲν ἀγαθοὺς ἅπαντας θαρρεῖν ὁρῶντας (71); so Pliny

---

96 Trisoglio (1972) 19f.
97 Trapp (1990) 143 and n. 2 lists many of the later Greek and Latin adaptations of the Choice of Heracles; cf. also Cairns (1989) 36, 51f.
98 For this test of royalty see Fears (1977) 156 and n. 42 and cf. Dio 4.18 with Moles (1983a) 268 {above, p. 91} and n. 64.

praises Trajan's *honor capitis et dignitas oris* (*Paneg.* 4.7) and *laetissima facies et amabilis uultus* (*Paneg.* 55.11); around Royalty πολλὴν ... εὐφημίαν τε καὶ ἡσυχίαν ἀθόρυβον κατέχειν τὸν τόπον (72), just as Pliny extols the *magna ante te, magna post te, iuxta te tamen maxima quies; tantum ubique silentium, tam altus pudor* (*Paneg.* 47.6).

Though Heracles can look straight at Royalty's shining countenance he feels αἰδώς, like that of a good son for a noble mother (73): to be a true king is to recognise an august responsibility, which is greater than oneself. The son–mother analogy also recalls the relationship between prophetess mother and her son (54) and suggests that for the good king moral qualities matter more than actual lineage (Heracles' 'true' mother is not Alcmene [59] but Royalty). On learning that this impressive lady is called Royalty Heracles acquires 'courage' (73), a quality required of Trajan (5): the true king needs a sense of αἰδώς towards his tremendous responsibility yet also 'courage' to carry it through. And 'courage' is no longer merely the military quality it appeared to be at the beginning of the speech. Heracles' response to Royalty also recalls the response of those who come into the presence of the good king (25, cf. 71): they feel not ἔκπληξις or φόβος but θάρσος and αἰδώς. In the earlier passage (25) the good king had Trajanic qualities and the bad king Domitianic qualities; again, a thoroughly ambiguous effect results: Trajan should regard Royalty as Heracles does, yet Trajan himself is apparently a paradigm of Royalty who evokes from his subjects the reaction of Heracles to Royalty.

Royalty has attendants: three women—Justice, Sound Law, Peace (again the implicit warning against warmongering; cf. 5, 27), and chief of all, a man, Νόμος, also known as Λόγος Ὀρθός, Σύμβουλος, Πάρεδρος (75):

> ὁ δ᾽ ἐγγὺς οὗτος ἑστηκὼς τῆς Βασιλείας παρ᾽ αὐτὸ τὸ σκῆπτρον ἔμπροσθεν ἰσχυρὸς ἀνήρ, πολιὸς καὶ μεγαλόφρων, οὗτος δὴ Νόμος, ὁ δὲ αὐτὸς καὶ Λόγος Ὀρθὸς κέκληται, Σύμβουλος καὶ Πάρεδρος, οὗ χωρὶς οὐδὲν ἐκείναις πρᾶξαι θέμις οὐδὲ διανοηθῆναι.

The stress on the transcendental λόγος and the Νόμος/Λόγος Ὀρθός equation are Stoic and another reminder (cf. 42–7) of powers greater than a Roman emperor, whom he cannot with impunity 〚328〛 ignore. In more mundane terms Νόμος is the antithesis of Tyranny (one of whose attendants is Lawlessness, 82) and the equation with Λόγος Ὀρθός re-emphasises Trajan's need for the λόγος which will lead him to all virtue (8).

Though formally the description of Royalty and her attendants is of abstract powers, some aspects suggest human counterparts: Royalty (in some ways) evokes Trajan, Tyranny will (in some ways) evoke Domitian. What of νόμος/λόγος, the dominant male figure in Royalty's entourage? To some extent the Arcadian prophetess, ἰσχυρά and with πλόκαμοί τινες πολιοί (53), seems a manifestation of the divine and transcendental λόγος. But she cannot wholly fulfil this role, the νόμος/λόγος being so emphatically male.

Should we think of Trajan, standing beside Royalty through his supreme merit, and might the οὐ ... διανοηθῆναι clause allude to the emperor's supremacy in human affairs?[99] Trajan was ἰσχυρός and has been described by the prophetess in the narrative enclosing the μῦθος as ἀνὴρ καρτερός (56), he was grey-haired (*Paneg.* 4.7), and at the beginning of the speech, Dio has described him as wishing to be an ἀνδρεῖος and νόμιμος ἡγεμών and sought the ἀνδρεῖοι καὶ μεγαλόφρονες λόγοι appropriate to his character (4f.). Restoration of the rule of law was also one of Trajan's great claims (cf., e.g., *Paneg.* 36.2, 65.1–3, 77.3). It is not a difficulty that Heracles (also) represents Trajan to some extent; this kind of (con)fusion of persons occurs throughout the narrative and the μῦθος. And in the present context Royalty already (on one level) stands for Trajan, so that to have Heracles/Trajan surveying Royalty/Trajan accompanied by Νόμος/Trajan is indeed (on the face of it) extremely illogical but not at all impossible.

Yet there is another interpretation: we should think of Dio himself. Dio was (presumably) πολιός, as a Cynicising philosopher[100] he assumed the role of ἰσχυρὸς ἀνήρ (despite his actual physical weakness at this time of his life);[101] if he was able to provide ἀνδρεῖοι καὶ μεγαλόφρονες λόγοι, that must reflect his own qualities, and he has several times suggested a parallel between Trajan and himself; he has earlier made a bid to be Trajan's philosophical counsellor and promised Trajan the all-sufficient λόγος; finally, the correspondingly dominant figure in Tyranny's entourage is Flattery, the corrupt adviser. On this interpretation Dio would be making an extremely strong claim, but that is already implicit in his Hermes role.

Given the (con)fusions of persons, it is perhaps not necessary to choose between these two interpretations; Trajan might anyway see [[329]] himself in the description of Νόμος. Nevertheless, the second interpretation is preferable: in context, stress on the unlimited power of the emperor (even a good emperor) is inappropriate, and the emphasis on the figure of Νόμος as Σύμβουλος, Πάρεδρος, and Λόγος Ὀρθός suggests Dio as representative of the transcendental λόγος which is the ultimate external check upon imperial power.

ταῦτα μὲν οὖν ἀκούων καὶ ὁρῶν ἐτέρπετο καὶ προσεῖχε τὸν νοῦν, ὡς οὐδέποτε αὐτῶν ἐπιλησόμενος (76): again (cf. 33) the necessity of the ruler not merely

---

99   [[372]] Cf. Brunt (1977).
100  Cf. above, n. 44.
101  References in Moles (1978) 95 {above, p. 51} and n. 141.

beginning well but following through to the end. Heracles' demeanour also indicates the spirit in which Trajan should receive Dio's admonitions. And again, there is a parallel with Dio himself, who was instructed by the prophetess (58) ἄκουε δὴ τοῦδε τοῦ μύθου σφόδρα ἐγρηγορώς τε καὶ τὸν νοῦν προσέχων, ὅπως διαμνημονεύσας ἀπαγγείλῃς ... Dio has fulfilled his role as philosopher/divine messenger in bringing Trajan the divine myth: it is now Trajan's responsibility to respond to it in the same spirit (cf. 2f., 8–10).

Hermes shows Heracles 'the other woman', Tyranny, whose character and appearance in several respects recall Domitian. The emphasis on familial feudings and killings in order to possess her recalls similar rumours about the Flavian house.[102] Peak Tyranny evokes what Tacitus and Juvenal describe as Domitian's *Albana arx* (*Agr.* 45.1; Juv. 4.145), with typical tyrannical associations.[103] Hermes leads Heracles not through the unseen and hidden corridors smeared with blood and filled with corpses but along 'the purer outside one, since he was, I think, to be an observer only' (77). The philosophical ideas—'the observer', the association of Heracles with 'purity'—are Cynic,[104] and there is also the practical implication that although Trajan was active during Domitian's tyranny, he was not besmirched by it. In these respects there is some parallel between Trajan and Dio, but there is also a difference, for Dio did not 'observe' Domitian's tyranny at first hand (50): Trajan has greater inside knowledge of the evils of tyranny and hence, Dio thinks (again the qualifying οἶμαι; cf. 5), he will be better able to avoid them in his own reign.

When (83) Hermes asks Heracles to choose between the two women he chooses Βασιλεία, averring that she is 'worthy of blessing': Royalty is what Trajan is if he is like the good king (36); as for Tyranny, Heracles would gladly dethrone Tyranny and destroy her. Hermes tells Heracles' choice to Zeus, who entrusts him with kingship over the human race. Hermes/Dio is again the direct link ⟦330⟧ between Heracles/Trajan and Zeus/Nerva. Ring structure thus binds together the μῦθος: 83 ~ 59f., 83 also ~ 11f. (Zeus gives the sceptre only to good kings): thus the whole of the expository section of the speech is bound together by ring structure and the myth is integrated with the straight exposition (another indication of the deceptiveness of the transition at 49).

Wherever Heracles saw tyranny and tyrants, among both Greeks and barbarians, he punished and overthrew them; wherever kingdoms and kings,

---

102   Domitian: cf., e.g., C. P. Jones (1978) 118; above, n. 53; rumours: e.g., Suet. *Tit.* 9.3; *Dom.* 2.3.
103   Cf. Courtney (1980) 227.
104   Cynic 'observer': above, n. 73; Cynic Heracles as 'purifier': cf. Dio 5.21, 23; 8.35; Epict. 2.16.44; 3.24.13, 26.32; Cairns (1989) 35, 101f. (the conception is also common outside Cynic contexts).

he honoured them and protected them. Hence Heracles is called Saviour of mankind—not because he defended them from wild beasts, but because he punished savage and wicked men and destroyed the power of overbearing tyrants. Thus ends Dio's report of the μῦθος/λόγος of the prophetess; with his last words he addresses Trajan directly: καὶ νῦν ἔτι τοῦτο δρᾷ, καὶ βοηθός ἐστι καὶ φύλαξ σοι τῆς ἀρχῆς ἕως ἂν τυγχάνῃς βασιλεύων (84).

This seemingly simple final section of the speech conveys conflicting messages. To the extent that Tyranny represents Domitian, Heracles correspondingly represents Trajan, as he has done earlier in the myth; this analogue is further supported by Heracles' status as Saviour, deriving from his destruction of tyrants, just as Trajan seemed to be the saviour of Dio and all mankind after Domitian's tyranny (55f.). Thus the myth ends firmly with Trajan himself and on an apparently complimentary note. The Heracles–Trajan analogy is again brought out by the rejection of the Cynic or mythical Heracles, destroyer of monsters, in favour of the political destroyer of tyrants. Heracles' right choice reflects, and compliments, Trajan's apparent preference for kingship over tyranny. The emphasis that Heracles destroyed tyrants not only among Greeks but among barbarians and mankind at large extends the destruction of tyrants beyond the confines of the Roman empire, thus again (cf. 63) allowing an allusion to external tyrants such as Decebalus. The characterisation of Heracles as Trajan's 'helper' looks back, through a further ring structure, to the initial description (8) of the λόγος of the prudent and wise as 'helper' of Trajan's 'persuadable and virtuous nature', thus suggesting a further allegory—that of Heracles and λόγος itself. (We recall that two other figures in the μῦθος have also been associated with λόγος—Hermes and Dio: 56, 58, 75.) Thus on a philosophical level the speech progresses from Cynicism to Stoicism[105]—from the simple to the sophisticated. This progression seems to suggest limitations to Cynic ethics.

⟦331⟧ All this may seem simply complimentary of Trajan. Yet the final sentence is challenging. The emphasis both of the whole speech and of the particular context, with its sharp distinction between kingship and tyranny, gives βασιλεύων the additional nuance 'being a true king', and τυγχάνω can mean not merely 'happen to be' but also 'hit the mark'; the latter implication is guaranteed by the stress in the myth on the moral choice facing Heracles/Trajan between Kingship and Tyranny and the right and wrong roads, and by the symbolic nature of Dio's own wanderings and loss of direction in 52 (with the words διαμαρτάνω, ἐπλανώμην, and ἐπετύγχανον). So the whole sentence means both 'Heracles is your protector so long as you are king' (i.e., as long as your natural

---

105   For such Stoic allegories of Heracles cf., e.g., SVF II.319.31ff.; I.115.16ff.

life) and 'Heracles is your protector so long as you are a good king'[106] (and he won't be if you aren't). Thus Dio's final approval of Trajan is conditional upon his continuing efforts to be a good king. To be sure, there is a parallel here with the *Paneg.* (e.g., 67.5, 68.1), but again Pliny is perfectly serious about this; and as in 42–7 Dio's feline obliquity gives his formulation still greater force.

There is more: the statement 'Heracles does this even to this day' seems vague, but 'this' refers precisely to Heracles' continuing capacity to overthrow tyrants—so if Trajan fails to be a good king, he will forfeit not only Dio's approval, but his office and life. The exegesis of the myth, therefore, reaffirms the lesson of 45–7. Heracles represents not only Trajan but something more than Trajan—a superior force whose continuing goodwill depends on Trajan's continuing to be a good king. This aspect of Heracles also makes a further parallel, or analogy, between Dio and Trajan: as Trajan–Saviour seems to be to Dio in 56, so Heracles here seems to be to Trajan himself.

What are the consequences of this analysis of Dio's First Kingship Oration? First, aesthetics. Dio's prose style was much admired in antiquity. When Menander commended the multifarious pleasures of the simple style (Men. Rhet. 390.2–4), he included Dio among its best exponents. On one level, this speech, especially the narrative enclosing the myth and the myth itself, seems to illustrate the style perfectly. The structure seems correspondingly firm and simple, consisting of a series of ever more weighty λόγοι, which climax in the μῦθος/λόγος which justifies Dio's claim to provide, and itself best represents, the λόγος of the prudent and wise men of the past. In fact, appearances are misleading; though the expression is sometimes rather ample, the content is extremely tight: everything relates to 〚332〛 everything else, and the structure is so organised as to suggest a series of interlocking and challenging parallels between Dio, Trajan, the prophetess, and Heracles.

Second, conception. As a first address to Trajan, the speech is excellently conceived in several respects: the skilful exploitation of the Timotheus–Alexander analogy, the intriguing self-characterisation, the Cynic framework round an evolving philosophical content, the relatively undemanding use of literary allusion, the judicious mixture of praise and exhortation, the switch in the final section from straight exposition to the apparently more entertaining 'set-piece' mode of continuous narrative and myth.

Third, Dio's purpose. One aim is to establish himself in Trajan's favour, against competition and opposition. Who are Dio's rivals? The reference in 61 to σοφίσμασι can partly be taken at face value, given Dio's general stance towards sophists; 'sophists' can also cover other philosophers, with whom Dio

---

106  Double meaning: Wirszubski (1950) 145 n. 5; Desideri (1978) 316.

might have felt professional rivalry; if these included Epicureans, as is likely given Plotina's sympathies, he was at the opposite end of the philosophical spectrum. Whether the rivals cover a still wider circle depends on more general considerations. Dio bases his claims on his status as a great Cynic/Socratic philosopher, as a sufferer of πόνοι (some inflicted by Domitian), as a messenger to Trajan of the divine wisdom of old (these three roles being interrelated), and as the confidant of Nerva (as represented by Hermes, Zeus' messenger).

What did Dio want from Trajan's favour? In general, to become one of Trajan's *amici* (cf. 33, 64), in which he succeeded (45.3; 47.22), as modern historians such as Crook and Millar recognise.[107] The natural assumption that he also wanted benefits for Prusa is supported by the end of the Second Oration and Dio's remarks in 45.2f. Here too he succeeded.

The First Kingship Oration also makes a bid for the position of Trajan's philosophical counsellor, as Dio himself elsewhere asserts: he played Nestor to Trajan's Agamemnon or Achilles (57.1–12; cf. also 56.8–16 and 49.4). Scholars such as C. P. Jones[108] who dismiss this claim as mere pretence fail to see how integral it is: not only is Dio a great Cynic/Socratic philosopher, but he is a model for Trajan, he offers Trajan further philosophical disquisitions, his ἔργον in instructing Trajan is the culmination of all his ἔργα and a fusion of λόγοι and ἔργα and the roles of philosophical teacher and pupil, his spiritual journey parallels the journey Trajan must make, he himself has some of the qualities of Heracles (who is both Trajan and [[333]] something greater than Trajan), he is Hermes, the link between Nerva and Trajan *qua* Nerva's adopted son, and between Zeus, representative of divine wisdom at its most august, and Trajan *qua* imperfect mortal, he seeks to be the philosopher behind the throne, the very embodiment of the transcendental λόγος (75). The bid for the role of philosophical adviser is itself an important part of the speech's meaning. And Dio envisages this role as involving both public performance and private exhortation (6f., 75).

How realistic was this bid? Dio's exile had removed him from political influence in Rome and Prusa, but his maternal grandfather had been an *amicus* of a Roman emperor (perhaps Claudius); in his youth Dio had been a pupil of Musonius Rufus, a staunch advocate of philosophical participation in politics, had supported Vespasian's expulsion of philosophers in 71, and had developed close ties with the Flavians, notably Titus and Flavius Sabinus;[109] his Eighteenth Oration provides a reading-list for some eminent politician (though probably a

---

107  Crook (1955) 162; Millar (1977) 114.
108  C. P. Jones (1978) 122.
109  Moles (1978) 82–8 {above, pp. 27–39}.

Greek).¹¹⁰ He also became a friend of Nerva, who on his accession recalled him from exile; illness prevented Dio from visiting Nerva before the latter's death.¹¹¹ Dio's exile under Domitian apparently won him fame (19.1), he supposedly quelled a mutiny after Domitian's assassination (Philost. *vs* 488), and then lost no time (when his health recovered) in immersing himself in Prusan politics and representing Prusan interests in Rome. All this makes his bid to be Trajan's philosophical counsellor not ridiculous, though such relationships always receive much more emphasis in Greek sources than Roman, a fact eloquent of the relative importance assigned them by the two races. And if the bid was to be made at all, it had to be early on, when the new emperor was still malleable.

When exactly? The usual dating of 100¹¹² rests on the parallels with Pliny's *Panegyricus*, on general reconstruction of this period of Dio's career, including the Prusan embassy he led to the new emperor, and on the movements of Trajan, who reached Rome in about October 99 and left it on March 25–26, 101.¹¹³ Dio's description of the path to Basileia in 1.67 (ἀσφαλῆ καὶ πλατεῖαν, ὡς ἀκινδύνως τε καὶ ἀπταίστως δι' αὐτῆς εἰσιέναι ἐφ' ἅρματος ἐλαύνοντα, εἴ τῳ δεδομένον εἴη παρὰ τοῦ μεγίστου θεῶν), surely alluding to an emperor's triumphal entry into Rome under the auspices of Jupiter Optimus Maximus Capitolinus, may suggest an earlier dating.¹¹⁴ Would Dio have written this after Trajan's much-bruited first entry on foot? From Pliny's remarks (*Paneg.* 22.1f.) there appears to ⟦334⟧ have been a theoretical possibility of Trajan's entering by chariot; it might also be relevant that Trajan shared the title Germanicus with Nerva and that Dio himself was earlier on the Danube frontier. On the other hand, Dio returned to Prusa after Domitian's assassination and lost time through illness, and his description in 45.2f. of his relations with Nerva and Trajan does not seem to allow any contact with Trajan before the embassy. On the whole, then, the First Oration cannot be much before 100 but may well antedate Trajan's entry into Rome; otherwise, 1.67 is a 'prophecy' of Trajan's triumph over Decebalus or a later insertion (like *Paneg.* 17.1–4?), neither of which seems likely.

---

110    Von Arnim (1898) 139f., followed by Moles (1978) 93 {above, p. 47} and n. 122 (I still think rightly); other suggested addressees: Cohoon I.209–11; Desideri (1978) 137–42, 185 n. 14.
111    Moles (1978) 86 {above, p. 35}; Dio 45.2f. with Moles (1984) 67f. {above, pp. 106f.}.
112    Hitherto the only dissentient voice has been Desideri (1978) 350 n. 1, arguing for late 99 (though his reconstruction of this period of Dio's career is inaccurate in detail: cf. n. 111 on Dio 45.2f. and Sheppard [1984]).
113    Trajan's movements: Halfmann (1986) 184.
114    The passage also links with 1.46 (Phaethon) and 1.71 (the true king can withstand the sun's brightness)—cf. above, n. 98.

Trajan at least made a show of accepting the proffered relationship. Though he had apparently never met Dio before,[115] he gave him audience, listened to three further Kingship Orations, received philosophical instruction, accepted Dio's representations on behalf of Prusa (45.2f.), and honoured him by having him in his chariot in one of his Dacian triumphs (Philost. *vs* 488). Hence Dio was able to claim (though not without opposition both in court and in the Greek world) that he was Trajan's 'friend' (45.3; 47.22), Trajan was one of those whom he made ὑπακούοντας καὶ πειθομένους to his exhortations (57.10), he played the role of Nestor and, more generally, 'knew the homes and tables of rich men, not only private individuals but also satraps and kings' (7.66).

What advantages did the relationship have for Trajan? Several may be surmised. No doubt Trajan was happy to discuss his imperial role with prominent individuals, which is presumably why we know his opinion of two of his predecessors.[116] It was good policy to honour a philosopher and intellectual victimised by Domitian, a personal friend of Nerva, a Greek who had some connections with the Roman ruling class. Dio could act as an unofficial imperial agent to Prusa and other Greek states of the east (he did so act) and as a Greek publicist of the Trajanic imperial programme (this he also did, delivering the Kingship Orations, which he likens to αἱ δημόσιαι εὐχαὶ ἢ κατάραι [57.12], in the Greek world; the parallels with the *Panegyricus* also raise the strong possibility of direct Trajanic input); Dio's recent travels in Dacia[117] would also have interested Trajan. Whether he was genuinely impressed by Dio and his philosophy is an important, but unanswerable, question; certainly he did not take the lessons of the Fourth Oration to heart.[118]

What else? On the above analysis the First Kingship Oration is not only complex but intentionally puzzling: various parallels between [335] Dio, Trajan, the prophetess, and Heracles are suggested, but their implications not spelled out; the exact relationship between μῦθος and λόγος in the μῦθος remains unclarified, which explains why Trajan is to think about it later (49). The speech is so organised, and so full of ambiguities and obliquities, as to

---

115   This is the clear implication both of the First Kingship Oration and of 45.2f.
116   Nero: Aurel. Vict. *Caes.* 5.2–4; *Epit. Caes.* 5.2–5; Domitian: SHA *Alex.* 65.5; cf. also the remark in Plin. *Ep.* 6.31.9.
117   Dio as imperial agent: apart from the obvious areas the neglected suggestion of Crosby IV.279 n. 1 that the τις who told Dio διάλλαξον τὴν πόλιν (48.5) was Trajan attracts me; Dio in Dacia: Dio 36.1 (with C. P. Jones [1978] 51; Sheppard [1984] 158); 12.16–21; the *Olympicus* is variously dated to 105 (von Arnim [1898] 405–7, followed by Desideri [1978] 267), 101 (C. P. Jones [1978] 53, 138, 176 nn. 70–4), and 97 (scholars cited by Desideri [1978] 279 n. 49; Cohoon II.1; Sheppard [1984] 159). In my view the arguments for 97 are decisive.
118   Cf. Moles (1983a) 277f. {above, pp. 101f.}.

force Trajan continually to ask himself questions and face up to the greatest question of all: what does it mean to be a Roman emperor? The speech is itself a moral test, and paradoxically its success is proved by the failure of almost all modern scholars to interpret it rightly—a sure σημεῖον of their irremediable moral depravity.[119]

A plea for the position of philosophical counsellor, a moral test: has this speech anything else to impart? Some modern historians take the apparent lack of specific governmental prescriptions (in contrast to Seneca's *De clementia* or Plutarch's *Politica Praecepta*, or even the *Panegyricus*) as proof that the speech has little practical content.[120] Yet it would have been very odd if Dio, particularly when he had never met Trajan before and needed to establish his credentials, had attempted in public performance to make precise recommendations such as 'cut the imperial bureaucracy', 'transfer two legions from the Rhine to the Danube', 'don't trust Titinius Capito'. Instead he takes the claims of Trajanic propaganda and either gives them a different emphasis and value, or transforms them, or, in a few cases, actually rejects them, so as to produce a series of propositions, which though general, have real practical import.

At the heart of the speech is the μῦθος/λόγος puzzle. One sense in which the μῦθος is a λόγος is that it encapsulates the λόγος of the past (8), yet the collocation μῦθος/λόγος also gives the term the meaning 'factually true account'; the 'factual truth' of the μῦθος of the Choice of Heracles is one reason for Trajan to take it seriously. But the story is also an allegory of Trajan's adoption by Nerva, of his rejection of Domitianic tyranny, and of his acceptance of Dio in the role of philosophical interpreter of divine wisdom. Some elements in this allegory are factually true: Nerva did adopt Trajan, Trajan has (so far) rejected Domitianic tyranny, Trajan in one sense 'is' Heracles; other elements are not: in another sense Heracles is different from Trajan, Trajan has not yet accepted Dio as philosophical counsellor; further, a persistent concern of the μῦθος as of the speech in general, is the relationship between appearance and reality, between the potential and the actual, between the past, the present, and the future. Hence the implications of the μῦθος/λόγος collocation also reverse themselves: the μῦθος will only truly be the ⟦336⟧ λόγος which will bring Trajan to all virtue (and λόγοι and ἔργα will only truly be reconciled), if he turns it into factual truth by becoming the ideal king under Dio's philosophical tutelage. Trajan, now potentially the divine Saviour, will then actually be the divine Saviour.

---

119  Any scholar who does not see the relationship between the myth and 8f. fails the moral test.
120  An extreme (and wholly untenable) formulation in Waters (1975) 429: 'I find the "Orations" of Dio almost totally lacking in reference to the contemporary political situation.'

Thus to the extent that Dio's ideal king is described in terms of Trajan's own imperial propaganda (reflecting Trajan as vicegerent of the gods, the new Hercules, etc.), the point is not merely to praise Trajan but so to praise him as to emphasise the need to translate his own propaganda, or those aspects of it approved by Dio, into full reality. Seneca signals a similar approach at the beginning of the *De clementia* (1): *Scribere de clementia, Nero Caesar, institui, ut quodam modo speculi uice fungerer et te tibi ostenderem peruenturum ad uoluptatem maximam omnium*; present slides into future and the mirror reflects both what is and what may be if Nero acts upon Seneca's prescriptions.[121] Dio's technique, though, is far more sophisticated and thought-provoking. So although it is true that Dio's material has many parallels with Pliny's, that, for the purposes of encouragement, he sometimes speaks as if Trajan is virtually already the ideal king, and that Pliny too strikes some cautionary notes, Dio's overall position is fundamentally different from that of Pliny, who (on the whole) is delighted with Trajan as he is.

The seriousness of Dio's plea to Trajan to improve is confirmed by several factors: the clear (though tactful) implication, especially at the beginning, that Trajan has not yet attained the ideal, the recognition that the ideal may be impracticable but must still be sought, the conditionality of Dio's approval of Trajan, the emphasis on the correct initial moral choice and on the necessity of maintaining it to the end, the insistence that there exists an authority superior to philosophical or divine λόγος, the stress on the need for good friends and advisers (especially Dio himself), because of emperors' vulnerability to corruption at the hands of bad ones, and the pointed reminders that if Trajan deteriorates in Domitianic fashion, he too will be killed. The implied parallels between the moral and spiritual journey which Dio has already made and that which Trajan has begun but not yet completed (84 τυγχάνῃς ~ 52 ἐπετύγχανον) are relevant here, for if Dio was morally 'lost' before he met first the priestess and then Trajan, there must be a theoretical possibility that Trajan himself is still in some sense 'lost', however promising the start he has made. Trajan's promising start corresponds to Dio's state at the beginning of the exile narrative (50f.): then 〚337〛 already potentially the great Cynic philosopher, Dio was yet capable of losing his way in 'rough country'.

Dio also modifies Trajan's imperial propaganda in several ways. The Trajan–Heracles link conveys not only compliment and encouragement but warning (84), as does the conception of the emperor as vicegerent of the gods (43–7). The legitimation of this conception by philosophical doctrine, whether Stoic (42ff.) or Cynic-Stoic (58ff.), reinforces the sense of an independent and superior

---

121  〚373〛 Cf. Adam (1970) 18f.; Desideri (1978) 333 n. 4.

authority. Dio also comes close to rejection of Alexander as a model for Trajan (1–7) and the general military ethos of the start of the reign, though conceding the desirability of specific action against Decebalus. To be sure, the preferred model—that of the Cynic exponent of πόνος represented by Dio himself, the prophetess, and Heracles—has points of contact with Trajanic ideology and imperial ideology generally, through Trajan's emulation of Heracles, the suggested parallels between Dio, the prophetess, and Trajan, and well-established notions of kingship as consisting of voluntary slavery and πόνος/*labor*,[122] of Heracles as a paradigm of the good king and the Roman emperor in particular, etc. These notions originate in philosophical kingship theory but by the imperial period had long been assimilated into less philosophical contexts. But Dio puts greater stress on the philosophical aspect and the result is to suggest an ideal of kingship different from that propounded by Roman emperors generally and Trajan in particular. Glamorous Alexandrian schemes of conquest and rank populism (33) are replaced by a generally Cynic code of unremitting individual moral struggle and by a Stoic conception of the position of the emperor within the κόσμος—privileged certainly, yet firmly subordinate to the ultimate λόγος.

The chronology, both relative and absolute, of the other three speeches is uncertain. I defer discussion of this question and take them in the order 2, 4, 3.

### 1.7    *The Second Kingship Oration*

In its casual, conversational, style, apparent obliquity of approach, and use of a χρεία, the start of the Second Oration closely parallels the start of the First. This λεγόμενον is of a dialogue between the young Alexander and his father Philip, concerning Homer and (in effect) kingship, subjects on which Alexander discoursed μάλα ἀνδρείως καὶ μεγαλοφρόνως (1)—a description which seems to recall [[338]] 1.4 and suggest that this speech, in contrast to the first, will focus largely on military matters and present them favourably. It also suggests Alexander's precocity (μειράκιον ~ ἀνδρείως). Given Trajan's imitation of Alexander, the fact that in the first speech Alexander to some extent represented Trajan, and the stress on a son–father relationship, corresponding to that of Heracles and Zeus in the first speech, one suspects that Alexander stands for Trajan and Philip for Nerva. Trajan's relationship to Nerva will be one of this speech's main concerns.

The characterisation of Alexander (1f.) sets the interpretative framework for the whole speech. Alexander was already campaigning with his father, although the latter tried to stop him: Alexander lacks self-control and can be

---

122    For a valuable summary of this voluminous material see now Cairns (1989) 10–38.

charged with excessive precocity and devotion to war. How does this reflect on Trajan in his triple role as son of Nerva, imitator of Alexander, and military emperor? The subsequent simile likens Alexander to οἱ γενναῖοι σκύλακες, and the simile itself echoes Plato, *Republic* 375a, where the γενναῖος σκύλαξ is a model of a good potential Guardian. Within the simile, however, the young dogs ἐνίοτε ... ταράττουσιν ἐν τῷ ἔργῳ, διὰ τὴν νεότητα καὶ τὴν ἐπιθυμίαν φθεγγόμενοι καὶ πρὸ τοῦ καιροῦ τὸ θηρίον ἀνιστάντες, which seems to confirm the negative implications of the narrative (cf. also *Rep.* 539b, where argumentative and disputatious youths are compared to puppies);[123] but then in turn ἐνίοτε ... εἷλον αὐτοὶ προπηδήσαντες, as at the battle of Chaeronea, τοῦ πατρὸς ὀκνοῦντος τὸν κίνδυνον. Honours are left ambiguously even: both Alexander's youthful energy and Philip's caution have positive and negative potential. Implicitly, the same applies to the contrasting qualities of Trajan and Nerva.

The occasion of the dialogue is described as a συνουσία (3);[124] Philip puts the first of a series of questions to Alexander about Homer and other poets, and a discussion develops: the speech takes the form of a philosophical dialogue about the relationship between literature and morality. To Philip's question why Alexander devotes himself exclusively to Homer, Alexander replies (3): ὅτι δοκεῖ μοι, ὦ πάτερ, οὐ πᾶσα ποίησις βασιλεῖ πρέπειν, ὥσπερ οὐδὲ στολή.[125] The subsequent debate concerns the usefulness of poetry solely to kings, and usefulness will be defined by τὸ πρέπον (cf. 1.9).

After enumerating the main categories of poetry by function, Alexander affirms that only Homer's poetry is 'really noble and great and kingly', hence suitable (πρέπει) for the attention of one who is going to be a universal ruler, who will have no leisure to read ⟦339⟧ anything but the best. Indeed, Alexander cannot bear to hear any poet but Homer (4–7). Philip greatly admires Alexander's μεγαλοφροσύνη (cf. 1), in that he has no base or lowly intentions but compares himself with, or rivals (παραβαλλόμενος), the heroes and demigods, yet still seeks to stimulate (κινεῖν) him with further questions (8). Trajan, too, possesses μεγαλοφροσύνη and seeks to emulate Alexander, just as Alexander seeks to emulate the Homeric heroes, and Trajan, like Alexander, will benefit from external stimulation. The thought parallels that of the First Oration, where Trajan had a good and persuadable φύσις and/but required further philosophical instruction.

---

123   I owe these Platonic parallels to Professor Russell.
124   With possible philosophical implications: cf. Dio 4.3 with Moles (1983a) 269 {above, p. 93} and n. 66.
125   The speech skilfully exploits the technique of 'suspension of thought' (cf. Woodman (1988) 122, 147 n. 13) or 'putting down a marker' (Moles [1985] 37f., 56 n. 29 {below, pp. 367–8 with n. 29}). Here ὥσπερ οὐδὲ στολή anticipates 2.49ff.; cf. also 2.9, 14, 15 (n. 127).

Dio's apparently artless narrative poses intriguing interpretative problems. To what extent does Alexander, rather than Philip, expound the correct view on these matters? Alexander does almost all the talking, his answers grow ever longer, and the latter half of the speech is virtually continuous exposition by him; but it is Philip who (on the face of it) performs the Socratic role and achieves some modifications in Alexander's views. To what extent does Alexander's view of Homer's absolute pre-eminence reflect the view of Trajan, lover of Homer? Surely very largely, for the historical Alexander's devotion to Homer was not so exclusive. But a certain tension (already latent in Alexander's ordered enumeration of other categories of poetry) arises from the fact that though Alexander argues Homer's unique importance, other poets, while formally 'rejected', are quoted at length. It is as if Dio, while concentrating on Homer as the best poet on kingship and Trajan's favourite, still wishes somewhat to broaden the emperor's literary horizons, rather as in Oration 36 he tries to show the Borysthenites that Phocylides is better than Homer in some things (36.10ff.). At any rate, Trajan's reading matter is one of this speech's central concerns, in which it invites comparison with the Eighteenth Oration, Dio's reading-list for an anonymous statesman.

Philip's next question (8) raises the rival merits of Hesiod. Alexander concedes Hesiod's usefulness to shepherds, carpenters, and farmers, but not to kings, nor Philip, nor himself, 'nor to Macedonians of the present, though to those of the past'—a seemingly obtrusive qualification which adumbrates the superiority of the present (9). He asserts Homer's superiority to Hesiod even concerning farming, quoting a Homeric simile comparing reapers to warriors cutting swathes through each other's lines. When Philip objects that Homer was defeated by Hesiod in Euboea, Alexander [[340]] replies that the defeat was just, because Homer should not have performed before farmers and ordinary people, still less before 'pleasure-lovers and softees' (Homer himself here violated τὸ πρέπον); Alexander amusingly maintains that Homer got revenge by calling the Euboeans 'long-haired', thus convicting them of effeminacy. Philip laughingly warns Alexander not to offend poets or τοὺς δεινοὺς συγγραφέας, ὡς κυρίους ὄντας ὅ τι βούλονται περὶ ἡμῶν λέγειν, to which Alexander replies that Stesichorus' fate shows that writers are not πάντως κύριοι (13).

Where does this exchange leave Dio, a δεινὸς συγγραφεύς about Alexander/Trajan? Συγγραφεῖς means 'prose-writers' in contrast to poets (cf. also 25), and the Kingship Orations are prose writings about Trajan, but one might wonder if Dio had already written, or was now writing, his *Getica*, a historical work which seems to have alluded to Trajan. At any rate, Dio seems to be suggesting that in the role of δεινὸς συγγραφεύς about the emperor he has a certain independence or authority, which Trajan must respect, but that Trajan's power limits it: he cannot criticise Trajan directly. To interpret the passage thus is not to over-interpret: Dio himself notes (17) the σπουδαιογέλοιον character of this section.

Alexander's contention that Hesiod acknowledged his inferiority to Homer by composing the *Catalogue of Women*, whereas Homer wrote about heroes (13f.), develops the female–male contrast and the idea of Alexander himself as ἀνδρεῖος (1), as Trajan also was. To Philip's next question—whether he would like to have been a Homeric hero or Homer (14)—he replies that he wants far to surpass Achilles and the others: ὑπερβάλλειν rather than παραβάλλειν, as Philip first interpreted his intentions (7). Is Alexander excessively ambitious? Not here at any rate, for Alexander immediately (15) develops the theme suggested in 9: he does not believe that Philip is inferior to Achilles' father Peleus, or Olympus to Pelion, or the education given by Aristotle to that given by Phoenix. If Alexander is Trajan and Philip Nerva, Aristotle must be Dio, whose presence in the speech has just been suggested in 13; but Dio now appears as a philosopher, not a δεινὸς συγγραφεύς, and his timely appearance seems to give decisive support to Alexander's insistence on the superiority of the present. Yet there is irony in the fact that on the one hand Alexander reveres Homer and the Homeric past, but on the other champions—apparently rightly—the superiority of the present, an irony sharpened by the First Kingship Oration's championship of the past. It looks as if Dio, while conceding much to Trajan's ⟦341⟧ imitation of Alexander (the remote past to him, just as Achilles is to Alexander), wants to some extent to direct him away from it.

Alexander's next argument (15) is that Achilles (the Homeric hero whom he most imitated) had to take orders from others and was not κύριος. The question of 'authority', applied in 13 to poets and prose-writers, now turns to politicians and military men. Indeed, Alexander himself refuses to be ruled by any man, including Philip (to the latter's annoyance): he accepts Philip's authority not as king but father (16) (in context ἀκούω also means less than ὑπακούω). There follows witty but edgy badinage concerning Alexander's mother Olympias, whom Philip ruefully admits to be οὐκ ἀνδρειοτέρα μόνον [sc. than the Nereids] ἀλλὰ καὶ πολεμικωτέρα. ἐμοὶ γοῦν οὐ παύεται πολεμοῦσα, after which Dio himself comments: ταῦτα μὲν οὖν ἐπὶ τοσοῦτον ἅμα σπουδῇ ἐπαιξάτην (16f.).

Another challenging passage: Alexander's statement of the terms of his allegiance to Philip clearly reflects the official Trajanic line of limited deference to Nerva; to that extent, Dio backtracks from the 'Nervan' account of the relationship in the myth of the First Oration; but the allusions to serious family feudings in Philip's house far exceed the official Trajanic line, for they suggest serious political dissension between Nerva and Trajan:[126] protected by the σπουδαιογέλοιον format, Dio is here hinting at thoroughly unconstitutional behaviour by Trajan and skating on very thin ice indeed. An Alexander/Trajan of this type will certainly need some binding external restraint (much stronger than the bonds which cannot contain Alexander the puppy [1]).[127]

Philip reverts to Alexander's admiration of Homer (17 ~ 3) and asks why, if he so admires Homer, he looks down on his art (by not writing poetry himself; this question is anticipated by the mention of Homer in 14). Alexander replies that while he takes pleasure in hearing other people's virtues proclaimed at Olympia, he would not himself wish to proclaim them but would rather hear his own proclaimed, a sentiment which Dio explains as meaning that Alexander regards himself as a competitor with the Homeric heroes in the contest of virtue (18). Alexander corrects himself somewhat and says that it would not be out of place if he were to be a good poet, should nature allow him to be, since a king might well require rhetorical skill. Dio is surely alluding delicately to Trajan's modest poetical efforts.[128]

A discussion follows on the usefulness of rhetoric to a king (18–24): Philip jokes that he would gladly have exchanged Amphipolis for [[342]] Demosthenes, and elicits Alexander's interpretation of Homer's views on rhetoric. Homer's admiration of rhetoric is first illustrated by Phoenix' statement that Peleus sent him to teach Achilles to be a speaker of words and a doer of deeds (19): given the earlier parallels between Phoenix and Aristotle (15) and between Aristotle and Dio, it looks as if Dio is either teaching, or bidding to teach, rhetoric (in some sense of the word) to Trajan (cf. again Oration 18). (Skill in speaking was expected of emperors on various public occasions, e.g., in responding to embassies).[129] Further, all the most kingly Homeric heroes were zealous orators, above all Nestor, so much so that Agamemnon prayed that he might have ten such elders rather than youths such as Ajax and Achilles (20f.): here, as in Orations 56 and 57 (56.8–16; 57.1–12), Dio is unmistakably boosting his own claims as a latter-day Nestor—as both counsellor and orator.

The final illustration of Homer's belief in the importance of oratory is the success of Odysseus, backed by Nestor, in dissuading the Greek army from

---

126   The circumstances of Nerva's adoption of Trajan are murky; for the malign interpretation (receiving some support from Dio here) see Aur. Vict. *Epit.* 13.6; Syme (1958) 35f.
127   Note the complex economy of effect achieved by the description of Phoenix as φυγάδος ἀνδρὸς καὶ διαφόρου τῷ πατρί (15), which (a) establishes Aristotle/Dio's superiority by contrast, (b) nevertheless helps the allusion to Dio as φυγάς, and (c) introduces the theme of father–son dissension.
128   Cf. n. 15.
129   Cf. in general Millar (1977) 203–6, 233ff., 277, 342, 570.

flight, demoralised as they were by the length of the war, the plague, dissension between the kings, and the turbulent activities of a demagogue (21–3). Given the identity of Nestor in the preceding illustration, another allusion to Dio himself seems clear, especially as the episode—marked by quarrels between kings and an army mutiny—surely reflects a notable (alleged) event in his own career, when he quelled a mutiny after Domitian's assassination by a dramatic Odyssean intervention (Philost. *VS* 488).[130] The conclusion is that both Homer and Hesiod hold 'true' rhetoric to befit the king (24). Whether the appeal to Hesiod indicates that Alexander's views are developing under Philip's stimulus, or Dio makes him speak out of character to emphasise a point, this again illustrates Dio's apparent desire that Trajan should not limit himself to Homer.

The subsequent statement that it is not wholly necessary for kings to compose epic or prose pieces like Philip's celebrated letters, unless when they are young and have leisure, like Philip at Thebes (25), has several points of interest. The exclusion of epic seems redundant after 17f. but follows neatly after the mention of Calliope in the quotation from Hesiod and balances the exclusion of prose pieces. The exclusion of prose pieces means that 'rhetoric' in 18–24 must have the sense 'practical persuasiveness'; there is surely also an allusion to the fact that Trajan did not write his own (formal) speeches.[131] The reference to letters suggests not that Trajan wholly or largely wrote, or dictated, his official letters himself, but that they were written for ⟦343⟧ him.[132] The reference to Philip's literary studies in his youth must allude to Nerva's.[133]

Alexander next describes the good king's attitude to philosophy (26). In its rejection of subtleties and emphasis on a life of simple virtue and on listening at appropriate moments to philosophical disquisitions that suit one's own character, the prescription is close to the First Oration's. There is also compliment of Trajan—both for the pleasure he shows in listening to Dio's philosophical speeches (cf. 3.2; 4.15) and for his generosity to Dio. But two things stand out: first, by comparison with 1.10 and 1.37–48 Dio seems to be downgrading the claims of philosophy as such (as opposed to general ethics): Trajan may

---

130   The authenticity of this story has been disputed, e.g., by C. P. Jones (1978) 51f., but can be defended with slight chronological adjustments (cf. Sheppard [1984] 158); whether true or not, the story looks Dionian (cf. Moles [1978] 97 {above, p. 53}; Desideri [1978] 261f.), as the present passage confirms (it is hard not to compare Musonius' behaviour [Tac. *Hist.* 3.81], in which case the Dio story is either a doublet or genuine imitation of Musonius by a pupil).
131   Julian, *Caes.* 327b; cf. SHA *Hadr.* 3.11.
132   Discussion in Sherwin-White (1966) 536–46; Millar (1977) 219–28. Sherwin-White's conclusions are closer to Dio.
133   Martial 8.70.7; 9.26.9f.

for the moment have had enough of it; second, the extension of theme, from a character 'lofty and brave' to one also 'humane, gentle, and just', mirrors the extension of theme at 1.4f. and suggests a similar message: Alexander's warlike virtues need supplementation with more general kingly virtues, though this thought is not fully developed until the end.

Alexander repeats the original prescription that the true king should not pay attention to all poetry but only Homer's (27 ~ 6 and 3), though he qualifies this by allowing καὶ τῶν Ἡσιόδου τὰ τοιαῦτα, καὶ εἴ τις ἄλλο τι λέγει χρηστόν, a qualification already explained.

The prescription as regards music is similarly minimalist (28–31): the king should not learn all music (contrast Domitian and Nero, cf. 1.8), but merely enough to sing hymns to the gods and encomia of good men, or among lyric poetry, not the erotic poems of Sappho or Anacreon, though perhaps those of Stesichorus or Pindar; Homer may suffice in this area too (this last a deviation from the generally Platonic prescription). Homer's virile poetry should be sung not to the kithara or lyre but the trumpet, to encourage to battle (in which it far surpasses Tyrtaeus), not to sound the retreat. Achilles' singing in *Iliad* 9 shows that the noble and kingly man should never forget valour or glorious deeds but always be performing or celebrating them. Thus the section ends on an extremely heroic and warlike note.

Dio now recapitulates the main points (32f.). His description of Alexander's attitude to Achilles is not without irony and links with the comments at the end of the section, which recall the remarks about poets and συγγραφεῖς in 13 and thus again allude ambiguously to one aspect of Dio's own role in relation to Trajan; moreover, ἄγαν φιλότιμος must raise the possibility that Alexander (and by implication Trajan) is excessively ambitious for encomiastic commemoration.

⟦344⟧ Two other points of interest are the stress on Alexander's philhellenism (33), which seems designed to forestall the danger that reaction against Domitian would involve rejection of Hellenic culture (rejection implicit in the *Panegyricus*),[134] and the allusion to Alexander's preservation of Pindar's house, which provides a paradigm for the rebuilding of Stagira/Prusa (79).

The dialogue resumes, with consideration of the true king's palaces and temples (34–43). The exposition grows increasingly leisurely and expansive, a general movement paralleled in the First and Fourth Orations. Alexander becomes a mouthpiece for Dio himself, the dialogue form being abandoned from 49 until the end. The seemingly innocuous content—the buildings should be decorated not with riches but enemy spoils, lavish descriptions of palaces in Homer

---

134   Cf. above, n. 13.

illustrate their owners' moral defects, soft and effeminate instead of manly—is in fact double-edged: while it conveys criticism of the sumptuous buildings[135] and incompetent military performance of Domitian/Sardanapallus (35), in contrast to the virile and military Trajan, it must also be cautionary, for Trajan was an equally extravagant builder. (It is interesting to compare Pliny's embarrassment over Trajan's building activities: *Paneg.* 50.4, 51.1–3.)[136] Thus Dio tries to direct Trajan away from external show towards internal virtue.

There follows Homer's advice on general way of life and diet (44–8); the emphasis on hardihood compliments Trajan and the approval of meat as opposed to fish implies that Trajan was a dedicated carnivore. The advice on dress (49–51) criticises the excesses of Domitian[137] and approves Trajan's habit. Description of a commander's appearance leads neatly to the subject of military discipline (52–4), which again combines reproof of Domitian with compliment of Trajan. The conclusion—that the two most kingly virtues are ἀνδρεία and δικαιοσύνη—re-emphasises the need for a broader conception of kingship than Alexander's first thoughts.

So far the focus has been on the king himself, but (55–64) he has a duty to improve others as well, which entails not only his personal rejection of vulgar music, language, and dance but banishment of them from his imperial city; Dio commends Trajan's banishment of mimes—a compliment certainly (as in *Paneg.* 46.2–4), but also a fair reflection of his own moralistic attitudes (cf., e.g., the *Euboicus*). Only war songs, whether triumphal songs or exhortations to battle, are permissible: the Second Oration must have been delivered just before one of Trajan's military campaigns. However, the martial ⟦345⟧ note is somewhat alleviated by full-length quotations, as examples of the sort of poetry which the king must reject, of a delightful poem by Anacreon and an Attic skolion. And given Trajan's interest in boys,[138] it is hardly accidental that the Anacreon poem is homoerotic. Dio's attitude here seems playfully dismissive rather than genuinely censorious.

Time forbids further exposition of the many other manly and kingly lessons and teachings in Homer, says Alexander (65), sounding very like Dio, ever anxious not to impose upon the emperor's limited leisure. The essence of Homeric teaching on kingship is summed up in the comparison of Agamemnon to the bull among the herd (65–77), whose implications are explored in detail

---

135  Cf. in general Suet. *Dom.* 5, 12.1; Garzetti (1974) 282f.
136  Cf. in general Syme (1958) 41, 226; Garzetti (1974) 313f., 330–4.
137  Cf., e.g., Suet. *Dom.* 4.4.
138  Cass. Dio 68.7.4, 10.2; Julian, *Caes.* 333b; SHA *Hadr.* 2.7; 4.5.

and with ingenuity and some humour. Like the First and Fourth Orations, the speech finishes with an elaborate set-piece.

Much of the material seems innocuous and/or simply complimentary of Trajan: like the bull the king is far superior to the rest in strength and size, and in gentleness of nature and zealous concern for his subjects; he does not abuse his strength, gets his sustenance by grazing not rapine, defends his herd from wild beasts, defeats the bull of rival herds (clearly Decebalus—cf. 71). The good bull (obviously to some extent Trajan) contrasts with the bad bull, which is savage, breaks the law of nature, despises and injures its herd, retreats before external plotters, brags when no danger threatens, gores the weaker, prevents his herd from pasturing in peace, and is justly killed by the herdsmen—a perfect description of Domitian. The polar contrast echoes that between Kingship and Tyranny at the end of the First Oration.

Yet things are not quite what they seem. Firstly, the emphasis moves away from the bull's strength to its peaceableness—the more pointedly because the necessity of waging war on external enemies is explicitly conceded, a movement which parallels the broadening of the king's role in the earlier exposition. Second, even the good bull is ἄφρων and, though supreme among animals, is subject to λογισμός and φρόνησις. So the king is subject to the higher authority of the gods (72); the gods are the masters and herdsmen of the bull, just as he is of his herd. They kill bad bulls, whereas the good bull can serve out his time with divine blessing, even when heavy with age; similarly with the tyrant and the true king; and if the true king dies a natural death before his time, he will at least have the reward of everlasting fame, and of heroisation or deification, as had Heracles.

No doubt the gods did approve of Domitian's assassination but ⟦346⟧ they did not carry it out themselves. Thus the message is the same as sections 43-7 and 84 of the First Oration. Dio slyly reaffirms the conditions of Trajan's office: if he continues to be a good bull, he will fulfil his role in the natural order, retain the approval of gods and men, and achieve posthumous heroisation or deification; if, however, he turns out to be a bad bull, his herdsmen, those possessed of superior λογισμός and φρόνησις, will kill him, as they did Domitian.

At the end of the speech (79) Alexander's exposition earns Philip's delighted approval as truly philosophical in reflecting the teaching of 'Aristotle', who has already been mentioned in 15, and who is an alias for Dio, beneficiary of the largesse of Nerva and Trajan, especially in the rebuilding of Prusa (cf. 40.5, 15; 45.3; 47.13). (The historical Aristotle also supposedly addressed a Περὶ Βασιλείας to the historical Alexander: FF 646-7 Rose.) As in the First Oration it is Dio who forms the real link between Nerva and Trajan and who (as it were) passes the torch from the former to the latter. But more, Philip/Nerva is now revealed to have less influence on Trajan's development as king than Aristotle/Dio. The shadowy figure of 15 takes centre stage. Philip's Socratic role has been something of an illusion. It is Dio who represents the superior λογισμός and φρόνησις of the gods, to which Trajan must submit himself. The point is softened, but not blunted, by the apparently warm mutual compliments of king and philosopher. The interpretation is confirmed by 49.4–6, where Philip, despite his own great παιδεία, entrusts Alexander's education to Aristotle.

Some concluding observations. First, date. Its martial tone led von Arnim to date the speech to the eve of the Second Dacian War in 104;[139] he is right to put the speech on the eve of a war (cf. 57–9), but wrong to put it so late. A dating at the start of Trajan's reign, just before the First Dacian War, is indicated by the facts that Dio is still partly basing his claim to influence with Trajan on his relationship with Nerva, that Nerva's adoption of Trajan still seems matter for debate, and that the benefactions to Prusa seem recently granted, and by the parallels with the *Panegyricus* and the sharp and seemingly topical contrast between Trajan and Domitian.

Second, interpretation. One concern of the speech is Trajan's reading matter: Dio seems to be trying to influence his choice, and interpretation, of literature. It looks as if Dio has put him on a reading programme (perhaps a scaled-down version of Oration 18); 3.3 does attest that, much to Dio's approval, Trajan has been reading edifying ancient literature. The Second Oration may also be a ⟦347⟧ demonstration of the progress Trajan has already made under Dio's inspiring tutelage.

Another concern is the relationship between Nerva and Trajan. While conceding something to Trajan's own line on this, Dio makes the relationship more important to Trajan's legitimacy as emperor than did Trajan himself.

Another concern is Dio's own role in relation to the emperor—partly that of a δεινός συγγραφεύς whose subject is Trajan, with the freedom and lack of freedom thus entailed, partly that of the external philosopher figure, who represents the philosophical and divine wisdom which is superior to Trajan's earthly power.

Another concern is Trajan's emulation of Alexander. The portrait of Alexander in this speech is not free of criticism; Dio makes some effort to underline Alexander's need for moral improvement and to suggest that there should be limits to Trajan's emulation of him, yet the portrait remains generally favourable, in some contrast to that in the First Oration and considerable contrast to that in the Fourth. Why? The answer must partly be that Alexander is being put to a legitimately different use—as kingly exegete of Homer, a role

---

139  Von Arnim (1898) 407.

to which he is well suited. But the contrast with the other treatments remains striking. This raises another of the speech's concerns: war. Again, while there are clear hints that Alexander is excessively warlike and the speech moves emphatically away from war and ends by stressing internal affairs, war looms large and seems to be regarded as more or less a good thing—again in contrast, in different degrees, to the First and Fourth Orations. Dio must to some extent be adjusting his prescriptions to immediate realities—conceding the inevitability, even the desirability, of the First Dacian War and granting more indulgence to Trajan's military ambition and emulation of Alexander than ideally he would, yet at the same time trying to direct Trajan's energies to more worthy and lasting goals. It must also be true that after the First Oration Trajan resisted Dio's attempt to steer him away from Alexander (a model that he never abandoned and that, on one view, led him to disaster) and Dio had to take some account of this obduracy.

The speech's form as a dialogue between Philip and Alexander concerning Homer and kingship provides the perfect vehicle for exploration of these various concerns. This skilful and resourceful piece, written with a notably light touch, conveys very much more than compliment of Trajan.

## [[348]] 1.8   *The Fourth Kingship Oration*

Of all the Kingship Orations this has aroused most controversy. I summarise the interpretation I argued in 1983,[140] relating it to the interpretations here advanced of the First and Second Orations.

The speech falls into three parts: introduction (1–15), dialogue (16–74), and continuous exposition (75–139), the structure resembling the Second Oration's. The dialogue is between Alexander the king and Diogenes the Cynic philosopher. Diogenes attacks Alexander's insane ambition, especially his ambition to conquer the Persians. Alexander is the complete opposite of the idealised figure of Plutarch's *De Alexandri fortuna*; that figure reflects the bowdlerised Cynic treatment of Onesicritus,[141] the obvious treatment had Dio wished to flatter Trajan. The continuous exposition consists of a lengthy 'set-piece' description by Diogenes of three spirits which dominate the majority of men—the spirits of avarice, pleasure, and ambition, followed at the very end (139) by a brief and unheralded allusion to 'the good and prudent spirit'.

As in the Diogenes discourses (6, 8, 9, 10), Diogenes represents Dio, an even bolder and more challenging assumption of the role of Cynic philosopher

---

140   Moles (1983a)—a paper I would write differently now but which I believe to be substantially right.

141   Moles (1983b) 115 {below, p. 337} and nn. 97f.

than that in Oration 1. Alexander should therefore represent Trajan, as in the First and Second Orations, and the use of a historical analogy with a king and philosopher representing Trajan and Dio would be closely parallel in all three speeches. This interpretation is supported by a literary reminiscence in the introduction: Dio's words (2) οἱ γὰρ ἄνθρωποι χαίρουσι φύσει πάντες τιμωμένην ὁρῶντες φρόνησιν ὑπὸ τῆς μεγίστης ἐξουσίας τε καὶ δυνάμεως echo Pseudo-Plato's in the Second Letter, 310e5ff.: πέφυκε συνιέναι εἰς ταὐτὸν φρόνησίς τε καὶ δύναμις μεγάλη ... ἔπειτα καὶ οἱ ἄνθρωποι χαίρουσιν. Plato and Dionysius the Younger, Dio and Trajan: the pattern is the same. To the usual points of contact between Alexander and Trajan—that Trajan imitated Alexander and was militarily ambitious—can be added the fact that Trajan wanted to defeat the Persians' contemporary equivalent (a parallel he himself emphasised during the Parthian War).

Diogenes' severe censure of Alexander's false conception of kingship, absurd ambition, and insane plans of eastern conquest, is a development, a hardening, of the criticisms contained in the First and Second Orations. But Dio stresses that Alexander's φύσις was good (like Trajan's in the First Oration) and Diogenes embarks on an educational crash course with him (15, 31, 38). The speech is not [[349]] merely an attack upon Alexander/Trajan: it is an attempt to show him the error of his ways and set him on the right road (the imagery of the two roads, in the First Oration used of the roads to Kingship and Tyranny, is now [33–7] applied to ignorance and knowledge). The educational crash course is the same as the First Oration's: a simple regimen under the guidance of Diogenes/Dio, total rejection of the false complexities of sophistic teaching, and assimilation of the Cynic ideal of moral kingship to the political kingship of the ordinary world.

This speech has clear reference to Trajan, was delivered before him, censures him, and attempts to educate him in true philosophical values. But Dio throws various sops to Trajan's self-esteem. Besides the stress on his good φύσις, Alexander is incongruously credited with virtues like Trajan's own (alleged)—for example, his love of frankness, which receives disproportionate emphasis in 15; as in the First and Second Orations one of the main functions of praise is to soften criticism. He is also given some vices like Domitian's, for example, his love of honours and titles and reliance upon bodyguards for personal safety (5, 8, 25). As in the First Oration, what is good about Alexander looks like Trajan, while some of what is bad looks like Domitian.

More subtly, the Cynic core of the speech, which contains the sharpest criticism of Alexander/Trajan, is introduced with a degree of irony, for in the introduction (2) Dio concedes that in their accounts of the meetings of great kings and great philosophers men 'not only relate the facts ... but add extravagant embellishments of their own'. It is also sandwiched between, and cushioned by, this somewhat ironic introduction and a blander Platonic final section. The latter contains the elaborate description of the three spirits, and Diogenes explicitly changes his style at this point (79), switching to sophistic rhetoric, in order to mollify Alexander. The description itself owes much to Plato's *Republic*, and it culminates, at the end of the speech, in the unexpected introduction of the fourth spirit (139):

ἀλλὰ δὴ μεταλαβόντες καθαράν τε καὶ κρείττω τῆς πρότερον ἁρμονίας τὸν ἀγαθὸν καὶ φώφρονα ὑμνῶμεν δαίμονα καὶ θεόν, οἷς ποτε ἐκείνου τυχεῖν ἐπέκλωσαν ἀγαθαὶ Μοῖραι παιδείας ὑγιοῦς καὶ λόγου μεταλαβοῦσι.

The philosophical concepts can be regarded as Platonic (ἁρμονία, παιδεία, λόγος) or Stoic (the δαίμων/θεός-within), but on another level Trajan could see a complimentary allusion to himself, as the saviour god who had rescued Dio and the world in general from [[350]] misery and sin under the tyranny of Domitian. In this, and in the blurring between Trajan as he now is (in the bulk of the speech) and as he ideally might be (at the end), the Fourth Oration again closely resembles the First.

The Fourth Oration is less sinewy than the First but of equally heroic temper, less feline than the Second but equally well conceived. In their different ways these three speeches are all excellent. The First and the Fourth are major speeches by any standards, the Second, while slighter, is immensely accomplished.

### 1.9    *The Third Oration*

By contrast, this speech is problematic in several respects. There are numerous textual difficulties and problems of organisation (scholars have felt it necessary to transpose sections, hypothesise doublets, or the intervention of an ancient editor working with an incomplete draft),[142] and even Dio's admirers have found the tone excessively complimentary to the emperor.[143] Thus Desideri, while acquitting Dio of 'squallida adulazione', sees 'un fare conciliato e tutto sommato ossequioso' and Dio himself as 'palesemente imbarazzato'.[144] The following analysis will try to show that neither the techniques nor the contents nor the quality of this speech are much different from those of the other three.

---

142   Desideri (1978) 344 n. 3a summarises the main problems and solutions proposed.
143   [[374]] Certainly Trajan; Desideri's view that it is Nerva is refuted in Moles (1984).
144   Desideri (1978) 303, 297, 299.

The speech begins in an ingenious and complex manner. The technique of analogy is given a fresh twist: this time the analogy for the relationship of Dio and Trajan is Socrates and (as it were) not the Persian king. Dio gives the ultimate boost to his own credentials; he is not the generalised Cynic philosopher nor the embryonic Socrates of the First Oration, nor the discreet Aristotle of the Second, nor even the brash Diogenes of the Fourth; he here assumes the full mantle of the great Socrates, πρεσβύτης ἀνὴρ καὶ πένης like Dio himself, the fount of all true moral philosophy and teaching about government and kingship (42); self-defence and self-justification will be even more important in this speech than in its companions. The Socratic model has further implication: the emphasis will be more on moral encouragement than criticism (though Socrates retains some mild Diogenic/Cynic features, such as πενία and generally iconoclastic attitudes); there will be some Socratic dialectic, and the style will be Socratic in its abundant use of τέχνη-analogies and illustrations from everyday life (a style maintained even after the [[351]] abandonment of the Socratic model in 42).

Trajan's role has been correspondingly upgraded: he is not the apprentice king of the First Oration, nor the brilliant but imperfect Alexander of the Second, nor the thoroughly flawed Alexander of the Fourth, but the very opposite of the Persian king. Since the latter is the type of the defective king, Trajan seemingly represents the ideal.

The question put to Socrates (whether he considered the Persian king εὐδαίμων: *Gorg.* 470e) introduces the basic theme: the relationship between the inner qualities of a king and externals, such as riches, imperial possessions, and other men (1). Socrates, whom Trajan 'knows' by hearsay (γιγνώκεις ἀκοῇ) to have lived many years ago, replies that the Persian king may be (τυχόν) εὐδαίμων, but that he does not 'know' (εἰδέναι) this, since he has not 'been with him' (συγγενέσθαι) and does not 'know' (γιγνώσκειν) his διάνοια. But, whereas Socrates 'happened to be' (ἐτύγχανεν) 'unacquainted' (ἄπειρος) with the Persian king's soul, and hence with his εὐδαιμονία, Dio has 'been with' (παραγέγονα) Trajan and 'happens to be' (τυχόν) as 'well acquainted' (ἔμπειρος) with his nature as anyone, that Trajan 'happens' (τυγχάνεις) to rejoice in truth and frankness rather than in flattery and deceit (2). This quality of Trajan's contrasts with the characteristic attitude of the Persian, or bad, king; and the emphasis prepares the full examination of truth and flattery in 12–25. Dio must also be alluding to the apparent pleasure with which Trajan has listened to his previous kingship speeches, which have conveyed some frank criticism or warning. However, any expectation that the emphasis prepares for, and softens, explicit criticism in this speech, as it does of Alexander/Trajan in the Fourth Oration (4.15), seems quickly squashed. For just as Trajan suspects flatterers, so does he suspect irrational pleasures and endure labours, taking them to be 'tests' of virtue; the contrast between pleasure and hardship will be another major theme. Indeed, when Dio sees Trajan ἐντυγχάνοντα τοῖς παλαιοῖς ἀνδράσι καὶ συνιέντα φρονίμων καὶ ἀκριβῶν λόγων, he declares him to be σαφῶς ἄνδρα ... μακάριον, since he has the greatest power after the gods and uses that power most nobly (3), i.e., he has both the worldly power of the Persian king and the moral excellence which makes him truly μακάριον (= εὐδαίμονα, cf. 5 *ad fin.*). The progression from the conditional μακαρισμός of the First Oration (36) is marked.

The sources of this moral excellence are two: first, Trajan's own φύσις (2), second the fact of his ἐντυγχάνοντα τοῖς παλαιοῖς ἀνδράσι καὶ συνιέντα φρονίμων καὶ ἀκριβῶν λόγων (3). Through reading, ⟦352⟧ Trajan can achieve the close association with, and knowledge of, παλαιοὶ ἄνδρες which will transmit their virtue to him. Dio reaffirms three main emphases of the other kingship speeches: on the excellence of Trajan's φύσις, on ancient wisdom in contrast to mere modern cleverness, and on the need to associate with good moral teachers and exemplars. These surely include Dio, the present-day equivalent of Socrates and both literally and spiritually a παλαιὸς ἀνήρ, and now apparently Trajan's constant companion. The sense of a philosophical 'succession' is reinforced by the intricate word patterning based on γιγνώσκω/οἶδα, συγγίγνομαι/παραγίγνομαι, τυχόν/τυγχάνω/ἐντυγχάνω, ἄπειρος/ἔμπειρος. Similarly, the 'prudent and precise words' are not only the words of great ancient philosophers such as Socrates but also those of Dio himself, who in his first Kingship Oration had sought to provide Trajan with 'the word of the prudent and wise', urged him to ponder the meaning of the myth, and then set him on a reading programme. If then Trajan now is, or very nearly is, the ideal king ('hitting the mark', as at the end of the First Oration Dio had hoped he would), the main reason is that he has accepted Dio's philosophical programme. While the compliment Dio pays Trajan is extreme, it has strings attached.

4f. elaborates on Trajan's moral qualities: though he can (ἐξόν) enjoy all pleasures, avoid all hardships, live a life of complete ease, do precisely as he wants, hindered by nobody, indeed praised by everybody—though he has supreme power in a worldly sense, he performs excellently in all his various roles, so that anyone must admit that his δαίμων is a good, not only to himself but also to everyone else. The 'inner–outer' contrast here takes a different turn: though a king's εὐδαιμονία depends on his own internal moral character, it necessarily affects the well-being of all his subjects, which in the case of a Roman emperor means all human beings. The cool observation that even if an emperor behaves badly, everybody still praises him commits Dio to defence of the twin propositions that Trajan behaves supremely well and Dio's praises are fully deserved.

Whereas the δαίμων of most men, whether private individuals or petty rulers, is small and affects its possessor alone, a universal ruler is necessarily πάντων ... ἀνθρώπων ... σωτὴρ καὶ φύλαξ, ἄνπερ ᾖ τοιοῦτος (6). Here, as in the First and Fourth Orations, Dio comes very close to hailing Trajan as σωτήρ and φύλαξ of the human race, and this suggestion is strengthened by the subsequent description of the ideal world ruler, which has some typically Trajanic features (e.g., the stress on πόνος). On the other hand, the ἄνπερ-clause formally ⟦353⟧ avoids complete identification, and this note of reserve sounds again at 9 (τοιοῦτος); admittedly, however, it is less strong than in the other three Kingship Orations.

The ideal ruler inculcates his own virtues into his subjects, ὁ γὰρ τοιοῦτος βασιλεὺς τοῖς μὲν ἄλλοις καλὸν κτῆμα τὴν ἀρετὴν νενόμικεν, αὑτῷ δὲ καὶ ἀναγκαῖον (9). The 'inner–outer' contrast takes yet another turn (the wording picks up, and contrasts with, 5 *ad fin.*): the king makes others like himself. But for him virtue is an absolute essential—Dio spells out the implications of the fact already alluded to (4), that to the Roman emperor πάντα ἔξεστι. Absolute power imposes its own moral imperative: virtuous behaviour on the part of the omnipotent ruler. The inextricable connection between the ideal ruler and his subjects and between his inner moral character and their well-being and the absolute necessity for the ruler to perform virtuous acts, are illustrated by the image of the sun, which πάντα ... τἆλλα ἀναφαίνων πρῶτον ἑαυτὸν ἐπιδείκνυσι (11). This constantly-recurring image will be another unifying theme.

Dio now provides a lengthy self-justification (12–28), beginning (12f.):

> λέγω δὲ ταῦτα οὐκ ἀγνοῶν ὅτι τὰ ῥηθέντα νῦν ὑπ' ἐμοῦ ἐν πλείονι χρόνῳ ἀνάγκη λέγεσθαι· ἀλλ' οὐκ ἔστι δέος μήποτε ἐγὼ φανῶ τι κολακείᾳ λέγων· οὐ γὰρ ὀλίγην οὐδὲ ἐν ὀλίγῳ χρόνῳ δέδωκα βάσανον τῆς ἐλευθερίας. εἰ δὲ ἐγὼ πρότερον μέν, ὅτε πᾶσιν ἀναγκαῖον ἐδόκει ψεύδεσθαι διὰ φόβον, μόνος ἀληθεύειν ἐτόλμων, καὶ ταῦτα κινδυνεύων ὑπὲρ τῆς ψυχῆς, νῦν δέ, ὅτε πᾶσιν ἔξεστι τἀληθῆ λέγειν, ψεύδομαι, μηδενὸς κινδύνου παρεστῶτος, οὐκ ἂν εἰδείην οὔτε παρρησίας οὔτε κολακείας καιρόν.

A preliminary problem: what is the implication of the ὅτι-clause of the first line? Is Dio referring to other, longer, performances of the speech which he must give in the future to a different audience, thus allowing more protracted examination of his motives? But, while he did deliver his kingship speeches before other audiences, meeting the same sorts of criticisms as at court (57 *passim*, especially 57.11), why should these performances necessarily have been longer? And would he not have said (e.g.) πάλιν λέγεσθαι? There is much in favour of Usener's ἐλέγχεσθαι,[145] linking with the idea of 'testing' conveyed by βάσανον, and alluding to the heated debate caused by the Kingship Speeches.

The main points, however, are clear. As in the First Oration Dio has to confront the charge of flattery because, even by his own admission, much of the preceding material is highly complimentary to Trajan. He defends himself by reference to his heroic stance [[354]] against Domitian. There are also interesting parallels between his situation and that of the ideal ruler/Trajan. The actions of both are exposed to public scrutiny (ἀναφαίνων ... ἑαυτὸν ἐπιδείκνυσι/φανῶ) and both are, as it were, 'on trial' (βάσανον, ?ἐλέγχεσθαι; cf. 11 θεατὰς καὶ μάρτυρας ... μηδὲν οἷόν τε λαθεῖν); there is also a contrast: whereas to Trajan πάντα ἔξεστι (10), which makes it all the more necessary for him to behave with supreme virtue, to everybody else (πᾶσιν), including Dio, ἔξεστι τἀληθῆ λέγειν about Trajan's virtue or lack of it, which means that there is no longer any excuse for flattery, not that Dio used it even before the tyrant Domitian. The moral status of Trajan the king and of his actions, and of Dio his philosophical counsellor and of Dio's speeches about Trajan, are interdependent. An important element of the Third Oration, then, is defence of Dio's relationship with Trajan but the defence takes the form of aggressive self-assertion and involves Trajan's moral status as much as Dio's (a point that Dio makes explicit at 25 and that might well deter critics).

Dio then further elides the distinction between actions (performed by the ruler) and words (performed by speakers about the ruler such as himself), by analysing flattery in terms of πράξεις (14ff.) and detailing the various motives of οἱ πράττοντες. The analysis begins with further self-defence (the arguments have force but are not necessarily convincing) but broadens into a lengthy general discussion of flattery, so that Dio seems not only to be defending himself but turning the tables and attacking others.

So far, he has defended himself on two grounds: examination of his words will reveal no flattery; and he has none of the usual motives for flattery. He now (25) seemingly changes tack, in a formulation similar to that of 1.15:

> ἵνα δὲ μήτε ἐγὼ κολακείας αἰτίαν ἔχω τοῖς θέλουσι διαβάλλειν μήτε σὺ τοῦ κατ' ὀφθαλμοὺς ἐθέλειν ἐπαινεῖσθαι, ποιήσομαι τοὺς λόγους ὑπὲρ τοῦ χρηστοῦ βασιλέως, ὁποῖον εἶναι δεῖ καὶ τίς ἡ διαφορὰ τοῦ προσποιουμένου μὲν ἄρχοντος εἶναι, πλεῖστον δὲ ἀπέχοντος ἀρχῆς καὶ βασιλείας.

---

145  Accepted also by Desideri (1978) 346 n. 8.

In fact the following description will not be purely abstract, for the good king will again, as at the beginning of the speech and in the other Kingship Speeches, have some recognisably Trajanic features, so that compliment is still implicitly being paid to Trajan. But this procedure also reverses itself: reactivating the question, is Trajan fully τοιοῦτος (6)?

Dio next disposes of two further, and related, charges against [355] himself (26–8): that of repetitiousness (Socrates also repeated himself and truth does not change) and that of sameness of theme (on the τέχνη-analogy speeches about kingship are the proper subjects for kings to listen to).[146] Obviously, the considerable overlap of material among the four speeches might well provide critics with further ammunition. He then returns to the conversation between Socrates and his interrogator about the Persian king (29): having defended his position against all possible attacks, he can re-establish his Socratic role.

In the conversation Socrates' interrogator reasserts the δύναμις of the Persian king (this development is simply invented by Dio). Various details both in the interlocutor's remarks and Socrates' response give the Persian king suspiciously Domitianic attributes, which as usual compliments Trajan by contrast.[147] On the other hand, the other speaker's stress on the vastness of the Persian king's imperial possessions and Socrates' demolition of this as a criterion of δύναμις suggests criticism of Trajan's own imperial ambitions. And this part of the speech reads very much as a milder version of the Fourth Oration, with the Persian king substituting for Alexander and Socrates for Diogenes, a factor which strengthens the interpretation (especially if the Fourth is earlier). The opposition between Trajan and Persian king (1f.) has proved less than absolute.

Dio now sums up the Socratic section of the speech: τοιαῦτα μὲν ἐκεῖνος εἰώθει λέγειν, προτρέπων ἀεὶ πρὸς ἀρετὴν καὶ βελτίους ποιῶν καὶ ἄρχοντας καὶ ἰδιώτας (42). Socrates/Dio is still operating at the level of protreptic; the philosophical effort on the part of both teacher and pupil needs to be constantly maintained; Trajan is still not the ideal king.

There follows (42–9) a brief theoretical survey, along Aristotelian and Polybian lines, of the various constitutions and their degenerate counterparts. Although skilfully linked to the Socratic section, and part of Dio's general programme of 'distinguishing' between types (43 διαφοράν ~ 25 διαφορά; cf. 1.15), the section is problematic in detail and of little moment, as Dio himself virtually

---

146  For the thought cf. 1.9f.; 2.3.
147  E.g., power over nature (31): n. 53; fear (34); universal acclamation as king (37f.): n. 53; tiaras and sceptres: n. 53.

admits at the end (49).¹⁴⁸ But it serves several functions. First, it creates the impression of a theoretically comprehensive treatment of the subject of ἀρχὴ καὶ βασιλεία (42), including other types of ἀρχή besides kingship. Second, it allows Dio to pay Trajan ambiguous compliments, which as usual sweeten the implied criticisms: what are the exact references of the descriptions μία μὲν ἡ πρώτη καὶ μάλιστα συμβῆναι δυνατή, περὶ ἧς ὁ νῦν λόγος, εὖ διοικουμένης πόλεως ἢ πλειόνων ἐθνῶν ἢ [[356]] ξυμπάντων ἀνθρώπων ἑνὸς ἀνδρὸς ἀγαθοῦ γνώμῃ καὶ ἀρετῃ (45) and περὶ δὲ τῆς εὐδαίμονός τε καὶ θείας καταστάσεως τῆς νῦν ἐπικρατούσης χρὴ διελθεῖν ἐπιμελέστερον (50)? Does ξυμπάντων ἀνθρώπων ἑνὸς ἀνδρὸς ἀγαθοῦ γνώμῃ καὶ ἀρετῃ assimilate the ideal form of world rule with Trajan's world rule? Is the εὐδαίμονός τε καὶ θείας καταστάσεως τῆς νῦν ἐπικρατούσης the Roman imperial system in general, the divine solution to the turmoil of the Late Republic (49), or the rule of the εὐδαίμων Trajan in contrast to that of Domitian? In both cases the reference is no doubt formally to the general type but compliment to the particular regime of Trajan can hardly be suppressed. Third, it creates an effective rhetorical build-up to the treatment of the best form of government—that of 'divine' kingship, which occupies the rest of the speech (50–138).

The ideal king has a position analogous to that of 'the first and best god' (50) and is himself θεοφιλής ('god-loving' rather than 'beloved of the gods'). The description of his religious observances (51–4) is generally compatible with Trajanic ideology, but there are interesting emphases. Religious observance is not just a matter of action and statement but of belief; this is yet another aspect of the 'inner–outer' contrast, and Dio again seems to take a position diametrically opposed to that of sophisticated modern scholarship.¹⁴⁹ And the ideal king believes in the gods ἵνα δὴ καὶ αὐτὸς ἔχῃ τοὺς κατ' ἀξίαν ἄρχοντας: because he has to assure himself that he is under the control of worthy rulers (just as he himself rules worthily over his subjects).¹⁵⁰ Yet again Dio rams home the existence of powers independent of, and superior to, the Roman emperor. Finally, the king's mortal nature is stressed, as in section 65 of the First Oration, but the carrot is extended of posthumous transition to a higher

---

148  This undermines Desideri's attempts ([1978] 300) to find 'il messaggio politico di questo terzo Sulla regalità' in this section. (I omit discussion of the various textual difficulties hereabouts.)

149  E.g., the formulations of Price (1984) 9–11 ('"Belief" as a religious term is profoundly Christian in its implications ... the question about the "real beliefs" of the Greeks is again implicitly Christianising', etc.) cannot cope with this passage (or countless other passages in Greek literature; an obvious example: Socrates and his accusers did not view the question of religious belief as a non-question).

150  Cohoon's translation (1.129) 'to the end that he too may have worthy governors under him' is wrong (cf. also Desideri [1978] 300).

state (54), as in section 78 of the Second Oration and more generally at the end of the First Oration. But this higher state explicitly falls short of full deification. Although the last sentence of 54 clearly alludes to the Roman imperial cult, Dio's assimilation of that cult to heroisation or 'demonology' seems pointedly minimalist.[151] The sentiments expressed in 51–4 are not those of a κόλαξ or of one to whom the ordered hierarchy of the universe and the position of the Roman emperor within it are matters for opportunistic modification.

The next topic is the king's ἐπιμέλεια for his subjects (55–7): this is his ἔργον to which he has been appointed by god, he willingly assumes πόνοι for others, his task is unending, his paradigm the sun, which he sees οὐκ ἀχθόμενον, εἰ σωτηρίας ἕνεκεν ἀνθρώπων καὶ [357] βίου τὸν αἰῶνα διαπράττεσθαι πάντα ὅσα πράττει (for the emphasis cf. 1.33, 45, 76, 84; 2.77f.).

Up to this juncture, despite textual problems, the speech is excellently put together, but the problem of organisation now becomes acute. I accept the radical transpositions of Emperius (also followed by Desideri),[152] so that the speech is ordered as follows: 1–57; 62–85; 58–61; 86–111; 128–32; 112–27; 133–8. While space precludes proper discussion, the analysis will indicate the logic of the transpositions. In the immediate context they mean that the sun's activity on behalf of men illustrates the universal divine principle that τὸ βέλτιον should rule over, and have ἐπιμέλεια for, τοῦ ἥττονος (62). They also give a pleasing and characteristic ambiguity to the switch from the third person ὁρᾷ in 57 (of the good king) to the second person ὁρᾷς in 62: is Dio now addressing Trajan as already the good king, or instructing him in his place in the cosmos by appeal to illustrations which he can easily see for himself?

The universal principle is illustrated in different spheres and at some length: it is difficult to resist the impression that hereabouts Dio is coasting. The illustrations culminate once more with the sun (73 ~ 57), whose activities exemplify both divine πόνοι on behalf of men and the Stoic conception of the harmony of the universe (as in the First Oration Dio seems concerned to give full philosophical sanction to the place of the emperor within the cosmos). The sun is also a common paradigm for kings and the parallel becomes particularly marked with the reference in 75 to the sun's δουλεία ἰσχυρά. The sun's activities do not simply illustrate the universal principles which also apply to kings: they allegorise the correct behaviour of a Roman emperor. Dio's development of Xenophon, *Memorabilia* 4.3.8, on the sun's role in bringing the right amount

---

151 Desideri (1978) 301 also seems to suggest this; again, Dio's position challenges the contentions of modern historians of the imperial cult (e.g., Price [1984] 33: 'the heroic system of classification was eschewed in ruler cult in favour of the divine system').

152 Cf. n. 142.

of heat at the right time of year (76–80), thus alludes to an acute practical problem which defeated so many emperors: that of striking the right balance between over- and under-participation in public affairs. Such allegory and allusion, and indeed the emphasis throughout the speech on the sun, surely reflect the Sol-cult under Trajan.[153] But as usual this aspect of the content is not mere compliment, but provides a point of departure for philosophical exposition.

The good king *qua* ἄνθρωπος θεοφιλής, seeing that the sun, the best and most conspicuous god, does not neglect his constant ἐπιμέλεια for ἄνθρωποι, strives to imitate it (82). As in the First Oration, the emperor, while a key element in the divine hierarchy, the [[358]] vicegerent of god on earth, and himself due for a higher state after death if he merits it, remains in the here and now emphatically human. (Cf. Dio 53.11: τοὺς ἀγαθοὺς βασιλεῖς δέον πρὸς ἐκεῖνον [sc. Δία] βλέποντας κατευθύνειν τὴν ἀρχήν, ἀφομοιοῦντας, ὡς δυνατόν ἐστιν ἀνθρώποις, θεῷ τὸν αὐτῶν τρόπον.) The good king toils incessantly and (by the usual philosophical casuistry) has a pleasanter life than the devotee of luxury (82–5).

This contrast introduces a contrast between the good king and the tyrant and a striking thought (58–60): the good king realises that qualities such as ἀνδρεία, ἐγκράτεια, φρόνησις, and toleration of πόνοι are needed even more by tyrants, if they are to survive; hence virtue is positively advantageous: the good king is praised and loved by men and by gods, whereas the tyrant is reviled and hated; man's present is short and incalculable (Dio attains almost Solonian solemnity), most of his life is filled with remembrance of the past and expectation of the future. His memories bring joy to the good king, grief to the tyrant, his expectations confidence to the good king, fear to the tyrant. No doubt Domitian is the tyrant and Trajan may be the good king, but, as in the First and Second Orations, Dio is still preoccupied with the question how Trajan will ultimately turn out and eager to remind him of the fate of tyrants. The conclusion again is that the good king has a pleasanter life (61).

From the king's inner qualities (58–60), Dio moves to his external possessions, of which the finest and holiest is friendship and friends (86), which topic occupies almost all the rest of the speech (86–111; 128–32; 112–22). The trustworthiness of friends is a surer guarantee of the king's εὐδαιμονία than his revenues, armies, or the rest of his δύναμις (~ 1).

For (the 'inner–outer' contrast is modified yet again) complete self-sufficiency is impossible for anyone, especially kings with their many and

---

153 See, e.g., Cumont (1940); Beaujeu (1955) 99–103; Fears (1977), index and 240–2, 250 for Trajan; Desideri (1978) 349 n. 25; Lane Fox (1986) 593; Dio's Third Oration itself strengthens the case for Trajanic Sol cult and early in the reign too; the silence of the *Panegyricus* presumably reflects cultural difference; cf. also n. 98 on the sun and true kingship.

diverse responsibilities (87); absolute εὐδαιμονία requires friends in addition to the perfection of one's own inner moral qualities. There is a point beyond which Cynic self-sufficiency, so vigorously expounded in the body of the Fourth Oration and recommended—with certain qualifications—in the First Oration, becomes inadequate. Then another aspect of the fact that kings are above the law (~ 10): not only must they discipline themselves but they have no real protection other than the loyalty of friends, especially οἱ ἐγγὺς τῶν βασιλέων καὶ τὴν ἀρχὴν συνδιοικοῦντες (89).

As in the First Oration, the long disquisition on friendship is to [[359]] some extent complimentary of Trajan, and in the present context there may well be an implicit contrast between Trajan's behaviour and Domitian's final, disastrous alienation of his immediate 'friends'. Dio later (116) contrasts the states of the good king and the tyrant with regard to friends and there the allusion to Domitian is plain. But compliment is not the sole function of 86–9. First, the topic of friendship is not gratuitously inserted but an essential element of the analysis of the relationship between inner and external. Second, as already emphasised, Trajan's choice of friends mattered, and in this speech the topic links with the earlier discussion of flattery; Dio is again bringing home to Trajan the importance of the right choice of friends and at the same time defending his own position (which is under attack) as one of the emperor's closest 'friends'—indeed, the phrasing of 89 seems to recall that of 1.75.

The topic of friendship is now explored from the point of view of pleasure *vs* utility: only friendship combines extreme usefulness with extreme pleasure (94). The sequel mixes praise of Trajan with positive moral exhortation in the usual Dionian manner. The description in 103 of the man who by virtue of his countless friends and their approval is τελέως εὐδαίμων echoes the earlier descriptions of the εὐδαίμων at 4 and 7, descriptions with at least some reference to Trajan. Yet to be τελέως εὐδαίμων Trajan will have to accept Dio's recommendations on friendship. A similar case is the observation in 109 concerning glory. This seems a concession to Trajan's love of glory, yet redefines glory as the praise of friends, which can only be bestowed if it is deserved (18, 110). The programme of friendship expounded in 128–32 also looks perfectly serious: friends must be carefully selected not merely from the narrow imperial circle but from all over the world—a broad-minded attitude paralleled elsewhere in Dio's writings.[154] The scope and emphasis of this section amount to more than compliment of Trajan's promotion of Eastern senators.[155] Again, the elevation of friendship over love of kin (113) is, to the excessively familial Trajan, a

---

154 Cf., e.g., Moles (1983c) 132 {above, p. 68} and n. 12.
155 Cf. the widely accepted figures of Hammond (1957) 77; Hopkins (1983) 200.

pointed emphasis (cf. again the competing claims of friendship and kinship in the early days of Vespasian);[156] true, Dio subsequently concedes love of kin to be a great good (119), but the concession is awkward and even then kinship is subsumed within the greater good of friendship.

The long discussion of friendship is followed by a summary description of the good king (123–7) in relation to the main moral criteria of the speech: luxury, virtue, endurance, security, usefulness and pleasure (here united), toil. The description closes with a ⟦360⟧ contrast between the activity of sensible ordinary people and the still more purposeful activity of the ruler (the allusion to ordinary people's physical activities anticipates the final section).

The speech so far has dealt with the king 'at work': the final section (133–8) concerns the recreations needed by a king, 'a human being by nature', as consolation for all his activities (133). The recreations of many kings damaged their souls and destroyed the dignity of kingship—witness the recreations of Nero and Ptolemy Auletes (both unnamed but clearly referred to). The good king never listens to such things, considering hunting the best recreation. Hunting in its true form provides valuable military ἄσκησις and unites καρτερία and ἡδονή (i.e., it is as near 'work' as any recreation can be),[157] whereas the Persian version is a mere charade, without πόνος or κίνδυνος, and comparable to the behaviour of those who claim to be warriors but put to death prisoners at home. There are unmistakable allusions to Trajan the true hunter and Domitian, a hunter who avoided the full rigours of hunting,[158] and a self-proclaimed warrior who imprisoned and killed his own people. The speech ends on a note of high compliment to Trajan, as do the First, Second, and Fourth Orations, but without the ambiguity of the other endings.

Close analysis reveals the Third Oration to be very much better than its reputation. The speech is not mere compliment but has some serious moral content. Yet its compliment-quotient is the highest of all the speeches. Why? Was the Third Oration an 'official-occasion' speech, like the *Panegyricus*? But it is hard to see how the occasion of the other three speeches could have been much different. Was it an early effort, before Dio had mastered the technique of addressing a Roman emperor?[159] That hypothesis could only work if the addressee was not Trajan but Nerva, but Trajan is the addressee, and on any viable chronology the Third Oration is later than the highly accomplished First

---

156   Tac. *Hist.* 4.7; Suet. *Vesp.* 25; Cass. Dio 65.12.1; cf. also (with a slightly different emphasis) Desideri (1978) 303.
157   A conventional view: Dickie (1985) 188–202.
158   Cf. the closely parallel *Paneg.* 81.1–3; also Suet. *Dom.* 19.
159   These two explanations are suggested by Desideri (1978) 297, 303.

Oration. Had Dio offended Trajan by his criticisms in an earlier speech (perhaps the Fourth) and was he now trying to re-ingratiate himself by excessive compliment? But Trajan claimed to be able to take criticism and why in that case would other people have accused Dio of flattery? The right explanation has already been suggested. The increased praise is the reward for Trajan's apparent acceptance of Dio's philosophical programme.

⋯

Two final topics. First, absolute and relative chronology. The only really fixed points are the priority of the First Oration and its date of ⟦361⟧ 99/100. But only in the case of the Fourth Oration are there serious arguments for a late dating and these arguments are finally untenable.[160] All four speeches have similar preoccupations and seem to be of the same period, very early in Trajan's reign. 49.4f. (date: 103)[161] even seems to provide a *terminus ante* for the Second Oration: Dio there cites as examples of king-philosopher relationships Agamemnon and Nestor, and Philip, Alexander, and Aristotle. Reconstruction of the Kingship Orations' relative chronology, therefore, will illuminate the progress of Dio's relationship with the new emperor and of his attempted philosophical programme rather than political developments.

The Fourth Oration, brimming with verve and self-confidence, comes after the Second, where Dio has begun a relationship with Trajan but does not stress it nearly so much; the Second is clearly earlier than the Third. Which is earlier of the Third and the Fourth? The manuscript order hardly signifies: the Fourth could have been 'attracted' into its present position in the collection by its similarity to the Diogenes discourses (6, 8, 9, 10). The higher compliment quotient of the Third argues for its being the latest of the speeches, as do apparent reworkings of material from the Fourth (e.g., 3.32–41 ~ 4.17, 46, 49–51) and the specific parallel between 4.17 and 3.2: whereas Diogenes does not know the mind of Alexander, Dio knows Trajan's through and through; it is hard to imagine Dio writing the former after the latter.

The order of the speeches is 1, 2, 4, 3, and the logic is plain. 1 combines moral exhortation and warning against Alexander-imitation with a bid to be Trajan's philosophical counsellor; 2 shows Dio newly accepted in that role, continuing the moral exhortation but focusing on Trajan's reading and making some concessions to the Alexander-model and the imminent First Dacian war; 4 returns with a vengeance to the problem of Trajan's Alexander-imitation and excessive

---

160  Moles (1983a) 277f. {above, pp. 101f.}.
161  Von Arnim (1898) 385; Sheppard (1984) 167.

military ambition, which had no doubt been overstimulated by the prospect, or actuality, of the First Dacian War; 3 handsomely acknowledges Trajan's apparently whole-hearted acceptance of Dio's philosophical programme but continues the philosophical effort.

Second, other works relevant to Dio's relationship with Trajan.

The Sixty-Second Oration (*On Kingship and Tyranny*) is addressed to an emperor, who is clearly Trajan (1, 3). There are obvious parallels with the Kingship Orations, especially the Third. The abruptness of the beginning and end and its brevity mark the speech 〚362〛 as incomplete. It has been variously considered a handbook of kingship *topoi*, the beginning of a lost speech on kingship, an alternative version of a section of one of the Kingship Speeches.[162] It looks to me a first effort at a Kingship Speech, which Dio himself may never have completed: by comparison with the surviving Kingship Speeches, the technique is crude and experimental (cf., e.g., 3 ὁ δὲ ἀγαθὸς ἄρχων, ὥσπερ σύ).

The Fifty-Seventh Oration (*Nestor*), which defends Nestor's boasting in *Iliad* 1 as necessary to secure the compliance of Agamemnon and Achilles, is clearly a προλαλία to a performance of one of the Kingship Speeches (presumably the Second) before a Greek audience.[163] It provides interesting evidence for the interpretation Dio himself wished to project: the Kingship Orations are 'helpful and useful' (11); his relationship with Trajan parallels that of Nestor with Agamemnon and Achilles; like them Trajan required moral correction.

In the Fifty-Sixth Oration (*Agamemnon*), a dialogue, Dio argues before an unnamed pupil that true kings are not unaccountable but take advice, as Agamemnon did from Nestor. The reference to his own relationship with Trajan is plain[164] and the piece emphasises the necessity for kings to have such advisers. It may be that the unnamed interlocutor is meant to be Trajan himself and this speech, along with Orations 53, 54, and 55, represents some of Dio's 'behind-the-scenes' teaching of Trajan. The Fifty-Third Oration (*On Homer*) summarises various philosophers' interpretations of Homer, combines literary criticism with moral exposition, especially of Homer's views on kingship, draws a clear analogy between Homer's life and Dio's own (9), and likens Homer to the prophets of the gods (10). The Fifty-Fourth Oration attacks sophists and praises Socrates and contrasts the loss of the sophists' writings with the continuing power of Socrates' λόγοι. The Fifty-Fifth Oration (*On Homer and Socrates*) argues that Socrates can be regarded as a pupil of Homer, since they were alike in character and σωφροσύνη, were moralists, scorned wealth, were masters

---

162  Von Arnim (1898) 416; Desideri (1978) 344 n. 1; Crosby v.23.
163  Von Arnim (1898) 410; Crosby IV.417.
164  〚375〛 C. P. Jones (1978) 122.

of similes and comparisons, and expounded moral lessons through various devices. The long discussion of Homer's practice instances Nestor's attempts to school Agamemnon and Achilles, and Odysseus' intervention when the Greeks fled to the ships (cf. 2.22f.), while the brief treatment of Socrates praises his adaptation of his material to his listeners' interests. The points of contact between all this and the Kingship Orations may well be significant.

[363] The Forty-Ninth Oration of 103 (cf. n. 161), which argues the philosopher's duty to take part in politics unless there is an ἀδύνατον, seems to allude (through the examples of Agamemnon and Nestor, and Philip, Alexander, and Aristotle, 49.4f.) to Dio's role as philosophical counsellor of Trajan.

Other possibly relevant works are the *Encomium of Heracles* against Plato,[165] *On the Virtues of Alexander*, and *Getica* (all lost). The first might be connected with Trajan's imitation of Hercules, but even if it is, need not have been written, in C. P. Jones' words, to 'gratify' Trajan.[166] Is the second connected with the general philosophical and literary debate concerning Alexander or with Trajan's *Alexandri imitatio*? Nothing is known of time or circumstances of composition, but a Trajan link is very plausible. The title indicates a favourable treatment and the work presumably imitated Onesicritus (cf. the eight-book format and the emphasis of Julian 7.212c Διογένης δὲ ... Ἀλέξανδρον ... ἥκειν ἐκέλευε παρ' ἑαυτόν, εἴ τῳ πιστὸς ὁ Δίων). None of this legitimates the conclusion that it was purely honorific of Trajan; Dio could have developed, and expanded upon, Onesicritus' thesis of Alexander-φιλόσοφος (cf. again Julian). The natural supposition is that the work post-dated the Kingship Orations, Dio wrote it because Trajan refused to abandon his *Alexandri imitatio*, but Dio made yet another attempt to divert this imitation into more philosophical channels.

Dio probably began research for his *Getica* on his travels in Dacia during his exile (cf. n. 117). If, as seems likely, the work alluded to Domitian's military failures, it presumably published under Trajan.[167] Whether it covered Trajan's campaigns is uncertain: 12.16–20 does not support the case that Dio was Trajan's *comes* in the First Dacian War, since Oration 12 dates to 97,[168] but Philost. *vs* 488 (Dio in Trajan's chariot) may do so. On the other hand, praise of Trajan cannot have been the main motive of the *Getica*, since Dio's interest in Dacia preceded Trajan's reign.

---

165   On this title see Gallavotti (1931).
166   C. P. Jones (1978) 122.
167   Ibid. 123.
168   *Pace* C. P. Jones (1978) 53: see above, n. 117.

Finally, the attempt to connect the *Euboicus* with a Trajanic 'back-to-the-land' programme[169] seems speculative, though it would not be to Dio's discredit.

I conclude with Syme's wonderful characterisation of Trajan:[170]

> The public and official façade exhibits a soldier emperor of the nobler sort, firm, just, and courteous. Behind it is something elusive and perhaps discordant, not easily to be estimated in words. Discipline and modesty concealed a devouring ambition that in youth made him eager for the military career—sharpened by [[364]] frustration, and later breaking out fiercely and proudly in wars of conquest. It might all end in anger, conceit, and obstinacy. The service of Rome meant less than the love of battle and the pursuit of fame.

That was what Trajan was like, Dio saw it, or was told it, and he tried to do something about it. Both in the public Kingship Speeches and in private tuition, he made a sincere effort to teach Trajan true philosophy and thereby make him a better emperor. He failed, but the failure was not his but Trajan's: in the last analysis there was something irremediably wrong with Trajan's φύσις.

## Bibliography

Adam, T. (1970) *Clementia Principis: der Einfluss hellenistischer Fürstenspiegel auf den Versuch einer rechtlichen Fundierung des Principats durch Seneca* (Stuttgart).
Ahl, F. M. (1976) *Lucan: an Introduction* (Ithaca and London).
Ahl, F. M. (1984a) 'The Art of Safe Criticism in Greece and Rome', *AJPh* 105: 174–208.
Ahl, F. M. (1984b) 'The Rider and the Horse: Politics and Power in Roman Poetry from Horace to Statius', *ANRW* II.32.1: 40–110.
von Arnim, H. (1898) *Leben und Werke des Dio von Prusa* (Berlin).
Attridge, H. W. (1978) 'The Philosophical Critique of Religion under the Early Empire', *ANRW* II.16.1: 45–78.
Balsdon, J. P. V. D. (1958) 'The Ides of March', *Historia* 7: 80–94.
Beaujeu, J. (1955) *La religion romaine à l'apogée de l'empire* (Paris).
Berry, E. L. (1983) 'Dio Chrysostom the Moral Philosopher', *G&R* 30: 70–80.
Bowie, E. L. (1982) 'The Importance of Sophists', *YCS* 27: 29–59.
Bowie, E. L. (1985) 'Dio of Prusa', in P. E. Easterling and B. M. W. Knox, edd. *The Cambridge History of Classical Literature: I. Greek Literature* (Cambridge) 669–72.

---

169  Mazon (1943) and scholars cited by Desideri (1978) 257 n. 28.
170  Syme (1958) 41.

Brancacci, A. (1980) 'Tradizione cinica e problemi di datazione nelle orazioni diogeniane di Dione di Prusa', *Elenchos* 1: 92–122.

Brancacci, A. (1986) Rhetorike Philosophousa: *Dione Crisostomo nella cultura antica e bizantina* (Naples).

Brown, T. S. (1949) *Onesicritus: A Study in Hellenistic Historiography* (Berkeley and Los Angeles).

Brunt, P. A. (1977) 'Lex de Imperio Vespasiani', *JRS* 67: 95–116.

Burkert, W. (1979) *Structure and History in Greek Mythology and Ritual* (Berkeley and Los Angeles).

Burkert, W. (1985) *Greek Religion* (Oxford and Cambridge, Mass.).

Cairns, F. (1972) *Generic Composition in Greek and Roman Poetry* (Edinburgh).

Cairns, F. (1989) *Virgil's Augustan Epic* (Cambridge).

Chilver, G. E. F. (1985) *A Historical Commentary on Tacitus' Histories IV and V* (Oxford).

Coleman, K. M., ed. (1988) *Statius: Silvae IV* (Oxford).

Combet Farnoux, B. (1981) 'Mercure romain, les "Mercuriales" et l'institution du culte impérial sous le Principat augustéen', *ANRW* II.17.1: 457–501.

Courtney, E. (1980) *A Commentary on the Satires of Juvenal* (London).

Crook, J. (1955) *Consilium Principis: Imperial Councils and Counsellors from Augustus to Diocletian* (Cambridge).

Cumont, F. (1940) 'Trajan "Cosmokrator"?', *REA* 42: 408–11.

D'Espèrey, S. F. (1986) 'Vespasien, Titus et la littérature', *ANRW* II.32.5: 3048–86.

Desideri, P. (1978) *Dione di Prusa: un intelletuale greco nell'impero romano* (Messina and Florence).

Dickie, M. W. (1985) 'The Speech of Numanus Remulus (*Aen.* 9.598–620)', *PLLS* 5: 165–221.

Douglas, A. E., ed. (1966) *Cicero: Brutus* (Oxford).

Dudley, D. R. (1937) *A History of Cynicism from Diogenes to the 6th century A.D.* (London).

Durry, M. (1938) *Pline le Jeune: Panégyrique de Trajan* (Paris).

Durry, M. (1947) *Pline le Jeune: Lettres IV* (Paris).

Fears, J. R. (1974) 'The Stoic View of the Career and Character of Alexander the Great', *Philologus* 118: 113–30.

Fears, J. R. (1977) *Princeps a diis electus: The Divine Election of the Emperor as a Political Concept at Rome* (Rome).

Fears, J. R. (1981) 'The Cult of Jupiter and Roman Imperial Ideology', *ANRW* II.17.1: 3–141.

Fehling, D. (1989) *Herodotus and his 'Sources'* (Liverpool); rev. trans. by J. G. Howie of *Die Quellenangaben bei Herodot* (Berlin and New York, 1971).

Fisch, M. H. (1937) 'Alexander and the Stoics', *AJPh* 58: 59–82, 129–51.

Fuhrmann, F. (1988) *Plutarque: Oeuvres morales III* (Paris).

Gallavotti, C. (1931) 'Sopra un opuscolo perduto di Dione Crisostomo', *RFIC* 59: 504–8.

Garzetti, A. (1974) *From Tiberius to the Antonines* (London); trans. by J. R. Foster of *L'Impero da Tiberio agli Antonini* (Bologna, 1960).
Giancotti, F. (1954) 'Il De Clementia', *RAL*[8] 9: 587–609.
Goodenough, E. R. (1928) 'The Political Philosophy of Hellenistic Kingship', *YCS* 1: 53–102.
Goulet-Cazé, M.-O. (1986) *L'Ascèce Cynique: un commentaire de Diogéne Laërce VI 70–71* (Paris).
Griffin, J. (1981) 'Genre and Real Life in Latin Poetry', *JRS* 71: 39–49; rev. version in id., *Latin Poets and Roman Life* (London and Baltimore, 1985) 48–64.
Griffin, M. T. (1976) *Seneca: a Philosopher in Politics* (Oxford; repr. with addenda, 1992).
Halfmann, H. (1986) *Itinera Principum: Geschichte und Typologie der Kaiserreisen im Römischen Reich* (Stuttgart).
Hamilton, J. R. (1969) *Plutarch, Alexander: A Commentary* (Oxford).
Hammerstaedt, J. (1988) *Die Orakelkritik des Kynikers Oenomaus* (Frankfurt).
Hammond, M. (1957) 'Composition of the Senate, 68–235', *JRS* 47: 74–81.
Hardie, A. (1983) *Statius and the* Silvae: *Poets, Patrons, and Epideixis in the Graeco-Roman World* (Liverpool).
Heuss, A. (1954) 'Alexander der Grosse und die politische Ideologie des Altertums', *A&A* 4: 65–104.
Höistad, R. (1948) *Cynic Hero and Cynic King: Studies in the Cynic Conception of Man* (Uppsala).
Hopkins, K. (1983) *Death and Renewal* (Cambridge).
Hunter, R. L. (1983) *A Study of Daphnis and Chloe* (Cambridge).
Jaczynowska, M. (1981) 'Le culte de l'Hercule romain au temps du Haut-Empire', *ANRW* II.17.2: 631–61.
Jones, B. W. (1973) 'Domitian's Attitude to the Senate' *AJPh* 94: 79–91.
Jones, B. W. (1979) *Domitian and the Senatorial Order: a Prosopographical Study of Domitian's Relationship with the Senate, A.D. 81–96* (Philadelphia).
Jones, C. P. (1971) *Plutarch and Rome* (Oxford).
Jones, C. P. (1975) 'An Oracle Given to Trajan', *Chiron* 5: 403–6.
Jones, C. P. (1978) *The Roman World of Dio Chrysostom* (Cambridge, Mass. and London).
Kennedy, G. (1972) *The Art of Rhetoric in the Roman World* (Princeton).
Kindstrand, J. F. (1973) *Homer in der zweiten Sophistik: Studien zu der Homerlektüre und dem Homerbild bei Dion von Prusa, Maximos von Tyros und Ailios Aristeides* (Uppsala).
Kindstrand, J. F. (1976) *Bion of Borysthenes: a Collection of the Fragments with Introduction and Commentary* (Uppsala).
Kindstrand, J. F. (1981) *Anacharsis: the Legend and the Apophthegmata* (Uppsala).
Lane Fox, R. (1986) *Pagans and Christians* (Hardmondsworth; New York, 1987).
Lepper, F. A. (1948) *Trajan's Parthian War* (Oxford).

Levick, B. M. (1980) 'Review of Jones (1978) and Desideri (1978)', *CR* n.s. 30: 192–4.
Luttwak, E. N. (1976) *The Grand Strategy of the Roman Empire* (Baltimore and London).
Macleod, C. W. (1973) 'Catullus 116', *CQ* 23: 304–9; repr. in id., *Collected Essays* (Oxford, 1983) 181–6.
Mazon, P. (1943) 'Dion de Pruse et la politique agraire de Trajan', *Lettres d'humanité* 2: 47–80.
Millar, F. (1977) *The Emperor in the Roman World (31 BC–AD 337)* (London and Ithaca; 2nd ed., 1992).
Moles, J. L. (1978) 'The Career and Conversion of Dio Chrysostom', *JHS* 98: 79–100 [above, Ch. 1].
Moles, J. L. (1983a) 'The Date and Purpose of the Fourth Kingship Oration of Dio Chrysostom', *ClAnt* 2: 251–78 [above, Ch. 3].
Moles, J. L. (1983b) '"*Honestius quam Ambitiosius*"? An Exploration of the Cynic's Attitude to Moral Corruption in his Fellow Men', *JHS* 103: 103–23 [below, Ch. 12].
Moles, J. L. (1983c) 'Dio Chrysostom: Exile, Tarsus, Nero and Domitian', *LCM* 8: 130–4 [above, Ch. 2].
Moles, J. L. (1984) 'The Addressee of the Third Kingship Oration of Dio Chrysostom', *Prometheus* 10: 65–9 [above, Ch. 4].
Moles, J. L. (1985) 'Cynicism in Horace *Epistles* I', *PLLS* 5: 33–60 [below, Ch. 14].
Moles, J. L. (1987) 'Politics, Philosophy and Friendship in Horace *Odes* 2.7', *QUCC* 25: 59–72 [vol. 2, Ch. 67].
Momigliano, A. D. (1950) 'Dio Chrysostomos' (Unpublished Lecture, 1950), in id., *Quarto Contributo alla Storia degli studi classici e del mondo antico* (Rome, 1969) 257–69.
Morr, J. (1915) *Die Lobrede des jüngeren Plinius und die erste Königsrede des Dio von Prusa* (progr. Troppau).
Mortureux, B. (1989) 'Les idéaux stoïciens et les premières responsabilités politiques: le "De Clementia"', *ANRW* II.36.3: 1639–85.
Münscher, K. (1920) 'Kritisches zum Panegyrikus des jüngeren Plinius', *RhM* 73: 174–98.
Nisbet, R. G. M. and M. Hubbard (1978) *A Commentary on Horace's Odes II* (Oxford).
Oliver, J. H. (1938) 'An Inscription Concerning the Epicurean School at Athens', *TAPhA* 69: 494–9.
Otto, A. (1890) *Die Sprichwörter und sprichwörtlichen Redensarten der Römer* (Leipzig; repr. Hildesheim, 1971).
Pearson, L. (1960) *The Lost Histories of Alexander the Great* (New York and Oxford).
Price, S. (1984) *Rituals and Power: the Roman Imperial Cult in Asia Minor* (Cambridge).
Radice, B. (1968) 'Pliny and the *Panegyricus*', *G&R* 15: 166–72; repr. in R. Rees, ed., *Oxford Readings in Classical Studies: Latin Panegyric* (Oxford, 2012) 77–84.
Rawson, E. (1989) 'Roman Rulers and the Philosophic Adviser', in M. T. Griffin and J. Barnes, edd., *Philosophia Togata: Essays on Philosophy and Roman Society* (Oxford) 233–57.

Reardon, B. P. (1980) 'Review of Jones (1978)', *Phoenix* 34: 174.

Reardon, B. P. (1983) 'Travaux récents sur Dion de Pruse', *REG* 96: 286–92.

Rostovtzeff, M. (1957) *The Social and Economic History of the Roman Empire*$^2$, rev. by P. M. Fraser, 2 vols. (Oxford).

Russell, D. A. and N. G. Wilson, edd. (1981) *Menander Rhetor* (Oxford).

Scott, K. (1929) 'Plutarch and the Ruler Cult', *TAPhA* 60: 117–35.

Sheppard, A. R. R. (1984) 'Dio Chrysostom: the Bithynian Years', *L'Antiquité Classique* 53: 157–73.

Sherwin-White, A. N. (1966) *The Letters of Pliny* (Oxford).

Sutherland, C. H. V. and M. Hammond (1970) 'Trajan', *OCD*$^2$: 1088f.

Syme, R. (1958) *Tacitus*, 2 vols. (Oxford).

Syme, R. (1968) *Ammianus and the Historia Augusta* (Oxford).

Talbert, R. J. A. (1984) *The Senate of Imperial Rome* (Princeton).

Trapp, M. B. (1990) 'Plato's *Phaedrus* in Second-Century Greek Literature', in D. A. Russell, ed. *Antonine Literature* (Oxford) 141–73.

Trisoglio, F. (1972) 'Le idee politiche di Plinio il Giovane e di Dione Crisostomo', *Il Pensiero Politico* 5 (1972) 3–43.

Vernant, J.-P. (1980) *Myth and Society in Ancient Greece* (Bristol); trans. by J. Lloyd of *Mythe et société en Grèce ancienne* (Paris, 1974).

Vessey, D. W. T. (1973) *Statius and the* Thebaid (Cambridge).

Wallace-Hadrill, A. W. (1987) 'Time for Augustus: Ovid, Augustus, and the *Fasti*', in M. Whitby, P. Hardie and M. Whitby, edd., *Homo Viator: Classical Essays for John Bramble* (Bristol) 221–30.

Waters, K. H. (1964) 'The Character of Domitian', *Phoenix* 18: 49–77.

Waters, K. H. (1974) 'Trajan's Character in the Literary Tradition', in J. A. S. Evans, ed., *Polis and Imperium: Studies in Honour of E. T. Salmon* (Toronto) 233–52.

Waters, K. H. (1975) 'The Reign of Trajan and its Place in Contemporary Scholarship (1960–72)', *ANRW* II.2: 381–431.

Weinreich, O. (1941) 'Ein Epigramm des Kaisers Traian und sein literarischens Nachleben', *Die Antike* 17: 229–48.

Williams, F. (1993) *The Sage, the Shepherdess, and Caesar* (Inaugural Lecture, Belfast, 1987; Liverpool).

Wirszubski, Ch. (1950) *Libertas as a Political Idea at Rome during the Late Republic and Early Principate* (Cambridge).

Wirth, G. (1976) 'Alexander und Rom', in *Alexandre le Grand: image et réalité* (Vandoeuvres-Genève) 181–221.

Woodman, A. J. (1988) *Rhetoric in Classical Historiography: Four Studies* (London, Portland, and Sydney).

CHAPTER 6

# Review

D. A. Russell, ed., *Dio Chrysostom: Orations VII, XII, XXXVI*. Cambridge Greek and Latin Classics, Imperial Library. Pp. viii + 266. Cambridge: Cambridge University Press, 1992. £37.50/$59.95 (Paper, £14.95/$22.95).

Does Dio deserve inclusion in *Cambridge Greek and Latin Classics*, even in the *Imperial Library*, new home for 'titles which fall outside the conventional canon but are works of genuine interest and literary quality'? Russell, one of the greatest living connoisseurs of Greek prose, claims Dio as 'the foremost Greek orator' of his time (p. 1), as possessor of 'a marvellous ear for the cadences and idioms of fourth-century prose' (p. 2), and as intermittent achiever of 'Longinan' sublimity (p. 3), even if his sometimes 'loose and untidy' style (p. 172), his penchant for improvisation (p. 12), the occasional nature of some of his pieces and their recycling in other contexts (p. 12; cf. now also {P.} Desideri, {'Tipologia e varietà di funzione comunicativa degli scritti dionei',} *ANRW* II.33.5 (1991) 3904–59 with earlier bibliography) creates major problems of structure and coherence. Russell's well judged selection presents some of the very best of Dio (though we should admit that most of the second half of *Euboicus* is irredeemably tedious and that even *Olympicus* and *Borystheniticus* have their *longueurs*, and one of Dio's directly political speeches would have been welcome). Russell aims to provide an attractive introduction not only to the multi-faceted Dio himself, but also to important aspects of first-century thought and literature in general, especially for students (hence the commentary's numerous translations and linguistic explanations, sometimes of elementary Greek). Such a readership being a lost cause, even in Oxbridge, Russell's success depends on other criteria.

The introduction to Dio's life and work (pp. 1–25) is worth anyone's while: broad, yet with revealing detail, artfully constructed, literate, humane, striking judicious distinctions and nice balances between philosophy and rhetoric, moral earnestness and entertainment, showing good judgement on crucial issues (e.g., the importance of Musonius' influence on Dio), and including valuable general discussions of each of the three works.

On essential interpretative problems, Russell's positions are as follows. The beginning and end of *Euboicus* are lost, and the surviving text exhibits alike omissions and over-long developments of topics, suggestive both of incompleteness and amalgamation of different versions; delivery of one version in

Rome is probable, though not certain. Granted the pastoral, novelistic, and other literary ingredients of the narrative, the element of play and entertainment for a sophisticated audience, the general topical concern of Dio's social and economic 'programme', and some precise contemporary parallels, it remains true that (a) the moral element is central, (b) the picture of social conditions is at least as much a product of literary tradition as a precise reflection of contemporary realities (pp. 8–13). In *Olympicus* (probable date 105 [Russell has missed A. R. R. Sheppard's strong arguments for 97 in {'Dio Chrysostom: the Bithynian Years',} *AC* 53 (1984) 157–73]) the introduction of 'the philosopher' as a fourth source of acquired religion is a major structural inconsistency; besides the speech's overt philosophical, theological, and aesthetic concerns, the portrayal of Zeus has contemporary political implication (pp. 14–19, 206). The 'Magian' myth in *Borystheniticus* is predominantly Greek with only superficial Persian colouring. The speech has two main concerns: (a) the implications and requirements of being truly 'Hellenic'; (b) the need for political concord and [[257]] regeneration within the overall context of the Roman empire (pp. 19–23). (Thus Russell's interpretation of these two speeches is basically Desiderian.)

Within the commentary Russell's greatest strength is his tremendous understanding of the grammar, syntax, and stylistic nuances of Greek prose and of the divergences from Classical practice by even so accomplished a classiciser as Dio. Time and again Russell's constitution, interpretation, and translation of the text are decisively superior to those of the Loeb (the edition which, if we are honest, most of us have used, primarily or exclusively, hitherto, and which had seemed serviceable enough). Russell is also predictably full and excellent on literary echoes, rhetorical techniques, and philosophical influences, particularly Stoic and Platonic.

There are weaknesses. Despite his general expertise in philosophy, rhetoric, and later Greek prose, Russell does not seem to me especially at home in Dio's distinctive world. 'Typical' (pp. 1, 4) is the last thing Dio was: indeed, it is above all his very shiftingness (or shiftiness) which makes him interesting and worthy of study. 'Broussa' is not the modern name for Prusa (p. 3); the idea that Dio could have been born as late as 60 (p. 3) is wholly untenable (or is this a misprint?); von Arnim's arguments for a provincial Greek addressee of *Or.* 18 (p. 8) are unassailable (or, if not, require proper attack); it is unwise to invoke Philostratus *VA* for orators and philosophers speaking about Zeus at Olympia (pp. 14–15), Dio himself being an important inspiration for Philostratus ({E. L.} Bowie, {'Apollonius of Tyana: Tradition and Reality',} *ANRW* II.16.2 (1978) 1668–9; Dio surely is (p. 110) including himself among the old at 7.1 (he *was* then 'old' and here, as at 12.15, the emphasis suits the fruitful equivocalness of Dio's ἦθος: old and foolish or old and wise?); the problems posed by the description of the owl as 'not at all wiser' than the other birds (12.1) and by the sudden intrusion of 'the philosopher' (12.47) invite characteristically Dionian solutions.

In general, Russell shows little interest in 'close reading'. Word-play is virtually ignored (e.g., 7.146 Πολυδώρας is certainly not a 'confusion' and Russell misses the point of the brilliant ἐποποιίας at 12.69), as are verbal parallels and correspondences and ring structures, essential though these are to the articulation of structure, with which in itself Russell is properly much concerned. Detailed analysis of such phenomena would establish a far higher degree of structural coherence in these speeches than Russell allows, as well as bolstering the case for Dio's literary excellence. One cannot help wishing that Russell had said just a little less about linguistic matters and a little more on both literary and historical questions. The parallels between the *Euboicus* narrative and the pastoral or novel, or between the *Euboicus* debate and the famous literary debates cited by Russell, could usefully have been spelled out (p. 9), and more than puzzlement should have been expressed about the ending of *Olympicus* (p. 211). There is much to say about the interplay between Socratic/Platonic and Stoic elements in *Borystheniticus* (cf. now M. Schofield, *The Stoic Idea of the City* [Cambridge, 1991] 57ff.). And some quite large literary topics pass unnoticed (e.g., the 'what-shall-I-talk-about?' τόπος of 12.21ff. [cf. Hor. C. 1.12.1ff.] or the τόλμα of 36.43 [cf. C. Macleod, *Collected Essays* (Oxford, 1983) 264 n. 14]). Similarly, one would like some comment on Dio's claim to have known (before his exile) the homes and tables of satraps and kings (7.66), bearing as it does both on Dio's ἦθος in *Euboicus* and on the important historical question of the degree, or indeed existence, of his relations with the Flavians at the highest level, and some documentation for the statement (p. 214) that 'there is evidence for fresh Greek settlements around Olbia after the crisis period'. And the discussion of the historical verisimilitude of Dio's description of Olbia (p. 22) would have greatly benefited from the pertinent observations of {C. P.} Jones, *The Roman World of Dio Chrysostom* {Cambridge, Mass., 1978} 61–3.

⟦258⟧ Yet a reviewer's complaints, while perhaps necessary, are churlish and ungrateful when so much has been given. Rather, we should praise Russell's enterprise in presenting so attractive an introduction to Dio and his success in analysing and explaining some of the best Greek prose of the later period in a manner which will delight and instruct all his readers, whoever they may be.

CHAPTER 7

# Dio Chrysostom, Greece, and Rome

Donald Russell's commentary on Dio happily unites the best Greek orator and the greatest connoisseur of Greek prose of their respective ages. No scholar has argued more persuasively for the literary, philosophical, and indeed moral excellence of *Euboicus*, *Olympicus*, and *Borystheniticus*.[1] I here offer a sketch of their attitudes to Rome.[2] While my interpretations differ from Donald's, they owe his scholarship an incalculable debt.

## 1

The extant *Euboicus* (*Or.* 7) is a patchwork of different versions but one version seems to have been delivered in Rome[3] (which Dio visited after his exile, the context of his Euboean adventure). Allusions to aqueducts (106), parks, suburban villas, and groves (145) indicate a large city; the sentiment 'we are criticising the things most important among the Greeks' (122) and some apparent harmless accommodation of Roman prejudices suggest a Roman audience,[4] as does a powerful counter-element: the final tirade against sexual exploitation and prostitution, which suggestively links the ideas of capture in war, literal enslavement, enslavement in the provision of degrading sex, enslavement of the human spirit, and depravity at the highest levels of ⟦178⟧ society (133–4).[5]

---

1   Russell (1992), with Moles (1993).
2   I thank Malcolm Schofield, Simon Swain, Tony Woodman, and the editors for valuable comment.
3   Russell (1992) 1, 13, 156; cf. 139–40, 146.
4   Brunt (1973) 17. For 'we' cf. *Or.* 79.4–5 (p. 191). Roman delivery of one version does not exclude, indeed it entails, delivery also elsewhere (some passages suggest a Prusan perspective, e.g. 83–90 on Odysseus' continued tribulations on his return home likely bear on Dio's troubles in Prusa [for Odysseus/Dio see p. 190]).
5   Note the ambiguous and defensive discussion of this passage in Jones (1978) 129. The reference to 'barbarian bodies or those of Greeks who previously were not at all slaves but now live in abundant and considerable slavery' makes these sex-slaves into a particularly degrading example of that moral and political slavery to which in Dio's view all non-Romans are subject under the empire (cf. *Orr.* 31.125; 34.39, 51; 12.85 (p. 194)). Of course the attack upon Roman sexual depravity is *also* an attack upon *any one's* sexual depravity.

Thus the speech has both general significance for great (Greek) cities and particular reference to Rome.[6]

Dio's message is plain: the rural Euboean hunters show that the poor can live a natural, self-sufficient, and virtuous life (81, 103), city life is potentially corrupting and frequently corrupt in practice (24–48), but even the urban poor can find occupations consistent with virtuous living (104–52).

Several areas, however, require sharper definition: (1) the balances between idealisation and realism and between fictionality and fact in the narrative; (2) Dio's own role; (3) the relationship to imperial policy; (4) Dio's attitude to Roman social mores.

(1) On the one hand, the narrative is set idyllically 'practically in the middle of Greece' (1), exploits pastoral topics and novelistic, New Comedy, and Odyssean plot-structures;[7] the description of the grazing (14–15) has Golden Age and *locus amoenus* resonances; the debate in the theatre (24–63) recalls famous literary debates;[8] the hunter's hospitality (65) is coloured by reminiscences of Plato's *Republic*; his naïveté provokes amusement (as he himself realises [21–2, 24–5, 43–4, 47–8, 59, 62]).

On the other hand, the narrative is 'authenticated' both by Dio's eyewitness testimony and personal experience (1) and by the parallels between the hunter's treatment of 'Sotades' (55–8) and his treatment of Dio (2–10, 64–80); the hunters suffer hardship when their master is killed by a Roman emperor (12); there are realistic allusions to transhumance (13), to an 'exchange economy' (69), to the Euboean city's economic decay (34, 38–9), and to *emphyteusis* arrangements (37) popular under Nerva and Trajan;[9] the terms of the honorific decree (60–1) are officially correct;[10] the hunter is several times allowed the last laugh (47–8, 50, 59, 63–4): his naïveté reflects a higher truth.

Thus the hunters' ideal life is presented with knowing irony and fictionality, but also seriously propounded and anchored in reality: hence Dio can reasonably propose that the principle of self-sufficiency be transferred into city life (103).

‖179‖ In the second half of the speech, while Dio's recommendations for the urban poor are practicable enough, parallels and disclaimed parallels with Platonic programmes (107, 110, 113, 118–22, 125, 130) create a rather similar balance between ideal and actuality.

---

6   *Pace* Swain (1994).
7   Russell (1992) 8–9.
8   Russell (1992) 9.
9   Russell (1992) 120–1.
10  Russell (1992) 126.

Within the whole speech, therefore, the balances between ideal and reality, between seriousness and entertainment, and between moral absolutism and accommodation of audience prejudice are finely judged for exposition of a message at once general and specific.

(2) Dio's philosophical persona compounds the Cynic (1, 9, 66, 75, 103), Socratic (81, 100), and Platonic (1, 102–3, 124–6),[11] with a corresponding progression from individual moral philosophy to Platonic social and political philosophy. As a Cynic and/or Odyssean figure (1, 3),[12] Dio himself exemplifies wandering, suffering, and poverty. He also suggests an analogy between his 'wandering' life and 'wandering' (philosophical) speech (1, 127): his own biography is interwoven into the discourse. There are also implicit parallels between Dio's life and experience and the hunter's (4, 9–10, 32). Consequently, Dio's comment at 81 acquires a double meaning: 'I have not *gone through* this whole account pointlessly, nor, as I might perhaps seem to some, because I wished to talk idly, but because I was setting out an example of *the life I undertook*[13] from the beginning and of *the way of life* of the poor, an example I *knew myself* ...'.[14] The example consists of Dio's life as well as the hunters'.

Further, 81 echoes 1:

> I shall now *relate at length* something which I saw *for myself* and did not hear from others. For wordiness and difficulty in rejecting any of the topics that *come one's way* are perhaps not only characteristic of an old man: they may possibly be just as characteristic of the wanderer as of the old man. The reason is possibly that both have had many *experiences* that they recall with some pleasure. So *I shall tell* of the sort of people I encountered virtually in the middle of Greece and *the sort of life* they lived.

These echoes suggest that the work's beginning is not lost[15] and unify 1–81 into a strong moral statement centring on the role of Dio himself as both observer and exponent of poverty.

⟦180⟧ (3) Date, location, echoes of Trajanic agrarian schemes, and Dio's friendship with Trajan might seem to make *Euboicus* a manifesto for Trajanic

---

11  Hardly the Stoic, despite the Cleanthes allusion (102) and general Stoic influence (Brunt (1973)).
12  Russell (1992) 8.
13  ὑπεθέμην = (i) 'propounded', (ii) 'undertook' (cf., e.g., Andoc. 6.19).
14  For the double sense, 'know of' and 'know through experience', cf. 65–6.
15  Discussion in Russell (1992) 109, 132; I think the Euripidean quotation has simply fallen out at 82, like the Sophoclean at 102.

'back-to-the-land' policy.¹⁶ But this interpretation fails against Dio's fierce attacks on Roman corruption and his brusque, Cynic-style, dismissal of imperial wealth by comparison with the hunters' poverty (66):

> and yet I knew the homes and tables of rich men, not only private individuals but also satraps and kings, who seemed to me at that time the most wretched of all, and though they seemed so before, they seemed still more so when I saw those men's poverty and freedom and saw that they lacked nothing of the pleasure of eating and drinking, but rather even in those respects effectively had the greater riches.

The Roman setting and Dio's past and present intimacy with Roman emperors give this sentiment enormous force. Dio can pronounce authoritatively on the relative value of poverty and riches, on the ideal of rural life, on contemporary rural and urban decline in Greece, and on the corruptions of Roman city-life because he has direct personal experience of all these different states.

(4) Granted the double focus of the attack on urban corruption (both general and Roman), Dio's condemnation of Roman luxury remains uncompromising. Poverty is simply superior to wealth; sexual exploitation is disgusting; there is no praise of the magnificence of Rome as a city, nor acknowledgement of the benefits of the Roman peace (note the casual 'just now there is peace' (49)); and the miserable economic conditions of the Euboean city are implicitly linked, in part, to Roman misrule (12).

In this unsatisfactorily preserved but excellently conceived speech Dio projects himself as a moral authority who attacks contemporary urban decline and corruption and Roman corruption in particular, and offers practical solutions. The speech coheres with his claim in *Oration* 13, delivered in Athens, that he had told the Romans that true happiness came from the practice of virtue, not from the acquisition of ever greater luxuries from the whole world, and that the poorer and more self-sufficient the Romans became, the happier they and their subjects would be (31–7). Similarly, *Oration* 79, a radical attack on urban luxury, seems both to envisage, and to have been delivered in, Rome and refers to 'us in Rome'.¹⁷

---

16   Desideri (1978) 257 n. 28 with bibliography.
17   Moles (1983).

⟦181⟧ 2

In the long *prolalia* to *Olympicus* (1–16), the sophists resemble the peacock in being beautiful, vain, and empty-headed, whereas Dio resembles the owl in being apparently no wiser than anybody else yet besieged by crowds, without eloquence and a mere complainer, scorned for his dowdiness but admired, a divine messenger and purveyor of wisdom, a warner whose warnings are spurned until too late, the embodiment of philosophy and ancient wisdom. The multiple ironies are transparent: in this triumphant come-back speech[18] delivered, just after his exile had ended, at the cultural and religious centre of Greece, the moral and philosophical claims that Dio makes for himself could not be greater.

Dio's analogy between his wanderings and wandering speech (16) introduces his recent visit to the Roman army as it prepared for war against the Dacians (16–20). Is Dio here 'wandering' from his subject?

The allusion to the Dacians' ancient and modern names (16) suggests their antiquity, in implicit contrast with the Romans. Dio himself appears in Cynic guise—'wanderer', 'alone', 'unarmed' and peaceable amongst armed men, yet 'fearless' and 'safe' from physical assault, an 'observer' of military 'sights' (16–20; cf. *Or.* 6.60-2).

Dio desired 'to see men contending for empire and power and the others for freedom and fatherland' (20). Within a Cynic perspective 'empire and power' are false values and 'freedom' a good. Other details reinforce this reading: the tart allusion to congratulatory embassies 'which join in prayers with the tongue only', a remarkable sentiment from Dio, intimate of emperors (17); the Roman army's lack of leisure (19) to listen to speeches (granted the formal moral ambiguity of 'leisure', Dio's present audience do have the leisure to listen, and rightly so, and a pupil of Musonius would surely have required even an army to make the leisure);[19] the statements that Olympia and the 'history' of Zeus are divine things better and more profitable, older and greater, than the Dacian war and Dacian history, however great these may be on the human plane (20–1). Finally, we recall that in Aesop's fables the ancient owl's wisdom consisted of warnings about devices to entrap and kill birds (7–8): if the Greeks are birds, what are the Romans?

⟦182⟧ In the introduction to Dio's grand main theme of the providential organisation of the universe (23–4), these ideas are sustained. Hesiod, poet of peace, is preferred to Homer, poet of war, and after 16–20 listeners might hear

---

18   I believe the date to be 97, *pace* Russell (1992) 16, 171, but cannot argue it here.
19   Cf. Tac. *Hist.* 3.81; Moles (1990) 373 {above, p. 159} n. 130.

in Hesiod's hymn to Zeus' omnipotence (*Erg.* 5–7: 'easily he makes strong, and easily he brings the strong man low', etc.) the possibility of Rome's humbling (cf. *Or.* 13.34: 'Rome's greatness is not very secure').

Dio also constructs a hierarchy of 'sights': having dismissed the 'sight' of the Roman army, he now depreciates the 'sights' of the games by comparison with the 'sight' of Phidias' great statue (25). The conception of Zeus as ruler of the universe and of the entire human race, Greeks and barbarians alike (27), so far from providing a heavenly paradigm for the Roman world-empire,[20] evokes a higher reality, which demotes that empire. And Dio locates true human wisdom in the ancients, the first men, who were closest to God and responded most freshly to heavenly 'sights' (27–8). Their current earthly representative is Dio himself, 'ancient' philosopher, not military man.[21] Further, Dio's comparison of the Epicureans' 'banishing' of the gods from the world to unfortunates banished to deserted islands (37) recalls the Roman emperor's merciless power, and the introduction of Phidias' 'contest' or trial (49–50) confirms the relative triviality of the 'contest' between Rome and Dacia. Phidias justifies his claim that this is the greatest 'contest' ever by the fact that it is *not* about empire or military resources but about Zeus' governorship of the universe and his own likeness of him (53). He insists that his god, unlike Homer's, is one of peace (74). Thus the Dacian episode is no 'wandering' from the true discourse but sets up a mirror which both by itself and through refraction with the rest of the discourse reflects negatively on Roman militarism.

Now *Olympicus*, like *Euboicus* and *Borystheniticus*, contains elements which in isolation might appear complimentary to Rome. Thus, as in *Euboicus*, allusion is made to peace in Greece (formally fifth-century Greece during the truce covering the games): 'our god is peaceful and altogether gentle, as befits the overseer of a faction-free and concordant Greece' (74).[22] But the 'mirror' deflects contemporary compliment of an aggressive imperialist power. Here, as at the end, the [[183]] Greeks are behaving rightly, not the Romans. Similarly, while the enumeration and exegesis of Zeus' titles (74–7) *can* be employed to promote links between Zeus and the emperor, as by Dio himself before Trajan (*Or.* 1.37–41), this analogy is excluded here, both by the 'mirror' of the section on Dacia and by the immediate context: Phidias again rejects Zeus' warlike aspects (78–9).

---

20   Desideri (1978) 331; Russell (1992) 14.
21   Russell (1992) 18 and 194 rightly stresses the sudden and undeveloped intervention of 'the philosopher' as the fourth and greatest interpreter of the divine (47–8): the point, I believe, is that he is making the speech.
22   Russell (1992) 206.

The speech ends (85) with a theatrical *coup*, testimony to the mimetic powers alike of Phidias the sculptor and of Dio the orator and philosophical and religious exegete: the statue of Zeus seems to look upon the Eleans and all Greece in goodwill and concern and to address them. Greece herself becomes the final 'sight' of the speech. After congratulating the Greeks for offering sacrifices as magnificent as their means allow, for maintaining as from their beginning the Olympic games, and for preserving inherited festivals and mysteries, Zeus expresses his anxiety for Greece by quoting the words of Odysseus to his father Laertes (*Od.* 24.249–50). Having congratulated Laertes on his care for his garden, Odysseus says: 'you yourself enjoy no good care, but you bear grievous old age, you are badly unkempt and unfittingly clothed'. What does this abrupt and pessimistic conclusion mean?

Clearly, Laertes represents old Greece and, as a lament for its present wretchedness, this conclusion fulfils Dio's description of the owl's song as 'mournful' (1). No doubt there is also an allusion to Dio himself,[23] old and unkempt like both Laertes and Greece and the embodiment of Greek philosophical and religious values. Such allegorising has been anticipated by Dio's remarks about Phidias' covert representations of himself and Pericles on Athene's shield (6). But there is another, barbed, point.[24] Odysseus next says that it is not because Laertes is lazy that his master has no care for him but because he is a slave (24.257). Greece therefore is suffering not through her own fault but because her master, Rome, treats her as a slave. The integralness of the Dacian section is again manifest: Greece is unfree under Roman rule. Allusion to Dio himself also yields criticism of Rome, his exile (cf. 37) having been inflicted by the merciless Domitian.

To describe *Olympicus* as an attack upon Roman imperialism would diminish a rich and profound speech. Nevertheless, criticism of Rome [[184]] must be integrated into any overall interpretation. Dio is telling the Greeks that Greek culture and religion are more important than the Roman empire, that the eternal divine governance of the universe is a far greater reality than that transient empire, and that Greece's decline is largely Rome's fault. He also proffers the divine governance as a source of deep spiritual comfort and joy to all men, Greeks and barbarians (who must logically include Romans). It remains true that it is Greek poets, artists, and philosophers (naturally, on this occasion, Dio

---

23   Reiske (1784) 1.418 n. 34; Geel (1840) 122–3. It is also Δίων who makes Δίω speak; for the significant association of names cf. *Or.* 4.27; such (con)fusion of roles is unproblematic: Moles (1990) 328 {above, p. 145}.
24   Argued, independently, in Simon Swain's forthcoming book, *From Plutarch to Philostratus* {= Swain (1996)}.

himself) who have most perfectly represented the divine, and that contemporary Greece is suffering from Roman misrule.

3

Donald Russell's and Malcolm Schofield's fine readings[25] have demonstrated *Borystheniticus'* complexity and subtlety, clarified difficulties, and proposed convincing solutions; but there is more to say.

As in *Olympicus*, a central concern is Greekness, focused here with peculiar sharpness by the city's marginal, perilous, and ruinous state. As in *Euboicus* and *Olympicus*, the narrative provides a mirror for the audience, here the Prusans. As in *Euboicus*, there is a mixture of the realistic and the literary, the serious and the humorous. While much of Dio's topography seems historically accurate, it has been influenced by literary accounts, especially Herodotus',[26] and, while the information about Dio's behaviour at Borysthenes seems circumstantial, details of both narrative and topography recall Plato's *Phaedrus*.[27] Moreover, Dio has greatly exaggerated the Borysthenites' poor Greek, ignorance of Greek culture and philosophy, and lack of contact with Romans.[28] One effect must be to amuse the sophisticated Prusans (cf. *Euboicus*).

After the initial description of place we learn that barbarians, Borysthenites, and Scythians buy salt from the same mines (3), and although Borysthenes is under continual barbarian attack (no Roman peace here),[29] after its most disastrous capture it was refounded with Scythian help in order to maintain trade between Greeks and barbarians. This contrasts with most of the Pontic cities, whose fate illustrates 'the dispersal of the Greek world into many places' (5). The [[185]] old city has been physically fragmented 'so that you would not surmise that the surviving towers once belonged to a single city', and not a single statue remains undamaged among the holy places (6).

The first of the two Borysthenite characters is well mannered but, like the Borysthenites generally, wears barbarian clothing. As his name Callistratus indicates, he is an excellent warrior. But he is also interested in oratory and philosophy and wants to sail away with Dio as his pupil. His military prowess and handsome 'Ionian' appearance attract many lovers. In their homosexuality

---

25    Schofield (1991) 57–92.
26    Russell (1992) 22, 212.
27    Trapp (1990).
28    Jones (1978) 63.
29    Whether Olbia was garrisoned in Dio's time is unclear (Russell (1992) 220): *if* it was, Dio's silence is eloquent.

at least the Borysthenites maintain ancestral tradition and are likely to win barbarian converts, leading to barbarian debasement of the practice (7–8). Notwithstanding Dio's general hostility to homosexuality, the allusion here is not overtly hostile (otherwise the practice could not be debased) but strengthens the dialogue's Platonic texture. Callistratus is a lover of Homer,[30] as are the Borysthenites generally because of their warlike nature and devotion to Achilles. Although, surrounded by barbarians, they no longer speak Greek clearly, almost all know the *Iliad* by heart (9). These details link warfare, homosexuality, love of Homer, and Achilles to create an image of Greekness rather like that espoused by Alexander the Great, but they also suggest a tension between that image and love of wisdom.[31]

Dio's challenging attempt to interest Callistratus in the gnomic poet Phocylides instead of Homer (10) has several implications: Dio himself will perform a provocative Socratic role; as Platonic *eromenos* and would-be pupil of Dio, Callistratus has good philosophical potential; like Achilles, Homer is an excessively warlike model (causing philosophical 'blindness'); Phocylides better inculcates civic virtue; Dio will eventually broach a philosophical mode analogous to Phocylides' severe poetic mode (i.e., a Stoic mode). The relative depreciation of Homer, Hellenic icon, illustrates how for Dio, custodian of Hellenism, the constituents of Hellenic παιδεία are negotiable according to particular moral and practical needs.[32]

Dio's analogy between sampling Phocylides' poetry and sampling a merchant's wares (11) suggests that virtue is not necessarily the exclusive preserve of Greeks (he himself had planned to observe the Getae [1]). Phocylides' poem shows that even a small city perilously ⟦186⟧ located (like Borysthenes) can be more truly a city than a great city foolishly and lawlessly governed (13; cf. both *Euboicus* and *Or.* 13). Dio soothes Callistratus over Homer and with a great crowd of Borysthenites they go, symbolically, within the city, in contrast to the fleeing Scythians of the previous day (evidently not true 'city' people [14–16]).

The Borysthenites' philosophical potential is emphasised by their Hellenic manner and enthusiasm to hear Dio, even though they are still under arms. The meeting takes place, again symbolically, within the temple of Zeus. The seating arrangements reflect respect for age, and the sight of so many long-haired and long-bearded Greeks of the ancient type would have delighted a philosopher (Dio teasingly suggests that he is not himself such). Greekness and philosophy

---

30   Also, presumably, 'thigh-lover': for such plays cf. Ach. Tat. 8.9.3; *Anth. Pal.* 11.218 (Crates).
31   *Or.* 2 offers interesting parallels: Moles (1990) 339 {above, p. 155}.
32   Similarly in *Orr.* 2 (cf. Moles (1990) 339 {above, p. 155}) and 18 (the reading-list for an unnamed Greek statesman).

are closely associated. Only one man was clean-shaven, through desire to flatter the Romans and advertise his friendship with them: he is rightly derided and hated (17).

The smug Prusan audience now has *its* preconceptions challenged. For Prusa had far closer dealings with Rome than had Borysthenes and Dio often mentioned his own friendship with Romans, including the emperors (e.g., *Orr.* 40.5, 13–15; 43.11; 44.6, 12; 45.2). The point must be that while such associations may be necessary, it is essential not to compromise one's cultural Greekness, as Dio himself visibly did not, or one's moral integrity, as Dio claimed not to have done. This passage, like the Dacian episode and the end of *Olympicus*, shows that there are occasions when Dio registers direct hostility to the encroachments of Roman imperialism and culture. The passage also reveals another function of his exaggeration of Borysthenite simplicity and lack of culture: to define the *essence* of Greekness. Despite their faults, the Borysthenites are here the Prusans' moral superiors.

After stressing the city's ancient and Greek character, Dio goes into Socratic mode, insisting on the importance of correct definitions. Those without this ability are like barbarians (18–19): true Greekness entails philosophical competence. By the Stoic definition of a city as a group of men dwelling in the same place under law (where 'man' = 'a mortal man endowed with reason'), there never has been, and never will be, a city on earth: only the community of gods merits the name. Nevertheless, it is worth distinguishing between fairly good examples (ruled by good persons) and utterly corrupt ones (20–1). This section need not disturb interpreters who detect complimentary allusions to the Roman empire or to the reigns of Nerva or Trajan:[33] while Dio [[187]] cannot commend the empire whole-heartedly, he might still commend it reservedly. Yet the allusion to the solitary shaven Borysthenite discourages such interpretations.

Dio's desire to discuss the fairly good communities (23–4), that is, to philosophise in the tradition of Plato's *Republic*, is now diverted by Hieroson's intervention into the long final exposition about the divine city or government. Is Hieroson abandoning hard political thought for cloudy abstractions?[34]

On the contrary, his old age, respected status, courtesy and frankness, awareness of the question of Greekness (which, like Dio, he partly defines in moral terms), consciousness of Dio's divine role, love of Plato (an advance upon the general love of Homer), metaphorical desire, though he is all but blind, to look upon the sun itself, name ('preserver of holy things'), and the 'erotic'

---
33   Desideri (1978) 318, 321–2; Russell (1992) 23.
34   Schofield (1991) 63.

excitement which he and his companions feel at the prospect of hearing about the divine government (24–6): all these factors validate his intervention. We have progressed from Callistratus, 'fine warrior', to Hieroson, 'preserver of holy things', from war to peace and to concern for the city and for the preservation of holy things currently neglected (6). *Olympicus* exhibits the same progression and fundamental concerns.

Hieroson now requests Dio to discuss the divine city, not the mortal (27); the restated distinction seems to exclude any allusion to the Roman empire. Dio's exposition will mix Stoicism (his own creed, but difficult) with Platonism (as more appropriate to the Borysthenites, because a few read him and he has some affinity with Homer), and will be marked by Platonic elevation (28–9). While this mixture of both doctrine and mode reflects the respective tastes of Dio and his internal audience, it must also appeal to Dio's Prusan audience and any other audiences. A Stoic exposition will persuade only those who are themselves Stoics or susceptible to Stoic arguments, whereas harmonisation of Stoic and Platonic positions, however forced,[35] must have larger appeal, especially given the greater attractiveness of Platonic modes of exposition.

Dio's initial assertions that the Stoics do not literally define the universe as a city but liken the present arrangement of the universe to a city and that this doctrine aims to harmonise the human race with the divine (29–31) may seem again to open the possibility of integration of the Roman empire within the universe, especially as he states that the term 'city' can be applied only to a kingdom in the proper sense, ⟦188⟧ as exemplified by the kingship of Zeus.[36] After arguing that poets offer partial insight into religious thought, Dio restates the 'account of the philosophers', whereby there exists a fellowship of gods and men which apportions citizenship to those possessed of reason (32–8).

He next, however, embarks on an 'amazing myth sung in secret rites by the Magi' (39), who learned it from Zoroaster. This myth concerns the physical organisation of the universe and its periodic conflagration and rebirth. The Magi, he says (42), stubbornly assert the truth of their myth, whereas Greek poets try to persuade their audience. At a critical point in the development Dio elaborately apologises (43): 'what follows concerning the horses and their driving I am ashamed to tell in the manner in which they say it in their exposition, not caring in the least whether their image is in all respects a good likeness. For I might perhaps seem absurd [lit., 'out-of-place'] singing a barbarian song to follow songs that were elegant and Greek [i.e., the 'city-of-the-universe'

---

35  Schofield (1991) 88 on 31–2.
36  Desideri (1978) 322; Russell (1992) 228.

section], but nevertheless I must dare to do so.' His final words to his Prusan audience excuse his imaginative flights as due to Borysthenite insistence (61).

Questions of Greekness and barbarian-ness again obtrude. Clearly, Dio aims to make both his audiences *think*. But to what effect?

There are two basic interpretative principles. (*a*) While the myth has a Mithraic veneer, its substance is solidly Stoic, with some of the imagery (the chariot and horses) derived from Plato's *Phaedrus* and some from Stoic contexts.[37] (*b*) One would expect Dio to approve that substance: his general philosophical position is Stoic, as he notes in *Borystheniticus* (29), and he says similar things in *Or.* 40.35–41. The length, power, and eloquence of Dio's treatment here suggest some sort of assent and he finally refers not to a 'myth' but to an 'account' (60–1), thereby blurring the distinction of 38–9.

Why, then, Dio's stress on the myth's 'barbarian', 'out-of-place' quality and on the Magi's 'stubbornness' in asserting their myth, despite their apparently inaccurate imagery, a stress which entails elaborate apologies? Is Dio seriously suggesting that truly Greek 'songs' are not only charming but sober and rational (43), thereby conveying a salutary warning against the Borysthenites' irrational barbarian tendencies?[38] This interpretation fails to account for the implicit approval of Hieroson's desire to learn about the divine city, the disingenuousness of describing as 'Mithraic' material that is essentially [[189]] Stoic and Platonic, and the fact that Dio himself would naturally approve such material.

To some extent the stress on the myth's bizarreness reflects Dio's stance towards the entire 'divine-city' material, which is one simultaneously of ironical disavowal and ironical assertion of his powers to scale such Platonic and Homeric heights (29). To some extent also, within the 'divine-city' material, the stress distinguishes, conventionally, between the rationalism of an 'account' (38) and the cloudiness of 'myth' (39). This again reflects Dio's double agenda: appeal both to Stoic and to Platonic material; the 'account' belongs to the 'more accurate philosophy' of Stoicism (26), the 'myth' deploys 'Plato's liberty of style' (27), its details necessarily less 'accurate' than Stoicism's. Appeal to Magian authority is also Platonic (*Alcib.* 122a; [*Axioch.*] 371a). These factors, however, do not fully explain why Dio describes as Mithraic what is not Mithraic but just as Stoic as the formally contrasting 'account'-material of 29–38, nor why he stresses its bizarreness so heavily.

One factor concerns the Borysthenites' status as would-be Greeks surrounded by barbarians. They are given both a Stoic account of the divine

---

37  Russell (1992) 22.
38  Russell (1992) 23.

city and a basically Stoic myth which is proclaimed as 'Mithraic', 'barbarian', and 'out-of-place' and which disputes Greek traditions (40–2, 48–9). This myth could not be more serious in its concerns—the organisation of the universe and its successive destructions and rebirths—nor more universal in its application—to all men, irrespective of race, at all times. Dio seems to say that virtue and true understanding of the gods and the universe can be found in unexpected 'places': as in *Olympicus*, Greek thought is especially honoured, but other human beings may contribute to the understanding of the highest truths of the universe—even the Iranians, represented by the Sauromatians (Sarmatians) with whom the Borysthenites are constantly at war (3, 8).

It is particularly pointed that Dio relates the 'Magian' myth in response to Hieroson. For the latter's observation (25) that, in contrast to Dio, visitors to Borysthenes are only nominally Greeks and are actually more barbarous than the Borysthenites themselves, with whom they exchange poor-quality goods, echoes Dio's earlier merchandise simile (11; cf. 5). But whereas Dio allowed the possibility of good-quality merchandise from any source, Hieroson assumes the impossibility of good-quality barbarian merchandise. Furthermore, he apologises for his request for a Platonic exposition on the ground that [[190]] 'it may be "out-of-place" for a barbarous speaker to delight in the most Hellenic of writers' (26).[39]

Dio's 'apology' for 'out-of-place' Magian material interacts with Hieroson's preconceptions in contradictory ways. *Qua* apology, it acknowledges Hieroson's request for impeccably Hellenic material. But Dio provides Hieroson with formally non-Hellenic material. Yet this formally non-Hellenic material is actually not non-Hellenic. Yet in turn, the rhetorical effect of providing formally non-Hellenic material is not erased, especially for the Borysthenites, who cannot penetrate the philosophical disguise. For them it remains both disconcerting and educative to receive the highest truths about the universe wrapped up in the teachings of their Iranian enemies. We may also recall Dio's own projected visit to the Getae, who here, as in *Olympicus*, are not necessarily despicable: they too may represent that 'alien wisdom' which may benefit even Greeks trying very hard to be Greeks. For Greekness is not just language and culture: it includes virtue.

Other factors concern Dio's external audience or audiences. As in *Euboicus* and *Olympicus*, one effect is to boost Dio's own claims as philosopher and embodiment of Greekness. There is also the question of philosophical doctrine. Not only non-Stoics but by Dio's day even some Stoics rejected the

---

39   On this sentence see Russell (1992) 224–5.

doctrine of the universe's cyclical destruction and rebirth.[40] Hence elaborately distancing irony might seem an appropriate rhetorical mode for exposition of such material.

How should the Prusans take the 'Magian' material? Just as the Borysthenites are racially challenged by Dio's giving them an 'Iranian' myth, the Prusans are also racially challenged (although differently): they, presumably, expect exotic tales from Dio the returning traveller, but the exotic material which Dio so flamboyantly produces turns out to be Greek.[41] The effect is disconcerting but also, apparently, ingratiating. Greek values seem to be affirmed and the Prusans can feel superior to the gullible Borysthenites as Dio passes off standard Greek philosophical material for Eastern wisdom. But the material's unexpected presentation and the earlier jolt to Prusan self-esteem must unsettle their self-satisfaction. Even for them, the rhetorical effect of the myth's 'barbarian' presentation remains. Its hybrid nature seems to suggest the ultimate harmony of Greek and barbarian peoples within the universe. Here again, the Borysthenites provide an ambiguous paradigm for the Prusans and other Greeks: in some ways [[191]] their barbarism prevents their fulfilment as true Greeks, in other ways it adumbrates the ultimate fusion of Greek and barbarian within the universal city ruled by God the king.[42]

What of the Romans? As in *Olympicus*, allusion to the Romans brings them within the interpretative framework. But nothing indicates that the cosmic city offers a paradigm for the Roman empire. While an analogy between Zeus, king of all, and the emperor is always a theoretical possibility, exploited, as we have seen, by Dio himself in addressing Trajan, it is here deliberately short-circuited by the sharp criticism of the single shaven man, which performs an 'exclusion' function analogous to that of the Dacian section in *Olympicus*. The attempt to interpret the 'regeneration' of the universe as a metaphor for the rebirth of the Roman empire under Nerva and Trajan[43] also founders on Dio's insistence that the newly created universe is 'far more resplendent than it appears today' (58). Rather, this periodic regeneration is an essential manifestation of divine providence. Moreover, before his regeneration and expansion of the universe the 'erect' divine Fire 'occupied as great a "place" as possible' (53): the 'place' that ultimately matters is not Borysthenes or Prusa, the Greek world (5), barbary, or the Roman empire: it is the 'place' of the universe. Dio's lengthy and

---

40   Rist (1969) 175–6, 202.
41   Russell (1992) 232.
42   Within Dio's interpretation of Stoic theology 'God' is a wholly appropriate term: Russell (1992) 14–15.
43   Russell (1992) 23, 233.

remarkably sexy description of the act of regeneration (55–7) is also integral to the whole speech. For the Borysthenites' homosexuality and 'sexual arousal' in anticipation of Dio's discourse (26) represent a striving, however imperfect, towards the true, divine, love that is at the heart of the universe. (The Platonic 'ladder of love' is also relevant here.)

As in *Olympicus*, Dio offers his audiences these great Stoic reflections on the workings of the universe not in order to reconcile them to the Roman empire but to give them a higher vision. Both in space and in time this vision dwarfs and transcends that empire, but it can provide a context and a standard for the expression of true Greekness, because it is Greek thinkers who have come closest to an understanding of the divine. Greekness, however, cannot be an exclusive thing, for Greeks may benefit from barbarian wisdom and we are all children of God (cf. *Euboicus* 138). This vision is at once what ought to be and what, ultimately, is, and the right way to handle problems of racial identity and conflict lies in emulation of the cosmic harmony. The 〚192〛 requisite adjustments of attitude and behaviour will naturally vary according to circumstances: the Prusans, beset by Romans, must desist from flattering them, the Borysthenites, beset by barbarians, should preserve, deepen, and in some ways redefine their Greekness, but should also become more receptive to barbarian religious thought. As in *Olympicus*, Dio is not 'anti-Roman' as such; he cannot be: the Romans are necessarily (potential) fellow-citizens of the Greeks (and of everybody else) in the cosmic state. What he pointedly resists is the universalising claim of the Roman empire, whether it proclaims itself the earthly instantiation of that state or encroaches upon the Greek way of life (17). Dio's warm and humane interpretation of Stoic cosmopolitanism encompasses concern for Greek cultural integrity, openness to barbarian wisdom, and a profound sense of kinship between all human beings and between humans and the divine. This is a fine and noble speech, as well as being an extraordinarily subtle one. Donald Russell is right to discern in both *Olympicus* and *Borystheniticus* that 'sublimity' whose 'cosmic dearth' was lamented by Dio's great contemporary, 'Longinus'.[44]

4

Dio, we agree, adjusts his message to his audience. He can criticise the Roman empire before Greeks (*Olympicus*, *Borystheniticus*); to the Romans (*Euboicus*)

---

44   Russell (1992) 2–3.

and to Trajan (*Orr.* 1–4)⁴⁵ he is the insider who delivers honest advice and warnings. This is a matter of practical moralism, not of inconsistency. Now in some respects Dio was, I still believe, a dreadful fraud,⁴⁶ hence his self-projection as a moral and philosophical paradigm was a double-edged ploy, which often encountered, and indeed created, resistance among his contemporaries (even though it is generally tempered by irony and wit). Yet, in Donald Russell's humane words, Dio is also, sometimes even at the same time, 'a moralist of convincing earnestness and charm'.⁴⁷ The greatness of these three speeches derives from their combination of literary excellence, profound moral seriousness, and intense engagement with the problems of being Greek in the Roman empire.

## Bibliography

Brunt, P. A. (1973) 'Aspects of the Social Thought of Dio Chrysostom and the Stoics', *PCPhS* 199: 9–33; repr. in id., *Studies in Stoicism*, edd. M. Griffin and A. Samuels (Oxford, 2013) 151–79.

Desideri, P. (1978) *Dione di Prusa: un intellettuale greco nell'impero romano* (Messina/Florence).

Geel, J. (1840) *Dio Chrysostomos: Olympicus* (Leiden).

Jones, C. P. (1978) *The Roman World of Dio Chrysostom* (Cambridge, Mass. and London).

Moles, J. L. (1978) 'The Career and Conversion of Dio Chrysostom', *JHS* 98: 79–100 [above, Ch. 1].

Moles, J. L. (1983) 'Dio Chrysostom: Exile, Tarsus, Nero and Domitian', *LCM* 8: 130–4 [above, Ch. 2].

Moles, J. L. (1990) 'The Kingship Orations of Dio Chrysostom', *PLLS* 6: 297–375 [above, Ch. 5].

Moles, J. L. (1993) 'Review of D. A. Russell, *Dio Chrysostom: Orations VII, XII, XXXVI* (Cambridge, 1992)', *CR* 43: 256–8 [above, Ch. 6].

Reiske, J. J. (1784) *Dionis Chrysostomi Orationes*, 2 vols. (Leipzig).

Rist, J. M. (1969) *Stoic Philosophy* (Cambridge).

Russell, D. A., ed. (1992) *Dio Chrysostom: Orations VII, XII, XXXVI* (Cambridge).

Russell, D. A. and M. Winterbottom, edd. (1972) *Ancient Literary Criticism: the Principal Texts in New Translations* (Oxford).

Schofield, M. (1991) *The Stoic Idea of the City* (Cambridge; repr. Chicago, 1999).

---

45   I here rely upon Moles (1990).
46   Moles (1978).
47   Russell–Winterbottom (1972) 504.

Swain, S. (1994) 'Dio and Lucian', in J. R. Morgan and R. Stoneman, edd., *Greek Fiction: the Greek Novel in Context* (London and New York) 166–80.

Swain, S. (1996) *Hellenism and Empire: Language, Classicism, and Power in the Greek World, AD 50–250* (Oxford).

Trapp, M. B. (1990) 'Plato's *Phaedrus* in Second-Century Greek Literature', in D. A. Russell, ed., *Antonine Literature* (Oxford) 141–73.

CHAPTER 8

# The Dionian *Charidemus*

The *Charidemus* attributed to Dio Chrysostom ostensibly commemorates a recently deceased pupil of Dio's named Charidemus.* As *Or.* 30 in the extant Dionian corpus the piece suitably follows *Orr.* 28 and 29, the two obituary encomia of the athlete Melancomas. On any reading, *Or.* 30 is adroitly conceived and executed and not without pathos. Yet the bibliography, despite recent and forthcoming items, remains inchoate,[1] its growth perhaps stunted by nervousness over the alleged problem of authenticity.[2] Authenticity is indeed not guaranteed by presence in the corpus. Thus *Orr.* 37 and 64 are generally agreed to be by Favorinus, one of Dio's most distinguished pupils. Nor does the piece's proximity to *Orr.* 28 and 29[3] significantly support authenticity: *Orr.* 37 and 64 are also appropriately contextualised. Might *Or.* 30, then, be 'school of Dio' rather than Dio himself? The piece also poses substantial interpretative problems, which have so far eluded resolution.

The general character of the work may best emerge from a summary interspersed with running comment, followed by direct engagement with the interpretative problems. Since the latter cannot [[188]] ultimately be detached from the authenticity question and since continual formulation of strictly non-prejudicial comment would be very laborious, the summary will adopt the genuineness of the piece as a working hypothesis and defer formal consideration of the question until the end. There, however, it will be argued that the case against authenticity is misconceived. Moreover, the commentary material will itself provide evidence for the defence. Consequently, the work's presence and position in the corpus, the material in the commentary, and the solutions offered to the problems will constitute a strong cumulative case for authenticity. We shall then be free to appreciate the work's quality without distraction.

---

* I thank: Simon Swain for inviting me; all who commented at the conference; Tony Woodman for comments on a written version; and Mike Trapp for a copy of his paper, Trapp (2000).
1 Hirzel (1895) II.111–14; Meiser (1912); Wilhelm (1918); Cohoon II.395–8; Kassel (1958) 48; Moles (1978) 95 {above, p. 50}; Bowie (1985) 671; Giner Soria (1990–1); Menchelli (1997); and Trapp (2000) 223–5 makes valuable observations; Menchelli's doctoral thesis is to be published {Menchelli (1999)}; Giovanni Schiavo is producing an Italian translation.
2 Hirzel (1895); von Arnim (1898) 283; Nilsson (1961) 401 n. 2; Desideri (1978) 185 n. 19, 248 n. 42; Moles (1978) 95 {above, p. 50}; Menchelli (1997) 67–73; note the uncertainty of Russell (1992): dubious (178), authentic (247).
3 Wilhelm (1918) 364: 'in Discourse 29 physical, in 30 intellectual excellence'.

The discussion will also explore a hypothesis which, if accepted, adds new dimensions alike to the work's emotional intensity, to its literary complexity, and to its philosophical coherence.

## 1  The *Charidemus*: Summary and Comment

Dio,[4] having heard of Charidemus' death, is condoling with Charidemus' father Timarchus and surviving brother, also called Timarchus, who are both rightly distraught: besides their personal loss, Charidemus would have been of immense benefit not only to his city but to all Greece (1–3). Dio's relations with his pupil were exceptionally close: he feels almost as much grief as do Timarchus father and son (2); the dying Charidemus kept naming Dio and bade his family tell Dio when they met him that he died thinking of him (4); in life, Charidemus had the same philosophical deportment as Dio, whether or not because he imitated him (4–5). Thus Dio already appears as both a lofty external and an intensely internal figure, an ambiguous status that is capable of rich development and one that is familiar from such Dionian works as the first, second, and fourth *Kingship Orations*, the *Euboicus*, and the *Olympicus*.[5]

The opening scene deftly sketches important themes. The elaborate circumstantial grounding in details of travel and informants and in terms such as ἀκούω, ἐπίσταμαι, γιγνώσκω, etc. sets up questions of truth, language, naming, and knowledge (1–2). There is a contrast [[189]] between the select and the ignorant majority (3). There is emphasis on the role of φύσις, both nature as a moral standard (here the natural feeling proper to familial relationships) and individual nature or character (3, 4–5); the latter emphasis already suggests that while philosophical teaching and teachers and their imitation have their place, it is the individual's deployment of his φύσις that mainly determines good or bad moral behaviour. The question whether Charidemus' deportment caused his family λύπη (5) neatly conveys the points that among all the λῦπαι of life, not least are the λῦπαι caused by others, and λῦπαι can be small as well as great. Charidemus' death, while the source of the greatest λύπη which human beings have to bear, is paradigmatic of all types of λῦπαι. As will become ever more

---

4  Donald Russell emphasises (in conversation) that the name Dio (in contrast to Charidemus and the two Timarchuses) does not appear in the text (the division of the dialogue by names is a modern convenience). But such 'namelessness' is the norm in Dio. Furthermore, it will be argued that Dio's name is *implicit*.

5  Cf. n. 49.

apparent, there are numerous skilful links between the opening scene, the main body of the work, and the final scene.

The question whether Charidemus' philosophical sobriety betokened cheerfulness or gloominess (5) anticipates the key question which informs the structure of the whole piece: did Charidemus die well? But first (6) Timarchus father declares that Charidemus said 'many spirit-like [δαιμόνια] things'. On his death-bed Charidemus is between life and death and approaches the mediating character of δαίμονες.[6] To the key question, the answer is that Charidemus died cheerfully and courageously, as proved not only by his death-bed behaviour but also by the work of consolation which he there dictated, which at Dio's request Timarchus father now reads aloud (8–44). The structure of the *Charidemus* thus echoes that of the *Phaedo*, Dio's favourite philosophical text, according to Philostratus (*vs* 488).[7] Both works use the device of an outer frame for the last words of a philosopher as reported by a witness or witnesses to a concerned friend or friends. Conceivably, the device of death-bed utterances transmuted into philosophical text may also reflect something of Dio's own knowledge of philosophical heroism at Rome in his youth, that heroism exhibited (for example) in the deaths of Seneca (Tac. *Ann.* 15.62–4) and Thrasea Paetus (*Ann.* 16.34–5), which were themselves partly modelled on the death of Socrates as transmitted in Platonic texts, while Seneca dictated to secretaries what were intended to be his last words and these were subsequently published as a separate work (*Ann.* 15.63.3).

⟦190⟧ In the inner text of the *Charidemus* Charidemus affirms calm acceptance of God's will, cites Homer (*Il.* 3.65) in support of the proposition that all things done by the gods are 'gifts' which should not be cast aside by mortals, and exhorts his loved ones not to yield to grief, since nothing terrible has befallen him, even if one were to 'go for' (ἔλθοι ἐπί) τὸν δυσχερέστατον τῶν λόγων (9): the most difficult, the most disagreeable, of the various λόγοι of the human condition (in effect, the worst-case scenario). This description, which interacts with 8 δυσχερῶς φέρειν ('we must not bear anything brought to pass by God with difficulty/disagreeably'), already suggests the suspect quality of such a λόγος, acceptable only to the δυσχερεῖς: one's personal disposition affects the sort of λόγος of the human condition that one goes for, but some λόγοι are better than others.

Charidemus' own text, therefore, is explicitly presented as a 'consolation' (6) which will consist of a series of λόγοι, providing progressively greater

---

6  At least on re-reading, this δαίμων-emphasis may be regarded as the first, light, evocation of Plato's *Symposium* (e.g., 202e).
7  For the *Phaedo* relationship cf. further Trapp (2000) 224.

consolation. Scholars customarily speak of the 'myths' of the *Charidemus*,[8] and indeed these λόγοι possess the conventional characteristics of 'myths': they claim to explain huge moral/theological problems, contain some narrative and much imaginative writing, and freely invoke the divine.[9] But they are formally presented as λόγοι in the first instance because they make greater truth claims than μῦθοι sometimes do,[10] and Charidemus' concern is above all with truth (9). Yet there remains an implicit challenge in the application of the term λόγοι to material which obviously contains at least some elements of the 'mythical', a challenge for which there are Platonic and Dionian parallels.[11]

The first 'account' (10–24), 'difficult' or 'disagreeable' as it is, is recognisably largely Orphic.[12] Thus the influence of the *Phaedo*, itself influenced by Orphism, continues into the inner text of the [[191]] *Charidemus*.[13] According to this first account, humans are descended from the blood of the Titans, the gods hate us, life is a punishment, lifted only by death, and the universe is a prison; so far from its organisation demonstrating beneficent divine providence, everything has been designed to punish and torture us, and most only escape into death when they have produced children to be 'left behind' as 'successors [διάδοχοι] to their punishment' (17). This conception of the function of children seems to reverse that of Plato, *Symposium* 207d: there '*mortal* nature' can pursue its quest for *immortality* only through begetting and 'always *leaving behind* something new in place of the old'; here men desire *death* and can only achieve this by *leaving behind* children to take over their punishment in *life*.

We are all in chains, but for a very few good people the chains are light (19). Charidemus now (20) digresses into an explanation of the chain which he once heard as a child from a beggar (ἀνδρὸς ἀγύρτου).[14] The chain is composed

---

8   E.g., Saïd (2000) 174 and Trapp (2000) 224; Cohoon II.395 ff. translates 'explanation'. I adopt 'account', as suggesting (*a*) rationalist pursuit of truth, (*b*) narrative content.
9   The Orphic *logos* is particularly 'mythical' in having something of 'the wonderful' about it (10 θαυμαστόν).
10  Although much recent scholarship (both on Plato and 'myth' generally) argues the slipperiness of μῦθος and λόγος as categories, λόγος certainly sometimes makes a stronger truth claim: cf., e.g., Plat. *Gorg.* 523a; *Tim.* 20d, 21a; *Crit.* 108c–d; Dio 1.49 (Moles (1990) 318–19 {above, pp. 134–5}); 5.3 (with Saïd (2000) 163 and Trapp (2000) 229; cf. Anderson (2000) 155–6).
11  As in the references in n. 10.
12  Meiser (1912); the much-discussed problematics of 'Orphism' hardly matter here.
13  Trapp (2000) 224.
14  Translation points: Cohoon's prejudicial 'wandering philosopher' subserves his interpretation of larger questions (below, pp. 218ff.); παῖς ὤν naturally goes with ποτε and the genitive ἀνδρὸς ἀγύρτου naturally depends on ἤκουσα (cf. also 25), so that Trapp's interpretation ([2000] 224–5), 'the teller of the myth [characterises himself] as the offspring of

of alternating pleasures and pains, great succeeding great, small small; death is the greatest pleasure, the pain before death the greatest pain. This thought obviously has consolatory force, though this is not spelled out. The digression then discusses the chains that are hopes (πήδας/ἐλπίδας): these come at the end of life, control men, and enable them to endure all tortures; they are very big for the stupid, loose and light for the more intelligent. Presumably (though this also is not spelled out), they bear on different conceptions of an afterlife: the stupid have unrealistically big hopes, the intelligent more subtle ones. Again, then, a thought with consolatory force, though hopes are insubstantial things. The digression continues with the idea of the file that is reason (superior to hope), which is hard to find but whose diligent and constant use enables a man to endure and leave his imprisonment easily (24 εὐχερῶς contrasts with 9 δυσχερέστατον and 8 δυσχερῶς). A digression within an 'account' (λόγος) which instates 'reason' (λόγος) as a source of consolation must have *something* 'reasonable' about it.

⟦192⟧ The digression now seemingly rejoins the main account, though the ending of the digression is not formally marked:[15] sometimes the gods actually make the virtuous and wise their coadjutants (πάρεδροι) in an afterlife: more solid consolation, though qualified by that 'sometimes'. There is another deft link between the introduction and the body of the work: Timarchus father rarely saw Charidemus laughing ἀνέδην (5: 'unrestrainedly'): philosophers are 'bound' to observe a certain 'restraint'. The sober picture of Dio himself (4) now finds a place within the overall argument[16] and the image of chains is revalued in a positive way.

Charidemus ends this first account with a provocative and problematic formulation, to which we must return: 'now this was said by a certain difficult-to-please man [δυσάρεστος ~ 9 τὸν δυσχερέστατον τῶν λόγων ~ 8 δυσχερῶς φέρειν], who had suffered many things in his life and only late had attained true education; but it is not true nor appropriate to the gods; there is another account better than this one, which I shall speak with much more enthusiasm' (25).

This better account (26–7) he heard from a worker of the land who spoke in very rustic style (another problematic formulation). This man hymned Zeus

---

some vagabond', is in itself forced; nevertheless, as we shall see, wider considerations give the collocation ἀνδρὸς ἀγύρτου παῖς teasing additional resonances.

15    19 ὑπὲρ ὧν αὖθις λέξομεν seems to be picked up by 24 ἐκ τούτων, 19 ἐπιείκειαν by 24 ἀρετὴν καὶ σοφίαν, though there is no resumptive οὖν (*uel sim.*).

16    This answers Donald Russell's observation (in conversation) that 'the philosopher in 4 does not much look like Dio but more like Aristotle's *megalopsuchos*' (cf. *EN* 4.3, 1125a12–14).

and the other gods and declared that they were good and loved us as their kin (herewith an emphatic Stoic rejection of the Orphic genealogy). The hymning of Δία is significant in another way. As part of the debate about the relationship between language and truth, the introduction played with the question of right and wrong naming, and the dying Charidemus kept naming Dio (1–2, 4, 8). The suggestive linkage between his own name and that of Zeus is exploited by Dio elsewhere to bolster his moral and religious authority: Zeus, father of all, is particularly the father of Δίων.[17] Mankind on earth is a divine colony, related to the gods' home city ⟦193⟧ but much inferior. For a time after the foundation the gods themselves visited or sent divine governors; they then left humans to themselves, whence sin and injustice. As a whole, this account is much more optimistic than its Orphic predecessor and already provides more substantive philosophical consolation.

The worker of the land also sang a second song (28–44): the universe is a very beautiful and divine house built by the gods, all its appurtenances designed for man's good cheer; a still more optimistic vision unfolds. This account must obviously be the most congenial to the cheerful and optimistic Charidemus (5) and indeed has been anticipated by his initial appeal to Homer (8). Man's life is like a splendid feast, banquet, or symposium, man's behaviour at which is conditioned by his individual nature (33 ~ 3). The symposiastic emphasis conveys a sly metatextual allusion to the influence on the *Charidemus* of Plato's[18] *Symposium*. The general conception of a beauteous and harmonious creation is acceptably Stoic and both Chrysippus and Epictetus use the symposium as an image for human life.[19] The contrast between porcine devotees of pleasure (33) and sober types who seek to understand the intelligent universe (41) makes a broad contrast between Epicureans (traditionally caricatured as pigs [Cic. *Pis.* 37; Hor. *Ep.* 1.4.15–16]) and Stoics. As in Dio's *Olympicus* (36.7), Epicureanism is polemically misrepresented, and despite the Platonic

---

17  E.g., *Or.* 4.27 and *Or.* 12.85 with Moles (1995) 183 {above, p. 194}. I suspect also further punning interaction between Δία and διάνοιαν (25), especially in the light of the prominence of Νοῦς in the third account, with large implications for the ultimate identity of the 'author' of the whole work (pp. 221ff.); and as the work becomes progressively more Stoic, as Δίων himself appears within the 'accounts' (p. 223), and as apparently separate identities become confused (pp. 223ff.), one might also recall the Hesiodic word play on Διός/δία (*Theog.* 465) and the Platonic word plays on νοῦς, διάνοια, and δαίμονες (*Laws* 713c–d).

18  Trapp (2000) 224 n. 32, sceptical of any influence of Plato's *Symposium*, hazards an echo of Xenophon's (*Smp.* 1.26) at 36.

19  *SVF* 768 (III.190); Epict. 1.24.20; 2.16.37; *Ench.* 15.

framework the existential choice of philosophy lies between Epicureanism and Stoicism (as is often the case also in Dio's fellow-Stoics, Seneca and Marcus Aurelius).

Gross sensualists spend their time acquiring possessions and when they have to depart from life 'leave these behind' to others (34). This detail parallels and contrasts with the anxiety of the majority in the Orphic account to 'leave behind a successor to their punishment' (17): there, what is 'left behind' consists of a child; here, what is 'left behind' consists of possessions left *to* dependants. The drink on offer at life's symposium is Pleasure and there are two cup-bearers, Intelligence (Νοῦς) (corresponding to reason in the Orphic account) and Intemperance (Ἀκράτεια). This contrasting pair evokes the two jars of Zeus in the *Iliad* and Prodicus/Xenophon's choice between Virtue and Vice/Pleasure. The majority of humans become drunk [[194]] on Intemperance, thereby insulting the gods' grace; by contrast the good temper their intake of pleasure with intelligence (42) and admire, observe, and try to understand the beauties of the house that is the universe (41). When they depart, they are anxious to be able to make some response to any enquirer about their observations (42).

The implications of this last detail are multiple and thought-provoking. The introduction's apparently trivial enquiry about people's well-being turns into profound philosophical enquiry (42 πυνθάνοιτο ~ 1 ἐπυνθάνομεν). The response of the good to this enquiry is obviously exemplified by Charidemus' work within the *Charidemus* and presumably also by the *Charidemus* itself. The situation of the good at the end of their lives corresponds with the situations both of the gross sensualists, who 'leave behind' to dependants mere material possessions (34), and of the majority of humans in the Orphic account who need to 'leave behind' a child as 'successor to their punishment' (17). These parallelisms create a sense that both Charidemus' text within the *Charidemus* and Dio's *Charidemus* itself are their respective 'children', an idea for which there are important Platonic parallels: *Symposium* 209d 'everyone would prefer children of this sort to be born to them rather than human children, looking at Homer, Hesiod, and the other good poets, and envying the sort of offspring they leave behind them' and *Phaedrus* 275e (words have 'fathers'). The hypothesis that the *Symposium* is an important conceptual influence upon the *Charidemus* seems confirmed.[20] Presumably, however, the *recipients* of these texts, which

---

20  The *Symposium* similarly provides the framework of the myth in the first *Kingship Oration*: Moles (1990) 319 {above, p. 135}.

are in one sense the 'bequests' of their 'fathers', are also to be regarded as 'children' or 'successors'.

The discussions of the virtuous recall Socratic dialectic: 'talking one to one, or peers in groups of twos or threes' (42). Further parallels are suggested: with Charidemus' death-bed dialectic with his loved ones (42 διαλεγόμενοι ~ 6 διελέχθη ~ 4 διαλέγεσθαι); with the Socratic dialogue that is the *Charidemus*; with the *Phaedo*, the Socratic dialogue behind the *Charidemus*; with the initial conversation between Dio and Charidemus' father and brother. And the interplay between Charidemus' παίζειν and ἐλευθέριοι παιδιαί (5) now suggests the Socratic/Platonic interplay between παίζειν/παιδιά/παιδεία (e.g., Plat. *Leg.* 2.656c; Dio 4.30). It now becomes clear ⟦195⟧ that ἐλευθέριοι also proleptically distances Charidemus from the Orphic account and marks the *Charidemus* as a text conducive to philosophical 'freedom'. This whole series of parallels, including the present exposition of the *Charidemus* to fellow-Dionians, means that to read and interpret the *Charidemus* is itself a philosophical activity: our interpretation of it is part of the business of a right interpretation of human life and living. Such an observation is nowadays almost a truism of Platonic criticism: it remains, nevertheless, important, and even more so in the case of a text such as the *Charidemus*, which is concerned not with first-order philosophical questions but with useful practical moralising about the most difficult and painful areas of life.

Appropriately both to their beliefs and behaviour Epicurean pleasure-enthusiasts cling in unseemly fashion to life and have nothing to leave behind them and no hope of an afterlife. By contrast, the virtuous depart exhibiting Socratic φαιδρότης, and those with whom God is particularly pleased (44 ἀρεσθείς contrasts with 25 δυσάρεστος) are called by him to be his fellow-symposiasts in an apparently everlasting bout of the nectar that represents the true sobriety. This apparent immortality is not Platonic, since *only* the elect survive, but reflects Stoic orthodoxy, though obviously no soul survives the next conflagration (in which Dio, unlike some contemporary Stoics, actually believed).[21] But in this generalised mythic context allusion to the conflagration would be inappropriate and perhaps insufficiently consolatory. The promise of immortality for the elect corresponds to the final section of the Orphic account (24). Clearly, Charidemus will belong in this company; hence a final consolation for his death (43–4).

Yet Dio's reaction to Charidemus' work is not unalloyed (45–6): while Charidemus has provided a wonderful ἐπίδειξις not of words but of great and

---

21   Euseb. *PE* 15.20.6 = *SVF* 809 (II.223) = Long–Sedley §53W; Moles (1995) 190 {above, p. 200}.

true manliness,[22] thereby validating his extraordinary promise and providing an inspiring παράδειγμα, Dio feels unable adequately to console his family, being unable indeed adequately to console himself. They all risk succumbing to Orphic pessimism (45 βαρέως φέρειν ~ 8 δυσχερῶς φέρειν). Here, as elsewhere, there is a sense that human beings can, as it were, to some extent 'write [[196]] their own λόγος' of the universe. While it makes a big difference to the constitution of the universe and to the human condition within it whether God hates us (as in the Orphic account) or loves us (as in the second and third accounts), our own attitudes and behaviour have some effect on the sort of universe we live in. The challenge implicit in describing as λόγοι what are in some obvious senses 'myths' here becomes acute: one of the functions of such a description is to suggest that these 'myths' are to some degree realisable and thus to pose the question: have we the moral strength to flip the categories and turn μῦθος into λόγος?[23]

As for Timarchus father, only Timarchus son can lighten his misfortune by showing himself akin to Charidemus in virtue (the value of genetic kinship is much enhanced by kinship in virtue). Thus again, while Charidemus' virtue is exhibited in, and proved by, his dictated work, that wonderful work does not quite succeed in its proclaimed aim of consolation (6). It is an unsettling ending, the strongly affirmatory characterisation of Charidemus (which corresponds to the final words of the *Phaedo*) segueing into only partial philosophical success on the key moral question of how we bear the terrible misfortunes inevitable in human life.[24]

## 2  Structural and Verbal Control

This summary already suggests some of the piece's considerable quality. Clearly, proper appreciation of the work would need to take greater account of its creative adaptation of the *Phaedo*, of its rich blending of Stoic and Platonic

---

22  The first *Kingship Oration* works a similar 'redefinition' of ἐπίδειξις: *Or.* 1.61 ~ 1.1 with Moles (1990) 326 {above, p. 143}.
23  The first *Kingship Oration* issues the same challenge: Moles (1990) 335–6 {above, pp. 151–3}.
24  Menchelli's ([1997] 73–80) interpretation (the moral of the *Charidemus* is Socratic/Dionian πραότης/ἐπιείκεια in the acceptance of destiny) takes inadequate account of the ending's complexities (of which more below).

(cf. *Euboicus*, *Borystheniticus*, and *Olympicus*),[25] and of its intermixing of genres: dialogue, encomium, and consolation.

More directly relevant to the present enquiry is the piece's structural control, keyed by detailed verbal relationships and their dense interpretative implications. These detailed verbal relationships are [[197]] everywhere, but the most marked examples occur between beginning and end, hence analysis of these relationships must form part of the interpretation of the end. Clearly, 45 Χαρίδημε ... τέθνηκας echoes 1 Χαριδήμου τελευτῆς and 2 Χαριδήμου ... τεθνηκέναι; 45 ὡς πολὺ ... ἔμελλες echoes 3 ἐπεὶ καὶ ... ἔμελλεν ἔσεσθαι with a significant expansion of context: Charidemus would have excelled not merely in all Greece but among mankind; 45 μεγάλης καὶ ἀληθίνης ἀνδρείας echoes 5 τὸ ... ἀνδρεῖον ... τοῦ σχήματος (before merely manliness of deportment, now full manliness of character); and 45 ἐγὼ μὲν ... φέρειν echoes 2 καὶ οἶμαι ... ἀδελφοῦ (here no change: Dio remains inconsolable).

More importantly, 45 ἱκανῶς echoes 1 πρὸ ἱκανοῦ, which means 'a considerable time before' but in juxtaposition with πρὶν ὑμᾶς ἰδεῖν and in collocation with the travel terminology παρέβαλον δευρί and the indication of place ἐν Μεσσήνῃ, suggests the association of ἱκανός with ἱκνέομαι. Then in 1 the man who knows nothing at all about Charidemus and his brother except their names[26] 'meets with Dio' (ἐντυχών); by contrast in 4 the dying Charidemus 'kept naming Dio' and gave his father and brother a significant message for when 'we should meet him' (ἐντύχωμεν). Thus the dramatic context of the *Charidemus* is itself the meeting that matters, in contrast to the chance and inchoate meeting of Dio and the man who knows nothing.

Time is similarly redefined: in 7 Timarchus father worries that Charidemus' dictated work may not be right, as having been spoken 'at such a time' (ἐν τοιούτῳ καιρῷ), whereas for Charidemus himself at 9 the fact that he is speaking at the καιρός of his death gives his words authority. At the end of the work, in 45 and 46, the ideas of significant travel and significant place recur, with the words ἱκανῶς, ἄτοπον, and προσήκων. Προσήκων means 'being kin' but it is a travel word ('having arrived'), linking with ἄτοπον and looking back to the notions of travel and place in 1. Travel and place become metaphors (of course very common) for moral progress; at the end Dio himself has not reached his destination of full philosophical consolation for Charidemus' death (οὐδὲ ...

---

25  *Euboicus*: Moles (1995) 179 {above, p. 190}, Trapp (2000) 219–21, Brenk (2000) 270–5; *Borystheniticus*: Schofield (1991) 57–64, Trapp (2000) 214–19; *Olympicus*: cf. now Trapp (2000) 227–8; Trapp (2000) is an important contribution to the general topic.

26  Οὐ πάνυ can mean both 'not quite' and 'not at all' (LSJ s.v. πάνυ 3), but context excludes Cohoon's 'not very well' (the man knows only the names).

ἱκανῶς); Timarchus son, by contrast, must put himself in the same moral topos as that achieved by Charidemus: his journey has yet to begin. Of course the ⟦198⟧ text is itself a journey and both a metaphor for, and a means to, the moral progress to which all must aspire.[27] The different temporal perspectives of 45 also have their force: the death-bed recitation of Charidemus was the original καιρός—the right time, but how should the various parties respond now? How of course also should we respond now? Is this, *now*, the topos, is this, *now*, the καιρός, when the problems of the *Charidemus* and of human suffering will be resolved? For the moment Dio himself is disconsolate and will be unable to console the Timarchuses; the future for Timarchus son lies in emulation of Charidemus. The control of topography and time is exceedingly skilful and paralleled not only in Plato but in such Dionian works as the first *Kingship Oration*[28] and the *Borystheniticus*.[29]

The ending is indeed extraordinarily well-judged. Charidemus' text does not fully succeed in its philosophical purpose, but Dio's text (the immediate life beyond Charidemus' text) goes on and holds out the possibility that Timarchus son may emulate Charidemus' virtue as established both in Dio's text (the frame) and in Charidemus' own. Timarchus son in fact corresponds to the διάδοχος left behind mentioned both in the Orphic-Pythagorean account and—implicitly—in the worker of the land's account. He has a double aspect: the literal child and the philosophical child. The influence of the *Symposium* is again felt, and in context τῶν καλλίστων ἐρασθῆναι (46) functions as a signal for the *Symposium*. And life goes on beyond the *two* texts: maybe in the future the combination of the two will bear real philosophical fruit—or maybe not. The ending dramatises alike the strengths and the limitations of philosophical texts and teachers (cf. 4–5) *and* the possibility both of human philosophical failure (Dio) and eventual success (Timarchus son). And the pain of loss is not alleviated but the possibility is opened that the continuing practice of virtue by those left behind affords some compensation. It is a magnificent ending (about which there is yet more to say) and the richness of the literary conception and the deft skill of its midwifery look very Dionian.

If the complexities of the ending derive largely from the relationships—the potentially oppositional relationships—between text(s) and context(s)/life, those complexities can also be analysed ⟦199⟧ in terms of the relationships between internal audiences and external audiences, in which respect the

---

27  Hence the dead/colourless metaphor 'go for' (9; LSJ s.v. ἔρχομαι B.1, 4) is brought to life.
28  Moles (1990) 322 {above, p. 138}.
29  Moles (1995); Trapp (1995).

multi-layered and ambiguous implications of the ending may fruitfully be compared with those of the *Borystheniticus*.[30]

## 3 Problems of Interpretation

All the interpretative problems interrelate but it is formally convenient to take them one by one.[31]

1. Is Charidemus a real person (so von Arnim, Wilhelm, and Jones;[32] *contra*, Bowie and Giner Soria)? Failing cogent epigraphic attestation,[33] the question is formally unresolvable but it remains crucial. Dio had pupils; on the other hand, he is adept at creating fictional situations for the exposition of philosophical doctrine (*Euboicus*, the μῦθος/λόγος section of the first *Kingship Oration*, etc.). The circumstantiality of the introduction could point towards truth or fiction: is it, like, say, that of the *Symposium*, so elaborate and so emblematic of wider themes as to convey its own artifice? The chances of Charidemus' reality would increase were there a significant disparity, whether philosophical or literary, between his exposition and Dio's own writings (as von Arnim, Nilsson, and Desideri believe there to be).

2. Is there then such a significant disparity? The answer is two-fold: if there is a disparity, it need not be significant (Charidemus expounds but rejects the Orphic account) and there is no real disparity in other respects, as the broadly Stoic colour of the 'worker of the land' section itself suffices to show[34] (there are obvious possible parallels with *Olympicus*, *Borystheniticus*, etc.).

3. Is Charidemus' work the transcript of the independent work that it purports to be? This already looks unlikely, and modern interpretations of parallels such as *Menexenus* and *Symposium* discourage such a simple reading, as do the intricate links between [[200]] Charidemus' work and the dialogue frame and the correspondence between Charidemus' work and Socrates' last words.

The ground is cleared for a return to the question of Charidemus' reality with probability already against it. Clearly, 'Charidemus' is a significant name, whose associations of pleasure, joy, grace, etc., suit his adoption of the most

---

30  Russell (1992) 22–3; Moles (1995) 188–92 {above, pp. 198–202}.
31  Cohoon II.395–8 and Menchelli (1997) 67–73 usefully survey the problems.
32  Jones (1978) 135.
33  Ewen Bowie once (letter 27/8/80) alerted me to *IGR* IV.1: K. Lollios Charidemos, who died aged 20 in Tenedos, a σοφιστής from Byzantium: coincidence, I think, especially as the Dionian Charidemus was 22 (6).
34  Wilhelm (1918) 364 well adduces parallels both philosophical and literary with Dio's works.

optimistic account of the human condition, where man and god can interact with reciprocal χάρις.[35] Such a person brings joy to his δῆμος: his particular δῆμος, the δῆμος of Greece and the human race within the κόσμος. The name-play plus the extensive imitation of the *Phaedo* discourages taking 'Charidemus' at face value. Subtleties in the text reinforce this, as we shall see in connection with the next problem.

4. Should we identify the figures of the 'beggar', the 'certain difficult-to-please man, who had suffered many things in his life and only late had attained true education', and 'the worker of the land' with specific philosophers? Thus Dümmler, Hagen, and Sonny thought the difficult-to-please man might be Antisthenes, late convert to philosophy and gloomy Cynic πόνος type, while for the 'worker of the land', Dümmler suggested Bion (who certainly used the symposium analogy (F 68 Kindstrand)) and Sonny suggested Cleanthes, who made a living by watering a garden and digging earth (D.L. 7.168, 169, 171) and famously hymned Zeus. In this vein one might also hazard Musonius, Dio's revered teacher and proponent of the simple country life.[36]

But is the quest for specific identifications right? It is true that Charidemus encourages the idea, not only by the mention of these various figures and their differentiation but also by the seemingly rather banal gloss at 26 on divine colonisation. Nor is it an objection that Charidemus in the early second century AD would be listening to philosophers of hundreds of years before: this is the timeless world of myth and such direct contact with earlier generations would reinforce the idea that choice of philosophical belief is much affected by individual personality. There is also the Stoic–Epicurean distinction in the third μῦθος. But that is much more broad-brush. The gloss could be an ironic allusion to pedestrian scholarly exegesis of a text, conveying a sophisticated double-edged irony: the reference [[201]] being primarily to Dio's own exegesis of the second account but secondarily to *our* exegesis of Dio.[37] Moreover, the text sometimes blurs who says what when. Chapters 10–24 mostly use ὅτι followed by accusative and infinitives, focalised by the difficult-to-please man and the beggar, with some harmless glosses by Charidemus, but 16 and 24 use straight indicatives: focalised by whom? The end of 19 is ὑπὲρ ὧν αὖθις λέξομεν: who sees, who speaks? Certainly not the difficult-to-please man. Moreover, while the beginning of the digression containing the teaching of the beggar is clearly

---

35   Cf. 3 (χαρίεντα), 10 (first λόγος not χαριείς), 41 (gods' χάρις); other 'pleasure'/'displeasure' words then become relevant too.

36   Musonius' influence on central aspects of Dio's thought is rightly stressed by Brunt (1973); Russell (1992) 4, and Brenk (2000) 262–4.

37   I suspect anyway neat reversal of Plat. *Symp.* 193a2: 'but now, because of our wickedness, we have been de-settled by god, like the Arcadians by the Spartans'.

marked, its ending is not, and 20–4 on the file of reason can hardly constitute a genuinely independent element: are the beggar and the difficult-to-please man therefore in some sense the same?[38] Again, Dio says of Charidemus (7): 'I do not yearn to know his style so much as his meaning'; Charidemus says (25): 'There is another account better than that, which I will say much more enthusiastically. I [first-person singular] heard it from a worker of the land in country rhythm and song; but perhaps I/we [first-person plural] do not need to imitate *that*: rather I/we shall try to recall his meaning.'[39] Who speaks? In the worker of the land's second song, 39 to the end uses straight indicatives. At the end Dio cannot adequately console the bereaved father and brother; but Charidemus' work was a consolation: was Dio, then, the real speaker?

The question of specific philosophical identities also involves the question of Dio's sources: are the various suggested identities likely sources for their respective sections, or are there other more plausible sources? The latter conclusion would tend against specific philosophical identities.

Wilhelm argued forcefully for overriding (though not exclusive) Posidonian influence. While some Posidonian influence remains likely,[40] more important are Dio's direct use of the *Phaedo* and of the *Republic*[41] in the first account and (I believe) of the *Symposium* ⟦202⟧ in all three accounts.[42] Most of the rest of the material could readily have been composed by anyone familiar (as Dio certainly was) with the comparison of the world to a feast or symposium and with standard arguments for and against design in the universe.

Platonic parallels, as nowadays read, also tell against the search for specific philosophical identities in such elusive figures. It is primarily their thematic functions that matter. Thus the beggar and worker of the land appropriately voice 'country wisdom' (cf. Diotima in the *Symposium* or the Arcadian shepherdess of Dio's first *Kingship Oration*), here reinforcing the damning portrayal of the great of this world, and the worker of the land naturally knows most about the physical world. The character of the spokesmen also underpins the link between personality/experience and choice of belief: the man who has

---

38    Cohoon II.396–7.
39    On the possible interaction of Δία, Δίων, and διάνοια see n. 17.
40    Mainstream modern scholarship has rejected elaborate earlier reconstructions of Posidonian material based on extensive *Quellenforschung* in favour of austere concentration on attested fragments (notably Edelstein–Kidd [1972] and Kidd [1988] and [1996] 1232). Wilhelm (1918) remains, however, a good example of the earlier approach, with some challenging detail (e.g., that both Posidonius and Dio use ἑστιάτωρ in the extremely rare sense of 'guest' rather than 'host').
41    Trapp (2000) 223–5.
42    Trapp notes other Platonic traces: (2000) 224 n. 32.

suffered much naturally goes for the account which most emphasises and least palliates suffering; as 'difficult-to-please', he is the opposite of the elect with whom God 'is pleased'. And the expression of philosophical doctrine through the mouths of representative figures helps to create that sense of distancing irony with which one must advance and regard myths about ultimate realities; irony that is explicit, for example, at 30.

Yet if the quest for specific philosophical identities is misconceived and thematic functions preponderate, the various figures may still be given identifying characters of a different kind. The beggar, author of part or whole of the first account, recalls the 'vagabond' Orphic priests (ἀγύρται) of *Republic* 2, 364b,[43] thereby 'signing' the Orphic/*Phaedo* provenance of that account, and when Charidemus retails the Orphic account he may appropriately characterise himself as 'child of a beggar'[44] (with another allusion to the *Symposium*'s idea of 'literary paternity'). Similarly, the worker of the land might evoke Hesiod, since the worker's 'rustic' songs contain many elements which could be regarded as Stoic interpretation of Hesiodic material.[45] An implicit appeal to Hesiod's poetic authority would nicely balance the initial explicit appeal to Homer (8).

The Loeb editor, Cohoon, however, had already made a more radical suggestion which showed a fine feeling for Dio's distinctive thought world[46] (even if the terms in which Cohoon formulated the [[203]] suggestion were too straightforwardly biographical). The suggestion, which falls somewhere in the middle of specific philosophical identities, generalised representative figures, and literary identifications, was that the beggar and the difficult-to-please man recall Dio himself and that Charidemus' work reflects Dio's own religious odyssey (real or alleged). This is surely right. The intensity of Dio's self-projection in other pieces marks the allusion to the difficult-to-please man who had suffered many things in his life and only late had gained true education as typically self-referential: beggary, suffering (the exile), the celebrated late conversion to philosophy (a construct for which Dio himself bears the ultimate responsibility).[47] Closely parallel passages are *Or.* 1.9: 'a wandering man and working in wisdom by myself, rejoicing for the most part as far as I can in labours and works, and uttering words for the sake of exhortation to myself and to those others whom I periodically encounter' and *Or.* 12.51 (on the effect of Zeus' statue at Olympia) 'of humans, whoever ... altogether labouring

---

43  Noted by Trapp (2000) 225 n. 33.
44  Cf. n. 14.
45  So Malcolm Schofield in conversation.
46  Cohoon II.396–8, followed by Moles (1978) 95 {above, p. 50} and n. 134.
47  Self-projection and conversion: Moles (1978).

in soul, having endured in life many disasters and griefs, not even wrapping himself in sweet sleep, even he, I think, standing before this image [as Dio was when delivering the *Olympicus*], would forget all the terrible and difficult things which occur for suffering in human life'. Moreover, in the first *Kingship Oration* (50) Dio describes himself during the exile period as, precisely, an ἀγύρτης. Within this sort of scenario he could also be dubbed a worker of the land.[48] All this would make 23 (on the beggar's 'manly' follow-through of the chain imagery) ironically self-referential in a literary sense, but this is a bonus, not a difficulty.

In the context of Charidemus' work the self-allusion suggests a move from Cynic pessimism to Stoic optimism (*mutatis mutandis* this can be paralleled elsewhere in Dio, e.g., in the aforementioned first *Kingship Oration*). The immodesty of such self-allusion would be characteristically Dionian and equally characteristically the self-allusion would not be merely immodest: Dio the seemingly external figure offers a paradigm of great internal relevance to the progression of the moral argument. The same is true in (e.g.) *Euboicus* and the first and fourth *Kingship Orations*.[49] The illogicality of Charidemus, ⟦204⟧ Dio's pupil, referring to Dio in this way is no objection, for, as we have seen, mythical time is not diachronic and the voice of 'Charidemus' is not univocal. Dio's own philosophical progression (real or alleged) powerfully underpins the cumulative and progressive persuasiveness of Charidemus' case. Cohoon also suggests, with some plausibility, that the lingering emphasis in 16–end on the long-lasting effects of disease glosses Dio's own experience.[50] This again puts Dio inside the Charidemus section.

5. How can Charidemus say that the Orphic account was given by a difficult-to-please man who had suffered much and only late attained true education and *then* claim that that account is not true and that there is another better account? There are two answers. First, there is truth and truth: the coda to the pessimistic Orphic account—the section on the file that is reason and on the gods' freeing of the virtuous and wise—adumbrates the fuller, more joyous, union of god and man promised by the worker of the land in 44; even the most pessimistic account gropes towards the truth. Secondly, since the description of the difficult-to-please man reflects the entire philosophical progression of Dio himself, the writer of the dialogue, the true education is represented not

---

48  Cf. Philostr. *VS* 488 (with Moles [1978] 95 {above, p. 50}) on Dio's alleged way of life during the exile.
49  *Euboicus*: Moles (1995) 179–80 {above, pp. 189–91}; first *Kingship Oration*: Moles (1990) 310–12, 319–29 {above, pp. 125–8, 135–46}; the fourth: Moles (1990) 348–9 {above, pp. 164–6}.
50  The emphasis is characteristic: Moles (1978) 95 {above, p. 50}.

by the Orphic account but by the conclusion of Charidemus' work, the Stoic affirmation of God's goodness and man's potential for virtue and happiness.

## 4 The Dionian *Charidemus*

The presence of Dio's philosophical progression in the text makes it reasonable to hypothesise another connection with Dio's life. This hypothesis has already been published by Ewen Bowie[51] but merits full-scale, if to some extent speculative, development.

The *Charidemus* looks like a late work: Dio is the great philosopher, widely so recognised, he has a pupil, who died aged 22. He alludes elliptically to his celebrated, if fraudulent, conversion. In ⟦205⟧ his late post-exilic phase Dio was old (60 or more) and sick (cf. 16). Like the difficult-to-please man he had suffered many λῦπαι. Despite everything, he maintained his Stoic belief in divine goodness and providence and man's capacity for virtue and happiness (*Olympicus, Borystheniticus*). In, or before, 110 his wife and one of his (probably two) sons died (Plin. *Ep.* 10.81–2). We do not *know* that this was the son who had been an archon in Prusa in 102 (*Or.* 50.2), that is, that son, then over 30, in whom Dio had had such great hopes and whose nature and virtue he claimed as equal to his own (*Or.* 40.2), but, for reasons that will emerge, we may strongly suspect it. Disdaining the Roman imperial cult, Dio buried his wife and son in a building beside a statue of Trajan (Plin. loc. cit.). To commemorate and eulogise his son and to console himself he wrote the *Charidemus*, which was one of his last works. But as a fundamentally good man (for so I increasingly believe), he wished to help others as well as himself (to 'leave something behind'), hence he tried to transmute his personal grief into a universalising exploration and explanation of the human condition in all its suffering in the shape of a literary work whose imaginative creativity and interpretative complexity would give pleasure as well as comfort, pleasure, indeed, that would itself reinforce the case for a fundamentally optimistic reading of life.

Thus the *Charidemus* is at once intensely personal *and* universalising and objective, and it is this doubleness of perspective which gives it its special poignancy and explains some otherwise puzzling emphases. On the one hand

---

51  Bowie (1985) 671: 'if Charidemus is fictitious, we may suspect that the tender pathos of the introduction derives its power from the attested early death of Dio's own son'. My battered second volume of the Loeb Dio has a pencilled 'Dio as father!?!' on p. 401, a scholion inserted on a Skopelos beach in August 1976, but neither Ewen nor I can remember who first advanced the hypothesis in our conversations about Dio in the 1970s.

are Dio's externalness and the transformation of his son into a μειράκιον of 22, poised between youthful promise and mature fulfilment, the extreme untimeliness of whose death maximises the pain of loss and poses the theoretical question of human suffering in its acutest form, but whose fictional name offers true hope.

On the other hand are Dio's intense internalness and the hints that he is suffering like a peculiarly close member of the family: 'I think that I myself was not much less pained than you; for to say "more pained" would not be right or proper for me, if someone loved him more than you, his father and brother did' (2); or at the end (45): 'I for my part do not know how to console you, bereft of such a man, so as not to bear it hard; for I am not able sufficiently to console myself for the present. You, Timarchus, alone can lighten the burden of this father'. 'This father': in a work so skilful in its blurring of focalisation, this father can also be Dio. So, too, [[206]] the dying Charidemus' anxiety to leave a message for Dio and his self-characterisation as 'child of a beggar' (20); the persistent (and not very Stoic) concern of the λόγοι with the possibility of immortality for the virtuous;[52] and the final inability of Charidemus' work to provide complete philosophical consolation; instead, the consolations of family and kinship, even if kinship reinforced by kinship in virtue. Thus Dio the philosopher sought ultimate consolation in his surviving son, who he hoped would fulfil the promise of the dead one. There is some move from philosophy to life, though philosophy is not abandoned.

On this hypothesis, Charidemus must be Dio's elder son, who must have died when Dio was away from Prusa, hence Dio's absence from the death-bed of 'Charidemus', a circumstance which must greatly have increased Dio's distress. Timarchus son must represent Dio's younger son. Charidemus: a significant name; Dio, too, a significant name. Why 'Timarchus' father and son? It would help if an inscription turned up showing that Dio's second son was called Dion;[53] other than that, Charidemus obviously needs a dramatic father; and since as a μειράκιον he can hardly have a legitimate son of his own, a younger brother is the next best thing; in terms of the 'logic' of the *logoi* it is important that he should have a διάδοχος of some kind, but this younger brother is also Dio's younger son, Dio's sole remaining genetic διάδοχος. Hence, just as Timarchus son is both a literal and a philosophical child, so 'Charidemus' is both the work of that name which is one of Dio's philosophical children and the literal son whom he had lost (doubly therefore 'child of a beggar'). The

---

52  This is insufficiently explained by Socrates' arguments in the *Phaedo* for the immortality of the soul, especially given *Charidemus*' restriction of immortality to the virtuous.
53  But cf. Salmeri (2000) 89 n. 176.

*Symposium* again underpins the implicit argument. Timarchus the father also of course (!) represents Dio the father of two sons. All this might seem to make the *Charidemus* like a 'soap' which has spiralled into absurdity under the progressive revelation of ever less plausible personal and family relationships. But such fusion/confusion of roles is not self-confuting:[54] witness the first *Kingship Oration*, the *Olympicus*—or the *Aeneid*.

As for the name *Timarchus*, Timarchus father tells Dio at the beginning (4): 'Charidemus seemed to me to προτιμᾶν [to honour more or before] you even before me, his father, not only before other [[207]] people ... and he did this till the very end'. Dio at the beginning and end of the work; at the beginning and end of Charidemus' life; Dio the philosophical beginning, the philosophical ruler, the philosophical writer, the genetic beginner of his own son. Dio, but also Zeus (Δία/Δίων): in a Stoic κόσμος Zeus is 'author' of *everything*. But Dio himself is also a 'Timarchus', because he Dio, philosophical ἄρχων, genetic and philosophical son of Zeus, *honours* the rule of the gods (27 ἄρχοντας). Gods and men are kin; the gods inevitably superior; human beings akin to one another in the shared kinship of humankind may also be akin in the genetic kinship of families; they should strive to promote the kinship of virtue which will maximise their shared kinship with God. Within these interlocking relationships, both horizontal and vertical, Dio is the great mediator (Δίων/Δία).[55] As always, his arrogance is superb (it is one of his most attractive qualities), but this arrogance also subserves the need to establish the essential relationships between man and God and to activate the links between them. And the arrogance is also tempered by the grief of a father for his son and by the larger allegorical implications.

Thus the hypothesis that Dio wrote the *Charidemus* in response to the death of his son is not simply an interesting external factor which might help to explain the work's intensity: the death of his son is inscribed in the text.

Such an allegorical interpretation does not restrict these allegorical figures to the personal and individual: they are all also generalised allegorical figures representing different aspects of a positive human response to God. Dio is also the representative of Zeus; Charidemus is also simultaneously Charidemus, a dramatic character in a Platonic dialogue; a latter-day Socrates; the messenger between god and man; 'Everyman'; Timarchus is also the honourer of ἀρχή in various senses. And given the general influence of the *Symposium* on the *Charidemus*, the names *Dio* and *Timarchus* must also be fragmentations of *Dio-tima*: this further name-play signalling not only the influence of the

---

54   Moles (1995) 183 {above, p. 194} n. 23.
55   Cf. also n. 17.

*Symposium* but the divine authority and the thoroughgoing piety of Dio's great text.

Yet the identification of Dio as the real grieving father at the end of the work enormously enhances its emotional power. Ideally, we should accept the optimistic Stoic account of the human condition, [[208]] but for real-life suffering humans the practical implementation of that account remains fitful and problematic. Even Dio, the great philosopher, the representative of Zeus, the almost mythic figure, whose philosophical biography underpins Charidemus' progressive exposition, even this Dio must suffer loss and pain like any human being, must find them hard to bear, yet strive to endure. Nowhere did Dio, master of the art, create a more persuasive or moving *persona* or ἦθος than at the end of the *Charidemus* and it is persuasive and moving precisely because it is true.[56] And when Dio wrote of the inheritance of Timarchus the son and the future death of Timarchus the father, he must have been conscious that his own death was near at hand. Thus Charidemus also represents Dio himself, 'father' of the discourse, and we, its readers, are his 'children', challenged as he himself is in the outer text, to translate philosophical text into moral reality in our own lives.

There is, however, another, intensely humanising, factor in play.[57] Though the ending suggests some philosophical failure, there is also a sense that such λύπη is natural and to a degree justifiable. For at the start of the work, which, as we have seen, rings with the end, the Opuntian's[58] cold reaction to the loss of his son, who is like Charidemus in being both χαρίεις and κόμψος, is roundly condemned. That is the sort of reaction commended by Dio's steely fellow-Stoic Epictetus.[59] Thus on another level, Dio moves away from the austerities of orthodox Stoicism to a more practical and humane Panaetianism. The travel imagery of 45–6 glosses Panaetian προκοπή (moral 'progress'), which is intrinsically ambiguous: alike formally second best to full Stoic σοφία and the real moral locus of life. Earlier ideas in the text, for example that different personalities accept different doctrines and that individual nature produces different behaviour, and the appeal to τὸ πρέπον (25) help to put Panaetius potentially in the frame from the very beginning. So if the ending exhorts us

---

56 This principle is sometimes recognised in ancient literary criticism, e.g. Arist. *Poet.* 9, 1451b16.
57 The *Charidemus* is one of several Dionian works which challenge the judgement of Jones (1978) 130 that 'Dio was not by nature warm or sympathetic'.
58 Donald Russell finds the text's allusion to τοῦτον τὸν Ὀπούντιον (3) problematic; but if so, it is problematic irrespective of the authorship of the *Charidemus*, and in any case it is explicable as the sort of studiedly untidy detail which promotes realism.
59 E.g., 3.24.85–6; 4.1.107, 111; *Ench.* 3.11.

to translate philosophical text into moral reality, there is some doubt about which text we should be reading, that [[209]] which expounds Stoic perfectionism or that which gives full dignity to the moral struggle. This, I repeat, is a wonderfully rich ending to what is surely a great work.

There is yet another aspect to the work's moral integrity. Dio was for decades the friend and adviser of powerful Romans, perhaps even of Roman emperors,[60] and his attitude to Roman power has been much discussed, not least in Simon Swain's magisterial recent study.[61] It might seem eccentric to canvass this question here. But the *Charidemus* is at once a universalising text, concerned with the whole human condition, so that worldly power inevitably comes into the theoretical frame, and an intensely personal text, which should give us access to what Dio 'really thought'. But the text is solidly Greek and when Dio reflects on what Charidemus might have achieved, it is in the context of his city or all Greece; yet Charidemus was going greatly to surpass the men of his generation, which must include non-Greeks (45 ~ 3). Moreover, the third account registers sharp contempt for worldly power and imperial struggles (35 [allegorised]). Thus in the time of his grief for his son Dio felt nothing for the Roman Empire and rejected its militaristic ethos, and he implicitly commended these attitudes to his readers (Roman as well as Greek).

∙ ∙ ∙

On this analysis the *Charidemus* is as good as anything that Dio wrote, in fact very much better than most of Dio's surviving works (at least as preserved):[62] it is of the same calibre as the first, second, and fourth *Kingship Orations*, the *Euboicus*, the *Olympicus*, and the *Borystheniticus*, the works on which Dio's claims to greatness, or sublimity, rest. Indeed, to my taste, in its sheer courage, its philosophical grip, its generalising power, and its literary virtuosity, the piece surpasses Plutarch's acclaimed *Consolation to his Wife*. Clearly, the *Charidemus* is by someone very familiar with Dio's works, with his ways of thinking, with his manner of self-projection, which is at once brash and subtle, and with the complex riches of his literary technique. It is far superior to anything produced by Favorinus, whose imitations of Dio in *Orr.* 37 and 64 are flat indeed. If it is [[210]] by a pupil, we have a single work of supreme quality by a pupil extremely close to Dio of whom we otherwise know nothing. The very

---

60  I do not accept the determined minimalism of Sidebottom (1996).
61  Swain (1996) 187–241.
62  For of course the relationship between the text as transmitted and 'the original(s)' is often particularly problematic in Dio.

possibility seems remote. But in any case, the view that the *Charidemus* may be spurious rests on a simple misconception, for neither of the two great scholars cited in favour of this view, von Arnim and Nilsson (who in fact merely follows von Arnim), denied that Dio wrote the frame of the work; they claimed only the independence of Charidemus' putative contribution. But that claim is, as we have seen, untenable, indeed quite naïve. Yet the *Charidemus* as a whole is anything but naïve.

Let us then unreservedly welcome the *Charidemus* back into the canon of Dio's works and salute its greatness: its immense literary resource, its profound philosophical seriousness, and its deep humanity.

## Bibliography

Anderson, G. (2000) 'Some Uses of Story-Telling in Dio', in Swain (2000) 143–60.
von Arnim, H. (1898) *Leben und Werke des Dio von Prusa* (Berlin).
Bowie, E. L. (1985) 'Dio of Prusa', in P. E. Easterling and B. M. W. Knox, edd. *The Cambridge History of Classical Literature: I. Greek Literature* (Cambridge) 669–72.
Brenk, F. E. (2000) 'Dio on the Simple and Self-sufficient Life', in Swain (2000) 261–78.
Brunt, P. A. (1973) 'Aspects of the Social Thought of Dio Chrysostom and the Stoics', *PCPhS* 199: 9–33; repr. in id., *Studies in Stoicism*, edd. M. Griffin and A. Samuels (Oxford, 2013) 151–79.
Desideri, P. (1978) *Dione di Prusa: un intelletuale greco nell'impero romano* (Messina/Florence).
Edelstein, L. and I. G. Kidd, edd. (1972) *Posidonius, I: the Fragments* (Cambridge; ²1989).
Giner Soria, M. C. (1990–1) 'Anotaciones a un dialogo consolatorio', *Faventia* 12–13: 293–305.
Hirzel, R. (1895) *Der Dialog*, 2 vols. (Leipzig).
Innes, D. C., H. Hine, and C. Pelling, edd. (1995) *Ethics and Rhetoric: Classical Essays for Donald Russell on his Seventy-fifth Birthday* (Oxford).
Jones, C. P. (1978) *The Roman World of Dio Chrysostom* (Cambridge, Mass. and London).
Kassel, R. (1958) *Untersuchungen zur griechischen und römischen Konsolationsliteratur* (Munich).
Kidd, I. G. (1988) *Posidonius, II: the Commentary*, 2 vols. (Cambridge).
Kidd, I. G. (1996) 'Posidonius', $OCD^3$ 1231–3.
Meiser, C. (1912) 'Über den Charidemos des Dion von Prusa', *SBBay.Akad.Wiss.* Jg. 1912, Abh. 3.
Menchelli, M. (1997) 'La morte del filosofo o il filosofo di fronte alla morte: ἐπιείκεια e πραότης nel discorso XXX di Dione di Prusa', *SIFC* 15: 65–80.

Menchelli, M. (1999) *Dione di Prusa: Caridemo (Or. XXX): testo critico, introduzione, traduzione e commenta* (Naples).

Moles, J. L. (1978) 'The Career and Conversion of Dio Chrysostom', *JHS* 98: 79–100 [above, Ch. 1].

Moles, J. L. (1990) 'The Kingship Orations of Dio Chrysostom', *PLLS* 6: 297–375 [above, Ch. 5].

Moles, J. L. (1995) 'Dio Chrysostom, Greece, and Rome', in Innes–Hine–Pelling (1995) 177–92 [above, Ch. 7].

Nilsson, M. P. (1961) *Geschichte der griechischen Religion*, $II^2$ (Munich).

Russell, D. A., ed. (1992) *Dio Chrysostom: Orations VII, XII, XXXVI* (Cambridge).

Saïd, S. (2000) 'Dio's Use of Mythology', in Swain (2000) 161–86.

Salmeri, G. (2000) 'Dio, Rome, and the Civic Life of Asia Minor', in Swain (2000) 53–92.

Schofield, M. (1991) *The Stoic Idea of the City* (Cambridge).

Sidebottom, H. (1996) 'Dio of Prusa and the Flavian Dynasty', *CQ* 46: 447–56.

Swain, S. (1996) *Hellenism and Empire: Language, Classicism, and Power in the Greek World, AD 50–250* (Oxford).

Swain, S., ed. (2000) *Dio Chrysostom: Politics, Letters, and Philosophy* (Oxford).

Trapp, M. B. (1995) 'Sense of Place in the Orations of Dio Chrysostom', in Innes–Hine–Pelling (1995) 163–75.

Trapp, M. B. (2000) 'Plato in Dio', in Swain (2000) 213–39.

Wilhelm, F. (1918) 'Zu Dion Chrys. Or. 30 (Charidemos)', *Philologus* 75: 364–83.

CHAPTER 9

# Dio and Trajan

In the ancient world, the paradigm of the philosophical counsellor of kings goes back to the very beginnings of Greek literature.* In Homer's *Iliad*, the old Nestor (himself, as it happens, a king) acts—or tries to act—as the counsellor of the hot-headed Achilles (another king) and of Agamemnon (the chief king). In the fifth-century historian Herodotus, Solon, one of the canonical 'Seven Wise Men', adopts a similar role in relation to Croesus, king (or tyrant) of Lydia (1.27–33), though Solon's role also has elements of a related type (also already found in Homer and tragedy): that of the wise warner.

These literary examples had their counterparts in real life. The great philosopher Plato attempted to turn Dionysius the Younger, tyrant of Syracuse, into a philosopher-king, and, although he failed, his attempt proved enormously influential upon subsequent philosophers. Kings certainly might honour philosophers: Archelaus invited Socrates to Macedonia, Philip entrusted the education of Alexander to Aristotle, Antigonus Gonatas had several philosophers at his court. Naturally, the relationship between philosophers and kings could be hostile, because some philosophers rejected the very notion of worldly kingship (Diogenes the Cynic abused Philip of Macedon) and some kings degenerated into tyrants (Alexander the Great executed Aristotle's nephew Callisthenes).

These various Greek models were played out equally in the Roman world, of course with especial intensity once the Republic was superseded by the effective monarchy of the Empire. Cicero envisioned for himself the role of counsellor of Pompey the Great and Seneca tried to philosophise the emperor Nero; Augustus honoured Areius of Alexandria. From the time of the Late Republic many leading Roman politicians (Lucullus, Cicero, Brutus, and Cassius among them) were pupils (in some sense) of philosophers. Yet under certain Roman emperors (the 'good' Vespasian as much as the tyrannical Nero and Domitian) friction between philosophers and rulers was considerable, whether because of Cynic abuse of kings or for other reasons, and there were sometimes mass expulsions of philosophers from Rome and Italy. The relationship between philosophers and the powerful was complicated by a factor not generally present

---

\* Versions of this paper were delivered to the International Plutarch Society in Chapel Hill on 25th June, 2000, and at the Mannheim conference on 30 April, 2001; I am extremely grateful to Professor Kai Brodersen for all his kindness, and Karen Piepenbrink for the translation of the paper {into German}.

in the Greek world: that of racial and cultural difference, for most philosophers in the Roman world were not Roman but Greek.[1]

At all times in the Greek and Roman worlds the real influence of philosophers and philosophy upon men of power is debatable: that there was sometimes real influence can hardly be denied (in the case of Brutus and Cassius, for example, as they debated the ethics of the assassination of Julius Caesar, or of the Stoic emperor Marcus Aurelius). Yet Seneca's pedagogic success with Nero was lamentably short-lived. Equally, the sincerity of philosophers in their formal attempts to influence kings could sometimes be doubted, and, as some philosophers combined other roles, it is not always clear—where there is no direct evidence—that their relations with men of power should be classified as primarily philosophical.[2]

As is well known, the ancient tradition continues into the modern era: witness the repeated attempts (however self-deluding) by Great Britain to play the role of Athens to the United States' Sparta as evidenced, for example, by the counselling role of Harold MacMillan in relation to John F. Kennedy or, today, of Tony Blair in relation to George W. Bush. No doubt, the tradition has always been a comforting one for intellectuals, who consequently celebrate it: as the writer of the second Platonic letter (not in fact Plato) puts it (310eff.), 'it is natural for wisdom and great power to associate together and they are forever pursuing and seeking each other and consorting together. Moreover, these are things which people delight in discussing themselves in private conversations and hearing discussed in poems'.

Within the whole ancient tradition, a particularly controversial figure is the Greek Dio of Prusa (*c.* AD 40/45–*c.*115), alike sophist, philosopher, literary critic, and local and perhaps also imperial politician.[3] For Dio's varied corpus includes four speeches on kingship; two of these (I and III) are formally addressed to an unnamed Roman emperor; the other two are in dialogue form: II a dialogue between Philip of Macedon and the young Alexander, IV a dialogue between Diogenes and Alexander. In recent years, these speeches have stimulated lively

---

1 Of course, these terms are themselves not necessarily unproblematic in the Empire, when some of the Greek philosophers themselves were Roman citizens: see below, §§2 and 3.
2 Out of a huge bibliography on these matters I cite a tiny representative selection: Goodenough (1928); Bischoff (1932); Lattimore (1939); Toynbee (1944); Höistad (1948); Brunt (1975); Griffin (1976); Wistrand (1979); Schofield (1986); Hahn (1989); Rawson (1989); Erskine (1990); MacMullen (1966); Sedley (1997); Schofield (2000b); (2000a) 446–56; Hahm (2000); Atkins (2000) 503–14; Gill (2000); Moles (1995a); (2000); Whitmarsh (2001a); (2001b) 134–246 (with useful bibliographies on 181–2 n. 3 and 184–5 n. 15).
3 Fundamental treatments: von Arnim (1898); Desideri (1978); C. P. Jones (1978); Moles (1978); Swain (1996) 187–241; (2000).

debate: were they delivered to Trajan,[4] or were they designed for performance in the Greek world, or both? Are they serious works of political morality, mere specimens of court flattery, or demonstrations to Greek audiences of the superiority of Greek culture to Roman or of the need to civilise Roman power with Greek culture?

The present paper is concerned with some of the contributions to this recent debate, with the methodological issues that they raise, and with the rich variety of interpretative questions that they also raise: concerning the relationships between texts and contexts, between primary and secondary audiences and between philosophical and sophistic writings; the possibility of different meanings for different audiences; the processes of reading Dio; of reading Philostratus, himself both a sophist and a biographer of sophists (including Dio); and of reading Philostratus reading Dio; the role of παιδεία ('education', 'culture', 'civilisation')[5] in the so-called 'Second Sophistic';[6] the figure of the Greek philosophical counsellor; Graeco-Roman relations; and Dio's ethnicity. This very variety attests the richness of the best of the literature of the Second Sophistic period. Of the methodological issues, the most crucial is the validity of the so-called 'cumulative argument', a type of argument which one is bound to employ in contexts where evidence is scarce (if, that is, one wants to say anything positive) but which is necessarily vulnerable to attack from sceptically-minded scholars. The paper is arranged in the following sections:

1. Dio's early Roman connections
2. Alternative perspectives on Dio and Trajan: the Roman imperial perspective and that of Philostratus
3. Dio's ethnicity
4. The Kingship Speeches: a distinctively Greek perspective?
5. The Kingship Speeches: conclusions.

This arrangement is itself designed to mount what I hope will constitute a convincing cumulative argument.

---

4  For a preliminary defence of the case for delivery see Moles (1983); (1990) 366 {= above, p. 114} n. 15.

5  Some recent discussions of this defining Greek concept: Reardon (1971) 3–11; Bowie (1970); Swain (1996) 18–64; Schmitz (1997); Whitmarsh (1998); (2001b) 5–9; 15–38 and *passim*; see also below, §§2 and 3.

6  This controversial term, which derives from Philostratus, *VS* 2.27 (481) and 21.27 (507), remains convenient, as applied to those elements of Greek literature from *c.* AD 50–250 which were produced by sophists (itself a controversial but convenient term) or those imitating them. For recent discussion of the problematics both of the Philostratean and (the various) modern usages see Whitmarsh (2001b) 42–5, with essential bibliography.

## 1 Dio's Early Roman Connections

The *terminus post* of the kingship speeches is AD 99:[7] if Dio had high Roman status at that time, it is easier to hypothesise circumstances for the Trajanic delivery of the speeches (which is not to say that Trajanic delivery absolutely depends on his having had such status). Consequently, it becomes necessary to consider Dio's early Roman career. There are a number of key questions:

(a) Had Dio, who was born into a rich family in about 40–45 and whose maternal grandfather had been an *amicus* of Claudius,[8] close Flavian connections?
(b) How did he get his Roman citizenship?
(c) Who was the eminent Roman whose fall under Domitian caused Dio's exile?
(d) Are the *Rhodian* and *Alexandrian* orations Vespasianic?

(a) According to the modern orthodoxy established by Arnaldo Momigliano and variously developed by Paolo Desideri, C. P. Jones, John Moles, and other scholars, Dio was an *amicus* to the Roman emperor Vespasian and his envoy to the Greek east, *amicus* to Vespasian's son Titus, and *amicus* and *sumboulos* ('counsellor') of T. Flavius Sabinus, son or grandson of Vespasian's brother, whose fall in the early years of Domitian's reign caused Dio's exile.[9] This orthodoxy has, however, been vigorously attacked by Harry Sidebottom.[10] Methodological issues arise: cumulative cases, the problems of reading Philostratus—the progenitor of the modern orthodoxy—and of reading Dio, who in the *Euboicus* (7.66) boldly asserts that before his exile he 'knew the homes and tables of rich men, not only private individuals but also satraps and kings' (i.e., Roman governors and emperors).

---

7  von Arnim (1898) 402ff.; Moles (1990) 333–4 and 360–1 {above, pp. 149–51 and 176–8}; Salmeri (2000) 90–1 n. 187.
8  46.3–4; 44.5; 41.6, with von Arnim (1898) 123.
9  Momigliano (1951) 152 = (1975) II.972; (1950) 258–60; C. P. Jones (1973) 307–8; (1978) 14–17, 44–5, 123; Desideri (1978) 138–9; Moles (1978) 84–5, 93 {above, pp. 31–4, 47}; (1990) 333 {above, p. 149}; Salmeri (1982) 24–6; cf. also B. W. Jones (1990) 348, 354–7; Fein (1994) 232; Verrengia (2000) 72–4. Whether Sabinus fell in 82 or some years later is disputed: discussion in Verrengia (2000) 70 n. 16 and 76–7, rightly preferring 82, the year of Sabinus' only attested consulship.
10 Sidebottom (1996); some counter-arguments (of varying quality) in Verrengia (2000) 72–4. It is important to stress that the modern orthodoxy does not accept all the ancient links between Dio and the Flavians (few, for example, believe in 'the constitutional debate' of Philostr. *VA* 5.27–38 (discussed on p. 235).

Sidebottom's scepticism is glib. The cumulative case of which the orthodoxy necessarily consists is not invalidated by constant appeals to the primacy of 'explicit evidence' (one attempts to construct a cumulative case precisely because the 'explicit evidence' is insufficient) or to tautological minimising formulations such as 'this perhaps should not be exaggerated' (it is always wrong to exaggerate but the question always is: what constitutes exaggeration?). That the young Dio unscrupulously backed Vespasian's purge of philosophers in 71 is supported by Dio's attested works *Against the Philosophers* and *Against Musonius*,[11] and by his own slippery autobiography;[12] that Musonius, one of the leading Roman philosophers of the time, had been Dio's philosophical teacher, as Fronto says, is supported by 'Rufus' as an addressee in letters attributed to Dio, by Musonius' clear influence on Dio's thought, and even by the *Against Musonius*.[13] That the highly *engagé* Musonius knew Vespasian is very likely, and in the philosophical purges Musonius attracted individual Flavian attention.[14] Dio's early acquaintance with top-level Romans, a natural consequence of his family tradition (above), is immediately confirmed by two key relationships: his friendship with Nerva, himself a major Flavian figure, whom at the start of Trajan's reign Dio describes as his 'friend of old' (45.2); this friendship, therefore, must predate Dio's exile and extend back into the early years of the Flavian era; and his hatred of Domitian (45.1–2),[15] which seems extremely personal.[16] As for Dio's assertion in the *Euboicus*, while it is widely recognised by modern scholarship that the *narratives* of the *Euboicus* are knowingly fictional, the assertion is of a different order, for it grounds Dio's right to pronounce on these great social questions and would have been risky if false, especially since the *Euboicus* was delivered, among other places, in Rome itself.[17]

As for (b), the arguments about Dio's Roman citizenship are complex, but I think that the hypothesis that Cocceianus Dio got Roman citizenship

---

11  Moles (1978) 82, 85–7 {above, pp. 28f., 32–9}.
12  Moles (1978).
13  Fronto II.50 Haines = p. 135 van den Hout; Hercher 259; Dio 31.122; Moles (1978) 82 and 86 {above, pp. 29 and 35}; Whitmarsh (2001b) 137 n. 16, 159.
14  Cass. Dio 66.13.2; Hieron. *Chron.* p. 189 Helm.
15  Not to mention the numerous implicit (but equally hostile) allusions to Domitian in the *Kingship Orations* and in the *Diogenics* (*Orr.* 6, 8, 9, and 10).
16  On most views, 13.1 attests another relationship with an eminent Flavian: see above, (c) (p. 231).
17  Assertion: Moles (1995b) 180 {above, p. 191}; delivery in Rome: Brunt (1975) 17 {= (2013) 160}; Russell (1992) 1, 13, 139–40, 146, 156; Moles (1995b) 177 {above, p. 188}.

for himself (and perhaps also for his father) as a pay-off for the *Against the Philosophers* in 71, when his 'old friend' Cocceius Nerva was consul, remains viable.[18] If so, (b) supports Dio's Flavian connections.

As for (c), Dio writes (*Or.* 13.1):

> When it came about that I was exiled because of the friendship alleged with a man who was not of low status but very near to those who at that time were Fortune's favourites and were ruling and actually lost his life because of the very things which made him seem blessed to many men, indeed to practically everyone, that is because of his relationship and kinship with those people, this charge having been brought against me, that I was friend and counsellor to the man.

This man has traditionally been identified as T. Flavius Sabinus.[19] Sidebottom's alternative suggestion of L. Salvius Otho Cocceianus, whom, following Syme,[20] he takes to be Nerva's nephew, is derived from Philostratus *VA* 7.8, on the ground that Nerva's unhistorical exile under Domitian is based on his nephew's historical fate as Philostratus raids the life of Dio for his largely fictional *Life* of Apollonius. This is neat—but a very long shot. Equally, B. W. Jones' M. Arrecinus Clemens, executed in 93, makes Dio's exile too short.[21] *Pace* Sidebottom, Dio's wording in 13.1 clearly implies a high-up Flavian, so T. Flavius Sabinus it should be.[22] What, however, is the force of the participle 'alleged' (λεγομένης)? Is Dio denying the existence of the friendship[23] or is he simply reproducing the legal wording of the charge against him? He is certainly doing the latter,[24] but he is, I think, also casting some doubt on the friendship,

---

18 Moles (1978) 86 {above, p. 35} and n. 59 (following an original suggestion of Ewen Bowie); useful overviews of the problem in Sidebottom (1996) 453; Whitmarsh (1998) 199 n. 35 (Whitmarsh (2001b) 156 and n. 83, however, is confused); Salmeri (2000) 66–7 n. 67.
19 So first Emperius (1847), followed by, e.g., Sonny (1896) 188; von Arnim (1898) 223; Desideri (1978) 188; C. P. Jones (1978) 46; Moles (1978) 93 {above, p. 47}; Verrengia (2000) 66–77 provides a useful overview of the debate.
20 Syme (1958) II.628.
21 Sidebottom (1996) 451–3; Salmeri (2000) 62 n. 41; M. Arrecinus Clemens: B. W. Jones (1990), but Dio's exile was long (40.2, 12); cf. Sidebottom (1996) 451 n. 33, and Jones makes other errors: Verrengia (2000) 72–3.
22 The objections raised to this identification by Verrengia (2000) 76–7 are insubstantial and some indeed are met in my main text.
23 Verrengia (2000) 68 and n. 8 comes close to this interpretation.
24 Λεγομένης corresponds to δέ in the definition of the αἰτία.

not, however, in the sense that he was not in fact friends with the man, but rather that the friendship, which was on a worldly political level, was not the optimal type of friendship.[25] Thus on any identification, (c) supports Dio's close Flavian connections and all the more so, if the man is indeed Sabinus.

What of (d)? The *Rhodian* and *Alexandrian* matter because they are major political speeches about Graeco-Roman relations, some modern scholars date one or both to Vespasian's reign, and *Alexandrian* (32) 21–2, where Dio compares himself to Hermes sent by Zeus, has been read as hinting at a commission from the emperor. The arguments concerning the *Rhodian*'s date are very complex, but I think the dating of both speeches is not resolved and the imperial reading of 32.21–2, which is brusquely dismissed by Salmeri, Sidebottom, and Swain, is certainly right.[26] Sidebottom's plausible suggestion that the *Alexandrian* inspired Philostratus' fiction of Dio's presence with Vespasian at Alexandria in 69 (*VA* 5.27–40) suggests that Philostratus too read that speech in an 'imperial' way and that he might even have read it as belonging to the Vespasianic era.[27]

---

25   The sequel of the speech will redefine *philia*, *eudaimonia*, *arche*, and *sumboulia* in the terms of the true philosophical politics that Dio is trying to promote: see my forthcoming study {Moles (2005)}.

26   Momigliano (1951) 151 (Rhodian Vespasianic); C. P. Jones (1978) 133 (Rhodian Vespasianic); (1973) and (1978) 36, 39, 134 (Alexandrian Vespasianic (restated in id. [1997])), followed by Desideri (1978) 68, 110; Moles (1978) 84 {above, p. 31}; Barry (1993), esp. 99–100; dissent: Kindstrand (1978) (Alexandrian Trajanic); Salmeri (1982) 97–8 n. 30 (Alexandrian Trajanic); Sidebottom (1992) (Rhodian and Alexandrian Trajanic); Swain (1996) 428–9 (Rhodian and Alexandrian Trajanic). 32.21–2 runs: 'A god, as I said [32.12], has given me courage' (long disquisition on Hermes and Zeus follows): 'imperial reading': C. P. Jones (1973) 307; (1978) 44; Desideri (1978) 109–10; Moles (1978) 84 {above, p. 32}; B. W. Jones (1990) 355; rejected by Salmeri (1982) 92–3; (2000) 80 n. 129; Sidebottom (1996) 449; Swain (1996) 217 n. 115. But the argument goes: 32.12: Socratic *daimon*, general *pronoia* of the gods, hierarchy of gods, *sumbouloi* and listeners, supporting appeal to Alexandrian Serapis; 32.21–2: repetition of 32.12 but with more precise divine model: Hermes, unwilling, sent by Zeus; 32.25: human hierarchy, with kings on top, kings who have been deified (which helps a god/emperor equation), in opposition to tyrants (if speech Trajanic, surely an allusion to Domitian); 95–6: explicit mention of emperor and *his emissaries* (surely including Dio), with prospect of emperor himself coming (combined carrot and stick); as often, Dio's thinking is much subtler than that of some of the scholars who seek to interpret him. Note also that 1.65ff., cited by Sidebottom and Swain as counter to the 'imperial reading', actually supports it, because Dio/Hermes is there the messenger of Zeus/Nerva (Moles (1990) 324–5 {above, pp. 140–2}).

27   Sidebottom (1996) 448; Philostr. *VA* 5.24–38 (on which see p. 235).

## 2    Alternative Perspectives on Dio and Trajan: The Roman Imperial Perspective and That of Philostratus

On Domitian's assassination, then, Dio did indeed have high status in Rome. He was recalled by Nerva, though news of Nerva's death prevented his actual return.[28] Trajan's lauded 'repatriation' of philosophers and intellectuals[29] could provide a context for the kingship speeches,[30] especially since Dio led a Prusan embassy to Trajan in 100.[31] The fairly substantive parallels with Pliny's *Panegyricus* seem to support the hypothesis of an imperial initiative.[32] Thus, it seems, the imperial perspective; what of the Greek one?

Philostratus' representations of Dio both in *The Lives of the Sophists* (VS) and in the *Life of Apollonius* (VA) have been stimulatingly analysed by Tim Whitmarsh. Whitmarsh's analyses are underpinned by a theory of the role of Greek παιδεία under the Roman empire, a theory which, as we shall see, also informs his reading of the speeches. The theory goes more or less as follows:[33] in the Second Sophistic period παιδεία had distinctive importance for the construction and consolidation of Greek cultural identity (certainly among the elite) and for ideals of manhood;[34] it was not a purely 'cultural' phenomenon,[35] nor primarily a form of self-consolation by the Greeks for their political impotence under Rome,[36] nor primarily a Roman-driven strategy for appeasing the Greek elite and thereby bolstering Roman power (though the Romans did try so to use it);[37] rather, it was an expression of the power of the elite,[38] a *locus*

---

28  45.2 with Moles (1984).
29  Plin. *Paneg.* 47.1–2.
30  C. P. Jones (1978) 53; Charles-Saget (1986) 128–9; Whitmarsh (1998) 201–2 (a position Whitmarsh has now abandoned: n. 59 below).
31  40.13; C. P. Jones (1978) 52–3; Salmeri (2000) 68 n. 78.
32  C. P. Jones (1978) 118; Moles (1990) 301–2 {above, pp. 115–17}.
33  It is difficult to summarise concisely; for a first statement see Whitmarsh (1998) 196–203; for development and refinement see Whitmarsh (2001b), esp. 5–9, 15–38, 88–9, 90–130, 181–246.
34  Gleason (1995); Whitmarsh (2001b) 113–14, 148, 180, 188–9, 193–4; cf. also n. 78 below.
35  *Pace* scholars such as Bompaire (1958).
36  *Pace* Bowie (1970); Whitmarsh (2001b) 20 does, however, concede, even emphasise, that 'the Greeks and Romans themselves were the authors of the culture-power polarity … and that 'Greeks were … keen to represent themselves as lacking in power but compensating for it with *paideia*'.
37  *Pace* scholars such as C. P. Jones (1971) 43 n. 25; Swain (1996) 71–2; for some of the evidence cited see Whitmarsh (2001b) 16–17, 23–4.
38  Bowersock (1969); Schmitz (1997) 50–63; Whitmarsh (2001b) 18, 96–108; dissent: Bowie (1982).

for power struggles within the elite,[39] and a *locus* for discussion and negotiation of power relationships between Greeks and Romans,[40] performed (a key concept)[41] in such rhetorically sophisticated forms (including 'figured speech')[42] as to be comprehensible only to other *pepaideumenoi* and to allow different meanings for different readers or audiences. Thus to read power properly requires powerful readers.[43]

Whitmarsh himself then reads Philostratus both as sophisticated writer and as sophisticated reader of Dio.

Philostratus' treatment of Dio in *VS* 488 runs as follows:

> [During his exile] while he planted and dug and drew water for baths and gardens and did many works like those for a livelihood, he did not neglect serious study but sustained himself with two books; these were the *Phaedo* of Plato and Demosthenes' *On the False Embassy*. And visiting the camps in the rags he was wont to wear and seeing the soldiers rushing to revolt at Domitian's assassination, he did not spare himself when he saw the disorder that had broken out, but stripped and leaped on to a high altar and began his speech thus: 'But Odysseus of much cunning stripped himself of his rags' [*Od.* 22.1]. And having said this and having revealed himself—that he was no beggar nor the person whom they believed him to be but Dio the *sophos*—he delivered a powerful and inspired indictment of the tyrant and he taught the soldiers to have better thoughts by doing what seemed good to the Romans.[44] For indeed the persuasiveness of the man was such as to bewitch even those who did not have precise competence in Greek matters. For example, Trajan the emperor set him on the golden chariot before Rome in which the kings

---

39   Cf. Gleason (1995) xxi–xxiv; Schmitz (1997), 26–31, 97–135.
40   Cf. Whitmarsh (2001b) 66–71; 131–294. This process may involve implicit challenges to Roman power: e.g., 66–71, 141, 151, 153–5, 164–5, 178–9, or the 'message' that Roman power must submit to Greek learning/philosophy, e.g., 186, 203–4, 206, 209–14, 218.
41   E.g., Whitmarsh (2001b) 188, 248, 301.
42   That is, rhetorical speech that invites audiences/readers to uncover hidden meaning(s) beneath the surface meaning; discussions of ancient theory and practice thereof in Ahl (1984); Moles (1990) 303–5 {above, pp. 119–21}; Bartsch (1994); Whitmarsh (2001b) 33, 69–71.
43   Whitmarsh (2001b) 81–3 and 100–8 (cf. also 124–6) also stimulatingly discusses texts which construct a dialectic between such urban, sophisticated *paideia* and older, rustic, forms of *paideia*/Greekness: a collocation obviously relevant to Dio's *Kingships*, esp. the First.
44   This is the normal interpretation of the participial phrase; for Whitmarsh's alternative rendering see the main text.

celebrate their triumphs in wars and turning to Dio would often say: 'I do not know what you are saying, but I love you as myself.'

Whitmarsh's reading of this passage may be summarised as follows.[45] Philostratus emphasises Dio's role-playing.[46] The *Phaedo* and *On the False Embassy* are programmatic of Dio's performing the role of martyred champion of Greek freedom (Socrates being the great Greek philosophical martyr, Demosthenes the great martyr of Greek freedom against Macedonian tyranny). In the drama itself, when Dio reveals himself to the mutinous legions as a latter-day Odysseus, how can he be 'revealing himself', when he is actually 'revealing' one of his favourite *personae*?[47] Does *sophos* mean 'truly wise' or merely 'clever', even 'sophistic'? And is Dio disowning Domitian, tyrant over Rome, or is he latently disowning the Romans *tout court*, tyrants over Greece? When Dio shares Trajan's triumphal chariot, is his role that of slave, flatterer, or warner? Does Trajan's apparent non-comprehension reflect tyrannical failure to recognise limits, intellectual failure to cope with Dio's ingenious rhetorical sophistication, or final inability to cash out Dio's rhetorical trickiness? Was Dio still, latently, denouncing tyranny? Does Trajan realise this? Is he dissembling: for in the theatre of imperial propaganda, any 'tyrannicidal' connotations must actively be ignored? ('Figured-speech' theory allows such obfuscations.) Intrinsic to the chariot scene is its interpretative undecidability, eloquent of such writing's being a focus for power negotiations.

The most important single question about Whitmarsh's interpretation is whether the 'anti-Roman' reading is viable at all. It is adduced from the *On the False Embassy*, from pressing the relevance of the *Odyssey* quotation (because Odysseus is confronting the suitors *qua* illegitimate pretenders to Odysseus' house and land); and from a rather forced 'subversive' reading of Philostratus' gloss: whereas, as Whitmarsh admits, the overt meaning of Philostratus' gloss on Dio's behaviour is: 'he taught the soldiers to have better thoughts by doing what seemed good to the Romans' (i.e., with the participial phrase epexegetic of 'to have better thoughts'), Whitmarsh suggests the 'subversive' reading: 'he taught the soldiers who were doing what seemed good to the Romans to have better thoughts' (i.e., with the participial phrase epexegetic of 'the [mutinous] soldiers'). Nevertheless, I wonder if one of the many constituents of this

---

45   Whitmarsh (1998) 204–10, reproduced, with modifications, in (2001b) 238–44; cf. also Schmitz (1997).
46   An important element, as Whitmarsh kindly notes, of the interpretation of Dio advanced in Moles (1978).
47   Dio ~ Odysseus: Höistad (1948) 94–102; Desideri (1978) 174–5 n. 2; Jones (1978) 46–8; Moles (1978) 97 {above, p. 54}; (1990) 319 {above, p. 135}.

admittedly fictional scene is Philostratus' reading of Dio's *Olympicus*, which would help Whitmarsh's interpretation in this respect (see below, §3).

Whitmarsh is at least right that the surface unity of the chariot scene is threatened by tensions: between Roman and Greek, power and philosophy, incomprehension and intelligence, equal status and higher or lower status. So if we accept Philostratus as a powerful and critical reader of Dio, we might expect to find these tensions in the kingship speeches themselves.

Whitmarsh's analysis of Philostratus' representation of Dio in the *Life of Apollonius* may be summarised as follows.[48] Dio appears as the holy man's closest friend but also serves to accentuate Apollonius' superior virtue. Apollonius regards Dio's philosophy as too rhetorical (5.40) and surpasses Dio as principled philosopher: an impression heightened by the fact that items of Apollonius' alleged biography such as his victimisation by Domitian and his speech in favour of kingship are clearly 'borrowed' by Philostratus from Dio's biography. Apollonius, however, also has sophistic traits and this ambivalence between philosophy and sophistry, mirrored in an ambivalence in the truth claims of the text itself, reflects a similar ambivalence in Dio. The fictitious constitutional debate before Vespasian at Alexandria (5.27–38) explicitly tackles the themes of philosophical counselling of kings and of the kingship speech. Whereas the other philosophers, Dio and Euphrates, are motivated by competitiveness and jealousy, Apollonius is disinterested and high-minded, although in the event he emerges victor in the competition for philosophical authority over Vespasian. His speech in favour of kingship borrows heavily from Dio's *Kingships* (historically, delivered a generation later and addressed to a different emperor), even as the Dio of the present narrative makes a speech in favour of oligarchy. Multiple effects accrue: Apollonius 'trumps' Dio as philosophical adviser of kings; Dio's thinking on kingship is revealed to be unoriginal and derivative; Dio himself appears as fickle and opportunist, beginning his career as an exponent of oligarchy and ending it as an encomiast of kingship, having simply purloined the views of Apollonius.

This analysis is brilliantly revealing about Philostratus' literary procedures, in particular the ways in which he plays upon real or perceived ambivalences in Dio's self-representation. But for us the key question is this: does Philostratus' representation of Dio raise the possibility that Dio did not actually deliver the *Kingships* to Trajan? And the answer is: no. Questions are raised about the quality of the *Kingships*, whether they are philosophical or sophistic, whether they are original, whether Dio's motivation was virtuous or opportunist, but

---

48  Whitmarsh (2001b) 227–38. At the risk of misrepresentation and over-simplification I focus on what is strictly relevant to the theme of this paper.

all these questions rest on the assumption that Dio actually delivered the *Kingships* to Trajan.

## 3     Dio's Ethnicity[49]

Moles and Swain have shown how radical Dio's ethnicity can be, especially in three of his most serious philosophical works, all post-exile. In the *Olympicus* a Cynic Dio observes the Roman armies' preparations against the Dacians and favours freedom over imperialism. The concluding *Odyssey* quotation casts Greece as Rome's slave (a thought found elsewhere in Dio).[50] The *Borystheniticus* sharply reproves Greek cultural and political flattery of the Romans; both works pointedly avoid any analogy between the Stoic *kosmos* and the Roman empire.[51] The *Charidemus*, both inspired by and commemorative of, the untimely death of Dio's brilliant son, looks for consolation only to Greek philosophy and culture and contemns worldly power.[52]

How does this radically, even defiantly, Hellenic Dio[53] fit with the kingship speeches?

---

49      Moles (1995b); Swain (1996) 187–24; Veyne (1999); Salmeri (2000) 86–92.
50      12.16–20, esp. 20: 'to see men contending for empire and power and the others for freedom and fatherland'; 12.85 and *Od.* 24.249–50 (Odysseus to Laertes, after congratulating him on his care for his garden) 'you yourself enjoy no good care, but you bear grievous old age, you are badly unkempt and unfittingly clothed', explained by the uncited sequel (24.257): it is not because Laertes is lazy that his master has no care for him but because he is a slave; exegesis: Moles (1995b) 181–3 {above, pp. 192–4}; Swain (1996) 200–2. Note the thematic parallels with the scene at Philostr. *VS* 488 (discussed on p. 236). Greeks as slaves: 7.133–4 (with Moles (1995b) 178 {above, p. 188} n. 5); 31.125; 34.39, 51.
51      36.17: 'a philosopher would have been much pleased at the sight, because all were after the old manner, as Homer describes the Greeks, long-haired and with flowing beards, but one of them alone was shaven, and they all abused him and hated him. And he was said to practise this not randomly, but flattering the Romans and showing off his friendship with them, so that one could have seen in his case the disgrace of the activity and its unseemliness for men'; exegesis: Moles (1995b) 186–92 {above, pp. 196–202}; Swain (1996) 216; Whitmarsh's dissent ([2001b] 215) fails: though 36.17 is first focalised by the Borysthenites, it is then endorsed by Dio; avoidance of analogy: Moles (1995b) 183, 191 {above, pp. 193, 201}; Swain (1996) 203; *pace* Russell (1992) 23, 233.
52      Moles (2000) 209 {above, p. 225}.
53      Whether or not it is possible to recover Greek writers' 'real beliefs' (about Greekness or Roman power) is disputed by recent scholars: Swain (1996) 71 and 412, e.g., argues that it is possible; Whitmarsh (2001b), by contrast, emphasises that 'literature can be sophisticated, ludic, self-ironizing, and/or irresponsible' (3), denies the possibility of identifying an author's 'true' feelings and insists that 'literary texts do not provide a clear window into the souls of their authors (22), etc. (29, 30–1, 215, 222, 250). These are difficult questions; I

## 4  The Kingship Speeches: A Distinctively Greek Perspective?

That Dio addressed Trajan on kingship is, I think, certain. In one of his works Dio makes the claim explicit: 57.11 '[it would be inappropriate] if we seem to be acting inappropriately, when you wish to hear *logoi*, in now reporting the ones spoken to the emperor, as if it were indifferent to know whether they were helpful and useful, both for you and for all other people, or trivial and unhelpful'.[54] There are other speeches where the claim is clearly implicit.[55] As literary critics too blithely ignore, Dio was not only a rhetorician and a sophist: he was also a practical politician,[56] who in Prusa and other Greek cities of the East often appealed to his imperial connections.[57] Before his frequently suspicious fellow-Greeks, he could not have risked so great a claim as this if it had been a lie. But did he make more than one speech? Would more than one have strained Trajan's patience? Or do the extant speeches represent more or less what was delivered to Trajan?

Some hold that the extant speeches were not delivered to Trajan;[58] and there are cognate views, for example, that they may all have been delivered to Trajan or only the first was delivered to Trajan, but anyway they were all delivered elsewhere (whether or not as well) and exhibit a distinctively Greek perspective. On one view (Sidebottom, partially Swain) what is driving the extant speeches is Dio's need to offer Greeks an idealised representation of his relationship with Trajan;[59] on another view (Whitmarsh), it is the competitive

---

tentatively suggest a *tertium iter*: we can talk of serious attitudes that writers can adopt, propound and integrate into the overall argument of a particular speech, while recognising that they can adopt different attitudes on other occasions. Thus the characterisation 'this radically, even defiantly, Hellenic Dio' (a) acknowledges that he is not always like this, but (b) claims that this is an aspect both of his self-presentation and of his thinking in the last period of his life.

54  *Or.* 57 is a *prolalia* (preparatory speech) to a performance of one of the *Kingships*, seemingly *Or.* 2: Crosby IV.417; note Dio's claim for Trajanic delivery of a kingship speech which does not use second-person addresses. *Pace* Whitmarsh (2001b) 187, the question over which Dio is defensive is not whether the *Kingships* were delivered to Trajan but whether they are 'profitable and useful' or 'trivial and unprofitable'.

55  Viz. *Orr.* 49, 53, 54, 55 and 56 with Moles (1990) 361–3 {above, pp. 177–9} and C. P. Jones (1978) 121–2. Hence it is misleading for Sidebottom, Swain, and Whitmarsh to assert that *Or.* 57 is the *only* Dionian evidence (outside the kingship speeches) for delivery before Trajan.

56  Whitmarsh's (2001b) discussions of the *Kingships* effectively ignore this aspect of Dio.

57  Cf., e.g., his use of imperial letters at 40.5, 44.12, and 47.13.

58  E.g., Waters (1974) 237; Swain (1996) 193–4 (ambiguous); Whitmarsh (2001b) 156, 186–216, 325–7 (not without ambiguity) and cf. also n. 31 above.

59  Swain (1996) 194–5.

sophistic παιδεία of the Greek East;⁶⁰ obviously, these two views can overlap and both stress the self-justification which suffuses the speeches.

These essentially non-Roman-context readings might seem not implausible. Those versions which allow at least some Trajanic delivery adduce the notorious practice of sophists of recycling their talks. The fourth speech already has alternative endings, one as it were imperial, one not;⁶¹ as we have seen (57.11), on Dio's own evidence he delivered the speeches in the Greek east as well as before Trajan; nor is it *a priori* excluded that Dio wrote with different audiences in mind, as he subtly does in other works. Dio did indeed appeal to the kingship speeches as evidence for his status with Trajan (57.11).

But we must respect the claims of context. It is a matter of emphasis: granted that speeches can travel, they may nevertheless perform better in their original context, or that context may explain more about them, or, when they are heard or read in other contexts, they may derive most of their meaning from the new audience's appreciation of their original context. The impact of the *Kingships* when re-performed in a sophistic context would actually be greatly increased by the audience's knowledge of an original Trajanic delivery. A strong cumulative case supports that original delivery of all four extant speeches: the certain delivery of one speech (57.11, above); Dio's own claims; the fact that emperors could listen to philosophers and to dialogues at court;⁶² Dio's presence in Rome in 100; a plausible political context (Trajan's 'repatriation' of philosophers and intellectuals); the Roman imperial perspective; the parallels with Pliny, which are not confined to the first speech; the internal implications of all four speeches (Christopher Jones and John Moles have stressed both Dio's persistent contact with Trajan's predilections and claims and the persistent (implicit) polemic against Domitian (both features which undermine the claim of a distinctively Greek perspective and which are paralleled in the *Panegyricus*));⁶³ the sense that the four speeches provide a unified—and

---

60   Whitmarsh (2001b) 186–216, 325–7.
61   4.75–139 has the 'imperial' ending of the long *daimones* section (and for 4.139 see n. 68 below); *Or.* 5, the 'Libyan myth', is cited as an alternative ending in 4.73. Whitmarsh (2001b) 326 is confused on this question of the alternative endings.
62   Tac. *Ann.* 14.16.2; Suet. *Aug.* 89.3.
63   C. P. Jones (1978) 115–21; Moles (1983) and (1990), *passim*. Whitmarsh's dismissal of this material ([2001b] 207, 326) is perfunctory, and his claim (212) that 'there is not a single allusion to Roman history in the *Kingships*, and no concession to specifically Roman means of conceptualizing monarchy' is tenable only with the insertion of the word 'explicit' (there are allusions, e.g., to Domitian's assassination, Nerva's adoption of Trajan, Trajan's accession, the Roman imperial cult: cf., e.g., Moles [1990] 317, 324, 326, 331, 345–6 {above, pp. 133, 140–1, 143, 148, 161–3}, etc.). Equally, Whitmarsh (2001b) ignores the parallels with the *Panegyricus*.

developing—moral programme for the emperor;[64] the readings (surely culturally informed) not only of Philostratus (both in the *Lives of the Sophists*[65] and in the *Life of Apollonius*) but also of the Roman emperor Marcus Aurelius[66] and of the practical politicians Themistius and Synesius, who made their own speeches to Caesars.[67] There are other signs. The brilliant convolutions of the end of the fourth speech are hard to decode on the page and would be hard in any performance in a Greek context; in Trajan's presence, however, they would have been readily comprehensible.[68] While there are ways of rescuing the moral integrity of the third speech,[69] it is far the least challenging of the four and far the most complimentary of Trajan; it reads like a more conventional court piece; if its primary motive were to advertise Dio's influence with Trajan or to defeat sophistic competitors in the Greek east, it is a failure.[70] As for Dio's elaborate self-justification, this can be explained by Dio's own temperament, by his rather spotty career, by the need to parade his anti-Domitian credentials, and by the court context (a context which, obviously, is just as competitive as the world of Greek sophistry).[71] But Dio also puts his self-presentation to positive use, as a general symbol of philosophy *qua* counterbalance to worldly power and as a concrete moral paradigm for Trajan. To this multi-pronged and multi-faceted cumulative case for the speeches' delivery before Trajan may

---

64  Denied by Whitmarsh (2001b) 325–7, but see Moles (1990) 338, 348–9, 351, 361 {above, pp. 154–5, 164–6, 167, 177}, and below, p. 245.

65  Whitmarsh (2001b) 237ff. argues that the no doubt fictitious *VS* 488 'does not allude specifically to the *Kingships*'; it does, however, allude to Dio's role as Trajan's counsellor, a role predicated upon the *Kingships*' having been delivered to Trajan.

66  Whitmarsh (2001b) 216–18 argues that the *Meditations*' interior dialogue represents an internalisation of Dio's collocation of principate and pedagogy; if so, and if 1.14.1 does allude to Dio of Prusa (as, persuasively, Desideri [1978] 16–19; Whitmarsh [2001b] 217), the natural inference is that Marcus read Dio's addresses to Trajan as real.

67  Scharold (1912) 9–40; Asmus (1900) 85–151; Brancacci (1986) 137–97; further, Whitmarsh (2001b) 183 n. 8.

68  The Greek of 4.139 is very intricate, but may be translated roughly as follows: 'But come let us take in exchange a pure harmony, better than the previous one, and let us hymn the good and prudent spirit and god, us to whom the good Fates once spun that we should attain him, when we had taken a share of sound education and reason'; exegesis: Moles (1983) 258–61 {above, pp. 80–4}; Trapp (2000) 226 n. 36 (decisively strengthening Moles); Whitmarsh (2001b) 209 suppresses the crucial allusion to the god-like emperor and his *genius*.

69  Moles (1990) 350–60 {above, pp. 166–77}; Konstan (1997).

70  Cf. Swain (1996) 193–4; Whitmarsh (2001b) 194–7 restricts his analysis to Dio's handling of the question of friendship as opposed to flattery without properly confronting this problem.

71  And indeed is not necessarily absolutely distinct from it: note Whitmarsh (2001b) 245.

perhaps be added an aesthetic argument: if the speeches are not regarded as having been delivered before Trajan, they become enormously less interesting.

But I briefly consider Whitmarsh's readings of the speeches[72] in order to provide some practical illustrations of the general arguments stated above. Whitmarsh privileges such elements in the speeches as the emphasis on critical reading and interpretation of signs, the analogies between physical, moral, intellectual, and textual wanderings, the attacks on defective sophistic education and defective literary exegesis, and Dio's own claims to intellectual virility. This combination looks very like the Whitmarsh model of Second Sophistic παιδεία[73] and the speeches thus become Dio's attempt to defeat his fellow-sophists in agonistic struggle in the Greek East.

A sequence in the fourth speech may serve as a test case (4.29–37). Diogenes (who here, as elsewhere, clearly represents Dio and who is explicitly distinguished from 'the sophists' [14]) is expounding philosophical doctrine to Alexander (who clearly represents Trajan, at least to some extent). Diogenes speaks of the 'double παιδεία', one part 'divine', the other 'human'. The former is inborn and effectively equals simple moral virtue; the latter includes knowledge of writing and the type of learning practised by sophists (29–36). The former is far the more important, though both are necessary and in fact the possessor of the former easily acquires the latter. The effect upon the kingly pupil of a good moral teacher is contrasted with that of a sophist (33):

> If he comes upon a man who, as it were, knows the road, this man easily displays (ἐπέδειξεν) it to him, and on learning this, the king immediately departs. If, however, he falls in with some ignorant and charlatan sophist, this fellow will wear him out by leading him hither and thither, dragging him now to the East and now to the West and now to the South, not knowing anything himself but merely guessing, after having been led far afield himself long before by imposters like himself.

The good moral teacher is manly and virile, the sophist like a 'licentious eunuch' (35), because, although licentious eunuchs have perpetual intercourse with women, 'nothing more comes of it' (36), that is, there is no moral product.

In Whitmarsh's interpretation, the distinction between the two forms of παιδεία is not directed at Trajan, as having the potential for kingly virtue without needing much in the way of conventional education, but at Dio and his rival sophists respectively: Dio is the virile philosopher, his sophistic rivals

---

72  Whitmarsh (2001b) 191–216.
73  See above, p. 231.

effeminate eunuchs; in 33 ἐπέδειξεν refers to sophistic ἐπίδειξις ('performance'); and the whole sequence enacts Dio's victory over his sophistic rivals.

Now the fact that the formal contrast in this sequence is not between superior and inferior forms of sophistry but between philosophy and sophistry does not in itself invalidate Whitmarsh's interpretation: one way for a sophist to defeat another sophist is to pretend that he is something different, in this case, to construct himself as a philosopher. Nevertheless, Whitmarsh's reading seems to me to miss crucial points. It is not the case that the 'divine' παιδεία must be associated with *either* Trajan *or* Diogenes/Dio: Diogenes/Dio functions as a moral paradigm for Alexander/Trajan (as Dio himself does in the *First Kingship*).[74] If the primary performance context really were a sophistic one, Diogenes/Dio's emphasis on 'ease' and 'speed' of teaching and learning would be inappropriate and inconsistent both with Whitmarsh's general model of παιδεία and with his repeated claims for the hermeneutic difficulty of the speeches (difficulty which in my opinion he in any case exaggerates). But the contrast in this sequence is not in fact between sophistry and philosophy *tout court*: it is between 'sophistry' (in some sense) and Cynicism as a particular philosophy: the emphases on 'ease' and 'speed' are characteristic of the thought of the dramatic speaker Diogenes the Cynic and consistent with the broader Cynic-Stoic prospectus that Dio himself has been offering Trajan, a prospectus which insists not on hermeneutic complexity but, precisely, on hermeneutic simplicity. It is also essential to register the fact that the human παιδεία, while depreciated by comparison with the 'divine', is not totally rejected. In effect, this human παιδεία equals the normal educational curriculum. It is necessary to have it but it is subordinate to the divine education. Consequently, 'sophists' are a metaphor for all those who uphold this normal educational curriculum at the expense of the 'divine' παιδεία. They are not restricted to 'sophists' in the technical sense: in effect, they represent any of Diogenes' (or Dio's) intellectual rivals (they could, for example, include the Epicurean philosophers favoured by Trajan's wife, but detested on principle by Dio). They do, however, *include* sophists in the technical sense, because sophists (in that sense) privilege a form of that human παιδεία which is least concerned with basic moral questions and represent it at its worst. The sophistic performance context claimed by Whitmarsh for this sequence is thus illusory.

Nor is it right to gloss ἐπέδειξεν as a *sophistic* performance. Within the road imagery, the term glosses Dio's own performance of the first speech to Trajan, a speech represented as an ἐπίδειξις (1, 69) but of a transcendent moral kind (8) and conceived as a journey, relaying Dio's own journeys (50) and climaxing

---

74   Moles (1990) 309, 311, 319–20 {above, pp. 124, 126–7, 135–7}, etc.

in the Choice of Heracles, Trajan's favourite hero, with its own road imagery (67); this linkage between these two speeches is one of several indications that Dio conceived the kingship speeches as a unified programme,[75] a context itself alien to individual sophistic contests. Ἐπέδειξεν also, very obviously, metatextually glosses Dio's current performance of the fourth speech before Trajan and it also proleptically glosses Diogenes' rhetorical performance before Alexander within the speech, in the long concluding *daimones* section (74–139); the form of that section is indeed represented as something of a sophistic concession to Alexander (or of course Trajan), but the content is philosophical—it is mostly straight Platonism[76]—and the form is explicitly a concession from within philosophy. In short, the implications of 4.29–37 are tied firmly to the internal philosophical world of the speeches and to their immediate context: Dio's attempt to direct Trajan towards a particular kind of philosophy and away from rival attractions. Moreover, this text insists on the virility of the correct kind of philosophy, virile because it can beget virtue in a receptive pupil. For Whitmarsh, this virility is the virility of the triumphant sophist; but it is not: it is the virility of a Cynic/Stoic type who impregnates his pupil with true moral virtue—dramatically, Diogenes and Alexander, in reality Dio and Trajan—and who does so by means of 'philosophical intercourse' (1). Philosophers 'perform' better.[77] Whitmarsh's sophistic interpretation puts far too much stress on the text *qua* text and not nearly enough on its moral product, that is, Trajan's hoped-for 'regeneration' under Dio's philosophical teaching. It is not obvious what this moral product would be were the performance context a purely Greek one.

## 5  The Kingship Speeches: Conclusions

When Dio agreed to deliver kingship speeches to Trajan in 100, like Pliny, he was told some of the things to put in (hence the parallels between the two authors). Also like Pliny, but with far greater *nous*, artistic resource, and moral refinement,[78] he used praise of Trajan as a spring-board for moral exhortation, even criticism, and he designed the speeches so that their interpretation was both itself a moral act and a stimulus for moral growth. In this post-exile stage,

---

75  Cf. above, n. 64.
76  Moles (1983), esp. 256–8 and 262–3 {above, pp. 77–80 and 84–6}; (1990) 348–50 {above, pp. 164–6}; Trapp (2000) 225–7.
77  For pedagogy and erotics see Gleason (1995); Simon (1995) 95–100; Whitmarsh (2001b) 94 and n. 12; 111–16.
78  Notwithstanding recent attempts to revalue the *Panegyricus*: e.g., Whitmarsh (2001b) 166.

and in contrast with his unscrupulous younger self, part of Dio felt nothing for the Roman empire, resisted its totalising tendencies and held that the Greeks were slaves. In this sense, perhaps, his conversion was not a fraud.[79] Aspects of this radically Hellenic and Philostratean[80] Dio lurk within the speeches: Dio the tyrannicide who can turn 'well done, Trajan, how different you are from the ghastly Domitian' into 'if after all you're like Domitian, we'll kill you too'. Dio the Hellenic opponent of Rome, the burden of whose fourth speech is the folly of Trajan's militarism and Alexander-fixation. But, if at this stage Dio was not, at heart, of the Roman world, he was in it, and he rightly sought gains from Trajan alike for himself, for Prusa, and for the Greeks generally (the third speech urges increased Greek recruitment in Roman government). These practical goals were underpinned by Dio's profound Stoic *philanthropia*: the Romans being the Greeks' fellow-citizens in the *kosmos*.[81]

Trajan must have detected the astringency—the harshness—of Dio's criticisms, but an autocrat, unless a naked tyrant like Domitian at the end, cannot afford to show resentment at criticisms proffered via figured speech. True, Trajan did not take the criticisms to heart, becoming one of the most populist of Roman emperors and pushing his Alexander-fixation to the point where the eastern empire nearly collapsed. Yet Dio's description of the speeches as being 'like public prayers or imprecations' (57.12) suggests that they became quasi-official public documents; if so, in the Greek east they functioned not only for Dio's self-advertisement but also as an advertisement of an ideal of interaction between the emperor and his subjects which allowed, even welcomed, honest disagreement and criticism (there are again parallels with the *Panegyricus*). In that sense, the speeches bring Roman and Greek together and bring credit upon Trajan as well as Dio.

## Bibliography

Ahl, F. M. (1984) 'The Art of Safe Criticism in Greece and Rome', *AJPh* 105: 174–208.
von Arnim, H. (1898) *Leben und Werke des Dio von Prusa* (Berlin).
Asmus, J. R. (1900) 'Synesius und Dio Chrysostomus', *BZ* 9: 85–151.
Atkins, E. M. (2000) 'Cicero', in Rowe and Schofield (2000) 477–514.

---

79  *Pace* Moles (1978) 100 {above, p. 59}.
80  That is, as in *VS* 488 (above, p. 236).
81  This is an essential backdrop to all Dio's thinking on the relationships between Greeks and Romans: see Moles (1995b).

Barry, W. D. (1993) 'Aristocrats, Orators and the "Mob": Dio Chrysostom and the World of the Alexandrians', *Historia* 42: 82–103.
Bartsch, S. (1994) *Actors in the Audience* (Cambridge, Mass. and London).
Bischoff, H. (1932) *Der Warner bei Herodot* (diss., Marburg).
Bompaire, J. (1958) *Lucien écrivain: imitation et création* (Paris).
Bowersock, G. W. (1969) *Greek Sophists in the Roman Empire* (Oxford).
Bowie, E. L. (1970) 'Greeks and their Past in the Second Sophistic', *P&P* 46: 3–41.
Bowie, E. L. (1982) 'The Importance of Sophists', *YCS* 27: 29–59.
Brancacci, A. (1986) Rhetorike Philosophousa: *Dione Crisostomo nella cultura antica e bizantina* (Naples).
Brunt, P. A. (1975) 'Stoicism and the Principate', *PBSR* 43: 7–35; repr. in id., *Studies in Stoicism*, edd. M. Griffin and A. Samuels (Oxford) 275–309.
Charles-Saget, A. (1986) 'Un miroir-du-prince au I$^{er}$ siècle après J.C.: Dion Chrysostome, Sur la royauté I', in B. Cassin, ed., *Le plaisir du parler: études de sophistique comparée* (Paris) 111–29.
Desideri, P. (1978) *Dione di Prusa: un intelletuale greco nell'impero romano* (Messina/Florence).
Emperius, A. (1847) 'De exilio Dionis', in id., *Opuscula philologica et historica* (Gottingen, 1847) 103–8; repr. in H. von Arnim, ed., *Dionis Prusaensis quem vocant Chrysostomum quae exstant omnia*, 2 vols. (Berlin, 1893–6) II.333–6.
Erskine, A. (1990) *The Hellenistic Stoa: Political Thought and Action* (London and Ithaca).
Fein, S. (1994) *Die Beziehungen der Kaiser Trajan und Hadrian zu den Litterati* (Stuttgart).
Gill, C. (2000) 'Stoic Writers of the Imperial Period' in Rowe and Schofield (2000) 597–615.
Gleason, M. W. (1995) *Making Men: Sophists and Self-Presentation in Ancient Rome* (Princeton).
Goodenough, E. R. (1928) 'The Political Philosophy of Hellenistic Kingship', *YCS* 1: 53–102.
Griffin, M. T. (1976) *Seneca: a Philosopher in Politics* (Oxford; repr. with addenda, 1992).
Hahm, D. E. (2000) 'Kings and Constitutions: Hellenistic Theories', in Rowe and Schofield (2000) 458–64.
Hahn, J. (1989) *Der Philosoph und die Gesellschaft: Selbstverständnis, öffentliches Auftreten und populäre Erwartungen in der hohen Kaiserzeit* (Stuttgart).
Höistad, R. (1948) *Cynic Hero and Cynic King: Studies in the Cynic Conception of Man* (Uppsala).
Jones, B. W. (1990) 'Domitian and the Exile of Dio of Prusa', *PdP* 45: 348–57.
Jones, C. P. (1971) *Plutarch and Rome* (Oxford).
Jones, C. P. (1973) 'The Date of Dio of Prusa's Alexandrian Oration', *Historia* 22: 302–9.
Jones, C. P. (1978) *The Roman World of Dio Chrysostom* (Cambridge, Mass. and London).

Jones, C. P. (1997) 'Egypt and Judaea under Vespasian', *Historia* 46: 249–53.

Kindstrand, J. F. (1978) 'The Date of Dio of Prusa's Alexandrian Oration—A Reply', *Historia* 27: 378–83.

Konstan, D. (1997) 'Friendship and Monarchy: Dio of Prusa's Third Oration on Kingship', *SO* 72: 124–43.

Laks, A. and M. Schofield, edd. (1995) *Justice and Generosity: Studies in Hellenistic Social and Political Philosophy* (Cambridge).

Lattimore, R. (1939) 'The Wise-Adviser in Herodotus', *CPh* 34: 24–35.

MacMullen, R. (1966) *Enemies of the Roman Order: Treason, Alienation and Unrest in the Roman Empire* (Cambridge, Mass.).

Moles, J. L. (1978) 'The Career and Conversion of Dio Chrysostom', *JHS* 98: 79–100 [above, Ch. 1].

Moles, J. L. (1983) 'The Date and Purpose of the Fourth Kingship Oration of Dio Chrysostom', *ClAnt* 2: 251–78 [above, Ch. 3].

Moles, J. L. (1984) 'The Addressee of the Third Kingship Oration of Dio Chrysostom', *Prometheus* 10: 65–9 [above, ch. 4].

Moles, J. L. (1990) 'The Kingship Orations of Dio Chrysostom', *PLLS* 6: 297–375 [above, Ch. 5].

Moles, J. L. (1995a) 'The Cynics and Politics', in Laks and Schofield (1995) 129–58 [below, Ch. 15].

Moles, J. L. (1995b) 'Dio Chrysostom, Greece, and Rome', in D. C. Innes, H. Hine, and C. Pelling, edd., *Ethics and Rhetoric: Studies Presented to Donald Russell* (Oxford, 1995) 177–92 [above, Ch. 7].

Moles, J. L. (2000) 'The Dionian *Charidemus*', in S. Swain, ed., *Dio Chrysostom: Politics, Letters, and Philosophy* (Oxford) 187–210 [above, Ch. 8].

Moles, J. L. (2005) 'The Thirteenth Oration of Dio Chrysostom: Complexity and Simplicity, Rhetoric and Moralism, Literature and Life', *JHS* 125: 112–38 [below, Ch. 10].

Momigliano, A. D. (1950) 'Dio Chrysostomos' (Unpublished Lecture, 1950), in id., *Quarto Contributo alla Storia degli studi classici e del mondo antico* (Rome, 1969) 257–69.

Momigliano, A. D. (1951) 'Review of Wirszubski (1950)', *JRS* 41: 146–53; repr. in id., *Quinto Contributo alla Storia degli studi classici e del mondo antico*, 2 vols. (Rome, 1975) II.958–75.

Rawson, E. (1989) 'Roman Rulers and the Philosophic Adviser', in M. T. Griffin and J. Barnes, edd. (1989) *Philosophia Togata: Essays on Philosophy and Roman Society* (Oxford) 233–57.

Reardon, B. P. (1971) *Courants littéraires grecs de II$^e$ et III$^e$ siècles après J.-C.* (Paris).

Rowe, C. and M. Schofield, edd. (2000) *The Cambridge History of Greek and Roman Political Thought* (Cambridge).

Russell, D. A., ed. (1992) *Dio Chrysostom: Orations VII, XII, XXXVI* (Cambridge).

Salmeri, G. (1982) *La politica e il potere: saggio su Dione di Prusa* (Catania).
Salmeri, G. (2000) 'Dio, Rome, and the Civic Life of Asia Minor', in Swain (2000) 53–92.
Scharold, J. (1912) *Dio Chrysostom und Themistius* (Burghausen).
Schmitz, T. (1997) *Bildung und Macht: zur sozialen und politischen Funktion der zweiten Sophistik in der griechischen Welt der Kaiserzeit* (Munich).
Schofield, M. (1986) '*Euboulia* in the *Iliad*', *CQ* 36: 6–31; repr. in id., *Saving the City: Philosopher Kings and Other Classical Paradigms* (London, 1999) 3–30.
Schofield, M. (2000a) 'Epicurean and Stoic Political Thought', in Rowe and Schofield (2000) 435–56.
Schofield, M. (2000b) 'Plato and Practical Politics', in Rowe and Schofield (2000) 293–302.
Sedley, D. N. (1997) 'The Ethics of Brutus and Cassius', *JRS* 87: 41–53.
Sidebottom, H. (1992) 'The Date of Dio of Prusa's Rhodian and Alexandrian Orations', *Historia* 41: 407–19.
Sidebottom, H. (1996) 'Dio of Prusa and the Flavian Dynasty', *CQ* 46: 447–56.
Simon, R. I. (1995) 'Face-to-face with Alterity: Postmodern Jewish Identity and the Eros of Pedagogy', in J. Gallop, ed., *Pedagogy: the Question of Impersonation* (Bloomington) 95–105.
Sonny, A. (1896) *Ad Dionem Chrysostomum Analecta* (Kiev).
Swain, S. (1996) *Hellenism and Empire: Language, Classicism, and Power in the Greek World, AD 50–250* (Oxford).
Swain, S., ed. (2000) *Dio Chrysostom: Politics, Letters, and Philosophy* (Oxford).
Syme, R. (1958) *Tacitus*, 2 vols. (Oxford).
Toynbee, J. M. C. (1944) 'Dictators and Philosophers in the First Century A.D.', *G&R* 13: 43–58.
Trapp, M. B. (2000) 'Plato in Dio', in Swain (2000) 213–39.
Verrengia, A., ed. (2000) *Dione di Prusa: In Atene, sull'esilio (or. XIII): Introduzione, testo critico, traduzione e commento* (Naples).
Veyne, P. (1999) 'L'identité grecque devant Rome et l'empereur', *REG* 112: 510–67.
Waters, K. H. (1974) 'Trajan's Character in the Literary Tradition', in J. A. S. Evans, ed., *Polis and Imperium: Studies in Honour of E. T. Salmon* (Toronto) 233–52.
Whitmarsh, T. (1998) 'Reading Power in Roman Greece: the *Paideia* of Dio Chrysostom,' in Y. L. Too and N. Livingstone, edd., *Pedagogy and Power: Rhetorics of Classical Learning* (Cambridge) 192–213.
Whitmarsh, T. (2001a) '"Greece is the World": Exile and Identity in the Second Sophistic', in S. Goldhill, ed., *Being Greek under Rome: the Second Sophistic, Cultural Conflict and the Development of the Roman Empire* (Cambridge) 269–305.
Whitmarsh, T. (2001b) *Greek Literature and the Roman Empire: the Politics of Imitation* (Oxford).
Wistrand, E. (1979) 'The Stoic Opposition to the Principate', *StudClas* 18: 93–101.

CHAPTER 10

# The Thirteenth Oration of Dio Chrysostom: Complexity and Simplicity, Rhetoric and Moralism, Literature and Life

From his own day on, Dio of Prusa has always been a controversial figure: variously characterised as sophist, philosopher (whether Cynic, Stoic, Platonist, or general Socratic), sophistic philosopher, philosophical and political turncoat, earnest moralist, relentless self-advertiser, friend and critic of Rome, counsellor of emperors, middling local politician, literary and philosophical bantam, of the same stature, among philosophers, as Plutarch or Epictetus, or, among literary figures, as Lucian and the novelists.* All these questions converge in *Or.* 13: in von Arnim's judgement, 'one of the most beautiful of Dio's pieces',[1] but also one of his most demanding.

## 1 Structure

The structure of the speech can be variously analysed.

There is a simple bipartite division between the Greek world (1–28) and the Roman (29–37). From a more detailed thematic perspective, the structure is tripartite. The first part (1–13) relates the decree of exile passed against Dio, his fluctuating responses, consultation of Delphi, embarkation on his wanderings, and beginning to be regarded as a philosopher. The second (14–28) summarises the philosophical teaching that he then dispensed: his virtual and admitted quotation of Socrates' teachings. The third (29–37) summarises the philosophical teachings, again avowedly Socratic, that he gave in Rome.

But if one analyses how the speech achieves its enormous progression from Dio's account of his exile to a philosophical programme for the salvation of Rome, a quadripartite structure emerges: (1) exile raises the problem of Dio's

---

\* Versions were given at the Newcastle Classics Seminar (5 December 2001), the International Plutarch Society (Nijmegen, 2 May 2002), and the colloquium 'Greek Bodies, Roman Control' (Corpus Christi College, Oxford, 18 May 2002). I thank: all who commented on those occasions; Paolo Desideri, Malcolm Schofield, and Mike Trapp for commenting on other versions; and *JHS*'s referees for stringent critiques. Surviving errors, and translations, are all my own work. The text is Cohoon's (11.90–120), cross-referenced with Verrengia (2000).

1 Von Arnim (1898) 334.

own moral response and triggers his wanderings (1–11); (2) on these wanderings, people ask Dio about good and evil and the duties of man (12); (3) in reply, he imitates Socrates, who discoursed about money, education, the city, the necessary connection of private and public, concord, the need for a good teacher, and the valuelessness of imperialism (13–28); (4) in Rome, he applies these Socratic categories to the case of corrupt contemporary Rome (29–37).

None of these analyses, however, adequately conveys the depth and detail of the speech's organic unity, which will gradually become clear.

There is one structural problem. The speech ends (37; Dio is summarising what he said to the Romans): 'I did not, however, say that it was difficult for them to be educated, "since" (I [[113]] maintained) "when you were better than nobody in the past, you learned easily all the other things that you wished: I speak of horsemanship, bowmanship, and hoplite warfare".' The original ending must be lost,[2] but analysis will show that the speech is substantially complete.

One problem with the progression of the argument must be deferred.[3]

## 2    Context and Date

That the place of delivery was Athens, focus of a third of the speech (14–28), cannot immediately be proved (the ancient title *In Athens Concerning Exile* may only be an inference), yet will seem persuasive. The speech was made after Dio was exiled (1). Most scholars date the speech after the *end* of the exile (AD 96), partly because the great majority of Dio's extant works are post-exilic and partly because of Dio's description in section 1:

> when it came to me to be exiled on account of a stated [λεγομένης] friendship with a man who was not base [ἀνδρὸς οὐ πονηροῦ],[4] but who was very close to those who were then fortunate and ruling [τῶν ... τότε εὐδαιμόνων τε καὶ ἀρχόντων] but who was put to death because of those things because of which he seemed blessed to many and indeed to practically everyone—because of his relationship and kinship with those people, this accusation [αἰτίας] having been brought against me, that indeed [δή]

---

2   Reiske (1798); von Arnim (1893) xxxivff.; Cohoon II.120–1; Desideri (1978) 254; Highet (1983) 80; Verrengia (2000) 169.
3   Below, p. 269.
4   Generally taken morally; Whitmarsh (2001) 160 and Moles (2003) 190 {above, p. 232} prefer the socio-political 'of no mean station'. The latter is guaranteed by the contrast between πονηροῦ and εὐδαιμόνων τε καὶ ἀρχόντων, the former is at least retrospectively implicit: 'not base' essays both.

I was the man's friend and counsellor, for this is the custom of tyrants, just as it is among the Scythians to bury cupbearers and cooks and concubines with their kings, so to those who are being put to death by them to add others for no reason [αἰτίας].

These scholars take 'those who were then fortunate and ruling' as an allusion to a now defunct Flavian dynasty,[5] and they believe in the Flavian contacts that Dio himself claimed.[6]

But in an influential attack upon that belief,[7] Sidebottom takes 'ruling' as referring merely to 'leading Romans', as sometimes elsewhere in Dio.[8] This seems impossible. The phrase should refer to a general category: close kinship to 'the then dynasty' makes sense (such kinship did undo some); close kinship to 'the then leading Romans' does not. The man's very high rank is further supported by his 'seeming blessed to many and indeed to practically everyone', by his being compared to 'kings', and by the clear allusions to Herodotus 1.5.3–4, 6.1, and 30.2–33 (the mutability of εὐδαιμονία, Croesus the 'tyrant', the deceptiveness of worldly εὐδαιμονία, and 'calling no man happy until he is dead'). As in Herodotus, 'the then fortunate' were 'fortunate' only in their self-estimation and that of the world, and the reality comes in 24, where Dio's transparent allegory[9] makes Domitian a δαίμων and his subjects κακοδαίμονες, and in 31, where Dio tells the Romans they need a good education 'if they are going to be fortunate [εὐδαίμονες] in actuality and in truth, and not, as now, in the opinion of the many'. In 33, the full phrase εὐδαίμονες καὶ ἄρχοντες is applied to the Romans in general, of the 'self-rule' [[114]] necessary for genuine good fortune and secure rule over others. In this hierarchy of fortune and ruling, the εὐδαίμονες καὶ ἄρχοντες of 1 should be at the top of the pile, and—as in Herodotus—correspond to the 'tyrants'. Moreover, as we shall see, complimentary allusions to Nerva and Trajan at the end of the speech create an implicit contrast between the bad rule of Domitian and the good rule of the former, a

---

5   Emperius (1847) 103–8; von Arnim (1898) 230; Desideri (1978) 189; C. P. Jones (1978) 138; Verrengia (2000) 74.
6   7.66: '[before the exile] I knew the homes and tables ... of satraps and kings'; development in Momigliano (1951) 152 = (1975) 972; id. (1950) 258–60; C. P. Jones (1973) 307–8; id. (1978) 14–17, 44–5, 123; Desideri (1978) 138–9; Moles (1978) 84–5, 93 {above, pp. 31–4, 47}; (1990) 333 {above, pp. 149–50}; (2003) 189–91 {above, pp. 231–4}.
7   Sidebottom (1996), himself influenced by Rawson (1989), followed by Claassen (1999) 271 n. 115, 291 n. 33; Salmeri (2000) 61 n. 33; Whitmarsh (2001) 156.
8   Sidebottom (1996) 451 and nn. 35–6, cf. Dio 1.44; 13.33 (not the same usage, though thematically related to 13.1: discussion in the text); 39.4; 79.1 and Mason (1974) 110–15; cf. Cohoon II.90: 'high officials'.
9   See n. 115 below.

contrast that suits the speech's general movement.[10] Hence 1 alludes to 'régime change'. Reconstruction of Dio's movements in the Trajanic period then makes 101 the likely delivery date.[11]

## 3   Generic Affiliations

Following the ancient title, scholars have taken *Or.* 13 as a Περὶ φυγῆς, and appreciation of Dio's handling of exilic *topoi* has grown steadily. Whereas Häsler and Doblehofer detect only one *topos*,[12] Verrengia sees that Dio covers some *topoi* by implication,[13] and Claassen that, in the opening, consolatory section, Dio refashions the usual writer/addressee relationship into an internal dialectic, with Dio himself both questioner and questioned.[14] Whitmarsh notes numerous *reversals* of *topoi*: creation of conversational immediacy through the omission of a formal prologue (1); failure to attribute the exile to philosophical παρρησία (1); apparently 'accidental' becoming a philosopher (3; 11–12); and the simplicity of the means by which Dio 'discovers' philosophical truths (2; 3; 7).[15]

More could be said. Exilic cosmopolitanism is reflected in Dio's claim that competent philosophical teachers can be Greeks, Romans, Scythians, or Indians (32). Exilic rejection of Athenian civic ideology[16] is additionally pointed when Athenians are both internal and external audiences. Whereas exile characteristically entails physical separation and philosophical alienation from 'the city', Dio the dramatic character ends up in Rome (29ff.) and Dio the speaker speaks in Athens. While Dio preserves the traditional cosmopolitan sentiment (32), he 'homes in' on Rome as the central place of the earth (36). These last examples illustrate the challenging-ness of Dio's response to

---

10   P. 270; this contrast is also structural in the *Kingships*: C. P. Jones (1978) 118–22; Moles (1983b) *passim*; (1990) *passim*.
11   Von Arnim (1898) 331, 334; C. P. Jones (1978) 53–4, 135; Sheppard (1984) 162, 173; further support for a post-exilic dating in sustained parallels with the *Kingships* (below, nn. 10, 101), especially *Or.* 1 (below, nn. 117, 122, 129, 135, 143, 183, 186, 189, 217, 220), crucial parallels with *Or.* 79 (p. 277), and points of contact with *Olympicus* (below, nn. 192, 219) and *Or.* 72 (below, n. 167); *contra*, n. 133.
12   Häsler (1935) 37, 55; Doblehofer (1987) 42.
13   Verrengia (2000) 87–8, 135.
14   Claassen (1999) 25, 166.
15   Whitmarsh (2001) 160–2.
16   Whitmarsh (2001) 142–5, 151 (Musonius); 172, 175–8 (Favorinus); Socrates'/Dio's rejection of the *epitaphios* tradition (23–6) is particularly relevant; on that tradition within exile literature: Whitmarsh (2001) 175–7.

the exile genre: the logic of the speech progressively moves away from it and finally 'rejects' it, the focus becoming ever more civic.

For numerous other genres also signify. Philosophical autobiography[17] and protreptic (16, 28) are obvious. There are also affinities with a Πολιτεία[18] and with a Περὶ παιδείας. Debate or dialectic between old and new types of παιδεία is a theme of non-philosophical works such as Aristophanes' *Clouds* (to which Dio alludes).[19] The speech also has features from epic[20] and tragedy,[21] with Dio 'hero' of both.[22] Herodotean and Thucydidean allusions[23] import a historiographical quality, as of a narrative formally 'true', imbued with high seriousness and moral ⟦115⟧ purpose, and having particular concern with 'the city', its authority deriving from the author's exilic status.[24] The σπουδαιογέλοιον ('serio-comic') tradition is also relevant.[25]

Generically, then, the speech is richly creative and complex.

## 4    Philosophical Material

Dio's consultation of Delphi reflects Chaerephon's consultation on behalf of Socrates. His reactions to the oracle largely imitate Plato's *Apology*.[26] There are other extended traces of that work[27] and nods also at the Socrates of the *Gorgias*.[28]

17   Jouan (1993b).
18   Similarly, the *Borystheniticus*: Schofield (1991) 57–92; Moles (1995b), esp. 191 {above, p. 201}; and the *Euboicus*: Moles (1995b) 178–9 {above, pp. 188–9}.
19   19, 23 ~ *Nub.* 965, 967, 985–6 (p. 278).
20   4 ~ *Od.* 1.48–59; 81; 10 ~ *Od.* 11.119–34; 10–11: p. 268 and n. 121.
21   Cf. the shrewd allusion of Dio's biographer Philostratus (*VS* 488) to 'the man's going off stage [*parodos*] to the Getic tribes'; 1 ~ Hdt. 1.32.1, 2–4 ~ D.L. 6.38 (Diogenes' tragic verses); 2, 20 (emphasis on δυστυχία); 5 ~ Soph. *El.* 233–6 (note τόπον for the MSS νόμον); 14 ('like a god from a machine'); 20–1 (disquisition on tragedy).
22   P. 269.
23   1 ~ Hdt. 1.32; 1 (Scythian royal burials) ~ Hdt. 4.71.4; 6–8 ~ Hdt. 1.55; 1 ~ Thuc. 5.26; 6 ~ Thuc. 1.70.3; 15 ~ Thuc. 1.22.
24   1 ~ Thuc. 5.26.
25   P. 284.
26   Detail in Moles (1978) 99 {above, p. 57}; cf. also von Arnim (1898) 227; Verrengia (2000) 137; Trapp (2000) 231; Whitmarsh (2001) 162 and n. 114; *contra*, Brancacci (2000) 249; Momigliano (1950) 261, followed by C. P. Jones (1978) 47, detects Xen. *An.* 3.1.5–8; implausibly: Verrengia (2000) 137.
27   14 ~ *Ap.* 29d (Cohoon II.101 n. 2; Whitmarsh [2001] 163 n. 116), perhaps also ~ *Clit.* 407e (Verrengia (2000) 147); 28 ~ *Ap.* 30a–b, 36c (cf. also 31b, 24d–25a); 33 ~ *Ap.* 36d.
28   E.g., 29; cf. 14 ~ *Gorg.* 509a (though also ~ Xen. *Mem.* 4.4.5–6, cited by Dio himself in 3.26–7).

The Delphic narrative also evokes the (pseudo-)biographies of Diogenes and Zeno.[29] Exile as the trigger of philosophising further recalls Diogenes,[30] and there are other plausible Diogenic traces.[31]

The Socratic *logos* (14–28) raises huge controversy. The closeness of 14–17 to the *Cleitophon*[32] makes many scholars think that Dio is following it directly,[33] but others that Antisthenes is the common source.[34]

This dispute is one of the key elements in the general debate concerning the presence or absence of Antisthenes in Dio, a debate which connects with two others: the extent of Cynic influence on Dio and the importance within the general Socratic tradition of Antisthenes himself. Brancacci has recently reaffirmed Dio's extensive use of Antisthenes, notably in the *Third* and *Fourth Kingships* and in *Or.* 13, whereas Trapp sees Plato as the dominant source. This disagreement concerns also the *kind* of Socrates projected in the sources and inherited by Dio, with Brancacci insisting on a distinctively Antisthenic/Cynic/Dionian Socrates *qua* dogmatic teacher of positive moral truths and Trapp denying that distinctiveness.[35] The dispute affects the interpretation of *Or.* 13 and cannot be evaded.

The verbal resemblances are as shown below.

| *Or.* 13 | *Cleitophon* |
|---|---|
| (1—description of Socrates) 'shouting and straining his voice' (14) | 'you hymned as you spoke' (407a) |
| (2—description of Socrates) 'like a god from a machine, as someone has said' (14) | 'like a god on a tragic machine' (407a) |
| (3—description of Socrates) 'censuring' (16) | 'when you censured' (407a) |

---

29   Moles (1978) 99 {above, p. 57}; C. P. Jones (1978) 47.
30   D.L. 6.21, 49.
31   E.g., 2–5 ~ D.L. 6.38; 33 ~ D.L. 6.29, with Höistad (1948) 116–26; Diogenes' writings survived and Dio read him: SSR IV.484; Moles (forthcoming, a).
32   Genuine?: hesitantly, Slings (1999) 215–34; no matter here: authenticity was anciently accepted.
33   Hagen (1891); Wegehaupt (1896) 56–64; Desideri (1978) 253 n. 3; Claassen (1999) 167; Slings (1999) 94 6; Trapp (2000) 231, 234; Verrengia (2000) 88–91; Whitmarsh (2001) 163–4.
34   Dümmler (1882) 8–11; (1889) 1–17; von Arnim (1898) 256–60; Caizzi (1966) 92ff.; SSR IV.350–3; cf. V A 208; Brancacci (1992) 3310 n. 3; id. (2000) 251–2.
35   Brancacci (2000); Trapp (2000), esp. 233 and n. 59.

⟦116⟧ (4—Socrates starts speaking) 'Where are you rushing to, human beings?' (16)

(5) 'Do you not know that you are doing none of the things that are necessary, in concerning yourselves with money and trying to acquire it in every way, in order that you may have it in abundance yourselves and may hand it down in even greater quantity to your children? But of the children themselves and before them of yourselves, their fathers, you have all alike had no concern, having found no adequate or helpful training whereby you will be able to use your money rightly and justly and not harmfully and unjustly and yourselves without penalty, which you should have considered a more serious matter than money and your sons and daughters and wives and brothers and friends, and they also you.' (16)

(6) 'But is it by learning from your parents—and teaching your sons—lyre-playing, wrestling, and letters that you think that you will inhabit your city in a more disciplined and better way?' (17)³⁶

'Where are you rushing to, human beings?' (407b)

'Do you not know that you are doing none of the things that are necessary, in as much as you make all your serious efforts at getting money but you have no concern if your sons, to whom you will be handing it down, will not know how to use it justly, nor do you find them teachers of justice, if it can be learned, or if it can be acquired by exercise or training, people who will train them or exercise them adequately, nor even before did you take care of yourselves in that way.' (407b)

'But seeing that both you yourselves and your children have learned adequately letters, music, and gymnastic, which things you hold to be a complete education for virtue, and then becoming no less bad concerning money, how do you not despise the present type of education and fail to seek those who will make you desist from this disharmony? It is actually because of this lack of tunefulness and negligence—and not because of the lack of co-ordination between foot and lyre—that brother behaves

---

36  Textual problems in 16 and 17 (Verrengia [2000] 149–53) are immaterial.

> towards brother and cities towards cities without co-ordination or harmony, engaging in strife and warring and doing and suffering the most extreme things.' (407c–d)

Items 2–5 are very close, and so is item 1.[37] Any πεπαιδευμένος must take Dio's 'as someone has said' (item 2) for a 'pointer' to the very popular *Cleitophon*.[38] Item 6 is also close. While the positive 'good teacher' theme of 407c–d does not appear in the Socratic *logos*, it does appear when Dio is speaking *in propria persona* (31ff.): seemingly, Dio himself has transferred it there,[39] to fit the speech's general movement from negative to positive.[40] Thus Dio is here following the *Cleitophon* directly.

The rest of the Socratic *logos* (17–28) enlarges on the inadequacy of conventional education. Dio is writing freely.[41] The refutation (23–7) of the claim that Athens' military victories showed her superior education controverts the *epitaphios*. The anachronistic allusion in 26 to Cnidus, taken by Cobet as illustrating the historical ignorance of later rhetoricians and sophists and by von Arnim and Giannantoni as showing Dio's uncritical reliance on a text written after 394 BC,[42] ⟦117⟧ is better explained as sophisticated imitation of Platonic anachronisms in the *Menexenus* and *Symposium*.[43]

If there is no Antisthenic influence on the Socratic *logos*, the final part of the speech certainly contains Antisthenic elements.

One is Archelaus' invitation to Socrates (30), only recorded in Antisthenes' *Archelaus*.[44] A second case, not noticed hitherto,[45] requires lengthy demonstration, but has important consequences.

---

37  Because Dio, [Plut.] *Mor.* 4E, and Epict. 3.22.26 all understand Socrates here to be 'shouting': Slings (1999) 95.
38  The formula in Dio: Slings (1999) 95 n. 174.
39  Slings (1999) 94.
40  P. 269.
41  Desideri (1978) 253 n. 3; Slings (1999) 94, 96; *pace* Trapp (2000) 234 n. 62 and Wegehaupt (1896) 57–63.
42  Cobet (1878) 65; von Arnim (1898) 258; *SSR* IV.350–1.
43  *Menex.* 244d–46a (including Cnidus) and *Symp.* 182b and 193a (which Dio noted: Moles (2000a) 201 {above, p. 218} n. 37).
44  Dümmler (1882) 8–11; *SSR* IV.350; Brancacci (2000) 249–50.
45  Höistad (1948) 171–3 argues a plausible *general* case for Antisthenes' 'double *paideia*' in *Or.* 13; cf. also n. 69.

The speech's closing words (already quoted) distinguish between true philosophical education, which is 'not difficult', and the Romans' military expertise, represented as a kind of education: 'I did *not*, however, say that it was *difficult* for them to be *educated*, "since" (I maintained), "when you were better than nobody in the past, you *learned easily all the other things* that you wished. I speak of horsemanship, bowmanship, and hoplite warfare".' Now, an Antisthenic fragment (Themist. *De virt.* p. 43 Mach) runs:[46]

> But if you wish truly to learn that wisdom is something lofty, I invoke neither Plato nor Aristotle as witnesses, but the wise Antisthenes, who taught this road. For he says that Prometheus spoke to Heracles as follows: 'Your labour is very cheap, in that your care is for human things, but you have deserted the care of those things which are of greater moment; for you will not be a perfect man until you have learnt the things that are loftier than human beings, but if you learn those things, then you will learn also human things; if, however, you learn only human things, you will wander like a brute animal.' For the man who studies human things and confines the wisdom and intelligence of his mind in such cheap and narrow things, that man, as Antisthenes said, is not a wise man but like to an animal, to whom a dung-pit is pleasing. In truth, all celestial things are lofty and it behoves us to have a lofty way of thinking about them.

This must come from Antisthenes' *Heracles*. The scene reworks the Prodican Choice of Heracles, with an admixture of the Aeschylean interpretation of the relationship between Prometheus (~ intelligence) and Zeus (~ power).[47] The choice is between 'human' and 'celestial' 'learning' and is not absolute: 'learning' only the former will leave Heracles in a bestial state; 'learning' the latter is far the more important, but will immediately secure the former; Heracles will then be a 'perfect man'.

A passage in Dio's *Fourth Kingship* (Diogenes the Cynic is the dramatic speaker) contains the following elements (29–33):
(i) the 'double *paideia*', one part of which is divine, the other human, the former superior and 'easy', the latter inferior, but both necessary for complete education;
(ii) the claim that knowledge of the divine *paideia* easily confers knowledge of the human;

---

46  Antisthenes F27 DC {= 96 Prince}; SSR V A 96; Moles (forthcoming, a) and (forthcoming, b).
47  Kitto (1961) 61.

(iii) Heracles as representative of divine education;
(iv) the sophists, including Prometheus, as representative of human education;
(v) road imagery (good and bad roads);
(vi) comparison between human education/sophists and animals.

Many have taken this passage as Antisthenic.[48] Trapp, however, holds that 4.29–33 is merely one of a series of items drawn from *Alcibiades I*, *ex hypothesi* the Platonic 'master-text' of the 〚118〛 *Fourth Kingship*.[49] The parallels adduced by Trapp prove that Dio is indeed so using *Alcibiades I*, though this hardly diminishes the Cynic extremeness of his own speech.[50]

Nevertheless, of the six itemised elements, (i), (ii), (iii), (v), and (vi) are found in the fragment, and the emphasis on philosophical 'easiness' is characteristically Cynic[51] (there is even a verbal parallel here). By contrast, *Alcibiades I* lacks not only the emphasis on 'easiness' but also the sharp distinction between human and divine education, the extended Heracles exemplum, the motif of the two roads, and the comparison of human education to animals.

*Or.* 4.29ff., then, reflects Antisthenes' double *paideia* and the verbal parallel shows that Dio had himself read the *Heracles*.

Now *Or.* 13.37 resembles Antisthenes' double *paideia* in the distinction between two types of education (the only two envisaged),[52] of which the first is the true education and the second is allowed only limited utility; the emphasis on the 'easiness' of the educational programme; and the thought that 'if you've got the one form of education, the other follows'. Antisthenic influence coheres with the implicit commendation of moral 'strength',[53] with Dio's earlier use of Antisthenes at 30, and with his use of the Antisthenic *paideia* in *Or.* 4.29ff. and elsewhere.[54]

The passage, however, differs from Antisthenes' double *paideia* in four respects. First, the two types of education are not distinguished in terms of 'divine' and 'human'. Second, the non-philosophical education is not conventional education but military expertise. Third, conventional education is

---

48   Dümmler (1882) 14; Weber (1887) 241; von Fritz (1926) 78; Höistad (1948) 56–9; Moles (1983b) 270 {above, p. 93}; Brancacci (2000) 254–5; SSR IV.312–13; Whitmarsh (2001) 191 n. 43.
49   Trapp (2000) 226–7, cf. 232–4; the authenticity of *Alcibiades I* (advocated by Denyer ([2001] 14–26) is here immaterial, authenticity being anciently accepted.
50   Höistad (1948) 213–20; Moles (1983b), esp. 268–9 {above, pp. 92–3} n. 65.
51   E.g., D.L. 6.44, 70; Antisthenes and Cynicism: p. 261; 'easiness' in *Or.* 13: p. 267.
52   Similarly 24, where the Persians have no education but some military 'training', a significantly parallel passage, as it emerges (nn. 115, 156).
53   P. 266; in Antisthenes, e.g., D.L. 6.2, 6.14–15.
54   Höistad (1948) 50–7, 86–94; note that *Or.* 4 is a year earlier than *Or.* 13 (nn. 11, 101).

accorded not slight value but, implicitly, no value at all. Fourth, whereas in Antisthenes possession of the philosophical education allows the 'easy' acquisition of the non-philosophical education, here the pattern is reversed.

But these differences are explicable. The true education is generally sanctioned by the divine in *Or.* 13.[55] As Dio addresses the Romans and substitutes their military supremacy for conventional education, he is trading on two assumptions: first, that the Romans do power, not culture, which is left to the Greeks;[56] second, that there is some affinity between Roman virtue and Cynic virtue.[57] Thus the Romans' military supremacy and the alleged 'ease' with which they acquired it indicate the 'ease' with which they can acquire the true philosophical education, and the reversal of the Antisthenic pattern has further protreptic force. The implicit dismissal of conventional education also accords with the more radically Cynic or Diogenic position[58] that the speech as a whole adopts on this issue. Finally, to increase the complications, I believe that *Or.* 13.37 also engages with *Aeneid* 6.847ff.[59] In sum, Antisthenes' double *paideia* underlies *Or.* 13.37 and Dio's adaptation of it shows great didactic resourcefulness.

So much for specific philosophical sources.[60]

The general 'feel' of the speech is Cynic:[61] witness the evocations of Diogenes; Dio's emphasis on his humble attire,[62] 'self-chastening', and 'wandering', and on others' calling him a vagabond and tramp as well as a philosopher (10–12);[63] the appeal to the Scythians[64] and ⟦119⟧ Indians;[65] the implicit cosmopolitanism;[66] the advocacy of philosophical 'strength';[67] the central philosophical claim that things are 'easy';[68] the savage attacks on material things;

---

55   P. 267.
56   Virg. *Aen.* 6.847–53; Petrochilos (1974) 58–62; Whitmarsh (2001) 9–17.
57   Griffin (1993) 251–8; (1996) 197–204 {= (2018) 480–5}.
58   D.L. 6.73, 103–4.
59   Space, however, precludes discussion of this possibility here: Moles (forthcoming, b).
60   Whitmarsh's claim that Dio is engaging with Musonius' Περὶ φυγῆς: p. 264; another possibility: n. 140.
61   Dudley (1937) 150–1; Moles (1978) 99–100 {above, pp. 56–8}; Jouan (1993a) 393.
62   Cf., e.g., Kindstrand (1976) 161–3; p. 286.
63   Dio's Cynicising representation of his wanderings: 1.9, 50–1; 4.1, 6–11 (Diogenes ~ Dio); 6.1ff. (Diogenes ~ Dio); 7.9, 81; 8.1 (Diogenes ~ Dio); 12.16–20; 19.1; 33.15; 36.1; 45.1; further Montiglio (2000) 98ff.
64   See, e.g., Martin (1996).
65   See, e.g., Brown (1949) 38–51; Moles (1995a) 146–9 {below, pp. 405–8}.
66   Moles (1993); (1996); *pace* Montiglio (2000) 99–100.
67   P. 266.
68   Above, n. 51 and p. 259.

and the basic philosophical message that individual and civic 'good fortune' is secured by 'self-sufficiency' (33–5).[69]

Dio's use of the *Apology* and the *Gorgias* hardly undermines this Cynic 'feel', since Socrates was generally appropriated within the Cynic tradition, and Dio's Socrates differs from Plato's in that he does not make the minimalising claim that his wisdom consists only in the fact that he does not know but appears as a forthright exponent of positive moral doctrine. Thus, rightly, Brancacci.[70]

Dio's deployment of the *Cleitophon* is also apposite. Whereas that work's Socrates is ironised by his inability to explain what virtue is,[71] Dio largely discards the irony and uses the *Cleitophon* image of Socrates as a representative of moral virtue at its most robust and uncompromising. This procedure, also adopted by Dio's fellow Stoic, Epictetus, in his *On Cynicism* (3.22.26), is philosophically justified, because the Socrates parodied in the *Cleitophon* was very like the Socrates championed by the Cynics and by Antisthenes. Use of the *Cleitophon* also underwrites the move from individual ethics to social and political ones.

Use of Antisthenes is also compatible with the Cynic 'feel' of the speech, since, whoever founded Cynicism, Antisthenes undoubtedly influenced it,[72] as Dio knew.[73] On the whole, *Or.* 13 inclines towards the 'soft', here Antisthenic, type of Cynicism, which (here) involves the acceptance of human beings' social and political obligations, however redefined, and an intense concern with the well-being of 'the city', rather than towards the 'hard' Diogenic version.

More generally, Dio's rich play with the metaphorical and moral implications of place and travel[74] can be regarded as Platonic[75] and/or Herodotean,[76] although such play is also found within Cynicism, albeit in less developed form.[77]

---

69  Though extant Dio does not use the word αὐτάρκεια, he often comes close, as at 34–5: ἐλαττόνων ... δεήσεσθε (virtually the standard definition). Dio's formulations hereabouts resemble D.L. 6.11 (Antisthenes); I suspect implicit punning on αὐτ/άρκεια/self-ἀρχή, as perhaps in Plato (e.g., *Rep.* 369b; *Polit.* 271d) and (surely) in lost Cynic material. Dio's thinking about this idea: Brenk (2000).
70  Brancacci (2000) 249.
71  Slings (1999) 209–12
72  Dudley (1937) 1–15, 54–5; *SSR* IV.223–33; Giannantoni (1993); Moles (2000b) 417 {below, p. 442} (all favouring Diogenes); D.L. 6.2; Höistad (1948) 10–11; Döring (1995); Goulet-Cazé (1996) (favouring Antisthenes); influence: von Fritz (1926); Döring (1995).
73  *Or.* 8.1, with Brancacci (2000) 256–7.
74  P. 266.
75  See, e.g., Pender (1999).
76  See, e.g., Redfield (1985).
77  D.L. 6.73 with Moles (1995a) 139–40 {below, pp. 398–400}; D.L. 6.37, 68.

Discussion of *Or.* 13's philosophical content must tackle the question of irony. A *certain* degree of ironisation is intrinsic alike to the model of the Cynicised Socrates and to the self-representation of the Cynic himself;[78] hence these elements are 'always already' present both in Dio's representation of Socrates and in his self-representation. Nevertheless, Dio has *somewhat* increased that irony by introducing the sorts of equivocation highlighted by Whitmarsh,[79] including the characterisation of Socratic doctrine and of himself, Dio, as 'old'/'old-fashioned' (*archaios*):

> (14) ... while I was upbraiding all the others and first and most of all myself in these and similar ways, sometimes through lack of resources I would go to a certain **old** *logos*, spoken by a certain Socrates ... [[120]] (29) ... so to all the others I used to say practically the same things [as Socrates did], things **old/old-fashioned** and stale,[80] and when they would not let me be at peace when I got to[81] Rome itself, I did not dare to speak any word of my own, fearing lest I be laughed to scorn and seem a fool, in as much as I was fully conscious of my own great **old-fashionedness** and lack of learning.

This irony requires further consideration,[82] but it is important to note here that Dio's appeal to an 'old *logos*' falls within a broad philosophical tradition which grounds itself in 'ancient wisdom'.[83] This move is often made by Cynics,[84] and repeatedly by Dio himself.[85]

From this survey *Or.* 13 emerges as philosophically erudite and resourceful.[86]

---

78  Cynic theatricality and exaggeration (both developments of Socratic characteristics) and their clear protreptic/paideutic justification: D.L. 6.35; Kindstrand (1976) 208–9; Moles (1983b) 274–6 {below, pp. 97–100}; (1983c) 108–9 {below, pp. 325–8}; p. 281 below; *contra* Branham (1996); cf. also the *spoudaiogeloion*: n. 204.
79  Whitmarsh (2001) 160–7.
80  ἕωλα (Capps) is certain: cf. *Or.* 12.12 (with Russell (1992) 169).
81  Translation: p. 269.
82  P. 281.
83  Boys-Stones (2001).
84  Moles (1983c) 116 {below, p. 339} and n. 103; Boys-Stones (2001) 7–8, 13–14, 24–5.
85  1.8, 53, 75; 3.1–3; 11.37; 12.12, 27–8; 36.34, 58–60; 72.11–12, 15–16; Desideri (1978) 351 n. 14; Moles (1990) 308, 321, 368 n. 40, 370 n. 79 {above, pp. 124, 137, 124 n. 40, 137 n. 79}; Swain (1996) 202–5.
86  *Pace* Long (2002) 123: 'Dio's recourse to Socrates is trite and self-serving.'

## 5    Historical Problems

There are three: (a) who was the Roman whose fall caused Dio's exile? (b) Where was Dio exiled from? (c) How reliable is Dio's account of his becoming a philosopher? All three historical problems have important interpretative implications.

(a) Possibilities are: Q. Iunius Arulenus Rusticus; M. Arrecinus Clemens; L. Salvius Otho Cocceianus; T. Flavius Sabinus; *non liquet*.[87]

The crucial passage has already been quoted.[88] There are two criteria: (i) the man must be closely related to the Flavians;[89] (ii) Dio's exile was long.[90] Rusticus, killed in, or shortly before, 93,[91] is excluded by (i) and (ii). Clemens, executed in 93, is excluded by (ii). Otho Cocceianus is excluded by (i). Sabinus, cousin of Domitian and *cos.* 82, the year of his death,[92] satisfies both criteria, as do also Dio's Flavian contacts.[93] The man's identity and the date of Dio's exile are worth (re-)establishing for the historical reconstruction of Dio's early career.

But a problem remains. Was Dio *in fact* Sabinus' φίλος/*amicus* and σύμβουλος/ *consiliarius*? Is Dio admitting this or merely recording the charge and then, while implying Sabinus' innocence, either leaving the truth of the alleged relationship between himself and Sabinus open or implying its non-existence? Verrengia takes λεγομένης as 'cosiddetta' and comments: 'da tale amicizia Dione intende prendere le distanze'.[94] On this reading, δή is presumably also distancing.[95] On the usual reading, however, these words merely gloss the charges as *stated*.[96]

Since Dio characterises Sabinus as 'not base' and compares himself to Scythian kings' cup-bearers, cooks, or concubines, he is not denying that he 'knew' Sabinus. He represents Sabinus (*qua* 'not base') as innocent; Sabinus' innocence necessarily makes Dio also innocent, but his innocence seems to

---

87  Respectively, Mommsen (1869) 84 n. 4; B. W. Jones (1990); Sidebottom (1996) 451–2; Emperius (1847) 103–8, followed by von Arnim (1898) 223ff; C. P. Jones (1978) 46; Desideri (1978) 189; Moles (1978) 93 {above, p. 47}; (2003) 190–1 {above, pp. 232–4}; *non liquet*: Schmid (1903) 852; Swain (1996) 189 n. 8; Verrengia (2000) 66–77 (useful overview).
88  P. 251.
89  P. 252.
90  12.16; 40.2, 12; 45.10.
91  Verrengia (2000) 70–1.
92  Verrengia (2000) 70 n. 16; 76–7.
93  Above, n. 6; my treatment meets Verrengia's difficulties ([2000] 76–7).
94  Verrengia (2000) 68 and n. 8.
95  Denniston (1954) 230.
96  Von Arnim (1898) 228; Cohoon II.91; Desideri (1978) 188; cf. Denniston (1954) 234–5.

exceed this: Scythian cup-bearers, cooks, and concubines are not kings' friends and counsellors, and the αἰτία made against Dio was without αἰτία (even on its own terms, 'without cause'). Thus λεγομένης and δή do have a distancing quality. Dio is representing himself as legally cleaner than clean, though the full implications of this dextrous passage only [[121]] become clear later.[97] As to the facts, Dio admits that he knew Sabinus; his implicit denial that he was his friend or counsellor, doubly motivated as it is, does not establish a historical negative. I conclude that Dio was close to Sabinus. Dio had the highest court contacts and his fall was mighty.

(b) Where was Dio exiled from? Prusa, certainly (*Or.* 19.1–2); on the usual forms of exile, also Bithynia, *qua* province, and Rome and Italy, *qua communis patria* of Roman citizens.[98] But Desideri has repeatedly maintained that Dio's exile took the lighter form of *ciuitate pellere*, since sections 29ff. have Dio philosophising in Rome.[99] These sections are usually read as referring to Dio's philosophising after his recall and return to Rome in 99/100,[100] when he philosophised before Trajan among others.[101] Resolution of this problem must be deferred.[102]

(c) How reliable is Dio's account of his becoming a philosopher?

Simple acceptance[103] is immediately threatened by the elaborate Socratic, Diogenic, Antisthenic, Zenonian, and Cynic associations which Dio invokes.[104] There is every reason to accept Fronto's testimony that Dio learnt philosophy from Musonius Rufus, i.e., before the exile.[105] Hence another reading of the speech: as a self-serving rewriting of Dio's autobiography. By post-dating his philosophising, Dio buries his early pupillage under Musonius, his unsavoury oscillations between philosophy and sophistry, and his collaboration with

---

97   Below, p. 267.
98   Verrengia (2000) 83.
99   Desideri (1978) 193, 241–2 n. 50; accepted by Whitmarsh (2001) 157 n. 89.
100  Von Arnim (1898) 256, 332; C. P. Jones (1978) 53, 128; Sheppard (1984) 162; Verrengia (2000) 79.
101  Reaffirmation of delivery to Trajan as the primary context for the *Kingships*: Moles (2003) 195–201 {above, pp. 195–201}; cf. Salmeri (2000) 89–91; *contra*, Whitmarsh (2001) 186–216, 325–7; the *a priori* plausibility of such contexts: Haake (2003); the dating 99/100: Salmeri, loc. cit.; Moles (2003) 196 {above, p. 242}; other philosophical contexts: p. 277.
102  Below, p. 269.
103  Nock (1933) 173–4; Kindstrand (1978); Blomqvist (1989) 225–6, 232.
104  Above, pp. 254–62.
105  Fronto 11.50 Haines = 135 van den Hout; Moles (1978) 82, 86 {above, pp. 28, 35}; below, nn. 108–9.

Vespasian's campaign against philosophers in 71.[106] From these perspectives, *Or.* 13 conveys a most misleading impression.

What, then, of Whitmarsh's claim that Dio is here engaged in a Freudian/Bloomian struggle for 'authority' with his teacher, Musonius?[107] Since another of Dio's works alludes obliquely to Musonius,[108] some other works show Musonian influence,[109] and Musonius' Περὶ Φυγῆς was in Greek, Dio 'the man' can hardly have been unconscious of his master's voice. But it is another question whether Musonius is 'in the text'. There are no significant parallels nor any 'contradictions' so sharp as to imply polemic. Any active presence of Musonius would sabotage the narrative's basic credibility.[110]

Thus on the general issue of when and how he became a philosopher Dio should still be convicted of disingenuousness. This, however, does not provide a sufficient explanation of the speech or even of the function within it of Dio's autobiography.[111]

The important question of the historicity of the consultation of Delphi involves so many other questions that I defer it.[112]

[[122]] 6 Main Themes

I here summarise main themes and note interconnections, without prejudging ultimate interpretative questions:

(a) Place. Like all exiles, Dio faces the question: where can the 'displaced' exile 'place' himself (5)? The speech ends with Rome as the central 'place' of the world's riches (36). Place can also be metaphorical: Apollo's oracular reply in 9 is ἄτοπος—seemingly, 'out of place'. Physical place is less important than moral place. Even at the end, Rome will not be truly 'strong' (34)—with the standard pun,[113] unless she 'renames' herself under Dio's philosophical programme by reducing her luxury, consumption, and very population, thereby

---

106   Moles (1978), esp. 96–100 {above, pp. 52–8}.
107   Whitmarsh (2001) 137, 164 ('the master–pupil relationship ... has been translated into a contest of the symbolic terrain of literary tropes and allusions').
108   31.122 with, e.g., Moles (1978) 82–3 {above, pp. 27–30}; Whitmarsh (2001) 137 n. 16.
109   Geytenbeek (1963) 14–15; Brunt (1973); Russell (1992) 150; Blomqvist (1995) 187; Houser (1998) 257–8; Hawley (2000) 136–7; Brenk (2000) 262–6.
110   The nearest 'parallel' is the rejection of the play 'Rome' ~ 'strength' (Musonius F 9, p. 44 Hense; below, with n. 113), but this move is commonplace. As to the *general* explanatory force of Whitmarsh's claim, I am sceptical.
111   Pp. 267 and 283.
112   P. 272.
113   Erskine (1995); Whitmarsh (2001) 21, 149; cf. n. 110 above.

becoming a smaller place (34–5). Places, too, are not what they seem: Rome under Domitian resembles Scythia at its most barbarous (1), or Athens rent by war or *stasis* (1, 6);[114] similarly, Socrates' description of Persia under Xerxes (24) eerily evokes Rome under Domitian.[115]

(b) Travel. Dio, like many exiles, must 'wander'. He consults Delphi because Apollo is a ἱκανὸς σύμβουλος (9): he can 'reach' the right advice or help humans to 'reach' the right goal (ἱκανός ~ ἱκνέομαι).[116] By contrast, ordinary politicians are not 'competent to give advice' (22). Τὸ ἱκανόν becomes one of the speech's philosophical *desiderata* (9, 16, 19, 22, 27, 32). Travel can be *both* literal and moral/metaphorical *or* simply metaphorical (13, 16, 19). The speech itself becomes a philosophical journey. When Dio starts his philosophical preaching (14), he 'goes to' an old, Socratic *logos*, and it is the 'old' *logos* of the Cynicised Socrates which enables the moral progress of Dio himself and of his individual listeners as he wanders and which is finally capable of saving Rome (29ff.).[117]

The horizontal movement of travel is matched by vertical movement downwards through time (16, etc.). The acme of the travel imagery is reached in 35, where Dio expatiates on the rewards the Romans will gain 'when you have reached the peak of virtue', a phrase which combines horizontal movement and vertical movement, and vertical movement in two senses: upwards to a peak of virtue and upwards in time.

The imagery of (a) and (b) is, indeed, almost all-pervasive, and, once established, energises ordinarily inert words. For example, in 13 'the present evils, great ignorance and disturbance' and in 32 'the unchastenedness and havingness' are, as it were, 'places' to get away from. Συμβαίνω, a *leitmotiv* of the speech (1, 6 [*bis*], 12, 26), is similarly energised: moral problems involve not only human beings as agents, who have to progress in the right way, but also as passive before challenges which come from the outside. Ultimately, therefore, exile, wanderings and travel, while literal enough, are also metaphors for moral states or aspirations. By contrast, place, while sometimes also metaphorical, retains important literal force in the case of Rome, though she too has to 're-place' herself morally.

---

114   Above, n. 23.
115   Domitianic are: (a) the Persian king (cf. *Orr.* 4 and 6; von Arnim [1898] 261–2; Desideri [1978] 202, 244 n. 5, 288); (b) the tiara (cf. 1.79; 3.41; 4.25, 61); (c) the evil *daimon* (cf. 45.1); (d) the alleged military incompetence.
116   Cf. 30.1, 45 with Moles (2000a) 197–8 {above, pp. 214–16}.
117   The same enabling role of *logos* in the *First Kingship* (Moles [1990] 311, 322, 325–6 {above, pp. 127, 138, 141–3}) and the *Charidemus* (Moles [2000a] 197–8 {above, pp. 214–16}); cf. the related 'wandering physically'/'wandering in words' (4.37; 7.1, 127; 12.16; Moles [1995b] 179 {above, p. 190}; Whitmarsh [2001] 160).

In this Dionian speech, as in others,[118] the relationships between literal, metaphorical, and textual places and travels present puzzles. Apollo's oracle to Dio, seemingly 'out of place', is (9) 'not easy to put together' (συμβαλεῖν). Apollo, *qua* ἱκανὸς σύμβουλος, tells Dio to keep on wandering until he comes to the last place on earth, just as—Dio reflects—Teiresias, *qua* σύμβουλος, told Odysseus to wander until he 'met together with' (συμβάλῃ) people 'who knew not the sea even by hearsay'. There are insistent and suitably oracular verbal plays. Apollo poses a prophetic puzzle both for Dio, *qua* dramatic character, and for Dio's audience/readers to 'put together'.

⟦123⟧ (c) The search for a competent philosophical counsellor. Τὸ βουλεύεσθαι is another *leitmotiv* (1, 6, 8, 9, 11, 19, 22, 23, 24). Right decisions require the help of a competent σύμβουλος: Apollo in relation to Croesus and Dio, Tiresias in relation to Odysseus (6–10). By the end, the σύμβουλος is transformed into a more explicit διδάσκαλος (32; cf. 17). This theme adds another dimension to Dio's veiled and equivocal allusion to Sabinus (1). Dio's implicit denial that their association extended to friendship and counsel *adumbrates* an *ideal* counsellor/friend relationship. Dio has now left behind the glittering, meretricious world of high-level politicking.

(d) The search for the right education. This theme first becomes explicit in the Socratic *logos* section, which it proceeds to dominate (16ff.; 23; 24–6). Similarly, Dio in Rome argues the need for good education and good teachers (31–3), and ends by expounding the Antisthenic double *paideia* (37). But the theme is latent from the very beginning of the speech, as Dio turns first to literature and then to the Delphic oracle for guidance on the correct response to exile.

(e) In this speech, apart from the puzzling oracle, what seems hard is actually easy, both hard and easy being used both of worldly states and of the intellectual and moral capacities required to cope with them. Exile and all other similar disasters seem hard: they are actually easy to deal with (2–8). And the speech ends (37) with the Antisthenic 'double *paideia*', both elements of which are 'easy'.

(f) A related idea is that true philosophical virtues are the opposite of worldly values, characteristically those held by the ignorant majority (2, 7, 31). Exile, etc. are not evils: they are, in a way, goods: πόνος ἀγαθόν (D.L. 6.2). The shape of the speech again instantiates this moral lesson. Sabinus seems very close to the 'fortunate rulers', but they were not *really* fortunate, and by the end the only 'good fortune' and 'rule' that matter are *philosophical* 'good fortune' and *self*-rule (31, 33).

---

118   P. 272.

(g) Divine authority is stressed throughout: the δαιμόνιον (3), the various oracles, including Delphi (2, 6–10, 36). This does not mean that 'religion' is more important than 'philosophy':[119] as in the Socratic–Antisthenic–Cynic philosophical tradition generally, the two are mutually implicated. The δαιμόνιον co-exists with human εὐδαιμονία. Xerxes/Domitian (24) is *alike* an 'evil spirit' *and* himself 'unfortunate' *and* the agent of 'misfortune' in others.

(h) As a dramatic figure within the text, Dio himself helps to knit together apparently disparate elements and to embody major themes. His unclarified relationship with Sabinus adumbrates the σύμβουλος and διδάσκαλος themes. His 'experiencing' of exile, his 'consultation' of Delphi, and his and Socrates' sermons on the 'use' of wealth are all interlinked by the verb χράομαι (3, 9, 16, 23):[120] the right 'use' of apparent misfortune, of oracles and of material things is always the same thing: the right individual and collective response to external things, and Dio's initial apparent misfortune anticipates all the other problems. His poverty in exile prefigures Socrates' attacks upon Athenian materialism and his own attacks upon Roman materialism. His 'wandering' is itself morally ambiguous: it can be a symbol of folly, a route to wisdom, or itself already a form of 'truth' (ἀλητεία ~ ἀλήθεια).[121] Dio dangles these alternatives in 10–11:

> exhorting myself in this way [according to the example of Odysseus] neither to fear nor to be ashamed of the thing, and putting on humble dress and in all other respects chastening myself, I began to wander [ἠλώμην] everywhere. And the people who chanced to meet me, when they saw me, some of them called me a wanderer [ἀλητήν], but certain others actually a philosopher.[122]

⟦124⟧ And not only do Dio's experiences and reactions anticipate Socratic teachings, but he himself becomes the σύμβουλος of everybody whom he meets in the speech, including the Romans at the end. Dio's own education, which the speech traces, equips him for this task. There is another level on which Dio's self-representation is not just about himself: through the comparisons with Odysseus, with tragic figures and with tragic plots,[123] his wanderings

---

119   *Pace* Brenk (2000) 269–70.
120   Similar play in *Or.* 10 (2ff.): both perhaps inspired by Hdt. 7.140–1 (p. 273 and n. 147).
121   The ambiguity: Moles (1990) 309, 322 {above, pp. 124, 138}; Montiglio (2000); Whitmarsh (2001) 162, 198–200; Hom. *Od.* 14.122–7; Hdt. 1.29.1–30.2; 4.76.2; Pl. *Apol.* 22a; Redfield (1985) 98–9.
122   Closely similar are 1.9 (Dio's self-introduction in the *First Kingship*), with Moles (1990) 309 {above, p. 124}, and 72.2, 11.
123   Above, n. 21.

acquire mythic status, and, though the effect is undoubtedly partly to sound Dio's own trumpet, it is also to shift the focus away from the personal towards the mythical and universalising. As in other works (notably the *First Kingship, Euboicus, Diogenics,* and *Charidemus*), Dio transmutes his own biography into rich philosophical myth.[124]

(i) As much of the above material already suggests, the speech enacts a general movement of 'correction' or 'redefinition' of several of its key themes: from false 'good fortune', 'counsel', 'rule', and 'education' to 'true', from 'hardship' and 'difficulty' to 'easiness'. This process is in fact thoroughly comprehensive.[125]

The sheer thematic density of Dio's writing, beneath its complaisant surface, is remarkable.

## 7  Specific Interpretative Problems

There are two: (a) sections 29ff.; (b) section 9.

(a) There are strong objections to Desideri's claim that sections 29ff. show Dio philosophising in Rome during the exile:[126]

> (1) Dio writes (29): 'so to the others I used to say practically the same things [as Socrates], things old-fashioned and stale, and when/since they would not let me be in peace when I got to Rome itself, I did not dare to speak any word of my own …' Here 'the others' means 'everybody other than the Romans' and 'when I got to Rome' refers to a later time.[127] The clear implication that sections 29ff. mark the culmination of Dio's exile wanderings hardly fits the hypothesis that Dio was never exiled from Rome.
>
> (2) In sections 30–1 Dio writes: 'Archelaus, king of the Macedonians … summoned [Socrates] with the inducement of gifts and fees, that he might hear him speaking these words. In the same way I too tried to speak to the Romans, when they summoned me and asked me to speak.' This

---

124  Cf., respectively, Moles (1990) 305–37 {above, pp. 120–3}; Jouan (1977), (1993a), and (1993b); Moles (1995b) 180 {above, p. 191}; (2000a) 202–4 {above, pp. 218–21}.

125  However, I failed to persuade Readers and Editor that the process is systematically 'keyed' by an elaborate series of ring-structures between beginning and end.

126  Above, p. 264 and n. 99.

127  Translation: Cohoon 11.115; Swain (1996) 212; *pace* Desideri (1978) 221; Verrengia (2000) 111; aorist of γίγνομαι + ἐν as 'arrive at' is Classical and suitably Herodotean (p. 253): Hdt. 1.105, 189; 2.107; Powell (1938) 69.

analogy between Archelaus' 'summoning' of Socrates and the Romans' 'summoning' of himself can hardly apply to Domitianic Rome.

(3) Dio elsewhere, in contexts where duplicity is unlikely and would have been risky (as damaging his credibility, or inviting ridicule, were his claims falsifiable), states, or implies, that, once exiled, he was absent from Rome for the rest of Domitian's reign and that his return was secured by Domitian's death and Nerva's accession.[128]

However, if sections 29ff. refer to Dio's *post*-exile philosophising in Rome, three questions arise: (i) how can Dio's exile narrative legitimately include allusion to his post-exilic philosophical activity in Rome? While it is easy to see that Dio might *want* to represent his philosophising ⟦[125]⟧ in Trajanic Rome as part of his whole philosophical project ever since he first became a philosopher, indeed as the culmination of his philosophical career,[129] how can he do this within the logic of this speech? (ii) How can Dio convey an allusion to his recall by Nerva and return to Rome under Trajan without explicitly alluding to them? (iii) How can he link the exile and post-exile phases of his career so as to imply both difference and continuity?

Question (i) is fundamental, and questions (ii) and (iii) concern Dio's technical skill. *If* sections 29ff. represent Dio's philosophising in Rome as the culmination of his exile wanderings, then, since Socrates is a figure for Dio, it is easy to read *Archelaus* ('ruler of the people'), who 'summoned' Socrates, as an analogue of either Nerva, who recalled Dio to Rome,[130] or of Trajan, for whom Dio performed the σύμβουλος role that Archelaus had solicited from Socrates, or indeed of both Nerva and Trajan, such 'allegory', whether simple or double, being thoroughly Dionian, in the *Kingships* and elsewhere.[131] The wording is suspiciously 'loaded': Archelaus 'knew many things and had associated with many of the wise' (like Nerva); 'he called him [Socrates] with presents and fees, in order that he might hear him saying these *logoi*'. 'These *logoi*', formally Socrates', can also be Dio's, 'now' or on similar occasions.[132] Hence another ring-structure and contrast: between Rome at the beginning under the tyrannical Domitian and Rome at the end under the 'good' 'ruler' of his people, Nerva and/or Trajan, whose function is to bring Dio's philosophical

---

128   1.50, with Moles (1990) 329 {above, p. 146}; 46.2–3, with Moles (1984) 67–8 {above, pp. 106–8}; cf. Philostr. *VS* 487–9.
129   Cf. the *First Kingship*: 1.56–8 (the Arcadian prophetess).
130   45.2–3 with Moles (1984) 67–8 {above, pp. 106–8}.
131   Moles (1990), e.g., 328 {above, p. 145}; (2000a) 206–7 {above, pp. 222–4}.
132   For the nicely blurred focalisation, cf. 'this father' in the *Charidemus* (30.45): Moles (2000a) 205–6 {above, pp. 221–3}.

teaching to the Romans at large. So 'the Romans summoned me' effectively implies: 'Nerva/Trajan gave me this huge philosophical commission'.[133] Hence also Dio's return becomes a metaphor not only for Trajan's celebrated 'repatriation' of philosophers and intellectuals[134] but also for the return from exile of the entire Roman world under Nerva and Trajan, and Dio's exile a metaphor for the exile of the spirit imposed on all his subjects by the 'evil δαίμων' Domitian, who frustrated his subjects' εὐδαιμονία (1, 24).[135]

As for (i), part of the answer lies in Dio's response to Apollo's oracle to go to the ends of the earth. In a way, he did: he penetrated deeply into Dacia, Scythia, and the Black Sea area, as presumably his audience knew and as he himself described in other works.[136] Such travel enhances his moral authority: as the wanderer *par excellence* who has travelled to the ends of the earth, he has done, and seen, it all. As the ultimate Cynic 'scout' (κατάσκοπος),[137] he is uniquely qualified to apply his experience to the task of reforming Rome, the central τόπος of the world (36). But it is not only a question of Dio's response to the oracle: it is also a question of the oracle's meaning.

(b) Apollo's oracle to Dio, seemingly 'out of place', was 'not easy to put together' (συμβαλεῖν). Apollo told Dio to go to the last place on earth, as Teiresias told Odysseus to wander until he 'met together with [συμβάλῃ] people who knew not the sea even by hearsay'.

〖126〗 Now *Or.* 13, a text that relates wanderings and journeys, is itself a journey which Dio (and his listeners) have been making. Although he was exiled from Rome, Dio's last destination, at the end of the text, turns out to be Rome. At the beginning of the text Rome was like Scythia in a bad sense. At the end,

---

133 A referee objects that 32–3 (on the ideal teacher to be established on 'the Acropolis') alludes both to Dio and Trajan and that 'it hasn't happened yet', hence an earlier Nerva/Trajan allusion in 30–1 is excluded and the speech is exilic. But: (i) other considerations make the speech post-exilic (p. 253; n. 11); (ii) 32–3 is future in relation to 31, where Dio is already in Rome, not (or not necessarily) in relation to the delivery context; (iii) in Domitianic Rome Dio could hardly be publicly arguing, however allusively, for Domitian's removal; (iv) how could Dio *then* know that *Trajan* would replace Domitian (and Nerva)? (v) nothing in the passage suggests violent change; (vi) Dio is surely alluding to himself (p. 283) but hardly also to Trajan (or any other potential emperor): this is a philosophical teacher. 'Establishment on the Acropolis' entails 'philosopher-ruler', but this is not 'Trajan as philosopher-king' but philosopher as philosopher-ἄρχων (= Dio as Trajan's court-philosopher), Trajan's ἀρχή having already been covered by 30 Ἀρχελάος.
134 Plin. *Pan.* 47.1–2.
135 The *First Kingship* enacts the same philosophical/political narrative of 'mass exile': 1.55, with Moles (1990) 321, 370 n. 82 {above, p. 137 with n. 82}.
136 12.10–20; 36.1; Philostr. *vs* 487–9.
137 D.L. 6.17–18, 43; Norden (1893) 373–85; Moles (1983c) 112 {below, p. 331}; Schofield (2004) 453–5.

if Rome is to be radically reinvented, she may need the services of a Scythian or Indian (32): she may need to become like the positive Cynic conceptions of Scythia and the Gymnosophists. Dio's real-life wanderings had taken him to the end of the earth: Dacia and Scythia. The end of the earth can be morally bad (Scythia as a tyranny) or morally good (Scythia as the location of Cynic perfection). But places and journeys are not only places and journeys: they are also metaphors. If Rome is to be morally regenerated, to become truly 'Rome', she must become like one of the 'good' countries at the end of the earth. From the point of view of Dio's *moral* journey, then, 'the last (bad) place on earth' is Rome itself.[138] Rome as the *end* of the earth is a thoroughly paradoxical conception, though not unparalleled,[139] but the provocative inversion of categories is characteristically Cynic and here facilitated by Scythia's switch from being morally bad to morally good.

It turns out, then, that Apollo was ultimately telling Dio to convert the Romans.[140] Hence the sense of fulfilment in 29 'when I got to Rome *itself*'. There is an important 'gap' in the text here: we must see that, after initial puzzlement (9), Dio eventually interpreted Apollo's oracle rightly. If, as a result of Dio's teaching, the Romans eventually 'come to the summit of virtue', this will be the vertical culmination of Dio's horizontal wanderings (the wording echoes 9 'until you come to the last place on earth').[141] The application to Rome of Socratic teaching is similarly apposite: the best form of education has been 'handed down' in the place where it can be most useful. For its recipients to 'come to the summit of virtue', they have to go back in time to the true ἀρχή (both 'beginning' and 'rule'). The horizontal and vertical movements of the speech converge in the central τόπος of the world.[142] The shape of the speech

---

138  Fittingly, therefore, the negative allusion to Rome at 36 ('all the possessions from everywhere have been gathered together into this one place ...') *inverts* an encomiastic *topos* about the greatest cities, especially Rome (e.g. Plin. *HN* 3.39; Dio 32.36; Aristid. 46.23).

139  See next n.

140  Remarkably, *Or.* 13 parallels Luke, Acts: (i) Jesus sends the apostles to the end of the earth ~ Apollo sends Dio on mission to the end of the earth; (ii) both texts instantiate these journeyings; (iii) in both, the end of the earth/text/ultimate missionary location turns out to be Rome (whether in Acts literally the end of the earth, as in ps.-Sol. 8.15, or—better—proleptically so). *Could* Dio have known Luke, Acts (certainly the earlier text and often conjectured to be Rome-orientated)?

141  The combination of horizontal (Dio's wanderings) and vertical (ascent to the 'heights' of virtue) and the relationship between the two (the former precursor of the latter) is paralleled in the *First Kingship* (1.66ff.).

142  A referee notes that Delphi also claimed to be the centre of the world, which presumably increases the piquancy of Dio's topographical playing.

again instantiates the philosophical trajectory: progression from Rome entails regression to Rome.

This play with seemingly 'atopic' topology as the central structuring device of a speech is paralleled in the *First Kingship, Olympicus, Charidemus*, and *Borystheniticus*;[143] and the use of the Delphic oracle to justify Dio's philosophical relationship with Nerva and Trajan is paralleled by the Arcadian prophetess as a device for bringing Dio before Trajan (1.49ff.).

What, at last, of the *historicity* of Dio's consultation of Delphi? Is this consultation—otherwise unattested in Dio—based on the Socrates, Zeno, and Diogenes paradigms? How does Dio's encounter with the Arcadian prophetess, itself obviously invented,[144] affect the question? Would invention of the consultation of Delphi, if detected, have damaged Dio's credibility, or would such a fiction have been smilingly accepted by his sophisticated audience?

Oracle experts and some Dionian scholars take Dio's consultation and Delphi's reply as historical.[145] Jones, however, suggests: 'since Dio was in fact "at the end of the earth" when he was [[127]] recalled, it might ... seem that this oracle was made up after the event.'[146] Moreover, 'the end(s) of the earth' is an exilic *topos*; Delphi told the Athenians in 481/80 to flee to the ends of the earth[147] (hence Dio's *Athenian* audience might be tickled by such an invention); and the phrase plays a crucial role in *Or.* 13's spatial and moral architecture.

Yet such invention might, even for Dio, be an invention too far. The 'coincidence' of Dio's being 'at the end of the earth' when recalled is only excessive if the oracle's response (9 'he told me to keep doing the very thing on which I was[148] engaged with all enthusiasm, as being a fine and useful activity, "until", he said, "you come to the end of the earth"') was to the question 'when will my exile end?'[149] Dio omits the question, but it is better understood as 'what should

---

143   1.49, 55, etc.; 12.1, 16; 30.1, 46; 36.43; Moles (1990) 322 {above, p. 138}; (1995b) 181, 188 (above, pp. 192, 199}; (2000a) 197–8 {above, pp. 214–15}.
144   Because of the Platonic evocations (Moles [1990] 320 {above, p. 136}; Trapp [1990] 143–4) and the obviously *post eventum* prophecy.
145   Parke–Wormell (1956) 1.409; Fontenrose (1978) 15 n. 4; 263; Moles (1978) 99 {above, pp. 57f.}; Desideri (1991) 3938–9.
146   C. P. Jones (1978) 47 (quotation), 51, 176 n. 57.
147   Hdt. 7.140 (which perhaps influenced Dio in another respect: n. 120), and, e.g., Ov. *Tr.* 1.2.85; 2.195; 3.3.3; Sen. *Ep.* 28.4.
148   'I *am* engaged' (Cohoon) could only be justified were Dio saying: 'to do the very thing on which I am [now] engaged' (post-96 Dio could still represent himself as wandering: 12.16ff.); but 'the very thing' implies 'more of the same', an implication reinforced by the Odyssean analogy; πράττειν means 'to keep doing' (thus also Cohoon); the present εἰμί is 'vivid'.
149   As Fontenrose (1978) 15 n. 4.

I do in my exile?' He then found the response 'out of place' and 'not easy to put together', because it was not easy to see how wandering was a fine and useful activity, nor to locate 'the end of the earth', nor to understand how attaining it was a solution to his problems. More positively, Delphi provides the ultimate divine and philosophical grounding for the speech, and it *would* be weakening, if that grounding were entirely groundless, especially, perhaps, given the very public association with Delphi of Plutarch and the rivalry between these two great Greeks.[150] Rather, when the sentence of exile was passed, Dio *immediately* began wandering,[151] and his inventiveness comes into play, not with the consultation itself nor with the oracular response (oracles, too, use τόποι),[152] but with the many philosophical associations that he thereby invokes and with the paradoxical twist that he gives to 'the end of the earth', using Apollo's instruction as the basis for a rewriting of his whole career, a rewriting which has the practical advantage of suppressing his pre-exile philosophising and related aspects of his disreputable past, but which, more importantly, gives divine sanction to his post-exile dealings with Nerva and Trajan and to his project of the conversion of Rome.

As to why Dio consulted Delphi, he may have been influenced by the motives that he adduces (8), commonplace though they are,[153] and, as a Stoic (mostly), he should have accepted oracles,[154] but he must already have been conscious of the philosophical associations of his action, must already have been stage-managing the drama of *Dio Socraticus et Cynicus*.

## 8  Interpretation

There is much to consider: the speech's wit, irony, and literary sophistication; its moral seriousness; its philosophical content; its view of *paideia*; Dio's own dramatic role; the representations of fifth-century Athenians, of contemporary Greeks other than the Athenians (11–15), and of the Romans; the apparently dominant focus on Rome at the end; the teaching that Dio gives the Romans; the relationship between internal audiences (especially the Romans) and external audience (Athenians).

I start with the last.

---

150  *Lamprias Catalogue* 204, 227; Desideri (1978) 4–5.
151  Had Dio *settled* elsewhere, he would have lost his Bithynian properties: von Arnim (1898) 235–6.
152  Fontenrose (1978) 166ff.; Hammerstaedt (1993) 405.
153  Verrengia (2000) 87–8, 136.
154  Contrast his more Cynic voice in 1.56 and 10.17ff.

## [128] 8.1 *Greeks and Romans*

On one level, Dio and his audience are Greeks and the Romans are Romans (despite Dio's own Roman citizenship and high imperial connections and the certainty of there being Roman citizens in Dio's audience). Dio consults Delphi 'in accordance with the ancient custom of the Greeks' (9), addresses the Romans as 'you' and talks of 'your city', alludes to the Roman empire as something external to himself (34ff.),[155] and distinguishes straightforwardly between Greeks, Romans, Scythians, and Indians (32). The latter half of the speech focuses on Roman vices, and the ending leaves the Romans entirely without *paideia* in the normal sense, their 'learning' confined to the military arts, not themselves commended,[156] while the Greeks seem to belong to the 'ruled' (33), which, given the 'succession-of-empires' motif (23–5, 34), effectively makes them the Romans' 'slaves'.

Is Dio, then, merely trying to convince his Athenian audience that he said appropriately critical and admonitory things to the Romans, thereby deflecting the charge that he was a mere flatterer of the Greeks' imperial masters?[157] True, self-justification is rarely absent from Dio's works; *Or.* 13 is at least self-justifying in its treatments of his relationship with Sabinus and of his philosophical career;[158] and Dio often had to deflect this charge.[159] But this reading leaves large tracts of the speech unexplained.

Might one, then, broaden the reading out and suggest that *Or.* 13 promotes Greek intellectual and philosophical identity as a bulwark against Roman power, at its most brutal under the Domitianic tyranny (1) but corrupted generally by materialism and luxury (31–7)? This reading *seems* to swab up a great deal of the speech, and one might compare Dio's *Olympicus*, a celebration of Greek religious culture that represents the Romans as militarists and the Greeks as their slaves.[160]

Superficially, there is much that appears to be intended to compliment the Athenians on their *paideia*. There are literary allusions a-plenty, nice literary turns, much skilful interweaving of different philosophical strands, and juicy interpretative challenges. There might also seem to be an appeal to

---

155  Contrast 3.34, 50; 41.9 (see n. 213) and 79.5.
156  37 ~ 32 ~ 24 (the Persians); also (?) ~ Virg. *Aen.* 6.847ff. (n. 59).
157  Swain (1996) 213.
158  Pp. 263 and 264.
159  E.g., 3.12–25; *Or.* 57.
160  Moles (1995b) 183–4 {above, pp. 193–4}; Swain (1996) 200–3; Klauck–Bäbler (2000) 158–9; *pace* Billaut (1999) 218–19; Greeks slaves of Rome: 31.125; 34.39, 51; Moles (1995b) 178 {above, p. 189} n. 5; Veyne (1999); *pace* Salmeri (2000) 86; Roman militarism: also 30.35 with Moles (2000a) 209 {above, p. 225}.

Athenians' sense of moral superiority, as they listen to Dio's attacks on Roman decadence;[161] amusing disparagement of Rome as 'the end of the earth'; and consolation in the thoughts that Roman power, apparently so strong, is fragile[162] and that the philosophical 'solution' is Greek.[163]

Yet any 'anti-Roman' reading fails in the face of the simple fact that the portrayal of the Romans is not finally negative. When Dio alludes to the Roman empire as something external to himself, he is appealing to the Romans' self-interest; the characterisation of the Romans as 'learned' in military matters (only) is made to the Romans themselves as well as to the Athenians and has protreptic force; and the fact that Dio ends up as philosophical 'ambassador' of Nerva and Trajan to the Romans and propounds a substantial philosophical programme indicates moral concern for them. Thus, in so far as the Romans are represented as different from the Greeks, ⟦129⟧ they are, paradoxically, both uneducated and easily educable, and the latter not only because of the intrinsic 'easiness' of the Antisthenic/Cynic education, but because the Romans' military expertise has already demonstrated their capacity for learning and because there is some analogy between Roman *uirtus* and Cynic virtue. The practicability of that virtue is further facilitated by the transition from Domitianic to Nervan and Trajanic Rome.[164]

Moreover, the *content* of Dio's teaching of the Romans is important. Despite modern scepticism,[165] his claim (29ff.) to have publicly exhorted the Romans to virtue is confirmed by *Or.* 79,[166] which attacks the city's materialism and argues that she will follow previous empires into oblivion, if she does not reform (cf. *Or.* 13); by *Or.* 72,[167] which wryly notes the unpopularity of philosophers' preachiness (9); and by the *Euboicus* (*Or.* 7), which tackles the question

---

161   Thus, e.g., Fuchs (1938) 18 n. 65; C. P. Jones (1978) 129 and 195 n. 26, comparing Lucian's *Nigrinus*, also set in Athens and seemingly critical of Roman morals; *contra*, Desideri (1978) 253–4 n. 10; sophisticated analysis in Whitmarsh (2001) 265–79 (though I do not agree that *Nigrinus* offers *no* moral *locus*).

162   34: 'but as for now [Rome's] greatness arouses suspicion and is *not at all* secure': thus rightly Swain (1996) 212, *pace* Cohoon and Verrengia; cf. Dio's brilliant reworking (36) of *Il.* 23.161–77.

163   Cf. the *Olympicus*, in which 'it is Greek poets, artists, and philosophers ... who have most perfectly represented the divine, and ... contemporary Greece is suffering from Roman misrule' (Moles (1995b) 184 {above, p. 195}).

164   Cf. Tac. *Agr.* 3.1, etc.

165   Swain (1996) 213; Whitmarsh (2001) 164, 215.

166   Schmid (1903) 857; Moles (1983a) 130–1 {above, pp. 63–6}; *contra*, Sheppard (1982) (exilic delivery in Tarsus) and Desideri (1978) 232–4 (exilic).

167   Von Arnim (1898) 276 (add 72.13–16 ~ 12.6–8); Crosby v.174–5; Russell (1992) 166; Desideri's exilic dating ([1978] 235; 259 n. 68) is untenable.

of suitable work for the urban poor, which was delivered, among other places, in Rome, and which, like *Or.* 13, has a certain Cynic underpinning.[168] Further, *Or.* 13 alludes to Dio's philosophical relationships with Nerva and Trajan, and it has repeated conceptual parallels with the *First Kingship*.[169] Thus *Orations* 1–4 (the *Kingships*), 7, 13, and 79 (and, in lighter vein, 72) all contribute to a post-exilic project for the moral reform of Rome, with the *Kingships* focusing on the new emperor, the others on the Romans *en masse*.

This suggests another context for *Or.* 13. Although most of Dio's works are speeches for oral delivery and many are occasional, some of the occasional pieces were recycled for other contexts;[170] Dio emphasises the paideutic value of reading; and some of his works are (also) reading works.[171] Hence, besides the primary audiences of speeches delivered in Rome and Athens, Dio may also have envisaged a 'reading audience',[172] which could contextualise *Oration* 13 alongside *Orations* 1–4, 7, and 79, and construct intertextual relationships. Certainly, such readings 'work'. One might hold that *Or.* 13's subtleties make private reading the 'ideal' reception context anyway. The moral teaching of 29ff. could have been directly available to Romans, as well as to Athenians and other Greeks.

But, if on any view Dio's moral teaching of the Romans is substantial, he is also saying profoundly uncomfortable things to his primary audience. Any cosy feelings of Greek superiority (cultural or other) are undermined on a number of levels. Athenian military successes of the fifth and early fourth centuries BC are summarily dismissed by Socrates (25–6)[173]—and the emphasis matters, because of the parallel dismissal by Dio of Roman power (32, 34). Greeks who yearned for the glory days[174] are granted no indulgence. Even more challengingly dismissed are the main constituents of traditional Athenian (and general Greek) *paideia*: music, athletics, the highest literary achievements. This dismissal cannot be sanitised as 'inert' repetition of 'historical' philosophical positions: in the Second Sophistic era, when Greece was, from one perspective,

---

168  Moles (1995b) 177–9 {above, pp. 188–90} (naturally not the *only* philosophical underpinning).
169  Above, n. 11.
170  Cf. 3.12; 4.73; *Or.* 5; *Or.* 7 (with Moles [1995b] 177 {above, p. 188}); 11.6; *Or.* 57.
171  *Or.* 18 is a reading-list for a politician and *Or.* 2 a reading-list for Trajan: Moles (1990) 346 {above, p. 162}; *Or.* 3.3 approves Trajan's reading of 'the ancients' (including Dio's own *Kingships*); and *Or.* 52 starts from Dio's reading of tragedy.
172  Intriguingly, Whitmarsh (2001) 162: 'the sophisticated reader'. Note also 15, where Dio's playful Thucydidean stress on the difficulty of recalling Socrates' λόγοι gains piquancy from his own reliance on a written text.
173  Similar in tone to *Charidemus* 30.35, with Moles (2000a) 209 {above, p. 225}.
174  Bowie (1970); (1974); Plut. *Praec. pol.* 814A–C.

under Roman rule (as this speech stresses), these were things that the Greek élite vigorously celebrated.

Dio in fact uses various devices to suggest the collapsing of time between Socrates and himself. One is to imply parallels between then and now (the triviality and impermanence of [[130]] fifth-century Athenian military successes ~ the triviality and impermanence of current Roman military supremacy). Another is simply to dissolve the distinction between 'then' and 'now' into a universalising 'always', hence Dio's own swift aside within Socrates' speech (26): 'and this has come not only to the Athenians but also to practically all human beings, both previously and now'.[175] Another is to suggest a distinction between education which is merely old and education whose oldness has genuinely validating force. Thus Socrates, as reported by Dio, satirically instances the ability to play Lamprocles on the lyre as proof for his Athenian audience of their political competence and defeat of the Persians as proof of the superiority of Athenian education (19; 23). These arguments were used by Right, to champion what to him was 'the old education' (Ar. *Nub.* 967, 985–6). But to *his* Athenian audience Dio projects *Socrates* as representative of 'the old *logos*' (14, 29)—a representation itself supported by the link between Socrates and Delphi (30) and the latter's association with 'the ancient custom of the Greeks' (9). Hence the standards of 'ancient Socrates' deconstruct the 'ancient' *paideia* both of Socrates' contemporary audience and of Dio's.

Thus Dio's Athenian listeners are given every incentive to see that Dio's account of Socrates' haranguings of fifth-century Athenians is a text that applies to them too, and that they are also in the same boat as the morally uninstructed Greeks whom Dio addressed during his wanderings (11–15): they must not take the fact that Dio is saying 'things which happen to have been said many years before' as an excuse for 'applying their minds the less' (15).

Hence the apparently dominant, and apparently problematic, focus on Rome at the end is on one level deceptive: the speech has quite as much to say to, and about, the external, contemporary Athenians. While it seems that the speech finally 'homes in' on Rome, this is not because Rome is its final concern, but rather because the physical place of Rome as it now is provides the best context for the promotion of the moral reform of *both* Romans *and* Athenians, both of whom are invited to *redefine* their moral place/space. For, if temporal boundaries are dissolved, so also are spatial (*cf.* 26).

Indeed, by the very end (37), the needs of both Roman and Athenian audiences paradoxically converge. The Athenians have lost their military power forever. Their vaunted *paideia* did not produce that evanescent military power,

---

175  Clearly Dio's own intervention: Desideri (1978) 221.

nor should it be a source of pride to them now in their subordination to Rome. The Romans never had any *paideia* in the Greek sense but had military *paideia* and still have empire, but that empire is fragile. Despite their apparent differences of status, then, the solution for both audiences is precisely the same: moral regeneration through Cynic *paideia* or 'self-sufficiency', though it is a solution to two rather different problems—for the Romans, the problem of materialism and luxury, for the Athenians, that of devotion to a culture which contributes nothing to moral virtue.[176]

Strikingly, in a speech addressed to cultured Athenians, the (alleged) fact that the Romans have no conventional culture has no moral significance and their military superiority proves their suitability for Cynic *paideia*. Here, as elsewhere, notably in *Or*. 18, the *Borystheniticus*, and the *Kingships*,[177] the highly πεπαιδευμένος Dio shows admirable flexibility in varying the dose of conventional *paideia* to suit particular moral needs. And as in the *Charidemus* and *Borystheniticus*,[178] Dio disconcertingly plays internal and external audiences off against each other.

This paradoxical convergence of need is pointed by structural patterning: just as Socrates ended his appeal to the Athenians by engaging with their national myth (the *epitaphios*), so Dio ends his appeal to the Romans by engaging with theirs (Romans do power, not culture); and the [[131]] Romans' moral problems, to which the Cynic educational programme is a solution (37), are climactically characterised as a form of 'unchastened licentiousness', just as Dio himself began the slow process of his own Cynic education by 'chastening himself' (10). And if Dio is the σύμβουλος of everybody he meets in the speech, he is necessarily also—because of the interplay between internal audiences and external audience—the σύμβουλος of the Athenians.

This explains another level of the speech. Analysis so far has proceeded on the basis of Greeks and Romans being different, but this difference is sometimes ignored. Dio's allusions to 'the man who was not base' and to 'those who were then fortunate and ruling' (1) do not imply: '*they* were Romans, *we* are not'. Similarly, the Scythian analogy (1) suggests Dio's membership of the same race/nation as everyone else (that is, as members of the Roman empire), and Dio's role as philosophical agent of Nerva and Trajan stresses his closeness to (good) Roman emperors, not his separateness from Rome. For ultimately in this speech, as in two other of his greatest works, the *Olympicus* and the

---

176  Of course, attacks on Roman luxury must also impact on wealthy Athenians.
177  Moles (1995b) 185 {above, p. 195}.
178  Russell (1992) 23; Moles (1995b) 184–92 {above, pp. 195–203}; Nesselrath–Bäbler-Forschner–de Jong (2003) appear uninterested in these interpretative aspects of the *Borystheniticus*.

*Borystheniticus*, Dio's moral concern is with nothing less than the whole world, because essentially the same moral prescription fits all human beings, though with necessary adjustments for local circumstances.[179] The Dio of these texts plays off the differences between Greek and Roman, but then subordinates them to the construction of virtue. Through Dio's 'redefinition' of 'Romanness', as implicit in the claim that, if the Romans follow his moral programme, they will become 'stronger' (34), the Athenians are also invited to become 'more roman', but this does not at all mean that they should become more *R*oman. For both groups, the apparent redefinition of 'ethnicity' functions as an encouragement to the acquisition of virtue. True, that virtue is conceived and exemplified by Greeks (Delphi, Socrates, Plato, Antisthenes, Dio), but it is not distinctively Greek: very few Greeks have it; Scythians and Indians might have it, and in the Cynic tradition, to which *Or.* 13 broadly belongs, some of them did have it; even Romans might have it; and it is open to everyone. In these respects, *Or.* 13 issues a profound challenge to Greeks' self-consciousness as Greeks, not because the constitution of Greekness is problematic, but because Greekness is not synonymous with virtue.[180]

## 8.2 *Philosophical Simplicity*

The speech issues an even more uncomfortable challenge to that most characteristic prejudice of sophisticated intellectuals (Greek and Roman, ancient and modern): that the more complex a philosophy, the better it is. But, for all its philosophical allusions, *Or.* 13's moral teaching is essentially simple, as Dio insists,[181] and it culminates in the exposition, directly to the Romans, implicitly to the Athenians, of a modified version of Antisthenes' 'double education', which is *explicitly* 'easy'. That the physical end of the speech which articulates that doctrine is also the end of the speech (in the sense of its ultimate meaning) is conveyed by numerous factors: the cumulative sense that Dio's 'wanderings' point towards 'the truth'; the status of Rome as the Apollo-inspired final destination of those wanderings; the status of the text itself as a journey; the sense of Dio as Nerva and Trajan's 'ambassador' to the Romans and as the

---

179  Here the *Charidemus is* different: Moles (2000a) 209 {above, p. 225}.
180  Hence another parallel with the subtly destabilising *Borystheniticus*: Russell (1992) 23; Moles (1995b) 190–2 {above, pp. 200–2}. Whitmarsh's claims ([2001] 20, 31) that '"Greek" and "Roman" … [are] constructed self-positions, idealised reifications rather than self-evident subjectivities' and that 'identity is not *expressed through* but *constituted by* social discourse' seem to me overwrought: Dio is interested in the 'construction' of *virtue*; he takes 'Romanness' and 'Greekness' (and 'Indianness' and 'Scythianness') as *givens*. Nor is his double typology—Greeks and Romans different, Greeks and Romans the same (as fellow members of the Roman empire)—problematic. Of course, one can decide which to emphasise in a given context, but that is not 'construction'.
181  P. 267.

ultimate σύμβουλος of the speech; and the sense that the Antisthenic 'double education' is the answer to the speech's quest for true education.

[132] **8.3 *Irony***

How, then, does Dio's elaborate irony play within this ultimately simple moral scenario? Irony's many effects undoubtedly include complicit pleasure between sophisticated audiences/readers and sophisticated speakers/writers. 'For a sophisticated reader, the thirteenth oration's conspicuous focus upon [Dio's] ... random discovery of philosophy must be offset against his knowing evocation of a deeply established narrative paradigm.'[182] But there is also *philosophical* irony, both Socratic and Cynic.

A main function of such irony is to challenge audiences' ability to discern underlying seriousness. Dio's 'random discovery of philosophy' is not *finally* random: *apparent* chance is *divine* chance.[183] The 'modesty' of his disclaimer of the title of philosopher is short-lived: such terminology was avoided by Socrates himself (28). A more involved example is Dio's characterisation both of Socrates' *logos* and of himself as 'old' (14/29).[184] There is much irony: the allusion to 'a certain Socrates' (14),[185] the characterisation of Socratic doctrine as 'old' and 'stale' (29), the very notion (especially in this highly sophisticated speech) of Dio himself as old-fashioned and unlearned. Still, it is 'not hard' to see that the 'old' (ἀρχαῖος) *logos* of 'old' Socrates and 'old' Dio (who in 101 was even literally 'old' and looked it)[186] *unites* such *apparently* varied themes as the superiority of old wisdom to new; the inversion of beginning and end; the associations between ancient wisdom, beginnings, endings, and ruling (ἀρχή), and ruling as self-rule, ruling others, and having good or bad rulers;[187] the association between *all* these things and 'good' and 'bad' fortune and 'good' and 'bad' 'chance';[188] and the idea that Dio himself is the mediator between past and present and between Greek and Roman and the instantiation of the

---

182 Whitmarsh (2001) 162–3.
183 Below, n. 188; the same play in the *First Kingship*: 1.9, 52; 'I chanced to find the right road', etc.; Moles (1990) 320, 323 {above, pp. 136, 139}.
184 Quoted on p. 262.
185 Whitmarsh (2001) 163.
186 The *First Kingship* similarly uses Dio's 'oldness' as visual validation: 1.53, 75 with Moles (1990) 321, 328 {above, pp. 137, 145}; cf. also p. 286.
187 1 ἀρχόντων, 6 ἀρχήν, 14 λόγον ἀρχαῖον, 29 ἀρχαῖα ... ἀρχαιότητα, 30 Ἀρχέλαος, 33 ἄρχοντες ... αὐτῶν ... καὶ τῶν ἄλλων ἀνθρώπων, 34 ἡ πόλις ... ἄρχουσα. This extended punning on ἀρχή-roots (whether inspired by Thucydides [1.1.1, 23.4–6], Herodotus [1.5.1, 3], or Hesiod [*Theog.* 1, 36]) is paralleled in the *Charidemus*: Moles (2000a) 206–7 {above, pp. 222–4}.
188 1 εὐδαιμόνων τε καὶ ἀρχόντων, 2 δυστυχές, 3 τοῦ δαιμονίου, 11 ἐντυγχάνοντες, 12 τυχόν, 20 ἀτυχήματα ... δυστυχεστάτῳ, 24 κακοδαιμόνων, δαιμόνων, 31 εὐδαίμονες, 33 εὐδαίμονες ... καὶ ἄρχοντες.

'old', 'beginning', 'ruling' *logos* which potentially solves all moral problems. Dio constructs a similar overriding architectural and thematic role for himself in other speeches, notably in the *First* and *Fourth Kingships*, *Euboicus*, *Olympicus*, *Borystheniticus*, and *Charidemus*.[189]

The move from formally depreciatory to positively assertive is underscored by several factors. The characterisation 'old and stale' (29) is elegantly 'pre-cut' by 15:

> I requested them … not to pay any the less attention just because I was saying the things which happened to have been said many years before, 'For', I asserted, 'perhaps you will be helped most in this way. For it is not at all likely that the words of old have evaporated like drugs and lost their power.'

The apparent equivocations about Socrates' *logos* are supplanted by the statements (30) that he was admired by all the Greeks for his wisdom and esteemed wisest by Apollo. The always implausible picture of Dio as an unoriginal and reluctant (!) performer (29) is undermined by the allusions to his relations with Nerva and Trajan (analogous to Socrates' with Archelaus) and to the Delphic oracle (another ring-structure), which reinforce the parallels between Socrates and Dio and the validation of 'ancient wisdom'. Existing admirers of Dio (who certainly got the invitations) will already know that appeal to such wisdom is one of his commonest moves.[190]

So much for irony as challenge to audiences' discernment of underlying seriousness.

⟦133⟧ Other functions of philosophical irony are more rhetorical. Ironic self-deprecation helps to soften otherwise uncompromising moral prescriptions.[191] Dio is adept at this technique. When disclaiming the title of 'philosopher' (11–12), he contrasts himself with 'the majority of the so-called philosophers [who] proclaim themselves such, just as do heralds at Olympia'—and not only with heralds, but also with Dio himself in the recent past.[192] Again, the protracted narrative (21) of the Greeks' stoning of Palamedes after he had taught

---

189  Cf. Moles (1990) 309, 314, 316, 319, 323–5, 328–33, 336, 349 {above, pp. 124, 130, 132, 135, 139–42, 144–50, 153, 165}; (1995b) 180–1, 183–92 {above, pp. 190–2, 193–203}; (2000a) 202–9 {above, pp. 218–25}.
190  Above, n. 85.
191  Cf., e.g., Demetr. *Eloc.* 261; D.L. 6.38 (Diogenes' self-description); Epict. 3.22.90; Dio 72.13.
192  12.12, 27–8, 47–8 (also 70.8), with Moles (1995b) 182 {above, p. 193} and n. 21; I adhere to 97 as the *Olympicus*' date (also Sheppard [1984] 159); 101 (C. P. Jones [1978] 53, 176 n. 69) might also allow *Olympicus*' priority; only 105 (far too late, I believe) would exclude it.

them literacy and the rudiments of military and regal skills has conflicting implications, but one of these is to recall *Socrates'* fate after his *unsuccessful* attempt to educate the Athenians and slyly to suggest: 'don't shoot the messenger on this occasion'.[193] This 'softening' effect is also secured by the rumbustious and typically Cynic combination of comic exaggeration, self-depreciation, and self-assertion[194] illustrated by Dio's elaborate proposal (32–3) that the Romans should find true philosophical teachers and install him (Dio shifts neatly from plural to singular) on 'the Acropolis', issuing an edict for all the young men and even the older men to associate with him and learn wisdom from him. This proposal, a sort of rhetorical blow-up both of Socrates' claim to free maintenance by the city[195] and of edicts honouring philosophers for associating with the young, makes Dio himself both obviously *not* such a man and—equally obviously—*exactly* such a man (at 34 Dio even assumes the man's voice).[196] And the proposal itself, like its Socratic original, is both comically exaggerated and serious.

### 8.4 Paideia

If Dio's supple and flexible irony does not threaten the simplicity of his moral teaching but on the contrary emphasises it, what of the speech's literary sophistication?

Of course, that literary sophistication, too, is to some extent pleasurable in its own right. Not only, however, do the literary allusions become progressively more sparing,[197] but there is a gathering sense of literature's inadequacy as a moral guide. Exiled from his glittering Roman world, Dio turns to epic and tragedy, Classical Greece's highest literary forms, but they counsel only despair (4–6). Later, Dio notes that 'no one has propounded a tragedy about anyone simply because he is poor' (20), pointedly underlining tragedy's incapacity as a vehicle for the Cynic philosophical solution propounded by the speech itself. Better the 'tragic performance' of Socrates (14)—or the tragic *metabasis* of Dio, returned from exile to Rome but as a chastened Cynic. Dio's is the 'true', Cynic, tragedy—the one that works, both for himself and as a paradigm for others.[198] Not conventional *paideia*, then, but the *paideia* of Cynicism, which

---

193  The *Palamedes* being one of Gorgias' most celebrated works, 21 also conveys anti-sophistic polemic.
194  Cf., e.g., D.L. 6.35, 38.
195  Pl. *Ap.* 36d.
196  On this clever passage cf. also n. 133.
197  Illustrative material in nn. 19–24, above.
198  Thus the implicit 'tragedy of Diogenes', archetypal poor philosopher (2–5; n. 21), is proleptic of the 'correct tragic solution'.

rejects conventional *paideia* and replaces it with a simple *moral* programme. If, at the beginning, the apparent simplicity of the speech is (on one level) deconstructed by its literary sophistication and complexity, by the end (metaphorically, literally, and literarily), that complexity itself is unwinding.

It is of course an acute paradox that a speech that rejects conventional *paideia* should itself contain such *paideia* and in such large quantities. But such paradox is not 'play' for its own sake.

Cynic rhetoric is again relevant. Paradox itself challenges audiences to think about essentials.[199] Cynics' use of sophisticated philosophical devices (for example, Diogenes' *Politeia* and syllogisms)[200] pre-empts intellectual contempt for the simplicity of Cynic moral teaching. His learned and deft mobilisation of different philosophical sources should prevent patronising disparagement ⟦134⟧ of Dio-*philosophus*.[201] Again, for all Cynicism's intellectual simplicity, leading representatives such as Diogenes and Crates were sharply intelligent. Dio's own sharpness comes through in unorthodox insights such as that the Peloponnesian War was won not by the Spartans but by the Persians[202] and that, even at its apparent height, the Roman Empire was enviously hated and fragile[203] (contrast the usual fatuities about Rome the Civiliser and *Roma aeterna*). Confronted with Cynics at their formidable best, audiences encounter the unsettling phenomenon of clever people who say simple things in clever ways. True, the commonest Cynic mode is one of direct attack and direct moral exhortation and this mode, too, is abundantly illustrated in *Or.* 13. But direct attack becomes wearisome without the leavening of entertainment, whence Cynic σπουδαιογέλοιον.[204]

More fundamentally, however, the very argument of the speech requires the presence of such *paideia*. Dio's Athenian audience needs to have the moral inefficacy of its sophisticated education systematically demonstrated to it, hence the massive presence of that education and its progressive retreat, and the blithe concluding implication that the Romans' complete lack of such education has no moral significance whatsoever.

---

199  Discussion in Moles (1993) 259–62 {below, pp. 259–62}; (1996) 105–7 {below, pp. 421–3}.
200  Moles (1995a) 129–43 {below, pp. 389–402} and (2000b) 423–32 {below, pp. 448–57}.
201  From this perspective, the classic Brunt (1973) reads rather datedly now.
202  Cf. Olmstead (1948) 371: 'Persia had won the second great war with the European Greeks.'
203  Starr (1982) 3: 'the Roman Empire ... was an impossibility'.
204  Kindstrand (1976) 47–8; *spoudaiogeloion* in Dio: *Or.* 72.13 (important); Moles (1983b) 274–5 {above, pp. 97–9}; Saïd (2000) 171, 180.

## 9  Performance Context and Moral Demand

Ever since Philostratus and Synesius,[205] critical discussion both of Dio's varied corpus and of his ambiguous career has revolved around the debate whether he should be classified as a philosopher or as a sophist, with such concomitant polarities as 'serious/playful', 'weighty/trivial', and 'sincere/insincere'. The post-exile Dio wrote some sophistic works and sometimes performed as a sophist and had pupils who became sophists.[206] He also wrote unequivocally philosophical works. And some of his works actively resist such pigeonholing.[207] 'Sophistic' is part of 'performance culture', but 'philosophy' can be too. Cynics were necessarily public performers,[208] though some also wrote. Dio himself was one of the biggest public performers of his age. But it is also a philosophical technique (going back to Socrates and Plato) to 'out-sophist sophists' as a preliminary, or adjunct, to the proper business of philosophising, or as a *reductio ad absurdum*.[209] Of course, the polarities 'philosopher/sophist', 'serious/playful', etc. are too sharp, particularly as applied to this period of Greek literature. Nevertheless, it may still be worth establishing the dominant propensity of a particular work, because that propensity may itself be part of the meaning of the work (and of other similar works, though not necessarily of the *oeuvre*). Where, then, within these competing but overlapping landscapes, should we locate *Or.* 13, performed in Athens (though arguably also a reading text)? Does it belong within 'the highly charged, highly agonistic space of sophistic performance' and demonstrate that 'literature can be sophisticated, ludic, self-ironising, and/or irresponsible' and that 'literary texts do not provide a clear window into the souls of their authors'?[210]

Dio's 'sincerity' does not ultimately matter, although in one respect he is being *insincere*,[211] and wedges between texts and authors can be excessively great (it would, for example, be highly counter-intuitive to deny that Dio had a colossal ego, apparent throughout *Or.* 13). But it is the text that counts, and between the polarity of 'ludic' and 'sincere' lies the crucial *tertium* [[135]] *quid* of 'serious'. This speech makes an *argument*, and, while that argument is ultimately simple, it is also *serious*, because practically *everything* in the speech

---

205  Philostr. *VS* 487–8; Synes. *Dion*.
206  Moles (1978).
207  Cf. Saïd (2000) 180 on the *Troicus*: 'there is no reason to think that these readings are mutually exclusive ... In a way this is "play", but really "serious play".'
208  Branham (1996).
209  E.g., Dio 4.79–81; Moles (1978) 81 {above, p. 27}; Saïd (2000) 171; Schofield (2000) 198–9.
210  Whitmarsh (2001) 215.
211  P. 264.

contributes to it. *Or.* 13's 'ludic' qualities positively reinforce its moral teaching, which is both overtly philosophical (once we discount Dio's tissue-thin equivocations) and implicitly anti-sophistic.[212] Nor are there 'contradictions' with other Dionian speeches explicable only in terms of 'the highly charged, highly agonistic space of sophistic performance'.[213] Rather, the speech takes its place in a series concerned with the Romans' moral status, though it simultaneously targets the Athenians. And it is actually its performance context (whether that in Athens or that which we as readers have to reconstruct) that provides the last proof of its radically philosophical claims.

Dio says that, as part of his 'self-chastening' in response to the Delphic oracle, he donned 'humble dress' (10 στολὴν ... ταπεινήν). In context, this dress is Cynic and Dio's donning of it symbolises proleptically his conversion to Cynicism.[214] Such Cynic dress is as 'undressy' as may be (short of 'Gymnosophy' or 'Cynogamy'). When the Cynicised Socrates appears, he is described as shouting 'altogether manlily and un-dressed-up-ly' ([16] ἀνυποστόλως). Dress now becomes a metaphor for style or type of performance,[215] and the contrast is between the simplest and the most elaborate types of dress, the latter of which conceals.[216] Both Socrates and the dramatic Dio of 10ff. are 'undressy' Cynic performers,[217] and there is the further implication that style and moral content must match. Nothing suggests that the dramatic Dio changed dress when he reached Rome (29ff.), and *Or.* 72 confirms that he at least sometimes 'dressed Cynic' when performing as a philosopher in Rome, as elsewhere.[218] Dio's self-representation in this speech would fail if he were wearing something different before his Athenian audience. Hence, just as Dio's

---

212  Above, n. 193.
213  Whitmarsh (2001) 215–16 takes the 'contradiction' between Dio's 'anti-Roman' attack on Roman decadence in *Or.* 13 and his apparent 'pro-Roman' pride in his Roman citizenship in 41.6 as deriving from 'shifts in rhetorical self-presentation ... [between the roles of] oppositionalist (the pose he adopts in his writings on exile) or ... adviser (the pose he adopts in the *Kingships*)'. But: (i) Dio's attack on Roman decadence in *Or.* 13 is not 'anti-Roman'; (ii) *Or.* 41 is a *political* speech delivered to a Roman colony; (iii) in *Or.* 13 Dio *begins* as 'oppositionalist' but *ends* as 'adviser' (both of Romans and Athenians). Here 'sophistic' is being made to explain too much.
214  This conversion motif: Kindstrand (1976) 163–4; the old debate whether/to what extent Dio 'really' became Cynic does not matter here: the *representation* is *serious in context.*
215  Douglas (1966) 201; Fantham (1972) 171–2 (I thank Jaap Wisse for advice).
216  LSJ s.v.
217  The *First Kingship* also plays with μῦθος ~ 'dress': 1.49, with Moles (1990) 319 {above, p. 135}; Whitmarsh (2001) 197; and the Arcadian prophetess' 'country dress' (1.53) emblematises that speech's rugged Cynic strand.
218  Cf. 1.50; 12.9, 85 (with Moles [1995b] 183 {above, p. 194}); 33.14–15; 34.2; 70.8.

'oldness' (metaphorical and literal) instantiates and validates the speech's 'old *logos*', so also his Cynic dress instantiates and privileges the Cynic narrative and moral voice (which is only another form of 'the old *logos*'). Style, content, man and appearance are one.[219] Although the speech itself is 'dressed up' in all sorts of sophisticated ways, in order to interpret it rightly we have, as it were, to 'undress' it to its Cynic 'underwear', itself of course a fittingly Cynic act, at least potentially.

But 'potentially' is itself another point. *Or.* 13 is a protreptic: its ultimate success or failure does not lie with Dio the speaker/writer, or with his audience's/readers' ability to decode his meanings, but rather with whether, inspired by Dio's rhetoric, impressive as it is, and following Dio's practical example, which has at least some moral substance, they accept their own moral responsibility and begin the process of enacting those meanings in their own lives. Hence the explicitly forward-looking exhortations to the Romans (35, 37) and the implicitly forward-looking exhortations to the Athenians and any other audiences/readers, all of whom are invited to 'write a better moral story' in the future than the dismal stories of their respective pasts and presents.[220]

[[136]] Imaginatively conceived and perfectly realised in unfailingly creative Greek, *Or.* 13 offers many pleasures. It also makes demands, some of which may seem to be 'purely literary'. But its final demands are moral and the literary demands are subservient to them. We should all appreciate the enormous resource and freshness with which Dio brings those demands to our attention. But perhaps even today a few may find that the 'simple' moral demands of 'ancient Dio' have not entirely lost their power.

## Bibliography

von Arnim, H. (1898) *Leben und Werke des Dio von Prusa* (Berlin).
von Arnim, H., ed. (1893) *Dionis Prusaensis quem vocant Chrysostomum quae exstant omnia*, vol. 1 (Berlin).
Billaut, A. (1999) 'Dion Chrysostome avait-il une théorie de la sculpture?', *BAGB*: 211–29.

---

[219] Similarly, in the *Olympicus*, the visibly old, unkempt, 'owlish', suffering 'Cynic' Dio instantiates Greece herself: Moles (1995b) 183 {above, p. 194}.

[220] Similar 'write-your-own-life' challenges in the *First Kingship* (esp. 1.49); the *Fourth Kingship*; the *Euboicus*; the *Borystheniticus*; and the *Charidemus*: Moles (1990) 335–6; 348–50; 372 n. 119 {above, pp. 152–3, 164–6, 152 n. 119}; (1995b) 178–9; 190–2 {above, pp. 188–90, 200–2}; (2000a), esp. 194–9, 207–9 {above, pp. 211–15, 223–5}.

Blomqvist, K. (1989) *Myth and Moral Message in Dio Chrysostom: A Study in Dio's Moral Thought, with a Particular Focus on his Attitudes towards Women* (Lund).

Blomqvist, K. (1995) 'Chryseïs and Clea, Eumetis and the Interlocutress: Plutarch of Chaeronea and Dio Chrysostom on Women's Education', *Svensk Exegetisk Arsbok* 60: 173–90.

Bowie, E. L. (1970/1974) 'Greeks and their Past in the Second Sophistic', *P&P* 46: 3–41; rev. version in M. I. Finley, ed., *Studies in Ancient Society* (London and Boston, 1974) 186–229.

Boys-Stones, G. R. (2001) *Post-Hellenistic Philosophy: A Study of its Development from the Stoics to Origen* (Oxford).

Brancacci, A. (1992) 'Struttura compositiva e fonti della terza orazione "Sulla Regalità" di Dione Crisostomo: Dione e l'"Archelao" di Antistene', *ANRW* II.36.5: 3308–34.

Brancacci, A. (2000) 'Dio, Socrates, and Cynicism', in Swain (2000) 240–60.

Branham, R. B. (1996) 'Defacing the Currency: Diogenes' Rhetoric and the *Invention* of Cynicism', in id. and Goulet-Cazé (1996) 81–104.

Branham, R. B. and M.-O. Goulet-Cazé, edd. (1996) *The Cynics: the Cynic Movement in Antiquity and its Legacy* (Berkeley and Los Angeles).

Brenk, F. E. (2000) 'Dio on the Simple and Self-sufficient Life', in Swain (2000) 261–78.

Brown, T. S. (1949) *Onesicritus: A Study in Hellenistic Historiography* (Berkeley and Los Angeles).

Brunt, P. A. (1973) 'Aspects of the Social Thought of Dio Chrysostom and the Stoics', *PCPhS* 199: 9–33; repr. in id., *Studies in Stoicism*, edd. M. Griffin and A. Samuels (Oxford, 2013) 151–79.

Caizzi, F. D. (1966) *Antisthenis Fragmenta* (Varese/Milan).

Claassen, J. M. (1999) *Displaced Persons: The Literature of Exile from Cicero to Boethius* (London and Madison).

Cobet, C. G. (1878) *Collectanea critica quibus continentur observationes criticae in scriptores Graecos* (Leiden).

Denniston, J. D. (1954) *The Greek Particles*, 2nd ed. rev. by K. J. Dover (Oxford).

Denyer, N., ed. (2001) *Plato: Alcibiades* (Cambridge).

Desideri, P. (1978) *Dione di Prusa: un intelletuale greco nell'impero romano* (Messina/Florence).

Desideri, P. (1991) 'Tipologia e varietà di funzione comunicativa degli scritti dionei', *ANRW* II.33.5: 3903–59.

Doblehofer, E. (1987) *Exil und Emigration: zum Erlebnis der Heimatferne in der römischen Literatur* (Darmstadt).

Döring, K. (1995) 'Diogenes und Antisthenes', in G. Giannantoni, et al., edd., *La tradizione socratica* (Naples, 1995) 125–50.

Douglas, A. E., ed. (1966) *Cicero: Brutus* (Oxford).

Dudley, D. R. (1937) *A History of Cynicism from Diogenes to the 6th century A.D.* (London).

Dümmler, F. (1882) *Antisthenica* (Bonn).

Dümmler, F. (1889) *Akademica: Beiträge zur Litteraturgeschichte der sokratischen Schulen* (Giessen).

Emperius, A. (1847) *Opuscula Philologica et Historica* (Göttingen).

Erskine, A. (1995) 'Rome in the Greek World: the Significance of a Name', in A. Powell, ed., *The Greek World* (London and New York) 368–83.

Fantham, E. (1972) *Comparative Studies in Republican Latin Imagery* (Toronto).

Fontenrose, J. E. (1978) *The Delphic Oracle, its Responses and Operation, with a Catalogue of Responses* (Berkeley and Los Angeles).

von Fritz, K. (1926) *Quellenuntersuchungen zu Leben und Philosophie des Diogenes von Sinope* (*Philologus Suppl.* 18.2; Göttingen).

Fuchs, H. (1938) *Der geistige Widerstand gegen Rom in der antiken Welt* (Berlin).

van Geytenbeek, A. C. (1963) *Musonius Rufus and Greek Diatribe* (Assen).

Giannantoni, G. (1993) 'Antistene fondatore della scuola cinica?', in Goulet-Cazé and Goulet (1993) 15–34.

Goulet-Cazé, M.-O. (1996) 'Appendix B: Who Was the First Dog?', in Branham and Goulet-Cazé (1996) 414–15.

Goulet-Cazé, M.-O. and R. Goulet, edd. (1993) *Le Cynisme ancien et ses prolongements* (Paris).

Griffin, M. T. (1993) 'Le mouvement cynique et les Romains: attraction et repulsion', in Goulet-Cazé and Goulet (1993) 241–58.

Griffin, M. T. (1996) 'Cynicism and the Romans: Attraction and Repulsion', in Branham and Goulet-Cazé (1996) 190–204 = ead., *Politics and Philosophy at Rome: Collected Papers*, ed. C. Balmaceda (Oxford, 2018) 475–85.

Haake, M. (2003) 'Warum und zu welchem Ende schreibt man *peri basileias*? Überlegungen zum historischen Kontext einer literarischen Gattung im Hellenismus', in Piepenbrink (2003) 83–138.

Hagen, P. (1891) 'Zu Antisthenes', *Philologus* 50: 381–4.

Hammerstaedt, J. (1993) 'Le cynisme littéraire à l'epoque imperiale', in Goulet-Cazé and Goulet (1993) 399–418.

Häsler, B. (1935) *Favorin über die Verbannung* (Berlin).

Hawley, R. (2000) 'Marriage, Gender, and the Family in Dio', in Swain (2000) 125–39.

Highet, G. (1983) 'Mutilations in the Text of Dio Chrysostom', in R. J. Ball, ed., *The Classical Papers of Gilbert Highet* (New York) 74–99.

Höistad, R. (1948) *Cynic Hero and Cynic King: Studies in the Cynic Conception of Man* (Uppsala).

Houser, J. S. (1998) '*Eros and Aphrodisia* in the Works of Dio Chrysostom', *ClAnt* 17: 235–58.

Jones, B. W. (1990) 'Domitian and the Exile of Dio of Prusa', *PdP* 45: 348–57.

Jones, C. P. (1973) 'The Date of Dio of Prusa's Alexandrian Oration', *Historia* 22: 302–9.

Jones, C. P. (1978) *The Roman World of Dio Chrysostom* (Cambridge, Mass. and London).

Jouan, F. (1977) 'Les thèmes romanesques dans l'*Euboïcos* de Dion Chrysostome', REG 90: 38–46.

Jouan, F. (1993a) 'Le Diogène de Dion Chrysostome', in Goulet-Cazé and Goulet (1993) 381–97.

Jouan, F. (1993b) 'Les récits de voyage de Dion Chrysostome: Realité et Fiction', in M.-F. Baslez, P. Hoffmann, and L. Pernot, edd., *L'Invention de l'autobiographie d'Hésiode à Saint Augustin* (Paris) 189–98.

Kindstrand, J. F. (1976) *Bion of Borysthenes: a Collection of the Fragments with Introduction and Commentary* (Uppsala).

Kindstrand, J. F. (1978) 'The Date of Dio of Prusa's Alexandrian Oration—A Reply', *Historia* 27: 378–83.

Kitto, H. D. F. (1961) *Greek Tragedy*³ (London).

Klauck, H.-J. and B. Bäbler, edd. (2000) *Dion von Prusa: Olympische Rede oder über die erste Erkenntis Gottes* (Darmstadt).

Long, A. A. (2002) *Epictetus: a Stoic and Stoic Guide to Life* (Oxford).

Martin, R. P. (1996) 'The Scythian Accent: Anacharsis and the Cynics', in Branham and Goulet-Cazé (1996) 136–55.

Mason, H. J. (1974) *Greek Terms for Roman Institutions: a Lexicon and Analysis* (Toronto).

Moles, J. L. (1978) 'The Career and Conversion of Dio Chrysostom', *JHS* 98: 79–100 [above Ch. 1].

Moles, J. L. (1983a) 'Dio Chrysostom: Exile, Tarsus, Nero and Domitian', *LCM* 8: 130–4 [above, Ch. 2].

Moles, J. L. (1983b) 'The Date and Purpose of the Fourth Kingship Oration of Dio Chrysostom', *ClAnt* 2: 251–78 [above, Ch. 3].

Moles, J. L. (1983c) '"*Honestius quam Ambitiosius*"? An Exploration of the Cynic's Attitude to Moral Corruption in his Fellow Men', *JHS* 103: 103–23 [below, Ch. 12].

Moles, J. L. (1984) 'The Addressee of the Third Kingship Oration of Dio Chrysostom', *Prometheus* 10: 65–9 [above, Ch. 4].

Moles, J. L. (1990) 'The Kingship Orations of Dio Chrysostom', *PLLS* 6: 297–375 [above, Ch. 5].

Moles, J. L. (1993) 'Le cosmopolitisme cynique', in Goulet-Cazé and Goulet (1993) 259–80 [English version below, Ch. 16].

Moles, J. L. (1995a) 'The Cynics and Politics', in Laks and Schofield (1995) 129–58 [below, Ch. 15].

Moles, J. L. (1995b) 'Dio Chrysostom, Greece, and Rome', in Innes–Hine–Pelling (1995) 177–92 [above, Ch. 7].

Moles, J. L. (1996) 'Cynic Cosmopolitanism', in Branham and Goulet-Cazé (1996) 105–20 [below, Ch. 16].
Moles, J. L. (2000a) 'The Dionian *Charidemus*', in Swain (2000) 187–210 [above, Ch. 8].
Moles, J. L. (2000b) 'The Cynics', in Rowe and Schofield (2000) 415–34 [below, Ch. 17].
Moles, J. L. (2003) 'Dio und Trajan', in Piepenbrink (2003) 186–207 [above, Ch. 9].
Moles, J. L. (forthcoming, a) 'Cynicism in Dio Chrysostom' [below, Ch. 11].
Moles, J. L. (forthcoming, b) '*Romane, Memento*: Virgil, Dio, and Antisthenes on the Education of the Strong', in A. J. Woodman and J. Wisse, edd., *Word and Context in Latin Poetry: Studies in Memory of David West* (Cambridge) 105–30 [below, Ch. 19].
Momigliano, A. D. (1950) 'Dio Chrysostomos' (Unpublished Lecture, 1950), in id., *Quarto Contributo alla Storia degli studi classici e del mondo antico* (Rome, 1969) 257–69.
Momigliano, A. D. (1951) 'Review of Wirszubski (1950)', *JRS* 41: 146–53; repr. in id., *Quinto Contributo alla Storia degli studi classici e del mondo antico*, 2 vols. (Rome, 1975) II.958–75.
Mommsen, T. (1869) 'Zur Lebensgeschichte des jüngeren Plinius', *Hermes* 3: 31–139; repr. in id., *Gesammelte Schriften* IV (Berlin, 1906) 366–468.
Montiglio, S. (2000) 'Wandering Philosophers in Classical Greece', *JHS* 120: 86–105.
Nesselrath, H.-G., B. Bäbler, M. Forschner, and A. de Jong, edd. (2003) *Menschliche Gemeinschaft und göttliche Ordnung: die Borysthenes-Rede* (Darmstadt).
Nock, A. D. (1933) *Conversion: the Old and the New in Religion from Alexander the Great to Augustine of Hippo* (Oxford).
Norden, E. (1893) 'Beiträge zur Geschichte der griechischen Philosophie', *Jahrbücher der classische Philologie*, Suppl. 19: 365–462.
Olmstead, A. T. (1948) *A History of the Persian Empire* (Chicago).
Parke, H. W. and D. E. W. Wormell (1956) *The Delphic Oracle*, 2 vols. (Oxford).
Pender, E. E. (1999) 'Plato's Moving *Logos*', *PCPhS* 45: 75–107.
Petrochilos, N. K. (1974) *Roman Attitudes to the Greeks* (Athens).
Piepenbrink, K., ed. (2003) *Philosophie und Lebenswelt in der Antike* (Darmstadt).
Powell, J. E. (1938) *Lexicon to Herodotus* (Cambridge).
Rawson, E. (1989) 'Roman Rulers and the Philosophic Adviser', in M. Griffin and J. Barnes, ed., *Philosophia Togata* (Oxford, 1989) 233–57.
Redfield, J. (1985) 'Herodotus the Tourist', *CPh* 80: 97–118.
Reiske, J. J. (1798) *Dionis Chrysostomi orationes* I–II² (Leipzig).
Rowe, C. and M. Schofield, edd. (2000) *The Cambridge History of Greek and Roman Political Thought* (Cambridge).
Russell, D. A., ed. (1992) *Dio Chrysostom: Orations VII, XII, XXXVI* (Cambridge).
Saïd, S. (2000) 'Dio's Use of Mythology', in Swain (2000) 161–86.
Salmeri, G. (2000) 'Dio, Rome, and the Civic Life of Asia Minor', in Swain (2000) 53–92.
Schmid, W. (1903) 'Dion (18)', *RE* V: 848–77.

Schofield, M. (1991) *The Stoic Idea of the City* (Cambridge; repr. Chicago, 1999).

Schofield, M. (2000) '*Gorgias* and *Menexenus*', in Rowe and Schofield (2000) 192–99.

Schofield, M. (2004) 'Epictetus: Socratic, Cynic, Stoic', *Philosophical Quarterly* 54: 448–56.

Sheppard, A. A. R. (1982) 'A Dissident in Tarsus? (Dio Chrysostom, Or. 66)', *LCM* 7: 149–50.

Sheppard, A. A. R. (1984) 'Dio Chrysostom: the Bithynian Years', *L'Antiquité Classique* 53: 157–73.

Sidebottom, H. (1996) 'Dio of Prusa and the Flavian Dynasty', *CQ* 46: 447–56.

Slings, S. R., ed. (1999) *Plato: Clitophon* (Cambridge).

Starr, C. (1982) *The Roman Empire 27 B.C.–A.D. 476. A Study in Survival* (New York and Oxford).

Swain, S. (1996) *Hellenism and Empire: Language, Classicism, and Power in the Greek World, AD 50–250* (Oxford).

Swain, S., ed. (2000) *Dio Chrysostom: Politics, Letters, and Philosophy* (Oxford).

Trapp, M. B. (1990) 'Plato's *Phaedrus* in Second-Century Greek Literature', in D. A. Russell, ed., *Antonine Literature* (Oxford) 141–73.

Trapp, M. B. (2000) 'Plato in Dio', in Swain (2000) 213–39.

Verrengia, A., ed. (2000) *Dione di Prusa: In Atene,* sull'esilio *(or. XIII): Introduzione, testo critico, traduzione e commento* (Naples).

Veyne, P. (1999) 'L'identité grecque devant Rome et l'empereur', *REG* 112: 510–67.

Weber, E. (1887) 'De Dione Chrysostomo Cynicorum Sectatore', *Leipziger Stud. z. Classichen Philologie* 10: 77–268.

Wegehaupt, I. (1896) *De Dione Chrysostomo Cynicorum sectatore* (Gottingen).

Whitmarsh, T. (2001) *Greek Literature and the Roman Empire: the Politics of Imitation* (Oxford).

CHAPTER 11

# Defacing the Currency: Cynicism in Dio Chrysostom

Twenty-eight and a half years ago my teacher Ewen introduced me to Dio *Chruso*stomos—one of many ways in which Ewen has enriched my life; and Dio introduced me to the Cynics.* I've never regretted either introduction: both have become old friends whom it is a pleasure to revisit from time to time. Whether these nostalgic reunions ever bear new fruit is another question, but one must trust the credit of one's author and—a rather taller order—one must trust the credit of the Cynics.

## 1 Introduction

Diogenes' most famous tag, 'deface the currency', encapsulates the extreme radicalism of Diogenic Cynicism: the imperative form and the play on νόμισμα/νόμος prescribe the rejection of all *nomoi*, including money itself and all *paideia* (at least as conventionally understood). Diogenic Cynicism appears, then, to be in polar opposition to the theme and values of a conference entitled 'Purse and *Paideia* in Plutarch and the Second Sophistic', the *pera* in which Cynics carried the scraps of food that they had stolen or begged, the very antithesis of the 'purse' of the conference's title. Dio Chrysostom happens to be one of the ancient authors to preserve this Diogenic tag and Dio has generally been regarded as an important Cynic source, alike by scholars interested in Cynicism for its own sake; by modern advocates of so-called 'Cynic kingship theory'; by those New Testament and Patristic scholars who see Cynic influence on Jewish and Christian thought; and by investigators of the Cynic-influenced literary form of 'diatribe'. Some scholars have even maintained that for a period of his career Dio himself actually was a Cynic.[1] Yet on most modern views, Dio is (or, is also) a key figure of 'Second Sophistic' *paideia*. The present topic, therefore,

---

\* This is a lightly-edited, -expanded and -annotated version of the paper given on June 30, 2001 (in particular, the notes have been kept to a minimum). I thank all those who made comments, both publicly and privately. All translations are my own.

1 The scholarly history of Dio 'Cynicus' up to 1978 is admirably surveyed in Desideri (1978) 537–47; post-1978 developments: Brancacci (2000), esp. 254–5; Moles (1983a); (1990); (1995a) 155–6 {below, pp. 413–15}; Gill (2000) 603ff.

both focuses on a central problem in Dio and interacts challengingly with the general theme of the conference.

Both Cynicism and Dio, indeed, pose huge problems: some scholars of philosophy are sceptical of Cynicism's very existence; some scholars of Dio (whatever their views on the status of Cynicism) are sceptical of Cynic influence on him. It is therefore impossible to treat the topic without making certain assumptions (for which I have elsewhere argued extensively).[2]

My basic assumption about Cynicism is that it was indeed an independent philosophy. Founded by Diogenes though influenced by Antisthenes, it entailed a distinctive way of life. Since works were written about Cynicism both by practising Cynics and by non-Cynics, we must distinguish between practical Cynicism and 'literary' Cynicism. Diogenic Cynicism projected a 'hard primitivism' which entailed rejection of all conventional social and political structures (παραχαράττειν τὸ νόμισμα) and of virtually all material possessions. Diogenes views everybody else as morally bankrupt but his attacks on others don't obscure a fundamental *philanthropia* and his 'cosmopolitanism' potentially embraces all human beings. While rejecting conventional religion as superstition, he believes in the gods, as paradigms of Cynic virtue, self-sufficiency and happiness. But we must distinguish between Diogenes' 'hard Cynicism' and the 'soft Cynicism' of those who make various compromises with conventional social and political structures (proleptically, Antisthenes, then Diogenes' follower Crates followed by Onesicritus, Alexander-historian, and Bion, court-philosopher of Antigonus Gonatas, and others). Hence implications for so-called Cynic kingship theory. If Cynic means 'hard Cynic' and 'kingship' means a political institution, Cynic kingship theory is a complete misconception: the much-touted 'Cynic king' is the very antithesis of a political king. But soft Cynicism could produce Cynic kingship theory in the required sense and Onesicritus, Bion, and, proleptically, Antisthenes, did indeed do so.

Since Zeno began as a follower of Crates, Cynic ethics entered Stoicism, though Stoicism developed far beyond Cynicism, but Cynicism as a separate movement did not die out in the last two centuries BC. Within the general Cynic tradition, some account has to be taken of Antisthenes, *qua* in some ways proto-soft-Cynic.

My basic assumption about Dio is that all four Kingships were delivered to Trajan, though repeated to Greek audiences.[3] Those who reject this latter

---

2  Moles (1995a), (1996), and (2000).
3  Momigliano (1950) 265; Moles (1983a) 277 {above, p. 40} n. 90; Trapp (2000) 226 n. 36 powerfully reinforces Trajanic delivery. Few would deny that Kingships 1–3 are of Trajanic *date* (Desideri (1978) 235, 259 n. 68 is untenable: Moles (1984)); Kingship 4 has sometimes been

assumption may regard this paper as being largely concerned with a fiction of the ways in which Cynicism *might* have been used, albeit a fiction created by Dio himself and (surely) represented by him as true.

The volume of material to be considered is necessarily controversial, partly depending on one's views about Cynicism, partly on one's analyses of Dio. Given all these controversies, the only correct way of proceeding is to work outwards from selected texts. This paper surveys the Kingships and the Diogenics, with forays into a few other pieces. The crucial questions are: Dio's knowledge of Cynicism; the different types of Cynicism being expounded; Dio's sources; the uses to which Cynicism is being put; the extent to which Cynicism is presented straight or is modified or adapted; the role of Cynicism within Dio's self-presentation; and the possible influence of Cynicism upon Dio's thinking, even perhaps upon his way of life. Within the source question an important sub-question is that of the use and influence of Antisthenes, for, although on the majority ancient and modern opinion (with which I concur) Cynicism was founded by Diogenes, not Antisthenes, the minority ancient opinion made Antisthenes both founder of Cynicism and teacher of Diogenes, and some aspects of Antisthenes' thought certainly influenced Diogenes, and (as we shall see) Dio himself is perfectly aware of these latter considerations.

## 2  The Kingships

Since, both implicitly and explicitly, the Kingships accept kingship as a political institution, they cannot contain any uncompromisingly 'hard' Cynicism,[4] which rejects all political structures as forms of *nomos*. Nevertheless, the Kingships do contain significant Cynic material. In the First Kingship of c. AD 100, Dio, who had probably never met Trajan before, introduces himself (1.9) as a 'wanderer and self-taught philosopher, who find pleasure … in toils [*ponois*] and works, but utter words for encouragement to myself and to such individuals as I meet from time to time'. Cynic here are the emphasis on wandering and *ponos*, viewed as intrinsically pleasurable, the idea that you've got to do it all by yourself, the inverted boasting, and the basic philanthropy (encouragement of others besides oneself). The phrase 'self-taught philosopher' is

---

dated to Dio's exile, as I believe, incorrectly: see Moles (1983b); (1990) 349 {above, p. 165}; (2003); of course, there are other views ….

4  The distinction is not absolute but remains useful; the 'hard-soft' opposition is exploited in Lovejoy–Boas (1935) but fits well with general ancient gendered discourse and is even implicit in Dio's *Or.* 8.1–2 (quoted below, p. 301).

Socratic but Cynics selectively appropriated Socratic ethical characteristics, as part of their claim to be the only *true* descendants of Socrates.[5] Dio here also fittingly evokes the contrast drawn by the soft-Cynic Bion of Borysthenes between himself *qua* wretched wanderer and king Antigonus Gonatas.[6]

The speech's core consists of Dio's retailing a prophecy he received on his exile wanderings from a prophetess in a place sacred to Heracles in deepest Arcadia. Cynicism locates virtue—or at least its origins—in the country: (1.51) 'arriving once in the Peloponnese I did not approach the cities at all, but spent my time in the country, as having much knowledge, mixing with herdsmen and hunters, noble and simple characters'; so in the *Euboicus* the Euboean hunters provide a paradigm to some extent transferable to the city.[7]

The prophecy was that he would one day meet a 'mighty man and ruler over very many lands and people' (who of course turns out to be Trajan *qua* imperial addressee) and it came with instructions that Dio should then retail the tale told by the priestess about Heracles. That tale is a reworking of the Prodican/Xenophontic Choice of Heracles (Xen. *Mem.* 2.1.21–33), with Virtue and Vice morphed into Kingship and Tyranny. The priestess, the meeting, and the prophecy are fictional and the reworking of Xenophon is Dio's own work, the purpose of all this being to ground Dio's exhortations to Trajan in the highest philosophical and divine authority and to imply analogies between the Cynic virtues of Dio, the prophetess, Heracles, and Trajan, known admirer of Heracles, with Trajan being urged to actualise his potential or inchoate virtues, to turn *muthos* into *logos*. Dio expertly walks the tight-rope between the Cynic framework and appropriate addresses to a Roman emperor. In delivering the prophecy Dio acts the role of the Cynic messenger from god.[8] Although Cynics rejected prophecy (as in *Oration* 10), they could appeal to the Delphic maxim 'know thyself' (*Orations* 4 and 10), and prophecy had been absorbed into the pseudo-biographies of Diogenes and of Dio himself (*Oration* 13). The device of prophecy naturally honours Trajan, especially as Trajan had himself

---

5   On Dio's Socratic *persona*, Moles (1978) 98, 99f. {above, pp. 55, 56–8}; on Dio, Socrates, and the Cynics see Brancacci (2000), esp. 254–5; (1990) 95–6, 104–9; (1992); Trapp (2000) 226–7; cf. 232–4.
6   Bion F16 K with Kindstrand (1976) 208.
7   *Euboicus* (7.)81: 'I have gone through this whole account not idly nor, as perhaps I might seem to some, wishing to spin a yarn, but setting forth a paradigm of the life I undertook from the start and of the way of life of the poor, a paradigm which I myself knew' (for the interpretation of this sentence, see Moles (1995b) 179 {above, p. 190}).
8   A conception most explicitly found in Dio's great Stoic contemporary, Epictetus (3.22.2, 23, 59, 69; with Billerbeck (1978) 78), but integral to Cynicism from the very beginning: Moles (1995a) 146 {below, p. 405} n. 56 and (1996).

received prophecies of his future elevation,⁹ yet Dio strikes an authentically Cynic note when he dismisses the histrionics of conventional prophets (1.56). The figure of Heracles is used with deft ambiguity. While emphasising his general Cynic aspects, Dio pointedly rejects the strong Cynic claims to *asphaleia* (safety in all circumstances) and self-sufficiency, because a great king needs armies.¹⁰ Dio's striking contention that Eurystheus was never king of Argos does double duty in making Heracles *always* king and in suggesting the illegitimacy of Domitian's 'kingship': even during Domitian's reign, Trajan was 'always' the true king.¹¹ The stress on Heracles' simple education alludes alike to Trajan's limited educational attainments and to the simplicities of the Cynic philosophical programme that Dio is now rolling out. The characterisation of Heracles as an 'observer' of the bloody interior of Mount Tyranny alike evokes the rich Cynic concept of the *episkopos*—the outsider figure who examines other people's wickedness, seeks to understand it and correct it—and conveys the point that Trajan, active under Domitian, was uncorrupted by Domitianic tyranny. The First Kingship, then, achieves a fine balance between compliment of Trajan as he was and hoped-for reformation of Trajan through a thorough-going individual Cynicisation under the tutelage of Dio, exile and Cynic sufferer extraordinary. Dio effectively appropriates the Cynics' typical arrogance, which, considering their worldly status, is strongly paradoxical and thus itself pedagogical in provoking thought about ultimate moral values.

Kingship 2 (the dialogue between Alexander and Philip of Macedon) is entirely devoid of Cynicism, but Cynicism reappears emphatically in Kingship 4, whose core is the meeting between Alexander and Diogenes: otherwise, Trajan, admirer of Alexander (as already suggested in Kingships 1 and 2), and Dio (like *Dio*genes an exile); Dio develops the Cynic *persona* of his first appearance before Trajan.

---

9    Dio 45.4; Tac. *Agr.* 44.5; Plin. *Pan.* 5.2–9; *Ep.* 10.1, 102; Cass. Dio 67.12.1
10   1.61–3: 'they say these things also about Heracles, that he went unclothed and unarmed ... the thing that they say is untrue, that he went about alone without an army. For it is impossible to have the power to overthrow cities and to cast down tyrants and to give orders to everyone everywhere without military power'. For parallel passages cf. pp. 307–8 below; note that these claims go back directly to Antisthenes' *Ajax* and *Odysseus*, if those works are authentic (as they are).
11   1.59: 'Heracles was, as all say, the son of Zeus by Alcmene, and king not only of Argos but also of all Greece. (The majority do not know that Heracles was away from home conducting campaigns and protecting his empire; but they say that Eurystheus was then king. This, however, is said falsely by them [text of this parenthesis corrupt; meaning clear].) And Heracles was king not only of Greece but held empire over every land from the rising to the setting sun and over all men among whom are found shrines of Heracles'.

Read by itself, this core comes very close to uncompromising hard Cynicism.[12] Diogenes undertakes to rid Alexander of his vices, which include general delusion (τῦφος), incontinent ambition, extreme materialism, foolish militarism, mad schemes of world conquest, and an obsession with defeating the Persian King (all charges which could be made against Trajan). This is rough stuff, especially as it is strengthened by contrasts with Kingship 1: there, as we've seen, Dio rejected the strong forms of Cynic self-sufficiency and ἀσφάλεια and conceded the necessity for imperial military power;[13] now, Cynic ἀσφάλεια easily trumps Alexander's militarism, as it does Roman militarism in the *Olympicus*.[14] Nevertheless, even within this Cynic core, there are elements which soften the blows. Further, the Cynic core should not be read by itself: it is sandwiched between a carefully ambiguous introduction[15] and a florid, quasi-sophistic, ἐπίδειξις, and the effect of this sandwiching is to suggest that the Cynic core offers an exaggerated moral prescription. As in the First Kingship, Dio's deployment of Cynic material is skilfully adjusted to the needs and sensibilities of his imperial addressee. It remains a powerful and impressive speech.

What of the sources for the Cynic core? Clearly, it rebuts Onesicritus' soft-Cynic revaluation of Alexander as 'the only philosopher under arms'.[16] Sections 29ff. form a recently sharply debated test-case for the whole question of Antisthenic influence on Dio. Brancacci, following older scholars, argues for Dio's extensive use of Antisthenes, notably in Kingships 4 and 3 and *Oration* 13, Dio's account of how he became a Socratic philosopher,[17] such use of Antisthenes forming one of the traditions through which Dio mediates the Socratic inheritance (the others being Plato and those sorts of Stoicism which bypass or reject Cynicism). But Trapp thinks that the Platonic tradition explains far more of Dio's philosophy. In the present case, Brancacci, like many, analyses the 'double *paideia*' expounded by Diogenes, one part human, the

---

12  Which is why Kingship 4 has sometimes been dated to Dio's exile: Höistad (1948) 219f.; Fears (1977) 157; Desideri (1978) 200ff.
13  The passage is quoted in n. 10 above.
14  4.8: 'but Diogenes [sc. in contrast to Alexander] went forth by himself in complete safety not only by day but also by night where he wished to go'; 12 (*Olympicus*, post-exile).17–20: 'I [Dio] went [among the Roman armies massing against Dacia] "unarmed, without helmet or shield, having no spear" [*Iliad* 21.50] ... I appeared quite alone among this great host, perfectly at ease and a very peaceful observer of war ...'; for the *Olympicus* as anti-Roman imperialism see Moles (1995b) 183–4 {above, pp. 193–4}; Swain (1996) 200–3.
15  On these 'softening' elements see Moles (1990) 303–4, 348ff. {above, pp. 118–19, 164ff.}
16  *FGrHist* 134 F 17A = Str. 15.1.63–5.
17  Brancacci (1990); 95–6, 104–9; (1992); (2000), esp. 254–5.

other divine, as deriving from Antisthenes' 'double *paideia*', whereas for Trapp it is only one of a series of items drawn from *Alcibiades 1*.[18]

4.29–35 (which is too long to quote here) contains the following elements:
(i) the distinction between the 'double *paideia*', one divine (*daimonios*), the other human, the former superior, the latter inferior, but both necessary;
(ii) the claim that knowledge of the divine *paideia* readily confers knowledge of the human also;
(iii) Heracles, *qua diogenes* (> Diogenes/Dio), as representing the divine education;
(iv) the sophists as representing human education;
(v) road imagery (good and bad roads);
(vi) a comparison between human education/sophists and erroneous dogs (sc. in contrast to the true Cynic dog).

The fragment which contains Antisthenes' double *paideia* (and which obviously comes from Antisthenes' *Heracles*) is quoted and interpreted by Themist. *De virt.* p. 43 Mach {= F 27 DC = F 96 Prince}:

> but if you wish truly to learn that wisdom is something lofty, I invoke neither Plato nor Aristotle as witnesses, but the wise Antisthenes, who taught this road. For he says that Prometheus spoke to Heracles as follows: 'your labour is very cheap, in that your care is for human things, but you have deserted the care of those things which are of greater moment; for you will not be a perfect man until you have learnt the things that are loftier than human beings, but if you learn those things, then you will learn also human things; if, however, you learn only human things, you will wander like a brute animal'. For the man who studies human things and confines the wisdom and intelligence of his mind in such cheap and narrow things, that man, as Antisthenes said, is not a wise man but like to an animal, to whom a dung-pit is pleasing. In truth, all celestial things are lofty and it behoves us to have a lofty way of thinking about them.

*Pace* Trapp, there are noteworthy correspondences between 4.29–35 and Antisthenes. The fragment contains elements (i), (ii), (iii), (v) and (vi) in Dio (creatively modified); Dio even seems to echo Antisthenes verbally: 'but if you learn those [loftier] things, then you will learn also human things' ~ Dio 4.31

---

18   Trapp (2000) 226–7 for the parallels between Kingship 4 and *Alcibiades 1*; cf. 232–4; for Trapp, in accordance with the modern consensus hitherto, *Alcibiades 1* is pseudo-Platonic; its genuineness is upheld by Denyer (2001), who has persuaded many; no matter here: its genuineness was accepted without question in the ancient world.

'whoever, then, being noble by nature, possesses that higher education, easily acquires this other also' (an echo the more striking because this piece of Themistius/Antisthenes is preserved only in an Arabic translation). It is *a priori* likely that Antisthenes also contained item (iv): Antisthenes, who began as a pupil of Gorgias, later attacked him (e.g., in the *Archelaus*). By contrast, *Alcibiades I* lacks the sharp distinction between human and divine education, the exemplum of Heracles, the motif of the two roads, and the comparison of human education to erroneous animals.

It is true that there are differences between Dio and Antisthenes, which have to be explained. In Kingship 4 the exponent of the double *paideia* is Diogenes, not Prometheus; the pupil is Alexander, not Heracles; and Heracles is the perfect paradigm of the double *paideia*, not a defective pupil who has yet to learn it; moreover, in Dio's *Oration* 8 (at a point where Diogenes is again the speaker), the teacher-pupil relationship is reversed when Prometheus appears as a sophist saved by Heracles. But these differences are easily explained once one allows for Dio's being not a passive reproducer but a creative adapter of his sources. In Kingship 4 Dio makes Diogenes the main philosophical exponent to Alexander and uses him as the voice both of Diogenic Cynicism and (to a degree) of Dio Chrysostom; Dio wants to include Antisthenes' doctrine of the double *paideia*, as particularly suitable for Trajan; that it should be Diogenes, not Prometheus, who expounds it is not only dramatically necessary, but also—in this more radically Cynic context—philosophically necessary. For in Diogenic (as opposed to Antisthenic) Cynicism Prometheus symbolises the falsities of civilisation, so Dio/Diogenes naturally cuts out Prometheus in Kingship 4 but in *Oration* 8 he preserves vestiges of the educational relationship between Prometheus and Heracles but with Heracles taking the lead. Heracles' 'promotion' from defective pupil to perfect paradigm is similarly both dramatically necessary (because the pupil role is already filled by Alexander), philosophically necessary (because Diogenic Cynicism mostly made Heracles the perfect hero), and pedagogically necessary (because Heracles was Trajan's personal hero). 4.29ff. therefore *is* Dio's development of Antisthenes and, as Höistad saw,[19] Heracles' education in Kingship 1 must also then be *basically* Antisthenic. But in both cases our emphasis should be on Dio's *creative* adaptation.[20]

---

19  Höistad (1948) 150–79.
20  On the other hand, the larger sequential parallels between Kingship 4 and *Alcibiades I* are also compelling and also need explanation. Either Dio *also* used *Alcibiades I* and/or *Alcibiades I* was itself influenced by Antisthenes, who wrote an *Alcibiades*, which on almost any view predated *Alcibiades I*. Here again likely *Platonic* interaction with Antisthenes helps to explain things.

Antisthenes in Kingship 4 and 1 leads to Kingship 3, where Brancacci, following older scholars, argues extensive imitation of Antisthenes. This raises an important methodological point of *Quellenforschung*. It might seem counter-intuitive to reject the notion that the initial questioning of Socrates and his reply derive from the *Gorgias* and that most of the rest of the speech is Dio's 'blow-up' of that exchange. But it's bad method simply to assume that an apparent parallel is *the* parallel; and the *Gorgias* itself interacts with Antisthenes' lost *Archelaus*. It may sometimes be right to go behind (as it were) the Platonic parallel in search of Antisthenes. 4.29ff. clearly illustrates this principle and so does Kingship 3, where Brancacci has made a strong case for sustained Antisthenic influence, despite the more obvious-looking parallel with Plato's *Gorgias*.[21] From my point of view, it's appropriate that Kingship 3, generally the blandest and least challenging of the Kingships, should derive from the proleptically soft-Cynic Antisthenes. The same problem arises in *Oration* 13, Dio's misleading and self-serving account of how his consultation of Delphi at the beginning of his exile gradually turned him into a philosopher. On the face of it, Dio leans heavily on the pseudo-Platonic or possibly even Platonic *Clitophon*, but again Brancacci argues for an Antisthenic basis. And again, *pace* Trapp, I think Brancacci is right. If many older scholars erred in seeing the much-read but now almost entirely lost Antisthenes practically everywhere in Socratic writings, it must equally be an error to see him nowhere, and Kingship 4.29ff. encourages prudent speculation in Antisthenes.

These findings are strengthened by Dio's account of the philosophical relationship between Diogenes and Antisthenes at the start of *Oration* 8 (1–2):

> When Diogenes the Sinopean was exiled from his fatherland, he arrived in Athens, no different at all from the very lowliest, and there he found a good many still of Socrates' companions: Plato, Aristippus, Aeschines, Antisthenes, and Eucleides the Megarian [otherwise unattested and chronologically impossible]; but Xenophon was still in exile because of the campaign with Cyrus [not true]. Now he quickly despised all the rest, but associated with Antisthenes [chronologically impossible], not approving the man himself so much as the words that he spoke, thinking them alone to be true and most able to help a human being. (2) When he compared Antisthenes himself with his words he sometimes criticised him as much weaker.

---

21  Brancacci (1992), esp. 3318–22; (2000) 252–3.

The anachronisms and factual misrepresentations of this account (as indicated in the square brackets) Brancacci rightly explains by Dio's desire to connect Diogenes back to Socrates through Antisthenes *qua* influential on the Cynics but flawed because of the disparity between his words and deeds.[22] This insight can be developed: the interplay between Ἀντισθένει and μαλακώτερον suggests that Antisthenes is untrue to his name, a telling blow against a philosopher who insisted on the correct use of *onomata* as the basis of philosophical truth, whereas, as in Kingship 4, *Diogenes* truly represents divine wisdom; further, *Oration* 8 is centrally concerned with the difference between good philosopher-follower relationships (the *sunousia* between Antisthenes and Diogenes) and bad master-pupil relationships (the sophists and their *mathetai*, so-called because they *manthano* nothing); again like Kingship 4. In *Oration* 8 Diogenes surpasses Antisthenes by uniting words and deeds, the latter exemplified by Heracles; again, like Kingship 4. And when Heracles frees Prometheus, Prometheus represents Antisthenes, ambiguous as he is between sophist and proto-/true philosopher. In effect, then, *Oration* 8, while connecting Diogenes to Antisthenes, *appropriates* Antisthenes' 'double *paideia*' to Diogenes, validating its attribution to him in Kingship 4 and giving Diogenic Cynicism real content. Too much content? I don't think so, because Diogenes Laertius 6.70 attributes to Diogenes a double *askesis*, which Höistad among others connects with Antisthenes' double *paideia*. True, Marie-Odile Goulet-Cazé argues that D.L. 6.70 is inauthentic,[23] but *Oration* 8 is full of Diogenic *askesis* and, as we have seen, it appropriates the Antisthenic double *paideia*. Dio understands authentic Diogenic Cynicism better than they do in the CNRS. *Oration* 8 is a very skilful piece: it ingeniously enacts both the diachronic relationship between Antisthenic and Diogenic Cynicism and the synchronic superiority of the latter: at the end the sophists' failure to understand the philosophical profundities of Diogenes' public defecation replays the relationship between Prometheus and Heracles but this time the sophist figures fail the Cynic test.

Some interim conclusions: Antisthenes *is* important in Dio; Dio uses Antisthenes creatively—in the ways in which he adapts Antisthenic philosophy to his own contexts—but this very creativity has serious moral and

---

22  Brancacci (2000) 256–7; I once wondered if 8.1–2 dramatises Dio's youthful arrival in Rome, with the exiled Xenophon representing some philosopher(s) exiled by some Roman emperor(s) and Antisthenes representing Dio's own philosophical master, Musonius. But I doubt if Dio would ever have criticised the virtuous Musonius in the terms he here uses of Antisthenes, and Brancacci's interpretation makes 8.1–2 far more organic to *Or.* 8's wider concerns.

23  Goulet-Cazé (1986).

philosophical goals; the Socrates–Antisthenes–Diogenes *diadochê* matters greatly to Dio, as one of several legitimate ways of mediating the Socratic inheritance; part of him rates Diogenic Cynicism more highly than Antisthenic.

So far, then, Diogenic Cynicism, Antisthenic Cynicism, and some 'soft-Cynicism' (as built into the Kingships and represented by Bion, Onesicritus, and—again—Antisthenes). Further Dionian soft Cynicism is found in the Alexandrian Oration, where Malherbe rightly argues that Dio adopts a fundamentally soft-Cynic *persona* as the 'reconciler', the *diallaktês*, a role particularly associated with Crates.[24] Dio's self-presentation in other Greek political speeches and Philostratus' representation of Dio in *Vitae Sophistarum* suggest the same Cratetean *diallaktês* pose.[25] Importantly, I think, this role had been assumed by Dio's teacher Musonius in the Roman civil wars of 69/70.[26]

## 3   The Diogenics

We have already considered some aspects of *Oration* 8, but the Diogenics need group treatment.[27] They are pure gold: finely written and structured, they tell us almost everything we need to know about Diogenic Cynicism: its grounding in a hard primitivist interpretation of living in accordance with nature validated by appeals to animals, Diogenes' life-style in detail, and all his characteristic roles—doctor, scout, overseer, etc.; his *spoudaiogeloion* style, his virulent abuse of the privileged, theatricality, outrageous subversions of convention, and shameless public behaviour. The main elements which some might regard as fake are Diogenes' evident 'philanthropy', his 'cosmopolitanism', and belief in the gods, but these, as we know from the Moles assumptions about Cynicism, are genuinely Diogenic. Some of Dio's material is simply an inflation

---

24   Malherbe (1970).
25   VS 488: 'Frequenting the military camps in the rags he was accustomed to wear and seeing the soldiers rushing to revolt at the slaying of Domitian, he did not spare himself when he saw the disorder that had broken out: stripped, he leapt on to a high altar and began his speech as follows: "Then Odysseus of much cunning stripped himself of his rags" [*Od.* 22.1], and saying this and revealing himself as no beggar, nor as whom they believed him to be, but as Dio the sage, he delivered an inspired indictment of the tyrant and he taught the soldiers to have better thoughts by doing what seemed good to the Romans'.
26   Musonius διαλλακτής: Tac. *Hist.* 3.81 'Musonius Rufus of the equestrian order had mixed with the legates, emulating the study of philosophy and the precepts of the Stoics, and, mixing with the maniples, he was beginning an attempt to admonish the armed men, discoursing on the goods of peace and the crises of war …'.
27   The Diogenics are: *Or.* 6 = 'Diogenes/On Tyranny'; *Or.* 8 = 'Diogenes/On Virtue'; *Or.* 9 = 'Diogenes/Isthmian'; *Or.* 10 = 'Diogenes/On Servants/House-Slaves'.

of well-known *dicta* attributed to Diogenes, e.g., Diogenes' various exegeses of what it is to be a dog; other items have more substantial provenance: the justification of incest by appeal to Oedipus derives from Diogenes' notorious tragedy; the anti-Prometheus primitivist myth goes back to the historical Diogenes; some items suggest that Dio had read Diogenes' *Politeia*; there are Antisthenic traces beyond those already discussed. Again I stress that Dio shows a shrewd understanding of Cynicism (better than many modern scholars): for example, he sees that Cynicism is fundamentally anti-*polis* but that the Cynic's missionary role entails his going among crowds. Not only, then, do the Diogenics provide an excellent guide to Diogenic Cynicism—certainly more authentic than Arrian/Epictetus' *Peri Kunismou*—but they show that Dio had read some of Diogenes' own writings and they confirm his familiarity with Antisthenes.

It is, then, legitimate to read the Diogenics as timeless expositions of hard Cynicism. Indeed, on *any* reading much of the material is timeless and non-context-specific. What conceivable specific audience, apart from one of pubertal boys, could explain Diogenes' long disquisition on the delights of masturbation? Moreover, as we have seen, *qua* historian, as well as exponent, of Socratic philosophy, Dio is interested in, and keen to reinforce, the Socrates–Antisthenes–Diogenes *diadochê*. But the Diogenics are not wholly abstract: von Arnim argued that they allegorise Dio's own experiences: both Diogenes and Dio were exiles; Diogenes repudiates the Persian King, who has tyrannical attributes; Dio was exiled by the tyrannical Domitian, Eurystheus also represents Domitian, etc. This interpretation, widely current nowadays, suits Dio's general practices of constructing *personae* out of famous philosophers or mythical figures (cf. already the Diogenes of Kingship 4) and of vilifying Domitian (everywhere in the Kingships), and it is clearly right.

It is then reasonable to seek a broad dating and context. For von Arnim, followed by most scholars, including Dudley, Desideri, Blomqvist, Moles, Brenk, and Brancacci, not only do the Diogenics allegorise Dio's own experiences but they were written during the exile and show Dio going through a Cynic phase in which he practised and celebrated Cynic poverty and rejected kingship; for Dudley the Diogenics were the vehicle of the *parrhêsia* against Domitian which in Kingship 3 Dio claims to have fearlessly exercised; others have seen them as a vehicle of self-therapy. On this exile dating, the Diogenics have inspired Dio's assumption of a Cynic role in Kingships 1 and 4, especially as that Cynic role is largely backward-looking and tied to Dio's exile. Jones, however, suggests that the Diogenics are Trajanic, generated by Dio's interest in the Diogenes–Alexander encounter as a way of approach to Trajan.[28] These

---

28   Jones (1978) 50, 122.

opposed reconstructions agree on a close thematic relationship between the Diogenics and the Kingships; but reverse their chronological relationship with profound interpretative differences. How to decide? The argument of von Arnim and his followers that Dio could not have endorsed extreme poverty, etc. after his exile because of the resultant credibility gap is unconvincing, because we can hypothesise different sorts of context for delivery, levels of irony, etc. The use of allegory as a vehicle for attacks on Domitian does not prove an exile context, such allegorical attacks being everywhere in the Trajanic Kingships. Although appeal to thematic parallels as a pointer to the same period of composition cannot be decisive, anyone sure that Kingship 4 is Trajanic should perhaps incline to regard the Diogenics as also Trajanic. Are there any sharper arguments? We need to consider a series of 'test' passages:

> (1) 6.39: 'he [the Persian King *qua* tyrant] suspected both his food and his drink and had people to test these in advance, like scouts on a road full of enemies; he did not even have confidence in his close relations, neither his children nor his wife'.

Since Darius III had excellent relations with his wife, the distrusted wife here clearly evokes Domitian's wife Domitia.[29] Now Dio himself was in exile from Rome from c.82[30] and the context of this passage concerns a developed tyranny, when the tyrant fears constantly for his life: is there an allusion here to Domitia's (alleged) part in Domitian's assassination? Cf. (2) and (3) below.

> (2) 6.45: 'it seems to me that the tyrant is happy only when he is struck down, as having been released from the greatest evil'.

This is a derisive Cynic take on Solon's 'call no man happy until he is dead', underpinned by the Cynic doctrine λόγος–βρόχος ('reason or the noose'). Might it allude to Domitian's assassination? Of course, Dio could have 'foreseen' that event.[31]

> (3) 6.57 'it seems that [the tyrant] would never live in safety, not even if he were to become bronze or iron, but even thus he would be destroyed by being broken into pieces or melted down'.

---

29   Blomqvist (1989) 235.
30   On Dio's exile see Jones (1978) 45–55.
31   Cf. 66.13.

Might this allude to Domitian's *damnatio memoriae*? Of course, Dio would know that this was the likely fate of 'bad emperors'.

> (4) 6.60 makes the strong Cynic claim to *asphaleia*: 'I, however [sc. in contrast to the fearful and unfree tyrant],' says Diogenes, 'go where I wish by night and I go by day by myself, and I have courage, if need be, even going through an army without the herald's staff and through the midst of brigands'.

Does it belong to the same temporal context, the same thought-world, the same sort of dramatic self-presentation as 4.8 'but Diogenes [sc. in contrast to Alexander] went forth by himself in complete safety not only by day but also by night where he wished to go'; 1.63 'he went about alone and did everything he desired single-handed'; 12 (*Olympicus*, post-exile).17–20 'I [Dio] went [among the Roman armies massing against Dacia] "unarmed, without helmet or shield, having no spear" [*Il.* 21.50] ... I appeared quite alone among this great host, perfectly at ease and a very peaceful observer of war ...'; and 7 (*Euboicus*).8–9 'I followed him gladly; for I did not at any time fear to be plotted against, since I had nothing but a shabby cloak. And often at other times, in as much as I was in continual wandering, and also on that occasion, I verified by experience the fact that poverty is in reality a sacred and inviolable thing, and no one wrongs you, much less than they do those who carry a herald's equipment'—all of which are post-exile?

> (5) 8.29–33 'they think that Eurystheus [= Domitian] had power over him and gave him orders, Eurystheus whom they considered worth nothing, nor did anyone ever pray or sacrifice to Eurystheus [denial of Domitian's excessive divine claims?]. But Heracles traversed Europe and all Asia ... [account of Heracles' labours] These things, then, he did, not at all as a favour to Eurystheus'; cf. 1.59: 'Heracles was, as all say, the son of Zeus by Alcmene, and king not only of Argos but also of all Greece. (The majority do not know that Heracles was away from home conducting campaigns and protecting his empire; but they say that Eurystheus was then king. This, however, is said falsely by them [text of this parenthesis corrupt; meaning clear].) And Heracles was king not only of Greece but held empire over every land from the rising to the setting sun and over all men among whom are found shrines of Heracles'.

Does 8.29–33 use Eurystheus and Heracles in the same way as 1.59, that is, to palliate Trajan's apparent *obsequium* of Domitian, to suggest Domitian's illegitimacy and to imply that Trajan was always the true king?

(6) There is a series of contrasts between Diogenes/Dio and sophists:

(a) 6.21: 'Such things, then, he used to say at times laughing at the puffed up and mindless; but most of all he abused the sophists who wished to be revered and thought that they knew more than other men.'

(b) 8.8: 'At that time, too, it was possible to hear around Poseidon's temple many accursed sophists shouting and reviling one another, and their so-called learners [*mathêtai*], fighting one with another.'

(c) 8.33: 'Prometheus, a sort of sophist, as it seems to me, he [Heracles] came upon being destroyed by reputation, his liver swelling and growing whenever he was praised but again shrivelling whenever they censured him, and he pitied him and taught him wisdom[32] and thus relieved him of his vanity and love of competition'.

(d) 8.36: 'When Diogenes was saying these things, many stood around and heard his words with complete pleasure. But, thinking, I suppose, of Heracles' action [in cleaning the Augean stables], he desisted from his words, and squatting on the ground he performed an action of ill repute. At once, then, the majority scorned him and said that he was mad, and again the sophists raised a din, like frogs in a pond when they do not see the water-snake.'

(e) 10.32: 'Whoever being ignorant persuade themselves that they are wise, these men are much more wretched than all others; such indeed is the tribe of the sophists'.

What is the context of 6(a)–(e)? Is it a Greek one, and if so, is it a struggle between Dio-*philosophos* and sophists or an internal sophistic struggle between Dio-*sophistês* pretending not to be a *sophistês* and other *sophistai*? If it is some sort of Greek context, that might make the Diogenics post-exile, on the grounds that (a) Dionian sophistic activity is less likely in the exile period; and (b) a pre-exile context might involve too great a chronological separation of thematically related works. But such reasoning cannot be sure.

Now items 6(a)–(e) find parallels in the Kingships, in 6(f)–(h).

(f) 1.57: 'The words of men and all their sophistries are worth nothing beside the knowledge and speech of the gods'.

(g) 1.61: 'He [Heracles] was educated simply, not multiply nor superfluously by the sophistries and knavish tricks of accursed men'.

(h) 4.33–8 [speaker Diogenes]: 'Furthermore, if he [the seeker after true education] falls in with a man who as it were knows the road, that man easily shows him the direction and he learns and at once departs.

---

32  Reading Cohoon's emendation φρενώσας.

But if he falls in with an ignorant and charlatan sophist, he will wear him out by leading him hither and thither ... you will sometimes find around the so-called sophists a large crowd of simple-minded men, and you will realise that a sophist is no different from a lecherous eunuch ... [you will gain no profit] even if you wear out your whole life sleeplessly and fasting among the accursed sophists ...'.

The contrast in 6(h) is between the unproductive relationship between sophists and their pupils and the truly productive relationship, the philosophical *sunousia*—union or intercourse—between Diogenes and Alexander, which, if Alexander is sufficiently receptive, will allow the virile Diogenes to impregnate him with virtue: or Dio to impregnate Trajan. But, as we have seen, *Oration* 8 seems to appropriate to Diogenes Antisthenes' double *paideia* as found in Kingships 4 and 1 and it also sketches the same pattern of right philosopher-follower relationships as does Kingship 4.

Furthermore, items 6(a)–(e) find another post-exile parallel, with the *Olympicus*, in which Dio (this time *in propria persona*) again contrasts himself with sophists (12.13–16). Given the strong element of autobiographical allegory in the Diogenics and Dio's general propensity for self-dramatisation, one might well wonder if *Or.* 8 (which includes strong Diogenes/Dio-sophist contrasts and shows Diogenes in action at the Isthmian games) and *Or.* 9 (the *Isthmian Discourse*, again set at the Isthmian games) dramatise Dio's triumphant appearance at the Olympic games, with the location of the games changed to fit the biography of Diogenes, who frequented Corinth as well as Athens.

No single one of these items can count for much; nevertheless, when account is also taken of the general resemblances between Kingship 4 and the Diogenics, the cumulative case that they provide for a Trajanic dating and context for the Diogenics seems strong. If so, the 'ideal reader' (useful concept) of the Diogenics is Trajan, who, after Kingships 4 and 1, needs more information about the Cynics and Diogenes and about the power of his philosophical example, and who in the Antisthenes–Diogenes *sunousia* is given a further paradigm of the *sunousia* between himself and Dio, as opposed to the unfruitful *sunousia* between himself and any other intellectuals whom Dio can dismiss as 'sophists', who include sophists in the usual sense but also such venal and impotent wordsmiths as Plutarch. This reconstruction does not deny that the Diogenics are also timeless and would also work in a purely Greek context, though ideally one cognisant of Dio's *sunousia* with Trajan. This reconstruction also enhances our appreciation of Dio's literary skill: his 'mapping' of Antisthenic *paideia* firstly on to Diogenes in his philosophical context (Kingship 4 and Oration 8), and, secondly on to himself in his philosophical and political context (Kingship 4 and *Oration* 8) provides yet another illustration of Dio's almost symphonic ability to create multiple layers of meaning.

## 4  Conclusions

How does all this cash out? As a Stoic (mostly), Dio was almost bound to engage with Cynicism, the progenitor of Stoicism. As Musonius' pupil, he was even likelier to do so, Musonius' ethics being strongly Cynic-influenced.[33] When the young Dio first visited Rome, he must have seen, even met, the great Cynic Demetrius. At this period, the Greek cities of the East swarmed with Cynics. Both practical and literary Cynicism were abundantly available to Dio.

Cynic ethics are good to teach with *qua* simple and strong and appropriate both for beginners in philosophy (Kingship 1) and for those whose moral state is so poor that only a fully-fledged Cynic assault will do (Kingship 4 and all the Diogenics). Modern philosophers often claim that ancient philosophical texts are 'good to think with', meaning that they raise many of the basic intellectual questions and can be brought into fruitful dialectic with modern concerns. Cynicism is also good to think with, primarily of course because of its elemental *moral* power, though I shall shortly dare to suggest that it has at least intellectual *potential* as well.

So Dio used Cynicism both to teach with and to think with and though you don't need much reading to understand Cynicism, Dio as a good lecturer did quite extensive reading, including Antisthenes, Diogenes, Onesicritus, and Bion. Cynic theatricality suited Dio the actor, with his varied and imaginative exploitation of *personae*. Diogenes provided a particularly fruitful parallel with Dio's own career. Cynicism is also fun: Diogenes was witty and Kingship 4 and the Diogenics make entertaining reads. But *spoudaiogeloion* is also a good way of doing philosophy. Was Dio ever seriously influenced by Cynicism? It's likely enough that he *sometimes* behaved as a Cynic during his exile wanderings when cut off from his normal sources of revenue; even on a Trajanic dating the Diogenics mostly look back to the exile period. Dio's *diallaktês* stance in the Greek cities of the East—reminiscent of his master Musonius in Italy—is in the Cratetean tradition. With his beard and *tribōn* Dio looked like a Cynic, though he sometimes found it politic to dissociate himself from them. It is also true and important that in simple ethical contexts Cynic ethics are largely acceptable to Stoics. More substantially, Dio shows a real interest in the

---

33  Dudley (1937) 193–6; cf. Lutz (1947) 28–30.

Socrates–Antisthenes–Diogenes *diadochê* as one important way (not the only important way) of deriving and preserving the Socratic tradition.

But I'm going to go the whole dog by closing with a case of really substantive Cynic influence, a case of the dog that did bark. Or perhaps I'm the one that's barking. Brunt is grudgingly perturbed by *Oration* 15:

> [Dio] goes further than any other writer of Roman times ... in subverting the legal institution of slavery; his argument ... tends to show that there are no natural slaves and no just way, i.e. no way according with natural law, of acquiring title to another human being.[34]

Now it is notoriously hard to find disapproval of slavery *per se* in Stoicism, even though some Stoic principles *could* have yielded this conclusion. But it's easy to derive such disapproval from Cynicism. The Diogenic Cynic should have no possessions beyond those necessary for physical survival. It was a defining moment in Diogenes' philosophical evolution when he realised that the loss of one of his slaves didn't matter. When the rich Crates became a Cynic, he gave away all his possessions with the words 'Crates has liberated Crates'. Dio's Diogenic 10th Oration explicitly argues that it's better not to have slaves. These items concern the virtue of the owner or non-owner. What of the slave? Of course, a Cynic will always argue that even on the rack (slavery at its worst) the wise man is free, hence the Cynic claim that Diogenes endured his entirely fictional slavery 'most nobly'. But although virtue is possible under such conditions, they are not optimal and do not represent the ideal Cynic condition, where the Cynic's freedom to move around at will (like Diogenes or Dio in military camps or Diogenes commuting between Athens and Corinth or Dio on his wanderings) or to enjoy the sun unblocked by the greatest of kings is part of his existential freedom. From the slave's point of view, as of the owner's, Cynicism is anti-slavery. In Oration 10 Dio argues this in Cynic mode; in 15 he argues it within a Stoic framework, but if he is indeed the only Stoic ever to argue this position, as Brunt claims, he does so because his thinking has been liberated—however temporarily—by Cynicism. Aristotle and the Stoics are no doubt incredibly smart, but when they fail to stagger as far as disapproval of slavery, it's not really very impressive. And their failure is not just (just!) moral and humanitarian, it is also intellectual, a direct result of their excessively vertical, compartmentalising, or 'convergent' modes of thought. As some might say, typical classicists. In this, as in other areas, Cynic thought is better—morally *and* intellectually.

---

34   Brunt (1973) 18 {= (2013) 162}.

Why do eminent scholars of ancient philosophy or ancient slavery ignore this clear Cynic evidence?[35] Partly ignorance, partly a precious (by which I mean, valueless) refinement, partly all the vices with which I have just tarred Aristotle and the Stoics, partly snobbery, partly the unthinking assumption, so often demonstrably false, that virtue is to be found among the intellectually sophisticated, as those scholars themselves are. But for 'intellectually sophisticated' read 'sophists': that true virtue is often rather to be found among the simple (Kingships 1 and 4, the *Euboicus*) and in the simple (Oration 10) is the single most important lesson of Cynicism, and to his enduring credit the highly sophisticated Dio, the sometimes sophist Dio, the Platonist Dio, the orthodox Stoic Dio, the Posidonian and Panaetian Dio, Dio the economist, Dio the tax expert—this Dio/these Dios sometimes recognised the truth of this most valuable Cynic lesson, sometimes taught it and sometimes also—I believe and trust—himself enacted it. For virtue, read also common sense. Trajan's Alexander obsession fructified in military disaster: we may doubt if such luminaries as Plinius Secundus, Sosius Senecio, or even L. Mestrius Plutarchus did much to restrain their rather unstable *dominus*; but in Kingship 4 Dio/Diogenes showed impressive moral concern and impressive practical prescience. Nothing could be more misconceived than to dismiss Cynicism as other-worldly, unconcerned with others or without practical value. Deface the currency. Woof! Or grr.

## Bibliography

Billerbeck, M. (1978) *Epiktet: vom Kynismus* (Leiden).
Blomqvist, K. (1989) *Myth and Moral Message in Dio Chrysostom: A Study in Dio's Moral Thought, with a Particular Focus on his Attitudes towards Women* (Lund).
Brancacci, A. (1990) *Oikeios logos: la filosofia del linguaggio di Antistene* (Naples).
Brancacci, A. (1992) 'Struttura compositiva e fonti della terza orazione "Sulla Regalità" di Dione Crisostomo: Dione e l'"Archelao" di Antistene', *ANRW* II.36.5: 3308–34.
Brancacci, A. (2000) 'Dio, Socrates, and Cynicism', in Swain (2000) 240–60.
Brenk, F. E. (2000) 'Dio on the Simple and Self-sufficient Life', in Swain (2000) 261–78.
Brunt, P. A. (1973) 'Aspects of the Social Thought of Dio Chrysostom and the Stoics', *PCPhS* 199: 9–33; repr. in id., *Studies in Stoicism*, edd. M. Griffin and A. Samuels (Oxford, 2013) 151–79.
Denyer, N., ed. (2001) *Plato: Alcibiades* (Cambridge).

---

[35] Honourable exceptions are Summers (1910) 210; Long (1974) 4; Brenk (2000) 276–7.

Desideri, P. (1978) *Dione di Prusa: un intelletuale greco nell'impero romano* (Messina/Florence).

Dudley, D. R. (1937) *A History of Cynicism from Diogenes to the 6th century A.D.* (London).

Fears, J. R. (1977) *Princeps a diis electus: The Divine Election of the Emperor as a Political Concept at Rome* (Rome).

Gill, C. (2000) 'Stoic Writers of the Imperial Period' in Rowe and Schofield (2000) 597–615.

Goulet-Cazé, M.-O. (1986) *L'Ascèce Cynique: un commentaire de Diogéne Laërce VI 70–71* (Paris).

Höistad, R. (1948) *Cynic Hero and Cynic King: Studies in the Cynic Conception of Man* (Uppsala).

Jones, C. P. (1978) *The Roman World of Dio Chrysostom* (Cambridge, Mass. and London).

Kindstrand, J. F. (1976) *Bion of Borysthenes: a Collection of the Fragments with Introduction and Commentary* (Uppsala).

Long, A. A. (1974) *Hellenistic Philosophy* (London; repr. with additional bibliography, 1986).

Lovejoy, A. O. and G. Boas (1935) *A Documentary History of Primitivism and Related Ideas in Antiquity* (Baltimore; repr. New York, 1965).

Lutz, C. E. (1947) 'Musonius Rufus, "The Roman Socrates"', *YCS* 10: 3–147.

Malherbe, A. J. (1970) 'Gentle as a Nurse: The Cynic Background to 1 Thess ii', *Novum Testamentum* 12: 203–17; repr. in id., *Light from the Gentiles: Hellenistic Philosophy and Early Christianity: Collected Essays, 1959–2012*, 2 vols, edd. C. R. Holladay et al. (Leiden and Boston, 2014) I.53–67.

Moles, J. L. (1978) 'The Career and Conversion of Dio Chrysostom', *JHS* 98: 79–100 [above, Ch. 1].

Moles, J. L. (1983a) 'The Date and Purpose of the Fourth Kingship Oration of Dio Chrysostom', *ClAnt* 2: 251–78 [above, Ch. 3].

Moles, J. L. (1983b) 'Dio Chrysostom: Exile, Tarsus, Nero and Domitian', *LCM* 8: 130–4 [above, Ch. 2].

Moles, J. L. (1984) 'The Addressee of the Third Kingship Oration of Dio Chrysostom', *Prometheus* 10: 65–9 [above, Ch. 4].

Moles, J. L. (1990) 'The Kingship Orations of Dio Chrysostom', *PLLS* 6: 297–375 [above, Ch. 5].

Moles, J. L. (1995a) 'The Cynics and Politics', in A. Laks and M. Schofield, edd. *Justice and Generosity: Studies in Hellenistic Social and Political Philosophy* (Cambridge) 129–58 [below, Ch. 15].

Moles, J. L. (1995b) 'Dio Chrysostom, Greece, and Rome', in D. C. Innes, H. Hine, and C. Pelling, edd. *Ethics and Rhetoric: Classical Essays for Donald Russell on his Seventy-fifth Birthday* (Oxford) 177–92 [above, Ch. 7].

Moles, J. L. (1996) 'Cynic Cosmopolitanism', in R. B. Branham and M.-O. Goulet-Cazé, edd., *The Cynics: the Cynic Movement in Antiquity and its Legacy* (Berkeley, 1996) 105–20 [below, Ch. 16].

Moles, J. L. (2000) 'The Cynics', in Rowe and Schofield (2000) 415–34 [below, Ch. 17].

Moles, J. L. (2003) 'Dio und Trajan', in K. Piepenbrink, ed. *Philosophie und Lebenswelt in der Antike* (Darmstadt) 186–207 [English version above, Ch. 9].

Momigliano, A. D. (1950) 'Dio Chrysostomos' (Unpublished Lecture, 1950), in id., *Quarto Contributo alla Storia degli studi classici e del mondo antico* (Rome, 1969) 257–69.

Rowe, C. and M. Schofield, edd. (2000) *The Cambridge History of Greek and Roman Political Thought* (Cambridge).

Summers, W. C., ed. (1910) *Select Letters of Seneca* (London).

Swain, S. (1996) *Hellenism and Empire: Language, Classicism, and Power in the Greek World, AD 50–250* (Oxford).

Swain, S., ed. (2000) *Dio Chrysostom: Politics, Letters, and Philosophy* (Oxford).

Trapp, M. B. (2000) 'Plato in Dio', in Swain (2000) 213–39.

# PART 2

*Studies in Cynic Philosophy*

∴

CHAPTER 12

# *'Honestius quam Ambitiosius'*? An Exploration of the Cynic's Attitude to Moral Corruption in His Fellow Men

Two important studies have recently appeared of the career and philosophy of the celebrated first-century Cynic Demetrius:* an article by J. F. Kindstrand and a monograph by M. Billerbeck.[1] Both scholars discuss Demetrius' defence of P. Egnatius Celer in AD 70.[2] The purpose of the present paper is threefold: (i) to argue that Kindstrand's and Billerbeck's interpretations of this incident, different as they are, must, like all previous interpretations, be rejected; (ii) to offer a new perspective, in the hope of showing that Demetrius' action can be understood as thoroughly honourable; (iii) to demonstrate that Demetrius' action can be understood as not only thoroughly honourable, but also profoundly Cynic. It may be objected that investigation of motive in such a case is intrinsically misguided. The only evidence is a short notice in Tacitus,[3] and it is of course true that we shall never be able to say for certain what Demetrius' motives were. Some modern historians, moreover, deprecate on principle analysis of motive, in the ancient world especially. It seems, nevertheless, both legitimate and worthwhile to attempt to understand the reasons why Demetrius, a Cynic philosopher of (on the normal view) high moral character, should have defended Celer, a Stoic philosopher who (again on the normal view) had revealed himself to be a complete scoundrel. The exercise may also serve to bring out some fundamental points about the Cynics' conception of man and their interpretation of human weakness. For reasons which will become clear below, Cynicism was vulnerable to misunderstanding and misrepresentation. Demetrius' defence of Celer, I shall argue, provides an instructive paradigm for the correct interpretation of Cynicism. In the formulation of the argument I make three major assumptions:

(1)  that it is possible to reconstruct early Cynic doctrine in some detail;
(2)  that Demetrius' philosophy was authentically Cynic;

---

\*  I am grateful to Professors G. B. Kerferd and A. A. Long for stimulating criticism of earlier drafts of this paper.
1  Kindstrand (1980); Billerbeck (1979).
2  Kindstrand (1980) 96ff.; Billerbeck (1979) 46f.
3  Doubtfully relevant is *Schol. in Iuv. vet. ad sat.* 1.33: see n. 20 below.

(3) that the Cynicism of the Imperial era was part of a continuing tradition of Cynicism and cannot be dismissed as merely a radical form of Stoicism, even though Cynic doctrine coincided in many respects with Stoic (because since Zeno Stoic ethics had been profoundly influenced by Cynic and because Late Stoicism in general took on an even more markedly Cynic character), and even though we can point to some Cynic texts which have been influenced in turn by Stoicism.[4]

(1) The reconstruction of early Cynic doctrine is naturally difficult. Cynic *testimonia* are comparatively few, and frequently take the form of anecdotes or *apophthegmata*. The personalities of early Cynics, especially Diogenes, were such as to inspire much apocryphal [[104]] material. Moreover, since Cynicism was essentially a practical, and rather simple, philosophy, it did not produce canonical writings like other philosophical systems. It is almost certain that Diogenes and other early Cynics did write philosophical works,[5] but if so, they seem to have lost currency quite early in the Hellenistic period. Most important, the Stoics had a vested interest in harmonising Cynic teachings, as far as possible, with their own, in order to support the claim that their philosophy derived ultimately from Socrates by the *diadochê* Socrates–Antisthenes–Diogenes–Crates–Zeno. Thus there is always the possibility that any 'Cynic' *testimonium* has been contaminated by Stoicism. This is demonstrable in some cases, debatable in others, and a theoretical possibility in nearly all. But total suspension of critical judgement would be wrong. There is some firm Cynic evidence: the fragments of the poems of Crates, the lengthy fragment of Onesicritus on Alexander and the Gymnosophists quoted by Strabo,[6] and (with qualifications) the fragments of Bion of Borysthenes and

---

4   Stoic influence is clear on (e.g.) Dio 4 (n. 110 below), the Geneva papyrus (n. 112), some of the Cynic letters (cf. Attridge [1976]; Malherbe [1977]; and Oenomaus' attack on prophecy and the theory of predestination (Eus. *PE* 6.7.10–19), which exploits Stoic sense-perception theory to support the argument (cf. Long [1980] 53 n. 1). But the Stoic influence is generally trivial—more a case of the use of convenient terminology or suitable *ad hoc* arguments than of change in philosophical orientation. (Diogenes himself seems to have exploited other philosophers' theories when it suited him—cf. D.L. 6.70 with the good discussion of Dudley [1937] 216ff.) Such works, if not 'pure', are *fundamentally* Cynic. It is harder to classify works like Epictetus' περὶ κυνισμοῦ (see n. 92) or Julian's *Orr.* 6–7, where sympathetic Stoics give their interpretations of the true meaning of Cynicism. Used critically, such works do seem to me to provide some useful evidence about Cynicism.
5   For Diogenes see von Fritz (1926) 55ff. The objections of Tarn and others lack force: cf. Ferguson (1975) 89f.
6   Str. 15.1.64–5 = Onesicr. *FGrHist* 134 F 17.

of Teles of Megara.⁷ Some Antisthenic *testimonia* are also arguably important,⁸ and Diogenes Laertius preserves some authentic material.⁹ It is also possible to interpret even doubtfully historical material as, in some instances, at least *ben trovato*, hazardous though this procedure may be. And finally, it is possible in certain cases to document differences in doctrine between 'Cynic' *testimonia* and Stoic,¹⁰ which in itself suggests that the Cynic *testimonia* in question may be authentic. Exploitation of the Cynic *testimonia* is therefore difficult, and sometimes involves judicious recourse to 'cumulative argument', but the reconstruction in some detail of early Cynic doctrine is not impossible.¹¹

(2) Since the main source for Demetrius' philosophy is Seneca, there are problems in disentangling Demetrian material from Senecan. But although some cases remain controversial, the work of Dudley, Kindstrand, and above all Billerbeck has shown that Demetrius' philosophy was authentically Cynic, at least in the sense of later Cynicism.¹²

(3) This assumption being far more controversial, I relegate formal discussion to an appendix, while hoping that the material in the main body of the paper will help to demonstrate the basic continuity of Cynicism from the fourth century BC to the first century AD.

## 1   The Historical Background to the Trial of Celer

The historical background is well known and has been much discussed in connection with the so-called 'philosophical opposition' to the emperors, but since treatment of the problem of Demetrius' defence of Celer must take it into account, I summarise it briefly.

---

7   Bion: Kindstrand (1976); Teles: Hense (1909), O'Neil (1977). Qualifications are necessary because although both writers are broadly Cynic their work is clearly a dilution of Diogenes', or even Crates', teaching, and also shows (I think) some Stoic influence.
8   The ancient tradition that Diogenes was Antisthenes' pupil was effectively refuted by Dudley (1937) 1ff. (*pace* Höistad [1948] 10ff.), but Antisthenic influence upon Diogenes has been widely accepted, and is patent (cf. esp. Xen. *Symp.* 4.34ff.).
9   Cf. esp. Höistad (1948) 16ff.
10  Cynic and Stoic attitudes to (e.g.) prophecy, political activity, and the meaning of the maxim κατὰ φύσιν ζῆν are *characteristically* different, even if individual Cynics and Stoics do not always adopt the characteristic positions of their respective philosophies.
11  The basic works on Cynicism are the books of Dudley (1937) and Höistad (1948). At the time of writing I have not seen Niehues–Proebsting (1979).
12  Dudley (1937) 125ff.; Kindstrand (1980) 89ff.; Billerbeck (1979) *passim*.

P. Egnatius Celer was a friend of Barea Soranus, the friend of Thrasea Paetus. All three men were Stoics and Celer had been Soranus' teacher in philosophy.[13] Soranus and his daughter were tried for *maiestas* in 66. There were three charges: (1) that Soranus had been a friend of Rubellius Plautus; (2) that he had planned a revolt in the province of Asia; (3) that he and his daughter had consorted with *magi*. Despite their former friendship Celer appeared as a witness for the [[105]] prosecution (according to Tacitus he had been bribed) and Soranus and his daughter were found guilty and condemned to death.[14] Soranus was, of course, only one of many men of a philosophical disposition to be persecuted (for whatever reasons) under Nero. On Nero's death the position of the *delatores*, whose activities had greatly contributed to the abuse of the *maiestas* law in the latter part of the reign, became a major political issue. Prominent senators, like the Stoic Helvidius Priscus, the son-in-law of Thrasea Paetus, and other associates of the 'philosophical martyrs', like the distinguished Stoic philosopher Musonius Rufus, wanted the *delatores* punished. In addition, the accession of Vespasian seems to have inspired some philosophically-minded politicians with the naïve hope of investing the new emperor with some of the characteristics of 'the good king'. Furthermore, there was a widespread desire among independently-minded senators to reclaim the senatorial *auctoritas* and *libertas* so seriously eroded by the Julio-Claudians in general and Nero in particular.

The lead was taken by Helvidius Priscus. Helvidius had been banished from Italy in 66 because of his relationship with Thrasea Paetus and returned to Rome under Galba, when he brought charges against Eprius Marcellus, the most notorious *delator* of all, who had informed against Thrasea. This action split the senate, Galba's attitude was ambiguous, and Helvidius was persuaded to drop the attack.[15] When Vitellius became emperor Helvidius quarrelled with him in the senate for reasons that are unclear.[16] On the day when the imperial power was voted to Vespasian Helvidius clashed with Marcellus over the question of the composition of the senatorial delegation to be sent to the new emperor.[17] When the consul designate proposed that the question of a reduction in public expenditure be left to Vespasian, Helvidius argued that this was a job for the senate. He also proposed that the Capitol should be restored at

---

13  Tac. *Ann.* 16.32.3; Juv. 3.116f.; Cass. Dio 62.26.2.
14  Tac. *Ann.* 16.21.1, 23.1, 30.1–33.2; Cass. Dio 62.26.13.
15  Tac. *Hist.* 4.6.
16  Tac. *Hist.* 2.91.
17  Tac. *Hist.* 4.6ff.

public expense, with the assistance of Vespasian.[18] None of these proposals of Helvidius came to anything.[19]

It was now that Musonius Rufus attacked Celer. The trial was an important test case from several points of view. It formed the back-drop to the continuing power struggle between Helvidius and Marcellus and it was intended to herald a general attack upon the *delatores*. Moreover, it had obvious implications for the problem of the relative status of emperor and senate. Celer, who did not defend himself, was defended by Demetrius in his only known appearance in a Roman court of law.[20] Celer was condemned. Tacitus comments (*Hist* 4.40.3):

> Sorani manibus satis factum. Insignis publica seueritate dies ne priuatim quidem laude caruit. iustum iudicium explesse Musonius uidebatur, diuersa fama Demetrio Cynicam sectam professo, quod manifestum reum ambitiosius quam honestius defendisset.

We are now in a position to attempt to answer the question: why did the great Cynic Demetrius, the friend of Thrasea Paetus and presumably also of Musonius Rufus, defend Celer, the Stoic who had apparently betrayed his pupil Barea Soranus?

## 2     Previous Interpretations of Demetrius' Behaviour

Before Kindstrand's and Billerbeck's discussions various suggestions had been made.

Dudley admits puzzlement, but suggests that Demetrius was motivated by a sense of fairness: 'Celer lacked the skill or the nerve to defend himself, and however guilty, had a claim to be represented.'[21] Toynbee offers a more detailed, though equally tentative, reconstruction: 'we ⟦106⟧ can only explain it as a case, possibly, of the proverbial "cussedness" and perversity of the Cynic extremists, here reacting against the official and respectable Stoicism represented

---

18    Tac. *Hist.* 4.9.
19    I hope that this summary is suitably uncontroversial. For authoritative discussion see Brunt (1975), esp. 28 {= (2013) 299–30}.
20    Roman advocates were not jurists or lawyers as such and could come from any social class in theory (cf. Schulz [1946] 43ff., 108f.). The suggestion sometimes made that *Schol. in Iuv. vet. ad sat.* 1.33 ('Demetrium causidicum dicunt, qui multos Neroni detulit') refers to our Demetrius may or may not be right, but even if it is, the allegation can only rest on hostile interpretation of Demetrius' behaviour in 70.
21    Dudley (1937) 134.

by Musonius, the defender of monarchy. Such "cussedness" would, indeed, be all of a piece with Demetrius' conduct in the next and final scene in his career—his collision with Vespasian in, or soon after, 71.'[22] Koestermann finds the explanation of Demetrius' conduct in a 'falsch verstandenem Korpsgeist'.[23] Griffin thinks that Tacitus' wording may indicate that Demetrius, an eloquent speaker, may have hoped to achieve a rhetorical *tour de force*.[24]

None of these interpretations is attractive. Dudley does not develop his case, and both Koestermann and Griffin attribute to Demetrius a relatively trivial motivation. Of course people—even philosophers—may do things for trivial motives, but before we attribute such motives, it is fair to look for some more creditable explanation, especially if they are well-respected philosophers, and perhaps particularly if they are Cynics, since Cynicism, to a degree greater than any other ancient system, demanded the unity of philosophical theory and philosophical practice.[25]

Toynbee's reconstruction requires careful consideration. The validity of her general thesis that Stoics and Cynics had profoundly different attitudes to monarchy as an institution is too large a question to discuss here.[26] Kindstrand argues that Toynbee's reconstruction is in any case self-contradictory: 'P. Egnatius Celer was a Stoic, like Musonius, and had acted in the emperor's interest. According to Toynbee's interpretation we should expect to find them on the same side, with Demetrius acting as prosecutor.'[27] But this criticism seems crude. Celer had indeed acted on behalf of an emperor, but the emperor was Nero, who might fairly, and certainly by serious philosophers, be regarded as a tyrant, so that there would be no inconsistency in an attack by Musonius, upholder of monarchy though he was, on one of Nero's collaborators. On the other hand, the apparent implication of Toynbee's reconstruction—that the condemnation of Celer was desired by the Flavians—seems questionable. It is true that Vespasian had been a friend of Soranus,[28] but the whole senatorial campaign was against the interests and wishes of the Flavians, as they soon indicated, and it is more likely that they were prepared to let the trial

---

22  Toynbee (1944) 53.
23  Koestermann (1968) 407.
24  Griffin (1976) 312 n. 2.
25  Hence the ancient dispute whether Cynicism was a αἵρεσις or merely an ἔνστασις βίου (D.L. 6.103).
26  The thesis has not won widespread acceptance (cf. Kindstrand (1980) 97), but is broadly endorsed by Momigliano (1951) 148f. = (1975) II.946f., and Brunt (1975) 29 {= (2013) 301} and n. 140. In my view it must be right in theory, but practice was more complex.
27  Kindstrand (1980) 97.
28  Tac. *Hist.* 4.7.

and condemnation of Celer go by default as a sop to senatorial sentiment than that Musonius should be regarded as actively representing the Flavian point of view. Moreover, Toynbee's reconstruction seems in general too schematic. None of these interpretations, therefore, seems satisfactory, although, as I shall argue, there may be elements of truth in all of them.

Kindstrand's approach appears more rigorous. He starts from the proposition that Demetrius must have acted in what he felt to be a just cause, and then follows R. S. Rogers[29] in inferring that Demetrius defended Celer in the knowledge that the accusations made against Soranus were true. The consequences of this approach, however, seem to make it highly implausible.

The initial contention, that Demetrius, a man of sterling moral character—to judge at least from Seneca's evidence[30] and Demetrius' association with Thrasea Paetus—must have acted in what he considered to be a just cause, is reasonable enough. No student of human nature will deny that a man of virtue may sometimes commit a wrong act, unless virtue be so defined as to [[107]] exclude the possibility of moral wrong-doing. But in a case like this it is clearly right to look for a sympathetic interpretation of the act before accepting the jaundiced verdict of Tacitus (not that even Tacitus is savagely condemnatory: see below). Nor is the conclusion that Soranus was guilty as charged in itself untenable. His friendship with Rubellius Plautus is certain, and if he did nothing to restrain the inhabitants of Pergamum from resisting the depredations of Nero this could indeed be considered an act of *maiestas*. Moreover, he and his daughter (Cassius Dio), or his daughter alone (Tacitus), had consulted *magi*. But to say that Soranus was guilty as charged, i.e., in a legal sense, is not to say that he was morally guilty. He had been a friend of Rubellius Plautus, but the condemnation of Rubellius Plautus had itself been an act of flagrant injustice.[31] And from a moral point of view his refusal to coerce the people of Pergamum was wholly commendable: had he coerced them, he would have been condoning the rapacity of the tyrant Nero. Finally, both Tacitus and Dio provide more or less reasonable *apologiae* for the consultation of *magi*. It is surely unlikely that Demetrius *qua* Cynic would have disapproved of Soranus'

---

29  Rogers (1952) 292ff. His main argument is Demetrius' probity, but he also contends that Tacitus' claim that the real ground for Soranus' prosecution was his failure to punish Pergamum for resisting Acratus' requisitions (*Ann.* 16.23.1f.) is refuted by chronology. But it is not necessary to convict Tacitus of ignorance or mendacity here (see Furneaux {1896–1907} and Koestermann {1968} *ad loc.*). Even if it were, the behaviour Rogers attributes to Soranus would not have troubled a true Cynic—see below.
30  Kindstrand (1980) 90; Billerbeck (1979) 12ff.
31  At least on any reasonable view (*pace* Rogers).

behaviour on political grounds.³² As a Cynic he might well have ridiculed the dabbling in divination, but he would certainly not have believed it to be a capital offence. In effect, Kindstrand's interpretation attributes to a Cynic philosopher a concern to uphold the (perhaps) legally correct but (almost certainly) morally repulsive machinations of what he must have regarded as a tyrannical regime.³³ There is more. Kindstrand's interpretation implies that if Demetrius was acting on behalf of a completely just cause, Musonius Rufus was doing the reverse.³⁴ Yet this is to attribute to a Stoic philosopher of high virtue, the 'Roman Socrates', nakedly dishonourable conduct. There is something wrong with the implied polarities: *either* Celer was completely innocent *or* there was nothing at all to be said in his defence, and *either* Musonius *or* Demetrius had absolute justice on his side. Rather than suppose that there was nothing against Celer (a supposition contradicted by the evidence) and that Musonius was acting with an utter lack of moral scruple (a supposition inconsistent with everything known about Musonius' character), it seems better to look for an alternative, and less simple, explanation.

Billerbeck, in contrast to Kindstrand, finds Demetrius' behaviour rather mysterious, impossible to reconcile with his philosophy, and such as to cast doubt upon his reputation for absolute incorruptibility. She tentatively suggests that the explanation may lie in 'persönliche Querelen oder Animositäten gegen Musonius', whose work shows that he rejected radical Cynicism of the type espoused by Demetrius. But there is no evidence for hostility between the two men, who seem to have moved in the same circles on amicable enough terms.³⁵ Moreover, as already argued, it is methodologically better to seek an explanation for Demetrius' behaviour consonant with his reputation for moral excellence.

---

32   I exclude the hypothesis that Demetrius was an informer under Nero—cf. n. 20.
33   Epict. 1.25.22; Philostr. *VA* 4.42; 5.19; 7.16; Kindstrand (1980) 94f. Of course the Philostratean material is highly suspect in detail: cf. Bowie (1978) 1657ff. But, given my working hypothesis that Demetrius was a sincere Cynic, it may be regarded as *ben trovato*. Bowie (1978) 1658 suggests, indeed, that 'Demetrius might not have been uncomfortable under Neronian rule', but the evidence he adduces is (1) Demetrius' defence of Celer, and (2) the anecdote of Lucian *de Salt.* 63, which, however, is surely fictitious (cf. Billerbeck [1979] 51f.).
34   In fact Kindstrand seems to offer two possibilities: (1) Celer was completely innocent; (2) though not completely innocent, he should not have been singled out when the greater transgressors were left alone. But his argument is loose and he evidently favours the first possibility.
35   Cf. Rogers (1952) 292; Philostr. *VA* 5.19 is, however, chronologically impossible (and, incidentally, untrue to Cynic thought): Kindstrand (1980) 88.

## 3 The Cynic Justification for Demetrius' Behaviour

### (i) *The Meaning of Tacitus' Criticism of Demetrius*

The proper starting point must be Tacitus' wording 'ambitiosius quam honestius'. Tacitus himself clearly endorses the charge, even though the 'quod'-clause is technically *oratio obliqua*. ⟦108⟧ But what exactly does he mean? 'Honestius' presents no problem, but 'ambitiosius' has been interpreted in two slightly different ways, as referring (1) to 'ambition', or (2) to 'ostentation' or 'publicity seeking'.

That Tacitus is suggesting that Demetrius was 'ambitious', presumably in some political sense, seems unlikely.[36] Such 'ambition' could only have been an attempt to gratify the Flavians, but Vespasian's representatives in Rome at the time, Domitian and Mucianus, did nothing to influence the course of the trial, though they moved quickly when it seemed that a general campaign against the *delatores* was imminent. Nor does such an interpretation square with Demetrius' career under Nero, or his later outspoken opposition to Vespasian.[37] Further, 'ambitiosius quam honestius' would, I think, be an unlikely description of Demetrius' conduct, had it been merely and flagrantly self-seeking: from Tacitus it would surely have earned much harsher criticism. Tacitean usage also supports the second interpretation. The reference to 'ambitio' comes immediately after the description of Demetrius as 'Cynicam sectam professo' and in context one thinks naturally of the typical 'ostentation' or 'publicity seeking' of philosophers. Such a charge was often made against Stoics, in Tacitus and elsewhere, but could be made even more speciously against Cynics (below). Tacitus' phraseology therefore implies that Demetrius acted 'ostentatiously rather than honourably'. It is a criticism of Demetrius because, from Tacitus' point of view, since Celer was manifestly guilty, Musonius' course was necessarily the more honourable, and because for Tacitus 'ostentation' was itself a fault, but it falls short of total moral condemnation of Demetrius.[38]

---

36    Cf. Dudley (1937) 134.
37    Cass. Dio 66.13; Suet. *Vesp.* 13; Kindstrand (1980) 95ff.; Billerbeck (1979) 47ff.
38    For other Tacitean attacks on 'ambitio' cf. *Agr.* 4.3; 42.4; *Hist.* 4.6.1. A referee objects that in *Hist.* 4.40.3 Tacitus is implying that Demetrius was unfaithful to his philosophical principles ('Cynicam sectam professus', he nevertheless acted 'ambitiosius quam honestius'). This is certainly Tacitus' view. My argument simply is that Tacitus is wrong, since to the Cynic 'ambitio' and 'honestum' are not opposed concepts: 'ambitio' is precisely the *vehicle* by which 'honestum' is advertised or performed. Tacitus, in short, does not understand Cynicism. The referee also points out that Tacitus is particularly outraged by Celer's betrayal of 'friendship' (*Hist.* 4.10) and argues that Cynicism, which set a high value on the concept of 'friendship' (see below), could not condone such a betrayal. But I do not argue that Cynicism could *condone* such behaviour, but rather that the Cynic concept of

We must now return to the basic question: on what grounds could a Cynic philosopher of high moral character like Demetrius defend P. Celer, manifestly guilty though he was? There are, it seems to me, several grounds on which Demetrius' stance could be held to be properly Cynic.

(ii)   *The Cynic Style of Demetrius' Intervention*
Ostentatious behaviour was a Cynic speciality. Of course it often degenerated into mere exhibitionism, but in theory it was a deliberate pedagogical device. The basic aim was to force people to recognise the meaninglessness of convention (in accordance with the Cynic principle παραχαράττειν τὰ νόμισμα), but there were others as well. One was simply to attract an audience. So, for example, when Diogenes found that nobody paid attention when he was talking seriously he began whistling and a great crowd gathered about him.[39] Another was to demonstrate a specific philosophical point. Thus on one level Diogenes' celebrated public performances of masturbation[40] were ludicrous, and deliberately so; on another they were intended to demonstrate in the most graphic manner the ease with which sexual needs, the source of such anguish to human beings, can be satisfied.[41] The frequently exaggerated, [[109]] sometimes ridiculous character of this ostentatious behaviour was itself a didactic ploy: 'Diogenes used to say that he followed the example of the trainers of choruses, for they too set the note a little high, to ensure that the rest would hit the right note.'[42] Often these displays would put the Cynic in a humiliating or degrading position. This too was deliberate: humiliation trained the Cynic's καρτερία and ἀπάθεια, but it was also a device by which he sought to ingratiate himself with his audience.[43] In this we can almost compare the role of the

---

φιλία on a large scale (including, in the last resort, φιλανθρωπία, or 'friendship' for *all* men) enabled Cynics to move from simple condemnation of those who committed morally wrong acts (including the betrayal of φιλία) to a more understanding attitude. There are always those (like Tacitus) who misunderstand, or refuse to accept, such an attitude. It remains significant that Tacitus does not use some harsher word than 'ambitiosius': he is uneasily aware that Demetrius' action was not simply 'inhonestum'.

39   D.L. 6.27.
40   D.L. 6.69, etc.
41   Dio 6.16ff. I here assume that Dio Chrysostom is (sometimes) a good source for Cynicism, with two *caveats*: (1) some of his works are obviously more relevant than others (many are not Cynic at all); (2) formal exposition of Cynic doctrine need not entail sincere or practical adherence to Cynicism. For Dio as 'Cynic' see von Arnim (1898) 245; Höistad (1948) 50–61, 86–94, 150–220; Moles (1978) 94–6 {above, pp. 48–52}; cf. also n. 110 below. The objections of Desideri (1978) 537ff. and Jones (1978) vi, 49f. seem to me misconceived in principle.
42   D.L. 6.35.
43   Cynic self-humiliation: Höistad (1948) 60f., 97, 101, 196f.; ingratiation: Demetr. *Eloc.* 261.

Cynic with that of a medieval court fool. If, then, we are prepared to consider the possibility that Demetrius was philosophically serious in his defence of Celer, there is no difficulty in the fact that Tacitus describes his action as 'ambitiosius'. A man who finds the typical Stoic suicide 'ambitiosa' would certainly find Demetrius' behaviour 'ambitiosius'. Demetrius himself could have agreed with this description, but have differed from Tacitus in insisting that the 'ambitio' could be justified.

Another aspect of Cynic teaching technique may be relevant. Cynics liked to express themselves in seemingly self-contradictory paradoxes. For example, they could equally describe the Cynic way of life as a life of 'toil' or of 'ease'. This use of paradox often involved the revaluation of concepts to which they were fundamentally opposed. They would vilify such things as 'glory', 'wealth', and 'pleasure', for example, and then claim to possess them themselves.[44] Naturally this process might involve the use of pungent rhetoric, an art of which many Cynics were master.[45] This technique could be extended to discussion of men's characters. The Cynics, for example, habitually criticised Alexander the Great for being the slave of ambition and τῦφος,[46] but Onesicritus, pupil of Diogenes, was able to present Alexander as the φιλόσοφος ἐν ὅπλοις, a deliberate, and paradoxical, contradiction in terms, since a Cynic philosopher by definition went without ὅπλα and regarded them as useless at best.[47] The attempt to 'revalue' as it were the character of the criminal Celer could therefore be Cynic, provided that something could be said in his favour. In this limited sense (but only in this limited sense) I think that Griffin may be right in suggesting that Demetrius may have hoped to achieve a rhetorical *tour de force*. Equally, such behaviour would seem to be part of the 'proverbial "cussedness" and perversity' of the Cynics emphasised by Toynbee, though Cynic behaviour at its best was never merely 'cussed'.

Finally, let us recall that Demetrius' intervention took place at a trial, at which passions on both sides must have been high. The role of the Cynic as Reconciler,[48] in both private and public spheres (a distinction meaningless to Cynics), a role which goes back at least to Crates, may well also be relevant.

---

44     Cynic 'revaluation' of concepts they vilified: cf. Kindstrand (1976) 65, 252.
45     Cf. Kindstrand (1980) 93 and n. 45.
46     Cynic portrayal of Alexander: see, e.g., Höistad (1948) 204ff.; Hamilton (1969) lvi, 34, 179; Fears (1974) 130; see also my forthcoming paper {Moles (1983)}.
47     Str. 15.1.64 = Onesicr. *FGrHist* 134 F 17; uselessness of ὅπλα: cf., e.g., Philodemus περὶ τῶν Στωικῶν, col. 14 = Crönert (1906) 61. Some scholars have failed to see the paradox in Onesicritus' 'Cynic' interpretation of Alexander.
48     Documentation in n. 73.

The general manner, or style, of Demetrius' intervention, then, is actually characteristically Cynic. But style without content is alien to Cynicism (at least in theory). How then might Demetrius have justified his apparently shocking decision to defend the repellent P. Celer?

(iii)   *The Relations of the Cynic with His Peers*
First of all, could Demetrius have been influenced by the fact that Celer was a φιλόσοφος? ⟦110⟧ We may usefully begin by considering the relations of the Cynic σοφός with his fellow men.

Among men the only φιλία that the Cynic recognised *unequivocally*[49] was with τῷ ὁμοίῳ. It is unclear how far, if at all, P. Celer, before he was corrupted, would have been regarded by a Cynic as a σοφός. Cynic σοφία was a much more practicable ideal than Stoic,[50] but Celer was, after all, from a different school, and his luxurious way of life was very far from the Cynic way of life as strictly defined and sometimes practised. Nevertheless, it is comprehensible that a Cynic might feel a certain philosophical kinship with a Stoic in theory (because of the debt that Stoicism owed to Cynic ethics, the admiration that many Stoics felt for Diogenes, and the 'Cynic' characteristics of radical Stoics), as many Cynics obviously did in practice, particularly at this period (as, e.g., Demetrius' relationship with Thrasea Paetus and Seneca). But would this sense of kinship lapse or be annulled if the σοφός lost his virtue, as Celer clearly had? In strict theory, the question should not arise, since for the Cynics, as for the Stoics, ἀρετή is ἀναπόβλητος and the σοφός is ἀναμάρτητος.[51] But in practice this Cynic position, like the corresponding Stoic position, was not maintained as absolutely as the strict theory would suggest. To take a clear example: it is evident that the suicide of Heracles, the Cynic paragon of virtue, which on the face of it was an act of cowardice, posed the Cynics awkward problems, and they devised various expedients to explain, or excuse, it.[52] Moreover, it is obvious that in practice the apparently uncompromising proposition ὁ σοφός φίλος τῷ ὁμοίῳ might be diluted in either, or both, of two ways: (1) some Cynics were prepared to extend their definition of φιλία. When, for example, Crates in his

---

49   I stress this qualification, because the Cynic did in fact recognise obligations towards others besides his ὅμοιοι, and this is an important aspect of Cynicism—see below. For the φιλία of the σοφός with his ὅμοιος, cf., e.g., D.L. 6.105.
50   I justify this statement, with a possible qualification, below (p. 335).
51   D.L. 6.105. The wording of this formulation may show Stoic influence (ἀναπόβλητος is a Stoic technical term, though ἀναμάρτητος is found earlier: LSJ s.v.), but the Cynics must have accepted the content on the old Socratic *per definitionem* argument.
52   Cf. Höistad (1948) 54f., 61, 66ff.

pleasant parody of Solon, prays ὠφέλιμον δὲ φίλοις, μὴ γλυκερὸν τίθετε,[53] he is clearly not restricting the use of φίλοι to οἱ ὅμοιοι in the purist Cynic sense. Demonax is even described by Lucian as φίλος ... ἅπασι[54] and Epictetus claims that Diogenes (of all people!) 'loved everybody', and although as a statement of fact that claim seems somewhat remarkable, what is significant for our purposes is that in a Cynic context (which this is) it could be made at all.[55] (These two passages in fact imply that the true Cynic is in a state of φιλία with mankind at large; I shall return later to the question of Cynic φιλανθρωπία.) (2) Not all Cynics claimed that they themselves were σοφοί or even that complete σοφία was possible. Crates apparently would have made neither claim.[56] The evidence is hardly good enough to decide Diogenes' position on this question. It is true that for Diogenes, as for all Cynics, the path to virtue was 'easy',[57] but extensive ἄσκησις was necessary,[58] and it may be that Diogenes did not himself claim perfection. Alternatively, it is possible that Crates here modified Diogenes' [111] views.[59] But, either way, it is the general point which is important. Interestingly, in the present case, Seneca's evidence indicates that Demetrius did not claim absolute 'sapientia'.[60]

Thus, as a Cynic, Demetrius could have felt a certain interest in the fate of Celer, either as a φιλόσοφος whose ἀρετή had been corrupted, or simply as a φίλος in an extended sense. Koestermann may therefore be partly right in

---

53  Crates F 1.5 Diehl; Solon F 13 *IEG*².
54  Lucian, *Demonax* 10. In several respects Demonax' Cynicism was impure, but his basic orientation was clearly Cynic: cf. Dudley (1937) 158ff. and Attridge (1978) 59f. In the anecdote of *Demonax* 21 (p. 333 below) Demonax tacitly accepts the label 'Cynic'.
55  Epict. 3.24.64. I cannot here discuss how far it is legitimate to extrapolate Cynic doctrine from Epictetus. There are contexts where it seems to me a truer emphasis to say that Epictetus has been influenced by Cynicism than that he is working with ideas which were indeed originally Cynic but have now been transmuted into Stoic.
56  D.L. 6.89: ἀδύνατον εἶναι ἀδιάπτωτον εὑρεῖν, ἀλλ' ὥσπερ ἐν ῥοιᾷ καὶ σαπρόν τινα κόκκον εἶναι. 'ἀδιάπτωτος' is a Stoic technical term, so this dictum *may* be contaminated by the Stoic tradition (though it is possible, here as elsewhere, that such terminology derives from Antisthenes, in which case it would have been available to early Cynics independently of Stoicism), but the sentiment is consistent with what is known of Crates' humane personality. It is true that the pomegranate analogy appears in Teles (55 Hense = O'Neil [1977] 63) and in Seneca (*Ep. mor.* 85.5): both reject it in favour of the more rigorous traditional Cynic-Stoic ideal of ἀπάθεια, and Seneca explicitly attributes the analogy to the Peripatetics. Moreover, Teles quotes Crates elsewhere for moderate Cynic views, but not here. But on the whole, I incline to regard the dictum as *ben trovato*.
57  Cf., e.g., D.L. 6.70.
58  Cf. D.L. 6.70f.
59  So Höistad (1948) 128.
60  *De Ben.* 7.8.2; perhaps also *Vit. beat.* 18.3 with Griffin (1981) 59, though Seneca's point is there obscure.

suggesting that Demetrius was influenced by 'Korpsgeist', though not necessarily by '*falsch verstandenem* Korpsgeist'. But he would still have had to say something in explanation, or mitigation, of Celer's behaviour.

One obvious line of justification suggests itself. Celer had played a relatively minor role in the trial of Soranus. He was merely a 'testis', whereas the prosecutor was Ostorius Sabinus. The attack in 70 on Celer, an insignificant figure, seems to have been an attempt by Musonius and his associates to 'test the water', while for the time being the great *delatores* like Eprius Marcellus were left alone. (Helvidius' direct attack upon Marcellus under Galba had failed.) It could therefore be reasonably argued that it was unjust to single out Celer.[61] Dudley may, then, be partly right in implying that Demetrius was motivated by a sense of fairness, for δικαιοσύνη was a great Cynic concept.[62] But there could have been more to Demetrius' defence than that.

(iv)    *The Relations of the Cynic with Ordinary Men*

I have discussed the relations of the Cynic, whether σοφός in the full sense or not, with his ὅμοιοι. The relationship and attitude of the Cynic to ordinary men present difficult problems, mostly because the evidence is defective. But I shall treat them in some detail, because they are, I think, relevant to the present case, in respect both of the Cynic's conception of his duty to ordinary men and of his understanding of human wrong-doing, and because they affect our interpretation of Cynicism at a fundamental level.

It is an idea basic to Cynicism that the true Cynic is on the one hand a solitary, self-sufficient, passionless figure (μόνος, αὐτάρκης, and ἀπάθης are standard epithets),[63] but on the other hand feels a concern for other men. In itself, this is not so much an inconsistency in Cynicism as a paradox: the wise man, though μόνος, is not an isolated, but rather an independent, individual.[64] He himself is self-sufficient, but he may have dealings with other men—on his own terms. But who, in this context, count as 'other men'? Other wise men

---

61   So, apparently, Kindstrand (cf. n. 34 above).
62   Documentation in Kindstrand (1976) 214f.
63   μόνος: cf., e.g., Antisth. *Od.* 2, 8 = F 15.2, 8 DC {= 54.2, 8 Prince}; D.L. 6.38; Dio 6.60; αὐτάρκης: cf., e.g., D.L. 6.78, 104; ἀπάθης: cf., e.g., D.L. 6.2 = Antisth. F 128a DC {= 12A Prince} (for Antisthenes as 'Cynic' cf. n. 8 above). Here, as elsewhere, I follow Höistad (1948) 94ff. (cf. also Decleva Caizzi [1966] 90ff.) in seeing serious philosophical content in Antisthenes' *Ajax* and *Odysseus*. A purely rhetorical approach, as, e.g., Kennedy (1963) 170–2, yields little.
64   Cf. Rist (1969) 61, correcting Baldry (1965) 111. In what follows, however, I go further than Rist in giving a positive value to Cynic φιλανθρωπία.

(or of course, women),[65] the wise man's ὅμοιοι, with whom he shares φιλία, obviously come into that category. But here an important question arises: is the category of 'other men' *restricted* to the wise? Several factors would seem to suggest this, notably: (1) the apparently absolute division among men that the Cynics made between 'the wise', who are 'few', and 'the foolish', who are 'many';[66] (2) the harsh descriptions the Cynics used of other men and of their own activities towards them;[67] (3) the Cynic doctrine ὁ σοφὸς φίλος τῷ ὁμοίῳ, which *seems*, with its apparent rejection of ordinary ties, to be thoroughly élitist in its implications;[68] (4) the strong Cynic sense sometimes given to the word ἄνθρωπος, which can be used to mean 'free man', or, in effect, Cynic 'wise [[112]] man'.[69] An ἄνθρωπος in this sense is apparently by definition a Cynic σοφός. Does this mean that those who are not ἄνθρωποι in this sense are of no account to the Cynic, as being un- or sub-human?

But there are serious objections to the view that to the Cynics 'other men' means simply and solely 'other wise men'. There is abundant evidence to show that Cynicism was a strongly missionary philosophy,[70] and it is obviously true that in practice Cynics did not confine their teaching to 'the wise'. Indeed, so far as their proselytising was concerned, it would have been absurd to do so, since the σοφός by definition does not require philosophical help: once he has his σοφία it is a permanent possession—his ἀρετή is ἀναπόβλητος.[71] Many Cynics seem to have conducted their teaching in two very different ways—both before a relatively small circle of followers and in public, before quite large crowds or any chance passer-by.[72] In the latter case such Cynics must have been exhibiting (or at least, affecting) a concern for 'other men' in the broader sense. That this cannot be dismissed as mere inconsistency is shown by the fact that the

---

65   Cynicism is basically non-sexist. Rist (1969) 61ff. discusses Cynic views on the relationship between the sexes excellently.
66   Cf., e.g., Kindstrand (1976) 157, 220.
67   E.g., οἱ πλεῖστοι are 'one finger removed from madness' (D.L. 6.35, etc.); the Cynic's activities are regularly described in such terms as ἐλέγχω/ἐξελέγχω, ἐπιτιμάω, κολάζω, λοιδορέω, μέμφομαι, ὀνειδίζω, etc.; for representative documentation see Gerhard (1909) 35–8.
68   This is Baldry's main argument (1965) 111.
69   Cf., e.g., D.L. 6.41, 60 (though note that ἄνθρωπος does not invariably have this connotation in Cynic texts: cf., e.g., D.L. 6.56); for the view that this implies that other men are sub-human see Baldry (1965) 111.
70   The view of De Witt (1954) 329, that Epicureanism was 'the *only* missionary philosophy produced by the Greeks' (my italics) is incorrect, unless of course Cynicism is not classed as a 'philosophy' (an arbitrary contention).
71   This argument holds even though Cynic insistence on the permanence of virtue was not always rigorously maintained (above). The argument is actually used, though in a different context, by Epict. 3.22.67.
72   Cf. Kindstrand (1980) 90; (1976) 138.

Cynic is regularly characterised by a range of terms which necessarily imply a concern for mankind at large. Thus, for example, the Cynic is a παιδαγωγός, a διδάσκαλος, an ἰατρός, a σωφρονιστής, a νουθετητής, a εὐεργέτης, an ἐπίσκοπος, a κατάσκοπος: he 'helps' others, he 'saves' them, he can be compared to the ἀγαθὸς δαίμων, and he sometimes even resolves quarrels and enters people's houses for that purpose.[73] He is, in short, φιλάνθρωπος, and the ἄνθρωποι in this context are not restricted to ἄνθρωποι in the strong Cynic sense.[74] (I discuss Cynic φιλανθρωπία further below.)

All this seems to indicate a profound concern for the well-being of men in general, not just 'wise men'. It is true that attempts have been made to distinguish between early Cynicism, in particular the Cynicism of Diogenes, and later Cynicism, which has been argued to be a humanised, even bowdlerised, form. There is, admittedly, some justification for this. Thus, for example, when Epictetus 3.24.64 describes Diogenes as ἥμερος καὶ φιλάνθρωπος (where φιλάνθρωπος takes a 'soft' colouring from the conjunction with ἥμερος), we must be dealing [[113]] with an attempt to alleviate and humanise the traditional

---

[73] I give fairly full documentation of these concepts in order to show that they are integral to Cynicism and not an apologetic Stoic refinement. Of course the evidence does not permit precise dating of all these concepts and it may occasionally be possible to distinguish between Diogenic and Cratetean Cynicism (though this can easily be overdone—see below), but the general picture is clear. παιδαγωγός: cf., e.g., D.L. 6.75, 30f.; [Diog.] Epp. 29.1; 40.5; Epict. 3.22.17; Lucian, Pisc. 45; Gerhard (1909) 35; Höistad (1948) 125f., 131, 138, 176ff., 210; Kindstrand (1976) 209; Billerbeck (1978) 71; διδάσκαλος: cf., e.g., Stob. 3.1.55; Gerhard (1909) 35f.; ἰατρός: cf., e.g., Antisth. Ai. 4 = F 14.4 DC {= 53.4 Prince}; D.L. 6.4, 6 = Antisth. FF 185–6 DC {= FF 169, 167 Prince}; D.L. 6.30, 36; Lucian, Vit. auct. 8; Höistad (1948) 101f., 118f.; Billerbeck (1978) 137; σωφρονιστής: cf., e.g., Str. 15.1.64 = Onesicr. FGrHist 134 F 17; [Socrat.] Ep. 12 (p. 618 Hercher–Simon to Aristippus on Antisthenes); Julian, Or. 7.213a; Gerhard (1909) 36; νουθετητής: cf., e.g., D.L. 6.86; Gerhard (1909) 35; εὐεργέτης: cf., e.g., Epict. 3.22.77; 4.6.20; M. Aurelius 7.36 = Antisth. FF 20A–B DC {= 86A–B Prince}; ἐπίσκοπος: cf., e.g., D.L. 6.102; Dio 9.1; Epict. 3.22.72; Max. Tyr. 15.9c–d; Billerbeck (1978) 136f.; κατάσκοπος: cf., e.g., D.L. 6.17, 18 = Antisth. F 1 DC {= F 41A Prince}; D.L. 6.43; Plut. quom. adul. ab amico internosc. 70C; de exil. 606C; Epict. 1.24.6–7; 3.22.24; Cynic 'help': cf., e.g., Crates F 1.5 Diels; Bion F 75 Kindstrand; [Diog.] Ep. 29.4; Lucian, Peregr. 33; Julian, Or. 6.201c; Cynic 'salvation': cf., e.g., Antisth. Od. 8, 10 = F 15.8, 10 DC {= F 54.8, 10 Prince}; Stob. 3.13.44, 3.8.20; Dio 1.84; 32.3 (with Höistad (1948) 160); Plut. quom. adul. ab amico internosc. 74C; de prof. in virt. 82A; de cap. ex inim. util. 89B = Antisth. F 77 DC {= F 109 Prince}; Cynic as ἀγαθὸς δαίμων: D.L. 6.74; Apul. Flor. 22; Julian, Or. 6.200b (arbitrarily deleted by edd. like Hertlein and Wright); Lucian, Demonax 63; this is perhaps a specifically Cratetean characteristic; Cynic as **reconciler**: cf., e.g., Xen. Mem. 4.64; Philod. Rhet. 223.12ff. (Sudhaus) = Antisth. FF 106–7 DC {= FF 69, 13A Prince}; Str. 15.1.65 = Onesicr. FGrHist 134 F 17; D.L. 6.86; Plut. Quaest. conv. 632E, cf. Brut. 34.5–8; Lucian, Demonax 9, 63; Apul. Flor. 22; Julian, Or. 6.201b. Cf. also Plut. de fort. Alex. 329C (discussed below, p. 337). The continuity of Cynic ideas over the centuries is indeed striking.

[74] Cf. n. 69 above.

character of Diogenes. But this line of argument can be taken too far. φιλανθρωπία in a broad sense is a concept already latent in Antisthenes[75] and implicit in the teaching of Diogenes,[76] and it seems to have found concrete expression in Crates' (alleged) giving of his wealth to the poor.[77] One must distinguish in this context between different aspects of φιλανθρωπία. Early Cynicism is not incompatible with the general concept—indeed, the Cynic's missionary zeal, which is attested from the first beginnings of Cynicism, and many of his traditional roles, the most important of which seem also to be integral to Cynicism (above), logically presuppose φιλανθρωπία, although it is very often not φιλανθρωπία in the 'softer' sense. Later Cynicism, or at least some branches of it, following the example of the humane and kindly Crates,[78] emphasised φιλανθρωπία in the 'softer' sense, but this is a difference of emphasis, and not of fundamentals. Concern for the well-being of one's fellow man is basic to Cynicism in all its forms, though this concern could be articulated in contrasting ways—harshly and aggressively, à la Diogenes, or humanely and benignly, à la Crates. A good example of the former type is the portrayal of Diogenes given by Dio Chrysostom in his *Orr.* 4, 6, 8, 9, and 10. In Dio Diogenes is the usual stern critic of the folly of mankind (a view no doubt much truer to the historical Diogenes than that offered by Epictetus 3.24.64), but his concern for the moral well-being of others is patent and a fundamental part of his philosophical activity. The essential point that even the harsh and aggressive type of Cynic must not withdraw completely from mankind at large is nicely brought out in the exchange between the fanatical Peregrinus and the humane Demonax recorded by Lucian.[79] To Peregrinus' accusation that Demonax is not a true Cynic because of the humanity and jocularity he deploys in his relations with his fellow human beings (οὐ κυνᾷς), Demonax replies that Peregrinus has taken his Cynicism to such extremes that he can no longer be counted a member of the human race (οὐκ ἀνθρωπίζεις).[80] It is important to realise that this is not an exchange between a Cynic and a non-Cynic about the merits of Cynicism, but an exchange between fellow Cynics (Demonax here implicitly accepts that he can be classified as a Cynic) about the real nature of Cynicism.

Thus φιλανθρωπία in a profound sense ('love of mankind'), as opposed to a trivial sense ('kindliness', 'gentleness') is integral to Cynicism. This conclusion

---

75  Cf., e.g., Decleva Caizzi (1966) 91 (on Antisth. *Od.*).
76  As even Baldry (1965) 111 admits.
77  D.L. 6.87–8.
78  Cf., e.g., Julian, *Or.* 6.201b–c.
79  *Demonax* 21.
80  For similar verbal jibes against Cynic/Stoic extremes cf. Plin. *Ep.* 8.16.3–4; Sen. *Ep. mor.* 99.5; and Cic. *ad Quint. fratr.* 2.10(9).3 (with Moles [1982]).

has, indeed, been disputed on three main grounds, and though these grounds are inadequate, it is worth analysing them to see where the error lies:

(1) it has been argued that Cynic φιλανθρωπία would be hard to reconcile with the élitism of the doctrine ὁ σοφὸς φίλος τῷ ὁμοίῳ;[81]
(2) explicit attestation of Cynic φιλανθρωπία is slight;[82]
(3) some texts actually contrast the Cynic attitude to other men with φιλανθρωπία.[83]

These difficulties look much more formidable than they are. (1) is a simple misconception, as I hope to show below. (2) and (3) go together. Explicit attestation of Cynic φιλανθρωπία is indeed slight, but in fact this proves nothing. Relative dearth of explicit attestation of a concept is not an argument against the existence of that concept, if other considerations seem to make its existence certain,[84] especially when the totality of the evidence is so defective. In any case it is easy to understand why φιλανθρωπία should be relatively seldom attributed to Cynics. From [[114]] the fourth century onwards φιλανθρωπία is very often used of 'mildness' or 'gentleness', a quality not possessed by those Cynics who practised the harsher brand of Cynicism represented by Diogenes. But this does not disqualify them from being considered φιλάνθρωποι in the more profound sense. By the same token, a Cynic who is harsh in his criticism of mankind can in turn be criticised for lack of φιλανθρωπία by those who believe that gentler teaching methods are likely to be more productive, but such a Cynic may nevertheless be motivated by 'love of mankind'. The general point is elementary and was indeed widely appreciated by ancient philosophers, both Cynic and non-Cynic.[85]

At this juncture, a further question arises: is there any inconsistency between these two aspects of traditional Cynicism—on the one hand the abuse, often vitriolic, of οἱ πολλοί, on the other the profound concern for all men, including οἱ πολλοί? At times there seems to be a certain awkwardness arising from these two opposing emphases, but fundamentally there is no real

---

81   So Baldry (1965) 111.
82   So, e.g., de Romilly (1979) 21f. For explicit references to Cynic φιλανθρωπία see, e.g., Dio 4.24; Epict. 3.24.64; Lucian, *Demonax* 11; scholarly discussion and bibliography in Kindstrand (1976) 247.
83   For useful documentation see Malherbe (1970) 210ff. Cf., e.g., Stob. 3.8.20 (? Demetrian—see Billerbeck [1979] 57ff.).
84   For this important methodological point (in quite different contexts) cf., e.g., Lloyd-Jones (1971) 13; Stinton (1975) 251 {= (1990) 181}.
85   Documentation in Malherbe (1970) 208ff.; cf. also Dickie (1981) 199ff.

inconsistency, because of the Cynic view of the nature of man.[86] The Cynic σοφός is a man in his ideal, or perfect, state—the only true ἄνθρωπος. But all men, whatever their culture or background (relevant factors here are the Cynic emphasis on the absolute meaninglessness of social distinctions, their rejection of conventional παιδεία, and their readiness to cite the practices of non-Greek peoples as standards of what is 'good' or 'natural'),[87] have a natural endowment of νοῦς or λόγος.[88] Their κακία is the product of ignorance, and virtue can be 'taught'.[89] The Cynic tries to remove their ignorance and to inculcate virtue. Moreover, the acquisition of virtue is 'easy'[90]—easy, admittedly, only along the lines of the Reagan aphorism 'it's simple, but it's not easy'; but it is important that Cynicism, which despised both conventional παιδεία and all theoretical speculation,[91] was unencumbered by the intellectual impedimenta of other philosophical schools, and was indeed 'easy' in an intellectual sense. Thus on the one hand ordinary men are not the Cynic's fellow men because they are not 'real' ἄνθρωποι, but on the other they are the Cynic's fellow men because all men have a natural capacity for the attainment of the Cynic state, itself an 'easy' matter. All men are therefore potentially ἄνθρωποι in the full Cynic sense. This kind of double attitude—the emphasis on the exclusiveness of Cynicism and the Cynic claim to help mankind at large—is illustrated in many Cynic texts, but perhaps nowhere more graphically than in Epictetus' περὶ κυνισμοῦ.[92] Epictetus, for example, insists vehemently on the purist Cynic

---

86  Arguments analogous to those that follow here have of course been widely used in relation to Stoicism (and even Epicureanism), but are generally ignored in discussion of Cynicism (owing, I believe, to failure to take Cynicism seriously).
87  Meaninglessness of social distinctions: e.g., D.L. 6.104; rejection of conventional παιδεία: e.g., D.L. 6.103–4; non-Greek peoples as standards: e.g., D.L. 6.73; Weber (1887) 127–33; a slightly less dismissive attitude to παιδεία appears in Antisthenes' doctrine of the διττὴ παιδεία (Antisth. F 27 DC {= F 96 Prince}; Dio 4.29ff.; Höistad [1948] 56ff.), which allowed human παιδεία a certain small value, but the concession was minimal, nor was this the usual Cynic view.
88  Cynic νοῦς: cf., e.g., Plut. de Stoic. repugn. 1039E = Antisth. F 67 DC {= 105 Prince}; [Diog.] Epp. 34.2, 40.5; Dio 10.28; Cynic λόγος: cf., e.g., D.L. 6.24, 73; indistinguishable from these is the γνώμη of Max. Tyr. 36.1.
89  E.g., D.L. 6.105.
90  D.L. 6.70 (and many other refs).
91  Cf. n. 87 above.
92  Epict. 3.22; how far this work is properly Cynic is of course debatable: discussion in Dudley (1937) 190–8 (very balanced) and Billerbeck (1978) 1–9; the rejection of Cynic ἀναίδεια and the use of some Stoic terminology excepted, there is, I believe, little that is not Cynic, although it is of course Stoic as well. Cf. also p. 348 below.

definition of φιλία[93] but his Cynic is the usual παιδευτής, παιδαγωγός (3.22.17), κατάσκοπος (3.22.24), etc., who has a strong sense of missionary duty towards his misguided fellow-men and feels φιλανθρωπία towards all (3.22.81).

If, then, these arguments are sound, we must conclude that the Cynics operated a double classification of the relations between the σοφός and the ignorant majority: on the one hand, as a matter of empirical fact, there was a vast gulf between the two, and the ignorant majority did [[115]] not even qualify as 'men' at all; but on the other hand, there was a bond of humanity between the two classes. As with Cynic φιλανθρωπία, it is unfortunately difficult to cite texts which make explicit the doctrine that all men are potentially ἄνθρωποι in the full Cynic sense. If pressed, I would be prepared to cite a number of *testimonia* where it seems to me that the idea is strongly implied. For example, Antisthenes is reported by Xenophon as saying: τούτους [τυράννους] πάνυ οἰκτίρω. This 'fragment' of Antisthenes is not authentic, in the sense that it can hardly reflect Antisthenes' actual words, but it may at least faithfully reflect Antisthenes' general attitude. Its relevance lies in the fact that in Greek thought 'pity' is an emotion that depends on a sense of kinship between the pitier and the pitied.[94] More strikingly, there is the famous statement in Plut. *de fort. Alex.* 329B that the main principle of Zeno's *Republic* was πάντας ἀνθρώπους ἡγώμεθα δημότας καὶ πολίτας. For various reasons, many scholars have shied away from taking this statement at face value, but if it is so taken (as I believe it should be), it is highly relevant to the present discussion. Zeno's *Politeia* was heavily influenced by Cynic thought, and the formulation πάντας ἀνθρώπους ... δημότας καὶ πολίτας looks essentially similar to the famous Cynic doctrine of 'cosmopolitanism': both formulations are paradoxes, in which the idea of a small political unit (the δῆμος or πόλις) is deliberately juxtaposed with the idea of the largest grouping possible. The paradoxical word play is characteristically Cynic and in itself another reason for taking πάντας ἀνθρώπους at face value. I think it likely therefore that Zeno was here reflecting the teaching of Diogenes and Crates.[95]

---

93  3.22.62ff. (Billerbeck's comments *ad loc.* are misconceived).

94  Antisthenes: Xen. *Smp.* 4.37 = F 117.22 DC {= F 82 Prince}; to Aristotle the arousal of pity depends on ὁμοιότης (*Rhet.* 1385b13, 1386a24), which is the normal Greek view: cf. in general Dover (1974) 195ff.

95  Zeno's *Politeia*: Baldry (1959) and (1965) 153ff.; Rist (1969) 64ff.; its Cynic character: D.L. 7.4 with the discussions of Baldry and Rist.

Against the 'universalist' interpretation of πάντας ἀνθρώπους here adopted, it has been urged that: (1) there is no evidence that Zeno held such a view (Rist [1969] 65). But this is just *petitio principii*. (2) a universalist principle would conflict with the élitism attested in D.L. 7.32–4 (Baldry). This is a misunderstanding of the Cynic–Stoic 'two-tier' classification of mankind: see Fisch (1937) 67ff. Nor (*pace* Fisch) need it be supposed that πάντας ἀνθρώπους are *actual* members of the state, especially if Zeno's *Politeia* describes both the

Finally, in this same passage of *de fort. Alex.* Alexander is described as διαλλακτής τῶν ὅλων (329C). Plutarch's argument here is that whereas Zeno's prescription was purely theoretical, Alexander actually put such precepts into practice. Thus each of Alexander's achievements is an analogue of some philosophical recommendation.[96] Now the notion of the philosopher as 'the reconciler' is very Cynic,[97] and the hypothesis that in the present context this is a Cynic analogy is supported by Plutarch's general reliance upon Onesicritus in this essay.[98] The description of Alexander as 'reconciler of the whole world' may therefore reflect a Cynic concept of the unity of mankind.

Needless to say, these interpretations are highly controversial and cannot in any case be fully [[116]] justified here. So, while I believe that these *testimonia*

---

ideal state and the attitude of the wise to the present (Murray [1966] 369). D.L. 8.32-4 can be regarded as a statement of fact, Plut. *de fort. Alex* 329A-B of the ideal or potential (as indeed Plutarch represents it). (3) a universalist principle is incompatible with the apparent form of the *Politeia*, which was jussive or prescriptive (Baldry [1965] 161ff.). This objection is met by the same argument as in (2) above.

The main suggested alternative interpretations to the 'universalist' interpretation are: (1) πάντας ἀνθρώπους only means 'everybody', 'all people' in a weak sense (Baldry [1959] 13). This seems highly unlikely. Not only are there difficulties in devising a suitably weak application for the phrase, but this interpretation is incompatible with (a) the international character of Zeno's prescriptions and (b) the strong paradox of πάντας ἀνθρώπους ... δημότας καὶ πολίτας. (2) πάντας ἀνθρώπους means 'all *wise* men' (Murray). On this hypothesis Plutarch is twisting Zeno's doctrine to suit his own argument. But this is very forced: Plutarch's wording is unequivocal: not only πάντας ἀνθρώπους (in paradoxical conjunction with δημότας καὶ πολίτας), but also εἷς δὲ βίος ᾖ καὶ κόσμος. Rist (1969) 65 suggests instead that Plutarch's account of Zeno's *wording* is correct, but that Zeno was using ἄνθρωποι in the strong Cynic sense. Again, this seems highly implausible. Elsewhere, the context makes clear when ἄνθρωπος has a strong sense. If Plutarch's rendering of Zeno's wording is remotely accurate, this did not apply to Zeno's use of ἄνθρωπος. Rist's interpretation also fails to give full value to the paradox in Zeno's words. In sum, I believe that Fisch and others are right to take πάντας ἀνθρώπους as 'all human beings'.

96 Cf. Fisch (1937) 66ff.
97 Cf. n. 73. The contention of Bosworth (1980) 4, that Plutarch's interpretation of Alexander stems largely from interest in the ideas of reconciliation and fusion in the Roman Empire, seems to me to disregard the philosophical background, which is Cynic/Stoic.
98 Cf. Hamilton (1969) xxxi. Bosworth (1980) 4 argues instead that Plutarch has 'totally transformed' Onesicritus' view, which was 'of an Alexander who still has sympathy for the search for wisdom even in the cares of empire', whereas 'for Plutarch Alexander not only sympathises with philosophical theories, he embodies and perfects them in his actions'. The centrality of the thesis 'Alexander philosophus' to Onesicritus' work is indeed debatable, but Fisch (1937) 129ff. makes (on the whole) a good case for supposing that the thesis was not incidental but expounded at length and illustrated in several different contexts. (Even in Strabo Alexander is φιλόσοφος ἐν ὅπλοις, i.e., 'he embodies and perfects philosophical theories in his actions'.) Note too that in Str. 15.1.65 the Gymnosophists are seen as reconcilers.

offer some support for the arguments put forward to show that the Cynics must have believed that all men were potentially full Cynic ἄνθρωποι, I hope that the case may stand without the support of such controversial items.

At this juncture, I must make another important point. My whole discussion of the Cynic conception of 'other men' has been framed on the assumption that we are talking of the true Cynic, the σοφός/ἄνθρωπος *par excellence*. But if, as already pointed out, not all Cynics claimed to be σοφοί in the strict sense, it must follow that such Cynics would find it even easier to feel φιλία with mankind at large. Some Cynics must surely have taken something like the position of humane Stoics like Panaetius.[99] This attitude, indeed, may well go back as far as Crates.[100]

I have prolonged this discussion, elementary though I fear it may be, simply in order to demonstrate that the élitism of Cynicism, which on one level is real enough, is in the final analysis less important than its 'philanthropy'. Cynicism is not just an inward-looking philosophy: the Cynic, at all phases of Cynicism, is not merely preoccupied with his own moral condition—he is also deeply concerned with the moral condition of others, even the most depraved.[101]

How might this apply to Demetrius and Celer? I have already argued that Demetrius could have been concerned with the corruption of Celer, if Celer is regarded as a φιλόσοφος. But in the light of the above analysis it should be clear that he could also have been concerned with the corruption of Celer, if Celer is regarded simply as the normal 'ignorant' human being. Moreover, Cynicism could have provided Demetrius with the justification not only for castigating Celer's vice but also for attempting to 'cure' it. Could it also have provided a justification for coming to Celer's defence in his time of trouble? The answer, I believe, is yes, and here again we must explore the implications of the Cynic understanding of vice.

### (v)   *The Cynic Understanding of Vice*

Vice is the product of ignorance, virtue of knowledge. In effect, the virtuous life is equated with τὸ κατὰ φύσιν ζῆν, and the phrase κατὰ φύσιν is given a very basic, primitivist meaning, as both the practice of the Cynics and their

---

99    Cf. especially Sen. *Ep. mor.* 116. 5 = F 114 {van Straaten}; discussion in Rist (1969) 187ff, 213ff.; Griffin (1976) 179ff.
100   Cf. n. 56.
101   Cf. especially the Christ-like sentiment of Antisthenes: D.L. 6.6 = F 186 DC {= F 167 Prince} (similarly Stob. 3.13.43 [Diogenes]). Such a 'fragment' may of course not be authentic, but is at least consistent with Antisthenes' *persona* in Xenophon (cf. Xen. *Smp.* 4.37 = F 117.22 DC {= F 82 Prince}, discussed above, p. 336 and n. 94).

characteristic appeals to animal behaviour reveal.[102] Man must live in his natural state. Broadly speaking (and the Cynic analysis of virtue and vice was nothing if not broad) the ignorance of vice is the result of the corrupting influence of civilisation. Hence the virtuous state in Cynicism is frequently described in Golden Age terms. Man is therefore seen as fundamentally innocent, before his corruption by civilisation and all the evils it brings with it—greed, love of glory, wars, addiction to pleasures, etc.[103] By virtue of [[117]] their natural endowment of νοῦς all men have the potential of achieving true self-knowledge,[104] that is, the knowledge of the essential nature of man, and of 'stripping off' the corruption wrought by civilisation and returning to their natural state.[105] Now this view of man ought to mean that the Cynic could take an understanding, if not an indulgent, view of human vice. Of course it may be said that the same applies, at least potentially, to any philosophical system which analyses vice in terms of ignorance. This is true, but there were particular elements in Cynicism, stemming admittedly from its very theoretical deficiencies, which logically imply a fundamentally rather optimistic view of man. In so far, for example, as Cynicism dealt with the problem of evil, it argued (a) that πόνος is good for man,[106] and (b) that evil in human beings resulted, ultimately, from the corrupting influence of civilisation. There was thus no place in Cynicism for the dualistic notions that are found in various strands of Platonic and even Stoic thought. Furthermore, Cynicism, unlike Stoicism, asserted the uselessness of conventional παιδεία for the acquisition of virtue, and unlike both Stoicism and Epicureanism did not require its doctrine to be supported by elaborate physical theories.[107] In a real, though paradoxical, sense Cynicism was 'easy' (above). The description of Cynicism as a 'short cut to virtue' may

---

102   E.g., D.L. 6.71; appeals to animal behaviour: D.L. 6.22; Dio 6.22, etc. Many scholars have failed to realise how far the Cynic identification of the 'good' life with life 'according to nature' depended upon the primitivist ideal. It is not true that Diogenes 'does not tell us what virtue is' (Rist [1969] 59): the Cynic answer to the question is (no doubt) inadequate, but it is explicit.
103   Basic texts for this kind of reconstruction: D.L. 6.44; Str. 15.1.64 = Onesicr. FGrHist 134 F 17; Dio 6.22f.; [Diog.] Ep. 32.3; Lucian, Fug. 17; Max. Tyr. Or. 36; discussion in Vidal-Naquet (1978) 135. More generally relevant are the fragments of Diogenes' Πολιτεία (conveniently, if carelessly, discussed by Ferguson [1975] 89ff.) and Crates' Pera (best discussion in Höistad [1948] 129 ff).
104   Cynic emphasis on self-knowledge: cf., e.g., D.L. 6.83; Dio 4.57; 10.22, 27; Epict. 3.22.53; Julian Orr. 6.183b, 185a, 188aff.; 7.211b–c.
105   Cynic 'stripping off': cf., e.g., Str. 15.1.64–5 = Onesicr. FGrHist 134 F 17; [Diog.] Epp. 24, 29.2; Dio 4.66; Lucian, Vit. auct. 9.
106   Cf., e.g., D.L. 6.71.
107   Cynics might exploit physical theories on an ad hoc basis (cf., e.g., D.L. 6.73), but by and large they were unimportant to Cynic thought.

be Stoic,[108] but it accurately reflects the Cynic attitude to the problem of the acquisition of virtue. And Cynic virtue is, in the last resort, merely a return to man's natural state.

Thus a Cynic ought, in theory, to be able to say of the undoubtedly corrupt P. Celer: 'He's undoubtedly corrupt, but underneath his corrupt exterior he is a human being and he can be saved'; and to regard his essential (or, from another point of view, his potential) humanity as a saving grace. It must be admitted that such an attitude is infrequently attested in Cynicism, partly, no doubt, because of the general dearth of reliable Cynic *testimonia*, mostly, one suspects, because of the other side of Cynicism—the emphasis on the castigation of vice, a procedure which many Cynics carried out with such gusto as almost to obscure the basically outward-looking and positive character of their philosophy. Nevertheless, there are some texts which expound a basically Cynic view and make such an attitude explicit. For example, Plutarch tells the story of how when Diogenes saw a child eating sweets he struck the child's παιδαγωγός, not the child himself, on the ground that the fault lay with him who had failed to teach, not with him who had failed to learn.[109] The historicity of such an anecdote may well be nil, but it may still be *ben trovato*. It is Cynic to condemn the eating of fancy food and the apparently bizarre, but in its own way logical, behaviour of Diogenes is also appropriately Cynic. If, as is the case, the thinking behind Diogenes' behaviour chimes with the theoretical analysis of Cynic attitudes argued for above, the story does have a certain modest evidential value. Or again, in the fourth kingship oration of Dio Chrysostom, the philosophical content of which is mainly Cynic, Alexander the Great is extensively criticised along standard Cynic lines.[110] But the defects in Alexander's character are put down to the facts that he is 'young' and has been brought up in a corrupt environment, and it is implied that, because of his innate φύσις or ἀγαθὸς δαίμων καὶ θεός, Alexander still possesses 'redeeming' characteristics.[111] It is true that there are Stoic and Platonic elements in the speech, but the main thrust is Cynic, and again the attitude to Alexander's corruption coheres with the theoretical arguments I have put forward. Similarly in ⟦118⟧ the Geneva papyrus which

---

108  It may stem from Apollodorus of Seleucia (D.L. 7.121 = Apoll. Sel. F 17 (*SVF* III.261), though the description is common in later Cynic texts (e.g., the Cynic letters) and 'road imagery' generally is also a Cynic τόπος.
109  Plut. *an virt. doc. poss.* 439E.
110  For recent discussions of this speech see Jones (1978) 120f. and Desideri (1978) 287ff. and my own forthcoming paper {Moles (1983)}. On the philosophical content (which is clearly Cynic) see Höistad (1948) 56–63, 154–8, 173f., 180f., 187, 202–22. For Cynic attitudes to Alexander cf. n. 46 and below.
111  Dio 4.6, 38, 139; cf. Bosworth (1980) 4 n. 27.

recounts the meeting between Alexander and the Gymnosophists we are given a standard Cynic interpretation of this incident.[112] But Alexander's reaction to Dandamis' long speech of criticism is interesting: ἡδέως ἤκουσε, καὶ οὐκ ἐθυμώθη· ἐνῆν τι καὶ ἐν αὐτῷ θεῖον πνεῦμα, ἀλλὰ ὑπὸ κακοῦ Ἑλλήνων ἔθνους εἰς κακὸν αὐτὸ ἔστησε.[113] As in Dio, the phraseology θεῖον πνεῦμα is Stoic-influenced, but the more important point is that in a generally Cynic context we are given a view of a man corrupted by civilisation,[114] yet not devoid of redeeming qualities thanks to his essential humanity. Finally, the Cynic Demonax is explicitly credited with the view ἀνθρώπου ... εἶναι τὸ ἁμαρτάνειν.[115]

Now it must be admitted that none of these texts is purely Cynic. It must also be admitted that the Stoics explained vice in terms of mistaken judgements and the corrupting influence of adverse environments[116] (as indeed did several other philosophical schools). But these factors do not invalidate my case. That few 'pure' Cynic texts have survived is not surprising. The works of early Cynics like Diogenes had soon passed out of circulation. Many later Cynics may have written nothing, or if they did, their works were not of sufficient interest to survive.[117] This makes extrapolation of Cynic doctrine from the orations of Dio Chrysostom or from a work such as Lucian's *Demonax* a task requiring nice judgement, but it does not invalidate the exercise entirely. It is clear that Dio's fourth kingship oration and other of his works are basically Cynic and that Demonax, while not a 'pure' Cynic, nevertheless owed most of his philosophical inspiration to Cynicism.[118] It is therefore legitimate to use the evidence from such sources to support a case based on more general theoretical arguments. Again, the fact that the analysis of human vice here argued to be

---

112 *Pap. Génèv. inv.* 271; published by Martin (1959); discussion by Photiadès (1959).
113 Col. ii, 45ff.
114 Here specifically Greek civilisation: for the defectiveness of Greek civilisation in Cynic texts, cf., e.g., Dio 8.12, 15; 9.16; 10.30; the theme seems also to be latent in Onesicritus' account of Alexander and the Gymnosophists—cf. Str. 15.1.65. Of course given that the Cynics condemned all civilisation, it is no surprise to find specific condemnation of Greek civilisation in Cynic texts.
115 Lucian, *Demonax* 7. Note, incidentally, that one of Demonax' teachers was our Demetrius (*Demonax* 3). We may note also, without overstressing, the fact that a lenient attitude to wrongdoers is quite frequently expressed in the Cynic Letters: cf., e.g., [Diog.] *Ep.* 28.3, 29.2–5; [Heraclit.] *Ep.* 5.3, 7.2.
116 Cf. Long (1968) 329ff.
117 Of later Cynic writings those of Dio Chrysostom, Oenomaus, and (in some ways) Lucian are most important. Demetrius probably wrote nothing (though cf. Kindstrand [1980] 93). What the evidential value of Lucian, *Vit. auct.* 9 and Juv. 13.121 (both attesting Cynic literature) is I am unsure.
118 Cf. n. 54.

Cynic is also found in Stoic texts (particularly those of the Imperial period)[119] does not necessarily indicate that the Cynics were influenced by Stoicism on this question, still less that Cynicism was only a branch of Stoicism. Rather, we should suppose that to a large extent Cynic and Stoic thinking on this question coincided, which, given the general Cynic influence upon Stoic ethics and the increasingly 'Cynic' emphasis of late Stoicism, is precisely what we should expect.

These passages, therefore, support the theoretical arguments already advanced for supposing that Cynicism could take an understanding, even sympathetic, view of human weakness.

### (vi)   *The Practical Application of the Cynic Understanding of Vice*

How can all this be related to the concrete historical situation of the trial of P. Celer in AD 70? Should we assume that, if Demetrius did take this kind of attitude to Celer's corruption, he must [[119]] have argued on a rather remote philosophical plane? Not necessarily, for it is not difficult to relate this kind of attitude to patterns of thought current in the contemporary political world.

Tacitus attributes a long speech in the senate to Eprius Marcellus in response to Helvidius Priscus' proposal concerning the composition of the delegation to be sent to Vespasian.[120] How far this speech represents τὰ ἀληθῶς λεχθέντα is naturally a ticklish question, but in view of Marcellus' great reputation as a speaker and the importance of the speech Tacitus' rendering may be relatively faithful to the original.[121] The speech is a defence of senatorial collaboration with bad emperors, and as good as concedes that a bad emperor may extort bad behaviour from an enslaved senate. To describe the speech as 'firm and statesmanlike'[122] is hardly accurate, since on any reasonable interpretation Marcellus was a very nasty piece of work. But such sentiments must have been

---

119  The great representative of such 'philanthropic' Stoicism is of course Panaetius (n. 99). Similar views can be found in Seneca, Epictetus, and Marcus Aurelius. Seneca: cf. Griffin (1976) 179ff. Epictetus: cf., e.g., Epict. 1.4, 13.3, 18, 28.10–11, 29.64–5; 3.22 *passim*, esp. 22.23, 22.72, 22.97f.; 3.24.66, 24.79; 4.4.27, 6.2, 12.19; F 71 Schweighäuser = 25 Oldfather. Marcus Aurelius: cf., e.g., 2.1, 13; 3.4, 11; 4.2; 5.28; 6.27, 47; 7.22, 26, 31, 63, 70; 8.8, 14; 9.11, 42; 11.18.3, 18.9; 12.12; discussion in Brunt (1974) 11f. {= (2013) 376ff.} Cf. also Thrasea Paetus' dictum: 'qui uitia odit, homines odit' (Plin. *Ep.* 8.22.3). Quint. 1.1.9 = Diogenes of Babylon F 51 (*SVF* III.220) is a clear example of a Stoic view that adverse environments are a mitigating (not, of course, a completely exonerating) factor. Note also that Celer's prosecutor Musonius could take a highly 'philanthropic' view of vice (F 39 Hense), but evidently chose not to in the case of Celer.
120  *Hist.* 4.8.
121  Cf. Syme (1958) 187f.
122  Syme (1958) 187.

widely canvassed at the start of Vespasian's reign and not only by scoundrels like Marcellus.[123] It is obvious that the corruption of P. Celer could readily have been explained, or excused, along these general lines. But, as I have tried to show, a Cynic like Demetrius, without going as far as Marcellus in his justification of collaboration with a bad emperor, could have argued in an essentially similar way. He could have maintained that although Celer's action was morally wrong and blameworthy, he had been corrupted by an evil political environment, and that his essential humanity should be considered as a mitigating factor.

To sum up. If we suppose (a) that Celer was guilty, as the evidence virtually obliges us to do, and (b) that Demetrius was acting sincerely, which is at least a reasonable starting point, it is perfectly possible to find Cynic justification for his defence of Celer. A Cynic could have felt an obligation to help Celer, either as a philosopher who had gone wrong, or simply as a normal, ignorant human being. The trial could also have provided a Cynic with the opportunity to make a striking and paradoxical demonstration of a philosophical truth and perhaps also to act in the role of Reconciler. A Cynic could have argued that it was unjust to single out Celer for prosecution, and—more important—that although Celer was guilty of a criminal act he had been corrupted by an evil political situation and deserved to be viewed with understanding because of his essential humanity. We cannot of course be sure that these were Demetrius' motives, but it should at least be clear that his defence of Celer *could* have been inspired by motives that were thoroughly humane and honourable, and Cynic through and through.

Two final points. It might be objected that the end result of this lengthy analysis of Cynic attitudes is really rather banal. But such is the nature of Cynicism. Cynic behaviour at its most typical frequently presents problems of precise interpretation, but the basic theoretical propositions of Cynicism are extremely simple. Secondly, is it just misconceived to attempt to analyse a single Cynic act—Demetrius' defence of Celer—in such detail? The answer to this is that in one important respect Cynicism was a very rigorous philosophical system, in that it insisted on the unity of philosophical thought and philosophical action. Hence, if we are prepared to consider the possibility that Demetrius defended Celer in his capacity as Cynic philosopher, we are entitled to expect that we shall be able to find good reasons in Cynicism for such an apparently shocking course of action. There were good Cynic reasons, and Demetrius may have been impelled by them (I like to think he was). At the least

---

123  As Syme emphasises, Marcellus' views substantially accord with Tacitus' own, in the *Agricola* and elsewhere.

we may hope to have clarified some difficulties in a philosophy which was, and is, widely misunderstood, but whose general outlook was in many ways admirable, although it must be admitted that the characteristic Cynic techniques of exposition often tended to obscure the fact. More specifically, we may hope to have shown how a philosophy whose theoretical basis was extremely limited could arrive at a humane and enlightened moral position. It is one of the many apparent paradoxes of Cynicism that for all its crudity it held progressive views on issues we today consider very important (e.g., the equality of the sexes, the breaking down of social barriers, the claims of internationalism over nationalism). In reality these progressive views were a function [[120]] of that crudity, but in the ancient world, as today, it was often not the cleverest and most sophisticated thinkers who held the most enlightened views.

### Appendix: The Continuity of Cynicism from the Fourth Century BC to the Roman Imperial Era

Bernays and Zeller believed that in the last two centuries BC Cynicism as a philosophical movement died out and when it revived in the first century AD it had been reborn out of Stoicism.[124] Dudley challenged this contention and argued that, while Cynicism went through an obscure period in the last two centuries BC, it was never entirely extinguished, so that the Cynicism of the first century AD was indeed part of a continuing tradition of Cynicism, more or less independent of Stoicism. Although the Bernays–Zeller position has been endorsed by a number of distinguished scholars, it is fair to say that most scholars who have recently written about late Cynicism have accepted Dudley's position.[125]

A third view has also been held: that, although Cynicism died out in the last two centuries BC, it revived in the Imperial era independently of Stoicism. This position too has been defended by some distinguished scholars, although it has been much less popular than the other two.[126] On the face of it, it seems implausible that a philosophy which had died out revived spontaneously *ex nihilo*, but the implausibility would be less in the case of Cynicism, which was

---

124 Bernays (1879) 27f.; Zeller (1923) 287f., 791f.
125 Followers of Bernays–Zeller: e.g., Marcks (1883) 13f.; Pohlenz (1959) I.170f.; A. A. Long (private letter to me and Long [1982]); followers of Dudley: e.g. (apart from Kindstrand and Billerbeck), Helm (1924) 5 (anticipating Dudley); Höistad (1948) *passim*; Brunt (1973) 9 {= (2013) 152}, id. (1975) 29 {= (2013) 301}; Griffin (1976) 306; Moles (1978) 94 {above, p. 49}; Jones (1978) 49; Attridge (1978) 56ff.; Malherbe (1976) 201ff. and (1977) 7.
126 Cf., e.g., von Fritz (1970).

not a 'school' as such, and whose simple tenets could be grasped by anyone, whether or not there was a continuing tradition to draw upon.

Dudley's case rests upon three main arguments: (a) that there are good reasons why Cynicism should have been eclipsed in the second and first centuries BC; (b) that there are good reasons why it should have revived in the early Imperial era; (c) that there is enough evidence for the continuing existence of Cynicism in the second and first centuries BC. Arguments (a) and (b) go some way towards meeting Bernays' and Zeller's case, though obviously (c) is critical.

(a) Dudley adduces several reasons for the eclipse of Cynicism in the second and first centuries BC:

(1) during that period Cynicism failed to produce any outstanding personalities, which was particularly damaging to Cynicism, since it was not a 'school' as such and lacked a comprehensive theoretical background;
(2) the essential features of the Cynic system, especially the αὐτάρκεια and ἀπάθεια enjoyed by the σοφός, could be found in the much more sophisticated systems of the Stoics and Epicureans;
(3) Cynicism necessarily made less of an impact with the passing of time because it had become familiar;
(4) most important, with the shift in the centre of gravity in the Mediterranean world from Greece to Rome, Cynicism inevitably lost much of its appeal, since it was uncongenial to Roman taste and the Romans already had their own tradition of *antiqua virtus*.

Of course one can question some of the details of this analysis or move the emphasis hither or thither,[127] but this is a reasonable set of explanations for the apparent decline of Cynicism in the second and first centuries BC, always provided that it is possible to produce some evidence for continuing Cynic ‖121‖ activity. One might also suggest that possibly Cynicism did not greatly decline during this period, but that we merely hear little about it, because of the almost total lack of contemporary Greek sources like Dio Chrysostom, Lucian, and Julian, who are so informative about later Cynicism.

(b) Dudley adduces several reasons for the revival of Cynicism in the early Imperial era:

(1) in general 'the conditions which had proved favourable for the growth of Cynicism after the death of Alexander were being repeated in the early years of the first century AD'. More specifically:
(2) the Imperial system had taken the interest out of politics, i.e., presumably, there was a greater need for individual reassurance and comfort;

---

127 Dudley (1937) 117ff.; more could obviously be made of the impact of Stoicism, which borrowed so extensively from Cynic ethics.

(3) there was a great increase in cosmopolitanism;
(4) luxury was more rampant than ever—even Stoicism had compromised with it—so Cynicism naturally came into its own.

Again, this is a fair case,[128] although again one could speculate that the apparent difference between the second and first centuries BC and the early Imperial period is in part a function of the vagaries of the source material. And, accepting that there is some difference, one could add other explanations, e.g., (5) late Cynicism did succeed in producing a number of outstanding individuals (Demetrius, Dio Chrysostom, Demonax, Peregrinus, Oenomaus, Sostratus, and Theagenes); (6) the increasingly authoritarian nature of the Imperial system, in some contrast with that of the Republic, provided Cynics with more specific targets for their political invective; (7) the possibility that some of the more striking Cynic manifestations can be explained in terms of the particular opposition of Alexandrian Cynics to the Flavians; (8) the personal and philosophical links of several leading Cynics with prominent figures of the 'Stoic opposition', which necessarily brought Cynicism more into the public eye.

(c) Dudley's handling of the evidence is generally quite rigorous. He distinguishes Cynic influence upon literature, which obviously might persist after the 'death' of the philosophy that had inspired it, from possible evidence for the continuing existence of Cynicism. Thus he excludes references to Cynicism in Roman comedy (in any case too early to bear on the crucial question) or the alleged 'Cynicism' of Varro. He also distinguishes Cynic mannerisms (exhibited by the street preachers whose existence is attested by Horace, and by Favonius, the follower of Cato the Younger) from Cynicism in the strict sense (both the street preachers and Favonius are described in the tradition as Stoics).[129] On the Roman side he finds two pieces of evidence that the κυνικὸς βίος was known in Rome, a reference in a mime of Laberius (c.106–43) to the 'Cynica haeresis' and an alleged reference in Cic. *Acad.* I–II to the Cynic 'habitus et consuetudo'. On the Greek side, Dudley adduces rather more evidence. He maintains that the 'Cynicism' of Meleager of Gadara is not simply 'literary' Cynicism. He argues that a passage in Diogenes Laertius, deriving probably from Diocles of Magnesia, contemporary and friend of Meleager,[130] refers to Cynics of Diocles'

---

128   Though it is hard to attach much meaning to (3).
129   Favonius is so described in Tac. *Ann.* 16.22.4. Geiger (1974) 167ff. argues that Favonius' philosophical allegiance is an open question, given the tendentiousness of the speech Tacitus attributes to Cossutianus Capito in *Ann.* 16.22. But on *a priori* grounds (strict Cynicism being incompatible with senatorship or public office) Favonius is best classed as a Cynicising Stoic (like, indeed, his friend and inspiration, Cato the Younger).
130   D.L. 6.104; the traditional identification of Diocles the doxographer with Meleager's friend is doubted by Gow and Page (1965) xvi, but unreasonably.

own day. He points out that an epigram of Antipater of Thessalonica on a degenerate Cynic shows that the 'Cynicus habitus' was known in Greece in the Augustan age. He also instances some of the papyrus literature and Cynic letters as evidence for continuing Cynic literary activity.

Assessment of these items is not easy. The Laberius reference certainly implies the continuing existence of Cynicism in some form or other,[131] as does the epigram of Antipater.[132] On the other hand, Dudley's inference from Diogenes Laertius is dubious, and the evidence of the various forms of Cynic literature [[122]] (none securely debatable) proves only the continuing existence of 'literary' Cynicism. More interesting is Dudley's analysis of Meleager. He is, I think, right to argue that to some extent Meleager adopted a Cynic *persona*. In particular, he correctly interprets Meleager's σκηπτροφόρος σοφία as a reference to Cynicism. If Meleager represented himself, tongue in cheek, as a Cynic philosopher conquered by Love, this implies the continuing existence of Cynicism in Meleager's lifetime.[133]

Such a haul (Laberius, Antipater, Meleager) may seem meagre, but given Dudley's case that Cynicism declined sharply in the last two centuries BC without being extinguished entirely, it seems sufficient. Moreover, Dudley could have made more of the Roman evidence. Three well-known passages in Cicero are important:

(1) *de Off.* 1.148: 'Cynicorum uero ratio tota est eicienda: est enim inimica uerecundiae, sine qua nihil rectum esse potest, nihil honestum.'
(2) *de Off.* 1.128, 'nec uero audiendi sunt Cynici, aut si fuerunt Stoici paene Cynici, qui reprehendunt et irrident, quod ea, quae re turpia non sint,

---

131 The implications of the term αἵρεσις are exhaustively analysed by Glucker (1978) 166ff. He shows that it does not mean 'school' in an institutional sense, but rather 'school of thought', 'persuasion'. Since the term can refer both to 'schools of thought' *within* different systems of philosophy and to separate systems of philosophy conceived as 'schools of thought' (one can talk, e.g., both of αἱρέσεις within Stoicism and of Stoicism as a αἵρεσις), the description of Cynicism as a αἵρεσις tells us nothing about its status in relation to Stoicism.
132 Laberius, *Compitalia* F 3 Ribbeck { = F 22 Panayotakis}; Antipater: *AP* 11.158 = Gow–Page (1968) Antipater no. 97.
133 Meleager as 'Cynic': cf. Athen. 157b, 502c; D.L. 6.99; his previous σκηπτροφόρος σοφία: *AP* 12.101 = Gow–Page (1968) no. 103. The phrase alludes (*pace* Gow and Page *ad loc.*) to the σκῆπτρον of Diogenes and his followers (a half-ironic, half-serious description of the Cynic's staff—the emblem of the Cynic 'king'): cf., e.g., [Diog.] *Ep.* 19; Epict. 3.22.34, 22.57, 22.63; 4.8.30, 8.34; Julian *Or.* 6.181b; Apul. *Apol.* 22. Consistent also with the Cynic *persona* are (1) the imitation of Menippus; (2) the cosmopolitan epitaph (*AP* 7.417 = Gow–Page no. 2); (3) the spoof Λεκίθου καὶ φακῆς σύγκρισις (Athen. 157b).

uerbis flagitiosa ducamus, illa autem, quae turpia sunt, nominibus appellemus suis.'

(3) *de Fin.* 3.68: 'Cynicorum autem rationem atque uitam alii cadere in sapientem dicunt, si qui eiusmodi forte casus inciderit ut id faciendum sit, alii nullo modo.'

In both *de Off.* and *de Fin.* Cicero is writing *in propria persona*. All three passages imply that Cynicism was an option still available at the time of writing. In the first Cicero is arguing against the flouting of custom. It is no justification of such behaviour to cite the example of Socrates and Aristippus, for they had 'great and almost superhuman personalities'; the Cynic rejection of convention is even worse and should be totally excluded. In the second Cicero is again arguing against Cynic ἀναίδεια. The formulation 'Cynici, aut ... Stoici paene Cynici' is absolutely incompatible with the hypothesis that *all* Cynicism was now part of Stoicism. Nobody denies that there were 'Cynic' Stoics,[134] but the wording 'Cynics, or Stoics who are almost Cynics' necessarily implies that there were *also* Cynics independent of Stoicism. The same applies to the third passage. Cicero has just been expounding the Stoic view that the wise man should engage in politics and marry and have children; as for the Cynic option (i.e., in context, rejection of politics and of marriage) some Stoics think this justifiable, others not. The argument here is compatible with the hypothesis that a Cynic option remained available to Stoics, but it is also implied that Cynicism still existed *separately* from Stoicism: there is a generic contrast between the mainline Stoic view and the Cynic view. It is true that in rejecting Cynic ἀναίδεια and upholding 'uerecundia' (αἰδώς), Cicero is closely following the teaching of Panaetius.[135] But in order to avoid the conclusion that these passages, particularly the second, attest the continuing *independent* existence of Cynicism, one would have to suppose that Cicero was following Panaetius so mechanically as to write about Cynicism anachronistically. There is no justification for refusing to accept the natural implications of the Ciceronian evidence.

In short, Dudley seems to have produced enough evidence to demonstrate that Cynicism continued to exist in the last two centuries BC. The Ciceronian evidence also seems to demonstrate that some Cynicism existed separately from Stoicism, although a type of Cynicism was of course also an option within Stoicism.

Finally, a brief look at the Imperial evidence. It is of course possible to adduce texts which make no distinction between Stoicism and Cynicism, as

---

134 For the most important *testimonia* see Billerbeck (1979) 4; also relevant are the Cynicising aspects of Zeno's and Chrysippus' teachings (particularly in their Πολιτεῖαι).
135 Cf. Billerbeck (1979) 3f.

for example Cassius Dio's description of the behaviour of the philosophers in AD 71.[136] It is also true that a Cynic option continued to be available within Stoicism: that is reflected in some of Seneca's and, perhaps to a greater extent, Epictetus' philosophy. But this does not prove that Cynicism was only an option within Stoicism. In a sense it is true that to Epictetus the true [[123]] Cynic is a Stoic, because the doctrine of περὶ κυνισμοῦ is Stoic. But the doctrine of that work is *also* (apart from Epictetus' rejection of the characteristic Cynic ἀναίδεια) Cynic, and it seems to me better to say that περὶ κυνισμοῦ shows how Cynicism could be interpreted by a sympathetic Stoic than to claim it as *evidence* that Cynicism was now only a branch of Stoicism.[137] It is not at all surprising that Stoics like Seneca and Epictetus should have admired, and to a certain degree, attempted to expound, Cynic doctrines: that had always been a possible position within Stoicism.

In the main, the Imperial evidence, like the evidence of the second and first centuries BC, suggests that Stoicism and Cynicism were generally regarded as distinct (subject to the usual reservation that this distinction might be blurred if Stoics 'Cynicised' either in their doctrine or their behaviour, or Cynics exploited some of the philosophical refinements of their sister philosophy).[138] So, for example, Diogenes Laertius attests a scholarly controversy concerning the status of Cynicism, but the controversy is not whether Cynicism is an offshoot of Stoicism, but whether it is a αἵρεσις or an ἔνστασις βίου. For Diogenes (or, more important, for his authorities), while there is a close κοινωνία between the two philosophies so that some Stoics can recommend Cynicism as a σύντομος ἐπ' ἀρετὴν ὁδός, the two are separate.[139] Similarly, in his *Philosophies for Sale*, Lucian includes both Cynics and Stoics.[140] And Juvenal can write: 'qui nec Cynicos nec Stoica dogmata legit | a Cynicis tunica distantia'.[141] The dividing line between the two philosophies is very thin (a mere 'tunica'), but the two are formally distinct (the thought recalls Cicero's in *de Off.* 1.128). Of course the 'authority' of Juvenal on such a point means little in itself, but we seem

---

136 Cass. Dio 66.13.1: ἄλλοι πολλοὶ ἐκ τῶν Στωικῶν καλουμένων λόγων ... μεθ' ὧν καὶ Δημήτριος ὁ κυνικός (but could this be a case of 'Telemachus and the other suitors'?).

137 As (e.g.) Prof. Long argues. We might also recall that Epictetus, like Dio Chrysostom (sometimes) and Julian, simultaneously upholds a Cynic ideal and attacks so-called 'degenerate' Cynics. In reality of course the behaviour of these 'degenerate' Cynics was truer to the original Cynic spirit than was the ideal Κυνικός of bowdlerising Stoics, and the attacks upon these Cynics might be taken to imply the existence of a type of Cynicism *outside* Stoicism.

138 Cf. n. 4.

139 D.L. 6.103–4 (αἱρέσεις meaning 'school of thought', but here referring to separate systems of philosophy: cf. n. 131).

140 *Vit. auct.* 7ff., 20ff.

141 Juv. 13.121–2.

to be dealing with a general, agreed, perception of the relationship between the two philosophies. (Elsewhere, we find Cynics attacking Stoic doctrine.)[142] The evidence of Seneca is also interesting. For all Seneca's exposition (on occasion) of 'Cynic' views, and his use of Demetrius as a philosophical ideal, he clearly regards Cynicism and Stoicism as separate. For example, in *de Ben.* 2.17 he discusses first the Cynic attitude to the receiving of money, but in 2.17.3 he expounds the view of 'Chrysippus noster': he is making (or implying) a generic distinction between two philosophies. Or, in *de brev. vit.* 14.2 he writes: 'disputare cum Socrate licet, dubitare cum Carneade, cum Epicuro quiescere, hominis naturam cum Stoicis uincere, cum Cynicis excedere'. The Socratic circle, the sceptical Academy of Carneades, Epicureanism, Stoicism, Cynicism—to Seneca Stoicism and Cynicism are distinct, even though the influence the latter had exerted, and continued to exert, upon the former, was profound. The evidence is decisive that this is the correct position.[143]

## Bibliography

von Arnim, H. (1898) *Leben und Werke des Dio von Prusa* (Berlin).
Attridge, H. W. (1976) *First-Century Cynicism in the Epistles of Heraclitus* (Missoula).
Attridge, H. W. (1978) 'The Philosophical Critique of Religion under the Early Empire', *ANRW* II.16.1: 45–78.
Baldry, H. C. (1959) 'Zeno's Ideal State', *JHS* 79: 3–15.
Baldry, H. C. (1965) *The Unity of Mankind in Greek Thought* (Cambridge).
Bernays, J. (1879) *Lucian und die Kyniker* (Berlin).
Billerbeck, M. (1978) *Epiktet: vom Kynismus* (Leiden).
Billerbeck, M. (1979) *Der Kyniker Demetrius: ein Beitrag zur Geschichte der frühkaiserzeitlichen Popularphilosophie* (Leiden).
Bosworth, A. B. (1980) 'Alexander and the Iranians', *JHS* 100: 1–21.
Bowie, E. L. (1978) 'Apollonius of Tyana: Tradition and Reality', *ANRW* II.16.2: 1652–99.
Brunt, P. A. (1973) 'Aspects of the Social Thought of Dio Chrysostom and the Stoics', *PCPhS* 199: 9–33; repr. in id. (2013) 151–79.
Brunt, P. A. (1974) 'Marcus Aurelius in his Meditations', *JRS* 64: 1–20; repr. in id. (2013) 360–93.
Brunt, P. A. (1975) 'Stoicism and the Principate', *PBSR* 43: 7–35; repr. in id. (2013) 275–309.
Brunt, P. A. (2013) *Studies in Stoicism*, edd. M. Griffin and A. Samuels (Oxford).
Crönert, W. (1906) *Kolotes und Menedemos* (Leipzig; repr. Amsterdam, 1965).

---

142   E.g., Oenomaus (cf. n. 4).
143   Note also that the Cynic Epistles consistently project Cynicism as a distinct 'philosophy' (cf., e.g., [Crates] *Ep.* 16.1, 29.1).

Decleva Caizzi, F. (1966) *Antisthenis Fragmenta* (Varese/Milan).
Desideri, P. (1978) *Dione di Prusa: un intelletuale greco nell'impero romano* (Messina/Florence).
De Witt, N. W. (1954) *Epicurus and his Philosophy* (Minneapolis).
Dickie, M. W. (1981) 'The Disavowal of *Invidia* in Roman Iamb and Satire', *PLLS* 3: 183–208.
Dover, K. J. (1974) *Greek Popular Morality in the Time of Plato and Aristotle* (Oxford and Berkeley).
Dudley, D. R. (1937) *A History of Cynicism from Diogenes to the 6th century A.D.* (London).
Fears, J. R. (1974) 'The Stoic View of the Career and Character of Alexander the Great', *Philologus* 118: 113–30.
Ferguson, J. (1975) *Utopias of the Classical World* (London and Ithaca).
Fisch, M. H. (1937) 'Alexander and the Stoics', *AJPh* 58: 59–82, 129–51.
Furneaux, H., ed. (1896–1907) *The Annals of Tacitus*, revised by H. F. Pelham and C. D. Fisher, 2 vols. (Oxford).
Geiger, J. (1974) 'M. Favonius: Three Notes', *RSA* 4: 161–70.
Gerhard, G. A. (1909) *Phoenix von Kolophon: Texte und Untersuchungen* (Leipzig and Berlin).
Glucker, J. (1978) *Antiochus and the Late Academy* (Göttingen).
Gow, A. S. F. and D. L. Page, edd. (1965) *The Greek Anthology: Hellenistic Epigrams*, 2 vols. (Cambridge).
Gow, A. S. F. and D. L. Page, edd. (1968) *The Greek Anthology: The Garland of Philip*, 2 vols. (Cambridge).
Griffin, M. T. (1976) *Seneca: a Philosopher in Politics* (Oxford; repr. with addenda, 1992).
Griffin, M. T. (1981) 'Review of Billerbeck (1979)', *CR* 31: 58–60.
Hamilton, J. R. (1969) *Plutarch, Alexander: A Commentary* (Oxford).
Helm, R. (1924) 'Kynismos', *RE* XII.1: 3–24.
Hense, O. (1909) *Teletis Reliquiae* (Tübingen).
Höistad, R. (1948) *Cynic Hero and Cynic King: Studies in the Cynic Conception of Man* (Uppsala).
Jones, C. P. (1978) *The Roman World of Dio Chrysostom* (Cambridge, Mass. and London).
Kennedy, G. (1963) *The Art of Persuasion in Greece* (Princeton).
Kindstrand, J. F. (1976) *Bion of Borysthenes: a Collection of the Fragments with Introduction and Commentary* (Uppsala).
Kindstrand, J. F. (1980) 'Demetrius the Cynic', *Philologus* 124: 83–98.
Koestermann, E. (1968) *Cornelius Tacitus, Annalen Band IV: Buch 14–16* (Heidelberg).
Lloyd-Jones, H. (1971) *The Justice of Zeus* (Berkeley and Los Angeles; repr. with addenda, 1983).
Long, A. A. (1968) 'The Stoic Concept of Evil', *PhilosQ* 18: 329–43.
Long, A. A. (1980) 'The Cynics in Translation [Review of L. Paquet, *Les cyniques grecs: fragments et témoinage* (Ottawa, 1975)]', *CR* 30: 53–4.

Long, A. A. (1982) 'Review of Billerbeck (1979)', *JHS* 102: 260.
Malherbe, A. J. (1970) 'Gentle as a Nurse: The Cynic Background to 1 Thess ii', *Novum Testamentum* 12: 203–17; repr. in id., *Light from the Gentiles: Hellenistic Philosophy and Early Christianity: Collected Essays, 1959–2012*, 2 vols, edd. C. R. Holladay et al. (Leiden and Boston, 2014) I.53–67.
Malherbe, A. J. (1977) *The Cynic Epistles: a Study Edition* (Missoula).
Marcks, J. F. (1883) *Symbola critica ad epistolographos* (diss. Bonn).
Martin, V. (1959) 'Un recueil de diatribes cyniques: Pap. Genev. inv. 271', *MH* 16: 77–115.
Moles, J. L. (1978) 'The Career and Conversion of Dio Chrysostom', *JHS* 98: 79–100 [above, Ch. 1].
Moles, J. L. (1982) 'A Note on Cicero, *ad Quintum fratrem* 2.10(9).3', *LCM* 7: 63–5 [vol. 2, Ch. 65].
Moles, J. L. (1983) 'The Date and Purpose of the Fourth Kingship Oration of Dio Chrysostom', *ClAnt* 2: 251–78 [above, Ch. 3].
Momigliano, A. D. (1951) 'Review of Wirszubski (1950)', *JRS* 41: 146–53; repr. in id., *Quinto Contributo alla Storia degli studi classici e del mondo antico*, 2 vols. (Rome, 1975) II.958–75.
Murray, O. (1966) 'The Unity of Mankind [Review of Baldry (1965)]', *CR* 16: 368–71.
Niehues-Proebsting, H. (1979) *Der Kynismus des Diogenes und der Begriff der Zynismus* (Munich).
O'Neil, E. N. (1977) *Teles: the Cynic Teacher* (Missoula, Mont.).
Photiadès, P. (1959) 'Les diatribes cyniques du papyrus de Genève 271, leurs traductions et élaborations successives', *MH* 16: 116–39.
Pohlenz, M. (1959) *Die Stoa*², 2 vols. (Göttingen).
Rist, J. M. (1969) *Stoic Philosophy* (Cambridge).
Rogers, R. S. (1952) 'A Tacitean Pattern in Narrating Treason-Trials', *TAPhA* 83: 279–311.
Romilly, J. de (1979) *La douceur dans la pensée grecque* (Paris).
Schulz, F. (1946) *History of Roman Legal Science* (Oxford; repr. with addenda, 1967).
Stinton, T. C. W. (1975) '*Hamartia* in Aristotle and Greek Tragedy', *CQ* 25: 221–54; repr. in id., *Collected Papers on Greek Tragedy* (Oxford, 1990) 143–86.
Syme, R. (1958) *Tacitus*, 2 vols. (Oxford).
Toynbee, J. M. C. (1944) 'Dictators and Philosophers in the First Century A.D.', *G&R* 13: 43–58.
Vidal-Naquet, P. (1978) 'Plato's Myth of the Statesman, the Ambiguities of the Golden Age and of History', *JHS* 98: 132–41.
von Fritz, K. (1926) *Quellenuntersuchungen zu Leben und Philosophie des Diogenes von Sinope* (Philologus Suppl. 18.2; Göttingen).
von Fritz, K. (1970) 'Cynics', *OCD*²: 305.
Weber, E. (1887) 'De Dione Chrysostomo Cynicorum Sectatore', *Leipziger Stud. z. Classichen Philologie* 10: 77–268.
Zeller, E. (1923) *Die Philosophie der Griechen* III.1 (Leipzig).

CHAPTER 13

# The Woman and the River: Diogenes' Apophthegm from Herculaneum and Some Popular Misconceptions about Cynicism

The apophthegm attributed to Diogenes* on a Herculaneum *graffito*, about a woman being swept away by a river, has been much discussed.[1] The usual transcription of the text runs as follows:

Διογένης ὁ κυνικὸς φιλόσοφος ἰδὼν γυναῖκα ὑπὸ ποταμοῦ φερομένην εἶπεν· ἄφες φέρεσσθαι τὸ κακὴν ὑπὸ κακοῦ.

The *graffito*, as befits its content, is written in an educated hand. The spelling φέρεσσθαι should not necessarily be considered a mere error, since in Hellenistic Greek unvoiced σ is often spelled σσ. κακήν is the normal interpretation of the original ΚΑΚΗΝ, though this interpretation has recently been challenged by Giangrande, as we shall see. κακοῦ appears to be the writer's own supralinear correction of his first effort κακιυς (*sic*).[2]

## 1 General Interpretation

The form of the combined anecdote and apophthegm is a familiar type: a philosopher sees something upon which he makes a trenchant observation. There are many such stories in the Diogenes tradition.[3] As scholars have seen, ΚΑΚΗΝ,

---

\* I am grateful to Professor Giangrande for his helpful criticism of an earlier draft of this paper and for kindly allowing me to see a paper containing his own second thoughts on the problem. It will be obvious that we disagree on essentials.

1 Della Corte (1958) 262 nr. 264 and plate II; Maiuri (1958) 435 and fig. 379; Schubring (1962) 240f.; Strohmaier (1967); Boegehold (1968); P. Ciprotti ap. *CIL* IV, Suppl. 3, fasc. 4, no. 10529; Lebek (1976); Gallo (1980) 311–24; Giangrande (1980).

2 I am indebted to Professor Giangrande for pointing out that 'Gemination' of sigma is found in Hellenistic Greek: cf. Mayser (1906) 219.

   That κακοῦ is the writer's own correction of κακιυς is the view of all scholars except Lebek and (now) Giangrande. Lebek argues that κακοῦ κακῶς (as in the *Gnom. Par.* version) should be read, but the lettering simply does not seem to allow this interpretation: cf. Gallo (1980) 322 n. 10.

3 Cf. Strohmaier (1967) 254; Rudberg (1935) 34f.

whether or not τό goes with it, and whether or not the word itself should be emended, refers to the woman (φέρεσθαι τὸ ΚΑΚΗΝ ὑπὸ κακοῦ/γυναῖκα ὑπὸ ποταμοῦ φερομένην), whom the philosopher describes as a 'bad thing'. The river is also described as a 'bad thing', because it is drowning the woman. The woman is 'bad' because (1) in Greek popular thought from Hesiod through to the Classical period women as a species could be regarded as a κακόν, and (2) Diogenes was sometimes represented in the tradition as a misogynist[4] (falsely, as I argue below). The apophthegm of the Herculaneum *graffito* is also found in the forms Δείξαντός ποτε αὐτῷ [Διογένει] γυναῖκά τινος ὑπὸ ποταμοῦ φερομένην καὶ εἰπόντος· 'σώσωμεν αὐτήν' φησίν 'ἔα τὸ κακὸν ἐκεῖνο τὸ πολυθρύλλητον φέρεσθαι ὑπὸ κακοῦ κακῶς' (from the *Gnomologium Parisinum*)[5] and 'Er sah eine Frau, die von der Flut weggetragen wurde, und sagte: Das Übel geht durch das Übel zugrunde' (an Arabic version).[6] Another very similar story is preserved in another Arabic version: 'Er sah eine kranke Frau und sagte: Das Übel wird durch das Übel abgewendet', though this story is told about Socrates.[7] The implication of these apophthegms (besides the obvious point that both river and women are κακά) must be that it is poetically just that one evil should receive its desserts at the hands of another. This idea is even more clearly implicit in the *Gnomologium Parisinum* version, the emphatic conjunction of κακός and κακῶς being common in contexts where the notion of retributive justice is stressed.[8]

## 2  The Text

The problem is of course to explain τὸ ΚΑΚΗΝ. Schubring, arguing that the apophthegm is more pointed if Diogenes regards the woman as a greater evil than the river, proposes ὑπὸ κακοῦ κάκιόν τι. Even allowing for the apparent incompetence of the writer, this seems, as Giangrande emphasises, too drastic an alteration of the text. Strohmaier, followed by Gallo, suggests simply κακόν,

---

4  Cf., e.g., D.L. 6.51, 52; other *testimonia* in Gallo (1980) 314 n. 10.
5  ⟦129⟧ Sternach (1893) 136 n. 3.
6  German translation of Arabic text cited by Strohmaier (1967) 254 n. 5. The Arabic text is *Cod. Monac. arab.* 651, f. 126ʳ *in marg.*; German translation and commentary in Loewenthal (1896) nr. 9.
7  *Cod. Monac. arab.* 651, f.5ᵛo 2f. = Loewenthal (1896) nr. 75. Attributions of such anecdotes are of course notoriously unreliable (cf. Strohmaier [1967] 255 n. 2), and moreover attribution of essentially similar anecdotes to both Diogenes and Socrates is frequent in the Cynic-Stoic tradition.
8  As, e.g., in the common curse formula κακὸς κακῶς ἀπόλοιτο ὅστις ... or Plut. *Brut.* 33.6; *De sera num. vind.* 552F.

but [[126]] Giangrande finds the postulated corruption of κακήν into κακόν 'neither phonetically nor palaeographically convincing'. Boegehold maintains that the text is defensible: it should be punctuated Ἄφες φέρεσθαι· τὸ κακὴν ὑπὸ κακοῦ, which Boegehold translates as 'let her go. It is a case of "Bad to get rid of bad ... woman"', the phrase κακὴν ὑπὸ κακοῦ, in Boegehold's opinion, alluding with a twist to the proverb μὴ κακὸν κακῷ ἰᾶσθαι. But, as Giangrande points out, this punctuation upsets the clear parallelism between the phrases ὑπὸ ποταμοῦ φερομένην and φέρεσθαι ὑπὸ κακοῦ, and the allusion to the proverb alleged would be intolerably obscure.[9] Lebek resorts to extensive emendation to support the implausible hypothesis that the text is based on an anecdote composed in comic trimeters. In the latest contribution to the discussion Giangrande suggests that ΚΑΚΗΝ should be retained but understood as κάκιν = κάκιον, 'spelled according to the current Hellenistic phonetic and graphic habit'.[10] But this solution, learned and ingenious as it is, also fails to convince. Schubring's view, which Giangrande follows, that the apophthegm is more pointed if the woman is described as a greater evil than the river seems misconceived. This false refinement spoils the idea that it is appropriate that one evil should be overcome by another—an idea effectively reinforced by the repetition of similar word forms, and it ignores the close parallels for the 'evil by evil' motif in the *Gnomologium Parisinum* and the two Arabic versions.[11] Nor are Giangrande's objections to the reading κακόν cogent. κακήν instead of κακόν would be quite a natural error for the writer to make (the more so if he was capable of κακιυς as his first try at κακοῦ), when his mind was running on the idea that the woman was 'evil' and he had just written γυναῖκα φερομένην. The parallels in the other versions of the apophthegm strongly suggest that κακόν is right.

## 3 Detailed Interpretation: The Assumptions behind the Anecdote

We should be in no doubt that the anecdote and apophthegm, in whatever form, are fictitious, but even fictitious anecdotes about famous philosophers may possess a certain historical value. Such anecdotes often travesty the

---

9   Professor Giangrande now accepts this alleged allusion, but his first reaction was (I believe) correct.
10  -ιν can represent -ιον in Hellenistic texts: cf. Mayser and Schmoll (1970) 130f.; η can represent ι: cf. ibid. 52f.
11  Cf. also Strohmaier (1967) 255. Schubring's argument that κακόν ... κακοῦ would be a weak formulation for a Cynic has no objective force in view both of these parallels and of the common idea 'like for like' in retribution contexts.

behaviour and attitudes of the philosophers with whom they are concerned and it is sometimes interesting and instructive to isolate the truths upon which these travesties are based. In what follows I shall briefly outline the ways in which our anecdote reflects some popular misconceptions about Cynicism and attempt to account for them, and I shall also suggest an interpretation of the Herculaneum version of Diogenes' apophthegm which gives it a clever additional point.

In general, the anecdote shows Diogenes behaving in a highly bizarre manner. Cynic behaviour was indeed often bizarre, but for good reason, its very outrageousness being an arresting device for imparting philosophical truths.[12] Our anecdote travesties the bizarreness of Cynic behaviour to the point of absurdity: we should not believe that the historical Diogenes would have behaved in this way.

The anecdote also shows Diogenes indifferent to, indeed positively enthusiastic about, the woman's death by drowning. Cynics were vulnerable to the general charge of misanthropy. This charge was based on such aspects of Cynicism as the Cynic's vehement insistence on his own self-sufficiency (his αὐτάρκεια) and his characteristically virulent abuse of the mass of mankind. The charge was misguided, because the true Cynic feels φιλανθρωπία, even towards the morally depraved, but it is easy to see why it should have been made.[13]

The explanation for Diogenes' behaviour in the anecdote is that he regards the [[127]] woman as a κακόν, hence her death can be viewed with equanimity, even satisfaction. Again, there might appear to be some justification for this implication in Cynic thought, as one of the most celebrated Cynic tags was 'Reason or the Noose' (λόγος ἢ βρόχος): human beings devoid of reason are better dead.[14] Hence, for example, we find the Diogenes of legend greeting the sight of women hanging from an olive-tree with the remark 'Would that every tree bore similar fruit' (D.L. 6.52). But the tenet λόγος ἢ βρόχος is a typical Cynic exaggeration, not to be interpreted with pedantic literalness,[15] and moreover it properly applies to the ethics of suicide (in fact it forms the basis of one of the Stoic justifications for suicide),[16] and it is wrong to infer from it that Cynics actually approved of the death of the morally corrupt. On the contrary, Cynics

---

12  On this aspect of Cynic teaching methods cf. D.L. 6.27, and see the discussions of Rist (1969) 69, and Kindstrand (1976) 138f. Cf. also my own paper forthcoming in *JHS* {Moles (1983)}, which deals in detail with the positive aspects of Cynicism.

13  I discuss these apparent contradictions in Cynicism in my *JHS* paper {Moles (1983)}.

14  Cf., e.g., Plut. *De Stoic. repugn.* 1039E = Antisthenes F 67 DC {= 105 Prince}; D.L. 6.24, 86; [Diog.] *Ep.* 28.6; *Gnom. Vat.* 386; Teles 83, 3 Hense.

15  On the function of Cynic exaggeration cf. D.L. 6.35.

16  Cf. Rist (1969) 237ff.; Griffin (1976) 376 and n. 2.

maintained that virtue was teachable (D.L. 6.105) and they tried to inculcate it in others, even—perhaps even especially—in those who lacked it most.[17]

The reason why Diogenes regards the woman as morally corrupt is the simple fact that she is a woman. Again, we can see several possible explanations why Cynics, and perhaps particularly Diogenes (after the celebrated κυνογαμία of Crates and Hipparchia the charge would have been more difficult to sustain), might be regarded as misogynists, even though this was a mistaken view. For one thing, the Cynics used such words as 'man' and 'woman' in approbation and derogation.[18] But for the Cynics these were simply convenient terms of moral evaluation and, while from a purist point of view we may regret their use (just as the modern feminist objects to such expressions as 'be a man'), it is important to grasp that they did not imply the moral inferiority of women. Far from it. The Cynics believed that the virtues of men and women were identical, that they should receive the same education, and that in the sphere of sexual relationships (the nub of male-female relations) they should both exercise complete freedom of choice.[19] No Cynic would have denied that Hipparchia possessed the Cynic virtue ἀνδρεία or that it was available to women in general. Another relevant factor must be the constant Cynic attacks upon Pleasure. Pleasure of course often involves sexual pleasure, hence association with women. But the Cynics did not condemn sex *tout court*. The Cynic ideal is τὸ κατὰ φύσιν ζῆν, the phrase κατὰ φύσιν being understood in a literal, primitivist way (rather different from the developed Stoic position). Thus to the Cynics sexual urges are natural and should be satisfied either by masturbation or by free association with a willing partner, whether female or male.[20] What the Cynics were really criticising was Pleasure in excess or the pursuit of Pleasure as an end in itself.[21] Hence, because women, for most men, are the vehicle of the greatest pleasure, the Cynics could be represented, quite wrongly, as misogynists. Again, Diogenes' views on the institution of marriage, as reflected in

---

17  Cf., e.g., D.L. 6.6 = Antisthenes F 186 DC {= 167 Prince}; Stob. 3.13.43 (Diogenes), and for fuller discussion see my *JHS* paper {Moles (1983)}. It is interesting to note that in [Diog.] *Ep.* 28.3 Pseudo-Diogenes argues that it would be better παιδεῦσαι malefactors than ἀποκτεῖναι. Although the philosophical content of the Cynic epistles is of generally low quality, this represents, I believe, the correct Cynic position.
18  Cf., e.g., Theon, *Progymn.* 35 = Antisthenes F 195 DC {= 7 Prince}; D.L. 6.59; D.L. 6.14 = Antisthenes F 135A DC {= 22A Prince}; D.L. 6.27, 33, 43.
19  Cf. D.L. 6.12 = Antisthenes F 72 DC {= 134r Prince}; D.L. 6.96; Philodemus, Περὶ τῶν Στωικῶν, col. IX = Crönert (1906) 64; D.L. 6.72, 96; for an excellent discussion of Cynic views on the relationship between the sexes cf. Rist (1969) 56ff.
20  Cf. Rist (1969) 60.
21  For Cynic views on Pleasure cf. Kindstrand (1976) 64ff.

two famous *dicta*,[22] might seem to imply a dismissive attitude to womankind. But this would be a simple misinterpretation. The Cynics criticised marriage as a social institution which restricted the freedom of the individual (his, or her, αὐτάρκεια and ἐλευθερία). No derogation of women is implied, for women were as free as men to participate in the sexual freedom the Cynics advocated.[23]

These then are the more obvious implications of our anecdote and some of the possible explanations for them. There may also be a rather more subtle point.

Diogenes' wording in the Herculaneum version repays closer investigation. One of the most celebrated Cynic ideas is that πόνος is ἀγαθόν: what appears to be a misfortune is in fact a Good, because misfortune trains and toughens the moral ⟦128⟧ character.[24] The Cynics habitually expressed this simple idea in striking rhetorical phrases. The formulation πόνος ἀγαθόν is itself practically an oxymoron. A *dictum* attributed to Bion of Borysthenes, whose philosophical standpoint is broadly Cynic, runs: μέγα κακὸν τὸ μὴ δύνασθαι φέρειν κακόν. Similar expressions become standard in the general Cynic-Stoic tradition,[25] and we can be confident that μέγα κακὸν τὸ μὴ [δύνασθαι] φέρειν κακόν (*vel. sim.*) was a well-known Cynic tag—a pithy variation on the general theme πόνος ἀγαθόν. Diogenes' wording in our anecdote is suspiciously similar: there is the repeated κακόν and the use of the same verb φέρω. Given that clever word play is a general Cynic speciality and one in which Diogenes was regarded as being particularly adept, I suggest that the apophthegm can be understood in two ways: (1)—the obvious application—'let the bad (woman) be borne (away) by a bad (river)'; and (2)—the more subtle application—'let the bad (experience, i.e. τὸ φέρεσθαι ὑπὸ ποταμοῦ) be borne (endured) by a bad (woman)' (with an ironic allusion to the tag κακὸν τὸ μὴ φέρειν κακόν). From the point of view of the woman, what is happening to her is a κακόν (and of course drowning was regarded as a particularly horrible death in the ancient world), but in Cynic thought what is apparently a κακόν is in fact an ἀγαθόν, hence Diogenes does not intervene because the woman's tribulations are actually good for her! This is of course an absurdity, even in Cynic thought. Although the woman's imminent death does not exclude the possibility of her 'bearing'

---

22   D.L. 6.29: ἐπῄνει τοὺς μέλλοντας γαμεῖν καὶ μὴ γαμεῖν and D.L. 6.54: ἐρωτηθεὶς ποίῳ καιρῷ δεῖ γαμεῖν, ἔφη, 'τοὺς μὲν νέους μηδέπω, τοὺς δὲ πρεσβυτέρους μηδεπώποτε'.

23   Cf. Rist (1969) 62. Philodemus' statement (col. IX–XI) that the Cynics advocated, and practised, indiscriminate heterosexual and homosexual rape is pure fabrication by a hostile witness.

24   Cf. e.g. D.L. 6.2 = Antisthenes F 19 DC {= 85 Prince}; D.L. 6.70–1; the idea is fully documented and discussed in the important work of Höistad (1948).

25   D.L. 4.48 = Bion F 23 Kindstrand; Sen. *Ep.* 85.28; 96.1; *De prov.* 3.2, 4.3, 4.16; M. Aurel. 4.49.2.

her ordeal successfully in a philosophical sense,[26] it obviously does exclude her from the continuous exposure to κακά—the unremitting ἄσκησις, which on the proper Cynic view is necessary if she is to progress from her current κακία to ἀρετή.[27] This, then, too is a travesty of the Cynic position, but like all travesties, it takes its departure from a truth—the Cynic doctrine πόνος ἀγαθόν. Thus from several aspects even such a trivial and unhistorical anecdote as the present one can tell us much about Cynicism and about some of the ways in which it was open to vulgar, if sometimes witty, misinterpretation.

## Bibliography

Boegehold, A. L. (1968) 'An Apophthegm of Diogenes the Cynic', *GRBS* 9: 59–60.
Della Corte, M. (1958) 'Le iscrizioni di Ercolano', *Rendiconti della Accademia di Archeologia Lettere e Belle Arte* 33: 239–308.
Gallo, I. (1980) *Frammenti Biografici da Papiri* II (Rome).
Giangrande, G. (1980) 'Diogenes' Apophthegm from Herculaneum', *AJPh* 101: 316–17.
Griffin, M. T. (1976) *Seneca: a Philosopher in Politics* (Oxford; repr. with addenda, 1992).
Kindstrand, J. F. (1976) *Bion of Borysthenes: a Collection of the Fragments with Introduction and Commentary* (Uppsala).
Lebek, W. D. (1976) 'Dichterisches über den "Hund Diogenes" (CIL IV suppl. 3 fasc. 4 10529)', *ZPE* 22: 293–6.
Loewenthal, A., ed. (1896) *Sefer musre haphilosophim (Sinnsprüche der Philosophen). Aus dem Arabischen von Honein Ibn Ishâk ins hebräische übersetzt von Jehuda ben Salomo Alcharisi* (Berlin).
Maiuri, A. (1958) *Ercolano: i nuovi scavi 1927–1958* I (Rome).
Mayser, E. (1906) *Grammatik der griechischen Papyri aus der Ptolemäerzeit* (Leipzig).

---

26  I cannot accept Professor Giangrande's counter-argument: 'the verb φέρω, in the sense "endure", means ... "endure successfully, without succumbing to" ... The woman can hardly be said to endure successfully her drowning: she obviously died'. This is a misconception. Cynics advocated 'endurance' of κακά/πόνοι. Certain κακά/πόνοι may be imposed by external forces (forces of nature, like our river, or the cruel dictates of tyrants—a favourite Cynic-Stoic example); the Cynics would [[130]] obviously never concede that in such cases death would rule out the 'successful endurance' of the κακά. Other κακά may be undergone voluntarily; in these cases too death is no impediment to *philosophical* 'endurance'; for example, Peregrinus billed his suicide as a lesson in ἐγκαρτερεῖν τοῖς δεινοῖς (Lucian, *Peregr.* 23).
27  We may compare (*mutatis mutandis*) the story that when Ariston of Chios denied any value to the 'indifferents', Chrysippus pointed out that if one rejects 'preferred indifferents' one will die and consequently not attain virtue (*SVF* III.27). For Cynic emphasis on ἄσκησις cf., e.g., D.L. 6.70–1.

Mayser, E. and H. Schmoll (1970) *Grammatik der griechischen Papyri aus der Ptolcmäerzeit* (Berlin).

Moles, J. L. (1983) '"*Honestius quam Ambitiosius*"? An Exploration of the Cynic's Attitude to Moral Corruption in his Fellow Men', *JHS* 103: 103–23 [above, Ch. 12].

Rist, J. M. (1969) *Stoic Philosophy* (Cambridge).

Rudberg, G. (1935) 'Zur Diogenes-Tradition', *SO* 14: 22–43.

Schubring, K. (1962) 'Epigraphisches aus kampanischen Städten', *Hermes* 90: 239–44.

Sternach, L., ed. (1893) *Gnomologium Parisinum Ineditum* (Cracow).

Strohmaier, G. (1967) 'ΤΟ ΚΑΚΟΝ ΥΠΟ ΚΑΚΟΥ: zu einem weiberfeindlichen Diogenesspruch aus Herculaneum', *Hermes* 95: 253–5.

CHAPTER 14

# Cynicism in Horace *Epistles* 1

A series of outstanding contributions in the sixties and seventies from scholars such as Stégen, Becker, Préaux, Maurach, Gordon Williams, McGann, Macleod, and Kenney has greatly advanced our understanding of the nature of *Epistles* 1.[1] It is now common ground[2] that the poems are not 'real' letters, that they all deal with questions of ethics (as understood in the ancient world), that many are linked by thematic correspondences and detailed cross-references, so that not only does the Book as a whole possess a complex formal unity but the full meaning of any single poem can only be grasped when it is read in conjunction with related poems, and that much the most important philosophical influence upon them is Panaetius.[3]

Yet on fundamental problems of interpretation disagreement persists. Maurach, McGann, and Macleod view the poems as, at bottom, morally serious, but for Williams and, to a lesser extent, Kenney, the ethical questions discussed provide simply the raw material for sophisticated poetic treatment, often ironic and humorous, and it is not the material itself that matters but the intricate play of ideas, the swift modulations of tone, and the corresponding demands made upon the alertness and sensitivity of the reader. Even scholars who agree on the seriousness of the poems disagree over the function of the philosophical language in which Horace habitually expresses himself. The traditional view holds that while Horace is indeed generally concerned with universal ethical questions, he sometimes writes from the standpoint of an

---

1 A version of this paper was given to the Liverpool Latin Seminar on 15th March 1985. I am grateful to all those who made constructive criticisms, both formally and informally, on that occasion, to my colleagues in Bangor for their comments on an earlier draft, and to Francis Cairns for his continued encouragement.
2 Stégen (1960b) and (1963); Becker (1963); Préaux (1968); Maurach (1968) 73–124; Williams (1968), esp. 1–30; McGann (1969); Macleod (1977) and (1979); Kenney (1977). This is of course merely a selection from many important recent contributions. For a useful overview of the *Epistles* and recent work on them see Dilke (1981) 1837–57, and for full bibliographies Dilke (1981) 1857–65 and Kissel (1981) 1515–28.
3 Letters: Morris (1931) 81ff.; Williams (1968) 7ff., 518ff.; McGann (1969) 89ff.; ethics: Macleod (1977) and (1979); unity of Book: Maurach (1968); Préaux (1968) 1–13; McGann (1969) 33–87; Kenney (1977) 229f., 237–9; Macleod (1979); Dilke (1981) 1839–42; for discussion of the general [[54]] phenomenon of linked poems within books see further Cairns (1983) 60ff. (with bibliography on 96f.); Panaetius: McGann (1969) 9–32 (summarised, rather inaccurately, by Dilke [1981] 1848f.).

adherent of a particular philosophical school (so, for example, La Penna sees the deflation of [[34]] the Stoic *sapiens* at *Epistles* 1.1.108 as sectarian polemic).[4] But for Macleod the relationship between formal philosophical expression and moral content is much less close, the philosophical language being merely a convenient vehicle for the ethical investigations. And for McGann there seems to be no necessary relationship between the two at all: though no scholar has done more to establish the philosophical sources of the poems, McGann pointedly disclaims the notion 'that the results which he has reached have any bearing on the *Epistles* as poetry.'[5]

The aim of the present paper is to analyse the use of Cynic material in *Epistles* 1 in the hope of contributing not only to the further documentation of Horace's philosophical sources and to a more exact understanding of individual poems and their place in the book, but also to the resolution of these more fundamental problems of interpretation. The idea that Cynicism should be an important element in the philosophy of *Epistles* 1 may strike some scholars as intrinsically implausible, but since 1.17 and 1.18 contain explicit discussion of *Cynic* views, the investigation is justified in principle.

I shall discuss 1.2, 1.10, and 1.17,[6] and at the end of the paper suggest some general reasons why Horace should have given such prominence to Cynicism in these poems.

1    *Epistles* 1.2[7]

This poem has several conventional features: it is a protreptic, it argues the philosophical claims of poetry in order to steer a young man towards philosophy,

---

4   La Penna (1949) 25, 29; for criticism of this view see McGann (1969) 37, and see also below.
5   McGann (1969) 5.
6   This does not exhaust the Cynic material of the book. Also relevant are 1.18.5–8 and 15–20 (which I discuss in relation to 1.17 in §3 below); 1.6.15–16: *insani sapiens nomen ferat, aequus iniqui | ultra quam satis est uirtutem si petat ipsam*, which must at least include criticism of the Cynics (for Cynic 'madness' cf., e.g., D.L. 6.54; Ael. 14.33; Plut. *Brut.* 34.4); 1.12 (to Iccius), esp. 7f., 11, 12ff.; Iccius was a follower of the eclectic Stoic Sextius (McGann [1969] 64), whose asceticism had Cynic aspects (cf. Billerbeck [1979] 15), and for the 'Cynic' Democritus (1.12.12ff.) see the references in McGann (1969) 17 n. 6 and Brancacci (1980) 411–25 (Crates' abandonment of his property is especially germane); 1.19.12–14 (the portrait of the Cynicising Cato—cf. §4 below). I am, however, sceptical of any general influence upon the *Epistles* of Cynic epistolography (*pace* Dilke [1981] 1844f.). *Epistles* 1.2, 1.10, and 1.17 contain what is really important in Horace's treatment of Cynicism in *Epistles* 1.
7   On the 'genre' of 1.2 see Luschnat (1963) (though I do not accept that the second half of the poem is based on a Greek *gnomologium*). Skalitzky (1968) well demonstrates the poem's

lines 6–31 exploit a rich tradition of Homeric interpretation, the style and content of 32ff. are typical of 'diatribe'.[8] The philosophical orientation of the poem is usually thought to be Stoic, or Stoic-Cynic.[9] In my opinion, a persuasive cumulative case can be made for classifying it as more particularly Cynic:

(a) 1–4. Though Horace gives specific grounds for the superiority of Homer as a philosophical teacher to Chrysippus and Crantor (4: *planius ac melius ... dicit*), they are philosophers of different schools and character, and the question of the relative worth of poetry and philosophy has already been raised in *Epistles* 1.1 at 1.1.10f.[10] Hence lines 1–4 amount to a general statement of Homer's superiority to all 'official' philosophers: a Cynic attitude.[11]

(b) Though most of the Homeric interpretation would be widely acceptable, there appear to be three distinctively Cynic touches:

⟦35⟧ (i) The portrayal of Nestor in 11f. Nestor may provide a paradigm for Horace vis-à-vis Lollius, but he also suggests the unlikely, but well-attested, Cynic concept of the philosophical reconciler, who rushes in to resolve disputes (*componere litis | ... festinat*).[12]

(ii) The portrayal of Odysseus in 19f. The stress on 'seeing' and 'insight' (*prouidus, inspexit*), which is the more emphatic because *prouidus* does not correspond precisely to anything in *Odyssey* 1.1–3, evokes the Cynic

---

thematic unity. In its use of poetry 1.2 invites comparison with such works as Zeno's Περὶ ποιητικῆς ἀκροάσεως, Chrysippus' Περὶ τοῦ πῶς δεῖ τῶν ποιημάτων ἀκούειν, and Plutarch's Πῶς δεῖ τὸν νέον ποιημάτων ἀκούειν. For very full documentation of the philosophical background to lines 23–31 see Kaiser (1964).

8   On the vexed question of 'diatribe' I am in broad agreement with the positions of Russell (1973) 29 and Gottschalk (1982); (1983) 91f.
9   Stoic: e.g., Courbaud (1914) 209f.; Becker (1963) 38, 83 n. 14; Maurach (1968) 88; Stoic-Cynic: e.g., Heinze (1890) 522; Skalitzky (1968) 444.
10  *Versus* (1.1.10) denotes poetry in general: cf. McGann (1969) 35; Macleod (1977) 360; Macleod (1979) 16.
11  Cf., e.g., [Diog.] *Ep.* 34.1; Dio 4.38; Max. Tyr. 1.3.2–4, 26.310f. On the Cynics' attitude to Homer see Kindstrand (1976) 35f.; their attitude to other philosophers: id. (1984) 170 (both with extensive bibliographies). Horace's position in *Epistles* 1.2 differs from those of Plutarch (n. 7), for whom Homer and poetry in general are a *propaedeutic* to philosophy, and Cleanthes (*SVF* 1.109.11—cited as a parallel by Dilke [1966] 80), to whom poetry is better than philosophical discussion at revealing the highest philosophical truths *about the divine*, from claims in Stoic and other philosophical texts that Homer is the first philosopher and that his poetry *foreshadows* later philosophical discoveries (cf., e.g., Heraclit. 4.1), or from claims in strictly non-philosophical texts that Homer contains *all* knowledge (e.g., in [Plut.] *De vita et poesi Homeri*).
12  For references see Moles (1983a) ⟦55⟧ 112 {above, p. 332} n. 73. The stress on the speed of the Cynic's intervention is characteristic: cf. Koniaris (1983) 238.

notion of the philosophical 'examiner' (ἐπίσκοπος) and 'spy' or 'scout' (κατάσκοπος).[13]

(iii) Since Odysseus' companions, the suitors, and the Phaeacians are all 'soft', in contrast to the one true *uir*, Odysseus (17: *uirtus ... possit*), Kiessling may well have been right to see in *sponsi Penelopae* (28) an allusion to Bion F 3 Kindstrand, where the suitors' inability to seduce Penelope is a metaphor for philosophical impotence.[14] The imputation of philosophical effeminacy and/or impotence and the Bionian colouring combine to produce a Cynic tone.

(c) 17–31. The contrast between a totally corrupt world (27: *nos numerus sumus*) and the single man of virtue (17ff.) is typically Cynic.[15]

(d) The phrase *aduersis rerum immersabilis undis* (22). Given the complex links among the poems of the book and the particularly close connection between *Epistles* 1.1 and 1.2, this must tie in with *mersor ciuilibus undis* (1.1.16), Horace's self-depreciating description of his unsuccessful attempts to find salvation in Stoicism. The parallels between the two phrases suggest that the two figures, Horace and Odysseus, belong to the same broad category, but the differences establish distinctions within that category. The ideal to which Horace aspires in 1.1.16 is orthodox Stoicism (*agilis fio ... ciuilibus undis*), though *mersor* amusingly conveys his own inadequacy and the consequent 'leakiness' of Stoicism as a *portus* (1.1.15) for him.[16] But the *undae*, which in 1.1.16 are those of public involvement, in 1.2.22 those of moral adversity, are objectively different. Thus the

---

13 For the Cynic ἐπίσκοπος and κατάσκοπος see Moles (1983a) 112 {above, p. 332} n. 73. Cynic colouring in 1.2.19f. is also detected by Kiessling–Heinze (1977) 27, who refer to 'die kynische Interpretation von ἀνδρα πολύτροπον als "Menschenkenner"'. It is a mistake to construe *prouidus* as a 'translation' of πολύτροπον (so Dilke [1966] 80) or πολύμητις (so Wilkins [1885] 100): Horace's treatment of the *Odyssey* is free (cf. n. 28 below).

14 ἀστείως δὲ καὶ Βίων ἔλεγεν ὁ φιλόσοφος ὅτι ὥσπερ οἱ μνηστῆρες τῇ Πηνελόπῃ πλησιάζειν μὴ δυνάμενοι ταῖς ταύτης ἐμίγνυντο θεραπαίναις, οὕτω καὶ οἱ φιλοσοφίας μὴ δυνάμενοι κατατυχεῖν ἐν τοῖς ἄλλοις παιδεύμασι τοῖς οὐδενὸς ἀξίοις ἑαυτοὺς κατασκελετεύουσι; Kiessling (1883) 2. Heinze (1890) 522 leaves it open whether this allusion is present (it is not mentioned in Kiessling–Heinze [1977]), while Kindstrand (1976) 186f. considers it 'very uncertain'. But, given the contrast between Odysseus' *uirtus* and the effeminacy of the other groups, it seems highly attractive. *Canis immundus* (1.2.26) does not, of course, rule out a Cynic interpretation of lines 17ff.: Cynic *testimonia* often contain disparaging references to 'false dogs' (cf. e.g. D.L. 2.66).

15 Cf. e.g. Dio 4.6f.; 6.34; Epict. 3.22.62ff.

16 Close connection between 1.1 and 1.2: Maurach (1968) 88–90; McGann (1969) 33–9; on the implications of *mersor* see Maurach (1968) 84 n. 33 (citing Sen. *Ep.* 22.12 *emerge ad meliorem uitam* and *Ep.* 24.16 *ut animum tuum non mergas in istam sollicitudinem*); Macleod (1979) 22 ('the metaphor here is a striking contrast to Epicurean γαλήνη or Stoic εὔροια');

second figure, Odysseus, is not the orthodox Stoic, who takes part in public life, but the Cynic, who rejects public life, courts adversity, and cannot be sunk by it.¹⁷ Two other elements in the description of Odysseus support this interpretation of the relationship between 1.2.22 and 1.1.16. First, 19f., as we have seen, allude to the Cynic ἐπίσκοπος and κατάσκοπος and the meaning of these two concepts is that the Cynic is concerned with society, in that he assesses it and criticises it, but is not himself part of it. Secondly, Odysseus' [36] purposeful and determined struggles with the *undae*, which contrast with the hapless Horace's involuntary immersion, are described in characteristic Cynic terminology (21f.: *aspera multa | pertulit, aduersis rerum immersabilis undis*) and reflect the fundamental Cynic doctrine πόνος ἀγαθόν.¹⁸

(e) *Epistles* 1.2 is addressed to Lollius, the *liberrime Lolli* of 1.18.1, a poem which explicitly discusses Cynic ethics (6-8, 15-20) and whose opening lines (1-4) emphasise that Lollius' character will not allow him to be a *scurra* within society. But Aristippus played that role in opposition to Diogenes in 1.17 (1.17.19ff.) and *libertas* is a Cynic quality (cf. 1.18.8: *dum uolt libertas dici mera ueraque uirtus*).¹⁹ The freedom-loving Lollius is thus temperamentally closer to Diogenes than to Aristippus. Hence in 1.18 there is a clear link between Lollius' 'Cynic' character and the philosophical content of the poem: there may be a similar link in 1.2.

If, then, we classify the philosophical orientation of 1.2 as Cynic, what are the consequences?

There are some minor gains. The Cynic tone fits Lollius' character. The directness and moral fervour of Cynicism suit an initial philosophical approach to a young man who is uninterested in philosophy and who is wasting his time on rhetoric. The simplicities of Cynicism perhaps also help to sustain the idea of 1.1.27 that Horace must make do *pro tempore* with philosophical *elementa*. A Cynic pose goes well with the debate in 1.1 and 1.2 about the value of poetry—in 1.1 all forms of poetry are seemingly dismissed as *ludicra* (1.1.10), in 1.2 Homer is

---

cf. also the sea imagery of Cic. *De fin.* 3.48 = SVF III.142.13ff. and Plut. *Mor.* 1063A = SVF III.143.39ff.; the oxymoron *agilis fio* also suggests the inefficacy of Horace's endeavours.

17    Cf. esp. Sen. *Ep.* 28.7: *dissentio ab his* [sc. *Cynicis*] *qui in fluctus medios eunt et tumultuosam probantes uitam cotidie cum difficultatibus rerum magno animo colluctantur.*

18    Cynic terminology: cf. n. 17 above and n. 67 below; πόνος ἀγαθόν: cf. n. 67 below. The Cynic interpretation of 21f. is guaranteed by the inverted imagery of 1.17.33–42 (§3).

19    On this link between 1.17 and 1.18 see McGann (1969) 79; for Cynic παρρησία and ἐλευθερία see Kindstrand (1976) 263.

a better teacher than all conventional philosophers, for the Cynics rejected all literature in one breath and asserted the didactic value of Homer in the next.[20]

But far more important are the implications for the philosophical structure of 1.2 as a separate poem, of 1.1 and 1.2 as a unit, and indeed of the whole book.

Lines 17–31 make a polarity between the active *uirtus* of Odysseus and the passive life of pleasure of the companions, suitors, and Phaeacians. At the end of the poem (70f.) there is another polarity:

> quod si cessas aut strenuus anteis,
> nec tardum opperior nec praecedentibus insto.

One of the poles of this second polarity (70: *cessas*) clearly corresponds to the Phaeacians' life of *cessatio* in the first polarity (30f.: *cui pulchrum fuit in medios dormire dies et | ad strepitum* ⟦37⟧ *citharae cessatum ducere curam*).[21] The two polarities therefore contain the same basic opposition. Hence the other pole of the second polarity should refer to Odysseus' Cynic way of life, which could indeed be described as *strenuus*. What, then, is the life of *cessatio*? The opposite of Cynicism is Epicureanism and the portrayal of the companions, suitors, and Phaeacians could in itself be a critical view of the Epicureans. For the Epicureans notoriously avoided 'rough seas' and were often seen as soft and effeminate, equated with the Phaeacians, described as pigs (26), and thought to be devoted to a life of *cessatio*.[22] This interpretation is in fact confirmed by two parallel passages later in the book. In 1.4.15f. Horace describes himself to Albius:

> me pinguem et nitidum bene curata cute uises,
> cum ridere uoles, Epicuri de grege porcum.

Here *bene curata cute* clearly echoes *in cute curanda* (1.2.29) and the association of softness, skin care, and piggery with Epicureanism is made explicit. Then in 1.15.24 Horace imagines his condition after a gastronomic tour:

---

20   Rejection of literature: cf., e.g., D.L. 6.27, 103–4; Dio 4.30; commendation of Homer: cf., e.g., D.L. 6.84; Dio 4.39; n. 11 above.

21   The text of l. 31 has been much discussed, but all 'emendations' (none, in my opinion, is called for) leave the verb *cessare* in place (in one form or another).

22   Avoidance of 'rough seas': cf., e.g., Plut. *Mor.* 778C = F 544 Usener; effeminacy: SVF II.284.38; Cic. *ND* 1.102; Sen. *Ep.* 33.2; Phaeacians: Heraclit. *Hom. Prob.* 79.2; Plut. *Mor.* 1087B, 1093C; Max. Tyr. 30.3D; pigs: Cic. *Pis.* 37 (with Nisbet {(1961)} *ad loc.*); Epicurean *cessatio*: Cic. *ND* 1.102; Nisbet-Hubbard (1978) 254; contrast the 'good' *cessatio* of *Epist.* 1.10.46; on the effeminate associations of *otium*, *cessatio*, etc. see Woodman (1983) 245.

pinguis ut inde domum possim Phaeaxque reuerti.

The description of himself as *pinguis* looks back to *pinguem* (1.4.15) and thus guarantees the equation of Phaeacians and Epicureans in 1.2.28ff.[23]

So when Horace writes *nec tardum opperior nec praecedentibus insto* (1.2.71), he means that he himself stands midway between the extremes of Epicureanism and Cynicism. And this is no throwaway remark, since it reverses a dictum attributed to Aristotle[24] (D.L. 5.20): ἐρωτηθεὶς πῶς ἂν προκόπτοιεν οἱ μαθηταί, ἔφη, 'ἐὰν τοὺς προέχοντας διώκοντες τοὺς ὑστεροῦντας μὴ ἀναμένωσι'. Contrary to Aristotle's prescription, Horace pointedly declines to 'press hard on those in front'. He thus appears half as *proficiens*, who would like to improve but cannot be rushed, half as positive advocate of the middle way.[25] What does this make him? On McGann's analysis of the general philosophical background to *Epistles* 1, he should be a follower of Panaetius.[26] And again, as with the lives of *uirtus* and *cessatio*, Horace in effect attaches the appropriate philosophical label. Line 3 (*qui quid sit pulchrum, quid turpe, quid utile, quid non*) reflects Panaetian categories,[27] hence an apparently general statement at the start of the poem about Homer's philosophical value is so phrased as to anticipate Horace's own final [[38]] position: the poem is enclosed in a Panaetian 'frame', 3 balancing 70f.[28] The technique is exactly the same as that of *Epistles* 1.1. There *quid uerum atque decens curo et rogo, et omnis in hoc sum* (1.1.11) looks like a statement of devotion to philosophy in general (as opposed to the *uersus et cetera ludicra* of 1.1.10), but *decens*, a Panaetian category, functions as a 'marker' for Horace's implicit rejection of extreme Stoicism at the end of the poem (1.1.106ff.):

---

23   [[56]] For these parallels see Maurach (1968) 92; McGann (1969) 44 (neither interprets them as I do). The Epicurean interpretation of 1.2.23ff. is further supported by the links between 1.2.30, 1.14.35, and 1.17.6 (the last two being clearly Epicurean contexts).

24   This is a much sharper parallel than Quint. 2.8.1–5 or *Epist.* 2.2.203f. (cited by Préaux (1968) 58; nor do I see how *Epist.* 2.2.203f. 'proves' Aristippean inspiration). It is immaterial that the attribution of the *dictum* to Aristotle is (surely) false.

25   On this ambiguity, which corresponds to an ambiguity in the position of Panaetius, see McGann (1969) 11, 14, 39.

26   Cf. in general McGann (1969) 9–32.

27   McGann (1969) 12 (cf. Cic. *de off.* 1.9; 3.7–10).

28   It is true that the Panaetian reference is partly sustained by *utile* (18, cf. 3) and *pulchrum* (30, contrast 3), but at the same time the Homeric passage employs all the characteristic distortions of Cynic-Stoic moralising, quasi-allegorical, Homeric interpretation, e.g., it is *not* the case in Homer that the companions drink Circe's potion through *stultitia* and *cupido* (24), that Circe is a whore (25), that her victims, once transformed, are *excordes* (25), that they become dogs (26), or that the Phaeacians think only of their physical appearance and sleeping (29–31) (on these distortions see Kaiser [1964] 109). In other words, lines 17ff. 'slide' from Panaetianism into Cynicism.

> ad summam: sapiens uno minor est Ioue, diues,
> liber, honoratus, pulcher, rex denique regum,
> praecipue sanus, nisi cum pituita molesta est.²⁹

Hence 1.2 puts Horace in a virtually explicit Panaetian position, halfway between Cynic and Epicurean.

The Cynic-Epicurean polarity of 1.2.17–31 and 1.2.70f. must also be related to the Stoic-Aristippean polarity of 1.1.16–19:

> nunc agilis fio et mersor ciuilibus undis,
> uirtutis uerae custos rigidusque satelles;
> nunc in Aristippi furtim praecepta relabor,
> et mihi res, non me rebus, subiungere conor.

Just as the parallel and contrast between 1.2.22 and 1.1.16 establish both the similarity and the difference between the Cynic individualist and the orthodox Stoic, so the Epicureans both correspond and do not correspond to Aristippus. On one level Aristippus stands for pleasure, luxury, and moral sloth (*furtim ... relabor* of 1.1.18 has similar implications to *cessatum* in 1.2.31),³⁰ but on another level for positive adaptability and mastery over widely different circumstances and modes of life.³¹ In this latter guise, indeed, he offers (in structuralist jargon) a potential mediation between Stoic-Cynic and Epicurean poles, and

---

29  Panaetian *decens*: McGann (1969) 10; Préaux (1968) 30. Note also how the difference between Cynic (extreme) *uirtus* and Panaetian (moderate) *uirtus* is further established by the parallel and contrast between 1.2.17 and 1.41f. (the latter a 'modest' Panaetian formulation: cf. McGann (1969) 11 and n. 1). *Epist.* 1.10 shows the same technique as 1.1 and 1.2: the opening lines (esp. l. 3) already contain the philosophical 'solution' of the poem, but this solution is only made explicit at the very end (by the parallel between 50 and 3—cf. §2).

30  For the implications cf. Cic. *Acad. pr.* 2.139: *uerum tamen uideo quam suauiter uoluptas sensibus nostris blandiatur; labor eo, ut assentiar Epicuro aut Aristippo. reuocat uirtus uel potius reprehendit manu*; Sen. *Ep.* 68.10: *otium, inquis, Seneca, commendas mihi? ad Epicureas uoces delaberis.* (I doubt, however, if *furtim* hints specifically at the Epicurean doctrine: λάθε βιώσας either in 1.1.18 or—still less—in 1.10.25, as Préaux [1968] 32 supposes.) In Horace, as in Cicero, both Aristippus and the Epicureans can represent Pleasure, even though they actually had quite different conceptions of the nature of pleasure and Epicurus polemicised against Aristippus' views (F 450 Usener), because Pleasure is set in generic opposition to Virtue. The linkage of Aristippus and the Epicureans in the *Epistles* is further eased by (a) the use in 1.1.18 of *relabor*, a verb which—to judge from Cicero and Seneca—normally alluded to the attractions of Epicureanism and (b) the fact that 1.2.23ff., 1.4.15f., and 1.15.24 all describe 'vulgar' Epicureans, devoted to sensual pleasures, and thus akin to Aristippus. (The true Epicureans will appear in 1.17 and 1.18.)

31  Cf. Stob. 3.17.17; D.L. 2.66–8; 75; Plut. *Mor.* 330C. It is of course true that adaptability is often credited to Odysseus in myth (cf., e.g., Stanford [1968] 87, 91, 118, 162), but it is significantly absent from the uncompromising Cynic Odysseus of 1.2.

Horace actually realises this potentiality in 1.17, where Aristippus can play the roles of both ascetic Cynic and lover of luxury (1.17.23ff., 1.17.27ff.).[32]

In 1.1, then, Horace sets up the polarity Stoic–Aristippus, in 1.2 the polarity Cynic–Epicureans. The two poems exhibit an identical philosophical structure. In each Horace finally adopts a Panaetian position midway between polar opposites. In each, too, he seemed at first to be endorsing as his philosophical ideal one of the polar opposites, orthodox Stoicism in 1.1, Cynicism in 1.2. Together, the two poems map out the whole philosophical area that is to be explored in *Epistles* 1. The map is plotted by reference to the basic polarity Virtue–Pleasure, but Pleasure is subdivided into Aristippeanism and Epicureanism, Virtue into orthodox Stoicism and Cynic individualism. The map coordinates are ideally set for the exploration of questions like: should one engage in social relations? [[39]] Is self-sufficiency possible? Which should be one's guide in life, virtue or pleasure? If virtue, Stoic or Cynic virtue? If pleasure, pleasure of a gross (Aristippean) or a higher (Epicurean) kind?—and so on, all questions that are in fact treated in *Epistles* 1. It is also significant that both 1.1 and 1.2 end with Horace in a recognisably Panaetian stance: his final philosophical 'solution' to all these questions is already anticipated. And from the point of view of the formal structure of the whole of *Epistles* 1 it cannot be accidental that at the start of the book we are introduced in turn to the orthodox Stoic, Aristippus, the Cynic, and the Epicureans, whereas at the end of the overtly philosophical part of the book we re-encounter orthodox Stoic (1.16), Aristippus (1.17 and latently in 1.18), Cynic (1.17 and 1.18.5–8, 15–20), and Epicureans (1.17.6–10; 1.18.102f.).[33]

## 2 Epistles 1.10[34]

At first sight the philosophical orientation of this poem seems Stoic. The central proposition (12) is:

---

32   In fact the mediation offered by Aristippus in 1.17 is rather different from what 1.1 and 1.2 lead one to expect—cf. §3. The implications of the polarities of 1.2.17–31 and 1.1.16–19 are indeed almost kaleidoscopically complex and I cannot follow them through to the last detail in the present paper.

33   Orthodox Stoic in 1.16: cf. Kiessling–Heinze (1977) 134; McGann (1969) 73ff. (and his [[57]] fuller discussion, McGann [1960]); Aristippus latently in 1.18: lines 2–4, 10–14 with McGann (1969) 79. For a basically similar analysis of the philosophical structure of the book (but without the Cynic and Epicurean elements) see Kiessling–Heinze (1977) 7 (on 1.18) and McGann (1969) 72f.

34   Stégen (1960a) gives an excellent analysis of the formal structure of 1.10; for interpretation, the discussions of Williams (1968) 593–600 and Macleod (1979) 24–7 are both important, widely different though their conclusions are.

> uiuere naturae si conuenienter oportet.

And Horace describes his feelings when he leaves Rome as follows (8f.):

> uiuo et regno, simul ista reliqui
> quae uos ad caelum effertis rumore secundo.

Though the primary meaning of *regno* is the colloquial 'I feel like a king', the connotation 'I am/become a philosopher-king' is also present. For there have been several earlier references in the book to philosophical kingship (1.1.59f.; 1.1.107; 1.2.10) and lines 32f. run:

> licet sub paupere tecto
> reges et regum uita praecurrere amicos.

These lines, which pick up *regno* in 8 and thus round off the first main section of the poem, make a standard contrast between worldly kingship and true philosophical kingship. Hence, while *simul* too in 8 has a simple colloquial meaning ('I feel like a king as soon as I leave town'), it also acquires a philosophical colouring, alluding (however ironically) to the idea of instantaneous philosophical conversion, again a Stoic idea. Finally, the paradoxes which apply to the philosophical ideal the language of worldly triumph (24f.: *naturam ... uictrix*; 49: *post fanum putre Vacunae*, with the play of *Vacuna/Victoria*)[35] and, conversely, that of slavery to worldly riches (39–41) [[40]] are commonly regarded as typically Stoic. In fact, however, there is nothing here that could not equally well be analysed as Cynic, and the tone of lines 10f. (*utque sacerdotis fugitiuus liba recuso, | pane egeo iam mellitis potiore placentis*), with their challenging association of worldly slavery and philosophical kingship, is Cynic rather than Stoic.[36]

Lines 12ff. pose the key interpretative problem of the poem:

---

35  Varro identified *Vacuna* with *Victoria* (ps.-Acro on 1.49); on the significance of this for the interpretation of the poem see Macleod (1979) 27; for other possible (but, in my opinion, implausible) implications see Préaux (1968) 121f.

36  The idea that philosophical kingship may be manifested through the condition of worldly slavery is fundamental to Cynicism: for full discussion see Höistad (1948) 91f., 100f., 121f., 201ff. The Cynics also claimed to live in accordance with nature (cf. n. 40), used striking paradoxes which confounded worldly values, and believed in instantaneous philosophical conversion (cf., e.g., Epict. 4.8.34; Apul. *Flor.* 14).

> uiuere naturae si conuenienter oportet
> ponendaeque domo quaerenda est area primum,
> nouistine locum potiorem rure beato?

How exactly does the superiority of the simple country life bear out the philosophical proposition of 1.12, which orthodox Stoics took to mean living in accordance with the whole natural order as divinely appointed?
Different answers have been given:
(a) Line 12 is a mere gesture to philosophy (McGann, Kenney).[37]
(b) The apparently logical philosophical argument is just an amusing *tour de force* (Williams).[38]
(c) The Stoic maxim of 12 is supported by an Epicurean preference for the country and the simple life (Kiessling–Heinze, Macleod).[39]

These three explanations, different though they are, all suppose a disjunction in Horace's thought in 13ff. But there is no such disjunction: what Horace is doing is taking the maxim 'live in accordance with nature' to entail poverty (cf. 32) and primitivism, which is precisely how it was taken by the Cynics and Cynicising Stoics.[40] The link between *rus* and Cynic poverty is further emphasised by the parallel between *potiorem* (14) and *potiore* (11). Thus Horace's initial stance (even if ironical) is one of uncompromising Cynic-Stoic self-sufficiency—that extreme form of self-sufficiency which claims that one needs neither worldly possessions nor other people ('country' implies solitude, an idea assisted by the mention of urban crowds in 9).

But a shift in the argument does occur at 42f.:

> cui non conueniet sua res, ut calceus olim,
> si pede maior erit, subuertet, si minor, uret.

This passage introduces a note of moral relativism by allowing that different people may have different material needs, which, like different shoe sizes, will

---

37  McGann (1969) 58; Kenney (1977) 237.
38  Williams (1968) 593ff. Williams' further idea (594) that l. 13 alludes, with mock pedantry, to Hes. *Op.* 405: οἶκον μὲν πρώτιστα, seems wholly implausible. In fact *primum* has two levels of reference: (1) the obvious 'first you must decide where to live' (a supremely natural sentiment); and (2) 'parodiant le τέλος des philosophes' (Préaux [1968] 118). The play on two levels of meaning is certainly humorous (as in 1.8), but it does not entail philosophical incoherence.
39  Kiessling–Heinze (1977) 93 (on 1.12); Macleod (1979) 25 and n. 46.
40  Cf., e.g., D.L. 6.71 (with Moles [1983a] 116 {above, p. 339}); Sen. *Epp.* 5.4; 90.16; *De Tranq.* 8.5; *De Provid.* 6.6; Epict. 1.9.9.

be 'natural' for them (always provided, of course, that they keep within due bounds). *Conueniet* (42) has a ⟦41⟧ Panaetian flavour and the parallel and contrast with *conuenienter* in 12, which seemed to entail poverty and primitivism, signal that Horace is now arguing for the Panaetian interpretation of 'living in accordance with nature', which was quite opposed to the Cynic.[41] In Cynicism *natura* is a moral absolute, but Panaetius believed that one should harmonise one's behaviour with both universal *natura* and one's own individual *natura*.[42] Line 44 (*laetus sorte tua uiues sapienter, Aristi*) maintains this note of moral relativism, Fuscus' *sors* being different from Horace's (cf. 1–3).[43] Thus Horace now dissents from strict Cynic-Stoic self-sufficiency in two respects: he concedes that (1) it is not a universal moral absolute, hence (2) others may legitimately enjoy greater material prosperity than himself. But he for his part, equally legitimately, right to the end of the poem (49: *fanum putre*) still adheres to the ideal of Cynic-Stoic material self-sufficiency: that is his choice, appropriate to his nature.[44]

Fuscus reappears in lines 44ff., partly, as we have seen, to stress the legitimacy of Panaetian moral relativism, partly to illustrate the need for contentment with one's lot, whatever it may be, and partly to 'punish' Horace if he becomes discontented and fails his ideal of material self-sufficiency (45f.). The implications of this last thought are complex. The Cynic-Stoic stance, which Horace himself is still trying to maintain, is at once broken, upheld, and deflated by ironic incongruity. It is broken in that, were Horace a true Cynic-Stoic *rex*, there would be no question of his losing that status (of course the transitory character of Horace's *regnum* is implicit in the whole 'plot' of the poem: he is only on holiday in the country, but Horace here emphasises the point to amusing effect). But it is upheld by the idea of the *liber amicus*. It is true that line

---

41  Lines 42f. are misinterpreted by Macleod (1979) 26 ('here there is another twist in the expression which makes the homely comparison more than a platitude; it is not the shoe that has to fit us, it is we who have to fit the shoe, our condition'). The parallel with 1.7.98: *metiri se quemque suo modulo ac pede uerum est*, which in turn echoes Cic. *De Off.* 1.110 = Panaetius F 97 {van Straaten}: *ut etiamsi sint alia grauiora atque meliora, tamen nos studia nostra nostrae naturae regula metiamur*, proves that lines 42f. are a statement of Panaetian moral relativism. Cf. also McGann (1969) 11, 13, 59.

42  Cic. *De Off.* 1.110.

43  The second persons of l. 44 are simultaneously appropriate to Fuscus and general (referring to how 'one' ought to behave).

44  Thus in strict philosophical terms what Horace has done in lines 42ff. is to make Cynic-Stoic self-sufficiency into one of the options which a man may choose if it suits his own *natura*. Panaetius himself would not have approved of this (cf. Cic. *De Off.* 1.148 for his rejection of Cynicism), but Horace is of course not a slavish follower of Panaetius.

45 contains a pleasant allusion to Fuscus the school-teacher,[45] that it is a good joke that a school-teacher should be requested to punish someone for doing too much and 'not slacking' (*non cessare*), and that the friend who helps by offering criticism is a familiar figure in ancient ethics generally.[46] But the activities 'doing too much' and 'not slacking' are, after all, lapses from Cynic-Stoic self-sufficiency, so that in context the picture of the teacher who punishes a wrong-doer for his own good must reflect the Cynic concept of the διδάσκαλος or the παιδαγωγός who punishes sinners (including, if need be, friends) to improve them.[47] In so far as Horace in 45f. falls short of the Cynic-Stoic ideal which he has set himself, it is philosophically proper that he should need the services of a critical friend to set him right. Naturally, once he has regained his ideal, he will no longer need his friend. But this serious Cynic concept ⟦42⟧ is in turn deflated by the comic incongruity of the role being performed by Fuscus, lover of the city (with all that that implies) and hitherto the philosophical pupil and recipient of the wise exhortations of Horace, Cynic-Stoic *rex*.[48] Hence 45f. further undermine the Cynic-Stoic model.

The last two lines of the poem find Horace himself still faithful to the ideal of material self-sufficiency (though with a question-mark hanging over his ability to sustain it). But what is his attitude to the other implication of Cynic-Stoic self-sufficiency—that, if one is truly self-sufficient, one does not need other people?

Line 50 (*excepto quod non simul esses, cetera laetus*) echoes line 3 (*multum dissimiles, at cetera paene gemelli*). That discussion of the two friends' characters makes an implicit challenge to the normal ancient assumption that friendship depends on 'likeness'.[49] Horace's remarks are potentially still more pointed because this assumption had been elevated to the status of philosophical doctrine by the Cynics and strict Stoics, who both argued that 'the wise man [or, on a lower level, the philosopher] is the friend of his like'.[50] True friendship can only exist with other wise men or philosophers and such friendships are freely chosen: the self-sufficient Cynic or Stoic does not actually need friends. Hence in Cynic and Stoic texts 'like' and 'unlike' are almost technical

---

45   Nisbet (1959) 74f. {= (1995) 3}.
46   Cf., e.g., Hor. *Sat.* 1.4.132; *Epod.* 11.25; Arist. *EN* 8, 1159b7ff.; Cic. *Amic.* 88; Plut. *Mor.* 50B, 51C, 59D; Macleod (1977) 375 and nn. 91–2.
47   For references see Moles (1983a) 112 {above, p. 332} n. 73; 111 {above, p. 331} n. 67; for the abrasive Cynic ⟦58⟧ conception of the usefulness of friends cf., e.g., Crates F 1.5 Diehl; Stob. 3.13.44; 3.8.20; Plut. *Mor.* 89B = Antisth. F 77 DC {= 109 Prince}.
48   Macleod's analysis at this point ([1979] 27) is too solemn.
49   Arist. *EN* 8, 1155a32ff., etc.
50   D.L. 6.105 (Cynics); *SVF* III.160.40–3, 162.2.

terms, denoting those with whom the wise man, or the philosopher, may legitimately be friends and those with whom he may not.[51] Line 3, therefore, by asserting close friendship with a *dissimilis*, sets up a potential conflict with this doctrine, a conflict which comes closer to realisation once Horace appears as Cynic-Stoic *rex* (as he does by 33, which, as we have seen, activates the latent philosophical implications of 8). Thus in 50, right up to the two final words of the poem, Horace poses the question: is it philosophically right for him *qua* Cynic-Stoic *rex*, to be friends with Fuscus? For, when he wishes that Fuscus *simul esses*, is he wishing the presence of a *dissimilis*, or would Fuscus become a *similis* by the mere fact of joining him in the country *simul* (50, 3, 8)?

But he answers the question himself—by finally changing his own philosophical position. His 'joy' (50: *laetus*), while real, is incomplete without Fuscus. This point seems to be emphasised by the repeated *laetus* (50, 44): Fuscus' more relaxed stance seems to provide something that in the last resort Horace's austere ideal cannot. To be completely happy, Horace needs Fuscus—this is not a matter of the free association of Cynic-Stoic *similes*—and he needs him, not as an abrasive Cynic παιδαγωγός (45f.) but as a friend [[43]] whom he loves and who loves him, despite their 'difference' (3ff.). And now at last we see that a plaintive message underlies all the high-flown philosophical arguments for the superiority of the primitive life: 'Dear Fuscus, it's much better in the country, but I'm feeling rather lonely, please come and see me.' So, in the very last line, Horace rejects Cynic-Stoic isolationism in favour of the Epicurean ideal of friendship: though the Epicureans, like the Cynics and strict Stoics, claimed self-sufficiency, they regarded friendship as indispensable for the truly happy life.[52]

The philosophical content of *Epistles* 1.10 has been greatly underestimated. Many of the effects stem from manipulation of philosophical ideas. The poem does have a philosophical argument and that argument, with Horace first adopting, and then, point by point, rejecting, extreme Cynic-Stoic self-sufficiency, in favour, initially, of Panaetian relativism and, finally, of Epicurean friendship, is tight. Moreover, as Préaux and McGann have shown, 1.10 functions as the corner-stone of, so to speak, the thematic architecture of the book.[53] But since it openly compares the merits of the Stoic, Cynic, Panaetian, and Epicurean

---

51 Cf., e.g., Sen. *Ep.* 5.2–6; 7.6–8; 18.3, and in Cynicism see Moles (1983a) 110–16 {above, pp. 328–38}.
52 Epic. FF 174–5.; BD 21–2; VS 13.23.52; for Epicurean views on friendship see recently Rist (1980); the difference between the Cynic-Stoic and Epicurean positions is well analysed by Sen. *Ep.* 9.1ff.
53 Préaux (1968) 4, 122; McGann (1969) 60; cf. Maurach (1968) 101ff.

positions, it also acts as the corner-stone of the philosophical architecture of the book, looking back to *Epistles* 1.1 and 1.2 and forward to 1.16, 1.17, and 1.18.[54]

## 3 Epistles 1.17[55]

1.10 has rejected the Cynic claim of emotional self-sufficiency, but not, or at least not unequivocally, that of material self-sufficiency. This is examined in 1.17.

The philosophical background here poses no difficulty. On McGann's analysis the endorsement of the principle *maioribus uti* and rejection of Cynic extremes should be Panaetian. Specifically Panaetian elements are the use of the criterion *decet* (2, 23, 26), the *persona* doctrine (28f.), the insistence that the virtuous man may legitimately seek *decus* and *pretium* (42), and, to some extent, the view of Aristippus (22f.),[56] though this may owe something to Xenophon's *Memorabilia*[57] and certainly draws upon the general Aristippus legend as well. The Aristippus-Diogenes anecdote was also used in the debate within Cynicism as to whether philosophers should associate with rulers.[58] Horace is right to suppose that true Cynicism spurns such associations[59] and can have no truck either with the moral relativism of the *persona* doctrine, even though that doctrine is found in Bion and Teles.[60]

The general interpretation of the poem is also relatively ⟦44⟧ straightforward. Though Horace points out that Aristippus can play the roles of both social

---

54  Cf. my discussion above.
55  The key discussions of this poem are Williams (1968) 14–17; McGann (1969) 75–7; Macleod (1979) 18f.
56  McGann (1969) 12, 22f.; Cic. *De Off* 1.128; 1.148 (rejection of Cynicism); 1.107ff. (*persona* doctrine); 2.31ff. (glory); 1.17; D.L. 7.128 (wealth); Cic. *De Off*. 1.148 (special status of Aristippus).
57  Cf. Nickel (1980).
58  Cf. Hock (1976) 49–52.
59  That is the single most important point of the various stories about Alexander's dealings with Diogenes; cf. also Diogenes' derisive description of Aristippus as a βασιλικὸν κύνα (D.L. 2.66). Kindstrand (1976) 14 completely misunderstands the proper Cynic attitude to this question.
60  Teles pp. 5.2–6.8 Hense = Bion F 16A Kindstrand; cf. also Teles p. 16.4–7; p. 52.2–5 Hense. Neither Kindstrand (1976) 206ff. nor De Lacy (1977) 165 finds it odd that a Cynic should expound such a doctrine, but true Cynicism, as Horace recognises here, in *Epist*. 1.10, and indeed in 1.2.17 (contrasting with 1.1.41f.—cf. n. 29 above), proclaims moral absolutes. Teles is simply following Bion (*suo more*) and Bion may well have got the doctrine from his Cyrenaic teacher Theodorus (cf. D.L. 2.66 for Aristippus and the πρόσωπον doctrine). It was well suited to the ambiguity of Bion's own career (both 'Cynic' and court-philosopher), as indeed it had been to Aristippus'.

dependent and Cynic (23ff., 29), the main purpose of the Aristippus-Diogenes debate is to arbitrate between the claims of social dependence and Cynic self-sufficiency. The argument goes decisively against the latter (17, 32) and the stock point is made that the Cynic claim to material self-sufficiency is anyway fraudulent, since Cynics have to beg (19f., 21). The fact that now, in contrast to *Epistles* 1.10, the Cynic appears as a city-dweller who relies on the charity of others further undermines the Cynic primitivist ideal. The initial sketch of the Epicurean position (6–10) seems to suggest that an individual may legitimately, if he pleases, reject social dependence, but if so, the Epicurean way is far superior to the Cynic. It is the Epicurean who lives in the country and is the true primitive. The Cynic is as much a dependent as those whose dependence he contemns.

All this is obvious enough. Scholars have, however, I believe, failed to appreciate quite how sustained and detailed the attack upon Cynicism is and have consequently misconceived Scaeva's role in the poem.

To the Cynic, Aristippus stands for luxury, decadence, and effeminacy, the Cynic himself being the only true *uir*. Lines 33ff. subvert this analysis in detail and do so by employing a standard polemical technique—that of appropriating one's opponent's terms of approval, reversing them, and using them to commend the very concepts that he most abhors. The statement (33ff.) that military success denotes god-like *uirtus* is immediately challenging,[61] for the Cynics completely rejected the claims of military success. To the Cynic the idea that successful association with *principes* is also a form of *uirtus* (35) is still more absurd: in his view such associations are tantamount to spiritual enslavement.[62] The Cynic counters Horace's assertions by arguing that the acquisition of material goods is a matter of pure chance (36: *contingit*),[63] so that one cannot base a moral claim upon it—quite the reverse:

---

61  There is no doubt also something in McGann's interpretation of the transition at lines 33ff. ([1969] 75: 'but with this ποικιλία he [Aristippus] is very much a Greek, and his qualities will not count greatly with anyone whose ideal is Roman *uirtus*. Horace therefore moves into a Roman context, speaking firstly of men whose *uirtus* is pre-eminent'), but the primary function of 33ff. is to attack the Cynic position.

62  Cf. n. 59 above. That Horace himself endorses l. 35 is further shown by the closely parallel 1.20.23: *me primis urbis belli placuisse domique* (on the parallel, which disposes of the arguments of Williams (1968) 17, see, e.g., Kiessling–Heinze (1977) 153; McGann (1969) 86; Macleod (1979) 19); cf. also *Sat.* 1.6.62f.: *magnum hoc ego duco | quod placui tibi* (Maecenas).

63  For this implication of *contingit* see Kiessling–Heinze (1977) 154 and Préaux (1968) 181 (and cf. 1.17.9 and 1.4.10). 36 is clearly spoken by Horace's Cynic opponent: see Kiessling–Heinze (1977) *ad loc.* (their analysis of lines 33ff. is generally perspicacious [[59]] though insufficiently detailed).

> non cuiuis homini contingit adire Corinthum.

'Corinth' has general implications of luxury and decadence but it is particularly relevant here that both Aristippus and Diogenes frequented Corinth and for very different reasons—Aristippus to patronise Lais, Diogenes to castigate vice.[64] Horace's reply (37) that failure to take part in the race for material goods may indicate cowardice attacks the Cynic belief that it is Cynic poverty that ⟦45⟧ requires 'bravery'.[65] The Cynic concedes Horace's point (37: *esto*: the concession is presumably only formal), but asks if the man who does enter this race can be a *uir*, which on the Cynic view he of course cannot be. He errs, however, in using the verb *peruenit* (38), which, in contrast to *contingit* (36), might seem to admit that such a policy entails purposeful action.[66] Horace agrees that this is indeed the crucial question and exploits his opponent's error by applying positive Cynic concepts ('burden', 'bearing', 'stamina') to the task of associating with *principes*, while ridiculing the Cynic claim to both moral and physical strength (38–41):[67]

> atqui
> hic est aut nusquam quod quaerimus. hic onus horret,
> ut paruis animis et paruo corpore maius,
> hic subit et perfert.

The reversal is complete: it is the successful social dependent who is the true *uir*, the Cynic the weakling. Horace now sums up the debate (41f.):

> aut uirtus nomen inane est,
> aut decus et pretium recte petit experiens uir.

---

64  Line 36 does not mean 'not everyone can reach his goal in life' (Dilke [1986] 134), nor 'not everyone can gain the prize of virtue' (Fairclough [1929] 363 n. d), but 'it does not fall to every man to attain the life of luxury', i.e., the meaning is very close to that of the original Greek proverb but with an implicit sneer at worldly riches. Cf. Wilamowitz (1893) II.24, who actually cites the Greek proverb before stating the different reasons why Aristippus and Diogenes went to Corinth (cf. D.L. 2.75; Dio 8.5).
65  Cf., e.g., D.L. 6.14; Dio 4.7.
66  Cf. the excellent comments of Kiessling–Heinze (1977) on l. 36 and Préaux (1968) on l. 38.
67  Cf. the basic Cynic doctrine πόνος ἀγαθόν (D.L. 6.2; 6.71; etc.); φέρω: cf., e.g., D.L. 4.48 = Bion F 23 Kindstrand (with Kindstrand [1976] *ad loc.*); Cynic ἰσχύς: cf., e.g., D.L. 6.11. Note how in lines 30ff. Horace leaves the reader with an impression of Diogenes in physical straits, thus preparing for 40: *paruo corpore*.

Either *uirtus* (that is, *uirtus* as understood by the Cynics) is a mere name without substance and without reward (*inane* has financial implications)[68] or the man who tries and suffers (that is, by associating with *principes*) is right to aim at honour and reward (both of which of course the Cynics totally rejected).[69] *Experiens* again subverts Cynic terminology.[70] So, even more pointedly, does the phrase *uirtus nomen inane est*. These words were spoken by the dying Heracles and were part of the Cynic debate about his moral decline and resort to suicide. The Cynic Heracles utters the words when he has failed to maintain Cynic standards and has succumbed to luxury:[71] Horace adroitly turns a Cynic condemnation of luxury into a criticism of Cynic poverty.

Even when he has made his case that one should associate with the great and has begun to analyse the best means of squeezing money out of one's patron, Horace continues to criticise Cynic behaviour. A *rex* is a *rex* in any context (43, 13ff.) and the same general principles of association apply. *Poscente* (44) picks up *poscis* (21): whether one claims to reject social dependence, like Diogenes, or accepts it, begging is a demeaning and ineffective technique of securing one's wants. Finally, what is the function of the story of the beggar who has broken his leg and vainly solicits help (58–62)? ⟦46⟧ Scholars generally have seen this as a discordant, even intrusive, element in the poem.[72] In fact, however, it represents Horace's final demolition of Cynic self-sufficiency and brings his argument to a triumphant conclusion. The beggar recalls the characteristic Cynic itinerant (59: *planum*), who 'mocks at' passers-by (58: *irrisus*), loiters at street-corners (58: *triuiis*), and has so alienated his fellow human beings that in his greatest need he can only beg for help, like Diogenes himself (19ff.).[73] Cynic

---

68  It can have such implications anyway (cf. *OLD*, s.v. 6), but they are brought out by the contrast with *decus* and *pretium*.
69  Cf. in general Kindstrand (1976) 60f.
70  It 'glosses' something like καρτερικός: cf., e.g., Ov. *Met.* 1.414: *genus durum sumus experiensque laborum*; 14.159: *experientis Ulixei*. Closely parallel to 1.17.42 is 1.18.86f.: *dulcis inexpertis cultura potentis amici*: | *expertus metuit* (cf. McGann [1969] 78)—another indication (cf. n. 62 above) of the seriousness of Horace's argument here.
71  Cf. Nisbet–Hubbard (1978) 114; *Trag. adesp.* 374N² {= *TrGF* 88 F 3 (1.256)} = Cass. Dio 47.49.1f.; cf. Florus 2.17.11; Zonaras 10.20; for discussion of the Cynic background to the lines see Wilamowitz (1895) 1.103 (n. 186 from p. 102); Höistad (1948) 54f., 61, 66f.; cf. also Moles (1983b) 778f. {vol. 2, pp. 31–3f.}.
72  Cf. the comments of McGann (1969) 77.
73  Cynic 'wanderers': cf., e.g., Bion F 16A Kindstrand with Kindstrand (1976) 208; on the actual status of the *planus* in Roman society see Préaux (1968) 183 and articles cited there; the classic description of 'street' Cynics is Dio 32.9; the beggar may invoke Osiris (l. 60) because he is an Alexandrian Cynic (cf. again Dio 32.9).

self-sufficiency is a sham. In the next poem (1.18.5–8, 15–20) Horace will turn his attack on Cynic behaviour *within* society.

Close analysis, therefore, proves, contrary to the views of Fraenkel, Williams, and other scholars,[74] that the question posed in 1.17—which is better, social dependence or Cynic self-sufficiency?—and the answer given—social dependence—are both wholly serious, otherwise Horace's detailed and sustained attack on Cynicism, couched as it is in the sharpest of philosophical polemic, would be pointless.

Where does Scaeva fit in this picture? On the usual view Scaeva is a careerist, who associates with the great but does so unsuccessfully because of social incompetence (signified by his name, Scaeva). Williams, by contrast, believes no criticism of Scaeva to be intended.[75] Neither interpretation convinces.

The opening lines present a Scaeva who is self-sufficient (1: *per te tibi*) and who knows all about how to associate with the great, whereas Horace appears as the bumbling *proficiens*, though he still claims friendship with Scaeva (3: *docendus ... amiculus*). Thus Horace is again concerned with the 'like–unlike' problem of friendship which has already been raised in 1.10, though there has been an amusing reversal of roles, for in the earlier poem it was Horace who seemed to be the man with the philosophical answers, his friend the beginner. Scaeva will thus find it hard to make *proprium* (5) the thoughts of the philosophically incompetent Horace. In reality, however, Scaeva is a brash youth, who needs sound advice from an older and more experienced man (16: *uel iunior audi*). The debate about the merits of social dependence and Cynic isolationism is, as we have seen, central to the poem. If Scaeva is already committed to social dependence, why does Horace discuss, and at such great length, the prior question whether it is justified at all, and why does he put this question directly to Scaeva (15ff.), if Scaeva already accepts his conclusion? The point is rather that the self-sufficient Scaeva, who wrongly regards Horace as his inferior, whose self-sufficiency [[47]] is illusory, and whose name means 'gauche', 'boorish', 'perverse'—all, for obvious reasons, epithets commonly applied to Cynics[76]—is to the Panaetian Horace as Diogenes is to the Panaetian Aristippus. He is a Cynic type, who simply does not accept that one should associate with the great and must be persuaded. The opening lines are therefore ironic, not because Scaeva associates with the great incompetently, but because the Panaetian concept of *decet*, with all its civilised social

---

74   Fraenkel (1957) 321f.; Williams (1968) 14ff.; Reckford (1959) 206 n. 21; for sensible observations on the other side see now J. Griffin (1984) 196f.
75   Careerist: Fraenkel (1957) 321; Williams (1968) 14ff.
76   Cf., e.g., Dio 4.18; Plut. *Brut.* 34.5; Sen. *Ep.* 5.2.

implications, is as alien to him (2) as it is to Diogenes (26). In a poem marked by rigorous philosophical argument the relationship between content and addressee is appropriately close.[77] The reversal of roles from 1.10 is thus even sharper than it first seemed: in 1.10 Horace stood for Cynicism, his friend for Panaetianism; here his friend stands for Cynicism, Horace for Panaetianism.

This analysis has shown some connections between 1.17 and 1.10. There are also important links between 1.17 and 1.2, whose significance must now be explored.

In 1.2 the central figure is Odysseus, in 1.17 Diogenes. Both are great Cynic exemplars, both represent *uirtus* and self-sufficiency at their most extreme. In 1.2 the contrast between Odysseus and his companions, the suitors, and the Phaeacians is expressed in terms of a contrast between Cynicism and Epicureanism; one side of Aristippus, the 'pleasure' side, is aligned with Epicureanism, though there is another side, that of supreme adaptability, which means that Aristippus can play any role assigned to him. In 1.17 Diogenes is contrasted with Aristippus and the Epicureans, both of whom reject the unremitting austerity of Cynicism. But the positions of Aristippus and the Epicureans are now also themselves distinct. Supremely adaptable though Aristippus in theory still is (1.17.23ff.), in practice his adaptability enables him to play the parts of both social dependent and ascetic Cynic (1.17, 29), not that of the Epicurean, who is associated with the quite separate world of the country. Between 1.2 and 1.17 there has been a great change in the portrayal of Epicureanism: in 1.2 Epicureanism stands for Pleasure in a gross sense, in 1.17 for the 'hidden life' (10) and only quiet and moderate pleasures (6). There has been a corresponding change in Aristippus: in so far as he still stands for Pleasure and material gratifications, his needs are satisfied through social dependence, not Epicureanism, but he is in any case less representative

---

77   Two questions therefore arise: (1) is Scaeva a real person? (2) is it plausible to posit criticism of an addressee? Some scholars have supposed Scaeva to be a fictional character (e.g., Kiessling–Heinze [1977] 147; Morris [1931] 101, 104, 108; Maurach [1968] 114 n. 127), partly indeed on the ground that he seems to be criticised (cf. Williams [1968] 14f.). But the indubitable historicity of most of the addressees in *Epistles* 1 tells against this (cf. Williams; Préaux's idea ([1968] 177) that Scaeva is the son of the famous centurion of Caes. BC 3.53, etc. has, however, little to commend it). (2) is therefore the critical question, to which different ⟦60⟧ scholars, in the *Epistles* as in the *Odes*, return different answers. Certainly, addressees may be *formally* criticised: cf., e.g., 1.1.3f. (Maecenas wants Horace to continue writing frivolous poetry); 1.2.2 (the folly of Lollius' rhetorical studies); 1.8 (to Celsus—cf. McGann (1969) 57); 1.12 (gentle mockery of Iccius' 'lofty' philosophical concerns and the gap between them and his actual behaviour—cf. *Odes* 1.29). We can therefore say that (a) an addressee may be formally criticised, though often in a humorous, ironical, way, and (b) this criticism may relate to more general concerns of the poem.

of Pleasure as such than of the Panaetian moderation which Horace himself espouses. To put it another way, Aristippus and the Epicureans begin at the same pole, ⟦48⟧ Pleasure, of the basic polarity, Pleasure–Virtue, but end up offering quite different, but equally viable, mediations of this polarity.

These philosophical relationships were keyed initially, as we have seen, by the parallel and contrast between the Cynic–Epicurean polarity of 1.2.17–31 and the Stoic–Aristippus polarity of 1.1.16–19. Their subsequent rearrangement is conveyed above all through the fact that 1.17.33–42 inverts the imagery of 1.2.17–31.

In 1.2.17–31 *uirtus* characterises the Cynic, effeminacy the Epicureans and Aristippus. The Cynic Odysseus is the independent individualist, the companions, suitors, and Phaeacians are all, in various ways, dependents: the companions depend on Odysseus (21) and even more, once thoroughly corrupted, on Circe (24ff.); the suitors sponge off Odysseus' estate and woo Penelope; the Phaeacians are quite commonly regarded as parasites.[78] But in 1.17.33–42 the Cynic claim to *uirtus* is comprehensively overturned, as we have seen, and Cynicism appears as an unmanly, cowardly thing. Contrary to the Cynic view, social dependence is not dishonourable *per se*: the role of dependent can be performed ignobly, as by the companions, suitors, and Phaeacians, or honourably, as by Aristippus and in accordance with Panaetian principles, in which case *uirtus* can be attained. But Epicureanism, too, allows a kind of *uirtus*. This idea is foreshadowed in 1.17.10:

nec uixit male, qui natus moriensque fefellit[79]

and reinforced by 1.17.36:

non cuiuis homini contingit adire Corinthum.

The wording of the Cynic's sneer at the fortuitous nature (as he sees it) of worldly success recalls Horace's own remark about the blessings of the Epicurean 'hidden life' at 1.17.9:

nam neque diuitibus contingunt gaudia solis.

To the Cynic Horace replies directly that worldly success is not restricted to those who are rich by accident of birth: it can be achieved by social dependents

---

78   Cf., e.g., Philodemus p. 35 Crönent; Lucian, *Parasit.* 10; [Crates] *Ep.* 19.
79   *Male* is ambiguous in the same way as *bene* in 1.6.56.

who make an honest effort. But the parallel between 1.17.36 and 1.17.9 unobtrusively suggests that Epicurean withdrawal offers something of equal value, similar to Panaetian social dependence in that one does not have to be rich to achieve it, but different from it in that success is not measured in material terms.

⟦49⟧ 4 Some General Observations and Conclusions

From this analysis Cynicism emerges as an important strand in the philosophical fabric of *Epistles* 1. It is a major component of the subject matter of not only 1.17 and 1.18 but also 1.2 and 1.10. Recognition of this fact greatly affects our interpretation of the individual poems, their interrelationships, and the philosophical structure of the book.

Horace has a sound general grasp of the meaning of Cynicism—he understands, for example, that it is absolutely opposed to any association with the great of this world and to the moral relativism of Panaetian *persona* doctrine. As one would expect of the poet of the *Satires*, he has also quite a detailed knowledge of favourite Cynic motifs and patterns of thought. His critique of Cynicism is preponderantly negative. Cynic φιλανθρωπία, which was certainly a significant element of Cynicism, is indeed acknowledged—in Horace's exhortation to Lollius (1.2), Nestor's efforts as reconciler (1.2.11f.), Odysseus' concern for his men (1.2.21), and perhaps also (and even if so, only with marked irony) in Horace's own attempt to 'convert' his friend Fuscus to the life of primitivism (1.10). But the emphasis is much more on Cynic independence and self-sufficiency. In the end, Horace seems not only to reject, but even to dislike, Cynicism—the natural response of a man who was genuinely proud *primis urbis belli placuisse domique* (1.20.23).[80]

This analysis of 1.2, 1.10, and 1.17 should also enable us to give some precise answers to the fundamental problems of interpretation mentioned at the beginning of the paper. These poems may properly be described as philosophical, in that they explore ethical and moral problems through the recognisable positions of the different philosophical schools: the reader has to recognise that, for example, 1.1.16f. refers to the ethical stance of the orthodox Stoic, that 1.1.11 and 1.2.3 use Panaetian criteria of moral assessment, and so on. The philosophical language matters for two main reasons. (1) Since the Hellenistic philosophies generally did address themselves to the problems of practical living, one's choice of philosophy should in theory affect how one actually lives

---

80  Cf. n. 62.

one's life. So the questions 'how should I live my life?' and 'which philosophy should I choose?' are simply different ways of asking the same thing: ethical investigations are thus fittingly conducted in formal philosophical language.[81] (2) In these poems the development of the argument is characteristically articulated by shifts in formal philosophical position, which act as 'signposts' for the reader, who must of course possess sufficient [[50]] knowledge of philosophical terminology to be able to detect them. Thus in 1.10 the reader has to see that 1.10.12 states a basic Stoic maxim, that this is subsequently given a Cynic interpretation, that 1.10.42 alludes (with deft economy) to the quite different Panaetian understanding of living in accordance with nature, and that each of these shifts marks a substantive change in the argument.

The philosophical language, then, fulfils a real function. At no point does Horace indulge in empty philosophical polemic: the attack on Cynic ethics in 1.17.33ff. is indeed polemical, but it is also essential to the whole meaning of the poem. It is of course true that Horace creates many humorous effects from the exploitation of philosophical ideas, as for example in the *simul–similis* pun of 1.10.3, 1.10.8, and 1.10.50, the comic absurdity of Fuscus being cast in the role of Cynic παιδαγωγός, (1.10.45), the jesting oxymoron *agilis fio* of 1.1.16. But these effects are not merely humorous, since they pinpoint real philosophical problems. The *simul–similis* play highlights the questions 'can one be true friends with someone who is fundamentally different from oneself?' and 'can one attain the status of philosopher-king simply by renouncing material things, as the Cynics claim?'. The ludicrous characterisation of Fuscus as παιδαγωγός enables Horace to reject the Cynic answer to the question 'what are friends for?' in favour of the Epicurean answer. And the *agilis fio* oxymoron introduces a theme of major significance in the *Epistles*: the sheer difficulty of translating philosophical belief into appropriate action.[82]

Are the poems which I have discussed, then, basically serious? To some extent the question should not be formulated in this way, since in the *Epistles* meaning is often created by the interaction of one poem with another. One might say that the question of seriousness hardly arises in the case of 1.2, a poem which, like 1.1, is essentially programmatic, in that its main concern is to give a sketch of the general philosophical landscape. But even these poems cannot really be considered in isolation from the rest of the book: both adumbrate concerns which will receive fuller treatment elsewhere. Nevertheless, some of the *Epistles* are clearly more weighty than others, and 1.10 and 1.17, for all their wit and humour, in the end do seem to make serious statements:

---

81  For a somewhat different emphasis see Macleod (1979) 17f.
82  For other functions of the humour of the *Epistles* see Macleod (1979) 18, 20f.

the endorsement of the Epicurean ideal of friendship in 1.10 seems unequivocal and the rejection of Cynic isolationism in 1.17 categorical. In both cases Horace's final position has been reached by sustained and (to a degree) trenchant argument, nor do these positions seem to be modified by any subsequent poems. [[51]] Horace the serious moralist may be an old-fashioned notion, but in these two cases at least I believe it to be correct.[83]

A final question: why does Horace give such prominence to Cynicism in Book 1 of the *Epistles*? Cynicism, after all, was never a formal philosophical school like Stoicism, Epicureanism, and the rest. Indeed, some scholars believe that as a philosophical movement it actually died out in the last two centuries BC and when it revived in the first century AD it had been reborn out of Stoicism.[84] Even if this were true, Horace's allusions to Cynics and Cynic beliefs in the *Epistles* could still be given point. Educated Romans had some acquaintance with written Cynic philosophy, such as it was, and were surely familiar with many of the sayings and exploits of Diogenes (however apocryphal). They would also have read some of the works of Greek writers influenced by Cynicism (Bion, Menippus, Teles, Meleager, perhaps Cercidas). Cynicism also had a direct influence upon some Latin literature, notably the satires of Lucilius, Varro, and Horace himself, to say nothing of the diffuse influence of the 'diatribe', a form originating in Cynic writings.[85] Thus Horace could have used Diogenes and the Cynic as a sort of timeless symbol of a particular set of philosophical attitudes, as he certainly does use Aristippus, from whom no active philosophical tradition survived in the first century BC. If so, he might have taken his inspiration from Panaetius, who campaigned against Cynic ethics in his Περὶ τοῦ καθήκοντος.[86]

In fact, however, scholars who assert the demise of Cynicism during this period have been misled by mistaken modern notions of philosophical 'significance': the mere fact that a philosophy fails to produce 'significant' figures in a particular era (as was undoubtedly true of Cynicism at this time) does not prove that there were no living adherents of the philosophy at all.[87] There

---

83  Macleod (1979) 18, 24–7 reaches the same general conclusion by a different route.
84  For this controversy see recently Billerbeck (1978) 1–3; (1979) 1–11; (1982) 151–5; Moles (1983a) 120–3 {above, pp. 344–50} (a position I still maintain).
85  I hope that as a general picture this may be broadly acceptable, though I cannot here substantiate the more contentious items. Cicero read Antisthenes extensively (*Ad Att.* 12.38a.2) and knew about Diogenes' life and views. For Cynic influence on Roman satire the works of Heinze (1889) and Fiske (1920) remain indispensable (however suspect many of their detailed claims).
86  Cf. n. 56 above.
87  So, for example, 'suivant nos sources, la première figure qui, à Rome, passa pour un cynique proprement dit fut Demétrius' (Billerbeck [1982] 158) seems to me a dangerous formulation of the problem.

is sufficient evidence to show that Cynicism still existed as a philosophical movement in the Late Republic and that Horace and his contemporaries were familiar with the Cynic type in real life. There are allusions to Cynics in Roman comedy and a mime of Laberius, and there were Cynics on the streets of Greek cities in the Augustan period. Brutus and Cassius saw in M. Favonius debased Cynic characteristics, Clodius mockingly described Cicero as the 'Cynic consular', and Horace himself gives the nickname *Canis* to Avidienus in *Satires* 2.2.56.[88] Moreover, in *Epistles* 1.17.58ff., as we have seen, the description of the beggar clearly recalls the typical Cynic and this episode has a Roman setting: Horace's readers must have been familiar with such figures from [[52]] their own experience (it is immaterial whether such beggars were 'true' Cynics or not—what matters is that they could plausibly be so regarded).

Furthermore, Cynicism admits of various degrees. First, there is the true Cynic, who acts out Cynic beliefs in his way of life. Second, there is the Cynicising Stoic, who from a position within Stoicism takes Cynic attitudes, which are sharply distinct from those of both orthodox and Panaetian Stoics, and/or adopts a Cynic way of life (wearing the simplest of clothing, going barefoot, etc.).[89] Into this category come, for example, the major Stoic philosopher Ariston of Chios in the middle of the third century BC, the *Stoici paene Cynici* attested by Cicero in the first century,[90] and even the younger Cato as described by Horace in *Epistles* 1.19.12f. (*uoltu toruo ferus et pede nudo | exiguaeque togae ... textore*). Third, there are individuals who possess particular characteristics (like Favonius, Cicero, Avidienus, or, in the *Epistles*, Lollius and Scaeva) which make them readily assimilable to the Cynic type. They themselves are of course very far from being true Cynics but in a philosophical context they may provide a convenient point of departure for examination of Cynic ethics.

Thus when Horace talks about Cynics and Cynic ideas in the *Epistles*, he is talking about something that was real in his own day. But this of itself does not explain the prominence he gives to Cynicism. Here the general character of the *Epistles* becomes important. Although these poems consider the claims of practically the whole gamut of philosophical schools (with a few striking exceptions),[91] they do so at a relatively simple level. The philosophy is all moral philosophy: so-called 'hard', technical philosophy has no place. And even within moral philosophy, complexities are avoided. This must be a deliberate omission: Epicurean, Panaetian, and, above all, orthodox Stoic ethics

---

88 Clodius on Cicero: Cic. *Ad Att.* 2.9.1; for the other material see Moles (1983a) 121 {above, p. 346}.

89 For Cynicism within Stoicism cf. e.g. Billerbeck (1979) 3f.; M. T. Griffin (1976) 297ff.

90 *De Off* 1.128 (with Moles [1983a] 122 {above, pp. 347–8}).

91 The Academy and the Peripatos, for example, are not given separate treatment, partly, indeed, because they are subsumed within Panaetianism (cf. McGann [1969] 17).

can be highly complex. Indeed it is remarkable how little attention Horace devotes to orthodox Stoicism, which features only really at *Epistles* 1.1.16f., 1.10.8 (before the reader sees that the maxim is interpreted along Cynic lines), and 1.16.52ff.[92] The reason for this exclusion of philosophical complexities is obvious. Whereas professional philosophers in search of ultimate truths, eager to make their systems watertight at every point, must be prepared to engage in detailed and complex argument, Horace is conducting an investigation of the everyday problems of living at a simple, practical level. Hence Epicurean and Panaetian ethics, both suitably simplified, and Cynic ethics, which are intrinsically ⟦53⟧ simple, provide appropriate media for his ethical investigations, but Stoic ethics, beyond a certain point, do not. Cynicism has the additional advantage that it offers the same general kind of conception of virtue as orthodox Stoicism: through Cynicism Horace can cover the same ground without becoming swamped by Stoic logic, Stoic paradoxes, and so on. There are two other main reasons for the prominence of Cynicism. First, it represents an extreme position and thus can well take its place in the polar opposition between Virtue and Pleasure which shapes Horace's arrangement of his formal philosophical material. Second, one of the most important single questions considered in the *Epistles* is: 'what place should philosophy play in our lives?'. Here the claims of Cynicism at least deserve a hearing, for of all ancient philosophies Cynicism most nearly brought philosophy and life together. From that point of view, if from no other, the Cynics are worthy opponents and Horace is right to take them seriously, even though in the end he condemns them.

## Bibliography

Becker, C. (1963) *Das Spätwerk des Horaz* (Göttingen).
Billerbeck, M. (1978) *Epiktet: vom Kynismus* (Leiden).
Billerbeck, M. (1979) *Der Kyniker Demetrius: ein Beitrag zur Geschichte der frühkaiserzeitlichen Popularphilosophie* (Leiden).
Billerbeck, M. (1982) 'La réception du Cynisme à Rome', *L'Antiquité Classique* 51: 151–73; repr. as 'Greek Cynicism in Imperial Rome', in Billerbeck (1991) 147–66.
Billerbeck, M., ed. (1991) *Die Kyniker in der modernen Forschung: Aufsätze mit Einführung und Bibliographie* (Amsterdam).
Brancacci, A. (1980) 'Democrito e la tradizione cinica', *Siculorum Gymnasium* 33: 411–25.
Cairns, F. (1983) 'Propertius 1.4 and 1.5 and the "Gallus" of the Monobiblos', *PLLS* 4: 61–103; repr. in id., *Papers on Roman Elegy (1969–2003)* (Bologna, 2007) 59–93.

---

92  Cf. McGann (1969) 75.

Courbaud, E. (1914) *Horace, sa vie et sa pensée à l'époque des epîtres: étude sur le premier livre* (Paris).
De Lacy, P. H. (1977) 'The Four Stoic "Personae"', *ICS* 2: 163–72.
Dilke, O. A. W. (1966) *Horace: Epistles Book I*³ (London).
Dilke, O. A. W. (1981) 'The Interpretation of Horace's "Epistles"', *ANRW* II.31.3: 1837–65.
Fairclough, H. R. (1929) *Horace: Satires, Epistles, Ars Poetica* (London and Cambridge, Mass.).
Fiske, G. C. (1920) *Lucilius and Horace: a Study in the Classical Theory of Imitation* (Madison).
Fraenkel, E. (1957) *Horace* (Oxford).
Gottschalk, H. (1982) 'Diatribe Again', *LCM* 7: 91–2.
Gottschalk, H. (1983) 'More on Diatribai', *LCM* 8: 91–2.
Griffin, J. (1984) 'Augustus and the Poets: *Caesar qui cogere posset*', in F. Millar and E. Segal, edd., *Caesar Augustus: Seven Aspects* (Oxford) 189–218.
Griffin, M. T. (1976) *Seneca: a Philosopher in Politics* (Oxford; repr. with addenda, 1992).
Heinze, R. (1889) *De Horatio Bionis imitatore* (Bonn).
Heinze, R. (1890) 'Ariston von Chios bei Plutarch und Horaz', *RhM* 45: 497–523.
Hock, R. F. (1976) 'Simon the Shoemaker as an Ideal Cynic', *GRBS* 17: 41–53.
Höistad, R. (1948) *Cynic Hero and Cynic King: Studies in the Cynic Conception of Man* (Uppsala).
Kaiser, E. (1964) 'Odyssee-Szenen als Topoi', *MH* 21: 109–36, 197–224.
Kenney, E. J. (1977) 'A Question of Taste: Horace, *Epistles* 1.14.6–9', *ICS* 2: 229–39.
Kiessling, A. (1883) *Coniectanea* (Stettin).
Kiessling, A. and R. Heinze, edd. (1977) *Q. Horatius Flaccus: Briefe*¹⁰ (Berlin).
Kindstrand, J. F. (1976) *Bion of Borysthenes: a Collection of the Fragments with Introduction and Commentary* (Uppsala).
Kindstrand, J. F. (1984) 'The Cynics and Heraclitus', *Eranos* 82: 149–78.
Kissel, W. (1981) 'Horaz 1936–1975: eine Gesamtbibliographie', *ANRW* II.31.3: 1403–1558.
Koniaris, G. L. (1983) 'On Maximus of Tyre: Zetemata (II)', *ClAnt* 2: 212–50.
La Penna, A. (1949) 'Schizzo di una interpretazione di Orazio, partendo dal primo libro delle Epistole', *ASNP* 18: 14–48.
Luschnat, O. (1963) 'Horaz Epistel 1.2', *Theologia Viatorum* 9: 142–55.
Macleod, C. W. (1977) 'The Poet, the Critic, and the Moralist: Horace, *Epistles* 1.19', *CQ* 27: 359–76; repr. in id. (1983b) 262–79.
Macleod, C. W. (1979) 'The Poetry of Ethics: Horace, *Epistles* I' *JRS* 69: 16–27; repr. in id. (1983b) 280–91.
Macleod, C. W. (1983b) *Collected Papers* (Oxford).
Maurach, G. (1968) 'Der Grundriss von Horazens erstem Epistelbuch', *AC* 11: 73–124.
McGann, M. J. (1960) 'The Sixteenth Epistle of Horace', *CQ* 10: 205–12.

McGann, M. J. (1969) *Studies in Horace's First Book of Epistles* (Collection *Latomus* 100; Brussels).

Moles, J. L. (1983a) '"*Honestius quam Ambitiosius*"? An Exploration of the Cynic's Attitude to Moral Corruption in his Fellow Men', *JHS* 103: 103–23 [above, Ch. 12].

Moles, J. L. (1983b) 'Some "Last Words" of M. Junius Brutus', *Latomus* 42: 763–79 [vol. 2, Ch. 33].

Morris, E. P. (1931) 'The Form of the Epistle in Horace' *YCS* 2: 79–114.

Nickel, R. (1980) 'Xenophon und Horaz', *Gymnasium* 87: 145–50.

Nisbet, R. G. M. (1959) 'Notes on Horace, *Epistles* 1', *CQ* 9: 73–6; repr. in id., *Collected Papers on Latin Literature*, ed. S. J. Harrison (Oxford, 1995) 1–5.

Nisbet, R. G. M., ed. (1961) *Cicero: In Calpurnium Pisonem Oratio* (Oxford).

Nisbet, R. G. M. and M. Hubbard, edd. (1978) *A Commentary on Horace's Odes II* (Oxford).

Préaux, J. (1968) *Horace: Epistulae, liber primus: Epîtres, Livre I* (Paris).

Reckford, K. J. (1959) 'Horace and Maecenas', *TAPhA* 90: 195–208.

Rist, J. M. (1980) 'Epicurus on Friendship', *CPh* 75: 121–9.

Russell, D. A. (1973) *Plutarch* (London and New York).

Skalitzky, R. (1968) 'Good Wine in a New Vase (Horace, *Epistles* 1.2)', *TAPhA* 99: 443–52.

Stanford, W. B. (1968) *The Ulysses Theme: a Study in the Adaptability of a Traditional Hero*[2] (Oxford and Ann Arbor).

Stégen, G. (1960a) 'L'Epître d'Horace à Aristius Fuscus (I, 10)', *Les Études Classiques* 28: 23–9.

Stégen, G. (1960b) *Essai sur la composition de cinq Épitres d'Horace (I, 1, 2, 3, 11, 15)* (Namur).

Stégen, G. (1963) *L'unité et la clarté des Épitres d'Horace. Essai sur sept pieces du premier livre (4, 6, 7, 9,13, 14, 16)* (Namur).

Wilamowitz-Moellendorf, U. von (1893) *Aristoteles und Athen*, 2 vols. (Berlin).

Wilamowitz-Moellendorf, U. von (1895) *Euripides: Herakles*, 2 vols. (Berlin).

Wilkins, A. S. (1885) *The Epistles of Horace* (London).

Williams, G. (1968) *Tradition and Originality in Roman Poetry* (Oxford).

Woodman, A. J., ed. (1983) *Velleius Paterculus: The Caesarian and Augustan Narrative* (Cambridge).

CHAPTER 15

# The Cynics and Politics

What was the Cynic attitude towards politics?[1] How did Cynics use the lexicon of politics? Was there a range of Cynic attitudes? Did Cynicism influence the political thought of others? Can one talk of Cynic political theory? My treatment of these questions will be chronological, to allow for development in Cynic thought, though Cynicism did not develop linearly (there were always Cynics who thought and behaved like Diogenes) and the notion of development is problematic (Cynicism was more a way of life than a system of thought). The treatment must also be selective: this essay presupposes the importance of the whole topic, and the more significance one attaches to Cynicism, the larger the topic will be, especially because in a fundamental sense, as we shall see, Cynic 'politics' are simply the Cynic way of life itself.

## 1   Diogenes

Since Antisthenes did not found Cynicism,[2] we begin with the problems of the 'cosmopolitan' sentiments anciently attributed to Diogenes. The two most important passages are in Diogenes Laertius. In 6.63 is recorded a saying: 'Asked where he was from, he said: "[I am] a citizen of the universe".' The word *kosmopolitēs* is extremely rare and is first attested in Philo of Alexandria (*De opif. mundi* 3; *Mos.* 1.157). The other passage comes in Diogenes' doxography in 6.72, which requires full quotation:[3]

---

[1] This essay complements Moles (1993) and (1996) but confronts the authenticity problem of D.L. 6.72, which the earlier paper sidestepped, covers much more ground, and can be read independently. I warmly thank Marie-Odile Goulet-Cazé, Margarethe Billerbeck, Malcolm Schofield, Jacques Brunschwig, and Tony Woodman for sharp criticisms of written versions, and members of the *colloquium* for salutary discussions of the oral version.
[2] Cf. Giannantoni (1993); *SR* IV.203–11; *SSR* IV.223–33; Dudley (1937) 1–15; I concede, and would myself emphasise, some Antisthenic influence on Cynicism: Moles (1983b) 104 {above, p. 319} n. 8.
[3] I use the translation and arrangement of Schofield (1991) 141–2 (Appendix H), with modifications.

⟦130⟧ (a) He said that all things belong to the wise, using the sort of arguments we have stated above [6.37]:
> All things belong to the gods.
> The gods are friends of the wise.
> The possessions of friends are held in common.
> Therefore all things belong to the wise.

(b) With regard to the law [*nomos*], he held that it was impossible for there to be political government [*politeuesthai*] without it. For he says:
> Without a city there is no profit in something civilised; and the city is civilised.
> Without law there is no profit in a city.
> Therefore law is something civilised.

(c) He would ridicule good birth and reputations and all those sorts of things, saying that they were the ornaments of vice [*prokosmemata kakias*].

(d) And he said that the only correct state [*politeia*] was the one in the universe [*kosmos*].

(e) And he said that women should be held in common, recognising no marriage, but saying that the man who persuades should go with the woman who persuades.[4] And because of this he thought that sons too should be held in common.

The syllogism in (b) has kindled fierce controversy. Like Goulet-Cazé and Schofield,[5] I believe that it will only work if the second 'without' is taken with 'law' rather than 'city' and that Diogenes the Cynic cannot have endorsed law or the city. Thereafter paths diverge. For Goulet-Cazé the syllogism is Stoic and has been inserted into Diogenes' doxography either (a) through confusion with the Stoic Diogenes, or (b) deliberately, to strengthen the affiliation between Cynicism and Stoicism. For Schofield the syllogism is authentic and shows Diogenes giving 'the civilised' a pejorative meaning (as it must have in Cynicism)[6] and attacking law, the city, and 'the civilised' as interconnected: 'Diogenes' argument is—as one would expect—*antinomian*, directed against those who sympathise with his aversion to the city and its manners, but who hold to the view rejected by him that the rule of law is indispensable.'[7]

---

4  On text and interpretation see Schofield (1991) 12 n. 21.
5  Goulet-Cazé (1982); Schofield (1991) 132–40 (Appendices F and H).
6  Schofield has reasons for rendering *asteios* as 'refined' but 'civilised' has more suitable political resonances.
7  Schofield (1991) 134.

Schofield's hypothesis makes better sense both of the syllogism itself and [[131]] of its relationship to a syllogism of Cleanthes (Stob. II.103.14–17 Hense = SVF 1.587 = Long–Sedley (1987) 67I {I.431; II.425}), which reads approximately as follows: 'If a city is a habitable construction to which people may have recourse for the dispensation of justice, then a city is surely civilised. But a city is that sort of habitation. So a city is civilised.' While text and interpretation are controversial, this syllogism is evidently intended as a riposte to Diogenes'. Schofield's hypothesis, as we shall see, also integrates Diogenes' syllogism into the overall logic of 6.72.

Whether Schofield is right that the introduction to Diogenes' syllogism is a misleading Stoicising gloss seems moot. In isolation the wording might suggest this. Yet the other items in 6.72 are anti-city, and the whole section is coloured by Diogenes' assertion in 6.71 of the superiority of nature to law. In context the introduction might imply rejection of law and the city.

The question whether, or how far, Diogenes' doxography has been 'Stoicised' affects interpretation of 6.72(d). Here ((b)), while I regard the second reading of the introduction as plausible, intervention by a Stoic doxographer would not necessarily damage the authenticity of the material itself.

From the assumption of the general correctness of Schofield's reconstruction of 6.72(b), two points emerge. First, the linguistic variation whereby 'without' is used prepositively in the first instance but postpositively in the second creates an elegant and paradoxical chiastic (ABBA) arrangement of material. Second, this syllogism has defeated many eminent scholars. These considerations caution us against underestimating the sharpness of Diogenes' intellect or verbal expression.

Most scholars assume the authenticity of 6.63. Their instinct is no doubt correct. Although the saying takes a typical *chreia* form and the *chreia* is much exploited within the general 'Diogenes-legend',[8] the question 'Where are you from?' was as standard in Greek life as in literature, and would have been particularly pointed for the notoriously stateless Diogenes.[9] The extreme rarity of *kosmopolitēs* does not impugn authenticity: Cynics were renowned for their verbal dexterity, including felicitous coinages,[10] and none more so [[132]] than Diogenes, and Philo's Stoic sources evidently got the word from somewhere. Numerous other ancient authors link Diogenes with 'cosmopolitan'

---

8   Documentation and discussion in SR IV.418–25; SSR IV.466–74; Goulet-Cazé (1992) 3978–97.
9   Tarn (1948) II.405, in a discussion which largely repeats Tarn (1933) and (1939).
10  Cf., e.g., Kindstrand (1976) 289–90.

sentiment.[11] The false attribution of 'cosmopolitan' sentiment to Socrates[12] is naturally explained as retrojection of Diogenic material upon the 'father' of the Cynic-Stoic 'succession'. And there is much evidence from Cynics and non-Cynics that 'cosmopolitanism' was a big Cynic claim, which presumably starts with Cynicism's true founder.[13]

But there have always been scholars sceptical, or dismissive, of the authenticity of 6.72(d); rejectionists have found it impossible to integrate into Diogenes' thought, and others, even upholders of its authenticity, have been perplexed.

While 6.63 and the other evidence adduced guarantee the association between Diogenes and 'cosmopolitanism', the case for giving that 'cosmopolitanism' philosophical weight is strengthened if 6.72(d) is authentic, especially if it derives, at some level, from a written *Politeia* of Diogenes. Discussion of the problem should also promote understanding of Diogenes' thought and style.

I here consider the most recent and fully developed case against 6.72(d), that of Schofield, which goes as follows.[14]

(1) Diogenes' doxography in 6.70–2 exhibits the same organisational principles as that of Diogenes' predecessor Antisthenes in 6.10–11:

(1) Virtue and its acquisition
(2) Goods—possessed by/common to the wise
(3) True and false goods—discussion of wealth, reputation, good birth
(4) Law and political activity
(5) Marriage

Similar principles underpin Stoic doxographies. The explanation is Stoic desire to present Antisthenes and Diogenes as philosophising like Stoics, in order to legitimate Stoicism within the great 'succession'. 〚133〛 The doxographies of 6.10–13 (Antisthenes) and 6.103–5 (the common doctrines of the Cynics) also show Stoic input.[15]

---

11  E.g., Dio 4.13; Epict. 3.22.45–8, 24.64–6; Plut. *De fort. Alex.* 332B–C; Lucian, *Vit. auct.* 8; Julian 6.201c; 7.238b–c; Max. Tyr. 36.5.
12  Cic. *Tusc.* 5.108; Musonius 42.1–2 Hense = Stob. 3.40.9, p. 749 Hense; Epict. 1.9.1; Plut. *De exilio* 600F–601A.
13  E.g., D.L. 6.93, 98 (Crates); Plut. *De fort. Alex.* 329A–D; Teles 3.21.1–22.7 Hense = Stob. 3.40.8, p. 738 Hense; [Heraclit.] *Ep.* 5.2; 9.2, 4, 7; *Anth. Pal.* 7.417 (Meleager); Max. Tyr. 36.4; Julian 6.201c; [Lucian] *Cyn.* 15.
14  Schofield (1991) 141–5, 133, 164. I arrange his arguments schematically.
15  On these see Mansfeld (1986), esp. 317ff., 328ff. (without consideration of 6.72); Goulet-Cazé (1986) 210–20, claiming the intervention of a Stoic doxographer in 6.70, with Mansfeld (1988) (I am not convinced of this claim), and Goulet-Cazé (1992) 3930–70.

(2) Although the assertion of the Epicurean Philodemus (*On the Stoics* XX.3–4 Dorandi) that 'it is their [the Stoics' and Cynics'] view that we should not think any of the cities or laws we know of to be a city or law' might seem to imply Cynic belief in an ideal city, there is no evidence that Philodemus has seen Diogenes' *Politeia* for himself; rather, his material derives from some general hotch-potch designed to discredit Zeno and Chrysippus.

(3) There is 'strong reason' for suspecting 6.72(d) as a Stoicised 'interpretation' of the 'cosmopolitan' saying of 6.63 in the doctrine reported by the Christian writer Clement of Alexandria (*Strom.* 4.26 = SVF III.327): 'the Stoics say that the *ouranos* is in the proper sense a city but that those here on earth still are not: for they are called cities, but are not. For a city or a people is something morally good, an organisation or group of men administered by law which is civilised.'

Note that Schofield does not take (3) and (1) to imply that the material of 6.72 is simply *invented*: rather, '6.72 as a whole constitutes an attempt to make Diogenes a constructive political philosopher of a proto-Stoic cast. It is best explained on the supposition that genuine Diogenean sayings have been converted into theoretical positions they were never designed to express.'[16]

(4) The proper interpretation of the sayings of 6.63 is indicated by the tragic verses applied to himself by Diogenes, quoted at 6.38 ('citiless [*apolis*], homeless, deprived of country [*patris*], a beggar, a wanderer, living life from day to day'): Diogenes is communicating merely 'un cosmopolitisme negatif' (Goulet-Cazé).[17]

These arguments are not persuasive.

(1) What precisely does the general correspondence of 6.70–2 to a Stoicising organisational scheme prove? Our concern is with the ⟦134⟧ items of 6.72, not those of 70–1, which present their own problems. And in 6.72 *all* the items apart from (d) are *certainly* Diogenic. Why should (d) be different? For Schofield, though the items apart from (d) are genuine, they have been given a theoretical weight which they did not originally possess, an inflation matched by the transformation of Diogenes' 'cosmopolitan' saying into the more pretentious formulation of (d). Yet the syllogisms of (a) and (b) are not mere sayings, but employ a formal philosophical mode, and on Schofield's own showing (b) is philosophically adroit; (e) also looks like a serious philosophical proposition, however shocking, and one appropriate to a serious philosophical context. Moreover, while the doxography of 6.70–3 shows an overall Stoic arrangement of material, it falls into several sections, whose material is derived from

---

16   Schofield (1991) 133.
17   Goulet-Cazé (1982) 231.

different sources. 6.72 is one of these sections and its general 'political' focus suggests Diogenes' lost *Politeia* as a source, which is anyway the natural home for (e).[18] This work, while doubtless partly a 'spoof' on the *Politeiai* of 'proper' philosophers like Plato, must have entailed more systematic exposition of Diogenes' thought. The relative philosophical weight and orderliness of 6.72 thus find another explanation. This does not exclude some Stoic intervention, but it restricts it, wholly or largely, to the overall arrangement of 6.70–3: the actual material of 6.72 remains full-blooded Cynicism. Even more important, however, as we shall see, 6.72 exhibits its own internal logic.

(2) While it would be rash to base a positive evaluation of Diogenes' 'cosmopolitanism' on the polemical and unscrupulous Philodemus alone, some scholars regard the detail of his account of Cynic ethics and its general convergence with the doxography of 6.72 as sufficient to make his acquaintance with Diogenes' *Politeia* likely.[19] More important, the substance (whatever its source) of Philodemus' report of Cynic views of the city consists both of a negative (rejection of the city in the conventional sense) and a positive (implied approbation of an ideal city), which corresponds formally to the material in Diogenes Laertius, who attributes to Diogenes both a negative 〚135〛 (6.38 ['I have no city'], 6.72 ['ordinary *politeiai* are "incorrect"']) and a positive (6.63, 72).

As stated, (3) is wholly unconvincing, since *ouranos* means not 'universe' (Schofield), but 'heaven'. Whether or not Clement's formulation has good Stoic ancestry, it is formally distinct from the doctrine that the universe is the city (even if the two doctrines are ultimately not irreconcilable), and the latter is at least the more orthodox Stoic claim.[20] Of course one might argue for the latter as the Stoic model for 6.72(d), but the hypothesis of thorough-going 'Stoicisation' of 6.72 has no greater intrinsic plausibility than the reverse: that

---

18   Authenticity of Diogenes' *Politeia*: e.g., von Fritz (1926) 54–5; Dudley (1937) 25–7; Ferguson (1975) 89–90; Dorandi (1982) 119, 122; SR IV.416–17; Goulet-Cazé (1986) 85–90; Schofield (1991) 10 n. 15 and 13; its presence in 6.72: e.g., von Fritz (1926) 54–5; Höistad (1948) 139, 141; Giannattasio Andria (1980) 148; Goulet-Cazé (1992) 3897.

19   E.g., Goulet-Cazé (1982) 228–30; SR IV.483; SSR IV.537. The case seems reasonable to me but not to Schofield: it is obviously unprovable.

20   Clement's formulation has been seen variously as orthodox Stoic (Schofield, but with the difficulty mentioned above); as a Christianising interpretation influenced by Pl. *Rep.* 592b, where the true city is not 'on earth' but 'in heaven' (Burnyeat in the conference discussion); or as reflecting Cercidas' play on the etymology of Diogenes in D.L. 6.76–7 (Margarethe Billerbeck in private communication). There is a near Stoic parallel in Dio Chrysostom's 36th oration (especially 36.22): Schofield (1991) 57–92, especially 61–2; Russell (1992) 19–23; 211–47, esp. 222; but Dio has his own, to some extent non-philosophical, agenda; two doctrines ultimately not irreconcilable: Schofield (1991) 78: 'Dio's solution is to see men not as full but potential citizens [of the *kosmos*], like children.'

6.72(d) itself is authentic and is the inspiration for the Stoic *kosmopolis*. The formulation 'the only *correct politeia* is the one in the universe' does not sound like a Stoic paradox, which would dispense with the qualification 'correct', but has an appropriately fourth-century air, making an implicit contrast between Diogenes' 'correct state' and those of Plato and Aristotle.[21] And if 6.72(d) is an 'interpretation' of the saying of 6.63, what more likely than that the 'interpreter' is Diogenes himself, fleshing out the implications of his saying in the more formal context of his *Politeia*? Would he not have been bound to discuss the *politeia* of the *kosmos*, to which his one-word saying had tantalisingly alluded, in a written *Politeia*?

(4) No matter what modern philosophers say, a negative ('I have no city') is not the same as a positive ('my city is the *kosmos*'): the latter entails a negative but should also entail a positive, and the conclusion that it does not could only be justified if in the final analysis it proved impossible to give that positive positive content. The apparent assumption (a very common one) that Cynicism is completely negative is misconceived: of course Cynic teaching is largely negative, because it aims to expose the falsity of conventional values, but the point is to isolate the only thing that matters: the Cynic way of life 'according to nature', which itself is positive.

[[136]] The case for the authenticity of 6.72(d) can be strengthened by analysis of the whole context.

*Ex hypothesi* 6.72 summarises the thought of Diogenes' *Politeia*, which encapsulated his 'political' thoughts. The first syllogism is indubitably Diogenic (cf. 6.37) and concerns legitimate possessions or needs. The second syllogism, interpreted as above, is also certainly Diogenic and concerns something that is conventionally regarded as necessary for civilised life but which the Cynic rejects, along with the city and civilised life itself. The rejection of 'the civilised', etc. is followed by a rejection of similar things within the city ('good birth and reputations and all those sorts of things') expressed by a characteristic Cynic attitude, 'ridicule'.[22] These similar things are designated 'ornaments of vice'. Then comes the disputed cosmopolitan sentiment, introduced by an 'and', which in context seems to imply a logical connection between the two sentences.

The verbal and logical links with the preceding material are indeed numerous. After the false political and social values of the second syllogism and of the 'good-birth' section we are told the correct political system (we find the same movement of thought in 6.93, where Crates' rejection of his country Thebes

---

21  Höistad (1948) 141.
22  Cf. in general Kindstrand (1976) 44–8.

is succeeded by his 'redefinition' of the term 'country'). After the plurality of false values we have the single correct value (a typical Cynic contrast); after the multitudinous manifestations of vice we are given (by clear implication) the single Cynic virtue.

The cosmopolitan sentiment is also humorous, which suits both the note struck in context by 'ridicule' and that most characteristic Cynic style of exposition. For it is a splendid joke that while earnest philosophers such as Plato and Aristotle spend their lives attempting to define, and then disastrously to implement, their conceptions of the 'correct *politeia*', the Cynic, who eats, drinks, urinates, farts, defecates, masturbates, and fornicates in public, even in the sacred space of the *agora*[23]—this incredible figure not only solves the theoretical problem instantly but immediately practises it in his way 〖137〗 of life. Of course, like most of Diogenes' jokes, this also has serious import, in accordance with the serio-comic aspect (*spoudaiogeloion*)[24] of Cynic discourse.

The term 'correct state' also illustrates the characteristic Cynic appropriation of the rhetoric of his opponents or of values that he rejects (just as he is 'rich', 'a ruler', 'a king', etc.). Nor does the Cynic merely unite theory and practice (itself no mean feat), but he unites exterior and interior, in contrast to those who pursue the 'ornaments of vice'. And whereas 'good birth', etc. are the *prokosmemata* of vice, the Cynic state is in the *kosmos*: false *kosmos* yields to true *kosmos*. It is another agreeable irony that the Cynic seemingly aligns himself with *kosmos* in the sense of 'order' or 'adornment' and also in the sense of *political* 'order'. A last point about the doxography of 6.72 is that the final item, on wives and sons 'in common', links by ring-structure to the first item, on possessions held 'in common'. This ring-structure seems to emphasise 'communism' as the alpha and omega of Diogenes' *politeia*, in implicit contrast with the exclusiveness of worldly possessions and of gradations of birth and reputation, etc. and in implicit parallel to the doctrine of 'cosmopolitanism', the *kosmos* being the 'common' home of everyone, as the Cynic writer of [Heraclit.] *Ep.* 9.2 describes it.

---

23  For the problems of private and public defecation and the removal of sewage in Athens see Owens (1983). Public defecation may or may not have been unusual, but was at least contrary to the sacral character of the *agora* (Owens [1983] 45; Parker [1983] 19) and surely consistent with Diogenes' assault on convention and his denial of 'sacred space' (below). The ancient tradition clearly regards Diogenes' practice of 'using any place for any purpose' (D.L. 6.72) as outrageous.

24  See, e.g., Kindstrand (1976) 47–8.

While there are other things to say about the brilliant style of expression of 6.72(d),[25] it should now be clear that not only is the sentiment integral to the whole context of 6.72, but in its verbal energy and virtuosity, its economy, its wit, its sense of the absurd, its superb effrontery, and indeed its taut logic, it has Diogenes the Cynic written all over it.

But what does it mean? Diogenes' cosmopolitanism unites a negative, rejection of the conventional city and *ta politika* ('politics'), with a positive, assertion of the primacy of the 'state in the *kosmos*'. Since rejection of the city promotes Cynic freedom (*eleutheria*) and virtue, by a typical re-evaluation, or appropriation, of terms, Cynics use the words *patris* ('country'), *polis*, *politeia*, etc. as metaphors for the Cynic way of life itself.[26] Consequently, the Cynic *politeia*, the Cynic 'state', is nothing other than the 'state' of being a Cynic, which is at once a ‖[138]‖ material or social state and a moral state (Cynic moral virtue being dependent on rejection of conventional social and political values). The Cynic 'state' is viewed as being co-extensive with the *kosmos* and in some sort of positive relationship with it and its various constituent elements (the natural world, the animal world, other Cynics, the gods,[27] humanity as a whole).

Cynic rejection of the conventional ('incorrect') *polis* is theoretically absolute, but in practice somewhat less so, because Cynics lived and begged in *poleis* and slept in baths and temples, etc. Such behaviour could be justified both by the Cynic principle 'use the things that are present', which permits a certain moral relativism (a strictly limited moral relativism, far stricter than the 'adaptability' or 'flexibility' (*poikilia*) of Aristippus the Cyrenaic),[28] and by the Cynic's missionary role. This slight misfit between theory and practice opens a window for the greater degree of accommodation with existing

---

25  For example, on its relationship to celebrated earlier 'redefinitions' of such terms as *patris*, *polis*, and *politeia*, particularly that of Aristippus in Xen. *Mem.* 2.1.12–13: Moles (1993) and (1996).

26  E.g., D.L. 6.85 (Crates' *Pēra*), 93; Epict. 3.22.84–5.

27  The question of Cynic attitudes to the gods and religion is too controversial to discuss here. Suffice it to say that in my opinion the apparent contradictions in the evidence are best explained by the hypothesis that Cynics generally accepted the existence of the gods but gave them only a limited role in the *kosmos*, in effect just as paradigms for the Cynic way of life. Cynics could thus be diversely interpreted as religious (because they accepted the gods' existence) or irreligious (because their position was minimalist and their attacks on superstition, which for them began at a much lower point than for others, could seem like attacks on religion in general). There are obvious parallels in the ancient reception of Epicureanism.

28  Hor. *Epist.* 1.17 provides an impeccable analysis of the differences between Diogenes and Aristippus: Moles (1985) 43–8 {above, pp. 375–82}. See also below.

political and social realities that we find in certain later developments of Cynicism, as we shall see.

The traditional question about 'ideal states' has always been: to what extent, if any, are they intended as practical propositions? Given that the essence (at any rate) of the 'Cynic state' is the 'state' of being a Cynic, this question has to be reformulated: is complete Cynic virtue intended as a fully practicable proposition?

On this question Diogenes and other Cynics seem to speak with two voices. To be sure, Diogenes proclaims himself a 'citizen of the universe' (D.L. 6.63, 72) and (presumably) one of 'the wise' (6.72), Crates is 'citizen of Diogenes' (6.93), which implies both that Diogenes is the embodiment of the ideal state and that Crates himself is too, Cynic virtue is 'easy', Cynicism is a 'short cut to virtue', the Stoic Seneca attributes 'wisdom' (*sapientia*) to his friend Demetrius the Cynic (as he would not have done to any contemporary ⟦139⟧ Stoic), etc.[29] Yet Cynic 'training' (*askēsis*) seems to be a continuous process, anecdotes portray Diogenes even after his conversion to philosophy as learning new ways of 'simplicity of life' (*euteleia*), Crates *may* have held that 'it is impossible to find a man without fault, but as in a pomegranate there is some seed that is rotten',[30] Demetrius disclaimed wisdom,[31] and the Cynic ideal state is an attempt to return to the age of Kronos, but obviously civilisation has supervened and still presents problems (in the age of Kronos there *were* no baths, temples, etc.), so that the Cynic's adaptation to the city, while limited, represents some compromise from the ideal.

Thus the question arises whether Diogenes proposed the actual dismantling of civic institutions. He certainly advocated the abolition of money (the suggested substitution of knuckle-bones is of course a joke),[32] but obviously the Cynic does not need, and rejects, money in the here-and-now (cf. Crates' giving away of his wealth). His advocacy of 'free sex' between consenting partners was a proposal for the here-and-now (famously enacted by Crates and Hipparchia) but also had future reference, in that the resulting children were to be brought up in common. There is no evidence that Diogenes' *Politeia* advocated the abolition of lawcourts, gymnasia, and temples,[33] as Zeno's certainly did; indeed, Diogenes' claim that there was nothing out of place in taking something from

---

29  'Easy': D.L. 6.70 (and many other references); 'short cut': Plut. *Amat.* 759D; Gal. *De cuiusl. anim. pecc.* 3; D.L. 7.121 (Apollodorus) = Apoll. Sel. 17, SVF III.261; Demetrius: Sen. *Ben.* 7.8.2.
30  D.L. 6.89 with Moles (1983b) 110 {above, p. 329} n. 56.
31  Sen. *Ben.* 7.8.2.
32  Athen. 4.159c; Philod. XVI.6–9 Dorandi.
33  Erskine (1990) 28, correcting Dudley (1937) 99.

a temple (D.L. 6.73) and his advocacy of gymnastics, including nude gymnastics by women,[34] seem to point in the other direction. Yet the bowdlerising Stoic Athenodorus seems to have felt that Zeno's abolition of public buildings, like other of his antinomian proposals, was unacceptably Cynic in spirit.[35] And Diogenes must certainly have condemned lawcourts.

Two points emerge. First, the proposal that children be raised 'in common' presupposes that Diogenes is envisaging some sort of community, or 'state', which does not yet exist and which must be a community of 'the wise' (cf. item (a)). Second, the saying about taking something from a temple is double-edged: it allows the [[140]] continued existence of buildings called 'temples', yet denies their *raison d'être*. If there is nothing 'out of place' in taking things from a temple, the whole notion of 'sacred space' is subverted. In sum, a Cynic must reject a social institution such as marriage, because it is an institution of *nomos* and an infringement of individual freedom. He will not advocate the dismantlement of buildings such as temples, even though they did not exist in the primitive era when man was uncorrupted, because they have a practical Cynic usefulness, but he will not use them in the conventional way.

There is another aspect to this question of the realisation of the Cynic state. The Cynic state is a cosmic state in various senses: the Cynic is at home anywhere in the world, he has a positive attitude to the natural world, the animals, the gods, and other wise men and women, there are no social, sexual, racial, or geographical barriers to this state, etc. But it is part of the Cynic's role (because of his profound 'philanthropy' (*philanthropia*) based on recognition of his kinship or potential kinship with all human beings) to try to convert others to Cynic virtue.[36] The more of these he converts, the larger the community or state of the wise will be. How far does this process go? Is there any possibility that the Cynic cosmic state, like the later Stoic conception, envisages, at least potentially, all human beings?

The Cynics' rejection of all the conventional barriers between human beings could have made it easy for them to recognise the unity of mankind, but did they in fact do so? This recognition is credited to them by later sources such as Epictetus and Julian,[37] but should we here distinguish between the views of the first Cynics and those of later times, or between the views of true Cynics and those of others intent on promoting a philanthropic and Stoicising

---

34   D.L. 6.70; Philod. XIX.17 Dorandi.
35   Schofield (1991) 13.
36   Kindstrand (1976) 61, 247; Moles (1983b) 113–16 {above, pp. 332–8} (arguing that this 'philanthropy' is integral to Cynicism from the start).
37   Epict. 3.22.81; Julian 6.201c; cf. also [Heraclit.] *Ep.* 9.2 (below).

model of Cynicism? My own view is that the unity of mankind is implicit in the Cynic missionary project and in the Cynic anti-Prometheus myth, which envisages mankind as a unity before the upsurge of vice.[38] And we can, I believe, glimpse traces of a Cynic cosmic state involving all human beings in early sources such as Onesicritus (whom I discuss below) and Zeno. Of course, Onesicritus' 'cosmic' vision can be dismissed both as un-Cynic and as simply a reaction to Alexander's conquest of the world, but it looks to me, rather, a [141] *distortion* of an already-existing Cynic conception of the *kosmopolis*. And it seems to me inconceivable that there is no connection between the Cynic *politeia* in the *kosmos* and what Plutarch claims as the 'main point' of Zeno's Cynic-influenced *Politeia*, namely that 'we should hold *all men* as members of the same people and *fellow-citizens* (*politas*), and there should be one way of life and one *kosmos*' (Plut. *De fort. Alex.* 329A–B).[39]

If, then, the Cynic cosmic state includes all human beings potentially, there is a sense in which it remains unfulfilled. The Cynic project of converting others must also have implications for the extent to which the Cynic will be driven to advocate the abolition, or the non-construction, of institutions characteristic of the traditional *polis*. The individual Cynic will avail himself of existing baths and temples, etc., but a fully realised universal Cynic state could not have them.

Two factors hamper reconstruction of Cynic thought: paucity of evidence and the likelihood that the Cynics themselves never articulated their thoughts with great precision. Nevertheless, it is worthwhile sketching what they 'must' have thought about the Cynic 'state'.

---

38   D.L. 6.44; Str. 15.1.64 (Onesicritus); Dio 6.22–5; [Diog.] *Ep.* 32.3.
39   Moles (1983b) 115–16 {above, pp. 336–7} and nn. 95–8; interpretation of this passage of course remains controversial: cf. Schofield (1991) 104–8 for a trenchant statement of the opposite view, that 'all men' means all *good* men. I do not deny that that is then said at 329c; my contention is that 'all men' pivots between 'all men [of any kind]' and 'all good men', an ambiguity found in many Stoic contexts and throughout Plutarch's speech, and one attributable to the variation of perspective between the ideal or potential and the actual. There is an exact parallel in the Cynic [Heraclit.] *Ep.* 9.2, where the good man is a citizen of the *kosmos*, and yet the latter is the common home of all, *including* malefactors. It is (I believe) equally mistaken to restrict the meaning of *kosmos* in the Plutarch passage to 'order', as if in a Stoic context 'order' in a microcosm could be divorced from the supreme 'order' that is the universal *kosmos*, and as if the ear can dissociate 'citizens' and '*kosmos*' from 'citizens of the *kosmos*'. Note that Sen. *De otio* 6.4–5, a passage overlooked in modern discussions of Zeno's *Politeia* yet clearly referring to it, claims that Zeno and Cleanthes passed laws for all humanity instead of for one state and addressed not a few citizens, but all mankind present and future.

The essence of the Cynic state is the virtue of the self-sufficient individual, a state certainly largely attainable in practice. This state involves rejection of the city-state and all its institutions, except those that have immediate practical utility. The minimalist Cynic requirements for subsistence mean that the Cynic can support himself by begging and 'living off the land'. His sexual needs he can satisfy by masturbation. Let us call this 'state 1'.

However, the self-sufficient Cynic recognises actual kinship with [[142]] other Cynics. Hence he may freely choose to have relations (sexual and other) with fellow-Cynics. If children result, a Cynic community will come into being. This too can easily support itself. Let us call this 'state 2'.

The self-sufficient Cynic, however, also recognises *potential* kinship with human beings in general, whom he attempts to convert to virtue. This constant missionary endeavour opens up the theoretical possibility of an ever-greater Cynic 'state', in principle bounded only by the *kosmos*.[40] Let us call this elastic and ever-expanding state 'state 3'. At some point begging and 'living off the land' will no longer suffice to sustain such a 'state'. Did Cynics therefore have anything to say about 'the means of production'? Not, it seems, very much, but there are Cynic, or Cynic-influenced, texts which endorse humble occupations[41] and we may perhaps get some idea of what a universal Cynic state would look like from the famous 'Golden Age fragment' of Diogenes of Oenoanda:

> then truly the life of the gods will pass to men. For everything will be full of justice and mutual love, and there will come to be no need of fortifications or laws and all the things which we contrive on account of one another. As for the necessaries derived from agriculture, since we shall have no [slaves at that time] (for indeed [we ourselves shall plough] and dig and tend [the plants] and [divert] rivers and watch over [the crops], we shall) ... such things as ... not ... time ..., and such activities, [in accordance with what is] needful, will interrupt the continuity of the [shared] study of philosophy; for [the] farming operations [will provide what our] nature wants.[42]

---

40  And including (in my view) the gods, as paradigms of the Cynic way of life (n. 27).
41  Cf. the material in Hock (1976); also Musonius' praise of farming (Stob. IV.381.20–1, 384.5–6 Hense).
42  NF 21 Smith = F 56 in Smith (1993), whose reconstruction and translation I gratefully follow.

Of course this Diogenes is an Epicurean and there are un-Cynic elements here (the utility of fortifications and laws in the present lapsarian state, the relatively elaborate agriculture envisaged, the implication that 'philosophy' is something beyond and above everyday life). But the Epicurean orthodoxy of the fragment is also problematic. Of the main elements, the true life like that of the gods, the ideal of mutual love, and the emphasis on minimalist levels of subsistence can be regarded as equally orthodox for Epicureans and Cynics. On the other hand, the very elements which have been felt to be unorthodox in Epicureanism—the rejection of fortifications and laws, the spirit of Golden Age primitivism, and the whole idea of [[143]] a *kosmopolis*—are precisely those which on my argument are integral to Cynicism. My view of this new fragment (F 56) is thus congruent with the interpretation of the well-known *kosmopolis* text (F 30 Smith = LS 22P) which finds Cynic influence there too.[43] We shall find another vision (albeit a distorted vision) of the Cynic *kosmopolis* of all mankind in Onesicritus.

The Cynic state, then, is a sort of 'rolling programme' and, for a variety of reasons, hovers between the actual and the ideal. Nevertheless, the Cynic state is much closer to reality and practical implementation than any other philosophical state in antiquity and, in order to boost their own claims and morale and their chances of converting others, Cynics sometimes talk as if they themselves actually possess this state and as if it is instantly available to mankind at large.

Two fundamental points emerge from this reconstruction of Diogenes' 'Cynic state'. First, the Stoic *kosmopolis* is not, as usually supposed, a *positive* interpretation of a *negative* Cynic *kosmopolis*: rather, it is an expansion, or development, of an original positive Cynic *kosmopolis*. Second, after Diogenes, the fundamental determinant of Cynics' attitudes to conventional politics must be whether or not they insist on the unique status of their own 'state'.

## 2   Crates

How far Diogenes' most famous follower Crates maintained Diogenes' philosophy is a large and difficult question.[44] My own answer would be that Crates' philosophy is essentially the same but to some degree modified, softened, and thus made (from one point of view) more practical. This answer seems to

---

43   E.g., Grilli (1950) 402.
44   Dudley (1937) 42–53; Rist (1969) 61–3; Kindstrand (1976) 65–6; SR IV.508–12, virtually = SSR IV.567–72. I am closest to Rist.

apply to 'politics'. On the one hand Crates is 'citizen of Diogenes', his country is not Thebes but the Cynic way of life itself (D.L. 6.85), which can be lived on the whole earth (D.L. 6.93), and he tried, no less energetically but more humanely than Diogenes, to convert others to this 'state'. On the other hand, it seems clear that he did not insist on the complete renunciation of wealth or that everybody should become a Cynic, and that he conceded a certain legitimacy to existing occupations. While the values of the Cynic philosopher are superior, [[144]] those of ordinary men are not damned. There seem here to be the seeds of the fully-developed moral relativism that we find in Bion. Crates' giving of his wealth to the poor (D.L. 6.87–8), while in the first instance an act of moral self-manumission, is also an act of philanthropy to others on the material plane, and raises the question (to which I shall return) of the extent to which the Cynic should be concerned to alleviate the poverty and hunger of other people and the means he may employ in doing so. But, clearly, Crates' action is something of a special case: one can give away one's wealth only once and one has this wealth in the first place only by accident of birth. Clearly, also, the Diogenic and Cratetean Cynic has no interest in the alleviation of poverty in general, since he regards it as a blessed state, provided that this poverty is sufficient to sustain life.

## 3    Onesicritus

With Onesicritus, we must face a question which does not apply to Diogenes or Crates: how strictly should we define Cynics? Some scholars argue that because Cynicism was more a way of life than a system of thought and at its most real when instantiated in the lives of individuals, it never had any fixed form: rather, at any one time or place, it was what the individual made of it.[45] This argument rests on a misconception of the idea of the individual. A Cynic is an individual in the sense that he claims to be completely self-sufficient and rejects the values of society at large. He is not an individual in the sense that he can embody any way of life that he chooses: no one who claimed to be a Cynic would have recognised the voluptuary Sardanapalus as a Cynic. At all periods, Diogenes is held up as the main 'standard' (*kanōn*) of Cynicism, even by those who had bowdlerised his behaviour and teaching (witness Epictetus' *On Cynicism*). It is equally misconceived to argue that because Cynicism was primarily a way of life, it was necessarily always tolerant of doctrinal diversity:[46]

---

45    E.g., Dudley (1937) 59; Baldry (1965) 106; Ferguson (1975) 97.
46    E.g., Malherbe (1982) 49–50 {= (2014) 635–7}.

the doctrines of original Cynicism were few and simple but they existed, were internally coherent, underpinned the way of life, and of course involved rejection of all the doctrinal impedimenta of conventional systems of philosophy. One can, then, usefully talk about 'true', that is Diogenic, Cynicism.

⟦145⟧ Nevertheless, in what follows I shall distinguish merely between 'hard' (Diogenic) Cynicism and 'soft' Cynicism. In practice it is important to take 'softer' developments into account, since they bear some relation to the 'harder' form and illustrate the spreading influence of 'hard' Cynicism, and we must give some weight to the fact that 'soft Cynics' are sometimes described in the sources as 'Cynics' *tout court*, even if such descriptions owe more to the ancient desire to attach labels and construct philosophical 'successions' than to describe accurately.[47]

Onesicritus, a named pupil of Diogenes, joined Alexander's army as steersman and praised this greatest of worldly kings. In itself steersmanship as an occupation might have been acceptable to Crates but hardly to Diogenes, and both would have condemned it in an army. What of the association with, and praise of, a worldly king? Kindstrand comments on Bion: 'it may at first be surprising to find a Cynic as court-philosopher, a position usually reserved for the Stoics, but this is due to a wrong conception of Cynicism as being a philosophy for the proletariat'.[48]

This observation raises fundamental questions. Of course Göttling's famous characterisation of Cynicism as a 'philosophy of the proletariat'[49] is misconceived in the sense that the 'hard' Cynic addresses his message to all men, including the rich. But the essence of his message to the rich is that they should become poor, so there is a sense in which 'hard' Cynicism champions the proletarian condition.[50] It has been rightly noted that among Diogenes' multifarious targets of attack, the poor are conspicuously absent. From a 'hard' Cynic perspective, the worldly king is defective in three respects (all deriving from Cynic exaltation of 'nature'): (1) he is rich; (2) his 'kingship' is a false 'external' state rather than an inner moral state; (3) his kingship is a form of

---

47  For similar distinctions cf. Gerhard (1909) 67ff., 165ff.; (1912); Malherbe (1970) and (1982) 50–9; Moles (1983b) 112–14 {above, pp. 331–6}. Such polarisations are easily exaggerated (talk of 'hedonistic Cynicism', for example, seems to me profoundly misleading) and within the 'hard'–'soft' polarisation Crates himself is an ambiguous figure, 'hard' in his general adherence to Diogenes' teaching, 'soft' in his modifications of it and in his highly philanthropic personal demeanour.
48  Kindstrand (1976) 14.
49  Göttling (1851) 251.
50  The problematics of the term 'proletarian' in an ancient context are of course another question.

*nomos*. The Cynic 'king', then, is the absolute antithesis of the worldly king and it is therefore self-contradictory for a self-professed Cynic to praise a worldly [[146]] king.[51] Cynic terminology can only be applied to such a king by the negation of an essential part of the 'hard' Cynic message. Hence both in joining Alexander's army as steersman and praising him, Onesicritus was fundamentally untrue to his master's philosophy.

Nevertheless, his work did have philosophical pretensions: it presented Alexander as 'philosopher in arms' and this theme was central.[52] From a Cynic perspective a 'philosopher in arms' is a paradox, and the paradox is heightened not only by the contrast with the normal Cynic rejection of worldly kingship but also by the fact that Diogenes, like other Cynics, contemptuously rejected 'arms'.[53] Thus Onesicritus, a heterodox Cynic, redeploys the Cynic trick of appropriating one's opponent's terminology in such a way as to gratify his worldly king, who has the best of both worlds, alike world conqueror and Cynic king. And not only was Alexander 'philosopher in arms', he was 'the only philosopher in arms', thereby presumably trumping Heracles himself, whose 'arms' were allegorised out of existence by his Cynic admirers.[54]

The key passage in Onesicritus' work was his description of his alleged meeting with the Gymnosophists (*FGrHist* 134 F 17a = Str. 15.1.63–5), which is too long to quote here.

Brown and Pédech have given excellent readings of this sparkling passage, without, I feel, gauging its full import.[55] Apart from the acknowledged Cynic character of the Gymnosophists themselves, the essential elements are the repeated emphasis on the fact that Onesicritus himself has been *sent* by Alexander and *sent* to hear the Gymnosophists' wisdom and *report it back* to Alexander (which makes Onesicritus himself a Cynic 'messenger' or 'scout'),[56] and the statements that Onesicritus had also heard Diogenes and that the Gymnosophists endorse the wisdom of both Diogenes and Alexander. All this creates a complex and reciprocal philosophical [[147]] 'succession'. The wisdom

---

51   I have no doubt that Diogenes' famous description of Aristippus as a βασιλικὸς κύων (D.L. 2.66) is derisive (= both 'royal poodle' and 'kingly Cynic', i.e. 'false Cynic', in associating with Dionysius), though many (e.g., SR IV.139 and SSR IV.151; Steiner [1976]) take it as complimentary; cf. also Diogenes' sneering description of courtesans as 'queens of kings' (D.L. 6.63) and his various attacks on royal dependants (D.L. 6.45, 57, 58).
52   Fisch (1937) 129–51; Brown (1949) 24–53; Pearson (1960) 85–111; Hamilton (1969) xxxi, lvii; Moles (1983b) 116 {above, p. 337} n. 98; Pédech (1984) 81–126; Giannantoni (1988) 82–3.
53   E.g., Philod. 15.31–16.4; D.L. 6.85; Dio 4.8, 53–4; 6.60; Epict. 3.22.94.
54   E.g., Dio 1.61; Epict. 3.26.33; [Lucian] *Cyn.* 13.
55   Brown (1949) 38–51; Pédech (1984) 104–14.
56   For discussion and documentation of these and other key Cynic roles see Norden (1893); SR IV.457–8 and SSR IV.507–8; Moles (1983b) 112 {above, pp. 331–2}.

of the east and the wisdom of the west, the internationalist claims of both Cynic philosophy and the Cynicised king Alexander, Alexander's imperialist policies and his philosophical mission are all mixed together in a rich stew of mutual validation and congratulation, with Onesicritus himself the chef who mixes together all these different ingredients. The effect would be distasteful were not the whole dish lightened with various pleasing dashes of irony, which have been well noted by Brown. What matters here is the centrality of the idea of Alexander as a Cynic philosopher-king and the deftly implied claim that Onesicritus himself is in some sense Alexander's philosophical 'counsellor' and emissary. Doubtless the claim was historically absurd, even if Onesicritus was once a favourite of Alexander, but a man who exaggerated his naval rank[57] would not have scrupled to present himself as Alexander's 'counsellor' (though his enemies regarded him as a mere 'flatterer';[58] the pattern of relations will recur with Dio Chrysostom and Trajan). Clearly, no credence should be given to the idea that Onesicritus simply misunderstood the teachings of the oriental sages and naively refashioned them according to the only stereotype he knew.

Onesicritus' contribution, while remote from historical truth, was considerable. As regards literary tradition, he was the second to incorporate Cynic ideas into historiography; the first was Theopompus, dubbed by G. Murray, not altogether unreasonably, 'the Cynic historian',[59] but Onesicritus' enterprise was far more systematic.[60] 'Cynic historiography' was not a major genre, but the use of Cynic concepts in historiographical assessment of political behaviour continues down to Pompeius Trogus[61] and beyond (though it is sometimes more accurate to talk of Cynic-Stoic concepts). As well as Arrian, *Anab.* 7.2 (on Alexander's relations with Diogenes and the Gymnosophists), there are lost works by Dio Chrysostom, i.e., the *Getica* and *On the Virtues of Alexander* (to which I shall return), and the later Alexander Romance. Plutarch's first speech *On the Fortune of* ⟦148⟧ *Alexander* (to which I shall also return) is broadly

---

57  Apparently: discussion in Pearson (1960) 83; Pédech (1984) 73–4.
58  *FGrHist* 134 T 7 = Lucian, *hist. conscr.* 40 (with Pearson [1960] 86–7).
59  Murray (1946); critical discussion in Pédech (1989) 231–41. The debate about Theopompus' 'Cynicism' began with the attack on Rohde (1876) by Hirzel (1892) and the former's responses in Rohde (1893) and (1894); cf. also Shrimpton (1991) 144–5.
60  I do not count the probable Antisthenic influence on Xenophon's *Cyropaedia* (Höistad [1948] 77–82), even though the *Cyropaedia* was Onescritus' own literary model, since Antisthenes was not a Cynic.
61  Oltramare (1926) 222–5; Malaspina (1976) 142–6.

relevant. Cynicising historiography may even have influenced such great figures as Posidonius and Sallust,[62] but these are murky waters indeed.

Still more important was Onesicritus' contribution to the general process of fudging a reconciliation between Cynicism and worldly power. On the practical level, there was Onesicritus' own example as philosophical counsellor or court philosopher, which must have influenced the Cynicising Bion in his relations with Antigonus Gonatas, and very likely influenced Dio in his relations with Trajan. It is true that in his first and fourth kingship orations Dio adopts tougher Cynic models than Onesicritus; in the first oration he presents himself as a Cynic 'wanderer', in the fourth he comes on as Diogenes himself, dispensing salutary admonitions to Alexander, Trajan's hero; indeed that speech, whose aim is to curb Trajan's military ambition, implicitly repudiates the very possibility of a 'philosopher in arms'. But Dio's lost *On the Virtues of Alexander* may well connect with Trajan, its title entails favourable treatment of Alexander, it was in eight books, like Onesicritus' work and Xenophon's *Cyropaedia*, and it utilised the motif, paralleled in Onesicritus' account of the Gymnosophists, that Diogenes would not come to Alexander but Alexander was to come to Diogenes. It looks therefore like a kind of halfway-house between the relatively robust Cynic critique of the Fourth Kingship oration and the extremely soft Cynicism of Onesicritus.[63]

On the theoretical level Onesicritus, himself following in the footsteps of Antisthenes and Xenophon, was the initiator of a general ideology which promoted an accommodation of sorts between Cynic philosophy and worldly power. This process culminated in Dio's First and Fourth Kingship orations. These orations contain much material which can be analysed equally as Cynic philosophy and as conventional rulership ideology (e.g., the glorification of 'toil' and 'philanthropy', the appeal to Heracles as a paradigm, etc.). Onesicritus' linkage of Alexander with Cynic ideas stimulated a series of accounts of the alleged contact between Alexander and Diogenes which allowed Alexander to emerge with honours even or at least as showing promise of moral improvement; [[149]] this stimulus will have been greater if, as seems virtually certain, Onesicritus himself included the meeting of Alexander and Diogenes. The completely implausible association of Diogenes with 'numerous politicians'

---

62   Cf., e.g., Laffranque (1964) 485ff.; Ferguson (1975) 90ff.; Lens (1986); García Moreno (1992) 134–6, 146–52. Africa (1961) 18–22 also argues for a Cynic Phylarchus, but without much plausibility: Pédech (1989) 450–2; Erskine (1990) 132–3.
63   Discussion in Moles (1990) 363 {above, p. 179} (with a slightly different emphasis).

(D.L. 6.76) is likely to have been stimulated by the Onesicritan tradition. The 'hard' Cynic view of Alexander was inevitably negative.[64]

The most arresting product of the Onesicritan tradition is Plutarch's first speech *On the Fortune of Alexander*, a rhetorical display speech which develops the thesis of Alexander as 'philosopher in arms' through an extended contrast between the mere 'words' of philosophers and Alexander's truly philosophical 'deeds'.[65] Though Diogenes is assigned to the category of 'words', he is the philosopher who most nearly approaches Alexander's achievements, so that the key contrast between Alexander and Zeno (329C) invests Alexander with distinctly Cynic features. In contrast to Zeno, Alexander translated philosophical ideals into action. He conceived of his role as that of a 'common heaven-sent governor and reconciler of the whole world'. 'Common', 'heaven-sent', 'governor', 'reconciler',[66] 'the whole world': Onesicritus' Alexander was the divine saviour and world-king of the Cynic *kosmopolis*. Tarn's view of Alexander as the originator of the idea of the unity of mankind was always a fantasy, but if he wanted ancient authority for it, he should not have invoked the ghost of Eratosthenes:[67] it was all there already in the resourceful and inventive Onesicritus.

## 4   Bion

The philosophical position of Bion, while largely Cynic,[68] marks a further stage in the adaptation of Cynicism to social and political realities. As one of the court-philosophers of Antigonus Gonatas he presumably said improving things to his master, one of the better Hellenistic monarchs. Direct influence, however, is unprovable: for instance, Antigonus' famous definition of kingship as 'glorious slavery' could reflect Bionian influence, in which case it would be ⟦150⟧ another example of the process whereby true Cynic appropriation of worldly terminology was redeployed in the service of worldly values, but the definition could equally reflect the Stoic influence of Persaeus.[69]

---

64    Cf. in general *SR* IV.397–411, virtually = *SSR* IV.443–51; Giannantoni (1988); Moles (1983a).
65    Pédech (1984) 92–5 is excellent on the Onesicritan provenance of *De fort. Alex.* 1.
66    A key Cynic role: Moles (1983b) 112 {above, p. 332}.
67    Tarn (1948) II.437–44; *contra*, Badian (1958).
68    Kindstrand (1976) 58–67, 73–8, though, as will become clear, I stop short of Kindstrand's claim, 'Bion can be called a Cynic without the usual reservations' (77).
69    Possible general Bionian influence on Antigonus is discussed by Tarn (1913) 235–6 and nn. 46–7; Kindstrand (1976) 15–16; Brunt (1975) 21 and n. 81 {= (2013) 292} assumes ἔνδοξος δουλεία to be Stoic.

Bion profited materially from his association with Antigonus, as Dio was to do with Trajan, and like Onesicritus, but unlike Diogenes and Crates, he found no theoretical difficulty in acknowledging the legitimacy of the worldly institution of kingship. The passage of Bion quoted by Teles which makes this explicit also uses a *prosopōn*-doctrine which foreshadows the *prosopōn* or *persona* doctrine of Panaetius and concedes the legitimacy of different social and political roles and therefore also of a considerable degree of moral relativism. While some of this may have been anticipated in Crates the Cynic, probably one of Bion's philosophical mentors, the main influence must have been another of his mentors, the Cyrenaic Theodorus.[70] He also adopted the Cyrenaic interpretation of the tag 'use the things that are present', whereby these can include riches as well as poverty, rather than the hard Cynic view of 'the things that are present' as the bare necessities. Nevertheless, Bion's influence as a model for the Cynic philosopher at court must have been considerable (rather as in literary satire *Bioneis sermonibus* (Hor. *Ep.* 2.2.60) must represent the tip of an iceberg even if it is impossible to discover what the iceberg is). For it is surely significant that when Dio Chrysostom made his first approach to Trajan he implicitly invoked the model of Bion and Antigonus (1.9).[71]

## 5   Cercidas[72]

Whereas Onesicritus was a military man and self-styled Cynic philosophical counsellor of Alexander, and Bion too was a court philosopher, Cercidas was himself an active politician. While [[151]] detailed reconstruction of his life and text is difficult, the general picture is clear enough. That Cercidas can fairly be categorised as Cynic, and perhaps even that he himself would have accepted that description, is indicated by several factors: the title given to the fragments of his poetry preserved on an Oxyrhynchus papyrus: 'the meliambic poems of Cercidas the Cynic', which at least reflects an ancient view of the matter; his

---

70   Teles F II, pp. 5.1–6.1 Hense = Bion F 16a Kindstrand with D.L. 2.66 (Aristippus); Hor. *Epist.* 1.17.29 *personamque feret non inconcinnus utramque*, and Moles (1985) 43, 58 n. 60 {above, p. 375}. On this matter and on 'present circumstances' (below) I am with von Fritz (1926) 44–5 as against Kindstrand (1976) 77; note also the importance of the figure of Aristippus in the debate within the later ('soft') Cynic tradition as to whether philosophers should associate with rulers: Hock (1976) 49–52. On the 'hard Cynic' attitude to Aristippus see also nn. 28 and 51 and above.

71   Dio's self-characterisation as 'wanderer' recalls Bion F 16a Kindstrand, which contrasts the roles of 'king' and 'wanderer': Moles (1990) 309 {above, p. 124}.

72   Dudley (1937) 74–84; Pennacini (1955–6); Livrea (1986).

praise of Diogenes (D.L. 6.77); his attacks on contemporary Stoics for useless logic-chopping and verbalising, in alleged contrast with Zeno (who of course began as Cynic); his advocacy of *parabilis uenus* (sex where you can get it); his attacks on music-making and general 'luxury'; and his apparent exploitation of Cynic terms in his political poetry. His philosophical self-consciousness is attested by his final moments (Aelian, *VH* 13.20; naturally imitation of Socrates is consistent with a Cynic stance).

From a Diogenic perspective Cercidas' activity as politician, general, negotiator with a Macedonian king, and law-maker is incompatible with Cynic status. For this activity entailed not only general recognition of worldly institutions but acceptance of monarchy (contrary to Cynic kingship) and law (contrary to the fundamental Cynic principle 'deface the currency' [*nomisma*]). Even if Cercidas' activity as law-maker restored freedom after tyranny (the less likely of the two suggested contexts), a Diogenic Cynic has no interest in freedom as a political institution, since such 'freedom' gives him rights which he does not want and imposes obligations which he must reject. Further, Cercidas' resolute defence of the interests of his fatherland is incompatible with Cynic cosmopolitanism. From that perspective the fate of Megalopolis *qua* Megalopolis should have been a matter of supreme indifference to Cercidas, as the fate of Thebes was to Crates (D.L. 6.93). Of course from the point of view of 'soft' Cynics who compromise, like Onesicritus or Bion, or Dio Chrysostom (in so far as Dio can be classified as a Cynic), it may be possible to pursue aims which are broadly consistent with Cynic beliefs within the constraints of existing political systems.

The extent to which this is true of Cercidas depends on the interpretation of the problematic F 4 Powell = F 1 Livrea. Dudley's reading still seems broadly convincing: the speaker (or one of the speakers) speaks not as one of the governing classes but as one oppressed by the current grossly unequal distribution of wealth, which makes him question the justice of conventional deities, ⟦152⟧ including Zeus. Better to act under the auspices of the gods Paean, Sharing, and Nemesis; the appeal to 'Sharing' (*Metados*) indicates the speaker's adherence to the reform party in Megalopolis which proposed to force the rich to give up a third of their land for redistribution amongst the poor.

How Cynic is this? The virulent moral indignation and the attacks on wealth and ignorant popular religion may seem Cynic enough; perhaps more specifically Cynic is the dismissal of theological speculation as irrelevant to practical living. One could also connect the goddess 'sharing' with Diogenes' famous syllogism on 'common possessions' (D.L. 6.72(a)). On the other hand, while Cynic attitudes to the gods are very controversial, I would regard the attack on Zeus's dispensation as inconsistent with Diogenes' teaching;[73] more important, however, poverty is regarded as a bad thing and the level of poverty which the speaker finds intolerable would to Diogenes and Crates have been not only tolerable but actually indispensable to the true life 'according to nature'. Cynicism, then, clearly inspired Cercidas with moral fervour, but although some of his poetry takes an apparently 'hard Cynic' stance, his behaviour was incompatible with that stance not only in his active political participation but also in his fundamental conception of what 'the good life' entailed.

## 6 The Roman Period[74]

After Bion, Teles (who is not sufficiently important to discuss here), and Cercidas Cynicism went into decline, without dying out. A famous instance of 'Cynic' political behaviour in the Roman context is Favonius' reconciliation of the quarrelling Brutus and Cassius, a scene described in detail by Plutarch (*Brut.* 34.4–7): Cynic here are the excessive, manic, philosophising (as Plutarch sees it), the 'frankness', 'harshness', and 'inappropriateness' of Favonius' behaviour, the appeal to Homer, the sumbouleutic role, the use of disarming humour, and the general role of reconciler (a role certainly performed by Crates but attributed to Diogenes, the Gymnosophists, and Cynics generally). Of course Favonius' role as senator, politician, ⟦153⟧ patriot, and gourmet was incompatible with Diogenic Cynicism (as Brutus recognised), but Favonius certainly here preserves something of the essential Cynic spirit. This is hardly surprising from such a close admirer of the younger Cato, who was of course a Stoic but a Cynicising Stoic in his personal deportment.[75] A similar case is Plut. *Crass.* 12 = *Pomp.* 23, where a Roman *eques*, described as 'rustic/boorish (*agroikos*) in his way of life and a private citizen', 'reconciles' the estranged Pompey and Crassus. Cratetean modes of behaviour were clearly well-known in Republican Rome.

Under the Empire another celebrated Cynic political intervention was the defence by Demetrius the Cynic of P. Egnatius Celer at his trial in AD 70, a test

---

73  See n. 27 above.
74  Rostovtzeff (1957) I.114–21 (notes in II.585–9); MacMullen (1966) 59–65; Billerbeck (1982); Goulet-Cazé (1990); Griffin (1993) and (1996); Moles (1983b) 120–3 {above, pp. 344–8} (on the survival of Cynicism from the Hellenistic period).
75  Tac. *Ann.* 16.22 makes Favonius Stoic; the incident is discussed by Geiger (1974) 167ff. and Griffin (1996) 193–4 {= (2018) 477}. It is at least clear that Plutarch's reference to Favonius' 'Cynicism' is not his own gloss, but goes back to an eyewitness account (almost certainly Messalla Corvinus).

case of the integrity of the greatest Cynic of his day. The argument[76] that the hitherto virtuous Demetrius was acting virtuously and completely in accordance with Cynic 'philanthropy' in defending the certainly guilty and deeply repulsive Celer has been strengthened by Miriam Griffin. She has recently noted that Thrasea Paetus, a philosophical friend of Demetrius, held it a moral duty to undertake 'desperate cases' (Plin. *Ep.* 6.29).[77]

More generally, Cynic political activity in this period can again be divided into the two main categories of 'hard' and 'soft'.[78]

Cynics are characteristically represented in imperial sources as invoking freedom and attacking 'monarchy' or 'tyranny' and even, sometimes, as advocating political revolution. What sense does this picture make? As I have already said, political 'freedom' is not the same as Cynic 'freedom' and political 'freedom' entails political obligations: anathema to Cynics. But it is comprehensible that Cynics should attack 'monarchs' or 'tyrants', as they had done since the days of Diogenes. For if all political systems and all politicians are deluded, tyrannies and tyrants are particularly so, because their devotion to false values is so extreme, and in certain cases (times of philosophical repression for example) their activities will directly infringe the freedom of Cynics. Of course there is a sense in which ⟦154⟧ that freedom is unaffected—thus Diogenes was able to bear his fictitious enslavement by pirates 'most nobly' (D.L. 6.74). Nevertheless, such conditions are not optimal for the Cynic free life 'according to nature', especially if they involve threat to life itself (as they sometimes did under Nero and the Flavians).

It is equally comprehensible that authoritarian regimes should persecute Cynics. Quite apart from the indignities that emperors suffered from Cynic abuse, there is an absolute ideological divide between the two parties. For the Cynic is bound to reject all forms of worldly authority: Roman imperial agents like Mucianus were quite right to see Cynics as fundamentally anarchic.[79] And in so far as the Cynic has a duty to try to convert fools to Cynicism, his

---

76  Moles (1983b).
77  Griffin (1992) 517 and (1996) {= (2018) 480}.
78  The omission of any discussion of the 'true Cynic' as portrayed by Epictetus and Julian (and to some extent also Seneca and Lucian) may strike some readers as cavalier, but in my view such portrayals are essentially prescriptive rather than descriptive, whereas the concern of this paper is with 'real-life' Cynicism.
79  This claim is disputed by scholars such as Dudley (1937) xi; Höistad (1948) 117 and n. 7; Gigante (1961); Baldry (1965) 112; Schouler (1973) 34 n. 3; Aalders (1975) 59, 61, 63; Kindstrand (1976) 14 and (1980) 97; it is upheld by (e.g.) Combes (1899); Joël (1921) 867; Toynbee (1944) 43ff.; Brown (1949) 48 and 151 n. 200; Momigliano (1951) 148–9 = (1975) II.946–7; Africa (1961) 18–20; Brunt (1975) 29 {= (2013) 301–2}; Moles (1983b) 106 {above, p. 322} and n. 26.

attacks on kings, magistrates, and tyrants are part of his philanthropic role. On the other hand, for a Cynic to advocate, or engage in, armed insurrection is a distortion of the original Cynic position, which is deeply opposed to arms, civil strife, and warfare. The Cynic should convert others by example and persuasion, not coercion. His strength is moral, not military. His 'virility' comes from personal toughness, not from the false *machismo* of armed might. The distortion is the greater if the armed insurrection is undertaken for nationalist reasons (as was the case with Agathoboulos and Peregrinus).

It may be helpful here to define more precisely the nature of hard Cynic 'anarchy'. For the hard Cynic, worldly 'power', 'rule', etc. is not merely indifferent: it is positively bad. He does not simply ignore it: he attacks it. He ought not to attack it physically (as we have just seen), but in attacking it with words, he is not thereby eschewing action. For he wants to persuade others to reject worldly power in just the same way as he himself does. Consequently, worldly power is quite right to see Cynicism as a threat.

These consequences flow from the hard Cynic view of worldly power as flatly contrary to nature. But Cynic attitudes to poverty and wealth also have consequences for Cynic 'anarchy'. Of course, as we have seen, the Cynic will not argue for social revolution in order to promote the more equal distribution of wealth. Yet, on the other hand, his attempts to persuade the rich to abandon their rich ⟦155⟧ way of life would, if successful on a large scale, inevitably result in a social and political revolution. In its attitude to worldly power and wealth, hard Cynicism differs radically from orthodox Stoicism, which of course explains why imperial agents who wish to discredit Stoics sometimes tar them with a Cynic brush. Of course, in the event, hard Cynicism proved little threat to worldly power and the reason for this is obvious: though Cynicism is in one sense 'easy', its practical demands upon its adherents are very tough, so that it never attained the status of a truly mass movement.

The most important manifestation of 'soft' Cynicism in this period is Dio Chrysostom's attempt to philosophise the worldly king Trajan, about which something has already been said. If Dio was ever in any sense a Cynic, he was certainly not one in AD 100, the date of delivery of his four Kingship Orations. Yet the first and fourth of these are heavily influenced by Cynic ideas (though admittedly qualified in various ways). Why? The idea that Dio 'wrote Cynic' in his kingship orations simply because there was a great mass of written Cynic kingship theory readily available for exploitation is dubious.[80] The real

---

80   A very brief over-view of the source question: the centre-piece of the first oration, the Choice of Heracles, comes straight from Prodicus/Xenophon (with suitable Dionian modifications), and while there is a Bionian allusion in 1.9 (n. 71), the rest of the speech's

reasons have to do with the personalities of Dio and Trajan and the needs of the situation. Dio had found in *Diogenes*—exile, Cynic wanderer, scourge of tyrants, etc.—a highly congenial *persona* for his self-presentation during his exile under Domitian and had already produced a series of discourses featuring Diogenes/Dio as hero. Trajan, for his part, was an admirer of Alexander (hence the appositeness of the dialogue between Diogenes and Alexander in Oration 4), an excessively ambitious soldier (hence in need of some robust Cynic deflation), and a novice in philosophy (hence the simplicities of Cynicism made a good starting-point). More generally, for any emperor philosophical technicalities are of small value: better to offer him a philosophy concerned [[156]] with moral improvement at a simple level. Further, as I have already noted, Cynicism was also suitable in that some of its ideas could be made to coincide with traditional kingly ideals. Finally, perhaps, while many in the ancient world ridiculed Cynics and others dismissed them as frauds, there remained a widespread recognition that of all philosophers the Cynics were profoundly *sérieux*: Cynicism therefore provides the appropriate moral fervour for Dio's sincere efforts to make Trajan a better man.[81] In one sense, therefore, Dio's kingship orations mark a high point in the history of Cynic political thought; but on the other hand we should not forget that their acceptance of monarchy, empire, and imperial ideals generally would have been regarded with contempt by the first greatest Cynic.

Another important representative of the 'soft'-Cynic stance was Demonax, the subject of Lucian's encomiastic essay.[82] Demonax participated in public life in Athens, even to the extent of becoming a magistrate (*Dem.* 11), and won great public acclaim as a true philosopher, but emphasised freedom of speech and moral independence (*Dem.* 11, 18, 38, 40, 50, 51); much of his practical philosophical activity (reconciling brothers and husbands and wives [9], behaving

---

Cynic material could surely have been composed out of Dio's head. The second oration is not Cynic at all. The 'spirits'/δαίμονες section of the fourth oration is essentially Platonic (Moles [1983a] 256–7 {above, pp. 78–9}) and the Cynic portion could again surely have been largely composed by Dio without specific 'sources', though he does exploit Antisthenes' διττὴ παιδεία at 4.29 and obviously knows of Onesicritus' conception of Alexander as 'philosopher in arms' (cf. also Dio's *On the Virtues of Alexander*). For the third oration (which, like the second, is essentially un-Cynic) Brancacci (1992) argues for Antisthenes' *Archelaus* as source. The general impression is that either there was not much formal 'Cynic' kingship literature available or if there was, Dio did not much use it.

81   For the highly favourable judgement of Dio's kingship orations here implied see Moles (1990).
82   Jones (1986) 90–8; Branham (1989) 57–63. I here assume (a) that *Demonax* is authentically Lucianic; (b) that it has a certain evidential value.

as friend to everybody [10], quelling political strife [64]) is in the Cratetean tradition and poses no new theoretical problems.

## 7   Conclusions

This survey has shown that from the time of Diogenes to the Roman imperial period there was a consistent 'hard'-Cynic tradition of rejection of the city and conventional politics, a rejection which was the direct and logical consequence of the Cynics' radically primitivist interpretation of life according to nature. Alongside this 'hard'-Cynic tradition there existed from the time of Onesicritus a 'soft-Cynic' option, which allowed substantial compromise with worldly institutions and thus involved the negation of an essential part of the 'hard'-Cynic position, but which nevertheless still proclaimed Cynic moral values such as personal integrity, superiority to luxury, devotion to toil, etc. By detaching them from their proper [[157]] context the 'soft'-Cynic interpretation of these values deprived them of their true significance. Nevertheless, they were not drained of all their Cynic content.

Are we, then, justified in talking of Cynic political theory, meaning by theory an ordered structure of propositions of general form designed to explain something? Here again we must distinguish between 'hard' and 'soft' Cynicism. One looks for theory in written contexts and the most promising candidate for 'hard'-Cynic political theorising must be Diogenes' *Politeia*, with its syllogisms and universalising propositions. Formally, the work is indeed theoretical and, as we have seen, its spirited humour does not preclude fundamental seriousness. Yet there is also a strong element of spoof of conventional philosophy. The *Politeia* is not Diogenes' favoured philosophical mode: it is in part a demonstration that Diogenes can play the conventional philosophical game yet deconstruct the political philosophy of conventional philosophers such as Plato and Aristotle. While Diogenes and other 'hard' Cynics do write voluminously and do use these written works to convey moral lessons, they prefer 'entertainment' genres such as tragedy, various types of poetry, 'diatribe', etc. to formal works of theory, and their projected readership includes fellow-philosophers only at the margins. Even more important, their use of written works surely takes second place to their practical philosophical demonstrations on the streets. Such practical demonstrations often involve mockery precisely of the theorising of conventional philosophers. There is an important sense in which Cynicism is anti-theory.

This is not to say that Cynic behaviour lacks philosophical grounding entirely. Here again, we must redefine the problem. If, as we have seen, the

Cynic state is essentially the state of being a Cynic, the question is whether the Cynic way of life is underpinned by anything that can be described as a theory. The nearest thing to such a theory is the Cynic anti-Prometheus myth which certainly goes back as far as Diogenes and which explains both why man declined from his original paradise state and why the majority of men are now unhappy. But the theoretical underpinning of Cynicism is minimalist: the essence of the Cynic message is that the good life is easy to understand and to practise: everything else, including elaborate education and philosophising, is not only irrelevant but inimical to this central message. The Cynic conception of the good life is given some justification in the form of the appeal to nature, [[158]] animal behaviour, the anti-Prometheus myth, and so on, but it does not require much justification of this kind, and indeed for the true Cynic his actual behaviour is self-justifying, hence his claim to be an 'example' of the good life in action.

'Soft' Cynicism also produced a large literature, some of which was directly concerned with politics and kingship. But its main representatives can hardly be described as producing political theory: Onesicritus offered a sort of spurious amalgam of the Cynic king and the worldly king, Dio Chrysostom's eclectic kingship orations were specifically angled towards the personality, strengths, and weaknesses of a particular worldly king, the Roman emperor Trajan. Reconstruction of Dio's sources does not disclose a hidden treasure of Cynic kingship literature. 'Cynic historiography' must have been even less theoretical than the Cynic philosophy it palely reflected, except to the extent that it contained theories of history which had nothing to do with Cynicism. Within the world of 'soft' Cynicism the most serious candidate for political theory is Antisthenes, who was not himself a Cynic but whose ethics and political thought were to a debatable extent absorbed within the general Cynic tradition. His works certainly survived into the Roman imperial era and exerted some influence (for example, on Dio). Yet within the totality of Cynic attitudes to politics, this influence was not great.

While 'soft' Cynicism made some contribution to conventional rulership ideology, it is the 'hard' Cynic position on politics which is the more individual and significant both in its own right and for its influence upon Stoic political thought. The relative lack of theoretical grounding in Cynicism did not prevent hard Cynics from making a powerful political, or anti-political, statement; indeed the reverse is true: their lack of theory was a main factor in their ability to reach so distinctive and radical a position. In politics, as in other areas, the Cynics bypass, but also transcend, philosophical theory, and their rejection of theory is at once their weakness and their strength.

## Bibliography

Aalders, G. J. D. (1975) *Political Thought in Hellenistic Times* (Amsterdam).
Africa, T. W. (1961) *Phylarchus and the Spartan Revolution* (Berkeley and Los Angeles).
Badian, E. (1958) 'Alexander the Great and the Unity of Mankind', *Historia* 7: 425–44.
Baldry, H. C. (1965) *The Unity of Mankind in Greek Thought* (Cambridge).
Billerbeck, M. (1982) 'La réception du Cynisme à Rome', *L'Antiquité Classique* 51: 151–73; Eng. tr., 'Greek Cynicism in Imperial Rome', in Billerbeck (1991) 147–66.
Billerbeck, M., ed. (1991) *Die Kyniker in der modernen Forschung: Aufsätze mit Einführung und Bibliographie* (Amsterdam).
Brancacci, A. (1992) 'Struttura compositiva e fonti della terza orazione "Sulla Regalità" di Dione Crisostomo: Dione e l'"Archelao" di Antistene', *ANRW* II.36.5: 3308–34.
Branham, R. B. (1989) *Unruly Eloquence: Lucian and the Comedy of Traditions* (Cambridge, Mass. and London).
Brown, T. S. (1949) *Onesicritus: A Study in Hellenistic Historiography* (Berkeley and Los Angeles).
Brunt, P. A. (1975) 'Stoicism and the Principate', *PBSR* 43: 7–35; repr. in id., *Studies in Stoicism*, edd. M. Griffin and A. Samuels (Oxford, 2013) 275–309.
Combes, L. (1899) *Un precurseur anarchiste (Diogene)* (Bibliotheque des 'Temps Nouveaux 19; Brussels).
Dorandi, T. (1982) 'Filodemo: Gli Stoici (*P. Herc.* 155 e 339)', *Cronache Ercolanesi* 12: 91–133.
Dudley, D. R. (1937) *A History of Cynicism from Diogenes to the 6th century A.D.* (London).
Erskine, A. (1990) *The Hellenistic Stoa: Political Thought and Action* (London and Ithaca).
Ferguson, J. (1975) *Utopias of the Classical World* (London and Ithaca).
Fisch, M. H. (1937) 'Alexander and the Stoics', *AJPh* 58: 59–82, 129–51.
von Fritz, K. (1926) *Quellenuntersuchungen zu Leben und Philosophie des Diogenes von Sinope* (Philologus Suppl. 18.2; Göttingen).
García Moreno, L. A. (1992) 'Plutarch's *Life of Sertorius*', in P. A. Stadter, ed., *Plutarch and the Historical Tradition* (London and New York) 132–58.
Geiger, J. (1974) 'M. Favonius: Three Notes', *RSA* 4: 161–70.
Gerhard, G. A. (1909) *Phoenix von Kolophon: Texte und Untersuchungen* (Leipzig and Berlin).
Gerhard, G. A. (1912) 'Zur Legende vom Kyniker Diogenes', *Archiv für Religionswissenschaft* 15: 388–408; repr. in Billerbeck (1991) 89–106.
Giannantoni, G. (1988) 'Cinici e stoici su Alessandro Magno', in G. Casertano, ed., *I filosofi e il potere nella società e nella cultura antiche* (Naples) 75–87.
Giannantoni, G. (1993) 'Antistene fondatore della scuola cinica?', in Goulet-Cazé and Goulet (1993) 15–34.

Giannattasio Andria, R. (1980) 'Diogene Cinico nei papiri ercolanesi', *Cronache Ercolanesi* 10: 129–51.

Gigante, M. (1961) 'Sul pensiero politico di Diogene di Sinope', *Parole del Passato* 81: 454–5.

Göttling, C. W. (1851) 'Diogenes der Kyniker oder die Philosophie des griechischen Proletariats', in id., *Gesammelte Abhandlungen aus dem classischen Alterthume*, 2 vols (Halle) I.251–77.

Goulet-Cazé, M.-O. (1982) 'Un syllogisme stoïcien sur la loi dans la doxographie de Diogène le Cynique: à propos de Diogène Laërce VI 72', *RhMus* 125: 214–40.

Goulet-Cazé, M.-O. (1986) *L'Ascèce Cynique: un commentaire de Diogéne Laërce VI 70–71* (Paris).

Goulet-Cazé, M.-O. (1990) 'Le cyniscisme à l'époque impériale', *ANRW* II.36.4: 2720–833.

Goulet-Cazé, M.-O. (1992) 'Le livre VI de Diogène Laërce: analyse de sa structure et réflexions méthodologiques', *ANRW* II.36.6: 3880–4048.

M. O. Goulet-Cazé and R. Goulet, edd. (1993) *Le Cynisme ancien et ses prolongements* (Paris).

Griffin, M. T. (1993) 'Le mouvement cynique et les Romains: attraction et repulsion', in Goulet-Cazé and Goulet (1993) 241–58.

Griffin, M. T. (1996) 'Cynicism and the Romans: Attraction and Repulsion', in R. B. Branham and M.-O. Goulet-Cazé, edd. *The Cynics: the Cynic Movement in Antiquity and its Legacy* (Berkeley and Los Angeles) 190–204 = ead., *Politics and Philosophy at Rome: Collected Papers*, ed. C. Balmaceda (Oxford, 2018) 475–85.

Grilli, A. (1950) 'I frammenti dell'epicureo Diogene da Enoanda', in V. E. Alfieri and M. Untersteiner, edd., *Studi di Filosofia Greca: Pubblicazion in onore di R. Mondolfo* (Bari) 347–435.

Hamilton, J. R. (1969) *Plutarch, Alexander: A Commentary* (Oxford).

Hirzel, R. (1892) 'Zur Characteristik Theopomps', *RhMus* 47: 359–89.

Hock, R. F. (1976) 'Simon the Shoemaker as an Ideal Cynic', *GRBS* 17: 41–53.

Höistad, R. (1948) *Cynic Hero and Cynic King: Studies in the Cynic Conception of Man* (Uppsala).

Joël, K. (1921) *Geschichte der antiken Philosophie* (Tübingen).

Jones, C. P. (1986) *Culture and Society in Lucian* (Cambridge, Mass. and London).

Kindstrand, J. F. (1976) *Bion of Borysthenes: a Collection of the Fragments with Introduction and Commentary* (Uppsala).

Kindstrand, J. F. (1980) 'Demetrius the Cynic', *Philologus* 124: 83–98.

Laffranque, M. (1964) *Poseidonios d'Apamée: essai de mise au point* (Paris).

Lens, J. (1986) 'Viriato, héroe y rey cynico', *Estudios de Filología Griega* 2: 253–72.

Livrea, E. (1986) *Studi Cercidei: P.Oxy. 1082* (Bonn).

MacMullen, R. (1966) *Enemies of the Roman Order: Treason, Alienation and Unrest in the Roman Empire* (Cambridge, Mass.).
Malaspina, E. (1976) 'Uno storico filo-barbarico', *Romanobarbarica* 1: 135–58.
Malherbe, A. J. (1970) 'Gentle as a Nurse: The Cynic Background to 1 Thess ii', *Novum Testamentum* 12: 203–17; repr. in id. (2014) 1.53–68.
Malherbe, A. J. (1982) 'Self-definition among Epicureans and Cynics', in B. F. Meyer and E. P. Sanders, edd., *Jewish and Christian Self-Definition* 3 (London and Philadelphia) 46–59; repr. in slightly different format in id. (2014) II.635–50.
Malherbe, A. J. (2014) *Hellenistic Philosophy and Early Christianity: Collected Essays, 1959–2012*, 2 vols (Leiden and Boston).
Mansfeld, J. (1986) 'Diogenes Laertius on Stoic Philosophy', *Elenchos* 7: 295–382.
Mansfeld, J. (1988) 'Review of Goulet-Caze (1986)', *CR* 38: 162–3.
Moles, J. L. (1983a) 'The Date and Purpose of the Fourth Kingship Oration of Dio Chrysostom', *ClAnt* 2: 251–78 [above, Ch. 3].
Moles, J. L. (1983b) '"Honestius quam Ambitiosius"? An Exploration of the Cynic's Attitude to Moral Corruption in his Fellow Men', *JHS* 103: 103–23 [above, Ch. 12].
Moles, J. L. (1985) 'Cynicism in Horace *Epistles* I', *PLLS* 5: 33–60 [above, Ch. 14].
Moles, J. L. (1990) 'The Kingship Orations of Dio Chrysostom', *PLLS* 6: 297–375 [above, Ch. 5].
Moles, J. L. (1993) 'Le cosmopolitisme cynique', in Goulet-Cazé and Goulet (1993) 259–80.
Moles, J. L. (1996) 'Cynic Cosmopolitanism', in Branham and Goulet-Cazé (1996) 105–20 [below, Ch. 16].
Momigliano, A. D. (1951) 'Review of Wirszubski (1950)', *JRS* 41: 146–53; repr. in id., *Quinto Contributo alla Storia degli studi classici e del mondo antico*, 2 vols. (Rome, 1975) II.958–75.
Murray, G. (1946) 'Theopompus or the Cynic as Historian', in id., *Greek Studies* (Oxford) 149–70.
Norden, E. (1893) 'Beiträge zur Geschichte der griechischen Philosophie', *Jahrbücher der classische Philologie*, Suppl. 19: 365–462.
Oltramare, A. (1926) *Les origines de la diatribe romaine* (Lausanne).
Owens, E. J. (1983) 'The *Koprologoi* at Athens in the Fifth and Fourth Centuries B.C.', *CQ* 33: 44–50.
Parker, R. (1983) *Miasma: Pollution and Purification in Early Greek Religion* (Oxford).
Pearson, L. (1960) *The Lost Histories of Alexander the Great* (New York and Oxford).
Pédech, P. (1984) *Historiens compagnons d'Alexandre: Callisthène, Onésicrite, Néarque, Ptolémée, Aristobule* (Paris).
Pédech, P. (1989) *Trois historiens méconnus: Théopompe, Duris, Phylarque* (Paris).

Pennacini, A. (1955–6) 'Cercida e il secondo cinismo', *Atti della Accademia delle Scienze di Torino* (Classe di Scienze morali, storiche e filofiche) 90: 257–83.

Rist, J. M. (1969) *Stoic Philosophy* (Cambridge).

Rohde, E. (1876) *Der griechische Roman und seine Vorläufer* (Leipzig).

Rohde, E. (1893) 'Zum griechischen Roman', *RhMus* 48: 110–39; repr. in id. (1901) II.9–39.

Rohde, E. (1894) 'Theopomp', *RhMus* 49: 623–4; repr. in id. (1901) I.345–6.

Rohde, E. (1901) *Kleine Schriften*, 2 vols. (Tübingen and Leipzig).

Rostovtzeff, M. (1957) *The Social and Economic History of the Roman Empire*$^2$, rev. by P. M. Fraser, 2 vols. (Oxford).

Russell, D. A., ed. (1992) *Dio Chrysostom: Orations VII, XII, XXXVI* (Cambridge).

Schofield, M. (1991) *The Stoic Idea of the City* (Cambridge; repr. Chicago, 1999).

Schouler, B. (1973) *Libanios: Discours moraux. Introduction, texte et traduction* (Paris).

Shrimpton, G. S. (1991) *Theopompus the Historian* (Montreal).

Smith, M. F. (1993) *Diogenes of Oenoanda: the Epicurean Inscription* (Naples).

Steiner, G. (1976) 'Diogenes' Mouse and the Royal Dog: Conformity in Non-Conformity', *CJ* 72: 36–46.

Tarn, W. W. (1913) *Antigonos Gonatas* (Oxford).

Tarn, W. W. (1933) 'Alexander the Great and the Unity of Mankind', *PBA* 19: 123–66.

Tarn, W. W. (1939) 'Alexander, Cynics and Stoics', *AJPh* 60: 41–70.

Tarn, W. W. (1948) *Alexander the Great*, 2 vols. (Cambridge).

Toynbee, J. M. C. (1944) 'Dictators and Philosophers in the First Century A.D.', *G&R* 13: 43–58.

CHAPTER 16

# Cynic Cosmopolitanism

How should we interpret Cynicism? A 1991 Paris conference laid the following stern injunction upon its participants:[1] 'The material demands both a very precise philological inquiry to take account of the fragments and testimonia and a rigorous philosophical approach to determine the exact originality of Cynic thought'. Of course, such traditional methods have their place, but in my opinion the most important thing is to penetrate the spirit of Cynic formulations, which are provocative, paradoxical, and ludic.

Cynic thought is simultaneously easy and difficult to interpret. The first Cynics, Diogenes and Crates, were obviously clever men, but they rejected intellectual subtlety in favour of simplicity, and they expressed this simplicity in paradoxical and ludic forms, which often seemed obtuse but in fact were not. Their aim was to challenge the preconceptions of their audience, and so-called wise men, philosophers, and sophists found themselves particularly targeted.

In the words of Saint Paul:[2] 'If any man among you seemeth to be wise in [[106]] this world, let him become a fool, that he may be wise'. Many modern scholars are too clever to interpret Cynicism correctly. And since the challenge posed by the Cynics is moral as well as intellectual, modern scholars who misinterpret Cynic cosmopolitanism are, from a Cynic point of view, not simply ignorant but wicked.

Consequently, anyone who tries to interpret Cynic cosmopolitanism should not be discouraged if he is not a philosopher. Indeed, it is an advantage not to be one, provided that one respects the extremely radical nature of Cynic thought and that one appreciates its ludic quality, never forgetting that in the case of Cynicism, because of the concept of the *spoudaiogeloion* or 'seriocomic', one can always uncover a deeper meaning.[3]

---

1 This paper is an English translation of Moles (1993), delivered at 'Le Cynisme Ancien et ses Prolongements: Colloque International du C.N.R.S.', Paris, 22–25 July 1991. I am grateful to the Comité Scientifique for inviting me to participate and particularly grateful to Marie-Odile Goulet-Cazé and Margarethe Billerbeck for numerous kindnesses. The published versions are close to the paper delivered on 23 July 1991 but incorporate some modifications, developments, and second thoughts. My subsequent paper, Moles (1995), contains further second thoughts on Diogenes, which, however, do not substantially alter my original conclusions.
2 1 Cor 3.18.
3 It is with regard to the fundamental seriousness (σπουδή) implicit in Cynicism that I find myself in disagreement with the otherwise excellent study of Branham (1996). On Cynic σπουδαιογέλοιον, see, for example, Kindstrand (1976) 47–8.

This study rests on the following assumptions. First, because Cynic philosophy is fundamentally simple, there comes a point beyond which it does not go. Second, because the evidence is so defective, there comes a point where we must employ the principle *ben trovato*. Third, there nevertheless comes a point beyond which our reconstruction of Cynic philosophy cannot go. Inevitably, therefore, my reconstruction of Cynic cosmopolitanism will be a 'story' (*muthos*) rather than a 'true account' (*logos*). Fourth, both the cosmopolitan 'saying' attributed to Diogenes in Diogenes Laertius (6.63) and the cosmopolitan 'thought' attributed to Diogenes in Diogenes Laertius (6.72) are authentic.[4] Fifth, the attribution of virtually identical formulations to Socrates and other philosophers before Diogenes lacks plausibility.[5]

In contrast to the ancient view, the current scholarly opinion of many years has been that Cynic cosmopolitanism, at least as regards Diogenes and the first ⟦107⟧ Cynics, is purely negative.[6] That is, when Diogenes answered the question 'Where are you from?' with the words 'I am "a citizen of the cosmos" [κοσμοπολίτης]', D.L. 6.63], and when he wrote, 'The only good government is that in the cosmos' (μόνην ... ὀρθὴν πολιτείαν τὴν ἐν κόσμῳ, D.L. 6.72), he meant only what he expressed elsewhere in tragic verses (D.L. 6.38): 'Without a city, without a house, without a fatherland, / A beggar, a wanderer with a single day's bread'[7]—namely, that he had no polis and rejected the polis as 'against nature' (παρὰ φύσιν).

---

4  I do not agree with the arguments of Schofield (1991) 141–5, 133, 64, against the authenticity of D.L. 6.72. My general reasons are implicit in this study as a whole, but one reason that seems to me virtually decisive in itself is the word play on προσχήματα and κόσμος. In fact, the testimonia that link cosmopolitanism to Diogenes are numerous. See, e.g., Dio 4.13 (*SSR* V B 582); Epict. 3.22.45–8 (*SSR* V B 263), 24.64–6 (*SSR* V B 290); Plut. *Fort. Alex.* 10.332B–C (*SSR* V B 31); Lucian, *Vit. Auct.* 8 (*SSR* V B 80); Julian, 6.201c (*SSR* V B 264); 7.238b–c (*SSR* V B 332); Max. Tyr. 36.5 (*SSR* V B 229). I deal directly with the so-called authenticity problem in (1995) 132–7. Also numerous are the passages that attest general Cynic cosmopolitanism. See, e.g., D.L. 6.93 (*SSR* V H 31; Crates), 98 (*SSR* V H 80; Crates); Plut. *Fort. Alex.* 6.329A–D (discussed below); Teles F 3, p. 21.1–22.7 Hense = Stob. 3.40.8, (p. 738 Hense); [Heracl.] *Ep.* 5.2, 36.9.2, 4, 7; *Anth. Pal.* 7.417 (Meleager); Max. Tyr. 36.4; Julian, *Or.* 6.201c; [Lucian] *Cyn.* 15.

5  Socrates: Cic. *TD* 5.108; Musonius, p. 42.1–2 Hense = Stob. 3.40.9 (III.749 Hense); Epict. 1.9.1; Plut. *Exil.* 6, 600F–601A; others: see, e.g., D.L. 2.7 (Anaxagoras); Democritus F 247 D–K {= Atom. D354 L–M}. I stress the terminology 'virtually identical *formulations*', for, as we shall see, *generally* cosmopolitan sentiments are widely attested before Diogenes, and this affects our interpretation of Diogenes' sentiments.

6  See, e.g., the altogether typical discussions of Giannantoni, *SR* III.483–92, virtually identical to *SSR* IV.537–47; Goulet-Cazé (1982) 229–31 (note her conclusion: 'par conséquent, un cosmopolitisme négatif'); Schofield (1991). Among the very few scholars to believe in a positive Cynic cosmopolitanism are Fisch (1937) 144; Höistad (1948) 138–52, esp. 141–3; Buora (1973–74) 247; Giannattasio Andria (1980) 148.

7  D.L. 6.38 (*SSR* V B 263).

In combatting this current opinion, I take my stand, like Diogenes himself, on the wisdom of old and not on the sophistry of the *savants de nos jours*; like Diogenes, I intend to deface the currency, and I appeal to an anecdote about Diogenes related by Dio Chrysostom.[8] In typically Cynic fashion, this anecdote shocks and instructs us at the same time. Both 'the many' and 'the sophists' despise Diogenes' teaching as κόπρος ('shit'), but in reality the sophists do not understand the 'opinions' of Diogenes, even though they are on the point of engulfing them, and it is their own false 'opinion' that is the κόπρος πολλῶν ἐτῶν ('the shit of many years'). I hope that my study will be the true κόπρος, the 'real shit' on Diogenes the Dog. No doubt some of my readers will consider it to be κόπρος pure and simple.

To begin with, can we accept that Cynic cosmopolitanism is negative to the extent that it rejects the polis? The tragic verses already cited, the slogan 'Deface the Currency', and numerous fragments and testimonia support the thesis that Diogenes and Crates and the Cynics in general considered the polis to be 'against nature'.[9] It is true that in the case of Diogenes the controversial passage concerning *nomos* ('law', 'custom') in Diogenes Laertius (6.72) poses a problem, but in my opinion those scholars who hold that this passage should not be taken at face value are certainly right.[10]

〚108〛 It is true also that the Cynics ordinarily lived in cities and exploited their amenities, including the opportunity of begging, but the principle 'use what is present' allows a certain moral relativism (compare the hypocritical behaviour of Western Marxists),[11] and to some extent also the Cynics' missionary role (to which I shall return) required their presence in the city.[12] The Cynics' hostility to the city is not fundamentally compromised by their behaviour in this context.

Another difficulty is posed by the existence of an apparently Cynic tradition that is less hostile to the polis and to political power in general. Antisthenes

---

8   Dio 8.35–6 (*SSR* V B 584): ἵνα μὴ δοκῇ ... τὸν ὕδρον οὐκ ὁρῶντες.
9   See, e.g., D.L. 6.20 (*SSR* V B 2), 29 (*SSR* V B 297); Epict. 3.22.45–7, 24.65–6; D.L. 6.85 (*SSR* V H 70; Crates' *Pēra*), 93 (*SSR* V H 31); Dio 6.25, 28, 31 (*SSR* V B 583); Philod. *Stoic. PHerc.* 339.10.4–6 Crönert = 20.3–4 Dorandi; Lucian, *Vit. Auct.* 9; Max. Tyr. 36.5; [Heraclit.] *Ep.* 5.2.
10  περί τε τοῦ νόμου ὅτι χωρὶς αὐτοῦ οὐχ οἷόν τε πολιτεύεσθαι· οὐ γάρ φησιν ἄνευ πόλεως ὄφελός τι εἶναι ἀστείου· ἀστεῖον δὲ ἡ πόλις· νόμου δὲ ἄνευ πόλεως οὐδὲν ὄφελος· ἀστεῖον ἄρα ὁ νόμος. For present purposes it matters little whether one follows Goulet-Cazé (1982), who sees Stoic influence on this passage or Schofield ([1991] 134), who sees a sarcastic note in the word ἀστεῖος. What is important is not to read the passage at face value. (My own preference now is to follow Schofield's interpretation: see Moles [1995] 130–1 {above, pp. 390–1}.)
11  See, e.g., Teles F 2, p. 6.5–8.5 Hense; Bion FF 16A, 17 Kindstrand, with Kindstrand (1976) 218–19.
12  See, e.g., Weber (1887) 126; Wilamowitz-Moellendorff (1893) II.24; Goulet-Cazé (1986a) 230.

compared the polis to fire—go too near and you burn; go too far away and you freeze[13]—and theorised about kingship. Onesicritus accompanied and eulogised Alexander.[14] Bion was court philosopher to Antigonus Gonatas, to whom he said, 'You rule well' (ἄρχεις καλῶς), thereby employing a relativist doctrine that allows considerable moral relativism.[15] The philosophical doctrine of Teles was even laxer. Cercidas was a 'politician' and 'lawmaker'. Dio Chrysostom addressed Cynic doctrines to a Roman emperor; and there are other examples.[16]

One must certainly distinguish the attitude of Antisthenes and his like from the more radical attitude of Diogenes and Crates. Should one then suppose that Antisthenes and his like are not true Cynics, or that they represent a less strict form of Cynicism, while still remaining Cynics? In the final assessment, this question is perhaps semantic and without much importance for the present study.[17] It is certain that the Cynicism of Diogenes and Crates, Cynicism at its most typical, rejected the polis.

⟦109⟧ But this does not make their cosmopolitanism purely negative. It also has positive implications, and I give five 'proofs' of this:

First, Diogenes did not say, in the context of D.L. 6.63, 'I am without a polis' (ἄπολίς εἰμι), nor did he write, in the context of D.L. 6.72, 'There is no good government' (οὐδεμία πολιτεία ὀρθή ἐστιν). His formulations were formally positive, a factor to which we must accord its full importance, since he could have answered, 'I am without a polis', as he did on other occasions. If in 1996 you are asked, 'Are you French or German?' and you reply, 'I am European', the reply entails both the rejection of a restrictive nationalism and the assertion of a larger loyalty.

Second, Diogenes' sentiments must be interpreted not in a vacuum but rather against a general tradition in which the polis or the 'fatherland' (πατρίς)

---

13  Stob. 4.4.28 (SSR V A 70). The attribution of this testimonium to Diogenes should be rejected.

14  See in general Brown (1949), and my own remarks in Moles (1983b) 109 {above, p. 327} and (1995) 144–9 {above, pp. 403–8}.

15  See Teles F 2, p. 5.1–6.1 Hense = Bion F 16A Kindstrand; and my own remarks in Moles (1985) 43, 58 n. 60 {above, p. 375}.

16  See my remarks in Moles (1983a) 268–9 {above, p. 92} n. 65 and Moles (1990), esp. 303, 309–11, 319–24 {above, pp. 118, 124–7, 135–41}.

17  In fact I agree with the arguments of Giannantoni (SR IV.203–11 = SSR IV.223–33; cf. Giannantoni [1993]) that Antisthenes was not the founder of Cynicism, though this conclusion requires slight modification, as follows: 'the ancient tradition that Diogenes was Antisthenes' pupil was effectively refuted by Dudley ... but Antisthenic influence upon Diogenes has been widely accepted, and is patent' (cf. esp. Xen. Smp. 4.34–44, as I wrote in Moles [1983b] 104 {above, p. 319} n. 8).

or some similar concept is rejected, or revalued, in favour of an internationalist or cosmopolitan ideal. Given that the various corresponding sentiments of Heraclitus, Euripides, Antiphon, Hippias, Alcidamas, and others have a positive value,[18] it cannot be justifiable to restrict the parallel formulations of Diogenes to a negative sense.

Third, not only do Diogenes' sentiments form part of a tradition: we must also take account of the philosophical rivalry between Diogenes and Aristippus, which I take to be historical, at least to the extent that there is a certain relationship between their philosophical systems and that Diogenes certainly criticised Aristippus.[19]

Scholars have noted a relationship between Diogenes' sentiments and those of Aristippus as reported by Xenophon. Their philosophical rivalry surely indicates some direct relationship, as Plutarch sensed.[20] Aristippus maintains his freedom by not shutting himself up in a πολιτεία ('state', 'government', ⟦110⟧ 'polity'), which seems to him 'against nature', and by maintaining his status of 'stranger' (ξένος) everywhere—that is, everywhere on earth, among all mankind. Like Aristippus, Diogenes maintains his freedom by rejecting the polis, which seems to him 'against nature', but whereas Aristippus is a 'stranger' (ξένος), Diogenes is a 'citizen' (πολίτης), and whereas Aristippus operates 'among human beings', Diogenes operates 'in the cosmos'. The attitude of Diogenes is much more positive than that of Aristippus: Diogenes substitutes the positive and the engaged (πολίτης, πολιτεία) for the negative and disengaged, and he extends his sphere of operations beyond the world of human beings. Clearly, Diogenes defeats Aristippus in the debate. In short, the relationship between the sentiments of Diogenes and those of Aristippus is itself sufficient to prove that Diogenes' sentiments have a positive content.

---

18  See, e.g., Heraclitus F 114 D-K {= D105 L-M}; Eur. FF 777, 902, 1047 N.² {= TrGF FF 777, 902, 1047}; Antiphon F 44 D-K; Hippias ap. Plat. Prot. 337c–d; Alcidamas ap. Arist. Rhet. 1373b18; Plat. Theaet. 173e1–174a1; Arist. EN 1155a21; see also Democritus F 247 D-K {= Atom. D354 L-M}; Thuc. 2.24.3; Tr. Fr. Adesp. 318 N.² {= [Men.] Monost. 735 Jaekel}; Ar. Plut. 1151, and ap. Stob. 3.40.2a; Lys. 31.6; see also the discussions of Lana (1951); Baldry (1965) 26–9, 35–45, 58–9; Guthrie (1969) 152–63; Schulz-Falkenthal (1979) 29–32; Kerferd (1981) 154–9.

19  On the problem of the relations between Aristippus and Diogenes, see Gigon (1956) 36; Giannantoni (1958) 47–9, 83–4; Mannebach (1961) 72; Guthrie (1969) 492; Steiner (1976) 36–46; Hock (1976); SR IV.138–40 = SSR IV.151–3; and my own remarks in Moles (1985) 43–8 {above, pp. 375–82}.

20  Xen. Mem. 2.1.12–13: ἀλλ᾽ εἰ μὲν ... καθίσταντες δούλοις χρῆσθαι ... [13] Ἀλλ᾽ ἐγώ τοι, ἔφη, ἵνα μὴ πάσχω ταῦτα, οὐδ᾽ εἰς πολιτείαν ἐμαυτὸν κατακλείω, ἀλλὰ ξένος πανταχοῦ εἰμι. It is significant that Plut. Exil. 5, 601A uses the word ἐνέκλεισεν in relation to the cosmopolitanism of Socrates.

Fourth, let us consider the precise form of these sentiments. They are paradoxes, which provoke and challenge us to find a meaning in apparent absurdities. How can a πολίτης, a member of so small a group as a polis, be a πολίτης ('citizen') of the *kosmos* ('cosmos'), the largest organism imaginable? How can the only true πολιτεία ('government'), a single small entity, be coextensive with the cosmos? This is the ultimate 'defacing' of 'the political currency'.[21] As in other celebrated Cynic formulations, the challenge to find a meaning is formulated in terms of polar oppositions. The answers suggested by the majority of modern scholars—'I am a citizen of no polis' and 'There is no good government'—are on the one hand intolerably banal and on the other hand take no account of these polar oppositions.

Fifth, the sentiments are paradoxical in another sense. For they seem to contradict Cynic doctrines themselves. How can the Cynic, severe critic of the polis, be a πολίτης ('citizen')? How can this savage outsider advocate a political *kosmos* ('cosmos')?[22] How can the apolitical man *par excellence* be *engagé*? How can the despiser of cosmology embrace the cosmos?[23] These paradoxes also demand substantive answers.[24]

These are my five 'proofs'. I submit that individually and cumulatively they prove that Diogenes' sentiments *must* have positive content. But they do not yet shed much light on this content.

Let us first recall what the cosmos consists of: the earth and the heavens; on ⟦111⟧ the earth, there is both animate and inanimate nature; animate nature consists of human beings and animals; human beings consist of Cynics and non-Cynics, Greeks and barbarians, men and women; the heavens contain the heavenly bodies and the gods who live in them.

Cynic cosmopolitanism has numerous positive aspects, which relate to each of these constituents of the cosmos:

*The Cynic, his virtues, and his way of life.* Cynic cosmopolitanism relates to Cynic 'freedom' (ἐλευθερία) because of the link with Aristippus's concept of 'hospitality' or 'rights of a foreigner' (ξενία), which was designed to secure his personal freedom, and because the polis, with all its attendant obligations, is equally an impediment to true Cynic freedom. It relates to Cynic 'virtue', a state

---

21  For this formulation of the great Cynic slogan, see D.L. 6.20 (*SSR* V B 2).
22  For this concept, see Bordes (1982) 493; and also LSJ s.v. κόσμος, I.4.iii.
23  See, e.g., D.L. 6.28 (*SSR* V B 374), 6.39 (*SSR* V B 371), 6.73 (*SSR* V B 370), 6.103 (*SSR* V A 135); Stob. 2.1.11 = Bion F 6 Kindstrand (with Kindstrand [1976] 192–3, 198–9), Stob. 2.1.11 (Demonax); in this respect, the position of Onesicritus in Str. 16.1.65 is altogether heterodox.
24  There is still more to be said about the verbal cleverness of Diogenes' sentiments: see Moles (1995) 136–7 {above, pp. 395–7}, which includes a detailed analysis of the whole of D.L. 6.72; but enough has been said here for the purposes of the essential argument.

defined as 'to live according to nature', because, as we have seen, the polis is 'against nature'. This link is implicit in Diogenes Laertius (6.72), where 'birth, reputation, and all such things' are linked with 'vice', and the 'one good government in the cosmos' is linked, by implicit contrast, with virtue; and also, as I have already noted,[25] the false cosmos of this world contrasts with the true cosmos of the Cynic 'state' (πολιτεία). Of course, Cynic freedom and virtue have negative aspects—freedom partly implies freedom *from* things, including the polis—but they are not *merely* negative: freedom from inessentials is a precondition of positive freedom.

Since rejection of the polis facilitates freedom and virtue, by a typical Cynic revaluation of terms, πατρίς, πάτρα, πόλις, πολιτεία, and so on ('fatherland', 'city', 'government', etc.), become metaphors for the Cynic way of life itself.[26] In other words—and this is an absolutely fundamental point—the Cynic πολιτεία, the Cynic 'state', is nothing other than a *moral* 'state': that is, the 'state' of being a Cynic. And since neither the polis nor racial distinction means anything to the Cynics, it is often claimed that one can live the Cynic life anywhere on earth, and that 'the whole earth' is the Cynic's home.[27] Positive or negative? Certain modern scholars hold that to say 'I am at home everywhere' is equivalent to saying 'I am a stranger everywhere'. This is only true if the word 'home' is given a narrow meaning, but the truth is that the Cynic expresses a positive allegiance to the whole earth. We may note in passing that this allegiance to the whole earth is sometimes linked to a sense of allegiance to all mankind.[28]

[112] *The natural world.* Cynic cosmopolitanism implies a positive attitude toward the natural world and all its riches (water, garlic, lupins, etc.!) as opposed to the world of the polis.[29] This positive attitude may extend to the heavenly bodies insofar as they affect the Cynic way of life on earth. (We recall Diogenes' pleasure in sunbathing.) It is true that the Cynic attitude towards the natural world is less lyrical, less developed, less integral to a total system than the corresponding Epicurean or Stoic attitude. It remains, nevertheless, a positive attitude.

---

25   See n. 4 above.
26   See, e.g., D.L. 6.85 (SSR V H 70; Crates' *Pēra*), 6.93 (SSR V H 31); Epict. 3.22.84–5.
27   See, e.g., D.L. 6.98 (SSR V H 80); Bion F 17.8–9 Kindstrand = Teles *ap.* Stob. 3.1.98 = F 2, p. 7.5–6 Hense; [Anacharsis] *Ep.* 5.3; Dio 4.13; Epict. 3.24.66; Max. Tyr. 36; [Lucian] *Cyn.* 15.
28   See, e.g., Dio 4.13; Epict. 3.24.64–6; of course, these are late testimonia, but, as we shall see, they are faithful to the true Cynic spirit.
29   See, e.g., D.L. 6.44 (SSR V B 332), 85 (SSR V H 70; Crates' *Pēra*), 98 (SSR V H 80); Bion F 17.7–9 Kindstrand = Stob. 3.1.98 = Teles F 2, p. 7.4–6 Hense; Dio 6.12–13, 25, 30 (SSR V B 583); Str. 15.1.64 = Onesicritus, *FGrHist* 134 F 17 (cf. Plut. *Fort. Alex.* 10, 332B); Max. Tyr. 36; [Lucian] *Cyn.* 15.

*Cynic cosmopolitanism implies a positive attitude to the animal world, in contrast with that of the majority of Greek philosophers.* As their willing acceptance of the abusive term 'dogs' shows, Cynics upheld animals as models of the true life 'according to nature'. Of course, Cynics generally ate animals,[30] but animals equally could eat human beings, and it is a notorious fact that Diogenes was even prepared to envisage cannibalism.[31] This mutual eating was supported by the theory of the kinship of human beings and animals,[32] and even by Anaxagoras' physical theory that 'there is a portion of everything in everything' and by Empedocles' theory of 'pores'.[33] We seem here to be verging on the idea (which would have very important consequences) that the universe is a unified physical organism. It is true also that man, or at least the ideal man, is distinguished by his possession of *logos* ('speech', 'reason'),[34] and in this regard he differs from the animals. We must therefore recognise the existence of a double attitude: human beings and animals are at once kin and not kin, but we must assess the kinship at its true value.

*Cynic cosmopolitanism has implications for the relations of the Cynic with his peers.* The Cynics recognised the kinship or community of the wise.[35] We ⟦113⟧ may recall, for example, the doctrine that 'the wise man is a friend to his kind';[36] and Diogenes' famous syllogism—'All things belong to the gods; the wise are friends of the gods, and friends hold things in common, therefore all things belong to the wise';[37] the 'like-mindedness' (ὁμονοία) that, according to Plutarch, was the basis of Diogenes' polity (πολιτεία);[38] and Crates' claim to be 'a citizen of Diogenes' (Διογένους πολίτης).[39] This kinship transcends the conventional barriers between men and women (cf. the relationship between

---

30  D.L. 6.34, 73, 76, 77 (*SSR* V B 93); Julian 6.190c–193c; Kindstrand (1976) 215; for Cynic food in general, see, for example, Lovejoy–Boas (1935) 133–4; Vischer (1965) 75–83.
31  See, e.g., D.L. 6.73 (*SSR* V B 132); Philod. *Stoic. PHerc.* 339.10.4–6 Crönert = 20.1–3 Dorandi.
32  D.L. 6.79 (*SSR* V B 101).
33  See D.L. 6.73 (*SSR* V B 132); discussion in Dudley (1937) 30; Höistad (1948) 143–4; Brown (1949) 37; *SR* IV.429–31 = *SSR* IV.479–81.
34  See, e.g., D.L. 6.24 (*SSR* V B 303), 73.
35  This is admitted by some scholars, for example Dudley (1937) 35–6; Baldry (1965) 110; Rist (1969) 62–3; *SR* IV.490 = *SSR* IV.545; see also my discussion, Moles (1983b) 109–11 {above, pp. 328–30}.
36  D.L. 6.105 (*SSR* V A 99).
37  D.L. 6.37, 72 (*SSR* V B 353).
38  Plut. *Lyc.* 31.2; I do not accept the arguments of Babut (1969) 201–2 for a reference to Diogenes the Stoic.
39  D.L. 6.93 (*SSR* V H 31).

Crates and Hipparchia)⁴⁰ and between the races (cf., for example, the relations between Diogenes and the gymnosophists described by Onesicritus).⁴¹

*Cynic cosmopolitanism has implications for the relations of the Cynics with the gods.* Since the polarised form of Diogenes' sentiments, their link with the thought of Aristippus, and Greek linguistic usage of the fourth century guarantee the word *kosmos* its full force of 'universe', Diogenes must be making a statement about the position of the Cynics vis-à-vis the heavens. As we have already seen, the heavenly bodies affect life 'according to nature' on earth. But we must also consider the position of the Cynics vis-à-vis the gods. (Here we venture upon dangerous territory that is fiercely contested by modern scholars.)⁴²

The gods, who are man's benefactors,⁴³ provide a paradigm for Cynic self-sufficiency;⁴⁴ the Cynic himself is godlike,⁴⁵ friend of the gods,⁴⁶ their messenger, their agent,⁴⁷ and, in being *agathos daimōn* ('tutelary god', 'guardian angel'),⁴⁸ he is himself virtually divine. We may recall too that 'Diogenes' [[114]] means 'Born of Zeus' and that Diogenes was hailed as an *ouranios kuōn* (a 'godlike [or 'heavenly'] dog').⁴⁹ This 'friendship' (*philia*) and 'affinity' (*homoiotēs*) between Cynic and gods should imply that the cosmos is the common home of gods and wise men, and this implication is substantially confirmed by the syllogism of Diogenes already cited. We may note in passing that there are Cynic fragments to the effect that everything is full of the divine—a contention consistent with the physical theories already mentioned⁵⁰—and that human beings in general are endowed by the gods with 'intellect' (*nous*),⁵¹

---

40  For sex in Cynicism see, e.g., D.L. 6.72 (*SSR* V B 353); Dio 6.19–20; the discussion in Rist (1969) 59–62, seems to me very convincing, despite the judgement of Giannantoni (*SR* III.482 {= *SSR* IV.534}) that 'non sembra necessario ... contestare il carattere genuino e originario della misoginia di Diogene'. See also Moles (1983c).
41  Str. 15.1.64–5 = *FGrHist* 134 F 17.
42  See especially Goulet-Cazé (1996), a rich and stimulating study, whose principal conclusions, however, I am unfortunately unable to accept.
43  See, e.g., D.L. 6.44 (*SSR* V B 322); Dio 6.25; [Lucian] *Cyn.* 7, 11, 18.
44  See, e.g., D.L. 6.51 (*SSR* V B 354), 104; Dio 6.31 (*SSR* V B 583); [Crates] *Ep.* 16; [Lucian] *Cyn.* 12.
45  See, e.g., D.L. 6.51 (*SSR* V B 354), 104, 105; Arist. *Pol.* 1.2, 1253a26–9.
46  See, e.g., D.L. 6.37, 72 (*SSR* V B 353).
47  See, e.g., Str. 15.1.63–4 = *FGrHist* 134 F 17 (cf. Plut. *Alex.* 65.2); D.L. 6.102 (*SSR* V N 1); Dio 1.58; 32.12, 21; Epict. 3.22.2, 23, 53, 69; [Heracl.] *Ep.* 9.3; see also the discussions of Billerbeck (1978) 78; Delatte (1953).
48  D.L. 6.74 (*SSR* V B 70); Apul. *Flor.* 22 (*SSR* V H 18); Julian 6.200b; Lucian, *Dem.* 63.
49  See, e.g., Cercidas *ap.* D.L. 6.76 (*SSR* V B 97); [Diog.] *Ep.* 7.1; for other testimonia and a large bibliography, see Kindstrand (1984) 161.
50  See D.L. 6.37 (*SSR* V B 344), 73 (*SSR* V B 132).
51  See, e.g., Dio 10.27–8 (*SSR* V B 586); [Diog.] *Ep.* 9.3.

or 'reason' (*logos*),⁵² or 'judgement' (*gnome*).⁵³ The possible implications of these two positions are obviously very important: they seem to weaken the ordinary distinctions between the animate and the inanimate and between gods and men.

*Cynic cosmopolitanism has implications for the relationship between the Cynics and mankind at large.* Cynicism presents itself as a missionary philosophy.⁵⁴ By his characteristically exhibitionist behaviour, the Cynic offers other human beings a model to imitate or a demonstration of the falsity of their own values.⁵⁵ In innumerable anecdotes and literary descriptions, we see the Cynic energetically trying to convert other human beings (whether one or two individuals, or vast crowds in cities)⁵⁶ to the Cynic life of virtue, and he is often followed by pupils.⁵⁷ He enjoys a vast range of titles that imply a didactic and proselytising [[115]] role towards others,⁵⁸ a role that seems to bear witness to a profound philanthropy (*philanthrōpia*),⁵⁹ 'love for mankind', 'benevolence'. These apparently altruistic aspects of the Cynic's behaviour cannot be dismissed as later embroideries inspired by the more humane character of Crates. They are all, or almost all, documented for Diogenes himself, and some indeed for his predecessor Antisthenes. It seems, therefore, that they form an integral part of Cynicism.

Does this mean that the Cynic recognises kinship with mankind in general? Admittedly, this conclusion presents difficulties, which a good number of

---

52  See, e.g., D.L. 6.24 (*SSR* V B 303 G), 73 (*SSR* V B 132).

53  See, e.g., Max. Tyr. 36.1 (cf. Str. 15.1.65 = *FGrHist* 134 F 17); see also the concept of the god within: e.g., Dio 4.139 (with Moles [1983a] 259–60 {above, pp. 81–3}); *PGénèv.* inv. 271.2.45–6.

54  Here I repeat some of the arguments of Moles (1983b), esp. 111–18 {above, pp. 330–42}, with some modifications and (I hope) some improvements also.

55  See, e.g., D.L. 6.78 = *Anth. Pal.* 16.334 (*SSR* V B 108); Sen. *Ep.* 20.9.; *Ben.* 7.8.3; Epict. 3.22.46, 86, 88; 3.24.112; Julian 6.187c, 201c; Strathmann (1942); Delatte (1953); Billerbeck (1978) 78, 107; Kindstrand (1980) 90; also relevant is the important παράδειγμα of Socrates: Pl. *Apol.* 23a12; Of course, the behaviour of the Cynics in this regard can be criticised as τῦφος or *ambitio*, etc.: see, e.g., D.L. 6.26 (*SSR* V B 55); Epict. 3.22.50–1; 4.8.34; Tac. *Hist.* 4.40.3; Sen. *Epp.* 5.2–4; 7.9; Lucian, *Vit. Auct.* 10–11.

56  See on this Kindstrand (1976) 138; id. (1980) 90.

57  Of course, this claim often depends on the meaning given to the word 'pupil': on this topic see von Arnim (1898) 37–43; Dudley (1937) 37–8; Kindstrand (1976) 10–11; (1980) 90; *SR* IV.205–8, 435–9, 504–8 = *SSR* IV.225–6, 485–9, 562–6; Goulet-Cazé (1986b).

58  κατάσκοπος, ἐπίσκοπος, εὐεργέτης, παιδαγωγός, διδάσκαλος, ἄρχων, ἰατρός, σωφρονιστής, νουθετητής, διαλλακτής, ἀγαθὸς δαίμων, σῴζειν, ὀφέλειν: for a representative documentation of these titles, see Moles (1983b) 112 {above, p. 332}. For the central and fundamental concepts of κατάσκοπος and ἐπίσκοπος, see especially Norden (1893) and *SR* IV.457–58 = *SSR* IV.507–8.

59  See especially Kindstrand (1976) 61, 247; Moles (1983b) 112–14 {above, pp. 331–6}.

scholars judge to be so great either that they vitiate the conclusion, at any rate in regard to the Cynicism of Diogenes, or at least that they render the Cynic position incoherent. What of the criticisms and insults that the Cynic directs at humanity in general, insults that are characteristic of the Cynicism of Diogenes but are far from absent from the type of Cynicism represented by Crates, which is universally admitted to be more moderate? What of the apparently disdainful fashion in which the Cynic divides humanity into a handful of sages and the mass of the foolish or insane? What of the apparent elitism as expressed in the doctrine that 'the wise man is a friend to his kind'?[60] And if the Cynic is totally self-sufficient and enters into the affairs of others only through his own free choice (as for example in the sexual sphere, where masturbation and 'free love' are equally legitimate), why should he concern himself with the moral state of others? It is true that the Cynics seem to recognise some virtues (for example, 'justice'),[61] which entail virtuous dealings with other people; but such virtues are marginal in Cynicism. It is true also that wrongdoing towards others obviously may form part of vice, but Cynic virtue—'life according to nature' in the most primitivist sense, a constant 'discipline' (ἄσκησις) of 'natural labours' (οἱ κατὰ φύσιν πόνοι)[62]—can surely be a very largely self-contained activity.

In my opinion, these difficulties have been exaggerated. Harsh criticism—even abuse—of the ignorant is not incompatible with a didactic purpose. Diogenes and Crates asserted this explicitly.[63] The apparent conflict between a philanthropic mission (φιλανθρωπία) and elitism is exactly paralleled in Stoicism, ⟦116⟧ and can be resolved by the hypothesis either of differing levels of reality, or of a distinction between the actual and the potential or ideal.

It is true that as a matter of fact there is a great gulf between the sage and the majority, who are victims of illusion, and that only the former is a human being in the fullest sense of the term.[64] Yet vice is a matter of ignorance, and virtue a matter of knowledge;[65] Cynic virtue is 'easy' and represents in effect the natural state of human beings;[66] and all men without exception are endowed with 'intellect', 'reason', or 'judgement'. Furthermore, many of the conventional barriers that separate human beings are demolished by the fact that the Cynic rejects the family and all distinctions based on sex, birth, rank,

---

60   D.L. 6. 105.
61   See, e.g., D.L. 6.16 (SSR V A 41), 12 (SSR V A 134), 5 (SSR V A 176); Crates F 10 D = 1 Diehl = SSR V H 84; Bion F 17.7 K. = Teles F 2, p. 7.3 Hense; Kindstrand (1976) 214–15.
62   See above all the remarkable study of Goulet-Cazé (1986a).
63   Stob. 3.13.44 (SSR V B 149); Crates F 10 Diels = 1 Diehl = SSR V H 84 G.
64   See, e.g., D.L. 6.41 (SSR V B 272), 60 (SSR V B 273).
65   See, e.g., D.L. 6.105.
66   See, e.g., D.L. 6.70 (SSR V B 291).

race, or education. Consequently, even the imbecilic masses can be regarded as potential human beings. In other words, for the Cynic other human beings are and are not *philoi* ('friends', 'kinsmen'). We may recall the Cynic's double attitude toward animals. Of course, this kind of complexity of attitude, based on differing perceptions of similarity and difference, is an integral part of Greek thought, as Claude Lévi-Strauss and other great French structuralists have shown us (or at least some of us). Consequently, the gulf between the Cynic and ordinary human beings, while still immense, is not insuperable. It is of course less great for Cynics like Crates, who (as it appears) held complete 'wisdom' (σοφία) to be an impossibility.[67]

It is the potential bond of humanity between the Cynic and the masses that explains several of his most characteristic roles. He is a 'teacher' (διδάσκαλος) because it is the fruitful application of Cynic doctrine that will bridge the existing gulf between the two groups. If this is not so, what is the good of Cynic teaching? He is a κατάσκοπος ('spy', 'inspector') because it is he who searches out the truth and reports it back to men. He is a 'mediator' (διαλλακτής) because he reconciles men, and, if this whole analysis is correct, he must also be a διαλλακτής because he reconciles men and gods. He is an ἀγαθὸς δαίμων (a 'guardian angel') because he is the mediator between men and gods.

Hence, when Epictetus describes Diogenes as 'dear to gods as to men', as 'loving all mankind',[68] this is not a late, propagandising, Stoicising view, but a conception integral to Cynicism from its beginnings. We must of course concede that in order to put Diogenes' profound 'philanthropy' (φιλανθρωπία) into relief, Epictetus implausibly attributes to him the 'soft' qualities of Crates, but the distinction between Diogenes' method of teaching and Crates' is one of means, not ends.[69] We must also concede the existence of a genuinely [[117]] misanthropic tendency, but this is not an integral part of Cynicism, nor was it ever more than a secondary tendency.[70]

There are other factors to support the thesis that the Cynics recognised at least the possibility of a common humanity: certain dicta of Diogenes and Demonax;[71] Diogenes' defence of cannibalism, which invokes not, as one might have expected, the differences between Cynics and their fellows, but their essential identity;[72] the Cynics' habit of appealing to the customs of

---

67  See D.L. 6.89 (*SSR* V H 36), with Moles (1983b) 110 {above, p. 329} n. 56.
68  Epict. 3.24.64 (*SSR* V B 290).
69  See Moles (1983b) 112–13 {above, pp. 331–3}.
70  See, e.g., [Heracl.] *Ep.* 4.2, 5.3, 7 *passim*; [Diog.] *Ep.* 27, 41; Plin. *HN* 7.19.79–80; Gerhard (1912), esp. 395 = (1991), esp. 94–5.
71  D.L. 6.56 (*SSR* V B 189); Lucian, *Dem.* 21, with Moles (1983b) 113 {above, p. 333}.
72  See D.L. 6.73 (*SSR* V B 132).

foreign countries;[73] the idea that all human beings are endowed with 'reason'; the Cynic anti-Promethean myth, which goes back to Diogenes himself and regards human beings as a unity before the insurgence of vice.[74]

Despite the arguments of certain scholars, I continue to believe that the celebrated passage in Plutarch's *De Fortuna Alexandri* reveals numerous details of the Cynic's attitude towards other men and of Cynic cosmopolitanism in general.[75] It is here that Plutarch develops Onesicritus' thesis of Alexander as a philosopher in action and that he contrasts the purely theoretical propositions of Zeno with the actual achievements of Alexander. Zeno wrote his *Republic* 'on the dog's tail' when he was still one of Crates' pupils,[76] and many of the Cynic elements of this work are generally recognised.

Like Diogenes, Zeno rejects the existing δῆμοι ('peoples', 'citizenries') and πόλεις ('states'), even though later Stoics did not agree. Zeno's ideal is that 'all human beings should be members of the same people and fellow citizens, and there should be one way of life and one cosmos' (πάντας ἀνθρώπους ἡγώμεθα δημότας καὶ πολίτας, εἷς δὲ βίος καὶ κόσμος, Plut. *De Fort. Alex.* 329A–B); Diogenes was himself a 'citizen of the cosmos' and in my view regarded all men as his potential φίλοι ('friends', 'kinsmen') and consequently [[118]] potential 'citizens of the cosmos', like himself. The sole divergence of opinion between the two philosophers is the importance that Zeno attaches to *nomos* ('custom', 'law'), but this has nothing to do with the existing *nomos*, which the Cynics scorned: it is the 'law' or 'reason' of nature, which interpenetrates the cosmos and which in consequence may be compatible with the Cynic principle of 'living according to nature'. (I shall return to this point.)

By contrast with Zeno, Alexander translated philosophical ideas into reality. On his view, his role was that of a 'universal divine governor and reconciler of all things' (κοινὸς θέοθεν ἁρμοστὴς καὶ διαλλακτὴς τῶν ὅλων, ibid. 329C). Like the Cynic, he is sent by the gods; like the Cynic, he is a governor of men; like

---

73   See, e.g., D.L. 6.73 (*SSR* V B 132); see further the discussions of Weber (1887) 117–33; *SR* IV.467 = *SSR* IV.518.

74   See, e.g., D.L. 6.44; Str. 15.1.64 = *FGrHist* 134 F 17; Dio 6.22–5; [Diog.] *Ep.* 32.3; Max. Tyr. 36; Brown (1949) 149 n. 152; Moles (1983b) 116 {above, p. 338}; Goulet-Cazé (1986a) 59–60.

75   Plut. *Fort. Alex.* 6, 329A–D: Καὶ μὴν ἡ πολὺ θαυμαζομένη Πολιτεία τοῦ τὴν Στωικῶν αἵρεσιν ... δι' αἵματος καὶ τέκνων ἀνακεραννυμένους. Of course this passage has been much discussed, with very varied conclusions. See, e.g., Fisch (1937) 66–9, 137–8; Tarn (1939) 65–9; (1948) II.417–24; Baldry (1959) 12–13; (1965) 159–60; Murray (1966) 369; Rist (1969) 64–5; Ioppolo (1980) 254; Moles (1983b) 115–16 {above, pp. 336–9} and nn. 95–8 (which already indicates the main lines of my interpretation); Long–Sedley I.429–30 (67A), 435; Erskine (1990) 20; Schofield (1991) 104–11.

76   The later dating proposed by Erskine ([1990] 9–15) conflicts with the ancient testimonia, which in my opinion should not be lightly discarded.

the Cynic, he is governor of all men; like the Cynic, he is a reconciler (and we note the presence of this idea in Onesicritus);[77] and he is reconciler not only of men, but also *tōn holōn*: that is to say, of everything that exists—the whole earth, the cosmos, men, and gods.

This passage also demonstrates the double classification of human beings that I have argued for: on one level, for Zeno 'all human beings' are 'members of the same people and fellow citizens', and for Alexander all men should consider 'the inhabited world' as 'home' or 'fatherland'; yet on another level, Zeno excludes the bad from his state,[78] and for Alexander humanity divides into the good, who are kin, and the bad, who have no kinship with the good. This double classification is also evident in another Cynic text, Pseudo-Heraclitus, *Epistle* 9.2, where the 'polity of the cosmos' is defined by virtue or vice, and yet the cosmos is the 'place common to all'.[79]

Let us come to our conclusion. The Cynic proclaims his allegiance to the cosmos. He can live a virtuous life anywhere: the whole earth serves as his home. He maintains a positive attitude toward the natural world and toward the animal world. He is himself godlike. He recognises his actual kinship with other sages and his potential kinship with human beings in general, whom he seeks to convert. He is a mediator between men and gods, and this mediation is an important part of his pedagogic activity.

Let me anticipate possible objections. Is this model Stoic rather than Cynic? No—it is the other way round. Stoicism is Cynicism, enriched of course with numerous refinements. Is it anachronistic to hypothesise such a model of cosmopolitanism before Alexander the Great, who, according to some scholars, was the first to give substance to the idea of the unity of mankind? No—the sense of the unity of mankind had already been expressed by Antiphon and Alcidamas (to say nothing of Homer and Herodotus), and Plutarch's thesis in *De Fortuna Alexandri* would founder if it was Alexander who had been the ⟦119⟧ initiator of such ideas. Does this model depend on physical theories, which the Cynics could not accept, given their rejection of physics? There are two possible answers to this question. First, whether logically or illogically, Diogenes did sometimes invoke physical theories. Second, although the physical theories of Anaxagoras and Empedocles serve to give the model coherence, they are not indispensable to it. The essentials of such a model go back to Homer, and

---

77 See Str. 15.1.65.
78 See D.L. 7.32–3.
79 ἀνὴρ δὲ Ἐφέσιος, εἰ ἀγαθός, κόσμου πολίτης. τοῦτο γὰρ κοινὸν πάντων ἐστὶ χωρίον, ἐν ᾧ νόμος ἐστὶν οὐ γράμμα ἀλλὰ θεός, καὶ ὁ παραβαίνων ἃ ⟨μὴ⟩ χρὴ ἀσεβείσει· μᾶλλον δὲ οὐδὲ παραβήσεται, εἰ παραβὰς οὐ λήσεται.

similar models were developed by certain of the Presocratics, whose physical explanations could readily have been discarded by non-intellectual philosophers like the Cynics.

Finally, what can one say of the importance, originality, and influence of Cynic cosmopolitanism? The concept clarifies the position of the Cynic in the universe and his relations with inanimate nature, the animals, other men, and the gods. It also offers us a partial answer to the question of why the Cynic should, despite his self-sufficiency, concern himself with the moral standing of other men. As κοσμοπολίτης ('citizen of the cosmos'), he recognises his potential kinship with others, and he has therefore a certain obligation to help them.

Claims for the originality of Cynic cosmopolitanism require careful formulation. Its most distinctive element—the primitivist, or animalistic, interpretation of the principle 'living according to nature'—has parallels in the fifth century, although in general these parallels dissociate animalism and 'philanthropy' (*philanthrōpia*).[80] Here again, Antisthenes was no doubt an important intermediary. One is, however, justified in crediting Diogenes with the invention of the word *kosmopolitēs*, a word that in itself marks an important stage in the history of ideas, and with expressing his cosmopolitan sentiments with that combination of verbal virtuosity and arresting exposition so characteristic of this great philosopher.

On my interpretation, Cynic cosmopolitanism influenced Stoic cosmopolitanism far more than current opinion recognises. The Cynics did not bequeath to the Stoics a purely negative concept to which the latter added a positive value: rather, Cynic cosmopolitanism already contained all the essential positive qualities that the Stoics endowed with a fuller exposition, and that they integrated into a fully developed physical system.

There remains a final problem—the precise degree of convergence between Cynic and Stoic cosmopolitanism. Cynic rejection of the polis contrasts with the Stoic orthodoxy that the polis had a certain value as an imperfect analogue of the true 'cosmic polity'. Precisely how far can one reconcile the Cynic and Stoic interpretations of the principle of 'living according to nature'? Primitivism and animalism remain available strategies within Stoicism at all periods, [[120]] although they are rejected, at least in their most extreme forms, by certain Stoics. Some modern scholars, notably Höistad, have seen in Cynic cosmopolitanism essentially the same fusion of 'nature' (*phusis*) and 'custom' or 'law' (*nomos*) and transcendental 'reason' (*logos*) that is found in Stoicism.[81]

---

80  See, e.g., Lovejoy–Boas (1935) 112–16; Sinclair (1951) 48 n. 4; Guthrie (1969) 104 and n. 4, 114 n. 4; Seaford (1984) 52–5.
81  See, e.g., Höistad (1948) 138–42; Anastasi (1972); Buora (1973–4).

One can then link the passage cited from Plutarch's *De Fortuna Alexandri* with certain passages in Philo and elsewhere. On this view, the Cynic and Stoic interpretations of 'living according to nature' are almost identical. Höistad's analysis, while flawed in detail,[82] is not thereby totally vitiated.

My own view is rather different. The Cynics and Stoics shared beliefs that could have led them both to the same conclusion—namely that 'to live according to nature' means to live in accordance with the whole natural order as divinely ordained. In practice, however, the Cynics gave greater weight to animalistic primitivism and individual self-sufficiency, because these ideas contributed to the simplicity and attractiveness of their message: What could be more natural than to live the life of animals? What more comforting than the conviction that self-sufficiency leads to happiness?

So much for the theory; what of the practice? Was the Cynic πολιτεία a reality, a utopia, an ideal, or a community of philosophers? The Cynics diverged from their primitivist fifth-century predecessors in that they practised their animalistic interpretation of 'life according to nature'. They also diverged from their cosmopolitan predecessors in that they practised their cosmopolitanism. The 'polity of the cosmos' is already a reality for the Cynics themselves, and they try to turn it into reality for others, who are potential fellow citizens. After all, in the time of Cronus, the 'polity of the cosmos' had already been a reality for all men. In its own bizarre fashion, Diogenes' polity was the most practical, the most universalist, and (let us not be afraid to say it) the noblest of all the philosophical states (πολιτεῖαι)—indeed, of all the political states—of all antiquity.

There remains a tension between the simplicity of the primitivist life and Cynic self-sufficiency, on the one hand, and the implications of Cynic cosmopolitanism, on the other hand. In my opinion, Julian appreciates this tension correctly when he writes that the 'end' (*telos*) of Diogenes and Crates was their own 'happiness' (*eudaimonia*), but that they also helped others as being their 'fellow citizens' (*sumpoliteuomenous*).[83] In any case, this tension does not allow us to deny the positive value of Cynic cosmopolitanism, a value that I hope to have established, contrary to current opinion.

---

82 For example, when he accepts the authenticity of the syllogism on νόμος in D.L. 6.72 (see n. 10 above).

83 Julian 6.201c: καὶ οὐ τοῦτο ... ἀλλὰ καὶ τοῖς λόγοις.

## Bibliography

Anastasi, R. (1972) 'Varia I: Diog. Laert. VI 72', in *Studi classici in onore di Quintino Cataudella*, 3 vols. (Catania) 1.367–70.
von Arnim, H. (1898) *Leben und Werke des Dio von Prusa* (Berlin).
Babut, D. (1969) *Plutarque et le stoïcisme* (Paris).
Baldry, H. C. (1959) 'Zeno's Ideal State', *JHS* 79: 3–15.
Baldry, H. C. (1965) *The Unity of Mankind in Greek Thought* (Cambridge).
Billerbeck, M. (1978) *Epiktet: vom Kynismus* (Leiden).
Billerbeck, M., ed. (1991) *Die Kyniker in der modernen Forschung: Aufsätze mit Einführung und Bibliographie* (Amsterdam).
Bordes, J. (1982) *Politeia dans la pensée grecque jusqu'à Aristote* (Paris).
Branham, R. B. (1996) 'Defacing the Currency: Diogenes' Rhetoric and the *Invention* of Cynicism', in id. and Goulet-Cazé (1996) 81–104.
Branham, R. B. and M.-O. Goulet-Cazé, edd. (1996) *The Cynics: the Cynic Movement in Antiquity and its Legacy* (Berkeley and Los Angeles).
Brown, T. S. (1949) *Onesicritus: A Study in Hellenistic Historiography* (Berkeley and Los Angeles).
Buora, M. (1973–4) 'L'incontro tra Alessandro e Diogene: tradizione e significato', *AIV* 132: 243–64.
Delatte, A. (1953) 'Le sage-témoin dans la philosophie stoïco-cynique', *BAB*[5] 39: 166–86.
Dudley, D. R. (1937) *A History of Cynicism from Diogenes to the 6th century A.D.* (London).
Erskine, A. (1990) *The Hellenistic Stoa: Political Thought and Action* (London and Ithaca).
Fisch, M. H. (1937) 'Alexander and the Stoics', *AJPh* 58: 59–82, 129–51.
Gerhard, G. A. (1912) 'Zur Legende vom Kyniker Diogenes', *Archiv für Religionswissenschaft* 15: 388–408; repr. in Billerbeck (1991) 89–106.
Giannantoni, G. (1958) *I cirenaici* (Florence).
Giannantoni, G. (1993) 'Antistene fondatore della scuola cinica?', in Goulet-Cazé and Goulet (1993) 15–34.
Giannattasio Andria, R. (1980) 'Diogene Cinico nei papiri ercolanesi', *Cronache Ercolanesi* 10: 129–51.
Gigon, O. (1956) *Kommentar zum zweiten Buch von Xenophons Memorabilia* (Basel).
Goulet-Cazé, M.-O. (1982) 'Un syllogisme stoïcien sur la loi dans la doxographie de Diogène le Cynique: à propos de Diogène Laërce VI 72', *RhMus* 125: 214–40.
Goulet-Cazé, M.-O. (1986a) *L'Ascèse Cynique: un commentaire de Diogéne Laërce VI 70–71* (Paris).
Goulet-Cazé, M.-O. (1986b) 'Une liste de disciples de Cratès le Cynique en Diogène Laërce 6, 95', *Hermes* 114: 247–52.

Goulet-Cazé, M.-O. (1996) 'Religion and the Early Cynics', in Branham and Goulet-Cazé (1996) 47–80.
Goulet-Cazé, M.-O. and R. Goulet, edd. (1993) *Le Cynisme ancien et ses prolongements* (Paris).
Guthrie, W. K. C. (1969) 'The World of the Sophists', in *A History of Greek Philosophy III: The Fifth-Century Enlightenment* (Cambridge) 3–319 = *The Sophists* (Cambridge, 1971).
Hock, R. F. (1976) 'Simon the Shoemaker as an Ideal Cynic', *GRBS* 17: 41–53.
Höistad, R. (1948) *Cynic Hero and Cynic King: Studies in the Cynic Conception of Man* (Uppsala).
Ioppolo, A. M. (1980) *Aristone di Chio e lo stoicismo antico* (Naples).
Kerferd, G. B. (1981) *The Sophistic Movement* (Cambridge).
Kindstrand, J. F. (1976) *Bion of Borysthenes: a Collection of the Fragments with Introduction and Commentary* (Uppsala).
Kindstrand, J. F. (1980) 'Demetrius the Cynic', *Philologus* 124: 83–98.
Kindstrand, J. F. (1984) 'The Cynics and Heraclitus', *Eranos* 82: 149–78.
Lana, I. (1951) 'Tracce di dottrine cosmopolitiche in Grecia prima del cinismo', *RFIC* 29: 193–216, 317–38.
Lovejoy, A. O. and G. Boas (1935) *A Documentary History of Primitivism and Related Ideas in Antiquity* (Baltimore; repr. New York, 1965).
Mannebach, E., ed. (1961) *Aristippi et Cyrenaicorum Fragmenta* (Leiden).
Moles, J. L. (1983a) 'The Date and Purpose of the Fourth Kingship Oration of Dio Chrysostom', *ClAnt* 2: 251–78 [above, Ch. 3].
Moles, J. L. (1983b) '"*Honestius quam Ambitiosius*"? An Exploration of the Cynic's Attitude to Moral Corruption in his Fellow Men', *JHS* 103: 103–23 [above, Ch. 12].
Moles, J. L. (1983c) 'The Woman and the River: Diogenes' Apophthegm from Herculaneum and Some Popular Misconceptions about *Cynicism*', *Apeiron* 17: 125–30 [above, Ch. 13].
Moles, J. L. (1985) 'Cynicism in Horace *Epistles* I', *PLLS* 5: 33–60 [above, Ch. 14].
Moles, J. L. (1990) 'The Kingship Orations of Dio Chrysostom', *PLLS* 6: 297–375 [above, Ch. 5].
Moles, J. L. (1993) 'Le cosmopolitisme cynique', in Goulet-Cazé and Goulet (1993) 259–80.
Moles, J. L. (1995) 'The Cynics and Politics', in A. Laks and M. Schofield, edd., *Justice and Generosity: Studies in Hellenistic Social and Political Philosophy* (Cambridge) 129–58 [above, Ch. 15].
Murray, O. (1966) 'The Unity of Mankind [Review of Baldry (1965)]', *CR* 16: 368–71.
Norden, E. (1893) 'Beiträge zur Geschichte der griechischen Philosophie', *Jahrbücher der classische Philologie*, Suppl. 19: 365–462.

Rist, J. M. (1969) *Stoic Philosophy* (Cambridge).
Schofield, M. (1991) *The Stoic Idea of the City* (Cambridge; repr. Chicago, 1999).
Schulz-Falkenthal, H. (1979) 'Ich bin ein Weltbürger: zum Kosmopolitismus in der Antike', *WZHalle* 28: 29–39.
Seaford, R., ed. (1984) *Euripides: Cyclops* (Oxford).
Sinclair, T. A. (1951) *A History of Greek Political Thought* (London).
Steiner, G. (1976) 'Diogenes' Mouse and the Royal Dog: Conformity in Non-Conformity', *CJ* 72: 36–46.
Strathmann, H. (1942) 'μάρτυς', *Theologisches Wörterbuch zum Neuen Testament* IV.477–520; Eng. trans. in G. Kittel and G. Friedrich, edd., *Theological Dictionary of the New Testament* (Grand Rapids, 1967) IV.474–508.
Tarn, W. W. (1939) 'Alexander, Cynics and Stoics', *AJPh* 60: 41–70.
Tarn, W. W. (1948) *Alexander the Great*, 2 vols. (Cambridge).
Vischer, R. (1965) *Das einfache Leben: Wort- und motivgeschichtliche Untersuchungen zu einem Wertbegriff der antiken Literatur* (Göttingen).
Weber, E. (1887) 'De Dione Chrysostomo Cynicorum Sectatore', *Leipziger Stud. z. Classichen Philologie* 10: 77–268.
Wilamowitz-Moellendorf, U. von (1893) *Aristoteles und Athen*, 2 vols. (Berlin).

CHAPTER 17

# The Political Thought of the Cynics

> Diogenes was a Greek philosopher who lived in a tub; one day he was sunning himself when Alexander the Great, smitten by desire to see the great philosopher, approached and asked if there was anything he could do for him, to which Diogenes responded: 'Get out of my light'.
>
> Cic. *Tusc.* 5.92; D.L. 6.38

∴

The Cynics[1] had no ideals of their own and assumed the worst of everybody else; hence the modern usages 'cynic' and 'cynical'.

Among non-classicists today these are perhaps the two dominant, although contradictory, images of Cynicism. The first projects Diogenes' behaviour, which some might regard as merely loutish, as illustrating a truly admirable independence of spirit; indeed, some versions add that Alexander delightedly exclaimed: 'Had I not been Alexander, I would have wished to be Diogenes' (Plut. *Alex.* 14.5; D.L. 6.32). The second projects the Cynics as, if not positively immoral, at least unpleasantly amoral. Neither seems to encourage claims that the Cynics made an important contribution to ancient political thought, and the contradiction between the two is but a pale reflection of the many difficulties involved in the attempt to uncover a true picture of Cynicism. Any assessment, therefore, of the Cynic contribution must begin by resolving these difficulties.

---

1 Texts/fragments/testimonia: Paquet (1988); SSR II.5.B–N; critical discussions: SSR IV.195–583; general books: Lovejoy–Boas (1935); Dudley (1937); Höistad (1948); Kindstrand (1976); Goulet-Cazé (1986); collections of papers: Billerbeck (1991); Goulet-Cazé–Goulet (1993); Branham–Goulet-Cazé (1996); my own views (which have fluctuated in detail): Moles (1983), (1993) {= (1996)}, (1995), with fuller documentation than is desirable here; potted accounts in my entries on the Cynics in OCD[3] and in Zeyl (1997).

## 1 The Problem of Evidence

Virtually all the writings of the Cynics themselves are lost, but a disparate mass of evidence survives: quantities of sayings and anecdotes; numerous 〖416〗 Cynic prose and poetic fragments, of greatly varying size; letters (Cynic in content but not written by the putative writers); the Diogenic discourses of Dio Chrysostom (c. AD 45–120), sophist and (mostly Stoic) philosopher; more or less systematic accounts of Cynicism by the Epicurean Philodemus (first century BC), the Stoic Epictetus ('On Cynicism';[2] early second century AD), and the biographer Diogenes Laertius (probably third century AD), Book 6 of whose *Lives of the Philosophers* treats the Cynics and remains the most important single source;[3] numerous allusions, with some discussion, in the Stoic philosopher Seneca (writing c. AD 55–65); several works of the rhetorician and satirist Lucian (second century AD); two speeches of the Roman emperor and intellectual Julian (fourth century AD); numerous Christian allusions to Cynicism; and a great quantity of Cynic-influenced literature, particularly that of the satiric tradition.

Within this mass, numerous different tendencies can be observed: the invention of sayings and anecdotes, a general phenomenon of ancient biography accentuated by the flamboyant and self-dramatising behaviour of leading Cynics; idealisation and bowdlerisation of Cynicism (Epictetus); making Diogenes look like Socrates; making the Cynics look like Stoics (Epictetus, elements of Diogenes Laertius), sometimes in order to legitimate a formal philosophical 'succession' (Socrates–Antisthenes–Diogenes–Crates–Zeno); projecting the Cynics as exemplars of primitive or simple virtue; projecting the Cynics as stern, but just, critics of the vices of human society; polemical misrepresentation (Philodemus); representing Cynics as frauds and hypocrites, hence suitable butts for comic ridicule (Lucian); portraying Cynics as threats to social and political stability (Roman imperial texts); appropriating a Cynic persona for self-portrayal (Dio; sometimes Lucian); contrasting early Cynics and their allegedly debased descendants; comparing, and contrasting, Cynics and Christian ascetics.

Of these tendencies, some are clearly distortions (many of Philodemus' claims are merely silly), although distortions help to define truths; some are not clearly distortions but conflict with others; some seem *a priori* reasonable but require the support of hard evidence. Thus any picture of Cynicism must be a synthesis of widely different types of material and of thousands

---

2 Billerbeck (1978).
3 Goulet-Cazé (1992).

of different items, each of which should, ideally, have been subject to exact scrutiny (by conventional criteria such as the attempt to distinguish between primary/early and secondary/late material). The ⟦417⟧ synthesis must also allow for the possibility of difference between different Cynics and different periods of Cynicism. And it will always be vulnerable to the accusation of circular argument. Nor is it merely a matter of establishing facts: Cynic behaviour, sayings, and writings themselves pose interpretative problems.

Unsurprisingly, therefore, the genesis, status, significance, value, and influence of Cynicism were all controversial in the ancient world and remain so. Nevertheless, the source problem can be exaggerated. The loss of nearly all Cynic writings does not matter as much as one would anticipate, and in any case we can get close to the most important written work in all Cynicism (Diogenes' *Politeia*). Even the volume and diversity of the surviving evidence has a positive aspect, as indicating the interest, importance, and vitality of the Cynic tradition.

## 2    Reconstructing Cynicism

The term 'Cynic' ('doggish') was certainly used from the fourth century BC of Diogenes, nicknamed 'the dog', and of his followers, hence the English 'Cynicism' ('Cynism' in ancient Greek and many modern languages) as the name of the general movement. There has, however, been controversy from ancient times as to whether Diogenes or Antisthenes (c.445–365 BC), one of Socrates' closest followers, was the first Cynic.[4]

The case for Antisthenes depends on Cynic-looking elements in his thought and in the attested titles of some of his works; on his having taught philosophy in Cynosarges, a gymnasium for non-Athenians whose name can be interpreted as including 'dog'; and on the ancient tradition that Diogenes was one of his pupils. But the whole ancient tradition agrees in calling Diogenes, not Antisthenes, 'the dog'; some elements of Antisthenes' philosophy (notably his study of language and logic) are emphatically un-Cynic; and direct association between Diogenes and Antisthenes is chronologically problematic (below). The case for Antisthenes should thus be attributed to the general ancient desire to construct traditions based on master–pupil relationships, to the specific project of tracing Stoicism back in unbroken succession to Socrates, and to Antisthenes' undoubted influence on Diogenes, transmitted not through direct association but through Antisthenes' writings.

---

4  SSR IV.223–33; Giannantoni (1993); Döring (1995).

In the reconstruction of Diogenes' life[5] and activity, the general distortions in the ancient traditions about Cynicism are exacerbated by the fact [[418]] that Diogenes was himself a flamboyant self-dramatist, who provoked extremes of admiration, hostility, and imaginative invention, thus inspiring a rich and varied Diogenes-legend. Ancient and modern reactions to Diogenes range from appreciation of his undoubted wit to admiration (often tinged with exasperation) for his supposed integrity, denial of his philosophical significance, revulsion at his cult of shamelessness, dislike of the threat he was thought to pose to conventional social and political values, and misguided attempts to make him respectable. All accounts, ancient and modern, are, therefore, necessarily controversial. But the picture is less obscure than one might fear.

Diogenes (c.412/403–c.324/321 BC) was a native of the Black Sea port of Sinope, where his father, Hecesias, was in charge of the mint; he was exiled; and he spent the rest of his life in Athens and Corinth. The date of his arrival in mainland Greece and the question of his relationship with Antisthenes remain disputed. On the most reasonable reconstruction, Diogenes and his father were accused, rightly or wrongly, of 'defacing the currency'—thus one of Diogenes' great slogans (D.L. 6.20) originated as an apologetic and metaphorical reinterpretation of a literal act; the literal 'defacement of the currency' caused Diogenes' exile; and both events occurred after Antisthenes' death. Hence Diogenes' exile was the catalyst for a dramatic change of life, and his pupilship under Antisthenes should be regarded as fictitious. In a similar spirit of rationalising minimalism, the stories of Diogenes' consultation of the Delphic oracle (clearly modelled upon Socrates') and of his capture by pirates (D.L. 6.21, 29–31, 74–5) should be rejected; on the other hand, the encounter with Alexander seems authentic (though it would have occurred before Alexander became 'the Great').[6]

The main outlines of Diogenes' activities in Athens and Corinth are clear. Over time he evolved a way of life which entailed the barest minimum of material possessions: coarse cloak, folded double for warmth in the cold (no under-tunic); staff for physical support and protection; knapsack for food; wine-jar for 'house' (the 'tub' of later tradition); no shoes. It also entailed the barest minimum of food: cold water from springs and fountains, not wine; vegetables, especially greens and lupins (though Diogenes was not committed to vegetarianism). These items were variously obtained by living off the land, begging, and stealing. Diogenes' life-style also involved the performance in public of all natural functions (eating, drinking, urinating, defecating, masturbating,

---

5 Goulet-Cazé (1994).
6 Hammond (1993) 28, 282.

and fornicating), ⟦419⟧ characteristically in the *agora*, a sacred area off-limits to such earthy activities. The main point of the appellation 'dog' is shamelessness, for which dogs were renowned.

Diogenes was highly vocal, launching verbal attacks upon a whole range of targets: all forms of convention, marriage, family, politics, the city, all social, sexual, and racial distinctions, worldly reputation, wealth, power, and authority, literature, music, and all forms of intellectual speculation; and upon their various human representatives. Many of these attacks exemplify the slogan 'deface the currency', 'currency' being a metaphor for law, custom, and convention. Diogenes' aggressiveness is another implication of his nickname. The attacks were generally witty, the wit often savage, often vulgar, often paradoxical, sometimes utilising literary parody and allusion. Diogenes' oral performances also included justifications of his peculiar way of life, a way of life which was adopted by countless Cynics over the centuries, down to the sixth century AD.

Fundamental questions arise. Was Diogenes a mere buffoon, a mere exhibitionist, as many ancient and modern critics claim? Is there anything here which is serious and implies thought? Can Cynicism be described in any useful sense as a philosophy?

That Diogenes was well educated might be inferred from his social background, and is confirmed by his knowledge of Homer and tragedy, his use of literary allusion and parody, and his own writings (below). He also shows familiarity with the life and thought of philosophers both earlier (the Presocratics, Socrates, Antisthenes, and the elder Aristippus) and contemporary (Plato). When he wants, he can indulge in technical philosophy, so much so that (as we shall see) one of his syllogisms defied solution until 1991. This last example indicates intelligence, as do many of his sayings and actions. Diogenes, then, illustrates a phenomenon that is always unsettling for clever intellectuals: that of the clever intellectual who rejects intellectualism in favour of some very simple creed or mode of life, in whose articulation, however, he continues to deploy cleverness. Any one (in the ancient or modern world) who dismisses Diogenes with patronising contempt is a fool, as many of his contemporaries learned to their cost. In the series of verbal skirmishes between Diogenes and the great Plato recorded by ancient tradition Diogenes typically comes off better (e.g., D.L. 6.25–6, 40, 58, 67).

What, then, of Diogenes' exhibitionism? Of course, if one holds that there is no shame in performing natural functions in public, some degree of what others will decry as mere exhibitionism is inevitable. But Diogenes' performance in public of natural functions often took the form ⟦420⟧ of full public performance, and masturbation was one of his star turns (D.L. 6.69). Later,

Diogenes' closest follower, Crates, achieved notoriety by having intercourse with his 'wife' Hipparchia in the *agora* (D.L. 6.96). How can such seemingly outrageous behaviour be justified?

And what of Diogenes' characteristic humour? Here the ancient tradition provides an immediate, though partial, answer: the Cynics specialised in the serio-comic (*spoudaiogeloion*), the exposition of serious thought through humorous means.[7] But what was the thought?

It is obvious that Cynicism was first and foremost how Cynics actually lived and behaved (even Diogenes Laertius, who presents Cynicism as a philosophy, attests ancient debate whether Cynicism was a philosophy or a way of life [6.103]). It was never a formal philosophical school: it never had, and obviously could never have, a physical school-building; equally, it never had, and could never have, any philosophical doctrine. Yet established philosophers of the time thought that Cynicism embodied some sort of philosophical project. Plato famously dubbed Diogenes a 'mad Socrates' (D.L. 6.54), Aristotle seems to allude to Diogenes in a serious ethical context (*Pol.* 1253a26–9), and Theophrastus certainly does so (D.L. 6.22). Diogenes and later Cynics do to some extent engage in philosophical debate with other philosophers. That debate mostly takes the form of verbal skirmishing but sometimes extends into written works, such as Diogenes' *Politeia* or the polemics between Cynics and Epicureans.[8] Diogenes himself claimed that his goal (*telos*) was virtue (D.L. 6.70, 72, 104), and this claim was taken seriously by reputable philosophers of different schools in succeeding generations. In popular philosophy, Diogenes often appears as the philosopher *par excellence*. Diogenes also claimed 'wisdom' (D.L. 6.72), had many personal followers (described in the ancient tradition as 'pupils'), and wrote numerous works,[9] some of which bear what look like conventional philosophical titles, and which evoked responses from established philosophers. (Denial of Diogenes' writing reflects the bowdlerising tendency, anxious to detach the great Diogenes from the disgusting propositions circulating under his name.)

Cynicism, then, is a way of life, but one which makes philosophical claims, and in this sense the polarity between 'way of life' and 'philosophy' is false (just as, conversely, one's philosophy should affect one's way of life). These philosophical claims are grounded in a criterion accepted by ⟦421⟧ practically all ancient philosophies: 'life according to nature' (D.L. 6.71). The crucial question is how this criterion is to be understood. It is certain that Diogenes gave it a

---

7  Kindstrand (1976) 47–8, López Cruces (1995) 77–84.
8  Gigante (1993) 198–203 (Menippus, Colotes, and Menedemus), 211–23 (Philodemus).
9  Goulet-Cazé (1994) 817–20.

'hard primitivist' interpretation: hence his constant appeals to animals, primitive man, uncivilised barbarians (all uncontaminated by civilisation), and the gods as moral standards, and his representation of the Cynic way of life in Golden Age terms (D.L. 6.44). This hard primitivism underpins all the characteristic Cynic modes of behaviour and attitudes. It is important to appreciate the extreme radicalism of the Cynic stance. When Diogenes says, 'I do not need material possessions (or whatever)', he is not saying, 'I do not *need* them but it is all right for me to have them', nor 'I do not need them, but it's all right for *you* to have them (because you have a legitimately different perspective)'. He is saying, 'these things are bad and prevent the attainment of virtue'.

As hard primitives, Cynics claim 'self-sufficiency' (D.L. 6.105), 'freedom' (D.L. 6.71), and 'passionlessness' (D.L. 6.2, 15), and they describe their way of life alike as 'simple', because natural in the most extreme sense, 'easy', because wholly anti-intellectual, and 'difficult', because of its enormous physical demands. Hence Diogenes' (highly selective) admiration of Sparta (D.L. 6.27, 59). Toil and suffering naturally acquire positive moral value in Cynicism, an idea expressed in the paradox *ponos agathon*: 'suffering is a good'. Overcoming these difficulties requires constant practice (*askēsis*).[10]

Of course, the core claim that virtue consists in living in accordance with primitivist nature is not self-evidently true, though it belongs to a long tradition of thought which reflects an understandable human desire that the world be a fundamentally good place and the problems of life merely a distortion of the natural order. Another obvious objection to the Cynic programme is that it is impossible. To both these difficulties the Cynic way of life itself provides some answer. That way of life *is* virtue in action, and it shows that the programme can be implemented. Like the appeal to 'living according to nature', this answer may be regarded as philosophically unsatisfactory, on the ground that Cynicism does not argue its position 'properly'. But that objection carried and could in principle carry little weight with Diogenes.

If the Cynic way of life shows that the programme *can* be done, Cynic exhibitionism immediately finds a creditable explanation: it is partly for the benefit of other people. This raises the question of the Cynic's relations with others.[11]

[[422]] It is clear that the Cynics recognised the kinship or community of the wise: they used the tag 'the wise man is the friend of his like' (D.L. 6.105), one of Diogenes' syllogisms appealed to 'wise men's being friends of the gods' and 'their having possessions in common' (D.L. 6.72 [below]), Diogenes himself had followers, and Crates claimed to be 'a citizen of Diogenes' (D.L. 6.93). This

---

10   D.L. 6.71; Goulet-Cazé (1986).
11   Moles (1983) 109–16 {above, pp. 328–38}; (1993) 269–77 {cf. above, pp. 428–34}.

kinship transcends the conventional barriers between men and women (as we shall see) and between races (hence Cynic appeals to the right behaviour of barbarian peoples).

More problematic is their relationship with mankind at large. Contrary, perhaps, to first impressions, Cynicism is a missionary philosophy. Cynic exhibitionism provides other human beings with a model to imitate or a demonstration of the falsity of their own values. By example and exhortation the Cynic energetically tries to convert others to the Cynic life of virtue. He claims a large range of titles ('scout', 'overseer', 'benefactor', 'teacher', 'ruler', 'doctor', 'reconciler', 'good spirit', 'helper', 'saviour', etc.) which imply a didactic and proselytising role towards others and indeed a profound concern for other human beings (*philanthrōpia*). These apparently altruistic elements of the Cynic's behaviour cannot be dismissed as later embroideries inspired by the more humane character of Crates. They are all, or almost all, documented for Diogenes himself and some for his predecessor Antisthenes.[12]

How, then, to explain the criticisms and insults which the Cynic directs at humanity in general, or the apparently disdainful fashion in which he divides humanity into an elite of sages and the mass of the foolish or insane? The explanation is simple enough. As a matter of fact there is a great gulf between the sage and the ignorant majority and only the former is a human being in the truest sense. Yet Cynic virtue is 'easy' and represents man's natural state. Consequently, even the imbecile masses can be regarded as *potential* human beings, and the gulf between the Cynic and ordinary human beings is not insuperable. Hence the common modern assumption that Cynicism is completely negative is misconceived: of course Cynic teaching is largely negative, because it aims to expose the falsity of conventional values, but the point is to isolate the only thing that matters, the Cynic way of life 'according to nature', which itself is positive—and to commend it to others. Epictetus (3.24.64) is thus right to describe Diogenes as 'loving all mankind'.

Thus far we have tried to reconstruct Cynicism as it were in a vacuum and without prejudice. Another approach is to plot Cynicism against 〖423〗 existing traditions. While Diogenes' way of life was original and distinctive, it can be seen to be constructed from many diverse, and mostly Greek, elements: the belief (espoused by certain types of holy men and wise men) that wisdom was a matter of action rather than thought; the principle (advanced by various sophists, fifth-century primitivists, and Antisthenes) of living in accordance with nature rather than law/convention; the tradition, perhaps sharpened by contemporary disillusionment with the polis, of promulgating ideal societies

---

12   Documentation in Moles (1983) 112 {above, p. 332} n. 73.

or constitutions, often with Golden Age associations; a tradition of 'shamelessness'(reflected by the symbol of the dog in literature and by the supposed customs of certain foreign peoples); Socratic rejection of all elements of philosophy except practical ethics; Socrates' pursuit of philosophy in the *agora* rather than in a school; an anti-intellectual tradition; the tradition (variously represented by Odysseus, Heracles, the Spartans, and to some extent by Socrates) of physical toughness as a requirement of virtue; the image of the suffering hero and the wanderer (Odysseus, Heracles, various tragic figures); the tradition of mendicancy (represented both in literature and in life); the life of asceticism and poverty (as represented by various wise men and holy men and labourers); the tradition of the wise or holy man who promises converts happiness or salvation; and various humorous traditions (the jester's practical and verbal humour; Old Comedy's outspokenness and crudity; Socrates' serio-comic wit).

Bizarre, perhaps repulsive, insufficiently grounded in philosophical theory, Cynicism nevertheless exhibits a coherence which in its own terms is quite powerful.

## 3  The Cynics and Politics

What room does this picture of Cynicism leave for conventional politics? Seemingly, none. But before we can accept this conclusion, we must consider the evidence regarding Diogenes' celebrated 'cosmopolitanism'.[13] That evidence may: (a) force us to modify our conclusion; (b) reveal an incoherence in Diogenes' position; (c) validate our conclusion but open up further perspectives.

The two key texts are in Diogenes Laertius. 6.63 records a saying: 'Asked where he was from, he said: "[I am] a citizen of the universe."' Although this saying comes in a literary form, the *chreia* (a brief anecdote including an apophthegm), which is much used in the 'Diogenes-legend', ⟦424⟧ the question was as common in life as in literature and had particular point for the stateless Diogenes. Nor does the extreme rarity of the word *kosmopolitēs* or its first being attested in Philo (*Opif.* 3; *Mos.* 1.157 [first century AD]) count against authenticity: Philo or his Stoic sources must have got the word from somewhere and the Cynics were renowned for their verbal resourcefulness, including coinages. Numerous ancient sources link Diogenes with 'cosmopolitan' sentiment. The false attribution of that sentiment to Socrates is naturally

---

13    This whole section reworks Moles (1993) and (1995) with some modifications and changes of emphasis.

explained as retrojection of Diogenic material upon the 'father' of the whole Cynic-Stoic 'succession'. There is much evidence from Cynics and non-Cynics that 'cosmopolitanism' was a big Cynic claim, which presumably starts with the first Cynic.

The other text comes in Diogenes' 'doxography' in 6.72, which requires full quotation:[14]

> (a) He said that all things belong to the wise, using the sort of arguments we have stated above (6.37):
> All things belong to the gods.
> The gods are friends of the wise.
> The possessions of friends are held in common.
> Therefore all things belong to the wise.
> (b) With regard to the law (*nomos*), he held that it was impossible for there to be political government (*politeuesthai*) without it. For he says:
> Without a city there is no profit in something civilised;
> and the city is civilised.
> Without law there is no profit in a city.
> Therefore law is something civilised.
> (c) He would ridicule good birth and reputations and all those sorts of things, saying that they were the ornaments of vice (*prokosmēmata kakias*).
> (d) And he said that the only correct citizen-state (*politeia*)[15] was the one in the universe (*kosmos*).
> ⟦425⟧ (e) And he said that women should be held in common, recognising no marriage, but saying that the man who persuades should go with the woman who persuades.[16] And because of this he thought that sons too should be held in common.

---

14  This section follows the translation and arrangement of Schofield (1991) 141–2, with modifications as in Moles (1995) 130 {above, p. 390}.

15  Translation of *politeia* is difficult. 'State' *tout court* misleads, but some reference to 'state' is desirable, because: (a) *politeia* alludes to the workings of the institution traditionally known as the 'city-state'; (b) 'state' can be used both of the political institution and of the individual, hence allowing a paradoxical transference of reference. The 'citizen' prefix attempts to give the term 'state' concrete political reference and also emphasises the closeness of the formulations of 6.72 and 6.63. The translation of the title of Diogenes' work as 'Ideal State' has disadvantages, but fewer than those of such translations as 'Republic' or 'Constitution', and makes the point that such a philosophical work aims to describe what ought to be rather than what is—though, as we shall see, the Cynic 'state' is not utopian.

16  On text and interpretation see Schofield (1991) 12 n. 21.

A preliminary problem is posed by the difficult syllogism in (b), which has occasioned considerable debate. Its authenticity is supported by two factors: its position in the doxography and its relationship to a syllogism of Cleanthes the Stoic (Stob. 2.103.14–17 [= *SVF* 1.587 = Long–Sedley §67.1]), which reads approximately as follows: 'If a city is a habitable construction to which people may have recourse for the dispensation of justice, then a city is surely civilised. But a city is that sort of habitation. So a city is civilised.' While text and interpretation are controversial, this latter syllogism, which defends the city and 'civilisation', clearly aims to refute (b). Diogenes, then, is giving 'the civilised' a pejorative meaning (as it must have in Cynicism) and attacking law, the city, and 'the civilised' as interconnected: 'Diogenes' argument is—as one would expect—*antinomian*, directed against those who sympathise with his aversion to the city and its manners, but who hold to the view rejected by him that the rule of law is indispensable'.[17]

Many scholars have supposed that the whole of 6.72 derives from Diogenes' lost *Politeia* ('Ideal State'). The content fits: a general 'political' focus; two syllogisms (a formal mode alien to Diogenes' oral philosophising); a specific allusion to 'the correct state' (a fourth-century term); and in (e) a radical proposal for sexual relations and the rearing of children suitable to a *Politeia* of radical cast. The arrangement also has a logic. The first syllogism, indubitably Diogenic, concerns legitimate possessions or needs. The second syllogism, also Diogenic, concerns something that is conventionally regarded as necessary for civilised life but which the Cynic rejects, along with the city and civilised life itself. The rejection of 'the civilised', etc. is followed by a rejection of similar things within the city ('good birth and reputations and all those sorts of things'), expressed by a characteristic Cynic attitude, 'ridicule'. These similar things are designated 'ornaments of vice'. Then comes the cosmopolitan sentiment, introduced by an 'and', which seems to imply a precise logical connection.

The links with the preceding material are marked. After the false political and social values of the second syllogism and of the 'good-birth' section comes the correct political system. After the plurality of false values comes the single correct value (a typical Cynic contrast). There is also an ⟦426⟧ implicit contrast between 'law' (and custom, etc.), as in the false things of (b) and (c), and the *natural* order of the *kosmos* in (d). The use of the term 'correct state' illustrates the Cynic technique of appropriating and reinterpreting the rhetoric of his opponents and values that he rejects (thereby 'defacing the currency' verbally). Nor does the Cynic merely unite theory and practice (itself no mean feat): he unites exterior and interior, in contrast to those who pursue the 'ornaments

---

17   Schofield (1991) 134.

of vice'. And whereas 'good birth', etc. are the *prokosmēmata* of vice, the Cynic state is in the *kosmos*: false *kosmos* yields to true *kosmos*. The final item, on wives and sons 'in common', links by ring-structure to the first item, on possessions held 'in common'. This ring-structure seems to emphasise 'communism' as the alpha and omega of Diogenes' *politeia*, in implicit contrast with the exclusiveness of worldly possessions and of gradations of birth and reputation and so on, and in implicit parallel to the doctrine of 'cosmopolitanism', the *kosmos* naturally being the 'common' home of everyone, as the Cynic writer of [Heraclit.] *Ep.* 9.2 describes it.

6.72, therefore, represents a coherent and close summary of Diogenes' *Politeia*. But what is this 'cosmopolitanism'? It seems to combine a negative and a positive.

The negative is the rejection of the city and *ta politika* ('politics'): cf. (b) and (d). This rejection coheres with the slogan 'deface the currency', with numerous fragments and *testimonia*, with the tragic verses applied by Diogenes to himself: 'cityless [*apolis*], homeless, deprived of country [*patris*], a beggar, a wanderer, living life from day to day' (D.L. 6.38, where Diogenes is not lamenting his condition, but boasting of it), and with our general picture of Cynicism: the Diogenic Cynic must reject the city as 'contrary to nature'.

The positive consists in the primacy of the 'state in the *kosmos*'. Once we have jettisoned the assumption that Cynicism is completely negative, interpretation becomes relatively easy. First, Diogenes' sentiment must be seen against the background of a general tradition, variously represented by proverbial wisdom, philosophers, and sophists, in which the polis or *patris* or some similar concept is rejected, or revalued, in favour of an internationalist or cosmopolitan ideal; some of these formulations are very similar to Diogenes'.[18] Second, since rejection of the city promotes Cynic freedom and virtue, by another re-evaluation of conventional terms, Cynics use the words *patris*, polis, *politeia*, and so on as metaphors for the Cynic way of life itself (D.L. 6.93; Epict. *Diss.* 3.22.84–5). This 〚427〛 idea is implicit in 6.72: items (c) and (d) contrast—(c) concerns things that produce vice, (d) concerns the thing that produces virtue. Consequently, the Cynic *politeia*, the Cynic 'state', is nothing other than the 'state' of being a Cynic,[19] which is at once a material or social state and a moral state (Cynic moral virtue being dependent on rejection of conventional

---

18   Documentation in Moles (1993) 264 {cf. above, p. 425} n. 18. For the specific interaction with Aristippus' claims in Xen. *Mem.* 2.1.12–13 see Moles (1993) 265 {cf. above, p. 425}.
19   There are earlier parallels for this kind of move, both implicit as in the general tradition already mentioned and explicit (notably Pl. *Rep* 9.592b3): Diogenes' version remains extremely arresting and radical.

social and political values). The point is clear in Crates' *Pēra*, a Homeric poetic parody, whose blend of wit, literary sophistication, and earthiness and elevation of sentiment perfectly illustrates the appeal of Cynic *spoudaiogeloion* (D.L. 6.85; Demetr. *Eloc.* 259; Clem. *Strom.* 2.20.121):[20]

> There is a city, Knapsack, in the midst of the winey sea of illusion,
> Fair and rich, surrounded by dirt, owning nothing,
> Into which sails neither foolish parasite,
> Nor glutton delighting in a prostitute's buttocks,
> But it bears thyme and garlic and figs and loaves,
> As a result of which they do not make war against one another for these things,
> Nor take arms for money, nor for glory ...
> Free from the slavery and torture of servile pleasure,
> They love immortal kingship and freedom ...

Diogenes' Cynic 'state' is viewed as being coextensive with the *kosmos* and in some sort of positive relationship with it and its constituent elements.[21] As a child of nature or noble savage, the Cynic regards the natural world as bountiful, and feels a sense of kinship with the animal world, which provides him with models for his way of life. He feels a sense of kinship also with other wise men, wherever they may be. He can live his natural life anywhere on earth. He even feels potential kinship with mankind at large. What of the gods? The evidence about Cynic attitudes to the gods raises problems.[22] Nevertheless, Diogenes and other Cynics can describe the gods as man's benefactors, because they have created a naturally good world (D.L. 6.44), and project them as a paradigm for Cynic self-sufficiency (D.L. 6.51, 104). Consequently, they can describe themselves as 'god-like' (D.L. 6.51, 104, 105), as 'friends of the gods' (D.L. 6.37, 72) and as their messengers and agents (Str. 15.1.63–4 [= Onesicritus, *FGrHist* 134 F 17a]; Plut. *Alex.* 65.2; D.L. 6.102; Epict. *Diss.* 3.22.2, 23, 53, 69). In 6.72 item (a) attests Diogenes' inclusion of the gods in his *kosmopolis*.

⟦428⟧ It will be useful to pose a series of specific questions about Diogenes' *Politeia*.[23]

First, what is its status? The Cynics rejected literature *tout court* (not merely 'bad' literature), but wrote more voluminously and variously than any ancient

---

20   Dudley (1937) 44, 56–7; Höistad (1948) 129–31.
21   For the following arguments see Moles (1993) 268–9 {cf. above, pp. 427–8}.
22   Goulet-Cazé (1996); Moles (1995) 138 {above, p. 397} n. 27.
23   For some of the following arguments see Moles (1995) 138–58 {above, pp. 397–416}.

philosophical school:[24] relatively formal philosophical treatises, dialogues, tragedies, historiography, letters, 'diatribes' (moral homilies in lecture form), various kinds of poetry and of literary parody, prose-poetry hybrids. This paradox reflects a familiar philosophical compromise: while written philosophy is a poor substitute for real philosophising, it may be a necessary vehicle for increasing one's audience. (The other customary motive, philosophical exploration, means little to Cynics, who in their own estimation have solved all philosophical problems.) With its syllogisms and universalising propositions, Diogenes' *Politeia* looks like a formal philosophical work and it is essentially serious. Yet there is also an element of spoof: Diogenes can play the conventional philosophical game yet deconstruct the political philosophy of conventional philosophers such as Plato and Aristotle. Furthermore, when Diogenes and other Cynics use written works to convey moral lessons, they prefer 'entertainment' genres to formal works, and their projected readership only includes fellow-philosophers at the margins. In short, within Cynic writings 'formal' works of philosophy take second place to 'entertainment' genres, and the whole business of writing takes second place to practical philosophising on the streets. Diogenes' *Politeia*, then, is important because it crystallises Cynic philosophy in a text to which subsequent philosophers could respond and which can serve as a bench-mark for our general reconstruction of Cynicism. But it cannot *add* much to Cynic philosophy, except insofar as it may have to cover events that have not yet occurred (such as babies).

Hence the second question, applicable to all 'ideal states': is Diogenes' 'state' intended to be practicable? Since Diogenes' 'state' is in the first instance the 'state' of being a virtuous Cynic, the answer must basically be 'yes', though with a few qualifications. Even Cynics sometimes admitted that they had not quite attained the pinnacle of virtue. Cynic 'free sex' might produce children, who would have to be reared, as in item (e). Cynics might consort, both sexually and otherwise, with other Cynics, so that the Cynic 'state' might acquire a plural dimension, which would obviously increase, the more converts the Cynics made, and potentially include all humankind.

〚429〛 Third, what implications does the Cynic 'state' have for existing civic institutions? Diogenes' claim that there was nothing out of place in taking something from a temple (D.L. 6.73) and his advocacy of gymnastics, including nude gymnastics by women (D.L. 6.70; Philod. *Stoic*. col. XIX.17), entail the continuing existence of these institutions. But the saying about taking something from a temple is double-edged: while it allows the continued existence of 'temples', it denies their *raison d'être*. If there is nothing 'out of place' in taking

---

24  Branham (1993).

things from a temple, the whole notion of 'sacred space' is subverted (as it is by Diogenes' 'using any place for any purpose' [D.L. 6.22]). A Cynic must reject a social institution such as marriage, because it is an institution of *nomos* and an infringement of individual freedom. He will not advocate the dismantling of buildings such as temples, even though they did not exist in the primitive era when man was uncorrupted, because they have a practical Cynic usefulness, but he will not use them in the conventional way. Of course if a universal Cynic state were ever to come to pass, many areas would lack such amenities, because they would never be built in the first place.

Hence the fourth question: is there a fundamental inconsistency, or even, as many, ancients and moderns, have claimed, a fundamental hypocrisy, in Cynicism? On the one hand, there is an absolute theoretical rejection of the conventional ('incorrect') polis; on the other hand, although we hear of occasional Cynics in the country,[25] the great majority, like Diogenes, lived and begged in poleis and slept in baths and temples and so on. In fact, there are several good answers to this question. (i) The Cynic's missionary role commits him to living among the foolish and immoral masses. (ii) He must demonstrate the immediate practicability of his way of life. The principle 'use the things that are present'[26] allows *ad hoc* use of certain existing civic institutions, coupled with denial of their status as civic institutions (above). (iii) Item (a) (p. 449 above) bears directly on the question of begging and exploiting already-existing material amenities. Fundamentally, the Cynic does not recognise private ownership or property at all: everything is 'his' because he has a stake in the *kosmos*. Thus to beg (or steal) something from someone or some place is to take something to which *qua* Cynic one has a right.

There is, then, a legitimate distinction between those who live in the city but do not accept the city *qua* city and those who live in the city and do accept the city *qua* city, although this distinction may become blurred in practice, thereby allowing the greater degree of accommodation with 〚430〛 existing political and social realities that we find in certain later developments of, or departures from, Diogenic Cynicism (developments which we may characterise alternatively as 'not truly Cynic' or as 'soft-Cynic').[27]

Fifth, does the Cynic state have social consequences? As far as the Cynics themselves are concerned, certainly. Marriage and the family are dead; sexual relations depend on reciprocal free choice; incest is permissible (as sanctioned by the 'natural' behaviour of animals). However unappealing some aspects of

---

25   Downing (1993) 287.
26   Bion FF 16–17 with Kindstrand (1976) 218–19.
27   Moles (1995) 144–5 {above, pp. 403–4}.

this package, it entails full sexual equality, an ideal realised in the celebrated 'dog marriage' of Crates and Hipparchia (D.L. 6.96–7). In the long and dismal litany of ancient philosophers' thoughts on the relations between the sexes the Cynic position is cause for celebration. As for other people, Diogenes does not attempt to enforce his social package: he employs a mixture of criticism and persuasion; on the other hand, the more converts he makes, the greater the social consequences. Otherwise, and quite understandably, Cynics were generally regarded as social nuisances.

Sixth, does the Cynic state have economic consequences? Item (a) (p. 449 above) has been interpreted by some as entailing the abolition of private property; Cynicism was famously described by Goettling as 'the philosophy of the proletariat',[28] and people described as Cynics later involve themselves in redistributionist schemes. So Cercidas of Megalopolis (end of the third century BC) invoked the (invented) god 'Sharing' in proposals for land redistribution (F 4 Powell [= F 1 Livrea]), perhaps with direct allusion to item (a).[29] In the light of everything argued hitherto, it is obvious that for the Cynics themselves there are serious economic consequences. Diogenes advocated the abolition of money (the suggested substitution of knuckle-bones is a characteristically derisive joke [Athen. 4.159c; Philod. *Stoic.* col. XVI.6–9]). Cynic virtue/self-sufficiency/freedom entails the renunciation of all but the most basic material possessions, as Crates famously demonstrated (D.L. 6.87–8). Cynic converts must act likewise, and the more numerous they are, the greater the economic upheaval. The description of Cynicism as 'the philosophy of the proletariat' would not be unreasonable, if taken to mean that Cynicism *champions* poverty, but not that it seeks to *alleviate* poverty. In this the Diogenic Cynic has no interest, since for him poverty is a blessed state, provided only that it suffices to sustain life.

Seventh, does the Cynic state have political consequences? Certainly, though they require careful definition. Since the Diogenic Cynic rejects the polis and all other political institutions (kingship, tyranny, etc.) as ⟦431⟧ contrary to nature, he is *committed* to anarchy. To the Cynic, worldly 'power', 'rule', etc. is not merely indifferent: it is positively bad. He does not simply ignore it: he attacks it. He attacks it with words, but in so doing, he is not thereby eschewing action. For he wants to persuade others (both rulers and ruled) to reject worldly power in just the same way as he himself does. Consequently, when worldly power sees Cynicism as a threat (as did the agents of Roman emperors), it is right to do so. Could a Diogenic Cynic justify violence in the

---

28   Göttling (1851) 251.
29   López Cruces (1995) 123–30.

pursuit of anarchy, as did Russian anarchists of the nineteenth century? The answer is surely no, even though we do hear later of self-styled Cynics involved in armed insurrection. For the Diogenic Cynic is deeply opposed to arms, civil strife, and warfare, which he attributes to the 'unnatural' greed for riches (D.L. 6.50, 85 [Crates' *Pēra*]). He should convert others by example and persuasion, not coercion. His strength is moral, not military. His 'virility' comes from personal toughness, nor from the false *machismo* of armed might. He will resist the attacks of kings and tyrants on his personal freedom, but not to the point of violence. In the last analysis, he will claim to be free even when enslaved, as Diogenes did in the fictitious story of his enslavement (D.L. 6.74), even though this ultimate inner moral freedom is something much more restricted than normal Cynic freedom.

Is there any way in which a Diogenic Cynic could support political freedom? We do hear of later Cynics doing this; it is true that Diogenic Cynics attack monarchs and tyrants with particular virulence (D.L. 6.43, 50; Dio 6.35–62; Plut. *An Seni* 783C–D). But a Diogenic Cynic has no interest in freedom as a political institution, since such 'freedom' gives him rights which he does not want and imposes obligations which he must reject. Indeed, there is adequate evidence that Diogenes and Cynics like him criticised democracy (e.g. D.L. 6.24, 34, 41). It is readily comprehensible that Cynics should attack 'monarchs' or 'tyrants': if all political systems and all politicians are deluded, tyrannies and tyrants are particularly so, because their devotion to false values is so extreme; in certain cases (times of philosophical repression for example) their activities will directly infringe the freedom of Cynics; and in general they will harm other people, for whom Cynics have philanthropic concern. In short, advocacy of political freedom is a distortion of Diogenic Cynicism.

What of kingship? Cynics described themselves as 'kings', 'rulers', and so on (D.L. 6.29; Clem. *Strom.* 2.20.121), and some scholars have argued for a more or less unified tradition of 'Cynic kingship theory' from Antisthenes down to Dio Chrysostom.[30] Onesicritus, follower of ⟦432⟧ Diogenes, wrote a history of Alexander which attested the encounter with Diogenes and represented Alexander as a 'philosopher in arms' and as the divine saviour and world-king of the Cynic *kosmopolis*. Bion of Borysthenes, whose philosophical orientation is largely Cynic, ended his days as one of the court-philosophers of the Macedonian king Antigonus Gonatas. Two of Dio Chrysostom's kingship

---

30  Notably Höistad (1948).

orations addressed to the Roman emperor Trajan (*Or.* 1 and 4) show clear Cynic influence, and for a time Dio, like Bion, played the role of court-philosopher.[31]

But for two reasons 'Cynic kingship theory', in the sense implied, is a mirage. (a) Although Antisthenes wrote about kingship and certainly influenced Diogenes, later Cynics, and Dio Chrysostom, he himself, as we have seen, was not a Cynic, and his general political stance, fairly represented by his comparison of the *politeia* to fire (go too close and you burn, go too far away and you freeze [Stob. 4.192.7–9]), is distinctly less radical than that of the Diogenic Cynic. (b) For the Diogenic Cynic the worldly king is defective in three respects (all deriving from Cynic exaltation of 'nature'): (i) he is rich; (ii) his 'kingship' is a false 'external' state rather than an inner moral state; (iii) his kingship is a form of *nomos*. The Cynic 'king', then, is the absolute antithesis of the worldly king, and it is therefore self-contradictory for a self-professed Cynic to recognise, still less praise, a worldly king. Diogenes' response to Alexander is the correct Cynic response. Cynic terminology can only be applied to a worldly king by the negation of an essential part of the Diogenic Cynic message. The works of Onesicritus and Dio accordingly represent an uneasy compromise between Cynic philosophy and worldly power. It is perfectly true that Cynic moral values such as personal integrity, superiority to luxury, devotion to toil, and so on can overlap with, and be pressed into the service of, certain elements of conventional rulership ideology. Cynics, Greek and Hellenistic kings, and Roman emperors can all agree upon the value of Heracles as a moral exemplar; Cynic emphasis upon toil and suffering finds some echoes in traditional Roman attitudes.[32] None of this, however, controverts the fact that 'Cynic kingship theory' in the Diogenic sense entails an absolute rejection of worldly kingship.

## 4  Significance and Influence

Since the Cynic 'state' is the 'state' of being a Cynic, there is a sense in which the influence of Cynic political thought means the influence of Cynicism generally. This was immense and wide-ranging, affecting Greek ⟦433⟧ and Roman philosophy, rulership ideology, literature, and (later) religion. The topic is unmanageably vast. But even within philosophy it is virtually impossible to isolate political thought from ethics in general. The very extremeness of Cynic positions on material possessions, individual ethics and politics in the

---

31  Moles (1995) 145–50, 155–6 {above, pp. 404–9, 413–14}. On Dio see further Gill (2000).
32  Griffin (1993) 252–8 {= (2018) 481–5}.

narrow sense catalysed the definition of other philosophies' positions. Stoic ethics are greatly influenced by Cynic: the link in the first instance being the master–'pupil' relationship of Crates and Zeno, founder of Stoicism. The legitimacy of Cynicism was debated within Stoicism, reactions ranging from nearly total acceptance (Aristo of Chios) to partial acceptance (Zeno, Chrysippus), to outright rejection (Panaetius), to a fluctuating mixture (Seneca), to bowdlerising and idealising redefinition (Epictetus).[33] Even Epicureanism was not untouched:[34] Epicurus' injunction that 'the wise man should not cynicise' (D.L. 10.119) conveys reluctant acknowledgment of the fact that key Epicurean values look embarrassingly like (and no doubt partly in origin were) diluted Cynicism.

The ancient tradition makes much of Diogenes' 'cosmopolitanism', and, while that cosmopolitanism was not itself a new concept, it became strongly associated with Diogenes and the Cynics, partly no doubt because of Diogenes' verbal inventiveness; partly perhaps because on a superficial view it seemed incongruous that Cynics should expound so elevated a conception; partly also because of the absoluteness of Diogenes' rejection of the polis, which far exceeded the partial withdrawal from politics of his predecessors Socrates and Antisthenes and thus gave his cosmopolitanism added force; and partly because of the concomitant boldness of his move in making his own way of life the instantiation of citizenship of the *kosmopolis*.

Thus the Cynics set the agenda for philosophical discussion of cosmopolitanism. In particular, Cynic cosmopolitanism influenced Stoic cosmopolitanism far more than current scholarly opinion[35] allows. The Cynics did not bequeath to the Stoics a purely negative concept ('we reject the city') to which the latter added positive value: rather, Cynic cosmopolitanism already contained all the essential positive qualities which the Stoics endowed with a fuller exposition, and which they integrated into a fully-developed physical system. The 'Golden-Age' cosmopolitanism of the later Epicurean Diogenes of Oenoanda (second century AD) also seems to show Cynic influence.[36] Diogenes' prescriptions for every-day life and his rejection of the conventional polis also greatly influenced the Stoics: [[434]] Zeno's *Politeia* has some clearly Cynic elements;[37] Cleanthes, as we have seen, was impelled to confute Diogenes' syllogism against law and the city; Chrysippus' *Politeia* retained some 'outrageous' Cynic

---

33   Dudley (1937) 96–103, 127, 190–8; Billerbeck (1978); (1979) 3–18, Goulet-Cazé (1986) 159–91.
34   Gigante (1993).
35   E.g., Goulet-Cazé (1982); Schofield (1991) Appendix H.
36   Moles (1995) 142–3 {above, pp. 401–2}.
37   Baldry (1959) 14; Schofield (1991) Ch. 1.

prescriptions.[38] The sheer starkness of the Cynic political, or anti-political, statement demanded a response, whether positive or negative. More generally, in asserting a 'cosmopolitanism' which rejected the city and transmuted the very notion of citizenship into a metaphor for the Cynic life according to universal nature, the Cynics provided the impetus for a crucial move in ancient political thought: that between theories based on the polis and those based on natural law.

Nor should we ignore the 'soft-Cynic' tradition represented by Onesicritus and Dio Chrysostom, whereby Cynic values were harnessed to conventional rulership ideology. If it is difficult to attribute moral value to Onesicritus' encomium of Alexander, it nevertheless has importance in being the first work to fuse Cynic philosophy with the ideology of world conquest, thereby creating a potent version of the Alexander myth, and influencing both subsequent interpretations of Alexander (notably Plutarch's two essays *On the Fortune of Alexander*) and Roman imperialist ideology (which had to accommodate, and outdo, the achievements of the greatest 'world-conqueror' of the past). By contrast, Dio Chrysostom's deployment of Cynic thought in his speeches to Trajan is subtle and nuanced, and yet, in the Fourth Oration at any rate, retains much of the elemental moral force of Diogenic Cynicism. In the end that is the significance of the Cynics: simultaneously magnificent and absurd, they set a standard of moral integrity which could not be ignored, whether by the general public, by other philosophers, or by the political powers to which they were so resolutely opposed.

## Bibliography

Baldry, H. C. (1959) 'Zeno's Ideal State', *JHS* 79: 3–15.
Billerbeck, M. (1978) *Epiktet: vom Kynismus* (Leiden).
Billerbeck, M. (1979) *Der Kyniker Demetrius: ein Beitrag zur Geschichte der frühkaiserzeitlichen Popularphilosophie* (Leiden).
Billerbeck, M., ed. (1991) *Die Kyniker in der modernen Forschung: Aufsätze mit Einführung und Bibliographie* (Amsterdam).
Branham, R. B. (1993) 'Diogenes' Rhetoric and the *Invention* of Cynicism', in Goulet-Cazé and Goulet (1993) 445–73.
Branham, R. B. and M.-O. Goulet-Cazé, edd. (1996) *The Cynics: the Cynic Movement in Antiquity and its Legacy* (Berkeley and Los Angeles).

---

38  Erskine (1990) 14.

Döring, K. (1995) 'Diogenes und Antisthenes', in G. Giannantoni, et al., edd., *La tradizione Socratica* (Naples) 125–50.
Downing, F. G. (1993) 'Cynics and Early Christianity', in Goulet-Cazé and Goulet (1993).
Dudley, D. R. (1937) *A History of Cynicism from Diogenes to the 6th century A.D.* (London).
Erskine, A. (1990) *The Hellenistic Stoa: Political Thought and Action* (London and Ithaca).
Giannantoni, G. (1993) 'Antistene fondatore della scuola cinica?', in Goulet-Cazé and Goulet (1993) 15–34.
Gigante, M. (1993) 'Cinismo e epicureismo', in Goulet-Cazé and Goulet (1993) 159–223.
Gill, C. (2000) 'Stoic Writers of the Imperial Period' in C. Rowe and M. Schofield, edd. *The Cambridge History of Greek and Roman Political Thought* (Cambridge) 597–615.
Göttling, C. W. (1851) 'Diogenes der Kyniker oder die Philosophie des griechischen Proletariats', in id., *Gesammelte Abhandlungen aus dem classischen Alterthume*, 2 vols. (Halle) I.251–77.
Goulet-Cazé, M.-O. (1982) 'Un syllogisme stoïcien sur la loi dans la doxographie de Diogène le Cynique: à propos de Diogène Laërce VI 72', *RhMus* 125: 214–40.
Goulet-Cazé, M.-O. (1986) *L'Ascèce Cynique: un commentaire de Diogéne Laërce VI 70–71* (Paris).
Goulet-Cazé, M.-O. (1992) "Le livre VI de Diogène Laërce: analyse de sa structure et réflexions méthodologiques', *ANRW* II.36.6: 3880–4048.
Goulet-Cazé, M.-O. (1994) 'Diogène de Sinope', in R. Goulet, *Dictionnaire des philosophes antiques II* (Paris) 812–23.
Goulet-Cazé, M.-O. (1996) 'Religion and the Early Cynics', in Branham and Goulet-Cazé (1996) 47–80.
Goulet-Cazé, M.-O. and R. Goulet, edd. (1993) *Le Cynisme ancien et ses prolongements* (Paris).
Griffin, M. T. (1993) 'Le mouvement cynique et les Romains: attraction et repulsion', in Goulet-Cazé and Goulet (1993) 241–58 {= 'Cynicism and the Romans: Attraction and Repulsion', in Branham and Goulet-Cazé (1996) 190–204; repr. in ead., *Politics and Philosophy at Rome: Collected Papers*, ed. C. Balmaceda (Oxford, 2018) 475–85}.
Hammond, N. G. L. (1993) *Sources for Alexander the Great: an Analysis of Plutarch's 'Life' and Arrian's 'Anabasis Alexandrou'* (Cambridge).
Höistad, R. (1948) *Cynic Hero and Cynic King: Studies in the Cynic Conception of Man* (Uppsala).
Kindstrand, J. F. (1976) *Bion of Borysthenes: a Collection of the Fragments with Introduction and Commentary* (Uppsala).
López-Cruces, J. L. (1995) *Les Méliambes de Cercidas de Mégalopolis: politique et tradition littéraire* (Amsterdam).

Lovejoy, A. O. and G. Boas (1935) *A Documentary History of Primitivism and Related Ideas in Antiquity* (Baltimore; repr. New York, 1965).

Moles, J. L. (1983) '"*Honestius quam Ambitiosius*"? An Exploration of the Cynic's Attitude to Moral Corruption in his Fellow Men', *JHS* 103: 103–23 [above, Ch. 12].

Moles, J. L. (1993) 'Le cosmopolitisme cynique', in Goulet-Cazé and Goulet (1993) 259–80.

Moles, J. L. (1995) 'The Cynics and Politics', in A. Laks and M. Schofield, edd., *Justice and Generosity: Studies in Hellenistic Social and Political Philosophy* (Cambridge) 129–58 [above, Ch. 15].

Moles, J. L. (1996) 'Cynic Cosmopolitanism', in Branham and Goulet-Cazé (1996) 105–20 [above, Ch. 16].

Paquet, L. (1988) *Les cyniques grecs: fragments et témoinage*$^2$ (Ottawa).

Schofield, M. (1991) *The Stoic Idea of the City* (Cambridge).

Zeyl, D. J., ed. (1997) *The Encyclopedia of Classical Philosophy* (London and Westport, Ct.).

CHAPTER 18

# Philosophy and Ethics in Horace

In his later poetry, Horace himself spins a narrative about these controversial topics. Poetry can be 'useful', 'delightful', or both (*AP* 333–4).* It has 'useful' ethical functions (*Epist.* 2.1.126–31). Writing 'well' (technically and morally) requires 'wisdom' sourced from Socratic and Platonic philosophy (*AP* 309–22): Socratic writings provide the poet's basic material; life is like a drama, but different social roles have appropriately different 'duties', 'parts', and 'characters'. Here the poetic representation combines the 'is' and the 'ought', and traditional Peripatetic literary theory is overwritten by the moral relativism of the Stoic philosopher Panaetius (who greatly influenced late Republican Roman philosophy).[1] 'Philosophy', both in its broadest sense and in the narrow sense of specific philosophies, informs Horace's own poetry.

*Epistles* 2.2.57–60 itemises Horace's range:

> What do you want me to do?
> Moreover, not all men admire and love the same things.
> *You* rejoice in lyric, this one delights in iambics,
> That one in Bionian 'conversations' and their black salt.

## 1 The *Satires*

Horace has written 'lyric', 'iambics', and 'conversations' (= 'satires'). Why the emphasis on Bion, the largely Cynic ('doggish') philosopher?[2]

The *Satires* parade numerous satiric predecessors, models, and exemplars without naming Bion,[3] but Horace here advertises his reading of Bion: 'black ⟦166⟧ salt' refers both to the salt fish sold by Bion's father and to Bion's 'abrasive' wit.[4] 'Conversations' glosses 'diatribes', or 'informal philosophical talks', a

---

\* Translations are mine. Presentation and documentation are minimalist, Moles (2002a) reworked. Nothing denies multiplicity of poetic meaning. Readers are assumed to want to read Horace. I thank Emily Gowers, Stephen Harrison, and Tony Woodman.
1 Cic. *De Off.* 1.107ff., 124ff.; McGann (1969) 10ff.
2 Kindstrand (1976) (useful but uncritical); Moles (1996a) (sharper).
3 E.g., 1.4; 1.6; 1.10; 2.1; 2.2; 2.3.11–12; 2.6.
4 D.L. 4.46; F 1a Kindstrand; TT 15–18 Kindstrand.

form associated with Bion.⁵ The Roman satirist Lucilius 'rubbed the city down with much salt' (*Sat.*1.10.4) and was 'of wiped [keen] nose' (1.4.8), just as Bion's father 'wiped his nose with his elbow':⁶ Lucilius is Horace's 'satirical father'.

Crucial is *Satires* 1.6 (beginning the second half of Book 1):

| Bion, FF 1, 2, 16 Kindstrand | Horace |
|---|---|
| The philosopher Bion addresses King Antigonus Gonatas (whose names imply 'high birth'). | The poet-philosopher Horace addresses Maecenas, himself of the noblest birth. |
| Antigonus asks Bion where he comes from and who his parents are. | At their first meeting, the question of Horace's background arises. |
| Bion, favourite of Antigonus, has been criticised by jealous rivals for low birth. | Horace, favourite of Maecenas, has been criticised by jealous rivals for low birth. |
| Bion gives much information about his father. | Horace gives much information about his father. |
| Bion admits that his father was a freedman and that he himself had been enslaved. | Horace repeatedly describes himself as son of a freedman. |
| Bion's father wiped his nose with his elbow. | Maecenas does not turn up his nose at unknowns (Maecenas is another 'literary father'). |
| Bion's father was branded on his face. | The highborn Laevinus was 'branded' by the Roman people. |
| Bion's mother was of dishonourable status: a prostitute. | Octavian's public supremacy prompts the question whether he was dishonoured by an unknown mother (Octavian is another 'father'). |
| Bion's father was a customs officer. | Horace's father was a tax-collector. |
| Bion's master bought him for sex. | Horace's father kept Horace pure. |

---

5   Moles (1996b) 463; T 8a–b Kindstrand; p. 465 below.
6   F 1 Kindstrand.

| | |
|---|---|
| Bion asks to be considered on his own merits; Bion tells Antigonus, in the case of friends, to examine not where they are from but who they are. | Maecenas holds that a man's father does not matter, provided he himself is a free man. |
| Antigonus chooses friends. | Maecenas chooses friends. |
| 〚167〛 Bion boasts of his parentage. | Horace will never regret such a father. |
| Bion: 'these are the things concerning me'. | Horace: 'now I return to myself'. |
| Antigonus rules many well, Bion himself. | Maecenas' ancestors commanded great legions, a Roman legion once obeyed Horace, and Horace now does as he pleases. |
| Bion rejects rhetoric. | Horace celebrates the education his father secured for him. |
| Bion rejects wealth and extravagance for simplicity and ease. | Horace rejects wealth and extravagance for simplicity and ease. |

Horace mobilises a whole series of items to accentuate the Bion analogy.[7] His reworking of Bion's father's 'branding' enlists Bionian diatribe under satire's 'branding' function (1.4.5, 106).

Readers are challenged to detect Bion's presence. The successful are retrospectively congratulated (*Epist.* 2.2.60), the unsuccessful re-challenged. The challenge is alike literary ('spotting the allusions') and moral/philosophical (discerning Horace's distinctive moral/philosophical stance).

Two passages in *Satires* 1.1 ambivalently acknowledge Cynic diatribe. In 13–14 (where Horace curtails examples), 'all the other examples of this *genre*, so many are they, could *wear out the talkative* Fabius', the italicised words gloss the Greek 'genre' of 'diatribe' (literally, a 'wearing away' of time in 'talk').[8] Lines 23–7 gloss Cynic 'pedagogic', 'serio-comic' didacticism:[9]

---

7  The historical circumstance of his father's being a freedman (Williams [1995]) will have contributed to Horace's inspiration.
8  Gowers (2005) 54.
9  Kindstrand (1976) 209, 47f.

Besides, not to run through the subject with a laugh like a writer of jokes—although what forbids telling the truth with a laugh? Just as coaxing teachers sometimes give little cakes to children, to make them want to learn the first elements—nevertheless, putting playfulness aside, let us seek serious matters.

A further Cynic 'marker' comes in 2.1.84–5: 'what if someone has *barked* at a man worthy of abuse, himself untouched by blame?' And the witch Canidia (*canis*) articulates another 'doggish' voice within the collection.[10]

⟦168⟧ Thus Horace presents his Satires as 'Bionian', 'Cynic', and 'serio-comic' 'diatribe'. Hence much basic Cynicism, of content and style;[11] jibing at pretentious Stoics;[12] and emphasis on 'unofficial' moral authorities such as Horace's father, Ofellus and Cervius.[13] Book 1.4, Horace's defence of his own milder satire, rejecting the 'blackness' of malevolent criticism (85, 91, 100) or himself as a biting dog (93), functions as a redefinition, rather than a negation, of such Cynicism (cf. Lucilius' 'wiped nose' and the 'branding' motif).

What of the strong Epicurean strand, both of doctrine and of allusions to Lucretius, greatest Epicurean poet of the previous generation?[14] Since Cynicism influenced Epicurean ethics and Epicureanism appropriated diatribe, Cynic and Epicurean positions sometimes intermix, as in 1.2 on 'easily available sex'. Elsewhere, they differ, Horace favouring the less extreme Epicurean position. In 2.2.53ff. Ofellus' simple living is the mean between gross, 'wolfish' gluttony and sordid, '*doggish*', parsimony. Book 1.1's gestures to Cynic diatribe are punningly redefined by the Epicurean moral '*sati*ety' which this Horatian '*sati*re' advocates and which its very length instantiates (119–21).[15] Horace's teasing citations, in an Epicurean erotic context (1.2.92–3, 121–2), of Philodemus, Greek poet, literary critic, and Epicurean philosopher, whose circle included Horace's friends and fellow poets Plotius, Varius, and Virgil (1.5.40; 1.10.81), look programmatic of that Epicurean strand. Horace actually *was* the fellow Epicurean of Plotius, etc. and of Maecenas,[16] a fact constantly alluded to, and reflected in, his poetry (however ironically). The extended punning on

---

10   Sat. 1.8.48; 2.1.48; 2.8.95; Muecke (1993) 293; Mankin (1995) 300; Oliensis (1998) 68f.
11   Esp. Sat. 1.1–4; 1.6; Freudenburg (1993) 8–27, 78–82, 216–29.
12   E.g., Sat. 1.1.120; 1.2.134; 1.3.96ff.; 2.3.
13   Sat. 1.4.105ff.; 1.6; 2.2; 2.6.
14   E.g., Sat. 1.1.74–5; 1.2.111–12; 1.3.76–7, 97–114; 1.5.44, 101–3; 1.6.128–31; 2.2.14–20, 25; 2.6.93–7.
15   Lucr. 3.938, 959–60; Epic. Sent. Vat. 88; F 69 Bailey; note that this criterion targets Lucretius as well as Cynics.
16   Armstrong (2004); Maecenas' Epicureanism: André (1967) 15ff; Maecenas' *Symposium* (C. 3.21) included Virgil and Horace.

his own name (*Horatius* ~ *hora*) in 2.6[17] makes Horace the personification of the Epicurean principle *carpe diem*, though Epicureans, too, can be satirised (2.4). And there are other important philosophical influences, including mainline Stoic, Panaetian Stoic, Peripatetic, and (in Book 2) Platonic dialogue.[18]

Philosophical programmes, then, can be presented piecemeal and unsequentially, implemented, Romanised, incompletely descriptive, ironised, redefined, subverted, etc.: but they must be recognised.

### [169] The *Epodes*

*Epodes* and *Satires*, contemporaneous and generically affiliated (both being 'blame poetry'), have many links, including the 'doggish' Canidia[19] and the Greek poet Archilochus, part of Horace's satirical reading (*Satires* 2.3.12) and the *Epodes*' main inspiration.[20]

Crucially, *Epode* 6 runs:

> Why do you worry unoffending strangers,
> A cowardly dog when facing wolves?
> Why not, if you really can, turn your empty threats here
> And attack me, who will bite back?
> For, like either the Molossian hound or the tawny Laconian, 5
> A force friendly to shepherds,
> I'll drive through deep snow with ear upraised,
> Whatever beast goes before.
> *You*, when you have filled the wood with fearful voice,
> Sniff at the food thrown you. 10
> Beware, beware! For I raise my ready horns most savagely against the wicked,
> Like the spurned son-in-law of faithless Lycambes or Bupalus' keen enemy.
> Or, if anyone attacks me with black tooth,
> Shall I weep unavenged like a child?

In this fable, one dog represents the malice of the iambic tradition's negative version (13), which attacks the innocent and defenceless (1) but is cowardly in the face of the strong (2–4, 10), becoming all bark and no bite (9f.). The

---

17   Reckford (1997); also *Sat.* 1.6.119ff.
18   Surveys: Muecke (1993) 6–7; Gowers (2005).
19   *Epod.* 3; 5; 17.
20   As *Epist.* 1.19.23–5 retrospectively reveals (cf. *Epist.* 2.2.60 on Bion).

other (Horace) bites back (4, 13–14), defends the community (6, 11), and, now also bull-like, charges the wicked (11). Its literary and moral ancestors are Archilochus and Hipponax (12), whose notorious aggressiveness is harnessed to Cynic moralising.[21] Thus the *Epodes* integrate Cynic 'doggishness' into the iambic tradition of 'biting', producing a genre which serves the common good, attacks the wicked and manifold forms of moral 'beastliness', and defends the weak, including the poet himself, but which is also serio-comic (Horace's '*upraised* ear' being deflated by his name *Flaccus* ~ 'floppy').[22]

As with the *Satires*, this Cynic programme does not make the collection solidly Cynic. Many of the poems deploy general 'hard–soft', 'public–private', 'business–leisure', 'manliness–unmanliness/womanliness', 'virtue–pleasure' (etc.) contrasts, which are sometimes given philosophical colouring. [[170]] In the *Epodes*, as elsewhere, 'soft' philosophical colouring denotes Epicureanism, 'hard' Stoicism, Cynicism, or both (Cynicism influenced Stoicism even more than it did Epicureanism, hence Cynic and Stoic ethics sometimes cohere, sometimes diverge).

Epode 1 introduces the contrasts:

| 'Virtue' (etc.) | 'Pleasure' (etc.) |
|---|---|
| Life 'oppressive' if Maecenas does not survive. | Life if Maecenas survives 'pleasant'. |
| Public engagement/'war'/'labour' | 'Leisure'/'unfitness for war' |
| | 'Leisure' only 'sweet' if Maecenas present |
| 'Men' | 'Softness' |
| Travelling to the extreme north, east and west | Staying put |
| 'Bearing labour' | Not bearing labour |
| 'Strength' | 'Insufficient strength' |
| Lack of fear | 'Fear' |

None of these is automatically philosophical, but the emphasis on 'labours' and travels to the Caucasus and extreme West evoke Hercules, Stoic hero. Consequently, 'pleasure', 'leisure', 'sweetness', 'softness', etc. are 'attracted' into the Epicurean colouring that they have in philosophical contexts. Exploration of the demands of friendship in crisis is underpinned by a contrast between

---

21    Dickie (1981) 195–203; *Epode* 6 resembles *Satires* 1.4 and 2.1 (esp. 47ff.).
22    Generally: Fitzgerald (1988); Oliensis (1998) 68ff.

Stoicism and Epicureanism, resolved by Horace's combining of public and private obligations.

Epode 2 has similar contrasts and lightly Epicureanises the countryside (19, 37–8, 40). Epode 3, on Maecenas' garlic, contrasts 'hardness' (4) and Hercules' sufferings (17) with Maecenas' girl. Epode 4, on the upstart, contrasts 'hardness' (4, 11) and 'softness' (1).[23] The boy victim of Epode 5 tries to 'soften' (14, 83–4) the witches' savagery (4) and 'labours' (31). In 8, Horace's 'strength' is 'unmuscled' (2), his impotence 'urged on' (7) by the woman's 'soft' belly (9); Stoic tracts fail to 'stiffen' Horace (who, symbolically, cannot 'sustain' his Cynic/Stoic 'hardness'), and the only useful 'labour' is *fellatio* (hardly a Herculean task).

*Epode* 9 reworks the contrasts of 1. The closing lines—37–8 'it is pleasurable to dissolve care and fear for Caesar's affairs in the sweet Loosener' (Bacchus)—give the celebratory symposium an Epicurean flavouring, hence [171] its opposites a Stoic one. In turn, 19–20 ('though *urged* to the left, the poops of the hostile ships *hide* in harbour') exploit Epicureanism's passive and negative associations. As in 1, Stoicism and 'good' Epicureanism coexist (hence Epicurean celebration of Octavian's Stoic valour), but 'bad' Epicureanism smears Antony and Cleopatra.

In 10, the shipwrecked Maevius emits 'unmanly' wailing (17). In 11, Horace no longer takes 'pleasure' in writing poetry, smitten by 'oppressive' love and fire for 'soft' boys and girls, a frequenter of 'hard' thresholds. Epode 12 finds Horace sniffing out odours more shrewdly than 'a keen dog where the pig [= vagina] lies hidden' (philosophical animal imagery—'dog' = Cynic, 'pig' = Epicurean—is again burlesqued: so much for poem 6), his penis 'dissolved', 'soft' for one act only, and 'inert'. Epode 13 Epicureanises the symposium (3–4, 9–10, 17–18). In 14, the 'soft inertia' of love for a freedwoman has prevented Horace from completing his promised iambics, just as Anacreon wept for love in 'unelaborated' feet. In 15, the unfaithful Neaera will suffer from Horace's 'manhood', 'if there is anything of the *man* in *Flaccus*' (pun). The politically escapist and extravagantly Epicurean 16 redeploys, in contrast to 1, the themes of 'manliness' (2, 5, 39), 'labours' (16), 'sweetness' (35), 'softness' (37), and 'womanliness' (39). Epode 17 finds Horace suffering 'labours' (24, 64) worse than those of Ulysses (16) or the dying Hercules (31–2), through the witchcraft of Canidia, in a final 'authority' struggle between the iambic tradition's 'two voices'.

The ingenious patterns Horace creates from these basic contrasts, philosophical and general, contribute substantially to the collection's poetic texture.

---

23   Read sympathetically, the upstart recalls Horace (cf. *Satires* 1.6) as (ironically) 'suffering Cynic-Stoic hero'.

## 2  Odes 1–3

Ode 1.1 programmatically weaves philosophical threads: the renewed Bion–Antigonus paradigm;[24] the 'choice of life' motif; structural imitation of *Satires* 1.1; evocations of the diatribe theme of 'discontent' and of 'endurance of poverty'; hinted reconciliation of public life/duty/reward/Stoicism and private life/pleasure/emotion/Epicureanism (Maecenas as Horace's 'sweet glory' [2]); and links between philosophical material and addressee.

Into this higher genre, diatribe sporadically injects low-life energy: heated moralism (serious or ironic), down-to-earth illustrations, mockery of pretension and folly, and paradoxical inversions of worldly values.[25] It suffuses 2.15 (encroachments of luxury-building), 2.18 (vanity of riches in contrast [[172]] to Horace's poverty) and 3.24 (futility and destructiveness of Roman luxury contrasted with Cynic primitivism).

Stoicism is the dominant philosophical presence in few odes. In 1.22 the sage's 'weaponlessness' is the paradigm for Horace's inviolability as lover/love-poet. Ode 1.29 twits Iccius for eyeing the treasures of Araby over those of Panaetius and the Socratics. Ode 2.2 contrasts Sallustius' 'tempered' use of wealth, self-rule, and philosophical kingship with Eastern potentates. In 3.2, military endurance and prowess, political greatness (especially that of Augustus), and political discretion (including Horace's) variously manifest Virtue. Ode 3.3 subsumes Augustus' political consistency under Stoic tenacity of purpose.

Epicureanism is the dominant presence in more than twice as many odes. Epicurean *carpe diem* feeling inspires symposia or holidaying as antidotes to wintertime, time passing (1.9; 3.29), preoccupation with the future (1.9; 1.11; 3.29), mortality (1.9; 2.3), hard times (2.3), cares (2.11; 2.16), anxieties over life's necessities or foreign wars (2.11; 3.8; 3.29), and luxury (1.38; 3.29), and as exhortations to love and pleasure (1.9; 1.11; 2.3). The simple Epicurean life is advocated in 1.31, 1.38, 2.16, and 3.1, where it is strikingly preferred to the lives—whether good or bad in their kind—of kings (who must include Augustus), politicians, and landowners (who must include Maecenas). By contrast, 1.34's spoof recantation of Epicureanism introduces reflections on Fortune's power.

Another important group juxtaposes Stoic and Epicurean, in varying relationships of tension. Ode 1.7 praises Plancus' 'virile' Stoic 'labours' in war and politics, while counselling periodic immersion in 'softening' Epicurean symposia. Ode 1.32 superimposes Stoic and Epicurean colourings on Horace's

---

24   Further *Odes* 2.18.12–14; 3.16.37–8.
25   E.g., *Odes* 1.3.9ff.; 1.16.9ff.; 1.31.6; 2.2.13ff.; 1.28.4ff.; 2.14.21ff.; 3.16.25–8; 3.29.55–6.

public and private[26] lyric voices (similarly 1.31; 2.13.25–8), warranting generalisations about public ~ Stoic and private ~ Epicurean. In 1.37 (a poem framed by legitimate Epicurean celebration), Cleopatra's base Epicurean association with 'un-men', 'sweet' fortune, and 'softness' (cf. Epodes 1 and 9) is succeeded by Stoic 'nobility', 'unwomanliness', rejection of 'the hidden', daring, serenity, bravery, and deliberated suicide. Ode 2.7 urges a returned Republican die-hard to forget a shared past of misguided Stoic 'virility' through Epicurean 'sweetness' of friendship and celebration. Ode 3.1, generally Epicurean, envisages a hierarchical Stoic universe. Ode 3.2, generally Stoic, piquantly mixes the two in the famous 'It is sweet and glorious to die for one's country' (cf. 1.32.13, 15; 1.1.2). Ode 3.16 combines Stoic incorruptibility, Epicurean satisfaction with little, gratitude to Maecenas, and teasing. In 3.21, tough Stoic types are not immune to wine and ⟦173⟧ the poem guys earnest philosophical Symposia, while simultaneously honouring both Maecenas' *Symposium* and Messalla's 'sweet' poetry. Horace's seduction campaign (3.28) deploys the Epicurean symposium against Lyde's 'Stoic citadel'.

Exceptionally, 2.10 advocates the Peripatetic golden mean as a remedy for political troubles.

Thus about a third of the *Odes* are varyingly philosophical, though their impact spreads further. The tone ranges from solemn (2.10; 3.2; 3.3) to flippant (1.22; 3.28). Proportionately, Stoicism lags far behind Epicureanism, which characteristically has the last word and with which, whether as temporary expedient or choice of life, Horace regularly identifies,[27] though not in a 'professional' way (cf. 1.34; 3.1; 3.2; 3.16). Epicureanism dominates 3.1 (the first 'Roman Ode'), a challenge redoubled by the corresponding, also Epicurean, 3.29. Yet, while Stoicism can be mocked (1.22), so can Epicureanism (1.34), and Stoicism generally receives great respect (1.7; 1.37; 2.2; 3.2; 3.3). 'Both—and' formulations (1.1.2; 1.32.13, 15; 3.1; 3.2.13; 3.16) further complicate the picture. Importantly, Epicureanism could celebrate stable rule as guarantor of Epicurean 'quiet' (something of this in 1.7, 2.7, and 3.1, as in the *Epodes*). Horace implicitly claims a 'Stoic voice' as well as an Epicurean (1.1.35; 1.31; 1.32; 2.13.25ff.; 3.2). There is, then, a strong pull towards the Epicureanism Horace had espoused since the 30s, but an avoidance of the exclusive commitment alien to his temperament (or its representations), to his role as Augustan *vates*, and to the collection's literary, political, social, and philosophical fecundity.

Other questions.

---

26 The punning 'Latin'/'latent' evokes Epicurean 'hiddenness'.
27 Again, *hora* ~ *Horatius*: *C.* 1.9.20; 2.16.32; 3.8.28; 3.29.48.

First, the relationship between content and addressee (including implicit addressees and referents). The two may complement—Stoic odes to Stoics (1.22 to Fuscus, 1.29 to Iccius, 2.2 to Sallustius), Epicurean odes to Epicureans (3.8 and 3.29 to Maecenas)—or contrast (2.7 Epicurean solution to Pompeius' 'Stoic' problems; 2.11 Epicurean exhortation to Stoic Quinctius). Other relationships are unclear (2.3 to Dellius; 2.10 to Licinius; 2.15 to Grosphus). If addresses are formally honorific, do philosophical exhortations function as concealed praise for what addressees are doing anyway, or as genuine admonitions? Admonition of other readers is always possible. Of addressees explicit and implicit, there is much concealed praise (Plancus in 1.7, Sallustius in 2.2, Augustus in 3.2 and 3.3, Messalla in 3.21). But there is also teasing (e.g., Iccius in 1.29, Quinctius in 2.11) and admonition: 2.7 ('forget the past'), or 2.10 (whoever its addressee). Slipperiest are odes addressed to, or implicitly referring to, Maecenas (1.1; ⟦174⟧ 2.18; 3.1; 3.16; 3.29). Granted encomium, affection, and gratitude, teasing is certain, jibing plausible, criticism—as morally protreptic—apparent. Such frankness was traditionally permitted to symposiastic companions and moralising poets, and demanded by Cynic and Epicurean[28] conceptions of friendship.

Second, integration of philosophy into the collection. As in the *Epodes*, Horace is consistently ingenious. Thus the non-philosophical 1.6 rejects, as a poetic theme, the wanderings over the sea of the duplicitous Ulysses. Ode 1.7 implicitly likens the mature Plancus to the sea-wandering and complex Ulysses, imbues him with Stoic virility and endurance, and recommends periodic Epicurean retreats to the shade.[28a] Ode 1.8 has the youthful Sybaris, hitherto enduring of dust and sun, lurking, unmanned in a shady brothel. *Odes* 1.9 and 11 reactivate 'good Epicureanism' in Horace's own erotic campaigns.

## 3  *Epistles* 1

The book begins (1.1–19):
Told of in my first Camena [Muse], to be told of in my last,
I've been spectated enough and already been given my discharge staff,
Maecenas, are you seeking to enclose me again in the old school game?
My age and mind are not the same. Veianius,
His arms fixed to Hercules' doorpost, lies low, hidden in the country,   5
So that he may not so often have to beg the people at the end of the arena.
There is one who constantly imparts loudly into my purified ear:

---

28   Armstrong (2004) 281f., 287f.
28a   {Fuller treatment of the Plancus ode in Moles (2002b).}

'If you're sane, loose the ageing horse in time, so that
He may not fail at the end laughably and strain his flanks.'
So now I put aside both verses and all those other games:  10
What is true and what befits is my care, this my question, this my whole concern:
I am laying down and putting together things that I can bring out presently.
And, in case by chance you question, under what leader, at what hearth I protect myself,
Not told to swear to the words of any master,
Wherever the storm snatches me, I am carried in as a stranger-guest.  15
Now I become active and drown myself in political waves,
Guard of true virtue and its rigid attendant,
Now I furtively slip back into the precepts of Aristippus,
And I try to subdue things to me, not me to things.  19

Horace, it seems, has retired from the 'old game' of 'verses', likened to gladiatorial games (1–10), and his 'new game', suiting his age (4), is 〚175〛 philosophy, which totally absorbs (11). As to philosophical master, he oscillates between Stoics (16–17) and Aristippus (18–19). The latter follower of Socrates may seem a surprising choice, because no 'Aristippean' school survived in Horace's day, but, as will emerge, the ambiguities of Aristippus' thought facilitate wide coverage of philosophical issues, and his chequered career, subject of amusing anecdotes, furnishes suggestive parallels with Horace's own.

The whole passage flaunts the poet's philosophical erudition. 'Game' (3) can apply to philosophical 'schools'; 5 glosses Epicurean 'hiddenness'; 7 evokes Socrates' 'divine voice', in its familiar 'deterrent' role. The verb translated as 'im*parts* loudly into' (*personet*) canvasses Panaetius' theory that individuals can play legitimately different 'parts' in life's 'drama'. The absoluteness of 11 suits philosophical conversion. 'What is truth?' is *the* philosophical question. 'What befits' glosses Panaetius' category of 'the appropriate'. Horace's and Maecenas' 'questions' (13) suggest Socratic dialectic. Philosophy is a 'storehouse' for the future (12). The sectarian religious imagery of 13 suggests philosophical exclusiveness. 14 echoes the Academic non-commitment of Cicero, *Tusc.* 4.7 ('but let each man defend what he feels; for judgements are free: we will maintain our principle and be bound to the laws of no single teaching'), and contrasts with Epicureans' oaths to Epicurus' doctrines. Horace's oscillations (15–19) recall Socrates' wanderings in search of knowledge (Pl. *Ap.* 22a). Line 15 echoes Cic. *Acad.* 2.8 ('carried in to whatever teaching, as if in a storm'). 'Stranger-guest' glosses Aristippus' claim to be a 'stranger-guest' everywhere (Xen. *Mem.* 2.2.13). Line 16 conveys Stoicism's commitment to political life, 17 its characteristic imagery of warfare and hardness. Contrastingly, 'drown myself in political waves' suggests the 'sea of troubles' rejected by the Epicurean. 'Guard' and 'attendant' (17) image Virtue as king, glossing Stoic 'kingship'. Line 18 adapts Cic. *Acad.* 2.139 ('I see how agreeably pleasure caresses our senses: I slip to the point of assenting to Epicurus or Aristippus'). 'Furtively' echoes 'lies low, hidden' (5), suggesting the side of Aristippus aligned with Epicureanism. Line 19 glosses, via the yoking metaphor, Aristippus' characteristic boast, 'I have, but I am not had' (D.L. 2.75). The combination of that yoking metaphor, of the horse metaphor for Horace's rejected verses (8–9), and of the name 'Aristippus' (= 'best at horses' or 'best horse') recalls the contrasting horses of Plato, *Phaedrus* 246bff. And beneath the general contrast of 16–19 lies Hercules' choice between Virtue and Vice/Pleasure and their corresponding roads, a choice put to Aristippus (Xen. *Mem.* 2.1.21–34) and alluded to in Cicero, *Academica* 2.139 (cf. also 6). Retrospectively, 'enclose' (3) glosses Aristippus' refusal to 'enclose himself' in any political state (Xen. *Mem.* 2.1.13).

⟦176⟧ First question: the status of the *Epistles*—self-evidently *philosophy*, are they *poetry*? Line 10 creates a key ambiguity. 'Verses' can mean '*lyric* poetry', a young man's game (4), 'the *old* school game' (3), 'enclosure' into which Horace avoids by writing philosophical hexameters. But 'verses' can also mean 'all poetry', 'philosophy' suits older men, and 'conversational' hexameters can be represented—archly—as prose.[29] Neither interpretation quite works, since, both in this poem and in later ones, Horace repeatedly brings the *Epistles* into relationship with other genres. The ambiguity/illogicality is fruitful: Horace both does and does not fulfil Maecenas' request; the *Epistles* both are poetry and are not poetry, but philosophy; they both are and are not a radical departure, whether in relation to Horace's earlier poetry in general or in relation to his earlier philosophical poetry; and philosophy itself is something that both can and cannot be dissociated from both texts and life. These ambiguities bear on central questions about social dependency or independence, the value of poetry and of books (including *Epistles* 1), and the practice and practicability of philosophy.

Second, figures in a philosophical landscape. Lines 16–19 construct a complex polarity between orthodox Stoicism/virtue/consistency/political involvement and Aristippus/adaptability/pleasure/political disengagement. Panaetian Stoicism (7), Socrates (7), and 'country' Epicureanism (5) are further possibilities. Subsequent poems unpack this complex polarity and feature these philosophical figures. For example, 1.2 contrasts Virtue/Wisdom/Ulysses/Stoics/Cynics (17–22) and Pleasure/Folly/Companions/Phaeacians/Epicureans (23–31), and

---

29   E.g., *Sat.* 2.6.17 and Harrison (2007).

ends with a practical Panaetian compromise (70–1). In 1.3 the addressee and his friends may be behaving like Phaeacians/vulgar Epicureans, and the unifying thought is that true wisdom involves concord/friendship with oneself, one's fellows, one's fatherland, and the universe (28–9), a Panaetian formulation. Epistle 1.4 again recycles the polarity but now favours Epicureanism. In 1.5, Augustus' birthday allows a busy man to implement Epicurus' advice.

Third, addressees and other characters. *Epistles* 1 is a philosophical drama (7), whose poems present a series of dramatic situations in which 'characters' 'play' the different philosophical parts outlined above (as in *AP* 309–22), in accordance with known philosophical preferences or psychological appropriateness, and whose purpose is 'right' or 'kingly' 'living' (1.60).

The most important character is Horace himself *qua* letter-writer. Of his stated parts, the orthodox Stoic is illustrated by Epistle 1 itself, with its ironic concluding endorsement of the 'sage'—a category that still includes Horace (106–8), and by 1.16 (where Horace the poet honours the magnificence [[177]] of the Stoic ideal), and Aristippus by 1.17,[30] while Horace's inconsistency appears repeatedly.[31] He has also unstated parts: that of Socrates and Panaetian relativist (7). The former is illustrated by further passages in Epistle 1 and elsewhere,[32] the latter throughout the collection.[33] Horace's appearance in later poems as an Epicurean[34] derives partly from the 'pleasure' side of Aristippus but also from the less explicit, but ultimately more substantial, Veianius analogy. Lines 14–19 and 7, then, introduce 'the dramatic Horace' at the start of the drama, the complexity of whose role allows the practical exploration of a wide range of philosophical possibilities, as on a first encounter with philosophy, whereas 4–6 adumbrate 'the real Horace', ever more drawn to Epicureanism.

Of other characters, Lollius, 'freest of men', receives one epistle (1.2) which is appropriately Cynic-Stoic, and in another (1.18) is warned against 'unmixed freedom' of manner. Both the sombre Albius (1.4) and the Epicurean Torquatus (1.5) get Epicurean letters. The Stoic Fuscus, city-lover, learns of Epicurean country pleasures (1.10). The Stoic Quinctius is shown the high stakes of Stoic conduct in Augustan Rome (1.16).

As with the *Odes*, the question arises whether addressees (as opposed to other readers), while honoured, are also admonished, even criticised. Granted Horatian irony, wit, and teasing, criticism is an indispensable element of

---

30  *Epist.* 1.17.35 ~ 20.23 (of Horace's own political career).
31  E.g., *Epist.* 1.76, 2.3–5, 7.1–2, 8.2–12, 10.49–50, 14.12–13, 15.
32  E.g., *Epist.* 1.18.96, 100.
33  E.g., *Epist.* 2.70–1, 7.98, 10.42–3, 14.44, 17.29.
34  E.g., 4.15–16, 5, 7.45, 10, 11.22ff., 16.15, 17.6–10, 18.104ff.

serious moralising addressed to individuals. Maecenas, Lollius, Florus, Albius, Iccius, Quinctius, and Scaeva all receive protreptic criticism: as, indeed, does Horace himself.

Fourth: philosophical conclusions. While high-falutin philosophy is predictably mocked (1.12), only one philosophy is strongly criticised: Cynicism, whether Diogenic (1.17) or modified within society (1.18.6–8), and, as against these, 1.2 is quite strongly Cynic (or Cynic-Stoic). Otherwise, two main strands. First, Socratic non-commitment and Academic, Panactian, and Aristippean relativism legitimalise not just flexibility within philosophies but choice between philosophies. This shrewd insight acknowledges that individual personality influences philosophical, political, and social choices. It becomes increasingly clear that Horace's personal choice is Epicureanism. But this is itself the second strand, for the Epicurean note sounds ever more insistently and comes at the end of 1.18, an analysis of the difficulties and dangers of friendship with the great, and the last strongly philosophical poem of the collection. When Horace tells Lollius, amid all his preoccupations, to [[178]] keep up study of philosophy, the list of alternatives (96ff.) resumes the main philosophical choices examined in earlier poems, and Horace then (104ff.) confesses his own, Epicurean, choice. But even within the list, there is an Epicurean bias, and the total emphasis recalls Veianius, in an Epicurean ring-structure similar to *Odes* 3.29 ~ 3.1. Even for Lollius, the Epicurean secret life seems the better way.

## 4   The Final Period

From Horace's first poems, and almost throughout his poetic corpus, the Epicurean life offers an alternative to public life. And from *Odes* 3.30 ('I have completed a monument more lasting than bronze') onwards, much of Horace's poetry seems valedictory. (Apparently) disappointed by the (apparent) fact that few readers—Augustus notably excepted—appreciated the *Odes* (*Epist.* 1.13; 1.19), and (apparently) pressurised by Maecenas (*Epist.* 1.1.3), Horace produced *Epistles* 1. The book ends with endorsement of Epicurean retreat, with thoughts about the remainder of life, and with retrospective glances at *Satires*, *Epodes*, *Odes*, and *Epistles* themselves.[35]

Whatever their relative chronology, the poems of Horace's last decade read similarly. To an importunate Florus (*Epist.* 2.2), Horace explains why he can no longer write poetry. There are retrospective glances at *Epistles* 1, *Odes*,

---

35   *Epist.* 1.18.104ff.; 1.19; 1.20.

*Epodes*, and 'Bionian conversations'.³⁶ But the poem is itself such a 'conversation', with internal Bionian diatribe and philosophical reminiscences. Thus 'I was nourished in Rome ['strength'] and learned philosophy in Athens' (41–5) echoes Bion's 'I am Borysthenite [= 'strong'] by birth and learned philosophy in Athens',³⁷ and '*Bio*nian' suggests 'bio-'. The poem ends with appeals to the Epicurean life, with the Bionian/Lucretian image of departure from the feast of life, and with renewed back-references to *Epistles* 1 and to the *Satires*, right back to Satire 1.1.³⁸ Like Satire 1.1, Epistle 2.2 is itself a feast (57ff.), but now the feast is nearly over. No more poetry, then, but philosophical poetry advocating a philosophical life for what remains of life and specifically both an Epicurean life and an Epicurean departure from it. A 'life-conversation', indeed.

〚179〛 At Augustus' request,³⁹ Horace added *Odes* 4: unphilosophical, except for the spring poem 4.12, which invites 'Virgil', 'client of noble youths', to 'wash away the bitterness of cares' in wine, to 'put aside the study of gain' and, 'mindful of the dark fires, mix, while you may, brief folly with your counsels; to be unwise in the right place is sweet'. Horace's 'sweet' 'unwisdom' is Epicureanism, the 'unwise wisdom' of 1.34.2. 'Virgil's' contrasting 'counsels' are public Stoicism. Naturally, this impossibilist vision of stealing time with the dead Virgil creates bitter-sweet pathos. But the serio-comic alignment of the Epicurean friend with Stoicism (through the *Aeneid*), with 'clientship to noble youths' (Octavian?) and with 'study of gain', ruefully recalls the philosophical, moral, and political compromises that Virgil had made in his life—and that Horace himself is still making. This perfectly poised philosophical focalisation could hardly be more disconcerting.

To a reproachful Augustus,⁴⁰ Horace explains why he is no longer writing poetry (*Epistles* 2.1), reviews the relationship between poets and rulers, especially that of his own poetry to Augustus *qua* world ruler, and emphasises their intertwined *Nachleben*.

The *Ars Poetica*, part response to a request, part general literary treatise, stresses the philosophical nature of poetry and ends with the end of life,

---

36   E.g., *Epist.* 2.2.1–19 (~ *Epist.* 1.20), 47 (~ C. 2.7.15f.), 55–7 (~ *Epist.* 1.1.4, 10), 59–60, 99, 141–2 (~ *Epist.* 1.1.3–4, 10–11), 175–9 (~ C. 2.3.17–24; ~ *Sat.* 2.2.132ff.), 199–200 (~ *Epist.* 1.1.15f.), 204 (~ *Epist.* 1.2.71).
37   F 1a Kindstrand.
38   *Epist.* 2.2.198; F 68 Kindstrand; *Epist.* 2.2.213–16 ~ *Sat.* 1.1.118–21 ~ Lucr. 3.938 and *Epist.* 1.1.2–4, 7–8, 10.
39   Suet. *Vit. Hor.* (Loeb edition, II.486).
40   Suet. *Vit. Hor.* (Loeb edition, II.486–8).

recalling both the end of the *Letter to Florus* and the end of *Satires* 1.1, the first poem of Horace's first published collection.[41]

Notwithstanding counter-factors (the *Carmen Saeculare*, the irony that disavowal of poetry occurs within writing what—on one level—obviously remains poetry, and Horace's apparent admission that, while claiming to be writing nothing, he is still writing),[42] the cumulative impression of Horace's last decade is that he would rather not write: he is old and tired, he would rather just live—or die. 'Enough' of poetry, of material things, and of life. That 'enough' is itself an Epicurean stance and one that looks back all the way to the close of the first Satire. In the end, it seems, living the philosophy he had favoured since the beginning of his poetic career was more important than writing, even than writing about the philosophy, and Epicureanism proved to be the main thread, not just of his poetry, or even of his philosophy, but of his life.

Spinning a yarn? Only a construction? With Horace, the boundaries between construction and life, while demanding exploration, are finally elusive.[43] But such questions do not—here—matter finally. Horace's representation of the role of Epicureanism in the pattern of his life is sufficiently [[180]] plausible to have protreptic force, a force enhanced, not diminished, by his constant ironies, playfulness, equivocations, and inconsistencies. He paints a far more realistic picture than most 'proper' philosophers of the ups and downs of practising philosophy in everyday life. Granted obvious differences of density and intensity, Horace's philosophising, essentially school-based, but broad-minded, benign, frequently humorous, and formally self-revelatory, can justly be compared with the philosophising of the two best philosophical teachers of pagan antiquity: Seneca, whom he influenced, and Plutarch.

## 5   Further Reading

The close, parallel-text translations of Bennett (1927), Fairclough (1929), Brown (1993) and Muecke (1993) are the best for non-Latinists. All relevant philosophical matters are fully covered in OCD³. Attractive accounts of Horace as moralist: Rudd (1993a); Russell (1993) (comparing Plutarch). 'Horace-*philosophus*' survey: Mariotti (1996–8) II.78–98. Scholarly controversy: 'pro'-philosophy: Macleod (1979); Harrison (1995); Moles (2002a); Armstrong (2004) (valuably linking Horace with Philodemus but, arguably, neglecting epistles' internal

---

41   *Ars Poetica* 476 'full' ~ *Epist.* 2.2.214 ~ *Sat.* 1.1.119–20 ~ Lucr. 3.938.
42   *Epist.* 2.1.111 (also ~ 2.1 itself).
43   See, e.g., Harrison (2007).

logic); 'anti'-philosophy: Mayer (1986); (2005); Rudd (1993). Of commentaries, on the *Satires*, Lejay (1911), Brown (1993), and Muecke (1993) are all philosophically responsive, Brown and Muecke especially helpful. On the *Epodes*, Mankin (1995) and Watson (2003), otherwise outstanding, minimise philosophy; on *Odes* 1–3, Nisbet–Hubbard (1970), Nisbet–Hubbard (1978), and Nisbet–Rudd (2004) excel, philosophically and otherwise. On *Epistles* 1, Mayer (1994) is unsympathetic to philosophy, but presents much evidence; similarly, Brink (1963, 1971, 1982) on the literary epistles. General studies include Fiske (1920) (controversial, but full of matter); McGann (1969) (seminal on *Epistles* 1); and Ferri (1993) (important on Horace and Lucretius).

## Bibliography

André, J.-M. (1967) *Mécène: essai de biographie spirituelle* (Paris).
Armstrong, D. (2004) 'Horace's *Epistles* 1 and Philodemus', in id., et al., edd. *Vergil, Philodemus, and the Augustans* (Austin) 267–98.
Bennett, C. E., ed. (1927) *Horace: the Odes and Epodes* (Cambridge, Mass. and London).
Brink, C. O. (1963) *Horace on Poetry I: Prolegomena to the Literary Epistles* (Cambridge).
Brink, C. O. (1971) *Horace on Poetry II: the Ars Poetica* (Cambridge).
Brink, C. O. (1982) *Horace on Poetry III: Epistles Book II* (Cambridge).
Brown, P. M., ed. (1993) *Horace: Satires I* (Warminster).
Dickie, M. W. (1981) 'The Disavowal of *Invidia* in Roman Iamb and Satire', *PLLS* 3: 183–208.
Fairclough, H. R. (1929) *Horace: Satires, Epistles, Ars Poetica* (London and Cambridge, Mass.).
Ferri, R. (1993) *I dispiacieri di un epicureo: uno studio sulla poetica oraziana delle Epistole (con un capitolo su Persio)* (Pisa).
Fiske, G. C. (1920) *Lucilius and Horace: a Study in the Classical Theory of Imitation* (Madison).
Fitzgerald, W. (1988) 'Power and Impotence in Horace's *Epodes*', *Ramus* 17: 176–91.
Freudenberg, K. (1993) *The Walking Muse: Horace on the Theory of Satire* (Princeton).
Freudenburg, K., ed. (2005) *The Cambridge Companion to Roman Satire* (Cambridge).
Gowers, E. (2005) 'The Restless Companion: Horace, *Satires* 1 and 2', in Freudenburg (2005) 48–61.
Harrison, S. J. (1995) 'Poetry, Philosophy, and Letter-Writing in Horace, *Epistles* 1', in D. C. Innes, H. Hine, and C. Pelling, edd., *Ethics and Rhetoric: Classical Essays for Donald Russell on his Seventy-fifth Birthday* (Oxford) 47–61.

Harrison, S. J. (2007) 'Horatian Self-Representations', in id., ed., *Cambridge Companion to Horace* (Cambridge) 22–35.

Kindstrand, J. F. (1976) *Bion of Borysthenes: a Collection of the Fragments with Introduction and Commentary* (Uppsala).

Lejay, E., ed. (1911) *Oeuvres d'Horace: Satires* (Paris).

Macleod, C. W. (1979) 'The Poetry of Ethics: Horace, Epistles I' *JRS* 69: 16–27; repr. in id., *Collected Essays* (Oxford, 1983) 280–91.

Mankin, D., ed. (1995) *Horace: Epodes* (Cambridge).

Mariotti, S., ed. (1996–8) *Enciclopedia Oraziana*, 3 vols. (Rome).

Mayer, R. (1986) 'Horace's Epistles I and Philosophy', *AJPh* 107: 55–73.

Mayer, R., ed. (1994) *Horace: Epistles Book I* (Cambridge).

Mayer, R. (2005) 'Sleeping with the Enemy: Satire and Philosophy', in Freudenburg (2005) 146–59.

McGann, M. J. (1969) *Studies in Horace's First Book of Epistles* (Collection *Latomus* 100; Brussels).

Moles, J. L. (1996a) 'Bion (1)', *OCD*[3]: 243.

Moles, J. L. (1996b) 'Diatribe', *OCD*[3]: 463–4.

Moles, J. L. (2002a) 'Poetry, Philosophy, Politics and Play: *Epistles* I', in T. Woodman and D. Feeney, edd., *Traditions and Contexts in the Poetry of Horace* (Cambridge) 141–57, 235–7 [vol. 2, Ch. 72].

Moles, J. L. (2002b) 'Reconstructing Plancus: Horace, *Odes* 1.7', *JRS* 92: 86–109 [vol. 2, Ch. 71].

Muecke, F., ed. (1993) *Horace: Satires II* (Warminster).

Nisbet, R. G. M. and M. Hubbard (1970) *A Commentary on Horace Odes I* (Oxford).

Nisbet, R. G. M. and M. Hubbard (1978) *A Commentary on Horace's Odes II* (Oxford).

Nisbet, R. G. M. and N. Rudd (2004) *A Commentary on Horace's Odes III* (Oxford).

Oliensis, E. (1998) *Horace and the Rhetoric of Authority* (Cambridge).

Reckford, K. J. (1997) 'Horatius: the Man and the Hour', *AJPh* 118: 538–612.

Rudd, N. (1993a) 'Horace as a Moralist', in id. (1993b) 64–88.

Rudd, N., ed. (1993b) *Horace 2000: A Celebration: Essays for the Bimillennial* (London).

Russell, D. A. (1993) 'Self-Disclosure in Plutarch and Horace', in G. W. Most, H. Petersmann, and A. M. Ritter, edd., *Philanthropia kai Eusebia: Festschrift ... A. Dihle* (Göttingen) 426–37.

Watson, L. (2003) *A Commentary on Horace's Epodes* (Oxford).

Williams, G. (1995) '*Libertino patre natus*: true or false?' in S. J. Harrison, ed., *Homage to Horace: A Bimillenary Celebration* (Oxford) 296–313.

CHAPTER 19

# *Romane, Memento*: Antisthenes, Dio, and Virgil on the Education of the Strong

This paper starts from propositions that are widely, though not universally, acknowledged:* Antisthenes, the first-generation Socratic who stands at the head of the Cynic tradition,[1] had a distinctive education doctrine, which was deployed by Dio of Prusa, the Greek sophist, philosopher, and politician of the first century AD, in at least two of his works.[2] The paper then proceeds to make two much more audacious claims: that Antisthenes' education doctrine underlies Virgil, *Aeneid* 6.847–53 (*excudent alii* …), with enormous consequences for the interpretation of that most controversial passage; and that Dio was aware of Antisthenic influence upon Virgil and incorporated this insight into one of his own reworkings of Antisthenes, in a way that crystallises currently much-debated questions about the knowledge of Roman culture possessed by Greek intellectuals in the early Empire, about the knowledge of that culture which those Greek intellectuals could assume in at least some of their contemporary (Greek)[3] audiences, and about the differing ways in which Greeks responded to the phenomenon of Roman power. The paper, then, may be regarded alternatively as falling into four more or less discrete parts or as unified by such themes as the whole ancient philosophical debate about the value of conventional education, the reception of Antisthenes, the

---

\* An earlier version of this chapter was given at a previous one-day conference at Newcastle in 2003. I thank A. J. Woodman for comments on a first draft; all those who commented at the conference; and David West for subsequent comment. Some of the material of the paper overlaps closely with that of two other papers: Moles (2005) and (2008). I thank M. Schofield for comments on the former and M. Trapp for comments on both. All translations are my own.

1 Whether Antisthenes was the actual 'founder' of Cynicism was disputed in the ancient world and remains so, but he at least influenced the Cynic tradition and could be co-opted into it, which is enough for present purposes. On this debate see, e.g., Giannantoni (1993), Moles (1995) 129 {above, p. 389} n. 2, Brancacci (2005) 10, 13, 85, 101, 145 n. 37. Of course, the ultimate 'head' of the Cynic tradition is Socrates himself, as was widely recognised by the Cynics themselves and by others.

2 For the terms of the debate about Dio, Antisthenes, and Cynicism see, e.g., Brancacci (2000), Trapp (2000), and Moles (2005).

3 I put this bracketed qualification because Dio, like Plutarch and other Greek philosophers and sophists, sometimes performed in Rome (though they spoke in Greek and their audiences in Rome will have included Greeks).

adaptation of Antisthenes to Roman contexts, and the general Graeco-Roman culture–power debate.

### [106] 1 Antisthenes' Education Doctrine

The relevant fragment of Antisthenes is embedded in a fragment from the *On Virtue* by Themistius, the Greek orator and philosopher of the fourth century AD:[4]

> But if you wish truly to learn that wisdom is something lofty, I invoke neither Plato nor Aristotle as witnesses, but the wise Antisthenes, who taught this road. For he says that Prometheus spoke to Heracles as follows: 'your labour is very cheap, in that your care is for human things, but you have deserted the care of those things which are of greater moment; for you will not be a perfect man until you have learnt the things that are loftier than human beings, but if you learn those things, then you will learn also human things; if, however, you learn only human things, you will wander like a brute animal'. For the man who studies human things and confines the wisdom and intelligence of his mind in such cheap and narrow things, that man, as Antisthenes said, is not a wise man but like to an animal, to whom a dung-pit is pleasing. In truth, all celestial things are lofty and it behoves us to have a lofty way of thinking about them.

Themistius' statement that he is 'invoking' Antisthenes *verbatim*—in the absence of any evidence to the contrary—has to be accepted as accurate. Since the fragment is preserved only in Syriac, it might be thought that we are operating at one remove from Antisthenes himself, but in fact there is good reason to suppose that the Syriac translation is very close to the original.[5]

Heracles' prominence in the fragment has led scholars generally, and no doubt rightly, to attribute it to Antisthenes' *Heracles*. The essential theme is Heracles' 'education' (note the repeated use of the word 'learn'). Prometheus criticises Heracles' care for 'human things', which are associated with the animal world, and his desertion of 'loftier things'. Acquisition of the loftier/celestial things guarantees acquisition of the human things; moral perfection needs both. This mythical paradigm concerning a choice set before Heracles naturally resembles the famous Choice of Heracles by Antisthenes' contemporary

---

4 Them. *De virt.* p. 43 Mach; Antisth. F 27 DC; SSR V A 96; F 96 Prince.
5 See on Dio 4.29–33 below.

Prodicus, but differs in that it has both a sort of 'either-or' quality (if the choice is between human and heavenly things, the heavenly are much preferable) and a 'both-and' quality (both are needed for perfection). The use of the term 'labour' in the criticism of Heracles' 'labour' as 'very cheap' inevitably recalls Heracles' Labours and suggests a contrast between misguided 'labour(s)' and true philosophical Labours. The mention of 'wandering' recalls Heracles' role as one of the great 'wanderers' of myth (here, of course, philosophical myth), but seems also to play 〚107〛 on the well-known relationship between literal and metaphorical wandering, the latter in its negative role of moral ignorance.

So much for the quoted words of Antisthenes within the fragment. The extent to which Themistius' introductory comments ('But ... road') and closing comments ('For the man ... about them') also reflect Antisthenes requires careful consideration. Though the explicit quotation from Antisthenes does not include a 'road' metaphor, this metaphor was of course extremely common in moralising and philosophical texts, both Cynic and other. It is part of the Prodican Choice, and it could be regarded as already implicit in metaphorical 'wandering'. Probably, therefore, Antisthenes used the 'road' metaphor elsewhere in the *Heracles*. Themistius' restatement of the lofty/celestial–human/animal contrast in terms of wisdom/intelligence and 'animalism' *might* simply be a restatement of Antisthenes' quoted words, with 'as Antisthenes said' merely picking up 'for he says' and 'cheap' merely echoing 'very cheap'. But the whole restatement is, I think, better read as a summary of Antisthenes' own exegesis of the story about Heracles and Prometheus, with Themistius' own gloss beginning at 'In truth ...', picking up the very beginning ('truly'). Antisthenes certainly lauded 'wisdom' and 'intelligence', and the former quality is given emphasis by another ring structure. The restatement generalises from the myth to human behaviour, uses a new image ('confinement' in 'narrow things') and ends on an appropriately crude Cynic note ('to whom a dung-pit is pleasing'). Consequently, we may infer that the connection between merely human wisdom/intelligence and animalism does indeed belong to Antisthenes' exegesis of the myth, in which case we may suspect here the influence of the Aeschylean (or pseudo-Aeschylean) representation of the relationship between Prometheus and Heracles' father, Zeus, as being between intelligence and (mere) power.[6] Antisthenes also seemingly used a 'virtue–pleasure' contrast, which is a feature of the Prodican myth and appears with extreme frequency in Cynic material, and seems here to be reflected in 'to whom a dung-pit is pleasing'.

---

6   Fitton Brown (1959); Kitto (1961) 61; cf. further p. 489 below.

Three other general factors must affect our interpretation of the fragment. First, Antisthenes certainly elsewhere projected Heracles as a paradigm of positive moral virtue: hence the fragment presents Heracles at the start of his philosophical learning-curve. Secondly, Antisthenes lauded philosophical 'strength' and *On Strength* is recorded as an alternative title to *Heracles*. 'Strength', therefore, must be part of the education package. Antisthenes *might* then here be making an implicit contrast between 'brute' strength and philosophical strength. It is even likely that Antisthenes played on the significance of his own name, as meaning 'strength'. And, given that ⟦108⟧ Antisthenes himself was a rough, tough moralist who wrote well, one might wonder whether he gave his educational doctrine metaliterary application in the *Heracles*, whether, that is, the work itself instantiated the doctrine. Thirdly, it may of course be plausible in some cases to infer additional elements from the Antisthenes-influenced texts, though this procedure naturally risks circularity.

Before we leave Antisthenes, it is worth registering—if only to dismiss—an objection made by certain modern Platonists: namely, that the fragment fails to provide any very distinctive doctrine. Now it is of course true that a contrast between the 'good' philosophical education and the inadequate conventional education is found everywhere in the Socratic/Platonic tradition and true also that this contrast may imply a distinction between 'divine' and 'human' education (as in the *Apology*, where Socrates' quest for wisdom is Apollo-driven, or in *Alcibiades I*,[7] where the Apolline precept 'know thyself' is taken to mean 'know one's god-like soul'). Nonetheless, in his *Heracles* Antisthenes, himself one of the earliest Socratics, evidently gave his own version of that divine–human educational contrast, and he and others, like the much later Themistius, evidently regarded that version as being sufficiently distinctive.

Since much of the rest of the paper will be taken up with the tracing of parallels between Antisthenes, Dio, and Virgil, it will be useful here to number the elements of the Antisthenic education doctrine in order of appearance as analysed above:

(A1)    Work as whole Cynic
(A2)    Education the general theme
(A3)    Immediate context an educational lesson

---

[7] For the direct relevance of *Alcibiades I* to the present enquiry see p. 485 below; the authenticity question concerning *Alcibiades I* (see, e.g., Giannantoni [1997] 365–6; Denyer [2001] 14–26), a dialogue anciently esteemed as one of Plato's most important pedagogic works (Trapp [2000] 226 and n. 37), matters little here; authenticity was unquestioned in antiquity and is now strongly advocated by Giannantoni and Denyer (*contra*, Trapp [2000] 226).

|     |     |
| --- | --- |
| (A4) | Philosophical teacher–pupil relationship |
| (A5) | Prometheus as teacher |
| (A6) | Heracles as pupil |
| (A7) | Education split into two parts |
| (A8) | One part 'human', the other 'lofty/celestial' |
| (A9) | 'Lofty/celestial' much more important |
| (A10) | 'Human' associated with animals |
| (A11) | Both parts needed for perfection |
| (A12) | Possession of the 'lofty/celestial' leads to possession of the human |
| (A13) | Evocation of Choice of Heracles |
| ⟦109⟧ (A14) | Myth has both 'either-or' and 'both-and' quality |
| (A15) | Evocation of Heracles' Labours |
| (A16) | Wandering literal and metaphorical |
| (A17) | Road metaphor |
| (A18) | Contrast between higher intelligence and brutishness |
| (A19) | Evocation of relationship between Prometheus and Zeus as in *PV* |
| (A20) | Confinement in narrow things |
| (A21) | Cynic scatology |
| (A22) | Virtue–pleasure contrast |
| (A23) | Heracles at start of philosophical learning-curve |
| (A24) | Fully-educated Heracles as philosophical paradigm |
| (A25) | Generalisation from myth to human behaviour |
| (A26) | Endorsement of 'strength' |
| (A27) | Contrast between mere 'brute' strength and philosophical strength (note that Cynic 'strength' combines physical and mental capacities) |
| (A28) | Pun on word/name 'strength' (Anti**sthenes**) |
| (A29) | Metaliterary application. |

I shall use these numbers (printed in bold) to identify parallels to Antisthenes in Virgil. Obviously, 'parallels' need to be numerous and sustained if real influence is to be proved and then analysed. We must now begin with Dio.

## 2     Antisthenes in Dio

I confine myself to two cases where Dio uses Antisthenes in what are, in some senses, Roman contexts. The first case occurs in Dio's *Fourth Kingship Oration*, which takes the form of a dialogue between Diogenes and Alexander. Whether the *Fourth Kingship* was actually delivered to Trajan is disputed,[8] but at least it dramatises an encounter between Trajan (~ Alexander) and Dio (~ Diogenes), i.e., between a Roman emperor and a (self-styled) Greek philosopher, which is enough for present purposes. As the use of Diogenes as main speaker implies, the general ethos and much of the doctrine of the speech are Cynic.[9] Sections 29–33 are commonly thought to reflect Antisthenes' [[110]] education doctrine as preserved in the *Heracles* fragment.[10] For Trapp, however, the doctrine of 29–33 is not Antisthenic but merely one of a series of items drawn from *Alcibiades 1*, which Trapp holds to be the Platonic 'master-text' of the whole of *Kingship 4*.[11]

The parallels between *Kingship 4* and *Alcibiades 1* are as follows:

| *Kingship 4* | *Alcibiades 1* |
|---|---|
| 1 Alexander's longing for world renown (4) | 1 Alcibiades' progressive ambitions for primacy, eventually extending to all mankind (105a–c) |
| 2 Alexander's long-standing desire to see Socrates and benefit from him (11) | 2 Alcibiades' previous desire to see Socrates (104c–d); Socrates' claim to have the power to crown Alcibiades' achievements (105d) |
| 3 Diogenes' insistence that Alexander, well-educated in a conventional sense, lacks the true education needed for kingship and is therefore premature in his ambitions (29ff.; 70) | 3 Socrates' insistence that Alcibiades, well-educated in a conventional sense, lacks the knowledge of statecraft and is therefore premature in his ambitions (118a; 106eff.) |
| 4 This education is a prerequisite for kingship (24–5, 53) | 4 This knowledge is a prerequisite for kingship (121a–124b, esp. 122a) |

---

8   See Moles (1983a) for discussion of this and related matters. The question of its dating involves the question of whether it was ever actually delivered and matters little here.
9   See, e.g., Höistad (1948) 213–20; Moles (1983a), esp. 268–9 {above, pp. 92–3} n. 65; and—rather uncritically—*SSR* IV.554–9; Jouan (1993) 387. Dio's use of *Alcibiades 1* (main text below) as his 'architectural' text does not make against this characterisation, since: (a) the characterisation of the speech as generally Cynic does not dispute Platonic 'wrappings' (Moles [1983b] 118–19 {above, pp. 341–3}); (b) *Alcibiades 1* is itself a strongly pedagogic/protreptic text; (c) Dio in any case 'radicalises' *Alcibiades 1*'s prescriptions.
10  Thus, e.g., Dümmler (1882) 14; Weber (1887) 241; von Fritz (1926) 78; Höistad (1948) 56–9; Brancacci (1990); 95–6, 104–9; (1992); (1997) 171–6; (2000), esp. 254–5; *SSR* IV.312–13; cf. also Moles (1983a) 270 {above, p. 94}; Whitmarsh (2001) 191 n. 43.
11  Trapp (2000) 226–7; cf. 232–4.

| | |
|---|---|
| 5 Diogenes' insistence on 'knowing thyself' (47) | 5 Socrates' insistence on 'knowing thyself' (124a–b, 128eff.) |
| 6 'Knowing thyself' requires knowledge of one's *daimon* (75) | 6 'Knowing thyself' requires knowledge of the god-like soul (129eff.; 133c) |
| 7 Diogenes' illustrations from Homer and the customs of the Persians (39ff.; 66ff.) | 7 Socrates' illustrations from Homer and the customs of the Persians (112b; 121cff.) |
| 8 Alexander's present slavish state (75) | 8 Alcibiades' present slavish state (135a–c) |
| 9 The dress of the *daimon* of hedonism (102) | 9 The sweeping robes of the Persians (122c) |
| 10 Finally, the need for the good *daimon* and 'sound culture and reason' (139) | 10 This is effectively the main theme of *Alcibiades I*. |

⟦111⟧ These parallels, which also include one clear verbal echo,[12] are compelling and prove that Dio is, indeed, using *Alcibiades I* as his 'architectural' text for the *Fourth Kingship*.[13] On Trapp's view, therefore, sections 29–33 are sufficiently explained in terms both of the broad thematic correspondences between the two speeches (items 3–4) and of that general Socratic/Platonic distinction already mentioned between the 'good' philosophical education and the inadequate conventional education. However, in my opinion, just as the general Socratic/Platonic distinction between the good and bad forms of education is insufficient to dispose of the distinctiveness of the Antisthenic version of it, so, here, these two factors are too general to explain the specifics of Dio 4.29–33, which now requires full quotation (for reasons that will emerge, I shall take the text as far as 38). Diogenes is addressing Alexander:

---

12  4.102 ἐσθήτων τε μαλακῶν ἕλξεις ~ *Alc. 1*. 122c ἐσθῆτας ἱματίων θ' ἕλξεις (Cohoon I.217 n. 1; Trapp (2000) 227 and n. 40).

13  This picture of the relationship between the two texts may, however, be complicated by the fact that Antisthenes also wrote an *Alcibiades* (and a *Cyrus minor* containing material on Alcibiades), which plausibly predated *Alcibiades I*, and there is therefore the possibility of Platonic, as well as Dionian, interaction with Antisthenes. There are certainly thematic parallels between *Alcibiades I* and Antisthenes' *Alcibiades*: see, e.g., Giannantoni (1997) 371–2; for possible interaction between Plato's *Gorgias* and Antisthenes' *Archelaus* see, e.g., Dodds (1959) 242; interaction between the pseudo-Platonic (or Platonic) *Clitophon* and Antisthenes is sure: see, e.g., Slings (1999) 94–6, 211–12; Brancacci (2000) 251; Moles (2005) 115–20 {above, pp. 336–44}.

(29) 'Do you not know that education is double, the one part divine [*daimonios*], the other human? Now the godlike [*theia*] part is great and strong and easy, but the human is small and weak and has many dangers and not a little deception; nevertheless, it is necessary for it to be added to the other, if there is to be a correct product. (30) But the majority call this human part 'education' [*paideian*], just—I suppose—like 'child's play' [*paideian*], and they think that the man who knows the most written languages, Persian and Greek and Syrian and Phoenician, and chances to read the most books is the wisest and most educated, but then again, when they chance upon scoundrels and cowards and money-lovers among these, they say that the fact and the man are worth little. The other kind they sometimes call 'education', sometimes 'manliness' and 'highmindedness'. (31) And it was for this reason that men of former ages called sons of Zeus those who successfully chanced upon the good education and were manly in their souls, having been educated like the famous Heracles. Whoever, then, being noble by nature, possesses that education easily becomes a possessor of this other one too, having heard only a few things on a few occasions, but those things that are the greatest and most authoritative, and he becomes initiated and guards them in his soul, (32) and no one could any more take any of these things away from him, neither time nor any sophist, not even one who wished to burn them out by fire; but even if someone burns the man, as they say that Heracles burned himself, his principles would remain in his soul, just as—I suppose—they say that the teeth of corpses that have [[112]] been utterly burnt remain intact, when the rest of the body has been consumed by the fire. (33) For he does not have to learn but merely to remember; afterwards, he immediately knows and recognises, as having had these principles in his mind from the beginning. In addition, if he falls in with a man who as it were knows the road, that man easily demonstrates it to him, and he learns it and departs immediately. But if he falls in with some ignorant and vagabond sophist, he will wear him out by leading him in circles, dragging him sometimes to the east, sometimes to the west, sometimes to the south, knowing nothing himself but merely conjecturing, and having wandered much himself under the lead of similar vagabonds. (34) Just as ignorant and unruly dogs in the hunt understanding nothing and failing to recognise the trail deceive others thoroughly by their voice and behaviour, as if they knew and saw, and many—chiefly the most foolish—follow these ones that make random sounds. (35) But of these some which make no sound and remain silent are only themselves deceived, but others, the most impetuous and

most mindless, imitating the ones at the front, make a din and zealously deceive others, such is the large crowd of simple-minded people that you would find sometimes following along around the so-called sophists. And you will learn that a sophist is no different from an unruly eunuch'. (36) Hearing this, Alexander wondered in what respect he had compared the sophist to a eunuch and asked him. 'Because', he said, 'the most wanton of the eunuchs say that they are men and have desire for women, and they sleep with them and pester them, but no further product accrues, even if they go with them for whole nights and days. (37) And among the sophists you will find many growing old, wandering in their speeches much worse than Homer says that Odysseus did upon the sea, and any one of them would sooner arrive in Hades, as that man did, than become a good man by speaking and listening. (38) And you, since your nature is such, if you chance upon a man who knows, one day is sufficient for knowing the thing itself and the art, and there will be no need thereafter for intricate sophistries or speeches. But if you do not chance upon a teacher who is a disciple of Zeus or another like him, who says speedily and clearly what must be done, there will be no profit for you, not even if you wear out your whole life sleepless and foodless among the accursed sophists.'

This lengthy, but sparkling and amusing, passage contains other elements, notably *ad hominem* appeals to Trajan and lashings of Dio's habitual polemics against (contemporary) sophists. Nevertheless, its essential philosophical provenance is clear from the numerous and sustained parallels with Antisthenes' *Heracles*, a text that contains the following elements:

(i) the idea of the 'double education', one part of which is divine, superior, strong, and 'easy', and which effectively equals moral virtue; the other part of which is human, inferior, and weak, and which effectively equals conventional education;
(ii) ⟦113⟧ the idea that both these parts are necessary for complete education;
(iii) the claim that knowledge of the divine education easily confers knowledge of the human;
(iv) the idea that Heracles represents the divine education;
(v) the idea that the sophists, of whom Prometheus is one, represent the human education;
(vi) road imagery (both good and bad roads);
(vii) a comparison between human education/sophists and errant dogs.

Elements (i), (ii), and (iii) are substantially represented in the fragment: although the latter does not use the term 'double education', it effectively divides 'education' into 'divine' and 'human'; it asserts the great superiority of the former but makes both necessary for moral perfection; it also says that acquisition of the heavenly education enables acquisition of the human. The emphasis in Dio on the 'easiness' of the educational programme, which is characteristically Cynic[14] and alien to the general Socratic/Platonic tradition, could have had Antisthenic precedent, Antisthenes being at the very least a proto-Cynic. Element (vi) could be Antisthenic, since his Prometheus–Heracles encounter has something of the flavour of the Prodican Choice of Heracles, which has the 'two roads' motif,[15] and Themistius' introductory 'the wise Antisthenes, who taught this road' might reflect this. The errant dogs of item (vii) may gloss Antisthenes' human education as animal/bestial. The association of human education with sophists is also plausibly Antisthenic: having begun as a pupil of Gorgias, Antisthenes later attacked him (e.g., in the *Archelaus*).[16] And—strikingly enough (in view of the fact that the Themistius fragment is preserved in Syriac)—there is even one apparent verbal parallel between Dio and Antisthenes: 4.31 'whoever, then, being noble by nature, possesses that higher education, easily acquires this other also' resembles the fragment's 'but if you learn those [loftier] things, then you will learn also human things'.

By contrast, *Alcibiades I* lacks not only the Cynic emphasis on 'easiness' but also the *explicit* distinction between human and divine education, the claim that acquisition of the heavenly education enables acquisition of the human, the motif of the two roads and the comparison of human education to errant animals. In all these respects, Dio is far closer to the Antisthenes fragment. Furthermore, although *Alcibiades I* does invoke Heracles (120e9), and the invocation is strategic,[17] it is wholly undeveloped, and there is no mention at all of Prometheus.

⟦114⟧ Now it is true that these last two factors themselves highlight a big difference between Antisthenes and Dio, a difference which Antisthenic and Dionian scholars have hitherto found hard to explain. This difference is the switch of roles between Heracles and Prometheus: in Antisthenes, Heracles represents human education and Prometheus divine; in Dio, Heracles represents divine education, Prometheus sophistic/human. But there is no cause for excitement. In Cynicism generally, and already in Antisthenes' *Heracles*, the educated Heracles is one of the great moral paradigms;[18] in the *Heracles* fragment Antisthenes is dealing with Heracles precisely at the point where he

---

14   E.g. D.L. 6.44, 70; further, p. 491 below.
15   Xen. *Mem.* 2.1.21.
16   Athen. 5.220d (Herodicus); Dodds (1959) 242; Decleva Caizzi (1966) 101; Brancacci (1990) 210–11.
17   Denyer (2001) 173.
18   Cf., e.g., Höistad (1948) 22–73.

has not been properly educated, whereas Dio is dealing with the developed, properly educated Heracles, because *this* is the Heracles he needs as an inspiring paradigm for Trajan, philosophical learner and devotee of Hercules.[19] Dio therefore correspondingly demotes Prometheus to the role of sophistic exponent of human education—a role Prometheus could fulfil from the *Prometheus Vinctus* on. And if the Antisthenic fragment already plays with the *PV*, as suggested above, Dio would also be playing games with Antisthenes' use of the *PV*, choosing the negative characterisation of Prometheus available there instead of the positive one chosen by Antisthenes. In short, once we accept the possibility of Dio's being not a passive reproducer, but a creative adapter, of his philosophical sources,[20] the switch of roles between Heracles and Prometheus does not disturb the general pattern of Antisthenic influence: it even reinforces it. Sections 29–38, then, are based on Antisthenes' double *paideia* and the apparent verbal parallel is revealed to be a true parallel and a sufficient indication that Dio had himself read Antisthenes' *Heracles*, as he had certainly read other texts of a Socratic whose works were widely read in the ancient world.[21]

The general pattern of Antisthenic influence once established, we may turn to other elements in Dio 4.29–33. Dio's emphasis on philosophical 'strength' is characteristically Cynic and already Antisthenic: Antisthenes' *Heracles* praised such virtues as *ischus*, and Antisthenes (I am sure) played on the *sthenos*-element in his own name.[22] Cynic philosophical strength has both mental and physical aspects. The strong–soft contrast suits a Choice of Heracles colouring[23] and was also exploited by the virile Antisthenes. Clearly, Antisthenes' Greek philosophical paradigm can usefully be transferred into a 〖115〗 Roman political context, even though Cynicism generally—and already, to some degree, Antisthenes—rejected worldly power. Finally, the double education has here some metaliterary application: the *Fourth Kingship Oration* itself embodies it, combining robust Cynic moralising with literary sophistication. This presumably also applied to Antisthenes, who was, as already noted, a rough moralist who wrote well. So, if the Roman emperor Trajan follows the teaching of the Greek philosopher, Dio, he will acquire both divine and human education and achieve perfection.

---

19  See Moles (2008).
20  This is now widely recognised: cf. e.g. Whitmarsh (2001) 156–67; Brunt's patronising dismissal of Dio's philosophical powers (Brunt [1973]) now seems very ill-judged.
21  This is wholly plausible: see, e.g., Brancacci (2000) 246.
22  Cf., e.g., D.L. 6.2, 14–15.
23  Cf. Xen. *Mem.* 2.1.21; Dio 1.70–84, Dio's own reworking of the Prodican *Choice of Heracles*, on which theme see in general Harbach (2010).

A year later, in *Oration* 13, Dio is telling his Athenian audience about his education of the Romans. The overall 'feel' of this speech, too, is Cynic;[24] as already noted, Höistad has plausibly argued for a general influence of Antisthenes' double *paideia*;[25] and there is one virtually certain Antisthenic trace at 13.30.[26] Now the closing words of the speech are as follows (37):[27] 'I did not, however, say that it was difficult for them [the Romans] to be educated, "since" (I maintained), "when you were better than nobody in the past, you learned easily all the other things that you wished." I speak of the arts of horsemanship, bowmanship, and hoplite warfare ...'. The theme of this passage is education (cf. 'educated', 'learned'). Education has two parts. The superior pertains to moral virtue, which the Romans do not (yet) have; the inferior embraces the arts of horsemanship, bowmanship,[28] and hoplite warfare, and consists, in effect, of the Romans' general military supremacy: their—allegedly—easy acquisition of that supremacy should make their acquisition of virtue 'not difficult'. The bipartite division of education, the Cynic emphasis on 'easiness', and the thought 'if you've got the one form, the other is easy'—these things show that Dio is again reworking Antisthenes for a Roman political context, though, as in the *Fourth Kingship*, with creative modifications.

He has taken the thought 'the superior form of education makes the inferior form easy' and inverted its terms—to obvious protreptic effect. He has discarded the ⟦116⟧ human–heavenly/divine terminology, presumably as being unnecessarily obtrusive in the present context. Nevertheless, throughout the speech the superior form of education, which produces true moral virtue, is validated by the divine. For Antisthenes' human education, Dio has substituted Roman military supremacy. One effect of this substitution is to leave the

---

24  Dudley (1937) 150–1; Moles (1978) 99–100 {above, pp. 57–9}; (2005) 118–19 {above, pp. 259–61}; Jouan (1993) 393.
25  Höistad (1948) 171–3; cf. also Höistad (1948) 50–7; 86–94 and Moles (2011) for this influence on other Dionian works.
26  This concerns Archelaus' attempt to persuade Socrates to come to Macedonia: the item, absent from Plato and Xenophon, was recorded in Antisthenes' *Archelaus*. Cf. Dümmler (1882) 8–11; *SSR* IV.350; Brancacci (2000) 249–50; Moles (2005) 124–5 {above, pp. 269–71}; Trapp (2000) 233 n. 57 concedes a 'non-Platonic' source here.
27  The ending is lost: first pointed out by Reiske (1798); then, e.g., von Arnim (1893) xxxivff.; Cohoon II.89, 120–1; Desideri (1978) 254; Highet (1983) 80; Verrengia (2000) 169; Moles (2005) 113 {above, p. 251} (arguing that the lost portion is small and insignificant).
28  This apparently odd illustration of Roman military supremacy is explained 'internally', that is, by the fact that it makes a parallel with the Persians of section 24: '[Socrates] would say that when the Persians came *they had not been educated in any education* nor did they know how to deliberate about public matters *but they had been trained to shoot with the bow, to ride horses*, and to hunt': Moles (2005) 118 {above, p. 259} n. 52.

Romans (sc. unlike the Greeks) without *any* conventional education. Here Dio is trading on a standard demarcation between Greeks and Romans: namely, that the Romans do war, not culture, which is left to the Greeks.[29] But the implicit dismissal of conventional education also accords with the more radically Cynic or Diogenic position on this issue[30] that the speech as a whole adopts rather than the Antisthenic view that conventional education has some, albeit minimal, value. But another effect of this substitution is to give greater elevation to this human education equivalent, thereby increasing its protreptic appeal. Earlier, Dio criticises the Romans' moral weakness, but says that if they choose the right education their city will become *strong* (34): this conventional pun on *Rome*[31] is well placed when *Romans* are being taught *Antisthenic* and Cynic educational doctrine, which teaches philosophical strength. Thus the Romans' military supremacy hovers, as it were, between mere strength (*rômê*) and philosophical strength, which itself has a physical element, and thus aspires towards the philosophical strength, which is the 'true' *Rome*. Here Dio is trading on another common assumption: namely, that there is some affinity between Roman virtue and Cynic virtue.[32] The emphasis on the alleged 'ease' with which the Romans acquired their supremacy further suggests their Cynic potential, as well, perhaps, as investing them, already, with something of the divine, 'ease' being an attribute of the gods.[33] (I shall return to this latter point.)

In sum, Antisthenes' double *paideia* doctrine underlies 13.37; Dio again shows considerable creativity in his reworking of it; and the doctrine itself again emerges as highly adaptable to a Roman political context, and one here, moreover, that compares and contrasts Romans and Greeks.

### [117] 3   Virgil and Antisthenes

Lines 847–53 of the sixth book of the *Aeneid* run as follows:

> excudent alii spirantia mollius aera
> (credo equidem), uiuos ducent de marmore uultus,

---

29   See, for example, Petrochilos (1974) 58–62; Whitmarsh (2001) 9–17.
30   Cf., e.g., D.L. 6.73, 103–4.
31   Erskine (1995); Whitmarsh (2001) 21, 149.
32   Cf. in general M. T. Griffin (1993) 251–58; (1996) 197–204 {= (2018) 480–5}.
33   Hes. *Op.* 5–8; some Cynic fragments associate Cynic 'easiness' with the divine, e.g., SSR V A 135; cf. Dio 4.29–33; Dio's representation of the Romans' ascent to world power, here and at 11.137–42, has something in common with the thesis of Plut. *Virt. Rom.*, with, e.g., Swain (1996) 151–61.

orabunt causas melius, caelique meatus
describent radio et surgentia sidera dicent:  850
tu regere imperio populos, Romane, memento
(hae tibi erunt artes), pacique imponere morem,
parcere subiectis et debellare superbos.

Others will hammer out bronzes breathing more softly (I certainly believe), they will mould expressions from marble that live, they will plead cases better, and the courses of the heavens they will write out with the rod and they will tell of the rising stars: you, Roman, remember to rule the peoples with power (these will be your arts), and to impose civilisation upon peace, to spare the subjected, and to war down the proud.

This epilogue—Anchises' culminating advice to Aeneas—is of course one of the most crucial passages in the *Aeneid*. It seems not only to define the Roman imperial mission but also to make a key statement about the respective geniuses of Greece and of Rome and to subordinate the Romans' pursuit of 'the arts' (in our usual sense of that term) to that mission, defined as 'arts' of a different kind. The description of war and imperialism in terms of arts is on one level paradoxical, in as much as it contrasts with 'the (liberal or fine) arts', on another level not so, because any pursuit demanding technical competence can be described as an art.[34] The passage has effectively three structuring elements: the first is priamel form; the second is the contrast between various 'fine arts' and the 'arts' of war and imperialism; the third is a contrast between Greeks and Romans, it being well understood that *alii* can refer only to the Greeks.[35] The second of these contrasts itself suggests other contrasts: between *otium* and *negotium*,[36] between pleasure and virtue, between soft and hard, between heavenly and earthly, between peace and war.

---

[34] Key discussions: Norden (1957) 334–9; Austin (1977) 260–4; Feeney (1986); Hine (1987); West (1993); Whitmarsh (2001) 15–17; Lyne (1987) 214–16; Race (1982) 121, Horsfall (2013) 577–86.

[35] As to why Anchises does not name the Greeks, two main explanations have been canvassed: (1) 'Virgil cannot bring himself to name the Greeks' [sc. because he is conceding their superiority in the arts]—so J. Griffin (1979) 66 = (1985) 169 and Jenkyns (1998) 666 n. 83; (2) Anchises is sparing Aeneas' feelings (Hine (1987) 174)—better. But account should also be taken of priamel conventions.

[36] To be sure, (forensic: p. 496 below) oratory does not sit with entire comfort within the category of *otium*, but it will become clear that *no* category within this complex passage is absolutely discrete, so a broad *otium–negotium* contrast may still be felt. The Lucretian echo in 851 (p. 499 below) 'helps' this contrast.

⟦118⟧ The first structuring element serves to privilege the Roman imperial mission among the various 'artistic' activities, though it is itself rather overtaken by the third element: in the hierarchy of values the arts of 847–50, although actually performed by different artists, are lumped together as the preserve of a generic *alii*. But when the passage is taken together with the immediately preceding 845–6 'tu Maximus ille es, | unus qui nobis cunctando restituis rem' (which quotes Ennius' famous judgement on Fabius Maximus, 'unus homo nobis cunctando restituit rem', *Ann.* 363 Sk.), a fourth element comes into play, that is, a ring structure concerning the 'arts' of war and empire. This ring structure further emphasises the pre-eminence of those arts, and the first member of the ring structure illustrates the defence and restoration of the state, the second its imperialist aggrandisement.

Most modern discussions see *Romane* (851) as having double reference: to each future Roman (Anchises as it were addresses the Romans down the generations) and to Aeneas, who is, so to speak, proleptically a Roman and, in being thus pregnantly addressed by his father, is yet further encouraged to make his own contribution to the Roman project. By contrast, E. Norden and R. Jenkyns argue that the reference is only to each future Roman.[36a] They claim that Anchises' long speech gradually moves away from Aeneas as addressee and that its contents must become progressively less real to him, so that *Romane* is Anchises' excited address to future Romans, in disregard of his son. This interpretation is wholly untenable. The whole passage has a sliding temporal focalisation: from 'now' in the heroic past, to 'the future', stretching down the generations, to 'now' in the Rome of Virgil's day, to 'the future' as from Virgil's day, a future that will extend for the duration of the Roman state. Consequently, the voice of Anchises is both the voice of Anchises the dramatic character and at least to some extent the voice of Virgil the poet speaking both to his contemporaries and to subsequent generations. Consequently also, *Romane* acquires *triple* audience reference: to Aeneas, to each future Roman 'in history', to Virgil's own audience/readership.

I shall now try to show that Antisthenes must be brought into the picture. In order to do so I will attempt to bring out some of the similarities between the words of Anchises and the Antisthenic education doctrine as outlined above. The numbers in bold refer to the elements there listed.

*Aeneid* 6 is a *katabasis*, whose main narrative purpose is the education of Aeneas ((**2**)); there is sustained comparison with Heracles, alike structural, explicit, and implicit ((**6, 13, 15, 23, 24**)).[37] Anchises, whose role plainly

---

36a {Norden (1957) 334; Jenkyns (1998) 666.}
37  Galinsky (1972) 134–6 = (1990) 279–82.

includes that of philosophical teacher, places before Aeneas a 'Choice' ((13)). This choice element is repeated, in a recognisably Herculean vein, in 892 ('fugiatque feratque *laborem*'), in the 〚119〛 *specific* 'spelling-out' of the *general* programme ((15)). The contrast between the activities of *alii* and those of *tu ... Romane* contains a direct contrast: between various 'fine' arts and the 'power' arts of warfare and politics. As in Dio 13.37 and in Greek and Latin generally, the term 'arts' can gloss the term 'education' ((2)). This, then, *could* be Antisthenes' 'double education' ((7)). The priamel form indicates that the 'power' arts of war and imperialism are preferred; in *Aeneid* 6 these arts are nothing if not divinely ordained; 'the whole tone of Anchises' expression of the Roman mission suggests an utterance of a divine sanction';[38] and these 'power' arts fulfil the moral demands of being *Romanus*, or 'strong' (both individual Romans in general and Aeneas in particular are exhorted to be both 'Roman' and 'strong': the one entails the other) ((26)).[39] Whence also a strong–weak/soft contrast: 847 *mollius*, which, in context, becomes slightly pejorative.[40] The 'power' arts themselves implicitly contain a contrast between 'mere power' and '*civilising* power' (852 *morem*) ((27)).[41] As in Dio 13, the larger bipartite (as it were) subject contrast goes with a bipartite ethnic contrast between Greeks (*alii*) and Romans, represented as potentially 'strong' ((26)).

Like the Greek Dio in his *Oration* 13, Roman Virgil is here evoking the standard trade-off, 'Romans do power, Greeks do culture'.[42] Nevertheless, the passage shows persistent points of contact with the Antisthenic educational doctrine as reconstructible from the extant fragment, from other Antisthenic fragments, from Dio 4.29–33 and from Dio 13.37. Clearly, then, Virgil, like Dio, is transferring the Antisthenic educational paradigm into a Roman political context, though substituting Roman power not (as Dio) for the human education, but for the divine one. He has elevated the 'power' or 'strength' arts to the status of full philosophical 'strength'. This Antisthenic background immediately disproves modern scholars' claims that 'philosophy' is significantly absent from these lines.

What are the consequences? There are several fairly obvious ones. From the point of view of *Quellenkritik*, it surely matters if Antisthenes is the main source of one of the most famous passages in Roman literature. This particular case also strengthens F. Cairns' thesis that the *Aeneid*'s general representation

---

38   Austin (1977) 263.
39   Cf. p. 492 and n. 31 above.
40   Even though *mollis* is *also* a term of art criticism (Austin [1977] 262; Hine [1987] 180).
41   For 852 *morem* ~ 'civilisation' see Austin (1977) 263–4.
42   Though he is of course modifying it: see p. 502 below.

of kingship and heroism is essentially Cynic.[43] Interpretatively, the apparent correctness of the Roman choice of the power arts is reinforced by the evocations of Heracles and of his Choice; by the implication that the choice made corresponds to the divine education; and by the [[120]] appropriation of philosophical 'strength'.[44] Further, this Cynic paradigm helps, I believe, to explain one of the items most frequently adduced in the 'further voices' approach to Virgil: namely, the apparent 'contradiction' between the Sibyl's statement about Aeneas' plucking of the Golden Bough (6.146–7 'ipse **uolens facilisque** sequetur, | si te fata uocant') and the actuality (6.210–11 'corripit Aeneas extemplo auidusque refringit | **cunctantem**').[45] For Cynicism itself is from one point of view 'easy' (as we have repeatedly seen), but from another point of view 'laborious', and Aeneas himself in his encounter with the Golden Bough is both Aeneas, the man of destiny who can 'easily' surmount the obstacle that others cannot surmount at all, and 'Romans in general' (6.851 *Romane*), for whom *cunctatio* is an inevitable constituent of the imperialist process (6.846 'unus qui nobis **cunctando** restituis rem').

One question cannot be ducked: can Antisthenes help with the question which has dominated recent discussion of *Aeneid* 6.847–53: namely, where, if anywhere, within this culture–power, Graeco–Roman, debate, is Virgil here locating the *Aeneid*? Anchises' whole protreptic of Aeneas imitates Ennius' *Annales*;[46] as already noted, the ringing echo of one of Ennius' most famous lines (846) immediately precedes the epilogue itself; and, while, on one level, lines 847–50 allude to different *types* of sculpture, to *forensic* oratory,[47] and to 'observational and theoretical astronomy',[48] on another level, they must be read as alluding to 'sculpture, oratory, and astronomy *in general*', even to 'the [fine] arts' *in general*, and this for a range of reasons: first, the Ennian allusions bring at least epic poetry into the picture; second, lines 847–53 *also* make a broad contrast between 'fine arts' and 'power arts'; third, as I have argued, the 'fine arts' correspond to Antisthenes' 'human education' and the 'power arts' to Antisthenes' 'divine education' (that is, there is a level on which the two groups combine to cover the whole of education); and, fourth, 'Aeneas has not

---

43   Cairns (1989) 33–8, building on Moles (1983b), (1985).
44   I am here talking only on the level of a first reading, without excluding the possibility of there being other considerations, both here and elsewhere in the *Aeneid*, which might entail that reading's having to be qualified, to a greater or lesser degree.
45   See the discussions of Lyne (1987) 214–16, West (1993), Horsfall (2013) 163–4.
46   Hardie (1986) 78.
47   Hine (1987) 179.
48   Hine (1987) 179.

encountered the observational and descriptive astronomy of 6.849–50',[49] and so has to take it as 'astronomy in general', which he has encountered (the Song of Iopas, 1.742–6). In short, like Ennian epic, like 'the arts in general', the *Aeneid* itself must come 'within the frame'.

⟦121⟧ Not a few scholars have herein detected a Virgilian disavowal of the importance of the arts, including poetry and the *Aeneid* itself, though their inferences, emphases, and methods of detection vary. Johnson has Virgil 'throwing doubt on the value and validity of the artistic process'.[50] J. Griffin states a typical 'cost of empire' case:[51]

> this unrivalled speech is at once a boast and a lament, a proud claim by a conqueror and a sigh of regret for the cost. Virgil, poet, philosopher, and aesthete, in the middle of his great poem, in which the Latin language and the Roman destiny alike were carried to a beauty which must have seemed impossible, yet must surrender to the Greeks (*alii*—he cannot bring himself to name them) the arts and the sciences. The traditional claim of the Roman patriot, that native morals outshone Greek accomplishments ..., is given a pregnancy and a pathos which transform it. '*Hae tibi erunt artes*': these are your arts, man of Rome—not the seductive beauties of Greece, which meant so much to Virgil as a man, and without which his poems could not have come into existence, but the hard and self-denying 'arts' of conquest and dominion. It is the price of empire that the Roman must abandon for this imperial destiny, splendid and yet bitter, so many forms of beauty.

For D. Feeney, 'the irony is not inert, as we hear Anchises proclaim that the Romans must abjure a faith in ideals of artistic attainment, when the very existence of the poem in which [Anchises] is a character is witness to the power of that faith'.[52] H. Hine, from this passage and others in the *Aeneid*, infers 'Virgil's pessimism about the role of the poet at Rome'.[53]

---

49 Hine (1987) 180; on the other hand, I do not think it is quite right to say, as Hine does, that 'forensic oratory plays no part in the action of the poem'; if (Hine [1987] 180) 'Highet ({1972} pp. 67–79, 310) finds only two "legalistic" speeches, Aeneas' at 4.33–61, and Juno's at 10.63–95', then at least Aeneas' at 4.33–61 does constitute some evidence, and Sinon's speeches in Book 2 surely have 'forensic' elements.
50 Johnson (1976) 108.
51 J. Griffin (1979) 66 = (1985) 169–70.
52 Feeney (1986) 15.
53 Hine (1987) 182.

R. O. A. M. Lyne writes in a similar vein to J. Griffin:[54]

> there is a striking paradox to notice, introducing ambiguity. Anchises' dismissal of art occurs, of course, within Rome's greatest work of art, the *Aeneid*. This is not a paradox of which Vergil will have been unaware, or thought that we should ignore. Anchises himself unwittingly calls attention to it by his ironical play on the word 'artes': claiming for the Romans the manly arts ('hae tibi erunt artes') he alludes also to the fine arts he disclaims: and in so doing surely reminds *us* that his disclaimer occurs within a work of consummate fine art. Another fact adds to the paradox: immediately preceding these art-eschewing lines, Anchises is made to include a resounding quotation from the poet Ennius. There is in fact a great irony to the passage, again a type of dramatic irony. Considered *in character*, as Anchises' speech, the lines require the clear, patriotic interpretation given to them above. Considered in *Vergil's* context, they have a different colour: to us, in this context, they [[122]] should mean something different. At the very least we could say that Vergil's context and the irony it produces suggest that Vergil cannot be at one with his character in his view of art, government, and the Roman mission. How much at odds with it we cannot, from this evidence, say. But the dramatic irony must make us wonder. It intrudes a striking further voice at this crucial part of the epic.

A more robust statement of 'the cost of empire' thesis (though with some close resemblances to Griffin's) is R. Jenkyns': 'the message [is] that the greater the price, the greater the reward must be. The splendour and the profundity of the passage are due to this: that Virgil counts the cost and counts it fully; and yet he accepts'.[55] Eloquent as these formulations are, they are all badly overstated. The comparatives of 847 ('*mollius*') and 849 ('*melius*'), which must carry over into 848 and 850, allow that Romans will achieve some competence in these arts, indeed, surely, that in them they will be second only to the Greeks.[56] Hence most scholars, while properly registering the force of these comparatives, have taken Virgil to be implying that the *Aeneid* must take second place, both to the superior importance of the 'Roman mission' and, in consequence, to the artistic achievements of the Greeks. Is it, however, possible

---

54  Lyne (1987) 215–16.
55  Jenkyns (1998) 668.
56  Hine's formulation is not open to this objection, though it will become clear that I disagree with it on other grounds.

to eliminate *any* depreciation of the *Aeneid*? A very few scholars have tried to do so. M. Wigodsky thinks that Virgil is implying that Ennius rivals the Greeks and that maybe he himself does too. D. West, in explicit repudiation of readings such as those quoted above, writes: 'this is not time ... to praise himself ... He leaves that to his readers. And they were saying it ... This is not a poignant disclaimer of artistic achievement ... It is a ringing boast which covers areas which it does not specify'.[57] Both these interpretations remain allusive and elusive, although I believe that they are both on the right general lines.

The starting-point must be that it is counter-intuitive to read this passage of the *Aeneid*, Virgil's greatest poem, as, on one level, encouraging/inculcating/stating and itself instantiating the Roman imperial mission and as, on another level, making a separation between that mission and its own status as epic poetry and, moreover, depreciating (however 'ironically', 'regretfully', etc.) that epic status. Several contextual considerations reinforce the implausibility of such a reading and combine to show that, on the contrary, Virgil is here making the highest possible claims for his epic, imperialist as it is.

First, as M. Wigodsky seems to sense, the quotation from Ennius (*Ann.* 363 Sk.), whom Virgil is here extensively imitating but—obviously—comprehensively outdoing, signals that Roman epic can be alike commemorative, protreptic, restorative, and itself ⟦123⟧ on the same level as that which it commemorates. Already, then, the *Aeneid* must be a *tertium aliquid*, distinct both from the liberal arts and from the power arts but partaking of both and thus transcending the apparent polarisation between 847–50 and 851–3. The point is further reinforced by the 'recapitulation' of 851–3 in 888–92, where Anchises performs the role of poetic historiographical paraenesist, again like Ennius and again like Virgil himself. H. Hine's conception of 'Virgil's pessimism about the role of the poet in Rome' thus seems badly misplaced.

Second, line 851 clearly echoes a phrase in Lucretius 5.1129f. 'ut satius multo iam sit parere quietum | quam regere imperio res uelle et regna tenere'. To what effect? Lucretius is asserting the superiority of Epicurean quietism to regal and imperial ambitions; Virgil controverts Lucretius by proclaiming the superiority of Rome's imperial mission. But this is a debate within poetry, indeed, again, within epic poetry, which, again, emerges not as distinct from political discourse but implicated within it.

Third, it is, I believe, impossible to deny the descriptions of 'the arts' in 847–50 some metaliterary application—as is true of almost all the *Aeneid*'s artistic descriptions—although the only previous scholar to argue this case seems to be W. R. Johnson. Obviously, both *describo* and *dico* can be used of

---

57   Wigodsky (1972) 7, 72f.; West (1993) 293.

literature, including poetry; further, the process *uiuos ducent de marmore uultus* must stimulate thoughts about debates concerning the relationship between *mimesis* and life, debates which obviously include poetry; further again, to the extent that the descriptions of the arts must be read as, on one level, general allusions to sculpture, oratory, and astronomy, even as glossing 'the arts' in general, the *Aeneid* itself obviously contains sculpture, oratory, and astronomy and indeed 'the arts' in general. Even when read as allusions to specific types of sculpture, oratory, and astronomy the *Aeneid* contains enough material to be adjudged as to some extent inclusive of them. There is, indeed, not much forensic oratory but there is some. There is, indeed, no technical astronomy but there are the philosophical cosmologies of Iopas and Anchises. As for sculpture, 848 would remind readers of Roman veristic portraiture of the second and first centuries BC.

Now it is true that H. Hine has argued that the specific arts of lines 847–50 are mainly absent from the *Aeneid* and that the reason for this is that they are implied not to be valuable in Roman public life or Roman imperialism. On both fact and explanation he is largely correct, though I would qualify the fact in two respects: first, 847–50 are not to be read only on the level of specific arts; second, there is somewhat more exemplification of the specific arts than he concedes. But to the extent that he is correct, the effect is not to detach the *Aeneid* from all the arts or from sculpture, oratory, and astronomy *tout court* but to emphasise those arts that are particularly compatible with the imperial Roman mission. And, again, the *Aeneid* contains them: it is the *tertium aliquid*.

⟦124⟧ Hence the fourth contextual consideration. In Book 6 itself, astronomy is represented by Anchises' philosophical cosmology; veristic sculpture by the parade of heroes; oratory by Anchises' whole speech, all of which surely 'trump' the precise forms of sculpture, oratory, and astronomy described in lines 847–50. Now it is true that Anchises' cosmology and philosophy are Greek-inspired, that all Roman oratory owed much to Greek oratory, and that so-called Roman veristic sculpture was probably modelled on the work of Greek artists, though the influence of early Roman portraiture may be disputed. Nevertheless, all these phenomena are here 'delivered' through the *Aeneid*, again, the *tertium aliquid* which preserves, inculcates, and instantiates the arts most valuable for the Roman mission. In short, all the considerations so far show that just as it is impossible to detach poetry, or epic poetry, from the Roman mission, so it is impossible to detach the arts, or at least the most important ones, from the *Aeneid*.

Fifth, given the fluidities of reference imported by the multiple and fluid focalisations, some space must at some point open up between Anchises the dramatic character—and indeed between Anchises' addressees: Aeneas and every future Roman—and Virgil the poet. Where and at what point? Precisely, with the *Aeneid* itself. Anchises' prophetic powers—and his artistic powers, that is, his ability to bring 'life' to the parade of dead heroes—extend extremely far—down to the death of Marcellus in 23; but they do not—and cannot—include the *Aeneid*, within which he is a character and which was written by Virgil, not Anchises. The words *credo equidem* (848) open the possibility that there might be other opinions about these artistic matters, and, as F. Bömer and H. Hine have pointed out,[57a] Anchises uses the technical artistic terms *excudo* and *duco* the wrong way round. Yet again, then, the *Aeneid* is the *tertium aliquid* which transcends Anchises' foreshortened polarities in 847–53. And Virgil the poet is himself *both* a 'Roman' in the sense of a 'strong' exponent of the Roman mission, *and* the master of the arts from which that strong Roman is to some extent excluded.

I now attempt to plot this highly complex relationship between 'arts' and the Roman mission in relation to Antisthenes. As before, I will attempt to bring out the similarities between the words of Anchises and the Antisthenic education doctrine by referring to the elements listed above on pages 483–4. Even by Anchises' imperfect aesthetics, the Romans in general will be second only to the Greeks in the specific arts of 847–50. Even on this level, therefore, the Romans, possessors, potentially and actually, of the 'arts' of imperialism, will be well on their way to *complete* education; and Virgil already preserves both his Antisthenic original's 'either-or' quality (the imperial arts are better than the artistic arts) and its 'both-and' quality (the truly educated are masters of both categories) ((14)). But the *Aeneid* itself transcends both Anchises' imperfect aesthetics and his one-sided focus on Roman power. The artistic arts—at least the most important of them—have been appropriated by the *Aeneid*, which unites ⟦125⟧ within itself, at the highest possible level, both forms of Antisthenic education, human as well as divine, and so achieves educational and philosophical perfection ((7–11)). This metaliterary enactment of the double education is, as we have seen, itself Antisthenic ((29)). But at this point we must factor in the full import of the Graeco–Roman debate embedded in 847–53. The *Aeneid* enacts Rome's military conquest of Greece (explicit in 6.836–40 and included in 851–3). But it also enacts a Roman cultural imperialism parallel to, and consequent upon, the Romans' military imperialism, exactly as in the Antisthenic paradigm possession of the human education follows from possession of the divine ((12)). *Pace* Anchises, in the *Aeneid* the Romans have defeated the Greeks both militarily and culturally. Thus the

---

57a {Bömer (1952) 118; Hine (1987) 180.}

'strength' of the Greek ANTISTHENES here yields to the 'strength' of Roman RHÔMÊ ((28)).

## 4 Dio, Virgil, and Antisthenes

Back, or forward, to Dio of Prusa. Dio's *Thirteenth Oration* cleverly plays external Athenian and internal Roman audiences against each other and past-time (Socrates' criticisms of his contemporary Athenians) against present-time (Dio's relations with his contemporary Athenians), exploiting double audience and double temporal focalisations and the whole Graeco–Roman cultural–political debate rather in the manner—one could say—of *Aeneid* 6.847ff. Socrates' criticisms of his contemporary Athenians culminate in an attack on the *epitaphios*, the Athenians' national myth; Dio's education of the Romans culminates with the thoughts that what is good about their existing education is their military supremacy, which they acquired easily (cf. the Sibyl on the Golden Bough) and which is one definition of 'Romanness'/'strength', and that they (unlike the Greeks) have no conventional education. The listening Romans might have recalled one of the most famous passages, even then, in Latin literature, as it were, their national myth. So the Greek Dio, a sharp literary critic, has seen what Virgil is doing in that passage, which means that he has seen something important that has escaped all modern Virgilian scholars. And, having seen it, he uses it in his own address to the Romans. He is implying: Virgil's message to you *qua* Romans was an imperial mission. My message to you is: you've done that, build on it and/but (it's both those) acquire moral strength (implement a higher definition of 'Roman-ness'). Further: Virgil high-jacked the Greek Antisthenes and made him subserve Roman imperialism. I am taking him back and reinstating his real philosophical message, which rejects worldly power in favour of true virtue. Further again, although Anchises left you second only to the Greeks in 'the arts', I am taking that away too, because, *pace* even Antisthenes, such education contributes nothing to virtue (this being the more radical Cynic view): you don't need it and nor do the listening Athenians, who are so foolishly proud of their education. Dio, that is, has chosen to interpret 847–50 in the mistaken way of J. Griffin, [[126]] R. Jenkyns, D. Feeney, and R. O. A. M. Lyne. Thus Dio pursues both with his Roman and with his Athenian audiences—and, in a way, with Virgil himself—the Graeco–Roman culture–virtue debate which underlies Anchises' advice to Aeneas.

Dio's attempt to reverse the clock and re-establish some distance between Antis*thenes* and *Roman* power was both a noble and a clever move, but, alas, a futile one: that attempt had already been comprehensively hollowed out by the most imperialist of Roman writers and indeed by the very progress of history.

### Appendix

In this Appendix, in which the argument of the paper is summarised schematically, **A** = Antisthenes, **D** = Dio, and **V** = Virgil.

**1. Antisthenic elements explicit in the fragment preserved by Themistius or inferable from other Antisthenic fragments** (i.e. A1–A29) are listed above, pp. 483–4.

**2. Antisthenic elements present in this passage of Dio and other related passages of *Or.* 13:**

| | |
|---|---|
| (A1) Work as whole Cynic | |
| (A2) Education the general theme | |
| (A3) Immediate context an educational lesson | |
| (A4) Philosophical teacher-pupil relationship | |
| (A7) Education split into two parts | |
| (A8) One part 'lofty/celestial' | [explicit elsewhere in speech] |
| (A9) 'Lofty/celestial' much more important | |
| (A11) Both parts needed for perfection | [explicit elsewhere in speech] |
| (A12) Possession of the one leads to possession of the other | |
| (A26) Endorsement of 'strength' | [elsewhere in speech] |
| (A27) Contrast between 'brute' (mere) strength and philosophical strength | |
| (A29) Pun on word/name 'strength' | [pun on Rome elsewhere in speech, with implication that Romans will become truly 'strong' once they're properly educated] |

⟦127⟧ 3. Five new and non-Antisthenic elements (also found in *Aeneid* 6.847–53) are:

(D36) Ethnic demarcation: Romans do war, Greeks culture
(D37) Romans have defeated Greeks militarily [implicit]
(D38) Affinity between Roman virtue and Cynic virtue
(D39) Glossing of 'education' in terms of 'arts'
(D40) Use of specific 'arts' to exemplify all the arts that make up the human education.

4. The essentials of Dio's reworking of Antisthenes in Dio *Or.* 13:

| ANTISTHENES | DIO, *OR.* 13 |
| --- | --- |
| Human education (= conventional education) | Human education *substitute* (Romans implicitly without any conventional education at all): Roman military supremacy |
| Human education weak, divine education strong | Human education substitute (Roman military supremacy) represents a sort of strength (affinity between Roman virtue and Cynic virtue), providing 'lift-off' for acquisition of true (divine) education |
| Divine education strong | True (divine) education will make the 'Romans' truly 'roman' (pun) |
| Possession of divine education leads to possession of human education | Possession of human education substitute (Roman military supremacy) leads to possession of true (divine) education [inversion for protreptic effect] |
| Acquisition of both forms of education 'easy' | Acquisition of both forms of education 'easy' |
| Acquisition of both forms of education leads to 'perfection' | Acquisition of both forms of education leads to 'perfection' |

## 5. Antisthenic elements in Virgil:

(A1) Work as whole Cynic(?) [Cairns (1989): *Aeneid*'s representation of kingship and heroism basically Cynic]
(A2) Education the general theme of Book 6 [759, 891, etc.]
(A3) Immediate context an educational lesson [cf. also 891 'docet']
(A4) Philosophical teacher–pupil relationship
(A6) Heracles as pupil [explicit and implicit parallels throughout Book 6]
(A7) 'Education' split into two parts ['arts' can ~ 'education', i.e., the '"arty" arts' correspond to Antisthenes' 'human' education, the imperialist arts to the 'divine']
⟦128⟧ (A9) 'Lofty/celestial' part much more important [for Antisthenes' divine education Virgil substitutes the Roman imperial mission and 'the whole tone of Anchises' expression of the Roman mission suggests an utterance of a divine sanction' (Austin ad loc.)]
(A13) Evocation of Choice of Heracles ['polar' choice between 'arts'; explicit at 892]
(A15) Evocation of Heracles' Labours [*labores* throughout Book 6; explicit at 892]
(A17) Road metaphor [900 'tum se ad Caietae ***recto*** [< 851 'regere'] ***limite*** portum']
(A22) Virtue–pleasure contrast
(A23) Heracles figure at start of philosophical learning-curve
(A25) Spelling-out of consequences of 'myth' for Aeneas' behaviour [890–2]
(A26) Endorsement of 'strength' [*Romane*]
(A27) Contrast between mere power and civilising power [852 *morem*]
(A28) Pun on word/name 'strength' [*Romane*]

I also argue for:

(A11) Both parts of education needed for perfection
(A12) Possession of the 'lofty/celestial' leads to possession of the human
(A14) Myth has both 'either-or' and 'both-and' quality
(A29) Metaliterary application

As it happens (maybe), the passage also includes:

(DV36) Ethnic demarcation: Romans do war, Greeks culture
(DV37) Romans have defeated Greeks militarily

(DV38) Affinity between Roman virtue and Cynic virtue
(DV39) Glossing of 'education' in terms of 'arts'
(DV40) Use of specific 'arts' to exemplify all the arts that make up the human education.

6. The essentials of Virgil's reworking of Antisthenes in *Aen.* 6.847–53:

| ANTISTHENES | VIRGIL |
| --- | --- |
| Human education (= conventional education) vs divine education | "Arty" arts vs. 'arts' of imperialism |
| Human education weak, divine education strong | "Arty" arts 'soft'/weak, 'arts' of imperialism 'strong' |

⟦129⟧ 7. The Antisthenic motifs used by Virgil and those used by Dio

| VIRGIL, *Aen.* 6.847–53 and context | DIO, *Or.* 13.37 and context |
| --- | --- |
| (A1) Work as whole Cynic (?) | (A1) Work as whole Cynic |
| (A2) Education the general theme | (A2) Education the general theme |
| (A3) Immediate context an educational lesson | (A3) Immediate context an educational lesson |
| (A4) Philosophical teacher–pupil relationship | (A4) Philosophical teacher–pupil relationship |
| (A6) Heracles figure as pupil | |
| (A7) 'Education' split into two parts | (A7) Education split into two parts |
| (A8) One part 'lofty/celestial' | (A8) One part 'lofty/celestial' |
| (A9) 'Lofty/celestial' part much more important | (A9) 'Lofty/celestial' much more important |
| (A11) Both parts needed for perfection | (A11) Both parts needed for perfection |
| (A12) Possession of the 'lofty/celestial' leads to possession of the human | (A12) Possession of the 'lofty/celestial' leads to possession of the human |
| (A13) Evocation of Choice of Heracles | |
| (A15) Evocation of Heracles' Labours | |
| (A17) Road metaphor | |

| | |
|---|---|
| (A22) Virtue–pleasure contrast | |
| (A23) Heracles figure at start of philosophical learning-curve | |
| (A25) Generalisation from myth to human behaviour, i.e., spelling-out of consequences of 'myth' for Aeneas' behaviour | |
| (A26) Endorsement of 'strength' | (A26) Endorsement of 'strength' |
| (A27) Contrast between mere 'brute' strength and philosophical strength | (A27) Contrast between mere 'brute' strength and philosophical strength |
| (A28) Pun on word/name 'strength' (Antisthenes) | (A28) Pun on word/name 'strength' (Antisthenes) |

[[130]] 8. Parallels between the two authors which are independent of Antisthenes:

| *Aen.* 6.847–53 and context | Dio, *Or.* 13.37 and context |
|---|---|
| (DV36) Ethnic demarcation: Romans do war, Greeks culture | (DV36) Ethnic demarcation: Romans do war, Greeks culture |
| (DV37) Romans have defeated Greeks militarily | (DV37) Romans have defeated Greeks militarily |
| (DV38) Affinity between Roman virtue and Cynic virtue [implicit] | (DV38) Affinity between Roman virtue and Cynic virtue [implicit] |
| (DV39) Glossing of education in terms of 'arts' | (DV39) Glossing of education in terms of 'arts' |
| (DV40) Use of specific arts to exemplify all the arts that make up human education | (DV40) Use of specific arts to exemplify all the arts that make up human education |

9. The ways in which Virgil and Dio 'cash out' the Antisthenic and non-Antisthenic motifs are sharply different:

| VIRGIL | DIO |
|---|---|
| 1) Roman military supremacy substituted for the divine part of education | Roman military supremacy substituted for the human part of education |
| 2) Roman military supremacy stands for true 'strength' (pun on 'Rome') | Roman military supremacy stands for an inferior sort of strength (pun on '*Rome*'), which yet provides an earnest of acquisition of true philosophical strength (pun on '*rome*') |
| 3) Antis*thenes*' philosophical 'strength' 'trumped' by Roman 'strength' | Philosophical 'strength' left unchallenged |
| 4) Romans left considerable competence (second only to Greeks) in 'fine arts' | Romans implicitly without any conventional *paideia* at all |

## Bibliography

von Arnim, H. (1898) *Leben und Werke des Dio von Prusa* (Berlin).
Austin, R. G., ed. (1977) *P. Vergili Maronis Aeneidos liber sextus* (Oxford).
Bömer, F. (1952) 'Excudent alii...', *Hermes* 80: 117–23.
Brancacci, A. (1990) *Oikeios logos: la filosofia del linguaggio di Antistene* (Naples).
Brancacci, A. (1992) 'Struttura compositiva e fonti della terza orazione "Sulla Regalità" di Dione Crisostomo: Dione e l'"Archelao" di Antistene', *ANRW* II.36.5: 3308–34.
Brancacci, A. (1997) 'Filosofia e "paideia" in Antistene', in Giannantoni and Narcy (1997) 153–77.
Brancacci, A. (2000) 'Dio, Socrates, and Cynicism', in Swain (2000) 240–60.
Brancacci, A. (2005) *Antisthène: le discours propre* (Paris).
Brunt, P. A. (1973) 'Aspects of the Social Thought of Dio Chrysostom and the Stoics', *PCPhS* 199: 9–33; repr. in id., *Studies in Stoicism*, edd. M. Griffin and A. Samuels (Oxford, 2013) 151–79.
Cairns, F. (1989) *Virgil's Augustan Epic* (Cambridge).
Decleva Caizzi, F. (1966) *Antisthenis Fragmenta* (Varese/Milan).
Denyer, N., ed. (2001) *Plato: Alcibiades* (Cambridge).

Desideri, P. (1978) *Dione di Prusa: un intelletuale greco nell'impero romano* (Messina/Florence).

Dodds, E. R., ed. (1959) *Plato:* Gorgias (Oxford).

Dudley, D. R. (1937) *A History of Cynicism from Diogenes to the 6th century A.D.* (London).

Dümmler, F. (1882) *Antisthenica* (Bonn).

Erskine, A. (1995) 'Rome in the Greek World: the Significance of a Name', in A. Powell, ed., *The Greek World* (London and New York) 368–83.

Feeney, D. C. (1986) 'History and Revelation in Vergil's Underworld', *PCPhS* 32: 1–24.

Fitton-Brown, A. D. (1959) 'Prometheia', *JHS* 79: 52–60.

Galinksy, G. K. (1972) *The Herakles Theme* (London).

Galinksy, G. K. (1990) 'Hercules in the *Aeneid*', in S. J. Harrison, ed., *Vergil's Aeneid* (Oxford Readings in Classical Studies; Oxford) 277–94.

Giannantoni, G. (1993) 'Antistene fondatore della scuola cinica?', in Goulet-Cazé and Goulet (1993) 15–34.

Giannantoni, G. (1997) 'L'*Alcibiade* di Eschine e la letteratura socratica su Alcibiade', in id. and Narcy (1997) 349–73.

Giannantoni, G. and M. Narcy, edd. (1997) *Lezioni socratiche* (Naples).

Goulet-Cazé, M.-O. and R. Goulet, edd. (1993) *Le Cynisme ancien et ses prolongements* (Paris).

Griffin, J. (1979) 'The Fourth *Georgic*, Virgil, and Rome', *G&R* 26: 61–80; repr. in id., *Latin Poets and Roman Life* (London and Baltimore, 1985) 163–82.

Griffin, M. T. (1993) 'Le mouvement cynique et les Romains: attraction et repulsion', in Goulet-Cazé and Goulet (1993) 241–58.

Griffin, M. T. (1996) 'Cynicism and the Romans: Attraction and Repulsion', in R. B. Branham and M.-O. Goulet-Cazé, edd., *The Cynics: The Cynic Movement in Antiquity and its Legacy* (Berkeley and Los Angeles) 190–204; repr. in ead., *Politics and Philosophy at Rome: Collected Papers*, ed. C. Balmaceda (Oxford, 2018) 475–85.

Harbach, A. (2010) *Die Wahl des Lebens in der antiken Literatur* (Heidelberg).

Hardie, P. (1986) *Virgil's Aeneid: Cosmos and Imperium* (Oxford).

Highet, G. (1972) *The Speeches in Vergil's* Aeneid (Princeton).

Highet, G. (1983) 'Mutilations in the Text of Dio Chrysostom', in R. J. Ball, ed., *The Classical Papers of Gilbert Highet* (New York) 74–99.

Hine, H. (1987) 'Aeneas and the Arts (Vergil, *Aeneid* 6.847–50)', in M. Whitby, P. Hardie, and M. Whitby, edd., *Homo Viator: Classical Essays for John Bramble* (Bristol) 173–83.

Höistad, R. (1948) *Cynic Hero and Cynic King: Studies in the Cynic Conception of Man* (Uppsala).

Horsfall, N., ed. (2013) *Virgil, Aeneid 6: A Commentary*, 2 vols. (Leiden and Boston).

Jenkyns, R. (1998) *Virgil's Experience: Nature and History: Times, Names, and Places* (Oxford).

Johnson, W. R. (1976) *Darkness Visible: a Study of Vergil's* Aeneid (Berkeley and Los Angeles).

Jouan, F. (1993) 'Le Diogène de Dion Chrysostome', in Goulet-Cazé and Goulet (1993) 381–97.

Kitto, H. D. F. (1961) *Greek Tragedy*³ (London).

Lyne, R. O. A. M. (1987) *Further Voices in Vergil's* Aeneid (Oxford).

Moles, J. L. (1978) 'The Career and Conversion of Dio Chrysostom', *JHS* 98: 79–100 [above, Ch. 1].

Moles, J. L. (1983a) 'The Date and Purpose of the Fourth Kingship Oration of Dio Chrysostom', *ClAnt* 2: 251–78 [above, Ch. 3].

Moles, J. L. (1983b) '"*Honestius quam Ambitiosius*"? An Exploration of the Cynic's Attitude to Moral Corruption in his Fellow Men', *JHS* 103: 103–23 [above, Ch. 12].

Moles, J. L. (1985) 'Cynicism in Horace *Epistles* I', *PLLS* 5: 33–60 [above, Ch. 14].

Moles, J. L. (1995) 'The Cynics and Politics', in A. Laks and M. Schofield, edd., *Justice and Generosity: Studies in Hellenistic Social and Political Philosophy* (Cambridge) 129–58 [above, Ch. 15].

Moles, J. L. (2005) 'The Thirteenth Oration of Dio Chrysostom: Complexity and Simplicity, Rhetoric and Moralism, Literature and Life', *JHS* 125: 112–38 [above, Ch. 10].

Moles, J. L. (2008) 'Defacing the Currency: Cynicism in Dio Chrysostom' [above, Ch. 11].

Norden, E. (1957) *P. Vergilius Maro Aeneis Buch VI*⁴ (Stuttgart).

Petrochilos, N. K. (1974) *Roman Attitudes to the Greeks* (Athens).

Race, W. H. (1982) *The Classical Priamel from Homer to Boethius* (Leiden).

Reiske, J. J. (1798) *Dionis Chrysostomi orationes* I–II² (Leipzig).

Slings, S. R., ed. (1999) *Plato: Clitophon* (Cambridge).

Swain, S. (1996) *Hellenism and Empire: Language, Classicism, and Power in the Greek World, AD 50–250* (Oxford).

Swain, S., ed. (2000) *Dio Chrysostom: Politics, Letters, and Philosophy* (Oxford).

Trapp, M. B. (2000) 'Plato in Dio', in Swain (2000) 213–39.

Verrengia, A., ed. (2000) *Dione di Prusa: In Atene,* sull'esilio (*or. XIII*): *introduzione, testo critico, traduzione e commento* (Naples).

von Fritz, K. (1926) *Quellenuntersuchungen zu Leben und Philosophie des Diogenes von Sinope* (*Philologus Suppl.* 18.2; Göttingen).

Weber, E. (1887) 'De Dione Chrysostomo Cynicorum Sectatore', *Leipziger Stud. z. Classichen Philologie* 10: 77–268.

West, D. (1993) 'The Pageant of the Heroes as Panegyric (Virgil, *Aen.* 6.760–886)', in H. D. Jocelyn and H. Hurt, edd., *Tria Lustra: Essays and Notes Presented to John Pinsent, etc.* (Liverpool) 283–96.

Whitmarsh, T. (2001) *Greek Literature and the Roman Empire: the Politics of Imitation* (Oxford).

Wigodsky, M. (1972) *Vergil and Early Latin Poetry* (Wiesbaden).

# Introduction to Part 3

*Jane Heath*

The eleven papers collected in this section span the decade up until John Moles' untimely death in 2015. The first six (Chs. 20–25) were published between 2006 and 2014; the last five (Chs. 26–30) are previously unpublished. Among them, one has been edited to completion by the careful work of Justin Allison; the remaining four are presented largely in the unfinished form in which Moles left them, polished by the painstaking labour of our indefatigable editor, John Marincola. Each of these papers is a gem that reveals something of Moles' wit, insight, and profound learning; collectively they stand not only as a monument to his scholarship, but as a summons to Classicists and New Testament scholars alike to embrace the kind of attention to New Testament texts that he models here. As a highly trained Classicist with breadth of expertise in philosophy, literature, and history, Moles in these papers recurrently announces a dual mission to Classicists and New Testament scholars respectively. To Classicists, he seeks to commend the texts of the New Testament for study as interesting and innovative receptions of Classical tradition; and to New Testament scholars he seeks to demonstrate that these texts are far more deeply rooted in Classical culture than they have allowed. He writes with sensitivity to the fact that the path he is treading is likely to be somewhat unfamiliar on both sides of the divide, and knowing that it will meet with questioning and resistance as a result. He inhabits that interface with humour, patience, and meticulous scholarship, and models the scholarly virtues of boldness in his claims, lucidity in his prose, delight in his material, and grace towards the interlocutors with whom he differs.

Moles always comes across as something of a loner when he brings his Classical learning to bear on the New Testament, and indeed at times cultivates this angular vision with a gleeful and almost Socratic irony, provoking his readers for their own edification. His solitude is both real and exaggerated: he *was* a pioneer, but in many ways his concerns and arguments are shared with others on both sides of the disciplinary divide. This enhances rather than dims the significance of his contribution, and some of the lines of enquiry to which he points have been more fully opened up in the years since these pieces were written, while others remain ripe for fuller study.

Moles' New Testament essays, which focus predominantly on Luke-Acts, can be understood as contributions to the scholarship on the Christian Second Sophistic. Occasionally he says as much, explaining that his purpose is to show that Luke-Acts deserves 'close and organic reading of the type now routinely accorded to Classical historiography or Second Sophistic prose works.'[1] More often he prefers to spell out what he means, and does so in disarmingly unpretentious terms:

> [This paper] has a range of aims: to prove organic engagement with philosophy; to demonstrate multiplicity of function; to provide new readings and to find new things; but also, much more generally, to commend to Classicists a marvellous Greek text which few explore, and to New Testament specialists a systematically 'classical' reading of it—whose validity not many accept.
>
> A 'classical' reading is one that applies the techniques that Classicists use in the interpretation of avowedly Classical texts. These techniques are in no way remarkable. They include the detailed analysis of structure, imagery, and wording, in the expectation that a Classical text should be a complex organic unity and that a Classical writer should have a high sensitivity to language, and the investigation of literary allusion, in the belief that the use of such allusion is a major feature of Classical texts. Naturally, it is not claimed that such a reading of the *Acts of the Apostles* displaces 'Jewish' or 'Christian' readings: only that it may usefully supplement them.[2]

At the time when Moles was writing, the study of the Second Sophistic was vibrant, but dominated by attention to literary and cultural features of 'avowedly Classical texts' from the late first to the early third centuries AD. The issues that were thematised were often specific to Classical culture, such as nostalgia for the language and literature of Classical Greece; reactions to Roman dominance articulated in Greek as a form of 'subaltern resistance through literature';[3] or the connection between politics, power, and *paideia*. However, even at this time, some scholars pointed out the relative paucity of attention to Christian engagement with the Second Sophistic and suggested that study of this area would be fruitful.[4] Some began to explore this interface, and scholarship on it was facilitated by the rise in American institutions of 'Early Christian Studies' as a field distinct from both Classics and Theology, which

---

1 Below, p. 786.
2 Below, p. 847.
3 The oft quoted phrase is from Whitmarsh (2013) 213.
4 E.g., König (2013); Henderson (2010). There was some engagement from the NT and patristics side of the fence: Winter (1997); Brent (2006).

drew methods from the historical, social-scientific, and literary approaches of non-theological disciplines.[5] Since the time when the essays collected here were written, the study of the Christian Second Sophistic has continued to develop apace, and has engaged the attention also of a growing number of scholars in New Testament and Patristics as well as those who name their specialism 'Early Christianity' or 'Late Antiquity'.[6] What stands out about Moles' contribution is not only that he was early in spotting the lacuna (although he was), nor just that he excelled in the Classical learning that he brought to it (although he did), but also the way he inhabited the interdisciplinary space, which he always conceived as a space between Classics and New Testament Studies (rather than, for example, a contribution to 'Early Christian Studies').

Moles cites very little of the leading scholarship on the Classical Second Sophistic,[7] and does not position his work in relation to Classical scholars working at the interface with Christian studies.[8] The distinctiveness of his approach emerges in at least two ways, which are 'organically' (one of his favourite words) connected: the texts that he focuses on are drawn from canonical Christian scriptures, and he engages with them from a seldom explicit but often implicit position of internally conflicted but deeply committed Christian faith.

His decision to focus on Luke-Acts and sometimes other New Testament texts was quite bold at the time that he was writing, both socially within the structure of the academy and intellectually in the claims that he was making. There has been a tendency even within Theology departments to fence off the 'New Testament' as a separate specialism that only professional New Testament experts get to pronounce upon. This derives historically from the way theology faculties were divided in the construction of the modern university in the 19th century, and it depends socially on the influence of ideas of canonicity in Christian and post-Christian culture. The segregation of NT studies has been fruitful in some ways, but distorting and destructive in many others. In any case, one consequence is that it is socially much easier even within the academy for a non-specialist to pronounce upon Christian texts that are not in the New Testament than to comment on the New Testament itself. Intellectually, it is also far more obvious that later Christian authors were steeped in Classical

---

5   For the rise of 'Early Christian Studies,' see Clark (2008).
6   E.g., see Nasrallah (2010); Eshleman (2012), and the inclusion of chapters on Christian texts in Richter–Johnson (2017); König–Langlands–Uden (2020).
7   E.g., Tim Whitmarsh does not appear in his notes to the New Testament papers (as opposed to the Classics papers); nor does Eshleman (2012), nor Nasrallah (2008), (2010); and of Jason König's work, only his essay on 'The Cynic and Christian Lives of Peregrinus' is cited.
8   But he does situate himself in relation to Classicists who had crossed the disciplinary fence into NT studies, such as Loveday Alexander. See below, p. 516.

rhetoric, literature, and philosophy than that the NT authors were. Especially at the time when Moles was writing, it would have been much easier to win an audience for a 'Classical reading' of Basil of Caesarea or John Chrysostom, rather than for texts in the New Testament.[9]

Moles' close attention to Luke-Acts and other NT texts appears to be motivated at least in part by his personal relationship to the Christian tradition, which he presents as both fraught and faithful. In the first essay in Part 3 (Ch. 20), he comments on this explicitly. On this occasion, he is writing about 'Cynic Influence upon First-Century Judaism and Early Christianity.' He begins by reflecting on the exhilaration and the challenge of interdisciplinary work: interfaces between disciplines are attractive as a release from well-worn inner-disciplinary debates, but one always feels inadequately proficient on the 'other' side of the disciplinary fence. When the interface is with scriptural studies, the material also presents a peculiar personal and existential challenge, which is in tension with scholarly commitment to critical distance.[10] Moles presents himself as an expert on Cynicism but one who 'has no professional competence in New Testament studies' (that should, of course, be taken with a heavy pinch of salt). He is, he says, 'an assiduously practising and intermittently (in some sense) believing Anglican; who in this scholarly context admits to a certain fideistic anxiety but seeks conscientiously to suppress it; and who, nevertheless, thinks that questions of value cannot ultimately be excluded.'[11] After arguing carefully that Cynicism was not only part of the early reception of the New Testament, but even part of Jesus' own formation, he urges that 'Jesus the Cynic to some extent' is important 'for the necessary refashioning of contemporary Christianity.'[12] His moving tailpiece adds a personal coda: 'in a rare and uncharacteristic expression of his "personal voice", the present writer confesses that at a time of acute depression many years ago he derived great, indeed decisive, solace from ancient Cynicism: he was saved not by Jesus but by *Dio-genes* (wrong god, wrong son)' and asserts that 'as in the first, so in the twenty-first, century AD, Christian Cynicism is the place to be.'[13]

This expression of the 'personal voice' is indeed 'rare and uncharacteristic' for Moles, but it is helpful for understanding his scholarship, because it suggests part of the way in which his deep commitment to the New Testament texts arises, while at the same time giving a glimpse of how he experiences the ironic

---

9   Henderson (2010) is an eloquent plea for more attention to 'non-elite speakers and the Second Sophistic', especially Christians.
10  Below, p. 523.
11  Below, p. 526.
12  Below, p. 543.
13  Below, p. 544.

distance he so often takes towards debates about the material. In chapter 28 on 'Greek, Roman, Jewish, and Christian Philosophy in Luke-Acts,' he promises that his 'expositions of Christian doctrine and ethics are Luke-focalised and value free.'[14] One would be hard put to find a New Testament scholar writing a phrase like that, even if they were trying to assert academic objectivity. This slightly flippant yet deeply attentive delight in the sophistication and power of the texts before him distinguishes the individual character of Moles' work. We might be tempted to compare and contrast another Christian Classicist whose principal contributions to scholarship on the NT took off from the time when Moles was taken from the field, namely, Teresa Morgan.[15] Like Moles, she has a real interest in close reading of the NT texts; like him, she has great intellectual confidence in the idea that Classics can contribute to understanding these sources. But her relationship to the texts is vastly different from Moles, and, as an ordained priest in the Anglican church, far less apparently conflicted. This diversity of perspective gives each a unique voice or, in NT terms, *charism* in their scholarship in this field.

Moles' choice of the New Testament as a focus for study is also bold relative to a long tradition of received wisdom that the New Testament texts are inferior to both Classical and patristic writings in literary and philosophical quality. Within the New Testament itself, Jesus' disciples are portrayed as illiterate fisherman; it is well-known that the earliest Christians were drawn extensively from lower social classes, thus less likely to be educated; the New Testament texts are written in *koinê* not in the sophisticated Attic prose that was cultivated by Greek-speaking *pepaideumenoi*; early Christians portrayed themselves as *simpliciores* and promoted their writings as unadorned in contrast to Hellenistic rhetorical style. At the time when Moles was writing, this stereotype of New Testament texts was even stronger than it is today, when more has been published on the philosophical, rhetorical, and cultural entanglement of the NT in the Classical world.[16] In his essays, he recurrently pleads with his readers not to assume *a priori* that Luke or his audience could not have been sophisticated. His own assumption, however, tends to be the reverse—and he does rely on it *as an assumption*. As he intimated in the passage on method quoted above, he works in the 'expectation' and 'belief' that these texts work

---

14  Below, p. 846.
15  Morgan (2015); (2020).
16  E.g., Engberg Pedersen (2018); Maier (2019); King (2020). But much work remains to be done: cf. Duncan (2015). For the trope of Christians as illiterate/uneducated, see Perkins (2012); Keith (2015).

like Classical texts. Often the proof of the pudding is in the eating: it is because the insights gleaned in this way are so rich that they carry conviction.

By contrast with the relative distance he maintains from Classical scholars with whom he might otherwise be compared, Moles is well-read in NT scholarship and often places his work in relation to it. As one might expect, he has an affinity for those NT scholars who are also trained in Classics (Loveday Alexander is prominent in his notes), or who are particularly sensitive to punning and other literary devices (Richard Bauckham is another frequent name in his work). But he also at times singles out less well-known NT scholarship for prominent attention: Manfred Lang's *Die Kunst des christlichen Lebens: Rezeptionsästhetische Studien zum lukanischen Paulusbild* (2008) appears to have made a particular impression on him. Moles sits lightly to consensuses in NT debates, confident in his Classicist's angle of vision and in the freedom afforded by approaching this as an outsider to the discipline. He adopts some positions that are not mainstream in NT scholarship, such as the view that John precedes Luke and Luke is partly inspired by it;[17] his acceptance that Luke was the healer and companion of Paul;[18] his rejection of gospel anonymity;[19] his confidence that Luke knew Classical texts and Dionysiac myth and ritual.[20] He often signals his independent perspective with an assertive, 'as I believe', or 'I suggest'; his versatility in the ways Classical authors think and write always adds credence to his positions; he has mastered the art of proportion, allowing his broader perspective on the Classical world to govern the proportion of attention he gives to different aspects of his argument. His style of argument is economical, precise, and systematic. He writes with the assurance of a sophisticated Classical reader who delights in recognition of familiar Classical patterns of thought and language, and he 'believes' against all sceptics that this text was also intended to entice a pagan audience in antiquity too.[21] It is telling that the final unfinished piece in this collection, 'Selling Christian Happiness to Pagans', gives attention to 'the pleasure of the text itself' in seducing ancient readers. This is an important point, too often overlooked, but abundantly vivid in Moles' own delight in this Classical Christian text.[22]

Whereas NT scholars in a similar period developed complicated criteria for ascertaining allusions, and for differentiating between echoes, allusions,

---

17  Below, p. 689.
18  Below, pp. 597, 692, 811.
19  Below, pp. 579, 592 n. 39, 832–5.
20  Below, Chapter 21, and p. 850.
21  Below, pp. 563, 615, 708, 710, 771.
22  Below, pp. 980–1002.

citations, and quotations,[23] Moles leans on his Classicist's confidence in the way ancient authors thought. He assumes rich intertextuality and conscious wit in playing with allusions to Classical as well as Christian texts. In Luke, he finds allusions to some Christian texts that many would hesitate to assume that he knew, such as Paul's letter to the Romans.[24] But mostly he focuses on allusions to Classical texts, and he casts his net wide. He finds Luke interacting not only with Greek Classics in different genres, including Plato, Euripides, Herodotus, and Thucydides, but also to some Latin ones, especially Vergil.[25] At one point, discussing the lack of early attestation for the title 'Acts of the Apostles', Moles affirms that it is original on grounds that it is 'so good it must be correct.'[26] Here speaks the voice of the sophisticated 'pagan' reader, who relishes the sophistication of this Greek author.

We should contrast this deep respect for the Classical brilliance of the evangelist with the tendency in some quarters of Classical scholarship to contrast 'playful pagans' with 'boring Christians', characterising the former as witty and subversive, the latter as pious, dull, and authoritarian.[27] In Moles, one gets a sense of his delight in the way Christian authors master and seek to 'trump' (one of his favourite words) pagan writing in ways that are characteristically pagan: 'educated pagans are being inducted—or seduced—by the subtlest of classical techniques', he writes.[28] 'Luke's staggeringly accomplished control of narrative space, narrative architecture, narrative road, and verbal interplay would have awed sophisticated pagans', he assures us on another occasion.[29] He makes it *exciting* to read these authors closely *as Classical authors*, in ways that also open up insights into their Christian purpose and message.

The sheer breadth of Moles' expertise as a Classicist emerges again and again in these essays; while most professional Classicists specialise in ancient philosophy *or* history *or* literature, Moles is manifestly master of all three, and that gives his work on the New Testament a many-layered fullness that is invaluable. In theme, Moles' essays are wide-ranging: he addresses Christian reception of Classical philosophy (chapters 20, 28); Christian adaptation of historiographical conventions (chapters 22, 24, 27); aspects of Christian socio-political history (chapter 24); the character of the Christian 'good news'

---

23  E.g., Hays (1989); (2016).
24  Below, p. 658.
25  Below, pp. 559; 562 n. 34; 568, and Chs. 27–8.
26  Below, p. 701.
27  For a nuanced interaction with this stereotype, König (2012) 141.
28  Below, p. 693.
29  Below, p. 695.

(chapters 20, 30); the theological rhetoric of punning (chapters 23, 26, 29), and of literary intertextuality with pagan texts (chapter 21).

The Moles whom we encounter through these essays is a *very* close reader of NT texts, and it is a poignantly occasioned privilege to have the opportunity to glimpse something of his working method in the unfinished papers. All of these papers, complete and otherwise, 'provide new readings and find new things' as Moles so simply puts it in the passage quoted—the understatement is typical. By way of *envoi* into the papers in this section, I would like to draw special attention to the three papers on punning, of which two are previously unpublished (chapters 23, 26, 29). These are among the most developed and original pieces of work in this book, and they deserve to be widely taken up in scholarship. They straddle literary, theological, and historical sensitivity and explore the way the NT sound-world interacted with the NT thought-world.[30] Whereas many other scholars have also pursued the relationship between NT and history, philosophy, and rhetoric, Moles' deep understanding of—and delight in—punning is unequalled. He shows that this is far from a *mere* game; it is a game, but a theologically and socially significant one. He thereby vividly conveys the rhetorical playfulness of the Christian Second Sophistic, not as a mere 'supplement' to its theological and social effect, but as integral to its form and character. In brief, Moles stands out as an early and significant voice expounding the reality and profundity of the Christian Second Sophistic, even within the New Testament itself, and as a wonderful example to all of us who seek to inhabit the exhilarating but complex space between disciplinary fields that are dear to us.

## Bibliography

Brent, A. (2006) *Ignatius of Antioch and the Second Sophistic: A Study of an Early Christian Transformation of Pagan Culture* (Tübingen).

Clark, E. A. (2008) 'From Patristics to Early Christian Studies,' in S. A. Harvey and D. G. Hunter, edd., *The Oxford Handbook of Early Christian Studies* (Oxford) 7–41.

Duncan, M. (2015) 'The Missing Rhetorical History between Quintilian and Augustine,' *Journal of the History of Rhetoric* 33: 349–76.

---

30    This is another area in which Moles could be seen to be ahead of the tide: soundscapes and the significance of orality and voice in the early empire are currently a growing area for research: Harrison (2013); Ruiz Montero (2019); Uden (2020). Also relevant is the exploration of voice and genre in Netz (2020).

Engberg-Pedersen, T. (2018) *John and Philosophy: A New Reading of the Fourth Gospel* (Oxford).

Eshleman, K. (2012) *The Social World of Intellectuals in the Roman Empire* (Cambridge).

Harrison, C. (2013) *The Art of Listening in the Early Church* (Oxford).

Hays, R. (1989) *Echoes of Scripture in the Letters of Paul* (New Haven).

Hays, R. (2016) *Echoes of Scripture in the Gospels* (Waco, Tex.).

Henderson, I. (2010) 'The Second Sophistic and Non-Elite Speakers', in P. Fleury and T. Schmidt, edd., *Perceptions of the Second Sophistic and its Times—Regards sur la Seconde Sophistique et son époque* (Toronto) 23–35.

Keith, C. (2015) 'The Oddity of the Reference to Jesus in Acts 4:13b,' *JBL* 134: 791–811.

King, F. J. (2020) *Epicureanism and the Gospel of John: A Study of their Compatibility* (Tübingen).

König, J. (2012) *Saints and Symposiasts: The Literature of Food and the Symposium in Greco-Roman and Early Christian Culture* (Cambridge).

König, J. (2013) *Greek Literature in the Roman Empire* (London).

König, J., R. Langlands, and J. Uden, edd. (2020), *Literature and Culture in the Roman Empire 96–235: Cross-Cultural Interactions* (Cambridge).

Maier, H. O. (2019) *New Testament Christianity in the Roman World* (Oxford).

Morgan, T. (2015) *Roman Faith and Christian Faith: Pistis and fides in the Early Roman Empire and Early Churches* (Oxford).

Morgan, T. (2020) *Being 'in Christ' in the Letters of Paul: Saved through Christ and in His Hands* (Tübingen).

Nasrallah, L. (2008) 'The Acts of the Apostles, Greek Cities, and Hadrian's Panhellenion', *JBL* 127: 533–66.

Nasrallah, L. (2010) *Christian Responses to Roman Art and Architecture: The Second-Century Church and the Spaces of Empire* (Cambridge).

Netz, R. (2020) *Scale, Space and Canon in Ancient Literary Culture* (Cambridge).

Perkins, J. (2012) 'Jesus was No Sophist: Education in Early Christian Fiction,' in M. P. Futre Pinheiro, J. Perkins, and R. Pervo, edd., *The Ancient Novel and Early Christian and Jewish Narrative: Fictional Intersections* (Groningen) 109–32.

Richter, D. S. and W. A. Johnson, edd. (2017) *The Oxford Handbook of the Second Sophistic* (New York and Oxford).

Ruiz Montero, C., ed. (2019) *Aspects of Orality and Greek Literature in the Roman Empire* (Newcastle-upon-Tyne).

Uden, J. (2020) 'The Noise-Lovers: Cultures of Speech and Sound in Second-Century Rome,' in König–Langlands–Uden (2020) 58–74.

Whitmarsh, T. (2013) *Beyond the Second Sophistic: Adventures in Greek Postclassicism* (Berkeley, Los Angeles, and London).

Winter, B. W. (1997) *Philo and Paul among the Sophists* (Cambridge).

# PART 3

## *Studies in the New Testament*

∴

CHAPTER 20

# Cynic Influence upon First-Century Judaism and Early Christianity?

Scholarship that moves within the interfaces between different subject areas and different disciplines is often exciting, as well as being personally energising for scholars who are at risk of becoming stale within their 'proper' fields.*  Such scholarship is also sometimes indispensable as a way of making progress in a particular area. But it has obvious dangers. Few scholars possess equal competence on both sides of any given interface, and the validity of any such interface may itself be in question ('did "a" really come into contact with "b"?'), as also the validity of one or other of its constituent elements ('was "b" of any real importance?').

For Christian and Jewish scholars the study of the historical Jesus and of the New Testament involves another kind of interface and one that is even more hazardous: that between scholarship and religious belief. Many such scholars are involved both in academic or scholarly and in religious or confessional spheres, and they struggle—with varying degrees of success or, indeed, of resolve—to maintain the necessary critical distances between these different types of activities.[1] Scholarly engagement with this kind of material should entail both a preliminary acknowledgement of interest and, in the analysis of the material itself, studious suppression of the 'personal voice'.[2] This does not

---

\*   [104] Versions of this paper under various titles were given at the 'Beyond Biography' conference in Dublin; at the New Testament Seminar in Durham (October 1998); at the *Hibernian Hellenists* in Maynooth (9th October 1998); at the New Testament Seminar in Sheffield (11th February 2002); and at the *Classical Association* in Durham (26th April 2002). My thanks to the respective organisers (Jimmy Dunn; Maureen Alden; Brian McGing and Judith Mossman (whose kindness beggars description); Loveday Alexander; and Gordon Cockburn); to all those who made helpful comments on those occasions; to Gerald Downing for helpful phone conversations over the years; and to Loren Stuckenbruck for advice on linguistic matters and for scrutiny of the penultimate draft.

1   [105] Of course, some dispute such formulations, e.g., Wright (1996) xiv: 'it is enough to say that I come to this work as a practising historian and as a practising Christian, and that my experience of both worlds suggests—to put it no stronger—that neither of them need feel compromised by intimate association with the other'. But, equally of course, *nothing* in this *apologia* is uncontentious.

2   A movement of that name within classical scholarship has been much savaged: Hanson–Heath–Thornton (2001).

mean that personal judgements about questions of quality or value are not ultimately appropriate.³

This paper treats claims, made particularly over the last few decades (though anticipated already in the late nineteenth and early twentieth centuries),⁴ that Greek Cynicism influenced both the representation and the reality both of first-century Judaism (of the kind exemplified by Jesus and his followers and by Paul) and of early Christianity.⁵ As it happens, these same decades have seen a renaissance of research on Cynicism by classicists.⁶ But, while there has been some scholarly traffic between the two groupings and some slight overlap of personnel, by and large the classicists have ignored this parallel movement in New Testament studies.

⟦90⟧ This Cynic–Jewish–Christian interface is sufficiently exciting, and, if it is valid, it brings new material and new scholarship into a field heavily over-worked and heavily oversubscribed. But it is of course highly problematic. Not only does it raise in an acute form the controversial general question of the extent of classical influence upon the world of the New Testament⁷ but its stakes for believing Christians are high. Thus if Jesus turned out to be a Cynic who made no real divine claims and for whom no such claims were made by his closest followers in the period immediately after his death, the doctrine of the Incarnation could be rescued only by such a radically 'Liberal' formulation as that of John Dominic Crossan, controversial New Testament scholar, former Roman Catholic priest, and still (at least in his own estimation) a Christian: 'to media or audience questions insisting, "Yes, yes, but was he *really* divine?" I answer again and again that, for the first as for the twenty-first century, Jesus was and is divine for those who experience in him *the* manifestation of God'.⁸ Again, a Cynic Jesus could be—and, indeed, has been—invoked by those who claim Jesus as a radical social reformer in (alleged) contrast to the (allegedly) bourgeoisifying tendencies of Paul, tendencies which rapidly came to

---

3  See p. 544 below.
4  E.g., Zeller (1893); Wendland (1895); (1912); Geffcken (1909); Bultmann (1910).
5  Select references in n. 16 below; for the refinement—no necessary Cynic influence on Jesus but 'objective' affinity—see p. 526 and n. 18 below; 'early Christianity' is a prejudicial term, but convenient.
6  Noteworthy contributions: Paquet (1988); Kindstrand (1976); Billerbeck (1978); (1979); (1991); Moles (1983a); (1993); (1995); (1996a); (2000); SSR II (fragments); IV (critical discussions); Goulet-Cazé–Goulet (1993); Goulet-Cazé (1986); (1990); (1993); (1994a); (1994b); (1996); (2003); Branham (1993); (1996); Branham–Goulet-Cazé (1996); Navia (1996); (1998); Luck (1997); Fuentes Gonzalez (1998).
7  For radical recent claims in favour of such influence cf. MacDonald (2000); (2003); Thiede (2004); Moles (2006).
8  Crossan (1995) 216.

dominate early Christianity.[9] From this point of view, a sentiment such as 'it is easier for a camel to go through the eye of a needle than for a rich man to enter the kingdom of God' (Mark 10.25) would be taken at face value and the consequences for contemporary Christianity would be challenging indeed.

But not only is there a question about the validity of the interface, there is even a question about the validity of the Cynic constituent itself. For the status of Cynicism—philosophy or way of life?—has been debated since antiquity,[10] and further, within the most recent classical scholarship, a profound divide seems to be opening up between those for whom the Cynics are genuine Socratics who articulate serious philosophical beliefs through their admitted public exhibitionism[11] and those for whom Cynic 'performance' and 'rhetoric' seem effectively to be the beginning and end of the Cynics' significance.[12]

Who, then, is competent to assess this Cynic–Christian interface? The model has been extensively discussed by more 'orthodox' New Testament scholars and largely rejected by them.[13] But its exponents have not been routed: they are nothing if not dogged, and the debate itself has been nothing if not repetitive. Furthermore, some of the model's most uncompromising opponents seem disturbingly ignorant about Cynicism. For example, Tom Wright's answer to the question (put to him at the Durham New Testament Seminar in 1996) 'what about the Cynic model?' was: 'its proponents have never been able to produce any good parallels for the Kingdom'.[14] And some curious cultural allusions in some of these responses bespeak defensiveness [[91]] and anxiety and a consequent failure to maintain due scholarly detachment.[15] Equally, however, the use of the Cynic material made by some of the model's exponents seems quite cavalier.

---

9  Cf., e.g., Downing (1987c); (1988a) ix–x; Ste. Croix (1981) 433 (using different terminology).
10 D.L. 6.103; cf. also p. 528 and n. 26 below.
11 E.g., Kindstrand (1976); Goulet-Cazé (1986); (1993); (1994a); (1994b); (1996); Moles (1983a); (1993); (1995); (1996a); (2000); Long (1996).
12 Cf. the influential Branham (1993); (1996).
13 E.g., Tuckett (1989); (1996) 368–91; Betz (1994); Robinson (1994), (1997); Eddy (1996); Wright (1996) 66–74; Aune (1997); Marshall (1997); Ebner (1998) 393–412; R. E. Brown (1997) 89, 822; Powell (1999) 68–73, 107; Maccoby (2003) 39–43; Dunn (2003) 154, 298–300 and index, s.v. 'Jesus: Cynic influence on'; Freyne (2004) 14, 136–7. These 'rejections' in fact vary considerably both in intensity and focus: Dunn (2003), for example, is far less dismissive than Wright (1996), while Maccoby (2003) 39 judges that the Cynic model 'does take account of certain authentic features presented in the Gospels'.
14 See p. 532 below.
15 Cf., e.g., R. E. Brown (1994) 677–8, with the response of Crossan (1995) 212ff.; van Beeck (1994) 97; cf. Wright (1996) 44: '[Crossan as] a rather skeptical New Testament professor with the soul of a leprechaun'; Theissen–Merz (1998) 11 ('the "non-eschatological Jesus" seems to have more Californian than Galilean local colouring').

Ideally, then, this interface should be assessed by a person who is equally expert in Cynicism and in New Testament and in related studies and who is completely objective in the contemplation of Judaism and Christianity. Naturally, no such person exists.

The present paper is written by someone who has made some contribution to the renaissance of classical scholarship on Cynicism and who thus hopes from that side to introduce into this debate some suitably Cynic rigour; who is committed to the view that the Cynics were serious moralisers and that they were important and influential; who (as will be obvious) has no professional competence in New Testament studies; who is an assiduously practising and intermittently (in some sense) believing Anglican; who in this scholarly context admits to a certain fideistic anxiety but seeks conscientiously to suppress it; and who, nevertheless, thinks that questions of value cannot ultimately be excluded.

The 'Cynic model' is associated with scholars such as Malherbe, Thiessen, Downing, Mack, Crossan, Kloppenborg, Vaage, and Seeley,[16] Mack and Crossan being prominent members of the famous—or notorious—American 'Jesus seminar'.[17] The model is applied in different ways and in different areas; these different applications can be regarded alternatively as free-standing or as constituting a cumulative case for general Cynic influence upon early Christianity and the sort of Judaism from which it sprang, back to, and including, Jesus himself. Downing is the leading exponent of this cumulative case: he is also the scholar who puts the Cynic case in its strongest form: that is: not all Cynics were Christians but all Christians were Cynics—more or less, or at least there was a recognised family relationship. This notion of the family is important to Downing, because it allows for diversity within a basic similarity. Even as restricted to Jesus, however, the model admits a considerable range: from a fully-fledged more-or-less secular Cynic, to a Cynic with a strong religious slant, to a Jewish rabbi more or less influenced by Cynicism, to a figure who need not actually have been influenced by Cynicism but for whom a Cynic model happens to provide the best ancient analogy.[18]

---

16   E.g., and very variously: Malherbe (1970); (1980); (1983a); (1983b); (1984); (1987); (1989); (1992); Theissen (1978) 14–15; (1992) 43–4; Downing (1984); (1987a); (1987b); (1987c); (1988a); (1988b); (1992); (1993); (1994); (1996); (1998a); (1998b); (2001); Mack (1988) 67–74, 179–92; (1993); (1997); (2001) 41–58; Crossan (1991) 72–88, 338–41; Kloppenborg (1987) 306–16, 326; (2000) 420–2; Vaage (1987); (1994); Seeley (1992); (1993); (1996).

17   Descriptions (largely hostile) in Wright (1996) 29–35; R. E. Brown (1997) 820–4; Dunn (2003) 58–62; self-presentation: http://religion.rutgers.edu/jseminar/ {dead link}.

18   E.g., Crossan (1994) 122; Kloppenborg (2000) 420–42.

This paper is less concerned with the model's different forms than with the fundamental prior question of whether it has anything to be said for it at all. Part I will try to establish the historical constraints on such a general model—in rather the same way as, a generation ago, A. E. Harvey tried to establish the historical constraints on the reconstruction of the historical Jesus.[19] Part II will survey the evidence adduced in favour of the model and Part III will attempt some conclusions.

## ⟦92⟧ 1  Problems about Cynicism and Their Methodological and Practical Implications for the Cynic Model

Space restrictions impose an appropriate dogmatism, though one that seeks to incorporate the methodological rigour absent from many modern reconstructions of Cynicism.[20]

### 1.1  *Was Cynicism a More or Less Uniform Philosophy/Way of Life?*

To be sure, some simple distinctions are needed: between Cynicism as lived, Cynicism as written, Cynicism as appropriated by other philosophies, and Cynicism as itself influenced by other philosophies. Within Cynicism as lived, one needs to distinguish—in adaptation of Lovejoy–Boas terminology[21]—between 'hard' Cynics (rigorous followers of Diogenes) and 'soft' Cynics (those who compromised with existing social or political structures, e.g., by marrying or engaging in political life—such as Demonax).[22] Beyond these distinctions, however, one should not go. Both advocates of the Cynic model such as Downing and opponents of it such as Betz and Wright greatly exaggerate Cynicism's diversity. Advocates do this because they want

---

19  ⟦106⟧ Harvey (1982).
20  I here reiterate, sometimes closely, my own published views on Cynicism but 'key' crucial points and arguments. Proper reconstruction of Cynicism must establish a hierarchy of evidence, as, e.g., von Fritz (1926); Höistad (1948) 5–21 (though weakened by mistaken rejection of the 'shameless' Diogenes); Goulet-Cazé (1986); (1994a) and (1994b); Moles (1983a) 104 {above, p. 318}; (1993); (1995); (1996a); (2000); *SSR* IV. Such rigour is effectively abandoned by (e.g.) Branham (1993); (1996); Navia (1996); (1998); cf. also n. 99 below. Throughout, I ignore the Cynic letters, much adduced by Downing, et al. and held important by Attridge (1976) and Malherbe (1977): since they are effectively impossible to date or contextualise, their utility is problematic.
21  Lovejoy–Boas (1935) 9–11.
22  Cf. Jones (1986) 90–8; Branham (1989) 57–63; Moles (1995) 156 {above, p. 414}; (1997); whether or not Demonax the man is a Lucianic fiction (as, e.g., Clay (1992) 3426, 3428), he represents a recognisable *type*.

to make the model as capacious as possible, so that practically any manifestations of Greek popular philosophy can be labelled 'Cynic'. Opponents do this because they want to undermine the very notion of 'a Cynic model'. Thus Tom Wright: 'who were the Cynics? The answers are always fuzzy, since it was of the essence of the movement that its adherents sat loose to formal structures. Everybody's definition, in the ancient as in the modern world, would carry some problematic aspects'.[23] On the contrary, what is striking about Cynicism is how little it changes over its thousand-year history or from place to place.[24] Why should it? Diogenes had solved all the problems of life.[25]

The belief in great Cynic diversity stems from two errors. The first is a misconception of the idea of the individual. A Cynic is an individual in the sense that he claims complete self-sufficiency and rejects the values of society at large. He is not an individual in the sense that he can embody any way of life that he chooses. The second is a misconception of the notion of (in Wright's words) 'sitting loose to formal structures'. This notion is often taken to imply that Cynicism's doctrinal base was flexible and indeterminate, but, while it is true that Cynicism's doctrines are few and simple and that they necessarily involve the rejection of all the doctrinal baggage of conventional philosophy, they nevertheless are internally coherent and they underpin the way of life.[26]

### 1.2   *The Range of Source Material and the Problem of Stoic Texts*

Why should it matter if Downing et al. cast their source net too widely? While such scholars are sometimes wrong to categorise their comparative material as 'Cynic', might it be reasonable to talk of the influence on Jesus 〚93〛 of 'Greek popular philosophy', abandoning the specific term 'Cynic', while maintaining the broad insight? But terminological exactitude does matter, for two reasons: first, Cynic positions are pretty distinctive and Downing et al. trade considerably on this distinctiveness; secondly, most scholars would find it implausible to posit the availability to Jesus of Greek philosophical material that goes beyond Cynicism.[27]

---

23   Wright (1996) 66.
24   Cf., e.g., Dudley (1937) 207; Moles (1983a) 112 {above, p. 332} n. 73; Krueger (1996) 73, 92.
25   Epicureanism is usefully parallel, that is, on the usual view that 'changes' introduced by Epicurus' followers and successors developed and refined Epicurus' original teachings in order to meet opponents' objections rather than radically to overhaul them.
26   Crucial are Diogenes' appeal to *phusis* (D.L. 6.71) and his Kronos/Zeus/anti-Prometheus myth: D.L. 6.44; Str. 15.1.64 = Onesicritus, *FGrHist* 134 F 17a; Dio 6.25; cf. 8.33; T. S. Brown (1948) 149 n. 152; Moles (1983a) 116 {above, p. 339} n. 103; T. W. Martin (1997).
27   See p. 541 below.

Stoic writers pose a particular problem: writers such as Seneca, Dio Chrysostom, and Epictetus are freely raided by Downing et al. for Cynic material.[28] Yet the legitimacy of this procedure varies: some Stoic contexts are essentially Cynic contexts (since Stoicism was born from Cynicism and Stoic ethics were greatly influenced by Cynic ethics); others are completely opposed to Cynicism.[29] Downing et al. often fail to make this vital context distinction. Use of Epictetus' *On Cynicism* (3.22) is particularly difficult. Epictetus offers a bowdlerised, Stoicised, and highly religious Cynic:[30] a gift to Downing et al., because you can then claim that there were real-life Cynics who did not urinate, defecate, masturbate, and fornicate in public (all characteristic Cynic activities),[31] and who also asserted a close personal relationship with God. But Epictetus' Cynic is a theoretical construct: there never were such Cynics, not even Epictetus himself. Yet it is a construct largely derived from Cynic realities: use of the *On Cynicism* is not wrong per se but it must be discriminating.

### 1.3 Cynic Literary Forms

Neither is appeal to *Cynic* literary material unproblematic. Three literary forms are crucial.

The first is 'diatribe', a form much canvassed in New Testament scholarship[32] but one whose boundaries and whose very existence have been fiercely debated in classical scholarship. It is certainly untenable to view diatribe as a tight literary genre with a whole series of formal elements; but classicists' obsessing over whether 'diatribe' exists has been equally unhelpful. We should agree that there was indeed a form called diatribe, that it describes the oral lecture, either in its original form or in a literary mimesis, and that it is particularly used of the popular sermon, itself particularly associated with, though not restricted to, the Cynics, who indeed probably invented it.[33]

---

28  The classification of Seneca and Epictetus as 'Stoic' is sure; Dio is more difficult: although heavily Plato-influenced (Trapp [2000]), he was caught by the Stoic philosopher Musonius Rufus; he sometimes classes himself as 'Stoic' (e.g., 30.30); his most substantial works are Stoic (Russell [1992] 6); and this is no doubt his most appropriate general classification; still, Cynic influence on him is also considerable: Brancacci (2000); Moles (forthcoming).
29  On Stoicism's appropriation of Cynicism see, e.g., Rist (1969) 54–80; Billerbeck (1978); Goulet-Cazé (2003); and n. 30 below.
30  Dudley (1937) 190–8; Billerbeck (1978) 1–9; (1993) 321–3; (1996) 207–8; Goulet-Cazé (1990) 2773–6; Long (2002) 58–61; rather differently: Schofield (2004) 451–5.
31  On this problem see p. 531 below.
32  Huge bibliography, but cf., e.g., Bultmann (1910); Stowers (1981); Schmeller (1987); Malherbe (1992) 313–20.
33  Moles (1996b).

The second literary form is the Cynics' collections of *chreiai*,[34] collections which could function as building-blocks of full biographies, as, for example, in Diogenes Laertius' *Lives of the Philosophers*.[35]

The third form, hypothetically, is 'Cynic biography', a form to which we shall return.[36]

### 1.4   Cynics and Religion

As we have seen, Epictetus' *On Cynicism* makes the Cynic a strongly religious ⟦94⟧ figure and Epictetus' conception of the Cynic as a divine messenger from God has been much invoked by exponents of the Cynic model. This raises the whole vexed question of Cynics and religion.[37]

In ancient philosophy generally, the inclusion of the wise man within the category of the 'holy man' is very widespread. Cynics, too, use such religious language extensively: they represent themselves as 'god-like', 'friends of the gods', 'sons of Zeus', etc.[38] What does such language mean? Certainly, it means that, if you are a Cynic, you can have the happiness, freedom, etc. traditionally attributed to the gods. But many distinguished scholars of Cynicism, including, recently, Marie-Odile Goulet-Cazé, have argued that Cynics generally were agnostic or even atheist.

Now it is true that Cynics ridicule conventional religion and that religion cannot be important to a Cynic: he has all his happiness and freedom (a freedom which includes freedom from superstition) right now. Nevertheless, appeal to the example of the gods obviously carries less force if you do not believe in them,[39] and there is strong reason to suppose that the gods were factored into Diogenes' *cosmopolis*.[40] Gods *plural*—what about God singular? From Homer onwards, classical polytheism always carries the potentiality of monotheism, and within Cynicism the conception of the Cynic as a divine messenger from god seems to go back to Onesicritus in *c*.320 BCE, probably back to Crates and perhaps even to Diogenes himself.[41]

---

34   Cf., e.g., Hock–O'Neil (1986–2002); Kindstrand (1986).
35   Cf. Goulet-Cazé (1992) 3978–90.
36   See p. 537 below.
37   Goulet-Cazé (1993); (1996); Moles (1995) 138 {above, p. 397} n. 27; (1996a) 113–14 {above, pp. 428–30}.
38   A list of references in Moles (1993) 270 {cf. above, p. 430}; (1996a) 113–14 {above, pp. 428–31}.
39   Epicureanism is again illuminatingly parallel (that is, on the orthodox and—I believe—correct view that the Epicureans believed in the gods).
40   D.L. 6.72 with Moles (1995) 138, 142 {above, pp. 398, 401}.
41   Moles (1983a) 112 n. 73, 115 {above, pp. 332, 336}; (1993) 270; (1996a) 113 {above, p. 429}.

Could a Cynic put God *singular* at the head of the universe? Ought he not to put Nature there?[42] Yet there are substantially Cynic texts which come close to equating nature with the divine principle that interpenetrates the cosmos.[43] These texts are Stoic-influenced, but the move they make is not a big one: Diogenes himself invoked 'right reason' as a cosmic principle,[44] and his anti-Prometheus myth[45] argued a fundamentally benign natural order as established by Zeus. Nevertheless, on balance it must be said that Cynicism's religious language has more to do with validation of the Cynic's philosophical role than with religious thought in any strong sense.

### 1.5   *Cynics and Other People*

Also controversial within classical scholarship on Cynicism is the extent to which Cynics have positive concern for others. How far are such things as Jesus' having disciples, his practice of 'commensality', and his moral concern for others compatible with Cynic ideas? The answer is that they are broadly compatible. Although the Cynic is independent and self-sufficient, he has a philanthropic concern for others:[46] he tries to convert them, he attracts followers or disciples,[47] and he has some conception of a Cynic community.[48]

### 1.6   ⟦95⟧ *The Cynic Way of Life*

As adherents of a primitivist conception of nature, Cynics are themselves poor, advocate poverty, and associate with the poor and the socially marginalised;[49] they wander,[50] and they promote and practise a basic economic egalitarianism.[51] All this, too, is broadly compatible with Jesus' way of life, though Jesus and his followers stop short of the outright begging that is one of the Cynics' trademarks. Even more alien to the celibate Jesus and his followers is that most distinctive of Cynic trademarks: the public performance of all natural functions, though it is interesting to note that such behaviour does find parallels in some stories in the Talmud.[52]

---

42   That is, given the primacy of 'life according to nature' as a Cynic principle (n. 26 above).
43   ⟦107⟧ Moles (1983a) 118 {above, p. 341}.
44   D.L. 6.73 with Dudley (1937) 33; Moles (1983a) 114 {above, p. 335}.
45   Cf. n. 26 above.
46   Cf. esp. Kindstrand (1976) 61, 247; Moles (1983a) 112–14 {above, pp. 331–6}; (1996a) 114–15 {above, pp. 429–31}.
47   Cf., e.g., D.L. 6.78–97.
48   Clearly evidenced in Diogenes' *Politeia*: Moles (1995) 140–1 {above, pp. 399–400}.
49   Good comment in Brenk (2000).
50   Cf., e.g., D.L. 6.38 (Diogenes' famous tragic verses); Montiglio (2000) 99.
51   Moles (1995) 137 {above, p. 396}; (2000) 426 {above, p. 451}.
52   Maccoby (2003) 107–8.

### 1.7 *Cynics and Politics*[53]

'Hard' Cynics reject all political institutions as unnatural and espouse anarchy. This does not make them political activists in any conventional sense: they need only a minimal level of subsistence and they reject armed conflict. There is no room here for 'Jesus the Zealot' (that is, leader of a patriotic, anti-Roman, revolutionary movement).[54] What, then, of 'Cynic kingship'? The concept was absorbed by conventional kingship ideology but its original point is to disavow conventional kingship in favour of Cynic kingship, which, as it were, flips the categories and is thus simply a metaphor for the Cynic way of life (with a range of easily derivable implications: self-mastery, total freedom to do as one likes, rejection of worldly power and pomp, etc.). So a 'hard' Cynic could certainly say 'the kingdom of god is at hand' or 'within you',[55] meaning that you—you yourself—can attain the perfect god-like state here and now. Such a Cynic interpretation underpins Crossan's single biggest idea about Jesus' ministry: that of 'the brokerless kingdom of god'.[56] This, of course, is not necessarily to say that Jesus' kingdom *is* the Cynic kingdom: but it is to say that a Cynic could speak in those terms. On the other hand, a 'hard' Cynic should certainly not say: 'Render to Caesar the things that are Caesar's' (Mark 12.17). But a 'soft' Cynic could say that, and indeed, in their respective relations with Antigonus Gonatas and Trajan, Bion of Borysthenes and Dio Chrysostom effectively did so.[57]

### 1.8 *Cynics and Eastern Wisdom*

Were there ever any real links, or overlap, between Cynics and eastern holy men, especially Jewish ones? Most scholars now discount eastern influence on Cynicism in favour of general resemblance (one ascetic type looks pretty much like another). Nevertheless, because of its elevation of Nature over Culture and its general iconoclasm, Cynicism is constitutionally welcoming to 'alien wisdom';[58] some leading Cynics came from the East; the legend of Diogenes was early contaminated by lore about the Indian gymnosophists;[59] ⟦96⟧ the

---

53  Moles (1993); (1995); (1996a); (2000).
54  Both this view of the historical Jesus and the prior assumption of a coherent 'Zealot' movement are nowadays generally discredited: see, e.g., Bammel–Moule (1984); Dunn (2003) 272–3; Freyne (2004) 135–6.
55  Extensive discussions of the Kingdom in Wright (1996) 198–472; Dunn (2003) 390–487.
56  Crossan (1991) 422.
57  Moles (1995) 149–50, 155–6 {above, pp. 408–9, 413–15}.
58  Cf., e.g., Romm (1996); R. P. Martin (1996); note especially for our purposes Dio Chrysostom's 'praise of the Essenes' (Crosby V.379), evidently written in Cynic 'alien wisdom' mode.
59  Onesicritus, *FGrHist* 134 F 17a; D.L. 6.23 with Höistad (1948) 137.

Cynic Oenomaus of Gadara (*fl.* 120 CE) is identifiable with the Jewish philosopher Abnimos of the Talmud,[60] and the great Jewish philosopher Philo of Alexandria (*fl.* 20 CE) was expert in Cynicism as well as Stoicism.[61] So there is a *general* possibility of two-way traffic here.

### 1.9   Hellenism in Jewish Palestine

This hugely controversial question[62] is obviously of some relevance to the present enquiry. Was such Hellenisation as there was limited to the city and upper-class? Yet this question is less important in relation to Cynicism, which, although sometimes practised by members of the élite who had lost, or abandoned, that status, was not in itself an élite activity.

### 1.10   The General Existence of Practical Cynicism at the Start of the First Century CE

Did practical Cynicism even exist at the time of Jesus' birth? (The question is framed in this way because, although the hypothesis that Jesus could have encountered Cynicism through the reading of Cynic texts is not theoretically falsifiable, few scholars would find it plausible.[63]) Such distinguished scholars of ancient philosophy as E. Zeller and J. Bernays maintained that Cynicism died out in the last two centuries BCE and that when it revived in the middle of the first century CE it had only been reborn out of Stoicism, and this view is still maintained by A. A. Long.[64] If such scholars are correct, that form of the Cynic model which claims direct Cynic influence is immediately vitiated, certainly as applied to Jesus and surely also as applied to Paul. Not only, however, do Malherbe's analyses prove Cynicism's vitality in Paul's lifetime in contexts which exclude 'rebirth from Stoicism' (as we shall see),[65] but the evidence on the classical side is also sufficient to validate this conclusion.[66]

### 1.11   Could Jesus Have Encountered Practical Cynicism?

But the case of Paul, born in the city of Tarsus in Cilicia, fluent both in spoken and in written Greek, and internationally travelled, is not the same as

---

60   Hammerstaedt (1990) 2836–9.
61   Wendland (1895); Dudley (1937) 186–7; Downing (1988a) 194.
62   Neusner (1986); Hengel (1974); (1989); Levine (1998); Collins–Sterling (2001); Freyne (2004) 14; Thiede (2004) 13–32.
63   *Pace* Mack (2001) 64: '[Jesus] may have read Meleager'. Thiede's very positive view of Jesus' Hellenic culture (n. 74 below) might also allow this.
64   Moles (1983a) 120–3 {above, pp. 344–8}; Long (2002) 59.
65   See p. 536 below.
66   Moles (1983a) 120–3 {above, pp. 344–8}; Goulet-Cazé (1990) 2723; (1996) 13–14.

that of Jesus of Nazareth. Could a Galilean villager have encountered practical Cynicism at the start of the first century CE?

Nazareth is about four miles from the Hellenistic city Sepphoris (with which Jesus is not recorded to have had any contact) and about twenty miles from the Transjordan Greek city of Gadara. On the current majority view, archaeological analysis of Sepphoris at the relevant time makes it, despite the Hellenism of its refounder Herod Antipas, both racially and culturally a very Jewish city.[67] Could there have been Greek Cynics or Jewish Cynics there? If there were, how could Jesus have encountered them? What sort of contacts were there between the Galilean cities and villages?[68] As a carpenter's son, might Jesus have visited Sepphoris to help his father in its rebuilding?[69]

⟦97⟧ In apparent contrast to Sepphoris, Gadara produced the Cynic Menippus in the third century BCE, the Cynicising poet Meleager in the 2nd/1st centuries BCE, and the Jewish Cynic Oenomaus towards the end of the first century CE. Might Gadara have had a Cynic community within Jesus' lifetime? If so, could he have come into contact with it? While Jesus visited the environs of Gadara during his ministry,[70] he began that ministry in the villages and countryside of Galilee and he is never recorded as having visited *poleis* in the full sense of that term, although he certainly visited the *chōrai* of such *poleis*.[71]

The question of 'village' and 'countryside' as opposed to 'city' in relation both to Jesus' upbringing and to his ministry is a difficult one. Might a useful distinction be drawn between attitude to cities (tension, even hostility, with practical consequences for Jesus' ministry: avoidance of *poleis* in the strict sense) and actual knowledge (whether as the result of the general commercial contacts that obtained between village and city, of hearsay, or of pre-ministry visits)? Agricultural and commercial contacts between Sepphoris and the surrounding villages are certain;[72] Jesus knew about city life, including Greek

---

67   Dunn (2003) 299–300; for a different emphasis see Thiede (2004) 21; the dating of the theatre is important: Dunn (2003) 299 n. 198; Thiede (2004) 131 n. 13.
68   See, e.g., Crossan (1991) 17–19 (Nazareth as 'satellite' of Sepphoris); Thiede (2004) 13–15; *contra*, Freyne (2000) 195–6, 205–6; Dunn (2003) 301–2 (both arguing 'tension' between city and village).
69   A common hypothesis: e.g. Batey (1991) 70, 103; Theissen–Merz (1998) 165–6; Thiede (2004) 15 (following the tradition that 'carpenter' underestimates Joseph's status).
70   Mark 5.1–20; Matthew 8.28–34; Luke 8.26–39, with the decisive arguments for Gadara of Thiede (2004) 44–7.
71   Ste. Croix (1981) 427–30; still more nuanced discussion in Dunn (2003) 319–21.
72   Dunn (2003) 301.

reclining at meals,[73] and he also knew something about pagan religion, both Greek and Roman.[74]

Might there also have been Cynics in the countryside of Galilee? Positive attestation of the phenomenon of 'country Cynics' in any cultural context is slight but not non-existent,[75] and there must have been such Cynics, because, although Cynics generally frequented the cities (in order both to beg and to maximise converts), they are fundamentally hostile to the city, *qua* contrary to nature, and they 'wander' from place to place, so must sometimes be found in the countryside. The existence of country Cynics, however, is obviously much less likely in contexts where there are no city Cynics, but the *chōrai* of *poleis* could afford a more plausible context.

To question 1.11, then, no final answer can be given. Those classicists (like the present writer) who believe in the widespread diffusion of Cynicism in the Hellenistic period, and who (again like the present writer) suspect that the much-touted 'decline' of Cynicism after the end of the third century BCE is more likely to reflect gaps in the evidence rather than any very substantial historical reality, will find it possible that the young Jesus could have encountered practical Cynicism, perhaps through pre-ministry visits to Sepphoris or Gadara or the latter's *chōra*. The notorious blank in Jesus' pre-ministry career makes one wonder if some of it was spent in travelling. John Dillon pleasantly sees Jesus' early career as similar to Socrates' in Plato's *Apology*, with Jesus searching for the truth—maybe visiting the Essenes, maybe the Gadarene Cynics—before striking out on his own.[76] Alternatively, of course, he may just have been working with his father. But even that would not provide a decisive [[98]] negative to the question. And, of course, if the evidence adduced in favour of the Cynic model is sufficiently solid, it itself constitutes evidence for the availability to Jesus of practical Cynicism.

### 1.12   *Could Jesus Speak Greek?*

This, surely, is highly desirable, perhaps even indispensable, for the Cynic model to work. Downing does not think it is indispensable, but it is not clear how a Greek-less Jesus could have acquired the Cynic-like social *langue* which Downing attributes to him. But in any case it is hard to believe that a first-century Jew—even a Galilean—whose life and sayings are almost exclusively recorded

---

73  Dunn (2003) 320.
74  See the exciting discussions of Thiede (2004) 66–72 and Freyne (2004) 55–6; cf. also the very positive view of Jesus' acquaintance with Greek culture in Thiede (2004) 13–32, a view that allows little distinction between 'city' and 'village'.
75  [[108]] Downing (1992) 82–3, 148–9.
76  So John Dillon in the discussion at the Dublin conference.

in Greek,[77] who is represented as talking directly to Romans and to a Greek woman (Mark 7.26), two of whose disciples have Greek names (Andrew and Philip), and who even *seems* to make bilingual Aramaic–Greek puns could not speak (at least some) Greek.[78] Probably a majority of New Testament and historical Jesus scholars now believe that Jesus could speak Greek, though many of these shirk what seems the natural consequence: namely, that Jesus must have had at least some knowledge of Greek culture. But this he anyway seems to have had.[79]

## 2 Evidence Adduced in Favour of the Cynic Model

The treatment here is anachronistic and designed to move progressively from the certain to the controversial and thereby to provide some controls for assessing the plausibility of the cumulative case.

### 2.1 *Cynic Influence on Paul*

Following Bultmann, several modern scholars, including Malherbe, Hock, Downing, Deming, have argued for various kinds of Cynic influence (alike on style and rhetoric, on thought and—to some extent—on way of life) upon Paul, though these scholars (Downing partially excepted) do not claim Paul as actually Cynic.[80] Not all of the parallels adduced with Cynic diatribe are convincing, but there are undoubtedly some convincing parallels, both of thought and of sentence structure, between Paul and Antisthenes[81] and Teles.[82] Malherbe also demonstrates Paul's frequent self-definition through, and against, Cynic

---

[77] Two possible exceptions: (1) Papias as quoted by Euseb. *HE* 3.39.16 says that Matthew 'put together' the *logia* of Jesus in 'the Hebrew dialect'; but this is best interpreted as an Aramaic collection of *sayings*: R. E. Brown (1997) 210–11; Thiede (2004) 148 n. 39; (2) an Aramaic Q (cf. n. 93 below), sometimes hypothesised, is rendered unlikely by the closeness of the verbal parallels between Matthew and Luke: Dunn (2003) 43.

[78] Sevenster (1968) 3–21; Hengel (1974) 56–106; Meier (1991) 255–68; Porter (1994); Wright (1996) 147 and n. 3; Dunn (2003) 315; Thiede (2004) 12, 68–71; if, as many now believe, the *Letter of James* is authentically by Jerusalem James and Jerusalem James was Jesus' (full or half-) brother, the case is yet further strengthened.

[79] See p. 535 and n. 74 above.

[80] E.g., Malherbe as cited in n. 16 above; Downing (1988a) 187–91 (with useful summaries of several of Malherbe's Pauline papers); (1998b); Barton (2003) 41–2; Deming (2004).

[81] Funke (1970); Malherbe (1983b).

[82] Two precise illustrations: Malherbe (1992) 315 (1 Cor 7.27 ~ Teles 10.6ff. Hense); Deming (2004) 157 (1 Cor 7.21 ~ Teles 2.10.65–80 O'Neil).

categories, and his analyses prove Pauline Christianity's engagement both with Cynic ethics and with real-life contemporary Cynics.

All these findings are of interest in themselves, but they might help the cumulative Cynic case: if a Jewish wandering rabbi and preacher, a follower and imitator of Jesus, who began his ministry in the decade after Jesus' death, comported himself in these ways, that might increase the possibility of the wandering[83] rabbi and preacher Jesus coming into some similar category. In any event, it is astonishing, and surely reprehensible, that these Cynic aspects ⟦99⟧ of Paul are entirely neglected in what might broadly be described as orthodox Christian treatments of Paul's theology.[84]

### 2.2    Cynic Influence on the Church Fathers

Downing, Dorival, and others have analysed how the Christian fathers often proclaimed, and often disclaimed, a link between Christian virtue and Cynic virtue.[85] There are also the concrete cases of Peregrinus, recorded—with derision—by Lucian[86] and Maximus.[87] If Christian virtue aims to imitate Jesus and sometimes does so in Cynic mode, was Jesus himself rather Cynic?

### 2.3    Cynic Influence on Pictorial Representations of Jesus

Some of the earliest pictorial representations of Jesus make him look like a Cynic.[88] Again the question: why?

### 2.4    Cynic Influence on the Gospels?

The case for Cynic influence on the Gospels depends partly on the subject-matter, partly on formal considerations. That the Gospels are generically biographies, always the obvious reading, has been comprehensively argued by Burridge and Frickenschmidt, and the overall case is decisive.[89] Of course, as Christopher Pelling has repeatedly taught us, ancient biography is a very flexible genre. The Gospels surely also fall slightly more specifically into the category of the biography of the 'holy man' (not that dissimilar from Philostratus' *Life of Apollonius of Tyana*, Apollonius for that very reason becoming a pagan

---

83    On Jesus as 'wanderer' see p. 539 below.
84    E.g., Wright (1991); Dunn (1998).
85    Downing (1993); (1996); Dorival (1993).
86    See König (2006).
87    Dudley (1937) 204–6.
88    Conceded even by Betz (1994) 461.
89    Burridge (1992); cf. also his restatement in (2006); Frickenschmidt (1997); Dunn (2003) 184–6.

rival to Jesus).[90] The Gospels also contain much *chreia* material, with standard narrative patterns. In a general way, then, the Gospels have something of the flavour of Cynic biography (like the reconstructible early biographical treatments of Diogenes, Diogenes Laertius' Book 6,[91] or Lucian's *Demonax*).[92] This seems true also of Q the hypothetical but (in the opinion of the present writer) certain second written source both of Matthew and of Luke (Mark being the first written source).[93] Does this light Cynic biographical flavouring say anything about the biographical hero?

The case for Jesus as Cynic in some sense (within, as we have seen, a considerable range) may invoke the individual items or the broad cumulative case already mentioned but within the New Testament it must depend on: (a) the general representation of Jesus' activities, teachings, and styles of exposition; and (b) certain specific parallels.

(a) The former may be most economically presented in list form: Jesus' 'wanderings' and 'homelessness';[94] high public profile; general low-life associations, including, strikingly, women and even women followers; 'free-loading' (not 'begging' in the strict sense); 'communism';[95] reversal/subversion [[100]] of normal hierarchies (the Sermon on the Mount); 'internationalism';[96] elevation of poverty and criticism of wealth; elevation of physical endurance as a moral test; ideals of voluntary self-abasement and suffering; at least partial rejection

---

90   Bowersock (1994) 96–7, 109–11; the relationship is admittedly complicated by the fact that Philostratus is registering pagan anxiety about Christianity and seems sometimes even to imitate or 'trump' Gospel miracles: Thiede (2004) 37–8.
91   Kindstrand (1986); Goulet-Cazé (1992).
92   References in n. 22 above.
93   Most New Testament scholars accept Q's existence (disagreement characteristically centring on boundaries and orientation, especially as regards alleged Cynic elements); some treatments: Kloppenborg (1987); (1988); (1994); (1995); (2000); R. E. Brown (1997) 116–22; Dunn (2003) 41–4, 147–60; Head–Williams (2003). Anyone trained in *Quellenforschung* in ancient historiography and biography would, I believe, regard Q's existence as certain, even though it is now rejected by Goodacre (2002) and Thiede (2004) 123 and 158 n. 6. The non-existence of Q would not destroy the present paper but would entail some modification. The significance of Q in this context is that it supports the case for a (partially) 'Cynic' Jesus in writing predating the Gospels (see p. 542 below). Neither does Dunn's distinction ([2003] 148–9) between 'oral q' and 'written Q' substantially affect this paper, provided 'oral q' also has Cynic elements.
94   'Foxes have holes, and birds of the air have nests, but the Son of Man has nowhere to lay his head' (Luke 9.57–8; Matt 8.19–20).
95   John 12.6; 13.29, cf. Acts 2.44–5; 4.32–7; 5.1–11.
96   E.g., 'nowhere in Israel have I found faith like this' (Matt 8.10); whether Jesus himself already envisaged a Gentile mission (Mark 13.10; Matt 28.18–19; Acts 1.8) is of course hugely disputed: arguments in favour in, e.g., Thiede (2004) 57; Freyne (2004) 111–13.

of conventional political structures (for the Kingdom of God is certainly far more important than the Kingdom of Caesar);[97] attacks on money-lenders and bigwigs; attacks on at least some aspects of institutionalised religion; fast, often abusive and aggressive wit; aphorisms; appeals to nature and animals ('consider the lilies of the field', etc.); vigorous, colloquial, non- or anti-intellectual style of exposition and concomitant rejection of 'cleverness'; general emphasis on practical, everyday virtue.

Naturally, not all scholars would agree with the inclusion—even for possible consideration—of all these elements. For example, Marshall claims that 'the strong presence of women among Jesus' followers has *no* Cynic precedent' (present writer's italics).[98] But the famous (and historical) case of the 'dog wedding' of Crates and Hipparchia, of Hipparchia's 'discipleship' of Crates, and of their subsequent fully-shared public 'living together' instantiates the Cynic principle of total sexual equality, a principle laid down by Diogenes himself.[99] If, as the very fame of Hipparchia's example suggests, few women in practice braved the extreme physical and societal demands of the 'hard Cynic' way of life, the principle remains important, as does the fact that Diogenes' ideal *Politeia* explicitly embraced women.[100]

The above list also raises a simple but important methodological point. Individual 'Cynic' items are often contested on the ground that other evidence tells against them. But the force of such objections requires precise calibration. For example, Crossan and his followers regularly adduce as one of Jesus' Cynic attributes his alleged 'itineracy'.[101] The seemingly correct insistence of Dunn and other scholars that 'Jesus made his base' in Capernaum, where he had 'his home',[102] has *some* force against a 100% *Jesus-Cynicus* model, yet even in this case its force is not absolute: Diogenes himself, the very type of the 'hard Cynic', who undoubtedly proclaimed his 'wanderings' and 'homelessness' and did indeed *sometimes* 'wander',[103] *largely* based himself in Athens; nor were all Cynics '*hard* Cynics'. And the insistence has *no* force against the model which

---

97   [[109]] Such implicit subversion of worldly power is becoming a major scholarly concern: cf., e.g., Wright (2003) 656; Thiede (2004) 66–8; Freyne (2004) 149.
98   Marshall (1997) 60, cited approvingly by Dunn (2003) 536 n. 231.
99   D.L. 6.96–7 with Rist (1969) 60–2; Moles (1983b) 126–7 {above, pp. 356–8}; (1995) 139 {above, p. 398}. Diogenes' principle: D.L. 6.72 (from his *Politeia*): such evidence overrides the *chreia* (and *graffito*) evidence too often taken by modern scholars as proving Diogenic misogyny (on the methodological point see n. 20 above).
100  D.L. 6.72.
101  E.g., Downing (1988a) vi, 43; Crossan (1991) 342–3; Crossan–Reed (2001) 125–8 (other references with polemical rejection in Dunn (2003) 159 and n. 96).
102  Dunn (2003) 317.
103  D.L. 6.38; Montiglio (2000) 99; Dio 6.1–7.

claims that even 'hard' Cynicism is (only) one of several influences upon Jesus, who, like Diogenes and other Cynics, undoubtedly *sometimes* represented himself as 'homeless'.

One should, then, allow this collection of items, or something like them, to be viable *possibilities*, but all one can really say about them is that, if one already knew that Jesus was a Cynic or was Cynic-influenced, most of this material would be Cynic or Cynic-influenced, but it does not itself prove the case or even establish much of a presumption in its favour.

⟦101⟧ (b) Most of Downing's 'parallels' are too generalised. Discussion is here restricted to five crucial cases adduced by Downing and others:

(i) 'Who is my mother, who are my brothers?' (Mark 3.21, 31–5; Matt 12.46–50; Luke 8.19–21; from Q).[104] This rejection and 'redefinition' of the family has no Jewish parallels, but is paralleled in the Cynic doctrine 'the wise man is the kin of his peer' (D.L. 6.105): Cynics, who do not marry, have no use for the family (D.L. 6.72) and they redefine 'kinship' in moral/philosophical terms.

(ii) 'Leave the dead to bury their dead' (Matt 8.21–2; Luke 9.59–60). This shocking dismissal of funeral rites is quite un-Jewish, but has Cynic parallels.[105]

(iii) 'You're not to carry a purse with you at all, nor a satchel, and don't wear sandals/ Take nothing for your journey, no satchel, no bread, no money, no change of shirt, no sandals, no staff' (Luke 10.4; Matt 10.9–10; Mark 6.7–13; variations of detail; from Q).[106]

Advocates of the Cynic model such as Kloppenborg, Mack, Vaage, and Downing take this as very Cynic. Thus Downing: 'if the first Christian missionaries obeyed instructions of [this] kind, they would have looked like a kind of Cynic, displaying a very obvious poverty ... a raggedly cloaked and outspoken figure with no luggage and no money would not just have looked Cynic, he would obviously have wanted to'.[107] Crossan is more cautious, finding both

---

104 Downing (1988a) 126 (without the crucial D.L. 6.105); 'softening' interpretation of Jesus' saying in Dunn (2003) 592–9, but the distinction between a '100% *Jesus-Cynicus* model' and a 'Cynic-influenced' model is again apposite.

105 Downing (1988a) 44; cf., e.g., Diogenes' derisive dismissal of conventional funeral rites (D.L. 6.79); for a thoroughgoing hunt for parallels, both Jewish and Greek, for this saying of Jesus see Hengel (1981) 3–13, allowing Cynic parallels (5–6 and n. 11), though contextually denying them, but such a Cynic sentiment could underpin both Jesus' offensive rejection of Jewish religious custom and his sense of urgency (Dunn [2003] 504–5), just as in Cynicism itself it ridicules both Greek religious custom and the inessential.

106 Downing (1988a) 47.

107 Downing (1988a) vi.

Cynic and non-Cynic elements.[108] Opponents of the Cynic model naturally stress the latter.

How to arbitrate? The absence of shoes, bread, and money (thereby entailing economic dependency on others) and the restriction to a single garment look Cynic; the exclusion of purse or satchel and staff looks un-Cynic, but pointedly so: in such exercises of self-definition you exclude the badges of groups to which you either are, or appear, close (characteristically, the man who says 'I'm not black' is not white but rather dark). Thus the mission passages seem to establish a recognition on the part of the New Testament of a certain resemblance between the disciples—and by extension Jesus—and the Cynics, a resemblance which Jesus himself is represented as acknowledging, though also as qualifying, taking the first Christians even farther down the ascetic road than the Cynics. These passages, which go back to Q, put the Cynic portrayal of Jesus very early; and they make Jesus himself aware of a certain kinship with the Cynics. From a reader-response point of view, also, the readerships both of Q and of the Gospels would surely have read these passages as, so to speak, 'modified Cynic'.

(iv) The temptation of Jesus (Matt 4.8; Luke 4.5–6; Q): 'The Adversary [*diabolos*] took Jesus up into a very high mountain and showed him all the world's kingdoms and their splendour, and said, I will give you all these'.[109]

⟦102⟧ Since Downing seems to be right that 'there is no Jewish parallel for this offer',[110] he is surely then also right in sensing two Cynic parallels: (a) the meeting between great worldly king and Cynic philosopher where the king offers the philosopher anything he likes and the philosopher rejects the offer with contempt (Alexander and Diogenes, Caligula and Demetrius); and (b) the existential choice between two opposed concepts—whether Virtue and Vice/Pleasure (the choice of Heracles) or Kingship and Tyranny, a choice sometimes offered at the top of a mountain. If so, and if the temptation is historical in the sense that Jesus told his disciples of some such visionary experience, he was familiar with this sort of Cynic temptation material which he then absorbed into his Jewish religious thinking (of course, Cynics do not believe in the Devil).

(v) The two-roads motif (Matt 7.13–14; Luke 13.23–4; Q): 'Enter by the narrow gate. There's a wide gate and a broad pathway leading to destruction, and lots

---

108 Crossan (1991) 338–9.
109 Downing (1988a) 15–16, 23.
110 Dunn (2003) 381 n. 193 hazards 'an echo of Moses on top of Pisgah looking over the Promised Land', but, if that is evoked, it is as a *contrast*.

of people use them. But it's a constricted gate and it's a narrow path that leads to life, and there aren't many who use those at all'.[111]

This looks very Cynic: the road imagery, the contrast between the wide destructive road used by the many and the narrow, difficult, road used by the few that leads to salvation. In Cynic texts the two-roads motif is often conjoined with the Choice between Virtue and Vice *vel sim*. Now it is true that 'the two roads' motif is widespread in sapiential Jewish-Christian literature and is also found in the Qumran material, and that it is elsewhere used by Jesus himself ('I am the Way', etc. [John 14.6]). But it is not the bare motif that counts: it is the detailed way in which the motif is developed. It is also true that 'the two roads' motif is everywhere in classical literature, from Hesiod on, often with development very similar to Jesus' here,[112] but few scholars now claim that Jesus was familiar with classical literature.[113] Hence another simple methodological consideration: where there is a range of classical parallels, the Cynic ones must trump the others.

## 3  Conclusions

The facts that Paul was influenced by Cynicism and sometimes himself assumed an ambiguous Cynic role and that early Christians saw a parallel between Christian and Cynic asceticism are not decisive. It could be that, once Christianity expanded beyond Palestine to include Gentiles and progressively detached itself from its Jewish base and personnel, it had to package itself for the wider world and one of the already available, and not altogether unsuitable, packagings was Cynicism. One might compare Christian theology's appropriation of some aspects of Stoicism.[114] But there seems sufficient evidence within the New Testament and—behind the New Testament—in Q to show that the Greek-speaking Jesus and his disciples (who included ⟦103⟧ Greek speakers who had Greek names and who had contacts with Greeks) already saw some parallels between themselves and contemporary Cynics. In which case, the ambiguous Cynic colouring of Paul and later Christians does reflect something about Christianity from its origins. In which case also, that colouring acquires a certain evidential value in its own right: it represents

---

111  Downing (1988a) 76–8.
112  As both Mike Trapp in Dublin and Peter Heslin in Durham insisted, against the present conclusion.
113  Always excepting Thiede (n. 74 above).
114  Or indeed Acts' appropriation of Dionysiac narrative patterns: Moles (2006).

*their* reading—not just *our* reading—of Jesus and the New Testament. Within the New Testament, if the detailed parallels are of sufficient weight, then the general representation of Jesus and his characteristic activities has also to be brought into the picture, and likewise the Gospels' lightly Cynic biographical character. So the present writer discerns Cynic influence on Jesus' way of life, social and political attitudes, general behaviour, and manner of teaching. Jesus must have seen and heard Cynics: he knew what they looked like, he knew some of their characteristic stories and narrative patterns. Of course, he eschewed the characteristic shamelessness of hard Cynicism, but, Jew though he was, he was able—like the later Abnimos/Oenomaus—to see through this shamelessness to the Cynics' real virtues.

Any attempt to reconstruct the complexity of the historical Jesus obviously has to factor in the many non-Cynic elements whose existence should not remotely be denied. These include (even on Downing's highly elastic conception of Cynicism) miracles, eschatology, and 'Christology'.[115] These are, of course, huge elements. To these should be added Jesus' strong *personal* sense of God and the strong religious piety. There are parallels for these latter elements in Stoics such as Epictetus and Musonius, as Downing stresses, Stoics who show clear Cynic influence in certain contexts. But not in these contexts, as has been argued above.[116] Unsurprisingly, all these non-Cynic elements focus on the strongly religious aspects of Jesus and raise the whole question of his situatedness within Jewish traditions. It is in these areas, then, that the Cynic model comes under intolerable strain. Conversely, however, the Cynic material seems sufficiently strong to challenge, even to undermine, the contention that Jesus is to be understood solely within Jewish traditions. Nor can this Cynic influence upon Jesus be sanitised within any model of a pre-existent Jewish form of Cynicism.

Jesus the Cynic *tout court*, then? Certainly not. Jesus the Cynic to some extent? Yes. The finding has large implications for the reconstruction of the historical Jesus, for the influence of Hellenism on first-century Judaism, for the history of the early Christian church, and for the necessary refashioning of contemporary Christianity.

---

115   Downing (1988a) viii, 36.
116   Above, p. 530.

## 4  Tailpiece

Notwithstanding its immensely rich and varied *Nachleben*, most classicist scholars of ancient philosophy have a low opinion of Cynicism, largely because ⟦104⟧ of Cynicism's very considerable theoretical inadequacies. But questions of quality or value cannot be brushed aside. From a modern perspective, we can see that, partly, though not wholly, because of those very theoretical inadequacies, Cynicism effortlessly attained some ethical positions that were qualitatively far superior to those of 'great' ancient philosophies such as Platonism, Aristotelianism, and Stoicism. Long, for example, has written:

> [Diogenes'] ethical values took no account of social status and nationality, and this emphasises the radical character of Diogenes' criticism of traditional attitudes. A study of Aristotle's painful defence of slavery in *Politics* Book I should make the point beyond doubt.[117]

Quite, and the insight cannot be exaggerated. Today, after decades of studious avoidance of such value judgements, due to embarrassment both over the ludicrously inflated claims that earlier generations made for the civilising benefits of classical culture and over the horrors highlighted by rigorous scholarly analysis of such central institutions of that culture as the Roman games, there seems to be renewed interest among classicists in arguing the value and utility of ancient philosophy for modern people.[118]

In a rare and uncharacteristic expression of his 'personal voice', the present writer confesses that at a time of acute depression many years ago he derived great, indeed decisive, solace from ancient Cynicism: he was saved not by Jesus but by *Dio-genes* (wrong god, wrong son). Admirable, however, as Cynic ethics are, they are greatly surpassed by Christian ones. Yet the latter turn out to have been influenced by the former. No doubt of it, then, as in the first, so in the twenty-first, century AD, Christian Cynicism is the place to be. The broad consequences of this are sufficiently clear. I leave it to Christian theologians and ethicists to work out the details.

Classical scholars of ancient philosophy who are less impressed by Cynicism than I am but who happen also to be Christians face an even greater moral and

---

117  Long (1974) 4; for similar claims cf. Moles (1983a) 119–20 {above, pp. 342–4}; (1995) 158 {above, p. 416}; (2000) 434 {above, p. 459}.
118  E.g., Long (2002) 259, 271–2.

intellectual challenge: of all the ancient pagan philosophies, Cynicism is the one most nearly endorsed by God.[119]

## Bibliography

Arnal, W. E. and M. Desjardins (1997) *Whose Historical Jesus?* (Waterloo).
Attridge, H. W. (1976) *First-Century Cynicism in the Epistles of Heraclitus* (Missoula).
Aune, D. E. (1997) 'Jesus and Cynics in First-century Palestine: Some Critical Considerations', in J. H. Charlesworth and L. L. Johns, edd., *Hillel and Jesus: Comparative Studies of Two Major Religions* (Minneapolis) 176–92.
Bammel, E. and C. F. D. Moule, edd. (1984) *Jesus and the Politics of his Day* (Cambridge).
Barton, S. C. (2003) 'Paul as Missionary and Pastor', in J. D. G. Dunn, ed., *The Cambridge Companion to St Paul* (Cambridge) 34–48.
Batey, R. A. (1991) *Jesus and the Forgotten City: New Light on Sepphoris and the Urban World of Jesus* (Grand Rapids).
van Beeck, F. J. (1994) 'The Quest of the Historical Jesus: Origins, Achievements, and the Specter of Diminishing Returns', in J. Carlson and R. A. Ludwig, edd., *Jesus and Faith: a Conversation on the Work of John Dominic Crossan* (Maryknoll, N.Y.) 83–99.
Betz, H. D. (1994) 'Jesus and the Cynics: Survey and Analysis of a Hypothesis', *Journal of Religion* 74: 453–75.
Billerbeck, M. (1978) *Epiktet: vom Kynismus* (Leiden).
Billerbeck, M. (1979) *Der Kyniker Demetrius: ein Beitrag zur Geschichte der frühkaiserzeitlichen Popularphilosophie* (Leiden).
Billerbeck, M., ed. (1991) *Die Kyniker in der modernen Forschung: Aufsätze mit Einführung und Bibliographie* (Amsterdam).
Billerbeck, M. (1996) 'The Ideal Cynic from Epictetus to Julian', in Branham and Goulet-Cazé (1996) 205–21.
Billerbeck, M. (1993) 'Le cynisme idéalisé d'Épictète à Julien', in Goulet-Cazé and Goulet (1993) 319–38.
Bowersock, G. W. (1994) *Fiction as History: Nero to Julian* (Berkeley, Los Angeles, and London).
Brancacci, A. (2000) 'Dio, Socrates, and Cynicism', in Swain (2000) 240–60.
Branham, R. B. (1989) *Unruly Eloquence: Lucian and the Comedy of Traditions* (Cambridge, Mass. and London).

---

[119] This formulation is intended to allow: (a) for the fact that I am not arguing 'a 100% *Jesus-Cynicus* model'; and (b) for *all possible* responses to the problems of the Incarnation and of 'kenotic theology'.

Branham, R. B. (1993) 'Diogenes' Rhetoric and the *Invention* of Cynicism', in Goulet-Cazé and Goulet (1993) 445–73.

Branham, R. B. (1996) 'Defacing the Currency: Diogenes' Rhetoric and the *Invention* of Cynicism', in id. and Goulet-Cazé (1996) 81–104.

Branham, R. B. and M.-O. Goulet-Cazé, edd. (1996) *The Cynics: the Cynic Movement in Antiquity and its Legacy* (Berkeley and Los Angeles).

Brenk, F. E. (2000) 'Dio on the Simple and Self-sufficient Life', in Swain (2000) 261–78.

Brown, R. E. (1994) *The Death of the Messiah: From Gethsemane to the Grave: a Commentary on the Passion Narratives in the Four Gospels*, 2 vols. (New York).

Brown, R. E. (1997) *An Introduction to the New Testament* (New York, London, Toronto, Sydney, and Auckland).

Brown, T. S. (1949) *Onesicritus: A Study in Hellenistic Historiography* (Berkeley and Los Angeles).

Bultmann, R. (1910) *Der Stil der paulinischen Predigt und die kynisch-stoische Diatribe* (Göttingen).

Burridge, R. A. (1992) *What are the Gospels? A Comparison with Graeco-Roman Biography* (Cambridge).

Burridge, R. A. (2006) 'Reading the Gospels as Biography', in McGing and Mossman (2006) 31–49.

Clay, D. (1992) 'Lucian of Samosata: Four Philosophical Lives (Nigrinus, Demonax, Peregrinus, Alexander Pseudomantis)', *ANRW* II.36.5: 3406–50.

Collins, J. J. and G. E. Sterling, edd. (2001) *Hellenism in the Land of Israel* (Notre Dame, Ind.).

Crossan, J. D. (1991) *The Historical Jesus: the Life of a Mediterranean Jewish Peasant* (Edinburgh).

Crossan, J. D. (1994) *Jesus: a Revolutionary Biography* (San Francisco).

Crossan, J. D. (1995) *Who Killed Jesus? Exposing the Roots of Anti-Semitism in the Gospel Story of the Death of Jesus* (New York).

Crossan, J. D. and J. L. Reed (2001) *Excavating Jesus: Beneath the Stones, Behind the Texts* (London).

Deming, Will (2004) *Paul on Marriage and Celibacy* (Grand Rapids).

Dorival, G. (1993) 'L'image des Cyniques chez les Pères grecs', in Goulet-Cazé and Goulet (1993) 419–43.

Downing, F. G. (1984) 'Cynics and Christians', *NTS* 30: 584–93.

Downing, F. G. (1987a) 'Interpretation and the "Culture Gap"', *Scottish Journal of Theology* 40: 161–71.

Downing, F. G. (1987b) 'The Social Contexts of Jesus the Teacher: Construction or Reconstruction', *NTS* 33: 439–51.

Downing, F. G. (1987c) *Jesus and the Threat of Freedom* (London).

Downing, F. G. (1988a) *Christ and the Cynics: Jesus and other Radical Preachers in First-Century Tradition* (Sheffield).

Downing, F. G. (1988b) 'Quite like Q—A Genre for "Q": the "Lives" of Cynic Philosophers', *Biblica* 69: 196–225; rev. vers. in Downing (1992) 114–42.

Downing, F. G. (1992) *Cynics and Christian Origins* (Edinburgh).

Downing, F. G. (1993) 'Cynics and Early Christianity', in Goulet-Cazé and Goulet (1993) 281–304.

Downing, F. G. (1994) 'A Genre for Q and a Socio-cultural Context for Q', *JSNT* 55: 3–26.

Downing, F. G. (1996) 'Word-processing in the Ancient World: the Social Production and Performance of Q', *JSNT* 64: 29–48.

Downing, F. G. (1998a) 'Deeper Reflections on the Jewish Cynic Jesus', *JBL* 117.1: 97–104; repr. in id., *Making Sense in (and of) the First Christian Century* (Sheffield, 2000) 122–33.

Downing, F. G. (1998b) *Cynics, Paul and the Pauline Churches* (London and New York).

Downing, F. G. (2001) 'The Jewish Cynic Jesus', in M. Labahn and A. Schmidt, edd., *Jesus, Mark and Q: the Teaching of Jesus and its Earliest Records* (*JSNTS* 214) 184–214.

Dudley, D. R. (1937) *A History of Cynicism from Diogenes to the 6th century A.D.* (London).

Dunn, J. D. G. (1998) *The Theology of Paul the Apostle* (Grand Rapids and Edinburgh).

Dunn, J. D. G. (2003) *Jesus Remembered: Christianity in the Making*, vol. 1 (Grand Rapids and Cambridge).

Ebner, M. (1998) *Jesus—ein Weihseitslehrer [sic]? Synoptische Weisheitslogien im Traditions-prozeß* (Freiburg and New York).

Eddy, P. R. (1996) 'Jesus as Diogenes? Reflections on the Cynic Jesus Thesis', *JBL* 115: 449–69.

Freyne, S. (2000) *Galilee and Gospel: Collected Essays* (Tübingen).

Freyne, S. (2004) *Jesus, a Jewish Galilean: a New Reading of the Jesus-Story* (London and New York).

Frickenschmidt, D. (1997) *Evangelium als Biographie: die vier Evangelien im Rahmen antiker Erzählkunst* (Tübingen).

Fuentes-Gonzalez, P. P. (1998) *Les diatribes de Télès* (Paris).

Funke, H. (1970) 'Antisthenes bei Paulus', *Hermes* 98: 459–71.

Geffcken, J. (1909) *Kynika und Verwandtes* (Heidelberg).

Goodacre, M. (2002) *The Case against Q: Studies in Markan Priority and the Synoptic Problem* (Harrisburg, Pa.).

Goulet, R., ed. (1994) *Dictionnaire des philosophes antiques II* (Paris).

Goulet-Cazé, M.-O. (1986) *L'Ascèse Cynique: un commentaire de Diogéne Laërce VI 70–71* (Paris).

Goulet-Cazé, M.-O. (1990) 'Le cynicisme à l'époque impériale', *ANRW* II.36.4: 2720–833.

Goulet-Cazé, M.-O. (1992) 'Le livre VI de Diogène Laërce: analyse de sa structure et réflexions méthodologiques', *ANRW* II.36.6: 3880–4048.

Goulet-Cazé, M.-O. (1993) 'Les premiers cyniques et la religion', in Goulet-Cazé and Goulet (1993) 117–58.
Goulet-Cazé, M.-O. (1994a) 'Cratès de Thèbes', in Goulet (1994) 496–500.
Goulet-Cazé, M.-O. (1994b) 'Diogène de Sinope', in Goulet (1994) 812–23.
Goulet-Cazé, M.-O. (1996) 'Religion and the Early Cynics', in Branham and Goulet-Cazé (1996) 47–80.
Goulet-Cazé, M.-O. (2003) Les Kynika du stoïcisme (Stuttgart).
Goulet-Cazé, M.-O. and R. Goulet, edd. (1993) Le Cynisme ancien et ses prolongements (Paris).
Griffin, M. T. (1993) 'Le mouvement cynique et les Romains: attraction et repulsion', in Goulet-Cazé and Goulet (1993) 241–58.
Griffin, M. T. (1996) 'Cynicism and the Romans: Attraction and Repulsion', in Goulet-Cazé and Branham (1996) 190–204; repr. in ead., Politics and Philosophy at Rome: Collected Papers, ed. C. Balmaceda (Oxford) 475–85.
Hammerstaedt, J. (1990) 'Der Kyniker Oinomaos von Gadara', ANRW II.36.4: 2834–65.
Hanson, V. D., J. Heath, and B. S. Thornton, edd. (2001) Bonfire of the Humanities: Rescuing the Classics in an Impoverished Age (Wilmington, Del.).
Harvey, A. E. (1982) Jesus and the Constraints of History (London).
Head, P. M. and P. J. Williams (2003) 'Q Review', Tyndale Bulletin 54.1: 119–44.
Hengel, M. (1974) Judaism and Hellenism: Studies in their Encounter in Palestine during the Early Hellenistic Period, 2 vols. (London and Philadelphia).
Hengel, M. (1981) The Charismatic Leader and his Followers (Edinburgh and New York).
Hengel, M. (1989) The 'Hellenization' of Judaea in the First Century after Christ (London and Philadelphia).
Hock, R. F. (1980) The Social Context of Paul's Ministry: Tentmaking and Apostleship (Philadelphia).
Hock, R. F. and E. N. O'Neil (1986–2002) The Chreia in Ancient Rhetoric, 2 vols. (Atlanta).
Höistad, R. (1948) Cynic Hero and Cynic King: Studies in the Cynic Conception of Man (Uppsala).
Jones, C. P. (1986) Culture and Society in Lucian (Cambridge, Mass. and London).
Kindstrand, J. F. (1976) Bion of Borysthenes: a Collection of the Fragments with Introduction and Commentary (Uppsala).
Kindstrand, J. F. (1986) 'Diogenes Laertius and the "Chreia" Tradition', Elenchos 7: 217–43.
Kloppenborg, J. S. (1987) The Formation of Q: Trajectories in Ancient Wisdom Collections (Philadelphia).
Kloppenborg, J. S. (1988) Q Parallels: Synopsis, Critical Notes & Concordance (Sonoma, Cal.).
Kloppenborg, J. S., ed. (1994) The Shape of Q: Signal Essays on the Sayings Gospel (Minneapolis).

Kloppenborg, J. S. (1995) *Conflict and Invention: Literary, Rhetorical, and Social Studies on the Sayings Gospel Q* (Valley Forge, Pa.).

Kloppenborg, J. S. (2000) *Excavating Q: the History and Setting of the Sayings Gospel* (Minneapolis).

König, J. (2006) 'The Cynic and Christian Lives of Lucian's *Peregrinus*', in McGing and Mossman (2006) 227–54.

Krueger, D. (1996) *Symeon the Holy Fool: Leontius' Life and the Late Antique City* (Berkeley, Los Angeles, and London).

Laks, A. and M. Schofield, edd. (1995) *Justice and Generosity: Studies in Hellenistic Social and Political Philosophy* (Cambridge).

Levine, L. I. (1998) *Judaism and Hellenism in Antiquity: Conflict or Confluence?* (Seattle).

Long, A. A. (1974) *Hellenistic Philosophy* (London; repr. with additional bibliography, 1986).

Long, A. A. (1996) 'The Socratic Tradition: Diogenes, Crates, and Hellenistic Ethics', in Branham and Goulet-Cazé (1996) 28–46.

Long, A. A. (2002) *Epictetus: a Stoic and Stoic Guide to Life* (Oxford).

Lovejoy, A. O. and G. Boas (1935) *A Documentary History of Primitivism and Related Ideas in Antiquity* (Baltimore; repr. New York, 1965).

Luck, G., ed. (1997) *Die Weisheit der Hunde: Texte der antiken Kyniker in deutscher Übersetzung mit Erläuterungen* (Stuttgart).

Maccoby, H. (2003) *Jesus the Pharisee* (London).

MacDonald, D. R. (2000) *The Homeric Epics and the Gospel of Mark* (New Haven).

MacDonald, D. R. (2003) *Does the New Testament Imitate Homer? Four Cases from the Acts of the Apostles* (New Haven).

Mack, B. L. (1988) *A Myth of Innocence: Mark and Christian Origins* (Philadelphia).

Mack, B. L. (1993) *The Lost Gospel: The Book of Q and Christian Origins* (San Francisco).

Mack, B. L. (1997) 'Q and a Cynic-like Jesus', in Arnal and Desjardins (1997) 25–36.

Mack, B. L. (2001) *The Christian Myth: Origins, Logic and Legacy* (New York).

Malherbe, A. J. (1970) 'Gentle as a Nurse: The Cynic Background to 1 Thess ii', *Novum Testamentum* 12: 203–17; repr. in id. (2014) 53–68.

Malherbe, A. J. (1977) *The Cynic Epistles: a Study Edition* (Missoula).

Malherbe, A. J. (1980) 'Medical Imagery in the Pastoral Epistles', in W. E. March, ed., *Texts and Testaments: Critical Essays on the Bible and Early Church Fathers* (San Antonio) 19–35; repr. in id. (2014) 117–34.

Malherbe, A. J. (1983a) 'Antisthenes and Odysseus, and Paul at War', *HTR* 76: 143–73; repr. in id. (2014) 135–66.

Malherbe, A. J. (1983b) 'Exhortation in First Thessalonians', *NT* 25: 238–56; repr. in id. (2014) 167–86.

Malherbe, A. J. (1984) '"In Season and out of Season": 2 Timothy 4:2', *JBL* 103: 235–43; repr. in id. (2014) 187–96.

Malherbe, A. J. (1987) *Paul and the Thessalonians* (Philadelphia).
Malherbe, A. J. (1989) *Paul and the Popular Philosophers* (Minneapolis).
Malherbe, A. J. (1992) 'Hellenistic Moralists and the New Testament', *ANRW* II.26.1: 267–333; repr. in id. (2014) 675–750.
Malherbe, A. J. (2000) *The Letters to the Thessalonians* (New York).
Malherbe, A. J. (2014) *Light from the Gentiles: Hellenistic Philosophy and Early Christianity: Collected Essays, 1959–2012*, edd. C. R. Holladay, J. T. Fitzgerald, G. E. Sterling, and G. W. Thompson (Leiden and Boston).
Marshall, J. W. (1997) 'The Gospel of Thomas and the Cynic Jesus', in Arnal and Desjardins (1997) 37–60.
Martin, R. P. (1996) 'The Scythian Accent: Anacharsis and the Cynics', in Branham and Goulet-Cazé (1996) 136–55.
Martin, T. W. (1997) 'The Chronos Myth in Cynic Philosophy', *GRBS* 38: 85–108.
McGing, B. and J. Mossman, edd. (2006) *The Limits of Ancient Biography* (Swansea).
Meier, J. P. (1991) *A Marginal Jew: Rethinking the Historical Jesus I: the Roots of the Problem and the Person* (New York).
Moles, J. L. (1978) 'The Career and Conversion of Dio Chrysostom', *JHS* 98: 79–100 [above, Ch. 1].
Moles, J. L. (1983a) '"*Honestius quam Ambitiosius*"? An Exploration of the Cynic's Attitude to Moral Corruption in his Fellow Men', *JHS* 103: 103–23 [above, Ch. 12].
Moles, J. L. (1983b) 'The Woman and the River: Diogenes' Apophthegm from Herculaneum and Some Popular Misconceptions about *Cynicism*', *Apeiron* 17: 125–30 [above, Ch. 13].
Moles, J. L. (1993) 'Le cosmopolitisme cynique', in Goulet-Cazé and Goulet (1993) 259–80.
Moles, J. L. (1995) 'The Cynics and Politics', in Laks and Schofield (1995) 129–58 [above, Ch. 15].
Moles, J. L. (1996a) 'Cynic Cosmopolitanism', in Branham and Goulet-Cazé (1996) 105–20 [above, Ch. 16].
Moles, J. L. (1996b) 'Diatribe', *OCD*$^3$: 463–4.
Moles, J. L. (1997) 'Demonax', in D. J. Zeyl, ed., *Encyclopedia of Classical Philosophy* (London and New York) 172–3.
Moles, J. L. (2000) 'The Cynics', in Rowe and Schofield (2000) 415–34 [above, Ch. 17].
Moles, J. L. (2006) 'Jesus and Dionysus in *The Acts of the Apostles* and Early Christianity' *Hermathena* 180: 65–104 [below, Ch. 21].
Moles, J. L. (forthcoming) 'Defacing the Currency: Cynicism in Dio Chrysostom' [above, Ch. 11].
Montiglio, S. (2000) 'Wandering Philosophers in Classical Greece', *JHS* 120: 86–105.
Navia, L. E. (1996) *Classical Cynicism: a Critical Study* (Westport, Conn.).
Navia, L. E. (1998) *Diogenes of Sinope: the Man in the Tub* (Westport, Conn.).

Neusner, J. (1986) 'How Much Hellenism in Jewish Palestine?', *HUCA* 57: 83–111.
Paquet, L. (1988) *Les cyniques grecs: fragments et témoinage*² (Ottawa; ³1992).
Porter, S. E. (1994) 'Jesus and the Use of Greek in Galilee', in B. Chilton and C. A. Evans, edd., *Studying the Historical Jesus: Evaluations of the State of Current Research* (Leiden) 125–54.
Powell, M. A. (1999) *The Jesus Debate: Modern Historians Investigate the Life of Christ* (Oxford).
Rist, J. M. (1969) *Stoic Philosophy* (Cambridge).
Robinson, J. M. (1994) 'The History-of-Religions Taxonomy of Q: The Cynic Hypothesis', in H. Preissler and H. Seiwert, edd., *Gnosisforschung und Religionsgeschichte* (Marburg) 247–65; repr. in id. (2005) 427–48.
Robinson, J. M. (1997) 'Galilean Upstarts: A Sot's Cynical Disciples?', in W. L. Petersen, ed., *Sayings of Jesus: Canonical and Non-canonical* (Leiden) 223–49; repr. in id. (2005) 535–58.
Robinson, J. M. (2005) *The Sayings Gospel Q: Collected Essays*, edd. C. Heil and J. Verheyden (Leuven).
Romm, J. (1996) 'Dog Heads and Noble Savages: Cynicism before the Cynics?', in Branham and Goulet-Cazé (1996) 121–35.
Rowe, C. and M. Schofield, edd. (2000) *The Cambridge History of Greek and Roman Political Thought* (Cambridge).
Russell, D. A., ed. (1992) *Dio Chrysostom: Orations VII, XII, XXXVI* (Cambridge).
de Ste. Croix, G. E. M. (1981) *The Class Struggle in the Ancient Greek World* (London and Ithaca).
Schmeller, T. (1987) *Paulus und die 'Diatribe': eine vergleichende Stilinterpretation* (Munster).
Schofield, M. (2004) 'Epictetus: Socratic, Cynic, Stoic', *Philosophical Quarterly* 54: 448–56.
Seeley, D. (1992) 'Jesus' Death in Q', *NTS* 38: 222–34.
Seeley, D. (1993) 'Rulership and Service in Mark 10:41–5', *NT* 35: 234–50.
Seeley, D. (1996) 'Jesus and the Cynics: a Response to Hans Dieter Betz', *JHC* 3: 284–90.
Seeley, D. (1997) 'Jesus and the Cynics Revisited', *JBL* 116: 704–12.
Sevenster, J. N. (1968) *Do You Know Greek? How Much Greek Could the First Jewish Christians Have Known?* (Leiden).
Stowers, S. K. (1981) *The Diatribe and Paul's Letter to the Romans* (Chico, Cal.).
Swain, S., ed. (2000) *Dio Chrysostom: Politics, Letters, and Philosophy* (Oxford).
Theissen, G. (1978) *The First Followers of Jesus: a Sociological Analysis of the Earliest Christianity* (London).
Theissen, G. (1992) *Social Reality and the Early Christians: Theology, Ethics, and the World of the New Testament* (Minneapolis).

Theissen, G. and A. Merz (1998) *The Historical Jesus: a Comprehensive Guide* (London); trans. by J. Bowden of *Der historische Jesus: ein Lehrbuch* (Göttingen, 1996).

Thiede, C. P. (2004) *The Cosmopolitan World of Jesus: New Findings from Archaeology* (London).

Trapp, M. B. (1990) 'Plato's *Phaedrus* in Second-Century Greek Literature', in D. A. Russell, ed., *Antonine Literature* (Oxford) 141–73.

Trapp, M. B. (2000) 'Plato in Dio', in Swain (2000) 213–39.

Tuckett, C. M. (1989) 'A Cynic Q?', *Biblica* 70: 349–74.

Tuckett, C. M. (1996) *Q and the History of Early Christianity: Studies in Q* (Edinburgh).

Vaage, L. E. (1987) *Q: the Ethos and Ethics of an Itinerant Intelligence* (diss., Claremont College).

Vaage, L. E. (1994) *Galilean Upstarts: Jesus' First Followers According to Q* (Valley Forge, Pa.).

von Fritz, K. (1926) *Quellenuntersuchungen zu Leben und Philosophie des Diogenes von Sinope* (*Philologus Suppl.* 18.2; Göttingen).

Wendland, P. (1895) 'Philo und die kynisch-stoische Diatribe', in P. Wendland and O. Kern, edd. (1895) *Beiträge zur Geschichte der griechischen Philosophie und Religion* (Berlin) 1–75.

Wendland, P. (1912) 'Die hellenistich-römische Kultur in ihren Beziehungen zu Judentum und Christentum: die urchristlichen Literaturformen', *Handbuch zum Neuen Testament*[2-3] (Tübingen) I.2/3: 75–96.

Wright, N. T. (1991) *The Climax of the Covenant: Christ and the Law in Pauline Theology* (London and New York).

Wright, N. T. (1996) *Jesus and the Victory of God* (London).

Wright, N. T. (2003) *The Resurrection of the Son of God* (London).

Zeller, E. (1893) 'Über eine Berührung des jüngeren Cynismus mit dem Christenthum', *Sitz. König. Preuss. Akad. Wiss. zu Berl.* 1: 129–32.

CHAPTER 21

# Jesus and Dionysus in the Acts of the Apostles and Early Christianity

Does Acts quote *Bacchae*?[1] Is Acts influenced by Dionysiac myth or ritual? These old questions, currently resurgent, remain acute.[2] If—as is still disputed—the answers are affirmative, what are the consequences? I argue a maximalist case.

## 1 The Evidence

### (A) Broad *Thematic Parallels between Acts and* Bacchae
These include:

> (A1) disruptive impact of 'new' god;
> (A2) (series of) judicial proceedings against 'new' god and his followers;
> (A3) 'bondage' of 'new' god or his followers;
> (A4) (series of) imprisonment(s) of 'new' god's followers;
> (A5) their generally miraculous escapes from prison;
> (A6) divine epiphany/ies (sometimes associated with (A4–5), sometimes not);
> ⟦66⟧ (A7) warning that persecution of 'new' god/'new' god's followers is 'fighting against god';
> (A8) direct warning by unrecognised 'new' god to persecutor;
> (A9) 'fighting against god' by 'new' god's persecutor(s);

---

[1] Oral versions were given, during 2004–6, at Newcastle, Durham, Dublin, Tallahassee, Princeton, Columbia, Charlottesville, and Yale. For much help (and, in some cases, wonderful hospitality), I thank: Loveday Alexander, John Barclay, Stephen Barton, Kai Brodersen, John Dillon, Jimmy Dunn, Sean Freyne, John Garthwaite, Albert Henrichs, Liz Irwin, Chris Kraus, Manfred Lang, Brian McGing, John Marincola, Damien Nelis, Susanna Phillippo, Richard Seaford, Rowland Smith, Tony Spawforth, Mike Tueller, and Tony Woodman. Translations and errors are mine, presentation and documentation minimalist.

[2] E.g., Nestle (1900); Smend (1925); Fiebig (1926); Rudberg (1926); Weinreich (1929), esp. 309–41; Windisch (1932); Voegeli (1953); Dibelius (1956) 190; Hackett (1956a) and (1956b); Funke (1965–6); Conzelmann (1972) 49; Colacides (1973); Pervo (1987) 21–2; Tueller (1992); Brenk (1994); Rapske (1994) 412–19; Seaford (1996) 53; (1997); (2006) ch. 9; Fitzmyer (1998) 341; Dormeyer–Galindo (2003) 49ff.; 95; 365; Hintermaier (2003); Lang (2003); (2004); Weaver (2004); Dormeyer (2005).

(A10) 'mockery' of 'new' god or his followers;
(A11) general human–divine conflict;
(A12) kingly persecutor(s);
(A13) kingly persecutor arrogates divinity to himself;
(A14) divine destruction of impious kingly persecutor(s);
(A15) rejection of 'new' god by his own, whom he severely punishes;
(A16) destruction of palace/destruction of Jerusalem and Temple;
(A17) adhesion of women to 'new' religion;
(A18) Dionysiac 'bullishness'.

While some of these parallels need justification, the two texts clearly share numerous important themes. From this perspective alone, the hypothesis that *Bacchae* influenced Acts is not implausible.

**(B)    Detailed *Thematic Parallels between Acts and* Bacchae**
There are three crucial cases:[3]

(B1) The three accounts of Saul's conversion on the road to Damascus (9.3–9; 22.6–11; 26.12–18) ~ *Bacchae* 576–641 (the epiphany of Dionysus and his escape from prison).

There are the following common elements: (i) light and lightning (the latter explicit at 9.3 and 22.6); (ii) people falling to the ground; (iii) invisible divine voice; (iv) divine voice addressing people by name; (v) people asking a question; (vi) ⟦67⟧ god identifying himself; (vii) divine command to stand up from the ground; (viii) seeing the god; (ix) conversion or reaffirmation of original conversion (Saul, the chorus in *Bacchae*) or non-conversion (Pentheus).

(B2) Herod Agrippa I's persecution of the Christians, his attempt to kill Peter, and Peter's miraculous escape from prison (12.1–10) also ~ *Bacchae* 576–641.

There are the following common elements: (i) ruthlessly persecuting king; (ii) imprisoned followers of the god; (iii) emphasis on the strength of the imprisonment; (iv) emphasis on the suddenness of the supernatural intervention; (v) divine light; (vi) divine instruction to stand up; (vii) confusion between vision and reality; (viii) miraculous, 'automatic' opening of the gate. Beyond the immediate sequences, the two narratives also have (ix) the death of the persecuting king.

---

3  See esp. Seaford (1997).

(B3) The miraculous deliverance of Paul and Silas from prison and the conversion of the gaoler (16.23–30) also ~ *Bacchae* 576–641.

There are the following common elements: (i) prayer by the god's followers; (ii) suddenness of the divine epiphany; (iii) earthquake; (iv) collapse of building; (v) miraculous release of prisoner's bonds and of doors; (vi) surprise and confusion of gaoler figure (the functionary in Acts, Pentheus in *Bacchae*); (vii) transition from darkness to light; (viii) gaoler figure's drawing his sword; (ix) gaoler figure's rushing into the interior; (x) gaoler figure's falling to the ground; (xi) conversion or reaffirmation of original conversion (the functionary in Acts, the chorus in *Bacchae*) or non-conversion (Pentheus); (xii) escaper's claim that he has not run away; (xiii) focus on the final religious response of the gaoler figure: since he has not actually lost his prisoner, will he accept the divine warning (the gaoler in Acts) or reject it (Pentheus)?

New Testament scholars, however, characteristically invoke Jewish material.

⟦68⟧ With 2 Maccabees 3,[4] where a divine epiphany prevents Heliodorus, officer of the Syrian king Seleucus, from plundering the Temple, the common elements are: (i) resplendence; (ii) person falling to the ground; (iii) darkness; (iv) person needing physical help from attendants; (v) conversion/religious transformation.

With *Joseph and Aseneth* 14.2–8 (on the conversion of Aseneth after a heavenly vision)[5] the common elements are: (i) heavenly light; (ii) human falling to the ground; (iii) divine figure (not actually the god) addressing human by name; (iv) human asking identity of divine figure; (v) divine figure identifying himself; (vi) divine figure telling human to stand up; (vii) conversion of human; (viii) divine instructions.

With Ezekiel 1.28–2.1 the common elements are: (i) heavenly light; (ii) human falling to the ground; (iii) god telling human to stand up; (iv) god giving human instructions; and with Daniel 10.5–11[6] the common elements are: (i) lightning (mentioned in a comparison); (ii) human falling to ground; (iii) angel addressing human by name; (iv) angel telling human to stand up; (v) angel giving instructions.

Also cited are such 'call of the prophet stories' as Isaiah 6.1–13 and Jeremiah 1.4–10.[7]

---

4  Wright (2003) 390ff.; Barrett (2004) 441.
5  Wright (2003) 392; Barrett (2004) 441.
6  Wright (2003) 392.
7  Barrett (2004) 442.

Rarely cited is 1 Samuel 26.17–18:[8] 'Saul recognized David's voice and asked, "David, is that you, my son?" "Yes, your Majesty", David answered. And he added, "Why, sir, are you still pursuing me, your servant?".

How to arbitrate? 1 Samuel 26.17–18, clearly important, concerns only one element in a complicated sequence. The 'call of prophets' narratives produce only very general parallels. The most substantial Jewish parallels are 2 Maccabees 3 and *Joseph and Aseneth* 14.2–8,[9] but the former contains some very discrepant elements, and the *Bacchae* passage produces more parallels than 2 Maccabees 3 and better parallels than both 2 ⟦69⟧ Maccabees 3 and *Joseph and Aseneth* (for example, the divine figure is the god himself, not his representative, and the light is lightning). Further, the Jewish material scarcely illuminates the narratives of Peter and of Paul and Silas, in relation to both of which, especially the latter, the *Bacchae* parallel is extremely strong. Moreover, all three narratives are thematically interrelated, and the parallels between Peter's and Paul's releases and the release of Dionysus in *Bacchae* were already noted by the Christian apologist Origen in c.249 CE (*Cels.* 2.34).

I conclude that, while there is some Jewish input into these narratives, the *Bacchae* parallel is far stronger. But what does it mean? Luke demonstrably uses *Bacchae* elsewhere in Acts, so *Bacchae* 576–641 may have provided some inspiration here as well, particularly in relation to 26.12–18 (cf. (C) below, esp. (C7)). But it seems unlikely that the three narratives were inspired by a single Euripidean passage or by any single intermediate source, now lost. Rather, there is a more general appeal to the patterns of initiation into Dionysiac cult that underlie *Bacchae* 576–641[10] and to prose works—such as the novel—that incorporate such Dionysiac patterns into their narratives.[11]

---

8   Haacker (2003) 32 n. 9.
9   Neither, probably, free of non-Jewish influences: 2 Maccabees seems to have 'Dionysiac' elements (p. 566 below), and some scholars regard *Joseph and Aseneth* (of very uncertain date) as Christian-influenced.
10  Discussion: Seaford (1996) 195–202.
11  Novelistic appropriation of 'mystery religion' elements: Pervo (1987) 21–2; Heever (2005); Acts ~ the novel: Pervo (1987).

## (C)  Verbal *Parallels between Acts and* Bacchae

| Acts | Bacchae |
|---|---|
| (C1) 5.39 'lest you be found *godfighters* [θεομάχοι]'. [The Sanhedrin has arrested Peter and other Apostles. The Pharisee Gamaliel argues for their release, on the ground that time will tell whether their movement comes from man or God. If the former, its falsity will soon be exposed; if the ⟦70⟧ latter, 'you will not be able to undo them, lest you be found godfighters', i.e., you will then be punished for impiousness.] | 45 'who *fights against god* in the matters regarding me'. [Dionysus in criticism of Pentheus, who rejects Dionysus' cult]; cf. also 325 'and I won't *fight against* god persuaded by your words' [Teiresias to Pentheus]; 540–4 'Pentheus ... who *fights against the gods*' [chorus]; 635–6 'for, ⟦70⟧ being a man, he dared to come to *a fight against a god*' [Dionysus on Pentheus]; 788 'suffering badly at your hands, nevertheless I say that you must not *raise up arms against a god*' [disguised Dionysus warning Pentheus]; 1255–6 'but that man is able only to *fight against god*' [Agave on Pentheus]. |
| (C2) 9.1 'Saul, still *breathing* threats and murder against the disciples of the Lord' | 620 '[Pentheus] *breathing* out his passion' |
| (C3) 12.7 'and the chains fell off their hands'; 12.10 '[the iron gate the one that bore toward the city] opened for them *all by itself*', of Peter and his companions' miraculous escape from prison<br>Cf. 5.19 'an angel of the Lord opened the prison doors' (of the second imprisonment of Peter and the Apostles) and 16.26 'and immediately all the doors were opened and the bonds of all were undone' (of the miraculous freeing of Paul and Silas and the other prisoners at Philippi) | 447–8 '*all by themselves* the chains were undone from their feet, and the bolts loosed the doors without mortal hand', of the miraculous escape of the imprisoned Bacchants. |

(C4) 17.18–21...–32 [Paul in Athens] 'others said, "he seems to be an announcer of *strange* [ξένων] *deities*." (For he was reporting the good news about Jesus and the Rising.) And they took hold of him and led him to the Areopagos, saying: ⟦71⟧ "May we know what this *new* teaching is which is spoken by you? For you are introducing to our ears certain *strange* [ξενίζοντα] things. So we want to know what these things mean". For all the Athenians and the *strangers* [ξένοι] that were staying there spent their time on nothing other than saying or hearing some *rather new* thing ... But when they heard the rising of corpses, some *mocked* ...'

(C5) 17.27–9 [Paul to the Athenians] 'to seek the Lord ... who is indeed not far from each one of us. For in him we *live and move and are*, as actually some of your poets have said: for we are his offspring.'

(C6) 17.34 'certain men joined him and believed, among whom was *Dionysios* the Areopagite and a woman by name *Heifer* [Damaris] and others with them' (of Paul's converts in Athens)

(C7) 26.14 'it is hard for you to kick against the pricks' [Jesus to Saul in the third telling of Paul's conversion]

216 'I hear of the *new* evils in this city'; 219–20 '*the new deity* Dionysus'; 247 'whoever the *stranger* is' [of the disguised Dionysus]; 256 '*introducing this new god* to men' [all spoken by Pentheus]; 272 '*this "new" god*, whom you *mock*'; ⟦71⟧ cf. 467; epithet '*stranger*' repeatedly applied to disguised Dionysus.
Cf. also Xen. *Mem.* 1.1.1 'Socrates acts unjustly, not believing in the gods that the city believes in but *introducing* other and *new* deities'; similarly Pl. *Apol.* 24b–c.

506 [Dionysus disguised as the stranger to Pentheus] 'you do not know *what you are living, nor what you are doing, nor who you are*.'

2 'Dionysos' (name constantly recurs), 100 (Dionysos as bull), many other 'bullish' allusions

794–5 'I would sacrifice to him rather than become angry and kick against the pricks, a mortal against a god' [Dionysus in disguise advising Pentheus]

⟦72⟧ Of these parallels, (C1), (C3), and (C7) are commonly cited; (C5) is due to Colaclides;[12] and (C2), (C4), and (C6) are, so far as I know, original suggestions. Some other suggestions occasionally made I have tacitly discounted.

These are, indeed, 'objective' verbal parallels, but are they accidental or 'real' (in the sense that they do things)?[13]

While the thought of (C1) is perfectly Jewish, it is also a common Greek religious concept, it is a *Leitmotiv* of *Bacchae*, the Greek compound 'fight against G/god' (and cognates) is distinctive, it is found only here in the New Testament,[14] and the item fulfils the same narrative and theological function in Acts and in *Bacchae*: that of the 'wise warning' disregarded by persecutors.[15] (Gamaliel's audience obeys here, but not later.) Interestingly, scholars debate the historicity of Gamaliel's intervention (certainly, some of his arguments are anachronistic).[16]

(C2) is in itself a slight verbal parallel, but its force depends on a larger question: whether Saul can be shown to 'play a Pentheus role' in the narrative.[17]

The specific parallel between 'all by itself' and 'all by themselves' hardly establishes (C3) as a significant verbal parallel, but in Classical texts such descriptions *are* associated with Dionysiac epiphanies.[18]

In (C4), Luke is casting Paul as Socrates, as the Platonic and Xenophontic parallels show.[19] But in Plato and Xenophon Socrates is accused of introducing not 'strange' deities, but 'new' ones, and Luke emphasises the notion of 'strangeness' three times. For its part, *Bacchae* represents Dionysus both as 'new' and as 'strange'. Further, *Bacchae* (date: *c.*405) sometimes creates the anachronistic impression of treating the accusation ⟦73⟧ made against Socrates (date: 399). This is because Euripides invests the introduction of Dionysus cult into heroic-age Greece with the anxiety response to new cults characteristic of late fifth-century Athens, a response which, historically, crystallised against Socrates.[20] Acts 17 also contains the *Bacchae* theme of 'mockery'

---

12  Colaclides (1973).
13  In the first instance, at any rate, the question should not be framed in terms of Luke's 'consciousness' or 'intention'.
14  Acts' adroit deployment of *hapax* material merits a study in itself.
15  Similarly Versnel (1990) 199; Tueller (1992) 36; Dormeyer–Galindo (2003) 95; Lang (2003) 7f.
16  Haenchen (1971) 256–8; Lüdemann (1989) 70–3; Barrett (2004) 282, 292–8.
17  P. 562 below; also relevant is Luke's intertextual engagement with 2 Maccabees: p. 566 below.
18  Weinreich (1929) 309ff.
19  I discuss Acts' engagement with pagan philosophy in 'Pagan Philosophy in the Acts of the Apostles' {below, Ch. 28} and flag here only the most important elements.
20  Cf., e.g., Dodds (1960) xxiv–v; Versnel (1990) 173–5; Seaford (1996) 51.

of the 'new' god (*Bacchae* 272). Luke's use of 'strange deities', therefore, combines an allusion to Plato and Xenophon with an allusion to *Bacchae*: he has seen, and is exploiting, this anachronistic conceptual relationship between the two apparently different types of material. The double literary allusion is deft and ingenious.[21]

(C5) is complicated. As commentators note, 'we are his offspring' is a quotation from the not in fact Athenian poet Aratus (*Phaenomena* 5), with an allusion also to the (poetic) *Hymn to Zeus* (line 4) of the Stoic philosopher Cleanthes, also not Athenian but at least Athenian by residence. But, as commentators also note, 'as actually some of your poets have said' could refer backwards as well as forwards or could indeed look both ways. 'Your' in what sense? Merely non-Jewish? That fits the allusions to Aratus and Cleanthes. But Paul is directly addressing the 'men of Athens' (17.22). Might then 'some of your poets' also gloss the Athenian Euripides and 'in him we live and move and are' also allude directly to *Bacchae* 506?[22] *Bacchae* is already in the air ((C4)). The contexts are similar. Paul is arguing that the Athenians are ignorant and do not realise the proximity of the one true god. Equally, Pentheus does not realise that Dionysus is 'near' (500) and the 'stranger' (Dionysus himself) upbraids Pentheus' ignorance. 'In him we live and move and are' represents the polar opposite of Pentheus' ignorance. This reconstruction attributes dense literary allusion, sliding phraseology, and decidedly fancy footwork to Luke:[23] ⟦74⟧ exactly as in (C4). The two items go together and are mutually reinforcing.

In (C6), Dionysios is a common Greek name and so is Damalis, but the unparalleled form Damaris[24] is arresting, and the names mean 'Dionysiac' and 'Heifer', and thus explicitly allude not only to Dionysus but to Dionysus *qua* bull god. Furthermore, even if Dionysios and Damaris are historical figures,[25] there is some historical distortion here, since they were not converted on this occasion.[26] As with the Gamaliel warning, a Dionysiac allusion has been purchased by historical distortion.

---

21 And rather in the manner of Persse McGarrigle's nicely provocative thesis concerning 'the influence of T. S. Eliot on Shakespeare', in David Lodge's international campus novel, *Small World*.
22 The traditional view that there is an allusion to the Cretan Epimenides (Bruce [1951] 338) is rejected by Colaclides (1973) 161f., but it hardly matters: the more allusions, the merrier!
23 Also of course to the dramatic Paul, who comprehensively outwits his stuck-up Epicurean and Stoic philosophical opponents and who is the real 'poet' here: below, Ch. 28.
24 Bruce (1951) 341.
25 Discussion: Lüdemann (1989) 193–4; Barrett (2004) 855; I think they are fictional (n. 91).
26 Not being among the 'first fruits of Achaea' (1 Cor. 16.15; Lüdemann [1989] 194).

(C7) is a Greek proverb, but, like (C1), it *is* Greek, it is not in fact a common proverb, it *is* used in tragedy,[27] it *is* used in *Bacchae*, this is its only occurrence in the New Testament, and the situation is exactly the same both in *Bacchae* and in Acts: the persecuted and unrecognised god uses the proverb in direct exhortation of his chief persecutor.

As individual parallels, (C1), (C4), (C5), (C6), and (C7) are all strong. The cumulative effect, particularly the concentration in Acts 17, is also compelling. Thus in my view the verbal parallels prove use of *Bacchae* and of more general Dionysiac material.

### (D)  *Other Dionysiac Material*

A fairly obvious case is the second arrest and imprisonment of the Apostles (5.19–25),[28] which comes within the sequence that begins at 4.1ff. (the arrest and examination of Peter and John) and that culminates in Gamaliel's warning at 5.39. The miraculous release of the Apostles by an angel of the Lord belongs to the same narrative pattern as 12.1–10 and 16.26–30 ((B2) and (B3) above). Indeed, 5.19–25 functions as a 'prequel' of Peter's more elaborate Dionysiac escape in 12.1–10.[29] One detail, the emphasis on the guards' discomfiture at the Apostles' ⟦75⟧ standing *outside* when they had been *im*prisoned, corresponds to *Bacchae* 644–6.[30]

Another possibility is the Pentecost episode,[31] where (2.13) the Apostles' glossolalia—enabling the widest international outreach—prompts the mocking 'they are filled with sweet wine'. 'Sweet' wine implies 'new' wine and commentators devise various expedients to explain the difficulty that new wine is not drunk at Pentecost, but Wallace and Williams sensibly infer: 'the phrase is a proverbial allusion to widespread drunkenness when the year's new wine first becomes drinkable'.[32] Peter denies the charge (15): 'these men are not drunk, as you take it, for it is the third hour of the day'.

Now, drunkenness is a feature of Dionysiac wine festivals such as the Anthesteria, Dionysiacs got drunk at night, they were divinely possessed, forms of glossolalia featured in pagan cult,[33] Dionysus cult was the most international of pagan cults, Pentheus accuses the Bacchanals of drunkenness and mocks

---

27  Aesch. *Ag.* 1624; *PV* 323; Eur. *IT* 1395f.
28  Dormeyer–Galindo (2003) 95.
29  Wallace–Williams (1993) 58; Dunn (1996) 67–8.
30  Tueller (1992) 33.
31  L. T. Johnson (1992) 44; Tueller (1992) 34; Dormeyer–Galindo (2003) 46, 50, 53.
32  Wallace–Williams (1993) 36.
33  Tschiedel (1975); 1 Cor. 14.22–3.

the new god, but the charge of drunkenness is denied by the Messenger,[34] and the Acts narrative opposes the mockery with an idealised description of the Christian life at 2.42 and 44–6, which includes 'the breaking of bread'. While scholars dispute whether in Acts 'the breaking of bread' refers to, or includes, the Eucharist,[35] given that Acts 2.42, 27.35, etc. ~ Luke 22.19 ~ 24.30, the allusion must at least be *included*, so that, although Acts does not specify wine-drinking at such meals,[36] a broad contrast remains between what is misapprehended as Dionysiac excess (2.13) and Christian table-fellowship.

Furthermore, the Holy Spirit, with which the Apostles are actually 'filled' (2.4) is imaged (*inter alia*) as a liquid (2.17–18, 33: 'I will pour out from my spirit'), as already implied in the prophecy of the risen Jesus at 1.5: 'John baptised in water, but after not many days you will be baptised in holy spirit'. The ⟦76⟧ function of the incorrect accusation of 2.13, therefore, is to imply a contrast between the 'bad' Dionysus of pagan religion and the 'good' Jesus who is the true wine. Moreover, since the Apostles are figured as drinking the equivalent of the true, *new* wine, the Pentecost episode looks back to three passages in Luke's former book, the Gospel (Acts 1.1). The first is the institution of the Lord's Supper (Luke 19–20): 'And having taken bread and having given thanks, he broke it and gave it to them, saying: "This is my body which is given for you. Do this with a view to my remembrance". And the cup similarly after eating, saying: "This *cup* which is *poured out* for you is the *new* covenant in my blood"'. The second is at 7.32, when Jesus, notorious as a wine-drinker, contrasts his own lifestyle with the Baptist's ascetic lifestyle: 'we piped to you and you did not dance', in apparent allusion to the devotees of Pan and Dionysus.[37] The third passage, at 5.33–8, also concerns the difference between John and Jesus:

> (36) He also said a parable to them: 'No one having torn a piece from a new garment puts it upon an old garment; otherwise, he will tear the new one and also the piece from the new one will not match the old. (37) And no one puts *new wine* into old wineskins; otherwise, the new wine will break the wineskins and it itself will be *poured out* and the skins will be destroyed. (38) But *new wine* must be put into new wineskins.'

---

34  *Bacch.* 221–2, 686–8, with Tueller (1992) 33.
35  Also 20.7, 11; 27.35; cf., e.g., Bruce (1951) 100, 465; Wallace–Williams (1993) 36; Dunn (1996) 268, 341; Dormeyer–Galindo (2003) 59; Barrett (2004) I.164–5; 950–1; 1208–10; II.xcii–xciii.
36  On the motive see p. 566 below.
37  Freyne (2000) 271–86; (2004) 56; cf. also Matthew 11.17.

This passage combines defence of the seemingly laxer behaviour of Jesus and his disciples with positive celebration of 'newness'.[38]

So the Pentecost narrative belongs within a complicated sequence—which extends back through Acts 1 and into the Gospel—concerned with the relationship, within first-century Judaism, Jesus' ministry, and early Christianity, between the old and the new, between Jesus and the Baptist, and between Jesus and wine, and within that sequence Dionysus plays an important role both of comparison and of contrast.

⟦77⟧ *Overall Conclusion*

The case for Luke's using both *Bacchae* and narrative patterns derived from Dionysiac myth or ritual is decisive. The following discussion assumes this conclusion but itself provides further evidence.

## 2   Consequences

I begin with *basic* consequences and work upwards.

Luke's culture is further illuminated (he knows *Bacchae* and about Dionysiac myth and ritual; he is sophisticated in a Hellenising sense). He expects reciprocal sophistication from at least a proportion of his readership/audience.[39] Origen's response justifies that expectation.[40] Within this sophisticated environment, *Bacchae* was an enduringly popular Greek tragedy, and it had already been exploited by Hellenistic Jewish writers as a way of exploring the relationships between Judaism and Dionysus religion and between religion and politics, and by Stoic and Cynic philosophers in philosophical/political contexts, and Luke knew about both these groups.[41] None of this is to *restrict* Acts' audience/readership to the sophisticated.[42]

---

38   Cf. also Matthew 9.14–15; Mark 2.18–20; discussion: Dunn (2003) 441–2; Luke 5.39 ('and no one having drunk old wine wants new; for he says: "the old is good"'), unparalleled in Matthew or Mark, is widely dismissed as a softening gloss.

39   Audience/readership of Acts, much disputed, can only be constructed from the text. As will emerge, I favour a considerable range. Although I believe that Acts is best 'received' as a reading text and some of my interpretations seem better suited to that context, in order to minimise controversy, I make no practical distinction between audience and readership.

40   Further, Dormeyer (2005) 167–70.

41   See 2 and *3 Maccabees* (p. 566 below); Hor. *Epist.* 1.16.73–9 with Moles (2002) 152–5 {vol. 2, pp. 716–20}; Epict. 1.1.22–4; 29.5–8 (Cynicising Stoic); Lucian, *Ind.* 19 (Demetrius the Cynic); Luke and philosophy: n. 19 above.

42   See n. 142 below.

Generically, the allusions to *Bacchae* and to Dionysiac myth and ritual bring new strands to Acts' highly varied literary texture. Within Acts' *primary* generic classification of historiography, tragedy is fully at home.[43] So, at least within *some* types of historiography (notably Herodotean) is myth.[44] Equally, tragedy goes well with Acts' Homeric material.[45]

⟦78⟧ The Dionysiac parallels highlight key elements of the narrative and of the earlier Jesus narrative, frequently recalled: the arrest, trial, and crucifixion of Jesus; the Pentecost event; the repeated trials (literal and figurative) of Jesus' followers; the Apostles' first escape from prison; the relative liberalism of Pharisees compared with Sadducees; Paul's conversion; the escapes from prison of Peter and of Paul and Silas; and the first converts from a rival religious movement.[46]

The main events of Acts are enacted against the template of *Bacchae*.[47] The Pentecost narrative and the second arrest and imprisonment of the Apostles set the scene. Gamaliel plays the wise warner, like Teiresias. The quotation from *Bacchae* functions as a 'signal' to the sophisticated reader. Gamaliel's warning deters the high priest and the Sadducees only temporarily. Structurally, his warning looks backwards, as well as forwards, colouring the miraculous escape narrative of 5.19–25 and the start of that sequence, 4.1, when the Apostles are first arrested and imprisoned. Indeed, the warning connects thematically as far back as Acts' opening words and implicates us as readers/audience.[48] Luke's addressee, *Theophilos* (Luke 1.3; Acts 1.1), has a doubly significant name: loved by God, we must love God.[49] We must be, as it were, '*theophiles*', not '*theomachs*'. And, given its emphatic placing near the beginning of the narrative, Gamaliel's warning seems to apply, poetically speaking, even to those who did not actually hear it. It is thus *structural* both within Acts and, as it were, *outside* Acts.

Stephen's arrest and death re-enact Jesus' (7.60 ~ Luke 23.34). Systematic persecution is inaugurated by Saul, complicit in Stephen's death, imprisoner of both men and women (8.1–3), 'still breathing threats and murder against the disciples of the Lord' and undertaking to bring those of the Way, whether men or women, in bonds to Jerusalem (9.1–2). Saul plays Pentheus,[50] and the

---

43 Cf., e.g., Saïd (2002).
44 Cf., e.g., Boedeker (2002).
45 Rutherford (1982); Homer in Acts: MacDonald (2003).
46 The last item anticipates pp. 568ff. below.
47 Lang (2003) 7ff.
48 Cf. Lang (2003) 9.
49 Discussion: Barrett (2004) 65–6; Theophilos' historicity is here immaterial.
50 Voegeli (1953) 418; Lang (2003) 8ff.; Dormeyer (2005) 166.

triple emphasis on his murderous 'breathing' (contrasting with the Holy Spirit or 'Breath'), on 'women' and 'bonds' further evokes *Bacchae*. Throughout, Acts, like *Bacchae*, ⟦79⟧ stresses the adhesion of women to the new religious movement. But on the Road to Damascus Saul, unlike Pentheus in *Bacchae* 576–641, acknowledges the divine epiphany. And the third version of the conversion adds psychological depth to Paul's character (26.14). In *Bacchae*, the use of the proverb is doubly 'pointed', first because the pricks are being administered by the bull (Dionysus); second, because, as is well recognised, Pentheus is himself secretly attracted by bullish things,[51] so Dionysus the bull who is doing the pricking is in effect saying: give in to your own bullish prickings. Pentheus (on this occasion) does not; Paul does. Luke's evocation of Euripides' use of the proverb suggests something crucial about the psychology of Saul the persecutor, as, no doubt, about the psychology of many persecutors. The message is both spiritually uplifting and practical: even some of the harshest persecutors can be converted. And Jesus' mercy—so different from Dionysus' implacability—is such that the conversion of the vengeful and hybristic king-figure to the humble servant of God—of the persecutor to the sectator—is in one sense a very small and easy change, a matter, almost, only of the change of a syllable. *Saoul* becomes *Paulus*, the *little* man who does *big* things among both *great* and *small*.[52]

Luke's subsequent elaborate detailing of Paul's physical blindness, his vision of Ananias, his new insight into his role, and his restoration to physical sight (9.8–18) can hardly fail to evoke both Pentheus, sighted but religiously blind, and Teiresias, the blind seer.

From being chief persecutor, Saul now becomes persecutee, at the hands of the Jews (9.23ff.), and the persecutor role is assumed by Herod Agrippa I, like Pentheus in that he is a persecuting king, and the next bad king in Luke–Acts' sequence ⟦80⟧ of bad kings.[53] As the narrative focus reverts to Peter, he also faces a 'god-fighting' moment: the vision at Joppa and the descent of the Holy Spirit upon Gentiles, and he decides: 'who was I that I had the power to *hinder God*?' (11.17). Thus the *Bacchae* template reinforces Acts' many parallels

---

51   Cf., e.g., Dodds (1960) 172–3; Seaford (1996) 213.
52   Scholars debate (Bruce [1951] 257; Wallace–Williams [1993] 26, 62; Barrett [2004] 609, 616) why at 13.9 Luke switches permanently (except for the transliterated Hebrew *Saoul* at 22.7 and 26.14) from *Saulos* to *Paulos*. But both in the OT and NT name changes can symbolise spiritual change; Acts is full of name-plays, including Roman ones; and the pun on 'Paulus' is virtually explicit at 26.22, 24. Thus Acts 13 stages a contest between different sorts of power: Paul is a 'small' person doing a 'big' thing, hence the 'strickenness' of his 'powerful' and 'intelligent' Roman namesake, the proconsul Sergius *Paulus*.
53   Cf. Luke 3.19–20; 9.7–9; 23.7–12; below, n. 114; below, p. 573.

between Peter and Paul. Herod, again Pentheus-like, imprisons Peter as the leader of the new movement (12.1ff.). Peter's miraculous escape from bondage and prison parallels the stranger's/Dionysus' escape in the *Bacchae*, and Herod, further like Pentheus in his impious aspiration to divinity,[54] is, like Pentheus, appropriately struck down by divine agency (12.20–3). Paul and Silas' miraculous escape from prison again re-enacts the stranger's/Dionysus' escape in the *Bacchae* and shows another persecutor—the gaoler—making the right choice of acceptance of the divine manifestation. Like the Road to Damascus narrative, all these 'miraculous-escape-from-prison' narratives show Dionysiac parallels providing a language and grammar for the description, in, as it were, an 'international' context, of the phenomena of divine epiphany and conversion or non-conversion. These narratives also imply a kind of religious liberation theology[55] more powerful than any worldly powers, whether Jewish or Roman.[56]

Subsequent trials—or their equivalents—help to keep the *Bacchae* parallel in play, and the parallel is strongly re-activated in Acts 17,[57] with its direct use of *Bacchae* motifs, its ambiguous allusion to 'your poets', and its explicit mention of 'Dionysios', and in the third telling of Paul's conversion, where the quotation from *Bacchae* (26.14) confirms the reader in reading that narrative in Dionysiac terms.[58] Clearly, the five pointers to *Bacchae* (5.39; 9.1; 17.28, 34; 26.14) are strategically distributed across the narrative. At the end of Acts, Paul is again under guard (28.16). Although the *Bacchae* template again 〚81〛 comes into play, interpretation of the end requires separate treatment.[59]

The Dionysiac parallels also create more general theological implications. The risen Jesus in Acts is a divine figure, and the miraculous releases from prison and the incident on the Road to Damascus prove this status, just as the corresponding events in the *Bacchae* prove Dionysus' divinity.[60] Like Dionysus, most epiphanic of pagan gods, the risen Jesus is epiphanic, and, again like Dionysus, Jesus is a divinity of tremendous physical powers. His followers and agents also have tremendous powers, partly in the healing of the sick, but partly also in the summary administration of justice. If the first category

---

54   *Bacch.* 318–21.
55   Weaver (2004).
56   Further pp. 567 and 578–80 below.
57   Whether or not Acts 17 describes a formal trial does not matter here: the proceedings are trial-*like*.
58   Similarly Dormeyer (2005) 166–7.
59   Below, p. 571.
60   Pervo (1987) 21–2.

clearly imitates Jesus, the second *seems* more like Dionysus.⁶¹ Jesus' disciples are to be feared. But in fact the same is true of Jesus himself. Like Dionysus, Jesus is a divinity who confronts people with the *choice* of *conversion*. To those who accept him, Jesus brings salvation,⁶² just as Dionysus was *the* great pagan 'saviour' god. But, given that Acts post-dates the destruction of the Temple and the sacking of Jerusalem,⁶³ Jesus is also like Dionysus in that he wreaks terrible vengeance on those who do not accept him, especially—history teaches—on his own people.⁶⁴ Dionysus also destroyed a palace, Jesus the Temple, since God does not inhabit temples made by hand.⁶⁵ As for worship, Dionysiac worship could take the form of a 'mystery', and, in whatever form, wine-drinking was important. So also for Jesus and his followers in Luke, and in Acts the descriptions of the Apostles at Pentecost and of the breaking of bread by Paul and his companions in Troas (20.7–12) characterise Christianity in somewhat similar terms,⁶⁶ though Acts, while presupposing such wine-drinking, ⟦82⟧ leaves it unspecified, no doubt as one way of creating distance between Dionysus religion and Christianity.⁶⁷

But, if the risen Jesus is a divine figure, during his earthly life he was also a human being, a point emphasised in Acts,⁶⁸ as in Luke. Again, the Dionysus parallel speaks, for, of all pagan gods, Dionysus looked and behaved most like a human being for the longest periods of time and was *deus praesentissimus*.⁶⁹ Dionysus is *the* pagan parallel—perhaps *the* parallel full stop—for the Incarnation.

From all this, it is already clear that Luke is extremely creative in his response to *Bacchae*, and that he expects at least a proportion of his readerships/audiences to recognise a complex intertextual relationship.⁷⁰ This conclusion should not surprise: similar intertextuality marks his engagement

---

61 5.5, 10 (of Ananias and Sapphira before Peter); 8.24 (Simon the Magus' fear of Peter); 12.23 (the angel's 'smiting' of Herod Agrippa I); 13.9–12 (Paul's blinding of Bar-Jesus); cf. Tueller (1992) 11 and Gamaliel's warning at 5.35, 38–9.
62 2.21, 41, 47; 4.12; 13.23, 26, 47; 16.30–1; 28.28.
63 Below, n. 106.
64 The vexed question of whether Acts is anti-Jewish (loosely, 'anti-Semitic') exceeds my brief.
65 17.24 > 7.48; 6.13–14.
66 Cf. Dormeyer–Galindo (2003) 308.
67 Cf. further p. 568 below.
68 Cf. 2.22; 17.31.
69 Henrichs (1982) 152; (1993); Tueller (1992) 14.
70 *Contra*, Alexander (2005), who remains sceptical of conscious *imitatio* of any of the poetic texts of the high literary culture.

with the Septuagint, or, among Classical authors, with Homer.[71] Hence, just as Classical texts are intensely 'imitative' in the sense of 'imitating' other Classical texts, so too is Acts.

Estimation of Luke's use of *Bacchae* and of Dionysiac material must also take account of 2 and 3 Maccabees,[72] which treat attempts by the Seleucids and Ptolemies to impose paganism, particularly the worship of Dionysus, on the Jews, whether in Judaea or in Egypt.

In 2 Maccabees 7.19 one of seven brothers being tortured to death warns Antiochus Epiphanes: 'As for you, do not think that you will be unpunished, having taken it in hand *to fight God*', and Antiochus is later described as 'breathing out fire, in his passions against the Jews' (9.7; cf. *Bacch.* 620 '[Pentheus] breathing out his passion'). As in Acts, *Bacchae* allusions in this strongly Hellenising text are persuasive,[73] and one 'god-fighter' is succeeded by another.[74] 3 Maccabees contains even more such ⟦83⟧ material.[75] In both texts, the *Bacchae* and Dionysiac material underpin powerful religious and political narratives of bondage and liberation, and a Dionysiac assault upon Yaweh is defeated by Yaweh's deployment of Dionysiac methods.

Now, Luke's Dionysiac material sometimes echoes Maccabean Dionysiac material. For example, just as the theomach Antiochus Epiphanes 'breathes fire in his rages against the Jews', so the theomach Saul 'breathes threats and murder against the disciples of the Lord' (9.1). Similarly, eating by worms characterises the deaths both of the theomach Herod Agrippa I (12.23) and of the theomach Antiochus (2 Maccabees 9.9),[76] and the kings share the hybristic aspirations to divinity (cf. 2 Maccabees 9.12) of which Pentheus also exhibits symptoms. Presumably, also, the use in 2 and 3 Maccabees of *Bacchae* both as a myth providing the backbone of the historical narrative and as a repeating mythical pattern influenced Luke more broadly, though allowance should surely also be made for the myth-historical narratives of Herodotus.[77] Luke's literary exploitation of Dionysiac material far exceeds anything in 2 or 3 Maccabees, but it is to some extent filtered through these texts and thus (again) involves a complex process of 'double allusion'. Luke's engagement

---

71　MacDonald (2003), with the judicious Lang (2004).
72　Vögeli (1953) 426 n. 44; Pervo (1987) 7, 119–20; Dormeyer (2005) 155 n. 8. There are also links—not directly Dionysiac—between Acts and 1 Maccabees: p. 579 below.
73　Cf. Dormeyer–Galindo (2003) 95.
74　Thus Nicanor: 14.32–3; 15.3, 32–3.
75　Cousland (2001).
76　Cf. also Dormeyer–Galindo (2003) 194.
77　Cf. p. 562 above.

with 2 and 3 Maccabees also has still larger religious and political implications, of which more later.

I turn now to other questions illuminated by the Dionysiac parallels in Acts.

### The Status of Christianity vis-à-vis Judaism

Christianity[78] is existentially problematic, partly Jewish, partly other, partly old, partly new. These problematics greatly exercised the early Christians.[79] Within the general context of Acts, Luke cannot say outright that Christianity is in some ways a 'new religion', because that would concede the Jewish claim that Christianity is the *bastard* child of Judaism, misbegotten by ⟦84⟧ the renegade Paul in unholy union with Gentiles.[80] So Acts contains much material designed to represent Christianity as the *fulfilment* of Judaism. This strand is protreptic for Jews within the historical narrative and, presumably, also protreptic for any Jewish readers/audience of Acts. The same applies to those elements, both in Acts and in Luke, which characterise Christianity in terms of *renewal*. As against this, the consistent narrative analogy in Acts between Jesus and Dionysus helps to *suggest* Jesus' 'newness', because, formally speaking, Dionysus is a 'new god'.[81] Moreover, Luke conveys this idea of 'newness' somewhat more explicitly, though still obliquely, in the Pentecost episode, with its allusion to 'sweet' wine and its links back to ambiguous claims to newness made by Jesus in the Gospel. As at least one of those examples shows—Jesus' celebration of the 'new wine' of his ministry—the implication of 'newness' may appeal even to Jews, but it has greater appeal to pagans, to whom Christianity *needs* to be presented as 'new', since they have already had much exposure to traditional Judaism. At the same time, even to pagans, it should not be presented as entirely new, otherwise it will lose much of its grounding. On this issue, early Christianity *has* to equivocate.

In Acts 17 Luke actually makes the idea of Jesus' newness explicit, but he focalises it through the Athenians, to whom Paul 'seems to be an announcer of strange deities' and who ask about 'this new teaching', even though Athens had a synagogue, only just mentioned in the text (17.17). As we have seen, the Athenians' comment recalls the accusation against Socrates and thus

---

78   Acts itself first attests 'Christians' (11.26; 26.28).
79   Harrisville (1955); (1960); Löning (1998); Lieu (2002); (2004); Buell (2005).
80   This might be called the 'Jewish' view of Christianity, e.g., Feldman (1996) 285; Vermes (2000) 63–4, 76, 80, 109–10.
81   Similarly, Lang (2003) 8; Dormeyer (2005) 154–5, 163–4; Dionysus is 'new' when in myth he introduces his cult into cities (as in *Bacchae*), or when in ritual his arrival is celebrated as of a new god, even though the ritual is annual. Thus this 'newness' is necessarily ambiguous.

amusingly wrong-foots the contemporary Athenians, who are further teased for their traditional obsession with newness. Yet, as we have also seen, the precise epithet 'strange' evokes more particularly Dionysus in *Bacchae*, and the Athenians', as it were, 'interrogation' of Paul evokes alike the trial of Socrates *and* Pentheus' judicial proceedings against Dionysus *and* the various judicial proceedings taken against the various Dionysus-substitutes—〖85〗 including Paul himself—in earlier episodes. Further, although the newness-obsessed Athenians look so different from allegedly tradition-loving Jews, the fact that the 'strangers' staying in Athens are also newness-obsessed helps to problematise the boundaries between Athenians and others, and between 'newness' or 'strangeness' and 'non-newness' or 'non-strangeness'.

Thus Acts 17 acts as a mirror for the narrative of Acts as a whole and as a space in which the ambiguous existential status of Christianity can be played out in a sanitised way but one that is relevant both to Jews and to Gentiles. Both parties can be enthused by the energy of this sort of new religious movement. The *ambiguity* of Dionysus' status—'new' or not, 'stranger' or not—suits Luke's purpose perfectly. In this crucial matter of the existential status of Christianity, the *Bacchae*/Dionysus intertext works hard.

### *The Relationship between Jesus-Religion and Dionysus-Religion*

If in Acts 17 the parallel between Jesus and Dionysus offers a way of exploring the relationship between Christianity and Judaism, it is also an important topic in its own right. Paul (16) is represented as being 'provoked' by the fact that 'the city was full of idols'. This is a transparent narrative device to cast him in the familiar role of 'outside innocent visits corrupt city'[82] (for the historical Paul surely knew that Athens, of all Gentile cities, would be like this). Conventionally, this scenario combines light fun at the expense of the innocent newcomer with censure of the city, which the sophisticated reader is invited to view with new eyes. Here the first element is absent and Paul at once plays the sterner figure of the outsider as observer and judge (16, 22), even as Cynic 'scout'. His initial characterisation of the Athenians to their face—'as being as fearful of divinities as it is possible to be in all respects' (22)—cuts two ways:[83] both parrhestiastically critical (you dreadfully superstitious lot!) and implicitly protreptic (you are so religious that you are fertile ground for the acceptance of the true god). Paul's appeal to the 〖86〗 Athenians' own religious and philosophical traditions follows a recognised Jewish proselytising technique,[84] but

---

82  Cf., e.g., Virg. *Ecl.* 1; Calp. Sic. *Ecl.* 7; Dio 7.22–63; Liban. 26.6; 27.6.
83  Similarly Klauck (2000) 81; Dormeyer–Galindo (2003) 266–7.
84  Below, p. 578 and n. 129.

again the *Bacchae* analogy plays a role. Clearly, in so far as Jesus is here, as earlier, being portrayed as like Dionysus, the latter is not being damned outright. Pagans are being led to the truth of the Jesus-god through the medium of the closest analogue to Jesus among their own gods. In this respect, too, Paul's performance in Athens functions as a sort of meta- or self-reflexive narrative for the whole narrative of Acts. There is a message here alike for potential pagan converts, led along the Dionysiac path to Jesus, for Christian proselytisers (this is the right way to approach pagans), and for the many Jews who compromised with paganism[85] (follow Jesus, not Dionysus). Earlier Stephen, who anticipates Paul in so many important ways, stressed how Moses had learned 'the whole wisdom of the Egyptians' (7.22). So there is a level on which Dionysus stands *also* for the *generality* of the pagan gods.

The end of Acts 17 even enacts the peaceful conquest of Dionysus religion, when Paul's named converts include 'the Dionysiac' and 'the heifer'. This allusion comes most appropriately in a sequence where there is stress on 'knowing' and 'not knowing'[86] and on bad and good divinities: 'recognition' of the true god is what this sequence is all about, and so followers of the bull god himself meekly come over to the right side. True, Luke lists Dionysios and Damaris as being among Paul's few converts on this occasion, but their coming over, like Paul's preaching in Rome at the end of Acts (shortly to be discussed), has proleptic force. The conversion of the Dionysiacs in general has not actually happened yet, but it will. And, indeed, in the fullness of historical time, it did.[87] Note also that climactic naming as a means of resolving implicit interpretative problems is a common trick in Classical literature, the best parallel here being the delayed dramatic appearance, in the Dionysiac novel *Daphnis and Chloe*, of a character named [[87]] *Dionysophanes*: 'Dionysus made manifest'.[88] But, as immediately emerges, this climactic naming has another aspect.

### *Definition of Jesus*
Acts 17 also contains significant puns. When Paul quotes Cleanthes and Aratus, 'we are his offspring' (28), the referent of 'his' is the 'unknown god' who has made heaven and earth. To a Jew this will be Yaweh, the God who, precisely, must not be named. To anyone who knows Cleanthes and Aratus, the implicit referent will be Zeus and the allusion to humans as his 'offspring' (γένος) will

---

85   Below, p. 576.
86   Note the similar stress in Peter's speech concerning Jesus in 2.14–36, where, similarly but more negatively, Dionysus is also the implicit comparator with Jesus (p. 561 above).
87   There had already been individual converts: p. 578.
88   Longus 4.13; Hunter (1983) 37–8.

recall the epithet 'Zeus-born' (Διογένης). Now, both in Acts and in Luke, the divinity of Jesus, son of a human mother, derives from his being 'the son of God'—in the strongest possible sense.[89] Similarly, *Dio*nysus, son of a human mother, is the son of Zeus, as his name signifies.[90] The appearance, at the end of the Athens sequence, of the name of *Dionysios*, therefore, clinches the process of definition: Dionysus, wrong son of wrong god: Jesus, right son of right God.[91]

Another pun signifies: Epicureans extolled the 'help' given to mortals by their 'divine' founder Epicurus, whose name means 'helper'.[92] But later, addressing Agrippa II (26.22), Paul invokes the '*help* that comes from God', the sole occurrence of ἐπικουρία in the New Testament. Thus the pagan 'helping' philosophers are helpless to help: help comes only from the Christian God. Similarly, the sign of the ship carrying Paul to Italy was the *Dios*curi (28.11), for pagans, 'sons of Zeus', as their name signifies, and divine 'saviours' and 'helpers',[93] the name Διόσκουροι being etymologically connected with ἐπικουρία,[94] [[88]] yet, like Jesus, gods of ambiguous human parentage. Hence again the question: which g/God, which son of which G/god, which divine 'helper', which 'saviour'?[95] Not the Dioscuri, not Zeus himself, but—again—the Christian god/God. Note also that in Acts 17, as earlier and later, 'Jesus' is etymologised as 'Healer',[96] so in this respect too Jesus bests Dionysus *qua* healing god.[97]

So much for the religious implications of Acts 17.[98] But it is also appropriate to register an aesthetic judgement. Acts 17 is quite brilliantly conceived, and it is very Classical in its problematising of boundaries, both spatial and temporal, its use of mirror technique, its self-reflexivity, its obliquity of implication, its

---

89  Explicitly at 9.20 and 13.33 (in both, Paul is the speaker), though many other passages are ambiguously relevant; Luke 1.32, 35; 10.22; 20.13–16; 22.29–30, 42, 70; discussion in (e.g.) Dunn (2003) 708–24.

90  The etymology (whether correct or not) is often clear, e.g., *Bacch*. 550–1.

91  The combination of at least some historical distortion (n. 26), of the climactic naming, and of the name's thematic density persuades me that 'Dionysios' and 'Damaris' are fictional.

92  Cf., e.g., Frischer (1982) 275–6.

93  Cf., e.g., Epict. 2.18.29.

94  E.g., Diod. 6.6 {= 6.5 Cohen-Skalli}: Διόσκοροι ... πολλοῖς ... δεομένοις ἐπικουρίας βεβοηθηκέναι.

95  Thus at 28.11 the deceptive associations of παράσημος as adjective (Barrett [2004] 1227–8) are very nicely judged.

96  10.38; 4.22 ~ 4.18; 28.27 > 28.31; the association is (re-)activated in Acts 17, (a) because this is how 'the philosophers' will naturally take the name at 17.18; (b) because of the earlier allusion (17.5–9) to a character called 'Jason', the Greek equivalent of the Jewish-Greek 'Jesus' and a name that *means* 'healer'. {Fuller treatment in Moles (2011).}

97  E.g., Soph. *Ant.* 1144.

98  There is also much to be said about the philosophical implications. {See below, Ch. 28}.

density of meaning, its clever punning, and its sheer overall poise. The next sequence, however, is even better.

### The End of Acts

> He [Paul] remained [in Rome] for a period of two years in a private hired lodging,[99] and he received all who came in to him, heralding the kingdom of God and teaching the things concerning the Lord Jesus Christ with all freedom of speech and unhinderedly (28.31).

Many scholars have found the end of Acts problematic, whether as being bathetic, pessimistic, evasive, or lacunose. From Luke's point of view, such judgements reveal their authors to be defective Christians. From a Classical point of view, the end of Acts is a very great end, on a par even with the end of Herodotus or the end of the *Aeneid*.[100]

How, broadly, does the end 'work'? At the beginning of Acts (1.8), the risen Jesus, after himself telling of the kingdom of [[89]] God to the Apostles, instructs them to bear witness to him in Jerusalem, all Judaea, and Samaria, and until the end of the earth. Paul, an Apostle since his conversion after the encounter with Jesus on the Road to Damascus,[101] is at the end of Acts telling of the kingdom of God and bearing witness to Jesus. So end and beginning link. Further, Rome itself can be focalised by Jews and Greeks as the end of the earth, or—better—mission to Rome, often conceived as the centre of the earth, *foreshadows* mission to the end of the earth.[102] 'He received *all* who came in to him' then becomes proleptic of that mission to all human beings.[103]

---

99 Translation: Hauser (1979) 153–7; Rapske (1994) 177–9.
100 Good discussions in Hauser (1979); Omerzu (2001); and Hooker (2003) 58–66, but there is much more to be said.
101 Many claim that Acts does not represent Paul as an apostle, except at the allegedly anomalous 14.4 and 14.14: Haenchen (1971) 114; Wallace–Williams (1993) 33, 66; Dunn (1996) 118, 188, 190; Barrett (2004) I.644, 671f., 1042; II.lxxxix. But Paul himself cites (13.47; cf. 26.23) the verse from Isaiah (49.6) underlying the risen Jesus' injunction at 1.8; he himself is now fulfilling that injunction; at 22.21 and 26.16–17 the risen Jesus applies the verbal form of 'apostle' to Paul; and at 23.11 he instructs Paul in words that echo 1.8. Acts' representation of Paul's apostleship parallels Paul's own; cf. Bruce (1951) 33, 405, 445; Brown (1997) 283 n. 8; Dormeyer–Galindo (2003) 31–2, 150, 179, 182, 287. Indeed, denial of Paul's apostleship misses a crucial invitation to all readers (p. 574 below).
102 The two interpretations: useful survey in Hauser (1979) 206ff.; the ideological geography of 1 Maccabees is also relevant: p. 581 and n. 146 below.
103 As elsewhere (bibliography in Hauser [1979] 160 n. 269; discussion: 160–5; Dunn [1996] 277ff., 323ff.), Paul's actions recall Jesus' (Hauser [1979] 157): 28.31 ~ Luke 9.11 'and he received them and talked to them concerning the kingdom of God'.

The question of reader knowledge, or of temporal frame, now becomes critical.

The inference that the end shows Acts to have been written before Paul's death[104] is untenable: that death is repeatedly foreshadowed within Acts,[105] and Luke alludes to the fall of Jerusalem and the destruction of the Temple in 70.[106] Thus readers/audience (ancient as well as modern) know that just beyond the end of the text Paul's current mild house arrest will itself end: he will stand trial and die a horrible death, albeit that [[90]] of a heroic witness or martyr.[107] For in Paul's case, Jesus' initial command (1.8) and Ananias' injunction, 'you will be a witness for him [the Just One] to all men of what you have seen and heard' (22.15), entail a crucial development of the concept of 'witness'—from 'witness' to 'martyr'. This development has already been illustrated by the example of Stephen, earlier described by Paul himself as 'Stephen the *martus*' (22.20).[108] The structural fulcrum between the beginning and end of Acts comes in Paul's valedictory speech to the Ephesian elders in Acts 20, with its unmistakable 'tragic foreshadowings'.[109] Verse 24 runs: 'But I do not make my life of any account as valuable to myself provided that I may end my race and the ministry which I received from the Lord Jesus, to bear witness throughly to the good news of the grace of God'. Here Paul's 'race' is the commission he received from Jesus, and the beginning of the sentence and the notion of completion in 'bear witness throughly' clearly convey that Paul's 'race' will be coextensive with his life.

Now, since *Paul*'s mission to Rome was cut short, it is up to readers/audience of Acts to take over the baton from Paul and in their turn assume Jesus' commission to mission to the ends of the earth—if, that is, they are willing to convert and themselves to become Apostles. The open-ended-ness of the end[110]

---

104  Thus, e.g., Bruce (1951) 10ff.; Hemer (1989) 365–410.
105  E.g., 9.16 [< 1.3, > 17.3]; 20.17–38 (with, e.g., Haenchen [1971] 566; Wallace–Williams [1993] 111; Dunn [1996] 269ff.; Brown [1997] 313); 21.4, 11–14; 23.3 (with, e.g., Wallace–Williams [1993] 117; Dormeyer–Galindo [2003] 342; Barrett [2004] 1059); 26.31–2; 27.24.
106  Though the historical Jesus perhaps predicted these things (Dunn [2003] 631–2), Luke 19.41ff. 'touches up' Mark 13.1–2 in the light of history: cf. e.g. Wallace–Williams (1993) 8; Dunn (1996) xi; Brown (1997) 273–4; Barrett (2004) II.xliii, cxiiff.
107  Since the mainline Christian tradition of Paul's martyrdom is foreshadowed in Acts (n. 105), the possible complications of Euseb. *HE* 2.22, 25, the Pastoral Epistles, and 1 Clem. 5.6–7 are interpretatively immaterial. The end of Acts also has many philosophical resonances. {See below, Ch. 28}.
108  For the explicit martyr sense, cf. Rev. 17.6.
109  See n. 105 above.
110  Cf. also Hauser (1979) 147; Dunn (1996) xv, 11, 278; Klauck (2000) 118; Omerzu (2001); Lang (2003) 10.

creates the space for readers'/auditors' acceptance or rejection of Jesus and, if acceptance, for their further acceptance of Jesus' commission to mission. And if that space is, as it were, completely filled by eager missionaries or Apostles, the space between Rome and the ends of the earth will also eventually be elided.

Thus the narrative that the end challenges 'us' to construct—the ways in which *we* 'write' Christianity—is more important than the narrative of Acts itself. This explains why Luke describes ⟦91⟧ (1.1) the Gospel as 'the *first* book':[111] if Acts is the *second* book, then the *third* 'book'—and all subsequent 'books'—is, or are, what *we* 'write'. Luke creates these implications by playing on the relationship between the book as space or journey, with a beginning and an end, and its theme as space or journey, with a beginning and an end that has yet to be reached. Again, this is a technique of Classical authors, especially historians, relevant to Luke, and especially among Luke's historian predecessors, of Herodotus and Livy (Herodotus surely being Luke's main model here).[112]

Now, how does this complex of endings and non-endings at the end of Acts involve *Bacchae* and Dionysus?

Readers/audience know that Paul will be killed and that the first Roman persecutions of Christians will begin shortly thereafter in Rome itself. Death; persecution; at the end of the narrative readers yet again face the Dionysiac choice: accept the new god and follow Paul's example, or persecute Paul and his fellow-Christians. The choice is for everybody, but since the final scene is set in Rome, it is particularly acute for a Roman audience.[113] But readers/audience also know that Paul's kingly persecutor Nero will die violently soon after: divine justice will overtake the new Pentheus.[114] Thus the *Bacchae* template helps to cover events beyond the narrative of Acts but past to first readers/audience. But such is the plasticity of myth that it can also cover events future to first readers/audience, the persecutions by Domitian, for example (if one puts Acts in the 80s), or by later Roman emperors. Nevertheless, the punishment of Nero, as of other *theomachs* within the narrative, serves to deter readers from

---

111  On the problem see, e.g., Barrett (2004) 65.
112  Cf. Moles (1996) 275–7 {vol. 2, pp. 264–7}; (1993) 158–9 {vol. 2, pp. 215–17}; intriguingly, Dio, *Or.* 13 (date 101 CE) performs the same geographical, moral, and, as it were, textual trajectory as Acts (Moles [2005] 126 {above, p. 272} n. 140); the parallel must mean something: exactly what, I am unsure. 'Write-your-life' challenges are posed by other genres besides historiography, notably philosophical protreptic (relevant to Acts, as to Dio 13 or Horace's *Epistles*).
113  Lang (2003) 10.
114  And Luke brilliantly anticipates Nero's death *within* the narrative: the acclamation of Herod Agrippa I's voice as 'the voice of a god' (12.22) recalls Nero: Klauck (2000) 43–4; Dormeyer–Galindo (2003) 193; note the important parallel at Dio 66.6, with Moles (1983) 133–4 {above, pp. 69–72}.

choosing to become persecutors. They should ⟦92⟧ instead follow Paul: but in full knowledge of what this may entail ('witness' in the form of 'martyrdom').

For here there is a decisive difference from *Bacchae*. Paul will not now be released. There will be no more prison-bursting Dionysiac epiphanies: instead, judicial murder. It is as if Luke is saying: bye-bye, miraculous divine interventions, hello, harsh reality. This change of tone partly registers the threat posed to Christianity by Rome herself.[115] Still another function of Luke's use of *Bacchae*, then, is to suggest a sort of transition from *muthos* to *logos*, almost from mythical time to real time or from myth to reality: a transition of frequent concern to ancient historiography.[116]

Such a transition does not necessarily—and in Luke's case obviously does not—deny the broad truth status of the *muthos* material. But the *broad* truth. No reader cognisant of the Dionysiac parallels can take the narratives of Peter's and Paul's and Silas' escapes from prison or of Paul's conversion as literally true.[117]

The move, at the end of Acts, away from, as it were, the age of miracles to harsh reality, however, does not mean that all is unrelieved gloom, both in regard to the general implications that we have already seen, in regard even to the reality of persecution (for Paul himself had been a great persecutor and yet had been converted), and in regard to Paul's own end.

Paul is left preaching and teaching 'with all frankness and unhinderedly'. Commentators generally take Acts' emphatic last word in a legal sense, as referring to Paul's *relative* freedom under house arrest.[118] This seems to be supported by 24.23: '[Felix] giving orders to the centurion that he [Paul] should be kept in custody and that he should have some relief and that *none* of his personal friends *should be hindered* from attending to him'.

⟦93⟧ But this interpretation trivially privileges the immediate dramatic situation and ignores the inevitable sequel (Paul's death), which, as we have seen, is interpretatively central. The relationship between 28.31 and 24.23 is one of contrast. The legal sense is 'trumped' by 'unhinderedly' as a metaphorical or spiritual term. Doubtless, as 2 Timothy 2.9 says—perhaps even glossing this passage—'the word of God is not bound',[119] but the paradoxical redefinition of imprisonment and liberty must also apply to human beings who proclaim that

---

115   Further p. 579 below.
116   Marincola (1997) 117–27; of concern also to ancient philosophy. {See below, Ch. 28.}
117   *Pace* many, e.g., Dunn (1996) xxi.
118   Hauser (1979) 144–50; also Bruce (1951) 481; Dunn (1996) 356; Barrett (2004) 1253. The important Platonic parallel (*Crat.* 415d)) brings further dimensions. {See below, Ch. 28, p. 931.}
119   Hauser (1979) 147; Klauck (2000) 118.

Word. Thus the end of Acts crucially redefines both imprisonment and liberty in Christian spiritual terms, thus providing powerful reassurance to those who choose as Paul did.

To understand the full theological implications of Paul's death, we again have to feed material from the rest of Acts into the 'spaces' between first, Paul at the end of Acts (very much alive) and Paul as we know he soon will be (dead), and second, between Paul dead and Paul's final state. Final justice will be restored by the resurrection of bodies at the end of time. Again, the 'gap' at the end of Acts is filled by the beginning, with its developing stress on resurrection (1.3; 2.24, 31–2; 3.15, 22; 4.2).

Thus on another level, the harshly realistic, even, in a sense, non-divine end of Acts, necessarily involves its own deconstruction, its own reversal: from real time and harsh reality—trans*cended* by Christian faith—to the literal fulfilment of the Christian *muthos* at the end of time.

There are again decisive differences from Dionysus-religion. *Bacchae* ends with misery for all the main characters, Dionysus' savagery made manifest, as he punishes even his followers because they were slow to accept him. He is merciless and his justice is partial.[120] Unlike *Bacchae*, however, Acts is not, finally, a tragedy. In contrast to Dionysus, Jesus forgave Saul the persecutor and the whole trajectory of Saul-Paul and of Paul's heroic progress to Apostleship, to spiritual freedom, to martyrdom, and to the general resurrection at the end of time illustrates both the perfect justice and the loving forgiveness of the one true God. That general resurrection at the end of time 〖94〗 itself decisively trumps Dionysus' promise of eternal life as made only to his initiates.

Acts, then, both enacts Jesus religion's peaceful appropriation of Dionysus and in the end demonstrates Dionysus' comprehensive inferiority. The latter purpose might seem *de trop*, since Luke obviously regards Christianity as true and Dionysus worship as false. But he is writing in a competitive religious market and needs to show that even the formal claims of Dionysus worship are inferior.

### *Larger Religious and Political Contexts*[121]

Jewish history and the geographical position of Palestine brought Jewish monotheism and pagan polytheism into constant contact, both within Palestine

---

120  Seaford (1996) 37–9, 44–52, and 252–3 convincingly argues that the punishment is restricted to the ruling family and that Dionysus benefits the polis as a whole. My remarks apply to the main *dramatis personae*.
121  Herewith extreme generalisation and simplification; essential background: Hengel (1974); critical assessment: Millar (2006) 32–90.

itself (and even within Judaea) and in the Diaspora. While the contact was generally hostile, there were complicating factors. Some Jewish religious symbols looked Dionysiac to non-Jews (some may well have been inspired by Dionysiac symbols[122]) and many Greeks and Romans[123] (and some Jews[124]) identified Yaweh with Dionysus. Pagan henotheism—which greatly benefited Dionysus[125]—could shade into practical monotheism. The 'Highest' God was widely, though not always, seen as Jewish.[126] Within Palestine some Greek cities honoured Dionysus and when Hellenistic kings sought to promote Dionysus among Jews they made converts. This is the background to 1–3 Maccabees.[127] There were always Jews who compromised (in varying degrees) with paganism.[128]

⟦95⟧ Law-observant Jews could either condemn paganism absolutely, or, while denying the pagan gods, seek to channel the underlying religious feelings into worship of the one true god. Thus definition and right naming become essential. Acts 17 starts from this Jewish proselytising tradition,[129] and definition and right naming are everywhere important in Acts.[130]

Both for Jews and non-Jews, the religious question was necessarily also political, and tensions necessarily worsened under Gentile rulers who claimed to be divine, especially when they claimed to be 'New Dionysuses'. Hence the concerns of 2 and 3 Maccabees. And, although the Dionysiac threat was particularly acute from Antiochus Epiphanes and Ptolemy Philopator, it was recurrent, because the role of 'new Dionysus' was claimed by many Gentile rulers, including—in the recent past—Mark Antony.[131]

The complexities of the relations between Yaweh and Dionysus increased with Jesus. In Luke, as in the other Gospels, parallels and contrasts are drawn between Jesus and Dionysus.[132] If the historical Jesus made divine claims for

---

122  Alföldi (1973) 138, with bibliography; Goodenough (1988) 60–1, 75–7, 138–9, 141–3; 251ff.
123  Val. Max. 1.2 ext. 3; Plut. *Quaest. Conv.* 4.6.1–2, 671C–672C; Tac. *Hist.* 5.5.5; Alföldi (1973) 137–8; Feldman (1996) 367–9; 540–6.
124  Smith (1975) 821–4.
125  Versnel (1990).
126  Mitchell (1999). Hence the ambiguities of the incident with the prophetic slave girl (Acts 16.16ff.).
127  Discussion: Hengel (1974) I.284–309; II.188ff.; Schäfer (2003) 42–4; Hacham (2005); S. Johnson (2005); Millar (2006) 67–90.
128  Hengel (1974) I.264; Barclay (1996) 130–2; Thiede (2004) 93–4.
129  Barrett (2004) 825.
130  The phenomenon can of course be analysed in Classical as well as Jewish terms.
131  Lane Fox (1973) 44–5, 508, 340–2, 339–400, 539–40; Rice (1983) 49–102, 189, 191–2; Cohen (1997) 158; Arr. *Ind.* 1.4–5; 5.12; Plut. *Ant.* 24; Sen. *Suas.* 1.6.
132  Tueller (1992) *passim*; John 2.1–11; 15.1; Keener (2003) 495; p. 560 above.

himself,[133] then, given the history of the relations between Yaweh, whom Jesus regarded as his father, and Dionysus, the *historical* Jesus *may* have drawn these parallels and contrasts, some of which seem to go back as early as Q.[134] They are certainly intrinsic to the Gospels' representation of Jesus' self-representation. From the Pentecost episode on, with its links back into Luke, Acts also recognises these ambiguous links between Jesus and Dionysus. The dramatic Paul also recognises them, because his third account of his conversion quotes *Bacchae*. How much the historical Paul knew about the historical Jesus is highly disputable, but unless Paul's account, in First Corinthians, of the institution of the Lord's Supper has no authority outside Paul ⟦96⟧ himself,[135] Paul must have known of the connection between Jesus and Dionysus, because the Lord's Supper, if not based on Dionysiac cult, inevitably invites comparison with it,[136] just as '*I* am the true Vine' (John 15.1) *includes* dismissal of Dionysus.[137]

Jesus' death and alleged resurrection further increased the parallels between the two gods, parallels widely recognised in the ancient world, both by pagans and by Christians.[138] The process began early. First Corinthians (in the 50s) runs a series of analogies between the Christian 'mystery' and pagan mysteries, especially Dionysus'.[139] Why? Negatively, Christianity has no choice but to acknowledge the parallels with Dionysus: they are so obvious that they have to be coped with. Positively, Paul clarifies the Christian mystery by comparison and contrast with its nearest pagan equivalent and thereby shows Christianity's superiority. One passage even implies that some of his addressees had come to Christianity through Dionysiac cult, as did later Christians such as Tatian.[140]

All these things in First Corinthians are also found in Acts. If Luke was Paul's companion,[141] was the *historical Paul* one of Luke's inspirations for his

---

133  Discussion: Dunn (2003) 718–24; Thiede (2004) 58–72 (decisive, I think).
134  Hypothetical but (in my view) certain source of the 50s; note esp. Luke 7.32 with n. 37 above.
135  The 'Jewish view' of 1 Cor. 11.23: Maccoby (1991); Vermes (2000) 73–4.
136  Cf. p. 560 above; the huge controversy whether there was actual Dionysiac influence is immaterial here.
137  Smith (1975) 818.
138  E.g., Orig. *Contra Cels.* 1.9; 2.34; 3.16; 4.10; 8.41f., 48; *Protrept.* 12; Just. Mart. *Ap.* 1.21.2, 54.6; *Dial.* 69.2; Clem. Alex. *Protr.* 2.19.3, 22.4; the *Christus Patiens*; Burkert (1987) 3; 134 n. 11. Dionysus is shockingly absent from Wright (2003) and Hurtado (2005).
139  Controversial but (in my view) certain (though several readers have warned me off these contentious areas). Cf., e.g., 2.6–7 with Héring (1949) 25; 10.14–22 with Collins (1999) 376; 12.2 with Dunn (2004) 298; 13.12 with Seaford (1984) (important).
140  Acts 12.2; Tat. *Or. ad Graec.* 29, with Sanders (2000) 113–14.
141  Still plausible: Bruce (1951) 2–3; Hemer (1989) 309–64; Dunn (1996) x, 118; Brown (1997) 267ff., 322–7.

Dionysicised Jesus? Did Paul actually quote *Bacchae* before Agrippa II and Berenice? Festus' reaction in 26.24—'Paul, you're mad. Your many-letteredness[142] is 〚97〛 turning you to madness'—seems to express exasperation at a virtuosic multicultural display. This seems to be a serious component of Luke's representation of Paul. Paul's knowledge of *Bacchae* can surely be assumed.[143]

Perhaps, then, in, so to speak, an international context, it was Paul who first mythologised his encounter with the risen Jesus as a Dionysiac event. Coming as it does three times, this encounter is the key conversion encounter with Jesus in Acts. The preoccupation of Acts, then, with Dionysus would have a double pedagogical significance. Not only would Acts emerge as a Christian teaching text which appropriated Dionysus to the new Jesus religion; it would also itself attest one of the ways—and a very important way—in which Paul and his companions actually did 'sell' Jesus: as the new Dionysus, whose virtues nevertheless eclipsed Dionysus' in every possible respect.

Such Pauline influence, however, would explain only a fraction of the immense riches of Luke's exploitation of Dionysiac material. Besides all the others discussed, there remains Acts' relationship—even dialectic—with 1–3 Maccabees.

In 2 and 3 Maccabees the Dionysicised Yaweh brings religious and political liberation from deranged Syrian and Egyptian kings who try to impose Dionysus upon the Jews. Nevertheless, 3 Maccabees advocates generic political loyalty to 'the kings'.[144] Now, many scholars see Acts as offering a broadly favourable portrayal of Roman power. Granted that Roman justice is better than Jewish lynch mobs and that there are 'good Romans', this general emphasis is hardly right.[145] In any case, there was bound to be a greater incompatibility between Christians and their Roman rulers than between Jews and their Syrian and Egyptian kings (and their Roman successors). Not only had Gentile rulers had plenty of time to reach broad accommodations with the Jews, unlike the Romans with the new Christian movement, but Christianity was a far more actively proselytising religion than Judaism and it was committed

---

142 Interpretation: Bruce (1951) 448; Barrett (2004) 1167. Contrastingly, Peter and John are perceived by the high priest and Sadducees as ἀγράμματοι (4.13). The point, presumably, is a 'both-and' one: the first Christian leaders embrace the 'unlettered' and the 'lettered'; while Christianity does not *need* great learning, it can hold its own in that world (cf. Klauck [2000] 94–5 on Acts 17); and the same is true of Acts itself. Luke deflects accusations (both pagan and Jewish) of Christian 'uneducatedness'.
143 Thiede (2004) 13–32.
144 3 Macc. 3.3–7; further Johnson (2005).
145 Useful correctives in Jervell (1996) 100–6; Brown (1997) 271; Klauck (2000) 43–4; and the essays in Labahn–Zangenberg (2002).

to proselytising throughout the Empire. Between Rome, with its kings (as the emperors were generally viewed), ⟦98⟧ polytheism, ruler-cult, and claims to an empire extending to the ends of the earth, and monotheistic Christianity, which aimed to extend 'the servant Kingdom' to the ends of the earth, there was a real conflict of power and of different kinds of power. Here again Luke seems to be developing a Maccabean motif, for 1 Maccabees makes play with the theme of 'the end(s) of the earth', as a marker both of imperial power and of religious power and in relation to different 'centres' (Alexandria, Judaea, Rome).[146] Luke's conceptualisation of the new religion—or new form of religion, in both its religious and its political aspects—is thus far more complex than anything in 2 and 3 Maccabees. Since Acts applies the process of Dionysification to Jesus rather than to Yaweh, Christianity emerges *both* as a freedom movement *and* as—in some sense—an imperialist movement, and these two things both *within* Judaism, *between* Christians and Gentiles, and *among* Gentiles. Luke fully apprehended the Dionysiac transgressiveness so emphasised by modern scholarship, and he appropriated it to the utmost: to the ends of the earth, in fact.[147]

Dionysius the Areopagite, pseudo-Dionysius the Areopagite, St Denis, Denis, Denise, Dennis the Menace, for Classicists, Denis Feeney ... Acts 17.34 is the single door by which all these names and personages come into the Christian, or post-Christian, world. But their very existence is due to an error in literary criticism.[148] Dionysius the Areopagite is an Orthodox saint, and on his feast-day of October 3rd Greek women decorate his icons with vine leaves. They think they know who he really is. They are right to be suspicious of Dionysius' identity and right also to intuit that the Acts of the Apostles is deeply permeated with the Dionysiac. The theology, however, is a little simple.

## Bibliography

Adams, E. and D. G. Horrell, edd. (2004) *Christianity at Corinth: The Quest for the Pauline Church* (Louisville and London).

Alexander, L. C. A. (2005) 'New Testament Narrative and Ancient Epic', in ead., *Acts in Its Ancient Literary Context: A Classicist Looks at the Acts of the Apostles* (London and New York) 165–82.

---

146  1.1–3; 3.9; 8.4; cf. 2.9.17.
147  Dionysus is one of the greatest 'international traveller' gods: cf. *Bacch.* 13–22 and the myth of Dionysus in India (quintessentially, an 'end of the earth').
148  P. 572 and n. 91 above.

Alföldi, A. (1973) 'Redeunt Saturnia regna II: an Iconographical Pattern', *Chiron* 3: 131–42.

Bakker, E. J., I. J. F. de Jong, and H. van Wees, edd. (2002) *Brill's Companion to Herodotus* (Leiden).

Barclay, J. M. G. (1996) *Jews in the Mediterranean Diaspora from Alexander to Trajan (323 BCE–117 CE)* (Edinburgh).

Barrett, C. K. (2004) *A Critical and Exegetical Commentary on The Acts of the Apostles, Volumes I and II* (London and New York).

Boedeker, D. (2002) 'Epic Heritage and Mythical Patterns in Herodotus', in Bakker–de Jong–van Wees (2002) 97–116.

Brant, J.-A., C. W. Hedrick, and C. Shea, edd. (2005) *Ancient Fiction: the Matrix of Early Christian and Jewish Narrative* (Leiden and Atlanta).

Brenk, F. E. (1994) 'Greek Epiphanies and Paul on the Road to Damascus', in U. Bianchi, ed., *The Notion of 'Religion' in Comparative Research* (Rome) 415–24; repr. in F. E. Brenk, *Relighting the Souls: Studies in Plutarch, in Greek Literature, Religion and Philosophy, and in the New Testament Background* (Stuttgart, 1988) 354–63.

Brown, R. E. (1997) *An Introduction to the New Testament* (New York, London, Toronto, Sydney, and Auckland).

Bruce, F. F. (1951) *The Acts of the Apostles: the Greek Text with Introduction and Commentary* (London).

Buell, D. K. (2005) *Why this New Race? Ethnic Reasoning in Early Christianity.* (New York).

Burkert, W. (1987) *Ancient Mystery Cults* (Cambridge, Mass. and London).

Cohen, A. (1997) *The Alexander Mosaic: Stories of Victory and Defeat* (Cambridge).

Colaclides, P. (1973) '*Acts* 17, 28a and *Bacchae* 506', *Vigiliae Christianae* 27: 161–4.

Collins, R. F. (1999) *First Corinthians.* (Collegeville, Minn.).

Conzelmann, H. (1972) *Die Apostelgeschichte*$^2$ (Tübingen).

Cousland, J. R. C. (2001) 'Dionysus Theomachos? Echoes of the *Bacchae* in 3 Maccabees', *Biblica* 82: 539–48.

Dibelius, M. (1956) *Studies in the Acts of the Apostles* (London and New York).

Dodds, E. R., ed. (1960) *Euripides: Bacchae*$^2$ (Oxford).

Dormeyer, D. (2005) 'Bakchos in der Apostelgeschichte', in Haehling (2005) 153–72.

Dormeyer, D. and G. Galindo (2003) *Die Apostelgeschichte: ein Kommentar für die Praxis* (Stuttgart).

Dunn, J. D. G. (1996) *The Acts of the Apostles* (Peterborough).

Dunn, J. D. G. (2003) *Jesus Remembered: Christianity in the Making*, vol. 1 (Grand Rapids and Cambridge).

Dunn, J. D. G. (2004), 'Reconstructions of Corinthian Christianity and the Interpretation of 1 Corinthians', in Adams–Horrell (2004) 295–310.

Feldman, L. H. (1996) *Studies in Hellenistic Judaism* (Leiden, New York, and Cologne).

Fiebig, P. (1926) 'Zu den Wundern der Apostelgeschichte', *Angelos* 2: 157–8.

Fitzmyer, J. A. (1998) *The Acts of the Apostles: a New Translation with Introduction and Commentary* (New York, London, Toronto, Sydney, and Auckland).

Frankemölle, H., ed. (1998) *Der ungekündigte Bund? Antworten des Neuen Testaments* (Freiburg).

Freyne, S. (2000) *Galilee and Gospel: Collected Essays* (Tübingen).

Freyne, S. (2004) *Jesus, a Jewish Galilean: a New Reading of the Jesus-Story* (London and New York).

Frischer, B. (1982) *The Sculpted Word: Epicureanism and Philosophical Recruitment in Ancient Greece* (Berkeley, Los Angeles, and London).

Funke, H. (1965–6) 'Euripides', *JAC* 8/9: 233–79.

Gill, D. W. J. and C. Gempf, edd. (1994) *The Book of Acts in its Graeco-Roman Setting* (Grand Rapids).

Goodenough, E. R. (1988) *Jewish Symbols in the Greco-Roman Period*, edited and abridged by J. Neusner (Princeton).

Haacker, K. (2003) 'Paul's Life', in J. D. G. Dunn, ed., *The Cambridge Companion to St Paul* (Cambridge) 19–33.

Hacham, N. (2005) '3 Maccabees: An Anti-Dionysiac Polemic', in Brant–Hedrick–Shea (2005) 167–83.

Hackett, J. (1956a) 'Echoes of Euripides in Acts of the Apostles?', *Irish Theological Quarterly* 23: 218–27.

Hackett, J. (1956b) 'Echoes of the *Bacchae* in Acts of the Apostles?', *Irish Theological Quarterly* 23: 350–66.

von Haehling, R., ed. (2005) *Griechische Mythologie und frühes Christentum* (Darmstadt).

Haenchen, E. (1971) *The Acts of the Apostles* (Oxford and Philadelphia).

Harrisville, R. A. (1955) 'The Concept of Newness in the New Testament', *JBL* 74: 69–79.

Harrisville, R. A. (1960) *The Concept of Newness in the New Testament: an Exegetical Inquiry into the Nature and Life of the New Order* (Minneapolis).

Hauser, H. J. (1979) *Strukturen der Abschlusserzählung der Apostelgeschichte (Apg 28,16–31)* (Rome).

van den Heever, G. (2005) 'Novel and Mystery: Discourse, Myth and Society' in Brant–Hedrick–Shea (2005) 89–114.

Hemer, C. J. (1989) *The Book of Acts in the Setting of Hellenistic History* (Tübingen; repr. Winona Lake, Ind., 1990).

Hengel, M. (1974) *Judaism and Hellenism: Studies in their Encounter in Palestine during the Early Hellenistic Period*, 2 vols. (London and Philadelphia).

Henrichs, A. (1982) 'Changing Dionysiac Identities', in B. F. Meyer and E. P. Sanders, edd., *Jewish and Christian Self-Definition III: Self-Definition in the Graeco-Roman World* (London) 137–60.

Henrichs, A. (1993) '"He Has a God in Him": Human and Divine in the Modern Perception of Dionysus', in T. H. Carpenter and C. A. Faraone, edd., *Masks of Dionysus* (Ithaca and London) 13–43.

Héring, J. (1949) *La première épître de Saint Paul aux Corinthiens* (Neuchatel and Paris).

Hintermaier, J. (2003) *Die Befreiungswunder in der Apostelgeschichte: motiv- und formkritische Aspekte sowie literarische Funktion der wunderbaren Befreiungen in Apg 5,17–42; 12,1–23; 16,11–40* (Berlin and Vienna).

Hooker, M. D. (2003) *Endings: Invitations to Discipleship* (London and Peabody, Mass.).

Hunter, R. L. (1983) *A Study of Daphnis and Chloe* (Cambridge).

Hurtado, L. W. (2005) *How on Earth did Jesus become a God?: Historical Questions about Earliest Devotion to Jesus* (Grand Rapids).

Jervell, J. (1996) *The Theology of the Acts of the Apostles* (Cambridge).

Johnson, L. T. (1992) *The Acts of the Apostles* (Collegeville, Minn.).

Johnson, S. (2005) 'Third Maccabees: Historical Fictions and the Shaping of Jewish Identity in the Hellenistic Period' in Brant–Hedrick–Shea (2005) 185–97.

Keener, C. S. (2003) *The Gospel of John: a Commentary*, 2 vols. (Peabody, Mass).

Klauck, H.-J. (2000) *Magic and Paganism in Early Christianity: the World of the Acts of the Apostles* (Edinburgh).

Labahn, M. and J. Zangenberg, edd. (2002) *Zwischen den Reichen: Neues Testament und römische Herrschaft* (Tübingen and Basel).

Lane Fox, R. (1973) *Alexander the Great* (London).

Lang, M. (2003) 'How a Roman Can Read Luke-Acts', unpublished paper given at the 58th SNTS-Meeting (Bonn) {cf. now Lang (2011)}.

Lang, M. (2004) 'Review of Macdonald (2003)', *BMCR* 2004.08.13.

Lang, M. (2011) 'The Christian and the Roman Self: The Lukan Paul and a Roman Reading', in C. K. Rothschild and T. W. Thompson, edd., *Christian Body, Christian Self: Concepts of Early Christian Personhood* (Tübingen) 151–74.

Lieu, J. M. (2002) *Neither Jew nor Greek?: Constructing Early Christianity* (Edinburgh and New York; second edition, 2016).

Lieu, J. M. (2004) *Christian Identity in the Jewish and Graeco-Roman World* (Oxford).

Löning, K. (1998) 'Eschatologische Krise und (Neuer) Bund: zum Stellenwert des Bundes-Motivs im Zusammenhang neutestamentlicher Soteriologien', in Frankemölle (1998) 78–116.

Lüdemann, G. (1989) *Early Christianity according to the Traditions in Acts* (Minneapolis).

Maccoby, H. (1991) 'Paul and the Eucharist', *NTS* 37: 247–67.

MacDonald, D. R. (2003) *Does the New Testament Imitate Homer? Four Cases from the Acts of the Apostles* (New Haven).

Marincola, J. (1997) *Authority and Tradition in Ancient Historiography* (Cambridge).

Millar, F. (2006) *The Greek World, the Jews, and the East* (Chapel Hill).

Mitchell, S. (1999) 'The Cult of Theos Hypsistos between Pagans, Jews, and Christians', in P. Athanassiadi and M. Frede, edd., *Pagan Monotheism in Late Antiquity* (Oxford) 81–148.

Moles, J. L. (1983) 'Dio Chrysostom: Exile, Tarsus, Nero and Domitian', *LCM* 8: 130–4 [above, Ch. 2].

Moles, J. L. (1993) 'Livy's Preface', *PCPhS* 39: 141–68; repr. in J. Chaplin and C. S. Kraus, edd., *Livy* (Oxford Readings in Classical Studies; Oxford, 2009) 49–86 [vol. 2, Ch. 50].

Moles, J. L. (1996) 'Herodotus Warns the Athenians', *PLLS* 9: 259–84 [vol. 2, Ch. 52].

Moles, J. L. (2002) 'Poetry, Philosophy, Politics and Play: *Epistles* 1', in T. Woodman and D. Feeney, edd., *Traditions and Contexts in the Poetry of Horace* (Cambridge) 141–57, 235–7 [vol. 2, Ch. 72].

Moles, J. L. (2005) 'The Thirteenth Oration of Dio Chrysostom: Complexity and Simplicity, Rhetoric and Moralism, Literature and Life', *JHS* 125: 112–38 [above, Ch. 10].

Moles, J. L. (2011) 'Jesus the Healer in the Gospels, the Acts of the Apostles, and Early Christianity', *Histos* 5: 117–82 [below, Ch. 23].

Moles, J. L. (2013) 'Greek, Roman, Jewish, and Christian Philosophy in Luke-Acts' [below, Ch. 28].

Nestle, W. (1900) 'Anklänge an Euripides in der Apostelgeschichte', *Philologus* 49: 46–57.

Omerzu, H. (2001) 'Das Schweigen des Lukas: Überlungen zum offende Ende der Apostelgeschichte', in F. W. Horn, ed., *Das Ende des Paulus: historische, theologische und literaturgeschichte Aspekte* (Berlin and New York) 128–56.

Pervo, R. I. (1987) *Profit with Delight: the Literary Genre of the Acts of the Apostles* (Philadelphia).

Rapske, B. M. (1994) *The Book of Acts and Paul in Roman Custody* (Grand Rapids).

Rice, E. E. (1983) *The Grand Procession of Ptolemy Philadelphus* (Oxford).

Rudberg, G. (1926) 'Zu den Bacchen des Euripides', *SO* 4: 29–35.

Rutherford, R. B. (1982) 'Tragic Form and Feeling in the *Iliad*', *JHS* 102: 145–60.

Saïd, S. (2002) 'Herodotus and Tragedy', in Bakker–de Jong–van Wees (2002) 117–47.

Sanders, J. T. (2000) *Charisma, Converts, Competitors: Societal Factors in the Success of Early Christianity* (London).

Schäfer, P. (2003) *The History of the Jews in the Greco-Roman World* (London and New York).

Seaford, R. (1984) 'Through a Glass Darkly', *JTS* 35: 117–20.

Seaford, R. (1997) 'Thunder, Lightning and Earthquake in the *Bacchae* and the Acts of the Apostles', in A. B. Lloyd, ed., *What is a God? Studies in the Nature of Greek Divinity* (London) 139–51.

Seaford, R. (2006) *Dionysos* (London and New York).

Seaford, R., ed. (1996) *Euripides: Bacchae* (Warminster).

Smend, F. (1925) 'Untersuchungen zu den Acta-Darstellungen von der Bekerung des Paulus', *Angelos* 1: 34–45.

Smith, M. (1975) 'On the Wine God in Palestine (Gen. 18, Jn. 2 and Achilles Tatius)', in S. Lieberman and A. B. Hyman, edd., *Salo Wittmayer Baron Jubilee Volume*, 3 vols. (Jerusalem) II.815–29.

Thiede, C. P. (2004) *The Cosmopolitan World of Jesus: New Findings from Archaeology* (London).

Tschiedel, H. J. (1975) 'Ein Pfingstwunder im Apollonhymnus (Hymn. Hom. Ap. 156–64 und Apg 2,1–13)', *ZRG* 27: 22–39.

Tueller, M. (1992) 'Literary Representations of the New God: Jesus and Dionysus' (B.A. thesis, Harvard).

Vermes, G. (2000) *The Changing Faces of Jesus* (London; New York, 2001).

Versnel, H. S. (1990) *Inconsistencies in Greek and Roman Religion, Vol. 1 Ter Unus* (Leiden).

Voegeli, A. (1953) 'Lukas und Euripides', *Theolog. Zeit.* 9: 415–38.

Wallace, R. and W. Williams (1993) *The Acts of the Apostles: a Companion* (London and New York).

Weaver, J. B. (2004) *Plots of Epiphany: Prison-Escape in the Acts of the Apostles* (Berlin).

Weinreich, O. (1929) 'Gebet und Wunder', in *Genethliakon Wilhelm Schmid* (Stuttgart) 169–452.

Windisch, H. (1932) 'Die Christusepiphanie vor Damaskus (Acta 9.22 u. 26) u. ihrer religionsgeschichtlichen Parallelen', *ZNW* 31: 1–23.

Wright, N. T. (2003) *The Resurrection of the Son of God* (London).

CHAPTER 22

# Luke's Preface: The Greek Decree, Classical Historiography, and Christian Redefinitions

Luke 1.1–4:

> Ἐπειδήπερ πολλοὶ ἐπεχείρησαν ἀνατάξασθαι διήγησιν περὶ τῶν πεπληροφορημένων ἐν ἡμῖν πραγμάτων, (2) καθὼς παρέδοσαν ἡμῖν οἱ ἀπ᾽ ἀρχῆς αὐτόπται καὶ ὑπηρέται γενόμενοι τοῦ λόγου, (3) ἔδοξε κἀμοὶ παρηκολουθηκότι ἄνωθεν πᾶσιν ἀκριβῶς καθεξῆς σοι γράψαι, κράτιστε Θεόφιλε, (4) ἵνα ἐπιγνῷς περὶ ὧν κατηχήθης λόγων τὴν ἀσφάλειαν.

[[462]] Since indeed many have set their hand to draw up a narrative guide about the things done which have been brought to fulfilment amongst us, (2) just as those who were from the beginning eyewitnesses and servants of the word gave them on to us, (3) it seemed good to me also, having closely followed all of them accurately from the up, to write/inscribe them down for you in order, most powerful Theophilos, (4) so that you may additionally know/experience/recognise the truth/security/safety about the words in which you have been orally instructed.

## 1 Preliminary Questions*

All agree that the Preface exhibits many formal features of Greek prose prefaces. Disagreement concerns generic claims, literary register, and quality; many find the Preface over-compressed, over-allusive, ambiguous, and obscure.[1]

While the Preface has generally been read as historiographical,[2] much recent discussion has been driven by Loveday Alexander's claims: there are strikingly close and numerous parallels, alike of thought, structure, rhetoric,

---

\* For diverse help I thank: Professors Loveday Alexander, Edward Harris, Peter Rhodes, and Tony Woodman; Drs Andrew Gregory and Todd Curtis; the anonymous reader and the Editor; none of these necessarily agrees with me. Translations are mine. This paper, while independent, has points of contact with: 'Luke-Acts as a Multimedia Text' (*Histos*, forthcoming) {never published}; Moles (2013); and Moles (2014).
1 E.g., Alexander (1993) 103–5, 175.
2 Seminally, Cadbury (1922).

and vocabulary, with the prefaces of scientific, medical, or technical works;[3] Luke's narrative exhibits similar 'professional-man' style[4] indicative of his general culture and social status and those of his projected readership/audience;[5] the Preface should accordingly be read as that of a technical/scientific work.

This last claim is critical—and counter-intuitive. As many observe and Alexander concedes,[6] not only is Luke, or Luke–Acts,[7] *narrative* but it is some sort of *historical narrative* (whether biography or Gospel does not affect the general point). Moreover, among numerous arguments (some given below) for ⟦463⟧ reading the Preface as historiographical, the first and decisive[8] is that, while διήγησιν (1) does not *necessarily* denote narrative, it must do so when it is a διήγησις of 'the things done which have been brought to fulfilment amongst us';[9] that is, a series of past events, and a 'narrative' of past events, especially one 'drawn up'/'written up' 'accurately' and 'in order', and with a beginning and an end, itself denotes historio*graphy*, history *itself* consisting of 'things that happened or that were done' (τὰ γενόμενα/*res gestae*). After this immediate generic 'signal', readers must read the rest of the Preface historiographically, as the narrative broadly confirms. This is to deny neither that Luke 1.1–4 *qua* historiographical preface has original and unusual features (some discussed here) nor the existence of parallels with 'professional' works (but appropriation of 'scientific' terminology was a staple of Greek historiography from the beginning).[10]

The secondary generic question of what *kind* of Greek historiography has also divided opinion, but I read the Preface as evoking primarily the 'Classical' historiography of Herodotus and Thucydides and their followers, including Polybius. Here I contest Alexander's claim that 'we should be looking for Luke's generic models not among the great classical historians ... Thucydides and Herodotus are probably the most difficult to square with the preface ...'[11] and align myself with Eckhard Plümacher, who has highlighted the Preface's

---

3   Selectively: Alexander (1978); (1993); (1986); (1999) 9–26; (2005) 1–6, 12–20, 161.
4   German 'Fachprosa': Rydbeck (1967); Alexander (2005) 3–4, 18–19, 231–52.
5   Alexander (1993) 176–84.
6   Alexander (1999) 23.
7   I accept the general consensus that one writer wrote Luke and Acts, which constitute a two-book unity, and, more controversially, that Luke 1.1–4 is a Preface for that unity, Acts 1.1 introducing a 'second preface'.
8   So, e.g., Green (1997) 1–6; Witherington (1998) 11, 13.
9   This, rather than 'most surely believed': Cadbury (1922) 495–6; Alexander (1993) 111, though the latter may be a secondary implication.
10  Cf., e.g., Thomas (2000); Raaflaub (2002); Hornblower (1987) 129–35.
11  Alexander (2005) 14.

Thucydidean quality.[12] This does not deny other historiographical influences, including later ones,[13] nor the suggestion of 'local history' in 'amongst us',[14] for 'local history' can accommodate Herodotean and Thucydidean influences (cf. Josephus' *Jewish Antiquities*). It is another question whether, or how far, Luke 'delivers' 'Classical' historiography (itself, of course, of considerable diversity and developmental potential), or whether it may not be his strategy to announce a work of [[464]] Classical historiography, while in some ways, already in the Preface and more radically in the narrative, reshaping readers' expectations. The adoption of similar strategies by Greek and Roman historians and biographers has been much discussed by Classicists.[15] Consequently, while the 'biography' model for Luke is persuasive,[16] biography can be subsumed within historiography. Similarly, Augustus' *Res Gestae* subsumes autobiography within historiography.[17] This does not deny that in Luke, as in Classical historians (including Augustus) and biographers, dexterous switching between historiography and biography itself creates meaning.

## 2 The Greek Decree and Lukan and Classical Historiography

My basic thesis is that, granted that Luke 1.1–4 is a formal preface of a common general type and that it announces a work of Greek historiography, the single type of writing that it resembles most is the Greek decree. Some existing treatments have noted relevant points, for example, that: the Preface's grammatical construction is parallel to the Apostolic Decree of Acts 15.24, 25;[18] ἐπειδή is *inter alia* decree language;[19] ἔδοξε κἀμοί is *inter alia* decree language;[20] and ἐπειδή paired with ἔδοξε is decree-like.[21] But these observations remain few and undeveloped.

---

12  Plümacher (2006) 2–9; cf. p. 604, below. I use 'Classical' in the same way as Alexander, as: (1) Greek (and Roman) rather than Jewish; (2) considered normative, both by ourselves and by the ancients. While (2) is less true of Polybius than of Herodotus and Thucydides, he remains in the 'great' Thucydidean tradition.
13  Cf. Bauckham (2006) 119–20.
14  Sterling (1992) 349.
15  E.g., Earl (1972) (on Sallust as 'philosopher'); Kraus (1999); McGing–Mossman (2006); Marincola (2007); below, p. 599.
16  Burridge (1992/2004); Frickenschmidt (1997).
17  P. 598 below.
18  Plummer (1901) 1; Creed (1930) 3.
19  Alexander (1993) 108.
20  Evans (1990) 128; Alexander (1993) 127.
21  Alexander (1993) 127.

The thesis has considerable interpretative implications, which I shall explore. It also validates the Preface's high literary quality. Such a judgement will seem implausible to some,[22] but there are no *a priori* criteria for what Luke could or could not do in these areas, especially in a Preface, a context where ancient authors deploy all their skill to impress readers. The language of great writers 〚465〛 can be very polysemous. The fact that a word, phrase, or image can be explained on one level does not exclude its operating on other levels; and in some contexts, the more levels the better, provided that each separate level retains sufficient definition, and the whole does not collapse into mess. Similarly, apart from the direct addressee, Theophilos,[23] Luke's target audience(s)/readership(s) can be (re-)constructed only from textual pointers ('the implied readership'), and *multiple* target audiences/readerships cannot *a priori* be excluded. If the Preface exhibits detailed allusions to the great Classical writers and densely associative language and imagery, Luke's target audience(s)/readership(s) should include 'Classical' readers, whether highly Hellenised Jews or highly educated Gentiles.[24]

The Greek decree has a standard format, with variations.[25] There are three key elements: a preambular 'since' (ἐπεί/ἐπειδή) clause, which gives the first justification for the decree, as relating to past or present circumstances; a main clause in which the decision is expressed by the impersonal 'it seemed good', plus dative of people or constitutional body; and a purpose (ἵνα) clause, which gives the secondary justification for the decree, as relating to the future. That Luke knows the format might be assumed but is proved by the Apostolic Decree, where an ἐπειδή clause is followed by a decision expressed by the impersonal 'it seemed good', plus a plural dative of person (Acts 15.25, 28). That the third standard element, the purpose clause, is there omitted shows that Luke need not echo the format slavishly: already, then, a sign of his literary sensitivity.

In the Preface, the first clause consists of an ἐπεί-clause, giving the first justification for Luke's work, as relating to past and present circumstances; the third clause is a main clause stating a decision and based on the impersonal 'it seemed good', plus dative; and the fourth clause is a ἵνα clause, giving the secondary justification for Luke's decision to write, as relating to the future. There are, then, objective parallels with the format and vocabulary of Greek decrees

---

22  E.g., Padilla (2009) 416–37.
23  Whoever or whatever Theophilos is (real person? patron? pseudonymous real person? ideal reader?, etc.), *qua* 'most powerful', he seems (many note) to be conceived as of similar worldly status to the Roman governors Felix and Festus: Acts 23.26; 24.3; 26.25.
24  Some educated second-century pagans besides Celsus did read Luke: Cook (1993); Bowersock (1994); König (2006) 230.
25  Rhodes–Lewis (1997) 4–5; Rhodes–Osborne (2003) xix–xx.

and no less than three quarters of the syntactical structure are closely parallel. Obviously, γράψαι ('inscribe') coheres with a decree allusion.[26]

⟦466⟧ This hypothesis does not deny other organising structures, nor that some of these overlap, and interweave, with that of the Greek decree, nor that there are other factors. Many formal prefaces begin with, or contain, 'since'-clauses (or their equivalents);[27] many make the move from 'many people have written about this' to 'I also';[28] and many end with a purpose clause, explaining the benefit to the reader.[29] But introductory 'since'-clauses and final-'so that' clauses acquire an *extra* dimension if they are *integrated* into an *overall pattern* that recalls the Greek decree. It is also true that the movement from an ἐπεί-clause to a decision of the writer's expressed by ἔδοξε is found in other formal prefaces, including 'professional' ones (for example, in Galen's medical and philosophical works).[30] But the fact that Luke's Preface and other formal prefaces share features with Greek decrees does not exclude an *active* decree colouring in Luke. The other formal prefaces may *also* possess decree colouring, and the pattern is more *fully* exemplified in Luke.

Again, there are elements that complicate the decree pattern. Greek decrees' preambular clauses do not properly begin with ἐπειδήπερ: paradoxically, however, that highly emphatic form highlights ἐπειδή as the first element of the text, thus alerting readers to a parallel with the Greek decree's preambular clause, especially as 'bureaucratic' -περ suffixes are common in Greek decrees. Within a Greek decree, it is also highly unusual for the impersonal 'it seemed good' to be followed by a singular person, as if of a people or a constitutional body, or by a first person, whether singular or plural, with similar implication. The usage, however, occurs. Thus a decree of Mausolus of Caria begins: 'it seemed good to Mausolus and Artemisia' (his sister/wife), and then switches to singulars of Mausolus alone,[31] and one of Augustus to the Asian Jews begins: 'it seemed good to me and my council' (Jos. *A.J.* 16.163). The singular is evidently the usage of 'kingly' figures. The Apostolic Decree also uses the first-person plural. In the Preface it is, naturally, *also* relevant that the decree format is being *adapted* to the characteristic first-person singular of writers of prefaces. Similarly, Greek decrees do not say: 'it seemed good to "x" *also*', but 'also' is explained by the fact that the decree format is being *combined* with the 'many have written, so I also' literary format.

---

26   LSJ s.v. II.2.
27   Alexander (1993) 107–8.
28   Alexander (1993) 107–9, 114–15, 126–7.
29   Alexander (1993) 75, 136.
30   Alexander (1993) 108, 127; Galen v.587; vi.816–18; vii.584–6 (Kühn).
31   Rhodes–Osborne (2003) 263–4 (no. 55).

Another marked difference from the decree is the omission of author's name, city, or other identifying information. Partly, this is, doubtless, a 'modest' pose, shared with the other Evangelists, as well as with many 'scientific' writers,[32] and it minimises distraction from the subject matter. But Luke's work cannot 〚467〛 have been formally anonymous: the first-persons would be left hanging; his name must have been inscribed on the *titulus* attached to the physical book.[33] The substitution of a first-person for people or constitutional body is itself thoroughly 'immodest', and in other respects the Preface (as we shall see) makes strong claims for Luke *qua* historiographer. Moreover, omission of one's name within a Preface *can* be paralleled in Classical historians (Xenophon, Sallust, Livy, Arrian, *et al.*), even among those who evoke decree language.[34] The effect is slightly coy: such historians do not memorialise *themselves* in the explicit manner of 'Hecataeus the Milesian' (*FGrHist* 1 F 1a), 'Herodotus the Halicarnassian' (*praef.*), 'Thucydides the Athenian' (1.1.1) or 'Appian the Alexandrian' (*praef.* 15.62) and implicitly rebuke the latter group's self-assertiveness; but they do not actually *conceal* their own identity.

More complex is the inserted clause, 'just as those who were from the beginning eyewitnesses and servants of the word gave them on to us' (2). There are 'scientific' parallels for its form and content.[35] The notion of 'giving on' is also 'school' terminology,[36] suitable both for a 'scientific' claim and for the representation (relevant, as we shall see) of Christianity as being like a philosophical school. But, beyond the fact that 'scientific' colouring can be subsumed within historiography, 'as' clauses epexegetic of the basic historical theme, announced in the first clause as the direct object of an initial verb of writing, are well paralleled in historiographical prefaces,[37] as is the notion of 'handing on'.[38] Luke, *qua* historian non-contemporary at least with the beginnings of his narrative,[39] 〚468〛 needs to appeal both to original eyewitnesses and to

---

32    Alexander (1993) 106 and n. 5.
33    *Pace* Droge (2009); arguments for original titles and names (Hengel [2000] 48–56; Bauckham [2006] 300) are particularly strong for Luke, which does not initially claim to be a Gospel, though of course it is *also* one.
34    Cf., e.g., Arr. *Anab.* 1.12.5, with Moles (1985) 167 {vol. 2, p. 144}; Liv. *praef.* 1, with Moles (1993a) 141 {vol. 2, p. 190}; generally: Marincola (1997) 271–5.
35    Alexander (1993) 117–18, 124.
36    Alexander (1993) 82–5, 118.
37    E.g., Thuc. 1.1.1; 5.26.1 (both, as will emerge, relevant here).
38    E.g., Jos. *c. Ap.* 1.8; note also the insistent παρα-compounds of Thucydides 1.21–2, with Moles (2001) 208 {vol. 2, p. 423}; on historiographical 'tradition' see Marincola (1997) 3–11, 103.
39    This even on the conservative view (which I accept) that Luke was—and implicitly claimed to be—Paul's companion.

reliable tradition. Alexander's denial that αὐτόπται is historiographical[40] is vulnerable both to simple logic—in so densely economical a passage, what single word could better convey historiographical emphasis on eyewitness testimony?[41]—and to the directly relevant examples of Herodotus (five times, both of himself and of figures within the text performing the historian's role),[42] Polybius (3.4.13: Polybius himself) and Josephus (*C. Ap.* 1.55: Josephus himself, imitating Polybius).[43] But 'just as' phrases or clauses are *also* common in Greek decrees, for obvious illustrative or justificatory reasons,[44] so the clause is *compatible* with the decree format.

There are also positive parallels in the narrative.

Acts 15.24–9, which imitates the Greek decree, objectively parallels Luke 1.1–4. Some early copyists evidently thought the parallel significant, because to Luke 1.3 'it seemed good to me' they appended 'and to the Holy Spirit', following Acts 15.28 'it seemed good to the Holy Spirit and to us'.

Another parallel comes at the beginning of the Jesus narrative (Luke 2.1), where the birth of Jesus is synchronised with a 'decree (δόγμα) of Caesar Augustus that all the inhabited world should be **written** out in a list' (ἀπογράφεσθαι). Both these parallels I discuss below.

There is another, very important, 'external', factor. 'Decree' language is intrinsic to the earliest Classical historiography: Hecataeus, Herodotus, and Thucydides all image their Histories as 'inscriptions' or 'monuments'. The tradition is maintained by Polybius, Dionysius, Arrian, and Appian, by the Jewish Josephus, Luke's contemporary,[45] and by the Roman Livy and Augustus.[46] Such historiographical 'decrees' can include the clause 'it seemed good to me'.[47] Of course, the epigraphic pose is found in other genres,[48] and there is also the general comparison of literary works to various prestigious physical objects: Pindar's odes a ⟦469⟧ 'treasury' (*Pyth.* 6.6), Horace's 'a monument' (*C.* 3.30). But the comparison of historiography to inscriptions or monuments seems to have

---

40  Alexander (1993) 120–3.
41  Generally: Marincola (1997) 63–86.
42  2.29.1 (Herodotus himself); 3.115.2 (no eyewitness); 4.16.1 (no eyewitness); 8.79.4 (Aristides); 8.80.1 (Aristides).
43  Cf. Bauckham (2006) 118–19.
44  Examples: Harris (2002) 5 n. 13.
45  Moles (1999) (bibliography at 26 {vol. 2, p. 383} n. 32); (1985) 166 {vol. 2, p. 142}; pp. 602–3 below; Jos. *c. Ap.* 1.3 (echoing Thuc. 1.22.4), 9–11, 21, 23; nothing here requires direct links with Josephus (cf. recently Mason [2005] 251–93), though these, if granted, would 'help' Luke's use of αὐτόπται and the inscription analogy.
46  Respectively, pp. 603 and 597 below.
47  E.g., D. Hal. *A.R.* 1.6.3; note Thucydides' elaborate 'playing' with the formula: 1.22.1–2.
48  Cf. recently Ramsby (2007).

begun independently and to retain independent value. The tradition comports a strong competitive element, with each successive historian implying: 'my inscription supersedes my predecessors' inscriptions', or 'this (my History) is the one possession you readers need'.

An allusion to the Greek decree is, therefore, supported by a combination of factors: the close parallels between the Preface and the decree; the close parallels between the Preface and decree contexts in the narrative; and the fact that Luke is writing Greek historiography, which characteristically exploits the analogy.

## 3 Implications of the Decree Format

Some of the implications are straightforward. Although Luke's knowledge of the decree format *could theoretically* be book-derived, for example, from the many antiquarian collections of decrees, it seems likelier that in this, as generally, he is well informed about the *Realien* of Hellenistic cities.[49] He knows too about the inscriptional inheritance of Greek historiography, and referencing it strengthens his own work's historiographical character. Imitation of the Greek decree implies the same sort of general claims as in the Classical historians mentioned: concrete memorialisation; formal weightiness; the 'authority' of this 'author' (= '*I* am the authority here'); the public nature, availability, utility, durability, and 'monumentality' of this work, parallel to, but exceeding, those of public decrees published on fixed and perishable media such as bronze or stone. Like those Classical historians, Luke hereby targets as wide a 'public' as possible. We should immediately applaud his skill in weaving the decree format into the many-stranded fabric of his Preface.

Other implications are more organic, though space restricts treatment.

## 4 The Christian *Politeia*

Luke's use of the decree format immediately implies that Christianity is a *politeia* (fruitful focus of recent Acts scholarship),[50] in parallel and contrast both with the Jewish *politeia*[51] and—through the address to 'the most powerful ⟦470⟧ Theophilos'—with the *politeia* of the Roman Empire. This suggestion

---

49  Cf., e.g., Wallace-Williams (1993) 26–7; Barrett (2004) cxiv.
50  Cf., e.g., Penner (2004); Rowe (2009) 4–5.
51  Jos. *A.J.* 1.2, etc.

becomes explicit in the Apostolic Decree sequence. When Paul and Barnabas go to Jerusalem to defend their Gentile mission and Pharisee opponents speak for circumcision and the Mosaic law, 'the apostles and the elders gathered together to *"see about* this speech"' (Acts 15.6): the phraseology echoes the Roman judicial formula *videre de*.[52] James, leader of the Jerusalem church, makes a formal 'judgement' (κρίνω, 19). Then (22), 'it seemed good to the apostles and the elders' to send messengers to Antioch, whereupon (24–9) they issue their δόγμα to the Gentile Christians. They are acting as an independent *politeia*, thereby giving concrete substance to the Preface's implication.

This same sequence illuminates another aspect of Christianity *qua politeia*. The Pharisees are described as a αἵρεσις (~ 'philosophical sect');[53] the debate about their 'doctrine' involves 'enquiry' (15.7, ζητήσεως);[54] Paul and Barnabas are 'our beloveds' (15.25, ἀγαπητοῖς)—the notion of 'beloved' disciples, very common in the NT epistles,[55] being one found in 'school' contexts;[56] and the Apostolic Decree enjoins only 'these necessary things' (15.28).[57] As elsewhere in Acts (and in Luke), Christianity is being strongly likened to a philosophical school. Thus the Preface *qua* decree again has an important proleptic function.[58]

Hence, too, another aspect of the 'decree' of Acts 15.24–9: *qua* the δόγμα of a *politeia* which corresponds to a philosophical *politeia*, it corresponds *also* to a *philosophical* δόγμα/'doctrine' (which can, as here, regulate food and sex). Although the term in Greek and Roman philosophy is often colourless, δόγματα can mark a philosophical community as a *politeia*. Epicurus divides δόγματα into 'one's own' (οἰκεῖα) and 'other people's' (ἀλλότρια), terms applicable to one's 'native' country and 'foreign' countries,[59] and characterises appropriation of 'other people's' δόγματα as 'colonisation' (ἀποικίζειν).[60] The philosophical biographer Diogenes Laertius (3.51) elucidates: 'to dogmatise is precisely to lay down *dogmata* as to legislate is to lay down laws'.[61] Again, then, the representation in Acts 15.22–9 of Christianity as a quasi-philosophical *politeia* which issues δόγματα is anticipated in the Preface.

---

52  North (1983).
53  Cf. Acts 5.17; 24.5, 14; 26.5; 28.22; Jos. *B.J.* 1.110; 2.162; *A.J.* 17.41; *Vit.* 189, 191; Mason (2005) 288–91.
54  LSJ s.v. 3.
55  Johnson (1992) 276.
56  Bauckham (2006) 397, 401.
57  LSJ s.v. ἀναγκαῖος, II.2.
58  Further p. 601 below.
59  LSJ s.v. οἰκεῖος; s.v. ἀλλότριος.
60  Epic. *Deperd. lib.* fr. 29.28.5–6, 11–12; fr. 29.30.16; fr. 30.31.1; fr. 31.2.4–6; fr. 36.10.3.
61  Similarly, Cic. *Acad.* 2.27.

〚471〛 5   Luke Himself as Legislator

If the status of Christianity as a *politeia* inevitably raises questions about its relationship to other *politeiai*, these are sharpened by Luke's own role as legislator: what of the powers within his narrative that legislate *literally*? Large and topical question:[62] are such analogies between Christianity and the Roman Empire and the latter's representatives oppositional or accommodationist, sometimes one, sometimes the other, or—even—both (initial accommodation subserving an eschatological perspective that is necessarily oppositional)?

6   Luke's Decree and Augustus'

Strikingly, the Jesus narrative itself *begins* with a 'decree' of Caesar Augustus[63] that 'all the inhabited world should be written out in a list': the thematic parallel between 1.1–4 (Preface) and 2.1–5 (narrative) is reinforced architecturally. In Augustus' alleged decree, there is, undeniably, huge divergence from historical fact,[64] whether this is analysed as simple error or (better) as creative rewriting (many Classicists so analyse similar cases in Classical historians and biographers).[65]

*Qua* 'legislators', Augustus, Roman emperor, and Luke, historian, are implicitly in contrast (on which level, Luke's 'it seemed good to me' is hugely assertive). Augustus' decree represents the Roman claim to world power at its most extreme. Seemingly subject to that power is the holy family, which has to be 'written out in a list' (2.1–5). But the angel Gabriel has just proclaimed that Jesus' 'kingdom' will be 'without end' (1.33), Mary's Magnificat that God has 'dragged dynasts down from their thrones and exalted the lowly' (1.52). Jesus' advent overturns worldly powers. Luke's 'writing' of the holy family surely also betters Augustus' 'writing out'. The relationship between the two decrees carries a message that, for any reader, though especially for such as 'the most powerful Theophilos', is implicitly oppositional: the Christian decree trumps 〚472〛 the Roman one, world-wide though the latter claimed to be. Or rather it does for the already Christian reader: for the non-Christian reader—whether Jewish or Gentile—yet to be persuaded of Christianity's truth, the effect is proleptic, and the narrative proves the case.

---

62   Recently: Kim (2008); Rowe (2009); Yamazaki-Ransom (2010).
63   Recently: Yamazaki-Ransom (2010) 72–4; Blumenthal (2011).
64   Precise treatment: Llewelyn (1992) 123–32.
65   Cf., e.g., the influential Pelling (1980); Moles (1993b).

Consideration of the inspirations of Luke's unhistorical world-wide Augustan census raises interesting perspectives. One inspiration is certainly[66] the census in Judaea in 6 CE under the governor of Syria, Quirinius, after the Romans had removed Herod's son Archelaus and created their own province, which was the catalyst of Jewish revolt.[67] The (probably) non-Jewish Luke hardly knew of this census through oral tradition:[68] better a written source, either Josephus or a common source. But might Luke also have been inspired by another written source, a massive inscription,[69] published in the name of Augustus, written by him in the first person, and entitled: 'Of the deeds of the divine Augustus, by which he set the whole world under the power of the Roman people, and of the expenses which he made for the Republic and for the Roman people, incised on two bronze pillars, which are placed in Rome, an exemplar has been set underneath'?

The original *Res Gestae* stood before Augustus' Mausoleum, which Luke, if companion of Paul,[70] could have seen. Copies were made round the Empire; the three surviving come from Galatia, including Pisidian Antioch, traditionally Luke's home city[71]—certainly one he knows about.[72]

Now why does Luke refer to the 'decree of Caesar *Augustus*', using the transliteration rather than Σεβαστός? R. L. B. Morris suggests avoidance of the Greek's quasi-divine associations.[73] But the very common transliteration 'Augoustos' has similar associations, as Luke's readers would have known. Nor are these associations inert: Christians must reject Augustus' 'divinity' in favour of the true divinity of God and Jesus. Further, Luke emphasises the sheer Roman-ness of the decree, an effect enhanced by mention of Quirinius, a quintessentially Roman name (~ 'Quirites'). Might 'Augustus', then, recall Augustus' own wording in the *Res Gestae*? Intriguingly, the Greek version of that inscription omits the clause 'by which he set *the whole world* under the power of the Roman people'. ⟦473⟧ Further, the *Res Gestae*, as the title proclaims, is a work of historiography, and contains specific generic markers of Greek (and Roman) historiography.[74]

---

66  Another, probably, Ps 87.6: Green (1997) 125 n. 19.
67  Acts 5.37; Jos. *B.J.* 2.117–18; *A.J.* 18.1–5; Mason (2005) 274.
68  *Pace* Syme (1973) 600 {= (1984) III.882–3}.
69  Recently: Scheid (2007); Cooley (2009).
70  Phil. 24; Col. 4.14; 2 Tim 4.11; Acts 28.16, etc.
71  Eus. *HE* 3.4.7; Jer. *vir. ill.* 7.
72  Acts 11.19–30.
73  Morris (1992).
74  Thus Woodman (2012).

Piquantly, then, whereas Luke presents his Greek historiographical work as an inscription, Augustus presents his inscription as a work of Greek historiography. Both, too, are 'exemplary' historiography. Luke–Acts' 'exemplary' character is obvious,[75] and the Latin 'exemplar' connotes both 'copy' and 'moral exemplar' (an important 'internal' theme). Another parallel intrigues. In his Preface Herodotus 'equates' his theme of 'deeds demonstrated' (ἔργα ... ἀποδεχθέντα) with his work, which is a 'demonstration' (ἀπόδεξις). Augustus' Preface imitates this by the repeated 'set under(neath)' ('subiecit'/'subiectum'). Luke's does too. Theophilos has already heard (oral) λόγοι about the λόγος: 'words'[76] about 'the word'; now Luke's *written* λόγος, his 'first *logos*' (Acts 1.1), gives a more authoritative version about/of the λόγος. Luke's Herodotean imitation, missed by NT scholars, is *triply* pointed, λόγος itself being Herodotus' own term for 'historiographical account' (e.g., 1.95.1).[77] There are other possible parallels and contrasts between Luke and Augustus.[78]

Given this series of objective parallels between Luke's and Augustus' historiographical works and given also that Luke 2.1–5 makes a parallel between Augustus' decree and Luke's prefatory 'decree', I suggest that Luke's substantially invented 'decree of Caesar *Augustus* that *all the inhabited world* should be written out in a list' recalls 'the deeds of the divine *Augustus*, by which he set *the whole world* under the power of the Roman people', 'recalls' meaning both 'Luke himself remembers' and 'he wants (some of) his readers to remember'. The very name 'Luke' is a Hellenisation of some Roman name,[79] and indicates familial *Romanitas*. From a Christian perspective, however, the 'examples' of Luke–Acts (Jesus, Peter, John, Stephen, Paul, Barnabas, et al.) far surpass Augustus'. And not only does Luke's 'decree' surpass Augustus', but Luke's inscriptional Greek historiography surpasses Augustus' Greek historiographical inscription, and Luke's Herodotean imitation also surpasses Augustus' (by a ⟦474⟧ factor of four to one!). Classical historians' customary implication that their 'inscriptional' historiography surpasses physical inscriptions here acquires new dimensions that are both ingenious and packed with meaning. No alert 'Classical' reader could fail to be impressed—and challenged.

---

75  E.g., Acts 26.29 (Paul to Agrippa and company).
76  The point disappears in RSV's 'things'; κατηχέω ~ orality: LSJ s.v.; Alexander (1993) 139, 141.
77  Even *quadruply* pointed, for Herodotus' text is also a 'road', just as Luke–Acts is a 'leading through' the 'road' of Christianity (p. 601).
78  E.g., common imitation of/rivalry with Livy's 'exemplary' History: for Augustus ~ Livy see especially Luce (1990); note also 'placed'/'exemplar' (*RG, Praef.*) ~ 'placed'/'example' (Livy *praef.* 10); for Luke ~ Livy see p. 604 below; for another possibility see p. 606 below.
79  Adequate survey: Plummer (1901) xviii.

Augustus' narrative, even theological, role as (inadvertent) facilitator of God's plan[80] cannot erase these systematic negatives.

## 7  Christian Appropriations and Redefinitions

Many commentators find the relationship between Preface and narrative problematic, on the ground that the Preface advertises a work of Classical or Hellenistic historiography, whereas the narrative is held to assume a distinctively Jewish tone and perspective.[81] This 'problem' disappears if one thinks in terms of Christian appropriation and redefinition: what matters is not the Roman *politeia* but the Christian, not the Greek philosophical *politeia* but the Christian philosophical *politeia*, not Augustus' decree, but Luke's Christian decree. The process of redefinition is organic and thoroughgoing and it begins in the Preface itself. The Preface in many respects looks extremely Classical, and Classical historiography is characteristically concerned with what is 'great',[82] a notion glossed by the phrase 'the things brought to *fulfilment*' (1) and consistent with the decree format, Greek decrees often being honorific. A Classical reader might recall Polybius' concern with the 'end' of his work as coterminous with the 'completion' of Roman power (3.1.5–4.1; cf. Polybius' use of αὐτόπτης and his programmatic emphasis on 'beginnings' and 'endings').[83]

But already there are elements suggestive of other perspectives: the Jewish/Christian religious emphases implicit in that same phrase 'the things brought to fulfilment' and in 'servants of the word'; the un-Attic form καθώς;[84] the address to the theophoric 'Theophilos'; the Preface's sheer 'smallness' by comparison with Classical historiographical prefaces, which are characteristically long and elaborate.[85] Then in the narrative, while elements congenial to Classical or Hellenistic taste continue all the way through,[86] the Classical reader (particularly the Gentile reader) progressively grasps that this Jewish-Christian perspective, which seems small and provincial, that of a mere ⟦475⟧ 'corner'

---

80  Blumenthal (2011) 19–21.
81  E.g., Cadbury (1922) 490.
82  Hdt. *praef.*; Thuc. 1.1.1–2, etc.
83  Bauckham (2006) 121–2.
84  So Phrynichus {399 Fischer}.
85  Alexander (1993) 103.
86  Thus, of the immediate narrative, rightly, Johnson (1991) 38: 'the prophecy of Jesus' birth would have made excellent sense to any Hellenistic reader'.

of the world,[87] actually extends both to the end of the earth and to the end of time (Acts 1.8), and is therefore the greatest of all possible historical themes, indeed, a very special, Christian, kind of universal history.[88] It is not therefore accidental that the 'hero' of most of Acts is a 'Mr Little', nor that this 'Mr Little' ends up in Rome, nor that the whole text should be 'small'.[89] Thus the Preface has a sort of proleptic bridging function, Luke's physically 'small' 'decree' 'pre-scribing' the supreme greatness of the seemingly 'small' Jewish-Christian perspective on the world. This interpretation seems implicit in Chrysostom's gloss on Acts 26.26 'not in a corner' (*Hom.* 52.4): 'the doctrine/decree [δόγμα] has been made everywhere in the inhabited world'. That gloss also connects Luke's 'decree' and Augustus'.

It is true that the move from 'big' to 'small' and the paradoxical revaluation of the latter can be found in Classical history-writing, both in historiography proper (especially Herodotus, but also Xenophon and Tacitus) and biography, and in the Socratic writings that influenced some of that history-writing[90] (as indeed they influenced Luke himself). But Luke uses that move to delineate a shift from the very notion of 'the Classical' to the Jewish-Christian.

## 8  The Multiple Implications of the Final Clause

Cadbury and Alexander give useful analyses of the final clause (1.4): ἵνα ἐπιγνῷς περὶ ὧν κατηχήθης λόγων τὴν ἀσφάλειαν.[91] But its full complexities, which are greatly intensified by the decree format, have not generally been appreciated.

## 9  General Implications

Certainly, 'know the truth' is part of the meaning. There are good parallels in Acts and elsewhere;[92] the sentiment is standard in historiography,[93] as in ⟦476⟧

---

87  Acts 26.26 'not in a corner', with Haenchen (1971) 689, cf. John Chrys. *Hom.* 52.4 (quoted in the main text); the phrase also has philosophical implications: Malherbe (1985–6).
88  See Moles (2013).
89  On the name 'Paul' see Moles (2006) 79 {above, p. 565}; Acts 26.22, 24, 28–29 ('meta' of Acts itself).
90  Hdt. 1.5.3–4; Xen. *Hell.* 2.3.56; 7.2.1; Tac. *Ann.* 4.32.1–2; Moles (1998); Nepos, *praef.*; *Pelop.* 1.1; Plut. *Alex.* 1.1–2; Xen. *Sym.* 1.1, etc.
91  Cadbury (1922) 508–10; Alexander (1993) 137–41.
92  Acts 2.36; 25.26; 21.34; 22.30 (the latter two with the simple rather than the compound verb); P. Giss. 1.27 (cited by Cadbury (1922) 509).
93  Thuc. 1.22.4; Moles (1993b); Marincola (1997) 160–2.

'professional' works.⁹⁴ Here, however, there is a double implication, because 'the truth' is not merely 'a true account of the events I have chosen to narrate' (the usual historiographical claim) but 'the Truth': everything readers need to know about 'life, death, and the whole damn thing'. Grammatically, the περί phrase can function as a periphrasis for a genitive,⁹⁵ and 'I shall tell the truth of Christianity' means both 'I shall give a true account of Christianity' and 'I shall show that Christianity is true' (genitive of definition).

Since κατηχέω is characteristically used of oral instruction,⁹⁶ Luke is also contrasting oral and written teaching modes, and ἀσφάλεια can specify 'truth' validated by writing.⁹⁷ But ἀσφάλειαν also falls within a vital image pattern ignored by commentators. The word literally means 'security from falling', can be applied to roads,⁹⁸ and goes with διήγησιν (literally, 'leading through') and παρηκολουθηκότι ('having closely followed') to create an organic 'road imagery' richly sustained in the narratives.⁹⁹ Thus ἀσφάλειαν conveys the 'security' or 'safety' that Theophilos or any reader derives from the truth both of the Christian narrative as related by Luke and of the True Christian Road¹⁰⁰ which that narrative describes, prescribes, and instantiates. Hence yet another vital link between Preface and narrative.

Furthermore, κατηχέω being a 'school' word,¹⁰¹ it is relevant both that 'road imagery' is common in Greek and Roman philosophical texts as well as Jewish/Christian ones and that various philosophical schools promised ἀσφάλεια.¹⁰² Hence ἀσφάλειαν also fits the philosophical representation of Christianity. From this perspective, 'know' the ἀσφάλεια implies both 'know as a fact' and 'experience as a reality'.

---

94  Alexander (1993) 137.
95  LSJ s.v., C.5.
96  See n. 76.
97  Cadbury (1922) 509; Alexander (1993) 140.
98  E.g., Xen. *Hell.* 5.4.51.
99  Cf., e.g., Luke 2.52; 9.51–19.41, with, e.g., Johnson (1991) 163–5; Green (1997) 396–9; Acts 8.30–31; full exploration in Moles (2013).
100 Acts 9.2; 19.9, 23; 22.4; 24.14, 22. 'Road' better conveys the interaction with the organic 'road' imagery than the traditional translation 'Way'.
101 LSJ s.v.
102 E.g., Plut. *Superst.* 171E; Just. Mart. *Dial.* 8.1, cf. Lucian, *Men.* 4; Mason (2005) 285; Dio *Or.* 4.8; Schofield (2000) 437–42; for Stoics, cf. the Lat. *constantia* and Epict. 2.13.7 ('writing a security' as an analogy for correct philosophical behaviour).

## 10  Looking at a Monument Which Cannot Fall

I now consider how the decree imagery affects the final clause, which corresponds both to the secondary justification for the Greek decree and to ⟦477⟧ the 'purpose' element of Classical historiographical prefaces that imitate the decree.

Herodotus' Preface begins:

Ἡροδότου Ἁλικαρνησσέος ἱστορίης ἀπόδεξις ἥδε, ὡς μήτε τὰ γενόμενα ἐξ ἀνθρώπων τῷ χρόνῳ ἐξίτηλα γένηται μήτε ἔργα μεγάλα τε καὶ θωμαστὰ τὰ μὲν Ἕλλησι, τὰ δὲ βαρβάροισι ἀποδεχθέντα ἀκλεᾶ γένηται.

> This is the demonstration of Herodotus of Halicarnassus, in order that neither should the things born from men become faded through time nor should great and wonderful deeds, some demonstrated by Greeks, some by barbarians, become without glory.

There is a strong visual directive (deictic 'this'; 'demonstration'; 'not faded') to a text imaged as an inscription or monument (deictic 'this'; 'not faded'; subsequent switch from third person to first (1.5.3)), which supersedes that of Herodotus' historiographical predecessor Hecataeus.[103]

Within his extended Preface (1.1.1–23.6), imitative of Herodotus', Thucydides states his History's purpose and function (22.4):

ὅσοι δὲ βουλήσονται τῶν τε γενομένων τὸ σαφὲς σκοπεῖν καὶ τῶν μελλόντων ποτὲ αὖθις κατὰ τὸ ἀνθρώπινον τοιούτων καὶ παραπλησίων ἔσεσθαι, ὠφέλιμα κρίνειν αὐτὰ ἀρκούντως ἕξει. κτῆμά τε ἐς ἀεὶ μᾶλλον ἢ ἀγώνισμα ἐς τὸ παραχρῆμα ἀκούειν ξύγκειται.

> But it will be enough that as many as will wish to look at the clear truth both of the things that happened and of those which, in accordance with the human thing, are going to happen again sometime like these and near the present ones should judge it useful. It is set down together as a possession for always rather than as a competition piece for present hearing.

The phrase 'will wish to look at' echoes the Athenian inscriptional formula 'for the person who wishes to look at' [the inscription],[104] and re-establishes

---

103  Moles (1999) 44–53 {vol. 2, pp. 382–91}.
104  Moles (1999) 32–3 with n. 5 {vol. 2, p. 370}.

the analogy, begun at 1.1.1, between History and inscription. The specificatory/restrictive 'as many as' recalls inscriptional terminology,[105] as does the emphasis on perpetuity.[106] Thucydides' readers 'look at' his History as at an imperishable inscription; their 'looking' involves a range of 'sight' processes, from quasi-literal 'looking' (as in 'reading', or in responding to Thucydides' highly 'visual' narratives), to ⟦478⟧ 'observation', to (ideally) true 'insight'.[107] Thucydides' 'inscription' variously supersedes Herodotus'.

Livy states his History's purpose and function, imitating Thucydides (*inter multos alios*), but arguing a much more directly moralising—and implicitly, a superior—value for history (*praef.* 10):

> hoc illud est praecipue in cognitione rerum salubre ac frugiferum, omnis te exempli documenta in inlustri posita monumento intueri: inde tibi tuaeque rei publicae quod imitere capias, inde foedum inceptu, foedum exitu, quod uites.

> This is the thing that is most takingly healthy and fruitful in the getting to know of history: that you look upon the lessons of every kind of example placed on a conspicuous monument: from these you may take for yourself and for your own (e)state—the public state, what you should imitate; from these, disgusting in the undertaking, disgusting in the outcome, what you should avoid.

Livy figures Roman History in general and his History in particular as a great monument, with, as it were, moral inscriptions or prescriptions. This 'monument' will restore the Roman State, previously imaged (9) as a falling/slipping/collapsing building.[108]

In the light, then, both of the general decree element of Luke's Preface and of these passages, which incorporate a 'decree element', from the prefaces of three of the greatest of Luke's historiographical predecessors and competitors, Luke's phrase can *also* be understood as creating the image of *looking at* an imperishable inscription/monument/artefact which *cannot fall*. ἐπιγι-γνώσκω often has a visual implication,[109] and σφάλλω and cognates, including

---

105  Examples in Harris (2002) 4.
106  Moles (1999) 46 {vol. 2, p. 383} n. 32.
107  Moles (2001) 213–15 {vol. 2, pp. 427–30}.
108  Moles (1993a) 153–4 {vol. 2, pp. 208–11}; id. (1999) 19–20 {vol. 2, pp. 402–3}.
109  LSJ s.v., esp. II; similarly, the simplex: LSJ s.v.

passives and negative forms, can be applied to buildings or such, literally and metaphorically.[110]

## 11 Direct Engagement with the Great Classical Historians?

Might Luke even be *intertexting* with Herodotus, Thucydides, or Livy?

Luke's Preface imitates Herodotus multiply in the 'equation' of theme and treatment. There are numerous other commonalities: use of λόγος for 'historical account'; characterisation of the theme as neuter 'things', followed by a middle/passive verb (Hdt. *praef.*);[111] concern with 'beginnings' (1.5.3); use of αὐτόπται; 'road imagery', including the idea of text as journey (1.5.3); claim to represent the Truth (1.5.4); and inversion of 'big things' and 'small things' (1.5.3–4). There is more than enough here to certify an ⟦479⟧ overall Herodotean colouring. But within the broad parallel of a visual inscription or monument there is no precise verbal parallel.

As for Thucydides, most discussions of Luke's speeches adduce Thucydides 1.22; the Luke–Acts narrative contains a brilliant Thucydidean allusion;[112] the Acts Preface plays (I believe) with Thucydidean categories, which favours a Thucydidean presence in the first Preface; and—beyond the broadly 'inscriptional' imagery—there are the following commonalities between Luke and Thucydides' Preface: 'equation' of theme and treatment (Thuc. 1.1.1); epexegetic ὡς-clause (1.1.1); emphasis on eyewitness testimony (1.22.3); 'it seemed to me' formula (1.22.1–2); emphasis on completeness (1.22.1–2); emphasis on ἀκρίβεια (1.22.2); emphasis on truth; claim to represent the Truth; notion that history consists of deeds and words (1.22.1–2); idea that the reader 'looks' at the historical work; visual element emphasised in two contexts: the testimony of the original eyewitnesses and the 'visualness' of the final text (1.22.3–4); contrast between the oral/aural and the written in favour of the latter; use of παρα-compounds; and concern with 'beginnings' (1.23.4). Also parallel, from Thucydides' 'second preface' in Book 5, are: epexegetic ὡς-clause (5.26.1); 'writing … in order' (5.26.1); a series of events from beginning to end (5.26.4); and a direct relationship between 'all' of them and the historian, productive of ἀκρίβεια (5.26.5). There is more than enough here to create a strong Thucydidean colour, which co-exists with, and enhances, the

---

110  E.g., LSJ s.v. σφάλλω, II; note Acts 5.23.
111  γίγνομαι in Herodotus can effectively = 'be done': LSJ s.v., I.2–3.
112  Haenchen (1971) 594 n. 5; Plümacher (1992); Barrett (2004) 983–4; *pace* Kilgallen (1993) and Padilla (2009) 427–9.

Herodotean. The double colouring immediately verifies Luke's mastery of literary allusion. It also reinforces the agonistic character of the Preface.

With Livy, there are the following commonalities: 'equation' of theme and treatment (Liv. *praef.* 1); association of 'knowing' and 'seeing'; cognate forms (ἐπιγνῷς ~ *cogn*itione); commemoration of the Truth in its strongest form; direct second-person-singular addresses (a remarkable effect in Livy); and the notion of *falling* or *not-falling*. Imperial Greek writers' use of Roman authors, formerly dismissed, is now topical in Classical scholarship. Luke himself dexterously 'caps' Virgil's *Aeneid*.[113]

Altogether, then, a 'Classical' reader would read ἵνα ἐπιγνῷς περὶ ὧν κατηχήθης λόγων τὴν ἀσφάλειαν as implying the superiority and greater importance of Luke's 'inscription', theme, and 'solution' to those of the greatest Classical historians, especially Thucydides and Livy.

## [480] 12 The Christian Contract between Luke and His Readers

The visual register immediately creates another implication: 'recognise an obligation',[114] for, while Luke–Acts constantly proffers readers the choice of accepting or rejecting Jesus, there is never any doubt that acceptance is obligatory. As in Thucydides 1.22.4, readers must 'want'—or be brought to want—the end product. Literary theorists regularly discuss the 'contract' between writers and readers. One such 'contract' is genre, characteristically pre-defined in prefaces, often thereafter re-negotiated (as is true of Luke's Preface). But 'contracts' can be much simpler: 'read this, get that'. Such 'contracts' are well conveyed in decree language, decrees characteristically commemorating agreements, alliances, etc. So, of our Classical historians, Thucydides 1.22.4, exploiting decree language, promises to those that 'contract' to read him with sufficient will contemplation and understanding of the Truth of human affairs: no mean reward. Livy's *Preface*, also exploiting decree language, stresses that public-interested behaviour by his readers is also in their interest, and the common goal is the restoration of the collapsing Roman state: a noble and magnificent project and reward.

For his part, Luke promises proof of the truth of Christianity and of the consequent 'safety' of the Christian Road. What, precisely, is that 'safety'? The

---

113 Acts 27.14, 17 ~ *Aen.* 1.102–12; further: Krauter (2009).
114 LSJ s.v., IV.2; note that this gives ἀσφάλειαν yet another image resonance (common in moral/theological contexts): a legal/financial one (LSJ s.v., 6), which makes a 'ring' with 1 πεπληροφορημένων, which can also be 'legal/financial' (LSJ s.v., I.2–3).

security of the truth, of course, meaning, as we have seen, both that this truth is securely true and that it provides security. What, *exactly*, is that security? ἀσφάλεια can be used of *physical* safety; it is regular Greek for 'safe conduct',[115] and in other contexts, including philosophical ones in Cynicism and Epicureanism, 'road imagery' implies this. But Luke–Acts scorns an apologetic alike so feeble and so implausible for contemporary Christians, reading Luke post-Pilate and post-Nero, and, on some datings, post-Domitian and post-Pliny. Rather, it glories in the deaths of Jesus, Stephen, Paul (proleptically), and others, and projects them as exemplary: precisely, examples that may have to be followed. But it repeatedly insists on the 'proven' Christian reward of ultimate resurrection.[116] True, readers have to read the whole text through to understand this final claim of Christian ἀσφάλεια. But that only shows how the Preface's decree imagery creates yet another organic link between Preface and narrative—and the most important link of all. In the last analysis, Christian ἀσφάλεια is underwritten by ἀνάστασις: the resurrection both of Jesus and of humankind: Christians cannot *fall* because they will *stand up*.

⟦481⟧ So also Luke's Preface plays with the notions both of 'up-ness' (ἀνατάξασθαι/ἄνωθεν) and 'down-ness'(καθὼς/καθεξῆς/κατηχήθης); these concepts inform both time and space, and are worked through in the narratives. The 'solution', the transcendental signifier beyond both time and space, is again the ἀσφάλεια of ἀνάστασις.[117]

How would Classical readers contextualise this Christian 'reward'? No Classical historiographical text, however great, and very few Gentile (or even Jewish) texts of any hue, can promise anything like as much. In particular, the *Res Gestae* is one of Luke's historiographical competitors, and, by its very nature, its readers 'look' at it as an inscription. When they read its title, or Preface, they find that, like many Roman 'inscriptions' or 'decrees', the work celebrates the Romans' '*sub*jection' ('subiecit … subiectum') of the whole world.[118] But Luke's readers learn that Luke is concerned both with down-ness and with 'up-ness', that his 'decree' trumps Augustus', and that, while Augustus claims to have set the whole world *under* the power of the Roman people, with Jesus' advent, God has 'dragged dynasts *down* from their thrones and *exalted* the lowly' (1.52). Whereas the *Res Gestae* celebrates the 'subjection' of the world, Luke–Acts

---

115  LSJ s.v., 2.
116  Luke 2.34; 14.14; 20.27, 33, 35, 36; 24.6–7, 34, 46; Acts 1.22; 2.31; 4.2, 33; 17.18, 32; 23.6, 8; 24.15, 21; 26.23, etc.
117  Further on these matters in Moles (2013) and (2014).
118  Cf. the archetypal 'Roman mission' of Virgil *Aen.* 6.847–53: 'you, Roman, remember to rule the peoples with power; your arts will be these: to *im*pose custom upon peace, to spare the *sub*jected and to war *down* the *up*pity'.

celebrates the world's 'security from falling' and its 'up-standing'. No judgement of Roman imperialism could be more damning, no commendation of Christianity more liberating.

More admirably than Augustus, Livy seeks only to reverse the 'fall' of the Roman state. But Luke asserts the ἀσφάλεια of the Christian *politeia* as opposed to the Roman, thereby emphasising the latter's fragility.[119] And for a fifth-century Classical, by now Christian, reader, Luke anticipates Augustine's *De Civitate Dei* by a good three hundred years.

## 13    Luke and His Christian Predecessors

Does the Preface imply that Luke's History surpasses not only the great Classical Histories but also the works of Luke's Christian predecessors? Christian anxiety from the Church Fathers onwards characteristically resists this [[482]] implication.[120] True, Luke avoids the self-naming and bragging of many Classical historians, and 'me also' (3) *formally* implies equality with the 'many' (1). But competitiveness is intrinsic to the decree format; 'many' naturally implies Luke's lateness in the sequence,[121] which augments his competitiveness; 'having closely followed all of them accurately from the top, to write them down for you in order' (3) raises the bar within the Christian tradition; the 'scientific' patina (absent from other Gospels or—surely—from Q) reinforces the claim of objectivity and reliability; the unabashed decision-making is very rare in the Bible (though common in pagan writings) and explains the early copyists' apologetic addition of 'to the Holy Spirit'; and the massive, climactic assurance of ἀσφάλειαν (4) trumps the tentative, initial ἐπεχείρησαν (1). There is also a telling general factor: while previous Evangelists can certainly be regarded as writing in a broadly historical tradition, in formal terms they are writing Gospels or biographies. Luke's Preface, however, co-opts them into 'great' Classical historiography, on which ground he is obviously their superior. Thus Luke's self-presentation as a historian of Christianity poises perfectly between 'I'm only one of many' and 'I'm the best' (a characteristic scholarly stance, Christians not excepted). His 'decree' supersedes the 'decrees' of the other Christian narratives circulating, including Q (to the extent that it was

---

119  I have suggested (Moles [2005] 126 {above, p. 272} n. 140) an organic relationship between Acts and Dio *Or.* 13 (Dio, I now think, influencing Luke). Interesting, therefore, is *Or.* 13.34: '[Rome's] greatness is not at all *secure from falling* [ἀσφαλές]'.
120  Typically: Green (1997) 37 and n. 20; *contra*, e.g., Alexander (1993) 110, 115–16, 133–4; Mason (2005) 254–6; Tyson (2006) 111–13; Strelan (2008) 153.
121  E.g., recently, Tyson (2006) 111.

narrative), Mark, and other Gospels. So too does his superior 'doctrine': Luke would stoutly resist all modern depreciation of his theology.

## 14    Overall Qualities of the Preface

I have treated Luke's Preface from only one aspect, although Luke's writing is so intricate here that this one aspect intersects with many. But I hope to have said enough to establish this Preface as one of the greatest of all Classical historiographical prefaces: masterly in its brevity, compression, complexity, depth of implication, and creative originality; in its aesthetic, literary, intellectual, political, philosophical, and religious demands; and in its organic and multi-functional interactions with the narrative.

### Bibliography

Alexander, L. C. A. (1978) *Luke-Acts in its Contemporary Setting with Special Reference to the Prefaces (Luke 1:1–4 and Acts 1:1)* (D.Phil. thesis, Oxford).

Alexander, L. C. A. (1986) 'Luke's Preface in the Pattern of Greek Preface-writing', *Novum Testamentum* 28: 48–74.

Alexander, L. C. A. (1993) *The Preface to Luke's Gospel: Literary Convention and Social Context in Luke 1.1.4 and Acts 1.1* (Cambridge).

Alexander, L. C. A. (1999) 'Formal Elements and Genre: Which Greco-Roman Prologues Most Closely Parallel the Lukan Prologues?' in D. P. Moessner, ed., *Jesus and the Heritage of Israel: Luke's Narrative Claim upon Israel's Legacy* (Harrisburg, Pa.) 9–26.

Alexander, L. C. A. (2005) *Acts in Its Ancient Literary Context: A Classicist Looks at the Acts of the Apostles* (London and New York).

Barrett, C. K. (2004) *A Critical and Exegetical Commentary on The Acts of the Apostles, Volumes I and II* (London and New York).

Bauckham, R. J. (2006) *Jesus and the Eyewitnesses: the Gospels as Eyewitness Testimony* (Grand Rapids and Cambridge).

Blumenthal, C. (2011) 'Augustus' Erlass und Gottes Macht: Überlegungen zur Charakterisierung der Augustusfigur und ihrer erzählstrategischen Funktion in der lukanischen Erzählung', *NTS* 57: 1–30.

Bowersock, G. W. (1994) *Fiction as History: Nero to Julian* (Berkeley, Los Angeles, and London).

Burridge, R. A. (1992) *What are the Gospels? A Comparison with Graeco-Roman Biography* (Cambridge; Grand Rapids, $^2$2004).

Cadbury, H. (1922) 'Commentary on the Preface of Luke', in F. J. Foakes Jackson and K. Lake, edd., *The Beginnings of Christianity: Part I The Acts of the Apostles*, Volume 2, *Prolegomena II: Criticism* (London) 489–510.

Cook, J. G. (1993) 'Some Hellenistic Responses to the Gospels and Gospel Traditions', ZNW 84: 233–54.

Cooley, A., ed. (2009) *Res Gestae Divi Augusti: Text, Translation and Commentary* (Cambridge).

Creed, J. M. (1930) *The Gospel According to St. Luke: the Greek Text with Introduction, Notes, and Indices* (London).

Droge, A. J. (2009) 'Did "Luke" Write Anonymously? Lingering at the Threshold', in Frey–Rothschild–Schröter (2009) 495–518.

Earl, D. C. (1972) 'Prologue-Form in Ancient Historiography', ANRW I.2: 842–56.

Evans, C. F. (1990) *Saint Luke* (London).

Frey, J., C. K. Rothschild, and J. Schröter, edd. (2009) *Die Apostelgeschichte im Kontext antiker und frühchristlicher Historiographie* (Berlin and New York).

Frickenschmidt, D. (1997) *Evangelium als Biographie: die vier Evangelien im Rahmen antiker Erzählkunst* (Tübingen).

Green, J. B. (1997) *The Gospel of Luke* (Grand Rapids).

Haenchen, E. (1971) *The Acts of the Apostles* (Oxford and Philadelphia).

Harris, E. M. (2002) 'Pheidippides the Legislator: a Note on Aristophanes' Clouds', ZPE 140: 3–5.

Hengel, M. (2000) *The Four Gospels and the One Gospel of Jesus Christ: An Investigation of the Collection and Origin of the Canonical Gospels* (London and Harrisburg, Pa.).

Hornblower, S. (1987) *Thucydides* (London and Baltimore).

Johnson, L. T. (1991) *The Gospel of Luke* (Collegeville, Minn.).

Johnson, L. T. (1992) *The Acts of the Apostles* (Collegeville, Minn.).

Kilgallen, J. T. (1993) 'Acts 20:35 and Thucydides 2.97.4', JBL 112: 312–14.

Kim, S. (2008) *Christ and Caesar: the Gospel and the Roman Empire in the Writings of Paul and Luke* (Grand Rapids).

König, J. (2006) 'The Cynic and Christian Lives of Lucian's *Peregrinus*', in McGing and Mossman (2006) 227–54.

Kraus, C. S., ed. (1999) *The Limits of Historiography: Genre and Narrative in Ancient Historical Texts* (Leiden, Boston, and Cologne).

Krauter, S. (2009) 'Vergils Evangelium und das lukanische Epos? Überlegungen zu Gattung und Theologie des lukanischen Doppelwerkes', in Frey–Rothschild–Schröter (2009) 214–43.

Llewelyn, S. R. (1992) *New Documents Illustrating Early Christianity: a Review of the Greek Inscriptions and Papyri published in 1980–81* (Marrickville, NSW).

Luce, T. J. (1990) 'Livy, Augustus, and the Forum Augustum', in K. A. Raaflaub and M. Toher, edd., *Between Republic and Empire: Interpretations of Augustus and his Principate* (Berkeley, Los Angeles, and London) 123–38.

Malherbe, A. J. (1985-6) '"Not in a Corner": Early Christian Apologetic in Acts 26:26', *Second Century* 5: 193-210; repr. in id., *Light from the Gentiles: Hellenistic Philosophy and Early Christianity*, 2 vols (Leiden and Boston, 2014) I.209-28.

Marincola, J. (1997) *Authority and Tradition in Ancient Historiography* (Cambridge).

Marincola, J., ed. (2007) *A Companion to Greek and Roman Historiography*, 2 vols. (Oxford and Malden, Mass.).

Mason, S. (2005) *Josephus and the New Testament*² (Peabody, Mass.).

McGing, B. and J. Mossman, edd. (2006) *The Limits of Ancient Biography* (Swansea).

Moles, J. L. (1985) 'The Interpretation of the "Second Preface" in Arrian's *Anabasis*', *JHS* 105: 162-8 [vol. 2, Ch. 46].

Moles, J. L. (1993a) 'Livy's Preface', *PCPhS* 39: 141-68; repr. in J. Chaplin and C. S. Kraus, edd., *Livy* (Oxford Readings in Classical Studies; Oxford, 2009) 49-86 [vol. 2, Ch. 50].

Moles, J. L. (1993b) 'Truth and Untruth in Herodotus and Thucydides', in Gill and Wiseman (1993) 88-121 [vol. 2, Ch. 49].

Moles, J. L. (1998) 'Cry Freedom: Tacitus *Annals* 4.32-35', *Histos* 2 (1998) 95-184 [vol. 2, Ch. 53].

Moles, J. L. (1999) 'ΑΝΑΘΗΜΑ ΚΑΙ ΚΤΗΜΑ: the Inscriptional Inheritance of Ancient Historiography', *Histos* 3: 27-69 [vol. 2, Ch. 54].

Moles, J. L. (2001) 'A False Dilemma: Thucydides' History and Historicism', in S. J. Harrison, ed., *Texts, Ideas and the Classics: Scholarship, Theory and Classical Literature* (Oxford) 195-219 [vol. 2, Ch. 55].

Moles, J. L. (2005) 'The Thirteenth Oration of Dio Chrysostom: Complexity and Simplicity, Rhetoric and Moralism, Literature and Life', *JHS* 125: 112-38 [above, Ch. 10].

Moles, J. L. (2006) 'Jesus and Dionysus in *The Acts of the Apostles* and Early Christianity' *Hermathena* 180: 65-104 [above, Ch. 21].

Moles, J. L. (2013) 'Time and Space Travel in Luke-Acts', in Dupertuis and Penner (2013) 101-22 [below, Ch. 24].

Moles, J. L. (2014) 'Accommodation or Opposition? Luke-Acts on Rome', in J. M. Madsen and R. Rees, edd., *Double Vision: Reflections of Roman Rule in Greek and Latin Writing* (Leiden) 79-104 [below, Ch. 25].

Morris, R. L. B. (1992) 'Why ΑΥΓΟΥΣΤΟΣ? A Note to Luke 2.1', *NTS* 38: 142-4.

North, J. L. (1983) 'Is Ἰδεῖν Περί (Acts 15.6 cf. 18.15) a Latinism?', *NTS* 29: 64-6.

Padilla, O. (2009) 'Hellenistic παιδεία and Luke's Education: A Critique of Recent Approaches', *NTS* 55: 416-37.

Pelling, C. B. R. (1980) 'Plutarch's Adaptation of his Source Material', *JHS* 100: 127-40; repr. in id., *Plutarch and History: Eighteen Studies* (London and Swansea, 2002) 91-116.

Penner, T. (2004) *In Praise of Christian Origins: Stephen and the Hellenists in Lukan Apologetic History* (New York).

Plümacher, E. (1992) 'Eine Thukydidesreminiszenz in der Apostelgeschichte (Acts 20,33–35–Thuk. II.97.3f.)' *ZNW* 83: 270–5.

Plümacher, E. (2006) 'Stichwort: Lukas, Historiker', *ZNT* 18: 2–8.

Plummer, A. (1901) *A Critical and Exegetical Commentary on the Gospel According to S. Luke*[4] (Edinburgh and New York).

Raaflaub, K. A. (2002) 'Philosophy, Science, Politics: Herodotus and the Intellectual Trends of his Time', in E. J. Bakker, I. J. F. de Jong, and H. van Wees, edd. *Brill's Companion to Herodotus* (Leiden) 149–86.

Ramsby, T. R. (2007) *Textual Permanence: Roman Elegists and the Epigraphic Tradition* (London and New York).

Rhodes, P. J. with D. M. Lewis, edd. (1997) *The Decrees of the Greek States* (Oxford).

Rhodes, P. J. and R. Osborne, edd. (2003) *Greek Historical Inscriptions 404–323 BC* (Oxford).

Rowe, C. K. (2009) *World Upside Down: Reading Acts in the Greco–Roman Age* (Oxford).

Rydbeck, L. (1967) *Fachprosa, vermeintliche Volkssprache und Neues Testament: zur Beurteilung der sprachlichen Niveauunterschiede im nachklassischen Griechisch* (Lund).

Scheid, J., ed. (2007) *Res Gestae Divi Augusti: Hauts faits du divin Auguste* (Paris).

Schofield, M. (2000) 'Epicurean and Stoic Political Thought', in C. Rowe and M. Schofield, edd., *The Cambridge History of Greek and Roman Political Thought* (Cambridge) 435–56.

Sterling, G. E. (1992) *Historiography and Self-Definition: Josephos, Luke-Acts, and Apologetic Historiography* (Leiden).

Strelan, R. (2008) *Luke the Priest: the Authority of the Author of the Third Gospel* (Aldershot).

Syme, R. (1973) 'The Titulus Tiburtinus', *Vestigia* 17: 585–601; repr. in id., *Roman Papers III*, ed. A. R. Birley (Oxford, 1984) 869–84.

Thomas, R. (2000) *Herodotus in Context: Ethnography, Science and the Art of Persuasion* (Cambridge).

Tyson, J. B. (2006) *Marcion and Luke-Acts: a Defining Struggle* (Columbia, S.C.).

Wallace, R. and W. Williams (1993) *The Acts of the Apostles: a Companion* (London and New York).

Witherington, B. (1998) *The Acts of the Apostles: a Socio-rhetorical Commentary* (Grand Rapids and Cambridge).

Woodman, A. J. (2012) 'Making History: the Heading of the *Res Gestae*', in id., *From Poetry to History: Selected Papers* (Oxford) 181–200.

Yamazaki-Ransom, K. (2010) *The Roman Empire in Luke's Narrative* (London and New York).

CHAPTER 23

# Jesus the Healer in the Gospel, the Acts of the Apostles, and Early Christianity

## 1    Contextualisations*

These are partly for readers new to the field, partly to delineate positions on basics. While the main analysis stands or falls on its own merits, these questions inevitably affect more detailed reconstructions. Informed readers (and doubtless others) may avert their gaze until p. 619.

### 1.1    *Jesus the Healer*

Within the writings of NT scholars, of 'historical Jesus' scholars, and of Christian theologians, 'healing' is seen as one of the central components of Jesus' ministry, and, often, as its defining characteristic (Jesus' 'healing ministry' is a summary formula, in English, as in other languages). On the basic facts, few scholars doubt that Jesus had a big contemporary *reputation* as a healer, and recent scholarship emphasises that much of his healing falls within the capacities of traditional healers, especially very gifted ones, as Jesus certainly

---

\*   'Early' = before c.110 CE (my outside limit for the Acts of the Apostles). Versions of this paper were given at the Newcastle Classics Research Seminar (19/01/2001) and Manchester Erhardt Seminar (24/02/2011). I thank: all who commented at the seminars; Professor George Brooke for tending and good advice; Professors John Barclay, Todd Penner, and Heather Vincent, and the anonymous *Histos* readers for comments on various written versions, and Todd Penner for a copy of a forthcoming paper; Professor Martin Karrer for copies of two of his papers; and, for help of various kinds, Professors Mark Goodacre, Robert Hayward, and John Marincola, Drs Livia Capponi, Andrew Gregory, Justin Meggitt, Thomas Rütten, Federico Santangelo, and Rowland Smith, and Mrs Jennifer Wilkinson of the Newcastle Medical School. Naturally, I take full responsibility for a literary exegesis which has historical aspects; for those (including myself) interested in theological matters, it surely also has theological (or, possibly, anti-theological [n. 42]) implications, but these are irrelevant to *Histos*. Translations (except Simonetti [2001]) are mine. For reasons of bulk, much of the treatment involves paraphrase; readers should consult full texts. Bibliography and annotations are correspondingly restricted, numerous corners/roads cut. The Greek text is Nestle–Aland (2001).

was.¹ Physical healings are of course implicated in much larger religious perspectives, most of which appear in this paper.

'Healing' powers are also attributed to Jesus' disciples, to Paul in the next generation, and to Christian saints down the ages. Jesus' healings were competitively imitated by pagans—seemingly as early as by Vespasian in 69/70,² certainly (I would say—many would not) by the time of Philostratus' ⟦119⟧ third-century representation of the first-century pagan holy man, Apollonius of Tyana. By a peculiar historical irony, the first great Roman persecutor of Christians, the emperor Nero, enjoyed several *Nachleben*, as Jesus' healing resurrection spawned (it seems) a series of *Nerones rediuiui*.³ The sudden first-century emphasis, within the Hippocratic tradition of medicine, on ethical healing might owe something to the impact of Christian healing.⁴ Once Rome became Christian, Jesus' healing acquired a status parallel to that of the Hippocratics. He also became celebrated as a 'physician of the soul', therein surpassing pagan philosophers. Conversely, Julian the Apostate maintained the overwhelming superiority of the pagan healing god Asclepius.⁵ Jesus-like healing powers have been attributed to—or claimed by—charismatic Christians down to the present day. Thus, for better or for worse, Jesus' 'healing' is fundamental to Christianity.

### 1.2  *The Texts: The Gospels and the Acts of the Apostles*

The earliest *extant* written sources for Jesus' 'healing ministry' are the canonical Gospels (a term I discuss below), Matthew, Mark, Luke, and John, and the Acts of the Apostles,⁶ the sequel to Luke which relates the growth of the

---

1    Cf., e.g., Vermes (1973) 58–82; Sanders (1993) 132–68; Theissen–Merz (1998) 296–315; Dunn (2003) 667–96; Casey (2010) 237–79; Eve (2008); (2009); Cotter (2010); Perrin (2010) 149–82; Theissen (2010); Penner (2012).
2    Mark 8.22–6; Tac. *Hist.* 4.81; Suet. *Vesp.* 7.2; Cass. Dio 65.8; Eve (2008) and (2009) 44–6 argues the reverse: Mark attributed spitting to Jesus to contrast Jesus' true messianic powers with Vespasian's false ones. That contrast is available anyway, but since Jesus' spit seems authentic (see, e.g., Dunn [2003] 683 n. 323; Casey [2010] 270), the influence should go from Jesus to Vespasian and his propagandists, especially given their physical location and exposure to Jewish messianic thinking (begun in Neronian Rome—p. 617); that this entails at least some fabrication in the biography and historiography of Vespasian is a bonus, not a problem, for our understanding of Flavian tradition. Penner (2012) takes the Vespasianic material straight.
3    Wright (2003) 68, 720.
4    This possibility was raised by Thomas Rütten. I cannot assess it medically but do not think it *a priori* implausible (n. 21).
5    See Appendix 2.
6    The traditional title (abbreviated to Acts), whose authenticity is disputed. I use it for convenience (while believing it authentic).

Jesus movement after the crucifixion of Jesus (*c.* CE 30)[7] until Paul's arrival and two-year stay in Rome (Acts 28.30), before his own martyrdom (somewhere in the period 62–4).[8] There are possibilities of *lost* written sources (below).

### 1.2.1  Generic Questions

Classicists might naturally read the Greek-language Gospels and Acts as falling into the categories of historiography or biography—or, certainly, historical writing of some sort (given the enormous elasticity of that Greek and Roman category). Within the specialist scholarship, however, there is much debate about their genre. Many hold that 'Gospels' are *sui generis* and that ⟦120⟧ Christians invented the form, as a Christian counter to imperial 'good news', in order to propagate the 'gospel/good news [εὐαγγέλιον] of Jesus Christ' ('of' meaning both 'about' and 'announced by').[9] But strong cases can be made: that the Gospels generally are (primarily) to be classified as Classical biographies,[10] especially given the non-existence of Jewish rabbinic biography,[11] though the nature of their subject matter puts them in competition with their pagan equivalents; that Luke and Acts, by the same author (Acts 1.1), form a unity (a 'double-work');[12] and that Luke-Acts is a work of historiography that incorporates biography and individual-orientated historiography (and, indeed, other genres such as various types of philosophical work).[13]

None of this confines any of these texts to generic strait-jackets, a point that needs emphasis, since, in this area, as in others, NT scholarship—in contrast to comparable recent Classical scholarship[14]—characteristically operates with excessively tight generic models. The hypothesised 'natural assumption' of Classicists—that all these texts fall into the broad category of Classical historiography—finds support in the Preface to Luke, which not only aligns

---

7   Detailed dating controversies about Jesus' biography do not affect this paper; recent discussion: Humphreys (2011) 61–79; 93–4.
8   The ending of Acts is controversial; see p. 653 below.
9   E.g., Barton (2006); Edwards (2006).
10  Burridge (1992); Frickenschmidt (1997); Keener (2009) 73–84.
11  P. S. Alexander (1984); Philo's *Life of Moses*, however, is an important and neglected Judaeo-Greek forerunner: McGing (2006).
12  Acts 1.1; Talbert (1974); Keener (2009) 85–94; separatists remain: Parsons–Pervo (1993); Gregory–Rowe (2010); Dupertuis–Penner (2013); Moles (2011), (2013), and the present paper assume, but also, I think, support, unity. For those who reject it, the papers may at least show, I hope, that the writer of Acts was a very good reader of Luke (though in my view because he wrote it).
13  Keener (2009) 85–94; Moles (2013). For a 'non-Classical' classification of the Gospels see now Troiani (2011) 115.
14  Kraus (1999); McGing–Mossman (2006); Marincola (2007); Miller–Woodman (2010).

that text with (Classical) Greek historiography but also impresses other Gospels (*sic*) into the same genre.¹⁵ For the separate classification of 'Gospels' is indeed viable (cf. Mark 1.1), provided it is taken to mean '*also* Gospels'.

### 1.2.2   ⟦121⟧ Readerships/Audiences

There is much debate, too, about the projected readership(s) or audience(s) of these texts. For Classicists, an important question is: does the readership or audience include, at least in an ideal sense, non-Christians and non-Jews? The very recourse to written texts written in Greek and in at least serviceable Greek (or, sometimes, certainly in the case of Luke-Acts, far better), and to texts which envisage certainly some readers,¹⁶ and the choice of Classical generic 'packaging', seem to open up this possibility, especially as Christians early became committed to evangelisation that included Gentiles, and even, at least theoretically, that extended to the ends of the earth (Matthew 28.19; Luke 24.47; Acts 1.8).

The weight given these various considerations is obviously affected by the degree to which one supposes Jews, both in the various parts of Palestine and in the various countries of the Diaspora, to have been Hellenised, a question which remains highly controversial, and by one's views on the speed and geographical distribution both of the general advance of Christianity¹⁷ and of the

---

15  Luke 1.1–4: 'Since indeed many have set their hand to draw up a narrative guide about the things done which have been brought to fulfilment among us, (2) just as those who became eyewitnesses from the beginning and servants of the word handed them along to us, (3) it seemed good to me also, having followed all of them closely from the up, to write them down for you in order, most powerful Theophilos, (4) so that you may additionally know/experience/recognise the truth/security/safety/un-slipperiness about the words in which you have been orally instructed'; of endless discussion of this (dense, complicated, and extremely Classical) preface see, e.g., Cadbury (1922); L. C. A. Alexander (1993); Moles (2011); (2013). I intend a general treatment {below, Ch. 27}.

16  Mark 13.14; Luke 1.3; John 21.24–25: 'this is the disciple who is bearing witness about these things and who wrote these things, and we know that his witness is true. (25) But there are also many other things which Jesus did, which, if they were written one by one, I do not think that the world itself could contain the books that would be written'. 'Reading' is important because it maximises both audience and interpretative complexity; but 'reading' and 'orality'/'aurality' are compatible, since even ancient private readers mostly read aloud (apparently), and the Gospels and Luke-Acts are also Christian 'performance texts'.

17  How far there is a unified phenomenon is massively controversial; brief remarks on p. 664; the term 'Christians' is also one-sided and anachronistic, since it was applied to Jesus' followers by others, including Romans (Acts 11.26; Tac. *Ann.* 15.44.2; 1 Peter 4.16), and not adopted by Christians before the second century. It is also misleading, in obscuring the complete Jewishness of the first generation and the still substantial Jewishness of the next generations. It remains fast and convenient.

so-called 'Parting(s) of the Ways' between Judaism and Christianity, both also highly controversial questions and far beyond the scope of this paper.

Few scholars have positively argued the possibility of the texts' including non-Christians and non-Jews in their projected readership/audience, but already in the second century some educated pagans *were* reading some of these texts,[18] which must mean something. 'Classical' elements beyond basic [[122]] genre have also been argued for all of them;[19] and I believe that Luke-Acts in particular contains enough 'Classical' material to suggest that it is partly designed to 'hook' educated pagans. Obviously, that claim cannot be substantiated here, though Acts 17 may stand as a test case.[20] Obviously, too, one could argue a less strong version of this case: these texts both commemorate and implicitly commend certain behaviours towards non-Christians and non-Jews. Thus, again, Acts 17 has often been read (rightly) as a 'how-to-talk-to-Greek-philosophers' guide. On any view, therefore, these texts are partly about 'converting pagans' and attest Christians' desire to 'speak to' pagans.

### 1.2.3 Christian Historiography and Jewish and Pagan Historiography

There is, then, a theoretical possibility that (some of) these texts were designed (partly) to function within a wider, public, and partly textual debate about the claims of Christianity. That possibility is strengthened, if one thinks that after Jesus' death (some) Romans were quick to inform themselves about the continuing Jesus, or Christ, movement,[21] reaching generally hostile conclusions (requiring rebuttal), and, if allowed, the possibility further increases the importance of our topic. And, given the texts' generic status as works of (to some degree) 'Classical' biography and historiography, that larger public, partly textual debate comes to include—at some point—the Jewish historian Josephus, the Roman historian Tacitus, the Roman biographer Suetonius, and the Greek satirist and biographer Lucian, all of whom reference Christianity.[22] Certainly, these writers mostly postdate the Christian texts under discussion, but this is

---

18  Cook (1993); (1994); (2000); (2010); König (2006); note also the widespread interest in resurrection (or similar phenomena) in pagan Imperial literature (Bowersock (1994) 99–113).
19  Cf., e.g., Pervo (1987); MacDonald (2000); (2003); L. C. A. Alexander (2005); Moles (2006b); Lang (2008); Moles (2011); (2013).
20  P. 647.
21  '(Some) Romans' = both the Roman authorities (in various places) and ordinary Romans (in various places); recent survey: Cook (2010); also Moles (2012).
22  Jos. *A.J.* 18.63–4; 20.9.1; Tac. *Ann.* 15.44.2–5; F 2; Suet. *Claud.* 25.4; *Nero* 16.2; Lucian, *Pereg.* (with König [2006]). Probably a majority of scholars accept a Josephan core at *AJ* 18.63–4, a Tacitean core at F 2, and the relevance of Suet. *Claud.* 25.4, in all cases, I believe, rightly; discussion: Moles (2012).

perhaps not true in all cases,[23] and at least they show that Christianity, theme of Christian historiography and biography, quite rapidly gained some attention in their Jewish and pagan counterparts. ⟦123⟧ This must surely also apply to attested but lost earlier works of Classical historiography and biography which covered the same material as Josephus, Tacitus, and Suetonius.

There is also the possibility, little known among NT scholars, that a text of a different, but not entirely unrelated, Classical genre, Petronius' *Satyricon* (not later than CE 65), alludes not to the text of Mark (which I regard as chronologically impossible—see below) but to the *story* of Jesus' Passion.[24] Such knowledge, at Nero's court, is utterly likely. Nero's wife, Poppaea, was a 'God-fearer' (Gentile follower of Judaism); before Paul's trial 'what has happened to me has eventuated to the advance of the gospel, so that my bonds are clearly known to the whole Praetorium and to all the rest as being for Christ' (Philippians 1.12–13 (written in Rome));[25] and Paul defended himself before Nero.[26]

### 1.2.4 Authorships and Places of Writing

The much-disputed questions of authorships and places of writing do not concern us (subsequent references to 'Matthew' et al. can be taken as merely traditional and convenient), except for three factors. First, there is the question of whether these texts are (at least primarily) 'community texts' (the majority view), or whether they (also) envisage an 'international' Christian audience or readership.[27] Clearly, the latter possibility becomes even more plausible, if they are (also) targeting pagans. Clearly, too, even the rather limited degree of traffic between the texts allowed by the modern consensus on the source picture (below) supports this possibility. Second, Bauckham has recently re-emphasised, with (for me) compelling arguments, that the Gospels and Acts

---

23  Following Mason (2005) 250–93, and with additional arguments, I think the author of Luke-Acts had read Josephus' *Jewish Antiquities* (CE 93). That Acts is a second-century text is quite a popular view (see, e.g., Dupertuis–Penner [2013]), usually involving a claim of the *disunity* of Luke-Acts (n. 12). My own view is that the unified Luke-Acts was written by 'Luke the beloved physician' (p. 618 n. 29; p. 657) in c.105 at the end of a long life.

24  Ramelli (1996), critiqued by Courtney (2001) 121 n. 67 (there is actually a large Italian bibliography on this and similar possibilities); the refinement of allusions to story, not text, protects the hypothesis; noteworthy also is the allusion to Jesus in the Syriac Letter of the Stoic Mara bar Sarapion to his son (19), of which the dramatic (and, if the letter is genuine, actual) date is 73: http://www.earlychristianwritings.com/text/mara.html.

25  Cf. 4.22: 'all the holy ones greet you, especially those from Caesar's household'.

26  Acts 27.24, with Lane Fox (1986) 430-2.

27  Bauckham (1998).

represent themselves as being the products of eyewitness testimony.[28] Third, there is the question of whether Luke's emphasis (greater than that of any of the other Evangelists) on Jesus' 'healing' reflects his own identity: if, that is, he is Luke 'the beloved physician' of Colossians 4.14, as [[124]] Christian tradition has generally maintained since about the middle of the second century.[29]

### 1.2.5 Datings and Relative Chronology

Most scholars rightly hold that Matthew, Luke-Acts, and John post-date, by some considerable time (fifteen years or more), the Romans' capture of Jerusalem and their destruction of the Temple in 70,[30] and that Mark falls within the period 66–73, with particularly strong arguments for c.70.[31] Mark's priority is further supported by the 'Two-source Hypothesis' (which is widely, though not universally, accepted): namely, that Matthew and Luke follow (at least largely) Mark and a second, hypothetical, sayings and anecdotes source (or sources) of the 50s or 40s, dubbed 'Q' (German 'Quelle') by modern scholarship. Any Classicist who believes in *Quellenforschung* and 'runs the parallels' would (I believe) find this hypothesis convincing, although it admits variations, gradations, and loose ends.[32] The subsidiary question of whether Q ever existed in Jesus' own language of Aramaic[33] need hardly concern us. That there were written *narratives* about Jesus before Mark remains a minority hypothesis, for which there are interesting arguments,[34] but which little affects the present paper.

Most scholars put John at, or near, the end of the sequence. Whether John has read all, or any, of the so-called Synoptics/'seeable-togethers'[35] (Matthew, Mark, and Luke) is disputed; I accept the arguments for his having read Mark and Matthew.[36] However, I hold the minority view that Luke-Acts comes at

---

28   Bauckham (2006); multiple reviews in *JSHJ* 6.2 (2008); *NV* 6.3 (2008); for Bauckham, they *are* the products of such testimony (hence, for Bauckham, reliable); for me, it is enough—and important—if they so *represent* themselves.
29   Not the only argument: cf. n. 168.
30   E.g. Davies–Allison (1988) 131–8; Brown (1997) 216–17; 273–4; Lampe (1984).
31   Brown (1997) 163–4; Telford (1999) 12–13; Boring (2006) 14–15; Collins (2007) 11–14; I cannot accept the very low date (c.40) argued for by Casey (2010) 71–4, following Crossley (2004).
32   See, e.g., Davies–Allison (1988) 98–114; Keener (2009) 131–2.
33   As, e.g., Casey (2002).
34   E.g., Allison (2010) 392–423.
35   The term refers in the first instance to the fact that the parallels between these three Gospels can be 'seen together' in parallel columns.
36   See, e.g., Barrett (1978) 15–17, 42–6.

the end, hence that Luke has read John, as well as the others.[37] That positioning is not essential to the analysis, although Luke-Acts contains the richest exploitation of our theme, which might reflect not only Luke's own qualities as a writer and religious thinker but also his having read all the [[125]] others. Both for these reasons, and for reasons of balance and proportion, Luke-Acts is here treated last. Some details of the analysis seem (to me) to make better sense if it really is last.

NT scholarship has little acknowledged the possibility of competitive intertextuality among these texts, but, unless one takes an implausibly reverential attitude to their writers or to Christianity itself, such a scenario is itself natural, largely consistent with the relative chronology and with the indications of who has read whom, and implicit alike in Matthew's expansions and corrections of earlier material and in editorial remarks made both by John and by Luke.[38]

### 1.2.6   Oral Traditions

Thus far, texts. Some prominent recent scholarship, however, has emphasised the role of continuing oral traditions about Jesus and their supposed influence upon the surviving written texts.[39] There must have been such traditions and some influence of this kind, but it seems insufficient to disturb the main patterns of written interaction, which leave little room for other material.[40] On the other hand, it is of course sometimes legitimate—even in a paper such as this—to raise the questions of what 'outside' knowledge (from whatever sources) readers (or, some readers) might be presumed (or reconstructed) to possess, and of how that knowledge might affect their reception of the texts, just as it is also legitimate to use the texts to reconstruct wider religious debates and perspectives, though at some point the latter process will exceed the *Histos* guidelines.[41] I have stretched these a little in this case, because the topic is so important and has so many different aspects.

---

37   Luke 1.1–3: 'since indeed *many* have set their hand to draw up a narrative guide ... it seemed good to me *also* ...'; Gregory (2006).
38   Sim (2011); Luke 1.1–3 (n. 15); John 21.24–5 (n. 16).
39   E.g., Dunn (2003); Bauckham (2006); Keener (2009) 138–61.
40   Sensible remarks in Eve (2009) 87–9. Classicists may compare the problematics—and limited explanatory power—of orality in Homeric and Herodotean scholarship.
41   Viz: 'it is not our intention to publish material which is per se historical, unless it illuminates the qualities of ancient historians or biographers (this will be a matter of balance and judgement)'.

### 1.3 Name Puns in Classical Literature and Culture

Much scholarship over the last four decades has demonstrated the importance of puns and name puns in Classical societies, cultures, and literatures, including historiography and biography. If individual cases and limits may obviously be debated, the general phenomenon is indisputable. Of the many levels on which such punning works, I cite four relevant to this paper. First, ⟦126⟧ bilingual punning is common. Second, it is not necessary for a word or name to interact with a cognate: a synonym or synonymous phrase suffices. I call this phenomenon 'punning by synonym'. Both these phenomena are illustrated by 'suis et ipsa Roma uiribus ruit' (Hor. *Epod*. 16.2), where 'Roma' glosses Greek ῥώμη = strength, and 'Roma'/ῥώμη interacts with 'uiribus' = 'strength'. Third, divine names are enormously significant and can have (or be understood to have) more than one meaning. Fourth, punning can be assisted by assonance or alliteration, though it requires neither. Punning in Classical historiography (and biography) naturally works in similar ways to that in other genres, but it may be even more organic and sustained, and etymological name punning may be particularly linked to the construction of genealogies and of early history.[42]

### 1.4 Names and Puns in the Jewish World

The above remarks about punning in the Classical world apply just as much to the Jewish world. Names are extensively punned on in the Hebrew Bible. 'As his name is, so is he' (1 Samuel 25.24).[43] Names can obviously be very significant and punned on in the Gospels and Acts ('thou art Peter', etc.), which, as we have seen, are themselves also (to some extent) Classical texts.

---

42  Huge bibliography, e.g., Woodhead (1928); Wiseman (1974); Cairns (1979) 90ff.; Snyder (1980); Ahl (1985); Maltby (1991); (1993); (2003); O'Hara (1996); Woodman–Martin (1996) 491–2; Paschalis (1997); Harrison (1998) 37 and n. 144; 38 and nn. 146–47; Moles (1998) 106 n. 14; 117–19, 134, 143, 153–9, 166, 168 n. 111 {vol. 2, pp. 283 n. 14, 295–7, 312, 321, 331–8, 344, 346 n. 111}; (2002) 44–7 {vol. 2, pp. 449–52}; (2007b) 253, 256, 259, 260 n. 80, 262, 264, 267 {vol. 2, pp. 470, 473, 477, 478 n. 80, 480, 482, 485}; (2010) 32, 34–35, 38 {vol. 2, pp. 507, 510, 513}; Michalopoulos (2001); Peraki-Kyriakidou (2002); Lateiner (2005); Booth–Maltby (2006); Hinds (2006); Henderson (2007); Irwin (2007); Elliott (2009); there is also a massive bibliography on punning and related sound effects in comic authors; on the general theory and a history of scholarship see also Attardo (1994). I thank Heather Vincent for expertise in this area. Some at Manchester registered unease at the term 'pun'. I use it as short, broad, and (unlike 'paronomasia') instantly comprehensible. There is no implication of triviality or of 'mere word play': quite the reverse (though grounds for Christian anxiety remain; possible alleviation on p. 665). Like Irwin (2007) 46 and n. 13, I am unconcerned with terminological exactitude or analytical precision, and think this pragmatic laxity appropriate to the topic.

43  Surveys: Metzger–Coogan (1993) 545–59; Ryken–Wilhoit–Longman (1998) 582–6.

Furthermore, in studying personal names in the Gospels, Bauckham has recently claimed: 'Names are a valuable resource for ancient historians, but one of which New Testament scholars have made relatively little use.' And: 'Onomastics (the study of names) is a significant resource for assessing the origins of Gospel traditions.'[44]

⟦127⟧ These principles must be right (however controversial Bauckham's use of them). But what if their single most crucial application is to the central figure of the NT?

### 1.5   The Name of Jesus; Factors Favouring the Pun on 'Jesus' ~ 'Healer'

The Palestinian Jewish Jesus bore the very popular name יֵשׁוּעַ ('Joshua'), which means something like 'Yahweh [or 'Yah'—shortened form] saves'.[45] The Jewish-Greek *form* of the name, found in the NT, is Ἰησοῦς, whence our 'Jesus'. Bilingual and etymological puns on the meaning of 'Joshua'/'Ἰησοῦς as 'Yahweh saves', alike in the Gospels and Acts (as we shall see), and in the letters of Paul and of others in the NT, are clear and acknowledged in some of the more linguistically alert scholarship.[46] But there is a crucial additional factor: Jews who bore the name יֵשׁוּעַ and wanted a straight Greek equivalent chose Ἰάσων (Ionic form Ἰήσων, modern 'Jason'): an equivalence attested in official and governmental contexts.[47] This Greek name actually means 'healer' (~ ἰάομαι) and readily produces etymological puns.[48] Jews who adopted Greek names generally tried to adopt ones nearest in form and meaning to the original. So not only do Ἰησοῦς, the Greek-Jewish form of 'Joshua' and the name of a renowned Jewish 'healer', and Ἰάσων, the Greek form of Ἰησοῦς/'Joshua' and a name which actually means 'healer', look similar and mean similar things: from a Hellenistic Jewish perspective, they are actually the same name, as any Jew with a modicum of Greek would have known.[49] For us it is of course completely immaterial in this sort of context whether they are *actually* the same name.

---

44   Bauckham (2006) 67, 84.
45   Cf., e.g., Williams (1995) 87; Karrer (1998) 47; (2000) 255. The precise meaning is in fact unclear, but the availability of 'Yahweh saves' is validated alike by the Gospels and Acts themselves, as we shall see, and by glosses both in other early Christian writers (nn. 46 and 86) and in Jewish writers (Karrer [1998] 47 n. 76); on the commonest male names among Palestine Jews in the period 330 BCE–200 CE see Bauckham (2006) 85–8; Joshua/Jesus is sixth; Diasporan patterns are significantly different: Bauckham (2006) 73.
46   E.g., Karrer (1998) 46–8; it remains true that many very distinguished NT scholars often miss this pun even in clamant contexts.
47   See Cohen (1984) 46–8; Williams (1995) 87; Jews and Greek names generally: Williams (1995); (1998) 113; Bauckham (2006) 83.
48   E.g., Pind. *Pyth.* 4.119, 270; Braswell (1988) 370–2; Mackie (2001).
49   As we shall see, this factor is crucial to the interpretation of Acts 17: p. 647 below.

There are also wider considerations. Not only was 'healing' by Ἰησοῦς a central part of his ministry, there was a much larger Jewish healing context in the period.[50] Solomon had a great first-century reputation as a healer (Jos. [[128]] *AJ* 8.45). The Essenes—frequent comparators of Jesus in modern scholarship—were celebrated as healers (Jos. *B.J.* 2.136), which their very name may mean.[51] While 'Therapeutae', the name of the Egyptian Jewish women philosophers, probably means 'attendants',[52] both the Jewish Philo (*Vit. contempl.* 2) and the Christian Eusebius (*H.E.* 2.16–17) readily connect it with 'healing' (which the Therapeutai certainly practised). A few years after Jesus, the Galilaean charismatic Hanina ben Dosa performed similar healings to Jesus'.[53] The Qumran community (pre-68 CE) expected an 'anointed one' who would 'restore sight to the blind, straighten the bent ..., heal the wounded, and give life to the dead' (4Q521, 2.1, 8, 12).[54] The 'healing' of Ἰησοῦς is thus writ all the larger, because he was certainly the greatest Jewish 'healer' of the time, and because from the Christian point of view, from the very beginning, and ever afterwards, he was the greatest healer of any race or culture at any time.

Obviously, the possibility of punning on the 'healing' aspect of Jesus' name is encouraged by the simple facts that the name of Jesus in its Jewish-Greek form was vitally important from the start to Christians who operated in Greek ('in the name of Jesus', etc.),[55] and that the NT is—through its very use of Greek—propounding a to some extent Hellenised Jesus. And where better to look for such punning than in Classical *biographies* of Jesus?

The further potentialities of the names also intrigue. The names Ἰάσων and Ἰησοῦς have similar divine associations. Not only does Ἰάσων, the Greek form of Ἰησοῦς, itself the Jewish-Greek form of 'Joshua', mean 'healer', but it derives from the pagan goddess of healing who is called Ἰάσω (Ἰήσω in Ionic).[56] Thus on the Greek side Ἰάσων is a human name derived from a god's: a theophoric name, just as on the Jewish side יֵשׁוּעַ is a human name derived from 'Yahweh'. Furthermore, for the early Christians, this Ἰησοῦς is in some sense, and to some degree, himself a divine figure.[57] There is also a simple matter of sound. Ἰησοῦς,

---

50 Vermes (1973) 59–63; Casey (2010) 244–5.
51 Vermes (1973) 59–63.
52 Taylor (2003) 55–73.
53 Casey (2010) 245.
54 Dunn (2003) 669; Casey (2010) 272.
55 Heitmüller (1903); Hartman (1997); Dunn (2009) 188–9.
56 *LSJ* s.v.; Meyer (1916).
57 Jesus' exact divine status in our various texts (and in the rest of the NT) is a very vexed issue: recently, Dunn (2010). I believe my material provides new arguments for a very 'high' Christology from very early on. See p. 664. Of course, the question cannot be dissociated from that of the historical Jesus' self-perception: also, of course, hugely controversial.

Ἰάσων, and Ἰάσω not only look very similar: [[129]] they sound very similar. And the sound of names is very important.[58] There is also a matter of extended meaning. There can be important links between 'saving', the basic meaning of 'Joshua', undeniably punned on in the NT, and 'healing', both at the levels of the divine and the quasi-divine and alike in medical, religious/social, and political contexts. Given these links and the sound factor, one even wonders whether the many Greek speakers who knew that the Jewish god was denoted by 'Yahweh' or 'Yah' could also 'hear' both Ἰη/σοῦς and Ἰά/σων as 'Yah saves' directly, because –σοῦς and –σων could evoke σῴζω and σῶς, and whether bilingual speakers could even regard the Greek σῴζω and the Hebrew verb[59] as cognates.

Another important linguistic factor is that by our period the commonest Greek translation—even transliteration—of Yahweh is Ἰάω ('Iao'),[60] which is instantly connectable by Greek-speakers to the verb ἰάομαι. 'Healing' is indeed one of Yahweh's/Iao's key attributes.[61] An interesting example from the Hebrew Bible is Exodus 15.26: 'For I am Yahweh [thus the Hebrew] the one that heals you', where the latter phrase is rendered in the Septuagint by the participle ἰώμενος, and where there must be a bilingual etymological association (which must have been perceived by the translators) between Yahweh, Ἰάω, and ἰάομαι. In this fundamental capacity of divine 'healing', as in many other things, like Father, like Son. This connection between Jesus' 'healing' and Yahweh's was instantly available to the NT writers (who variously used the Septuagint version of the Hebrew Bible) and to Diaspora Jews (who used the Septuagint and who would certainly have known of the Greek form Ἰάω).

If these considerations seem rather theoretical (not my own view), there are also the simple (though little-known) facts that Ἰησοῦς is directly glossed [[130]]

---

58  Cf. pp. 648 and 655.
59  Root ישע (Y-Sh-Ah, Strong's #3467); see further p. 628 below. As many have found, and many others have observed, investigation of name puns is a road whose ultimate destination is madness. In that spirit, one speculates (uninspired by the considerable and ill-disciplined Internet material on the matter) on an etymological association between 'Iovis' (~ 'iuvare' (Maltby [1991] 319)) and the similar-sounding/looking 'Yahweh', who is also a 'helper' (Renn [2005] 486–7), hence also between 'Iovis' and Ἰησοῦς, hence also whether a bilingual etymological *frisson* occurs whenever people ask Ἰησοῦς to 'help' them, as they not infrequently do (e.g. Matthew 15.25; Mark 9.22; Luke 9.38, 18.38; cf. also p. 628 below). There seems to be no ancient attestation, or implication, of 'Iovis' as cognate with 'Yahweh', although I would be astonished if there were not ancient people who 'heard' that association, especially as 'Jupiter'/'Iovis' is one of the two main pagan equivalences of 'Yahweh' (the other being Dionysus). But I do not *argue* any of this.
60  van Kooten (2006) 126–8; I thank John Barclay for suggesting Iao's relevance to this paper.
61  Renn (2005) 472–4.

as ἰώμενος by the fourth-century Greek bishop Cyril of Jerusalem (*Cat. Myst.* 10.13) and that it is clearly sometimes so understood by other Greek Church Fathers from as early as Ignatius of Antioch (? early second century), that is, in the same period as the Gospels and Acts, or only slightly later.[62] Church Fathers themselves also make the pun.[63] This etymology is also known to the Greek-speaking and Christian-raised Roman emperor Julian.[64] Thus a punning association between Ἰησοῦς and ἰάομαι was both seen and actively exploited, by native Greek speakers and readers, both Christian and pagan, of the Gospels, and (?) from as early as the early second century. Some of these readers, needless to say, were extremely good readers (and I sometimes cite them),[65] and they certainly knew their texts. Food, surely, for thought.

Given all this, I would even claim that, within their cultural context(s), Christians would have missed an obvious trick, if they had not availed themselves of this available, extremely useful, and obviously rich pun, especially if they were also punning fruitfully on Jesus' 'other name', Χριστός (*Chreestos*), while with equal energy pagans were punning negatively on it,[66] and while competing and widely different authority figures—above all Roman emperors—were also claiming to be 'healers'.

There is, then, a mass of considerations commending a Ἰησοῦς-ἰάομαι pun in our texts.

Within existing NT scholarship, however, only a small minority of commentators on only one of our texts, Acts, sees a maximum of about four such puns.[67] Few, if any, commentators on the Gospels; few, if any, historical Jesus books; few, if any, books about, or discussions of, Jesus' healing, or of his attitude and conformity to the Jewish purity laws, or of NT representations of these things; few, if any, studies of the influence of Isaiah on the NT 〚131〛 or on Jesus and the

---

62   Ignatius, *Ad Ephes.* 7.1–2 (contrasting deceitful Christian Cynics, who carry around 'the name', 'bite secretly', and are 'hard to tend', and the 'one healer ... Jesus Christ, our Lord'); later, Euseb. *Demonstr. Ev.* 4.10; Epiphanius, *Haer.* 29.4. Cf. also pp. 631 and 635. Note, however, that some scholars date the letters attributed to Ignatius to the late second century.
63   E.g., Just. *2 Apol.* 6.6; Orig. *c. Cels.* 1.25; F 54 *in Jo.*; Clement of Alexandria, *Str.* 3.17; *Paed.* 1.2.
64   See Appendix 2.
65   Conversely, Church Fathers' apparent silences in contexts where I find puns are no discouragement: most of their comments come not from systematic exegeses but from homiletics, which have selective and rather simple concerns.
66   Moles (2012).
67   Thus, for example, Page (1918) 142; Bruce (1951) 210, 333; Barrett (2004) 481; the cases variously cited are 4.30; 9.34; 10.38; 17.18; cf. also Moles (2006b) 88 {above, p. 572} n. 96 (slightly supplementing the list); (2013) (on the end of Acts).

early Christians;⁶⁸ and few, if any, histories of early Christianity even consider this possibility. That, certainly, is my impression of the admittedly endless bibliography, and it has been confirmed by several distinguished NT scholars whom I have consulted, as well as by a leading NT seminar. Indeed, one of the most linguistically accomplished and linguistically self-conscious of contemporary NT scholars, Maurice Casey, has recently written: 'healing was central to Jesus' ministry', and then asked: 'why is Jesus never called a healer …?'.⁶⁹ (On the other hand, it must be admitted that there is a fair amount of more or less ignorant speculation about the etymological connection on the Internet [not my inspiration], as readers can check for themselves.)

It will be a necessary implication of my analysis that failure to see or hear the pun is not only a literary but also a theological failure. For these texts are highly coercive, or 'imperialist', in their demands.⁷⁰ Of course, it is open to readers, particularly modern readers, to respond: 'No, thanks, we don't want to play that particular game'. But they can only legitimately do so, if they first see what that particular game is.

But the proof of the pudding lies finally in the eating.

## 2    Textual Analyses

I translate ἰάομαι and cognates as 'heal' and cognates; καθαρίζω and cognates as 'cleanse' and cognates; σῴζω as 'save'; and θεραπεύω as 'tend'. I choose the latter in order to open the possibility that Jesus' 'tending' of the sick links to his role as 'servant' or '*attendant*', in the same way as outsiders could view the Therapeutai as both 'attendants' and 'healers'/'medical attendants'.⁷¹ I do not think this possibility *a priori* excluded by the fact that the main NT word for 'servant', 'attendant', 'slave' is δοῦλος, not θεράπων, which actually occurs only once (and the ambiguous παῖς is characteristically used of Jesus). The aim is to maintain consistency (as standard translations lamentably do not). From time to time, I leave Ἰησοῦς in Greek, so as to re-emphasise linguistic points. I am not concerned with the much-studied questions of whether NT usage corresponds either to ordinary, or to specialised, medical usages. My first and overriding concern is to demonstrate that the pun is there. I explore the interpretative

---

68   The relevance of this category will become clear.
69   Casey (2010) 271; cf. 275.
70   For similar irritating claims (*mutatis mutandis*) in pagan contexts see Moles (1998) 130–2, 159, 169–76 {vol. 2, pp. 307–310, 337, 347–55}; (2007b) 267–8 {vol. 2, pp. 484–5}.
71   P. 622.

implications to some extent, but ⟦132⟧ I am well aware that many of the episodes discussed demand far more detailed and refined interpretation even on the basis of the pun—to say nothing of the many other bases that there often are. My method is 'sequential reading', and for comparative purposes it includes material where the pun does not occur. Thematic treatment might be more digestible and would certainly be less bulky, but it would be less rigorous, nor would it convey the distinctive rhythms, qualities, and techniques of these texts, which are both like and unlike Classical texts and which also differ interestingly among themselves. I hope that the sheer mass of material will prove persuasive but at the same time that the result is not a shapeless mass.

### 2.1   *Mark*

In this first Gospel, Jesus' name is announced in the opening words (1.1): 'The beginning of the good news of Jesus Christ'. It then comes three times (9, 14, 17) before the healing of the man with 'an unclean spirit' (23), who hails Jesus as 'Jesus the Nazarene' (24) (remarkably and significantly, no introduction is needed), and is rebuked by the named Jesus (25). The 'unclean spirit' (26) departs and the people commend Jesus' new and authoritative teaching, including his authority over 'unclean spirits' (27). Several healings follow, one group of which is described in terms of 'tending' (34), while 'cleansing' is used of the man with a skin-disease (40, 41, 42, 44). The sequence already illustrates how healing often involves other areas, notably those of purity and impurity. In the subsequent healing of the paralytic (2.1–12), Jesus is twice named (5, 8), though there is no (other) significant vocabulary.

Many Classicists nowadays, I think, would already feel that Mark's dramatic and emphatic foregrounding of Jesus' 'healing ministry' is underpinned by the very name of Jesus, which seems to be deployed both strategically (1.1, 9, 14, 17) and locally (1.24–5; 2.5, 8) in a telling way.[72] The logic would be that the combination of Jesus' much-repeated name, which means 'healer', with the lexicon of 'tending' and 'cleanness' and 'uncleanness' effects 'punning by synonym', a process further helped by the intrinsic importance attached to names (both of exorcist and demon) in exorcisms, whether Jewish or pagan.[73] Certainly, in Mark, as in the others, use of Jesus' name increases—sometimes dramatically—in healing contexts. By comparison with Classical texts (with which, as we have seen, Mark has some affinities), such punning would be quite elementary, naïve even, by comparison with a text ⟦133⟧ such as Pindar's

---

72   Note also that Ἰησοῦς is quite well attested at 1.41, though not printed by Nestle–Aland.
73   Dunn (2003) 675–6.

*Fourth Pythian*, which puns in subtle and allusive ways on 'Jason' as 'healer'.[74] Sceptics might object that, since 'Jesus' was this Palestinian Jewish person's name, since the name was very common, and since this person performed (allegedly) 'healings', 'collisions' between name and 'healings' are inevitable and signify nothing. Such facile scepticism, already strained (I believe) by the disposition and economy of the material, cannot survive the sequel.

In the NT illness is characteristically linked to sin. So 'healing' can also apply to sin itself, as in the healing of the paralytic (2.5, 9), and as when, to criticisms of his eating with undesirables, the named Jesus replies (2.17): 'those who are strong have no need of a healer but those who are ill' (οὐ χρείαν ἔχουσιν οἱ ἰσχύοντες ἰατροῦ ἀλλ' οἱ κακῶς ἔχοντες). In this self-definitional context, Ἰησοῦς characterises himself as an ἰατρός, and the whole apophthegmatic formulation employs strong assonance and alliteration, reinforcing the association between Ἰησοῦς and ἰατροῦ. The pun seems clear, and crystallises the implications of the preceding material, in accordance with the knowing 'solution-to-a-problem' technique common (I believe) in Classical texts.

The 'tending' (3.2, 10) of a man with a withered hand is inserted into a variety of material before healing returns as a major theme in chapter 5. Another man possessed by an unclean spirit (2, 8) hails the named Jesus (6) by name (7); the man's own name is 'Legion, for we are many' (9). The unclean spirits enter the pigs and drown in the sea. The local people come to the named Jesus (15). At the end of this long episode the demoniac proclaims in the Decapolis all that the named Jesus has done for him (20). In this episode, there are at least climactic naming and a degree of ring structure (20 ~ 6) based on this naming.

In the healings of Jairus' daughter and the woman with the flow of blood (5.22–43), Jairus requests that his daughter 'be saved' (23), the woman has 'suffered many things by many healers' (26), the verb ἰάομαι and the name Jesus are juxtaposed (29–30), and there is emphasis on the woman's 'being saved' (28, 34) and being 'in sound health [ὑγιής, 34] from her scourge'.[75] There is significant overlap between 'healing' and 'saving'. The juxtaposition of the verb ἰάομαι and the name Ἰησοῦς, proximity of cognate noun (ἰατρῶν), and proximity of alternative etymology ('saved') are telling. The punning on Ἰησοῦς and ἰάομαι is clear. The named (36) Jesus' then 'raises up' (41–2) Jairus' apparently dead daughter. Since both these episodes involve questions about 'cleanness' and 'uncleanness', and since Ἰησοῦς here appears, etymologically, both as 'saviour' ~ 'healer' and as 'healer' *simplex*, ⟦134⟧ there is some sense, at least just

---

74  See n. 48.
75  I choose 'sound' (and cognate phrases) for 'consistency' reasons.

below the surface, that the 'healing' done by Ἰησοῦς transcends, or sublates,[76] the complex problematics of the Jewish purity laws. This sense becomes explicit when, in chapter 7, Jesus (unnamed) is arrestingly described as 'making all foods clean' (7.19).

Amidst his general failure of power at Nazareth (6.1–6), the named Jesus (4) 'tends' a few infirm people (5). In the part of Jesus' commissioning of the Twelve Disciples (6.7–13) which deals with healing, there are allusions to 'unclean spirits' (7) and 'tending' (13). In the healings at Gennesaret, the sick 'are saved' (6.56). In the healings of the Syrophoenician woman's daughter (7.24–30) and the deaf and dumb man (7.31–37), no significant vocabulary is used. In the healing of a blind man at Bethsaida (8.22–6), there is again no significant vocabulary. In the healing of the boy with an unclean spirit (9.14–29), Jesus is thrice named (23, 25, 27). In the healing of the blind Bartimaeus (10.46–52), Jesus is directly addressed (47), in the narrative Jesus' name is repeated five times (47, 49, 50, 51, 52), and Bartimaeus' faith 'saves' him (52). There is here at least punning on Ἰησοῦς ~ σῴζειν in its medical application. This seemingly prepares for the next item (which, if so, illustrates Mark's unobtrusive literary skill).

At the crucifixion, mockers exhort Jesus to 'save yourself'; similarly, the chief priests: 'he saved others, he cannot save himself' (15.30–1).

As we have seen, Mark clearly puns on Ἰησοῦς/ἰάομαι (and synonyms). His representation of Jesus as 'saviour' also stresses his 'saving' in healing contexts;[77] Mark also knows and exploits the association between the name of Jesus and 'saving'. Here, since Jesus' 'healing' can include 'saving' from death (5.23, 28, 34), the double mockery at the crucifixion *inter alia*, but primarily, rejects the claims of Ἰησοῦς as ἰατρός, so that there is a broad ring structure between 15.30–1 and 2.17.

There is perhaps further ironic punning when the named Jesus 'cries for help' (15.34 ἐβόησεν).[78] At any rate, from a superficial, non-Christian view, in this, his seemingly most wretched situation, the gulf between 'Jesus' = 'The Healer' and 'Yahweh saves', the Son, and the Hebrew God, his Father, seems absolute, because 'Yahweh' does not 'save' him. Some readers might perhaps

---

76   'Sublate' is a useful theological term (less aggressive than 'cancel' or 'annul') implying 'absorb and transform'.

77   Since this claim, especially in this context, aroused discussion at Manchester, I emphasise that I am not saying that Jesus' 'healing' and 'saving' are formally the same: only that there can be significant overlap, and that it is important to recognise this overlap where it occurs (as numerous commentators on this passage and on others do not, but Church Fathers sometimes do [pp. 631 and 635]).

78   See n. 59 above.

also 'hear' Ἰησοῦς (34) as 'Yah saves' directly.[79] Then some of the [[135]] bystanders hear Jesus' 'cry for help' as a cry to Elijah (35), and one individual exhorts them to 'see if Elijah comes to take him down (36). And/but [more the latter] Jesus [named] let out a great cry and breathed his last' (37). The allusions to Elijah[80] are triply significant. First, Elijah, like Jesus, (allegedly) raised people (precisely, one person) from the dead (1 Kings 17.17–24; 2 Kings 4.34–5). Second, in the earlier narrative Elijah functions as an anticipatory paradigm for Jesus himself (Mark 6.15; 8.28; 9.4–13). Third, the name Elijah (Eli-Jah), which means 'Yahweh is God', is cognate with Ἰησοῦς. There is another significant pun. Jesus' 'cry for help' (15.34) takes the form of the question from Psalm 22.2 'My God, my God, why hast thou forsaken me?'. Jesus himself cries in the Aramaic version of the psalm, which Mark quotes and then translates into Greek. The Greek word for 'God' (θεός) interacts punningly with 'Jesus' (~ 'Yahweh'), but the punning interaction is even stronger in the Aramaic version, where the word for God (transliterated into Greek as ελωι) interacts also with 'Elijah' ('Ηλίας), hence some of the bystanders even interpret Jesus 'cry for help' as 'calling Elijah' (35).

The effect of this intense and varied punning is to ratchet up the identity and theodicean problems of the crucifixion to the very highest pitch. Is 'Yahweh' 'God'? Does he 'help'? Does he 'save'? Can the crucified 'Jesus' bring/be the 'salvation' of 'Yahweh'?

But of course all these problematics are resolved by the wider Christian narrative. Practising Christians who use Mark already know, and new readers who read Mark to the end learn, that the horrible mockery is refuted by the resurrection (16.1–7), when Jesus 'rose' (ὁ ἠγέρθη), just as some of those he himself 'saved' in 'healing' 'rose' or 'were raised' by him (1.31; 2.9, 11–12; 5.41–2; 9.27), and in some cases from death or effective death. So Jesus' resurrection is the greatest 'healing' of all, the 'healing' of death itself. Mark's soteriology of the crucifixion is rammed home by a whole series of significant name plays.

Mark's general treatment of Jesus' 'healing' acquires extra force from a special feature of his narrative technique: his very extensive use of present tenses,[81] which also occurs in healing contexts.[82] Jesus' healing in all its aspects remains 'present' to all readers and 'present' both in space and time. Thus Mark integrates the puns on the name of Jesus into the most essential Christology, or perhaps in this context one should rather say 'Jesusology'. That word exists but

---

79  See p. 623 above.
80  I thank John Barclay for suggesting Elijah's significance to my theme.
81  Boring (2006) 1, 24.
82  1.21, 41, 44; 2.3, 4, 5, 8, 10; 3.3, 4, 5; 5.9, 15, 19, 22, 23, 36, 38, 39, 40, 41; 7.32; 8.22; 9.19; note their profusion in the chapter 5 material.

is usually pejorative. I use it descriptively and neutrally. In the present context, it seems unarguably the *mot juste*.

⟦136⟧ Although the Greek of Mark, himself apparently bilingual in Greek and Aramaic and perhaps even also Latin-speaking, is certainly rough enough, and is apparently sometimes technically distorted by imperfect efforts to render Aramaic into Greek[83] and by the sometimes inappropriate incursions of Latinisms,[84] its creativity *qua* Greek should also be recognised, and Mark's deployment and exploitation of the Ἰησοῦς–ἰάομαι pun (and of related puns) is an excellent example of this. There are marked felicities (as noted) in this Gospel's literary handling and disposition of this material, too.

## 2.2 Matthew

Like Mark (whom he has read), Matthew foregrounds Jesus' name (or names): 1.1 'The book of the genealogy of Jesus Christ, the son of David, the son of Abraham'; 1.18 'the birth of Jesus Christ was like this'; 1.21 'you [Joseph] shall call his name Jesus'; 1.23 'and his name shall be called Emmanuel'; 1.25 'and he [Joseph] called his name Jesus'. There is already heavy emphasis on the process of naming and on the particular names, and chapter 1 is ring-structured by Jesus' name. Two of these references are etymological: 1.21 'you shall call his name Jesus, *for he will save his people himself from their sins*'; 1.23 'and his name shall be called Emmanuel, which is translated, "God with us"'. Such etymological punning on the name of the central figure of the particular narrative has many parallels both in Jewish and in Classical historiography (and biography), and it is particularly appropriate to histories of beginnings. There is a basic point here: the name of Jesus matters not just because of the person who bore it but also because of its meaning(s)—or, rather, the point is that in this case person and name are a complete and already complex unity.

The first of the etymological references spells out what Mark had left implicit (albeit heavily implicit), that 'Jesus' means 'Yahweh saves', although Matthew does not directly relate this meaning to the Hebrew, as he explicitly does with 'Emmanuel'. The natural inference is that early Christians who operated (whether entirely or partly) in Greek knew this meaning of 'Jesus' without necessarily deriving it actively from the Hebrew, an inference that is consistent not only with Mark but also with Paul[85] and with later Christian, 'Hellenistic' allusions.[86] In so far as 'saving' can include 'healing' and the latter also can

---

83   Casey (2010) 63–5, 74–6, 112–14, 323–4, 418–19.
84   Winn (2008) 81, 82, 235.
85   See n. 46 above.
86   Davies–Allison (1988) 209.

be described as 'saving', the way lies open for puns on Ἰησοῦς ~ ἰάομαι. In any case, the occurrence of two explicit etymologies presumably [[137]] allows the possibility of more than two. That this is not lax 'modernist' literary thinking is proved by the comment of the anonymous Christian commentator, *Opus imperfectum in Matthaeum* 1:[87]

> The Evangelist here interprets the meaning of Jesus in the Hebrew language, saying, 'He shall save his people from their sins'. Therefore, while a *doctor*, who has no real power over human *health*, is unashamed to call himself a *doctor* simply because of his ability to prepare herbs, how much more worthy is the one who is *called Saviour*, through whom all the world is *saved*?

Note how easily a qualified ancient reader 'slides' between the etymologies of 'saving' and 'healing'. Importantly, the etymology of 1.21, a quotation from Isaiah (7.14), foregrounds Isaiah as central 'proof text' of Matthean Jesusology. The emphasis of 'himself' (astonishingly untranslated in many versions) is also significant: here, as often, αὐτός implies 'by himself' or 'alone', and Ἰησοῦς the son looks very like his father Yahweh.[88]

Jesus' healing ministry is first mentioned, in general terms, in chapter 4, where the term 'tend' is twice used (23, 24). In 8.2–4, a leper is 'cleansed' (2, 3) and Jesus is named (4). As in Mark, Jesus' sublates Jewish 'purity' laws.

In 8.5–13, the healing of the centurion's slave, Jesus is twice named (10, 13) and the verb ἰάομαι twice used (8, 13), once in the same verse as the name of Jesus (13). As in Mark, these juxtapositions speak. There is also allusion to Jesus' 'tending' (7). Here the punning combines direct etymological punning ('Ἰησοῦς ~ ἰάομαι) with 'punning by synonym'. The combination serves to validate the earlier and subsequent 'punnings by synonym alone'. Characteristically, Matthew here 'plugs a gap' in Mark's less developed techniques. Given the emphases on the centurion's 'slave' (6, 8, 9, 13), on the centurion's authority and ability to give orders (9), and on his acknowledgement of Jesus' superior authority (8), one immediately wonders if a contrast is being suggested between worldly 'service' and Jesus' healing 'attendance', a form of 'serving' which actually *manifests* Jesus' superior 'authority'. Another important theme here is the extension of Jesus' ministry, including his healing ministry, to Gentiles (cf. 10–12).

The episode may also be fruitfully read as a Socratic-style exchange about Jesus' true identity, which the centurion perceives and challenges Jesus to

---

87   Simonetti (2001) 18 = PG 56.634.
88   Further, France (2007) 53.

admit but which Jesus only admits indirectly, through puns.[89] The centurion, who obviously already knows of Jesus' healing powers (that is, that 'Jesus' is 'the Healer'), addresses Jesus as Κύριε (6), which, as in modern Greek, can mean simply 'sir', although even that, as coming from a Roman [[138]] centurion to a non-elite Jew, implies unexpected deference.[90] But it can also of course mean 'Lord' in a religious sense, being the regular Greek 'substitution' for 'Yahweh', and it is also the Greek equivalent of the Latin 'dominus', meaning 'master', and thus suits the centurion's explicit acknowledgement of Jesus' superior authority, as well as his implicit disavowal (in this context) of Roman 'domini' such as Roman emperors.[91] Jesus, named (7), replies: 'I will come and tend him'.[92] 'Tend' (θεραπεύσω) glosses 'heal' without uttering that word. The expressed 'I' ('Εγώ) is, however, highly emphatic, and 'I will come' is also challenging, since, as the centurion immediately points out, with a renewed address to Jesus as Κύριε, there can be no question of the Jewish Jesus' literally 'coming' under the Gentile centurion's roof. The punning phrase, in short, points to Jesus' divine credentials as 'the coming one'.[93] The centurion's renewed appeal 'caps' Jesus' oblique θεραπεύσω with an explicit ἰαθήσεται, and uses an equally emphatic ἐγώ to assert both his own authority and its inferiority to Jesus'. The astonished Jesus proclaims that he has never found such 'belief' (πίστιν) even in Israel and says to the centurion: 'as you have believed, so shall it be to you'. This commends the centurion's true belief without making explicit what that belief is and without explicitly using the word ἰάομαι. Readers and listeners are left to infer that the 'true belief' is that 'Jesus' is 'Healer' is 'Lord'. A final point: if the incident has any claim to historicity,[94] the exchange must have taken place in Greek, not only because of the Roman interlocutor but also because the linguistic games would not otherwise work.

When Jesus then cures Peter's mother-in-law, he is again named (14), so that his name comes in adjacent verses, further emphasising the punning relationship between Ἰησοῦς and ἰάομαι. She then 'arises' and 'serves' (διηκόνει) him (8.14–15). The last detail seems to confirm that the healing of the centurion's

---

89  I follow (with modifications) a valuable suggestion of Heather Vincent's.
90  Discussion: Davies–Allison (1991) 20.
91  A parallel: it is well understood that Thomas' unhistorical acclamation of the risen Jesus as 'my Lord and my God' in John 20.28 subverts Domitian's claim to be 'dominus ac deus' (Suet. *Dom.* 13).
92  Many commentators think Jesus' reply much better as a question. I think a statement (*qua* ironic) subtler, but the point hardly affects my analysis.
93  Discussion of this concept, arguably accepted by the historical Jesus as applying to himself, in (e.g.) Allison (2010) 274–8; the 'divine' ἔρχομαι and 'uenio' provide pagan parallels comprehensible to the centurion.
94  Affirmative: e.g., Dunn (2003) 212–16.

slave is concerned with inversions of 'service' and 'authority'. Jesus' 'tending' (16) fulfils (17) the prophecy of the named Isaiah (53.4) that 'he himself took our infirmities and bore our diseases'. That prophecy is immediately succeeded by another episode, in which Jesus is both named [[139]] and gives orders (18): details which maintain the themes of 5–17. The perfectly placed Isaiah prophecy casts Ἰησοῦς both as medical scapegoat (foreshadowing Jesus' 'healing' Passion) and (again) as 'attendant' or 'servant'. Thus both 8.7 and 8.16–17 confirm that Jesus' 'healing' and 'tending' can be part of his role as 'the Suffering Servant'.[95] Some Christian readers would also certainly have known the sequel to Matthew's restricted quotation of Isaiah: 53.5 τῷ μώλωπι αὐτοῦ ἡμεῖς ἰάθημεν ('we were **healed** by his weal') and found there, already, a prophecy of Jesus' very name. We should also recall that the name Isaiah (Isa/iah), which means 'God is salvation', is closely cognate with the name of Ἰησοῦς, and that the name of Ἰησοῦς is the very opposite of 'disease' (17): the clash here could not be more elemental.

In the abbreviated story of the healing of the Gadarene demoniacs (8.28–34), Jesus is climactically named (34). In the healing of the paralytic, Jesus is twice named (9.2, 4). In the healing of the ruler's daughter and the woman with the flow of blood (9.18–26) Jesus is thrice named (19, 22, 23), and the woman's healing is thrice described as her 'being saved' (21, 22 [*bis*]). There is at least climactic punning on Ἰησοῦς as 'Yahweh saves', and, again, the implication that 'Jesus' sublates the purity laws.

In the healing of the two blind men (9.27–31), Jesus is thrice named (27, 28, 30). In the healing of the dumb man (9.32–4), no significant vocabulary is used. In the generalised description of Jesus' ministry at 9.35–7, mention is made of the named Jesus' 'tending' (35). Ἰησοῦς is again the opposite of 'diseases' (35), and this 'opposition' is reflected in the very structure of the sentence, with 'Jesus' at the beginning and 'disease' at the end. Here, too, there is significant stress on Jesus' 'all-ness' ('and Jesus went around all the cities and the villages, teaching in their synagogues and heralding the good news of the kingdom and tending all disease and all physical weakness'). In the named Jesus' commissioning of the Twelve (10.1–15), mention is made of 'unclean spirits' (1), 'tending' (1, 8), and 'cleansing' (8). Jesus' boasts to John the Baptist of his healing miracles are introduced by the named Jesus (11.4–5). In the healing of the man with the withered hand (12.9–13), mention is made of Jesus' 'tending' (10) and the hand is made 'sound'. The named Jesus (15) then 'tended all who followed him', and the following referenced Isaiah quotation (Isaiah 42.1–4; 41.9) emphasises that 'the races [= the Gentiles] will hope in his *name*' (21). And

---

95  On which, cf., e.g., Dunn (2003) 809–18.

Ἰησοῦς and Isaiah are again conjoined. Jesus' 'healing' powers are thus now *formally* extended to the Gentiles. Jesus' 'tending' (22) of a blind and dumb demoniac leads to a long disquisition against the Pharisees and the present wicked generation (24–43).

After much material bearing on the question of people's acceptance or rejection of his teaching, Jesus explains (13.13–17):

> it is for this reason 〚140〛 that I speak to them in parables, that seeing they do not see and hearing they do not hear. [14] And to them is fulfilled the prophecy of Isaiah [6.9ff.] that says: 'you will hear with your hearing and you will not understand, and seeing you will see and will not see. [15] For the heart of this people has grown dull, and they hear with their ears heavily and they have closed their eyes, lest ever they should see with their eyes and hear with their ears and understand with their heart and turn and I will heal [ἰάσομαι] them'.

In order to avoid overload and because the question matters less in the present context, I defer discussion of the syntax of ἰάσομαι until Acts 28.27,[96] although, since the immediate discussion takes the positivity of ἰάσομαι as read, linguistically keen readers may like immediately to correlate the two discussions.

There is supposedly a major textual problem here, in that some scholars reject verses 14–15 as a very early interpolation, perhaps 'imported' from Acts 28.27.[97] Probably most disagree, but, as always, it is the quality of the arguments, not a head count, that counts. The arguments, unfortunately, are too detailed for proper appraisal here. In brief, however, I think the text correct for the following reasons: (1) there is little or no manuscript disturbance to support, or suggest, deletion; (2) the verses are indeed attested very early (below); (3) the notion of 'importation' from Acts founders on our general relative chronology, and perhaps also on specific indications that in this area it is Luke who is taking material from Matthew's text, not the other way round;[98] (4) there is also the question of where John 12.38–40[99] (substantially the same as the Matthew text) fits in the sequence; *prima facie*, it supports the extant text; (5) whatever minor difficulties—and there are some[100]—the verses have great, and, I would say, decisive, positive strengths.

---

96   P. 653.
97   Full range of arguments in Davies–Allison (1991) 393–4.
98   P. 658.
99   P. 639.
100  Implicit riposte to Davies–Allison (1991) in France (2007) 513–14.

In Isaiah, the speaker is God. Here what is at issue is the teaching of Jesus, who is now speaking, and who is in some sense the son of God. Should readers not connect 'I will heal them' (ἰάσομαι) with 'Jesus'/'Ἰησοῦς, the pre-eminent 'healer'? Should they not 'hear' Ἰησοῦς as punning on his own name?[101] Why ever not? The connection is further helped (again) by the naming of the cognate 'Isaiah' and by the simple fact that Jewish unresponsiveness is here being characterised in terms of physical malfunction: that is, of spiritual *sickness*. Further, Matthew's first use of Isaiah at 1.23 is etymological; [[141]] the use at 8.17 refers to 'tending' by Ἰησοῦς and is implicitly etymological; the present use is climactic and also etymological. These three etymological contexts bring out central things about Jesus' name, identity, and function. The explicit naming of Isaiah is also climactic and could not be better placed. Further again, the identification of ἰάσομαι with Ἰησοῦς in the present passage has been anticipated by the Isaian 8.17.

Eloquent here are the comments of the fifth-century Cyril of Alexandria (F 166):[102] 'he speaks in this way in order to *save* them, since he ought rather to have said nothing but have been silent, except that it is not for his own glory's sake but for their *salvation* that *Jesus* does everything'. There are several noteworthy points. Cyril is evoking the etymology of Jesus ~ 'saviour', which he associates with the etymology of Jesus ~ 'healer'; he clearly connects ἰάσομαι with Ἰησοῦς; and he takes ἰάσομαι positively. Although more complex, his thought process is essentially the same as that of the anonymous commentator on Matthew 1.[103]

Now, a very big interpretative question is whether Matthew (writing, we have agreed, after the disasters of 70) regards the Christians' general Jewish mission as over and the Jews in general as having been finally punished by the Jewish war and the destruction of the Temple.[104] My obviously far too quick answer to this question would be that 'I [Ἰησοῦς] will heal [ἰάσομαι] them' in the present passage, of the currently visually and aurally impaired 'people' of Israel, combines with 1.21 'you shall call his name Jesus [Ἰησοῦς], *for he will save his people himself from their sins*', to assure readers (of whatever kind) that the Jewish war is not God's last word on the Jews in general and that they will eventually be 'healed' by the Healer. Admittedly, scholars debate the scope of 'his people' in 1.21: the Jewish people in general, or Jesus' 'own people' (redefined as

---

101  Thereby effectively acknowledging his own identity, as he did not explicitly do in his fencing exchange with the centurion (8.5–13).
102  Simonetti (2001) 272.
103  Quoted on p. 631.
104  On this question of anti-Judaism (more loosely, yet, I believe, justifiably, 'anti-Semitism') in Matthew, see recently Donaldson (2010) 30–54.

those that accept him), or, proleptically, 'all people'? In the immediate context of 1.21 and at first reading, the first is surely the most natural interpretation. While the developing narrative brings in the other two possibilities, and while the crucifixion sequence (which I discuss below) stages Jesus' rejection by 'the Jewish people' in general,[105] it also intersects with the beginning (1.21) to pose the question of the salvation of the Jews in general, and 1.21 and 13.17 *combine* to convey their 'salvation' and 'healing' *beyond* the disasters of the Jewish War. If this interpretation is accepted, Matthew's handling of the problem of Jewish rejectionism is not 〚142〛 only morally commendable (up to a point),[106] but also very adroitly executed. And in both respects, the 'Jesus'–'healer' pun, coupled with the 'Jesus'–'saviour' pun, plays a key role.

The narrative proceeds.

In the Feeding of the Five Thousand (14.13–21), Jesus is twice named (13, 16) and performs 'tending' (14). The healing of the sick at Gennesaret (14.34–6) is described as 'saving' (36), which is etymologically emphatic because of the explicit etymology of 1.21, of the naming of Jesus at 14.29 and 31, and of the collocation with Jesus' 'saving' of Peter on the sea at 14.30.

The healing of the Canaanite woman's daughter (15.21–8) juxtaposes the verb ἰάομαι and Jesus' name in the same verse (28), and the whole episode is ring-structured by the name of Ἰησοῦς (28 ~ 21). Here the theme of the extension of the 'healing' power of Ἰησοῦς to Gentiles receives even greater emphasis.

At 15.30 the named Jesus (29) again performs general 'tending'. The healing of an epileptic boy (17.14–20) names Jesus thrice (17, 18, 19) and speaks twice of his 'tending' (16, 18). The generalised notice about Jesus' healing juxtaposes Jesus' name with his 'tending' (19.1–2). So, too, 21.14. The healing of the two blind men (20.29–34) names Jesus thrice (30, 32, 34).

As in Mark, the crucifixion narrative (27.32–50) crystallises the most important 'healing'/'saving' elements and their punning expressions from the preceding narrative. Passersby mock: 'save yourself!' (40); similarly, the chief priests: 'he saved others, he cannot save himself' (42); and others wait to see if 'Elijah comes to save him' (49), itself a punning query, because Elijah means 'Yahweh is God', and 'saving' evokes both Yahweh and Jesus. Matthew's technique here is reminiscent of that of 8.17, 12.21, and 13.14 (the naming of Isaiah in juxtaposition with Jesus). As in Mark, the 'introduction' of Elijah at this point above all in the narrative recalls Elijah's 'saving' of people from death, Elijah's role as anticipatory paradigm for Jesus himself (16.14; 17.3–12), and the

---

105  On these interpretatively demanding 'slides' see, e.g., France (2007) 53, 1057–8, 1112–13; Donaldson (2010) 41–2.

106  The discussion of the end of Acts explores the issues more fully (p. 653).

apparent absoluteness, in the present situation, of the gulf between Ἰησοῦς and Yahweh. But Matthew has intensified these effects by three deft modifications of Mark. First, the mockings (40, 42) of these representatives of the Jewish people acquire even nastier irony from the direct contrast with Matthew's first explicit etymology of Jesus at 1.21: 'he himself will save his people from their sins'. Second, into Jesus' otherwise Aramaic quotation of Psalm 22.2, he puts the Hebrew form of the word for 'God', transliterated into the Greek letters ηλι. This makes the punning interaction with Elijah (47 Ἠλίαν) sharper and more obvious. Third, at 49 he juxtaposes the name 'Elijah' with the verb 'save' (instead of Mark's more ⟦143⟧ prosaic 'take down' [Mark 15.36]), thereby further heightening the problematics of the crucifixion's 'soteriology'.

As in Mark, however, these punning conundra are resolved by the wider Christian narrative: existing Christians know, readers of Mark know, and new readers learn, that the sneers are refuted by Jesus' 'rising' (28.6) from the dead, in the ultimate healing—that from, and of, death itself, just as he himself 'raised' others in his 'healing' (8.15; 9.5–7, 25; 10.8; 11.5 [all the synonymous ἐγείρω]). And the nasty subversion of the 1.21 etymology of Jesus is overcome by a deeper, positive, irony: it is precisely Jesus' crucifixion and death (that is, his apparent failure to 'save himself') that will 'save' all 'his people'—that is, ultimately, all people, including the Jewish 'people'—'from their sins'. Matthew's extremely deft footwork again enacts profound *'soterio*logy' or *'iatro*logy'—or, in a single, but meaning-packed, word, *'Jesus*ology'. Here again he seems to be 'plugging a gap' in Mark. For anti-Jewishness is also a problem in the first Gospel,[107] and, although Mark's anti-Jewishness is less emphatic and less developed than Matthew's, his own text provides no obvious palliative for it.[108] It is Matthew who makes the necessary move: despite everything, the 'Healer' and 'Saviour' will indeed 'save his people himself from their sins'. And in this context, that 'himself' acquires a distinctive further resonance: that of freely bestowed divine grace.

Like Mark, Matthew clearly connects Ἰησοῦς and ἰάομαι (and similar terms) and Ἰησοῦς and σῴζειν/ἰάομαι and, again like Mark, he integrates these related puns into the most essential Jesusology. As usual, his more explicit and more elaborate treatment presumably aspires to 'defeat' Mark's, although the latter's, as we have seen, has its own virtues and power and, indeed, its own felicities. Nevertheless, on this showing, as on others, Matthew remains markedly the more intricate and sophisticated writer, as well as the superior theologian.

---

107    Telford (1999) 234–41; Donaldson (2010) 139–40.
108    This may partly be to do with his own situatedness—precisely, in 70, in the midst of the Jewish War (n. 31 above).

## 2.3 John

In John's majestic Prologue (1.1–18), the name 'Jesus Christ' acquires tremendous, cumulative, weight from the characteristic hymnic and prooemial device of 'late-naming' (17), as commentators do not say. John's account of the healing of the official's son (4.43–54) juxtaposes Jesus' name and the verb ἰάσηται (47), with supportive assonance.

⟦144⟧ The healing of the man at the pool (5.1–18) demands fuller treatment.[109] The named Jesus (6), who already *knows* (somehow) of the man's condition, asks him if he *wants* to be made sound. He offers healing without being asked for it, though the need for reciprocal volition is stressed. The man replies that he finds it difficult to get to the pool, because he has no man to help him and others get there first. While his use of the address Κύριε (6) can mean simply 'sir', readers are bound to consider the possibility that the man speaks more truly than he *knows*, especially given the juxtaposition Κύριε, ἄνθρωπον. Jesus tells him to rise, take up his pallet and walk. The man is immediately made sound (9) and takes up his pallet and walks (9 ~ 8, 6). But this apparently strong closure is at once short-circuited when the Jews criticise the man for doing this on the Sabbath and he answers that he was told to do so by the one who made him sound. The latter phrase itself provides an epexegetic etymology of 'Jesus', but the man of course does not yet *know* this. They ask who this was, 'but the man who was healed (ἰαθείς) *did not know* who it was, for Jesus (Ἰησοῦς) had turned aside, there being a crowd in the place' (13). There is the by now very familiar juxtaposition of Ἰησοῦς and ἰάομαι in the same verse. 'After these things, Jesus [again named, again juxtaposed with a naming in the previous verse] finds him in the temple and said to him: "See, you have been made sound. Go wrong no more, in case something worse is done to you (14). The man went away and announced to the Jews that it was Jesus [Ἰησοῦς] who had made him sound' (15). The man somehow now *knows* Jesus' identity, rather as Jesus himself had *known*, without being told, of the nature of the man's illness (< 6), somehow now *knows* the meaning of the epexegetic phrase 'who had made him sound', and in effect himself becomes an evangelist (~ 'announced') of Jesus. The Jews persecute Jesus for doing these things on the Sabbath and for calling God his own father, making himself equal to God (16–18).

Certain things are clear. There is more than enough here to establish the pun Ἰησοῦς ~ ἰάομαι, especially for readers of earlier gospels. Ἰησοῦς here sublates Jewish purity laws. Jesus' (and Christian) baptism (literal and metaphorical) trump any ordinarily therapeutic immersion in any pool. The episode puts Ἰησοῦς on a divine level, equal with God. There is some link between sickness

---

109  I thank Heather Vincent for sharp comments.

and sin. There is some sort of testing and criticism of the healed man going on, even though he is healed and even though the healing is freely offered. The whole narrative has wide symbolic application.

More specifically, like Matthew 8.5–13, by which it was presumably influenced, this sharply written episode is about Jesus' identity as 'Lord' and 'Healer' ('Lord' *because* he is 'Healer') and about people's success or failure in apprehending this. The Jews understand that Ἰησοῦς is claiming divine identity ⟦145⟧ and parity with God; they do not understand the basis and justification of the claim. The man, object of the Healer's freely offered healing, initially responds to Jesus sufficiently at least to 'obey orders'. When challenged by the Jews for his behaviour on the Sabbath, he understands that the one who made him sound has sufficient authority to condone it but does not *know* his identity. He has some further impulse to virtuous behaviour in that when Jesus finds him he is in the temple. Nevertheless, Jesus there upbraids him. On what basis? The fact that he has been healed proves something, but what? What is the point of Jesus' adjuration, 'go wrong no more'? It is not simply a matter of a general association between illness and sinfulness: the point is that the man has not so far grasped the true identity of Ἰησοῦς as Healer and Lord, so he is still 'going wrong'. In essence, Jesus says that the man's wellness was the key to the question he missed.[110] The man then gets question and answer right by announcing that it was Jesus who had made him sound. The whole episode also functions as a sort of metaliterary test of readers' onomastic skills, of their ability to integrate name and Jesusology, and of their grasp of just what is at stake (acceptance or rejection of Ἰησοῦς in the full meaning of the name). It is a test that (seemingly) all modern commentators have failed.

The long treatment of the death and raising of Lazarus (11.1–44) shows Jesus moving between death and life, pre-echoes Jesus' own death and resurrection, and demonstrates his powers over death and resurrection. There is etymological punning here between the repeatedly, almost incessantly, named Jesus (4, 5, 9, 13, 17, 20, 21, 23, 25, 30, 33, 35, 38, 39, 40, 41, 44!) and 'saving' (12). From a 'pure' literary point of view, the repetitions seem altogether excessive, but they can be justified in other ways.[111] More generally, the episode reinforces the essential connection between 'resurrection' and Jesus' 'healing'.

Like Matthew, John uses the named Isaiah quotation with reference to Jewish unbelief, characterised in terms of defective sight and hearing, at 12.38–40, with the further gloss (41): 'Isaiah said these things, because he saw his glory and spoke concerning him'. Given that the whole question is about recognition

---

110   I owe this sentence to Heather Vincent.
111   P. 665.

of Jesus, who is repeatedly named hereabouts (30, 35, 36, 44), are not readers expected to connect ἰάσομαι and Ἰησοῦς and to see that 'the Healer' is punning on his own name? Again, why ever not, especially given (again) the naming of the cognate Isaiah and given Matthew's precedence? The gloss 'Isaiah said these things, because he saw his glory and *spoke concerning him*' functions as a not particularly subtle 'prompt'. Uniquely (seemingly) among commentators, Barrett here connects prophecy and speaker: 'John ⟦146⟧ may have made use of these words with an allusion to the inner meaning of Jesus' miracles of healing', though he does not connect Jesus' 'healing' with his name.[112]

There is the same big question with John as with Matthew: where ultimately—after the disasters of 70—do the Jews in general stand in relation to God?[113] I think that John, through the Ἰησοῦς ~ ἰάσομαι play, gives the same answer as Matthew, though the case is admittedly much harder to argue in his case (because of some extremely nasty elements in his treatment of 'the Jews').[114]

So far, John's use of the pun, though still theologically crucial, is considerably less than those of Mark and Matthew. Perhaps this reflects a desire to minimise vulgar 'Jesusology', which would be consistent with John's rather elevated concerns. But although John's narratives of Jesus' healings (in the normal sense of the word) stop half-way through the Gospel and although his exploitations of the direct pun Ἰησοῦς ~ ἰάομαι stop at 12.40, he extends the theme most richly in his long account of the Last Supper (13.1–17.26). At the start, in the washing of the disciples' feet (13.1–20), Jesus is four times named (1, 7, 8, 10), and the activity makes them 'clean' (11), in a symbolic pre-enactment of the 'cleansing' effects of the crucifixion.[115] Here Jesus' sublation of Jewish purity laws already acquires, proleptically, its sublimation. At the crucifixion (19.17, 18, 19, 20, 23, 25, 26, 28, 30, 33, 38, 40, 42!), and in the post-resurrection appearances (20.2, 12, 14, 15, 16, 17, 19, 21, 24, 26, 29, 30, 31; 21.1, 4, 5, 7, 10, 12, 13, 14, 15, 17, 20, 21, 22, 23, 25!), Jesus is insistently and repeatedly named, to a degree reminiscent of the proleptically resurrection Lazarus episode (11.1–44). John does not make explicit that Jesus' crucifixion and resurrection constitute the greatest 'healing' of all and 'save' all people: he does not need to (or not to readers who have read him aright). His treatment of the pun is a mixture of the sophisticated, the profound, and the clunky (though the latter, again, can at least largely be explained and excused in other than 'pure' literary terms).

---

[112] Barrett (1978) 431.
[113] Discussion: Donaldson (2010) 81–108.
[114] On which see Casey (1996), esp. 116–26; 223–6.
[115] Barrett (1978) 436–7.

## 2.4 Luke

Like the other Gospels, Luke handles the introduction of Jesus' name distinctively and creatively. In the Preface Jesus is only mysteriously glossed as, or ⟦147⟧ included within, 'the word' (1.2),[116] and in the narrative he is only first named at the visitation of the angel Gabriel (1.31 'you [Mary] will call his name Jesus'), and then again at the end of the birth narrative (2.21 'his name was called Jesus, the one called by the angel before he was conceived in the womb'). There is therefore great initial emphasis on the name Jesus as such, though, in contrast to Matthew, no etymology is given. The effect is to create suspense, before the name is 'resolved'. This sense of unresolvedness about Jesus' full identity continues in the early episodes up to chapter 4 (the divine baby of 2.1–40, the boy in the temple of 2.41–52, the baptised Jesus of 3.21–2, the tempted figure of 4.1–13), and use of Jesus' name remains correspondingly sparse (2.27, 43, 52; 3.21, 23; 4.1, 4, 12, 14), certainly by comparison with later developments. Then in the episode of Jesus' reception (and rejection) at Nazareth (4.16–30), while Jesus himself is not named, there are allusions to healings (18) and cleansing (27); the question of Jesus' identity is raised (22) and he is referred to as 'Joseph's son' (22); and he himself (23) anticipates his audience's challenging use of the proverb 'healer [ἰατρέ], tend [θεράπευσον] yourself'. That proverb itself exploits 'punning by synonym'. There is surely enough here already to suggest the pun on Jesus as 'healer' (the more so, of course, for readers of Mark, and of Matthew and John, if they too precede Luke).

In subsequent healings (4.31–41), Jesus himself is named (34), and there are allusions to 'uncleanness' (33, 36) and 'tending' (40). 5.12–26 recounts Jesus' healings of a leper and a paralytic. In the first case (12–16), Jesus himself is named (12), the word 'healing' is not used, and the process is described as 'cleansing' (12, 13, 14) and 'tending' (15). In the second case (17–26), the verb ἰάομαι is used (17). At 6.18–19, although Jesus himself is not named, there are allusions to 'unclean spirits' (18) and 'tending' (18) and the verb ἰάομαι is used twice (18, 19). As in Mark and Matthew, 'Jesus the Healer' sublates Jewish purity laws.

In the healing of a centurion's slave (7.1–10), Jesus is named four times (3, 4, 6, 9), the centurion sends messengers to ask Jesus to 'save' the slave (3) and he himself requests: ἰαθήτω (7). Jesus, named, responds favourably (9), and the slave is found 'in sound health' (10). There is thus double punning on 'saving' and 'healing', as well as the now familiar association between 'Jesus' and '*sound* health'. In 8.43–8 (Jesus' healing of the woman with the flow of blood), the name of Jesus occurs at 45 and 46, the verb ἰάομαι at 47, with clear

---

116   Full quotation: n. 15; for Jesus here ~ 'the word' see John 1.1–17; Dunn (2003) 178 n. 29; Moles (2013).

punning. In 9.1–6 (Jesus' mission to the twelve), the verb occurs ἰάομαι at 9.2. At 9.11 'tending' and the verb ἰάομαι are conjoined. In the healing of the boy with the unclean spirit (9.37–43), Jesus is named twice (41, 42), and ⟦148⟧ name and verb ἰάομαι occur in the same verse (42), the punning effect here being reinforced by assonance.

In the second commission, of the Seventy-two, Jesus' instructions include 'tending' of the sick (10.9) and the returning disciples announce that even the demons are subject to them 'in your name' (10.17). In the healing of the crippled woman on the Sabbath, the name of Jesus is conjoined with the verb for 'tend' (13.14).

Jesus' contemptuous message to Herod Antipas proclaims his casting out of demons and fulfilling of healings (13.32): the self-description, the self-proclaimed job description, of Ἰησοῦς is ἴασις ('healing'). The latter word acquires extra force because Luke is the only Evangelist to use it. There is a sort of 'implicit' assonance here (Ἰησοῦς [unstated] ~ ἴασις), which assists the punning association. *Could* any early Christian who heard the noun ἴασις, in practically any context, but especially this one, *not* think of Ἰησοῦς?

The healing of the man with dropsy (14.1–6) uses the name Jesus (3) and the verbs 'tend' (3) and ἰάομαι (4), with, again, assonantal punning. In the healing of the Ten Lepers (17.11–19), Jesus is addressed (13), they are 'cleansed' (14, 17), the verb ἰάομαι is used (15), and one is 'saved' (19). There is thus double punning, on 'saving' and 'healing'. In the healing of the blind beggar near Jericho (18.35–43), Jesus is addressed (38) and thrice named (37, 40, 42), and the beggar 'saved' (42). The pun on Ἰησοῦς ~ 'saviour' (as 'medical' saviour) is clear.

At the crucifixion (23.33–43), the rulers mock Jesus (34), saying (35): 'he saved others, let him save himself', as, similarly, the soldiers (37) and one of the criminals crucified with Jesus (39). Their mocking *inter alia*, but importantly, denies the etymology Jesus ~ saviour (and specifically its medical sense). Luke helps this etymological play, by naming Jesus in the immediate context of 34, as the other Evangelists do not, and, by omitting Jesus' quotation of Psalm 22 and any mention of Elijah, he keeps the focus on this central pun. Of course, as in Mark and Matthew, existing Christians know, and new readers learn, that these mockings are refuted by Jesus' 'rising', the ultimate healing, just as his own healings caused others to 'rise' (4.39; 5.25; 5.23–4; 7.14, 22; 8.54 [the last three with ἐγείρω]). Differently from Mark and Matthew (and, indeed, from most Classical biography), Luke's whole biography of the mortal Jesus is bookended by apparent failure and by apparent Jewish rejection (< 4.16–30), thus giving Jesus' 'rising' even greater weight.

Although his treatment of the crucifixion is (from the point of view of our theme) simpler than those of Mark and Matthew, Luke's general treatment of the Ἰησοῦς ~ ἰάομαι pun is much more emphatic and much more voluminous than those of the other Evangelists. One might even think it excessive and, sometimes, flat-footed, except that commentators miss it, and one might explain this greater emphasis as a riposte to the (in this respect) [[149]] more minimalist John (if John is earlier), or as preparation for Acts, where, importantly, the post-Ascension Jesus' healing continues, or indeed in other ways.[117]

In any case, readers of the second book of Luke's unified 'double-work' have already been sensitised to puns on Ἰησοῦς ~ ἰάομαι and on related terminology. Or, if they have not been, it is not Luke's fault.

### 2.5  Acts

Like the Luke narrative, Acts begins by emphasising the name of Jesus: 1.1 'The first *logos* I made about all the things, Theophilos, that Jesus began to do and teach'. Indeed, the Acts Preface is ring-structured by Jesus' name (1.11 ~ 1.1). The arresting statement that Luke, a biography of Jesus, concerned what 'Jesus *began* to do and teach' makes an essential *Jesus*ological point: the risen and ascended Jesus is still *alive* and active in the world, both within the narrative of Acts and within all subsequent narratives up to the Last Judgement (17.31) and beyond. Hence, generically, Acts *combines* historiography with biography—biography of Peter, Paul, and the rest, but also the *continuing* biography of Jesus himself.

The narrative begins. Peter's Pentecost speech (2.14–36) names Jesus (22) and then claims (24): 'God raised him up, having loosed the pangs of death, because it was not possible for him to be overpowered by it'. The description involves double action: an active God and an also active Jesus, who 'could not be overpowered by death'. The terminology is partly 'medical' ('raised up', 'pangs'), and re-emphasises that the resurrection was the ultimate 'healing'. The use of 'pangs' suggests also 'rebirth'.[118] Peter continues (31–2): 'He [David] foresaw and spoke of the rising of the Christ, that he was not left behind in Hades nor did his flesh see corruption. This Jesus God raised up, of which all of us are witnesses'. The speech also plays on the etymology of Jesus as saviour (22 ~ 21). Peter quotes an eschatological prophecy of Joel, which ends (21) 'and it will be that everyone who calls on the name of the Lord shall be saved', and

---

117  P. 665.
118  The phrase's biblical parallels (Bruce (1951) 92; Barrett (2004) 143) do not diminish its force within the continuing imagery. The precise interpretation of the phrase (Barrett [2004] 143–4) does not affect the present analysis. On the general theme of miracles in Acts see now Penner (2012) with much useful bibliography.

he then begins his own 'words' with the name of Jesus (22), effecting a neat 'slide' between God as Lord and Jesus as Lord.

In the healing of the lame man at the Gate of the Temple (3.1–10), the healing powers of Jesus' followers, adumbrated in Luke, first acquire narrative weight proportionate to those of Jesus himself in the Gospel. This is part ⟦150⟧ of the general 'succession' pattern of Acts rightly stressed by Charles Talbert.[119] The healing is effected as follows: Peter commands (6–7): '"In the name of Jesus Christ the Nazarene, walk." He took him by the right hand and raised him up, and immediately his feet and ankles were made firm.' Later (12–16), Peter states that the man walks and has perfect health because of the name of Jesus, 'the author of life, whom God raised from the corpses' (15). Here Jesus' healing powers acquire cosmic significance ('the author of life'). Peter stresses that the man has been made strong through 'his name' (ring-structuring with 6).

Peter and John continue 'proclaiming in Jesus the raising, the one from the corpses' (4.2)—'healing' vocabulary is maintained and resurrection is Jesus' greatest 'healing'—and they are therefore arrested and brought before the Council. Peter proclaims that the lame man was 'saved' (9) and is 'in sound health' (10, ὑγιής) 'by the name of Jesus Christ the Nazarene ... whom God raised from the corpses' (10), 'and there is salvation in no one else, for there is no other name under heaven given among human beings in which we must be saved' (12). While the name of 'Christ' also signifies here, the main emphasis is on 'Jesus' as both 'healer' and 'saviour'. The use of ὑγιής, in close association with Jesus' name, is reminiscent of John 5.15[120] and suggests the etymology, '*Jesus* makes people *sound*'. That, surely, is what *healers do*. Again, Jesus' 'healing' is now, emphatically and explicitly, unique among humans, and inferior only to God's. So much for the Caesars. And this 'healing' unites simple physical healing and *salvific* healing. The importance of the name of 'Jesus' is re-emphasised (18), and the episode closes by ring structure with a summary allusion to the 'healing' (ἰάσεως) of the lame man (22). The pun is clear, and it is structural. I have already noted Luke's distinctive use of the noun (Luke 13.32). Luke's use of language can be diamond-sharp. (Where it is not, as in the constantly repeated association of Ἰησοῦς and ἰάομαι in Luke, there should be other explanations).[121]

In the collective prayer of the Believers (4.23–31), there is an allusion to 'Jesus, whom [God] anointed' (27), referencing 'Jesus' as (also) 'Christos' (the 'Anointed'), and a request that they be enabled 'to speak your [God's] word

---

119  Talbert (1974).
120  P. 638.
121  Again, p. 665.

with all freedom of speech (29), while you stretch out your hand for healing [ἴασιν] and signs and portents are done through the name of your holy servant/child [παιδός] Jesus ['Ἰησοῦ]' (30). As elsewhere, the two etymologies help each other. In the second, 'healing' etymology, God's and Jesus' healing activities are combined, and Jesus' own are emphasised by the punning [[151]] ring-structure ἴασιν ... Ἰησοῦ. As in Exodus 15.26,[122] there is an implicit bilingual pun on Yahweh, Ἰάω, and ἴασιν, and one sees how readily early Christians who operated in Greek could connect 'healing' by Ἰάω with that by his son Ἰησοῦς. Here also Jesus' 'healing' seems to be connected with his wider 'service', in as much as παιδός equivocates between 'servant' and 'child'.

In chapter 5, Peter performs 'tending' (16) on the 'sick' (15) and on those afflicted by 'unclean spirits' (16), and, when the High Priest reminds Peter and the apostles that they had been ordered not to teach in this name [implicitly, that of Jesus], the punning reply is that 'God ... raised Jesus (30), who is leader and *saviour*' (31).

8.7–8 records generalised 'tending' of 'unclean spirits', and in 9.17 Ananias names Jesus as commissioning Saul's recovery of sight, which immediately occurs (18), and at 9.34, Peter heals Aeneas with the words: 'Aeneas, *Jesus* Christ *heals* you' (Αἰνέα, ἰᾶταί σε Ἰησοῦς Χριστός), whereupon Aeneas 'arises' and makes his bed. The ἰᾶται ~ Ἰησοῦς pun is helped by assonance. Luke is also here dramatising, proleptically, Jesus'—and Peter's—'healing' of a 'sick' Rome. At least some of Luke's Christian readers (and, indeed, some of his non-Christian readers) will know that, like Paul, Peter did get to Rome,[123] and that the 'healing' of Rome is part of the Christian prospectus. And, while Αἰνέα is on one level a Greek transliteration of the 'Roman' name Aeneas, no doubt Luke, like Virgil at *Aen.* 12.946–7,[124] recalls the literal meaning of the original Greek name: 'terrible', thereby creating a novel, Christianised version of the stereotypical contrast between Roman fierceness and Greek culture. This Christian bid to supplant (or, perhaps, sublate) Greek culture acquires more flesh in Acts 17.

Peter's restoration to life of Tabitha/Dorcas (parallel to Jesus' restoration to life of several people), employs the vocabulary of 'arising' (40–1). Luke uses the two names, Jewish and Greek, both of which mean 'gazelle'; the meaning 'gazelle' derives from the animal's large, bright eyes; and when the dead Tabitha is told to 'arise', she 'opens her eyes' (40). The effect is lovely. Restoration of life coincides with reactivation of name. There are thus further puns on 'Dorcas'

---

122   P. 623.
123   I take this tradition—although distorted in detail—to be basically sound. The crucial evidence is 1 Clem. 5.4–5 (90s–early 100s).
124   O'Hara (1996) 242.

as 'the seeing one' (Δορκάς ~ δερκόμαι) and 'Dorcas' as 'the living one', because to see is to live,[125] hence, as in the narrative of Paul's healing, 'healing' involves restoration of sight, in Paul's case both literal and (surely) metaphorical or spiritual.

⟦152⟧ Peter's vision from the Lord rescinding Jewish food laws (a vision paralleling Paul's on the road to Damascus [9.1–9]) and Peter's consequent association with the centurion Cornelius (10.1–30) show that no food is 'unclean' (14, 15), nor is any man 'unclean' (29). Is this profound 'insight' of Peter's, deriving from a vision 'seen', the result of the continuing 'healing' activity of Ἰησοῦς? Many things in the text (including Luke) so far support the answer 'yes', and it is further supported by Peter's summary of Jesus' ministry to Cornelius (38): 'As for Jesus (Ἰησοῦν), the one from Nazareth, how God anointed him with holy spirit and power, who went about doing good and healing (ἰώμενος) all those overmastered by the Devil, because God was with him'. Here the statement that God 'anointed' Jesus glosses his other name Χριστός and (as elsewhere) re-alerts readers to other punning possibilities. As before, Jesus' 'healing' is further illustrated by his 'being raised from the corpses' (41, 40). The whole sequence shows Ἰησοῦς decisively sublating Jewish purity laws.

A series of instances from chs. 2 to 10 shows that allusion to Jesus' healing' ministry comes naturally within extended expositions of doctrine. So, in Paul's speech to the synagogue at Pisidian Antioch (13.16–41), 'Jesus' is named 'Saviour' (23), with the by now familiar pun, and he is 'raised from the corpses' (30), 'raised' (33), 'raised from the corpses, no longer going to return to corruption' (34), and, as the one 'whom God raised up he saw no corruption' (37). Subsequently at Lystra, Paul's healing of a cripple (14.8–10) involves 'saving' (9) and 'standing up' (10).

Before the Jerusalem Christian Council (15.1–29), Peter argues that God has 'cleansed' the hearts of the Gentiles (9), and ascribes the 'saving' both of Christians and Gentiles to the grace of 'the Lord Jesus' (11), with double punning, on Jesus as 'saviour' and as 'healer'.

Paul's journeys include exorcism of a slave girl (16.16–18). Over a period of days she shouts: 'These men are servants of the Most High God, who proclaim ... the way of salvation'. Paul exorcises her in the name of Jesus Christ. Here the true 'healing' and 'salvation' of 'Jesus' overcome the false 'salvation' of the pagan monotheistic god, the Hypsistos.[126] In the subsequent imprisonment at Philippi and the disorder caused by Paul and Silas' miraculous release,

---

125   LSJ s.v. δέρκομαι.
126   On whom: Mitchell (1999); Mitchell–Van Nuffelen (2010). Mitchell rightly emphasises the Hypsistos as *the* pagan parallel to the Jewish and Christian monotheistic god.

the terrified gaoler asks (30): 'Sirs/Lords (κύριοι), what must I do that I may be saved [in the sense of 'saved from immediate death']?', and they reply (31): 'believe in the Lord [κύριον]¹²⁷ Jesus Christ and you yourself ⟦153⟧ will be saved and your household also' ['saved' (also) in the religious sense]. Since this is one of several passages in Acts where the post-ascension Jesus' activity evokes the activities of Dionysus, Jesus' 'saving' activity (emphasised by etymological punning) is implicitly preferred to that pagan god's.¹²⁸

The narrative of Paul in mainland Greece builds up to his encounter with the philosophers and his speech to the Areopagus (17.1–34), which is one of the greatest sequences in Acts (and in Luke-Acts) and one of the most complicated, and which can here be treated only selectively and summarily.¹²⁹

Paul preaches about Jesus (3) to the synagogue in Thessalonica with some success, but majority Jewish hostility results in attacks, both physical and judicial, on 'Jason' ('Ιάσων) and Paul and Silas. 'Jason' is introduced quite out of the blue, he is named four times (5, 6, 7, 9), and once in the same verse as Jesus (7), whose own name 'rings' the whole episode (3, 7). Any reader or listener hitherto blind or deaf to the symbiotic relationship between divine 'healing' and Jesus' name is here being hit over the head. The effect is intensified by assonance. One might even criticise Luke's technique as crude—were it not that commentators unerringly miss this connection between 'Jason' and 'Jesus'. In Luke's defence, Paul's success with a Jew named 'Ιάσων illustrates the progressive advance of the 'Ιησοῦς movement within Judaism, just as the naming of the first '*Christians*' in 11.26 marks their 'succession' to *Jesus* as '*Christ*'. This is part of the general 'succession' quality of Acts, which Luke underlines with many deft touches such as this one. Jason's responsiveness also contrasts markedly with the rejectionism of (some of) the philosophers. There may also be another point (below). At any rate, as the narrative moves to Acts' central engagement with rival pagan wisdom, Jesus' 'healing' is very much in the air. More particularly, the *sound* of 'healing' is already in readers' or listeners' ears—or should be.

---

127   There is something of the same play/ambiguity as in Matthew 8.6, 8 and John 5.6, as from the gaoler's point of view Paul and Silas can now, after the earthquake, be both 'sirs' (deserving of courtesy) and 'divine men' (because obviously divinely protected), and from Christian readers' point of view, they are Christ-*like*, though the apostles themselves then (re)define 'Ιησοῦς as the true κύριος.
128   Moles (2006b) 67, 80 {above, p. 554, 566}.
129   For some earlier observations, see Moles (2006b) 71–4, 80–8 {above, pp. 559–61, 565–73}; recent NT treatment: Rowe (2011). I intend a general treatment {= below, Ch. 28}.

As, Socratically,[130] Paul dialogued with chance passersby in the *agora*, 'some of the Epicurean and Stoic philosophers encountered him, and some said: "What would this seed-collector be wanting to say?" But others said: "He seems to be an announcer of foreign divinities"—because he announced as good news Jesus and resurrection' (18).

So the philosophers, too, are *listening* to Paul, and while one group finds his teaching in the *agora* incomprehensible, the other produces a tentative ⟦154⟧ interpretation which on one level is quite obtuse, in that they miss Paul's true Socratic credentials, but which on another level shows a dim apprehension of difficult theological truths about the ambiguous status of Ἰησοῦς.[131] There is also the usual interplay between internal and external audiences, with the latter facing, yet again, the same question as the philosophers: 'What do the words/names/sounds "Jesus" and "resurrection" mean to you?'[132] This whole emphasis on sound and its interpretation reflects alike: the conceptualisation of divine action as God's 'word' (John 1, etc.); the orality/aurality of Christian exposition[133] and of Christian reading;[134] the specific requirement to interpret these particular names/sounds rightly; and the representation of human responsiveness or unresponsiveness to God's word (as focused on Ἰησοῦς)[135] in terms of seeing and hearing, that is, of spiritual health (as in the familiar Isaiah prophecy).

The external audience also has to decode aurally the tentative response of the less blinkered philosophers, so as to understand them better and thus speak to them better, in just the same way as Paul himself moves from his '[visual] observation that the city was full of images' (16) and from his 'discovery of an altar on which was inscribed "To the Unknown God"' (23) to his '[visual and verbal] observation' that his audience are 'completely fearful of divinities in all respects' (22). Thus 'Jesus' and 'resurrection' must be making some sort of sense to the less blinkered philosophers, even if defective sense, as sounding like foreign divinities. 'Resurrection' (Ἀνάστασις) might suggest an abstract female divinity, and there is the additional possibility that they hear the word/name

---

130   Paul ~ Socrates: Sandnes (1993); Barrett (2004) 828–89; L. C. A. Alexander (2005) 62–8.
131   See further Moles (2006b) 83–5 {above, p. 568–70} and n. 57 above.
132   A similar aural demand occurs at Acts 11.26 χρηματίσαι τε πρώτως τοὺς μαθητὰς Χριστιανούς, where it is crucial that readers/listeners 'hear' Χριστιανούς as cognate with χρηματίσαι: see Moles (2012). I take it this 'aurality' is Luke's particularly intense version of Thucydidean 'vividness' (ἐνάργεια), for I believe that Luke 1.3 'recognise [etc.] the un-slipperiness [etc.]' includes in its many resonances allusion to Thucydides' (1.22.4) 'look at the clearness': Moles (2011).
133   Cf. Romans 10.17 'belief comes from hearing, but hearing by the word of Christ'.
134   See above, n. 16.
135   The emphasis is the same as Luke 1.2 (n. 116).

as similar to, though (as being 'foreign') different from, the ἀναστατήρια, sacrifices on recovery from *sickness* attested by Hesychius.¹³⁶ More disturbingly, they might also 'hear' 'resurrection' as akin to 'insurrection', for earlier in the chapter Paul and his companions have been accused of 'overturning the world' (17.6, with the cognate active participle ⟦155⟧ ἀναστατώσαντες).¹³⁷ What sort of στάσις, then, is this ἀνάστασις? Does it bring 'stability', or world-wide *stasis*? The philosophers' interest in political theory—and law and order—is piqued. As for Ἰησοῦς, having read so much before, and being here comprehensively softened up by the four times named 'Jason', readers must naturally suppose the philosophers to be connecting the name, albeit, again, in some distorted way, with ἰάομαι.¹³⁸ There is, again, a more particular distorted possible association, the goddess of healing, Ἰάσω,¹³⁹ who was 'at home' in Athens. Is this Ἰησοῦς, then, a political 'healer', or is he an 'insurrectionist'?

Within Paul's speech to the Areopagus,¹⁴⁰ some scholars¹⁴¹ see in 28 ('for in him we live and move and are') a quotation from a poem attributed to the (legendary) Cretan philosopher and holy man Epimenides, and, though the

---

136   See, e.g., Bruce (1951) 333.
137   Similar play at 24.5, 12, 15; as far as I can see, NT scholars miss these verbal interplays, which define Christian 'politics' (Christians are not 'revolutionaries', but the ἀνάστασις 'revolutionises' the world).
138   See, e.g., Bruce (1951) 333.
139   See, e.g., Bruce (1951) 333.
140   The question of whether this is an actual trial, undergone by the historical Paul—or whether, at any rate (whatever about actual historicity), it is so *represented* by Luke—is hugely controversial; useful surveys in Wallace–Williams (1993) 91–4; Barrett (2004) 831–2. Given the Socratic analogy, the conjecture that Paul is introducing foreign divinities, the question of 'insurrection', the role of the Areopagus (in whatever sense of the term), the request for elucidation of Paul's 'new' religious teaching, the 'silent' allusion to Aeschylus' *Eumenides* (n. 142), and Paul's own appeal to the Last *Judgement* (32), we should agree that Luke represents Paul's appearance before the Areopagus as *trial-like*, and that this is important on several interpretative levels; on the other hand, I think it clear (*pace* Barnes [1969]; Rowe [2011] 37) that Luke does not *definitely* represent it as a trial and there are obviously incongruous elements. The overall effect is of an iconic, 'mythic' trial, an effect which fits Luke's larger narrative, theological, and philosophical purposes. In any case, the question cannot be dissociated from the larger question of the historicity or fictionality of the whole episode of Paul in Athens as represented by Luke (n. 149), due account taken of the fact that the historical Paul did visit Athens (1 Thessalonians 3.1). {Cf. further below, Ch. 28.}
141   Lake (1933) 249–51 (followed by many); cf. also Bruce (1951) 338; Colaclides (1973) rejects this in favour of an allusion to Eur. *Bacch.* 506; the latter is, I believe, persuasive (see Moles (2006b) 73–4 {above, p. 559–61}), but does not preclude the former. It will be clear from my discussion that, and why, I reject the minimalising view of Luke's *paideia* in Padilla (2009).

arguments are complicated and often nowadays evaded, they remain (I believe) decisive. The allusion is in fact self-justifying: no allusion could be more apt, since the outsider Epimenides effected the purification of Athens from plague (a 'medical' activity); had contact with the Areopagus; instituted altars to unknown gods; and, in the quotation alluded to, had Minos address his father Zeus, falsely entombed as dead, as 'alive', thereby paralleling and anticipating the allusion to the (entombed and then) resurrected Jesus. The 〚156〛 last parallel creates a delicious irony, for Epimenides' championing of Zeus as 'alive' rather than 'dead' (the latter being the orthodox Christian view of the matter) is necessarily deconstructed by his famous claim that 'all Cretans are liars', a claim that was known to some Pauline Christians (Titus 1.12).

Paul's speech is short-circuited by the hubbub that arises when, in the context of the Last Judgement, he mentions the resurrection (31), surely (again) the healing to end all healings, as readers already know (or, by now, should know), and as the context reinforces. At this point, the philosophers again divide into two groups, and again it is a question of 'hearing'—of how one 'hears' or interprets (32): 'but when they *heard* of the resurrection of corpses, some jeered, but others said: "We will *hear* you again about this"'. In context, it is natural to take these 'some'/'others', the first group contemptuously dismissive, the second at any rate still formally open-minded, as corresponding to the original 'some'/'others' of 18, and the two groups as corresponding in turn to the there separately named 'Epicureans' and 'Stoics'. This also makes philosophical sense, as Paul's own speech implies, and it complicates interpretation of the whole encounter. Outside the philosophers' world, however, some individuals did accept Paul's teaching (34), 'among them, Dionysios the Areopagite'. The pagan theophoric name crystallises the subliminal textual presence of the pagan god Dionysus,[142] just as the pagan theophoric name 'Jason' emphasises the truth of the monotheistic Jewish-Christian god 'Yahweh' and the true credentials of Ἰησοῦς.

The whole episode, then, establishes the superiority of the healing of Yahweh and Ἰησοῦς (and also of course of the Epimenidean Paul, healer of Athens, if she responds) in the field of healing (as, of course, in all else) to a series of pagan targets.

One of these targets is Ἰάσω, goddess of healing, whose name is so like that of Ἰησοῦς. Another is Dionysus, referenced both in this chapter and in chapter 16, and also a 'saving' or 'healing' god. Another is the greatest pagan god Zeus, whose apparent supreme and saving powers do not include the raising of

---

142  Moles (2006b) 85–7 {above, pp. 570–3}.

corpses, as had been established at the very first trial before the Areopagus.¹⁴³ Another is the *poets* who celebrated those gods in this field: namely, Epimenides, Cleanthes (28), Aratus (28), Euripides (*Bacchae*), and Aeschylus (*Eumenides*). Another, surely, is Asclepius, son of Iaso, himself the most distinctive pagan healing god, and credited both in myth and in reality with raising people from the dead, and thus Jesus' greatest natural pagan rival, as Julian recognises.¹⁴⁴ Another, certainly, is the Hypsistos. As we have ⟦157⟧ seen, he was referenced in the immediately preceding ch. 16 (in the incident with the prophetic slave-girl). Whatever the notorious problematics (which need not here detain us) of Paul's appeal (23) to an inscription to 'the unknown god' (or, possibly better, 'to unknown god' without the article), the description objectively fits the Hypsistos, whose followers included 'God-fearers' (mentioned as one of the groups dialoguing with Paul in the Agora [17]); the 'unknown god' is formally here being adduced as a pagan monotheistic god amidst the forest of pagan polytheism; and the Hypsistos was certainly paganism's closest approximation to the Jewish and Christian monotheistic god, while in Athens he was also a healer.¹⁴⁵ One should also presumably think of the *hero* 'Jason', whose name means healer, because of the four-times-named Jason in this episode, and because Jason is a hero who in various ways overcomes death, but in myth—not history—unlike Jesus (Christians claim).

What of the philosophers themselves? Philosophers in general, of course, promise philosophical therapy, healing, and medicine, and the claim is naturally made both by Epicureans and Stoics, the latter of whom are further referenced by the well-known quotations from the Stoics Cleanthes and Aratus (28).¹⁴⁶ As we have seen, Paul's speech has little or nothing to offer Epicureans (nor could it have), and it is the Epicureans who initially dismiss Paul as a 'seed-collector' and then jeer at his mention of resurrection. So we should not forget that 'Epicurus' means '(divine) helper', that Epicureans celebrated Epicurus' name, and that 'Epicurean healing' is therefore one of Luke's specific

---

143   Aes. *Eum.* 647–8 ἀνδρὸς δ᾽ ἐπειδὰν αἷμ᾽ ἀνασπάσῃ κόνις / ἅπαξ θανόντος, οὔτις ἐστ᾽ ἀνάστασις. Cf., e.g., Bruce (1951) 340 for this 'silent' allusion.
144   See Appendix 2.
145   Mitchell (1999) 122; (2010) 176 n. 44; more generally (2010) 189–96; Parker (1996).
146   We should add Posidonius (Hommel [1955] and [1957]) and Luke's Stoic contemporary Dio Chrysostom, whose *Olympian Oration*, earlier than Luke-Acts in my view (n. 23; Moles [1995] 181 {above, p. 192}), and concerned, from a pagan point of view, with analogous issues, including the value of religious 'images', contains (12.28) a close verbal parallel to 17.27, and whose *Alexandrian Oration* uses the word 'seed-collecting' of disreputable 'street philosophers' (32.9). The noble and profound *Olympian Oration* is surely a most worthy pagan 'opponent' for Paul/Luke.

targets here.[147] By contrast, the door is left open to the Stoics—although only if they become followers of Jesus and the Jewish-Christian God, only if, for practical purposes, they define themselves out of existence. That is why it is Paul, not the Stoics or Epicureans, who is here—and, indeed, elsewhere in Acts—the true heir of Socrates.[148]

What of the political questions raised by the resurrection? Ἰησοῦς the 'healer', the man whom God 'stood up [ἀναστήσας] from the corpses' will be God's agent on the day that God 'has stood up' [ἔστησεν] for the judgement ⟦158⟧ of the world (31). So Jesus' healing dwarfs by the widest possible margin all judicial or political 'healings' by bodies such as the Areopagus itself or by any rulers, including world-wide rulers such as Roman emperors.

The Areopagus episode poses huge and fascinating interpretative problems. But even with the focus solely on 'healing', Luke's exploitation of the pun on Ἰησοῦς ~ ἰάομαι shows enormous literary and theological creativity, as well as dazzling economy (an economy, indeed, at odds with, and enhanced by, much of the rest of his treatment of the pun, including the first sections of chapter 17 itself). His creativity will be all the greater the more fictional we believe the episode to be. Presumably, it is the natural inclination of most *Histos* writers and readers to regard this episode as being more or less fictional, and there are good arguments for this position.[149] 'Felt' fictionality would import further levels of implication. But such considerations take us too far from our theme.

The narrative proceeds.

When Paul is at Ephesus (19.1–41) and various healings are done, itinerant Jewish exorcists unsuccessfully attempt to imitate them by invoking Jesus' name (13–17); the episode is ring-structured by the name of Jesus (13, 17), which again emphasises, though in a more practical religious context, the contrast between false healers and the one true healer. In the second version of Paul's conversion narrative (22.6–16), Ananias tells Paul: 'rise up and be baptised and wash away your sins, calling upon his name'. Jesus is again being glossed as 'healer'. In Malta, Paul performs more 'healing' and 'tending' (28.7–9). Jesus' name is not mentioned, for the simple reason that Paul and his companions are not trying to convert these benevolent but primitive people.

Finally, we come to the end of Acts (28.30–1), which, like the episode of Paul in Athens, is a very great piece of writing, with many different layers of meaning and of implications, and with the challenging 'unresolvedness' that

---

147   Moles (2006b) 87–8 {above, p. 571–3}.
148   Ignatius (n. 62), was presumably thinking—*mutatis mutandis*—of this aspect (false philosophers vs true) of Acts 17.
149   E.g., Barrett (2004) 824–6.

is a feature of the endings of so much of the most thought-provoking ancient historiography.[150] I again keep the focus on 'healing'.[151]

> And he [Paul] remained [in Rome] a whole two years in a private lodging, and he received all who came in to him, (31) heralding the kingdom of God and teaching the things concerning the Lord Jesus Christ with all freedom of speech and unhinderedly.

⟦159⟧ The end follows Paul's attempt—largely unsuccessful—to persuade the leaders of the Roman Jews about Jesus (28.23–8; 28.17–22). This attempt culminates in Paul's quotation of the familiar passage from Isaiah, cited by name; he has already twice alluded to it before unresponsive Jewish audiences (13.46–7; 18.6); and he now quotes it *in extenso*:

> Go to this people [the Jews] and say: 'You shall hear with your hearing and you will not understand; and seeing you will see, but you will not see. (27) For the heart of this people has thickened, and they have heard with their ears heavily, and they have closed their eyes, lest they should see with their eyes and hear with their ears and understand with their heart, and turn and I [God] will [or: would] heal them'.

It is unnecessary to rehearse manuscript detail here: suffice that at 27 there is a massive ⟦160⟧ textual split between ἰάσομαι and ἰάσωμαι.

To the Isaiah quotation Paul adds (28): 'Be it known then to you that this salvation of God has been sent to the races [= Gentiles]; they themselves will listen'.

Undoubtedly, Luke is here justifying the Christian Gentile mission, but for us the key interpretative question, which, as we have seen, also arises with Matthew and John and which has again prompted endless scholarly debate, is whether Luke (writing, we have agreed, after 70) represents the Christian mission to the Jews as finally over and whether he is in some strong sense of the term anti-Jewish or even anti-Semitic,[152] because in the disasters of 70 (foreshadowed in Luke-Acts and only a few years after the present dramatic situation) the Jews receive divine punishment for their rejection both of Jesus himself and of the renewed Jesus movement after his death. That was how the

---

150  Marincola (2005).
151  I treat some other aspects in Moles (2006b) 88–94 {above, p. 573–7}; (2013).
152  Recent survey: Donaldson (2010) 55–80; useful bibliography in Popkes (2009) 614–15.

early Christian Fathers understood the Jewish War,[153] and their understanding was underpinned by an interpretation of the Gospels, including Luke-Acts, which I think essentially right (though beyond our scope here).

The reading of 27 has recently attracted scrupulous technical debate.[154] On the one hand, Martin Karrer upholds ἰάσομαι and claims that Luke constructs a 'Bollwerk gegen jeden Anti-judaismus'. On the other hand, Enno Edzard Popkes regards the textual problem as insoluble.[155] Indeed, the massive textual split presumably reflects (some) early Christians' dubiety about how to read the scene. The textual split in fact goes back to the Septuagint itself, where ἰάσομαι is the majority reading but V has ἰάσωμαι, and the majority reading is itself a 'softening' of the uncompromising Hebrew. But there is a crucial situational difference between Isaiah and Luke-Acts. Neither Jews who used the Septuagint version of Isaiah nor Jews who used the original Hebrew can have regarded God's alienation from the Jewish people (which, after all, is a consequence of their 'turning away' from him) as irremediable. That possibility (whether from a Christian or Jewish point of view) only becomes acute with the rise of the Jesus movement, with its rejection by the majority of Jews, and with the disasters of the Jewish War, including the destruction of the Temple. So the difference between ἰάσομαι and ἰάσωμαι is of *some* import in the present context.

Expert linguists such as Karrer and Popkes debate the nuances of the difference. It seems, *mirabile dictu*, that within such subjunctive clauses (some) Hellenistic Greek can adopt a 'vivid' indicative, and there are even parallels for this in the NT.[156] Presumably, however, the general associations of the indicative make the possibility envisaged less 'remote' and more real. Presumably also, it is possible to regard καὶ ἰάσομαι as an admittedly very abrupt main clause. My own view (for what it is worth) is that, however one construes the Greek, the indicative is the better reading, for the following reasons: (a) it is always the *lectio difficilior*; (b) it is the majority reading in the Septuagint; and (c) Matthew and John both read the indicative.[157] They are using the passage from Isaiah in essentially the same context as Acts, that is, the question of where the Jews in general stand in relation to God, when they have rejected Jesus, although the *dramatic context* is even more acute in Acts, in that the Jews have now rejected

---

153   Lampe (1984); the fact that this theology—or theodicy—is ridiculous and disgusting is no reason for denying its existence.
154   Karrer (2000); Popkes (2009).
155   Karrer (2000) 271; Popkes (2009) 615.
156   Including (I believe) Philippians 2.10 (p. 657 below).
157   See pp. 634 and 639.

the *continuing* Jesus movement, and the Jewish War is only a few years away, as all readers know and as Luke-Acts has frequently reminded them.

But there are also important considerations *beyond* the textual problem.

First, Luke is explicit that *some* of the Jews who heard Paul were persuaded by the things being said (28.24). There is, then, *some* sense of a repetition (albeit with differences) of his reception by the philosophers in Athens (17.32, 34). If that episode leaves some 'openness' about future responsiveness, so also should this one.

Second, Paul's own martyrdom (which informed readers know about anyway) has been heavily foreshadowed in the text,[158] and with the implication ⟦161⟧ that this martyrdom, while great and glorious and the gateway to heaven, like Stephen's explicitly described martyrdom (7.55-9), is also the just punishment of his own earlier murderous persecution of the followers of Jesus, including Stephen.[159] Thus Paul himself seems to furnish an inspiring parallel for the Jews in general, whose punishment in the Jewish War is indeed here foreshadowed but also, proleptically, already discounted, as not being God's last word for the Jews.[160] We have seen (I believe) similar thinking in Matthew and John.

Third, not only does the emphasis on 'all' in 28.31 logically include (some) Jews, as well as Gentiles, but the 'all' is proleptic of the Christification of the whole earth. Obviously, I cannot argue that now,[161] but note that in 30-1 'all' comes twice, reinforcing the sense of 'all-ness'.

Fourth, seemingly no commentator registers that the entire sequence is book-ended by the name of Jesus (28.30; 28.23). That name gets even greater emphasis on the second occasion: the very last sentence of Acts, where it both ring-structures with the start of Acts (1.1) and contrasts eloquently with Jesus' 'namelessness' in the Luke Preface, at the very beginning of the double work Luke-Acts. The name of 'Jesus' sounds and resounds through this sequence and, as often elsewhere, chimes also with the cognate 'Isaiah'. As in Matthew and John, Jesus' name must interact with 28.27, *irrespective* of whether ἰάσομαι or ἰάσωμαι is read (even though I have argued the superiority of the former), especially given (once again) that Jewish unresponsiveness to Jesus is characterised in terms of visual and aural impairment: of spiritual *sickness*.

---

158   Discussion, with references and bibliography: Moles (2006b) 88-94 {above, pp. 573-7}; (2013); few scholars resist this implication.
159   Barrett (2004) 457 on 9.16: 'Patitur Paulus quae fecerat Saulus'; Moles (2013) develops this.
160   I do not suggest this theology is tenable: see n. 153.
161   Moles (2013).

By contrast, the thrice named Jews (28.17, 19, 21) are 'not of a united voice [ἀσύμφωνοι] to one another' (28.25). The word ἀσύμφωνοι itself gains tremendous force from being *hapax* not only in Luke but also in the whole of the NT. I translate it thus, because, although the sense of social or political (or musical) 'discord' is important, even more important, as we shall see, is the notice of 'voice'. The Jews' 'lack of a united voice' is the present lamentable reality—and 'present' alike in the sense of the 'present' dramatic situation within the text, in the sense of 'the present' of Luke's time of writing, and, even, in the sense of all 'presents', until …? Is there an 'until'? Will the 'present' *always* be 'present', or will it be replaced by some different reality? It seems to me that it would be incompatible with the tremendous and *all*-enveloping emphasis on the 'healing' powers of 'the Healer', if the implication were: 'The Jews have had their chance and "the Healer" won't heal *them*'. Rather, like Paul himself and like Tabitha/Dorcas, they will get their ⟦162⟧ 'sight' back: 'Jesus' is the ultimate 'healer' of 'all' (28.30): his 'healing ministry' has universal and timeless power, including the still un-persuaded and (from the points of view of writer and readers) already heavily punished Jews.

And fifth and last, when the Jews here are described as 'not of a united voice to one another', the formulation makes one of many ring-structures linking the end of Acts to the beginning.[162] Christian mission in Jerusalem began with Pentecost, the coming of the Holy Spirit, and Jesus' followers' speaking in different tongues which were comprehensible to Jews from all over the known world and yet caused general perplexity as to the meaning of the event (2.1–12). Mission is there confined to Jews, but universal mission is projected, both because the Jews concerned come from all over the world and because the event proleptically reverses the curse of Babel (Genesis 11.1–9):[163] before that curse 'the whole world was one lip, and there was one *voice* to all' (1); after it, 'each [could not] hear the *voice* of his neighbour' (7).

At the end of Acts, the Jews in Rome are 'not of a united *voice* to one another' in their response to Jesus. Here again (as in Acts 17), what is at stake is one's 'response' (a verbal term) to the 'word' of God, as here *said* by Paul (24), and as instantiated in *Jesus*, the *name* of the divine 'word'. But the universal Christian mission, having got as far as Rome, centre of the temporal world, is now well under way. Jewish disagreement over Jesus is unfinished business within this universal mission—but it is business that will be finished, and not by the Jewish War, but by the universal and timeless power of the Healer. At that point, the Jews will 'assent' to 'Jesus' as 'Lord'. As the (probable, and, probably,

---

162  See again Moles (2013).
163  Bruce (1951) 86.

pre-Pauline) hymn in Philippians 2.9–10 (written shortly after the dramatic situation at the end of Acts) puts it, 'God has exalted him above and graced him the name ['Lord'] above every name, (10) in order that every knee should bend at the name of Jesus, of those in heaven and of those on earth and of those under the earth, (11) and every tongue will say out loud together [ἐξομολογήσεται] that Ἰησοῦς *Chreestos* is Lord, to the glory of God the Father'. Almost inevitably, it seems, there is here a textual question as to whether ἐξομολογήσεται (future) or ἐξομολογήσηται (subjunctive) should be read, but the hymn itself reworks Isaiah 45.23 ἐξομολογήσεται, where we note the straight, uncontested, indicative. Thus the hymn, like the end of Acts when read in combination with the Pentecost episode at the beginning, undoes the curse of Babel, and anticipates a future where 'all' 'together' will 'say' or 'voice' that 'Jesus is Lord'.

Now there are interesting parallels between the end of Acts and this Philippians passage: both base themselves on Isaiah; both exhibit crucial textual [[163]] confusion between subjunctive and indicative; both use the word 'all' twice ('every' and 'all' being the same word in Greek); and both have a 'prison' context (in Acts, Paul is currently under house arrest in Rome and proleptically in prison; Philippians was written shortly afterwards when Paul was actually in prison in Rome).

Whether Luke knows, uses, or alludes to any of Paul's epistles is disputed among scholars, with perhaps a majority arguing the contrary. There are, however, sensible positive arguments,[164] and subtle evocation of the Philippians hymn is an extremely attractive possibility, made even easier if the hymn existed independently of Paul. The hymn's sentiments would trump the current unresolvedness of the Jews being 'not of a united voice to one another' in their response to Jesus. One might even say that the hymn *qua* hymn is the universal divine 'music' which will overcome current Jewish 'discord' (which can be a musical term) about Jesus. In any case, there is a sense here (as in Acts 17) that the name/sound of 'Jesus' transcends all sounds.

Having gone so far, we may revisit the actual Philippi narrative in Acts. Paul and Silas' imprisonment was miraculously ended in response to their 'hymning God' (16.25). What 'hymn' were they singing in prison? There may (especially just before chapter 17) be Socratic resonances,[165] but they would be a bonus, not a main explanation. A smart suggestion[166] is that, just as the narrative is a foundation narrative of the Philippian church, so the 'hymn' is an aetiology

---

164 See, e.g., Witherington (1998) 430–8, 568, 610–17; Mason (2005) 264; Dunn (2009) 77–9.
165 Barrett (2004) 793 and others.
166 Which I owe to a sermon by the Reverend Jonathan Roberts; the hymn's focus on Jesus does not prevent its being a hymn addressed to God and directed, explicitly, to his glory.

of the great Philippian hymn. And the Philippi narrative culminated in the Gentile gaoler's being 'saved' through his 'believing' in 'Jesus as Lord' (31–4). That is the 'gap', on the Jewish side, that remains to be filled at the end of Acts, but it is a gap that will certainly be filled.

One may speculate still further about the sources of Luke's stupendous creativity, alike literary and theological, at the end of Acts. As we have seen with Paul and the Athenian philosophers, the historicity of much of the Acts narrative polarises scholarly responses, some regarding it as extremely historical, others as more or less fiction. In this case, one should hardly doubt that, on his arrival in Rome as everywhere else, and despite his being under house-arrest, Paul did attempt to preach to non-Christian Jews, and that, if he did, his success was at best mixed.[167] And on the conservative view (with which on this issue I happen to agree), Luke was with him (28.14 'that was ⟦164⟧ how we came to Rome'), hence an eye-witness of Paul's attempt(s).[168] It is possible that Paul would have used the famous Isaiah passage on that occasion (or those occasions), especially as the historical Paul uses a truncated version of it in his letter to the Romans (Romans 11.8), precisely in the context of the discussion of the majority of Jews being 'hardened' against acceptance of Jesus. It is also possible—and, I would say, altogether likelier—that Luke, knowing of the importance of this Isaiah passage from the earliest days of Christianity, having read Paul's use of it in Romans, and (I believe) having also read how it was used in Matthew and John, 'transferred' it to the present context to achieve the effects here discussed. On this interpretation, his engagement with Matthew had particular point. Whereas Matthew used the beginning (1.21), middle (13.13–17), and end (27.32–50) of his Gospel to convey the notion that the Jews as a people would be 'saved' and 'healed' by 'Jesus, Saviour and Healer', Luke kept this notion to the end of his unified double-work, thus elucidating that this 'healing' would take place even after the apparently crushing divine punishment of the Jewish War, a punishment that came less than a decade after the end of his narrative.

The possibility that Paul is among Luke's direct inspirations here again deserves consideration. The complicated and difficult Romans 11 argues that the Jews in general will be saved after the full complement of the Gentiles comes in (25, 30–2).[169] That seems consonant with the end of Acts, as here interpreted. The two writers use the same Isaiah quotation and stress God's

---

167  Measured discussion: Barrett (2004) 1237.
168  I discuss the notorious (and endlessly discussed) 'we'-passages and their implications for authorship and other interpretative matters in Moles (2013).
169  I am aware there are other interpretations.

'all-ness' (11.26, 32). Paul supports his claim (26) that 'all Israel' will be 'saved' by another passage from Isaiah (59.26): 'The Deliverer [ὁ ῥυόμενος] will come from Zion. He will turn away irreverence from Jacob'. Paul does not then name 'Jesus' but he is making an *implicit* pun on Ἰησοῦς ~ 'saviour'. Thus broad consonance between the end of Acts and Romans 11 is supplemented by detailed parallels. Acts' use of the 'healing' etymology instead of the historical Paul's 'saving' one partly reflects the overall economy of Luke's punning on 'Jesus', partly his need to clarify Matthew (above), but also the intrinsic needs of the post-Jewish War situation, in which 'healing' was more appropriate than 'saving', especially as compared with the situation faced by Paul in the early 60s.

Thus Acts' use of the pun on Ἰησοῦς ~ ἰάομαι is wholly organic to the developing narrative of early Christianity in all its expansions and complexities, and Luke brings the Jesusology of the pun to a triumphant climax at the very close of his unified double-work. His use of the pun is undoubtedly ⟦165⟧ both richer and subtler in Acts than it is in Luke, with the latter's almost excessive collocation of Ἰησοῦς ~ ἰάομαι.

## 3   Conclusions

Of the texts under consideration, Mark, Matthew, John, and Luke-Acts all exploit the pun on Ἰησοῦς and ἰάομαι (and on cognate and related terms), and they all derive profound 'Jesusology' from it. All the others do well, but Luke uses the pun the most extensively, the most illuminatingly, and the most creatively, gives it its widest application, and takes it to its greatest heights (especially in Acts 17 and 28). Those who believe 'Luke' to be 'the beloved physician' may find a personal interest here (as have many), and they may speculate on some sort of psychological affinity between Luke the healer and this aspect of 'Jesusology'. But that is cod psychology, and in fact Luke's interest is far more in 'the cure of souls'. He is interested in physical healings primarily because they validate Jesus' wider 'healing' credentials and because such healings always have eschatological import (for Luke). But since I myself am one of those who believe Luke to be 'the beloved healer', I would not exclude the possibility that Luke's greatly increased emphasis on 'healing' functions (also) as a sort of subtextual autobiographical *sphragis*, in something of the same way as the constant puns on 'hours', 'flaccidity', and 'ears' in the poetry of the Roman poet Horatius Flaccus,[170] or the Russian composer Shostakovich's inscribing his own initials in some of his symphonies and string quartets. Alternatively, one

---

170   Moles (2007a) 168, 169, 171, 173 {above, pp. 465, 466, 468, 470}.

might hypothesise that the extreme Lukan emphasis reflects both a time (at the end of the sequence of the canonical gospels) and a cultural context in which Jesus' healing (and general Christian healing) was coming into increasing competition with Asclepius', although there seems little or no control over such a hypothesis.[171]

As for the datings of the pun and for the religious and cultural contexts in which it was deployed, the examples of Mark, Matthew, John, and Luke-Acts indicate widespread Christian awareness of it, by, say, the last third of the first century. I say 'widespread', because it is not a matter only of the authors involved but also of their readers and listeners, nor is it a matter only of direct punning ('Ἰησοῦς ~ ἰάομαι) but also of 'punning by synonym'. Those readers and listeners (in contrast to modern readers and listeners) cannot possibly have been blind or deaf to the insistent phenomenon, which was evidently thoroughly embedded in early Christian consciousness. Mark specifically 〚166〛 takes the pun back to c.70. But these findings must be further retrojectable. The occurrence of the pun in Matthew and Luke in common-source contexts independent of Mark indicates its presence already in Q, in, say, the 40–50s. Even if one does not believe in Q, these shared contexts indicate some sort of past material, older than Mark, which had the pun. And if one admits a written Greek *narrative* about Jesus before Mark,[172] that narrative must also have had it.

Further back again, given Jesus' tremendous reputation for healing, the punning association must have been made as early as the first use of the Greek-Jewish form of his name, whether already in Jesus' lifetime (by Greeks or Romans or by monoglot Hellenist Jews or in communication with Greek-speakers in Greek),[173] or soon after his death, as the renewed Jesus movement began its mission in Greek-speaking contexts. Indeed, it is likely that Jesus himself would have known of it, even used it: there are good grounds for supposing that he knew and spoke (some) Greek;[174] he surely referred to himself as a 'healer'; he was fond of puns; and he seems to have been capable of making bilingual ones.[175]

---

171   For the parallel (suggested here by Todd Penner): Wells (1998) 227–8; Telford (1999) 90; Penner (2012); and, indeed, Julian (see Appendix 2).
172   See n. 34.
173   Note John 12.20–2, where 'Greeks' (certainly 'Greek-speakers', whatever their other identity) negotiate with Philip and Andrew (both Greek names) about 'seeing' Jesus.
174   Cf., e.g., Dunn (2003) 315; Moles (2006a) 98 {above, p. 535}, with references; cf. also p. 632 above.
175   Cf., e.g., Keener (2011) 180, with references.

The whole area of 'active' bilingualism (as opposed to passive knowledge that Ἰησοῦς was the Jewish-Greek form of a name that in Hebrew meant 'Yahweh saves') opens up further perspectives. Just as there must have been Jews who saw a bilingual pun behind the Septuagint translation of Exodus 15.26,[176] and who found piquancy in the same translation's version of 2 Chronicles 16.12–13 ('in the thirty-ninth year of his reign, *Asa* developed a serious foot disease. Yet even with the severity of his disease, he did not seek the Lord's help but turned only to his *healers*. So he died in the forty-first year of his reign', because '*âsê*' is Aramaic for 'healer' and 'Asa' is generally supposed to be derived from it),[177] so there must have been educated bilingual Jews who heard of Jesus' self-representation as an ἰατρός in the apophthegm recorded in Mark 2.17 and then thought: 'Is that not uncannily like the apophthegm attributed to the Greek Cynic philosopher Antisthenes?'.[178] If so, not only does the potential for the dissemination of the basic pun on 'Jesus' ~ 'healer' increase, but so also does the potential for 'competition' between [[167]] 'healing' by Ἰησοῦς and that by other groups (in this case, Greek philosophers). Of the canonical Gospels, it is Mark that most registers this bilingual (even trilingual!) context, but it is also present in Matthew, John, and Luke-Acts.

Similarly, even on a minimalist acceptance of continuing oral traditions about Jesus, there must have been plenty of such material about his 'healing', and about its intrinsic link to his name, in the years following his death, and for as long as the lifetimes of those oral witnesses, lifetimes which in a few cases seem to have extended to the end of the century.[179] This circumstance supports both the actual historicity of the link between name and activity and the historicity of at least some of the material bearing on that link in the Gospels and Acts, texts which admit of *some* influence from oral traditions. More generally, Allison's sensible criterion for broad historicity, 'the larger pattern' (of which the Classical equivalent is Chris Pelling's equally sensible criterion of 'true enough'),[180] supports both the persistence of the tradition linking Jesus' healing and his name and some degree of historical reality behind it.

All this, so far, of Greek, or Jewish-Greek, or bilingual contexts. But some such punning would have been possible already in Jesus' lifetime even in purely Jewish contexts and with the Jewish form of Jesus' name, because 'saving' can

---

176 See p. 623.
177 And of course one then wonders about a bilingual connection between '*âsê*' and ἰάομαι, especially in its aorist and future forms; cf. n. 59 above.
178 D.L. 6.6 (with Collins [2007] 195–6).
179 John 21.24–5; Bauckham (2006) 384–411 on 'the Beloved Disciple' (of whom Casey (2010) 524–5 is over-hastily dismissive).
180 Allison (2010) 18–19, and the whole of the first chapter; Pelling (1990).

include 'healing'. If, as is generally supposed, the popularity of 'Joshua' as a name in Jewish Palestine reflects Jewish patriotism (the biblical Joshua having originally conquered the land of Israel),[181] then emphasis on 'salvific' healing would suit Jesus' (and the first Christians') general 'redefinition' of 'salvation' from *political* salvation in a narrow sense to *eschatological* salvation.[182] Such considerations provide further grounds for supposing that the basic pun goes all the way back to Jesus' lifetime. Thus this paper supports Geza Vermes' central claim about the historical Jesus: that he was a Jewish charismatic, the core of whose activity was healing.[183] 'Jesus the Jewish charismatic' does not, however, exclude other models, readings, or interpretations, for example, 'Jesus the eschatological prophet', 'Jesus the Suffering [[168]] Servant', or 'Jesus the eschatological King', in *all* of which Jesus' healing plays an essential proleptic role.

Of these other Jesuses, 'Jesus the Suffering servant' introduces another telling factor. One particularly rich and insistent context of the pun within the Gospels and Acts is Isaiah (itself, as we have seen, a significantly cognate name), a book which seems to have been used both by the early Christians (and from very early) and by Jesus himself.[184]

We may conclude, then, that the pun is very early, and I would say as early as Jesus' own life-time.

As for the significance of the pun, there are many things to be said, as we have seen, and the topic is a very large one, which touches on practically all aspects of Jesus' ministry and of his religious significance as seen by himself, by his disciples, and by early Christians. I here attempt as brief a summary as I can, sticking to punning contexts, building up from basics, and moving from the relatively secular (none is absolutely so) to the religious and the divine, and from Jesus' lifetime to the next, Christian, generations.

The pun emphasises Jesus' key role as healer. Within Jesus' life-time, and in the next generation and subsequent generations, when Christians perform healings 'in the name of Jesus', the pun connects in the first instance with Jesus' actual or perceived healings of physical maladies. Even in this category,

---

181  E.g., Bauckham (2006) 76.
182  This distinction can, of course, be exaggerated. As Casey (2010) 444 (cf. 215) nicely puts it: 'Jesus was at Passover hoping that God would finally establish his kingdom. Where would that leave the Romans? Not in the land of Israel, and perhaps not on the earth at all'. The degree to which Jesus—and the different works of the NT—are 'accommodationist' or 'oppositionalist' is currently—and rightly—a topic of intense interest in NT studies. {Cf. further Moles (2014).}
183  Vermes (1973) 58–82.
184  Endless discussion: e.g., Bellinger–Farmer (1998); Dunn (2003) 448–50, 516–17; Childs (2004) 1–31; Moyise–Menken (2005); Boring (2006) 33–41; Allison (2010) 113–15, 263–6.

however, Jesus is not just any healer: he is 'the Healer'. The union of name and healing gives an extra dimension to the stories of the key encounters between Jesus and the various demoniacs: the responsible demons intuitively know that they are going up against 'the Healer' himself (in which respect their theology surpasses that of most of Jesus' human contemporaries). The fact (presumably) that few or no *Histos* readers believe in demons is irrelevant: Jesus and his contemporaries did. Similarly, Ἰησοῦς is the polar opposite of 'disease'. The struggle between the Devil and the healing God (as represented by Ἰησοῦς) could hardly be more elemental. Jesus' healing role in this physical sense already has eschatological implications and already forges a necessary connection between Ἰησοῦς ('Yahweh saves') and Yahweh himself.

The Jesus–healer pun necessarily overlaps with the Jesus–saviour pun. Again, within Jesus' life-time, and in the next generation and subsequent generations, the latter pun connects in the first instance with healings or perceived healings of physical maladies, and Jesus' saving role in this physical sense also already forges a necessary connection between Ἰησοῦς and Yahweh.

⟦169⟧ Both the Jesus–saviour and the Jesus–healer puns occur in the Isaiah material, thus already in Jesus' lifetime creating the claim that he was to be the saviour/healer (in some senses) of Israel (in some senses).

Mark and Matthew have Jesus *qua* healer sublating the Jewish purity laws, and this is also an important concept in Acts. It naturally justifies the exemptions granted by Jewish Christians to the new Gentile Christians in the post-Jesus generations. Does the concept go back in any form to Jesus' own lifetime and might it then apply even to Jews? Jesus' attitude to, and practice of, the Jewish purity laws have been much discussed, but it seems at any rate obvious that he was at the liberal end of the wide spectrum of possible attitudes and practices, and that *qua* eschatological prophet who thought that the end was imminent and who may even have supposed that death in Jerusalem would accelerate that end,[185] he cannot have attached much importance—or much permanence—to the purity laws. On the other hand, the disputes among post-Jesus Christians about the applicability of those laws indicate either that Jesus did not clarify the question in his lifetime or that he was not remembered as having done so. As in other areas, the non-Parousia forced new clarifications of earlier ambiguities.

Both the Jesus–healer and the Jesus–saviour puns necessarily put Jesus, already in his lifetime, into competition and opposition with other individuals or groups who claimed powers of healing and saving. After Jesus' death,

---

[185] Serious historical Jesus scholars argue this: e.g. Dunn (2003) 818–24; Allison (2010) 221–304; Casey (2010) 377–81.

and as the renewed Jesus movement grew and expanded geographically, these competitors increased in numbers and in kind. In general, they included other Jewish healers and exorcists; official 'doctors'; pagan philosophers; Roman emperors; pagan healers, whether religious or secular, whether professional or kingly; and pagan healing gods. There can be debate about which particular competitors go back to Jesus' lifetime. Other Jewish healers and exorcists and 'official' doctors, surely, yes. I would also include pagan philosophers, both because of the close parallel between Jesus' apophthegm at Mark 2.17 and that attributed to Antisthenes (above) and because I believe (unfashionably) that there is *some* truth in the 'Jesus Cynicus' model.[186] Post-Jesus, as we have seen, the competitors certainly included other Jewish healers and exorcists, pagan philosophers, pagan healing gods, and Roman emperors, of whose salvific and healing claims followers of the true Healer are wholly dismissive (Acts 4.12).

In the post-Jesus phase, the Jesus–healer and the Jesus–saviour puns also underpin the claim that the ultimate healing, saving, and cleansing is the resurrection. There are natural accompanying claims—that baptism ⟦170⟧ cleanses and heals, that the resurrection brings rebirth, that Jesus is the author of life. Many Christian scholars have of course argued that the historical Jesus foresaw his own resurrection, in which case Jesus himself would have made the connection between healing and resurrection and might have told his disciples (though, if so, they did not in the first instance understand it). This is not a road I wish to pursue in a scholarly context.

All the material surveyed so far yields another important conclusion: while scholars hitherto have thought of Jesus as the name and then the assorted titles as predicates: Son of Man, Son of God, etc., for the early Christians Jesus the name was also a title: Healer and Saviour. This may conceivably also be true of Jesus himself.

Alike the related names of Ἰησοῦς and Yahweh, their shared activities (healing and saving in various applications), the union in Ἰησοῦς of name and activities, and the frequent sense that Ἰησοῦς looks and acts very like his father Yahweh: all these factors bring Ἰησοῦς and Yahweh into a very close relationship.

In this connection (as in others), the prophecy of Isaiah must have played a crucial role: when the early Christians read ἰάσομαι at Isaiah 6.10 and τῷ μώλωπι αὐτοῦ ἡμεῖς ἰάθημεν at Isaiah 53.5, they must have felt (*mutatis mutandis*): 'Eureka!/Bingo! Our Ἰησοῦς is (in some sense or senses) the instantiation and fulfilment of Yahweh'. This may conceivably also be true of Jesus himself (although in Hebrew or Aramaic).

---

186   Critical discussion in Moles (2006a).

All of this material yields another important conclusion: the name of Jesus,[187] with all the implications so far surveyed, was crucial for Christian self-definition. Much recent scholarship has argued the indeterminacy, or multiformity, of 'early Christianity'.[188] The argument can be overplayed: from very early on, 'Jesus Christ is Lord' is a Christian confessional and self-definitional formula, as we have seen. In this context, the name of Jesus actually made Jesus more useful than Yahweh, the supposedly unpronounceable divine name.

Given the links between the bearer's name and his characteristic healing activities (characteristically viewed as miraculous); given the power attributed to the name; given the repetitiveness and emphasis of its deployment both in relevant religious narrative (the Gospels and Acts) and in cult practice (as in the Philippian hymn); given the ways in which the name is used to blur Father and Son, it seems implausible to deny that 'Jesus' effectively functions as a divine name (although it is sometimes also, of course, just a 'narrative name').

[[171]] But it was even more than a divine name: for the early Christians the name 'Jesus' was a 'transcendental signifier'.[189] The early Christians '*knew*' that Ἰησοῦς would 'heal' (and 'save') everything and everyone. They also '*knew*' that the curse of Babel would finally be undone by universal acceptance, and proclamation, of the name of Ἰησοῦς (cf. Phil. 2.9–10). 'Jesus' was the 'name' above all names; 'Jesus' was also the incarnate 'word' of God; 'Jesus' was the *sound* that would resolve all discord. Again, the totalising linguistic unity of 'Jesus' as supreme 'name' and 'Jesus' as *logos* generated a religious energy and intensity quite unavailable through 'Yahweh' or through Greek or Latin words for 'G/god'.

Consequently, 'Jesus' had irresistible 'healing' power to 'heal' the Jews beyond their historical rejection of him, beyond their rejection of the renewed Jesus movement, beyond their punishment in the Jewish War, beyond all their future rejections of him. Thus the early Christian historiographical theodicy of the Jewish War is both like and distinctively different from the theodicy of Josephus, Jewish historian and (eventual) supporter of Rome.[190]

All of the above observations are the more paradoxical for the very commonness of 'Jesus' as a male Palestinian Jewish name. This paradox itself requires explanation. The explanation must be that those of his followers who accepted *Jesus*' resurrection (some, of course, did not) found in it decisive validation of his entire *healing* ministry.

---

187   As also, of course, the name of 'Christ', though Christians themselves avoided the precise form of 'Christians' till later on (p. 615 above).
188   E.g. King (2008); Lössl (2010) 13–24.
189   I say 'a', because the name/title 'Chreestos' was too: see Moles (2012).
190   Roughly, that the catastrophes of 70 were God's punishment for revolt against Rome; cf. Mason (2005) 21, 85–6.

So much for the significances of the pun on the level of meaning. But the phenomenon also illustrates things on the level of praxis.

Not least is the effect of the sheer repetitiveness of the naming and the associated punning: like Classical education, Jewish and Christian education emphasised the importance of memorising tags as a way of dinning in basic truths. No reader or listener of Luke-Acts or of the other Gospels should come away without knowing that Ἰησοῦς is 'the Healer' and 'the Healer' of everything. Such repetitiveness of naming is also part of religious ritual. But even for the already Christian reader or listener the texts are not only commemorative and ritualistic: at every reading and listening, they challenge the reader to encounter 'Jesus' and accept him (as 'Healer' and 'Saviour') anew. Our texts also illustrate the early Christians' immense linguistic resourcefulness, as, within their overall mission, they energised and invested with deep meaning one of the commonest of Jewish male names and made the name of 'Jesus the healer' into a distillation of all that he represented.

⟦172⟧ And they also illustrate the early Christians' eagerness to engage with, and persuade, the pagan world, including educated pagans. In the specific context which I hypothesised at the beginning of this paper, that of the public, Christian–pagan, partly textual and historiographical debate about the merits of Christianity, how would pagan readers react to the Jesus–healer punning of these texts? They would certainly see it and hear it. They would register its organic and its structural significances, its especial appropriateness to histories of beginnings and its sheer expansiveness and range of application. They would recognise its totalising religious and political claims—especially its competitiveness with the healing claims of Rome and the Caesars, especially as articulated in public media and in Greek and Roman historiographical and biographical texts.[191] They could hardly fail to grant all these Christian writers some skill in the deployment of the pun. They might find the insistence of the phenomenon in Luke and in parts of John a little trying, though they would understand its didactic purpose and its religious significance, but they would find also much to appreciate in its deployment and progressive expansion of range in Acts. They could hardly fail to admire Luke's handling of Paul among the philosophers or the end of Acts. In none of these Christian writers would they find anything as neat as (say) Herodotus' punning on 'Themistocles' or on 'Socles', as dense and probing as Thucydides' punning in Book I of his History, or as clever and multi-layered as (say) Tacitus' punning in the Cremutius Cordus

---

191  E.g., Liv. *praef.* 9; Tac. *Ann.* 1.9.4; 4.17.3; Plut. *Brut.* 55.2; Sen. *Ad Polyb.* 13.1; 14.1. Weinstock (1971) 167–74, 238–9, 317 n.; Cotter (1999) 39–42; Carter (2000) 123–7; 200–4.

episode of *Annals* 4.[192] But, overall, they would be impressed—and so should we be, as connoisseurs of ancient historiography in all its richness, flexibility, range, and moral demandingness.

### [173] Appendix 1: 'Jesus' Elsewhere in the New Testament

At Manchester Gerald Downing asked the inevitable question: what of Paul, who puns on 'Jesus' ~ 'saviour',[193] but not obviously on 'Jesus' ~ 'healer'? That he puns on 'Jesus' ~ 'saviour' (as do other NT letter-writers) weakens—without altogether refuting—any 'genre defence' (that, arguably, such 'healing' punning is likelier in biography/historiography than in epistolography). A radical defence to the question would be that this 'healing' punning is a phenomenon of the last third of the first century and later. But not only would that jettison the bulk of my conclusions (which I would not wish): it also seems itself untenable for reasons there given. So my reply was: that one does not need Paul because one has the earlier Q,[194] and that in this respect, as in others, Paul may be allowed to be different, especially as his energies are so hugely engrossed in exploring the implications of Jesus' 'other name', that of 'Christ'; also, that one could find *some* punning on Ἰησοῦς ~ 'healing' in Paul.

It must be admitted that, outside the Gospels (and behind them, Q) and Acts, active NT punning on 'Jesus' as 'healer' is not so easily demonstrable, but for comparative purposes here is a brief and, I am sure, incomplete survey.

If my analysis of the Gospels and Acts is right, practically any allusion to the 'resurrection' of Jesus will include a punning allusion to the 'healing' of, and by, Ἰησοῦς. That applies to 1 Peter 3.21: 'baptism ... now *saves* you, not as a putting away of dirt from the flesh but as a request to God for a good conscience, through the resurrection of Jesus Christ'. Here the pun on 'Jesus' as 'saviour' is latent, and there is an allusion to Jesus' 'cleansing' power via his 'resurrection'. Should the reader/listener not also 'hear' 'healing' by Ἰησοῦς 'the Healer'? While some conservative scholars defend the authorship of Jesus' disciple, 1 Peter is best dated towards, or at, the end of the century.[195] A similar pattern appears in Paul himself, in 1 Thessalonians 4.14 (date: early 50s): 'for if we believe that Ἰησοῦς died and rose again, so also God will bring with him those who have fallen asleep, through the agency of Ἰησοῦς'. Again, in Romans 5.6–21 (date:

---

192 See Moles references in n. 42.
193 See above, n. 46.
194 And possibly early written narratives about Jesus: n. 34.
195 Conservative: Dunn (2009) 1148–57, with adequate bibliography on the other side.

57), when Paul discusses Christ's death on behalf of human beings, 'when we were still *infirm*' (6 [medical imagery]), and argues its role in bringing *life out of death*, should we not 'hear' the Ἰησοῦς of the repeated 'Jesus Christ' (15, 17, 21) as 'healer'? In 1 John 1.7.5 (end first century/beginning of second) 'the blood of Jesus his ⟦174⟧ [God's] son cleanses us from all sin'. The long disquisition on '*sound* doctrine' in Titus 2.1–15 (last third of the first century) climaxes (13) in the naming of 'our saviour Jesus Christ', with (surely) the double etymology of 'Jesus': 'saviour' and 'healer'. In Hebrews (post-Paul), 'we see Jesus, for a little while made inferior to the angels, crowned with glory and honour because of the suffering of death, so that he might taste death for every man by the grace of God' (9). Is not this 'Jesus' 'healing' death itself?

More generally, since Ἰησοῦς, to Hellenising Jews and Greek Christians, actually *means* 'healer', the puns I have argued for throughout this paper will *always* be there, whether actively or only just below the surface. The category of 'material where the pun does not occur', which must of course form part of the initial analysis,[196] is finally illusory.

## Appendix 2: Julian on Jesus

I discuss two cases.

The first is from Julian's *Against the Galileans*, preserved in excerpts by Cyril of Alexandria. Reconstruction of the text is not certain, but there was clearly a sustained comparison between Jesus and Asclepius. At 191d–e '*Jesus* has been *named* for little more than three hundred years and during the time he lived he worked nothing worth hearing about, unless any one supposes that *to heal* cripples and blind persons and to exorcise demoniacs in the villages at Bethsaida and Bethany are among the greatest works'. By contrast (200a–b), 'Asclepius, having visited earth from the heavens, appeared at Epidaurus in the body of a man ... but afterwards he multiplied himself by his visits and reached out his *saving* right hand over all [the earth].... He is present everywhere on earth and sea ... he *raises up* afflicted souls and sick bodies.' Then (235b–238d), 'Asclepius *heals* our bodies, and with his and Apollo's and Hermes the learned's help the Muses train our souls ... consider then whether we are not your betters in the art of *healing* derived from Asclepius, whose oracles are everywhere on the earth. ... He often *healed* me when I was *ailing*, prescribing *cures*'.

---

196   P. 626.

The etymology of 'Asklepios' is obscure. One modern conjecture is the Hittite *assula(a)* ('well-being') and *piya* 'give'.[197] Whatever the objective truth, ⟦175⟧ it is possible that 'Asklepios' was 'felt' as meaning *something* like this, which would reinforce Julian's statement that 'the art of *healing*' 'derives' from Asclepius and his sustained contrast between 'Asclepius' and Ἰησοῦς. For Julian accepts the Jesus ~ healer etymology and is prepared to concede that Jesus did perform some healings and exorcisms in villages in Palestine, but he claims that Asclepius is much the greater 'healer', so that the vocabulary he applies to the latter systematically undermines Jesus' claims: see the italicised words and add 'oracles' (because χρηστήρια trumps 'Chreestos').

The second case comes at the end (336a–c) of Julian's *Caesares*, Menippean satire with historiographical elements,[198] hence part of the wider Christian–pagan historiographical debate about the merits of Christianity. When the various emperors are told to choose their guardian god, with whom henceforth to live, Constantine, unable to find the archetype of his life among the gods, runs to Luxury (Τρυφή), who dolls him up and leads him to Profligacy (Ἀσωτία), where he finds Ἰησοῦς proclaiming to all:

> He that is a seducer, he that is a murderer, he that is sacrilegious and loathsome, let him come with confidence. For, washing him with this water [of baptism], I will show him forth as clean, and, even if he be guilty of those same things a second time, I shall grant him, if he strikes his breast and beats his head, to become clean.

Constantine and his sons gladly join Jesus but are punished by the avenging gods for their atheism, until Zeus gives them a respite for the sake of Claudius and Constantius. As for Julian himself, Hermes has granted him to know his father Mithras, who, if he keeps his commandments, will provide him security in life and good hope in the afterlife.

Here the pun Ἰησοῦς ~ ἰάομαι is implicit (~ 'washing', 'clean' x2). So also is the pun on Ἰησοῦς ~ 'saviour', for Jesus' protection of Constantine and his sons is thwarted by the avenging deities; it is Jesus' great rival Mithras who will grant Julian security in life and good hope in the afterlife; and Jesus himself associates with Ἀσωτία, Profligacy, the 'inability to save' in a financial or material sense, but also, proleptically, his own 'inability to save' those (such as Constantine) whom he claims to protect: Julian out-puns those notorious Christian punsters.

---

197   Szemerényi (1974) 155.
198   For historiography within Menippean satire see Damon (2010).

Thus the apostate Julian was a maliciously good reader of the first Christian biographers and historians, though by his time the pagans had substantially lost the debate.

## Bibliography

Ahl, F. M. (1985) *Metaformations: Soundplay and Wordplay in Ovid and Other Classical Poets* (Ithaca).

Alexander, L. C. A. (1993) *The Preface to Luke's Gospel: Literary Convention and Social Context in Luke 1.1.4 and Acts 1.1* (Cambridge).

Alexander, L. C. A. (2005) *Acts in Its Ancient Literary Context: A Classicist Looks at the Acts of the Apostles* (London and New York).

Alexander, P. S. (1984) 'Rabbinic Biography and the Biography of Jesus: a Survey of the Evidence', in C. M. Tuckett, ed., *Synoptic Studies: the Ampleforth Conferences of 1982 and 1983* (Sheffield) 19–50.

Allison, D. (2010) *Constructing Jesus: Memory, Imagination, and History* (London and Grand Rapids).

Attardo, S. (1994) *Linguistic Theories of Humor* (Berlin and New York).

Barnes, T. D. (1969) 'An Apostle on Trial', *JTS* 20: 407–19.

Barrett, C. K. (1978) *The Gospel According to St John: An Introduction with Commentary and Notes on the Greek Text*[2] (London and Philadelphia).

Barrett, C. K. (2004) *A Critical and Exegetical Commentary on The Acts of the Apostles*, 2 vols. (London and New York).

Barton, S. C., ed. (2006) *The Cambridge Companion to the Gospels* (Cambridge).

Bauckham, R. J. (2006) *Jesus and the Eyewitnesses: the Gospels as Eyewitness Testimony* (Grand Rapids and Cambridge).

Bauckham, R. J., ed. (1998) *The Gospels for All Christians: Rethinking the Gospel Audiences* (Edinburgh and Grand Rapids).

Bellinger, W. H. Jr. and W. R. Farmer, edd. (1998) *Jesus and the Suffering Servant: Isaiah 53 and Christian Origins* (Harrisburg).

Booth, J. and R. Maltby, edd. (2006) *What's in a Name? The Significance of Proper Names in Classical Latin Literature* (Swansea).

Boring, M. E. (2006) *Mark: a Commentary* (Louisville, Ky.).

Bowersock, G. W. (1994) *Fiction as History: Nero to Julian* (Berkeley, Los Angeles, and London).

Braswell, B. K. (1988) *A Commentary on the Fourth Pythian Ode of Pindar* (Berlin).

Brown, R. E. (1997) *An Introduction to the New Testament* (New York, London, Toronto, Sydney, and Auckland).

Bruce, F. F. (1951) *The Acts of the Apostles: the Greek Text with Introduction and Commentary* (London).
Burridge, R. A. (1992) *What are the Gospels? A Comparison with Graeco-Roman Biography* (Cambridge).
Cadbury, H. (1922) 'Commentary on the Preface of Luke', in F. J. Foakes Jackson and K. Lake, edd., *The Beginnings of Christianity: Part I The Acts of the Apostles*, Volume 2, *Prolegomena II Criticism* (London) 489–510.
Cairns, F. (1979) *Tibullus: a Hellenistic Poet at Rome* (Cambridge).
Carter, W. (2000) *Matthew and the Margins: a Sociopolitical and Religious Reading* (Sheffield; Maryknoll, N.Y., 2001).
Casey, M. (1996) *Is John's Gospel True?* (London).
Casey, M. (2002) *An Aramaic Approach to Q: Sources for the Gospels of Matthew and Luke* (Cambridge).
Casey, M. (2010) *Jesus of Nazareth: an Independent Historian's Account of his Life and Teachings* (London).
Childs, B. S. (2004) *The Struggle to Understand Isaiah as Christian Scripture* (Grand Rapids and Cambridge).
Cohen, N. G. (1984) 'The Names of the Translators in the Letter of Aristeas: A Study in the Dynamics of Cultural Transition', *JSJ* 15: 32–64.
Colaclides, P. (1973) '*Acts* 17, 28a and *Bacchae* 506', *VigChr* 27: 161–4.
Collins, A. Y. (2007) *Mark: A Commentary* (Minneapolis).
Cook, J. G. (1993) 'Some Hellenistic Responses to the Gospels and Gospel Traditions', *ZNW* 84: 233–54.
Cook, J. G. (1994) 'The Protreptic Power of Early Christian Language: from John to Augustine', *VigChr* 84: 105–34.
Cook, J. G. (2000) *The Interpretation of the New Testament in Greco-Roman Paganism* (Tübingen).
Cook, J. G. (2010) *Roman Attitudes Toward the Christians: From Claudius to Hadrian* (Tübingen).
Cotter, W. J. (1999) *Miracles in Greco-Roman Antiquity: a Sourcebook* (London and New York).
Cotter, W. J. (2010) *The Christ of the Miracle Stories: Portrait through Encounter* (Grand Rapids).
Courtney, E. (2001) *A Companion to Petronius* (Oxford).
Crossley, J. G. (2004) *The Date of Mark's Gospel: Insight from the Law in Earliest Christianity* (London).
Damon, C. (2010) 'Too Close? Historian and Poet in the *Apocolocyntosis*,' in Miller and Woodman (2010) 49–70.
Davies, W. D. and D. C. Allison (1988) *Matthew 1–7* (London and New York).

Davies, W. D. and D. C. Allison (1991) *Matthew 8–18* (London and New York).

Donaldson, T. L. (2010) *Jews and Anti-Judaism in the New Testament: Decision Points and Divergent Interpretations* (London and Waco, Tex.).

Dunn, J. D. G. (2003) *Jesus Remembered: Christianity in the Making*, vol. 1 (Grand Rapids and Cambridge).

Dunn, J. D. G. (2004), 'Reconstructions of Corinthian Christianity and the Interpretation of 1 Corinthians', in E. Adams and D. G. Horrell, edd., *Christianity at Corinth: The Quest for the Pauline Church* (Louisville and London) 295–310.

Dunn, J. D. G. (2009) *Beginning from Jerusalem: Christianity in the Making*, vol. 2 (Grand Rapids and Cambridge).

Dunn, J. D. G. (2010) *Did the First Christians Worship Jesus? The New Testament Evidence* (London and Louisville).

Dupertuis, R. and T. Penner, edd. (2013) *Engaging Early Christian History: Reading Acts in the Second Century* (Durham and Bristol, Ct.).

Edwards, M. (2006) 'Gospel and Genre: Some Reservations', in McGing and Mossman (2006) 51–62.

Elliott, J. (2009) 'Ennius' "Cunctator" and the History of a Gerund in the Roman Historiographical Tradition', *CQ* 59: 532–42.

Eve, E. (2008) 'Spit in Your Eye: The Blind Man of Bethsaida and the Blind Man of Alexandria', *NTS* 54: 1–17.

Eve, E. (2009) *The Healer from Nazareth: Jesus' Miracles in Historical Context* (London).

France, R. T. (2007) *The Gospel of Matthew* (Grand Rapids/Cambridge).

Frickenschmidt, D. (1997) *Evangelium als Biographie: die vier Evangelien im Rahmen antiker Erzählkunst* (Tübingen).

Gregory, A. (2006) 'The Third Gospel? The Relationship of John and Luke Reconsidered', in J. Lierman, ed., *Challenging Perspectives on the Gospel of John* (Tübingen) 109–34.

Gregory, A. and C. K. Rowe, edd. (2010) *Rethinking the Unity and Reception of Luke and Acts* (Columbia, S.C.).

Harrison, T. (1998) 'Herodotus' Conception of Foreign Languages', *Histos* 2: 1–45.

Hartman, L. (1997) *'Into the Name of the Lord Jesus': Baptism in the Early Church* (Edinburgh).

Heitmüller, W. (1903) *'Im Namen Jesu': eine sprach- und religionsgeschichtliche Untersuchung zum Neuen Testament, speziell zur altchristlichen Taufe* (Göttingen).

Henderson, J. (2007) *The Medieval World of Isidore of Seville: Truth from Words* (Cambridge).

Hinds, S. (2006) 'Venus, Varro and the *Vates*: Towards the Limits of Etymologizing Interpretation', *Dictynna* 3: http://journals.openedition.org/dictynna/206.

Hommel, H. (1955) 'Neue Forschungen zur Areopagrede Acta 17', *ZNW* 46: 145–78.

Hommel, H. (1957) 'Platonisches bei Lukas. Zu Acta 17,28a (Leben–Bewegung–Sein),' *ZNW* 48: 193–200.

Humphreys, C. J. (2011) *The Mystery of the Last Supper: Reconstructing the Final Days of Jesus* (Cambridge).

Irwin, E. (2007) '"What's in a Name?" and Exploring the Comparable: Onomastics, Ethnography, and *Kratos* in Thrace (5.1–2 and 3–10)', in Irwin–Greenwood (2007) 41–87.

Irwin, E. and E. Greenwood, edd. (2007) *Reading Herodotus: a Study of the* Logoi *in Book 5 of Herodotus' Histories* (Cambridge).

Karrer, M. (1998) *Jesus Christus im Neuen Testament* (Göttingen).

Karrer, M. (2000) '"Und ich werde sie heilen": das Verstockungsmotiv aus Jes 6,9f. in Apg 28,26f.', in id., W. Kraus and O. Merk, edd., *Kirche und Volk Gottes: Festschrift ... J. Roloff* (Neukirchen-Vluyn) 255–71.

Keener, C. S. (2009) *The Historical Jesus of the Gospels* (Grand Rapids and Cambridge).

Keener, C. S. (2011) *Miracles: the Credibility of the New Testament Accounts*, 2 vols. (Grand Rapids).

King, K. L. (2008) 'Which Early Christianity?', in S. A. Harvey and D. G. Hunter, edd., *The Oxford Handbook of Early Christian Studies* (Oxford) 66–84.

König, J. (2006) 'The Cynic and Christian Lives of Lucian's *Peregrinus*', in McGing and Mossman (2006) 227–54.

Kooten, G. H. van (2006) *The Revelation of the Name YHWH to Moses: Perspectives from Judaism, the Pagan Graeco-Roman World, and Early Christianity* (Leiden).

Kraus, C. S., ed. (1999) *The Limits of Historiography: Genre and Narrative in Ancient Historical Texts* (Leiden, Boston, and Cologne).

Kraus, C. S., J. Marincola, and C. Pelling, edd. (2010) *Ancient Historiography and Its Contexts: Studies in Honour of A. J. Woodman* (Oxford).

Lake, K. (1933) 'Note XX: "Your Own Poets"', in F. J. F. Jackson and K. Lake, edd., *The Beginnings of Christianity: Part I: The Acts of the Apostles, Vol. V: Additional Notes to the Commentary*, edd. K. Lake and H. J. Cadbury (New York) 246–51.

Lampe, G. W. H., (1984) 'A.D. 70 in Christian Reflection', in E. Bammel and C. F. D. Moule, edd., *Jesus and the Politics of His Day* (Cambridge) 153–71.

Lane Fox, R. (1986) *Pagans and Christians* (Hardmondsworth; New York, 1987).

Lang, M. (2008) *Die Kunst des christlichen Lebens: rezeptionsästhetische Studien zum lukanischen Paulusbild* (Leipzig).

Lateiner, D. (2005) 'Signifying Names and Other Ominous Accidental Utterances in Classical Historiography', *GRBS* 45: 35–57.

Lössl, J. (2010) *The Early Church: History and Memory* (London and New York).

MacDonald, D. R. (2000) *The Homeric Epics and the Gospel of Mark* (New Haven).

MacDonald, D. R. (2003) *Does the New Testament Imitate Homer? Four Cases from the Acts of the Apostles* (New Haven).

Mackie, C. J. (2001) 'The Earliest Jason: what's in a Name?', *G&R* 48: 1–17.

Maltby, R. (1991) *A Lexicon of Ancient Latin Etymologies* (Leeds).

Maltby, R. (1993) 'The Limits of Etymologising', *Aevum Antiquum* 6: 257–75.

Maltby, R. (2003) 'The Role of Etymologies in Servius and Donatus', in C. Nifadopoulos, ed., *Etymologia: Studies in Ancient Etymology (Proceedings of the Cambridge Conference on Ancient Etymology 25–27 September 2000)* (Münster) 103–18.

Marincola, J. (2005) 'Concluding Narratives: Looking to the End in Classical Historiography', *PLLS* 12: 285–320.

Marincola, J., ed. (2007) *A Companion to Greek and Roman Historiography*, 2 vols. (Oxford and Malden, Mass.).

Mason, S. (2005) *Josephus and the New Testament*² (Peabody, Mass.).

McGing, B. (2006) 'Philo's Adaptation of the Bible in his *Life of Moses*', in id. and Mossman (2006) 117–140.

McGing, B. and J. Mossman, edd. (2006) *The Limits of Ancient Biography* (Swansea).

Metzger, B. M. and M. D. Coogan, edd. (1993) *The Oxford Companion to the Bible* (New York and Oxford).

Meyer, H. (1916) 'Iaso (1)', *RE* XI.1: 758–9.

Michalopoulos, A. (2001) *Ancient Etymologies in Ovid's Metamorphoses: A Commented Lexicon* (Leeds).

Miller, J. F. and A. J. Woodman, edd. (2010) *Latin Historiography and Poetry in the Early Empire: Generic Interactions* (Leiden).

Mitchell, S. (1999) 'The Cult of Theos Hypsistos between Pagans, Jews, and Christians', in P. Athanassiadi and M. Frede, edd., *Pagan Monotheism in Late Antiquity* (Oxford) 81–148.

Mitchell, S. (2010) 'Further Thoughts on the Cult of Theos Hypsistos', in Mitchell and Van Nuffelen (2010) 167–208.

Mitchell, S. and P. Van Nuffelen, edd. (2010) *One God: Pagan Monotheism in the Roman Empire* (Cambridge).

Moles, J. L. (1995) 'Dio Chrysostom, Greece, and Rome', in D. C. Innes, H. Hine, and C. Pelling, edd., *Ethics and Rhetoric: Classical Essays for Donald Russell on his Seventy-Fifth Birthday* (Oxford) 177–92 [above, Ch. 7].

Moles, J. L. (1998) 'Cry Freedom: Tacitus *Annals* 4.32–35', *Histos* 2 (1998) 95–184 [vol. 2, Ch. 53].

Moles, J. L. (2002) 'Herodotus and Athens', in E. J. Bakker, I. de Jong and H. van Wees, edd., *Brill's Companion to Herodotus* (Leiden and Boston) 33–52 [vol. 2, Ch. 56].

Moles, J. L. (2006a) 'Cynic Influence upon First-century Judaism and Early Christianity?', in McGing and Mossman (2006) 89–116 [above, Ch. 20].

Moles, J. L. (2006b) 'Jesus and Dionysus in *The Acts of the Apostles* and Early Christianity' *Hermathena* 180: 65–104 [above, Ch. 21].

Moles, J. L. (2007a) 'Philosophy and Ethics', in S. Harrison, ed., *Cambridge Companion to Horace* (2007) 165–80 [above, Ch. 18].

Moles, J. L. (2007b) '"Saving" Greece from the 'Ignominy' of Tyranny? The "Famous" and "Wonderful" Speech of Socles (5.92)', in Irwin–Greenwood (2007) 245–68 [vol. 2, Ch. 57].

Moles, J. L. (2010) 'Narrative and Speech Problems in Thucydides Book 1', in Kraus–Marincola–Pelling (2010) 15–39 [vol. 2, Ch. 58].

Moles, J. L. (2011) 'Luke's Preface: The Greek Decree, Classical Historiography and Christian Redefinitions', NTS 57: 1–22 [above, Ch. 22].

Moles, J. L. (2012) 'What's in a Name? Χριστός/χρηστός and Χριστιανοί/χρηστιανοί in the First Century AD' [below, Ch. 29].

Moles, J. L. (2013) 'Time and Space Travel in Luke-Acts', in R. Dupertuis and T. Penner, edd., *Engaging Early Christian History: Reading Acts in the Second Century* (Durham and Bristol, Ct.) 101–22 [below, Ch. 24].

Moles, J. L. (2014) 'Accommodation, Opposition or Other: Luke-Acts' Stance towards Rome', in J. M. Madsen and R. Rees, edd., *Roman Rule in Greek and Latin Writing: Double Vision* (Leiden) 79–104 [below, Ch. 25].

Moyise, S. and M. J. J. Menken, edd. (2005) *Isaiah in the New Testament* (London and New York).

Nestle, E., B. and K. Aland, edd. (2001) *Greek–English New Testament*[8] (Stuttgart).

O'Hara, J. J. (1996) *True Names: Vergil and the Alexandrian Tradition of Etymological Wordplay* (Ann Arbor; expanded edition 2017).

Padilla, O. (2009) 'Hellenistic παιδεία and Luke's Education: A Critique of Recent Approaches', NTS 55: 416–37.

Page, T. E. (1918) *The Acts of the Apostles* (London).

Parker, R. (1996) 'Hypsistos', OCD[3]: 739.

Parsons, M. and R. Pervo (1993) *Rethinking the Unity of Luke and Acts* (Minneapolis).

Paschalis, M. (1997) *Virgil's Aeneid: Semantic Relations and Proper Names* (Oxford).

Pelling, C. B. R. (1990) 'Truth and Fiction in Plutarch's Lives', in D. A. Russell, ed., *Antonine Literature* (Oxford) 19–51; repr. in id., *Plutarch and History: Eighteen Studies* (London and Swansea, 2002) 143–70.

Penner, T. (2012) '*Res Gestae Divi Christi*: Miracles, Early Christian Heroes, and the Discourse of Power in *Acts*,' in D. F. Watson, ed., *Miracle Discourse in the New Testament* (Atlanta) 125–73.

Peraki-Kyriakidou, H. (2002). 'Aspects of Ancient Etymologizing', CQ 52: 478–93.

Perrin, N. (2010) *Jesus the Temple* (London and Grand Rapids).

Pervo, R. I. (1987) *Profit with Delight: the Literary Genre of the Acts of the Apostles* (Philadelphia).

Popkes, E. E. (2009) 'Die letzten Worte des lukanischen Paulus: zur Bedeutung von Act 28,25–28 für das Paulusbild der Apostelgeschichte', in J. Frey, C. K. Rothschild, and J. Schröter, edd., *Die Apostelgeschichte im Kontext antiker und frühchristlicher Historiographie* (Berlin and New York) 605–25.

Ramelli, I. (1996) 'Petronio e i Cristiani: allusion al vangelo di Marco nel Satyricon?', *Aevum* 70: 75–80.

Renn, S. D. (2005) *Expository Dictionary of Bible Words: Word Studies for Key English Bible Words Based on the Hebrew and Greek texts* (Peabody).

Rowe, C. K. (2011) 'The Grammar of Life: the Areopagus Speech and Pagan Tradition', *NTS* 57: 31–50.

Ryken, L., J. C. Wilhoit, and T. Longman III, edd. (1998) *Dictionary of Biblical Imagery* (Downers Grove, Ill.).

Sanders, E. P. (1993) *The Historical Figure of Jesus* (London).

Sandnes, K. O. (1993) 'Paul and Socrates: The Aim of Paul's Areopagus Speech', *JSNT* 50: 13–26.

Sim, D. C. (2011) 'Matthew's Use of Mark: Did Matthew Intend to Supplement or to Replace his Primary Source?' *NTS* 57: 176–92.

Simonetti, M. (2001) *Ancient Christian Commentary on Scripture: New Testament 1: Matthew 1–13* (Downers Grove, Ill.).

Snyder, J. M. (1980) *Puns and Poetry in Lucretius' De Rerum Natura.* (Amsterdam).

Swain, S. (1996) *Hellenism and Empire: Language, Classicism, and Power in the Greek World, AD 50–250* (Oxford).

Szemerényi, O. (1974) 'The Origins of the Greek Lexicon: Ex Oriente Lux', *JHS* 94: 144–57.

Talbert, C. H. (1974) *Literary Patterns, Theological Themes, and the Genre of Luke-Acts* (Missoula).

Taylor, J. E. (2003) *Jewish Women Philosophers of First-Century Alexandria: Philo's 'Therapeutae' Reconsidered* (Oxford).

Telford, W. R. (1999) *The Theology of the Gospel of Mark* (Cambridge).

Theissen, G. (2010) 'Jesus and his Followers as Healers: Symbolic Healing', in W. S. Sax, J. Quack, and J. Weinhold, edd., *The Problem of Ritual Efficacy* (Oxford) 45–65.

Theissen, G. and A. Merz (1998) *The Historical Jesus: a Comprehensive Guide* (London); trans. by J. Bowden of *Der historische Jesus: ein Lehrbuch* (Göttingen, 1996).

Troiani, L. (2011) 'Storia antica e storia classica: il caso dell'oriente Greco-romano', *Histos* 5: 107–16.

Vermes, G. (1973) *Jesus the Jew: A Historian's Reading of the Gospels* (London).

Wallace, R. and W. Williams (1993) *The Acts of the Apostles: a Companion* (London and New York).

Weinstock, S. (1971) *Divus Julius* (Oxford).

Wells, L. (1998) *The Greek Language of Healing from Homer to New Testament Times* (Berlin).

Williams, M. H. (1995) 'Palestinian Jewish Personal Names in Acts', in R. Bauckham, ed., *The Book of Acts in Its Palestinian Setting* (Grand Rapids) 79–114.

Williams, M. H. (1998) 'The Structure of the Jewish Community in Rome', in M. Goodman, ed., *Jews in a Greco-Roman World* (Oxford) 215–28.

Winn, A. (2008) *The Purpose of Mark's Gospel: an Early Christian Response to Roman Imperial Propaganda* (Tübingen).

Wiseman, T. P. (1974) 'Legendary Genealogies in Late-Republican Rome', *G&R* 21: 153–64; repr. in id., *Roman Studies, Literary and Historical* (Liverpool, 1987) 207–18.

Witherington, B. (1998) *The Acts of the Apostles: a Socio-rhetorical Commentary* (Grand Rapids and Cambridge).

Woodhead, W. (1928) *Etymologizing in Greek Literature from Homer to Philo Judaeus* (Toronto).

Woodman, A. J. and R. H. Martin, edd. (1996) *The* Annals *of Tacitus, Book 3* (Cambridge).

Wright, N. T. (2003) *The Resurrection of the Son of God* (London).

CHAPTER 24

# Time and Space Travel in Luke-Acts

To us, the first and second centuries mark different epochs. Whether in relation to the Christian or Roman worlds, this periodisation is problematic.* Even on a 'rational' modern dating of *c.*85 CE, Acts in some areas may resonate as much with the second century as with the first. One such area is the burgeoning 'Second Sophistic'. This paper discerns strong classical elements as co-existing with Jewish and Christian, with the corollary that our author envisages pagan readers and listeners, as well as Jewish, Christian, and 'God-fearing'.[1] Early Christian writings, including Luke-Acts, did make some impact upon second-century pagan writers, including the philosopher Celsus and the satirist Lucian,[2] hence upon their readers. But in the case of 'political' texts, the modern periodisation finds an ancient analogue: contemporaries contrasted Nerva's and Trajan's 'new age' with Domitian's 'tyranny'. Thus in 100 Rome could be said to be at a crossroads (Tac. *Agr.* 3.1; Plin. *Paneg.* 2.2–3; Dio 1.61). If, then, Acts actually belongs to the second century (specifically, I believe, to the first decade),[3] this contextualisation should be eloquent, alike in the contexts of the Second Sophistic, of Roman persecution,[4] especially under Domitian,[5] and of Christianity's growth.

Acts can provisionally be read alone, as second-century Christians characteristically did, and as this volume, like many others, mostly does. But if Luke-Acts forms a two-book unity,[6] there must be important things in one

---

\* [121] For much conversation, I thank Loveday Alexander, John Barclay, and Tony Woodman; for exemplary forbearance and helpfulness, the editors. {*Editor's note: A number of in-text references to ancient and modern sources in the original publication have been moved to the footnotes; the footnote numbers do not, therefore, correspond to those of the original publication.*}

1 The bibliography and documentation are minimalist and the theology is Luke-focalised. Also, translations, respecting Greek verbal plays and patterns, are mine. It should become clear why this requirement matters.

2 Cook (1993); König (2006) 230.

3 For me the coordinates are: (a) Josephan priority, well argued by Mason (2005) 273–93, 164, 178, 251, 300 (the arguments can be strengthened); (b) use of John (see n. 20); (c) use of Dio Chrysostom; (d) most Roman historians' judgement that Acts represents a first-century Roman world; (e) authorship by Luke, companion of Paul.

4 Historians nowadays resist the notion of 'persecution', certainly in the first two centuries: my use is Christian-focalised.

5 Lane Fox (1986) 433.

6 See the recent surveys on this subject by Bird (2007) and Rowe (2007).

text that cannot be properly comprehended without the other. One such is my theme. Treatment provides new arguments for unity, or—to separatists—new evidences of the quality of the author of Acts as a reader of Luke.

Everybody recognises the importance of 'road imagery' in the gospels generally, including Mark,[7] one of our author's main sources, and of travel throughout Luke-Acts.[8] Jesus' journey to Jerusalem is the main organising structure of the second half of Luke.[9] Acts, following Jesus' instruction (1.8),[10] ranges from Jerusalem to all Judaea, to Samaria, to Ethiopia (symbolically), from Asia, to Europe, to Rome, [[102]] and—somehow—to 'the end of the earth'. It also contains one of the best ancient sea narratives.

Everybody also recognises that journeys in Luke-Acts are characteristically freighted with non-literal meaning. Jesus' physical journey is metaphorical, spiritual, and Christological, and, for the disciples, intendedly, formative. Again, in an extended stretch of Acts, an angel tells Philip 'to go ... to the road that goes down from Jerusalem to Gaza' (Acts 8.26). He meets the eunuch and answers his plea (8.31) to 'lead him along the road' (of scriptural interpretation); they then literally go along the road; the eunuch is baptised and 'went on his road rejoicing' (8.36–9). Saul begins persecuting 'those of the Road' (a more organic translation than 'the Way'), is converted on the road to Damascus (9.2–8, 27), a sequence told thrice, and found by Ananias, told by the Lord to 'go', on 'Straight Street' (9.11), location doubly apposite: Paul (as he becomes) is now on 'the straight road', and 'turning' (15.19) from the wrong road to the right one can always be a 'straightaway' event. And there are ever more sophisticated studies of the geography and 'spatiality' of Acts.[11]

For all this many scholars nowadays find parallels in contemporary pagan literature, including the novel, with its travelogues and quest narratives, sometimes at least formally religious;[12] epic;[13] the travel element of much historiography; the overlaps between historiography and geography;[14] travel narratives which mimic historiographical modes; sub-genres such as the *periegesis* of a site or the visit of sophisticated outsiders to primitive lands, or of outside

---

7   Ryken–Wilhoit–Longman (1998) 631; Boring (2006) 37–8.
8   Baban (2006); Morgan (2013).
9   Johnson (1991) 163–5; Green (1997) 396–9.
10  D. R. Schwartz's claim ([1986]; [2009] 122 n. 11) that γῆς means 'end of the land', later *reinterpreted* by Paul as 'end of the earth', misconceives the entire geography of Acts (and of Luke-Acts).
11  See Sleeman (2009).
12  Cf. L. C. A. Alexander (2005) 69–96, 97–119, 153–63; König (2009) 11–26.
13  Cf. Bonz (2000); L. C. A. Alexander (2005) 165–82; Krauter (2009).
14  Clarke (1999); Mossman (2006).

innocents to big cities; and the extensive exploitations of travel imagery, or of the interplay between physical travel and moral progress, in Greek philosophy. To these I would add the very common analogy between travelling and the acts of writing and reading.

This essay, however, pushes such perspectives to the limit, arguing that: travel in time and space is the text's central theme; 'the road' is the master metaphor; so focalised, the thorniest interpretative problems attain clearance; and our author's handling of this theme, in its almost infinite complexities and consequences, represents a culmination of classical literary procedures, well calculated to appeal to Second Sophistic tastes.

The preface draws the reader in and gives provisional guidance, naturally subject to redefinition, re-reading, and reinterpretation (Lk. 1.1–4):[15]

> Ἐπειδήπερ πολλοὶ ἐπεχείρησαν ἀνατάξασθαι διήγησιν περὶ τῶν πεπληροφορημένων ἐν ἡμῖν πραγμάτων, (2) καθὼς παρέδοσαν ἡμῖν οἱ ἀπ᾽ ἀρχῆς αὐτόπται καὶ ὑπηρέται γενόμενοι τοῦ λόγου, (3) ἔδοξε κἀμοὶ παρηκολουθηκότι ἄνωθεν πᾶσιν [[103]] ἀκριβῶς καθεξῆς σοι γράψαι, κράτιστε Θεόφιλε, (4) ἵνα ἐπιγνῷς περὶ ὧν κατηχήθης λόγων τὴν ἀσφάλειαν.

> Since indeed many have set their hand to draw up a narrative guide about the things done which have been persuasively brought to fulfilment amongst us, (2) just as those who became from the beginning eyewitnesses and servants of the word gave them down to us, (3) it seemed good to me also, having closely followed all of them from the up, to write them down for you in order, most powerful Theophilos, (4) so that you may additionally know/experience/recognise the truth/security/safety/un-slipperiness about the words in which you have been orally instructed.

The theme is 'the things done which have been persuasively brought to fulfilment amongst us'/'the word'/'the words in which you have been orally instructed'. But this does not mean that 'the *Preface* never speaks of God'.[16] 'Brought to fulfilment' and 'servants of the word' have divine implications for Jews, God-fearers, and Christians, as 'fulfilment' can have for pagans. Moreover, regardless of his reality, 'Theophilos" name is theophoric: *God* is 'spoken of'.

---

15   Cadbury (1922); L. C. A. Alexander (1993); Bauckham (2006) 116–24; Dunn (2009) 73–5; Moles (2011); Wolter (2009).
16   L. C. A. Alexander (2005) 223.

Indeed, Origen, Ambrose,[17] and Bede detected a doubly 'speaking' name: 'loving God' and 'loved by God', reflecting the reciprocity of divine–human relations. The name then has universalising force, including all Christians, actual (like Theophilos) and potential. This highly attractive reading is validated (I believe) in the narrative.

Further, in the Prologue to John, the Word is instantiated in Jesus. Is it here? Some moderns think so.[18] So, already, Irenaeus in the second century, Cyril, and Ambrose.[19] They had read John. Had our author?[20] The idea of Jesus as Word, anyway, is not difficult for Christians, and even necessary, once he was claimed as the fulfilment of Scripture. Further, if the eyewitnesses are eyewitnesses only of the word as usually understood, the clash of visual and aural/oral media is challengingly synaesthetic. But if the Word is instantiated in Jesus, this eyewitnessing finds concrete focus (as Ambrose sees). The implication would escape non-Christians, for whom the phrase would have 'read-on' appeal. The Preface, then, implicitly claims to be a treatment of 'Christianity' centred on Jesus Christ himself. This promise is concretised in the term 'Christian' in Acts 11.26 and 26.28.

What medium is our author using? 'Writing', of course, contrasted with oral instruction, but the Preface sketches a range of possible media. Its overall structure imitates that of a Greek inscription.[21] This format is a variant of the common analogy between texts and prestigious physical objects, including buildings (see, for example, Pind. *Pyth.* 6.8; Thuc. 1.22.4; Hor. *C.* 3.30). There is also an implicit comparison with artefacts ⟦104⟧ (again common in classical literature): cf. 'set their hand to', which can be used of artists,[22] 'closely' (or 'accurately'), which can be applied to works of art,[23] and ἀσφάλειαν (lit., 'security from falling', applicable to buildings and cities).[24] The reader contemplates different media and their respective merits. While 'writing' is our author's chosen medium and the analogy between text and physical object favours the former (as transportable, more complex, more durable, etc.), there is some sense

---

17   Just (2003) 4.
18   Dunn (2003) 178 n. 29; (2009) 74 n. 83.
19   Eus. *HE* 5.20.6; Just (2003) 3–4.
20   See Gregory (2006), with bibliography; 'many' (Lk. 1.1) naturally makes Luke last of the canonical gospels; hence 'the word', in Luke's remarkably concentrated Preface, also targets John's very 'wordy' Foreword about the Word.
21   Moles (2011).
22   LSJ s.v. χείρ, VI.b.
23   LSJ Suppl. s.v. ἀκριβόω.
24   LSJ s.v. σφάλλω, II.

that media interpenetrate ('eyewitnesses of the word') and that *logos* ('word') triumphs over all possible media.

But there is another medium. While everybody recognises the importance of travel in the narratives, no one seems to recognise the dominant image of the Preface, explicit in 'having followed closely', implicit or 'activated' in διήγησιν (lit. 'leading through'), 'brought to fulfilment', and ἀσφάλειαν (itself applicable to roads: e.g., Xen. *Hell.* 5.4.51). This road image is particularly 'conducive' to 'drawing' readers 'in' to a text. But it is also organic, creating, immediately, several different, though interconnecting, roads: (a) the text, 'drawn up' by the author, traversed by the reader; (b) the events themselves ('brought to fulfilment'); (c) the tradition ('given on') about those events; (d) Christianity as a road (this written road about Christianity will guarantee the ἀσφάλεια of 'the words'); (e) the road as metaphor for moral or religious 'progress'; and (f) the 'road of life', as best 'navigated' by the Christian road (reprised at Acts 2.28: 'the roads of life'). Particularly important are the notions of the text as a road (reprised, as we have seen, in Acts 8.31) and of Christianity itself as 'The Road'. Within the New Testament this notion, certainly in its basic form, is peculiar to our author,[25] though the term was historically applied to first-century Christians, both by themselves and others (Acts 9.2; 24.14, 22). There is thus a strong parallelism between theme and treatment: Luke-Acts is 'the road' to 'the Road' of Christianity—a 'Road' which can surely also be Jesus himself, as in John 14.6. In the Christian context, this parallelism seems our author's own twist, though there are classical parallels, including philosophical epitomes ('short-cut' texts to 'short-cut' solutions) and Herodotean historiography (below).

Within the medium of writing, what genre does our author propose? L. C. A. Alexander's repeated claim[26] that the Preface reads like that of a 'professional work' (of medicine, science, etc.) fails. Classical history consists of 'things that happened/were done' (the term used, for example, by Herodotus and Livy in the very first sentences of their Prefaces), here rendered by 'the things done that have been brought to fulfilment amongst us'. The highly energised Greek repays consideration. Πραγμάτων means 'things done', from the verb πράσσω. Πράσσω and πληροφορέω are similar in meaning but not synonymous, and the extension of meaning created by πεπληροφορημένων exemplifies the classical stylistic device dubbed 'amplificatory pleonasm'.[27] [105] Historiography 'writes' such 'things' up—compare with 'draw up', 'write', and 'narrative guide'.

---

25   Acts 9.2; 19.9, 23; 22.4; 24.14, 22; see Pathrapankal (1979).
26   L. C. A. Alexander (1978); (1986); (1993); (1996); (1999); (2005) 1–6, 12–20, 161.
27   By Diggle (2005).

Further, from Hecataeus, Herodotus, and Thucydides through to the Roman republican historians and the Greek and Roman imperial historians, it frequently exploits the inscription analogy.[28]

What sub-genre of historiography? 'Amongst us' suggests 'local' history.[29] What of primary historiographical influences or allusions? For Alexander, 'Thucydides and Herodotus are probably the most difficult to square with the *Preface*',[30] and even scholars who cite historiographical parallels characteristically cite later ones.[31] But differences from Herodotus and Thucydides (immediate theological implication, suggestion of 'local' history, anonymity of historian) do not preclude parallels. Among the many Herodotean prefatory, or programmatic, 'signals' are: the double imitation, in 'road about the Road' and 'word(s) about the Word', of the influential Herodotean parallelism, in his Preface, between treatment and theme ('demonstration ... deeds demonstrated'); the use of *logos* for 'historical account' (Hdt. 1.5.3); the analogy between text and road (1.5.3); and the term 'eyewitness'.[32] There are also many parallels with Thucydides' chapters on method.[33] These include: 'as' (ὡς-clause epexegetic of the historiographical theme, itself stated as the object of a verb [Thuc. 1.1.1; 5.26.1]); emphasis on eyewitness testimony (1.22.3); 'it seemed to me' formula (1.22.1–2); emphasis on 'accuracy' (ἀκρίβεια) (1.22.2); emphasis on truth (1.22.4); notion that history consists of deeds and words (1.22.1–2); idea that the reader 'looks' at the historical work;[34] visual element emphasised in two contexts: the testimony of the original eyewitnesses and the 'visualness' of the final text (1.22.3–4); contrast between the oral/aural and the written in favour of the latter (1.22.4); 'writing ... in order' (5.26.1); a series of events from beginning to end (5.26.4); and a direct relationship between 'all' of these and the historian, conducive to ἀκρίβεια (5.26.5).

None of this is narrowly restrictive. There is much internal variety both in Herodotus and in Thucydides, who differ greatly from each other. Both traditions are also richly hospitable to development and redefinition. Our author

---

28  Moles (1999).
29  Sterling (1992), e.g., 349.
30  L. C. A. Alexander (2005) 14.
31  Aune (2002); Bauckham (2006) 116–24.
32  Hdt. 2.29.1 (Herodotus applies the term to himself); 3.115.2 (he remarks that there is no eyewitness); 4.16.1 (the same); 8.79.4 (the term is applied to Aristides, an 'internal' historian figure); 8.80.1 (the same).
33  Plümacher (2006); cf. Frey (2009) 21; Schröter (2009) 41.
34  ἐπιγιγνώσκω often means 'recognise': LSJ s.v., esp. II; similarly, the simplex: LSJ s.v.; cf. Luke 18.34.

also references later historians.³⁵ Historiography itself is a very capacious genre and easily accommodates other generic elements, as three recent classicists' collections amply demonstrate.³⁶ Contrary to some assumptions, the presence of other genres—novel, epic, myth, tragedy,³⁷ philosophical treatise or 'Apology', and so on—does not threaten Luke-Acts' status as historiography. 'Great historiography' had always included most of these genres—or anticipated and influenced the others. Conversely, generic 'generosity' does not render genre meaningless: generic 'inclusions' and generic shifts 'generate' meaning.

[106] As with Herodotus (*praef.*), Thucydides (1.1–3, etc.), and their successors, although implicitly ('brought to fulfilment') rather than explicitly, the particular subject is claimed as supremely great. Consistently thus historiographical is the theme of 'beginnings and endings': 'set their hand', 'brought to fulfilment', 'from the beginning', and 'from the up';³⁸ moreover, 'the truth/security/safety/unslipperiness' is 'the end' both in position and in some logical sense. The theme applies alike to the work of writers, to the role of eye-witnesses, to the historical events themselves, and to the 'end' (as 'ultimate benefit') for the reader. It naturally fits road imagery and the sort of historiography which uses it, notably Herodotean.

This sense of traditional historiographical greatness is, however, problematised both by the notion of 'local history' and by a series of inversions. First, that, precisely, of great and small. This is a provocatively short *Preface*, especially compared with classical historiographical Prefaces, characteristically very long. Luke-Acts itself, *qua* work of 'great' historiography, is also very short. Yet, as concepts, greatness and smallness, the relationship between the two, and the paradoxical revaluation of the latter are intrinsic to classical history-writing, both historiography proper (especially Herodotus, but also Xenophon, Polybius, and Tacitus) and biography, and to the Socratic writings that influenced some of it.³⁹ Roads, too, can be 'short' or 'long'. Paul's conversion was 'straightaway', Luke-Acts a correspondingly 'short road': 'in short', a historiographical epitome.⁴⁰ The fact that in early Christianity Jesus himself

---

35  These include Polybius (see Bauckham [2006] 120–1), Josephus (see n. 3 above), and (I believe) Livy and Augustus' *Res Gestae*.
36  Kraus (1999); McGing–Mossman (2006); Marincola (2007).
37  Moles (2006).
38  See further Bauckham (2006) 119–23.
39  See, for example, Hdt. 1.5.3–4; Xen. *Hell.* 2.3.56; 7.2.1; Tac. *Ann.* 4.32.1–2 (with Moles [1998]); Nepos, *praef.*; *Pelop.*1.1; Plut. *Alex.* 1.1–2; Xen. *Symp.* 1.1; Eckstein (1995).
40  Note Acts 24.4 συντόμως (*hapax*, and synonymous with ἐπιτόμως): actually, not Tertullus, but Paul speaks συντόμως about, *concisely*, the Road to Damascus: that 'straightaway'

can be conceptualised in epitome terms (e.g., Eph. 1.10; 4.20) helps this parallel between treatment and theme. But also, *qua* 'guide', 'road', and 'short-cut', Luke-Acts functions as the indispensable 'Vade mecum' for all Christians. Here again, our author connects with contemporary classical culture, in which epitomes were an extremely popular form,[41] though it is also relevant that 2 Maccabees, a text I think known to our author,[42] is an earlier Jewish historiographical epitome (cf. 2 Macc. 2.26, 28).

Second, and relatedly, that of power. 'Brought to fulfilment' implies both control and teleology, implicitly God's. But there is a contrast between 'servants of the word' and Theophilos, who is 'most powerful' in a worldly sense. There is even internal conflict in Theophilos *qua* thus 'most powerful'. This conflict of powers occurs in classical historiography, especially Herodotean historiography as influenced by epic and tragedy, where it is mediated by such motifs as 'the wise warner', or the clash between wisdom/religion and worldly power (as in the programmatic encounter between Croesus and Solon, 1.29–33).

Third, and also relatedly, that of 'upness' ('draw up', 'from the up') and 'downness' (καθώς/καθεξῆς/κατηχήθης). These concepts characteristically [[107]] stand for arbitrary reversals of fortune; the power of the pagan gods, particularly Zeus;[43] and the rise and fall of states or individuals. Here, however, they are positive concepts; they apply both to time and to space; and in different areas (one can go 'up' and 'down' roads or other physical things, such as mountains, and one can oneself go 'up' or 'down' in various senses). Moreover, very paradoxically, their end product is *stability*. Worldly 'ups-and-downs' are transvalued. This picture is strikingly different from Herodotus, for whom human *good* fortune never remains in the same place (1.5.3–4), or Thucydides, whose central concern is *change* (1.1.3).

So far, then, Luke-Acts programs a challenging historiographical journey through Christianity, a journey which alike includes, redefines, and subverts Herodotean and Thucydidean canons. The text is the 'vehicle' which will transport the reader to the Christian 'destination' of 'truth/security/safety/un-slipperiness', provided he first 'recognises' the rightness of this destination and then gets himself 'on board'.

The implications of 'truth/security/safety/un-slipperiness' require unpacking. Historiographically, ἀσφάλειαν inevitably includes 'truth'.[44] But there is

---

event; Acts 26.2–29 (Paul and Agrippa II) also functions as a metaliterary epitome. Luke-Acts as (also) a *philosophical* epitome exceeds my scope.

41   Silk–Kaster (1996).
42   Moles (2006) 82–3 {above, pp. 567–9}.
43   LSJ s.v. ἄνω, II.2.b. Aesch. *Eum.* 651 (latent in Acts 17.31–2).
44   Cf. Acts 2.36; 21.34; 22.30; 25.26; *P. Giss.* 1.27; for discussion, see Cadbury (1922) 509.

also the much larger implication: Christianity is the Truth about everything. This Truth is like a 'safe' road on which one cannot 'fall', or a building which itself cannot fall. How does Christian Truth produce 'security', 'safety', and so on? Although ἀσφάλεια can denote physical safety and Acts (and, to some extent, Luke) is often read as showing that Christianity poses no threat, hence that Roman persecution is misguided, post-Jesus, post-Paul, post-Nero, and post-Domitian, our author cannot be promising *that*. The narrative, indeed, celebrates Christian martyrdom (Jesus and Stephen, and, implicitly, Paul and all Christian martyrs), so ἀσφάλεια must be something which takes account of Christians' always possible *lack* of safety. For 'recognition' of the full implications, the reader must read on. The narrative will turn out provocatively small both in size (a mere epitome) and compass: in the first instance from (roughly) 4 BCE (the birth of Jesus) to 62 CE (Paul in Rome), sixty-five years or so. One then has to add the years between 62 CE and the time of writing, known to the first readers, only reconstructible by us (for me, forty plus years). Yet this doubly brief narrative, extending into eras of persecution, can bring the reader to 'security/safety'.[45]

No educated pagan of the second century (least of all the highly erudite anti-Christian author of *How to Write History*) could fail to be impressed by the density, economy, and creativity of our author's historiographical allusions and of his manipulations of historiographical conventions. But the generic inventiveness continues. Luke turns out to be a classical biography of Jesus. It looks like one,[46] and is so described (admittedly, with provocative paradox) in the Acts Preface (below). The effect (for Jewish or Jewish-Christian readers) is enhanced by the absence ⟦108⟧ of rabbinic biographies,[47] and it is simultaneously challenging and pointedly logical. Classical historiography concerns 'the greatest story ever told' (according to the particular historian). Since that, to our author, is the Jesus event, historiography is properly pursued through biography. Interestingly parallel are second-century (and later) Greek historians' and biographers' treatments of Julius Caesar.[48] Educated pagans would recognise our author as doing similar things, and thereby adumbrating an ideological contest between Christianity and Caesarism. Then Acts, concerning Jesus' immediate followers, reverts to historiography[49]—more precisely, individual-orientated historiography, a *via media* between historiography and

---

45  Is the Preface, then, (also) riffing on Jn 14.6: 'I am the Road, the Truth, and the Life'?
46  Burridge (1992); (2004); Frickenschmidt (1997).
47  P. S. Alexander (1984).
48  Pelling (2006).
49  Dunn (2009) 68 and n. 57; Frey (2009) 2.

biography exactly suited to the new subject-matter. These, as it were, 'pagan' generic turns acquire still further meaning when superimposed upon the Jewish-Christian perspective of 'the word' (Lk. 1.2). In so far as 'the word' is God's 'narrative' for humans as communicated by true prophets and signs, it is historiographical; in so far as it is instantiated in Jesus, it is biographical. God's 'word' (Lk. 1.3; collective singular) necessarily consists of individual 'words' (Lk. 1.4), including Jesus himself and Luke's own 'word'.[50] But there is another classical layering. These multiple perspectives do not obviate Charles Talbert's thesis that Luke-Acts imitates a pattern of Greek philosophical biography: a Life of the Founder followed by Lives of his Successors.[51] Under classical historiography's generous umbrella, 'both-and' is generally a far better generic principle than 'either-or'.

The work's title should forward these effects. Martin Hengel claims 'The Gospel according to "x"' as the original title of all four Evangelists.[52] But that would obliterate our author's creative and pointed generic shifts. Better 'To Theophilos, on Security', with *logos* either understood or explicit, and with several implications, immediate or latent, that: Luke-Acts is a Herodotean historiographical text; it is (also) a philosophical text (outside my scope); and it is a divine *logos* (cf. Lk. 1.2, 4) about 'Security'.

Within Luke, itself a road, roads, of all sorts, proliferate and intersect. There is almost endless 'following', 'going', and 'turning', especially in the imperative mood (further pressuring readers to 'take the ride'). The boy Jesus himself 'progressed in wisdom and maturity' (Lk. 2.52). At the Transfiguration, just before Jesus' climactic journey begins, Moses and Elijah tell of 'his exit road (*exodos*), which he was going to *fulfil* in Jerusalem' (Lk. 9.31). Jesus' own 'road' is central to 'the things done which have been persuasively brought to fulfilment amongst us'. Inversions of power, space, and size, abound: 'he has dragged down dynasts from their thrones and exalted the lowly' (Lk. 1.52), the Beatitudes, and so on. Further pointers are given to the implications of 'security from falling'. 'Falling' is combined with road imagery in one parable (Lk. 6.39), with house-building in another (Lk. 6.48–9). Jerusalem will be razed to the ground (Lk. 19.44) and trodden down (Lk. 21.24), and every 〚109〛 stone of the Temple thrown down (Lk. 21.5). By contrast, belief in Jesus is like a house that cannot fall (Lk. 6.49), and Jesus, the stone which the builders rejected, has become the head of the corner (Lk. 20.17). The 'opposite' of 'falling' is 'standing' (Lk. 2.34), under which come: (a) allusions to the general 'standing-up' (resurrection) at the end of

---

50    Squires (1993); Dunn (2009) 73–4.
51    Talbert (1974), esp. 89–98; (1977); (1978); Talbert–Stepp (2003).
52    Hengel (2000) 48–56.

time; (b) prophecies of Jesus' own 'standing-up'; and (c) apparently more mundane exhortations to healed or helped people to 'stand up', which, thus contextualised, acquire eschatological depth. Hence Jesus' 'standing-up', which is both anticipatory and confirmatory of the general 'standing-up' at the end of time, forms the bedrock of 'security from falling'. In structuralist terms, both Preface and narrative conceive of time and space along horizontal and vertical planes, and 'security from falling'/'up-standing' is the transcendental signifier that mediates all.

Equally 'inductive' is the Acts Preface, which 'blurs' into narrative (Acts 1.1–3):[53]

τὸν μὲν πρῶτον λόγον ἐποιησάμην περὶ πάντων, ὦ Θεόφιλε, ὧν ἤρξατο Ἰησοῦς ποιεῖν τε καὶ διδάσκειν (2) ἄχρι ἧς ἡμέρας ἐντειλάμενος τοῖς ἀποστόλοις διὰ πνεύματος ἁγίου οὓς ἐξελέξατο ἀνελήμφθη. (3) οἷς καὶ παρέστησεν ἑαυτὸν ζῶντα μετὰ τὸ παθεῖν αὐτὸν ἐν πολλοῖς τεκμηρίοις, δι' ἡμερῶν τεσσεράκοντα ὀπτανόμενος αὐτοῖς καὶ λέγων τὰ περὶ τῆς βασιλείας τοῦ θεοῦ.

The first word I did/made about all the things, Theophilos, that Jesus began to do/make and to teach, (2) until the day when, having given instructions through the Holy Spirit to the apostles whom he had chosen, he was taken up. (3) By whom indeed after his suffering he stood himself present alive in many indications, being seen by them and speaking on the things of the kingdom of God.

The 'first word' recalls the play on 'word(s) about the Word' of the Luke Preface. Acts, too, is a specific 'word' within the collective and ongoing divine 'word'. The parallelism between work and theme is strengthened by the application of 'do/make' both to Luke and Jesus. 'Make' reactivates the artefact analogy. 'To do and to teach [and, in 1.3, 'speaking']' also recalls Jesus as Word in action (Lk. 1.2). But why 'first', rather than 'former'? Readers must read on. The emphasis of 'stood himself present alive' echoes Luke 24.36 ('he stood in the midst of them'), and reinforces the dependence of Christian 'security from falling' on Jesus' 'standing-up'. The emphasis of 'many indications' signposts Acts as 'proof text' of Jesus' resurrection. The 'speech–action' and 'active–passive' contrasts, legal terminology, and ⟦110⟧ emphasis on 'sight' as historical validation are Thucydidean (1.22.1–23.1; 1.1.3, 20.1, 22.4), echoing Thucydides' presence in the Luke Preface.

---

53  L. C. A. Alexander (1993) 142–6; (2005) 21–42; Dormeyer–Galindo (2003) 32–3; Mason (2005) 257; Dormeyer (2009) 453–5; Wolter (2009) 490–94; Sleeman (2009) 63–5.

All this is powerfully dense and economical (as the Luke Preface has schooled readers to expect) but relatively straightforward. The statement, however, that Jesus' earthly ministry was what he 'began to do' stops the reader short. Whereas mortal movement from 'beginning' to 'end' is bounded by death, Jesus continues to live after the resurrection and even after the ascension, partly through the Holy Spirit and partly through his own continuing activity.[54] There is a similar, though more generalised, effect in the Mark Prologue (Mk 1.1): 'The beginning of the good news/gospel of Jesus Christ'.[55] Matthew 1.1,[56] and John 1.1–18 (both of which, I believe, Luke had read) also do similar things. Further, as in Mark, the 'beginning' associated with Jesus and all his works is a *new* beginning within the developing divine plan from the original 'beginning' (Gen. 1.1). But our author's deployment of the motif at the beginning of the second book of his project marks an important difference from Mark.

Dextrous generic manipulation again creates meaning. The Acts Preface has a double function, as Preface to Acts and second preface within the unified Luke-Acts. Classical 'second prefaces' redefine the original project and emphasise the sequel's greater importance, in effect 'demoting' the earlier material and 'internalising' the 'external' rivalry that writers have with other writers.[57] Here our writer's first logos is 'demoted' to the category of 'beginning' history, in order to emphasise the history that matters *now*: the working-out of Jesus' ministry in Acts, as inspired/directed by the Holy Spirit and by Jesus himself. This shift of narrative gear is underpinned by a subtle allusion. Luke is what our author wrote 'first', and it was a logos about 'beginnings'. Acts 1.3 paradoxically juxtaposes the Thucydidean criteria of 'sight' and 'indications'. Luke is thus redefined as the *archaiologia*, the 'beginning-' or 'before-logos', of, or before, the main history (Thuc. 1.1.3, 20.1, 21.2), itself now redefined as Acts. Of classical historians' many and creative recontextualisations and redefinitions of Thucydides' 'Archaeology', our author's is the neatest, the sharpest, and far the shortest. Brevity again speaks volumes. Our author potently combines 'internal' rivalry (by surpassing his earlier self), 'external' rivalry (by surpassing Thucydides, all the many classical historians who had redefined Thucydides' 'Archaeology', the Jewish-classical Josephus (the 'endless' twenty-book *Jewish Antiquities*!), and all the many previous Christian gospel-writers who had failed to write Acts), and solid meaning.

---

54   See Sleeman (2009) 66–7, 219–21.
55   Boring (2006) 31.
56   Davies–Allison (1988) 149–60.
57   Conte (1992); Kraus (1994) 83; Virg. *Aen.* 7.37–44 and Liv. 6.1.1–3 are good examples.

Hence the Acts narrative acquires a quadrifocal temporality. On the one hand, it is a more 'now' narrative than Luke, especially in its gathering emphasis on persecution. On the other, it journeys even farther back in time, contextualising the Jesus story within God's 'word' from the beginning of ⟦111⟧ Israel (e.g., Acts 7.2–53; 13.17–41) and from the creation (17.24–31). Yet there is much also that echoes both the Luke Preface and narrative. Stephen's martyrdom re-enacts Jesus', Paul's journey to Jerusalem (to the threat of death) re-enacts Jesus' journey to Jerusalem (to actual death) and prefigures Paul's own (un-described) death in Rome. The inversion of powers is illustrated by the realisation of the 'intelligent' Roman governor Sergius Paulus that Paul's power is superior to his (Acts 13.12) and by Paul's invocation, both before the Areopagus (Acts 17.31) and the conscience-stricken Roman governor Felix, of the Last Judgement (Acts 24.25). Paul (lit., 'little') himself, central (human) figure of Acts, instantiates the inversion of 'great and small' (Acts 13.12; 26.22). Appeal to the 'standing-up' of Jesus or of all men is twice juxtaposed with the charge, or assumption, that Christians are political agitators and 'stand the world upside down' or 'foment risings' (Acts 17.6, 18, 31; 24.5, 12, 15). The juxtaposition conveys that Christians are not political revolutionaries, but Jesus' 'up-rising' 'revolutionises' everything. Through 'upness' and 'downness' again comes the 'security' of Jesus' 'standing-up'. By contrast, the Jewish Temple is (again) doomed to 'down-ness' (Acts 6.14), and Jesus is (again) the cornerstone (Acts 4.11; cf. 26.26). Christ and Christianity displace temple-based Judaism. As some of this material already suggests, the fourth temporal focus is that of the future—a future that extends to the Last Judgement.

As in the Luke Preface and narrative, roads are everywhere in Acts (cf. this paper's beginning), which brings us, unavoidably, to the 'we passages' (Acts 16.10–17; 20.5–15; 21.1–18; 27.1–28.16). Interpretation must satisfy: (a) the application, to the author, of first-persons singular and plural in the Luke Preface and of first-person singular in the Acts Preface; (b) the necessary inclusion of the 'we passages' within the overall road imagery of Luke-Acts; (c) the first announcement of that imagery in the Luke Preface; (d) the inclusion of the author within that imagery; and (e) the precise application of 'having closely followed' to the author. Only the 'conservative' interpretation—going back at least to Irenaeus towards the end of the second century—that the author is including himself in the 'we passages', fulfils these requirements.[58] But adherents, like opponents, miss a crucial subtlety.

---

58  Irenaeus, *Adv. haer.* 3.1.1; 14.1–3; among moderns, e.g., Bruce (1951) 2–3; Lane Fox (1991) 129, 210–11; Thornton (1991); Fitzmyer (1998) 50, 98–103; Witherington (1998) 52–9, 484–5, 605, 626–9; Frey (2009) 8; Dunn (2009) 75–7; Droge (2009) 506–8; the 'we passages' imitate,

The wording of Luke 1.3 requires revisiting. Grammatically, 'all' can be either masculine or neuter. If it is read as masculine, as by Eusebius (*HE* 3.4.1), then, since the author 'followed' Paul in some of the travel narratives and Paul himself was a primary eyewitness (Acts 26.15, echoing Lk. 1.2), the author too is claiming to be a 'follower' and an 'eyewitness' of (some of) the 'things done' (in Acts). The claim promotes the character qualifications (*ethos*) of the historian, and emphasises his 'eyewitness' authority.[59] It forges yet another strong link between the Luke Preface and the Acts narrative. Luke-Acts begins and ends with travel, and our author himself has 'walked the Christian Road', even into Rome, in the most literal of senses. But he is also a 'follower' in the Christological sense. This use of [[112]] 'follow' is everywhere in the gospels, and, as here, literal and Christological 'following' often combine.[60] Our author's technique invites comparison with, and was, I suggest, influenced by, John's techniques for privileging the 'authority' of the Beloved Disciple, which also play on this double sense of 'following'.[61] John's techniques in turn respond to Mark's (also exploiting that double sense) for grounding his authority in the witness of Peter.[62] Thus our author grounds his authority not only in his 'following' of Paul but also in a textual succession of 'followers' of Jesus down the generations, a succession which is hardly uncompetitive, as Luke 1.1–3 already ambiguously suggests. Such competitiveness is only what pagan readers would expect.

But what to make of our author's prefatory anonymity, especially as contrasted with the so emphatically named Peter? Within the Christian textual succession, the anonymity corresponds to the anonymous 'Beloved Disciple', as also the other anonymous gospel-writers. But there is also classical precedent. While many great classical historians name themselves, characteristically in the first words of the Preface, some (for example, Xenophon, Sallust, Livy, Tacitus, and Arrian) do not.[63] Such anonymity diverts attention from the historian to his theme, but does not exclude, from Preface(s) or narratives, use of first persons, claims to individuality and superiority over predecessors, or relevant autobiographical information. Hence our author is imitating the practice of classical historians who do not inscribe their names within the text. Readers

---

and better, Mark's 'they passages', themselves conveying a 'we' perspective (on them: Bauckham [2006] 156–64); their abrupt introduction (Acts 16.10), like the abrupt direct speech of Acts 1.4, creates 'vividness' (a historiographical requisite).

59   On *ethos*, see Marincola (1997) 128–45; on autopsy, ibid. 63–86; for 'eye-witness' as central to the gospels' claims, see Bauckham (2006).
60   Johnson (1991) 89; Green (1997) 235 n. 31; Boring (2006) 59, 80.
61   Bauckham (2006) 127–9.
62   Ibid. 124–7.
63   For discussion, see Marincola (1997) 146, 227, 230, 250–2, 273–5.

of such historians, however, know who they are reading, not least because the 'titulus' of ancient books gave the author's name. If, contrary to the norm, there was no name on the 'titulus' of Luke (or Luke-Acts) and the work was wholly anonymous,[64] the allusions to the author's companionship with Paul would lose their authority and could not plausibly provide 'security' in the strong and serious senses required. If, on the other hand, the 'titulus' to Luke (and Acts) followed the norm,[65] the first Christian readers would have been given a name and some would have known who that name referred to. Consequently, although the Christian tradition that the author was Luke, companion of Paul, including in Rome, is only first attested in the late second century,[66] it must go back to the first Christian readership, in which case it should be accepted. If, as I believe, other factors indicate a *terminus post* of the middle 90s–early 100s, Luke wrote in old age: not implausible, imminent mortality having inspired other gospels, including John,[67] one of Luke's inspirations—and Luke was younger than the Beloved Disciple. Consequently also, informed contemporaries know of Luke's relationship with Paul, already read Luke 1.3 thus, and already expect something like Acts.[68] Consequently also, Luke's autobiography is inscribed in 'how the text works' and in the 'security' it gives ⟦113⟧ readers, and the 'now' of 'the things ... brought to fulfilment among us' is post-Domitian and early Trajan: a time of persecution—like the situation at the end of Acts.

So much for 'all' read as masculine. But 'all' also makes excellent sense read as neuter (in which it is even echoed by Acts 1.1: 'all the things ... that Jesus began to do/make and to teach'). 'Following' Jesus in the flesh; 'following' Paul literally, 'following' the accounts of the first eyewitnesses, or, like Theophilos, 'following' Luke's text, are all legitimate 'roads' into the Christian 'succession' of 'followers'. This ambiguity between literal and literary, in a 'travel' word ('following') within the Luke Preface, is clamantly pre-echoed in Herodotus' Preface, when he blurs text and travels: 'I will advance forwards in my *logos*, going through small and great cities of men alike' (1.5.3). Hence a lovely contrast between Herodotus' self-confident and tautologous 'advancing forwards' and Luke's formally modest, but extremely 'packed', 'following'. But piquantly also, while Luke is a 'follower' of Jesus, Paul, and earlier evangelists, he is *also* the *historiographical* 'follower' of Herodotus. As often, while Christianity 'trumps' paganism, there is some sense that it fulfils paganism's best manifestations

---

64   Droge (2009).
65   Bauckham (2006) 301.
66   See Dunn (2009) 65.
67   Bauckham (2006) 420–3.
68   *Pace* L. C. A. Alexander (2005) 224: 'there is no way the reader could predict the plot of the second volume from the prologue to the first as it stands'.

(cf. Acts 17). Educated pagans are being inducted—or seduced—by the subtlest of classical techniques.

This smartest of literary allusions takes us to the problem of the end of Acts and of its relationship both to Acts 1.8 and to the Luke Preface. The instruction to the apostles to bear witness, through a range of places, 'to the end of the earth' is part of the Acts Preface, and 'maps' the geographical progression and expansion of the narrative road at least a certain distance. Of several influences behind this instruction, Herodotus should be one, as prominent in the corresponding Luke Preface and main influence upon Luke's parallelisms between treatment and theme and between physical and textual travel. Thus, just as in the Luke Preface, the two great historiographical influences in the Acts Preface are Herodotus and Thucydides.

And so to the end (Acts 28.30–1): 'He [Paul] remained [in Rome] for a period of two years in a private hired lodging, and he received all who came in to him (31), heralding the kingdom of God and teaching the things about the Lord Jesus Christ with all freedom of speech and unhinderedly'.[69] Genre again speaks. Challenging, 'unresolved' endings are a speciality of classical historians, including Herodotus, Thucydides (unfinished), Xenophon (*Hellenica*), and Sallust (in both monographs).[70] Herodotus again seems the obvious historiographical model, especially as his 'unresolvedness' is in tension with multiple closural devices,[71] which (as we shall see) also applies to Luke. Internally too, Luke-Acts has constantly presented interpretative and religious challenges both to characters and readers. These challenges include abrupt suspensions of exposition after interpretative failure or unresponsiveness by audiences, such as the Athenian philosophers (Acts 17.32), Felix the governor (Acts 24.25), and Agrippa II (Acts 26.28).[72] How, then, should readers respond now?

[114] The connections between end and beginning of Acts (both Preface and narrative) are far from being 'rather weak'.[73] Both Paul and Jesus 'teach' (cf. Acts 1.1); Paul 'teaches' about Jesus, main figure of Acts 1.1–11; Jesus 'speaks' about 'the kingdom of God' (Acts 1.3); the apostles ask if the Kingdom is to be established now and Jesus elliptically says 'no' (Acts 1.6–7); Paul 'heralds' 'the kingdom of God' (it is getting nearer). Similarly, Paul's 'private' location (not public, not synagogue) echoes the view of the Jerusalem hierarchy that Peter

---

69  Moles (2006) 88–94 {above, pp. 573–7} overlaps slightly. Holloway (2009) sidesteps proper analysis.
70  Marincola (2005).
71  Moles (1996); Dewald (1997).
72  Agrippa's reaction ('with little ...') sneeringly misconstrues the 'little–big' inversions of 'little' Paul.
73  L. C. A. Alexander (2005) 211 n. 113.

and John are unqualified 'private individuals' (Acts 4.13), and Paul's 'frankness' matches that of Peter and John (Acts 4.13). 'Frankness' to non-Christians frames the Acts narrative (cf. Acts 2.29). So does 'road imagery': the detailed itinerary of Acts 28.13–16 on the journey of Paul and his companions (including Luke) to Rome and Paul's appeal to Isaiah (Acts 28.26: 'Go to this people') and the question within Isaiah whether or not the Jews will 'turn' (Acts 26.27) respond (somehow) to Acts 1.8 (Jesus' geographical instruction to the apostles). Paul, himself, is also (somehow) at the end of his own road (Acts 20.29). When Paul 'witnesses throughly' to the 'kingdom of God' (Acts 28.23), he is fulfilling Jesus' instructions to the first apostles (Acts 1.8). Finally (for now), the narrative 'fade-out'[74] at the end of Acts parallels the 'blurring' of Preface and narrative at the beginning.

There are also very strong connections with the Luke Preface. The last word of Acts (and of Luke-Acts), 'unhinderedly' (ἀκωλύτως), is a four-syllable alpha-privative compound, echoing sonically the last word of the Luke Preface, Christianity's desired 'destination' at the 'end' of the 'road': 'unslipperiness' (ἀσφάλειαν). The Luke Preface introduces road imagery; the end of Acts (somehow) closes it. Luke-Acts ends with Paul—who is already anticipated in the Luke Preface, partly through the interaction of 'having closely followed' and Luke's travels with Paul. But also, as readers discover, Luke's use of πληροφορέω (1.1) is hapax within Luke-Acts. It primarily means 'bring to fulfilment'. But, with its cognate noun, it is used in the Septuagint, Paul, and elsewhere in first-century Christianity to mean 'fully convince', 'assure'.[75] It is so understood here by Origen.[76] Thus another point of ἀσφάλειαν is to extract the full implications of πεπληροφορημένων: 'brought to fulfilment in such a way as to provide assurance' (hence my inserted 'persuasively'). Classically, this interaction between two elements exemplifies the rhetorical figure (Quint. 8.6.20) of 'from preceding things following things, from following things preceding things' (itself, inevitably, a road metaphor). The meaning of 'following things' is refined by 'preceding things' and vice versa, and complete meaning is created by see-sawing interaction between the two. 'Amplificatory pleonasm' works similarly. The distance between Christian narrative and Christian belief is thereby collapsed: the former compels the latter (no 'leap of faith' required). For readers aware of Pauline usage,[77] this 'extension' of meaning 'signposts'

---

74  Dunn (1996) 356.
75  Verb: Rom. 4.21; 14.5; noun: 1 Thess. 1.5; see also Col. 2.2; 4.12; 2 Tim. 4.5, 17; Heb. 6.11; 10.22.
76  Just (2003) 3.
77  [[122]] I think Luke knew and used Paul's letters; see, for example: Witherington (1998) 430–8, 568, 610–17; Mason (2005) 264; Dunn (2009) 77–9.

Pauline travel on the narrative road, abundantly [[115]] 'fulfilled' in Acts. Even more fundamentally, the see-sawing interaction, within the Luke Preface, between πεπληροφορημένων, at the beginning, and ἀσφάλειαν, at the end, is replayed in the interaction between ἀκωλύτως at the end of the whole text and ἀσφάλειαν both at the beginning of the text and at the end of the first Preface.

Further, the repeated emphasis, within the Isaiah quotation (Acts 28.26–7) on Jewish failure of sight contrasts with the 'destination' of Luke 1.4: 'recognise the security [etc.] of the words'. The mention of 'God' (Acts 28.31) echoes Theophilos (Lk. 1.3); the emphasis of 'all' (Acts 28.30) echoes 'all' (Lk. 1.3 and Acts 1.1). The triumphant and closural naming of 'the Lord Jesus Christ' clarifies the un-named 'word' (or 'name') of Luke 1.2, and contrasts with Luke's suppression of his own name in the Luke- and Acts Prefaces. The stress on Paul's freedom even under house arrest emphasises the fact that in the Christian 'polity' (Lk. 1.1–4), unlike the Roman (Lk. 2.1–5), 'service' (Lk. 1.2) is 'perfect freedom' (Gal. 5.13; 1 Pet. 2.16; Jas 1.25). Luke's staggeringly accomplished control of narrative space, narrative architecture, narrative road, and verbal interplay would have awed sophisticated pagans. Numerous and complex formal links, then, signpost Acts 28.30 as (seemingly) the end of Luke's narrative road, begun in the Luke Preface. They also create immediate meaning: Paul is Jesus' greatest 'successor'; the on-going Gentile mission fulfils Jesus' instruction; the Kingdom progresses; Jews are 'blind', Christians 'see'; God/Jesus is 'all in all to all'.

The interaction between ἀκωλύτως and ἀσφάλειαν spurs further thoughts, which must, ultimately, be optimistic. Not only do the closing 'with all frankness' and 'unhinderedly' echo earlier positives in narrative and Prefaces, they also contrast eloquently with Mark's abrupt conclusion: 'for [the disciples] were afraid' (Mk 16.8). Markan problematics (doubtless, latently positive) are peremptorily skewered. Judgements that the end of Acts is 'a tragic story',[78] 'tragic', and a 'downbeat tragedy'[79] bypass Acts 28.30–1 and stop at the preceding scene (23–8), where, for the third and last time (cf. Acts 13.46–7; 18.6), Paul challenges Jews with the thought that their failure to 'turn' (Acts 28.27) justifies the 'turn' to the Gentiles (cf. Acts 15.3). Dupont and Alexander[80] have shown how this final focus on the Jewish mission connects with the rest of Luke-Acts, from the very beginning. Indeed, in one respect things look even grimmer, because of a major implication of the Luke-Acts narrative (as of the other gospels), unblinkingly perceived by Church Fathers from the second century onwards: the predicted fall of Jerusalem and the destruction of the Temple,

---

78   Tannehill (1985).
79   L. C. A. Alexander (2005) 226–7.
80   Dupont (1979); L. C. A. Alexander (2005) 207–30.

which all readers know to have happened and which are the very 'opposite' of Christian 'security from falling', were God's punishment for the Jews' having killed Jesus and having then rejected the apostles' renewed ministry.[81] Second-century readers can profitably contrast this Christian theodicy of the Jewish War with Josephus' Jewish one.

[116] Johnson and Karrer,[82] however, rightly emphasise that the Isaiah quotation ends with the word 'I will heal them' (Acts 28.27: ἰάσομαι). Although this is precisely not what is currently happening, it acquires decisive proleptic force from the wider context. Paul's teaching in Rome focuses on Jesus and is framed by allusions to him (Acts 28.23 Ἰησοῦ and 28.31 Ἰησοῦ), the second of which is a climactic final naming at the very end of the text, as Paul 'received all who came in to him'. The name Jesus can be understood as 'healer' (from ἰάομαι), and the punning etymology is used in Luke-Acts, as in the other gospels, as a way of signalling Jesus' 'healing ministry' (see, for example, Lk. 5.17, 19; 7.7, 9; 8.46–7; Acts 4.30; 9.34; 10.38; 17.18 (interacting with 17, 5, 7, 9); Mt. 8.13; 15.28; Mk 5.29–30). Thus Acts 28.23 (Ἰησοῦ), 28.27 (ἰάσομαι), and 28.3 (Ἰησοῦ) energise one another, in another version of 'amplificatory pleonasm' or 'from preceding things following things, from following things preceding things', and in a way, indeed, that makes yet another ring with the Luke Preface. Divine healing comes only from Jesus; Jesus' role is above all that of the healer.[83]

Hence, despite their rejection of Jesus and despite the disasters of 70, Jews will ultimately be brought within the 'all-ness' of God and 'healed' by God/'Jesus'. For those not absolutely dismissive of the very possibility, Lukan use of, even highly apposite allusion to, Romans 11.25–6 is very attractive (there are telling resemblances), with Luke developing Paul's thinking in the light of the Jewish War. There is anyway here a crucial parallel between the Jews and Paul himself, also healed by Jesus (Acts 9.17) and shown by the Lord 'all the things he must suffer on behalf of my name' (Acts 9.16). The latter emphasis answers Ananias' complaint about 'all the bad things [this man] did to your holy ones in Jerusalem' (Acts 9.13). Further, before his conversion, Saul was 'breathing threats and murder to the disciples of the Lord', as befitted his 'witness' at the 'martyrdom' of Stephen (Acts 7.58; 8.1). Now Paul's own martyrdom is repeatedly foreshadowed in the text. Here he looks like that great pagan 'martyr', the Socrates of the *Phaedo* on the night before he died.[84] Thus, while the post-conversion Paul serves Jesus devotedly and has a glorious martyrdom,

---

81   Lampe (1984); cf. also Moles (2006) 81 {above, p. 567}.
82   Johnson (1991) 472 and Karrer (2000).
83   {Cf. Moles (2011)}.
84   Moles (2006) 90 {above, p. 574} n. 107; L. C. A. Alexander (2005) 66.

that martyrdom is also just recompense for participation in Stephen's martyrdom and former persecution of 'the Road'. Paul, who, like Jesus, knows he must die (Acts 9.16; 20.18–35), thus achieves surpassing tragic grandeur: an extra Christian dimension to the recurrent *Bacchae* pattern[85] within (and beyond) Acts. But Paul, like Stephen (Acts 7.55–6, 59), will then be received into heaven. Similarly, the Jews' punishment for rejection of Jesus—their 'falling' (Lk. 2.33) in 70 CE—is not final. Ultimately, the 'roads' of Paul, Jewish (and Roman) persecutor turned Christian, of the still persecuting Romans, and of the rejectionist and horribly punished Jews will converge in Jesus. 'Tough love', undoubtedly: love, nevertheless, and another echo of 'Theophilos', as 'loved by God'.

For all 'Theophiloses', the link between 'unhinderedly' and 'unslipperiness' conveys a clear message: even in utmost danger, even (proleptically) 〚117〛 on the point of martyrdom, Paul is completely free because of the 'security from falling' provided by the Christian 'upstanding'. The end of Luke-Acts provides the final proof of the claim of 'security'. No end could better prove that claim. It follows that, although the explicit narrative ends in 62 CE, the implicit narrative extends to the general resurrection and the Last Judgement. That is the ultimate destination to which Luke-Acts transports the reader and at which it ensures him a 'not guilty' verdict—if, of course, he cooperates.

So much, for the moment, for time travel, which already involves spatial elements ('upness' and 'downness') and even 'space travel': the dead in the first instance go 'up' to heaven, and at the last Jesus will descend from heaven (Acts 1.11). But spatial travel requires further investigation, even beyond the important emphasis of Sleeman that Acts' spatiality is substantially directed by Jesus' post-ascension heavenly location.[86] How does Jesus' instruction to the apostles to witness to 'the end of the earth' (Acts 1.8) relate to the end of the text, especially given the text's own status as a road? It is true that, as focalised from Jerusalem, Rome can be 'the end of the earth' (cf. Pss. Sol. 8.15), that that interpretation might be natural to the still 'short-sighted' apostles, and that the arrival of Paul and his companions in Rome is somehow climactic (Acts 28.14 'and that was how we came to Rome'; cf. 28.16). But is this last because Rome is 'the end', or because 'Theophilos' and Luke are together in Rome (if 'Theophilos' is real, which I doubt), or because Rome, as the acknowledged centre, is appropriate departure point for mission to the 'end' (including Spain, target of the historical Paul [Rom. 15.24])?

At this point, sophisticated second-century pagan readers would register unsettling parallels between Acts and the *De Exilio* (*Or.* 13) of Dio Chrysostom

---

85  Moles (2006).
86  Sleeman (2009).

(date: c.101 CE): both texts describe travels and are themselves journeys (both literal and formational); the resurrected Jesus tells the apostles to be his witnesses to the end of the earth; the god Apollo tells Dio to go to the end of the earth; both texts end in Rome, and both endings pose difficult interpretative challenges.[87] While Dio's speech is brilliantly conceived and executed and is indeed a magnificent and noble work, which envisages nothing less than the moral reform of Trajanic Rome, Luke-Acts surpasses it in interpretative complexity and grandeur of vision, thereby 'trumping' one of the best works of one of the greatest Greek philosophers and rhetoricians of the age.

In Acts, unlike Dio, Rome cannot, ultimately, be 'the end' spatially. In the biblical passages which underlie Jesus' instruction, Isaiah 49.6 (later quoted by Paul and Barnabas at Acts 13.47) and Psalms 2.8 (later utilised by the believers at Acts 4.25–6), 'the end(s) of the earth' does not denote any one place but world-wide outreach, as Cyril, Theodoret, Chrysostom, and Ambrose see.[88] Further, 'end' can be used both of space and time, and the exchange between apostles and Jesus (Acts 1.6–7) implicitly links them. The apostles ask: 'will you re-establish the kingdom to Israel at this time?' Jesus replies: 'it is not for you to know the time. I will give you ⟦118⟧ power [at Pentecost]. Witness to the end of the earth'. A conception of the kingdom restricted both in space ('Israel') and in time ('now') is extended to the end of the earth and the end of time. An important foreshadowing is the eschatological parable of Luke 13.29–30, where 'they will come from east and west and from north and south, and they will recline in the kingdom of God. And look, there are last who will be first and there are first who will be last'. Here 'end' links place, time, and status.

The link between 'end' of place and time is reinforced by Peter's claim that Pentecost marks 'the end days' (Acts 2.17). Thus the 'end' of the text is an 'end' within the overall, eschatological, 'end', rather as Jesus' earthly ministry was a 'beginning' within the overall 'beginning' (Acts 1.1), but it is not the end of the Lukan story, which is the end of time and which will come when Christian mission has reached the ends of the earth.[89] Luke thus decisively betters Mark (9.1) and John (21.22–3), by avoiding all embarrassment over the non-occurrence of the Parousia. Beyond the end of the text, the divine *logos*, the divine narrative spoken by the incarnate *logos* (Lk. 1.2; Acts 1.1–3, 8), goes on to 'the end' (both of time and of space), indeed, farther: into 'timelessness' (cf. Lk. 1.33: 'of his kingdom there will not be an end'). Luke-Acts, a component of the divine *logos*, which 'grows' throughout Acts (6.7; 12.24; 19.20), now 'blurs' back into it. Just as

---

87   Moles (2005) 126 {above, p. 272} n. 140; (2006) 91 {above, p. 575} n. 112.
88   Just (2003) 114; Martin (2006) 9–10.
89   Dinkler (1967) 334.

Luke was redefined as 'archaeology', so here Acts subsumes itself into the final divine narrative.

Obviously, any contemporary reader knows—or can presume—that the historical apostles did not reach the *end* of the earth, nor did the historical Paul 'witness to all human beings' (Acts 22.15). Yet Paul's preaching to 'all who came into him' (Acts 28.30) is proleptic of just that witness. As elsewhere (especially Acts 26.29), Paul is an exemplar, and one of those who 'gave down' the Christian tradition (Lk. 1.2). Now, readers must 'give it on' themselves (another implicit link between beginning and end). The challenge to readers, to all 'Theophilos-es', is individually to contribute to the actualisation of Paul's proleptic preaching to 'all human beings'. In continuing the Christian mission, they themselves will become apostles, 'sent-out ones', like Jesus himself (Lk. 4.18, 43; 9.48; 10.16; Acts 3.20, etc.), like the twelve, like Paul and Barnabas earlier in the narrative,[90] and the process will snowball until the textual, not the historical, Paul will 'witness to all human beings'. For 'Paul', read also 'Luke', follower and successor of Paul, author of this greatest of all histories, who now leaves it to his readers—all his readers down to the end of time—to 'write' the 'third' and 'final' 'book' of the divine *logos*, a book to which Luke-Acts (including Luke himself) will be their comprehensive and infallible guide (thus Acts 1.1 'my first *logos*' is mathematically precise).

Hence another hugely significant generic claim: Luke-Acts, in form a local history, is in substance a 'universal history',[91] and that in the strongest possible sense: it bestrides all time and all space, and it describes—and [119] prescribes—the 'Christification' of the whole world, of all peoples ('us' [Lk. 1.1] becomes 'all' [Acts 28.30] and vice versa). Luke-Acts (along indeed with the other gospels) refutes Van Nuffelen's recent claim that Christians did not write universal history,[92] although obviously their 'universalism' has both distinctive omissions and distinctive inclusions and, in contrast to the cyclicity of the classical form, a decisive teleology.[93] This contrast, too, is adumbrated in the Luke Preface: not worldly 'ups' and 'downs' but 'fulfilment' and 'security'. Hence too another addition to the roster of Luke's classical rivals: Velleius' *Roman History*, universal history in two-book epitome form, encomium of Caesarian 'succession',[94] and 'journey' (*Hist. Rom.* 2.1.1, 55.1, 86.1, 99.4). Not least of the obvious contrasts between the two historians is that between Velleius' closing

---

90   Acts 4.14, 14.1–3; Moles (2006) 89 {above, p. 574} n. 105.
91   Cf. Frey (2009) 17; Schwartz (2009) 128–9; Dormeyer (2009) 455–6, 459, 469, 475.
92   Van Nuffelen (2010).
93   Fear (2010).
94   Dormeyer–Galindo (2003) 33; Dormeyer (2009) 443.

prayer for the Roman Empire (2.13.1–2)—necessarily unresolved[95] and—as it happens!—textually lacunose—and Luke's closing and triumphant foreshadowing of the Christification of the whole world by the Christian succession, and not its Romanisation by the Caesarian succession.

Luke-Acts thus also falls into the category of 'imperialist texts':[96] texts that inculcate a particular form of imperialism, but also, more broadly, themselves 'give orders', allow readers no interpretative 'freedom', strive to 'conquer' all other texts, and so on. In different ways and degrees, Herodotus' *Histories*, Thucydides' *Peloponnesian War*, and Virgil's *Aeneid* fit the pattern. Such 'conquest' may involve the appropriation of the 'wealth' of ancestral knowledge (Thucydides, esp. 1.22.4),[97] or of a whole rival culture (the *Aeneid*), or of all other artistic media (the *Aeneid*, esp. 6.847–53 with *Georg.* 3.10–36). Beyond even the characteristic generic capaciousness of 'great historiography', Luke-Acts appropriates—and 'conquers'—as many texts, genres, and media as subserve its stupendously great 'imperialist' goal. These texts include rival Christian ones. But Luke-Acts necessarily battles particularly with the pagan Herodotus and Thucydides, Luke's main models in the Luke- and Acts Prefaces. Both those historians aspire to universality and immortality of theme, Thucydides explicitly so (1.22.4: '[my work is] a possession for always'), and they convey this aspiration through the analogy between text and artefact, including decree or inscription (Hdt. *praef.*; 1.5.4; Thuc. 1.1.1, 22.4), but, 'great' as they are, they cannot remotely compete with Luke. As for Roman and Virgilian imperialism, 'of [Jesus'] kingdom there will no end', a prophecy that 'trumps' *Aen.* 1.278–9: 'I have given empire without end';[98] God has 'dragged dynasts down from their thrones and exalted the lowly' (Lk. 1.52); the Christian polity enjoys 'security from falling', the Roman does not; and Paul's voyaging 'trumps' Aeneas'.[99]

At the end of Luke-Acts, then, readers have a great deal to absorb, but, if they are to become 'apostles' like Paul, they must not only read and 'recognise': they must act (yet another link to the Luke Preface: 'eyewitnesses and ⟦120⟧ servants of the word'). When classical historiography and biography commemorate 'things done', or 'acts', the aim is that readers should read these 'acts' and themselves 'act' appropriately (e.g., Liv. *praef.* 10–12; Plut. *Per.* 1.4). Both Lukan Prefaces play with the interplay between 'word' and 'deed'/'act'. In the ancient world, individual works can have more than one title, and individual books

---

95  Schultze (2010).
96  Tomlinson (1991); Thieme (2001).
97  Cf. Moles (1999) 32–5 {vol. 2, pp. 370–3}.
98  Bonz (2000) 133.
99  L. C. A. Alexander (2005) 178.

within plural unities can have separate titles. A title of *To Theophilos Book Two* allows alternatives. The title of Acts of the Apostles, first attested in church writers from our context, the second century,[100] now defended by few,[101] is so good that it must be correct. It signposts the book as individual-orientated historiography; nicely anticipates 'do' in the Preface; echoes 'things done' (cognate) from the Luke Preface; conveys that Luke was about what Jesus 'began to do', Acts about what his first 'sent-out ones' did and about what, post-ascension, he himself, first apostle of the kingdom, continued to do; and commends the acts—especially those of Jesus, Peter, Paul, and Luke himself—that all future apostles should act/re-enact: it is the 'word' that readers must 'do' (being itself one 'word' of the divine 'word'). Luke's control of the relationship between theme and treatment is again perfect.

Lastly, what is the relationship between Acts' end and all the ends that it envisages, up to, and including, the end of the world, and the Luke Preface's 'things brought to fulfilment amongst us' (Lk. 1.1)? Is that 'fulfilment' only provisional, and radically extended by the end of Acts? Or does that end make readers, as they read and re-read, think through the 'full' implications of 'fulfilment'? Luke-Acts repeatedly situates its narrative in 'the end time'. Especially, Jesus' 'standing-up' is both proof and anticipation of the general 'standing-up' at the end of time. Peter, Paul, Luke, Theophilos, and all contemporary and all subsequent readers are 'always already' living in 'the end time'. On this dimension, 'fulfilment' is now.[102] The end of time and the end of space coincide. Jesus' road, 'fulfilled' in Jesus and in Paul, leads to eternity. All that Christians have to do is to walk it and to persuade everybody else, down the generations, to walk it with them. In that way, everybody will reach the destination of 'security from falling'.

The requisite 'persuasiveness' or 'creditworthiness' of that claim (Lk. 1.1, 4)[103] is underwritten by Luke's own apostolic example; by the absoluteness of his Christian conviction and by the universality of its benevolence; and by his mastery of narrative space, narrative time, and 'words' (in several senses), that mastery representing God's/Jesus' mastery of those very same things. Luke-Acts, then, presents a perfect synthesis of theme, treatment, and roads, of prose and poetry (Acts 17.24), of all possible media and 'words', of literary maker (Lk. 1.1; Acts 1.1) and God as maker (Acts 17.24, 26). Thus, while the dense and complex

---

100   For details, see Dunn (2009) 64.
101   E.g., Fitzmyer (1998) 47–9; Dormeyer–Galindo (2003) 33.
102   For inaugurated eschatology in Acts, see Wright (2008) 7–10, 32–3.
103   Both πεπληροφορημένων and ἀσφάλειαν can have financial/legal resonances (L. C. A. Alexander [1993] 140), reinforcing Luke's 'credit'.

formal mastery of Luke-Acts fits excellently within its second-century context, its real purpose is to underline, even to instantiate, its status as a text for all time, in every possible sense of that latter term.

## Bibliography

Alexander, L. C. A. (1978) *Luke-Acts in its Contemporary Setting with Special Reference to the Prefaces (Luke 1:1–4 and Acts 1:1)* (D.Phil. thesis, Oxford).

Alexander, L. C. A. (1986) 'Luke's Preface in the Pattern of Greek Preface-Writing', *NovT* 28: 48–74.

Alexander, L. C. A. (1993) *The Preface to Luke's Gospel: Literary Convention and Social Context in Luke 1.1.4 and Acts 1.1* (Cambridge).

Alexander, L. C. A. (1996) 'The Preface to Acts and the Historians', in B. Witherington III, ed., *History, Literature and Society in the Book of Acts* (Cambridge) 73–103.

Alexander, L. C. A. (1999) 'Formal Elements and Genre: Which Greco-Roman Prologues Most Closely Parallel the Lukan Prologues?' in D. P. Moessner, ed., *Jesus and the Heritage of Israel: Luke's Narrative Claim upon Israel's Legacy* (Harrisburg, Pa.) 9–26.

Alexander, L. C. A. (2005) *Acts in Its Ancient Literary Context: A Classicist Looks at the Acts of the Apostles* (London and New York).

Alexander, P. S. (1984) 'Rabbinic Biography and the Biography of Jesus: a Survey of the Evidence', in C. M. Tuckett, ed., *Synoptic Studies: the Ampleforth Conferences of 1982 and 1983* (Sheffield) 19–50.

Aune, D. E. (2002) 'Luke 1:1–4: Historical or Scientific Prooimion?', in A. Christopherson, B. Longenecker, J. Frey and C. Claussen, edd., *Paul, Luke, and the Graeco-Roman World: Essays in Honour of Alexander J. M. Wedderburn* (Sheffield) 138–48.

Baban, O. D. (2006) *On the Road Encounters in Luke-Acts: Hellenistic Mimesis and Luke's Theology of the Way* (Milton Keynes).

Bauckham, R. J. (2006) *Jesus and the Eyewitnesses: the Gospels as Eyewitness Testimony* (Grand Rapids and Cambridge).

Bird, M. F. (2007) 'The Unity of Luke-Acts in Recent Discussion', *JSNT* 29: 425–48.

Bonz, M. P. (2000) *The Past as Legacy: Luke-Acts and Ancient Epic* (Minneapolis).

Boring, M. E. (2006) *Mark: a Commentary* (Louisville, Ky.).

Bruce, F. F. (1951) *The Acts of the Apostles: the Greek Text with Introduction and Commentary* (London).

Burridge, R. A. (1992) *What are the Gospels? A Comparison with Graeco-Roman Biography* (Cambridge; second edition Grand Rapids, 2004).

Cadbury, H. (1922) 'Commentary on the Preface of Luke', in F. J. Foakes Jackson and K. Lake, edd., *The Beginnings of Christianity: Part I The Acts of the Apostles*, Volume 2, *Prolegomena II Criticism* (London) 489–510.

Clarke, K. (1999) 'Universal Perspectives in Historiography', in Kraus (1999) 249–79.
Conte, G. B. (1992) 'Proems in the Middle', *YClS* 29: 147–59.
Cook, J. G. (1993) 'Some Hellenistic Responses to the Gospels and Gospel Traditions', *ZNW* 84: 233–54.
Davies, W. D. and D. C. Allison (1988) *Matthew 1–7* (London and New York).
Dewald, C. J. (1997) 'Wanton Kings, Pickled Heroes, and Gnomic Founding Fathers: Strategies of Meaning at the End of Herodotus' *Histories*', in D. Roberts, D. Fowler, and F. Dunn, edd., *Classical Closure: Reading the End in Greek and Latin Literature* (Princeton) 62–82; repr. in R. Munson, ed., *Herodotus*, 2 vols. (Oxford, 2013) 1.379–401.
Diggle, J. (2005) 'Tibullus 2.1.45–6 and "Amplificatory Pleonasm"', *CQ* 55: 642–3.
Dinkler, E. (1967) *Signum crucis: Aufsätze zum Neuen Testament und zur christlichen Archäologie* (Tübingen).
Dormeyer, D. (2009) 'Die Gattung der Apostelgeschichte', in Frey–Rothschild–Schröter (2009) 437–75.
Dormeyer, D. and G. Galindo (2003) *Die Apostelgeschichte: ein Kommentar für die Praxis* (Stuttgart).
Droge, A. J. (2009) 'Did "Luke" Write Anonymously? Lingering at the Threshold', in Frey–Rothschild–Schröter (2009) 495–518.
Dunn, J. D. G. (1996) *The Acts of the Apostles* (Peterborough).
Dunn, J. D. G. (2003) *Jesus Remembered: Christianity in the Making*, vol. 1 (Grand Rapids and Cambridge).
Dunn, J. D. G. (2009) *Beginning from Jerusalem: Christianity in the Making*, vol. 2 (Grand Rapids and Cambridge).
Dupont, J. (1979) 'La conclusion des Actes et son rapport à l'ensemble de l'ouvrage de Luc', in J. Kremer, ed., *Les Acts des Apôtres: Traditions, rédaction, théologie* (Leuven) 359–404.
Eckstein, A. M. (1995) *Moral Vision in the* Histories *of Polybius* (Berkeley and Los Angeles).
Fear, A. (2010) 'Orosius and Escaping from the Dance of Doom', in Liddel–Fear (2010) 176–88.
Fitzmyer, J. A. (1998) *The Acts of the Apostles: a New Translation with Introduction and Commentary* (New York, London, Toronto, Sydney, and Auckland).
Frey, J. (2009) 'Fragen um Lukas als "Historiker" und den historiographischen Charakter der Apostelgeschichte: eine thematische Annäherung', in Frey–Rothschild–Schröter (2009) 1–26.
Frey, J., C. K. Rothschild, and J. Schröter, edd. (2009) *Die Apostelgeschichte im Kontext antiker und frühchristlicher Historiographie* (Berlin and New York).
Frickenschmidt, D. (1997) *Evangelium als Biographie: die vier Evangelien im Rahmen antiker Erzählkunst* (Tübingen).

Green, J. B. (1997) *The Gospel of Luke* (Grand Rapids).
Gregory, A. (2006) 'The Third Gospel? The Relationship of John and Luke Reconsidered', in J. Lierman, ed., *Challenging Perspectives on the Gospel of John* (Tübingen) 109–34.
Hengel, M. (2000) *The Four Gospels and the One Gospel of Jesus Christ: An Investigation of the Collection and Origin of the Canonical Gospels* (London and Harrisburg, Pa.).
Holloway, P. A. (2009) 'Inconvenient Truths: Early Jewish and Christian History Writing and the Ending of Luke-Acts', in Frey–Rothschild–Schröter (2009) 418–33.
Johnson, L. T. (1991) *The Gospel of Luke* (Collegeville, Minn.).
Just, A. A., ed. (2003) *Ancient Christian Commentary on Scripture: New Testament III Luke* (Downers Grove, Ill.).
Karrer, M. (2000) '"Und ich werde sie heilen": das Verstockungsmotiv aus Jes 6,9f. in Apg 28,26f.', in id., W. Kraus and O. Merk, edd., *Kirche und Volk Gottes: Festschrift … J. Roloff* (Neukirchen-Vluyn) 255–71.
König, J. (2006) 'The Cynic and Christian Lives of Lucian's *Peregrinus*', in McGing and Mossman (2006) 227–54.
König, J. (2009) *Greek Literature in the Roman Empire* (London).
Kraus, C. S., ed. (1994) *Livy: Ab Urbe Condita Book VI* (Cambridge).
Kraus, C. S., ed. (1999) *The Limits of Historiography: Genre and Narrative in Ancient Historical Texts* (Leiden, Boston, and Cologne).
Krauter, S. (2009) 'Vergils Evangelium und das lukanische Epos? Überlegungen zu Gattung und Theologie des lukanischen Doppelwerkes', in Frey–Rothschild–Schröter (2009) 214–43.
Lampe, G. W. H., (1984) 'A.D. 70 in Christian Reflection', in E. Bammel and C. F. D. Moule, edd., *Jesus and the Politics of His Day* (Cambridge) 153–71.
Lane Fox, R. (1986) *Pagans and Christians* (Harmondsworth; New York, 1987).
Lane Fox, R. (1991) *The Unauthorized Version: Truth and Fiction in the Bible* (London and New York).
Liddel, P. and A. Fear, edd. (2010) Historiae Mundi: *Studies in Universal Historiography* (London).
Marincola, J. (1997) *Authority and Tradition in Ancient Historiography* (Cambridge).
Marincola, J. (2005) 'Concluding Narratives: Looking to the End in Classical Historiography', *PLLS* 12: 285–320.
Marincola, J., ed. (2007) *A Companion to Greek and Roman Historiography*, 2 vols. (Oxford and Malden, Mass.).
Martin, F. ed. (2006) *Ancient Christian Commentary on Scripture: New Testament V: Acts* (Downers Grove, Ill.).
Mason, S. (2005) *Josephus and the New Testament*[2] (Peabody, Mass.).
McGing, B. and J. Mossman, edd. (2006) *The Limits of Ancient Biography* (Swansea).
Moles, J. L. (1996) 'Herodotus Warns the Athenians', *PLLS* 9: 259–84 [vol. 2, Ch. 52].

Moles, J. L. (1998) 'Cry Freedom: Tacitus *Annals* 4.32–35', *Histos* 2 (1998) 95–184 [vol. 2, Ch. 53].

Moles, J. L. (1999) 'ΑΝΑΘΗΜΑ ΚΑΙ ΚΤΗΜΑ: the Inscriptional Inheritance of Ancient Historiography', *Histos* 3: 27–69 [vol. 2, Ch. 54].

Moles, J. L. (2005) 'The Thirteenth Oration of Dio Chrysostom: Complexity and Simplicity, Rhetoric and Moralism, Literature and Life', *JHS* 125: 112–38 [above, Ch. 10].

Moles, J. L. (2006) 'Jesus and Dionysus in *The Acts of the Apostles* and Early Christianity' *Hermathena* 180: 65–104 [above, Ch. 21].

Moles, J. L. (2011) 'Luke's Preface: The Greek Decree, Classical Historiography and Christian Redefinitions', *NTS* 57: 1–22 [above, Ch. 22].

Morgan, J. M. (2013) *Encountering Images of Spiritual Transformation: The Thoroughfare Motif Within the Plot of Luke-Acts* (Eugene, Or.).

Mossman, J. M. (2006) 'Travel-writing, History, and Biography', in McGing–Mossman (2006) 281–303.

Pathrapankal, J. (1979) 'Christianity as a "Way" according to the Acts of the Apostles', in J. Kremer, ed., *Les Acts des Apôtres: Traditions, rédaction, théologie* (Leuven) 533–9.

Pelling, C. B. R. (2006) 'Breaking the Bounds: Writing about Julius Caesar', in McGing–Mossman (2006) 255–79.

Plümacher, E. (2006) 'Stichwort: Lukas, Historiker', *ZNT* 18: 2–8.

Rowe, C. K. (2007) 'Literary Unity and Reception History: Reading Luke-Acts as Luke and Acts', *JSNT* 29: 449–57.

Ryken, L., J. C. Wilhoit, and T. Longman III, edd. (1998) *Dictionary of Biblical Imagery* (Downers Grove, Ill.).

Schröter, J. (2009) 'Zur Stellung der Apostelgeschichte im Kontext der antiken Historiographie', in Frey–Rothschild–Schröter (2009) 27–47.

Schultze, C. (2010) 'Universal and Particular in Velleius Paterculus: Carthage versus Rome', in P. Liddell and A. Fear, edd., *Historiae Mundi: Studies in Universal Historiography* (London) 116–29.

Schwartz, D. R. (1986) 'The End of the ΓΗ (Acts 1:8): Beginning or End of the Christian Vision?', *JBL* 105: 669–76.

Schwartz, D. R. (2009) 'Circular or Teleological, Universal or Particular, With God or Without?: On 1–2 Maccabees and Acts', in Frey–Rothschild–Schröter (2009) 119–29.

Silk, M. S. and R. A. Kaster (1996) 'Epitome', *OCD*[3]: 549.

Sleeman, M. (2009) *Geography and the Ascension Narrative in Acts* (Cambridge).

Squires, J. T. (1993) *The Plan of God in Luke-Acts* (Cambridge).

Sterling, G. E. (1992) *Historiography and Self-Definition: Josephos, Luke-Acts, and Apologetic Historiography* (Leiden).

Talbert, C. H. (1974) *Literary Patterns, Theological Themes, and the Genre of Luke-Acts* (Missoula).

Talbert, C. H. (1977) *What is a Gospel?* (Philadelphia).

Talbert, C. H. (1978) 'Biographies of Philosophers and Rulers as Instruments of Religious Propaganda in Mediterranean Antiquity', *ANRW* II.16.2: 1619–51.

Talbert, C. H. and P. Stepp (2003) 'Succession in Luke-Acts and in the Lukan Milieu', in C. H. Talbert, ed., *Reading Luke-Acts in Its Mediterranean Milieu* (Leiden) 19–55.

Tannehill, R. C. (1985) 'Israel in Luke-Acts: A Tragic Story', *JBL* 104: 69–85.

Thieme, J. (2001) *Postcolonial Con-Texts: Writing Back to the Canon* (New York).

Thornton, C.-J. (1991) *Der Zeuge des Zeugen: Lukas als Historiker der Paulusreisen* (Tübingen).

Tomlinson, J. (1991) *Cultural Imperialism: A Critical Introduction* (New York).

van Nuffelen, P. (2010) 'Theology versus Genre? The Universalism of Christian Historiography in Late Antiquity', in Liddel–Fear (2010) 162–75.

Witherington, B. (1998) *The Acts of the Apostles: a Socio-rhetorical Commentary* (Grand Rapids and Cambridge).

Wolter, M. (2009) 'Die Proömien des lukanischen Doppelwerks (Lk 1,1–4 und Apg 1,1–2)', in Frey–Rothschild–Schröter (2009) 476–94.

Wright, N. T. (2008) *Acts for Everyone, Part 1: Chapters 1–12* (London and Louisville, Ky.).

CHAPTER 25

# Accommodation, Opposition, or Other? Luke-Acts' Stance Towards Rome

This contentious topic needs working assumptions.*

The Gospel according to Luke and Acts of the Apostles constitute a unified 'double-work'.[1] Titular authenticity, authorial identity, ethnicity, and location matter little; Christian tradition visible from the late second century makes 'Luke' a convenient name, intriguing here because basically Roman.[2]

Written c.100,[3] Luke-Acts covers the life, death, and alleged resurrection of Jesus (c.30 CE) and the Jesus movement until two years after Paul's arrival in Rome (Acts 28.30–31), culminating in his trial and death in 64 (narratively foreshadowed). While the term 'Christian' is controversial, the fact that Acts uses it twice (11.26; 26.28) and once transitionally—employed by Romans but acceptable to Christians (11.26)[4]—sufficiently justifies it here. The crucifixion of Jesus, Jewish riots in Rome under Claudius (occasioning expulsions of Christians), widespread Jewish hostility, Neronian and Domitianic persecutions, and general Roman and Greek antagonism, both elite and popular, generated considerable Christian anxiety.[5] The antagonism originated in Jesus' conviction as pretender king of a Roman province, which labelled his followers quasi-revolutionaries. Christian mission produced incomprehension and hostility as well as conversion.

The Roman capture of Jerusalem and destruction of the Temple in 70 accelerated Christians' detachment from Judaism.[6] Luke-Acts traces the progressive [[80]] failure of the Jewish mission and assumes a largely Gentile future,

---

\* I thank all at Odense, the Editors, John Barclay, Manfred Lang, Tony Spawforth, Francis Watson, and Bill Telford. Space restrictions and endless bibliography dictate economy and selectivity. Textual paraphrase implies neither historical nor theological reliability. This paper has local overlaps with others but remains substantially independent. Translations are mine.
1  Talbert (1974); Tannehill (1986–90).
2  Plummer (1901) xviii.
3  Moles (2011a) 124 {above, p. 618}.
4  See below p. 723.
5  Cook (2010).
6  Goodman (2007) 512–61.

although envisaging the Jews' eventual 'healing'.[7] The audience/readership[8] includes Christians and (still) Jews. Are there others? 'God-fearers' (Gentile followers of Judaism who had not converted), surely.[9] Other Gentiles are targeted at a remove, because Luke provides Christians 'fair copies' for key situations[10] (addressing superstitious pagans [Acts 14.15–17] and philosophers [Acts 17.18–31]; defending oneself before Roman governors, emperors,[11] or client kings). But a text aiming for the Christianisation of the world (Acts 1.8) should address it directly.[12]

Although Luke's language—basically functional, 'professional' Greek[13]—is straightforward, his literary merits include verbal economy and creativity; intertextual allusiveness, explicit or implicit, both to biblical and classical material; vivid story-telling and scene-painting; psychological realism; sustained imagery; elaborate narrative patterning; and density and intensity of effects. This Greek-Christian-Jewish text has Classical pretensions,[14] attracted 'Classical' readers from the second century,[15] and resonates challengingly with the Classical texts considered elsewhere in this volume.

### Luke-Acts and Rome

Luke is well-informed about Roman provincial government, legal procedures, army officers, the geography of the Roman East and Greece, and Rome's topography,[16] and has some acquaintance with Roman literature.[17] But Rome is not merely the inevitable or neutral historical background: she looms large, characteristically in charged contexts far beyond the crucifixion narrative. Why?

---

7    Moles (2011a) 159–64 {above, pp. 653–9}.
8    Lang (2008) 15–95; Moles (2011a) 121–2 {above, pp. 615–17}.
9    See below p. 718.
10   Sterling (1992) 382–6.
11   Since Acts foreshadows Paul's trial in Rome (p. 727), Paul's various 'apologies' (19.33; 22.1; 24.10; 25.8, 16; 26.1, 2, 24) anticipate his 'apology' before Nero; Still (1923) 11.
12   Streeter (1930) 535–9; Lang (2008); Moles (2011a) 121–2 {above, pp. 615–17}; (2011b) 465 {above, p. 590}.
13   Alexander (2005) 231–52.
14   Pervo (1987); MacDonald (2003); Moles (2006); (2011a); (2011b); (2013); Alexander (2005); Lang (2008).
15   Moles (2011a) 121 {above, p. 615}; also 123 {above, p. 617} for knowledge of the Passion at Nero's court.
16   Wallace–Williams (1993).
17   E.g., *Res Gestae* (p. 715), Livy's *Preface* (p. 712) and *Aeneid* (p. 728).

⟦81⟧ NT scholarship, like Classical, probes 'attitudes to Rome', broadly considered (rule, emperors, officials, culture, inhabitants, and subjects), as major drivers of Greek texts, whether explicit or implicit. Traditionally, most hold Luke-Acts accommodationist, favourable to Roman power, and anxious to demonstrate (to Christians or Romans) that Christianity is compatible with Rome;[18] others hold it existentially hostile, arguing that Jesus as Lord and Saviour and Christian 'good news' decisively trump Roman equivalents.[19] Three important books were unavailable in 2009 or published later: Manfred Lang's *Die Kunst des christlichen Lebens: Rezeptionsästhetische Studien zum lukanischen Paulusbild*; Kavin Rowe's *World Upside Down: Reading Acts in the Graeco-Roman Age*; and Kazuhiko Yamazaki-Ransom's *The Roman Empire in Luke's Narrative*.[20]

Lang, adducing comparative material from Seneca, Plutarch, and the like, and developing parallels between Euripides' *Bacchae* and key episodes, explores the *possibility* that Acts could be read by Romans (particularly in Rome) as a protreptic to the Christian 'philosophical way'. Rowe argues that '[Acts] is a highly charged and theologically sophisticated political document that aims at ... the construction of an alternative total way of life ... that runs counter to the life-patterns of the Graeco-Roman world' and is 'culturally destabilising', hence the danger (realised) that 'outsiders ... [would] ... construe Christianity as sedition or treason', hence Luke's 'negating the charges of [Paul's] opponents on the basis of a revisionary reading of Roman law', hence 'profound tension ... at the heart of Luke's ... program', 'new culture, yes—coup, no', 'not ... sedition or treason but ... the light and forgiveness of God'.[21]

Yamazaki-Ransom holds that Luke redefines the people of God as 'those who follow Jesus as Lord, not those who belong to ethnic Israel' and concomitantly redefines 'the opponents of the people of God', mapping his representations of relations between Roman and Jewish rulers and this people of God onto Jewish models of the relations between God, Israel, and, where relevant, Gentile rulers;[22] religion and politics, the divine and the worldly cannot be separated, and the Roman Empire is under demonic control, hence inevitable and existential conflict between the kingdom of God and that of Satan.[23] ⟦82⟧

---

18  E.g., Cadbury (1921); Walaskay (1983); Alexander (2005) 183–206 surveys helpfully.
19  Cassidy (1978); (1987); Horsley (1989) 107–23; (2011) *passim*; Hendricks (1996).
20  M. Lang (2008); (2011); Rowe (2009), esp. 53–89; critical debate on Rowe's claims in *JSNT* 33 (2011) {317–46}; Yamazaki-Ransom (2010).
21  Rowe (2009) 4–6.
22  Yamazaki-Ransom (2010) 3–4.
23  Yamazaki-Ransom (2010) 69–70.

For both Rowe and Yamazaki-Ransom, Romans lack both the language and the lived Christian experience to understand the truth of Christian claims.

My reading has significant contact with both Lang's and Rowe's and some with Yamazaki-Ransom's. Nevertheless, large differences remain. Neither Lang nor Rowe considers Luke-Acts as a unity. Lang's approach neglects many non-philosophical elements of Acts. While Yamazaki-Ransom's claim (which I cannot pursue) for Luke's 'mapping' is important (if schematic), focus on restricted categories and cases yields limited results. If Luke can be *shown* to include Romans within his audience/readership, all three readings are greatly extended. Lang's 'thought experiment' immediately becomes reality. Luke-Acts *gives* Romans the language and lived Christian experience that they currently lack. The revisionary reading of Roman law finds its proper readers. The category of 'good Romans', for which neither Rowe nor Yamazaki-Ransom can account, is explained. And beyond all this, there are simply many new things to say.

I combine sequential reading with thematic accumulations. The former establishes Rome's integralness to Luke's developing Christian story, the diverse logics of her inclusion, and the relevant interpretative frameworks; the latter the insistence and density of the material.

The Preface (Luke 1.1–4)[24] leads us in:

> Since indeed many have set their hand to draw up [ἀνατάξασθαι] a narrative guide [διήγησιν] about the things done which have been persuasively brought to fulfilment [πεπληροφορημένων] amongst us, (2) just as those who became from the beginning eyewitnesses and servants of the word gave them on to us, (3) it seemed good to me also, having closely followed [παρηκολουθηκότι] all of them accurately from the up [ἄνωθεν], to write them down for you in order [καθεξῆς], most powerful Theophilos [κράτιστε Θεόφιλε], (4) so that you may additionally know/experience/recognise [ἐπιγνῷς] the truth/security/safety/unslipperiness [τὴν ἀσφάλειαν] about the words in which you have been orally instructed.

Which elements matter here?

First, unobserved by scholars, 'road imagery'[25] ('narrative guide', 'brought to fulfilment', 'having closely followed', 'security'/'safety' [applicable to roads]) figures both Luke-Acts and Christianity as 'roads'. Consequently, 'the road to Jerusalem' taken by Jesus (Luke 13.33–19.44) is the major structuring and ⟦83⟧

---

24  Moles (2011b); (2013) 102–9 {above, pp. 679–88}.
25  Moles (2013).

Christological device of *Luke*; Acts, a 'quest narrative' (1.8), commemorates Christianity as 'the Road' (9.2); Paul's journeys (including the thrice-narrated 'Road to Damascus' [9.3–9; 22.6–16; 26.12–17]) dominate Acts, which closes with 'roads' into Rome (28.15). The geography of the Roman world fits organically within this imagery.[26] But also, since the text is a road, and the road of, or to, the Road of Christianity, everyone who reads it, 'induced' by the Preface, is already, to some extent, willy-nilly 'walking the road' of Christianity. If they reach the end of the textual road, they face a choice.[27]

Second, again unobserved by scholars, the Preface imitates a Greek decree.[28] Luke's community (1.1–2 'us') is a 'polity', himself its 'legislator'. What is its relationship to other 'polities', including Rome? But also, the 'polity' implication, plus the 'succession' vocabulary (2 'gave on') and the stated goal (4 'security'), figures Christianity, like Judaism, as a 'philosophy',[29] thus somewhat normalising it and soliciting philosophically-minded readers.

Third, generically, Luke-Acts announces Classical historiography,[30] which does many other things besides simply commemorating the past. Interpretation of any item involves consideration of function. Is it recorded 'just because it happened'? Is it exemplary? Does it validate present practice? Is it imaginative projection? The Preface also contains allusions to historians, including Herodotus and Thucydides,[31] suggestive of 'Classical' readers, and Livy,[32] suggestive of Romans.

Fourth, 'us' (1–2) casts Luke-Acts *also* as a 'local' history or history of a 'people',[33] with two effects. Christians are a distinct 'people', with, we have seen, their own 'polity', and cut across, and supersede, normal ethnicities. And, if Christians are characteristically constructed as 'other',[34] the outside reader is now invited to become 'one of us/them', and, ultimately, when the world-wide Christian mission succeeds, the 'them–us' polarity will dissolve and everybody will become 'us'.

Fifth, the complicated final clause includes the notion of 'looking at a monument that cannot fall'.[35] That suits allusions to Herodotus, Thucydides, and

---

26  Acts' 'geography': diversely, Alexander (2005) 69–131, 207–29; Sleeman (2009).
27  See below p. 727.
28  Moles (2011a).
29  Lang (2008) 304 n. 228; Moles (2011b) 470 {above, p. 595}.
30  Moles (2011b) 462–4 {above, pp. 587–9}.
31  Moles (2011b) 476–9 {above, pp. 601–5}.
32  Moles (2011b) 478–9 {above, pp. 603–5}.
33  Sterling (1992) 349.
34  Cook (2010) 2.
35  Moles (2011b) 476–8 {above, pp. 601–4}.

⟦84⟧ Livy, who all use the inscriptional analogy to represent their Histories as solid, permanent things in an uncertain world, but also figures Christianity itself as such—in contrast both to Livy's *History* and the collapsing building which Livy is shoring up: Rome herself.[36] Further appeal to Romans: security lies *here*, not *there*; further reassurance for *all* readers: despite all appearances, despite persecutions, often deadly, Christianity provides *security from falling*; but also, potentially, further contrast: Christianity is unlike Jerusalem and the Temple, destroyed, as all readers know, by the Romans, but whose destruction Luke-Acts blames on the Jews:[37] further Christian self-definition, further appeal to Romans, distinguishing Christians from justly punished Jews.

Sixth, Theophilos. Whether its bearer is real or fictional, the name (repeated at Acts 1.1), inculcates a right religious attitude, emphasised throughout Luke-Acts, and signifies both 'loving God' (of all who seek God) and 'loved by God' (as all humans are):[38] further indication of the universality of Luke's readership. But the emphasis on active 'theophiles' suggests their opposite, the 'theomachs'[39] who are a major concern of Acts. But also, the epithet attached to 'Theophilos', 'most powerful', suggests considerable status for the addressee conceived as an individual. Two Roman governors are also thus addressed, by a centurion and Paul (Acts 23.26; 24.3; 26.25), one of whom 'knows rather accurately the things about the Road' (sc. Christianity [24.22]), just as Theophilos has been orally instructed in Christianity, figured as a road. No matter, again, whether Theophilos is real or fictional, he is represented as of similar status to Roman governors, thereby included in Luke's readership.

Seventh, beyond the 'us–them' contrast, is a series of pregnant contrasts or inversions. First, that between divine power and worldly power: 'brought to fulfilment', sc. by God; 'servants of the word'; '*Theo*philos' and 'most powerful'; and *qua* 'most powerful', '*Theo*philos' himself embodies that contrast, and anticipates powerful officials within the narrative who face the challenge of divine power. Second, that between 'down-ness' and 'up-ness': 'draw up'/'from the up'/'to write them down'; this includes the contrast implicit in the fifth element: 'falling'–'not falling'. Third, that between 'small' and 'great': the arresting literal smallness of the Preface; the greatness of the theme: 'the things brought to fulfillment [by God]'. All three contrasts readily bear on the relationship between Christianity and Rome; the second on the centrality to Christianity of resurrection (ἀνάστασις ~ 'standing-up'): ultimate guarantee

---

36   Moles (2011b) 478 {above, p. 603}.
37   See below, p. 720.
38   Some deny the second meaning, but the double reference was seen by Church fathers (Just [2003]) 4; Martin (2006) 2).
39   Moles (2006) 78 {above, p. 564}.

⟦85⟧ of Christian 'security from falling'; the second also links with the other two. The idea of 'smallness' connects both to road imagery and to philosophical colouring to create another generic implication: as a 'small' 'road' to the 'road' of Christianity as the best 'road' through the 'road' of life, Luke-Acts is a philosophical 'epitome' (or 'vade mecum'): a 'short-cut road' containing the essentials about Christianity, philosophy, and life.

After the magnificently complex Preface, the pregnancy/birth sequences have mythical aspects: 'the prophecy of Jesus' birth would have made excellent sense to any Hellenistic reader'.[40] The angel Gabriel (1.33) foregrounds the first of the Preface's contrasts or inversions: 'And he will be king over the house of Jacob for the ages, and of his kingdom there will be no end'. Might Romans (and some Greeks) hear direct challenge of 'King' Jupiter's prophecy about the Roman imperium early in the first book of the *Aeneid* (1.278–9): '*his* [*Romanis*] *ego nec metas rerum nec tempora pono;* | *imperium sine fine dedi*' ('To them I put no limits nor temporal restrictions of their power: I have given them empire without end')? Towards the end of Luke-Acts, competitive allusion to *Aeneid* 1 seems convincing,[41] as, earlier, does another, more general allusion to Aeneas.[42] Links between beginning and end of the double-work are themselves plausible (as repeatedly emerges). Further, we soon find another Roman/Caesarian allusion in the narrative. From the beginning, 'Christian imperialism' competes with Roman; similarly, and framingly, Jesus' own injunction at the start of Acts (1.8): 'you will be my witnesses … to the end of the earth'.

The pregnant Mary (1.46–55) exultantly celebrates all prefatory contrasts:

> My soul *magnifies* the Lord,
> And my breath has rejoiced in God my *saviour*;
> Because he has looked upon the *lowliness* of his slave,
> For look! From now on all generations call me blessed,
> Because *the mighty one* has done *great things* for me,
> And holy is his name,
> And his pity extends to the generations
> He has done *power* with his arm,
> He has scattered the *uppity* in the false thinking of their hearts,
> He has dragged dynasts *down* from their thrones and raised *up* the *lowly*,
> He has filled the poor with good things and the rich he has sent away empty.

---

40  Johnson (1991) 38.
41  See below p. 728.
42  See below pp. 731–2.

⟦86⟧ This 'programme' looks organically 'programmatic', unambiguously revolutionary, radically hostile to 'dynasts' (including Roman emperors), and unequivocally punitive. Precision, however, is needed. The perspective is that of 'all generations' 'from now on'. The present flows into the future and as far as 'last things': this is Christian 'inaugurated [sc. by Jesus' birth] eschatology' which retrojects absolute eschatological principles on to 'present' realities and projects 'present' realities on to absolute eschatological principles, the 'present' itself consisting of a long series of 'presents' extending to 'last days'. Romans could comprehend Christian 'inaugurated eschatology': pagan prophecy can represent the future as having happened (cf. *Aen.* 1.279), Sibylline prophecy can forecast eschatological futures,[43] and *Roma aeterna* competes with Christian eschatology.

Practically, the 'programme' does not announce immediate 'systems collapse' or validate *human* revolutionary activity. Nevertheless, 'inaugurated eschatology' proclaims ultimate realities, effected by God, mandating universal alignment with Christianity and the erasure of Roman power, the Preface has already deconstructed *Roma aeterna*, and individuals, including 'present dynasts', should put themselves in the right by accepting Jesus, thereby promoting the already 'inaugurated' eschatology. The eschatological perspective presses even harder when allied to the theme of divine justice.[44]

In the historical narrative proper, Rome takes the foreground. Both the Jesus birth-narrative and Baptist mission-narratives are prefaced by wide-ranging Roman contextualisations and synchronisms (deftly echoed in Acts 11.28; 18.2): 'And it came to pass in those days there went forth a decree from Caesar Augustus that all the inhabited world should be written up' (2.1–3); 'In the fifteenth year of the reign of Tiberius Caesar, Pontius Pilate being governor of Judaea, and Herod being tetrarch of Galilee, and his brother Philip tetrarch of the land of Ituraea and Trachonitis, and Lysanias tetrarch of Abilene, (2) in the high-priesthood of Annas and Caiaphas, the word of God came to John the son of Zechariah in the desert' (3.1–2). The whole narrative movement of the double-work is towards Rome: Augustus' decree begins the *Luke* narrative, which ends with Pontius Pilate (23.1–25). In Acts (19.21), Paul proclaims, 'I must also see Rome'; the Lord exhorts (23.11), 'As you have testified the things about me to Jerusalem, so must you testify them to Rome also'; Paul's trials before Roman governors occupy much of Acts; his travels and voyages end with the words (28.14), 'That was how we came to Rome', as if the goal of all Paul's wanderings, and there the narrative closes (28.31).

---

43   Momigliano (1988); Virgil's *Fourth Eclogue* is relevant.
44   See below p. 718.

⟦87⟧ Augustus' unhistorical world-wide decree demands investigation. Rather than convict Luke of incompetence, it is better to credit him—as 'literary' scholars would a Classical historian—with purposeful invention.[45] Clearly, the item contextualises Jesus' birth within Roman, and world, history. Moreover, unnoticed by scholars, Augustus reappears, subliminally, at the end of Luke-Acts: the humane Roman centurion in Paul's shipwrecked voyage is '*Julius* of the *Augustan* Cohort' (Acts 27.1)—another instance of Rome's 'book-ending' the double-work. Augustus' decree also fulfils a vital narrative and theological function, enabling the Davidic Jesus' prophetic birth in Bethlehem: Augustus is thus an agent of the Christian god;[46] Romans have a stake here. This functionality, however, does not guarantee virtue, since God can use non-good, even bad, people for good. But Christian apologists could represent Augustus positively.[47] Were they right? Did they so read Luke? Is another of Augustus' functions to introduce the category of 'the good Roman'? Does 'Julius of the Augustan Cohort' validate Augustus' virtue? Is Augustus the paradigm of 'a good emperor', who does not persecute Christians, indeed, promotes Christianity? Is this possibility strengthened by the presence in the text of the great persecuting emperor Nero, who is referred to, though unnamed, in the speeches of Paul's later trials,[48] and whose violent, premature death is narratively encoded?[49]

But there are strong negatives. A second main function of Augustus' fictional world-wide decree is to bring the Preface's Christian 'polity' and Rome into direct relationship.[50] As the Preface already stages a contrast between divine power and human power, that contrast intensifies here. Within the developing text, there can be no doubt that Jesus is Lord (2.11), not Augustus. Roman *power* is further diminished by the Preface's implication that Christianity, not Livy's *History*, not Rome itself, is 'the monument that cannot fall'. Further, the use of the name 'Augustus', the term 'the whole world', and the commonalities of inscription/decree imagery, of self-identification as Greek historiography, and of imitation of Herodotus (in 'equation' of theme and treatment)[51] bring Augustus' *Res Gestae* and Luke-Acts into competition, again to the detriment

---

45  Moles (2011b) 471 {above, p. 596}.
46  Blumenthal (2011).
47  Millar (1977) 555–66.
48  Acts 25.8, 10–11, 21, 26.
49  See below p. 718.
50  Moles (2011b) 471 {above, p. 596}.
51  Moles (2011b) 473 {above, p. 598}; Woodman (2012) 198–200.

⟦88⟧ of the Roman text, particularly because of their contrasting ultimate visions: Luke-Acts raises people up, Augustus' *Res Gestae subjects* them.[52]

Thus the balance tells against a positive reading of Augustus and Rome. Yet the long-range link between 'Augustus' and 'Julius of the Augustan Cohort' raises the *possibility* of better things. Meanwhile, although 'Julius' treats his prisoner Paul humanely and saves the prisoners' lives, he wrongly prefers the captain's advice to Paul's (Acts 27.11), so Paul remains the *superior* 'authority figure'.

Joseph takes Mary to Bethlehem: Christians obey imperial decrees. And the aged Simeon's '*nunc dimittis*' eulogises 'my salvation, which you have prepared in the face of all peoples, a light for revelation of the races, and glory of your people Israel' (2.30–2). The Romans are included within 'all peoples' and 'the races'. In Luke-Acts any visceral anti-Roman feeling is excluded by the Gentile 'outreach' proclaimed from the start of Luke and systematically implemented throughout Acts, following the risen Jesus' injunction (1.8); by the category of 'the good Roman'; by exhortations such as Jesus' 'Love your enemies, do good to those who hate you' (Luke 6.27), and by the Christian claim that 'God is impartial' as between races (Acts 10.34; cf. 15.9).

The Baptist's ministry is validated by a prophecy (3.4–6 = Isaiah 40.3–5) announcing further inversions: 'a voice of one shouting in the desert, Prepare the road of the Lord, make his paths straight. Every valley will be filled, and every mountain and hill will be made low, and the crooked will be made straight, and the rough made smooth, and all flesh will see the salvation of God'. The perspective is again that of inaugurated eschatology. The Romans are necessarily included in the salvific prospectus—'all flesh shall see the salvation of God', and there is no implication that they will *reject* it.

That Romans belong within Luke's 'catchment area' is further indicated by the presence, among the groups who thronged to the Baptist, of Roman soldiers, by their question: 'what shall we too do?', and by John's reply: 'do not shake anyone down or bear false witness and be content with your wages' (3.13–14). This obviously fictional item speaks directly to Roman soldiers and more generally to any Romans seeking reassurance that Jesus' immediate predecessor was no revolutionary but supported good provincial governance and contented soldiers.[53] Christian readers are given a 'proof text' of John's (and, consequently, Jesus') peaceful prospectus and confirmation that Romans—even soldiers—can be included within the Christian project. Thereafter, Luke-Acts consistently shows Jesus and his followers associating with imperial ⟦89⟧

---

52  Moles (2011b) 481 {above, p. 606}.
53  Kinman (1993).

functionaries: Jesus enlists Levi the tax-collector among his disciples, fraternises with tax-collectors (Luke 5.27–30),[54] and in Jerusalem dines with Zacchaeus the tax-collector (19.1–30). As sinners (5.30; 19.7), they come under Jesus' salvific prospectus. In a development and intensification of the theme, once the Gentile mission gathers pace, Acts emphasises Peter's and Paul's free association with Romans of status, whether centurions, governors, or Asiarchs. As with 'the most powerful Theophilos', Christianity is 'aiming high' by appealing directly to Roman authority figures: not merely passively responding to them as investigators or instigators of persecution.

Narratively, the soldiers who throng to John anticipate the category of 'good Romans'. The first substantial example comes with the centurion at Capernaum, whose slave Jesus heals (7.2–10).[55] He seems to be a God-fearer (5), addresses Jesus as 'Lord' (6), recognises Jesus' superior authority (6–8), and prompts Jesus' acclamation (9): 'I say to you: not even in Israel have I found such belief'. The episode marks a significant advance upon the Roman soldiers and John. Being a Roman soldier, even an officer, is no obstacle to responding to Jesus, indeed, to becoming a Christian: 'Jesus is Lord' is a Christian confessional formula. Clearly, the centurion will not stop soldiering; equally clearly, he recognises that Jesus is superior 'Lord' to Caesar. This centurion's responsiveness to Jesus finds further (surely fictional) expression from another centurion at the crucifixion (23.27): 'And ... having seen what had been done, [he] praised God, saying: "This man was just indeed"'. The Capernaum episode is further paralleled and developed in Acts (10.1–48), in Peter's encounter with the centurion Cornelius, who is a God-fearer, devout, and an alms-giver, whose goodness is attested by the whole Jewish nation, and who receives direct prompting from an angel. For his part, Peter learns that Jewish food and cleanliness laws can be suspended in dealings with Gentiles and God is impartial. Cornelius and his household speak in tongues and are baptised. The episode fleshes out the practical implications of the conversion of Roman officers to Christianity.

In a further development (Acts 13.7–12), the proconsul Sergius Paulus, 'an intelligent man', actively summons the apostles Barnabas and Saul in order to hear the word of God. When a magician tries to turn the proconsul away from the faith, Saul/Paul blinds him and the proconsul believes, thunder-struck at the teaching of the Lord. Again, the gaoler at Philippi (16.16–40) responds to Paul and Silas' miraculous release by intended suicide, is dissuaded by Paul, asks, ambiguously (30), 'Lords, what must I do in order that I be saved?', is

---

54   That Levi is a tax-collector for Herod Antipas, not Rome, is immaterial (see p. 722).
55   Functionally, *pace* some, he is Roman, even if (which I doubt) Luke envisages Antipas' army.

baptised [[90]] along with his family, and provides the apostles hospitality. The roll-call continues: Titius Justus, God-fearer, with whom Paul lodges in Corinth (18.7); the Asiarchs, friends of Paul, and city official who restrain Ephesian hostility (19.31, 35); the humane Julius (27.1–43); and the hospitable Publius, Malta's first man (28.7).

Since Luke-Acts functions as exemplary historiography and biography (Acts 26.29), these 'good Romans' exemplify for Romans good ways in which they should respond to Christians, the responses ranging from simple kindness to absolute conversion. For Christians, they exemplify the *possibility* of favourable Roman responses, despite the dreadful events of 64 and other occasions, despite the intrinsic problems. The most substantial figures, the centurions in *Luke* and Acts, are both also God-fearers, and Luke repeatedly emphasises that (somewhat elastic) identity,[56] which suggests both direct appeal to 'God-fearer' readers and implicit exhortation to Christian readers to target this category particularly among Romans.

All this positive material about Romans is counterbalanced by constant emphasis, established from the beginning, on eschatological divine justice. John prophesies concerning Jesus (Luke 3.17): 'his winnowing fork is in his hand, to clear his threshing floor, and to gather his wheat into his repository, but the chaff he will burn with unquenchable fire'. Thereafter, great emphasis is placed on the Second Coming, with its rewards and punishments (Luke 12.35–48, 54–6; 17.24, 30–37; 19.11–27; 21.27–36); Jews and Jewish cities are condemned (10.12–15; 11.29–32; 13.24–8; 21.20–4), in contrast to Gentiles (13.29–30), who must include Romans; all will perish unless they repent (13.3, 5); the just will resurrect (14.14) and be vindicated (18.1–8), or the disciples will be enthroned as judges of Israel (22.30), or everyone who calls upon the name of the Lord will be saved (Acts 2.20). Sometimes, eschatological divine justice is invoked in contexts of human justice, to the latter's diminishment: Paul proclaims Jesus judge on the Last Day when he is addressing the Areopagus (17.31) and when Roman justice is also on trial, because of earlier political charges against the Christians (17.6–7); the governor Felix grows fearful when Paul dialogues on the judgement to come (24.25).

Divine justice can also be immediate. When the impious Herod Agrippa I ascends the tribunal to announce terms to Tyre and Sidon, 'immediately an angel of the Lord struck him, because he had not given God the glory, and he breathed his last eaten by worms' (Acts 12.23). Since the emphasis on his people's acclamation of the king's 'divine voice' evokes Nero, punished for

---

56   Also Acts 13.16, 26, 43, 50; 16.14; 17.4, 17.

persecution ⟦91⟧ of the Christians by untimely death,⁵⁷ this episode acquires timeless paradigmatic application to the clash between unjust human power and just divine power. The Apostles have similar power: Peter 'executes' the dishonest Ananias and Sapphira (5.5, 10), and Paul blinds the magician before Sergius (13.11). All readers see writ large the perils of resisting the Christian god.

When the narrative turns to Jesus, the Temptation (4.1–13), Jewish-Christian equivalent of the Choice of Hercules,⁵⁸ is readily 'translatable' by Gentile readers. The episode is programmatic both for Jesus within the narrative and for readers. It describes 'all the kingdoms of the world' as the fiefdom of the Devil, underlining the commandment (Deut. 6.13): 'You will worship the Lord your god and you will serve him alone' (4.1–8): within the totality of 'kingdoms', the Roman empire, Roman 'kings', and imperial cult are firmly enrolled 'on the other side'. The 'either-or' choice is emphasised throughout Luke-Acts, for example, in the sayings 'He who is not with me is against me and he who does not gather with me scatters' (11.23) and 'No servant can serve two masters' (16.13), and the terminology sometimes implicates Rome, as in the question 'what does it profit a man who gains the whole world but loses or punishes himself?' (9.25), the rival kingdoms of the devil and of God (11.14–23), Peter's pronouncement 'and there is salvation in no one else, nor is there any other name under heaven given among human beings in which we must be saved' (Acts 4.12), his application of Psalm 2.1 to Jesus' trial—'the kings of the earth stood together and the rulers were gathered together against the Lord and against his Anointed' (4.26), and Jesus' commission to Paul (26.18) 'open [the Gentiles'] eyes, to turn them from darkness to light and from the power of Satan to God'.⁵⁹ At the end of Acts, readers still face that choice (28.31).

Jesus' first sustained teaching, the Beatitudes (6.20–37; 'blessed are you poor, for the Kingdom of God is yours', etc.), continues the inversion/subversion of worldly power structures and values, and there are other similar sayings (9.24; 13.30; 14.11; 18.14). Romans could easily read these paradoxical ethics and economics as counter-cultural 'Cynic'.⁶⁰

In the Temptation of Jesus, 'the kingdoms of the world' oppose the kingdom of God—or of Jesus himself, as prophesised by Gabriel. This takes various forms. There is Jesus' own teaching about the Kingdom,⁶¹ carried on in ⟦92⟧ Acts,⁶² and the Lord's Prayer (Luke 11.2–4). There is the prostitute who anoints

---

57   Klauck (2000) 43–4; Moles (2006) 91 {above, p. 575} n. 114.
58   Downing (1988) 15, 23.
59   Pragmatic compromise is rare, e.g., Luke 6.37; 9.50; cf. also p. 730.
60   Downing (1988) 19–21; Moles (2006a).
61   Luke 10.9–11; 11.18–20; 22.30.
62   Acts 1.3, 8.12; 19.8, 25, 28.30–1.

Jesus (7.36–50). Among other implications, one is that Jesus is being 'anointed' as 'Christ' or 'Messiah', such 'anointing' marking Jewish kings, though Luke diplomatically 'pulls his punches' by using the verb ἀλείφω, not χρίω. And, climactically, there is his triumphal entry into Jerusalem, when 'the whole multitude of his disciples' hail him (38): 'Blessed is the coming one, the king coming in the name of the Lord; peace in heaven and glory in the highest', and Jesus himself accepts the salutation: when some of the Pharisees ask him to rebuke his disciples, he replies: 'if these are silent, the very stones will cry out'. This, again, is the perspective of 'inaugurated eschatology', of divine 'peace' as opposed to immediate, earthly strife.

As the narrative builds towards 'the Road to Jerusalem', there is strong emphasis on Jesus' prophecies of his death (9.22; 17.25; 18.32). These include mention of Romans: 'The son of man will be handed over to the Gentiles, and will be mocked and violently mistreated and spat upon' (18.32), which duly happens: 'The soldiers also mocked him ...' (23.36). They also emphasise the persecution of his followers: 'and when they bring you before the synagogues and the rulers and the authorities, do not be anxious how or what you answer in defence or say' (12.11); 'They will lay their hands on you and persecute you, handing you over to the synagogues and prisons, dragging you before kings and governors for the sake of my name' (21.12–17). The persecutors include Roman authorities and governors, and 'for the sake of my name' foretells trials of 'Christians' *sub nomine*. Useless to deny that Romans crucified Jesus and sometimes persecuted Christians. Jesus even emphasises that he will cause violent strife (12.49–51): 'I came to cast fire upon the earth ... Do you think that I came to give peace on earth? No, I tell you, but rather division' (body politic metaphor). This disturbing material is offset by the Christological dimension, and there is another level on which Romans could read Jesus' death positively: as a king who heroically sacrifices himself for his people, like Leonidas of Sparta (Hdt. 7.220), or Roman generals who 'devoted' themselves to secure victory.

Jesus' prophecies of the destruction of the Temple (19.42–4; 21.5–7, 20–4) have several aspects. There is Jewish failure to recognise Jesus' salvific function and ignorance of how to maintain peace (19.44): the Jewish revolt is prophetically condemned and Christians exonerated. The Romans appear as God's agents, as Augustus had been: further encouragement to Romans. But 'the times of the Gentiles' will yield to the Second Coming. The *eschatological* message for Romans remains the same as Mary's.

⟦93⟧ Jesus' riposte to the challenge of Jewish spies, 'Give to Caesar the things that belong to Caesar and to God the things that belong to God' (20.25), seems to justify payment of tribute and warrant some sort of wider 'Church–State demarcation', somewhat blurring the polarity 'no man can serve two masters'. Simultaneously, however, it implies sharp questions: *what* things (besides tribute) belong to each? Is it not blasphemous that Jews (or Christians) use coins bearing the *image* and inscription ('son of the divine Augustus', *'pontifex maximus'*) of Gentile/pagan kings who claimed divinity and made other strong religious claims? Is this not collusion with the imperial cult and the divinisation of humans—collusion already damned in the Temptation narrative and roundly excluded in Acts: the death of the impious Herod Agrippa I ~ Nero (12.20–3); Peter's rejection of such addresses by Cornelius (10.25–6); Paul and Barnabas' rejection of the same at Lystra (14.8ff.); and Paul's rejection of the whole category of 'images' or 'idols' (17.16, 23)?[63]

The plot against Jesus (Luke 22.2ff.) is initiated by chief priests and scribes; the fictional absence of Roman soldiers at Jesus' arrest (22.47) conciliates Roman readers; only at 23.1 is Jesus brought before Pilate. Romans can read the interim aetiological institution of the Last Supper (22.14–23) as analogous to cult meals in pagan mysteries, especially those of Dionysus, just as they can read Jesus' death and resurrection as parallel to Dionysus'.[64] The debate about greatness (24–7) inverts worldly values, but Jesus' phraseology—

> (25) the kings of the races lord it over them, and those in authority over them are called benefactors. (26) But not so with you; rather let the greater among you become as the younger and the leaders as the server. (27) For which is the greater, the one who lies at table or the server? Is it not the one who lies at table? But I am among you as the server

—could be heard by Classical readers as resembling Cynic 'redefinitions' of kingship.[65] At the arrest Jesus curtails armed resistance by his disciples (22.49–51); later (23.25), '[Pilate] released the one thrown into prison for *stasis* and murder ...'; Christianity's commitment to peace is again underlined. There remain the tense ambiguities of Jesus' status as 'Messiah' and 'seated at the right hand of God' (22.67–70), that is, as eschatological king.

Before Pilate, the Jews accuse Jesus of misleading the nation, forbidding tribute to Caesar (untrue), and claiming himself as anointed king. When Pilate asks Jesus if he is the king of the Jews, Jesus sidesteps: 'that's what you say',

---

63  Acts 28.6, where the Maltesers say Paul is a god without being rebuked, seems to be indulgent characterisation of 'philanthropic', credulous people.
64  Generally, Moles (2006); Seaford (2006) 120–30; Shorrock (2010) 54–5; note Luke 7.32 (with Moles [2006] 76 {above, p. 562}), 'trailing' the Dionysus parallel.
65  Höistad (1948).

and ⟦94⟧ Pilate finds no fault. Is this alleged 'kingdom' a threat to the Roman empire or Roman rule over Palestine? The answer is: ultimately, most certainly; immediately, ambiguously. The Temptation has already shown that Jesus' kingdom does not involve dramatic physical gestures, and all readers know that Jesus must die. Contextually, Pilate's instant dismissal of such a charge lacks any historical credibility. Luke has already palliated the charge's seriousness by emphasising it more in the entry into Jerusalem. The Jews next accuse Jesus of 'stirring *up* the people' throughout Judaea. Pilate sends Jesus to Antipas, as being within his jurisdiction; these buck-passings remind readers that, while the Herodians are Jewish (or half-Jewish), they are thoroughly Hellenised and Romanised, and, as client kings, agents of Roman power. In Luke-Acts they are categorisable as 'Roman'.[66] When Jesus remains silent before Antipas' curious questioning and Antipas and his soldiers have mocked and abused him, Antipas returns him to Pilate and the two former enemies cynically become friends. Pilate wants to release Jesus after beating, but under Jewish pressure releases Barabbas and consigns Jesus to crucifixion.

Four obvious points: first, Pilate's repeated conclusion that Jesus has done nothing wrong emphasises Jesus' innocence; second, Pilate, while not faultless,[67] is unhistorically white-washed; third, 'the Jews' are unhistorically 'black-washed'; fourth, Antipas is portrayed more hostilely than Pilate. The first of these is driven home by the centurion's reaction (23.47). The second and third are Luke's general line.[68] The second contrasts starkly with Luke's earlier representation of Pilate's bloodthirstiness (13.1). There is much less inconsistency with the earlier representation of Antipas,[69] sexual sinner, evil-doer, imprisoner (3.19) and executioner of John (9.9), would-be killer of Jesus, who calls him 'that fox' (13.31), and gross and heartless sybarite (16.19–31).[70] Clearly, the first three elements appeal both to Christian and Roman readers.

Acts, focusing on Jesus' followers as well as Jesus himself, both earthly and risen, develops the notion of the Christian community, people, and polity. Romans, already sensitised by Cynic colouring in the representation of Jesus, would naturally read the 'communism' of the Jerusalem community (2.44–6; 4.32–7) as Cynic-like.[71] The Jerusalem decree (15.19–20, 24–9), defining Gentile ⟦95⟧ Christians' relationship both to Jewish food and purity laws and (partially)

---

66  Similarly, Rowe (2009) 54; Yamazaki-Ransom (2010) 71–9.
67  Yamazaki-Ransom (2010) 110–14 exaggerates negatives.
68  Luke 24.20; Acts 2.22–3, 36; 3.13–15, 17; 5.30; 10.39; 13.27–9; *contra*, 4.25ff. (everybody against Jesus).
69  Yamazaki-Ransom (2010) 166–70.
70  Horsley (2011) 147.
71  D.L. 6.72.

to imperial cult, substantiates the 'polity' implications, both political and philosophical, of the Preface. And, climactically (11.26) and brilliantly, 'in Antioch the disciples were first called [χρηματίσαι] Christians'. Precision is needed. Χρηματίσαι is passive in meaning: other evidence shows that, in the first century, 'Christians' is other people's term: Christians call themselves other things.[72] The term is intrinsically pejorative, recalling that 'Christ' was executed as a political subversive, that Christians were 'political' and could be prosecuted *sub nomine*. Furthermore, as sounded identically to a word cluster differing only by the vowel 'e' and sometimes itself so spelled, it allows hostile puns ('the so-called "Goodies" are "baddies", "Christians" are "dead"', etc.).[73] The negatives are on one level operative here, because Luke sandwiches this notice between persecutions (11.19; 12.1). But he registers this first naming of Christ's followers with appropriate historiographical solemnity. Further, within the unity of Luke-Acts the notice recalls Luke 21.17, establishing 'Christians" legitimacy as true followers of 'Christ'.[74] Further still, Luke subverts the negative associations of the name by the pun (registering the eta spelling): *χρηματίσαι ~ Χριστιανούς*: 'Christians' are 'useful': 'Christians' are 'the real thing'. Thus Romans are invited radically to reevaluate 'Christians', Christians to find positives in the term.[75]

Acts also develops the Jesus–Dionysus analogy, to rich and diverse effect: ambiguously characterising Jesus as a 'new' and, undoubtedly, disruptive divinity; appealing to pagans generally and to Dionysians in particular by the closest parallel to Jesus in the pagan pantheon; boosting Luke-Acts' 'Classical' qualities by deft and architectural use of *Bacchae*; and exploiting the Dionysian myth to emphasise alike the tremendous physical powers of the risen Jesus (doubtless contrasting with the bogus Dionysian powers of Roman kings), the ever-present choice between acceptance or persecution of Jesus and his followers, and the recurrent pattern of Christian persecution, divine punishment of the persecutors, and Christian liberation.[76]

Saul/Paul unites many themes. Foreshadowed in the Lukan Preface,[77] and introduced into the narrative as accomplice to the murder of Stephen, first Christian martyr (Acts 7.58–8.1; 22.20), the 'whoreish' Saulos[78] becomes lead ⟦96⟧ Jewish persecutor of the Christians, imitating Pentheus against Dionysus and his followers (8.3; 9.1–2; 22.4–5; 26.9–11). On the Road to Damascus (9.3–9;

---

72    Tac. *Ann.* 15.44.2; 1 Peter 4.16; Acts 26.28 (p. 726).
73    Karrer (1991) 82–3; Cook (2010) 49. {Further treatment below, Ch. 29.}
74    P. 720.
75    *Contra*, Rowe (2009) 15.
76    Moles (2006); Lang (2008) 201–50; 376–7; 382, 385–6.
77    Moles (2013) 111–12 {above, pp. 690–1}.
78    LSJ s.v.

22.6–20; 26.12–18), he encounters the risen Jesus himself at his most Dionysian. Jesus reveals that persecution of his followers is the same as persecuting himself; Christians are now further defined: as 'the body of Christ': 'Persecutors, beware!'

Saul/Paul chooses rightly, as, later, does, the Roman gaoler at Philippi, but Herod Agrippa I does not. Paul now finds himself at the receiving end of persecution. A series of episodes both echo Jesus' own trial and exemplify the trials and prosecutions Jesus prophesised for his followers. Luke's subtle representations of the complex legalities and power relationships of provincial government have been well studied. I comment briefly.

At Philippi, after Paul exorcises in the name of Jesus Christ the slave girl whose prophesying enriched her owners, the latter accuse Paul and Silas of disturbing the city as Jews and proclaiming customs unlawful for Romans. The crowd joins in, and the magistrates strip, beat, and imprison the apostles. After their miraculous release and the gaoler's positive response, the magistrates order their release and peaceful departure. Paul's insistence on their proper vindication as Roman citizens (cf. 22.25–9; 25.10–12; 28.17–20) alarms the magistrates, who come and beseech their departure (16.16–40). Several points emerge. The apostles stand out as Jews who (unlike most) 'make trouble' by opposing paganism, which often has economic implications;[79] Christianity is generally assumed to be illegal (cf. 11.26); but the magistrates register the miraculous release and have qualms about rough treatment of Roman citizens (as Jesus was not).

When Gallio, proconsul of Achaea (18.12–17), dismisses the Jews' ambiguous accusation against Paul ('this man is trying to persuade people to worship God contrary to the law') as a matter of 'word' and 'names' and internal Jewish law, without allowing Paul to speak, the response suits the historical context, but would not have been plausible after 64 (when Christians were persecuted, but Jews were not), still less 70, so does not herein have paradigmatic value. While better than punishment, it is premature, contemptuous of Judaism, and unsubtle ('word' and 'names' matter, especially in this context).[80] When 'all' the Jews beat up Sosthenes, ruler (presumably Christian) of the synagogue, in front of Gallio's tribunal, he does nothing. He represents Roman governors with only elementary concern for law, civic or religious, and a short attention span.

⟦97⟧ In the riot at Ephesus following Demetrius the silversmith's charge that Paul's preaching will harm trade (cf. 16.16) and destroy the temple of Artemis

---

79  Similarly, Rowe (2009) 26–7.
80  Similarly, Yamazaki-Ransom (2010) 129–31.

and her worship, there are sharp ironies:[81] Demetrius' demagoguery risks *stasis* and Roman intervention (19.38–40), averted by the Asiarchs, Paul's friends, and the city official; yet Demetrius sees the existential threat posed by Christianity, as they do not (19.37). They represent a particular 'good Roman': well-meaning, humane, and public-spirited but, unlike Sergius Paulus, rather unintelligent. Demetrius' picture of the effects of Paul's teaching of course exaggerates greatly: the historiographical narrative is here ideally or futuristically true.

The proceedings in Jerusalem involving the tribune, Claudius Lysias (21.27–23.33), are still more complicated and ambiguous. On the one hand, Lysias calms civil disturbance, saves Paul from death, allows him to address the crowd and Sanhedrin, fearfully recognises his rights as Roman citizen, releases him temporarily, protects him from renewed Jewish violence and murderous plots, and sends him under escort to Felix the governor, with a letter in which he judges Paul innocent of any charge worthy of death or chains. On the other, he immediately arrests and chains him, examines him by scourging, and when the chains are removed does not finally release him, passing the buck to Felix, taking the same view of the issues as the crass Gallio, and white-washing his own treatment of a Roman citizen. No reader should miss *Lysias'* ironic failure finally to *release* Paul. The *Bacchae* paradigm reinforces a generic contrast between Christian 'freedom' and Roman 'unfreedom'.

Felix (23.33–24.27) also exhibits ambiguities, though rather different ones. After Jewish accusations and Paul's defence, Felix puts them off, 'knowing rather accurately the things about the Road', says he will make a decision when Lysias comes (mutual buck-passing between superior and inferior), ensures Paul's custody be as free as possible, summons Paul and listens to him about belief in Christ Jesus (compare Sergius, contrast Gallio), fears Paul's teaching about justice, self-control, and the coming judgement, protracts things in the hope that Paul will bribe him, and keeps Paul chained in order to secure favour with the Jews. The general point is clear: Felix has the requisite knowledge, but cannot commit himself, cannot finally treat Paul rightly, cannot become a true Theophilos (24.22 ~ Luke 1.1–4).

His successor Festus (25.1–26.32) keeps Paul at Caesarea, thwarting a Jewish murder plot, and hears charges against Paul, who asserts his innocence regarding Jewish law, the Temple, and Caesar. Wishing to do the Jews a favour, Festus offers Paul trial at Jerusalem, but Paul appeals to Caesar and Festus agrees. The arrival of Agrippa and Berenice prompts him to consult them. Festus asserts ⟦98⟧ the Roman tradition of proper trial and, like Gallio, regards the dispute as an internal Jewish matter but again accepts the appeal to Caesar. Agrippa's

---

81   Similarly, Rowe (2009) 49.

curiosity (reminiscent of his grandfather's about Jesus [Luke 23.8]) prompts a further hearing; Paul proclaims Jesus and his conversion within the context of ancestral Judaism. Festus exclaims that Paul is mad, but privately they agree his innocence. Festus seems paradigmatic of three governmental types: those whose conduct is a mixture of good and bad; those who think Christians simply mad; and those who think them innocent. Agrippa's 'verdict' (26.31), 'this man could have been freed, if he had not called upon Caesar', chillingly underlines the double-edgedness of Roman justice.

As for Agrippa, the unexplained introduction of Berenice, the emphasis on 'appearance' (25.23), and the general 'oriental' colouring recall the scandalous incest, rendering the 'whole trial ... a comedy'.[82] Both this last Herodian, towards the end of the narrative, and Antipas, towards the beginning, are sexually defiled. And, challenged by Paul to answer his claim that the prophets prove Jesus' messiahship, Agrippa resorts to the sneering 'Roman' sense of the term 'Christian'. Nevertheless, he and the others are not too corrupted to acknowledge Paul's innocence: it is worthwhile to persist in attempting to convert even the very immoral. There is always hope—as Paul himself demonstrated. More, the juxtaposition of sneer and 'verdict' of innocence (26.28, 32) undermines prosecution 'sub nomine': as if Luke answers the dubiety of Roman governors whether to punish Christians for their name or their crimes.[83] In Luke's Christian narrative, even so corrupt a character as Agrippa can serve good purposes. The name 'Christian' is now completely decontaminated (cf. 11.26).[84] Roman readers, aware that in 64 Christians were put to death for being Christians, are encouraged to rewrite the history next time.

The end of the text (28.30–1), one of ancient historiography's greatest, purveys complex and powerful messages:

> And he remained there for a whole two years in a private lodging and received all those who came in to him, (31) heralding the kingdom of God and teaching the things about the Lord Jesus Christ with all frankness and unhinderedly.

⟦99⟧ Readers know—and have been repeatedly reminded[85]—that just beyond the end of the narrative road in Rome lie Paul's trial before Nero, conviction, and death, and the events of 64. The climactic stress on Jesus' Lordship and

---

82  Mason (2005) 164.
83  Plin. *Ep.* 10.96.2.
84  Similarly, Rowe (2009) 132.
85  Acts 9.16; 20.17–38; 26.31–2; 27.24.

God's kingdom rings with the start of Luke (1.33; 2.11) and commemorates their diametric opposition to the Neronian and Caesarian equivalents.[86] Paul will suffer a martyrdom like Stephen's (9.16 'I [God] will show him how much he must suffer for my name'), noble and exemplary: that is, precisely, an 'example' that Christians may always have to follow, but which will unite them with Jesus. So, under house arrest and destined for martyrdom, Paul enjoys full 'frankness' and 'unhindered-ness', the earlier Christian Dionysian-style physical 'freeings' now redefined at a far profounder level. Paul's whole protracted 'Road to Rome' in Acts (19.21–28.13) parallels Jesus' protracted 'Road to Jerusalem' in Luke, and the choice for the Roman reader at the end of that road is the same as at the beginning, in the Temptation of Jesus, as at Jesus' trial, and always: do you persecute Jesus/the Christians or accept Jesus and become Christian yourself? But it acquires particular force here, through the reminiscences of the original fate of Jesus and the subsequent fate of Paul: need we go through this yet again? Given the plasticity of myth, that question resounds through the later persecution (before the time of writing) of the tyrannical Domitian, divinely punished like Nero, the persecution of Trajan (whose beginnings coincided with the time of writing), of Decius, Diocletian, and the rest.

But there is even tougher theology. Jewish, then Christian, and still Jewish, Paul is also Roman (13.9; 16.37; 22.25–8), and his inclusion, along with Nero, within the Penthean persecutor paradigm makes him also representative of Roman persecutors. So his noble martyrdom is also reparation for his role as persecutor (9.16): persecutors get theirs. But Paul also shows that even the greatest persecutors can become Christians—and great Christians. Legally innocent, Paul also encapsulates another key Lukan claim: Christians' right to protection under Roman law, but, while, as Festus insists, that law is a wonderful thing, it is also a terrible thing, when it condemns and executes innocent Christians. A final twist. Paul knows that he will fail to persuade Nero (9.16; cf. 20.24–5).[87] Yet go to Rome he must. His 'appeal to Caesar' is one way of 'hitching a ride'. Christians must bear witness, whatever the costs, for themselves or for fellow-Christians. This is a text of steel, demanding the respect of Romans, Paul the greatest of tragic heroes.

[[100]] The end comports another dimension. Paul, not in prison but under house arrest, yet discoursing 'with all frankness' and 'unhinderedly' about ultimate realities, looks not only like Jesus himself but also like Socrates the night before he died. Roman readers are further encouraged to approve of Paul through the comparison not only with Socrates but also with Seneca and the

---

86   Similarly, Yamazaki-Ransom (2010) 159.
87   Moles (2013) 116 {above, p. 696}.

various 'Stoic martyrs' of the Empire, especially under the dramatically contemporaneous tyrant Nero and the recent tyrant Domitian. 'Paulus Socraticus' crystallises Christian 'philosophy'. More: this culminating scene combines with Acts 17 to convey Christians' claim that they—not Epicureans or Stoics or the rest—are Socrates' true heirs.[88]

Paul also serves to define the relative 'geometry' and 'geography' of Christianity and Rome. That 'Saul' also possesses the Roman name, 'Paul', by which he is called for the remainder of the narrative, emerges in his encounter with Sergius Paulus (13.9). 'Good Roman' as the latter is, the encounter stages the superiority of divine to Roman justice. Can any reader miss that 'Paulus' means 'little', that 'Paulus' is here the 'bigger' man? The pun becomes even sharper when Paul, before Agrippa, Berenice, and Festus, 'testifies both to small and great' (26.22). The relationship between the 'great' of this world and the 'little' Christian Paul is absolutely inverted, again recalling Mary's programmatic Magnificat.

Paul's climactic (and brilliant) assertion to Agrippa (26.26), 'this [the whole Jesus story] was not done in a corner' has a triple function: it inverts the 'small–great' relationship geographically: Bethlehem/Judaea is the 'great' sphere, not Rome or the empire;[89] Rome is only superficially, only provisionally, the 'end' of the narrative; it extends Christian philosophy's outreach from the narrow school context to the whole world;[90] and 'architecturally', it signals the supersession of the Temple by the Christification of the 'temple' of the world.[91] The first of these implications is further developed when Paul's shipwreck evokes Aeneas'[92] (another telling ring structure between beginning and end of Luke-Acts), the Aenean foundation of Rome (*Aen.* 1.11) superseded by Paul's 'refoundation' of a Christian Rome subservient to a Christian world.

⟦101⟧ Paul also provides some mediation between Christianity as both 'new' and 'old'. If the Dionysian Jesus looks 'new', as dimly perceived by the Athenian philosophers (17.18–21),[93] the last third of Acts repeatedly stresses Paul's Jewishness (21.20–6; 24.14; 28.17). That of course reflects the historical Paul, but it combines with the explicit separate provision for Gentile Christians to convey a continuing truth about Christianity and to give all readers, whether

---

88  Sandnes (1993); Alexander (2005) 62–8; Lang (2008) 251–314; 316–37; 344–55; 361–86; 386–407.
89  John Chrys. *Hom.* 52.4.
90  Malherbe (1985–6) 210; cf. Plat. *Gorg.* 485d.
91  Cf. Acts 3.11 ('This is the stone, the one rejected by you builders, the one that has become the corner-stone').
92  27.13–14 (winds, sand-bank) ~ *Aen.* 1.102–12.
93  Moles (2006) 84–5 {above, pp. 569–71}.

Christian or Roman, reassurance that Christianity is the legitimate fulfilment of Judaism combined with the energising excitement of 'the new'.

Paul also defines Christian 'politics'. There is turmoil in Thessalonica when Jason and other Christians are accused by Jews of 'standing the world upside down' (ἀναστατώσαντες) and 'acting against the decrees of Caesar, saying that there is another king, Jesus' (17.6–7), which disturbs the crowd and the city rulers. The scene replays Jesus' own trial in Luke. Then both in the Athenian *agora* and before the Areopagus Paul proclaims 'the standing up' (ἀνάστασις [17.18, 31]). Similarly, at the start of a long sequence (21.38), Lysias takes Paul as the Egyptian who 'made an uprising' (ἀναστατώσας); at the end of the sequence (23.6), Paul claims to be on trial concerning the 'rising (ἀνάστασις) of corpses'. Again, before Felix, the prosecutor Tertullus alleges that 'this man sets in motion risings [κινοῦντα στάσεις] among all the Jews throughout the world' (24.5), to which Paul responds that he has never been found 'creating a rising' (ἐπίστασιν ποιοῦντα, 24.12), even as he continues to proclaim the 'rising' (ἀνάστασις) of both just and unjust (24.15) and of the corpses (24.21). This crucial pun,[94] unnoticed by scholars, clarifies: Christians are not revolutionaries, but the resurrection 'revolutionises' everything throughout the world. And only this *inversion/resurrection/revolution*, with all its implications, produces *security from falling* (Luke 1.4)—or divine peace.[95] Classical readers should admire Luke's Christian inversion of Thucydides' *stasis* analyses. All readers should note how the Christian lexicon of 'standing' systematically undermines Rome's boasts of her own 'standing' as a 'state' and her 'subjection' of the world.[96] And all this fundamentally affects Luke-Acts' 'stance'[97] towards Rome.

[[102]] Conclusions

Luke highlights contradiction.[98] Christians obey Rome, pay tribute/tax, embrace peace, reject violence, insist on their compatibility with Judaism and with Roman law, decrees, and the Caesars, and on their entitlement to Roman legal protection; Romans repeatedly judge Jesus and Paul innocent. But Jesus brings fire and division; Jesus, not Caesar, is Lord and King;[99] Christian mission repeatedly produces disorder, alike social, political, and economic, and alike in

---

94  Moles (2011a) 154–5 {above, pp. 648–50}.
95  Acts 10.36; 24.2; Rowe (2009) 152; Yamazaki-Ransom (2010) 37.
96  *OLD* s.v. 'sto' 14, 15, 16; 'status', 8; p. 716 above.
97  LSJ s.v. στάσις, B.I.2.e; 3; *OLD* s.v. 'status', 3.
98  Similarly, Rowe (2009) 54–5.
99  Similarly, Yamazaki-Ransom (2010) 151, 158–60.

Jewish, pagan, Roman, and mixed contexts; opponents' accusations, whether Jewish, pagan, or Roman, have some purchase; Romans execute Jesus and Paul. Pragmatic obfuscations (rare) and palliations (more substantial but localised) do not erase the contradiction.

Luke represents conflict as inevitable. Christian exclusivist monotheism and pagan polytheism are irreconcilable, polytheists wrong, their gods non-existent. The religious debate could not be acuter, admits only one answer, and is unavoidable. Beyond Judaea, polytheism pervades public space, and has social, economic, and political, as well as religious, consequences. All coalesce in the growing imperial cult, which Christians must reject. Christianity proselytises—far more than Judaism or any form of polytheism.[100] Christian mission first targets fellow-Jews, generally unreceptive, defensive of their contrary interpretation of Judaism, and anxious about their own position vis-à-vis Rome and local pagans. Similarly, paganism's apparent pluralist tolerance has its own boundaries[101] and economic anxieties. Disorder inevitably results, illimitably, because Christians must 'witness until the ends of the earth', whatever the cost. Rival world empires must collide. 'Witnessing' entails both 'telling' and 'living' the story, hence construction of the Christian life (service, healing, poverty, communism, peace, and partial separatism), inevitably and radically opposed to pagan ways of life and Roman conceptions of power and empire, hence relentless and implacable Christian inversions. The clash of values and authority is elemental. And if pagans misinterpret the 'revolutionary' implications of Jesus' 'resurrection' and kingship, their misinterpretation is largely chronological. For Christianity will win, polytheism lose, the Roman empire, demonic, like all worldly empires, fall, and the Ephesian silversmiths go bust. The eschatological perspective cannot be parked: it is already inaugurated and Christians must cooperate with God in promoting and realising it.

[[103]] But Luke seeks to persuade Romans (and everybody). To the interrelated charges of Christians' causing *stasis*, being revolutionary, and being 'new', he makes a range of replies. (1) Disorder is caused by others, as they react with physical hostility to Christian mission. (2) Christians themselves reject revolution and violence (though not the 'divine violence' of Jesus/God), and embrace peace, so they are entitled to the protection of Roman law, which should have acquitted Jesus and Paul, hence prosecution 'sub nomine' is unjust. (3) Christians participate in Roman life as far as possible (they pay taxes, ply trades,

---

100  Rightly, Rowe (2009) 118.
101  Acts 17.19; Rowe (2009) 168.

welcome, 'serve', and heal others). (4) Christianity is both profoundly[102] new and profoundly not-new. Jesus is a new manifestation of God, the resurrection a new and decisive event in world history which sets the clock ticking towards 'end times' (Acts 3.17–26; 17.30), Christians a new race, and pagans must adopt a new way of life, but Christianity *fulfils ancient* Judaism and Christian eschatology is eternally true. (5) Paradoxically, only Jesus' 'up-rising'/'standing-up' brings *everybody* peace and 'security from falling'. (6) Human unity will be achieved when all the world becomes 'the Christian people'. (God's 'impartiality' is not liberal pluralism, *Roman* unity is rejected.)

Luke's persuasion involves appeal through Roman traditions (literary, philosophical, religious, and legal). All should admire his Classicising skills. Positive exemplarities are extended. Clothing Christianity philosophically builds bridges (strictly one-directional) and justifies dogmatism, missionary zeal, and heroism under persecution. Casting Jesus as Dionysian conveys many truths. Aesthetics and exemplarities aside, such appeals are tactical and provisional (good Romans are 'good' if they accept Christianity; the Christian story triumphs over Classical historiography; pagan philosophical schools will close; Dionysus does not exist). It also involves some anti-Jewishness. This also, however unpleasant, is (mainly) tactical: all humans are sinners. It combines the serious stick (the threat of divine justice, immediate and eschatological) with the serious carrot (everybody's need for 'security from falling', guaranteed by Jesus' 'proven' resurrection, promise of universal 'healing', and 'peace'). This persuader is (mostly) unflinchingly honest about the issues and stakes, and essays that most difficult persuasive task: that of maintaining peace and cooperation with the target, while emphasising fundamental incompatibilities, and arguing the certainty of an outcome which will save the target but which ultimately requires his abandoning practically all defining aspects of his identity except his humanness. Unsurprisingly, Paul did not persuade Nero and his court. But Luke aims to do better.

[104] It is not naïve to ask of Classical historiography whether, in what senses, and to what degree it is true. It is not true that first-century Christians risked their lives, or Romans persecuted, continuously, nor did all Christians take absolutist religious or political stances. To a debatable degree, Luke combines an 'ideal' analysis of Christian–Roman relations with 'true history'. But Classical historiography also probes generals, universals, and futures (Acts 9.34–5):

---

102   Contrast the trivialising curiosity of Antipas (Luke 23.8), Agrippa (Acts 25.22), and Athenians (17.21).

> Peter said to him: 'Aeneas, Jesus Christ heals you. Stand up and make your bed.' And immediately he stood up. And all the inhabitants of Lydda and Sharon saw him, who indeed turned to the Lord.

Peter, of course, like Paul, reached the sick Rome, as all Christian readers (and some Romans) knew. He here heals 'Aeneas' in the name of 'the Healer'; as elsewhere, the healed person's 'standing-up' anticipates (and in a way already instantiates) his final 'standing-up' at the Last Days. This is another 'futuristic', multi-temporal, indeed, ultra-temporal, historiographical narrative.[103]

Whereas Herodotus (1.5.3–4) 'knew' only that human good fortune never remains in the same place and Thucydides (1.1.3; 22.4) could only 'conjecture' on the basis of 'the human thing', Luke 'knew' that his own amazingly ambitious and self-confident text would eventually convert Rome. He proved right. Such was the power of the Christian version of Classical historiography. Luke also 'knew' that conversion of Rome was only a step—albeit major—on the eschatological road. That, however, is a story Classicists may leave to theologians. This paper's conclusion is that Luke-Acts' stance towards Rome is radically different from anything in contemporary Greek literature or thought.[104]

## Bibliography

Alexander, L. C. A. (2005) *Acts in Its Ancient Literary Context: A Classicist Looks at the Acts of the Apostles* (London and New York).

Blumenthal, C. (2011) 'Augustus' Erlass und Gottes Macht: Überlegungen zur Charakterisierung der Augustusfigur und ihrer erzählstrategischen Funktion in der lukanischen Erzählung', *NTS* 57: 1–30.

Cadbury, H. (1921) 'The Purpose Expressed in Luke's Preface', *The Expositor* 21: 431–41.

Cassidy, R. J. (1978) *Jesus, Politics, and Society: A Study of Luke's Gospel* (Maryknoll, N.Y.).

Cassidy, R. J. (1987) *Society and Politics in the Acts of the Apostles* (Maryknoll, N.Y.).

Cook, J. G. (2010) *Roman Attitudes Toward the Christians: From Claudius to Hadrian* (Tübingen).

Downing, F. G. (1988) *Christ and the Cynics: Jesus and other Radical Preachers in First-Century Tradition* (Sheffield).

Goodman, M. (2007) *Rome and Jerusalem: The Clash of Ancient Civilizations* (London and New York).

---

103  Moles (2011a) 151 {above, p. 645}.
104  The nearest parallels, still very distant, are perhaps Dio's *Orations* 13 and 36.

Hendricks, H. (1996) *The Third Gospel for the Third World. Vol. 1: Preface and Infancy Narrative (L. 1:1–2:52)* (Collegeville, Minn.).

Höistad, R. (1948) *Cynic Hero and Cynic King: Studies in the Cynic Conception of Man* (Uppsala).

Horsley, R. A. (1989) *The Liberation of Christmas: the Infancy Narratives in Social Context* (Eugene, Or.).

Horsley, R. A. (2011) *Jesus and the Powers: Conflict, Covenant, and the Hope of the Poor* (Minneapolis).

Johnson, L. T. (1991) *The Gospel of Luke* (Collegeville, Minn.).

Just, A. A., ed. (2003) *Ancient Christian Commentary on Scripture: New Testament III Luke* (Downers Grove, Ill.).

Karrer, M. (1991) *Der Gesalbte: die Grundlagen des Christustitels* (Göttingen).

Kinman, B. (1993) 'Luke's Exoneration of John the Baptist', *JThS* 44: 595–8.

Klauck, H.-J. (2000) *Magic and Paganism in Early Christianity: the World of the Acts of the Apostles* (Edinburgh).

Lang, M. (2008) *Die Kunst des christlichen Lebens: rezeptionsästhetische Studien zum lukanischen Paulusbild* (Leipzig).

Lang, M. (2011) 'The Christian and the Roman Self: the Lukan Paul and a Roman Reading', in C. K. Rothschild and T. W. Thompson, edd., *Christian Body, Christian Self: Concepts of Early Christian Personhood* (Tübingen) 151–73.

MacDonald, D. R. (2003) *Does the New Testament Imitate Homer? Four Cases from the Acts of the Apostles* (New Haven).

Malherbe, A. J. (1985–6) '"Not in a Corner": Early Christian Apologetic in Acts 26:26', *Second Century* 5: 193–210; repr. in id., *Light from the Gentiles: Hellenistic Philosophy and Early Christianity* (Leiden and Boston, 2014) 209–28.

Martin, F. ed. (2006) *Ancient Christian Commentary on Scripture: New Testament V: Acts* (Downers Grove, Ill.).

Mason, S. (2005c) *Josephus and the New Testament*² (Peabody, Mass.).

Millar, F. (1977) *The Emperor in the Roman World (31 BC–AD 337)* (London and Ithaca; 2nd ed., 1992).

Moles, J. L. (2006) 'Jesus and Dionysus in *The Acts of the Apostles* and Early Christianity' *Hermathena* 180: 65–104 [above, Ch. 21].

Moles, J. L. (2011a) 'Jesus the Healer in the Gospels, the Acts of the Apostles and Early Christianity', *Histos* 5: 117–82 [above, Ch. 23].

Moles, J. L. (2011b) 'Luke's Preface: The Greek Decree, Classical Historiography and Christian Redefinitions', *NTS* 57: 1–22 [above, Ch. 22].

Moles, J. L. (2013) 'Time and Space Travel in Luke-Acts', in R. Dupertuis and T. Penner, edd., *Engaging Early Christian History: Reading Acts in the Second Century* (Durham and Bristol, Ct.) 101–22 [above, Ch. 24].

Momigliano, A. D. (1988) 'From the Pagan to the Christian Sibyl: Prophecy as History of Religion', in A. C. Dionisotti, A. Grafton, and J. Kraye, edd., *The Uses of Greek and Latin: Historical Essays* (London) 3–18; repr. in id., *Nono contributo alla storia degli studi classici e del mondo antico* (Rome, 1992) 725–44.

Pervo, R. I. (1987) *Profit with Delight: the Literary Genre of the Acts of the Apostles* (Philadelphia).

Plummer, A. (1901) *A Critical and Exegetical Commentary on the Gospel According to S. Luke*[4] (Edinburgh and New York).

Rowe, C. K. (2009) *World Upside Down: Reading Acts in the Greco-Roman Age* (Oxford).

Sandnes, K. O. (1993) 'Paul and Socrates: The Aim of Paul's Areopagus Speech', *JSNT* 50: 13–26.

Seaford, R. (2006) *Dionysos* (London and New York).

Shorrock, R. (2010) *The Myth of Paganism: Nonnus, Dionysus and the World of Late Antiquity* (London).

Sleeman, M. (2009) *Geography and the Ascension Narrative in Acts* (Cambridge).

Sterling, G. E. (1992) *Historiography and Self-Definition: Josephos, Luke-Acts, and Apologetic Historiography* (Leiden).

Still, J. I. (1923) *St. Paul on Trial: a New Reading of the History in the Book of Acts and the Pauline Epistles* (London).

Streeter, B. L. (1930) *The Four Gospels: A Study of Origins* (London).

Talbert, C. H. (1974) *Literary Patterns, Theological Themes, and the Genre of Luke-Acts* (Missoula).

Tannehill, R. C. (1986–90) *The Narrative Unity of Luke-Acts: a Literary Interpretation*, 2 vols. (Philadelphia).

Walaskay, P. W. (1983) *'And So We Came to Rome': The Political Perspective of St Luke* (Cambridge).

Wallace, R. and W. Williams (1993) *The Acts of the Apostles: a Companion* (London and New York).

Woodman, A. J. (2012) 'Making History: the Heading of the *Res Gestae*', in id., *From Poetry to History* (Oxford) 181–200.

Yamazaki-Ransom, K. (2010) *The Roman Empire in Luke's Narrative* (London and New York).

CHAPTER 26

# Matthew the Mathete: Sphragis, Authority, Mathesis, Succession, and Gospel Truth

*Edited by Justin Reid Allison*

## Introduction*

Mark Kiley's hypothesis[1] that the author of 'The Gospel according to Matthew' (hereafter Matthew—and similarly for the other gospels) puns on the name of 'Matthew' (Μαθθαῖος) in Matthew 9.9 so as to emphasise the theme of discipleship (μαθητής being the Greek for 'disciple') has variously been noted neutrally, accepted, rejected, and ignored;[2] other scholars have made similar proposals about other passages in Matthew;[3] overall, it is fair to say that such readings have made relatively little impact. This paper presents new considerations in favour of these readings, brings them together, and argues that the author of the gospel uses systematic and organic punning devices in order to

---

\* A first version of this paper was given at the Durham New Testament Seminar on 7th May 2012; I thank Professor John Barclay as chair and all who commented. The paper is a spin-off from Moles (2011a). I thank the anonymous readers, Professors Mark Goodacre and Mark Kiley, and my fellow-editor for help of various kinds; Professor A. J. Woodman and Dr Clemence Schultze for stimulating conversations; and Dr Ed Kaneen for bibliographical alerts. I have raided Professor Scott E. Noegel's valuable bibliography at http://faculty.washington.edu/snoegel/Wordplay-Bibliography.pdf. {dead link; cf. now Noegel (2021)}. The paper tries to be as economical as possible, but, since it seeks both Classicist and NT readers, on each side it provides 'excess' documentation for the benefit of the other side. Translations are original.

1  Kiley (1984).
2  Thus, e.g.: Luz (2001) 32 n. 21, Bauckham (2006) 111 and Sand (1986) 196 reject it; Davies–Allison (1991) 99 are ambivalent to Kiley's proposal ('there could be truth' in it); Hagner remarks ([1993] 237) that Kiley's hypothesis 'remains … ingenious speculation'; Nolland (2005) 384 notes Kiley's article in the bibliography for his treatment of 9.9–13, but never cites it directly; similarly, Turner (2008) 252; Harrington (1991) 126, 130 notes Kiley's hypothesis as a possibility; Carter (1996) 26–8 notes Kiley and the hypothesis approvingly as a possibility; Boxall (2015) 34 notes Kiley's article approvingly; France (2007) 352 seems to ignore the article and the suggestion.
3  Robert Gundry, for example, links the introduction of the name Peter in Mt 4.18 against Mk as part of the same phenomenon as 9.9, to avoid the pre-conversion name and use the post-conversion name to emphasize discipleship (Gundry [1982] 166); see also Rastoin (2002).

convey the claim that he was the disciple of Jesus who bore that name, a claim which forms the basis of other important claims and which underpins the whole didactic thrust of this gospel, though the primary claim is not itself true. If accepted, this argument has wide implications, alike for the reading and appreciation of Matthew and of the author's creative rewritings of Mark, for the questions of gospel anonymity or titulature, of pseudepigraphy (currently a hot topic both in NT and in Classical scholarship),[4] of gospel community, of rivalry among the evangelists, of 'gospel truth', and of the Greekness of the gospels. On this last question, while the importance of the Hebrew bible cannot be overestimated, the texts' Greekness can very easily be underestimated, because so many scholars are more interested in 'the historical Jesus' who lies (somewhere) behind the gospels than in the texts themselves. Yet it is clear in this case, as in others,[5] that important meanings are being thought through, even created, in the Greek.

At this stage, I make no assumptions about the author beyond the fact that he is cross-cultural (writing in Greek, knowing Aramaic and Hebrew, and deeply versed in the Hebrew bible; it matters little for my argument whether he is Jewish or Gentile; obviously, if he is Gentile, he cannot be Jesus' disciple Matthew, but this question, for which the text itself is the only worthwhile evidence, cannot easily be resolved).[6] Other assumptions will be added as necessary. For the sake of convenience, and for the time being, I call this author, without prejudice, 'Matthew' (and similarly for the other evangelists).

The name 'Matthew' in Hebrew (מַתִּתְיָהוּ, *mattityāhû*) means 'gift of Yah[weh]',[7] but this is of minor relevance to this paper,[8] whose central concern is with the Greek form Μαθθαῖος (which comes with unimportant variations). In my own title the noun 'mathete' (~ μαθητής) does not really seem to exist, although it is a South African name (both a Christian name and surname),[9]

---

4   E.g., Classical Pseudepigraphy: Speyer (1971); von Fritz (1972); Brox (1977); R. E. Brown (1997) 585–9 (bibliography on 588–9), 630, 668–71; Baum (2001); Rosenmeyer (2001); Parsons (2012); Pseudepigraphy in the New Testament: Metzger (1972); Lane Fox (1991) 126–36; Frey–Rothschild–Schröter (2009), esp. the introduction by Janßen–Frey (3–16); Ehrman (2011), esp. 22–5; 219–50; Porter–Fewster (2013).
5   Cf. Moles (2011a).
6   Cf., e.g., Davies–Allison (1988) 7–58; Meier (1992) 625–7.
7   Discussion: Williams (1995) 91–2; for discussion of the Greek name Μαθθαῖος generally, see Bauckham (2006) 107.
8   Ancient readers able to think bilingually in Greek and Hebrew (or Aramaic) might find some relevance in the Hebrew meaning at Matthew 1.21 and 27.32–50 (see Moles [2011a] 127, 142–3 {above, pp. 621, 636–7}).
9   See, e.g., http://za.linkedin.com/pub/mathete-maeteletja/2b/523/a99; http://za.linkedin.com/pub/solomon-mathete/14/887/194. 'Mathete' is an African version of 'Matthew'.

and it has been used in computing, business, and popular religious contexts (in the latter case, sometimes ignorantly).[10] There is, however, no reason why it should not exist, on the analogy of such words as 'aesthete' (~ αἰσθητής) or 'athlete' (~ ἀθλητής). 'Mathete' naturally allows 'matheteship' (the state of being a mathete). I also use 'mathete' as a transitive verb (in the sense of 'make [someone] a disciple'). I coin the verb 'math', meaning 'learn'. The noun 'mathesis' does exist, although it is archaic. I use it both in its general sense of 'learning' and also, innovatively, in the specific sense of 'lesson'. The adjective 'mathetic' also exists; I use it in senses appropriate to our context. The point of these easy extensions of language is to reflect in the English translation persistent verbal relationships in the original language[11] that are unregistered in the standard translations, either because they have not been seen, or because they are accorded no significance, or because they are thought impossible to reproduce.

## 1 Gospel Titles and the Classical *Sphragis*

I begin with general questions of titulature, because the presence or absence of a *titulus*[12] on our text has direct bearing on the enquiry, and because these questions raise more general issues of authorial anonymity or identity and authority.

Majority opinion in NT scholarship holds that the four so-called canonical[13] Gospels were originally anonymous texts, for use in individual church communities,[14] and it is of course true that, in contrast to many ancient texts, none of them contains *explicit* 'internal' self-naming. According to this majority opinion, *any* self-naming by the author, explicit or implicit, external or internal, would be intrusive and would impede the proclamation of the Gospel *tout court*, since 'the Gospel [εὐαγγέλιον] of Jesus Christ' (Mark 1.1) is a Gospel that is not only 'about' Jesus Christ but also 'proclaimed by' him. The thus anonymised gospels are supposed to be following the 'Near Eastern Tradition'

---

10  E.g., http://www.infosreda.com/en/projects/mathete/; http://www.yellowusapages.com/ks/city-wichita/company-146417-mathete-company.html; http://www.stevesweetman.com/disciple/whatis.htm.
11  On the translation principles: Moles (1988) 16–18; Woodman (2004) xxii–vi.
12  The mechanics: Capponi (2011) 262; Bauckham (2006) 303; a telling recent example of their interpretative consequences: Capponi (2011) 247–50; the difference between papyrus rolls and (Christian) codices is here immaterial.
13  On the gospel 'canon' see, e.g., Streeter (1930); Watson (2006); Hill (2010), with the review of Wimmer (2012).
14  Representative discussions: Streeter (1930) 500–1; Lane Fox (1991) 126–9; Ehrman (2011) 223–5; see now the review of discussions in Gathercole (2018).

of anonymous authorship,[15] or even to be representing their texts as more or less seamless continuations, or fulfilments, of anonymous books about the history of the Jewish people in the so-called Old Testament.[16] A partial Classical parallel for this would be Xenophon's *Hellenica*, if, as seems to be the case, that work represents itself as being part of the same text as Thucydides' incomplete *Peloponnesian War*.[17] The majority opinion also appeals to allusions, in the earliest Christian *testimonia*, to 'the Gospel' *simplex*.[18]

Now the titles of 'The Gospel according to "x"' can be traced back to somewhere in the second century (the different scholarly datings within that century need not concern us),[19] but on the majority opinion these titles are later additions, added to supply apostolic authority in an age of proliferating and competing gospels and themselves implicated in the process of constructing a 'canon' of Gospels. Martin Hengel, however, persistently argued that the generic title 'the Gospel according to "x"' is original;[20] some have accepted his arguments;[21] most have not. Certainly, in the ancient world, absence of internal self-naming does not automatically entail anonymity, because many such texts were clearly not received by readers as anonymous, either because they already knew who the author was, or because his name was contained in the external titulus, or both.

Hengel and others who advocate the name of an evangelist as being part of an original title counter the argument of 'intrusive individualism' by emphasising various circumstances: the positive advantages of having named witnesses as sources of authority; the fact that the name formula 'according to "x"' is very unusual in ancient titles and falls significantly short of the simple genitive of possession or source normally used to designate authorship, thus preserving the key notion of 'the Gospel' as being essentially about, and proclaimed by, Jesus himself, and conveying authenticity through its very distinctiveness; the contrasting need to distinguish one Gospel-writing from another; and the fact that even in the period when the titles are undoubtedly available Christian writers can still speak of 'the Gospel' *simplex*,[22] as of course they still can today. Moreover, some scholars hold that the Gospels were not, or were

---

15  E.g., Lane Fox (1991) 127.
16  Thus, e.g., Ehrman (2011) 223–5.
17  Discussion, e.g., Gray (1989) 1–9; D. Thomas (2009) xxiv–v.
18  E.g., Ignat. *Philad.* 8.2; *Didache* 8.1–2; 11.3–4; 15.3.
19  Davies–Allison (1988) 8; Hill (2010) 207–25.
20  Hengel (1985) 65–72; (2000) 48–56.
21  E.g., Stanton (1974) 78; Luz (2007) 59; Bauckham (2006) 111; 300–5.
22  Hengel (1985) 71.

not only, 'community' texts but were, or were also, 'international' Christian texts, whence an additional stimulus towards differentiating Gospels by their human authors.[23]

A further circumstance is that, while the Gospels are undoubtedly Gospels, they are also—and, it has been well argued, primarily—Classical biography,[24] a genre of which it is less plausible to posit authorial anonymity. Further again, Luke is—it is generally (though not universally) agreed—part of a two-book unity (Luke-Acts), which—it has been persuasively argued—represents itself as Classical historiography,[25] also a genre of which it is less plausible to posit authorial anonymity. Moreover, the author of that double work rests part of his claim to authority on his own alleged experiences—experiences that at least some of his first readers are expected both to know about and to find exemplified within the developing text.[26] He also implicitly glosses other gospels as Classical historiography, and, if this may be thought tendentious, it at least shows that it is a *possible* generic classification of them by a highly competent Christian reader.[27] Hence, again, anonymity becomes less plausible. Advocates of the titles as original also argue that the Gospels, like ancient books in general, would *naturally* have had *tituli*, and that anonymous Gospels would have posed early Christians awkward and embarrassing questions of provenance and—precisely—of authority. Consideration must also be taken of the evidence of Papias, bishop of Hierapolis (1st–2nd century), as transmitted by Eusebius, bishop of Caesarea (260–340 CE; *HE* 3.39). This evidence, difficult and disputed as it is, and, on practically any view, certainly not of unimpeachable reliability,[28] nevertheless appears to establish an early Christian perception (say, by 90 CE), deriving apparently from one of Jesus' longest-lived mathetes, of two named Gospels written by Matthew and Mark, the former, it seems, being taken as Jesus' disciple of that name. There is no consensus among NT scholars over the Mark claim; the Matthew claim is certainly garbled. But in a

---

23  E.g., Bauckham (1998); critique, e.g., Boring (2006) 15–16.
24  Burridge (1992); (2013); Frickenschmidt (1997).
25  E.g., Plümacher (2006); Moles (2011b) 464–9 {above, pp. 589–94}; cf. also Moles (2011a) 119–23 {above, pp. 613–17}.
26  This is a controversial view, but see Luke 1.1–4, with Moles (2011b); the crucial point is that παρηκολουθηκότι ('having closely followed') covers *both* 'the events' *and* 'the eye-witnesses', and that the latter application *anticipates* the author's *physical* following of Paul in the famous, or notorious, 'we-passages' of Acts.
27  Luke 1.1–4 with Moles (2011b) 461–9 {above, pp. 587–94}.
28  Endless discussion: e.g., Streeter (1930) 17–22; Hengel (1985) 47–50, 69–70; Davies–Allison (1988) 8–17; Sanders–Davies (1989) 8–16; Bauckham (2006) 12–38, 202–39, 412–37; Hill (2010) 207–25.

general way Papias supports the notion of named Gospels, and this fairly close to the time of their actual composition.

Clearly, claims, or denials, concerning the title may naturally also involve both claims, or denials, that our Gospel goes back—in some way or other—to the disciple of Jesus named Matthew, and datings of the Gospel (obviously, the later the dating, the more difficult authorship—or at least direct authorship—by one of Jesus' own mathetes). And with the Gospels, as with many other NT texts, there is of course also the possibility of so-called 'pseudepigraphy', however that admittedly diverse category is understood and evaluated. A pragmatic and non-prejudicial gloss on the term would be: 'writing of which the named author is not the real author'.[29] The phenomenon of course also occurs in the Greek and Roman worlds, and in relevant historiographical and biographical contexts, for example, the Athenian Xenophon's original attribution of his own *Anabasis* to 'Themistogenes of Syracuse',[30] the Hellenistic Hegesianax' attribution of his own *Troica* to the fictitious Cephalon of Gergis,[31] or the teasing claim to plural authorship by the single author of the late fourth-century *Historia Augusta*.[32]

It is worth noting, however, that on one account the hypotheses of originally anonymous Gospels and of originally named Gospels are not as incompatible as they at first sight seem. To quote Streeter:

> a poem or a pamphlet may lose little by being anonymous—sometimes, indeed, it may gain in effect; but a record of events, many of them of a marvellous description, purporting to give an authentic account of one whose deeds, words, and divine nature were a matter of acute controversy, would carry no weight at all if by an unknown author. In a work of this kind, therefore, anonymity implies that it was originally compiled for the use of some particular church which accepted it at once as a reliable authority, simply because it knew and had confidence in the person or committee who produced it.[33]

---

29  See references in n. 4 above.

30  Xen. *Hell*. 3.1.2; Plut. *Glor. Ath.* 345E; Gray (2004) 131–2; Erbse (2010) 494–5; 'Xenophon of Athens' is, I think, playing a knowing and ambiguous game: on the one hand, choosing the pseudonymous authorial name, Themistogenes, 'Rightly born', to bat away the 'strange'/'foreign' implications of his own name and of his own conduct in joining a *Spartan* expedition; on the other hand, locating his fictional historian in Syracuse, tomb of the Athenian Empire.

31  Farrow (1992) 339.

32  Syme (1968) 176–91.

33  Streeter (1930) 500–1 (I discount the possibility of 'committee authorship'); cf. Bauckham's arguments against anonymous community authorship of gospel traditions in Bauckham

On this account, it is possible to have gospels which are formally anonymous but whose communities know—or think they know or claim they know—who their author (in some sense)[34] is or was. No matter whether the so-called 'epilogue'[35] to John is part of the original text or was added later, the 'we' of the John community presumably know—or claim to know—the identity of the 'author' (in some sense) of that text. On the Streeter account, therefore, if an outsider asked a particular Christian community: 'what is the authority of your Gospel?', the reply presumably would have had to be: 'it's the Gospel according to "X"'. In this way, the apparent polarities between anonymous and named Gospels and between first and second centuries can be resolved. Given that the canonical Gospels were written by individuals, it seems difficult to exclude the possibility that at the moment of their first production some other people knew, or thought they knew, or claimed they knew, who had authored them (in some sense of that term).

The case for anonymity is, I believe, further challenged by three circumstances.

Firstly, in many ancient literary contexts, competition with one's predecessors is a recognisable and important phenomenon and one that entails assertion, explicit or implicit, of one's own individuality. It seems psychologically implausible to exclude the gospel-writers from this tendency, Christians though they are. In the case of Matthew, competition with Mark indeed seems sufficiently demonstrable.[36] The author of Luke-Acts is even more competitive in relation to 'many' earlier Gospel-writers.[37] Such competitiveness does not look naturally hospitable to anonymous authorship, certainly in the extreme sense of 'no one knows who is supposed to have written it'.

Secondly, both in the Classical and in the Christian/Jewish contexts names are very important, and may be punned upon.[38] Such punning may be freely creative, that is, etymologies may be suggested that are untrue but that are felt, or made, to be significant.

---

(2006) 290–318; Ehrman rejects the possibility that the gospels were anonymous because the authors were well-known to their recipients (Ehrman [2011] 247–53).

34  I insert this qualification here and elsewhere, because the term 'author' can be used alike of 'original writer', 'original source' (not himself the writer), and 'ultimate authority of a particular tradition'.
35  Which I discuss below, n. 73.
36  See recently Sim (2011).
37  Luke 1.1–4 with Moles (2011b) 481–2 {above, pp. 606–7}.
38  Basic Classical bibliography in Moles (2011a) 125–6 {above, pp. 619–21}; Jewish material at n. 63 below.

Thirdly, and consequently, and for our purposes very germanely, both in the Classical and in the Jewish contexts, writers sometimes inscribe their names within the text. In the Classical context this is done by the device known as the *sphragis* or 'seal', whose original purpose, as the term itself suggests, was to protect authorship in predominantly oral performance contexts, but which subsequently became a sophisticated literary *locus* in texts which had *tituli* bearing their authors' names.[39] The resultant self-naming may be explicit or implicit (by punning). Such authorial self-inscription in Classical texts characteristically takes place at nodal points in the text (the beginning and end of works; the beginning and end of individual books within a multi-book work, and other significant points), and it may involve more or less elaborate punning.

Consideration of some Classical examples of this practice may help to set the scene for the present enquiry. Most of these examples are well known to literary Classicists familiar with the texts concerned, whereas biblical scholars generally fail to acknowledge the very phenomenon, still less possible individual examples of it. I cite alike examples where the author gives his name and puns on it, examples where the author does not give his name but implicitly puns on it, and examples where authority is conveyed without self-naming, because all three forms may be relevant to our Gospel (according to whether there was an original *titulus* with a named author and whether a given community thought it knew its author (in some sense of the term)). I shall then consider some Jewish examples, because, although 'Matthew' is writing in Greek, he could here be 'thinking' in Hebrew. Or indeed he could here be 'thinking' both in Greek and in Hebrew.

The Boeotian poet Hesiod (composing in the 720s BCE) is the first Greek poet to name himself, towards the beginning of his long proem to his great epic about the gods, the *Theogony* (*Theog.* 23–4):

αἵ νύ ποθ' Ἡσίοδον καλὴν ἐδίδαξαν ἀοιδήν,
ἄρνας ποιμαίνονθ' Ἑλικῶνος ὕπο ζαθέοιο.

Who [the Muses] once taught Hesiod beautiful song, when he was shepherding lambs under holy Helicon.

---

39  General discussion: e.g., Kranz (1961); Nisbet–Hubbard (1978) 335–6; McKeown (1987) 93; Rutherford (1997) 46–8; Nisbet–Rudd (2004) 364–5; Roberts (2012); Peirano (2014); further discussion below.

In these and subsequent verses Hesiod puns, rather elaborately, on his name, as meaning 'sending forth ['Ησί-] song [οδον ~ ἀοιδήν]'.[40] Hesiod here refers to himself in the third person, but he immediately switches to the first person (which is the norm but, as we here see, not essential). The general account was of course hugely influential as a Classical account of a poet being inspired by the Muses or other gods of poetry.[41] The account provides a narrative justification for the direct appeal to the Muses to inspire the poet later used by Hesiod himself (*Theog.* 104–15), and by Homer (*Il.* 1.1; *Od.* 1.1) and countless later poets at the beginning of their works. The narrative form has clear parallels in biblical material concerning the divine empowerment of prophets and law-givers.[42] Such Classical poetic appeals to gods and the biblical narratives of divine empowerment also share the claim that the human poet or speaker is operating as the mouth-piece of the god. This could surely provide a parallel for named gospels: the 'good news' proclaimed by the divine Jesus but in different human voices.

The Alexandrian poet Aratus begins his *Phaenomena* as follows (1–5):

Ἐκ Διὸς ἀρχώμεσθα, τὸν οὐδέποτ' ἄνδρες ἐῶμεν
ἄρρητον. μεσταὶ δὲ Διὸς πᾶσαι μὲν ἀγυιαί,
πᾶσαι δ' ἀνθρώπων ἀγοραί, μεστὴ δὲ θάλασσα
καὶ λιμένες· πάντῃ δὲ Διὸς κεχρήμεθα πάντες.
τοῦ γὰρ καὶ γένος εἰμέν.

Let us begin from Zeus, whom we men never leave unspoken. All the streets are full of Zeus, all the agoras of humans, the sea and harbours are also full [of him], everywhere we all have need of Zeus. For we are actually his offspring.

Most scholars nowadays see in 2 ἄρρητον an allusion to Aratus' own name, which would have been on the titulus, in the form ΑΡΑΤΟΥ ΦΑΙΝΟΜΕΝΑ. The effect of the allusion is immediately clever (such is Zeus' all-pervasive presence that the 'unspoken'/'unspeakable' author cannot leave Zeus 'unspoken'). It is noteworthy that this name pun was seen and alluded to by some of Aratus'

---

40   Most (2018) xii–xiv; earlier references in West (1966) 161.
41   West (1966) 151–2.
42   West (1966) 159–61.

fellow-Alexandrian poets[43] and, bilingually, by the Roman poet Virgil,[44] that is, by some of his most sophisticated ancient readers.

Aratus' fellow Alexandrian poet Apollonius begins his *Argonautica* as follows (1–2):

Ἀρχόμενος σέο, Φοῖβε, παλαιγενέων κλέα φωτῶν,
μνήσομαι.

Beginning with you, Phoibos, I shall recall the famous deeds of humans born long ago.

Most scholars today suppose that the immediate invocation of the god Apollo ('Phoibos') contains an allusion to Apollonius' own name (which would have been on the titulus).[45] Again, the allusion is clever, because it is mediated not directly through the name 'Apollo' but through one of Apollo's 'other names'.

Towards the end of the first book of his four-book didactic poem *The Georgics* the Roman poet Virgil is discussing signs from the moon (1.424–37):

> Si uero solem ad rapidum lunasque sequentis
> ordine respicies, numquam te crastina fallet        425
> hora, neque insidiis noctis capiere serenae.
> luna reuertentis cum primum colligit ignis,
> si nigrum obscure comprenderit aëra cornu,
> maximus agricolis pelagoque parabitur imber;
> at si uirgineum suffuderit ore ruborem,              430
> uentus erit; uento semper rubet aurea Phoebe.
> sin ortu quarto (namque is certissimus auctor)
> pura neque obtunsis per caelum cornibus ibit,
> totus et ille dies et qui nascentur ab illo
> exactam ad mensem pluuia uentisque carebunt,        435
> uotaque seruati soluent in litore nautae
> Glauco et Panopeae et Inoo Melicertae.

---

43  Bing (1990) 282–4.
44  Several scholars identify Virgil's reception of Aratus' *leptos* acrostic (e.g., E. L. Brown [1963] 102–3; R. F. Thomas [1988] 139; Feeney–Nelis [2005]), whereas Bing and Katz argue further that Virgil shows signs of having recognized the earlier ἄρρητον pun (Bing [1990] 284; Katz [2008] 111f.). {Further discussion vol. 2, Ch. 73.}
45  E.g., Albis (1996) 22–3.

But if you look back in order at the ravishing sun and the following moons, never will the morrow's weather deceive you, nor will you be caught by the plots of a clear night. When first the moon collects the returning fires, if she collects black air obscurely on her horn, very great will be the rain prepared for farmers and the deep sea; but if she pours virginal redness on her face, there will be wind: golden Phoebe always reddens at the wind. But if at her fourth arising (for this is the most certain authority) she goes through the heavens with her horns unblunted, that whole day and the days which will be born from it will lack rain and winds until the end of the month, and the saved sailors will discharge their vows on the shore to Glaucus and Panopea and Inoan Melicerta.

Here Virgil inscribes and puns on his own name (Publius Vergilius Maro).[46] For (433) 'pura neque obtunsis per caelum cornibus ibit' renders PU-, (431) 'uentus erit; uento semper rubet aurea Phoebe' renders VE-, and (429) 'maximus agricolis pelagoque parabitur imber' renders MA-, the 'backwards' reading according with the initial instruction (425) 'ordine respicies' = 'look back in order'; there are also allusions to 'Virgil''s 'virginity' (430–1) as conveyed by his Greek nickname 'Parthenias'; and the whole process is 'keyed' by the reference to 'the most certain authority', in the first place the lunar 'sign', in the second place the 'most certain author' Aratus, Virgil's direct source here, and in the third place 'the most certain author' of *this* text, Publius Vergilius Maro himself. This is an implicit, and a third-person, *sphragis*. The punning was seen—and imitated—by Virgil's poet friend Horace.[47]

Virgil also closes the fourth and final book of the *Georgics* as follows (4.559–66):

> Haec super aruorum cultu pecorumque canebam
> et super arboribus, Caesar dum magnus ad altum        560
> fulminat Euphraten bello uictorque uolentis
> per populos dat iura uiamque adfectat Olympo.
> illo Vergilium me tempore dulcis alebat
> Parthenope studiis florentem ignobilis oti,
> carmina qui lusi pastorum audaxque iuuenta,          565
> Tityre, te patulae cecini sub tegmine fagi.

---

46   Various treatments: E. L. Brown (1963); R. F. Thomas (1988) 139–40; Feeney–Nelis (2005).
47   Hor. C. 4.12.1, with R. F. Thomas (2011) 228. {Cf. further vol. 2, Ch. 73.}

> I was singing these things about the cultivation of fields and cattle and about trees, while great Caesar is thunderbolting at the deep Euphrates in war and as victor is giving laws throughout willing peoples and is assaying a path to Olympus. At that time sweet Parthenope was nourishing me as I flowered in the studies of ignoble leisure, I who played the poems of shepherds and daring in youth sang of you, Tityrus, under the cover of a spreading beech.

The bilingual pun on 'Parthenope' and 'Vergilium' is again helped by Virgil's own nickname of 'virgin' ('Parthenias').[48] The allusion to 'virginity' helps the contrast between 'Virgil' and 'great' Caesar (to double effect: 'virginity' as opposed to 'potency', and 'femaleness' as opposed to 'maleness'). The combination of the allusion to 'youth' and the 'flowering' imagery may also evoke the Latin etymologies which connected 'uirgo' both with with 'green-ness' ('uiridis') and with 'spring' ('uer').[49]

Similarly, the Roman poet Q. Horatius Flaccus puns on all three of his names;[50] *any* such punning implies a *sphragis*, though some of the contexts are more typical of the developed *sphragis*.[51]

The examples so far have come from poetry. But there is no generic ban on the operation of such practices in prose. The Greek historian Herodotus begins the proem of his great *Histories* as follows:

> Ἡροδότου Ἁλικαρνησσέος ἱστορίης ἀπόδεξις ἥδε, ὡς μήτε τὰ γενόμενα ἐξ ἀνθρώπων τῷ χρόνῳ ἐξίτηλα γένηται, μήτε ἔργα μεγάλα τε καὶ θωμαστά, τὰ μὲν Ἕλλησι τὰ δὲ βαρβάροισι ἀποδεχθέντα, ἀκλεᾶ γένηται.

> This is the production of Herodotus of Halicarnassus, in order that neither should the things born from men come to an end through time, nor should great and wonderful deeds, some produced by Greeks, some by barbarians, be without name/fame.

The basic pattern—author's name plus adjectival form of city of origin—begun by Herodotus' predecessor Hecataeus (*FGrHist* 1 F 1a), remained a norm. In the case of Hecataeus, Herodotus, and Thucydides (1.1.1), it may be thought to

---

48  R. F. Thomas (1988) 139.
49  Maltby (1991) 635, 648. {For Virgil's 'virginity' see vol. 2, Ch. 73.}
50  Reckford (1997); Moles (2007a) 168, 171 {above, pp. 465, 468}.
51  E.g., Hor. C. 4.6.44.

derive directly from epistolary and inscriptional practice,[52] which reminds us that the literary *sphragis* is simply a particular version of a wider complex of imagery based on 'seals', 'signings', and 'buildings'. Further, Herodotus derives organic significance from his own name, which means 'Gift of Hera', because Hera is the goddess of procreation and marriage, and the dominant imagery of the Preface is biological: thus 'Herodotus' is indeed the 'Father' of History, as subsequent 'generations' hailed him.[53]

The Roman historian Tacitus, master of innuendo and the unsaid, vindicator of heroism from silence and oblivion, several times puns on his own name (= 'silent') as historically and historiographically significant and as emblematic of his own historical and historiographical roles. This is, as it were, historiography's 'answer' to the Alexandrian poet, the 'unspeakable'/'unspoken' Aratus.

The proem of Tacitus' *Agricola*, the encomiastic biography of his father-in-law, contains two such puns.[54] In the first case, Tacitus is lamenting the silences imposed by the tyranny of the emperor Domitian, before the present allegedly happy age of Nerva and Trajan (2.3):

> dedimus profecto grande patientiae documentum; et sicut uetus aetas uidit quid ultimum in libertate esset, ita nos quid in seruitute, adempto per inquisitiones etiam loquendi audiendique commercio. memoriam quoque ipsam cum uoce perdidissemus, si tam in nostra potestate esset obliuisci quam *tacere*.

> We have indeed given a huge proof of submission; and just as the former age saw what was the ultimate in liberty, so have we seen what was the ultimate in servitude, even the exchanges of speaking and hearing having been taken away through the inquisitions. We would have lost also memory itself as well as voice, if forgetting had been as much in our power as *tacitness*.

The second case again reviews the effects of Domitian's fifteen-year rule (*Agr.* 3.2):

---

52   Porciani (1997) 3–78; Moles (1999) 44–53 {vol. 2, pp. 382–91}.
53   Moles (2007b) 267 {vol. 2, p. 485}. Like Classical poets, Classical prose writers could also represent themselves as inspired by gods. This includes historians, e.g., Livy, *Praef.* 13; Cass. Dio 73.23.
54   Hedrick (2000) 153–70.

> quid, si per quindecim annos, grande mortalis aeui spatium, multi fortuitis casibus, promptissimus quisque saeuitia principis interciderunt, pauci et, ut sic dixerim, non modo aliorum sed etiam nostri superstites sumus, exemptis e media uita tot annis, quibus iuuenes ad senectutem, senes prope ad ipsos exactae aetatis terminos *per silentium* uenimus?

> What, if over fifteen years, a huge span of mortal life, many have fallen dead by chance befallings and the most energetic by the savagery of the Prince, and a few of us are survivors not only of others but also, so to say, of ourselves, so many years having been taken from the middle of our life, in which young men have come to old age and old men have come to the very bounds of extreme age *in silence*?

In both cases, the effects of Domitianic tyranny are crystallised in the last words of the section, and the first-person plurals, of Domitian's terrorised senatorial subjects, *include* the historian writing the Preface, the 'silent' Tacitus himself. And even now, when Tacitus is free to speak, the use of a verb ('tacere') and a noun ('silentium') which evoke his name when that name is not actually stated maintains a certain piquancy.

In another of his works, the *Annals*, Tacitus justifies his selective account of senatorial business in the light (it is usually thought) of his main historiographical purpose (3.65):[55]

> Exequi sententias haud institui nisi insignis per honestum aut notabili dedecore, quod praecipuum munus annalium reor ne uirtutes *sileantur* utque prauis dictis factisque ex posteritate et infamia metus sit.

> I have decided not to follow through senatorial motions, unless conspicuous through honourableness or of notable dishonour, which thing I regard as the highest function of annals, that virtuous actions *not be left in silence* and that to wicked words and deeds there should be fear from posterity and infamy.

---

55   Moles (1998) 101f. {vol. 2, pp. 278f.}, as opposed to Woodman (1988) 76–101, 180–5; Martin–Woodman (1989) 1–10, esp. n. 4, where they note differences in their view of Roman historiography compared to those of S. Usher, M. Grant, C. W. Fornara. See critique of Woodman's thesis in Henderson (1990) 196–7 n. 16.

Here again, the historiographical statement is both general and specific to 'Tacitus', who cannot remain 'silent' about extremes of moral behaviour in the politics of the Tiberian age.

The pun recurs in Tacitus' treatment of the trial and death of the historian Cremutius Cordus under the by now tyrannical emperor Tiberius (*Ann.* 4.34–5). Tacitus gives the 'damned' his own *sphragides*.[56]

Tacitus' great successor, the fourth-century Ammianus Marcellinus, ends his *History* as follows (31.16.8–9):

> His diebus efficacia Iulii magistri militiae trans Taurum enituit salutaris et uelox. Comperta enim fatorum sorte per Thracias, Gothos antea susceptos, dispersosque per uarias ciuitates et castra, datis tectioribus litteris ad eorum rectores, Romanos omnes, quod his temporibus raro contingit, uniuersos tamquam uexillo erecto, uno eodemque die mandauit occidi, exspectatione promissi stipendi securos ad suburbana productos. Quo consilio prudenti sine strepitu uel mora completo, orientales prouinciae discriminibus ereptae sunt magnis. (9) Haec ut miles quondam et Graecus, a principatu Caesaris Neruae exorsus ad usque Valentis interitum pro uirium explicaui mensura: opus ueritatem professum numquam, ut arbitror, sciens silentio ausus corrumpere, uel mendacio. Scribant reliqua potiora, aetate doctrinisque florentes. Quos id, si libuerit, aggressuros, procudere linguas ad maiores moneo stilos.

> During those days the efficiency of Julius, master of the soldiery across the Taurus, shone forth as salutary and swift. For on learning of the ill-fated events in Thrace, by rather concealed letters to their rulers, who were all Romans (a thing that happens rarely in these times), he gave orders that the Goths who had been admitted before and were scattered through the various cities and camps, should be enticed to come without anxiety into the suburbs in the hope of receiving the pay that had been promised them, and there, as if on the raising of a banner, should all be slain on one and the same day. Which prudent plan having been completed without confusion or delay, the eastern provinces were snatched from great dangers. (9) These things, beginning from the principate of Nerva Caesar down to the death of Valens, I, as a soldier once and a Greek, have expounded to the measure of my ability, never (as I believe) knowingly daring to corrupt through silence or through falsehood a work which professed truth. Let abler men write the rest, who are in the prime of life and

---

56   See Moles (1998) 155–6 {vol. 2, pp. 333–4}.

learning. But those who, if it pleases them, will undertake such a task, I advise to beat their tongues to greater styles.[57]

The start of section 9, the very last section of the History, functions as a *sphragis*. The combination of the historiographical starting-point (the era of Nerva, which Tacitus himself, despite several promises, never got on to),[58] of the Tacitean style, and of the use of the noun 'silence' 'sign' him as a historiographical 'successor' of 'Tacitus'; the failure to give his own name (which would of course have been on the *titulus*) further imitates 'Tacitus', though *qua* Marcellinus' (~ 'marceo' = 'to be withered, flabby, weak' > 'macer' = 'thin') Ammianus puns ironically against his name ('prime of life', 'greater'). On the other hand, the claim that he had 'never ... knowingly dared to corrupt through silence ... a work which professed the truth' could be read as bettering the Tacitus of the *Agricola*. The 'revelation' of his identity as a 'Greek' (further pointed by the emphasis in the previous section on true Romans) contributes to the ironic self-depreciation and elaborate ironies of the last two sentences.

So much for Classical poetry and historiography. The *sphragis* technique is also found among philosophers, including Antisthenes, Plato, Aristotle, Bion, Epicurus, and Dio Chrysostom (and, again, Horace, to the extent that his *persona* is sometimes philosophical).

The *sphragis* technique can include 'hostile take-overs' of rivals' names: so Hesiod 'out-Homers' Homer (*Theog.* 39 ὁμηρεῦσαι), Virgil 'out-fights' 'Calli*machus*' (*Georg.* 3.46 'pugnas'), Horace will be more 'perennial' than Ennius (*C.* 3.30.1 'perennius'), Ammianus rejects 'Tacitean' 'silence' (above).

And it hardly needs stressing that a *sphragis* can be pseudonymous.[59] Much more could be said, but this is more than enough for present purposes.

Classical authors can be creative and ingenious in inscribing their names, explicitly or implicitly, inside their texts, and Classical authors can here include ancient historical writers. When John Marincola comments on the practices of the imitators of Thucydides and Herodotus who were castigated by Lucian,[60] 'this mindless imitation reveals that no new conventions were being utilised, and suggests the exhaustion of what, after all, hardly lent itself to much creative imitation', the latter judgement seems to understate the

---

57   Discussion: e.g., Matthews (1989) 454–6, 461–4, 551 n. 23; Barnes (1998) 65–6; Kelly (2008) 318–21 (with bibliography in his n. 2).
58   E.g., Tac. *Hist.* 1.1 with Kraus–Woodman (1997) 90–2.
59   Cf. nn. 30–2 above.
60   Marincola (1997) 271–5 ('Appendix 11: Name and Nationality') at 275.

creative potential of the device in historiography, at least in the pens of its most inventive practitioners.

From such Classical possibilities there is no *a priori* reason to exclude Matthew. Not only can that Gospel be classified as Classical biography, but it also falls more generally into the category of ancient historical writing.[61] It can also reasonably be read as possessing affinities with Classical philosophical writing (through the representation of Jesus and his mathetes), and it was indeed sometimes so read in the ancient world.[62] Thus the Classical philosophical *sphragis* can also be relevant. It is worth noting that the opening lines of Aratus' *Phaenomena* were known to some Jewish and Christian writers, because line 5 is used both by the Jewish Aristobulus (F 1) and by the (probably) Gentile author of Acts of the Apostles (17.28) in their proselytising and philosophical appeals to Gentiles.

One might not expect a Gospel-writer to display the same degree of creativity and ingenuity as some of the Classical authors considered above, but there can of course be reasonable qualitative variation between authors in this area, as in others, and in the event, as I shall try to demonstrate, our Gospel-writer will show himself to be quite sufficiently creative for his particular purposes.

Nor of course need we confine ourselves to Classical parallels. Word play, puns of all kinds, name puns, acrostics, implicit etymologies and the like are abundantly attested in the Jewish material (as also of course in much other Near Eastern material).[63] Some of this verbal playing is as complex as anything in the Classical material. And name puns can be used to convey authorship.[64] General use of *sphragis* imagery is common in the Old Testament.[65] It so happens that OT scholars do not use the term *sphragis* of the phenomenon of literary self-naming,[66] but the phenomenon itself frequently occurs (and the term might indeed usefully be introduced into OT scholarship). For example, Jewish tradition held that the Pentateuch (the first five books of the Hebrew bible) was written by Moses. A series of passages within the Pentateuch itself describe Moses, who receives a 'call' from God of the same general type as Hesiod's, writing down commands from the Lord (Exodus 17.14; 24.4; 34.27; Deuteronomy 31.9,

---

[61] See n. 25 above.
[62] See, e.g., *The Gospel of Thomas* 13 (second century).
[63] See, e.g., Casanowicz (1893); Guillame (1964); Glück (1970); Garsiel (1995); Noegel (2000).
[64] E.g., in Isaiah 12.1–3; 35.3–5; Micah 7.18; Malachi 3.1; Hosea 1.7; Song of Songs 1.1, 4; 8.10–11, as argued by Garsiel (1995).
[65] E.g., σφράγις: LXX Ex 28.11, 21; Sir. 17.22; Sol. 8.6; Hag. 2.23; Hebrew *ḥôtām*: Ex 28.11, 21; Jer 22.24; Ezek 28.12; Job 38.14; 41.7.
[66] So I am reliably informed by members of the Durham Department of Theology and Religion.

24–6), thrice explicitly in a book (*Exodus* 17.14; Deuteronomy 31.9, 24–26). Later books of the bible then refer to Moses as having written the relevant books (Joshua 8.31–4; 2 Chronicles 34.14). The NT then assumes Moses' authorship of the Pentateuch (Matthew 19.7–8; 22.24; Mark 7.10; 12.24; Luke 24.44; John 1.17; 5.46; 7.23; Acts 26.22; Romans 10.5), the 'NT' here consisting of the figures of John the Baptist, Jesus, Paul, and the evangelists, including our 'Matthew'.

A similar case is the alleged authorship of 1–2 Samuel by the prophet Samuel, accepted, for example, by the Jewish historian Josephus (*Ap.* 1.37–43). In these books not only does Samuel receive a divine 'call' (again like Hesiod's) but his name is repeatedly and richly punned upon as that of the central character in the narrative.[67] Similarly, *Isaiah*, which begins 'The vision which Isaiah, son of Amos, saw, which he saw against Judaea and against Jerusalem, in the kingship of Ozias, and of Joatham, and of Achaz, and of Ezekias, who were kings over Judaea. Hear, heaven, and hearken, earth, because the Lord has spoken …' (1.1–2), and which includes an account of Isaiah's vision of the Lord and his subsequent 'call' (6.1–13). Even more explicit is the example of the prophet Hosea:[68] Hosea 1.1–2 'The word of the Lord, which came to Hosea the son of Beeri, in the days of Ozias, and Joatham, and Achaz, and Ezekias, kings of Judah, and in the days of Jeroboam son of Joas, king of Israel. (2) The beginning of the word of the Lord to Hosea. And the Lord said to Hosea …'. Similarly, Joel: Joel 1.1 'The word of the Lord, which came to Joel, the son of Bathuel. (2) "Hear these things, elders, and hearken all you who inhabit the land"'. OT scholars tend to refer to such prologues as 'superscriptions' or 'titles'. They illustrate how 'titular' material can 'migrate' to the start of the actual text in the hands of later editors.[69]

This OT material seems to problematise the notion of OT anonymity, at least as regards our context. For to object that the original OT texts were anonymous or not actually written by the people regarded as their authors by later tradition is beside the point, which is precisely that they could be—and were—read by competent later Jewish readers as composed by particular figures, those readings resting on *sphragis*-like literary indications within the texts themselves. Indeed, one could argue that the 'prophetic' *sphragis* at the beginning of some of the prophetic books, where 'the word' is always the Lord's but its direct human recipient is named, furnishes a direct parallel for the Gospel titles,

---

67  See Garsiel (2000).
68  On this type of 'superscription' or 'title' see, e.g., Andersen–Freedman (1980) 143–9; MacIntosh (1997) 1–6.
69  As discussed in Andersen–Freedman (1980) 143–149; MacIntosh (1997) 1–6; Wolff (1974) 3–6; Wildberger (1991) 1–6.

where the Good News is always Jesus' but it is in the version of the particular evangelist. That parallel could support the titles' authenticity. It is true that many scholars make a distinction between OT narrative texts as being anonymous and OT 'wisdom' texts as carrying authors' names, and they then apply this distinction to the NT, hence the gospels' anonymity (according to them),[70] but the distinction itself is hardly a firm one.

As in the OT, so in the NT, general use of *sphragis* imagery is widespread (especially in Paul's letters and in Revelation).[71] Are there, however, direct parallels for the use of the 'literary' *sphragis*? The letters of Paul, the letters pseudepigraphically attributed to Paul, and the letters attributed, whether pseudepigraphically or genuinely, to others all begin with the name of the claimed author (excluding Hebrews and 1 John). This is epistolary convention, but to deny it *sphragis* status is arbitrary, because, as we have seen, the *sphragis* may itself have an epistolary character.[72]

Otherwise, there are two cases. First, the non-Pauline 2 Timothy 2.19, where the word itself is used and the *sphragis* is subordinated within overriding foundation/building/inscription imagery and applied to the Lord:

ὁ μέντοι στερεὸς θεμέλιος τοῦ θεοῦ ἕστηκεν, ἔχων τὴν σφραγῖδα ταύτην· Ἔγνω κύριος τοὺς ὄντας αὐτοῦ, καί, Ἀποστήτω ἀπὸ ἀδικίας πᾶς ὁ ὀνομάζων τὸ ὄνομα κυρίου.

The firm foundation of God stands, however, having this seal: 'The Lord knows those who belong to him', and, 'Let everyone who names the name of the Lord stand apart from injustice'.

Second, the end of John (21.24): 'this is the disciple who is witnessing about these things and who wrote these things, and we know that his witness is true'. Here, admittedly,[73] the *sphragis* is supplied not by the author himself but

---

70   So, e.g., Lane Fox (1991) 90–8, 127; Ehrman (2011) 248–50.
71   E.g., σφράγις: Rom 4.11; 1 Cor 9.2; 2 Tim 2.9; Rev 5.1; 6.1; 7.2; 8.1; 9.4; σφραγίζω: Mt 27.66; Jn 3.33; 2 Cor 1.22; Eph 1.13; Rev 7.3; 10.4; 20.3; 22.10.
72   See discussion of Virg. *Geo.* 4.559–66 above, pp. 745–6.
73   I do not accept Bauckham's convoluted claim ([2006] 369–83) that 'we' in Jn 21.24 in fact stands for 'I', as a '"we" of authoritative testimony', based on his readings of Jn 3.11; 1 Jn 1.1–5; 4.14; and 3 Jn 9–10, 12. Bauckham holds this position in his larger effort to retain the 'beloved disciple' as substantially responsible for the content of the whole gospel, including ch. 21. Bauckham has also intriguingly argued that the names of Peter and John are numerologically embedded at the end of John, the two apostles representing different but complementary Jesus traditions (Bauckham [2002]). I am totally incompetent to evaluate that claim; some NT scholars whom I have consulted describe it as 'interesting'.

by other people, but the more important point is that formally it remains a *sphragis*.

Like the Classical material, then, the biblical material, whether from the Jewish bible or from the NT, indicates that the *sphragis* technique was perfectly at home in the world of our author.

Let us now return to the specific question of gospel titles. As we have seen, that debate involves many variables and many imponderables. It will be apparent that I personally am sceptical of general gospel anonymity, and I certainly do not believe it in the case of Luke-Acts (though I do not believe either that that was the work's title).[74] Gospel anonymity has been too easily assumed, partly, no doubt, because of the general conservatism of NT scholarship, partly also, no doubt, because of Christian scholars' anxiety to 'abnormalise' early Christianity (hence Christian 'good news' needs a 'new' form of writing). Formally, the case cannot be proved one way or the other, but I think that the three further circumstances that we have just considered (i.e., the inherent competition in gospel writing, the importance of names, and the *sphragis* tradition, together introduced on pp. 737–54 above) help to tilt the balance of probability away from anonymity. They also have importance in their own right as considerations which may well affect our reading of Matthew, *whether or not* it originally had a title. In the end this paper's conclusions do not depend on Matthew having had a titulus, though they would be enhanced by it and do themselves, I think, further support it.

As we go into the textual analysis, then, we should not close our minds to the possibility that Matthew originally had a titulus, and we should systematically test how the text would read if it had.

## 2   Analysis of Matthew 9.9–14

We begin our analysis with the account of Jesus' 'call' of the tax-collector in Mark 2.14–18, because the difference between 'Mark' and 'Matthew' over this incident is crucial to the enquiry:

καὶ παράγων εἶδεν Λευὶν τὸν τοῦ Ἀλφαίου καθήμενον ἐπὶ τὸ τελώνιον, καὶ λέγει αὐτῷ· Ἀκολούθει μοι. Καὶ ἀναστὰς ἠκολούθησεν αὐτῷ. (15) Καὶ γίνεται κατακεῖσθαι αὐτὸν ἐν τῇ οἰκίᾳ αὐτοῦ, καὶ πολλοὶ τελῶναι καὶ ἁμαρτωλοὶ

---

74  See discussion of the early titles of Luke and Acts in, e.g., Fitzmyer (1981) 35–8; (1998) 47–51. {Cf. below, Ch. 30, p. 993 for the suggestion that the title may have been Πρὸς Θεόφιλον περὶ ἀσφαλείας.}

συνανέκεινto τῷ Ἰησοῦ καὶ τοῖς μαθηταῖς αὐτοῦ, ἦσαν γὰρ πολλοὶ καὶ ἠκολούθουν αὐτῷ. (16) καὶ οἱ γραμματεῖς τῶν Φαρισαίων ἰδόντες ὅτι ἐσθίει μετὰ τῶν
ἁμαρτωλῶν καὶ τελωνῶν ἔλεγον τοῖς μαθηταῖς αὐτοῦ· "Ότι μετὰ τῶν τελωνῶν
καὶ ἁμαρτωλῶν ἐσθίει; (17) καὶ ἀκούσας ὁ Ἰησοῦς λέγει αὐτοῖς ὅτι Οὐ χρείαν
ἔχουσιν οἱ ἰσχύοντες ἰατροῦ ἀλλ' οἱ κακῶς ἔχοντες· οὐκ ἦλθον καλέσαι δικαίους
ἀλλὰ ἁμαρτωλούς. (18) Καὶ ἦσαν οἱ **μαθηταὶ** Ἰωάννου καὶ οἱ Φαρισαῖοι νηστεύοντες. Καὶ ἔρχονται καὶ λέγουσιν αὐτῷ· Διὰ τί οἱ **μαθηταὶ** Ἰωάννου καὶ οἱ **μαθηταὶ** τῶν Φαρισαίων νηστεύουσιν, οἱ δὲ σοὶ **μαθηταὶ** οὐ νηστεύουσιν;

And going along he saw **Levi the son of Alphaeus** sitting at the tax-office, and he says to him: 'Follow me'. And he stood up and followed him. (15) And it happened that he was lying at table in his house, and many tax-collectors and sinners were lying at table with **Jesus** and his **mathetes**, for there were many and they followed him. (16) And the scribes of the Pharisees saw that he was eating with the sinners and tax-collectors and said to his **mathetes**: 'why does he eat with the tax-collectors and sinners?' (17) And hearing, **Jesus** says to them that 'Those who are strong do not have need of a **healer** but those who are in a bad way. I did not come to call just men but sinners'. (18) And there were the **mathetes** of John and the Pharisees fasting. And they come and say to him: 'Why do the **mathetes** of John and the **mathetes** of the Pharisees fast, and your **mathetes** do not fast?'

The salient factors are as follows:

(1) Although commentators generally 'cut round' 2.14–17 as a separate episode,[75] 2.18 is thematically linked to it by the overriding theme of mathete-ship which is heavily emphasised (no less than six references).

(2) The 'call' of Levi is narratively parallel to the earlier 'calls' of Simon and Andrew (1.16–18) and of James and John (1.19–20):

(16) Καὶ παράγων παρὰ τὴν θάλασσαν τῆς Γαλιλαίας εἶδεν Σίμωνα καὶ Ἀνδρέαν
τὸν ἀδελφὸν Σίμωνος ἀμφιβάλλοντας ἐν τῇ θαλάσσῃ, ἦσαν γὰρ ἁλιεῖς· (17)
καὶ εἶπεν αὐτοῖς ὁ Ἰησοῦς· Δεῦτε ὀπίσω μου, καὶ ποιήσω ὑμᾶς γενέσθαι ἁλι-
εῖς ἀνθρώπων. (18) καὶ εὐθὺς ἀφέντες τὰ δίκτυα ἠκολούθησαν αὐτῷ. (19) καὶ
προβὰς ὀλίγον εἶδεν Ἰάκωβον τὸν τοῦ Ζεβεδαίου καὶ Ἰωάννην τὸν ἀδελφὸν
αὐτοῦ, καὶ αὐτοὺς ἐν τῷ πλοίῳ καταρτίζοντας τὰ δίκτυα, (20) καὶ εὐθὺς ἐκά-
λεσεν αὐτούς. καὶ ἀφέντες τὸν πατέρα αὐτῶν Ζεβεδαῖον ἐν τῷ πλοίῳ μετὰ τῶν
μισθωτῶν ἀπῆλθον ὀπίσω αὐτοῦ.

---

75  *Pericope* is in fact a t.t. used by NT scholars.

(16) And going along the sea of Galilee, he saw Simon and Andrew the brother of Simon casting in the sea, for they were fishermen. (17) And Jesus said to them: 'Come here behind me, and I will make you become fishers of human beings. (18) And straightaway leaving their nets they followed him. (19) And going forward a little he saw James the son of Zebedee and John his brother, they themselves also preparing their nets in the boat, (20) and straightaway he called them. And leaving their father Zebedee in the boat with the hired men they went off behind him.

(3) 'Mark''s subsequent List of the Twelve Mathetes (3.13–19) does not include Levi the tax-collector, but does include the 'called' Simon, Andrew, James, and John, '*James* the son of Alphaeus', and a Matthew, who does not seem to be/is not described as a tax-collector:

(13) Καὶ ἀναβαίνει εἰς τὸ ὄρος καὶ προσκαλεῖται οὓς ἤθελεν αὐτός, καὶ ἀπῆλθον πρὸς αὐτόν. (14) καὶ ἐποίησεν δώδεκα, ἵνα ὦσιν μετ' αὐτοῦ καὶ ἵνα ἀποστέλλῃ αὐτοὺς κηρύσσειν (15) καὶ ἔχειν ἐξουσίαν ἐκβάλλειν τὰ δαιμόνια· (16) καὶ ἐποίησεν τοὺς δώδεκα, καὶ ἐπέθηκεν ὄνομα τῷ Σίμωνι Πέτρον, (17) καὶ Ἰάκωβον τὸν τοῦ Ζεβεδαίου καὶ Ἰωάννην τὸν ἀδελφὸν τοῦ Ἰακώβου (καὶ ἐπέθηκεν αὐτοῖς ὀνόματα Βοανηργές, ὅ ἐστιν Υἱοὶ Βροντῆς), (18) καὶ Ἀνδρέαν καὶ Φίλιππον καὶ Βαρθολομαῖον καὶ Μαθθαῖον καὶ Θωμᾶν καὶ Ἰάκωβον τὸν τοῦ Ἀλφαίου καὶ Θαδδαῖον καὶ Σίμωνα τὸν Καναναῖον (19) καὶ Ἰούδαν Ἰσκαριώθ, ὃς καὶ παρέδωκεν αὐτόν.

(13) And he went up into the mountain and called to him those whom he himself wanted, and they went to him. (14) And he made Twelve, that they might be with him and that he might send them out to proclaim (15) and to have power to cast out the demons. (16) And he made the Twelve, and he added to Simon the name Peter, (17) and James the son of Zebedee and John the brother of James (and he added to them the names Boanaerges, which is: Sons of Thunder), (18) and Andrew and Philip and Bartholomew and Matthew and Thomas and James the son of Alphaeus and Thaddaeus and Simon the Canaanite (19) and Judas Iscariot, who actually handed him over.

(4) 'Luke''s account of Jesus' 'call' of a tax-collector has the same name as 'Mark' does, that of Levi, and includes neither Levi nor a tax-collector in the Twelve. His account of the 'call' looks to be based on 'Mark''s (Luke 5.27–33), which also accords with the usual source reconstruction, whereby Mark is the first gospel

and the main source both of Matthew and of Luke;[76] as before, I extend the quotation of Jesus' 'call' of the tax-collector, to include the incident with the mathetes of John and the Pharisees:

(27) Καὶ μετὰ ταῦτα ἐξῆλθεν καὶ ἐθεάσατο τελώνην ὀνόματι Λευὶν καθήμενον ἐπὶ τὸ τελώνιον, καὶ εἶπεν αὐτῷ· Ἀκολούθει μοι. (28) καὶ καταλιπὼν πάντα ἀναστὰς ἠκολούθει αὐτῷ. (29) Καὶ ἐποίησεν δοχὴν μεγάλην Λευὶς αὐτῷ ἐν τῇ οἰκίᾳ αὐτοῦ· καὶ ἦν ὄχλος πολὺς τελωνῶν καὶ ἄλλων οἳ ἦσαν μετ' αὐτῶν κατακείμενοι. (30) καὶ ἐγόγγυζον οἱ Φαρισαῖοι καὶ οἱ γραμματεῖς αὐτῶν πρὸς τοὺς μαθητὰς αὐτοῦ λέγοντες· Διὰ τί μετὰ τῶν τελωνῶν καὶ ἁμαρτωλῶν ἐσθίετε καὶ πίνετε; (31) καὶ ἀποκριθεὶς ὁ Ἰησοῦς εἶπεν πρὸς αὐτούς· Οὐ χρείαν ἔχουσιν οἱ ὑγιαίνοντες ἰατροῦ ἀλλὰ οἱ κακῶς ἔχοντες· (32) οὐκ ἐλήλυθα καλέσαι δικαίους ἀλλὰ ἁμαρτωλοὺς εἰς μετάνοιαν. (33) Οἱ δὲ εἶπαν πρὸς αὐτόν· Οἱ μαθηταὶ Ἰωάννου νηστεύουσιν πυκνὰ καὶ δεήσεις ποιοῦνται, ὁμοίως καὶ οἱ τῶν Φαρισαίων, οἱ δὲ σοὶ ἐσθίουσιν καὶ πίνουσιν.

And after these things he went out and he saw a tax-collector Levi by name sitting at the tax-office, and he said to him: 'Follow me'. (28) And leaving everything he stood up and followed him. (29) And Levi made a great reception for him in his house, and there was a great crowd of tax-collectors and others who were with them lying at table. (30) And the Pharisees and their scribes muttered to his mathetes saying: 'Why do you eat and drink with the tax-collectors and sinners?' And Jesus answered and said to them: 'Those who are healthy do not have need of a healer but those who are in a bad way. (32) I did not come to call just men but sinners to repentance'. (33) But they said to him: 'The mathetes of John fast frequently and make prayers, and likewise the mathetes of the Pharisees, but your mathetes eat and drink'.

Luke's account of Jesus' gathering of the Twelve (6.12–16) is as follows:

(12) Ἐγένετο δὲ ἐν ταῖς ἡμέραις ταύταις ἐξελθεῖν αὐτὸν εἰς τὸ ὄρος προσεύξασθαι, καὶ ἦν διανυκτερεύων ἐν τῇ προσευχῇ τοῦ θεοῦ. (13) καὶ ὅτε ἐγένετο ἡμέρα, προσεφώνησεν τοὺς μαθητὰς αὐτοῦ, καὶ ἐκλεξάμενος ἀπ' αὐτῶν δώδεκα, οὓς καὶ ἀποστόλους ὠνόμασεν, (14) Σίμωνα ὃν καὶ ὠνόμασεν Πέτρον καὶ Ἀνδρέαν τὸν ἀδελφὸν αὐτοῦ καὶ Ἰάκωβον καὶ Ἰωάννην καὶ Φίλιππον καὶ Βαρθολομαῖον (15) καὶ Μαθθαῖον καὶ Θωμᾶν καὶ Ἰάκωβον Ἀλφαίου καὶ Σίμωνα

---

76  Basic references: Moles (2011a) 124–5 {above, pp. 618–20}.

τὸν καλούμενον Ζηλωτὴν (16) καὶ Ἰούδαν Ἰακώβου καὶ Ἰούδαν Ἰσκαριὼθ ὃς ἐγένετο προδότης.

(12) And it came to pass in these days that he went out into the mountain to pray, and he was spending all night in prayer to God. (13) And when day came, he called to his mathetes, and choosing from them twelve, whom he also named apostles, (14) Simon, whom he also named Peter and Andrew his brother and James and John and Philip and Bartholomew (15) and Matthew and Thomas and James the son of Alphaeus and Simon the one called Zealot (16) and Judas the son of James and Judas Iscariot who became his betrayer.

We are now in a position to turn to 'Matthew''s version. For ease of consultation I first juxtapose the Greek of Mark and Matthew and then give 'Matthew''s version with an English translation. As before, I extend the context to include the mathetes of John and the Pharisees:

Mark 2.14–18

(14) καὶ παράγων εἶδεν Λευὶν τὸν τοῦ Ἀλφαίου καθήμενον ἐπὶ τὸ τελώνιον, καὶ λέγει αὐτῷ· Ἀκολούθει μοι. Καὶ ἀναστὰς ἠκολούθησεν αὐτῷ. (15) Καὶ γίνεται κατακεῖσθαι αὐτὸν ἐν τῇ οἰκίᾳ αὐτοῦ, καὶ πολλοὶ τελῶναι καὶ ἁμαρτωλοὶ συνανέκειντο τῷ Ἰησοῦ καὶ τοῖς μαθηταῖς αὐτοῦ, ἦσαν γὰρ πολλοὶ καὶ ἠκολούθουν αὐτῷ. (16) καὶ οἱ γραμματεῖς τῶν Φαρισαίων ἰδόντες ὅτι ἐσθίει μετὰ τῶν ἁμαρτωλῶν καὶ τελωνῶν ἔλεγον τοῖς μαθηταῖς αὐτοῦ· Ὅτι μετὰ τῶν τελωνῶν καὶ ἁμαρτωλῶν ἐσθίει; (17) καὶ ἀκούσας ὁ Ἰησοῦς λέγει αὐτοῖς ὅτι Οὐ χρείαν ἔχουσιν οἱ ἰσχύοντες ἰατροῦ ἀλλ᾽ οἱ κακῶς ἔχοντες· οὐκ ἦλθον καλέσαι δικαίους ἀλλὰ ἁμαρτωλούς. (18) Καὶ ἦσαν οἱ μαθηταὶ Ἰωάννου καὶ οἱ Φαρισαῖοι νηστεύοντες. Καὶ ἔρχονται καὶ λέγουσιν αὐτῷ· Διὰ τί οἱ μαθηταὶ Ἰωάννου καὶ οἱ μαθηταὶ τῶν Φαρισαίων νηστεύουσιν, οἱ δὲ σοὶ μαθηταὶ οὐ νηστεύουσιν;

Matthew 9.9–14

(9) Καὶ παράγων ὁ Ἰησοῦς ἐκεῖθεν εἶδεν ἄνθρωπον καθήμενον ἐπὶ τὸ τελώνιον, Μαθθαῖον λεγόμενον, καὶ λέγει αὐτῷ· Ἀκολούθει μοι· καὶ ἀναστὰς ἠκολούθησεν αὐτῷ. (10) Καὶ ἐγένετο αὐτοῦ ἀνακειμένου ἐν τῇ οἰκίᾳ, καὶ ἰδοὺ πολλοὶ τελῶναι καὶ ἁμαρτωλοὶ ἐλθόντες συνανέκειντο τῷ Ἰησοῦ καὶ τοῖς μαθηταῖς αὐτοῦ. (11) καὶ ἰδόντες οἱ Φαρισαῖοι ἔλεγον τοῖς μαθηταῖς αὐτοῦ· Διὰ τί μετὰ τῶν τελωνῶν καὶ ἁμαρτωλῶν ἐσθίει ὁ διδάσκαλος ὑμῶν; (12) ὁ δὲ ἀκούσας εἶπεν· Οὐ χρείαν ἔχουσιν οἱ ἰσχύοντες ἰατροῦ ἀλλὰ οἱ κακῶς ἔχοντες. (13) πορευθέντες δὲ μάθετε τί ἐστιν· Ἔλεος θέλω καὶ οὐ θυσίαν· οὐ γὰρ ἦλθον καλέσαι δικαίους ἀλλὰ ἁμαρτωλούς. (14) Τότε προσέρχονται αὐτῷ οἱ μαθηταὶ Ἰωάννου λέγοντες· Διὰ τί ἡμεῖς καὶ οἱ Φαρισαῖοι νηστεύομεν πολλά, οἱ δὲ μαθηταί σου οὐ νηστεύουσιν;

Matthew 9.9–14:

(9) Καὶ παράγων ὁ Ἰησοῦς ἐκεῖθεν εἶδεν ἄνθρωπον καθήμενον ἐπὶ τὸ τελώνιον, **Μαθθαῖον λεγόμενον**, καὶ λέγει αὐτῷ· Ἀκολούθει μοι· καὶ ἀναστὰς ἠκολούθησεν αὐτῷ. (10) Καὶ ἐγένετο αὐτοῦ ἀνακειμένου ἐν τῇ οἰκίᾳ, καὶ ἰδοὺ πολλοὶ τελῶναι καὶ ἁμαρτωλοὶ ἐλθόντες συνανέκειντο τῷ Ἰησοῦ καὶ τοῖς **μαθηταῖς** αὐτοῦ. (11) καὶ ἰδόντες οἱ Φαρισαῖοι ἔλεγον τοῖς **μαθηταῖς** αὐτοῦ· Διὰ τί μετὰ τῶν τελωνῶν καὶ ἁμαρτωλῶν ἐσθίει ὁ διδάσκαλος ὑμῶν; (12) ὁ δὲ ἀκούσας εἶπεν· Οὐ χρείαν ἔχουσιν οἱ ἰσχύοντες ἰατροῦ ἀλλὰ οἱ κακῶς ἔχοντες. (13) πορευθέντες δὲ **μάθετε** τί ἐστιν· Ἔλεος θέλω καὶ οὐ θυσίαν· οὐ γὰρ ἦλθον καλέσαι δικαίους ἀλλὰ ἁμαρτωλούς. (14) Τότε προσέρχονται αὐτῷ οἱ **μαθηταὶ** Ἰωάννου λέγοντες· Διὰ τί ἡμεῖς καὶ οἱ Φαρισαῖοι νηστεύομεν πολλά, οἱ δὲ **μαθηταί** σου οὐ νηστεύουσιν;

(9) And going along from there **Jesus** saw a man sitting at the tax office, **called Matthew**, and he **calls** to him: 'Follow me'. And he stood up and followed him. (10) And it happened that he was lying at table in the house, and see! many tax-collectors and sinners came and lay down beside **Jesus** and his **mathetes**. (11) And when the Pharisees saw they said to his **mathetes**: 'why does your teacher eat with tax-collectors and sinners?' (12) But he heard and said: 'those who are strong do not have need of a **healer** but those who are in a bad way'. (13) Go and **math** what this is: '"I want pity[77] and not sacrifice"'. For I did not come to call just men but sinners'. (14) Then there came to him the **mathetes** of John saying: 'why do we and the Pharisees fast much, but your **mathetes** do not fast?'

The salient factors now are as follows:
(1) Unlike 'Mark' and 'Luke', 'Matthew' names the tax-collector 'called' by Jesus as Matthew, not Levi.
(2) 'Matthew' inserts the instruction and quotation 'Go and math what this is: "I want pity and not sacrifice"' (9.13).
(3) His account of the Twelve (10.1–4) does not include Levi but includes 'James the son of Alphaeus' and 'Matthew the tax-collector':

(1) Καὶ προσκαλεσάμενος τοὺς δώδεκα μαθητὰς αὐτοῦ ἔδωκεν αὐτοῖς ἐξουσίαν πνευμάτων ἀκαθάρτων ὥστε ἐκβάλλειν αὐτὰ καὶ θεραπεύειν πᾶσαν νόσον

---

[77] The standard translation of 'mercy' suits the implicitly judicial context (which is more explicit at 12.1–8 [below p. 770]), as well, of course, as the larger Christian conception of God, but 'pity' can also have judicial resonances (cf. 'a pitiless judge'), it is a more general term, and this breadth of application better suits the context (see pp. 771–2 below).

καὶ πᾶσαν μαλακίαν. (2) τῶν δὲ δώδεκα ἀποστόλων τὰ ὀνόματά ἐστιν ταῦτα· πρῶτος Σίμων ὁ λεγόμενος Πέτρος καὶ Ἀνδρέας ὁ ἀδελφὸς αὐτοῦ, Ἰάκωβος ὁ τοῦ Ζεβεδαίου καὶ Ἰωάννης ὁ ἀδελφὸς αὐτοῦ, (3) Φίλιππος καὶ Βαρθολομαῖος, Θωμᾶς καὶ Μαθθαῖος ὁ τελώνης, Ἰάκωβος ὁ τοῦ Ἁλφαίου καὶ Θαδδαῖος, (4) Σίμων ὁ Καναναῖος καὶ Ἰούδας ὁ Ἰσκαριώτης ὁ καὶ παραδοὺς αὐτόν.

(1) And calling to him his twelve mathetes he gave them power over unclean spirits to cast them out and to tend every sickness and every weakness. (2) And of the twelve apostles, these are the names: first Simon who is called Peter and Andrew his brother, James the son of Zebedee and John his brother, (3) Philip and Bartholomew, Thomas and Matthew the tax-collector, James the son of Alphaeus and Thaddaeus, (4) Simon the Canaanite and Judas Iscariot the one who actually handed him over.

(4) 'Mark', 'Luke' and 'Matthew' at least agree that a 'Matthew' was one of the Twelve, and this is presumably historical (whatever else, a Matthew was always one of the Twelve).

(5) By the same token, the Twelve presumably also always included a 'son of Alphaeus'.[78]

Now, the quality of 'Mark''s narrative of these events is variously assessed by scholars. On one reading, a very common one, both in the ancient and modern worlds, the fact that Levi does not appear in Mark's list of the Twelve is narratively surprising, because (a) he has been given a major narrative 'call'; (b) it looks as if he should be one of the 'mathetes' of 2.15–16; (c) his 'call' is narratively parallel to those of Simon and Andrew and James and John, all of whom do appear in the list of the Twelve. A defence is to argue that Levi's 'call' illustrates the proposition that *anyone*, even a tax-collector, can be a 'mathete' of Jesus, and Jesus' 'mathetes' are not restricted to the Twelve.[79] This defence makes the narrative more coherent, without, surely, making it entirely smooth, because one has to work to find the 'defence', and, while the 'defence' deals to some extent with (a) (because Luke also gives Levi a major 'call' but does not include him in the Twelve), it hardly deals with (c). There is a further disconnect between Levi's 'call' and the list of the Twelve, because Levi is 'the son of Alphaeus' and the Twelve include a 'James son of Alphaeus'. It is possible to

---

78  Recent discussion of the composition of the Twelve: Bauckham (2006) 93–113; Burnet (2014). A sixth factor might be added, that Matthew and Mark both have significant emphases on discipleship in and around the passage, but Luke does not.

79  So, for example, Boring (2006) 80.

argue that they must have been brothers, but 'Mark' certainly does not help his readers (or listeners) on this point. On most views, then, 'Mark''s narrative is narratively messy. Is he, however, informationally sound? That would have to mean, historically: (1) Levi the tax-collector was 'called' by Jesus; (2) Levi was son of Alphaeus; (3) Levi was not one of the Twelve, so he belonged to a wider group of Jesus' followers; (4) James, son of Alphaeus, a member of the Twelve, was (that is, must have been) Levi's brother.

At which point, we must return to the counter-narrative of Matthew. In 'Matthew''s narrative this is the first occasion when a 'Matthew' is mentioned. It is therefore immediately a significant moment, especially as this Matthew, it turns out, is the only apostle, apart from Judas and the two pairs of brothers, James and John and Peter and Andrew, of whom any incident is recorded in this Gospel.[80] That latter factor is the more striking for the seeming insignificance of the person Matthew in the actual history of the early Christian movement.[81] Matthew the character is being emphasised here (and the emphasis will of course seem greater to any readers/listeners who have read/heard Mark).

In assessing 'Matthew''s account, a key source question immediately arises. Both from the indications of this episode itself and from general source reconstructions, it seems virtually undeniable that 'Matthew' (like 'Luke') is here using 'Mark' as his source. The question then is: is he using *only* 'Mark', or is he using 'Mark' *plus* other information?[82]

*Could* he have had other information? A *general* reply is that 'Matthew' generally follows 'Mark' extremely closely, but that he *sometimes* supplements him with genuinely other information (genuinely, that is, as opposed to apparent other 'information' which derives solely from 'Matthew''s free 'redactional' activity).[83] The source question of course crystallises on the fact that 'Matthew' writes 'Matthew' for the tax-collector's name rather than 'Levi'. For this name-difference a whole range of suggestions has been, or can be, made (I here introduce some of my own), with a range of different logics besides the hypothesis of 'Matthew''s having genuinely extra information. Some of

---

80    Streeter (1930) 501, who omits Judas.

81    See discussion in Burnet (2014) 545–90; note also (as Mark Bonnington reminded me) the 'Matthew' of Acts 1.23–6 (Μαθθίας).

82    The details of 'Matthew''s 'redaction' of Mark are helpfully set out by Davies–Allison (1991) 97–8; on the problem of Mk 2.14/Mt 9.9 see also the influential analysis of Pesch (1968); Duling (1992) is very useful on the 'Matthew' instead of 'Levi' problem, though far from exhaustive. I am excluding the possibility that the solution is to be found in the MSS variants, which simply represent early Christians' attempts to solve the problem by force; discussion: Duling (1992) 619–20.

83    Discussion in, e.g., Davies–Allison (1988) 97–127.

these suggestions are individual, some can be combined, some are ancillary to others, some are merely facilitatory of other possibilities. I group them by their different logics and generally in (as it seems to me) ascending order of probability, and I provide *immediate* assessments of some of them, although *fuller* assessments would require their being weighed 'in competition' with other suggestions, and *comprehensive* assessments require consideration of the *whole* literary picture regarding this topic (to which the rest of the paper aspires). The 'list' format is not beautiful but it is functional.

1. 'Matthew' has genuine extra information.

1(a) Levi and Matthew are the same person, and both 'Mark' and 'Matthew' are retailing correct, albeit incomplete, information. This is the 'traditional' 'Christian' solution, which goes back at least to (some of) the Church Fathers.[84] But there are great difficulties, which most NT scholars have regarded as individually or cumulatively insuperable: (i) 'Mark', earlier than 'Matthew', does not say this, even though he has a Matthew in his Twelve: he surely would have said so, if he had thought, or known, the two to be one individual, and he would surely have labelled his Matthew as a tax-collector too; (ii) 'Luke' does not say so, even though he too has a Matthew in his Twelve; this difficulty has increased force if we regard 'Luke' as having read 'Matthew', which would mean that he is actively *rejecting* 'Matthew''s naming;[85] (iii) although nomenclature is a difficult technical area, most NT and Jewish scholars agree that for a Palestinian Jewish male of this period to possess two *common* Jewish names (as both 'Matthew' and 'Levi' are) lies on the range of difficult to impossible.[86]

1(b) Matthew is, as it were, Levi's 'Christian name', either conferred by Jesus when he called Levi, or assumed by Levi himself, when he accepted Jesus' call; so 'Mark' records Jesus as giving extra names to Simon, James, and John (Mark 3.16–17). This runs into difficulties 1(a)i and 1(a)ii above. More importantly, 'called Matthew' in Matthew 9.9 goes decisively against it: Matthew is already Matthew before Jesus calls him. For λεγόμενον cannot be given a loose 'future' sense, as the interplay between λεγόμενον and λέγει shows (below).

1(c) John Chrysostom, *The Gospel of* Matthew, *Homily* 30.1, comments: 'in his account he freely adds his own name and his own bad profession, while the other Gospel writers had generously protected him under another name';

---

84  See, e.g., Luz (2001) 32; note, however, that the Patristic tradition is not unanimous on this (Luz cites as dissenters Heracleon in Clement of Alexandria, *Strom.* 4.9 and Origen, *Cels.* 1.62).
85  For more on this possibility see pp. 777–8 below.
86  Bauckham (2006) 108–10.

similarly, Jerome, *Commentary on* Matthew 1.9.9.[87] This works from the *assumption* that 'Matthew' the author is Matthew the disciple of Jesus; more importantly, in the interests of achieving Gospel 'harmony',[88] it turns its back on the avowed theology of the episode, which is, precisely, that through Jesus 'bad' people can become good. Were 'Matthew' Matthew, he himself would perfectly exemplify that theology, and the point (emphasised of course both by the historical Saul/Paul and by the literary Saul/Paul of Acts) could not be better made.

1(d) 'Matthew' knew that it was Matthew, either through tradition, or because he himself was the man. Unlike the others so far, this explanation entails 'Mark''s actually being wrong. 'Luke' disagrees (and, again, his disagreement has greater force if he has actually read 'Matthew', because he is actively rejecting his version). And the hypothesised sources of 'Matthew''s allegedly superior knowledge are unappealing: with 'tradition', we enter the unverifiable world of 'oral' tradition;[89] with 'he himself was the man', we have 'Matthew' telling the story of his own call using the words of 'Mark' except for the change of name and some small additions (additions which, as we shall see, themselves point in the direction of fictionality).[90]

2. The substitution reflects the interests of 'the Matthew community'. (1(d) is leaning towards this category but differs in that it is making a stronger truth claim.)

(2a) Levi was of no interest to the author of the First Gospel and his readers did know of a Matthew connected with their community and its tradition; thus the substitution. There are no particular arguments against this hypothesis (unless one is—implausibly—so committed to 'Matthew''s historical honesty that one regards it as cynical), though it again enters the unverifiable world of 'oral tradition', and it becomes positively unconvincing when weighed against other considerations (such as 3a–s below).

(2b) If Matthew's identity as a tax-collector (Matthew 10.3) derives from 'Matthew' community tradition, 'Matthew' might have been encouraged to identify 'Matthew the tax-collector' with 'Levi the tax-collector', especially as Jesus' 'mathetes' (at least in the broader sense of the term) did include tax-collectors. The same comments apply as to (2a).

---

87  Simonetti (2001) 177.
88  For this general concern see Watson (2013) 13–61.
89  Cf. in general Eve (2013); Moles (2011a) 125 {above, p. 619}.
90  Meier (1992) 627.

3. 'Mark''s account is a mess and needs cleaning up.

Given that there always was a Matthew in the Twelve, 'Matthew''s substitution of Matthew for Levi, combined with the characterisation of Matthew as a tax-collector in the List of the Twelve, achieves a completely smooth narrative. As a literary scholar (with a literary scholar's characteristic attitudes to 'how texts work' and in particular to 'how ancient historiography works'), I take this broad explanation to be self-evidently true. It also accords with 'Matthew''s general 'redactional strategy' in relation to Mark. 'Literary' in this sense does not mean 'trivially literary', nor does it exclude other 'literary' purposes, nor does it exclude other dimensions, such as 'theological'.

(3a) It is awkward that the tax-collector of Mark 2 is not one of the known Twelve; therefore one of the known Twelve must have been the tax-collector; 'Matthew' chose Matthew *exempli gratia*, or because only Matthew, Mattathias, carried a Levite name (as, of course, did Levi himself).[91] '[T]he apologetic motive, of supplying an apostle's name for one called, seems the obvious solution, rather than supposing that the evangelist knew better than Mark'.[92] This version is not merely 'literary': it involves 'Matthew''s thinking about the data and coming to a rewrite that best fits the facts.

(3b) The episode has a basic character of 'the wandering anecdote' (Jesus 'calls' someone from their day job),[93] so the 'substitution' of Matthew for Levi is relatively easy. This observation seems helpful, though it is 'ancillary'.

(3c) 'Transference of items' (from one historical figure to another) is a common device in Classical biography,[94] so the substitution is relatively easy. On the Classical side, the device does not seem to have disturbed readers, which provides some counterbalance to the perturbation of (some) Christian readers of Matthew. Again, this observation seems helpful, though 'ancillary'.

(3d) Jesus is said to associate with tax-collectors *plural*, whom he is 'calling', so the substitution is relatively easy.

(3e) The presence of several 'twos of a kind' in Mark (two sons of Alphaeus, two Simons, two Jameses) helps the creation of 'a second tax-collector'.

---

91    Goulder (1974) 142; cf. 325: 'The presence of Levi the publican in Mark 2, called just like the first Four Apostles in Mark 1, is an embarrassment when his name does not occur in the list of Twelve in Mark 3. One of the Twelve then must have been the tax-collector, and only Matthew, Mattathias, carries a Levite name. The publican, then, will have been Matthew, son of Alphaeus, a Levite: such logic was congenial to the Chronicler, and many after him'.
92    Goulder (1974) 142.
93    On the type see, e.g., Bultmann (1963) 55–61; Butts (1987).
94    Pelling (1980) 129 = Pelling (2002) 93–4; Moles (1988) 32–45.

(3f) Jesus' conferring of 'names' in Mark 3.16–17 perhaps helped to inspire 'Matthew''s own re-naming of Levi.

(3g) That Matthew is a Levite name also helps (cf. (3b) above).

(3h) 'If ... the First Gospel was originally a pseudepigraphon with the title "According to Matthew" placed above it ... 9.9 could be an attempt to inform the readers about the fictitious author ...'[95] This could be put more strongly: if the protasis is granted, the apodosis would *certainly* follow. That is, readers or listeners would surely infer that what is being described here is the enrolment among Jesus' mathetes of the author (in the most direct sense) of the Gospel. But of course the protasis itself raises many questions. (3h) also necessarily generates the less prejudicial (3i).

(3i) If Matthew had an *original* title of 'The Gospel according to Matthew', *whether or not* that title was genuine or pseudepigraphical, 9.9 makes a claim, *whether or not* genuine, pseudepigraphical, or formal, about the author's identity. In the case of both (3h) and (3i), when, shortly afterwards in the narrative, readers or listeners found 'Matthew the tax-collector' in the list of Jesus' twelve mathetes (10.3), they would find that enrolment had further significance as being the last such and hence climactic. That sense of fulfilment would also seem to favour implicit authorial self-identification.

(3j) It is important to get someone who is recognisably numerate and literate into the Twelve, so that the literary tradition concerning Jesus seems to go back to his own life-time and so that this text acquires its full 'authority' (as deriving from an 'author' who was one of the Twelve). The substitution helps this, because on 'Mark''s account Levi was not one of the Twelve.

(3k) 9.9 might anyway be read as a *sphragis*, the divine 'call' being not only to 'follow' but also, implicitly, to *write*. Such a reading might involve recognition of a significant Christian religious modification—or appropriation—of a pagan poetic or prose trope, though Jewish readers could also read the scene 'Jewishly'.

(3l) 'Matthew' was chosen because, through assonance, the name helps stress the theme of matheteship.[96] As already indicated in the Introduction, this suggestion of Mark (*sic*) Kiley is crucial but I leave it aside for the moment

---

95   Davies–Allison (1991) 98.
96   Kiley (1984); Luz (2001) 32 n. 21, Bauckham (2006) 111, and Sand (1986) 196 reject it; see further references in n. 2 above for other scholarly reactions to Kiley's hypothesis. Luz and Bauckham's rejections will be taken up presently; Sand's remarks concerning Kiley's proposal are very brief, and thus less important (Sand [1986] 196): 'Doch kann dieser Lösungsvorschlag nicht überzeugen (der Verweis auf 1,21.23 (die Deutung des Namens Emmanuel) stützt keineswegs die vorgetragene These)'.

in order to sketch in some ancillary possibilities. Note immediately also that it significantly enhances possibilities (3h)–(3k).

(3m) 'Matthew' presumably noticed the heavy emphasis in Mark on 'matheteship'.

(3n) 'Matthew' noticed that 'Mark' was already punning on Ἰησοῦς/ἰατροῦ (Mk 2.17, and earlier in 2.5, 8, 9).[97]

(3o) In Classical historical texts, when main figures are introduced, there may be significant punning on their name; Matthew itself puns significantly on Jesus' own name from the very beginning of the narrative, and does so also at 9.9, 10 ~ 9.12.[98] Hence it is additionally appropriate that the now-introduced 'Matthew' should generate similar punning. If it is objected that he is not a 'main figure' in the narrative, the answer is that, while he is not a 'main figure' in the immediate Gospel narrative, he has a much larger representative function as mathete *par excellence* and he is also a 'main figure' in the wider 'narrative' that surrounds this particular Gospel in being (allegedly) its direct author. Nor—as before—need we confine ourselves to Classical parallels: the Hebrew bible also furnishes examples.[99]

(3p) The pun would reinforce the proposition that even tax-collectors can become mathetes.

(3q) The overall context—that is, the combination of 9.9–12, 9.13, and 9.14—suggests a rival 'school' 'philosophical' context (the 'mathetes' and 'schools' of Jesus, John, and the Pharisees; the subsequent 'symposium' setting), where the goal is 'mathing'. A pun on 'Matthew' would intensify and crystallise this effect.

(3r) The pun might dramatise the 'institution' of a 'Matthew' school, deriving directly from Jesus himself.

(3s) The pun—within what is obviously a teaching text—might emphasise the point that 'mathetes' should themselves in turn become 'teachers'.

Let us return to (3l), which formed the starting-point of this paper, which is obviously the most critical of all the 'literary' explanations, and upon whose correctness or otherwise several other possibilities depend. The pun is explicitly rejected by two highly distinguished NT scholars, Ulrich Luz and Richard Bauckham.

After introducing Kiley's hypothesis, Luz argues: 'Nowhere else, however, do the names of the twelve disciples have symbolic meaning (with the exception

---

97   See discussion in Moles (2011a) 132–3 {above, pp. 626–7}.
98   E.g., Mt 1.21, 23; 8.5–13; Detailed discussion in Moles (2011a) 136–43 {above, pp. 630–7}.
99   See n. 64 above.

of Matt 16.18, where Peter's name is explained)'.[100] There are several things wrong with this argument (apart, that is, from the strength of the positive arguments for the pun). An allegedly universal principle cannot be allowed to decide a particular case for which there are counter-arguments. The admitted 'exception' logically allows the same possibility here. Lack of explanation does not preclude a pun: writers sometimes explain things, sometimes not. Matthew itself, as we have seen, puns extensively on 'Jesus'–'healer', and that pun is operative here.[101] As elsewhere, one pun may help another.[102] 'Matthew' does not explicitly explain the Μαθθαῖος–μαθήτης connection.[103] Lack of explanation may serve to stimulate readers' interpretation. In *sphragis* contexts, punning is implicit.

Bauckham argues[104] that the idea of punning '[makes] no connection between the occurrence of the name Matthew and the fact that the Gospel is called "according to Matthew"'. But clearly that 'fact' cannot be assumed, still less made the basis of an argument; moreover, there is no logical reason why an original title could not co-exist with, or even be enhanced by, the punning (see already the discussion of Aratus' *Phaenomena* above, pp. 743–4).

Since these objections fail, let us turn to the positives.

'*Matthew*', in answering Jesus' call, clearly becomes one of Jesus' '*mathetes*'. It is irrelevant (or, for those readers with Hebrew, marginally relevant at most) that the Jewish name מַתִּתְיָהוּ, *mattityāhû*, means 'gift of Yah(weh)'.[105] It is the Greek form Μαθθαῖος, used here and throughout the NT (with small variations), which concerns us. Clearly and undeniably, the sound 'math' is being repeated: 9 Μαθθαῖον, 10 τοῖς μαθηταῖς αὐτοῦ, 11 τοῖς μαθηταῖς αὐτοῦ, 13 μάθετε, 14 οἱ μαθηταὶ Ἰωάννου, οἱ δὲ μαθηταί σου. Note how the repetitions are increased when one includes 9.13 and 9.14 in the context, as neither Kiley nor his critics do. Note how the 'call' *peritome*[106] itself is ring-structured by Μαθ/μάθ. Note also that 'Matthew''s 'redaction' of 'Mark' itself increases the repetitions: by the critical substitution of Μαθθαῖον for Λευίν and by the sandwiching of the 'go and math ...' (μάθετε, 9.13) saying between the 'call' narrative and the contrast

---

100  Luz (2001) 32 n. 21.
101  Missed in Moles (2011a) 139 {above, p. 633}.
102  Moles (2011a) 136–7 {above, pp. 630–1}, on Mt 1.21 (the connection between the name of Jesus (Ἰησοῦς) and the salvation (σῴζω) of God's people through him prepares for the Ἰησοῦς, ἰάομαι connections further on in Matthew).
103  Though he does explicitly link Ἰησοῦς and ἰάομαι, which 'helps' the Μαθθαῖος–μαθήτης association, since ἰάομαι can be used medically (Moles [2011a] 127–31 {above, pp. 621–5}).
104  Bauckham (2006) 111.
105  Williams (1995) 91–2; Bauckham (2006) 107.
106  {Presumably a deliberate pun by JLM; cf. n. 75.}

between Jesus' mathetes and those of John and the Pharisees. One can only say: do the maths!

Such punning falls completely within the parameters both of Classical and of NT name-punning and within the parameters of Classical *sphragis* technique, especially as 'Matthew', following 'Mark', is already punning on Ἰησοῦς/ἰατρός. It is also completely at home in Jewish writing, or thinking, mediated through Greek, both sonic punning and name-punning being widespread in Hebrew and in equivalent Jewish *sphragis* contexts.

I conclude that Kiley's hypothesis is correct. But there is another point, seemingly missed by all translators and all commentators, the interaction between 'called' and 'calls'. The man 'called' Matthew, always the *potential* 'learner'/'disciple', is here *activated* by Jesus' 'call' to 'matheteship'. Such is Jesus' power over language and its potentiality: such the potential of names. 'Get in touch with your inner Matthew. Live into your name.' On its own level, Matthew's response to the responsibilities of his name reflects Jesus' response to the responsibilities of the names 'saviour', 'healer', and 'Emmanuel'/'God with us'. Or Peter's response to his name—beyond the text. But 'called' and 'calls' (λεγόμενον/λέγει) also interact with Jesus' *dictum* 'follow me', where the verb ἀκολουθέω is used. Like καλέω, λέγω can mean both 'call' in the sense of 'name' and 'call' in the sense of 'summon'. This further 'punning by synonym' interaction reinforces the thought that *everyone* can become a 'Matthew', *everyone* can become a 'mathete'.

At this point we must again revisit the question of titulature. Two of the possible explanations for 'Matthew''s substitution of 'Matthew' for 'Levi', (3h) and (3i), hypothesise that the title was original. In that case, any competent ancient reader or listener is going to say 'bingo' at this point. But of course it can be argued the other way round: an originally title-less gospel acquired its title precisely on the basis of the present passage, read as signalling authorial self-reference.[107] Kilpatrick, followed by Bauckham, argues against this hypothesis: 'Even after the changes of Matt. 9.9, 10.3, Matthew is a much less important figure than Peter and if an apostolic name was to be sought from the contents of the book, it would be expected that Peter would be chosen. The fact that it is not so makes against the possibility that the title of the book was subsequent to its production and arose out of Matt. 9.9, 10.3'.[108] This objection has some force but it is obviously not decisive: one could suppose, for example, that the person, or persons, who (*ex hypothesi*) subsequently attached the title decided against Peter, because his Apostolic authority had already been

---

107  So, e.g., Luz (2007) 59.
108  Kilpatrick (1946) 138–9.

enlisted for Mark, or even that they read Matthew's importance in the gospel in similar ways to the present paper! But in any case, this permutation does not preclude original readers from reading the passage by itself as an implicit authorial self-identification and their being right to do so. And if an originally title-less Gospel got that title (*ex hypothesi* in the early or middle second century), all subsequent ancient readers would rightly connect this passage with the title.[109] One could even say that, if Matthew lacked an original title, the *subsequent* addition of a title represented a correct reading of this passage and of its larger claims and associations. For the time being, then, we should again leave the question of titulature formally open, even if the arguments against an original title are coming to seem less and less plausible.

Let us turn now to the mathesis ('lesson') itself being expounded in this passage. The question is obviously germane to our enquiry. Since 9.13 quotes Hosea 6.6,[110] there is a sense in which Jesus' immediate interlocutors, the Pharisees, already know the lesson,[111] and the content itself seems simple enough. But a series of factors makes the mathesis weighty and gives it complexity.

First, the mathesis has already been adumbrated in Matthew 5.7 (one of the Beatitudes: μακάριοι οἱ ἐλεήμονες, ὅτι αὐτοὶ ἐλεηθήσονται, 'Blessed are those who pity, because they themselves will be pitied'), so 9.13 immediately acquires extra force.

Second, the mathesis is obviously implicated in the overall contextual emphasis on matheteship, in the Μαθθαῖος–μαθητής punning, and in the sense of different 'schools' and their 'mathetes': this is a core mathesis, and it is characteristic of Jesus' mathetes, not of John's nor of the Pharisees (nor, indeed, of *Gentile* philosophical schools, but I shall return to that), and characteristic also, of course, of the 'school' of 'Matthew' whose institution is here being commemorated and validated.

Third, this is the first of three occasions in the gospel where 'Matthew' uses the verb 'math', makes Jesus the speaker, and uses the verb in the imperative mood (cf. 11.29; 24.32). This is the first of a *series* of matheses, and acquires its full value when contextualised within that series. Of course, I am not claiming that these matheses encompass *all* the 'teaching/learning' of Matthew, but the thrice-repeated 'math', linked as it is to the name 'Matthew', gives this series particular force.

---

109   Cf. n. 20 above.
110   Other OT parallels: Davies–Allison (1991) 104.
111   So, e.g., Luz (2001) 34; Davies–Allison (1991) 104–5.

Fourth, in 9.13 there are two senses in which the Pharisees do not know the particular mathesis: (a) one could of course cite other OT passages to contrary effect: *choice* of *appropriate* quotation is part of correct biblical exegesis; (b) *they* are not actually *implementing* the mathesis. 'Math', then, means: 'really math', and the strong, 'proleptic' usage corresponds to the 'proleptic' usage of 'Matthew' ('live into your name').

Fifth, when they subsequently (12.2) claim Jesus' disciples' plucking of heads of corn on the Sabbath as unlawful, they show that they have not 'internalised' the mathesis of 9.13, as Jesus' reply emphasises (12.7): 'But if you had *known* (ἐγνώκειτε) what this means: "I want pity and not sacrifice" [same quotation], you would not have condemned the guiltless'.

Sixth, the meaning of 'I want pity and not sacrifice' requires consideration. Does Jesus' use of it[112] absolutely exclude sacrifice, or is the emphasis rather: 'pity is *more important* than sacrifice', or 'unless informed by a spirit of mercy, observance of the Torah can become uninformed slavery to the traditions of men'.[113] NT scholars debate the meaning (as indeed OT scholars debate Hosea's original meaning), and I cannot do justice to the intricacies of the debate.[114] Suffice to say that in my opinion the context naturally favours the absolute sense,[115] in just the same way as Jesus sits with tax collectors and sinners, but the Pharisees do not, as Jesus heals not the strong but those who are in a bad way, and as Jesus calls not the righteous but sinners. The absolute sense is also supported by the next two factors.

Seventh, the sheer brachylogic power of the quotation needs to be recognised. Human beings must of course worship God, but that worship should take the form not of sacrifice but of pity. One cannot of course pity God; one should pity one's fellow human beings, including—especially—sinners. It seems paradoxical that pity for one's fellow human beings should constitute the true worship of God, but the paradox is resolved by two facts: in pitying one's fellows, one will be behaving like God (cf. 5.7), or like (the divine) Jesus himself (significantly, in the subsequent narrative, sick people regularly appeal

---

112  By which I mean the dramatic Jesus' use of it, our interest being interpretation of the text, not establishment of facts about the historical Jesus.
113  Davies–Allison (1991) 105, citing Matthew 15.5–6.
114  Representative discussions: Davies–Allison (1991) 104–5; Luz (2001) 33–5; France (2007) 354.
115  I do not exclude the possibility that 'the absolute sense' may be qualified by other elements in the gospel; on the other hand, the destruction of the Temple in 70 also favours the absolute sense.

to Jesus to 'have pity' [ἐλέησον], and in pitying one's fellows, one will earn God's pity) (cf. 9.27; 15.22; 17.15; 20.30–1; 18.33).[116]

And eighth, since, as we have seen, I hold Matthew to include Gentiles among its ideal readership or audience, and since the context (redolent of 'philosophical school' rivalries) seems to support this perspective, the sentiment, 'I want pity, not sacrifice' acquires tremendous double force in its pagan application: complete rejection of sacrifice to the pagan gods (so-called), and, in very considerable contrast to pagan philosophical equivocation concerning, or outright dismissal of, 'pity', the enthronement of 'pity' as the central principle of human relations and of God's attitude to human beings. Collapse of boundaries—God near—and erasure of withholding of pity on ground of 'unlikeness'.

In sum, the first mathesis of Matthew is a very great one, and its authority is guaranteed by the testimony of Matthew the mathete of Jesus himself.

The next explicit mathesis comes at 11.28–30: 'Come to me all who are weary and heavily burdened, and I will give you rest. (29) Take my yoke upon you, and math from me, that I am gentle and lowly in heart, and you will find rest for your spirits. (30) For my yoke is kind, and my burden is light'. Here the word 'pity' is not used but the general theme is the same, it is now applied directly to the divine Jesus himself, and it is given significant developments. The operation of pity raises questions of power relations. The 'weary' and 'heavily burdened' are oppressed by their masters, social and political (cf. Mt 5.10–12). Jesus, as master, will give them rest, for his rule is kind and gentle. 'Matthew' reframes the familiar Christian trope of 'Jesus is Lord' and, implicitly, 'Caesar is not', within the overriding 'pity' discourse.

The third and final explicit mathesis occurs within Jesus' prophecies and warnings of his second coming (24.32–5):

> Math the parable from the fig tree; when its branch already becomes tender and puts forth its leaves, you know that summer is near. (33) So you too, when you see all these things, know that he is near at the gates. (34) Amen, I say to you that this generation will not pass away until all these things come to pass. (35) Heaven and earth will pass away, but my words will not pass away.

Since this mathesis concerns last things and people's preparedness for them it could hardly be more momentous.

---

116   Cf. Luz (2001) 34–5.

Next, let us turn our attention to the verb μαθητεύω. A common enough verb in itself, it does not occur before the Christian writers in the transitive sense 'make a disciple'. It occurs three times in this sense in Matthew, and elsewhere in the NT only in Acts (14.21, a passage to which we shall return);[117] this use of a verb cognate with μαθητής is distinctive to 'Matthew', and in 9.9 the name of 'Matthew' has been brought into punning relationship both with 'mathete' and with 'math'. 'Suggestive' is a useful word. Note immediately also that 'Matthew' uses both the verb 'mathete' and the imperative 'math' three times.

The first occurrence of the verb 'mathete' is at Matthew 13.52 (I put the crucial exchange between Jesus and his mathetes in bold type):

(47) Πάλιν ὁμοία ἐστὶν ἡ βασιλεία τῶν οὐρανῶν σαγήνῃ βληθείσῃ εἰς τὴν θάλασσαν καὶ ἐκ παντὸς γένους συναγαγούσῃ· (48) ἣν ὅτε ἐπληρώθη ἀναβιβάσαντες ἐπὶ τὸν αἰγιαλὸν καὶ καθίσαντες συνέλεξαν τὰ καλὰ εἰς ἄγγη, τὰ δὲ σαπρὰ ἔξω ἔβαλον. (49) οὕτως ἔσται ἐν τῇ συντελείᾳ τοῦ αἰῶνος· ἐξελεύσονται οἱ ἄγγελοι καὶ ἀφοριοῦσιν τοὺς πονηροὺς ἐκ μέσου τῶν δικαίων (50) καὶ βαλοῦσιν αὐτοὺς εἰς τὴν κάμινον τοῦ πυρός· ἐκεῖ ἔσται ὁ κλαυθμὸς καὶ ὁ βρυγμὸς τῶν ὀδόντων. (51) Συνήκατε ταῦτα πάντα; λέγουσιν αὐτῷ· Ναί. (52) ὁ δὲ εἶπεν αὐτοῖς· Διὰ τοῦτο πᾶς γραμματεὺς μαθητευθεὶς τῇ βασιλείᾳ τῶν οὐρανῶν ὅμοιός ἐστιν ἀνθρώπῳ οἰκοδεσπότῃ ὅστις ἐκβάλλει ἐκ τοῦ θησαυροῦ αὐτοῦ καινὰ καὶ παλαιά. (53) καὶ ἐγένετο ὅτε ἐτέλεσεν ὁ Ἰησοῦς τὰς παραβολὰς ταύτας, μετῆρεν ἐκεῖθεν.

(47) 'Again the kingdom of the heavens is like a net that was thrown into the sea and that gathered from every kind. (48) When it was full, they conveyed it to the shore and sat down and collected together the good ones into vessels, but threw away the bad. (49) So it will be at the completion of the age; the angels will come and will separate the wicked from the just, (50) and throw them into the furnace of fire; there there will be weeping and gnashing of teeth. (51) **Have you understood all these things?' They say to him: 'Yes'. (52) And he said to them: 'Because of this every scribe who has been matheted to the kingdom of the heavens is like a master of a house who brings forth from his treasury new and old things'.** (53) And it happened that when Jesus had completed these parables, he went away from there.

'Matthew''s dense patterns of 'math' sounds and implications immediately encourage us to take this passage together both with 9.9–14 and with 11.28–30.

---

117  See below pp. 777–8.

Further encouragement to link it with 9.9–14 is given by the theme of 'new and old things' (13.52), which Jesus applies to himself in the immediate sequel to 9.9–14 (15–17):

> And Jesus said to them: 'The sons of the bridechamber cannot mourn as long as the bridegroom is with them. But the days will come, when the bridegroom is taken away from them, and then they will fast. (16) But no one puts a piece of unshrunk rag upon an old cloak. For the patch lifts from the cloak itself and a worse tear is made. (17) Nor do they put new wine into old wineskins; otherwise, the skins are rent and the wine pours out and the skins are destroyed. But they put new wine into new wineskins, and both are kept safe together'.

We note also that the 'mathing' in 13.47–52 primarily concerns eschatological lore, just like the third and final mathesis at 24.32–5, and as adumbrated in 9.15.

Jesus' mathetes' surely rather unexpected understanding of his parable and Jesus' surely also rather unexpected commendation of their understanding invest Jesus' mathetes with an additional role—that of 'scribes'. This passage, then, firms up one of 9.9–14's potential implications—that mathetes should also teach—and teach also in writing. The plurality envisaged (13.52) is implausible in relation to Jesus' own mathetes as a group, but the highly unusual use of 'mathete' as a verb and its punning quality renew the focus on 'Matthew the mathete', alleged author of this gospel. Thus the passage also functions as a further *sphragis*. At the same time, the emphasis on a plurality of competent mathetic scribes seems to situate Matthew in a context of a school of Christian scribes—the 'school' implications of 9.9–14 now applied also to a 'Christian writing school'. This school's special qualifications consist in their correct interpretations of Jesus' parables (and of his general mathesis), in their creative combination of 'new and old', a combination which reflects Jesus' own qualities, and in their alleged descent from 'Matthew'. Clearly, the combination also well characterises Matthew the text; and particularly for Classical readers the emphasis on 'newness' suits both the *sphragis* context and the implicit literary programme. The same is true of the image of the 'treasury'.

The second occurrence of 'Matthew''s distinctive use of 'mathete' as a verb comes in the aftermath of the crucifixion at 27.57:

> (57) Ὀψίας δὲ γενομένης ἦλθεν ἄνθρωπος πλούσιος ἀπὸ Ἀριμαθαίας, τοὔνομα Ἰωσήφ, ὃς καὶ αὐτὸς ἐμαθητεύθη τῷ Ἰησοῦ· (58) οὗτος προσελθὼν τῷ Πιλάτῳ ᾐτήσατο τὸ σῶμα τοῦ Ἰησοῦ. τότε ὁ Πιλᾶτος ἐκέλευσεν ἀποδοθῆναι.(59) καὶ λαβὼν τὸ σῶμα ὁ Ἰωσὴφ ἐνετύλιξεν αὐτὸ σινδόνι καθαρᾷ, (60) καὶ ἔθηκεν αὐτὸ

ἐν τῷ καινῷ αὐτοῦ μνημείῳ ὃ ἐλατόμησεν ἐν τῇ πέτρᾳ, καὶ προσκυλίσας λίθον μέγαν τῇ θύρᾳ τοῦ μνημείου ἀπῆλθεν.

(57) And when evening had fallen, there came a rich man from Arimathaea, Joseph by name, who himself also had been **matheted** to Jesus; (58) this man approached Pilate and asked for the body of Jesus. Then Pilate ordered it to be given to him. (59) And taking the body Joseph wrapped it in clean linen, (60) and he placed it in his own new tomb which he had hewn in the rock, and rolling a great stone on the door of the tomb he went away.

'Matthew', it is well recognised, is again using 'Mark' (15.42–6):

(42) Καὶ ἤδη ὀψίας γενομένης, ἐπεὶ ἦν παρασκευή, ὅ ἐστιν προσάββατον, (43) ἐλθὼν Ἰωσὴφ ὁ ἀπὸ Ἀριμαθαίας εὐσχήμων βουλευτής, ὃς καὶ αὐτὸς ἦν προσδεχόμενος τὴν βασιλείαν τοῦ θεοῦ, τολμήσας εἰσῆλθεν πρὸς τὸν Πιλᾶτον καὶ ᾐτήσατο τὸ σῶμα τοῦ Ἰησοῦ. (44) ὁ δὲ Πιλᾶτος ἐθαύμασεν εἰ ἤδη τέθνηκεν, καὶ προσκαλεσάμενος τὸν κεντυρίωνα ἐπηρώτησεν αὐτὸν εἰ πάλαι ἀπέθανεν· (45) καὶ γνοὺς ἀπὸ τοῦ κεντυρίωνος ἐδωρήσατο τὸ πτῶμα τῷ Ἰωσήφ. (46) καὶ ἀγοράσας σινδόνα καθελὼν αὐτὸν ἐνείλησεν τῇ σινδόνι καὶ ἔθηκεν αὐτὸν ἐν μνημείῳ ὃ ἦν λελατομημένον ἐκ πέτρας, καὶ προσεκύλισεν λίθον ἐπὶ τὴν θύραν τοῦ μνημείου.

And evening having already fallen, since it was the Preparation, which is the day before the Sabbath, (43) there came Joseph from Arimathaea, a well-regarded councillor, who was himself also expecting the kingdom of God; taking courage he went in to Pilate and asked for the body of Jesus. (44) But Pilate wondered if he had already died, and calling the centurion he asked him if he had long died. (45) And learning from the centurion he gave the body to Joseph. (46) And he bought some linen and taking him down wrapped him in the linen and put him in a tomb which had been hewn from rock, and he rolled a stone to the door of the tomb.

Joseph of Arimathea is another 'mathete', whose adhesion to the Jesus movement further illustrates its 'successional' quality. The distinctive use of the verb ἐμαθητεύθη also provides further *sphragis* endorsement of the authority of 'Matthew the mathete'. Note how 'Matthew' secures these effects by a single deft change from 'Mark': the 'firming-up' of 'Mark''s vague 'who was himself also expecting the kingdom of God' into the precise 'who himself also had been **matheted** to Jesus'. The inspiration for the use of μαθητεύω may have come from Joseph's origin in Ἀριμαθαία. In Matthew anyway that place seems to be appropriately redefined as a 'very mathetic' place.

The third and last occurrence of 'Matthew''s distinctive use of μαθητεύω comes right at the end of the Gospel with the risen Jesus' commission to his mathetes at 28.16–20:

> (16) οἱ δὲ ἕνδεκα μαθηταὶ ἐπορεύθησαν εἰς τὴν Γαλιλαίαν εἰς τὸ ὄρος οὗ ἐτάξατο αὐτοῖς ὁ Ἰησοῦς, (17) καὶ ἰδόντες αὐτὸν προσεκύνησαν, οἱ δὲ ἐδίστασαν. (18) καὶ προσελθὼν ὁ Ἰησοῦς ἐλάλησεν αὐτοῖς λέγων· Ἐδόθη μοι πᾶσα ἐξουσία ἐν οὐρανῷ καὶ ἐπὶ τῆς γῆς· (19) πορευθέντες οὖν μαθητεύσατε πάντα τὰ ἔθνη, βαπτίζοντες αὐτοὺς εἰς τὸ ὄνομα τοῦ πατρὸς καὶ τοῦ υἱοῦ καὶ τοῦ ἁγίου πνεύματος, (20) διδάσκοντες αὐτοὺς τηρεῖν πάντα ὅσα ἐνετειλάμην ὑμῖν· καὶ ἰδοὺ ἐγὼ μεθ' ὑμῶν εἰμι πάσας τὰς ἡμέρας ἕως τῆς συντελείας τοῦ αἰῶνος.

> The eleven **mathetes** went to Galilee to the mountain where Jesus had directed them, (17) and seeing him they reverenced him, but some stood apart. (18) And coming towards them Jesus spoke to them saying: 'All power in heaven and on earth has been given to me. (19) So go and **mathete** all the nations, baptising them in the name of the Father and of the Son and of the Holy Spirit, (20) teaching them to keep all the things that I have commanded you; and see! I am with you all the days until the completion of the age.'

There is already a pun: 'I am with you' (20) echoes the angel's prophetic quotation from Isaiah about Jesus to Joseph at 1.23: 'they will call his name Emmanuel, which is interpreted: God with us'; as elsewhere, the presence of one pun makes other puns even easier than they would otherwise be. There is also a punning interaction between ἐνετειλάμην and συντελείας, emphasising the eschatological permanence of Jesus' 'ordinances'. Clearly, also, then, the designation of the eleven 'mathetes' punningly interacts with 'mathete', and the passage takes the 'successional' quality of the Jesus movement (Jesus, his mathetes, and all the nations as mathetes until the completion of the age) to its ultimate extent both in space and in time. And the use of 'mathete' as verb 'seals' the 'authority' of 'Matthew the mathete' in *the* most characteristic position for a *sphragis*: the end of the work. If the gospel also has an original title of 'The Gospel according to Matthew', there is a thoroughly satisfying ring structure or 'inclusio'. Certainly, as soon as the gospel acquires that title, all readers should register this culminating name pun. Note also that such a ring structure parallels the 'Emmanuel' pun and ring structure (and other ring structures, as we shall soon see). In all this, of course, there is no parallel in Mark, and

'Matthew' is being freely creative. Finally (for the moment), since Jesus' mathetes here include 'Matthew', 'author' of this text, and since, as we already know, Jesus' mathetes include 'mathetic' *scribes*, there is a clear implication that where the mathetics take the form of writing, Matthew is the 'prescribed text'.

Although we have come to the end of the narrative, three more general textual factors are worth adducing:

First, in his versions of Jesus' parables, 'Matthew' sometimes specifies very large sums of money, as Jeremias notes. Lane Fox suggests that this procedure might suggest, or be intended to suggest, the 'finger-print' of 'Matthew the tax-collector'.[118] This suggestion seems attractive and thoroughly consistent with everything in this paper. One might compare the great emphasis in Luke-Acts (greater than in any of the other evangelists) on Jesus' 'healings', evocative (it may be argued) of 'Luke the beloved healer'.[119]

Second, there are various ring structures/parallels/contrasts between the end of Matthew (27.57–61; 28.16–20) and the beginning (1.1–25): (no doubt more could be added):[120]

| Beginning | End |
| --- | --- |
| Jesus' genealogy and birth | Jesus' death |
| Jesus' genealogy/Jesus in time | Jesus throughout time until the completion of the age (28.20) |
| Jesus in his Jewish context | Jesus throughout all the nations (28.19) |
| Jewish history from Abraham down to Jesus' birth | After Jesus' death and resurrection world history till the end of the world |
| Emmanuel = God with us (1.23) | The divine Jesus has been given all power in heaven and on earth; Jesus is with his mathetes until the completion of the age (28.18, 20) |
| Joseph, husband of Jesus' mother | A Joseph buries Jesus (Jesus died untimely, buried by a 'father-figure') |

---

118  Jeremias (1954) 210; Lane Fox (1991) 128.
119  Moles (2011a) 146–65 {above, pp. 641–60}. Note that this is a different point from 'Luke''s use (or non-use) of medical language, nor does it matter here whether 'Luke the beloved healer' is the *real* author of Luke-Acts or merely the pseudonymous one.
120  See, e.g., Bauer (1988); Frankemölle (1973) 321–5.

| | |
|---|---|
| Jesus' ancestors include the twice-mentioned Matthas (1.15, a name cognate with 'Matthew') | Jesus' mathetes include a Joseph from a very mathetic place; Jesus tells his mathetes to mathete all the nations (the 'math' pun comes twice in two different locations); 'Matthew' seals his narrative with his name |
| Beginnings (in two senses: the beginning of the Jewish race; the beginning of Jesus' life) | Endings (in two senses: the end of Jesus' human life; the end of the world) |

The general effect seems clear enough: the beginning charts Jesus' genetic inheritance from Abraham; the end adumbrates the conversion of the world by Jesus and his mathetes, past, present and future; there is a broad movement between influences on Jesus and Jesus' 'succession' till the end of time. Within this movement, the influences on Jesus include a twice-named 'Matthas', and the Joseph of Arimathaea incident and the 'succession' blue-print both include two 'math' plays which evoke the names of 'Matthew' and 'Matthas'. The *sphragis* quality of all the 'math' plays, especially that at the end of Matthew, is powerfully underpinned by these great ring structures, and 'Matthew' even contrives to insert himself into Jesus', as it were, 'spiritual genealogy'.

Third, in discussion of our topic the question of the relationship between Matthew and Luke deserves at least some consideration. Of course, huge general source problems immediately arise. Are parallels between Matthew and Luke (or Luke-Acts as a two-book unity) to be explained by the two evangelists' using Mark and (the hypothetical) Q, that is, by the widely accepted 'two-source hypothesis'? Or: whether as a supplement to, or a substitute for, the 'two-source hypothesis', has 'Matthew' read 'Luke', or vice versa? My own view is that the 'two-source hypothesis' is sound but that 'Luke' has also read 'Matthew'. Now clearly one cannot base an argument on such a source reconstruction. Nevertheless, one can look at the relevant parallels between Matthew and Luke and see how they *might* play out and whether they *might* tend to support the overall argument of this paper.

As we have seen, 'Luke', following 'Mark', names the tax-collector called by Jesus as Levi. Either he has not read Matthew, or, for whatever reason, he implicitly rejects 'Matthew''s substitution of Matthew for Levi.

As we have also seen, 'Matthew' thrice uses the verb μαθητεύω in the transitive sense and does so in ways that reinforce the 'authority' of 'Matthew the mathete'. The only other NT parallel for this usage comes in Acts 14.21:

εὐαγγελισάμενοί τε τὴν πόλιν ἐκείνην καὶ μαθητεύσαντες ἱκανοὺς ὑπέστρεψαν εἰς τὴν Λύστραν καὶ εἰς Ἰκόνιον καὶ εἰς Ἀντιόχειαν.

And having announced the good news to that city [Derbe] and having matheted sufficiently many, they returned to Lystra and to Iconium and to Antioch.

Is 'Luke''s use of μαθητεύω influenced by 'Matthew''s, or vice versa, or is the usage of both evangelists to be explained simply as shared Christian usage? One could hypothesise that 'Luke''s usage is distinctive, caught 'Matthew''s eye, and, together with 'Mark''s emphasis on 'matheteship', inspired him to his elaborate 'math' punning. Equally, one could hypothesise that the highly competitive and agonistic 'Luke', bound as he was to reject 'Matthew''s claim to 'mathetic' authority, saw what 'Matthew' was doing with μαθητεύω, and crisply and economically appropriated the verb in a context which could be read as metaliterary ('having announced the good news'). In so doing, he would automatically also be pointedly and hostilely appropriating 'Matthew''s *name*.

As we have seen, Jesus' genealogy plays an important role in the parallels and contrasts between the end of Matthew and the beginning, and hence in the 'math' plays which underpin 'Matthew''s claims to mathetic authority. 'Luke', of course, unlike 'Mark', gives his own genealogy of Jesus (3.23–4.11):

23 Καὶ αὐτὸς ἦν Ἰησοῦς ἀρχόμενος ὡσεὶ ἐτῶν τριάκοντα, ὢν υἱός, ὡς ἐνομίζετο, Ἰωσὴφ τοῦ Ἠλὶ 24 τοῦ **Μαθθὰτ** τοῦ Λευὶ τοῦ Μελχὶ τοῦ Ἰανναὶ τοῦ Ἰωσὴφ 25 τοῦ **Ματταθίου** τοῦ Ἀμὼς τοῦ Ναοὺμ τοῦ Ἐσλὶ τοῦ Ναγγαὶ 26 τοῦ Μάαθ τοῦ **Ματταθίου** τοῦ Σεμεῒν τοῦ Ἰωσὴχ τοῦ Ἰωδὰ 27 τοῦ Ἰωανὰν τοῦ Ῥησὰ τοῦ Ζοροβαβὲλ τοῦ Σαλαθιὴλ τοῦ Νηρὶ 28 τοῦ Μελχὶ τοῦ Ἀδδὶ τοῦ Κωσὰμ τοῦ Ἐλμαδὰμ τοῦ Ἢρ 29 τοῦ Ἰησοῦ τοῦ Ἐλιέζερ τοῦ Ἰωρὶμ τοῦ **Μαθθὰτ** τοῦ Λευὶ 30 τοῦ Συμεὼν τοῦ Ἰούδα τοῦ Ἰωσὴφ τοῦ Ἰωνὰμ τοῦ Ἐλιακὶμ 31 τοῦ Μελεὰ τοῦ Μεννὰ τοῦ **Ματταθὰ** τοῦ Ναθὰμ τοῦ Δαυὶδ 32 τοῦ Ἰεσσαὶ τοῦ Ἰωβὴλ τοῦ Βόος τοῦ Σαλὰ τοῦ Ναασσὼν 33 τοῦ Ἀμιναδὰβ τοῦ Ἀδμὶν τοῦ Ἀρνὶ τοῦ Ἑσρὼμ τοῦ Φαρὲς τοῦ Ἰούδα 34 τοῦ Ἰακὼβ τοῦ Ἰσαὰκ τοῦ Ἀβραὰμ τοῦ Θάρα τοῦ Ναχὼρ 35 τοῦ Σεροὺχ τοῦ Ῥαγαὺ τοῦ Φάλεκ τοῦ Ἔβερ τοῦ Σαλὰ 36 τοῦ Καϊνὰμ τοῦ Ἀρφαξὰδ τοῦ Σὴμ τοῦ Νῶε τοῦ Λάμεχ 37 τοῦ **Μαθουσαλὰ** τοῦ Ἐνὼχ τοῦ Ἰάρετ τοῦ Μαλελεὴλ τοῦ Καϊνὰμ 38 τοῦ Ἐνὼς τοῦ Σὴθ τοῦ Ἀδὰμ τοῦ θεοῦ.

How does one construe the facts that 'Matthew', as an element in his whole elaborate 'math' playing, twice mentions a single 'Math' person in Jesus' genealogy, and that 'Luke' has a whole roster of such named persons in his version of Jesus' genealogy? Does the more precise common element, that Mary's husband, Joseph, had a grandfather with a 'math' name, indicate a solid historical basis for this single item? That inference would seem arbitrary, given the vast divergences in the rest of the material.[121] Does this more precise common element not rather indicate a direct connection (in whichever direction) between the two texts? And *if* other parallels *may* suggest some interaction (in whichever direction), who is following whom here? Has 'Matthew' been inspired by 'Luke''s great emphasis on 'Maths' among Jesus' ancestors (as also, hypothetically, by 'Luke''s distinctive use of μαθητεύω and by 'Mark''s emphasis on matheteship) to concoct his own elaborate 'math' plays? Or is 'Luke' concocting a *reductio ad absurdum* of 'Matthew''s 'math' plays and pointedly and hostilely appropriating 'Matthew''s name, as, hypothetically, again at Acts 14.21, as much as to say, in a children's game of hide-and-seek, 'I can see you, Matt!'?

It may be added that, as with everything else considered in this paper, these three items acquire extra edge if Matthew had an original title of The Gospel according to Matthew.

Nothing is sure here, but it seems to me that their respective handling of Jesus' call of the tax-collector, of the verb μαθητεύω, and of Jesus' genealogy does indicate a direct relationship between the two evangelists, and, if so, that 'Luke' comes after 'Matthew', and that 'Luke''s treatment of these items is designed to overturn the mathetic authority both of Matthew the text and of 'Matthew' the man, just as 'Matthew' himself had set out to supersede Mark and indeed (if that work originally had a title) 'Mark' himself. If that is so, 'Luke' read the 'mathetic content' of Matthew in the same ways as this paper has tried to do.

## 3   Conclusions

Let us summarise our conclusions about this passage, Matt 9.9–14.

Here we can see 'Matthew''s mind at work. The passage is brilliantly written, achieving its multiple effects by minimal rewriting of Mark and by extreme verbal economy.

Whether or not it was originally entitled 'The Gospel according to Matthew', Matthew is certainly not anonymous. The fingerprint of 'Matthew the mathete' is clearly and systematically visible, a circumstance which—as already noted—makes 'The Gospel according to Matthew' a jolly good title, whether original or not, and which itself also undermines most of the arguments for titular non-existence. In particular, the argument that Gospels must be

---

121   See, e.g., R. E. Brown (1993) 57–95, esp. 84–95.

anonymous because the Gospel is of Jesus, not of any human being, is refuted. It is true that the systematic punning encourages all readers—including those from 'the nations'—to become mathetes of Jesus, to respond to our inner Matthews—our desire to math in a religious sense. But it also underpins the unique authority of *this* Christian text, presents it as *the* vehicle for informed scribal and mathetic representation and interpretation of the Gospel of Jesus Christ, and creates a corresponding mathetic community, although one apparently based on an existing community of Christian scribes. Claims to authority often invoke legitimate succession, and here we have Jesus, his 'school' of mathetes, John similarly, Matthew the mathete's own 'school' which has produced this text, and the countless mathetes inspired by it until the end of the age.

However, unless one has overriding faith commitments to 'Matthew' as Matthew the disciple of Jesus, this text is pseudepigraphical. The punnings and *sphragides* are very adroitly executed, and one can see 'Matthew''s mind at work as he deftly transmutes primitive Mark into something much smarter. This of course raises huge questions of how we read NT pseudepigraphy, including the question of why second-century church fathers—pretty good NT readers, on the whole—accepted our Gospel's genuineness. Were they deceived, were they cheated, was 'Matthew' a fraud and a liar? That would be the Ehrman view of the consequences (even though in the case of the Gospels, he accepts the majority view of their anonymity). Well, faced with a few goodies in the Gospel literature amidst a mass of indifferent material, those church fathers had to make decisions and they surely chose the four best of the bunch. They *chose* to accept Matthew's claims. One can choose to believe, in this area as in others, and once the choice is made, it has to be maintained, at least in official contexts. When has anyone here heard a sermon based on a reading from Matthew which included the observation: of course, Matthew isn't 'Matthew'? On his side, is 'Matthew' being dishonest? He is being careful, in choosing as an 'authority' a disciple of Jesus who seems to have made little historical impact and who surely did not gather round himself any sort of Matthew community. But what is truth? someone asked, and it is a good question about all ancient historical writing, even including foundational Christian historical writing. 'Matthew''s deviations from the truth fall—just—within the elasticity classical historians and biographers permit themselves (think 'transference of items', think Xenophon and Themistogenes). Such elasticity serves many purposes, but one is 'the larger truth or truths'.[122] 'Matthew' could reasonably suppose that he would write a far better Gospel than Mark or Q and perhaps others and that this Gospel would mathete far more people to Jesus. History proved him

---

122  See, e.g., Moles (1993); Pelling (1990).

right—Matthew was by far the most popular Gospel. Do we here observe the 'Matthew' effect? Such larger truths could reasonably be underpinned by deft rewriting of Mark and a degree of dramatic fiction. That fiction is anyway alleviated by the fact that while Matthew the mathete is allegedly Matthew disciple of Jesus, he is also a mathete in various other important senses. There must have been Christian readers sufficiently sophisticated to see what 'Matthew' was doing. I think 'Luke' was one of them. Honesty and dishonesty do not really seem appropriate categories. But of course I write as a Classicist.

## Bibliography

Albis, R. V. (1996) *Poet and Audience in the* Argonautica *of Apollonius* (Lanham, Md. and London).
Andersen, F. I. and D. N. Freedman (1980) *Hosea* (Garden City, N.Y.).
Barnes, T. D. (1998) *Ammianus Marcellinus and the Representation of Reality* (Ithaca and London).
Bauckham, R. (2002) 'The 153 Fish and the Unity of the Fourth Gospel', *Neotestamentica* 36: 77–88.
Bauckham, R. (2006) *Jesus and the Eyewitnesses: the Gospels as Eyewitness Testimony* (Grand Rapids and Cambridge).
Bauckham, R., ed. (1998) *The Gospels for All Christians: Rethinking the Gospel Audiences* (Edinburgh and Grand Rapids).
Bauer, D. R. (1988) *The Structure of Matthew's Gospel* (Sheffield).
Baum, A. D. (2001) *Pseudepigraphie und literarische Fälschung* (Tübingen).
Bing, P. (1990) 'A Pun on Aratus' Name in Verse 2 of the *Phainomena*?', *HSCPh* 93: 281–5.
Boring, M. E. (2006) *Mark: a Commentary* (Louisville, Ky.).
Boxall, I. (2015) *Discovering Matthew: Content, Interpretation, Reception* (Grand Rapids).
Brown, E. L. (1963) *Numeri Vergiliani: Studies in 'Eclogues' and 'Georgics'* (Brussels).
Brown, R. E. (1993) *The Birth of the Messiah* (New Haven and London).
Brown, R. E. (1997) *An Introduction to the New Testament* (New York, London, Toronto, Sydney, and Auckland).
Brox, N., ed. (1977) *Pseudepigraphie in der heidnischen und jüdisch-christlichen Antike* (Darmstadt).
Bultmann, R. (1963) *The History of the Synoptic Tradition* (Oxford); trans. by J. Marsh of *Geschichte der synoptischen Tradition*[5] (Göttingen, 1961).
Burnet, R. (2014) *Les Douze Apôtres: Histoire de la réception des figures apostoliques dans le christianisme ancien* (Turnhout).
Burridge, R. A. (1992) *What are the Gospels? A Comparison with Graeco-Roman Biography* (Cambridge; second ed., Grand Rapids, 2004).

Burridge, R. A. (2013) 'Graeco-Roman Biography and the Gospels' Literary Genre', in B. Estrada et al., edd., *The Gospels: History and Christology* (Rome) 151–98.

Butts, J. R. (1987) 'The Voyage of Discipleship: Narrative, Chreia, and Call Story', in C. A. Evans and W. Stinespring, edd., *Early Jewish and Christian Exegesis* (Atlanta) 199–219.

Capponi, L. (2011) 'Hecataeus of Abdera and a New Conjecture in Josephus, *Contra Apionem* 1.189', *Histos* 5: 247–65.

Carter, W. (1996) *Matthew: Storyteller, Interpreter, Evangelist* (Peabody, Mass.).

Casanowicz, I. M. (1893) 'Paronomasia in the Old Testament', *JBL* 12: 105–67.

Davies, W. D. and D. C. Allison (1988) *Matthew 1–7* (London and New York).

Davies, W. D. and D. C. Allison (1991) *Matthew 8–18* (London and New York).

Duling, D. C. (1992) 'Matthew', *ABD* IV.618–22.

Ehrman, B. (2011) *Forged: Writing in the Name of God—Why the Bible's Authors Are Not Who We Think They Are* (New York).

Erbse, H. (2010) 'Xenophon's *Anabasis*', in V. J. Gray, ed., *Xenophon* (Oxford, 2010) 476–501; Eng. trans. of 'Xenophons Anabasis', *Gymnasium* 73 (1966) 485–505.

Eve, E. (2013) *Behind the Gospels: Understanding the Oral Tradition* (London).

Farrow, J. G. (1992) 'Aeneas and Rome: Pseudepigrapha and Politics', *CJ* 87: 339–59.

Feeney, D. C. and D. Nelis (2005) 'Two Virgilian Acrostics: *Certissima Signa*?', *CQ* 55: 644–6.

Fitzmyer, J. A. (1981) *The Gospel According to Luke I–IX* (Garden City, N.Y.).

Fitzmyer, J. A. (1998) *The Acts of the Apostles* (New York).

France, R. T. (2007) *The Gospel of Matthew* (Grand Rapids and Cambridge).

Frankemölle, H. (1973) *Jahwe-Bund und Kirche Christi* (Münster).

Frey, J., C. K. Rothschild, and J. Schröter, edd. (2009) *Die Apostelgeschichte im Kontext antiker und frühchristlicher Historiographie* (Berlin and New York).

Frickenschmidt, D. (1997) *Evangelium als Biographie: die vier Evangelien im Rahmen antiker Erzählkunst* (Tübingen).

von Fritz, K., ed. (1972) *Pseudepigrapha I: Pseudopythagorica, Lettres de Platon, littérature pseudépigraphique juive* (Vandoeuvres-Genève).

Garsiel, M. (1995) 'Puns upon Names: Subtle Colophons in the Bible', *Jewish Biblical Quarterly* 23: 182–7.

Garsiel, M. (2000) 'Word Play and Puns as a Rhetorical Device in the Book of Samuel', in S. B. Noegel, ed., *Puns and Pundits: Word Play in the Hebrew Bible and Ancient Near Eastern Literature* (Bethesda, Md.) 181–204.

Gathercole, S. (2018) 'The Alleged Anonymity of the Canonical Gospels' *JTS* 69: 447–76.

Glück, J. J. (1970) 'Paronomasia in Biblical Literature', *Semitics* 1: 50–78.

Goulder, M. D. (1974) *Midrash and Lection in Matthew* (London).

Gray, V. J. (1989) *The Character of Xenophon's Hellenica* (London and Baltimore).

Gray, V. J. (2004) 'Xenophon', in I. de Jong, R. Nünlist, and A. Bowie, edd., *Narrators, Narratees, and Narratives in Ancient Greek Literature: Studies in Ancient Greek Narrative* (Leiden) 129–46.

Guillaume, A. (1964) 'Paronomasia in the Old Testament', *Journal of Semitic Studies* 9: 282–90.

Gundry, R. H. (1982) *Matthew: A Commentary on His Literary and Theological Art* (Grand Rapids, Mich.).

Hagner, D. A. (1993) *Matthew 1–13* (Dallas).

Harrington, D. J. (1991) *The Gospel of Matthew* (Collegeville, Minn.).

Hedrick, C. W., Jr. (2000) *History and Silence: Purge and Rehabilitation of Memory in Late Antiquity* (Austin).

Henderson, J. (1990) 'Tacitus/The World in Pieces', in A. J. Boyle, ed., *The Imperial Muse: Ramus Essays on Roman Literature of the Empire: Flavian Epicist to Claudian* (Victoria) 167–210; revised version in id., *Fighting for Rome* (Cambridge, 1998) 257–300.

Hengel, M. (1985) *Studies in the Gospel of Mark*, translated by John Bowden (Philadelphia).

Hengel, M. (2000) *The Four Gospels and the One Gospel of Jesus Christ: An Investigation of the Collection and Origin of the Canonical Gospels* (London and Harrisburg, Pa.).

Hill, C. E. (2010) *Who Chose the Gospels? Probing the Great Gospel Conspiracy* (Oxford).

Jeremias, J. (1954) *The Parables of Jesus* (London); trans. by S. H. Hooke of *Die Gleichnisse Jesu*³ (Zurich, 1954).

Katz, J. T. (2008) 'Vergil Translates Aratus: *Phaenomena* 1–2 and *Georgics* 1.1–2', *MD* 60: 105–23.

Kelly, G. (2008) *Ammianus Marcellinus: The Allusive Historian* (Cambridge).

Kiley, M. (1984) 'Why "Matthew" in Matt 9.9–13?', *Biblica* 65: 347–51.

Kilpatrick, G. D. (1946) *The Origins of the Gospel According to Matthew* (Oxford).

Kranz, W. (1961) 'Sphragis: Ichform und Namensiegel als Eingangs- und Schluss-motiv antiker Dichtung', *RhM* 104: 3–46, 97–124; repr. in id., *Studien zur antiken Literatur und ihrem Nachwirken* (Heidelberg, 1967) 27–78.

Kraus, C. S. and A. J. Woodman (1997) *Latin Historians* (*Greece & Rome* New Surveys in the Classics 27; Oxford).

Lane Fox, R. (1991) *The Unauthorized Version: Truth and Fiction in the Bible* (London and New York).

Luz, U. (2001) *Matthew 8–20*, translated by J. E. Crouch (Minneapolis).

Luz, U. (2007) *Matthew 1–7*, rev. ed., translated by J. E. Crouch (Minneapolis).

MacIntosh, A. A. (1997) *A Critical and Exegetical Commentary on Hosea* (Edinburgh).

Maltby, R. (1991) *A Lexicon of Ancient Latin Etymologies* (Leeds).

Marincola, J. (1997) *Authority and Tradition in Ancient Historiography* (Cambridge).

Martin, R. H. and A. J. Woodman, edd. (1989) *Tacitus: Annals IV* (Cambridge).
Matthews, J. F. (1989) *The Roman Empire of Ammianus Marcellinus* (London and Ithaca).
McKeown, J. (1987) *Ovid: Amores Volume I. Text and Prolegomena* (Leeds).
Meier, J. P. (1992) 'Matthew, Gospel of', *ABD* IV.622–41.
Metzger, B. (1972) 'Literary Forgeries and Canonical Pseudepigrapha', *Journal of Biblical Literature* 91: 3–24.
Moles, J. L., ed. (1988) *Plutarch: The Life of Cicero* (Warminster).
Moles, J. L. (1993) 'Livy's Preface', *PCPhS* 39: 141–68; repr. in J. Chaplin and C. S. Kraus, edd., *Livy* (Oxford Readings in Classical Studies; Oxford, 2009) 49–86 [vol. 2, Ch. 50].
Moles, J. L. (1998) 'Cry Freedom: Tacitus, *Annals* 4.32–35', *Histos* 2: 95–184 [vol. 2, Ch. 53].
Moles, J. L. (1999) 'ΑΝΑΘΗΜΑ ΚΑΙ ΚΤΗΜΑ: the Inscriptional Inheritance of Ancient Historiography', *Histos* 3: 27–69 [vol. 2, Ch. 54].
Moles, J. L. (2007a) 'Philosophy and Ethics', in S. Harrison, ed., *Cambridge Companion to Horace* (Cambridge) 165–80 [above, Ch. 18].
Moles, J. L. (2007b) '"Saving" Greece from the 'Ignominy' of Tyranny? The "Famous and "Wonderful" Speech of Socles (5.92)', in E. Irwin and E. Greenwood, edd., *Reading Herodotus: a Study of the* Logoi *in Book 5 of Herodotus' Histories* (Cambridge) 245–68.
Moles, J. L. (2011a) 'Jesus the Healer in the Gospels, the Acts of the Apostles and Early Christianity', *Histos* 5: 117–82 [above, Ch. 23].
Moles, J. L. (2011b) 'Luke's Preface: The Greek Decree, Classical Historiography and Christian Redefinitions', *NTS* 57: 461–82 [above, Ch. 22].
Most, G. W., ed. (2018) *Hesiod: Theogony, Works and Days, Testimonia*, revised edition (Cambridge, Mass. and London).
Nisbet, R. G. M. and M. Hubbard (1978) *A Commentary on Horace's Odes II* (Oxford).
Nisbet, R. G. M. and N. Rudd (2004) *A Commentary on Horace's Odes III* (Oxford).
Noegel, S. B., ed. (2000) *Puns and Pundits: Word Play in the Hebrew Bible and Ancient Near Eastern Literature* (Bethesda, Md.).
Noegel, S. B. (2021) *'Wordplay' in Ancient Near-Eastern Texts* (Atlanta).
Nolland, J. (2005) *The Gospel of Matthew: A Commentary on the Greek Text* (Grand Rapids).
Parsons, P. J. (2012) 'Pseudepigraphical Literature', *OCD*[4]: 1232–3.
Peirano, I. (2014) '"Sealing" the book: the *sphragis* as paratext', in L. Jansen, ed., *The Roman Paratext: Frame, Texts, Readers* (Cambridge) 224–42.
Pelling, C. B. R. (1980) 'Plutarch's Adaptation of his Source Material', *JHS* 100: 127–40; repr. in id. (2002) 91–116.
Pelling, C. B. R. (1990) 'Truth and Fiction in Plutarch's Lives', in D. A. Russell, ed., *Antonine Literature* (Oxford) 19–51; repr. in id. (2002) 143–70.
Pelling, C. B. R. (2002) *Plutarch and History: Eighteen Studies* (London and Swansea).
Pesch, R. (1968) 'Levi-Matthäus (Mc 2,14–Mt 9,9; 10,3): ein Beitrag zur Lösung eines alten Problems', *ZNW* 59: 347–51.

Plümacher, E. (2006) 'Stichwort: Lukas, Historiker', *ZNT* 18: 2–8.
Porciani, L. (1997) *La forma proemiale: storiografia e pubblico nel mondo antico* (Pisa).
Porter, S. E. and G. P. Fewster, edd. (2013) *Paul and Pseudepigraphy* (Leiden).
Rastoin, M. (2002) 'Pierre "fils de la colombe" en Mt 16,17?', *Biblica* 83: 549–55.
Reckford, K. J. (1997) 'Horatius: the Man and the Hour', *AJPh* 118: 538–612.
Roberts, D. H. (2012) 'Sphragis', *OCD*[4]: 1394.
Rosenmeyer, P. A. (2001) *Ancient Epistolary Fictions: the Letter in Greek Literature* (Cambridge).
Rutherford, I. (1997) 'Odes and Ends: Closure in Greek Lyric', in D. H. Roberts, F. M. Dunn, and D. Fowler, edd., *Classical Closure: Reading the End in Greek and Roman Literature* (Princeton) 43–61.
Sand, A. (1986) *Das Evangelium nach Matthäus* (Regensburg).
Sanders, E. P. and M. Davies (1989) *Studying the Synoptic Gospels* (London).
Sim, D. C. (2011) 'Matthew's Use of Mark: Did Matthew Intend to Supplement or to Replace His Primary Source?', *NTS* 57: 176–92.
Simonetti, M., ed. (2001) *Ancient Christian Commentary on Scripture. New Testament Ia: Matthew 1–13* (Downers Grove, Ill.).
Speyer, W. (1971) *Die literarische Fälschung im heidnischen und christlichen Altertum* (Munich).
Stanton, G. N. (1974) *Jesus of Nazareth in New Testament Preaching* (Cambridge).
Streeter, B. L. (1930) *The Four Gospels: A Study of Origins* (London).
Syme, R. (1968) *Ammianus and the Historia Augusta* (Oxford).
Thomas, D. (2009) 'Introduction', in R. B. Strassler, ed., *The Landmark Xenophon's Hellenika* (New York) ix–lxvi.
Thomas, R. F., ed. (1988) *Virgil: Georgics. Volume 1: Books I–II* (Cambridge).
Thomas, R. F., ed. (2011) *Horace: Odes Book IV and Carmen Saeculare* (Cambridge).
Turner, D. L. (2008) *Matthew* (Grand Rapids).
Watson, F. (2006) 'The Four-fold Canonical Gospel', in S. Barton, ed., *The Cambridge Companion to the Gospels* (Cambridge) 34–52.
Watson, F. (2013) *Gospel Writing: a Canonical Perspective* (Grand Rapids).
West, M. L., ed. (1966) *Hesiod: Theogony* (Oxford).
Wildberger, H. (1991) *Isaiah 1–12*, translated by T. H. Trapp (Minneapolis).
Williams, M. H. (1995) 'Palestinian Jewish Personal Names in Acts', in R. Bauckham, ed., *The Book of Acts in Its Palestinian Setting* (Grand Rapids) 79–114.
Wimmer, L. (2012) 'Review of Hill (2010)', *Histos* 6: 359–66.
Wolff, H. W. (1974) *Hosea*, translated by Gary Stansell (Philadelphia).
Woodman, A. J. (1988) *Rhetoric in Classical Historiography: Four Studies* (London, Portland, and Sydney).
Woodman, A. J., trans. (2004) *Tacitus: The Annals* (Indianapolis and Cambridge).

CHAPTER 27

# Luke and Acts: Prefaces and Consequences

## 1     Initial Questions*

Although these Prefaces have prompted endless discussion amongst New Testament scholars (many of whom are Classics-trained), their interpretation remains disputed and there are many new things to say.

While it is always worthwhile to advance the interpretation of challenging individual passages, particularly famous ones, ancient Prefaces characteristically fulfil programmatic functions, hence these Prefaces affect some of the biggest interpretative questions about the two works, such as the following: the extent to which, if at all, they should be read as historiography; the extent to which they can, or should, be read as Classical texts, and seek to include 'Classical' readers/listeners (that is, readers/listeners, whether Jews, Gentiles, Christians, God-Fearers[1] or pagans, familiar with 'high' Greek—or even high Greco-Roman—culture); and whether they constitute a two-book unity.[2]

On the penultimate question, one of this paper's aims is to demonstrate that these texts deserve the attention of any literary Classicist, particularly specialists in Greek historiography or in Imperial Greek prose. A concomitant aim is to demonstrate that proper interpretation requires close and organic reading of the type now routinely accorded to Classical historiography or Second Sophistic prose works. Such claims may seem implausible to some, but there are no *a priori* criteria for what the author could or could not do, especially in his Prefaces, a context where ancient authors characteristically strut their stuff. Nor are they short-circuited by the author's expertise in the Septuagint: there is no theoretical bar to proficiency both in the Jewish and in the Classical.

The titles and authorship of the two works are also disputed, and the Prefaces are part of those debates. I adopt, *pro tem.*, and without prejudice, the conventional titles of 'Luke' and 'Acts', and 'Luke' as the name of the author or authors. I also refer initially to Luke(-Acts), leaving open the question of whether the Luke Preface is a Preface only to Luke or to a two-book unity of

---

* For many helpful conversations I thank Loveday Alexander, John Barclay, and Tony Woodman. None is responsible, etc. Bibliography is deliberately minimised. Translations are mine.
1 Gentile followers of Judaism who had not formally converted: see Fitzmyer (1998) 449–50 (with earlier bibliography).
2 Pro-unity scholars: e.g., Talbert (1974); (2003). The problematics of the notion of the 'unity' of Luke-Acts are probed by Alexander (2005) 207ff.

Luke-Acts. I make a single initial assumption—very widely, though not universally, agreed—that Luke(-Acts) postdates the fall of Jerusalem and destruction of the Temple (AD 70).[3]

It is generally agreed that the Luke Preface exhibits many formal features of the Prefaces of Greek prose works. Disagreement concerns generic claims, literary register, and literary quality. Many find the Preface over-compressed, over-allusive, ambiguous, obscure, and clumsy.[4] Some of these criticisms connect with the generic problem.

As for the latter, the Preface has traditionally been read, and is still now generally read, as a Greek historiographical Preface, the 1922 study of H. J. Cadbury having been especially influential.[5] 'Greek' here means not merely 'written in Greek', but also 'belonging to the Greek literary tradition'. Since at least 1986, however, scholarly discussion has largely been driven by the claims of the Classicist Loveday Alexander. She argues that there are strikingly close and strikingly numerous parallels, alike of thought, structure, rhetoric, and vocabulary, with the Prefaces of scientific, medical, technical, or—generally—'professional' works;[6] that Luke's narrative exhibits similar 'professional-man' style,[7] which should be indicative of his general culture and social status and those of his projected readership/audience;[8] and that the Luke Preface should accordingly be read as that of a technical/scientific work.

The generic debate is not restricted to the interpretation of the Luke Preface: many scholars have produced generic classifications other than historiography, whether applying a single generic classification to Luke-Acts (considered as a unity) or different generic classifications to the two books.[9] A particularly persistent classification has been that of biography. The case has recently been restated for *all* the Gospels by Richard Burridge and Dirk Frickenschmidt,[10]

---

3   Luke(-Acts) uses Mark, which is c.70 (Boring [2006] 14–15, 363–64, 367–68), or slightly later; Matthew, on most views roughly contemporary with Luke(-Acts), on some views earlier, is certainly post-70: Davies–Allison (1988) 127–38. {Cf. Moles (2006b) 89 {above, p. 574} n. 106.}
4   Representative criticisms in Alexander (1993) 103–5, 175.
5   Cadbury (1922).
6   Selectively: Alexander (1978); (1986); (1993); (1999); (2005) 1–6, 12–20, 161 (responding to critics).
7   German 'Fachprosa': Rydbeck (1967); Alexander (2005) 3–4, 18–9, 231–52.
8   Alexander (1993) 176–84.
9   E.g., Parsons–Pervo (1993) hold the first to be biography, the second historiography; Alexander ([2005] {133–63}) that different generic classifications are not automatically excluded.
10  Burridge (1992/2004); (2006); Frickenschmidt (1997).

and has won wide assent.[11] A sophisticated variant is Charles Talbert's much-discussed hypothesis that Luke-Acts (*qua* unity) imitates the pattern found in Diogenes Laertius—but (arguably) traceable back to the BC era: a *Life of the Founder* followed by *Lives of his Successors*.[12] Thus Jesus and his disciples would be likened to a philosophical school, and a main aim of the double work would be to legitimise the Twelve, plus Paul and Barnabas, as Jesus' *successors*.

In order to reflect the interpretative demands on first-time readers, my treatment of the Luke Preface is followed by discussion of its consequences in the Luke narrative; the Acts Preface is then discussed both in its own right, in relation to the Luke Preface, and in relation to Luke; its consequences in Acts are then discussed; the Luke Preface is then brought into the overall perspective. Attention is then paid to more general issues. The correlation of Prefaces and narratives is functional and ruthlessly abbreviated, aiming only to establish essential follow-through and organic interlocking of basic elements. Allowance is also made for the possibility that readings of the Prefaces may be enhanced by subsequent reading—and re-readings—of the narratives.

My appeal, here and elsewhere, to 'readers' does not exclude oral delivery and oral reception, but Luke 1.3-4 explicitly privileges reading by an existing Christian—and, clearly, private reading—over orality,[13] which would also be the natural context for any non-Christians and non-Jews. That is not to deny that a preponderantly oral/aural context, before Christian congregations, rapidly became important; such a context includes the illiterate, who were thus open to Christian mission.

Notoriously, any question in Luke(-Acts) involves numerous others, so I keep *all* interpretative questions (except the post-70 dating) formally open as long as possible—until the points where the most relevant factors are already in place, even though this procedure causes toing and froing and organisational strain. Throughout, I construct arguments by moving from the incontrovertible, or relatively incontrovertible, to the more controversial.

---

11   E.g., Dunn (2003) 184–6.
12   Talbert (1974), esp. 89–98; (1977); (1978a); (1989); (1997); Talbert–Stepp (2003); Dormeyer–Galindo (2003) 32–3; critical overview in Alexander (2005) 43–68 (in my view excessively formalist); Taylor (2006) 77–80.
13   The early reception of New Testament texts is endlessly controversial. While orality and texts must co-exist (Bauckham [2006] 287, 309), Mark was evidently composed for reading to a Christian congregation (Boring [2006] 1). But Luke is different (see also p. 816 below).

## 2 The Luke Preface

### 2.1 *Greek and Translation Issues*

Luke 1.1–4:

> Ἐπειδήπερ πολλοὶ ἐπεχείρησαν ἀνατάξασθαι διήγησιν περὶ τῶν πεπληροφορημένων ἐν ἡμῖν πραγμάτων, (2) καθὼς παρέδοσαν ἡμῖν οἱ ἀπ' ἀρχῆς αὐτόπται καὶ ὑπηρέται γενόμενοι τοῦ λόγου, (3) ἔδοξε κἀμοὶ παρηκολουθηκότι ἄνωθεν πᾶσιν ἀκριβῶς καθεξῆς σοι γράψαι, κράτιστε Θεόφιλε, (4) ἵνα ἐπιγνῷς περὶ ὧν κατηχήθης λόγων τὴν ἀσφάλειαν.

> Since indeed many have set their hand to draw up a narrative guide about the things done which have been persuasively brought to fulfilment amongst us, (2) just as those who became from the beginning eyewitnesses and servants of the word gave them on to us, (3) it seemed good to me also, having closely followed all of them from the up, to write them down for you in order, most powerful Theophilos, (4) so that you may additionally know/experience/recognise the truth/security/safety/un-slipperiness about the words in which you have been orally instructed.

There are no significant textual variants, and not usually thought to be any textual problems.[14] I make some preliminary observations on my translation.

In 1.1 ἐπεχείρησαν, it is important to retain the notion of 'hand'. I take two words for διήγησιν, both because in context the term entails 'narrative', and is itself a 'travel' word (lit., 'leading through'). Unusually, Alexander takes πεπληροφορημένων as middle voice ('which have come to fruition'), not passive.[15] This is strained. πληροφορέω (and the simple πληρόω) can of course be used in the passive, the 'opposite' of the active. Greek historians generally refer to their themes in the active or passive. Even Herodotus' formally middle γενόμενα with reference to his theme (*Praef.*)—which I hold relevant to Luke[16]—can be understood as effectively passive.[17] Here, once one grasps that this is a religious text, and the further into the text that one reads, 'brought to fulfilment

---

[14] Tony Woodman, however, suggests reading in 1.4 ἀλήθειαν ('truth') instead of ἀσφάλειαν. As a standard historiographical term, often found in prefatory or programmatic contexts, ἀλήθειαν would, as we shall see, be natural enough here; nevertheless, ἀσφάλειαν, while including the meaning of ἀλήθειαν, is immeasurably richer in implication, and must stand. {Cf. below, p. 801 with n. 77.}

[15] Alexander (1993) 111.

[16] See below, p. 799.

[17] LSJ s.v. I.2–3.

*by God/Jesus/the Holy Spirit*' is readily understood.[18] My further rendering '*persuasively* brought to fulfilment' seeks to include an ambiguity of the word in context. The translation of πραγμάτων as 'things done' covers: (a) the noun's basic meaning (from the verb πράσσω = 'do'); (b) the fact that historical themes are often described as 'things done' (*vel sim.*); (c) the fact that Luke is playing with the verbal interaction between πραγμάτων and πεπληροφορημένων: these 'done' things have not only been 'done', but 'brought to fulfilment'.

In 1.2 most interpreters take γενόμενοι with the whole phrase, and not as marking a temporal distinction between 'eye-witnessing' and 'becoming' 'servants of the word'.[19] This seems easier, but matters little: the emphasis on 'eye-witnesses' is here strongly positive: such people are naturally also 'servants of the word'.

In 1.3 scholars debate the 'meaning' of παρηκολουθηκότι (does it 'mean' 'investigate'? etc.). This confuses meaning and application.[20] The root meaning is 'follow closely' (or 'follow beside', to do justice to the παρά-compound), which, naturally, can be understood in different ways, but both writer and reader think first of 'following'. Retention of the root meaning does not prejudge the questions of whether the 'following' is literal or figurative, and of whether what is being 'followed' is personal or inanimate, and, like 'narrative guide', the root preserves a vital image.

In 1.3, the words 'of them' and 'them' do not occur in the Greek. I have inserted 'them' both to balance 'of them' and because the word 'write' naturally takes an implied object. I have inserted 'of them', because the form πᾶσιν can be neuter or masculine, and the reader must ask which. It is therefore wrong immediately to translate 'all things'. As a form, πᾶσιν can be either neuter or masculine, and scholars have divided over this question, though the great majority now read it as neuter.[21] This is doubtless better, because 'all' then balances 'the things which have been brought to fulfilment amongst us' and 'the words in which you have been orally instructed'; because it would seem excessive if Luke were claiming outright to have 'closely followed' 'all' 'those who were from the beginning eyewitnesses and servants of the word'; because ἀκριβῶς does not naturally refer to literal 'following'; and because πᾶσιν as neuter seems to be echoed in the Preface to Acts (below). Nevertheless, these are interpretative moves that the reader has to make and s/he has at least to consider the

---

18  'Brought to fulfilment': Cadbury (1922) 495–6.
19  {So, e.g., Alexander (1993) 119; Fitzmyer (1981) 294; Bauckman (2006) 29–30; cf. the warning of Kuhn (2003) 239 n. 8.}
20  Cf. Stinton (1975) 225–6 {= (1990) 148–50} on the principle, and Creed (1930) 4–5 here.
21  An exception: Barrett (2004) 1.59.

possibility that πᾶσιν is masculine. Hence I have avoided the explicit 'all things' and inserted 'of them' to maintain the grammatical ambiguity (whereas 'following all' without 'of them' would *have* to mean 'following' 'all' 'those who were from the beginning eyewitnesses and servants of the word'). Similarly, 'to write them ... in order' is acceptable Greek for 'to write *about* the eyewitnesses and servants of the word in order'.[22]

In 1.3 ἄνωθεν literally means 'from above', whether of space or of time.[23] It can be used as equivalent to 'from the beginning',[24] and clearly (on one level) means this here (in so far as Luke is saying that he has followed the whole story 'from the start' of the narrative). The slightly odd 'from the up' better preserves the double notion of space and time.

Κράτιστε is usually rendered 'most excellent', which, suggestive of the English title 'Your Excellency', well conveys the term's social elevation.[25] But 'most powerful' (Κράτιστε ~ κράτος) is better in context, because it registers the clear contrast with '*servants* of the word'.

In 1.4, the multiple alternatives for ἐπιγνῷς and ἀσφάλειαν require extended justification.[26] 'Additionally' is an available implication of the prefix ἐπι-,[27] and, though strictly redundant here, serves to emphasise the contrast between ἐπιγνῷς and κατηχήθης. Λόγων is standardly (as by the *Revised Standard Version*) translated by 'things'. This dreadful rendering destroys an important implication. Finally, I have inserted 'orally' before 'instructed', because, although there is no Greek adverb, κατηχήθης itself implies 'oral instruction',[28] and, since Luke talks of his own 'writing', there is an implicit contrast between oral and written instruction; without 'orally', this contrast would elude the Greek-less reader.

### 2.2    *Basic Generic Classification: Greek Historiography*

Given the Jewish/Jewish-Christian religious elements (a series of events 'brought to fulfilment', 'servants of the word'), most scholars read this preface as announcing some variety of *Greek* historiography ('Greek' meaning not merely 'written in Greek', but 'written in the tradition of Greek historiography').[29] There is considerable debate about what variety of Greek historiography, but it is the broad interpretation that matters here. Alexander, however, has

---

22  LSJ, s.v. γράφω II.3.
23  {Cf. Moles (2011) 481 {above, p. 606} with n. 117.}
24  Fitzmyer (1981) 298.
25  See, e.g., Fitzmyer (1981) 300.
26  See below, pp. 797, 804.
27  LSJ s.v. G.5.
28  κατηχέω ~ orality: LSJ s.v. II; Alexander (1993) 139, 141.
29  Classic is Cadbury (1922), generally followed until Alexander's challenge.

demonstrated numerous close parallels, both conceptual and linguistic, with the prefaces of scientific or technical works.[30] Luke's narrative uses similar language. This 'scientific' patina surely helps to reinforce the narrative's truth claims. What of Alexander's stronger contention that Luke-Acts thus becomes generically a technical/scientific work? I am among the dissenters.[31]

While διήγησις does not *necessarily* denote narrative, it must do so when it is a διήγησις of 'the things brought to fulfilment amongst us', and a narrative of past events, especially one 'drawn together' 'accurately' and 'in order' and one that has a beginning and an end, *itself* denotes historiography, history itself being 'things that happened or were done' (τὰ γενόμενα/*res gestae*). The reader then naturally takes most of the other elements of the Preface as historiographical (even though some *also* evoke scientific/technical/medical works):[32] the many previous treatments; their (certainly) implied inferiority; the narrative about 'things' that are the subject of either a middle or a passive verb; the retracing of events to 'the beginning' or 'the start'; the 'eyewitness' testimony; the division of material into 'things' and 'words'; the emphasis on traditions ('gave on'); the claim concerning the author's own place in the tradition and own contribution to it; the phrase 'it seemed good to me'; the emphasis on the author's 'closeness' to his subject matter and on his extensive research; the claim to completeness; the implicit claim for the superiority of 'writing' to (spoken) 'words'; the final purpose clause; and the emphasis on the solidity of the project.

To return to the initial qualification of my generic analysis of the Luke Preface: 'given the Jewish/Jewish-Christian religious elements'. Clearly, already within the Luke Preface and, still more, within the Luke and Acts narratives, that is a huge qualification of Luke-Acts' claim to be a work of Greek historiography. There certainly were Greek and Roman works of historiography which gave religion a prominent role, for example, on the Greek side, Herodotus, Xenophon, and Plutarch; and on the Roman, Livy and Ammianus. But, obviously, none of them makes it the central narrative that Luke-Acts does. There are also many scholars who regard the religious world of Luke-Acts as so alien to classical historiography that there simply cannot be anything here for sophisticated non-Christian or non-Jewish readers. Should one, then, while accepting the broad classification of 'Greek historiography', insert the specification

---

30  See above, n. 6.
31  Cf., variously: Witherington (1998) 2f.; Green (1997) 1–6; Johnson (1999) 213–19; Aune (2002); Mason (2005) 254–8; Bauckham (2006) 116ff.
32  For 'technical' features of Greek historiography cf., e.g., Thomas (2000); Raaflaub (2002); Hornblower (1987) 129–35.

'Greek historiography written in the manner of such Jewish-Greek historiography as I–III Maccabees'?[33] Acts does, indeed, show some narrative influence from that quarter.[34] But classicising elements, if proven, do provide something for non-Christian and non-Jewish readers; the alien is itself an important concern of classical historiography, and often involves bizarre supernatural material; and the religious alien-ness of Luke-Acts can anyway be exaggerated. By way of comparison, the rich cross-cultural and 'syncretist' stew of the Greek magical papyri—with their quite prominent Jewish ingredients—was primarily for Greek consumption,[35] and in our case, to take a single example of Lucan narrative, 'the prophecy of Jesus' birth [Luke 1.26–38] would have made excellent sense to any Hellenistic reader'.[36] If, to non-Christians, 'servants of the word' rings strangely, the 'wondrous' is an important concern of classical historiography (Hdt. *praef.*, etc.), and often involves religious matters. On the basis of the Preface, there is no reason to put Luke(-Acts) in some specialist and minority historiographical slot (which is not to deny subsidiary colourations from such sources).

Rather than invoking the historiographical sub-genre of Jewish-Greek historiography, then, it is better to say that telling the story of Jesus and early Christianity through the generic medium of Classical Greek historiography is part of Luke's literary creativity, extending the boundaries of that historiography and, obviously, extending also the literary and religious sensibilities of its usual readers.

The second large issue comes with the question of Luke's practical performance as a historian. The great Roman historian Ramsay famously judged the writer of Acts to be 'among historians of the first rank', and Alexander is no doubt right to argue that some of the analyses of the Luke Preface that claim Luke-Acts as historiography are registering anxiety that Luke should be a reliable historical source.[37] Whether he is or not is far too big a question for the present context. I merely observe that: (a) Luke's claim to historical reliability is conventional and necessarily relative; (b) there has, nevertheless, to be some historical reliability, otherwise the project will fail;[38] (c) this reliability is not always to be measured in terms of strict historical accuracy; (d) personally,

---

33  This was argued—on somewhat different grounds—by Loveday Alexander at a Durham New Testament Seminar.
34  Moles (2006b) 95–8 {above, pp. 578–81}.
35  Pachoumi (2007).
36  Johnson (1991) 38.
37  Ramsay (1895) 4; Alexander (2005) 12.
38  See p. 808 below.

I accept more fiction in Acts than many;[39] and (e) my understanding of the factual licence possible even within the most rigorous of Greek historiography permits such fictions.[40] In short, what happens in the narratives cannot prescribe the interpretation of the generic claims that Luke makes in the Prefaces.

We may now consider the question of how the above conclusions about Luke's generic claims impact upon the other generic hypotheses mentioned as possibly relevant to philosophy in Acts. Obviously, they exclude their strongest forms (that Acts—or Luke-Acts—*is* a biography, etc.). But too much New Testament scholarship applies excessively tight generic criteria and too much also assumes that one generic identification precludes another. Classical historiography is a flexible and capacious genre,[41] so Acts can readily accommodate other generic strands. These can include the scientific/technical/medical (historiographical possibilities ever since Herodotus and Thucydides),[42] the novelistic[43] and the biographical.[44] In any case, individual-centred historiography mediates between 'events-driven' historiography and biography (yet another reason why Acts is a good title).

As for Talbert's hypothesis, a two-book historiographical unity, or a stem narrative followed by a succession narrative, this can be explained in many other ways: a subsequent work (by the same author or another) which resumes where the first ended; 'Alexander the Great' works followed by 'Successor' works; or the example of Velleius, whose two-book work on Roman history is centrally concerned with the Caesarian 'succession' from Julius Caesar, to Augustus, to Tiberius.[45]

### 2.3 The Preface and the Greek Decree

While the Preface introduces a work of Greek historiography, the single type of writing that it resembles most, as I have shown elsewhere,[46] is the Greek decree. Essential to the syntactical structure of the Preface are an ἐπεί- subordinate clause, introduced by the very emphatic form ἐπειδήπερ, and a main clause based on the impersonal construction 'it seemed good' (ἔδοξε) plus dative of person. The only slightly less emphatic form ἐπειδή is used in the preambles

---

39  Cf. pp. 817–18.
40  Moles (1993b) 115–21 {vol. 2, pp. 181–6}.
41  Illuminating recent explorations of this theme: Kraus (1999); McGing–Mossman (2006).
42  {Cf., e.g., Hdt. 2.19–33 (inundation and sources of the Nile); Thuc. 2.47–53 (great plague at Athens).}
43  For references, see below, n. 231.
44  Cf., e.g., Homeyer (1962); Pelling (2006).
45  See below, p. 838, for the suggestion that Luke may also be seeking to outdo Josephus.
46  Moles (1999).

of Greek decrees, in which the main decision is characteristically expressed by the impersonal construction 'it seemed good' (ἔδοξε) plus dative of person, people, or constitutional body. Luke uses virtually the same syntactical pattern as the Preface's in Acts 15.24ff., where we have an ἐπειδή preamble clause, followed by a decision expressed by the impersonal 'it seemed good' (ἔδοξε) plus dative of person (15.25, 28). That is explicitly a 'decree' context—that of the so-called Apostolic decree—and it shows that Luke knows the preambular decree use of ἐπειδή. Hence, the Luke Preface should be read as imitating the pattern and vocabulary of governmental decrees. The use of the word γράφω is consistent with this, since γράφω can mean 'inscribe' as well as 'write'. Luke even helps this, as it were, 'decree' reading by using the form ἐπειδήπερ, which emphasises the ἐπειδή. The link between historiography and inscription is also exploited by the Roman historian Livy and by the emperor Augustus in his *Res Gestae*.[47] Historiographical imitation of the decree can include the 'it seemed good to me' element.[48]

Luke's imitation of the Greek decree conveys acknowledgement of the great Greek historiographical tradition and implies the same sort of general claims as those of the other historians mentioned: praise of the subject matter; 'concrete' memorialisation; formal weightiness; the 'authority' and 'power' of this 'author' (= '*I* am the authority here'); solid truth; the text as a highly visual medium (hence historiographical *enargeia*, 'the gaze', etc.); the public nature, availability, utility, durability, and 'monumentality' of this work. The imitation also makes the reader think of different media, and their respective merits. Those of historiographical texts are parallel to, but—obviously—exceed, those of public decrees published on fixed and perishable media such as bronze or stone. Texts are longer, more complex, more portable and more durable. Such implications suggest that Luke seeks as wide and as long-lasting a 'public' as possible.

It is, however, noteworthy that the decree element accounts for proportionately more in the Luke Preface—more than three quarters—than it does in any of the comparable Prefaces of Greek or Roman historians. This must have implications.

For the moment, I signal two. The Preface casts Luke in the role of legislator. The decree imagery naturally follows through to 1.4 'the truth/security/safety/un-slipperiness' (as of big physical objects which do not fall, for ἀσφάλεια literally means 'security from falling').

---

47   Respectively, pp. 803 and 819 below.
48   E.g., Thuc. 1.22.1–2; D. Hal. *AR* 1.6.3.

Another important historiographical motif is the implied unity of the subject matter and its treatment. Theophilos has already been orally instructed in 'words' about 'the word'. It is an easy move to apply this unity also to Luke's present *written logos*. This move is confirmed in the Preface of Acts by the allusion to 'my first *logos*' (Acts 1.1). As with Herodotus (*praef.*), Thucydides (1.1.1), and Livy (*praef.* 1), among many (other) Classical historians, Luke's work and theme are one—so much so, that, for its continued survival, theme depends at least to some extent on work. 'Classical' readers might well read Luke's 'word(s) about the word' as nice variation on Herodotus' 'demonstration' (ἀπόδεξις) of 'achievements demonstrated' (ἀποδεχθέντα) (*praef.*).[49] I use the term 'Classical readers' to denote both hypothetical non-Christian and non-Jewish readers *and* modern readers who happen to be Classicists.

### 2.4 Road Imagery

New Testament scholars neglect the single most important image pattern of the Preface, explicit in παρηκολουθηκότι ('having followed closely'), implicit or 'activated' in διήγησιν ('leading through'), πεπληροφορημένων ('*brought* to fulfilment'), and ἀσφάλειαν: that of the road. The last term can itself be applied to roads (e.g., Xen. *Hell.* 5.4.51). Clearly, the dynamic image of a road is particularly 'conducive' to 'drawing' the reader 'into' a text. Within the Preface, it is an organic image, creating several different, though interconnecting, roads: (a) the text, 'drawn up' by the author, traversed by the reader; (b) the historical events themselves ('brought to fulfilment'); (c) the tradition ('given on') about those events; and (d) Christianity as a road (Luke's written road about Christianity will guarantee the ἀσφάλεια of 'the words'). To these one can surely add: (e) the general 'road of life', as best 'navigated' by the Christian road.

'Road imagery' is of course common in historiography, Herodotus leading the way.[50] But Luke's use of it here is both more complex and more organic.[51]

Our analysis is already illustrating a simple, but important, truth. Language and imagery can be very polysemous. The fact that a word, phrase, formula, or

---

49  Discussion: e.g., Nagy (1987) 176–80; Moles (1993b) 92–4 {vol. 2, pp. 161–4}; Bakker (2002).

50  E.g., Hdt. 1.5.3. The 'text-as-journey' trope is also found in 'technical' texts and is a commonplace in Galen (e.g., *De constit. art. med.* 1–9; *Ord. lib. prop.* 19.51–2), where it has undoubted paedeutic force; nevertheless, it remains less organic than in historiography: 'technical' texts are not narratives of past events, nor concerned with physical journeys (as is Luke(-Acts)). The trope is also found in philosophical texts, e.g., Epicurus' letters (n. 111 below), which is relevant here.

51  {For the connection between road imagery and philosophy, see below, Ch. 28, pp. 856–8.}

image can be explained on one level does not exclude its operating on other levels, and, in some contexts, the more levels the better, provided that each separate level retains sufficient individual definition, and the whole does not collapse into pointless obscurity.

### 2.5 Beginnings and Endings

This theme is explicit in 'set their hand', 'the things done which have been persuasively brought to fulfilment', 'from the beginning', and 'from the up', and implicit in other elements; for example, 'the truth/security/safety/unslipperiness' is 'the end' not only by position within the Preface but also in some strong logical sense. The theme applies alike to the work of writers, to the role of eye-witnesses, to the historical events themselves, and to the 'end' (in the sense of 'purpose' or 'ultimate benefit') of the reader. The theme is also basic to historiography and road imagery (roads begin and end)—and to the sort of historiography which uses 'road imagery' (above).

### 2.6 Up and Down

New Testament scholars also fail to register that the Preface plays with the notions of 'up-ness' ('draw up', 'from the up') and 'down-ness' (καθώς/καθεξῆς/ κατηχήθης);[52] these apply both to time and to space. Obviously also, one can go 'up' and 'down' roads or other physical things (such as mountains), and one can oneself go 'up' or 'down' in various senses. There is a more general implication: these notions can stand for arbitrary reversals of fortune or for the supreme power of the pagan gods, particularly Zeus;[53] here, however, they are positive concepts, and, moreover, paradoxically, their end product is *stability*. Thus worldly ups and downs are transvalued.

### 2.7 Big and Small

'Brought to fulfilment' implies the traditional 'big-ness' of the historiographical theme (Hdt. *Praef.*; Thuc. 1.1.1–2, etc.), but scholars note that this is an outstandingly short Preface, especially by comparison with Classical historiographical Prefaces, which can be very/over- long and elaborate.[54] Nevertheless, as concepts, bigness and smallness, the relationship between the two, and the paradoxical revaluation of the latter are fundamental concerns of Classical

---

52  Note how Luke accentuates this by the use of rather uncommon (ἀνατάξασθαι, καθεξῆς) or un-Attic words (καθώς, condemned by Phrynicus, though Luke can roll out optatives when appropriate: Acts 17.17, 27).
53  LSJ s.v. ἄνω II.2.b. cf. Aes. *Eum.* 650.
54  E.g., Alexander (1993) 103.

history-writing, both of historiography proper (especially Herodotus, but also Xenophon and Tacitus) and of biography, and of the Socratic writings that influenced some of that history-writing.[55] Obviously, roads, too, can be 'short' or 'long'.

## 2.8 Power

'Brought to fulfilment' implies both control and teleology. There is also a contrast between the first '*servants* of the word' and the addressee, Theophilos, who is '*most powerful*', sc. in a worldly sense. There is an inversion of powers here, corresponding to the inversions of 'up-ness' and 'down-ness' and of 'bigness' and 'smallness'. Such ideas can be found in Classical historiography, especially Herodotean historiography as influenced by epic and tragedy, where they are mediated by such motifs as 'the wise warner' or the clash between wisdom/religion and power.[56]

## 2.9 The School Analogy

The notion of 'giving on' (παρέδοσαν), readily paralleled in historiography,[57] is also characteristic 'school' terminology.[58] 'School' texts often also have individual addressees.[59] Luke here contrasts (preliminary) oral and written teaching modes within a 'school' context.[60] Schools may also use 'road imagery'; hold out 'ends' for their adherents; and expound their material in 'small' compass (in epitomes, for example). Consequently, Luke(-Acts) presents itself as a 'school textbook'.

So far, so uncontroversial (I hope). I now enter controversial areas.

---

[55] Hdt. 1.5.3–4; Xen. *Hell.* 2.3.56; 7.2.1; Tac. *Ann.* 4.32.1–2; Moles (1998); Nepos *Praef., Pelop.* 1.1; Plut. *Alex.* 1.1–2; Xen. *Symp.* 1.1, etc.

[56] Hdt. 1.29ff. (Solon and Croesus); Lattimore (1939); etc.

[57] E.g., Jos. *Ap.* 1.8; note also the insistent παρα-compounds of Thuc. 1.21–22, with Moles (2001) 208 {vol. 2, p. 423}; on historiographical 'tradition' generally see Marincola (1997) 12–9, 103.

[58] Alexander (1993) 82–5, 118.

[59] {Alexander (1993) 59–63.}

[60] κατήχησις is of course the source of Christian 'catechism'. Whether that precise implication was established in Luke's time (whenever ...) is disputed (Green [1997] 45–6); if it was, Christian readers would find it here (further, p. 805 below). But 'catechism' is itself a development of the 'school' usage, Christians *ex hypothesi* are not Luke's only readers, and, moreover, since 1.1–4 makes a broad contrast between the 'written' and the 'oral', 'school' usage must anyway apply.

## 2.10  *Herodotus*

Alexander states a big claim: 'we should be looking for Luke's generic models not among the great classical historians ... Thucydides and Herodotus are probably the most difficult to square with the Preface ...'.[61] However, many of the scholars who read the Preface historiographically think similarly, for they characteristically seek parallels among later Greek historians.

But Luke provides an *instant* Herodotean 'marker' (seemingly missed by New Testament scholars). Herodotus (*Praef.*) characterises his broad theme as 'deeds demonstrated' (ἔργα ... ἀποδεχθέντα) and his treatment as a 'demonstration' (ἀπόδεξις): there is an exact parallelism between theme and treatment.[62] This striking conceit was imitated by several of Herodotus' successors as historians, for example, Thucydides, Livy, Dionysius of Halicarnassus, and Augustus.[63] Now, Luke's subject matter concerns 'the word' (1.2),[64] and Theophilos has been (orally) instructed in 'words' (1.4): 'words' about 'the word'. There is an immediate parallelism between theme and (one form of) treatment. Further, Herodotus' characteristic term for historical 'account', whether oral or written, is λόγος ('word'; e.g. 1.95.1), which became perfectly normal for a historiographical 'work'.[65] Thus Luke's written text is also a 'word'.

Having noted this 'marker', the reader finds other Herodotean elements: the characterisation of the theme as neuter 'things', followed by a middle or passive participle (Hdt. *Praef.*); the concern with 'beginnings' (Hdt. 1.5.3); the term αὐτόπται (below); the 'road imagery', which extends to the idea of the text as a journey (Hdt. 1.5.3); the claim to represent the Truth (Hdt. 1.5.4); and the inversion of 'big things' and 'little things' (Hdt. 1.5.3–4). Here Alexander's attempt to deny αὐτόπται historiographical force[66] seems particularly perverse. In so densely economical a passage, what single word could better convey the characteristically historiographical emphasis on eyewitness testimony?[67] Specifically, the term occurs five times, within Herodotus, both of himself and of figures within the text who perform a role analogous to that of the historian;[68] once in Polybius (3.4.13: Polybius himself, presumably imitating Herodotus); and once in Josephus (*Ap.* 1.55: Josephus himself, presumably imitating Herodotus and

---

61  Alexander (2005) 14.
62  Discussion: e.g., Moles (1993b) 92–4 {vol. 2, pp. 161–4}.
63  {See Moles (2011) 473 (above, p. 598)}.
64  Theological discussion: p. 807 below.
65  {See Moles (1982)}.
66  Alexander (1993) 120–3.
67  Generally: Marincola (1997) 63–86; on the Gospels, Bauckham (2006).
68  2.29.1 (Herodotus himself); 3.115.2 (no eyewitness); 4.16.1 (no eyewitness); 8.79.4 (Aristides); 8.80.1 (Aristides).

Polybius).⁶⁹ The 'Classical' reader will naturally also recall Herodotus' use of 'inscriptional' imagery.

### 2.11     *Thucydides*

The claim that Thucydides is absent from the Preface is equally misguided. Beyond the shared 'inscriptional' imagery, there are the following commonalities between Luke's Preface and Thucydides' First Preface (1.1–23): 'equation' of theme and treatment (Thuc. 1.1.1); 'as' (ὡς)-clause epexegetic of the historiographical theme, itself stated as the object of a verb (1.1.1);⁷⁰ emphasis on eyewitness testimony (1.22.3); 'it seemed to me' formula (1.22.1–2); emphasis on completeness (1.22.1–2); emphasis on 'accuracy' (ἀκρίβεια) (1.22.2); emphasis on truth (1.22.4); claim to represent the Truth; notion that history consists of deeds and words (1.22.1–2); idea that the reader 'looks' at the historical work; visual element emphasised in two contexts: the testimony of the original eyewitnesses and the 'visualness' of the final text (1.22.3–4); contrast between the oral/aural and the written in favour of the latter; use of παρα-compounds; and concern with 'beginnings' (1.23.4). If one also considers Thucydides' 'second Preface', there are the following commonalities: epexegetic 'as' (ὡς)-clause (5.26.1); 'writing … in order' (5.26.1); a series of events from beginning to end (5.26.4); and a direct relationship between 'all' of them and the historian, productive of the requisite ἀκρίβεια (5.26.5). Naturally, not all of these elements are exclusively Thucydidean, but there is more than enough here to create a strong Thucydidean colouring. This Thucydidean colouring co-exists with, and enhances, the Herodotean colouring. The double colouring from the two pioneers of Greek historiography reinforces Luke's basic generic claim and further illustrates the richness and dexterity of his literary allusions.

### 2.12     *Polybius*

Of course, 'great' Greek historiography did not end with Thucydides. Another towering figure is Polybius. Given Luke's echo of Herodotus' equivalence of theme and treatment and his programmatic emphasis on beginnings and endings, a Classical reader might well recall another version of the equivalence of theme and treatment: Polybius' concern with the 'end' of his work as co-terminous with the 'completion' of Roman power (3.1.5–3.4.1).⁷¹ Also then

---

69    Cf. Bauckham (2006) 118–19.
70    'Just as' phrases or clauses are *also* common in Greek decrees, for obvious illustrative or justificatory reasons (examples in Harris [2002] 5 n. 13), so the clause is also compatible with the decree format.
71    Cf. Bauckham (2006) 119–21.

Polybian (as well as Herodotean) is the use of αὐτόπτης (3.4.13 (above)). As with Herodotus and Thucydides, we have here another example of 'double allusion' and yet further proof of Luke's 'Classical' literary sophistication.

If Polybius' version of the equivalence between treatment and theme is relevant, there is another aspect to the inversion of powers: the power of the Word vs. the power of Rome.

### 2.13  *Later Greek Historiography*

David Aune has adduced parallels between Luke's Preface and the historiographical stance struck by Plutarch in the preface of the *Septem Sapientium Convivium*.[72] I shall argue subsequently[73] for active parallels with the Roman historian Livy, with Augustus' *Res Gestae* (which imitates Greek historiography), and with the Jewish historian Josephus, but these claims require more material to have been put in place.

### 2.14  *Historiographical Implications of 1.4*

While both Cadbury and Alexander provide useful interpretative surveys of this last clause, neither they nor other New Testament scholars grasp its complexity.[74] I stress *historiographical* implications (there are others). I begin with simple things.

*Pace* many, the apparently straightforward 'know the truth' must be part of the meaning. The reader expects this: the sentiment is standard in historiography,[75] as in 'professional' works;[76] and there are excellent parallels for ἀσφάλεια (and cognates) with the implication of 'truth'. In this application the term plays on notions of truth as stable, unequivocal, unchanging, etc.[77] Even on this level, however, there is a double implication, because 'the truth' is not merely 'a true account of the events I have chosen to narrate' (the usual historiographical claim) but 'the Truth': everything readers need to know about 'life, death, and the whole damn thing'. Grammatically, the περί phrase can function as a periphrasis for a genitive,[78] and 'I shall tell the truth of Christianity' means both 'I shall give a true account of Christianity' and 'I shall show that Christianity is true' (genitive of definition). On this level, also, Luke's

---

72  Aune (2002) 144–7; cf. Bauckham (2006) 119–20 {= Bauckham (2017) 107–8}.
73  Below pp. 803, 822ff.
74  Cadbury (1922) 508–10; Alexander (1993) 137–41.
75  Thuc. 1.22.4; Moles (1993b); Marincola (1997) 160–2.
76  Alexander (1993) 137.
77  Acts 2.36; 25.26; 21.34; 22.30 (the latter two with the simple verb rather than the compound); *P. Giss.* 1.27 (cited by Cadbury [1922] 509).
78  LSJ s.v. C.5.

term for 'truth' is particularly felicitous, because ἀσφάλεια can specify 'truth' validated by writing.⁷⁹

The next task is to consider 1.4 'architecturally', that is, as corresponding to the secondary justification for the Greek decree and to the 'purpose' element within the programmes of Classical historians that imitate the decree. Here it is important to remember the root meaning of ἀσφάλεια as = 'security from falling'.

Herodotus' Preface begins:

Ἡροδότου Ἁλικαρνησσέος ἱστορίης ἀπόδεξις ἥδε, ὡς μήτε τὰ γενόμενα ἐξ ἀνθρώπων τῷ χρόνῳ ἐξίτηλα γένηται μήτε ἔργα μεγάλα τε καὶ θωμαστὰ τὰ μὲν Ἕλλησι, τὰ δὲ βαρβάροισι ἀποδεχθέντα ἀκλεᾶ γένηται.

This is the demonstration of Herodotus of Halicarnassus, in order that neither should the things born from men become faded through time nor should great and wonderful deeds, some demonstrated by Greeks, some by barbarians, become without glory.

There is a strong visual appeal (deictic 'this'; 'demonstration'; 'not faded') to a text imaged as an inscription or monument (deictic 'this'; 'not faded'; subsequent switch from third person to first [1.5.3]) which supersedes that of Herodotus' great historiographical predecessor, Hecataeus.⁸⁰

Within his extended Preface (1.1.1–23.6), which is in part an imitation of Herodotus', Thucydides states his History's purpose and function (22.4):

ὅσοι δὲ βουλήσονται τῶν τε γενομένων τὸ σαφὲς σκοπεῖν καὶ τῶν μελλόντων ποτὲ αὖθις κατὰ τὸ ἀνθρώπινον τοιούτων καὶ παραπλησίων ἔσεσθαι, ὠφέλιμα κρίνειν αὐτὰ ἀρκούντως ἕξει. κτῆμά τε ἐς ἀεὶ μᾶλλον ἢ ἀγώνισμα ἐς τὸ παραχρῆμα ἀκούειν ξύγκειται.

But it will be enough that as many as will wish to look at the clear truth both of the things that happened and of those which, in accordance with the human thing, are going to happen again sometime like these and near the present ones should judge it useful. It is set down together as a possession for always rather than as a competition piece for present hearing.

---

79   Cadbury (1922) 509; Alexander (1993) 140.
80   Moles (1999) 44–53 {vol. 2, pp. 382–91}.

The phrase 'will wish to look at' echoes the Athenian inscriptional formula 'for the person who wishes to look (at)' [the inscription],[81] and re-establishes the analogy, begun at 1.1.1, between the History and an inscription. The specificatory/restrictive 'as many as' recalls inscriptional terminology,[82] as does the emphasis on perpetuity.[83] Thucydides' readers 'look at' his History as at an imperishable inscription; their 'looking' involves a range of 'sight' processes, from quasi-literal 'looking' (as in 'reading', or in responding to Thucydides' highly 'visual' narratives), to 'observation', to (ideally) true 'insight'.[84] In various telling ways, Thucydides' 'inscription' supersedes Herodotus'.

The Roman historian Livy states his History's purpose and function, imitating Thucydides (*inter multos alios*), but arguing a much more directly moralising—and implicitly, a superior—value for history (*Praef.* 10):

> hoc illud est praecipue in cognitione rerum salubre ac frugiferum, omnis te exempli documenta in inlustri posita monumento intueri: inde tibi tuaeque rei publicae quod imitere capias, inde foedum inceptu, foedum exitu, quod uites.

> This is the thing that is most takingly healthy and fruitful in the getting to know of history: that you look upon the lessons of every kind of example placed on a conspicuous monument: from these you may take for yourself and for your own (e)state—the public state, what you should imitate; from these, disgusting in the undertaking, disgusting in the outcome, what you should avoid.

Livy figures Roman History in general and his History in particular as a great monument, with, as it were, moral inscriptions or prescriptions. It is this 'monument' which will restore the Roman State, just previously imaged (9) as a falling/slipping/collapsing building.[85]

In the light, then, both of the general decree element of Luke's Preface and of these passages, which incorporate a 'decree element', from the Prefaces of three of the greatest of Luke's historiographical predecessors and competitors, Luke's phrase should *also* be understood as suggesting the image of *looking at* an imperishable inscription or monument, which *cannot fall*. Ἐπιγιγνώσκω

---

81   Moles (1999) 32–33 with n. 5 {vol. 2, pp. 370–1}.
82   Examples in Harris (2005) 4.
83   Moles (1999) 26 {vol. 2, p. 383} n. 32.
84   Moles (2001) 213–5 {vol. 2, pp. 427–30}.
85   Moles (1993a) 153–4 {vol. 2, pp. 208–10}; (1999) 64–5 {vol. 2, pp. 402–3}.

often has a visual implication of 'recognition',[86] and σφάλλω and cognates, including passives and negative forms, can be applied to buildings or the like, whether literally or metaphorically.[87]

Might, then, 1.4 be *echoing* Herodotus, Thucydides, or Livy?

As already argued, Herodotus is present in the Preface,[88] and readers should recall his use of 'inscriptional' imagery. They may also note that Luke's 'so that' clause corresponds to Herodotus' 'in order that' clauses. Beyond that, however, there are no specific verbal parallels for 1.4.

Thucydides is also present, and readers should recall his use of 'inscriptional imagery', as also the correspondence between Luke's 'so that' clause and Thucydides' statement of purpose in 1.22.4 (despite different syntax).

Between Livy and Luke there are the following commonalities: 'equation' of theme and treatment (Livy, *praef.* 1); association of the processes of 'knowing' and 'seeing'; cognate forms (ἐπιγνῷς ~ *cognitione*); commemoration of the Truth in its strongest form; direct second-person singular addresses (a remarkable effect in Livy); and the notion of *falling* or *not-falling*. The possibility of Imperial Greek writers' using Roman authors, in the past generally dismissed, is actively canvassed in current scholarship.[89]

Altogether, then, a 'Classical' reader would read ἐπιγνῷς περὶ ὧν κατηχήθης λόγων τὴν ἀσφάλειαν as bringing Luke's 'inscription', theme, and 'solution' into relationship with those of the greatest Classical historians, especially Thucydides and Livy. The initial consequences of this relationship I discuss below. The Livian allusion also fits within the 'inversion of powers' motif, specifically the contrast between divine power and Roman power.

### 2.15 Seeing and Recognising

Since 1.4 ἐπιγνῷς includes the notion of 'recognising' visually, both literally and metaphorically, and 1.2 emphasises 'eye-witness' as both validating and actioning ('servants of the word), the Preface implies a familiar but complex historiographical discourse of various 'seeing' processes as conducive to historical accuracy and reader understanding, participation, and energisation.

### 2.16 Buildings, Artefacts, and Media

The analogy between historiographical work and decree is a particular form of a larger analogy: between literary text and big physical object, especially

---

86  LSJ s.v., esp. II; similarly, the simplex: LSJ s.v., cf. Luke 18.34.
87  E.g., LSJ s.v. σφάλλω II.
88  See above, p. 802.
89  {See, e.g., the papers in Torres Guerra (2011).}

a building. So Pindar's *Odes* are a 'treasury of song' (*Pyth.* 6.7), Thucydides' *History* a 'possession for always' (1.22.4), Horace's *Odes* a 'monument more lasting than bronze' (*C.* 3.30.1). The larger analogy is suggested here by the Livian analogy between the Roman state and a collapsing building (above) and by the terminology 'set their hand to', 'accurately',[90] and ἀσφάλειαν (above). The broad implications are similar to those of the decree analogy. The reader again thinks of different media and their respective merits. Here there is a strange sense that *logos* infuses and triumphs over all possible media.

### 2.17 Religious Elements

Alexander states: 'the Preface never speaks of God'.[91] The claim is extraordinary. Even if literally true, it is true only in the narrowest sense and extremely misleading. As many emphasise,[92] 'brought to fulfilment' and 'servants of the word' (that is, the Jewish-Christian concept of the Word of God)[93] have direct religious import for Christian readers such as Theophilos. Even for non-Christian readers, the notion of 'fulfilment' often has religious implications. Another item is unclear: whether κατηχήθης specifically denotes Christian catechism.[94]

Obviously important also is the addressee, 'Theophilos'. Whether or not he is a real person,[95] the name is *theo*phoric: *God* is '*spoken* of'. Following the Christian Fathers, Bede (*ad loc.*) took 'Theophilos' as a *doubly* 'speaking' name, meaning both 'loving God' and 'loved by God'. The former meaning is certain, the latter immediately available to Christians, who believe they are loved by God. On Bede's interpretation, the name has generalising force, including *all* who aspire to be 'lovers of God'.[96] Given the other religious elements in the Preface and given early Christianity's general concern with proselytism, this is highly attractive. The reciprocity of 'loving God' and 'loved by God' also fits the reader's 'contractual obligations'.[97]

One item requires further discussion. In the Prologue to The Gospel according to John, the Word is instantiated in Jesus. Is it here? Some scholars think

---

90  {Cf. Moles (2013) 104 = above, p. 682.}
91  Alexander (2005) 223 (and frequently elsewhere).
92  E.g., Johnson (1991) 27–8; Green (1997) 39–42.
93  See, e.g., Ryken–Wilhoit–Longman (1998) 90ff.
94  See above, p. 791.
95  See below, p. 816.
96  {Cf. Moles (2013) 103 = above, p. 681.}
97  See below, p. 809.

so.[98] So also, among the Church Fathers, did Irenaeus[99] and Ambrose.[100] They, of course, had read John. That Luke had is heterodox in modern scholarship, even if some reputable scholars suppose it.[101] No matter, the *idea* of Jesus as Word is not difficult and even necessary, once Jesus was claimed as the fulfilment of the Old Testament. More substantially, if the eyewitnesses are eyewitnesses only of the word as usually understood, the clash of visual and aural/oral media is challengingly synaesthetic. But if the Word is instantiated in Jesus, this eyewitnessing finds concrete focus (as indeed Ambrose notes). The patristic interpretation, therefore, seems to me right, though the implication would escape non-Christian readers. For them, 'eyewitnesses of the word' would have a certain 'read-on' quality.

### 2.18 The Philosophical Aspect

As we have seen, the Preface has a 'school' aspect.[102] We may then ask: what sort of 'school': medical, rhetorical, philosophical, religious, or whatever? Clearly, neither of the first two. The religious elements must be given value. Further, within a Jewish-Christian context, the representation of a religious group as a 'school' already involves a comparison between religion and philosophy: thus there is already a philosophical aspect to the Preface. The general representation of Christianity as a 'philosophy' was in fact commonplace.[103]

But there is more. As we have seen, elements of the Preface's complex road imagery apply to the reader. Luke(-Acts) is itself a 'narrative guide' that has to be 'traversed'; but it is a 'guide' to a 'road', so that Theophilos 'may know the truth/security/safety/un-slipperiness concerning the words in which you have been orally instructed'. This is a 'road' to which Luke and the 'many' have written 'guides' because they themselves have, in some sense, 'done the journey' and so can now pass on the requisite information to others. Luke's particular narrative road unites historiographical 'truth' and (moral) 'reliability': you can

---

98  Though a goodly minority: cf., e.g., Dunn (2003) 178 n. 29; (2009) 74 n. 83.
99  Euseb. *H.E.* 5.20.6: 'having *received* them [Jesus' works and teaching] from *the eyewitnesses of the life of the Logos*'.
100 {*Exp. euag. Luc.* prol. 4, 1263A.}
101 E.g., Gregory (2006); for brief observations on Luke's date see p. 839 below; they allow Luke to have read John, in which case, 'the word' here includes a glancing—and, surely, critical—allusion to John's very long *Prologos*.
102 See above, p. 798.
103 Much discussed: e.g., Jaeger (1961); Millar (1977) 561–6; Lane Fox (1986) 304–8; Stead (1994); Mason (2005) 285–92; Sorabji (2000) 343–417; Alexander (2002); Barnes (2002); Louth (2007). Acts 24.5, 24.14 and 28.22 show that non-Christians could characterise Christianity as a form of philosophical sect at the time of writing (whenever ...), and even—presumably—as early as the dramatic date (*c.*60).

trust its truthfulness and 'rely' on it to keep on the straight road and not to fall. The word 'know' covers both 'know' as fact and 'know' as 'experience'; the latter is in the first instance the *vicarious* experience of the reader, but the double sense already conveys that the reader is both a reader and at least potentially an actor.

Ἀσφάλειαν, then, while acceptably historiographical, also leads into another discourse, and, clearly, some sort of moral discourse. Imagery based on good and bad roads (vel sim.) is common in Jewish writings.[104] But it is also common in Greek and Roman moral philosophy.[105] And, among Greek philosophers, Platonists, Cynics, Stoics, and Epicureans (especially, perhaps) all promised ἀσφάλεια.[106] A philosophical resonance would also suit a work addressed to a named individual, a circumstance which, while not exactly anti-historiographical,[107] is more at home in a philosophical address. Philosophically speaking, then, Theophilos is being required to make a transition between oral and written modes and between belief and knowledge. If, then, ἀσφάλειαν (also) evokes a Greek philosophical goal, the implication is not just the objective: 'you won't fall morally', but also the hortatory: 'you'll be safe, if you follow this road'. To discover what that 'safety' actually consists in, the reader, as already noted, has to read on.

There are other readily available philosophical implications. If Luke and the 'many' have (in some sense) 'done the journey', they must also (in some sense) be moral exemplars for Theophilos and other readers. And if all their works are 'guides', and if Luke's own work is 'small', then perhaps it is an *epitome*: a 'short-cut road', like the philosophical *epitomes* produced by Epicurus and (presumably) the Cynics before him,[108] and in Epicurus' case, with direct addressees.

Given this overall philosophical colouring, Luke's central theme, the λόγος of 1.2, must also be considered. In the first instance, this is the Word of God, in the second, arguably (above), Jesus. But Hellenised Jews or Gentiles familiar

---

104 Ryken–Wilhoit–Longman (1998) 630–2 ('path'); cf. also n. 174 below.
105 Cf. also n. 175 below.
106 E.g., Plut. *De Superst.* 171E; Justin Mart. *Dial.* 8.1, cf. Lucian, *Men.* 4; Mason (2005) 285; Dio 4.8; Schofield (2000) 437–42; for Stoics, cf. the Lat. *constantia*.
107 Alexander (1993) 27–8 and (2005) 31–2 slightly exaggerates the 'exceptionalism'; more balanced Marincola (1997) 53–7.
108 'Presumably', because, although there is no evidence as such, Cynics did write some philosophical works; these were (necessarily) short; some of them must have expounded the Cynic 'short-cut' to virtue (σύντομον ἐπ' ἀρετὴν ὁδόν, D.L. 7.121; συντόμως and ἐπιτόμως are synonyms); and, although Epicurean and Cynic 'short-cuts' differ in that the former is genuinely an abbreviated form, the latter an assertion that anything more is superfluous and detrimental, Cynicism certainly influenced Epicurus in some things.

with philosophical concepts could read this Word as (also) being equivalent to, or trumping, the Stoic or Platonic *Logos*. This idea is widespread in Philo;[109] the Preface to the Gospel according to John has often been interpreted in this 'double' way;[110] and such a mode of interpretation was, from the analogy with 'philosophy', readily available to educated Christians such as Luke.

How does all this affect Luke(-Acts) *qua* historiography? It becomes a *historiographical epitome* as well as a philosophical one. More generally, one now has to categorise Luke(-Acts) as a type of historiography that incorporates (some sort of) philosophy. Herein Luke(-Acts) aligns itself with a long tradition of Classical historiography: Onesicritus, Posidonius, Sallust, and Plutarch are obvious 'strong' cases, Herodotus, Thucydides, Xenophon, any more general 'Cynic historiography' that exists, and Polybius more arguable ones. Moral exemplarity is of course also a marked feature of Classical historiography (and biography).

Given that the Preface exhibits some Jewish-Christian colouring, the reader may also align Luke(-Acts) as 'philosophical historiography' with Jewish tradition. Here the obvious parallel is 4 Maccabees, a rhetorical-philosophical address on the superiority of religious reason to the emotions, which buttresses its philosophical argument with examples from Maccabean history, and whose primary purpose is to celebrate martyrdom as a response to Gentile political and religious oppression. This work, which seems to date before 70 CE, had great influence upon early Christianity, the first agreed case being the Pastoral Letter to the Hebrews. Immediate parallels with Luke's Preface include the direct address to readers or listeners, the elevation of λόγος, the philosophical goal, and the representation of Judaism as a philosophy.

There is, however, another generic implication of this philosophical material. Since the various religious elements are connected with a community ('us'), and, as we have seen, Luke uses 'decree language', the community therefore is being figured as a 'polity', and Luke(-Acts) is like a philosophical *Politeia*, expounding the *dogmata* of a philosophical community, in the style of Greek philosophers such as Diogenes, Crates, or Epicurus.[111] Some readers will already know of this analogy as applied both to Judaism[112] and to Christianity.[113]

---

109   Winston (1985); Runia (1986) 446–51; Tobin (1992).
110   See, e.g., Moloney (1998) 34–43; Thompson (2006) 186.
111   D.L. 3.51; 6.72; Cic. *Acad. Pr.* 2.27; Epic. *Deperdit. libr. reliq.* FF 29.28.5–6, 11–12; 29.30.16; 30.31.1; 31.2.4–6; 36.10.3 with Moles (2011) 470 {above, p. 594}; relevant also is the more general, attenuated sense of *politeia* as (way of) life (LSJ s.v. 2); cf. Mason (2005) 284–91.
112   Jos. *AJ* 1.2, etc.
113   See p. 831 below.

There is ancient warrant for reading Luke(-Acts) 'philosophically'. Papias and Justin the Martyr characterise Mark as Peter's 'memoirs' of Jesus, like Xenophon's of Socrates. Justin so characterises the Gospels generally. The *Gospel of Thomas* interprets Matthew as comparing Jesus to 'a wise philosopher'.[114] Galen views the Gospels as morally useful in encouraging a philosophical attitude to death and as Platonically true.[115]

### 2.19   *Financial/Legal Imagery; the Contract*

Πληροφορέω, ἐπιγιγνώσκω, and ἀσφάλεια can all be financial/legal terms, meaning, respectively, 'pay in full', 'come to a judgement', and 'security/bond', and financial/legal imagery is common in moral or theological contexts, both Jewish and Classical. The imagery seems useful here, underlining a sense of moral reciprocity: since certain things 'have been brought to fulfilment', producing 'security', readers should 'recognise' the 'pledge' and 'buy in' fully to Christianity. The imagery also creates a morally and aesthetically satisfying ring structure (πεπληροφορημένων ~ ἀσφάλειαν).

There are wider effects. Literary theorists make much of the 'contract' between writers and readers. One such is genre, characteristically pre-defined in Prefaces, as in Luke. But 'contracts' can be much simpler: 'read this, get that'. Such 'contracts' are well conveyed in decree language, decrees characteristically commemorating agreements, alliances, etc. Thus we return to Luke's relationship with his great Classical predecessors.

Thucydides (1.22.4) promises that those who 'contract' to read him with sufficient care will obtain the stability that resides in contemplation and understanding of the Truth of human affairs: no mean reward. Livy (*praef.* 10) stresses that public-interested behaviour by his readers is also in their own interest, and the common goal is the restoration of the collapsing Roman state: a noble and magnificent project and reward. Luke's 'so that' clause outlines his readers' reward, which must be better than those on offer by Thucydides or Livy. This reward is the security of the truth, meaning, as we have seen, both that this truth is securely true and that it provides security. What is that security? ἀσφάλεια can be used of *physical* safety; it is regular Greek for 'safe conduct',[116] and some philosophical contexts (especially Cynic and Epicurean ones) dangle an ἀσφάλεια that is physical as well as mental.[117] But post-Pilate and post-Nero, and, on some datings, post-Domitian and post-Pliny, Luke(-Acts) cannot be

---

114   Bauckham (2006) 211–13; 236–7.
115   Galen in Walzer (1949) 15–16; Alexander (2002) 245–6; (2005) 158 n. 82.
116   LSJ, s.v. 2.
117   See above, p. 807 with n. 106.

offering that. To discover the distinctive and supreme value of Christian ἀσφάλεια, the reader has to read on.

### 2.20 Further Implications of πεπληροφορημένων; Pauline Traces

As it happens—and the reader will eventually discover for himself—Luke's use of πληροφορέω here is *hapax* within Luke-Acts. To what ends? Analysis so far has given πεπληροφορημένων multiple and important significations within the discourses of beginnings and endings, bigness and smallness, power, the overall road imagery, and the financial/legal imagery. But the verb and the cognate noun are found in the Septuagint, in Paul, and elsewhere in First-Century Christianity in the sense of 'fully convince', 'assure'.[118] So here Origen, who glossed πεπληροφορημένων as 'surely believed'. He is followed by the *Authorised Version* and a few modern scholars.[119] Another point of ἀσφάλειαν, therefore, especially given the already existing financial ring structure, is to bring out the full force of πεπληροφορημένων: 'brought to fulfilment in such a way as to provide assurance'. Classically, this interaction between πεπληροφορημένων and ἀσφάλειαν exemplifies the rhetorical figure of *e praecedentibus sequentia, e sequentibus praecedentia* (Quint. 8.6.20): 'from preceding things following things, from following things preceding things'. That is, the meaning of 'following things' is refined by 'preceding things' and vice-versa, and fuller meaning is created by a sort of see-sawing interaction between the two.[120] The effect here is to convey that there should be no gap between Christian narrative and Christian belief: the former compels the latter.[121] Further, for readers aware of the Pauline usage, this 'elongation' of meaning functions as an implicit 'marker' of a Pauline presence in this text, whether in literary resemblance (religio-philosophical texts with direct addressees) or in religious thought (exposition of Pauline versions of Christianity). Also latently Pauline is 'servants of the Word', for which the closest parallel is Paul's self-description as 'slave of Christ'.[122] Such 'signalling'/'putting down a marker'/'suspension of thought' is itself a Classical technique.[123]

---

118  Lampe, *Patristic Greek Lexicon* s.v. 4–6. Verb: Rom. 4.21, 14.5; noun: 1 Thess. 1; 'pastoral' references: Col. 4.12, 2 Tim. 4. 5, 17; Col. 2, Heb. 6.11, 10.22.
119  Orig. *Hom. in Luc.* 1; {Rengstorf (1962) ad loc.; cf. Bromiley, et al. (1964–74) VI.309–10}.
120  Williams (1980) 23–4.
121  Modern notions of 'faith' as something short of absolute conviction are unLukan.
122  Rom. 1.1: Παῦλος δοῦλος Χριστοῦ.
123  Moles (1985a) 37–8, 56 n. 29 {above, pp. 367–8}; (1990) 373 {above, p. 155} n. 125.

## 2.21 *The Ambiguity of 1.3*

Is πᾶσιν masculine or neuter or—even—both?[124] Few scholars nowadays favour the first,[125] none (seemingly) the last. But the first was the interpretation of the early Church Fathers.[126] Notoriously, ancient readers (especially biographers and commentators) often make illegitimate biographical inferences from writers' works. This early Christian reading presupposes: (a) the unity of Luke-Acts; (b) a known author: 'Luke'; and (c) the identity of this 'Luke' and a known companion of Paul's called 'Luke'.[127] All contentious. There is clearly also a hardening, 'orthodox' trajectory. Nevertheless, the reading deserves consideration. There are arguments on both sides. On the one hand, 'all' seems to balance both 'the things done which have been persuasively brought to *fulfilment* amongst us' and 'the words in which you have been orally instructed'; on the other, 'from the up' seems to balance 'from the beginning'. Further, 'following' is a highly resonant concept in 'master-pupil' relationships, alike within Christian[128] and within philosophical contexts, and the possibility must arise here. I conclude, therefore, that, in the absence of decisive contrary 'external' data (for example, were the author known by contemporaries to be far too young for any such personal contacts), the reader simply cannot at this point resolve the question of the gender of πᾶσιν.

## 2.22 *Historiography and Biography*

As already noted, one of the great divisions in the scholarly debate is between those who hold Luke(-Acts) to be historiography and those who hold it to be biography. But, if 'the word' is understood by Christian readers as being instantiated in Jesus (above), this immediately connects the 'things' that are the stuff of Greek (and Roman) historiography and the life of Jesus.[129] More: since οἱ ἀπ' ἀρχῆς αὐτόπται καὶ ὑπηρέται γενόμενοι constitute, as it were, Herodotean γενόμενα, this blurring between historiographical stuff and biography extends to the lives of Jesus' followers. The notorious programmatic distinctions between biography and historiography drawn by Nepos and Plutarch have content and are useful, but they can also be over-drawn, and they can also

---

124 {Cf. Moles (2013) 111–13 = above, pp. 690–3.}
125 A notable exception: Barrett (2004) 1.31.
126 E.g., Justin, *Dial.* 103.8; Eus. *H.E.* 3.4.1; Jerome, *De vir. ill.* 7.
127 Further, pp. 832ff. below.
128 Cf., e.g., Harrington (1991) 72; Boring (2006) 59, 80; Johnson (1991) 89; Green (1997) 235 n. 31; Moloney (1998) 59.
129 Cf. Irenaeus' reading (p. 806 above).

allow fruitful generic inter-penetration or even mutual generic subversion.[130] The Luke(-Acts) Preface also illustrates a phenomenon sometimes found in Classical historiography at its most innovative: an 'external' genre of one kind (here historiography) and a formally different 'internal' genre (here biography). One may compare Xenophon's *Cyropaedia* (a study of constitutions illustrated by a biography of Cyrus the Great),[131] or Sallust's *Jugurthine War* and *Catilinarian Conspiracy* (works of philosophy explored through historical narratives).[132] For the historiography–biography pattern in particular one may compare the biographies enclosed within Herodotus' *Histories*,[133] and the various versions of Julius Caesar offered by the biographer Plutarch and by the historians Appian and Cassius Dio.[134] Simply put, this asymmetrical relationship between external and internal can work in opposite ways; as providing specific illustrations of general processes (Xenophon, Sallust), or as reflecting competition between historical 'things' and overweening human agents. Thus biography seems too 'small' a genre to 'contain' Caesar, who 'becomes' the historiography of his period. This last example seems particularly relevant to Luke(-Acts). Luke has a historiographically 'great' subject: 'the things that have been brought to fulfilment amongst us': that is, the life of Jesus. Because that life is so important, is, indeed, 'the greatest story ever told', historiography is expressed through biography—but also vice-versa.[135]

If, then, Luke(-Acts) is a generic hybrid of this sort, Talbert's hypothesis immediately acquires some plausibility. There is a biographical focus on the historiographical theme; emphasis on 'handing on'; and emphasis on 'following' (even if the reader cannot as yet resolve the grammatical ambiguity of πᾶσιν).

For Luke(-Acts) *qua* Jewish-Christian philosophical biography, the best parallel is Philo's *Life of Moses*,[136] though wider philosophical biographical parallels may also apply.[137] Obviously, within a Jewish-Christian context, 'the philosophical biography' includes not only the religious but also the political,

---

130 Kraus (1999); McGing–Mossman (2006); cf. also Augustus' *Res Gestae*, autobiography within historiography.
131 {D.L. 3.34 puts Xenophon's *Cyropaedia* alongside Plato's *Republic*.}
132 Earl (1972).
133 Homeyer (1962) 76ff.
134 Pelling (2006).
135 To appeal at this point to 'individual-orientated' historiography (Lives of Kings, Alexander, etc.) as a *via media* between historiography and biography blurs and trivialises these significant generic negotiations.
136 Excellently treated by McGing (2006).
137 Burridge (2006) 137.

as both Moses and Jesus immediately illustrate. Within Luke (and the other *Gospels*), Moses is of course also a significant paradigm for Jesus.

Notwithstanding the Moses parallel, it is important to take consideration of the fact that, as Philip Alexander has demonstrated, 'there were no rabbinic biographies'. It was therefore inevitable that Luke (like the other Evangelists) would reach for Classical biography as one of his generic models.

## 2.23   *Self-Effacement and Self-Assertion*

Scholars generally find Luke's self-presentation in the Preface equivocal. Is he implying that he is 'only one of many' narrators of the Christian story, or that he is the *best* of many? Is 'set their hand' neutral or pejorative (= 'tried' but did not succeed, whether they never finished, or their finished efforts were defective)? The claim, 'I am the best', is certainly the characteristic 'Classical' historiographical stance,[138] but Christian anxiety—going back to the Church Fathers—often resists that implication here.[139] What are the pros and cons?

On the one hand, 'me also' (1.3) formally implies parity with the many previous Christian narrators. Luke's failure here to name himself is also noteworthy. This 'modest' pose, shared with the other Evangelists, as well as with many 'scientific' writers,[140] *can* be paralleled in great Classical historians (Xenophon, Sallust, Livy, Arrian, *et al.*), even among those who evoke decree language, though the omission is never inert, and it is never implied that the reader is simply not meant to know the name of the writer.[141] The effect is to minimise distraction from the subject matter, and there is a sharp contrast with—and an implicit rebuke to—the intra-textual self-memorialisation of Classical historians such as 'Hecataeus the Milesian' (*FGrHist* 1 F 1a), 'Herodotus the Halicarnassian' (*praef.*), 'Thucydides the Athenian' (1.1.1), or 'Appian the Alexandrian' (*praef.* 15.62). Luke's manifold competitiveness with the great Classical historians in other respects (extensively discussed above) is not 'immodest' within a Christian context, because that context obviously must maintain its superiority to the pagan world.

On the other hand, 'having closely followed all of them accurately from the top, to write them down for you in order' (3) ups the stakes (there may even be implicit specific criticism of the 'oral' Mark);[142] the 'scientific' patina (absent

---

138   Livy's 'modesty' is unusual: Moles (1993a).
139   Typically: Green (1997) 37 and n. 20; contra, e.g., Alexander (1993) 110, 115–6, 133–4; Mason (2005) 254–6; Tyson (2006) 111–3; Strelan (2008) 153.
140   Alexander (1993) 106 and n. 5.
141   Cf., e.g., Arr. *Anab.* 1.12.5 with Moles (1985b) 167 {vol. 2, p. 144}; Liv. *praef.* 1, with Moles (1993a) 141 {vol. 2, p. 190}; generally: Marincola (1997) 271–5.
142   See n. 13 above.

from the other Gospels or—surely—from Q) reinforces the claim of objectivity and reliability; Luke's work cannot have been anonymous in the sense that the reader is simply not meant to know the writer's name; the first persons of the Preface would then be left hanging; Luke's name must have been inscribed on the *titulus* attached to the physical book(s).[143] The unabashed decision-making ('it seemed good to me') is very rare in the Bible;[144] and the substitution, within a decree format, of a first person for people or constitutional body is itself highly 'immodest'. The massive, climactic assurance—and self-assurance—of ἀσφάλειαν (4) trumps the tentative, initial ἐπεχείρησαν (1). Finally (so far), the Herodotean equivalence of theme and treatment—especially given the special nature of that theme (the Word of God)—is also anything but modest.

Thus Luke's self-presentation as a historian of Christianity poises perfectly between 'I'm only one of many' and 'I'm the best' (a characteristic scholarly stance, Christians included), and his 'decree' supersedes the 'decrees' of the 'many' other Christian narratives circulating, including Q (to the extent that it was narrative), Mark, and other Gospels. 'Many' naturally implies Luke's relative lateness in the sequence,[145] which augments his competitiveness. The same applies to his superior 'doctrine' (philosophical/religious): Luke would resist modern depreciation of his theology.

### 2.24  *Historiography, Gospel, Title, One Book or Two?*

If Luke is historiography—in all the many aspects analysed—as delivered through the medium of biography, is it also a *Gospel* (εὐαγγέλιον)? This term for the Christian 'good news' appears as early as Paul[146] (and perhaps even with Jesus himself).[147] Mark, one of Luke's main sources, begins (1.1): 'the beginning of the gospel of Jesus Christ', and in ancient practice titles can be derived from texts' first words or key elements within the Preface. Luke himself does not, within the Prefaces or narratives, apply that term directly to his own work, but he uses the verb εὐαγγελίζομαι frequently in Luke, when Jesus and others 'evangelise',[148] and one might infer a certain 'meta-' transference to Luke's own work, especially given the equivalence of theme and treatment. Luke's name evidently appeared in the title (above); the longer title 'The Gospel according

---

143  Bauckham (2006) 300; by this I mean (at this stage), 'the author's name' (whether or not it was Luke).

144  The Western Text's addition, in 1.3, of 'et spiritui sancto' imitates Acts 15.28 (Moles [2011] 468 {above, p. 593}), so as to soften the first-person assertiveness.

145  E.g., recently, Tyson (2006) 111.

146  {Rom. 1.1, 9, 16; 1 Cor. 4.15; Gal. 1.6; Eph. 1.13; etc.}

147  {Luke 4.43; 7.22.}

148  {E.g., Luke 1.19; 2.10; 3.18 (John the Baptist); 4.18, 43; 7.22; 8.1; 9.6; 16.16; 20.1.}

to Luke' (vel sim.) is attested from the second century; and Martin Hengel has repeatedly argued that 'The Gospel according to Matthew/Mark/Luke/John' must all be original.[149] If so, while there were four named 'evangelists', there was always one 'Gospel'.

How would this conclusion—so constitutive of Christian orthodoxy—affect the argument so far? Clearly, despite Luke's self-naming, it would add weight to the 'self-effacement' side of Luke's self-presentation (above). It would provide an arresting, though 'collective', title: the Christian 'good news' as opposed to that of Roman governors or emperors. It would imply *some* narrative ('good news' in that such-and-such has happened). It would have a 'generic' implication in signalling Luke as a Christian text comparable to Mark and other Gospels (whatever their identity) but nothing more.

Nevertheless, I doubt the conclusion. Luke's Preface, as analysed, strongly suggests that Luke was announcing his work as being distinctively *different* from Mark and other Gospels: as a work of Classical historiography with an implicit Jewish-Christian religious and biographical focus. This focus then takes centre stage in the narrative. Actually to entitle the work a *Gospel* would spoil the effect of this thought-provoking trajectory. This is not to deny that, within the narrative, Luke's extensive use of the *verb* signals some affinity with other Gospels.

But the question of whether the word 'Gospel' was included in the original title also involves another hotly contested question: is the Luke preface a preface just to Luke, or does it *already* envisage—even *signal*—Luke-Acts as a unity? If the latter, that would be another reason for rejecting 'Gospel' in the original title, because the term would not obviously, or immediately, cover Acts. Now Alexander has pronounced: 'there is no way the reader could predict the plot of the second volume from the prologue to the first as it stands'.[150] This is unsubtle. As some note,[151] 'the things done which have been brought to fulfilment amongst us' seems to anticipate 'the whole story', and 'the whole story' as applying 'now' (perfect tense) to the, or to one, Christian community, a point strengthened by the 'redefinition' of 'brought to fulfilment in such a way as to provide assurance'. Further, as I have argued, Luke's use of γενόμενοι, glossing Herodotus' γενόμενα, extends the biographical element to Jesus' followers.

Failing some implausible papyrological discovery, Luke's original title is irrecoverable. Justice would be done alike to ancient practice, to Luke's strategy for the Luke narrative (above), and to the preface's anticipation of Luke-Acts

---

149 Hengel (2000) 48–56.
150 Alexander (2005) 224.
151 E.g., Johnson (1991) 27.

(not just Luke), if the original title were (e.g.) *To Theophilos on Security*, a title which would strengthen the philosophical aspect of the work and add a challenging further layer to the interrelationship of Preface and narrative(s). Such a hypothesis requires that the original title was lost, or normalised, during the second century, neither of which is implausible.

Finally, since the author's name must have appeared in the title (above), the title of 'The Gospel according to Luke' does at least attest the second-century view of that author's identity.

### 2.25  Readers, Insiders, and Outsiders

The author Luke is a member of a (or the) Christian community (1.1 'us').[152] As for the addressee, scholars debate whether he is real or fictional, and, if the former, whether Theophilos is his real name or a pseudonym.[153] Regarding his racial or cultural background and social or political status, whether real or imaginary, he is represented as Greek or Jewish; a Roman citizen; a fledgling Christian; and as having some social standing: sufficient to be the author's addressee or patron and to be addressed as 'most powerful'. The theophoric name 'Theophilos', of a type popular among Jews as matching Jewish theophoric names,[154] might make him Jewish, but there is no guarantee of this (unless the target readership is provably restricted to Jews, which it is not). Other elements (the tone and basic content of 'the things done which have been persuasively brought to fulfilment'; the implications of 'servants of the word'; Luke's competitiveness with other Gospels) make fullest sense to Christians. On the other hand, there is plenty to interest, impress, and, indeed, in various ways, to test sophisticated 'Classical' readers; the name 'Theophilos' seems to extend the potential readership to *all* 'lovers of God'; and the 'road imagery' leads *everybody* in. The only restriction is literacy in Greek, though oral reception, while inferior to reading, is obviously also feasible. The Preface reads best as targeting as wide a readership as possible—Christian, non-Christian, learned and unlearned, for, obviously, the Preface makes *sufficient* sense for those unequipped to detect its Classical sophistication, including those familiar with 'professional' texts.

---

152  On that 'us': Johnson (1991) 27; Green (1997) 40.
153  Streeter (1930) 539 famously conjectured that Theophilos 'was the secret name by which Flavius Clemens [the cousin of Domitian] was known in the Roman Church'.
154  Bauckham (2006) 100.

## 3 The Luke Preface: Consequences in Luke

I summarise these according to the main headings above, re-ordered and collapsed into larger categories.

### 3.1 Basic Generic Classification: Greek (Classical) Historiography Delivered through the Medium of Biography

Luke is a historiographical narrative, 'in order', of a person's life from birth (2.1ff.) to death (23.46), including his *Nachleben* (24.1–53), with standard items, e.g., parentage, birth narratives, prophecies of greatness, precocious childhood behaviour, etc. This biographical material extends—to some degree—to Jesus' followers.

Herodotean are the technique of biography inserted within historiography; the interest in 'the other'; the extensive 'road imagery' (below); and the concerns with different sorts of power (Luke 1.33; 1.52), with 'beginnings and endings' {(1.2, 33)} and with 'bigness and smallness' (see below).

Thucydidean are the generally 'accurate' and 'ordered' narrative; the relatively 'free' speech material; and the synchronisations of 3.1–2 and 2.1–2, which combine religious and political datings (this is also Polybian).

Why, then, do so many regard Luke's religious world as alien to classical historiography, and/or—on various different grounds—perceive a 'disjunction' between Preface and narrative (greater than normal differences between formal preface and 'flatter' main text)?[155] This 'disjunction', of course, is sometimes predicated—as by Alexander—on the claim, here excluded, that the Preface is not historiographical.[156] The question then becomes: is there a 'disjunction' between historiographical Preface and narrative(s) as delivered? Doubtless, some scholars have confessional 'anxiety issues' here, but they are unscholarly.

In general, scholars who register these misgivings have unduly high—or, indeed, misguided—expectations of Classical historiography. Not all Classical historians are Thucydides or Polybius—not even Thucydides and Polybius themselves! Luke's prefatory claim to historical reliability is conventional and necessarily relative. Of course, there should be some such reliability, otherwise his project will fail (more on this later). But this reliability is not to be assessed by strict historical accuracy as many moderns conceive it. Personally, I accept more fiction in Luke-Acts than many,[157] but my understanding of the factual

---

155   Cadbury (1922) 490; Alexander (1993) 93, 175, 202; (1999) 23.
156   Alexander (2005) 35–6.
157   See above, n. 40.

licence possible even within the most rigorous of Greek historiography readily allows such fiction,[158] as we shall rapidly see.

More concretely, such scholars underestimate the amount of material in Luke that can be considered 'Classical', or: 'Jewish, but also Classical'. Some I have outlined above. More will follow. But, of an example which some would consider 'un-Classical', Luke Johnson well comments: 'the prophecy of Jesus' birth [1.26–38] would have made excellent sense to any Hellenistic reader'.[159] Or, indeed: 'to any reader of Herodotus, Ctesias, Xenophon, or Livy'. They also neglect the fact that Classical historiography is itself of considerable diversity and developmental potential. They also underestimate the genre's interest in, precisely, 'the alien'. They also ignore the possibility that Luke is *redefining* Classical historiography, announcing a work of Classical historiography, while in some ways, already in the Preface, and more radically in the subsequent narratives, reshaping readers' expectations. The adoption of similar strategies by Greek and Roman historians and biographers (as, of course, by authors in all genres) has prompted much illuminating discussion.[160] Here we are dealing particularly with Christian appropriation and redefinition, of which more later. Nor has Luke's basic generic 'trick' as between Preface and Luke been understood: that which, historiographically, is 'the greatest story ever told' must necessarily be delivered in biographical form and be situated in the world of Judaism, because 'the greatest story' is the Jesus event.

That biographical form is, as we have seen, quite standard, except that Jesus' *Nachleben* is of course special, but it can be viewed as an *extension* of the normal concerns of Classical biography, particularly where the *Nachleben* includes the supernatural (deification, 'Caesar's Ghost', etc.).[161] Similarly, the Ascension, both in Luke and in Acts, invites comparison with 'apotheosis' descriptions about (e.g.) Augustus.

### 3.2    *The Greek Decree and Other Inversions*

At the very beginning of the Jesus narrative (2.1), his birth is synchronised with a 'decree of Caesar Augustus that all the inhabited world should be written out in a list': an immediate thematic and architectural parallel between Preface and narrative. This unhistorical[162] decree (Luke is fictionalising in the best manner of Classical historians and biographers[163]) creates sharp con-

---

158   {Cf. Moles (1993b).}
159   Johnson (1991) 38.
160   E.g., Earl (1972) (on Sallust as 'philosopher'); Kraus (1999); McGing–Mossman (2006).
161   See Pelling (1997) for the way this works in Plutarch's biographies.
162   Precise treatment: Llewelyn (1992) 123–32.
163   Cf., e.g., the influential Pelling (1980); Moles (1993b).

trasts between Roman 'world' rule and cosmic divine power, between Roman 'world' rule and between the tiny Judaean village of Bethlehem, between the Roman and the Christian 'polities', between falsely divine Roman emperors and the truly divine God and Jesus, between apparent 'bigness' and apparent 'smallness', between Luke and Augustus as 'legislators' and 'authors', between Luke-Acts and Augustus' *Res Gestae* as texts, and between Roman and Christian 'exemplars'.

Luke illustrates many other such 'inversions'. One is the whole idea of religious 'service', whether in the form of 'ministry'[164] or 'slavery'.[165]

### 3.3 *School and Philosophical Aspects*

Many things make Jesus and his disciples look like a philosophical school: the very word 'disciples' (μαθηταί); Jesus' (most un-Jewish) calling of his disciples;[166] their 'following' him;[167] the listing and naming of the disciples;[168] Jesus' 'mission statements'; all the 'teaching' that he gives the disciples; his disciples' rivalry for primacy in his affections or after him; the position of the beloved disciple; and his own privileging of the leadership of the disciple Peter.[169] Jesus himself looks somewhat Cynic-like.[170] Luke promotes a sense of 'school rivalry' by (implausibly) attributing 'pupils'/'disciples' to the Pharisees (5.30–33).[171]

Other philosophical colourings include the Socratic symposium, inter-school philosophical polemic (7.36–50; 11.37–53; 14.1–24),[172] Plato's *Phaedo* (in the account of the Last Supper: 22.14–38),[173] and philosophical 'road imagery' (below).

All this increases the proportion of 'Classical' material.

---

164 8.3 (of women to Jesus and the Twelve); 12.37 (God in relation to faithful slaves); 17.8 (slaves serving master/God); 22.26–27 (Jesus as 'minister'/'servant').

165 2.29 (Simeon); 12.37, 43 (in parable—Master will 'minister' to them in turn); 14.17ff. (of Jesus as slave of God within parable); 17.7ff. (of apostles within parable); 19.13ff. (sim); 20.10ff. (of predecessors of Jesus within parable); verb: 15.29 (son to God within parable); 16.13 (in relation to God).

166 Cf. Boring–Berger–Colpe (1995) §§27–8. {Cf. above, Ch. 26}.

167 See pp. 820, 832ff. below.

168 Shiner (1995) 91 (on Mark 3.16–19—Luke's source here).

169 On the whole topic see Talbert (2003).

170 Moles (2006a).

171 Green (1997) 248 n. 82.

172 Steele (1984); Johnson (1991) 191–2; Witherington (1998), 161 n. 115; de Meeus (1961); Johnson (1991) 225; cf. also n. 1 above.

173 Kurz (1985); Johnson (1991) 348; Kloppenborg (1992).

## 3.4 Road Imagery and 'Following'

As is well recognised, the main organising structure of the second half of Luke (9.51ff.) is Jesus' journey to Jerusalem—a journey alike literal, metaphorical, spiritual, and Christological.[174] Thus Jesus himself is brought within the philosophical/historiographical road imagery of the Luke Preface. Jesus' 'road' is mentioned as early as 2.52 (of the boy Jesus in the Temple): 'And Jesus advanced [προέκοπτεν] in wisdom and maturity and grace before God and men'. The use of προκόπτω of moral advance (very rare in the New Testament and—again—significantly Pauline)[175] glosses the Stoic concept of 'moral progress' (προκοπή), reinterpreted to fit Jesus' status as Son of God (2.49)—or *logos* (1.2). All followers of Jesus are called to 'follow' Jesus' road (5.27; 9.23, 57–61; 10.37; 14.27), reinforcing the application of road imagery to readers such as Theophilos. Within the Preface, the application of 'following closely' is thus further problematised.

## 3.5 Sight

Luke runs the whole gamut of 'sight' discourse: e.g., 2.30 (Simeon's song); 6.39 (parable of blind men); 6.41 (failure of insight into oneself); 10.23–4 (blessed eyes of the disciples); 18.34 (meaning of prophecy 'hidden' from the disciples); 18.35 (healing of blind man who does recognise Jesus); 19.42 (blindness of Jerusalemites to things that make for peace); etc.

## 3.6 Security from Falling, Buildings, and Financial Imagery (ὀφείλω, etc.), Standing

'Falling' is combined with road imagery in one parable (6.39), with house-building in another (6.48–9). Jerusalem will be razed to the ground (19.44) and trodden down (21.24), and every stone of the Temple thrown down (21.5). By contrast, belief in Jesus is like a house that cannot fall (6.49), and Jesus, the stone which the builders rejected, has become the head of the corner (20.17). The opposite of 'falling' is 'standing', under which come: (a) allusions to the general 'standing-up' (resurrection) at the end of time (2.34; 14.14; 20.27, 33, 35, 36); (b) prophecies of Jesus' own 'standing-up' (18.33); and (c) more mundane exhortations to 'stand up', which, thus contextualised, seem to acquire an eschatological perspective (6.8).

---

174   Johnson (1991) 163–5 (with bibliography); Green (1999) 396–9; 'road imagery' is also very important in the other Gospels, including Mark: Ryken–Wilhoit–Longman (1998) 631; Boring (2006) 37–8.
175   Otherwise: verb: Galat. 1.14; 2 Tim. 2.16 (ironic); 3.9 (ironic), 13 (ironic); noun: Phil. 1.12, 25; 1 Tim. 4.15.

## 3.7 Fulfilment

Just before the start of Jesus' journey to Jerusalem, at the Transfiguration, Moses and Elijah tell Jesus of 'his exit road (ἔξοδος), which he was going to *fulfil* (πληροῦν: simpler form of πληροφορέω) in Jerusalem' (9.31), confirming Jesus' Road as central to the 'things done which have been brought to fulfilment amongst us'. The verb is also used of an angel's words (1.2), of scripture about Jesus (4.21), of the Passover in the kingdom of God (22.16), of everything written about Jesus in the Old Testament (24.44).

Related are the verb 'bring to the appointed end', whether τελειόω (13.32, of Jesus on his own mission) or τελέω (12.50, 18.31, 22.37, fulfilment of scriptural tradition), and the adjective 'full' (4.1, of Jesus).

## 4 The Acts Preface[176]

### 4.1 Greek and Translation Issues

> Τὸν μὲν πρῶτον λόγον ἐποιησάμην περὶ πάντων, ὦ Θεόφιλε, ὧν ἤρξατο ὁ Ἰησοῦς ποιεῖν τε καὶ διδάσκειν, (2) ἄχρι ἧς ἡμέρας ἐντειλάμενος τοῖς ἀποστόλοις διὰ πνεύματος ἁγίου οὓς ἐξελέξατο ἀνελήμφθη. (3) οἷς καὶ παρέστησεν ἑαυτὸν ζῶντα μετὰ τὸ παθεῖν αὐτὸν ἐν πολλοῖς τεκμηρίοις, δι' ἡμερῶν τεσσεράκοντα ὀπτανόμενος αὐτοῖς καὶ λέγων τὰ περὶ τῆς βασιλείας τοῦ θεοῦ (1.1–3).

> The first word (λόγος) I did/made about all the things, Theophilos, that Jesus began to do/make and to teach, (2) until the day when, having given instructions through the Holy Spirit to the apostles whom he had chosen, he was taken up. (3) By whom indeed after his suffering he stood himself present alive in many indications, being seen by them and speaking on the things of the kingdom of God.

The verb παρέστησεν includes the notions of 'standing beside as a support'[177] and 'present as evidence';[178] the first *can* have legal colouring; the second certainly does. So also ἐν πολλοῖς τεκμηρίοις. My rendering privileges the root meaning of 'stand' and the important implications of παρά. The reasons for other choices will emerge.

---

176 Discussion: Alexander (1993) 142–6; (1999); Dormeyer-Galindo (2003) 32–3; Mason (2005) 257.
177 LSJ s.v. B.I.2.
178 LSJ s.v. C.1.

## 4.2 Links with Luke Preface and Luke; Unity of Luke-Acts; Historiography; Thucydides; Historiography and Biography

The passage asserts that Luke and Acts were written by the same person, an assertion which is falsifiable only by the strongest counter-evidence and which the large majority of scholars readily accept. It connects the two closely: Luke is the 'first word', or 'book'; Acts the second. 1.1–3 summarises Luke, resuming the chronological limits of the first *logos*; glossing the chronological precision of proper historiography; and thereby glancing at the Luke Preface's claim to an 'orderly' narrative. The emphases on completeness ('all the things'/'until the day') and on 'beginnings', and the implicit division of matter into 'things done' and 'things said', again echo the Luke Preface and are again historiographical. 'All the things' specifically picks up 'all' (Luke 1.3), interpreted as neuter. The word 'do' picks up on the Luke Preface's 'things done', because πράσσω and ποιέω are effectively synonyms. 'To do [act] and to teach [and, in 1.3, 'speaking']' also recalls Jesus as Word in action (Luke 1.2). 'Teach' recalls Jesus' role in passages such as 4.15, 31; 5.17; 6.6; 11.1; etc. The parallelism between 'The first *logos* I *made*' and 'Jesus began to *do/make*' reaffirms the unity of subject matter and Luke's own treatment of it.

The emphasis on the Holy Spirit as mediator echoes numerous passages in Luke;[179] that on Jesus' choice of apostles specifically echoes Luke 6.13: 'he called to his disciples, and chose from them twelve, whom he named apostles'. The general theme of 'Apostles' (= 'sent-out ones') is already important in Luke, applying not only to the twelve but also to the angel Gabriel, the Baptist, Jesus himself, and earlier prophets,[180] and thus reinforcing a cascading 'succession'. 1.3 'suffering', while alluding in Christian terms to Jesus' Passion in Luke,[181] also glosses the historiographical notion of πάθη, both as 'sufferings' in a strong sense and as 'things that happen to people', as opposed to what they 'do'. Thus 1.1–3 contains the historiographical 'active-passive' contrast familiar from Thucydides 1.22–3 and Aristotle, *Poetics* 9, 1451b11. παρέστησεν echoes the παρά emphases of the Luke Preface. The emphasis on 'standing' relates to the 'security from falling' of Luke 1.4; fulfils prophecies made in Luke about Jesus' own 'standing-up'/resurrection/ἀνάστασις (24.7; cf. 9.22) and about

---

179  1.15 (cf. 17), 35, 41, 67; 2.25, 26, 27; 3.16, 22; 4.1, 14, 18; 10.21; 11.13; 12.10, 12.

180  Apostles: 6.13; 9.10; 11.49; 17.5; 22.14; 24.10; verb: 1.19, 26 (Gabriel); 4.18 (Jesus and Isaiah), 43 (Jesus); 7.27 (the Baptist); 9.2, 48 (Jesus), 52; 10.1, 3, 16; 11.49 (etymological link between noun and verb, of persecuted prophets generally); 13.34 (of murdered prophets generally); 14.17 (Jesus in parable); 19.29, 32; 20.10 (prophet in parable), 22.8, 35; 24.49 (of the promise of the Father).

181  Besides the actual narrative (22.1–23.46), cf. the prophecies of 9.22, 17.25, 22.15, 24.26, and 24.46.

the general resurrection at the end of time (2.34; 14.14; 20.27ff.),[182] and specifically echoes 'he [the post-resurrection Jesus] stood in the midst of them' (24.36). 1.3 also evokes two great historiographical criteria: 'indications' (τεκμήρια: *hapax* in Luke and in the New Testament generally) and eyewitness testimony; 'being seen by them' also echoes the Luke Preface's 'eyewitnesses of the word' (the Greek words are cognate). And it evokes those two historiographical criteria with neat paradox, because the evidence of 'sight' and 'indications' can be opposed, as in Thucydides' distinction between his account of the Peloponnesian War based on eyewitness testimony (1.22.2–3) and his reconstruction of the 'Archaeology' ('ancient'/'beginning' things) based on 'indications' (1.1.3; 20.1; 21.1). The authenticity of Jesus' post-resurrection appearances is thus historiographically over-validated.

The 'speech-action' and 'active-passive' contrasts, the use of legal terminology, and the emphasis on 'sight' as historical validation are Thucydidean and echo Thucydides' presence in the Luke Preface. The legal terminology also echoes that of the Luke Preface and confirms Luke as a 'proof text'.

Of course, the detailed content and vocabulary of 1.1–3, while suitably historiographical, are also biographical; 1.1–2 effectively summarises Jesus' βίος; and 1.3 explicitly covers Jesus' post-resurrection βίος. The status of Luke as biography under the overall umbrella of historiography is thus reaffirmed.

Scholars debate how far the Preface extends, as it fades into the narrative (a 'fade' which is itself another indication of Luke's literary creativity). To what effects? One is that the historiographical motifs of 1.1–3, most of which look back formally to Luke, also acquire forward reference to Acts, just as the ends of 1.2 and 1.3 push forwards into the Acts narrative (the ascension described more fully in 1.9–11; the generalised 'speech' about the Kingdom replaced by the more specific instructions of 1.4–8). Clearly, also, Acts will be like Luke in being an orderly narrative of past events (1.1–2 ὧν ἤρξατο ... ἄχρι ἧς ἡμέρας ~ Luke 1.3 παρηκολουθηκότι ἄνωθεν ... ἀκριβῶς καθεξῆς), in which respect, too, it qualifies as historiography according to the prescriptions of the Luke Preface.[183] It will also be like Luke in being a 'proof text', thereby (again) validating Luke 1.1, 'persuasively brought to fulfilment amongst us', as including Acts.

---

182  I restrict myself to 'stand' stems; fuller exposition would also involve the important use of ἐγείρω.
183  There is thus no case for different generic classifications of Luke and Acts, *pace* Parsons–Pervo (1993), who hold the first to be biography, the second historiography.

## 4.3 A 'Second' Preface; Luke 'Redefined' as Thucydidean 'Archaeology'; More on Beginnings and Endings

Within Luke-Acts as a unity, this Preface is, however, also a 'second Preface', whose characteristic functions are to direct the emphasis to the following events, to imply their greater importance, and to redefine the continuing project.[184] One aspect of this is the increased emphasis on 'proof'. Even more striking is the statement that Jesus' earthly ministry was what he '*began* to do'. Ordinarily, the movement from 'beginning' to 'end' in relation to an individual is bounded by that person's death. Here, however, not only does Jesus live after the resurrection, but he continues to live after the ascension. The Holy Spirit, which inspires the apostles to bear witness to Jesus, is a continuation of Jesus by other means. There is a similar effect in the Prologue to Mark (1.1): 'The beginning of the good news/gospel of Jesus Christ ...'. Both writers are also alluding to Gen. 1.1 'In the beginning'. The 'beginning' associated with Jesus and all his works is a *new* beginning within the developing divine plan from the original beginning.[185] Mark may very well have been a direct inspiration for Luke, and the Christian reader is presumably supposed to recall Mark 1.1.

Nevertheless, Luke's use of the motif at the beginning of the second book of his avowedly historiographical project makes an important difference from Mark. Luke 'demotes' his first *logos* to the category of 'beginning' history, in order to emphasise the history that matters *now*: the working-out of Jesus' ministry in the Acts of the Apostles/acts of the apostles, as inspired by the Holy Spirit (or Jesus). Further, this working-out of Jesus' ministry will involve *ends*,[186] so that the contrast between Luke and Acts is not only between 'beginning' and 'now' but also between 'beginning' and 'end'. It is true that the movement from 'beginning' to 'end' is (also) foreshadowed within Luke (not least in the Preface), but it is Acts which works that 'end' through.[187]

These decisive shifts of narrative emphasis are underpinned by an ingenious historiographical allusion. Luke is what Luke wrote 'first', and was a *logos* about 'beginnings'. 1.3 paradoxically juxtaposes the Thucydidean criteria of 'sight' and 'indications' (Thuc. 1.2: ἐκ τεκμηρίων ... σκοποῦντι). Luke is thus redefined as the ἀρχαιολογία, the 'beginning-' or 'before-'λόγος, of, or before, the main history, itself now redefined as Acts. For 'Archaeologies' are not necessarily, or not exclusively, concerned with '*ancient* things', rather with 'beginning'

---

184   Conte (1992).
185   Boring (2006) 31. John (1.1ff.) also 'redefines' Genesis 1.1, but to rather different effect; Matthew 1.1 'the book of the *genesis* of Jesus Christ, the son of David, the son of Abraham' has similar implications to Mark and Luke: Davies–Allison (1988) 149–60.
186   P. 821 above.
187   Cf. pp. 825, 827ff., 837 below.

things. Luke will implement further ingenious redefinitions of Acts itself at the end of Acts.[188] Of Classical historians' many and creative re-contextualisations and re-definitions of Thucydides' 'Archaeology', Luke's is one of the neatest and sharpest and, certainly, the shortest. For the sophisticated reader, these Thucydidean 'traces' confirm a Thucydidean presence in the Luke Preface.

Thus both Luke and Acts are works of Greek historiography; together, they constitute a single historiographical work; but within that single work Acts now 'trumps' Luke as the more important historiographical narrative.

Of course, the Acts Preface has far more overt religious content than the Luke (Jesus, Holy Spirit, Ascension, Resurrection, Kingdom of God): having read Luke, the reader by now realises that 'the greatest history ever told' is the Jesus event and its sequel. The address to 'Theophilos' thus acquires still greater force. Having read the first 'word' (both 'first book' and 'word of God'), the 'God-lover/God-beloved' is now drawn still further into, still further encircled within (note the ring structure), the kingdom of God.

Generically, then, Acts, even more than Luke, is labelled as 'religious historiography' under a Jewish-Christian umbrella.

### 4.4 A Two-Book Work of Historiography?

The Acts Preface *seems* to label Luke's work as a two-book history. (Nor does the subsequent 1.8 encourage thoughts of more than two books.) For Classical readers, the obvious parallel is the two-book history of Rome by the Tiberian historian Velleius Paterculus, and the parallel seems useful:[189] both Velleius' *History* and Luke-Acts are epitomes, centrally concerned with kingly figures and 'succession'—Velleius with the Caesarian 'succession' from Julius Caesar, to Augustus, to Tiberius, Luke with the 'succession' from Jesus to his disciples, to the Apostles more generally, and to all legitimate Christian converts. The effect is to intensify the sense of parallelism and competition between Christianity and Caesarism, and to match Luke himself against another Roman author (besides Livy and Augustus). Readers might also recall other historiographical versions of 'succession': functionally, a subsequent work (by the same author or another) which takes up where the first ended; thematically, Alexander the Great and his 'successors', or the philosophical biographical model (as advocated by Talbert).

So much on the *seeming* two-book format. Fastidious philologists, however, might ponder 'first' (Acts 1.1): should Luke not have written 'former'? Or is this mere pedantry?

---

188  Moles (2013) 113–18 {above, pp. 693–9}.
189  Dormeyer–Galindo (2003) 33.

## 4.5  *Titulature*

The title Acts [Πράξεις], or Acts *of the Apostles*, is first evidenced in church writers from the late second century.[190] Individual books of plural unities can have separate titles. Most scholars regard the title Acts as inauthentic and inapposite, a minority as apposite enough.[191] If the title is genuine, πράξεις neatly anticipates ποιεῖν in the Preface, neatly picks up on πραγμάτων from the Luke Preface, and nicely conveys, Talbert-style, that Luke was about what Jesus did, Acts about what his successors did. The title also labels Acts not precisely as straight events-driven historiography, nor precisely as biography, but more as that 'tertium quid': individual-orientated historiography. The title, then, is fitting, but it seems (to me) unlikely to be authentic. The 'Hengel defence' of authenticity—that of distinctive unusualness—does not apply, and, if Luke's title was not *The Gospel according to Luke* but something like *To Theophilos on Security*, not only does Acts not need a separate title, but it would 'shut down' the central theme of 'security' prematurely. Better, therefore, simply *To Theophilos Two*.

## 4.6  *Acts 1.8 as Part of Acts Preface: Travel; Herodotus; Historiography; Philosophy*

When the apostles ask whether the risen Jesus will now restore the kingdom to Israel (1.6), he replies that it is not for them to know times or seasons fixed by the Father by his own authority. Instead (1.8): 'you will receive power when the Holy Spirit has come upon you and you will be my witnesses in Jerusalem and in all Judaea and Samaria and until the end of the earth'. Then follows an ascension narrative (1.9–11) elaborating Luke 24.50–3. Only at 1.12ff. does the narrative advance. Thus 1.8 belongs to the prefatory material.

The direct allusion to 'the kingdom' reprises a main theme of Jesus' ministry in Luke.[192] The instruction to witness world-wide from Jerusalem echoes Luke 24.47–8, the promise of power 24.49; the precision of the Holy Spirit fills out the vaguer 24.49. Clearly, even more than Luke, Acts will be a 'travel' narrative, and one already anticipates an intermixing of different kinds of 'travel': literal, metaphorical, religious, textual, as in the Luke Preface and Luke itself. Herodotus is again the obvious paradigm from Classical historiography, so that, like the Luke Preface, the extended Acts Preface features the two greatest Greek historians. A conception of the kingdom restricted in time and membership (Israel)

---

190  Details: Bruce (1951) 1; Haenchen (1971) 3–14; Fitzmyer (1998) 47–9; Barrett (2004) 1.30–48.
191  Fair comment in Barclay (1976) 227–8; Fitzmyer (1998) 47–9 and Dormeyer–Galindo (2003) 33.
192  {Fitzmyer (1981) 153–8; Green (1997) s.v. 'Kingdom of God'; Fitzmyer (1998) 203.}

is superseded by a commission for Christian witness not just 'to the Gentiles' generally but to the end of the earth.

With extraordinary economy and complexity, the 'end of the earth'-motif evokes: (a) two biblical passages: Isaiah 49.6 and Psalm 2.8;[193] (b) a persistent theme of Maccabees 1 and 2, applied both to world conquerors and religious leaders;[194] (c) several passages from Luke (11.31–2; 13.22–30; 2.32); (d) the claims of self-styled 'world empires'; and (e) the claims of Cynic-Stoic (or even Epicurean) philosophers, who go to 'the ends of the earth' literally or metaphorically and 'witness' their discoveries (in implicit competition with 'world conquerors' such as Alexander; Onesicritus' Cynicised Alexander harmonises the two).

Like the Luke Preface, 1.8 appropriates Maccabean historiography and Cynic-Stoic philosophy, to (by now) obvious effects.

(a) and (c) are harder. Luke 2.32 (Simeon's prophetic 'a light for revelation of the Gentiles') also echoes Isaiah 42.6; 49.9, 6; and 46.13. Hence Acts 1.8 rings with the beginning of the Luke narrative and specifically that of the Jesus narrative. The effect is at once aesthetically satisfying, confirmatory, and finely discriminatory. On one level, as we have seen, there is a contrast between the 'beginning' that is Luke and the 'now' that is Acts, but Acts will also advance the *future*. Again, the Luke narrative, while tracing 'beginnings', *also* contains prophecies about 'ends', and 'ends' both of space and time (2.32; 13.30); similarly, the Luke Preface outlines a movement from 'beginnings' to 'fulfilment'. But when Jesus answers the apostles' question '*when* will the Kingdom come?' with the instruction to witness to the *end* of the earth, the implication is clear: *when* you have done that, the *end* will come. Thus Acts, like Luke, combines geographical and temporal ends, but promises resolution to the movement outlined in the Luke Preface.

(d) implies competition between Roman and Christian imperialism. Further, the exchange between the two parties clearly implies that the apostles will be witnessing to Jesus as king. Whence yet another retrojection to the beginning of Luke: Gabriel's prophecy to Mary (1.32–3): 'the Lord God will give him the throne of his father David, and he will be king over the house of Jacob for the ages, and of his kingdom there will no end'. The parallel reinforces the moves from Israel to the end of the earth and from 'end' in a temporal sense to 'end' as combining time and space. But also, the beginning of Jesus' birth narrative in Luke casts Jesus as 'king'—and king over the house of David and Jacob; the end

---

193  Isaiah 49.6 is explicitly cited later in Acts 13.47.
194  1 Maccabees 1.1; 3.9; 8.4; 2 Maccabees 9.17; Moles (2006b) 82–3, 94–5, 97–8 {above, pp. 567–9, 577–9, 580–1}.

of the Jesus narrative finds Jesus condemned to death as 'king' and 'king of the Jews' (23.2–3; 23.38), even though Pilate judges him innocent. The beginning of Acts similarly casts Jesus as king. These parallels and structural correspondences and contrasts emphasise the problem of the relationship between Jesus' 'kingdom' and Roman 'kingdom' and reactivate the contrast, or competition, of powers introduced in the Luke *Preface* and the start of the Luke *Narrative*.

Finally, while the apostles are Jesus' direct addressees, they can hardly themselves complete the mission to the end of the earth (nor did they, as all readers know). The 'you' slides into any and all readers of Luke-Acts: all 'lovers of God' until the 'end' is achieved. Luke-Acts the text is also everlasting.

## 5 Consequences of Acts Preface in Acts

### 5.1 *Teaching*

Acts greatly emphasises this aspect of Christianity *qua* 'school'.[195] The description, at the very end, of Paul 'heralding the kingdom of God and teaching the things about the Lord Jesus Christ' (28.31) rings with the Preface (1.2 ['teach'], 3 ['kingdom of God'], 6 ['the kingdom']), underlining Paul as Jesus' 'successor' (cf. the Talbert hypothesis) and Acts itself as systematic school 'teaching text'.

### 5.2 *Holy Spirit*

With Jesus' Ascension, the Holy Spirit becomes a (indeed, the) central 'character' in Acts.[196] Paul's appeal to the Holy Spirit, nearly at the end (28.25). makes another ring with the Preface (1.2, 5, 8).

### 5.3 *Apostles*

The term, used extensively of the original, and reconstituted, twelve,[197] expands to Paul and Barnabas (14.4, 14): pointedly, because the risen Jesus '*sends* [Paul] *out* far to the Gentiles' (22.21; 26.17). That 'sending-out' is part of the mission to the end of the earth delegated to the original apostles but not fully realisable by them. Thus any reader who joins that mission becomes an 'apostle'.

---

195  Verb: 4.2, 18; 5.21, 25, 28, 42; 11.26; 15.35; 18.11, 25; 20.20; 21.21, 28; 28.31; noun: 2.42; 5.28; 17.19; cf. 13.12; noun 'teacher': 13.1.

196  1.16; 2.4, 17, 18, 33, 28 [Pentecost]; 4.8, 25, 31; 5.3, 9, 32; 6.3. 5, 10; 7.51, 55; 8.15, 17, 18, 19, 29, 39; 9.17, 31; 10.19, 38, 44, 45, 47; 11.12, 15, 16, 24, 28; 13.2, 4, 9, 52; 15.8, 28, 29; 16.6, 7; 19.2, 6; 20.22, 23, 28; 21.4, 11; 28.25; cf. 18.25, 19.21, 23.8–9.

197  {1.2, 26; 2.37, 42, 43; 4.33, 35, 36, 37; 5.2, 12, 18, 29, 34, 40; 6.6; 8.1, 14, 18; 9.27; 11.1; 14.4, 14; 15. 2, 4, 6, 22, 23, 33; 16.4; Fitzmyer (1998) 196–7.}

## 5.4  *Suffering*
Jesus' 'suffering' (3.18; 17.3; 26.23) prefigures those of Stephen (7.54–60) and Paul (9.16).[198]

## 5.5  *Witnessing*
Following the 'programme', 'witness' is borne firstly by the original, and reconstituted, twelve, and primarily to Jesus' resurrection (1.22; 2.32; 3.15; 5.32; 10.41–2; 13.31). But it expands to 'all that Jesus did', echoing 1.1, and to Jesus' *future* role as judge of all men (10.41–2 > 17.31). The echo neatly conveys Luke's own 'witness' and Luke-Acts as being the textual vehicle of mission to 'the end'; the latter elaborates on what will happen at that 'end'. The risen Jesus also enjoins 'witness'—of his appearance on the road to Damascus and of future visions (cf. 22.17–21)—on Paul (22.15; 26.16), thereby further validating both the resurrection and Paul's role as legitimate 'apostle'. Paul's own description, to the visionary Jesus, of his presence at the murder of Stephen 'your witness' (22.20) neatly conveys that Christian 'witness' may entail 'martyrdom', that Stephen was the first Christian martyr, and that Paul too will suffer martyrdom (partly in expiation of Stephen's). This steady expansion of 'witness', paralleling that of 'apostle', makes all readers potential 'witnesses', a status both honourable and demanding—and also potential 'martyrs': a topical topic, wherever we date Luke-Acts.

## 5.6  *Travel*
Jesus' instruction in 1.8 anticipates the geographical movement of the narrative.[199]

## 5.7  *Historiography*
Clearly, the narrative is broadly historiographical, with historiographical formulae such as 'this was the first time' (11.26), and elements of sub-historiographical genres, such as individual-orientated historiography, biography, and Jewish historiography.

## 5.8  *Thucydides*
Acts being a 'proof' text, Thucydides, with his strong interest in truth and proof, is a suitable archetype. Acts being also greatly concerned with the question of civil strife, Thucydides is again most appropriate. Acts also, and more than Luke, contains numerous speeches, for which Thucydides 1.22 is

---

198  {It seems clear that JLM would have expanded this section further.}
199  {In the absence of further discussion, cf. Moles (2013).}

the obvious classical paradigm, automatically cited by most Acts scholars. As if to verify the Thucydidean allusions in the Acts (and the Luke) Preface and Thucydidean input both into the speeches and into the representation of civil strife, Luke provides a brilliant Thucydidean allusion in Paul's farewell speech to the Ephesian Elders (on Paul's own victim-hood and the future sufferings of the Church), when Paul converts an observation of Thucydides about the euergetism of the Persian King into a *dictum* of Jesus (20.35 ~ Thuc. 2.97.4).[200] Discussion of Herodotus I defer to §8.

### 5.9 *Lettered and Unlettered*

The Acts Preface, like the Luke, is alike in its verbal intricacy and use of allusion highly sophisticated and basically comprehensible to the unsophisticated. Similarly, the High Priest and Sadducees wonder at the frankness of Peter and John (4.13): 'perceiving that they were unlettered', whereas the Roman governor Festus is exasperated by Paul's 'many-lettered-ness' (26.24). Christianity embraces both.[201]

### 5.10 *Standing/Politics/Up and Down*

The theme of 'standing-up' (1.22; 2.24, 31, 32; 3.22, 26; 4.2, 33; 7.37; 9.41; 13.32, 34; 17.18, 31, 32; 23.6, 8; 24.15, 21; 26.23) naturally strengthens in Acts, 'proof text' of the resurrection.

The cognate transitive verb ἀναστατόω (= 'stand upside down') is used by the Jews of Thessalonica to accuse Christians of world-wide revolution (17.6), and by the Roman tribune when he mistakes Paul for the Egyptian revolutionary (21.38); similarly, Tertullus, spokesman for the Jerusalem Jews, accuses Paul of fomenting *staseis* among all the Jews throughout the inhabited world (24.5, cf. 24.12). The juxtaposition of these accusations with Paul's expositions of Jesus' 'standing-up' helps to define the nature of Christian 'politics': non-revolutionary as ordinarily construed, completely revolutionary metaphysically and eschatologically because of Jesus' 'standing-up' and the general 'standing-up' thus validated. These bad and good applications of 'up' recall, and 'answer', the 'up-down' movement of the Luke Preface.

The opposite of 'standing-up' is falling (thus, explicitly, Luke 2.34).

---

200  Haenchen (1971) 594 n. 5; Plümacher (1992); Barrett (2004) II. 983–4.
201  Moles (2006b) 96–7 {above, pp. 579–80}.

## 6 Consequences of Luke Preface in Acts

### 6.1 *Christianity as a Polity*
The general representation of Christianity as a polity in Acts,[202] finds concrete expression in the Jerusalem decree (15.6, 19, 22, 24ff.), which thus echoes the Luke Preface.

### 6.2 *Philosophical Elements*
Among the vast material here, may be mentioned: (a) the emphasis on the Apostles' παρρησία;[203] (b) the Cynic-like 'communism' of the Jerusalem church (2.44–5; 4.32, 34–5); (c) the 'Socratisation' of Peter, John, and, especially, Paul;[204] (d) the representation of both Pharisaism and Christianity as 'sects' (Gk. αἵρεσις);[205] (e) Paul's speech to the Athenian philosophers (17); (f) sustained exploitation of Plato's *Phaedrus* in connection with Paul's (implicit) martyrdom.[206]

### 6.3 *Road Imagery*
In an exchange in Acts which could hardly be more 'meta', Philip asks the Ethiopian eunuch who is reading the Scriptures, 'Do you understand what you are reading?', and the latter replies, 'How would I be able to, if someone does not lead me along the road?' (ὁδηγήσει 8.30–1). Again, in 18.23 Paul is described as '*going through* the land of Galatia and Phrygia *in order*'. More substantially still, the whole narrative of Acts, a narrative itself substantially concerned with journeyings, is conceived as a journey. This notion of narrative as journey is frequently found in Greek and Roman historiography, most notably in Herodotus, whose narrative, like Acts', is itself full of journeyings (1.5.3–4, etc.). The Herodotean colourings and the very narrative/geographical movement of Acts (1.8) help to characterise the latter work as (also) a *Periegesis*.[207] Thus this travel imagery further intensifies the general historiographical colouring and the specifically Herodotean tincture.[208]

---

[202] Cf., e.g., Penner (2004).
[203] 2.29; 4.13, 29, 31; 9.27–8; 13.46; 14.3; 18.26; 19.8; 28.31.
[204] 4.19, 5.29 ~ Plat. *Ap.* 29d; Sandnes (1993); {Alexander (2005) 63–8}.
[205] 5.17, 24.5, 24.14, 26.5, 28.22; Jos. *BJ* 1.110; 2.162; *AJ* 17.41; *Vit.* 189, 191; Mason (2005) 288–91; Witherington (1998) 229; Alexander (2002) 232–3; Dunn (2003) 265 n. 44.
[206] {For fuller treatment of the philosophical material in Luke-Acts, see below, Ch. 28.}
[207] A circumstance very germane to Alexander (2005) 97–131.
[208] See above, p. 799.

### 6.4 *The 'We'-Passages and the Luke Preface*

How to interpret the series of passages about journeys made by Paul that switch into the first-person plural (16.10–17, 20.5–15, 21.1–18, 27.1–28.16). Is the author including himself? This 'conservative' interpretation goes back at least to Irenaeus (c.180).[209] Is there a literary convention of first-person plurals in travel narratives, especially sea-voyages?[210] Are the passages excerpted by the author from a diary or itinerary of a companion of Paul?[211]

Given (a) the use of first persons (both singular and plural) in the Luke Preface (and the use of the first-person singular in the Acts Preface); (b) the fact that these passages fall within the sustained, organic, and multivalent road imagery of Luke-Acts; (c) that this imagery is first announced in the Luke Preface; (d) that that imagery includes the author; and (e) the word 'having closely followed' is there applied to the author, the 'conservative' interpretation seems to me right. Πᾶσι *can* be understood as masculine (which is not to say that it *cannot* also be understood as neuter).

Luke is a 'follower' and an 'eyewitness' of some of the 'things' in Acts, in as much as he 'followed' Paul in some of the travel narrative. This claim contributes to Luke's historiographical emphasis on eyewitness testimony,[212] and underwrites the character qualifications (*ethos*) of himself *qua* historian.[213] Since the Pastorals attest the existence of a follower of Paul named Luke; since Luke-Acts cannot have been formally anonymous; and since the 'we passages' are specific and restricted, the present claim must have some plausibility, otherwise the narrative cannot give Theophilos (real or fictional), or any contemporary reader, the required 'assurance' of the truth of the Christian narrative down to their own time.[214] True, a writer such as Dio Chrysostom can fiction-

---

209  Irenaeus, *Adv. haer.* 3.1.1, 14.1–3; among moderns, e.g., Bruce (1951) 2–3; Fitzmyer (1998) 50, 98–103; Lane Fox (1991) 129, 210–11; Thornton (1991); Witherington (1998) 52–9; 484–5, 605, 626–9.
210  Robbins (1978).
211  E.g., Dibelius (1956) 198–206.
212  Cf. esp. Bauckham (2006), though without discussion of the 'we passages' and their interaction with the Luke-Acts Preface.
213  On the general topic see Marincola (1997) 128ff.
214  Hence some readers are already presumed to know Luke's relationship with Paul; will already read thus 1.3; and will already expect the Acts narrative, or something like it: Luke-Acts is always already a unity from the start of Luke; *contra*, Alexander (2005) 224: 'there is no way the reader could predict the plot of the second volume from the prologue to the first as it stands'; Johnson (1991) 27 also stresses 'brought to fulfilment amongst us' as covering Acts, a point strengthened by the 'redefinition' of 'brought to fulfilment in such a way as to provide assurance'; note also that, at the end of Luke, 24.49 clearly 'requires' the explanation of Acts 1.4–5, 8: Johnson (1991) 405.

alise his early autobiography to a disturbing degree,[215] but Luke is not Dio, and the claim of 'some plausibility' would only be falsified if the 'we narratives', connected as they are with the Preface, were wholly or substantially fictional.

Luke is also a 'follower' in the technical sense of being a 'follower' of Jesus.[216] This use of the verb 'follow' is everywhere in the Synoptics and in John, and, as here, literal and Christological 'following' are often combined.[217] The term (and cognates) can also be used of 'followers' of a philosopher,[218] which (whether with regard to Luke's relationship to Jesus or to Paul) further supports the Preface's philosophical colouring.

Luke also has been a 'follower' 'from the start'. The latter emphasis recurs early in the Acts narrative at 1.21–2 ('so of the men who accompanied us during all the time that the Lord Jesus went in and out amongst us, (22) *beginning from the baptism of John* until the day when he was taken up from us, one of them should become a witness with us of his resurrection'); and in John 15.26–7 ('But when the Paraklete comes, he will witness on my behalf; (27) and you also are witnesses, because you have been with me *from the beginning*').[219]

In as much as Luke is the author of the Luke-Acts narrative, or *logos*, he is surely also himself—to some extent—a 'servant of the word' (*logos*).

Luke's claim also has 'successional' aspects. The word 'follow' (and cognates) can be a 'school' word and can be applied to 'succession'. And Luke's teacher Paul was mandated by the risen Jesus in the following words (26.15), 'I *appeared* to you for this purpose—to *put you in hand* as a *servant* and *witness* both of the things that *you have seen* and of those in which I shall *appear* to you', which clearly echo Luke's Preface. Qua Paul's 'follower', therefore, Luke insinuates himself into the 'handing on' of Luke 1.3. Again, there is a 'school' flavour, as Luke constructs a 'succession' of 'followers' down the generations, includes himself, and legitimises his own 'school text'.[220]

Many scholars have found Luke's categories in 1.1–3 frustratingly woozy, but this wooziness (particularly that of 'following', 'all', and 'from the start') has a

---

215   Moles (1978); (2005).
216   Bauckham (2006) 15 n. 17, and 203 n. 4 objects to the rendering 'follower', as implying (a) temporal posteriority; (b) discontinuance of the disciple-teacher relationship. But neither implication is *necessary*, and the positive associations outweigh any disadvantages.
217   Cf., e.g., Harrington (1991) 72; Boring (2006) 59, 80; Johnson (1991) 89; Green (1997) 235 n. 31; Moloney (1998) 59.
218   {See, e.g., Just. *Dial.* 103.8 (PG VI.717C).}
219   Dunn (2003) 177–80, 353; Bauckham (2006) 116–17, 123–4; on the strong parallel between Luke and John see Bauckham (2006) 389–90 (without suggesting—as I would—intertextuality).
220   Note (again) that in the phrase 'write them in order', 'them' can denote both 'things' and people.

function. There are levels on which Luke insinuates himself into *all* the categories of 1.1–3, while resting his main claim on being a follower of Paul and without claiming to be one of Jesus' own *direct* 'followers'. This, of course, is not to suggest that the claims are *mere* self-advertisement—as we have seen, they have organic import.

It is interesting to see how early Christians responded to this passage. It seems fairly clear that Papias' Prologue incorporates elements of Luke's.[221] Again, Justin, *Dial.* 103.8, referring to the ἀπομνημονεύματα [of Jesus] as '*put together* by his apostles and those who *followed* them', makes Luke a 'follower' in some direct sense, perhaps specifically a 'follower' of the 'apostle' Paul.[222] Similarly, Eusebius (*HE* 3.4.6):

> Luke ... was very frequently in the company of Paul, and had no merely casual acquaintance with the rest of the apostles ... [His two inspired books are] the Gospel, which also he testified that he penned in accordance with what they delivered unto him, who from the beginning were eye-witnesses and ministers of the word, all of whom, he also goes on to say, he had followed closely from the first; and the Acts of the Apostles, which he composed, no longer from the evidence of hearing but of his own eyes.

And Jerome, *De vir. ill.* 7:

> Luke ... the *follower of the apostle Paul, and his companion in all his journeying* ... Some suppose that ... Luke had learned the Gospel not only from the apostle Paul, who had not been with the Lord in the flesh, but also *from the other apostles. This he also himself declares, saying at the beginning of his book, 'As they who from the beginning themselves saw and were ministers of the word handed down to us'. The gospel therefore he wrote as he had heard; but the* Acts of the Apostles *he composed as he had himself seen.*

Modern scholars often accuse ancient writers of making illegitimate biographical inferences about writers of earlier generations from their writings. There are negatives about these early Christian readings. They were all presumably influenced by the allusions to Luke in the Pastorals (a link made explicitly by Jerome). They all take *parēkolouthēkoti* physically and *pasi* as masculine,

---

221  Euseb. *HE* 3.39.14–16; Bauckham (2006) 203ff.
222  Interpretation of this passage (without specific focus on Luke): Bauckham (2006) 213.

whereas the better interpretation is: 'having followed all the things'. There is clearly also a hardening, 'orthodox' trajectory. Nevertheless, these early Christian readings correctly connect the 'we passages' to the Preface, and their inference that Luke is claiming to be a follower of Paul shows a good feel for his self-representation.[223]

Scholars generally tend to describe Luke the man in terms such as 'kindhearted', descriptions supported by some aspects of his writing. Nevertheless, ancient historiographical prefaces are characteristically agonistic and self-promoting, and, while Luke is less egregious in this respect than some Classical historians, he is here making extremely strong individual claims. He is certainly saying, for example, 'I am better than Q'; 'I am better than Mark'. This, of course, is not to suggest that the claims are *mere* self-advertisement—as we have seen, they have organic import. Nevertheless, Classical readers would certainly register and appreciate this aspect of Luke's Preface.

### 6.5    *Moral Exemplarity*

To begin with, there is Theophilos. But he also connects with narrative themes. *Qua* 'most powerful', he seems of similar status to the Roman governors Felix and Festus,[224] and just as he 'has been orally instructed' in Christianity, so has the Jewish Christian Apollos (18.24), and Felix 'knows rather accurately about the Road' (24.22; sc. that of Christianity). Theophilos is thus paradigmatic of a high-level Roman supporter of Christianity whose knowledge as yet is rudimentary. The Epicureans and Stoics are 'philosophers' in a simple and recognisable sense: Greeks who '*love* wisdom' and debate how it is to be found. But the *term* (17.18) is *hapax* in Luke and the whole New Testament. In context, therefore, it has force. The philosophical aspect of Luke's own Preface sharpens the question about the value of the 'philosophy' of *these* 'philosophers'. Luke-Acts, itself with philosophical elements, is addressed to *Theophilos*, 'lover of God'/'*loved* by God'. A central theme of Acts is that one should 'love God' and not 'fight God'. One should be a 'theophile', not a 'theomach'.[225] Later, we learn that '*love of human beings*' (*philanthropia*) is intrinsic to the Christian

---

223   Most scholars call the author 'Luke', whether as a name of convenience, or as the real name of a follower of Paul attested by Philemon, Colossians, and 2 Timothy. Sceptics find in Coloss. 4.14 'Luke the beloved doctor' (? ~ John 21.20 'the disciple whom Jesus loved') and 2 Tim. 4.11 'Luke is the only one with me' a certain over-egging of the connection, with the Pastorals modelling Paul and Luke on Jesus and the Beloved Disciple, in a teacher-pupil 'school' relationship (Bauckham [2006] 397, 401).
224   Acts 23.26; 24.3; 26.25; Lane Fox (1986) 430; Mason (2005) 205, 258.
225   Moles (2006b) 78 {above, p. 564}.

mission.[226] Earlier, Stephen the Hellenist emphasised that Moses, patriarch of the Jews, had been educated in 'the whole wisdom [*sophia*]' of the Egyptians.

Now, if Luke-Acts *qua* Herodotean-Thucydidean historiography accommodates, among its subsidiary generic elements, the philosophical treatise addressed to a named individual, one should expect direct, as well as generalised, philosophical (as well as other) exemplarity.[227] There is plenty. Luke himself offers Theophilos a positive paradigm, while the 'most powerful' Felix and Festus offer predominantly deterrent paradigms. Acts 18.24ff. extends the process of positive exemplarity. The Jew Apollos, having been '*orally instructed in the road* of the Lord ... spoke and taught [like Jesus: ~ 1.1] *accurately* the things about Jesus ... Priscilla and Aquila took him and set out *the road of God more accurately* ... And when he wished to go over into Achaea, the brethren *turned him to it* [προτρεψάμενοι, which can cover philosophical 'protreptic'] ...'. Apollos is like Theophilos, Jesus, and Luke; Priscilla and Aquila are like Luke; philosophical and literal roads intersect; implicitly, Theophilos himself is 'protrepticised' to become a teacher and evangelist; and Judaeo-Christianity again appropriates Greek philosophical modes. The passage also illustrates the process of philosophical 'succession', so that Luke-Acts emerges as centrally concerned with 'succession': Jesus, his disciples, Judas' replacement, Paul, Barnabas, Luke himself, Theophilos, any whom Theophilos converts, 'us', and so on. The basic logic of Talbert's hypothesis seems ever more deeply inscribed.

### 6.6 *Big and Little*

The Classical reader (particularly the Gentile reader) progressively grasps that this Jewish-Christian perspective, which seems small and provincial, that of a mere 'corner' of the world,[228] actually extends both to the end of the earth and to the end of time, and is therefore the greatest of all possible historical themes. It is thus not accidental that the 'hero' of most of Acts is a 'Mr Little', nor that this 'Mr Little' ends up in Rome, nor that the whole text should be 'small'.[229] In this respect, then, the Preface has a sort of proleptic bridging function, Luke's physically 'small' 'decree' 'pre-scribing' the supreme greatness of the seemingly 'small' Jewish-Christian perspective on the world. This interpretation seems

---

226  Witherington (1998) 760–1.
227  Exemplarity in the Gospels: e.g., Davies–Allison (1997) 713–18; Burridge (2006) 42–3; note the recurrent 'Handlungsmodelle' of Dormeyer–Galindo (2003).
228  Acts 26.26 'not in a corner', with Haenchen (1971) 689; cf. John Chrys. *Hom.* 52.4 (quoted in the main text); the phrase also has philosophical implications: Malherbe (1985–6).
229  On the significance of 'Paul' see Moles (2006b) 79 {above, p. 565}; Acts 26.22; 24; 28–9 ('meta' of Acts itself).

implicit in Chrysostom's gloss on Acts 26.26 'not in a corner' (*Hom.* 52.4): 'the doctrine [δόγμα] has been made everywhere in the inhabited world'.

### 6.7  *Fulfilment and Endings*

For the sense of fulfilment in Acts see 1.16 (scripture); 3.18 (prophecy); 12.25 (ministry); 13.25 (John 'fulfilling his course'); 13.27 (prophecies); 14.26 (work of mission). As in Luke, the adjective 'full' (6.3, 5, 8; 7.55; 9.36; 11.24) is part of this process.

## 7  Other Genres in Acts

Luke-Acts, while predominantly historiographical, accommodates several other genres, including Classical biographies[230] and the novel.[231] While this accommodation contributes to the work's aesthetic richness (a quality both of value in itself and morally attractive),[232] it also functions as an act, or series of acts, of appropriation. Luke-Acts promotes 'Christian imperialism'; it is thus itself appropriately an 'imperialist' text; and imperialist texts characteristically aspire to engulfing all other texts and all other genres. And its character as an imperialist text is generically 'appropriate' both to historiography[233] and to philosophy,[234] and perhaps even to epic.[235] So Acts can readily accommodate other generic strands.

---

230  See, e.g., Talbert (1974); Alexander (1993); Taylor (2006).
231  Huge bibliography; Pervo (1987) 86–135 and Alexander (2005) 97ff. suffice.
232  Pervo (1987).
233  See Moles (2010) 29 {vol. 2, p. 504} with n. 44.
234  Cf., for example, Cynic 'cosmopolitanism' or Epicurean 'world conquest'.
235  Suggestions that Acts appropriates *Odyssey* and *Aeneid* (very varying emphases in Bonz [2000]; Alexander [2005] 165–82; Wright [2008] 11.126) are attractive, especially given Acts' 'imperialist' character, and epic would be another suitable genre for philosophical freight.

## 8   Herodotus

There are clear affinities with Herodotus: there is the importance of travel,[236] an interest in the exotic,[237] the presence of the historian within the text,[238] including the preface with its ring structure.[239]

## 9   Luke and Josephus

There are also objective commonalities between the Luke Preface and the work of the Jewish historian Josephus, especially his *Jewish Antiquities*, published, in Rome, in 93. There has been a long-running debate about the significance of these, which occur mainly when Luke is setting Christianity within large political contexts or contrasting it with revolutionary Jewish religio-political movements, though also when he is representing Judaism as a philosophy. Do these correspondences arise merely through shared subject matter, or do they indicate Josephus' use of Luke or Luke's use of Josephus?

The arguments for Lukan use of Josephus are cumulative and have been vigorously restated by Mason.[240] The notion of 'creative rewriting' of sources (demonstrable in other CE biographical/historical writers such as Plutarch, Appian, Dio, etc.)[241] meets the objection[242] that Luke cannot have used Josephus because he would then emerge as a consistent bungler. I agree with Mason and earlier advocates of the case that there are too many 'coincidences'.

One should think of debate, or rivalry, with Josephus. Mason has made interesting comments on this rivalry,[243] and I will add my own: precedent,[244] with Luke 'trumping' his predecessor in an appropriate way: both Josephus and Luke address two works to individuals with theophoric names, but whereas Josephus the Jew colludes with non-Jewish religion by honouring

---

236   {Paul's travels from ch. 13 onwards; cf. also the end-of-the-earth motif, above §4.6.}
237   {E.g., 11.5–10; 10.1–16; 28.1–6.}
238   {The well-known 'we' passages.}
239   {See above, §4.3.}
240   Mason (2005) 273–93; 164, 178, 251, 300; earlier discussions i.a.: Holtzmann (1873); Krenkel (1894); Barrett (2004) I.294–6.
241   Classic is Pelling (1980), with many followers.
242   E.g., Bruce (1951) 25.
243   Mason (2005) 251–93.
244   Something of this in Mason (2005) 257–9.

Epaphroditus ('Aphrodite-like'),[245] Luke the Christian does not so collude, because 'Theophilos' underpins Acts' monotheism.[246]

Luke's procedure in representing the Jewish movement of Jesus and his pupils in Luke, both internally and externally (in its relations with rival groups), is beginning to look rather like Josephus' 'philosophisation' of Judaism and its constituent sects.

## 10  Authorship and Writing Context

The context for Luke-Acts is the first-century world. Luke's status is dependent on the fact that he was Paul's follower. But since Luke used Josephus, the *terminus post* becomes 93, and Luke is with Theophilos (real or imaginary) in Rome in the 90s and an old man. Similarly, Luke's younger Greek contemporaries Dio Chrysostom and Plutarch both wrote into high old age. Mild encouragement for this context comes from several factors: the last 'we passage' concerns Paul's journey to Rome itself (27.1–28.16), where the narrative ends (28.31); 2 Tim. 4.11 puts Luke with Paul in Rome; the second-century Christian tradition made Luke live till eighty-four;[247] the Gospel according to John seems to have had a similarly old author (in some sense of the term);[248] Luke's theology and view of the Church seem to suit the end of the century; and his allusion (Luke 1.1) to 'many' previous narratives about Jesus, while doubtless rhetorically exaggerated, implies more than 'one, two, or three'—the most allowed by traditional relative chronologies of the Gospels. I put Luke-Acts at *c*.105. Presumably, the later Luke-Acts is dated, the more necessary it becomes to hypothesise particular motivations (beyond general 'evangelism'). One might be old age itself (publish before one perishes—something of that is apparently behind the Gospel according to John); another is rivalry with and/or response to Josephus.

## 11  Conclusion

Luke offers one of the greatest of all Classical historiographical Prefaces, masterly in its brevity, compression, complexity, implication, and creative originality; in its aesthetic, literary, intellectual, political, philosophical, and religious

---

245  Jos. *AJ* 1.8.
246  Dormeyer–Galindo (2003) 33.
247  {Aland (1967) 533.}
248  John 21.21–4.

demands; and in its organic and multi-functional interaction with the subsequent narratives.

## Bibliography

Aland, K. (1967) *Synopsis Quattuor Evangeliorum*[4] (Stuttgart).

Alexander, L. C. A. (1978) *Luke-Acts in its Contemporary Setting with Special Reference to the Prefaces (Luke 1:1–4 and Acts 1:1)* (D.Phil. thesis, Oxford).

Alexander, L. C. A. (1986) 'Luke's Preface in the Pattern of Greek Preface-Writing', *NovT* 28: 48–74.

Alexander, L. C. A. (1993) *The Preface to Luke's Gospel: Literary Convention and Social Context in Luke 1.1.4 and Acts 1.1* (Cambridge).

Alexander, L. C. A. (1999) 'Formal Elements and Genre: Which Greco-Roman Prologues Most Closely Parallel the Lukan Prologues?' in D. P. Moessner, ed., *Jesus and the Heritage of Israel: Luke's Narrative Claim upon Israel's Legacy* (Harrisburg, Pa.) 9–26.

Alexander, L. C. A. (2002) 'Foolishness to the Greeks: Jews and Christians in the Public Life of the Empire', in Clark–Rajak (2002) 229–50.

Alexander, L. C. A. (2005) *Acts in Its Ancient Literary Context: A Classicist Looks at the Acts of the Apostles* (London and New York).

Aune, D. E. (2002) 'Luke 1:1–4: Historical or Scientific Prooimion?', in A. Christopherson, B. Longenecker, J. Frey, and C. Claussen, edd., *Paul, Luke, and the Graeco-Roman World: Essays in Honour of Alexander J. M. Wedderburn* (Sheffield) 138–48.

Bakker, E. J. (2002) 'The Making of History: Herodotus' *Historiēs Apodexis*', in id., I. de Jong, and H. van Wees, edd., *Brill's Companion to Herodotus* (Leiden and Boston) 3–32.

Barclay, W. (1976) *The Acts of the Apostles* (Edinburgh).

Barnes, J. (2002) 'Ancient Philosophers', in Clark–Rajak (2002) 293–306; repr. in J. Barnes, *Method and Metaphysics: Essays in Ancient Philosophy I* (Oxford, 2011) 1–16.

Barrett, C. K. (2004) *A Critical and Exegetical Commentary on The Acts of the Apostles*, 2 vols. (London and New York).

Bauckham, R. J. (2006) *Jesus and the Eyewitnesses: the Gospels as Eyewitness Testimony* (Grand Rapids and Cambridge; second edition, Grand Rapids, 2017).

Bonz, M. P. (2000) *The Past as Legacy: Luke-Acts and Ancient Epic* (Minneapolis).

Boring, M. E. (2006) *Mark: a Commentary* (Louisville, Ky.).

Boring, M. E., K. Berger, and C. Colpe (1995) *Hellenistic Commentary to the New Testament* (Nashville).

Bromiley, G. W., et al. (1964–74) *Theological Dictionary of the New Testament*, 10 vols. (Grand Rapids).

Bruce, F. F. (1951) *The Acts of the Apostles: the Greek Text with Introduction and Commentary* (London).

Burridge, R. A. (1992/2004) *What are the Gospels? A Comparison with Graeco-Roman Biography* (Cambridge; second edition, Grand Rapids, 2004).

Burridge, R. A. (2006) 'Reading the Gospels as Biography', in McGinn–Mossman (2006) 31–49.

Cadbury, H. (1922) 'Commentary on the Preface of Luke', in F. J. Foakes Jackson and K. Lake, edd., *The Beginnings of Christianity: Part I The Acts of the Apostles*, Volume 2, *Prolegomena II Criticsm* (London) 489–510.

Clark, G. and T. Rajak, edd. (2002) *Philosophy and Power in the Graeco-Roman World: Essays in Honour of Miriam Griffin* (Oxford).

Conte, G. B. (1992) 'Proems in the Middle', *YClS* 29: 147–59.

Creed, J. M. (1930) *The Gospel According to St. Luke: the Greek Text with Introduction, Notes, and Indices* (London).

Davies, W. D. and D. C. Allison (1988) *Matthew 1–7* (London and New York).

de Meeus, X. (1961) 'Composition de Luc XIV et genre symposiaque', *ETL* 37: 847–70.

Dibelius, M. (1956) *Studies in the Acts of the Apostles* (London and New York).

Dormeyer, D. and G. Galindo (2003) *Die Apostelgeschichte: ein Kommentar für die Praxis* (Stuttgart).

Dunn, J. D. G. (2003) *Jesus Remembered: Christianity in the Making*, vol. 1 (Grand Rapids and Cambridge).

Dunn, J. D. G. (2009) *Beginning from Jerusalem: Christianity in the Making*, vol. 2 (Grand Rapids and Cambridge).

Earl, D. C. (1972) 'Prologue-Form in Ancient Historiography', *ANRW* I.2: 842–56.

Fitzmyer, J. A. (1981) *The Gospel According to Luke I–IX* (Garden City, N.Y.).

Fitzmyer, J. A. (1998) *The Acts of the Apostles* (New York).

Frickenschmidt, D. (1997) *Evangelium als Biographie: die vier Evangelien im Rahmen antiker Erzählkunst* (Tübingen).

Green, J. B. (1997) *The Gospel of Luke* (Grand Rapids).

Gregory, A. (2006) 'The Third Gospel? The Relationship of John and Luke Reconsidered', in J. Lierman, ed., *Challenging Perspectives on the Gospel of John* (Tübingen) 109–34.

Haenchen, E. (1971) *The Acts of the Apostles* (Oxford and Philadelphia).

Harrington, D. J. (1991) *The Gospel of Matthew* (Collegeville, Mn.).

Harris, E. M. (2002) 'Pheidippides the Legislator: a Note on Aristophanes' Clouds', *ZPE* 140: 3–5.

Hengel, M. (2000) *The Four Gospels and the One Gospel of Jesus Christ: An Investigation of the Collection and Origin of the Canonical Gospels* (London and Harrisburg, Pa.).

Holtzmann, H. J. (1873) 'Lucas und Josephus', *ZWT* 16: 85–93.

Homeyer, H. (1962) 'Zu den Anfängen der griechischen Biographie', *Philologus* 106: 75–85.

Hornblower, S. (1987) *Thucydides* (London and Baltimore).

Jaeger, W. (1961) *Early Christianity and Greek Paideia* (London and New York).

Johnson, L. T. (1991) *The Gospel of Luke* (Collegeville, Minn.).

Johnson, L. T. (1999) *The Writings of the New Testament: An Interpretation*, revised edition (Minneapolis).

Kloppenborg, J. S. (1992) '*Exitus clari uiri*: the Death of Jesus in Luke', *Toronto Journal of Theology* 8: 106–20.

Kraus, C. S., ed. (1999) *The Limits of Historiography: Genre and Narrative in Ancient Historical Texts* (Leiden, Boston, and Cologne).

Krenkel, M. (1894) *Josephus und Lucas: Der schriftstellerische Einfluss des jüdischen Geschichtschreibers auf den christlichen* (Leipzig).

Kuhn, K. A. (2003) 'Beginning the Witness: The αὐτόπται καὶ ὑπηρέται of Luke's Infancy Narrative', *NTS* 49: 237–55.

Kurz, W. S. (1985) 'Luke 22:14–38 and Greco-Roman and Biblical Farewell Addresses', *JBL* 104: 289–305.

Lane Fox, R. (1986) *Pagans and Christians* (Hardmondsworth; New York, 1987).

Lane Fox, R. (1991) *The Unauthorized Version: Truth and Fiction in the Bible* (London and New York).

Lattimore, R. (1939) 'The Wise-Adviser in Herodotus', *CPh* 34: 24–35.

Llewelyn, S. R. (1992) *New Documents Illustrating Early Christianity: a Review of the Greek Inscriptions and Papyri published in 1980–81* (Marrickville, NSW).

Louth, A. (2007) *The Origins of the Christian Mystical Tradition*[2] (Oxford).

Malherbe, A. J. (1985–6) '"Not in a Corner": Early Christian Apologetic in Acts 26:26', *Second Century* 5: 193–210; repr. in id., *Light from the Gentiles: Hellenistic Philosophy and Early Christianity* (Leiden and Boston, 2014) 209–28.

Marincola, J. (1997) *Authority and Tradition in Ancient Historiography* (Cambridge).

Mason, S. (2005) *Josephus and the New Testament*[2] (Peabody, Mass.).

McGing, B. (2006) 'Philo's Adaptation of the Bible in his *Life of Moses*', in id. and Mossman (2006) 117–140.

McGing, B. and J. Mossman, edd. (2006) *The Limits of Ancient Biography* (Swansea).

Millar, F. (1977) *The Emperor in the Roman World (31 BC–AD 337)* (London and Ithaca; 2nd ed., 1992).

Moles, J. L. (1978) 'The Career and Conversion of Dio Chrysostom', *JHS* 98: 79–100 [above, Ch. 1].

Moles, J. L. (1982) 'Plutarch, *Crassus* 13.4–5, and Cicero's *de consiliis suis*', *LCM* 7: 136–7 [vol. 2, Ch. 31].

Moles, J. L. (1985a) 'Cynicism in Horace *Epistles* I', *PLLS* 5: 33–60 [above, Ch. 14].

Moles, J. L. (1985b) 'The Interpretation of the "Second Preface" in Arrian's *Anabasis*', *JHS* 105: 162–8 [vol. 2, Ch. 46].

Moles, J. L. (1990) 'The Kingship Orations of Dio Chrysostom', *PLLS* 6: 297–375 [above, Ch. 5].

Moles, J. L. (1993a) 'Livy's Preface', *PCPhS* 39: 141–68; repr. in J. Chaplin and C. S. Kraus, edd., *Livy* (Oxford Readings in Classical Studies; Oxford, 2009) 49–86 [vol. 2, Ch. 50].

Moles, J. L. (1993b) 'Truth and Untruth in Herodotus and Thucydides', in Gill and Wiseman (1993) 88–121 [vol. 2, Ch. 49].

Moles, J. L. (1998) 'Cry Freedom: Tacitus *Annals* 4.32–35', *Histos* 2: 95–184 [vol. 2, Ch. 53].

Moles, J. L. (1999) 'ΑΝΑΘΗΜΑ ΚΑΙ ΚΤΗΜΑ: the Inscriptional Inheritance of Ancient Historiography', *Histos* 3: 27–69 [vol. 2, Ch. 54].

Moles, J. L. (2001) 'A False Dilemma: Thucydides' History and Historicism', in S. J. Harrison, ed., *Texts, Ideas and the Classics: Scholarship, Theory and Classical Literature* (Oxford) 195–219 [vol. 2, Ch. 55].

Moles, J. L. (2005) 'The Thirteenth Oration of Dio Chrysostom: Complexity and Simplicity, Rhetoric and Moralism, Literature and Life', *JHS* 125: 112–38 [above, Ch. 10].

Moles, J. L. (2006a) 'Cynic Influence upon First-century Judaism and Early Christianity?', in McGing–Mossman (2006) 89–116 [above, Ch. 20].

Moles, J. L. (2006b) 'Jesus and Dionysus in *The Acts of the Apostles* and Early Christianity' *Hermathena* 180: 65–104 [above, Ch. 21].

Moles, J. L. (2010) 'Narrative and Speech Problems in Thucydides Book 1', in Kraus–Marincola–Pelling (2010) 15–39 [vol. 2, Ch. 58].

Moles, J. L. (2011) 'Luke's Preface: The Greek Decree, Classical Historiography and Christian Redefinitions', *NTS* 57: 461–82 [above, Ch. 22].

Moles, J. L. (2013) 'Time and Space Travel in Luke-Acts', in R. Dupertuis and T. Penner, edd., *Engaging Early Christian History: Reading Acts in the Second Century* (Durham) 101–22 [above, Ch. 24].

Moloney, F. J. (1998) *The Gospel of John* (Collegeville, Mn.).

Nagy, G. (1987) 'Herodotus the Logios', *Arethusa* 20: 175–84.

Pachoumi, E. (2007) *The Greek Magical Papyri: Diversity and Unity* (Newcastle).

Parsons, M. and R. Pervo (1993) *Rethinking the Unity of Luke and Acts* (Minneapolis).

Pelling, C. B. R. (1980) 'Plutarch's Adaptation of his Source Material', *JHS* 100: 127–40; repr. in id. (2002) 91–116.

Pelling, C. B. R. (1997) 'Is Death the End? Closure in Plutarch's *Lives*', in D. H. Roberts, F. Dunn, and D. Fowler, edd., *Classical Closure: Reading the End in Greco-Roman Literature* (Princeton) 228–50; repr. in id. (2002) 365–86.

Pelling, C. B. R. (2002) *Plutarch and History: Eighteen Studies* (London and Swansea).

Pelling, C. B. R. (2006) 'Breaking the Bounds: Writing about Julius Caesar', in McGing–Mossman (2006) 255–79.

Penner, T. (2004) *In Praise of Christian Origins: Stephen and the Hellenists in Lukan Apologetic History* (New York).
Pervo, R. I. (1987) *Profit with Delight: the Literary Genre of the Acts of the Apostles* (Philadelphia).
Plümacher, E. (1992) 'Eine Thukydidesreminiszenz in der Apostelgeschichte (Acts 20,33–35—Thuk. II.97.3f.)' *ZNW* 83: 270–5.
Raaflaub, K. A. (2002) 'Philosophy, Science, Politics: Herodotus and the Intellectual Trends of his Time', in E. J. Bakker, I. J. F. de Jong, and H. van Wees, edd., *Brill's Companion to Herodotus* (Leiden and Boston) 149–86.
Ramsay, W. M. (1895) *St. Paul the Traveller and the Roman Citizen* (London).
Rengstorf, K. H. (1962) *Das Neue Testament deutsch, III: Das Evangelium nach Lukas* (Göttingen).
Robbins, V. K. (1978) 'By Land and by Sea: The We-Passages and Ancient Sea-Voyages', in C. H. Talbert, ed., *Perspectives on Luke-Acts* (Macon, Ga. and Edinburgh) 215–42.
Runia, D. T. (1986) *Philo of Alexandria and the Timaeus of Plato*$^2$ (Leiden).
Rydbeck, L. (1967) *Fachprosa, vermeintliche Volkssprache und Neues Testament: zur Beurteilung der sprachlichen Niveauunterschiede im nachklassischen Griechisch* (Lund).
Ryken, L., J. C. Wilhoit, and T. Longman III, edd. (1998) *Dictionary of Biblical Imagery* (Downers Grove, Ill.).
Sandnes, K. O. (1993) 'Paul and Socrates: The Aim of Paul's Areopagus Speech', *JSNT* 50: 13–26.
Schofield, M. (2000) 'Epicurean and Stoic Political Thought', in C. Rowe and M. Schofield, edd. *The Cambridge History of Greek and Roman Political Thought* (Cambridge) 435–56.
Shiner, W. T. (1995) *Follow Me! Disciples in Markan Rhetoric* (Atlanta).
Sorabji, R. (2000) *Emotions and Peace of Mind: From Stoic Agitation to Christian Temptation* (Oxford).
Stead, C. (1994) *Philosophy in Christian Antiquity* (Cambridge).
Steele, E. S. (1984) 'Luke 11.37–54: A Modified Hellenistic Symposium?', *JBL* 103: 379–94.
Stinton, T. C. W. (1975) '*Hamartia* in Aristotle and Greek Tragedy', *CQ* 25: 221–54; repr. in id., *Collected Papers on Greek Tragedy* (Oxford, 1990) 143–86.
Streeter, B. L. (1930) *The Four Gospels: A Study of Origins* (London).
Strelan, R. (2008) *Luke the Priest: The Authority of the Author of the Third Gospel* (Aldershot).
Talbert, C. H. (1974) *Literary Patterns, Theological Themes, and the Genre of Luke-Acts* (Missoula).
Talbert, C. H. (1977) *What is a Gospel?* (Philadelphia).
Talbert, C. H. (1978) 'Biographies of Philosophers and Rulers as Instruments of Religious Propaganda in Mediterranean Antiquity', *ANRW* II.16.2: 1619–51.

Talbert, C. H. (1989) *Reading Luke: A Literary and Theological Commentary on the Third Gospel* (New York).

Talbert, C. H. (1997) *Reading Acts: A Literary and Theological Commentary on the Acts of the Apostles* (New York).

Talbert, C. H. (2003) *Reading Luke-Acts in Its Mediterranean Milieu* (Leiden).

Talbert, C. H. and P. Stepp (2003) 'Succession in Luke-Acts and in the Lukan Milieu', in Talbert (2003) 19–55.

Taylor, J. (2006) 'The Acts of the Apostles as Biography' in McGing–Mossman (2006) 77–88.

Thomas, R. (2000) *Herodotus in Context: Ethnography, Science and the Art of Persuasion* (Cambridge).

Thompson, M. M. (2006) 'The Gospel According to John', in S. C. Barton, ed., *The Cambridge Companion to the Gospels* (Cambridge) 182–200.

Thornton, C.-J. (1991) *Der Zeuge des Zeugen: Lukas als Historiker der Paulusreisen* (Tübingen).

Tobin, T. H. (1992) 'Logos', *ABD* IV.348–56.

Torres Guera, J. B., ed. (2011) *Utroque sermone nostro: bilingüismo social y literario en el Imperio de Roma/Social and Literary Bilingualism in the Roman Empire* (Pamplona).

Tyson, J. B. (2006) *Marcion and Luke-Acts: a Defining Struggle* (Columbia, S.C.).

Walzer, R. (1949) *Galen on Christians and Jews* (Oxford).

Williams, G. (1980) *Figures of Thought in Roman Poetry* (New Haven).

Winston, D. (1985) *Logos and Mystical Theology in Philo of Alexandria* (Cincinnati).

Witherington, B. (1998) *The Acts of the Apostles: a Socio-rhetorical Commentary* (Grand Rapids and Cambridge).

Wright, N. T. (2008) *Acts for Everyone*, 2 vols. (London and Louisville, Ky.).

CHAPTER 28

# Greek, Roman, Jewish, and Christian Philosophy in Luke-Acts

Within the Acts of the Apostles, which is a very problematic text, few problems are more problematic than the role of Greek philosophy,* especially as, whether by Jews, Christians, or others, both Judaism and Christianity could themselves be called 'philosophies'.[1] Scholars such as Talbert and Mason hold that Jesus, his disciples, and the apostles are represented as philosophers.[2] Loveday Alexander argues that the Acts *of the Apostles* plots 'the complex sectarian groupings of first-century Judaism on to a philosophical grid'.[3] Malherbe, Adinolfi, Sandnes, and Alexander find significant analogies between Paul and Socrates.[4] Johnson believes that the author 'recognises [Greek philosophy] as a legitimate conversation partner in the approach to God'.[5]

Big claims—all controverted. Thus Witherington: '[The] ... attempt to relate the Pauline material in Acts to the biographical traditions about Socrates relies on too little data. Acts 17 should not be overpressed. [The] argument especially fails to convince since Paul's death is not related in Acts'.[6] While Paul in Athens is the most discussed episode in the whole work, interpretations have diverged widely. Lane Fox pronounces: 'the author of Acts ... has ... been *mistaken* for ...

---

\* Earlier versions with different titles were delivered at the Lampeter Celtic Cycnos Conference (30 August 2006) and the Durham New Testament Seminar (30 April 2007); to avoid unnecessary controversy, I here eschew the term 'pagan'; I thank John Morgan, John Barclay, and Bill Telford for invitations; all who then commented; Loveday Alexander (who has provided constant inspiration and kindness), John Barclay, Andrew Gregory, and Philip van der Eijk as readers; and Todd Curtis, Susanna Phillippo, Rowland Smith, James Wilberding, and Tony Woodman for valuable discussions. Translations are mine. Expositions of Christian doctrine and ethics are Luke-focalised and value-free. The enormous scholarship, the paper's length, and my own amateurism prescribe bibliographical economy.

1 Within a New Testament context, talk of 'Christianity' (as of a separate religion) is of course too simple, though Acts is itself concerned with such problematics. I use the term for convenience, of those who accepted Jesus as Lord.
2 Talbert (1974), esp. 89–98; Mason (1995) 130–3, 153–6.
3 Alexander (2002) (quotation from 233).
4 Malherbe (1989) 150ff.; Adinolfi (1990); Sandnes (1993); Alexander (2002) 233–4, 239–44; (2005) 62–8; of course, all commentators touch on this, especially in relation to Acts 17, though with very varying emphases, as Witherington (below) illustrates.
5 Johnson (1992) 319.
6 Witherington (1998) 105 n. 2.

a man of considerable ... culture' (my italics).[7] Wallace and Williams, authors of a very useful historical guide, aver that the writer 'shows no knowledge of philosophy'.[8] Worse: numerous 'orthodox' treatments of Jesus, of Paul, and of Luke handle these controversies by mentioning them little, or—even—not at all.

This paper focuses on the Acts of the Apostles, but also treats both the Gospel according to Luke and Luke-Acts as a unity. It has a range of aims: to prove organic engagement with philosophy; to demonstrate multiplicity of function; to provide new readings and to find new things; but also, much more generally, to commend to Classicists a marvellous Greek text which few explore, and to New Testament specialists a systematically 'classical' reading of it—whose validity not many accept.

A 'classical' reading is one that applies the techniques that Classicists use in the interpretation of avowedly Classical texts. These techniques are in no way remarkable. They include the detailed analysis of structure, imagery, and wording, in the expectations that a Classical text should be a complex organic unity and that a Classical writer should have a high sensitivity to language; and the investigation of literary allusion, in the belief that the use of such allusion is a major feature of Classical texts. Naturally, it is not claimed that such a reading of the Acts of the Apostles displaces 'Jewish' or 'Christian' readings: only that it may usefully supplement them.

Since our topic repeatedly intersects with some of the biggest problems in Acts, I begin with a detour, starting with basics and signalling passing relevance.

I

The title Acts [Πράξεις] of the Apostles, first evidenced in church writers from the late second century,[9] is now a title of convenience. Most scholars judge it inauthentic and inapposite: over-hastily, I think, and I give reasons periodically.[10] The same person wrote the third Gospel (hereafter Luke; Acts 1.1).[11]

---

7   Lane Fox (1986) 305.
8   Wallace–Williams (1993) 90.
9   Details: Bruce (1951) 1; Haenchen (1971) 3–14; Fitzmyer (1998) 47–9; Barrett (2004) 1.30–48.
10  Fair comment in Barclay (1976) 227–8; Fitzmyer (1998) 47–9 and Dormeyer–Galindo (2003) 33. Hengel's arguments for the authenticity of the Gospel ascriptions (n. 12 below) could presumably be tweaked for Acts.
11  To refer to the Gospels thus abbreviated by the names of their alleged authors may be misconceived, but in this paper brevity matters.

The author gives no name (though the texts cannot be formally anonymous).[12] He addresses both to 'the most powerful [κράτιστε] Theophilos' (Luke 1.3; Acts 1.1). A title of *To Theophilos* would not exclude other titles.

Scholars debate whether Theophilos is real or fictional, and, if the former, whether Theophilos is his real name or pseudonymous. As for racial or cultural background and social or political status, whether real or imagined, he can immediately be inferred to be Greek or Jewish; a Roman citizen; to have received oral instruction in Christianity (Luke 1.4);[13] and to have sufficient standing to be the author's addressee or patron. But he also connects with narrative themes. *Qua* 'most powerful', he seems of similar status to the Roman governors Felix and Festus,[14] and just as he 'has been orally instructed' in Christianity, so has the Jewish Christian Apollos (18.24), and Felix 'knows rather accurately about the Road' (24.22; *sc.* that of Christianity).[15] Theophilos is thus paradigmatic of a high-level Roman supporter of Christianity whose knowledge as yet is rudimentary. The parallel with Apollos and the theophoric name 'Theophilos', of a type popular among Jews as matching Jewish theophoric names,[16] might make him Jewish, but this is unsure and—surely—interpretatively immaterial (unless one holds that Luke's main target readership/audience is Jewish).[17]

The Venerable Bede (*ad loc.*) took 'Theophilos' as a doubly 'speaking' name, meaning both 'loving God' and 'loved by God'. Rightly so, for a series of *philo-* and *theo-*compounds in Acts conveys essential theological messages.[18] While Theophilos' Christianity implies a Christian readership/audience,[19] his name should include *any* who aspire to be 'lovers of God' (cf. again Bede). These obviously might include the Gentile 'God-fearers', well-informed about Judaism, hence ripe for conversion to Christianity (as Acts itself illustrates), but also

---

12  Bauckham (2006) 300; p. 850 below (Luke as Paul's 'follower'); cf. Hengel (2000) 48–56.
13  Cf. n. 19 below.
14  Acts 23.26; 24.3; 26.25; Lane Fox (1986) 430; Mason (2005) 205, 258.
15  I prefer this to the traditional 'the Way', because it better recalls the general 'road' imagery with which I shall be much concerned.
16  Bauckham (2006) 100.
17  P. 863 below.
18  See p. 889 below.
19  In this latter respect, as in all others, the early reception of New Testament texts is endlessly controversial. While orality and texts must in some senses co-exist (Bauckham [2006] 287, 309), it is generally agreed that Mark was composed to be read to a Christian congregation (Boring [2006] 1). Nevertheless, the Preface to Luke(-Acts) seems to envisage a 'performance' context of 'private reading', even for an existing Christian, and this is surely the natural context for non-Christian and non-Jewish readers. But I have no wish to alienate those who uphold a preponderantly oral/aural context, especially before Christian congregations.

Hellenised.[20] The hypothesis that the text makes any appeal to non-Christians or non-Jews beyond the 'God-fearers' is harder and needs to be argued. Of course, absolute proof is impossible; nevertheless, the more numerous the demonstrable classical elements, the more plausible the hypothesis becomes, especially if those elements sometimes seem to function as illustrations—even, in a sense, as invitations—for non-Christians and non-Jews. The text also (I believe) contains other signals that point the same way.

Of course, many existing Christians or Jews (and, among the latter, Diaspora Jews in particular) would also have been Hellenised, not only in the minimal sense that they had to have Greek to understand Luke-Acts, but that they had some acquaintance with Greek culture. The 'most powerful Theophilos' must have been one such. Classical allusions *per se* do not indicate a wider, non-Christian or non-Jewish readership: the question must be decided by their density and function. Conversely, if Luke is indeed writing for the widest possible range of readers, the Classical allusions and elements should not be so dense or, as it were, so autonomous as to oppress, alienate, or confuse those who do not possess that sort of knowledge. In other words, a 'simple', non-Classical reading should always be available. The favourable response to Luke of ordinary Christians in modern times suggests that any Classical elements are not thus oppressive, alienating, or confusing. I shall return frequently to this question of Classical allusions and readership.

The attribution of the two books to 'Luke' is first found in the second half of the second century, when 'Luke' is identified with the companion of Paul of that name mentioned in Philemon 24, Colossians 4.14, and 2 Timothy 4.11.[21] The value of such Christian traditions is disputed.[22] Of these letters, scholarship mostly accepts Philemon's authenticity, mostly dismisses 2 Timothy, and splits over Colossians.[23]

Another complication is the 'we passages' (16.10–17; 20.5–15; 21.1–18; 27.1–28.16), concerning journeys made by Paul. Is the author including himself? This 'conservative' interpretation goes back at least to Irenaeus (c.180).[24] Is there a literary convention of first-person-plural narrative in travel narratives,

---

20  On the problem of the 'God-fearers' as a category see Barrett (2004) I.499–501; they are Luke's 'target' according to Tyson (1992) 36.
21  Details: Bruce (1951) 1; Haenchen (1971) 9–14; Barrett (2004) I.30–48.
22  Doughty defence: Byrskog (2000) 272–92; Bauckham (2006) 12ff., 202ff., 413ff., 438ff.
23  Stuckenbruck (2003); Hultgren (2003).
24  Irenaeus, *Adv. haer.* 3.1.1, 14.1–3; among moderns, e.g., Bruce (1951) 2–3; Fitzmyer (1998) 50, 98–103; Lane Fox (1991) 129, 210–11; Thornton (1991); Witherington (1998) 52–9; 484–5, 605, 626–9.

especially of sea voyages?[25] Are the passages from a diary or itinerary of a companion of Paul other than the author that the latter has excerpted?[26]

Most scholars call the author 'Luke', whether as a name of convenience, or as the real name of a follower of Paul attested by Philemon, Colossians, and 2 Timothy. Sceptics find in Coloss. 4.14 'Luke the *beloved* doctor' (? ~ John 21.20 'the disciple whom Jesus *loved*') and 2 Tim. 4.11 'Luke is the *only* one with me' a certain over-egging of the connection, with the Pastorals modelling Paul and Luke on Jesus and the Beloved Disciple, in a teacher–pupil 'school' relationship.[27] Luke is certainly a follower in larger senses: Paul is the 'hero' of Acts; his Gentile mission is justified and celebrated; and the text sometimes adopts Pauline formulations. As for background, Luke's name is a Graecisation of Lucius; his Greek is respectable *koine* of a 'professional-man' kind,[28] frequently heightened by more or less elaborate Septuagint allusions, but he can 'write Classical', and he knows (controversially, but, I believe, certainly) great Classical texts such as Homer, Thucydides, and Euripides,[29] and more contemporary Classical literature such as the Greek novel;[30] he also (controversially, but, I believe, certainly) knows about Dionysiac myth and cult.[31] His errors about Jewish religious practice indicate a 'God-fearer' who embraced Christianity.

On the relationship between Luke and Acts there is broad consensus that not merely is Acts the sequel to Luke but the two constitute some sort of unity (whence Luke-Acts). This paper supports that consensus. How unified is much more controversial.[32] This paper supports a very high degree of unity.

As regards date, Paul's death (64 CE)[33] is repeatedly foreshadowed in the narrative and the speeches,[34] and Acts' prequel, Luke, is undoubtedly post-70.[35]

---

25 Robbins (1978).
26 E.g., Dibelius (1956) 198–206.
27 The relationship: Bauckham (2006) 397, 401.
28 '"Professional-man" kind' glosses the German 'Fachprosa': Rydbeck (1967); Alexander (2005) 3–4, 18–19, 231–52.
29 Moles (2006b); such 'knowledge' is of course only inferable from the text, interpretation of which is itself controversial.
30 Cf. p. 837 above.
31 Moles (2006a).
32 On the problematics of the notion of the 'unity' of Luke-Acts, cf. above, Ch. 27, pp. 822–3.
33 I regard the hypothesis that Paul died during Nero's attack on the Christians following the Great Fire as certain.
34 P. 895 below.
35 The general consensus, which I accept: references and standard arguments in Moles (2006b) 89 {above, p. 574} n. 106; if Mark is c.70 (cf. recently Boring [2006] 14–15, 363–4, 367–8), Luke-Acts is necessarily later, because Luke uses Mark as a source.

Otherwise, scholarly datings range from c.80–c.150.³⁶ Lower dates are favoured by those who believe that Luke was Paul's companion, or that Acts shows no knowledge of Paul's letters³⁷ (available as a collection seemingly by the 90s),³⁸ or that it represents the governmental and political world(s) of the first century. Contrarily, some slot Luke-Acts into Christian debates of as late as the 140s or 150s.³⁹

Another relevant consideration is the series of correspondences between Luke-Acts and Josephus, whose *Jewish Antiquities* appeared, in Rome, in 93. These mainly occur when Luke is setting Christianity within large political contexts or contrasting it with revolutionary Jewish religio-political movements, though also when Judaism is being represented as a philosophy.⁴⁰

The arguments for Lukan use of Josephus are cumulative and have been vigorously restated by Mason.⁴¹ The notion of 'creative rewriting' of sources (demonstrable in other CE biographical/historical writers such as Plutarch, Appian, Dio, etc.)⁴² meets the objection⁴³ that Luke cannot have used Josephus because he would then emerge as a consistent bungler. I agree with Mason and earlier advocates of the case that there are too many 'coincidences', and offer my own ha'p'orth (which has, indeed, some purchase on our topic).

A test example is Acts 5.36–7, where the Pharisee *Gamaliel* deters extreme action against the Apostles by arguing that time should be the judge of the divine credentials of the new movement: rapid failure condemned the recent movements of Theudas and Judas the Galilean. Josephus' accounts of these latter are closely parallel but indicate multiple errors in Gamaliel's/Luke's chronology. Josephus also notes that Judas came from *Gamala*, cognate noun (*AJ* 18.1.4). Coincidence? No: the geographical detail inspired Luke to 'father' a

---

36  Useful surveys: Barclay (1976) 244–58; Brown (1997) 273–4; Barrett (2004) I.48; II.xlii–xlv.
37  The usual view, with some dissenters (whom I think correct), e.g., Witherington (1998) 430–8, 568, 610–17; Mason (2005) 264.
38  1 Clement (c.96).
39  E.g., Baur (1831); Knox (1942); O'Neill (1970); Townsend (1984); other criteria—the relative chronology of Acts and 1 Clem.; the possibility of an intertextual relationship between Luke-Acts and the Gospel according to John, special emphases, interest in Church organisation, etc.—exceed my scope, though my (very heterodox) sense is that Luke-Acts uses John (as argued by Morgan [1994]); and Goodspeed (1937) 191–6 (cf. Barclay [1976] 249–50) makes a good case for the last decade of the first century, a period for which I would like a few years' extension.
40  P. 852 below.
41  Mason (2005) 273–93; 164, 178, 251, 300; earlier discussions: Holtzmann (1873); Krenkel (1894); {Streeter (1930) 556–7;} Barrett (2004) I.294–6.
42  Classic is Pelling (1980), with many followers.
43  E.g., Bruce (1951) 25.

creative rewriting of history on Gamaliel, with the further advantage of instituting a 'succession' between Gamaliel, leading Pharisee of his generation, and Paul, pupil of Gamaliel (22.2) and Christian convert from Pharisaism (26.5), and between Pharisees and Christians generally. The notion of 'succession' will rapidly emerge as a key concern of Acts.

Regarding Acts' genre, many suggestions have been made, but at least four could accommodate philosophical material: Greek historiography; the novel; biography; and Talbert's hypothesis of a pattern found in Diogenes Laertius' *Lives of the Philosphers*.[44] In this last, Jesus and his disciples would be likened to a philosophical school, and a main aim would be to legitimise the Twelve, plus Paul and Barnabas, as Jesus' *successors*.[45]

Classical authors can always describe exotic foreign religious movements in philosophical terms. Greeks from Aristotle on so characterise Judaism.[46] So do Jewish writers (Artapanus, Aristobulus, Aristeas, Ben Sira, Philo, and Josephus). These representations rest on commonalities such as distinctive, partly separatist, relatively ascetic way of life; canonical texts; focus on theology and related questions such as theodicy, afterlife, immortality, etc; relative doctrinal coherence; and concern with preservation of authentic traditions and successions, often within 'school' contexts. For non-Jews, such representations help to illuminate and normalise; for Jews, they promote 'conversation' with non-Jews, demonstrate religious fundamentals across races, or bolster Judaism's superiority, particularly that of Jewish Wisdom to Greek '(love of) wisdom'. The process allows a wide range of accommodation, from apparent, or near, parity of esteem to polemical contrast.

With Christianity, there are the same commonalities, plus an important difference that, paradoxically, might accentuate the parallel: the lack of public religious practice. When the process starts is debated. Some put it in the second century, with the so-called Christian Apologists. Thus Lane Fox: 'in the early second century, the picture changes importantly'.[47] But Jesus himself may have compared himself to the Cynics and seems (as early as Q)[48] to have been represented as (somewhat) Cynic-like.[49] Paul was influenced by Cynicism and Stoicism, sometimes represents himself in Cynic guise, and invites various

---

44  For these see above, Ch. 27, p. 788.
45  See above, Ch. 27, pp. 832ff.
46  Judaism ~ 'philosophy': much discussed, e.g., Mason (1995) 130–3; (2005) 111–16; Alexander (2002) 230–3, 244–8; more generally, Hunter (2006).
47  Lane Fox (1986) 305.
48  Hypothetical and enormously controversial second written source behind Matthew and Luke (the first being Mark), whose existence and conventional dating (the 50s) I accept.
49  Moles (2006a).

comparisons with Greek and Roman philosophers.[50] True, he can transvalue Christian 'foolishness' against Greek and Roman 'wisdom' (1 Cor. 2.1–5, cf. also the Pauline Colossians 2.8, the only New Testament case of the *word* 'philosophy'). Such dismissal by Christians is always possible: Tertullian, writing c.200, expostulates, evidently with an eye to Acts 17: 'What is there in common between Athens and Jerusalem?' (*De praescr. haer.* 7) and 'What likeness is there between a philosopher and a Christian?' (*Apol.* 46.18). But such sentiments are dwarfed by the formally positive material.

Christians can call themselves and their religion 'philosophers' and 'philosophy'; compare their life with that of (other) philosophies; recognise 'kinship' with Greek and Roman philosophers; admit the best Greek philosophy as a sign of divine providence, and a legitimate precursor of, and propaedeutic for, Christianity; hail Socrates and others as Christians *avant la lettre*, since they followed the *logos* incarnated in Jesus; and claim that Christians, Platonists, and Stoics are saying essentially the same things. The motives, attitudes, functions, and benevolence range enormously, encompassing an unselfconscious claim to philosophical status, genuine admiration for (some) Greek philosophy, acknowledgement of common concerns or conclusions or of influence, appropriation of Greek philosophical sophistication, attempt to normalise Christianity, appeal to Greek philosophers or educated Greeks and Romans generally through their own traditions and conceptual frameworks, defence of Christianity's intellectual respectability, the claim that Christianity fulfils or supersedes Greek philosophy, and outright dismissal of its allegedly excessive ratiocinations and moral hypocrisies. Greeks and Romans also can represent Christianity as a philosophy, whether disparagingly ('the barbarian philosophy'), patronisingly ('the simple philosophy'), neutrally, or positively.

This general phenomenon *could* provide Talbert's hypothesis with a plausible background. But Luke-Acts itself would have to illustrate the phenomenon and in content as well as form. I have elsewhere offered a full analysis of the prefaces of both Luke and Acts, and the claims made in that earlier analysis are assumed here.[51]

Since Luke's work is (to some extent) philosophical and has an addressee, one could compare it to a philosophical letter, like those written by Plato (allegedly), Epicurus, the great Cynics (allegedly), Horace, Seneca, or even

---

50   Malherbe (1989); Alexander (1994); (2001); Engberg-Pedersen (2000); Stowers (2001); Sampley (2003); brief discussion and bibliography, especially of the important findings of Malherbe, in Moles (2006a) 98 and 105 n. 16 {above, p. 526}.
51   See above, Ch. 27.

by Paul, whose letters show signs of such influence.[52] Here, commentators generally omit to note that 'bring to fulfilment' (*hapax* within Luke) and the cognate noun are Pauline words,[53] with the implication of 'assurance'. Another point of *asphaleian*, therefore, is, by implicit redefinition, to bring out the full force of *peplerophoremenon*: 'brought to fulfilment in such a way as to provide assurance'. Interestingly, this implication seems to have been sensed by Origen, who glossed *peplerophoremenon* as 'surely believed';[54] the gloss neglects the objective claim—'brought to fulfilment'—but correctly registers the nature of the religious belief. From a Classical point of view, this interaction between *peplerophoremenon* and *asphaleian* exemplifies the rhetorical figure of *e praecedentibus sequentia, e sequentibus praecedentia* (Quint. 8.6.20): 'from preceding things following things, from following things preceding things'. That is, the meaning of 'following things' is refined by 'preceding things' and vice versa, and fuller meaning is created by a sort of see-sawing interaction between the two separate elements.[55] Luke thus subtly conveys the link between Paul's religio-philosophical letters and his own historiographical-philosophical-epistolary *Pros Theophilon*, as well as signalling (to readers who know Pauline vocabulary) Paul's centrality to this version of Christianity.[56] Such 'signalling' is itself a technique of Classical writers, and is sometimes also described as 'putting down a marker' or as 'suspension of thought'.[57]

If Luke's philosophical *Pros Theophilon peri asphaleias* can be compared to Paul's religio-philosophical letters, it can also be compared to 4 Maccabees, a Jewish rhetorical-philosophical address on the superiority of religious reason to the emotions, which buttresses its philosophical argument with examples from Maccabean history, intended above all to celebrate martyrdom as a response to Gentile political and religious oppression. This work, which seems to date before 70 CE, had great influence upon early Christianity, the first agreed case being the Pastoral Letter to the Hebrews. Parallels with Luke include the

---

52  Malberbe (1989) 71–6.
53  Verb: Rom. 4.21, 14.5; noun: 1 Thess. 1; 'pastoral' references: Col. 4.12, 2 Tim. 4. 5, 17; Col. 2, Heb. 6.11, 10.22.
54  Orig. *Hom. in Luc.* 1; he was followed by the *Authorised Version*.
55  Williams (1980) 23–4.
56  Against Luke's association with, or even real knowledge of, Paul is often urged Acts' failure to mention Paul's writing letters. To which the answers may be: (a) Paul's letters may be far more important to us than to certain first- or early-second century Christians; (b) explicit mention of Paul's writing letters might interfere with the economy of the narrative of Acts/acts; (c) here and elsewhere there may be *implicit* allusions for those who know the Epistles.
57  See Moles (1985) 232–8 {above, pp. 367–8}.

direct address to readers or listeners, the praise of *logos*, the philosophical goal, the representation of Judaism as a philosophy, the combination of philosophy and historiography, and the influence of the earlier Maccabees texts. Anyone who knew 4 Maccabees would find certain analogies in Luke-Acts.

We have already noted the effective equivalence of theme and treatment: words about the Word of God. But Hellenised Jews or Gentiles familiar with philosophical concepts of *Logos* could read this Word as also being equivalent to, or trumping, the Stoic or Platonic *Logos*. This idea is widespread in Philo;[58] the Preface to the Gospel according to John has often been interpreted in this 'double' way;[59] and such a mode of interpretation was, from the analogy with 'philosophy', readily available to educated Christians such as Luke.

It seems perfectly reasonable to claim that a philosophical reading of the Luke Preface is strengthened if the narrative of Luke contains philosophical elements.[60]

After the implied comparison in the Preface between Christianity and a philosophical school, it immediately becomes easy for ancient readers to read allusions in the Luke narrative to 'Jesus and his disciples', Jesus' (most un-Jewish) calling of his disciples,[61] their 'following' him,[62] the listing and naming of the disciples,[63] Jesus' 'mission statements', all the 'teaching' that he gives the disciples, his disciples' rivalry for first place in his affections or after him, the position of the beloved disciple, and his own privileging of the leadership of the disciple Peter as comparable to the patterns of philosophical schools. For modern readers, the notion of 'Jesus and his disciples' has acquired such independent power that we forget that *mathētai* is the normal Greek term for 'pupils', which would, indeed, be a less loaded translation.[64] Of course, Jesus is *also* being represented as a broadly familiar type of Jewish rabbi, but this does not destroy the philosophical analogy. Herewith a simple but crucial methodological point: to argue for philosophical influences and allusions is *not* to claim that these alone 'drive' the text; conversely, however, biblical parallels do not exclude philosophical ones. As often, 'both-and' reading represents the better way.

Two factors indicate that Luke is actively promoting the philosophical school analogy within the narrative. First, there is the rather peculiar implication that

---

58   Winston (1985); Runia (1986) 446–51; Tobin (1992).
59   See, e.g., Moloney (1998) 34–43; Thompson (2006) 186.
60   Cf. above, n. 3.
61   Cf. Boring, et al. (1995) §§27–28.
62   See p. 871 below.
63   Shiner (1995) 91 (on Mark 3.16–19—Luke's source here).
64   {See above, ch. 26.}

the Pharisees have 'pupils'/'disciples', just as do John the Baptist and Jesus (5.30–3). (Pharisees did not in fact have 'pupils' unless they were also rabbis).[65] Luke's source at this point, Mark (2.16–17), does not have this implication, which Luke has imported in order to reinforce the impression of rival schools. Second, it is difficult for 'Classical' readers to read of some of Jesus' activities without mentally attaching a Greek philosophical label to them. I believe that Jesus is represented in (to some extent) recognisably Cynic terms.[66] For example, upon Jesus' 'mission statement' in Lk 9.1–5: 'take nothing for the journey, etc.', Downing has famously commented: 'if the first Christian missionaries obeyed instructions of [this] kind, they would have looked like a kind of Cynic, displaying a very obvious poverty ... a raggedly cloaked and outspoken figure with no luggage and no money would not just have looked Cynic, he would obviously have wanted to'.[67] Luke's procedure in representing the Jewish movement of Jesus and his pupils in Luke is beginning to look rather like Josephus' 'philosophisation' of Judaism and its constituent sects.

Other philosophical influences on the narrative adduced by some scholars include the Socratic symposium, inter-school philosophical polemic (7.36–50; 11.37–53; 14.1–24),[68] and Plato's *Phaedo* (in the account of the Last Supper: 22.14–38).[69] These readings are not particularly controversial and convince me.

Perhaps the most direct and important philosophical link between narrative and Preface is the 'road imagery'. For example, 2.52 (of the boy Jesus in the Temple): 'And Jesus advanced [προέκοπτεν] in wisdom and maturity and grace before God and men'. The use of προκόπτω of moral advance (very rare in the New Testament and—again—significantly Pauline)[70] glosses the Stoic concept of 'moral progress' (προκοπή), here reinterpreted to fit Jesus' status as Son of God (2.49). While the Stoics promoted 'moral progress', they effectively denied the practical attainability of 'wisdom'. By contrast, Jesus' 'moral progress' already shows 'wisdom', and he lacks *complete* 'wisdom' only because of his age. The suggestions that the 'road imagery' of the Preface should be seen as philosophical and that Jesus as the Word of God includes, or trumps,

---

65    Green (1997) 248 n. 82; the passage thus anticipates Acts 22.3 (Paul's 'pupillage' under Gamaliel) and Pharisees as a *hairesis*.
66    Moles (2006a).
67    Downing (1988) v–vi, with the mild correctives of Moles (2006a) 101–2 {above, pp. 540–2}.
68    Steele (1984); Johnson (1991) 191–2; Witherington (1998) 161 n. 115; de Meeus (1961); Johnson (1991) 225; cf. also n. 1 above.
69    Kurz (1985); Johnson (1991) 348; Kloppenborg (1992).
70    Otherwise: verb: Galat. 1.14, 2 Tim. 2.16 (ironic), 3.9 (ironic), 13 (ironic); noun: Phil. 1.12, 25; 1 Tim. 4.15.

the Stoic *Logos* seem confirmed. Noteworthily, moral/theological advance also here occurs within a context of *literal* travel (2.51). Further, as is well recognised, the main organising structure of the whole second half of Luke (9.51ff.) is Jesus' journey to Jerusalem—a journey alike literal, metaphorical, spiritual, and Christological.[71] And just before the start of that journey, at the Transfiguration, Moses and Elijah tell Jesus of 'his *exodos* [= the Ascension], which he was going to *fulfil* (πληροῦν) in Jerusalem' (9.31). Similarly, Luke's second version of the ascension explicitly uses 'travel' terminology (Acts 1.10–11). Thus Jesus himself is brought within the philosophical/historiographical road imagery of the Luke Preface, and such roads may be among the 'things *brought to fulfilment*'. And, as in Stoic writers such as Seneca and Dio Chrysostom,[72] such road imagery can combine horizontal and vertical movements (whether of ascending or of falling).

All this fits the application of road imagery to readers such as Theophilos, because all followers of Jesus are called to follow Jesus' road (Luke 9.23, 14.27). Other figures also come within the imagery. Besides the Ethiopian eunuch, there is Jesus' parable in Luke 6.39: 'Can a blind man lead a blind man along the road? Will they not both *fall* into a pit?' (no ἀσφάλεια there). And at the very beginning (1.6–7): '[Zacharias and Elizabeth] were both just before God, *journeying* in all the commandments and just ordinances of the Lord blamelessly. (7) And they had no child, because Elizabeth was sterile, and both were *advanced* in their days'. Road imagery and philosophical (and, of course, related) roads, therefore, are everywhere in Luke-Acts.

Since philosophical, related, and literal roads characteristically cross, I now revert to the 'we passages'.

Formally, whether 'real' or 'literary', they claim some person's participation in Paul's journeys. Moreover, some of the contexts in which they occur are much less obviously 'literary' than an exciting sea voyage, storm, and shipwreck. Further, as Fitzmyer argues,[73] that they occur only where they do (and not in other contexts where they would be expected, were their motivation *merely* 'literary') suggests sporadic participation in those journeys. Here 'suggests' means both 'allows as a historical inference' and 'conveys as part of the overall meaning of the text'.

---

71  Johnson (1991) 163–5 (with bibliography); Green (1997) 396–9; 'road imagery' is also very important in the other Gospels, including Mark: Ryken–Wilhoit–Longman (1998) 631; Boring (2006) 37–8.
72  Seneca: e.g., *Ep. mor.* 21.1–2; Dio: Moles (2005) 126 {above, pp. 271–3}.
73  Fitzmyer (1998) 98, 103.

To assess that part, their introduction requires consideration. At 16.8, Paul and Timothy are at Troas, when:

> (9) a vision was seen by Paul during the night: there was a Macedonian man standing and calling upon him and saying: 'Cross into Macedonia and come to *our* aid'. (10) And when he saw the vision, immediately *we* sought to go out into Macedonia, concluding that God had called to *us* to *bring the good news to them*. (11) Putting out from Troas *we* ran down immediately to Samothrace ... etc.' (my italics).

At this crucial juncture, Paul and his companions carry the Gospel from Asia into Europe.[74] The precision of the geography, the switch from third-person narrative to first-person, and the emphasis on the different pronouns or persons emphasise alike the current separations and the desired Christian unity of an all-embracing 'us' (the introduction of the 'we narrative' immediately after the appeal 'come to *our* aid' is peculiarly apposite). Now the use of the verb *bring the good news* (εὐαγγελίζομαι) has a 'meta'-implication, recalling a central function of Luke-Acts itself, as being a *Gospel*, or εὐαγγέλιον. True, Luke himself does not apply that term directly to his work, but he uses εὐαγγελίζομαι frequently in Luke-Acts in 'evangelising' contexts; the Gospel according to Mark, one of his main sources, explicitly so describes itself (Mark 1.1); and Luke was so called by later Christians, from ancient times to today. Hengel, indeed, has argued quite persuasively that the titles 'The Gospel according to Matthew/Mark/Luke/John' must be original.[75] Thus one can add εὐαγγέλιον to Luke-Acts' bristling generic panoply, and Acts 16.10 returns the reader yet again to Luke's first preface.

Scholars who read the 'we passages' as including Luke connect them with the first-persons (singular and plural) of the Preface. Fair enough—but they miss something of Luke's subtlety. Luke includes himself in an all-embracing Christian 'us'.[76] The narrative extends down to the present and culminates in 'fulfilment'. Luke 'has closely followed ... from the start'. While the reference of 'closely followed' is formally to Luke's 'closely following' the traditional accounts, the language evokes the imagery of physical travel. The 'we passages' intersect with this general road imagery, which, like much road imagery, combines metaphorical and literal. Even if those passages did not include Luke, this interaction helps to validate the authenticity of the overall narrative. But

---

74  Crucial, that is, in the light of the programmatic 1.8 (discussed below).
75  Hengel (2000) 48–56 (arguing the authenticity of the Gospel titles).
76  On that 'us': Johnson (1991) Green (1997) 40.

the interaction must also include the phraseology 'closely followed all things from the start', and 'followed closely' of research slides into literal 'following'. Πᾶσι, while mainly neuter, can also be understood as masculine.

Given Luke's general use of 'road imagery' in the Luke-Acts narrative and given the presence of that imagery already in the Luke Preface, we should always have expected that the 'we narratives' can be integrated into the general 'road imagery' and that they should have been anticipated in the Preface.

More can be said about Luke's literary artistry in this matter. A distinctive feature of Mark's narrative composition, rightly emphasised by Turner and Bauckham, is a series of 'they passages', where third-person plurals are used of Jesus and his disciples, followed by singulars, of Jesus alone. These passages both indicate and claim eyewitness testimony, which must have been in an original 'we' format.[77] The parallel with Acts' 'we passages' (where plurals also give way to singulars, of Paul) is rather striking. Now Bauckham observes that 'Matthew and Luke have a clear tendency to prefer a singular verb to Mark's plurals encompassing both Jesus and the disciples'.[78] It seems, then, that Luke's 'we passages' were partly inspired by Mark's 'they passages'. Luke has taken note of Mark's usage, simplified and normalised it in Luke, but transferred it in its original immediate form to Acts. Within the Acts narrative, the immediacy of the effect can be compared with, and is perhaps even anticipated by, the sudden switch from Jesus' indirect speech into direct speech at 1.4 ('and when he was taking salt with them he announced to them not to depart from Jerusalem but to await the announcement of the Father, "which you heard from me …"'). If the parallel between Mark's 'they passages' and Acts' 'we passages' can be given interpretative weight (that is, if some readers see what Luke has done in relation to Mark), there is an implicit and entirely suitable parallel between Jesus and his followers in Mark and Paul and his followers in Acts.

The whole notion of Luke as successor or follower of Paul returns us to the question of date. On the majority judgement of historians, Acts reflects a first-century world. I put Luke-Acts at c.105.[79]

Such are my views on some of the biggest problems. Although they inevitably and repeatedly intersect with our topic, they do not affect everything that follows, and informed (or prejudiced) readers may pick and mix.

One basic point emerges: philosophy is written in to the whole project of Luke-Acts. Further, there are *numerous* good subsidiary reasons for *expecting* significant philosophical elements in Acts. Encouragingly, some ancient

---

77    Bauckham (2006) 156ff.
78    Turner (1925); Bauckham (2006) 157; illustrative table on 181.
79    {For the reasons, cf. above, Ch. 27, p. 839.}

readers read the Gospels 'philosophically'. Papias and Justin the Martyr characterise Mark as Peter's 'memoirs' of Jesus, like Xenophon's of Socrates. Justin so characterises the Gospels generally. The Gospel of Thomas interprets Matthew as comparing Jesus to 'a wise philosopher'.[80] Galen views the Gospels as morally useful in encouraging a philosophical attitude to death and as Platonically true.[81] Conversely, some Greek philosophical (or related) texts show signs of appropriation of the Gospels: Lucian's *Peregrinus*, Porphyry's *Life of Plotinus*, Philostratus' *Life of Apollonius*.[82] All this said, the treatment of philosophy in Acts requires sequential reading, in order to verify organic depth, range, development, and multiplicity of function.

Two final *caveats*. In an attempt to keep the analysis as rigorous as possible, I restrict the focus to philosophical material in a strong sense, a procedure which, as we have seen, includes the possibility of 'both-and' reading. But what might be described as 'transferred reading' (where one reads originally non-philosophical material in philosophical terms) may sometimes be a legitimate response of Greek or Roman readers. 'Transferred reading' goes a step beyond 'both-and' reading (though the line between the two may sometimes be rather hazy), and I shall return to it at the end.[83]

II

Acts begins (1.1–8). To his existing apostles the risen Jesus speaks of the kingdom of God, and tells them to await the Holy Spirit in Jerusalem. They ask: 'Lord, will you re-establish the kingdom to Israel at this time?' He replies:

> It does not belong to you to know times or seasons which the Father has set by his own authority. But you will receive power when the Holy Spirit has come upon you, and you will be my witnesses in Jerusalem and in all Judaea and Samaria and *to the end of the earth.*

A conception of the kingdom restricted in time and in membership is superseded by a commission for world-wide Christian witness—implicitly to Jesus as king. As in Luke, the kingdom is at once something already happening and

---

80   Bauckham (2006) 211–13; 236–7.
81   Galen in Walzer (1949) 15–16; Alexander (2002) 245–6; (2005) 158 n. 82.
82   König (2006); Edwards (2000); Bauckham (2006) 137–54; de Labriolle (1950) 180–8.
83   Cf. below, p. 924.

something to be completed in the future. And Jesus' commission will determine the entire narrative trajectory of Acts.

Readers must take account of several biblical passages. The 'stem' is Isaiah 49.6 (explicitly cited later in Acts 13.47):[84] 'see, I have given you for a covenant of a race, for a light of the nations, that you should be for salvation *until the end of the earth*', but also relevant are Psalm 2.8 (the Lord to his son)—'Ask from me, and I will give you as your inheritance the nations and as your possessions the ends of the earth',[85] and Maccabees 1 and 2, which exploit the 'ends of the earth'-motif, as applied alike to great conquerors (1 Maccabees 1.1), to kings who come *from* the ends of the earth against Rome (8.4), and to great religious leaders (3.9; 2 Maccabees 9.17 [of a penitent Antiochus Epiphanes]), and these texts, too, had some influence on Acts.[86] Lukan Christianity, therefore, 'trumps' the claims of Maccabean Judaism.

Three passages within Luke are also recalled.

In 24.45–8 the risen Jesus admonishes his disciples:

> (46) so it has been written, that the anointed one should suffer and on the third day rise from the dead (47) and that repentance for the release of sins should be proclaimed in his name to *all the nations, beginning from Jerusalem.* (48) *It is you who will be witnesses of these things.*

11.31–2 reverses this trajectory: Jesus says:

> the queen of the South will rise at the judgement with the people of this generation and condemn them, because she *came from the ends of the earth* to listen to the wisdom of Solomon, and see, something greater than Solomon is here!

13.22–30 comes within Jesus' climactic journey to Jerusalem:

> And he journeyed through towns and villages, teaching and making the journey to Jerusalem. (23) And someone said to him: 'Lord, are those who are saved few?' And he said to them: (24) 'Struggle to enter by the narrow door, because many, I say to you, will seek to enter and will not have the strength. (25) From the time that the master of the house rises up and shuts the door, you will begin to stand outside and to knock at the door,

---

84  And looking back to Luke 2.32.
85  Luke uses *Psalm* 2 further in Acts 2.25ff. (~ Luke 23.7, 12).
86  Moles (2006b) 82–3, 94–5, 97–8 {above, pp. 567–9, 577–9, 580–1}.

saying: "Lord, open to us". And he will answer and say: "I do not know where you are from". (26) Then you will begin to say: "We ate and drank before you and you taught in our streets". (27) And he will say to you: "I do not know where you are from. Go away from me, all you workers of injustice". (28) There will be weeping and gnashing of teeth, when you see Abraham and Isaac and all the prophets in the kingdom of God and you yourselves being thrown outside. (29) And they will come from east and west and from north and south, and they will sit in the kingdom of God. (30) And look! There are those at the end who will be first and there are first who will be at the end'.

This passage richly and complexly combines literal and metaphorical travel; road imagery, door imagery, and house imagery; travel, 'end of the world', and 'eschatological' imagery; and worldly status ('those at the end', 'first'), theological pretensions, and geographical position (in the kingdom of God, as finally realised in the End Time, Gentiles from the ends of the earth will displace Jews). The representation of Jesus as a 'street teacher' and his utilisation of the 'two-roads'/'two-gates' motif have a Cynic air.[87]

Readers of Acts 1.8 should also register that the Christian mission to 'the end of the earth' 'trumps' the claims of empires—such as the Roman Empire—to extend their boundaries to the end(s) of the earth.[88] That theme is already signalled at the start of Luke in the angel Gabriel's prophecy to Mary that Jesus' 'kingdom will be without end' (1.33). Christian 'kingship' and 'imperialism' trump all other forms.

Might readers also sense an appropriation of the claims of the Cynic-Stoic philosopher to be a 'witness' (μάρτυς), to be cosmopolitan, and to go—whether literally or metaphorically—to the ends of the earth?[89] Again, there would be pointed 'trumping': contrast between what is being witnessed to; and contrast between going to the end of the earth, really just in order to come *back* and report to the centre (the Cynic-Stoic philosopher), and taking the message *out* to the end of the earth (the apostles).

Might a sophisticated reader even detect an intertextual relationship with the *Thirteenth Oration* of Dio Chrysostom?[90] The full force of the main parallels between that speech and Acts only becomes apparent once one has read

---

87  Downing (1988) 76–8; Moles (2006a) 102 {above, p. 541}.
88  Cat. 11.10–12; Hor. *C.* 1.12.55–6; Virg. *Aen.* 1.287; etc.
89  'Witness': Billerbeck (1978) 78, 148; Cynic cosmopolitanism: Moles (1996a); 'ends of earth': Sen. *Ep. mor.* 28.4; Dio 13.9; etc.
90  Embryonically: Downing (1988) 3; Alexander (2005) 64; more fully Moles (2005) 126 {above, p. 272} n. 140.

both texts through and, indeed, 'decoded' both, but, cumulatively, the main parallels are spooky:

| Acts | Dio, *Or.* 13 |
|---|---|
| The risen Jesus tells his disciples to mission *to the end of the earth*. Paradoxically, the end of the earth turns out to be Rome (or: mission to Rome, centre of the earth, is an important staging-post for mission to the end of the earth).[91] | The Delphic Oracle tells Dio to wander *to the end of the earth*. Paradoxically, the end of the earth turns out to be Rome. |
| The 'space' of the literary work reflects the 'space' to be traversed. Readers must 'write their own narrative' in their lives for the text's full programme to be achieved. | The 'space' of the literary work reflects the 'space' to be traversed. Readers must 'write their own narrative' in their lives for the text's full programme to be achieved. |

Moreover, the resemblances between Luke and Dio are not restricted to these parallels. (I here anticipate.) Dio *Or.* 13 is a philosophical speech influenced by Cynicism and Platonism and delivered in Athens (just as Paul performs in Athens), but also envisages a Roman audience (just as Luke does with Theophilos). Both texts draw extensively on Plato's *Apology*, and the protagonists of both (Paul, Dio himself) are heavily 'Socraticised'. Both texts employ extensive 'road imagery', and both are concerned with spatial and temporal trajectories from 'beginning' to 'end'. Dio *Or.* 13 dates to 101 (I think: others put it earlier).[92] Could Luke have read, and be exploiting, Dio, famous Greek philosopher/sophist?

Might later, Latinate readers note parallels between Acts and Apuleius' *Metamorphoses*[93] (written in the period 150–180 and probably towards its end)?[94] Both texts are (in varying degrees) novelistic, philosophical, and concerned with the promulgation of a religious 'mystery'; the protagonists of both texts—and the texts themselves—end up in Rome. Apuleius is, of course, on most views, much too late for Luke. Nevertheless, the parallels support the notion that Acts has contact with contemporary or near-contemporary Classical religious and philosophical quest narratives.

---

91  Discussion: p. 919 below.
92  Moles (2005) 114 {above, p. 251}.
93  I owe this suggestion to Christina Kraus.
94  Cf. Harrison (2000) 9–10.

All this suggests that 1.8 should indeed be read as *including* the appropriation and 'trumping' of Cynic-Stoic claims to 'witness' and world-wide philosophising. Moreover, the foregrounding of philosophical allusion at the introduction of the narrative looks like an important 'signal', re-emphasising the philosophical strand that stretches all the way through Luke from the Preface.

Once the narrative gets on the road, the apostles are repeatedly and emphatically credited with παρρησία. The noun is used at 2.29, 4.13, 4.29, 4.31, and 28.31; the verb at 9.27, 9.28, 13.46, 14.3, 18.26, 19.8, 26.26 (and only twice elsewhere in the New Testament [Eph. 6.20, 1 Thess. 2.2]).

The process begins, characteristically enough in Luke, with the impulsive Peter, but rapidly snowballs. The High Priest and the Sadducees are surprised by the παρρησία of Peter and John, the believers generally pray for all παρρησία, and receive a validating earthquake, and thereafter Barnabas, Apollos, and, especially, Paul have it. The apostles deploy it when preaching Christianity to Jews, with one full exception (the end of Acts when Paul is preaching to 'everybody') and one partial exception (Paul's performance before Agrippa II—Jewish,[95] but a king, and very Hellenised). The quality is necessary—but also remarkable—for two reasons: it takes courage to proclaim Jesus, and the apostles generally, Paul excepted, are not highly educated or professionally qualified as religious (or other) teachers. The latter point is explicit in the reaction of High Priest and Sadducees (4.13): 'observing the παρρησία of Peter and John and apprehending that they were unlettered and private individuals'.

Παρρησία, then, is an essential characteristic of the preaching of Jesus' followers, and it extends beyond explicit mentions (Paul in Athens, for example, is on one level speaking parresiastically to the Greek philosophers).[96] The concept is Greek, and—within the New Testament—deployed with unusual density by Luke. Are Jesus' followers here being invested in Socratic or Cynic guise, as many suppose?[97] There are obvious parallels. Socrates and the Cynics were associated with *parrēsia*, they were predominantly 'open-air' philosophers, some of the apostles' parresiastic activity takes place in the open,[98] and Cynics, who rejected education, could be regarded as 'unlettered and private individuals'.[99] Indeed, of all the great Greek philosophies, Cynicism provides

---

95   See pp. 900ff. below.
96   Pp. 871ff.
97   Cf., e.g., Johnson (1992) 78; Mason (1995) 133; (2005) 288; Witherington (1998) 195; Fitzmyer (1998) 302; Barrett (2004) I.233, 234.
98   See p. 892 below.
99   Education: D.L. 6.73; 'unlettered': e.g., Lucian, *Fug.* 13; *Vit. Act.* 11; 'private': e.g. Dio 12.16.

the best analogy for the first apostles' 'open-air' missionary activity and for their 'uneducatedness'. So the answer should be affirmative.

Luke's emphasis on the economic 'communism' of the first Christian community in Jerusalem closely follows Peter's 'parresiastic' speech and the first mass conversions (2.44–5):

> And all who believed were in the same place and had all things in common. And they sold their possessions and belongings and shared them out to all, according as any had need.

The emphasis recurs (4.32–7):

> There was one heart and soul of the crowd of those who believed, and not one of them said that anything of his belongings was his own but all things were common to them. And the apostles gave their witness to the resurrection of the Lord Jesus with great power, and great grace was upon them all. For there was not a needy person among them, for as many as were possessors of lands or houses sold them and brought the prices of what was sold and laid them at the apostles' feet, and it was given to each according as any had need. And Joseph ... sold a field belonging to him, and brought the money and laid it at the apostles' feet.

Commentators note that this 'communism' can be paralleled by Jesus and the disciples; Qumran; the Essenes; the Pythagoreans; and Plato's *Republic, Critias*, and *Laws*; that the repeated 'all things in common' evokes the Greek proverb 'the things of friends are common'; and that this proverb is cited to justify the 'communism' of Pythagoreans and Plato's *Republic* and *Laws*.[100]

Of these, Jesus and the disciples are obviously relevant: our descriptions show the apostles developing Jesus' own paradigm as the first actual Christian communities are being created. If the Qumran parallel applies, it must be as contrast, since in Luke Jesus himself had already implicitly contrasted his own 'open' fellowship with Qumran or Essene restrictiveness (Luke 14.13, 21).[101] In any case, Qumran, destroyed in the Jewish War, effectively no longer counted. In terms of Luke's rivalry with Josephus, Josephus barely mentions Jesus

---

[100] Cf., e.g., Witherington (1998) 162–3; Fitzmyer (1998) 270–1; Dormeyer–Galindo (2003) 60–2; Barrett (2004) 1.163–70, 251–2; Qumran: 1 QS 5.1–3; CD 9.1–15; Essenes: Jos. *BJ* 2.122; Pythagoreans: Timaeus, *FGrHist* 566 F 13a; Iambl. *Vit. Pyth.* 167–8; Kirk-Raven-Schofield (1984) 227–8; Taylor (2006) 78; Pl. *Rep.* 4.424a, 449c; *Leg.* 5.739c.

[101] See Dunn (2003a) 604.

or the Christians,[102] Luke does not explicitly mention the Essenes, and the implicit point here, as in Luke, is that Christian 'communism' is more important and more generous than Essene. But the proverb stimulates thoughts of some Greek paradigm. The Pythagoreans and Plato's *Laws* seem long shots. The *Republic* is better. But there is better still. The 'ideal state' of Diogenes, founder of Cynicism, had made 'commonness' its central principle, and had underpinned this 'commonness' with the proverb 'the things of friends are common'.[103] Moreover, Diogenes' greatest follower, Crates, sold his property and gave the proceeds to the poor (D.L. 6.87). For the latter item, there is again a parallel in Luke, Jesus' exhortation to his disciples at 12.33, 'sell your possessions, and give alms', but this parallel itself coheres with the Cynic elements in the representation of Jesus in Luke.[104] The Cynic parallel for the apostles' 'communism' is not generally cited by scholars, whether owing to general underestimation of Cynicism or to erroneous belief in the unavailability of Diogenes' works, known by Philodemus, Dio Chrysostom, and Oenomaus but Luke, too, knows of this Cynic programme and expects (some of) his readers to recognise it.

There are further points. The precise wording of 4.32 evokes another Greek philosopher, Aristotle, according to whom true friends 'hold everything in common and are of one soul' (*EN* 1168b1ff.).[105] The descriptions of 2.44–5 and 4.32–7 are, obviously, idealised, but equally, they represent both some sort of reality and a goal. But they are also idealised in the sense that elements in the surrounding narratives challenge, even contradict, them (see below). It is thus particularly fitting that they should evoke a philosophical 'state', an ideal, but one to be pursued, and especially the Cynic 'ideal state', because of all philosophical states this was the most practicable,[106] and because Luke gives Jesus himself Cynic features. Such idealised philosophical descriptions are often set in the remote past (or imitate its alleged virtues), and thus Luke's descriptions have an appropriate flavour of the 'foundation story',[107] or 'foundation myth'. Importantly, too, philosophical 'states' are necessarily in tension, or competition, with worldly states.

Next, as commentators note, 4.19 ('But Peter and John answered and said to them, "Whether it is just in the face of God to listen to you rather than God, you decide"') and 5.29 ('But Peter and the apostles answered and said: "we must

102   *AJ* 18.63–64 (where most scholars accept a small Josephan core); 20.200.
103   D.L. 6.72, with Moles (2000) 424–32 {above, pp. 448–57}.
104   Moles (2006a) 99–100 {above, pp. 537–9}.
105   Witherington (1998) 205; Barrett (2004) I.254.
106   Argument: Moles (2000) 428 {above, p. 453}.
107   Johnson (1992) 62.

obey God rather than men'") echo Plato, *Apology* 29d ('I will obey God rather than you', spoken by Socrates). The parallel is both verbal and situational: Socrates too had been urged to desist from his characteristic behaviour in case of death (28b–29d).

There are thematic and structural points. The echo marks the apostles as Socratic figures and enlists Socratic philosophy to support the proposition that, where a choice has to be made, Christians obey God, not man—and among men, neither Jewish rulers nor Roman, and this to the point of death. If the motif of the end of the earth at 1.8 adumbrates a power struggle between Christianity and the Roman Empire, this issue is already resolved: Christianity always takes precedence. The *Apology* also, of course, is spoken by someone who will be killed by the state—as Peter eventually was. The evocation of the *Apology* near the beginning of the Acts narrative may also have a programmatic significance (subject to verification). And within the larger unity of Luke-Acts, just as Jesus himself was likened to Socrates,[108] so now also are his apostles. Again, the essential logic of the Talbert hypothesis has ever-increasing attractiveness.

Some scholars find it surprising that 'unlettered and private individuals' (4.13) quote Plato's *Apology*. Is Luke uninterested in consistent characterisation? No: the Spirit gives the apostles power over speech itself. At Pentecost the apostles 'began to speak in other tongues, according as the spirit granted them to make utterance' (2.4). At 2.29, introducing the apostles' *parrēsia*, Peter immediately constructs an elegant *figura etymologica*: 'it is *allowed to say with permission to speak*'. So the apostles effortlessly master the appropriate Classical allusion. In all this they validate Jesus' (clearly *post eventum*) prophecy in Luke 21.12–15 (cf. 12.12):

> But before all these [Last] things, they will lay hands upon you and persecute you, handing you over to the synagogues and prisons, led away to kings and governors for the sake of my name. It will come down to witness for you. Settle it therefore in your hearts not to practise beforehand [προμελετᾶν] to defend yourselves [ἀπολογεῖσθαι]. For I will give you a mouth and wisdom which all those set against you will not be able to withstand or speak against.

The promise of 'I will give you a mouth and wisdom' is fulfilled by the Holy Spirit (cf. 12.12), and the words 'not withstand or contradict' are echoed in Acts 4.14 (the priests, et al. 'had nothing to speak against' the reality of Peter's

---

108 {See Ch 27, p. 809.}

healing of the lame man) and 6.10 (below). Jesus' injunction combines rhetorical terminology ('not to practise beforehand') with legal/Socratic terminology ('to defend yourselves', also at 12.11). The promised 'wisdom' includes the ability to hold one's own philosophically, as in the *Apology* quotation.

The cluster of philosophical allusions in the early narrative introduces a large question. At 5.17–18 'the High Priest rose up and all those with him, the existent sect (αἵρεσις) of the Sadducees, and they were filled with zeal (18) and laid hands upon the apostles and placed them in public custody'. This is the first of a series: 15.5 (Council of Jerusalem; narrative allusion to 'the sect of the Pharisees'); 24.5 (Tertullus accusing Paul before Felix calls him 'a leader of the sect of the Nazarenes'); 24.14 (Paul to Felix: 'But I admit to you this: that according to the Road, which they call a sect, that is how I serve the God of our fathers'); 26.5 (Paul to Agrippa: 'I have lived according to the most precise [ἀκριβεστάτην] sect of our religion as a Pharisee'); 28.22 (the first men of the Jews in Rome to Paul; 'concerning this sect it is known to us that it is spoken against everywhere').

The basic meaning of αἵρεσις is 'choice'. 'Sect', although from a different, Latin root, preserves the key idea of volition. In all cases, the term is applied to a different 'choice' within Judaism, whether Sadducees, Pharisees, or Christians. Αἵρεσις can be used of political 'factions' (e.g., App. *BC* 5.2), which in a Jewish context may be appropriate as *one* of the term's resonances. But several factors encourage a 'philosophical reading'. First, the initial occurrence comes where there are other philosophical elements and where a philosophical implication would fit (the 'philosophical' Sadducees are being 'out-philosophised' by the Socratic and Cynic apostles). Second, in philosophical contexts, the word is the regular term for different 'sects'. Third, it is so used by Josephus in his characterisation of Judaism as a philosophy with different 'philosophical' 'sects'.[109] Fourth, Paul's characterisation of the Pharisees as 'the most precise sect' is closely paralleled in Josephus, when (again) he is likening Pharisaism to a philosophical sect.[110] Thus the cumulative case for philosophical colouring is strong and, indeed, quite widely accepted.[111]

There are interesting implications, both historical and literary. 24.5, 24.14, and 28.22 constitute fair historical evidence that non-Christians, both Jews and Gentiles, could regard Christianity as a form of philosophical sect at Acts' time of writing. These references also indicate the availability of this attitude

---

109  *BJ* 1.110; 2.162; *AJ* 17.41; *Vit.* 189; bibliographical references in Dunn (2003a) 265 n. 44.
110  Jos. *Vit.* 191; *AJ* 17.41; *BJ* 2.162.
111  Cf., e.g., Mason (1995) 133; (2005) 288–91; Witherington (1998) 229; Alexander (2002) 232–3.

as early as the dramatic date (c.60), for, though they come in the historically unreliable area of speeches, they cohere with the narrative allusions to other religio-philosophical 'sects' in 5.17–18 and 15.5; with Josephan usage with regard to Jewish 'sects'; and with external considerations such as the representation/self-representation of Jesus and Paul. Josephus, the only extant writer before Luke thus to use the term, can hardly be Luke's sole inspiration:[112] the usage is natural once Judaism is conceptualised in philosophical terms, and Josephus scarcely refers to Christianity, still less to its being a αἵρεσις.

24.14 could be read as showing that the characterisation was completely rejected by first-century Christians, for Paul's point is that the Christian 'Road', as 'the only way', trumps any possible implication that there can be legitimately different 'choices'. But 26.4–5 points the other way: if Paul regards Pharisaism, his first affiliation, to which he still to some extent adheres, as a αἵρεσις within Judaism, then it retains some validity and Christianity also counts as a Jewish αἵρεσις. The difference between 24.14 and 26.4–5 presumably reflects Christians' flexibility, depending on whether they wished to represent themselves as being the *only* legitimate 'choice' within Judaism or as being *a part of it*.[113] Conversely, other Jews' regarding Christianity as a sect reflects their underestimation of the stronger Christian claim.

From the point of view of Luke's rivalry with Josephus, the characterisation of Christianity as a αἵρεσις again 'corrects' Josephus' scant treatment of Christianity. From the point of view of the larger unity of Luke-Acts, Luke's inchoate inter-school rivalries as Jesus debated with Pharisees and Sadducees are now firmed up as Jesus' disciples and apostles become an identifiable 'sect' in their own right. From the point of view of Acts itself, there could be no clearer 'marker' for 'reading' the early Christians 'philosophically'.

So much for αἵρεσις. We back-track.

The Cynic-like idealism of the first Christians' way of life is threatened, both externally (4.1–21; 5.17–40) and internally, especially by dissension between 'Hellenists' and 'Hebrews',[114] as the formers' widows are overlooked in the daily distributions (6.1ff.). Matters are resolved by the appointment of 'Hellenist' leaders, 'full of the Spirit and of wisdom', including Stephen. Stephen's performance of miracles among the people leads to debates with the members of a Hellenist synagogue, 'but they could not withstand the wisdom and the Spirit

---

112 *Pace* Mason (2005) 289.
113 Cf. also Mason (2005) 289. Of course, one emphasis easily slides into the other. Here, while Pharisaism is formally allowed parity, the very juxtaposition can suggest that Christianity 'succeeds' or 'supersedes' it.
114 Terminology: Witherington (1998) 240–7; Fitzmyer (1998) 346–48.

with which he spoke' (6.10 ~ Luke 21.15: Jesus/the Spirit gives Stephen also invincible eloquence). The word for 'debate' is συνζητέω, literally 'seek together with', a characteristic term for philosophical 'enquiry',[115] already used in Luke 22.23 and 24.15 of 'dispute' or 'debate' among Jesus' disciples. There follows Stephen's trial before the *Sanhedrin*, his long speech about Jewish history from Abraham to Jesus, and his stoning (6.11–7.60). The speech notes (7.22) that 'Moses was educated in all the wisdom [σοφίαι] of the Egyptians, and he was powerful in his words and deeds'. This philosophical representation, paralleled in Philo and Josephus,[116] is particularly striking because Moses' 'education' is solely Egyptian. In effect, alien wisdom, its own value conceded, is benevolently appropriated; the antiquity of Egyptian wisdom saluted; and legitimacy extended to quite strongly 'Hellenising' tendencies within Jewish Christianity. The phrase 'powerful in his words and deeds' recalls Jesus as 'a prophet powerful in deed and word' (Luke 24.19) and confirms that Jesus' own 'wisdom' can be compared with—and includes—philosophical wisdom (cf. Luke 12.12 and 21.15 above).

Stephen's martyrdom, the only martyrdom actually described in Acts, has obvious parallels with Jesus'.[117] But there are also suggestive parallels with Socrates: instantiation of wisdom (including an element of 'Hellenist' wisdom), philosophical debate, arrest, trial, great speech, condemnation, imperturbable demeanour before death, shining face (Stephen's 'angelic' face before death [6.15, 7.55] is like Socrates' 'shining' eyes, appearance, and gait before death [Xen. *Apol.* 27]), and paradigmatic power.

Subsequently, both Paul and Peter, when missioning, sometimes look like activist, no-doors-barred, Cynic preachers. Thus 9.28–9 'And he [Paul] was with them, going in and out,[118] in Jerusalem, speaking with παρρησία in the name of the Lord', and 10.25 'When Peter entered [un-Jewishly], Cornelius met him ... (27) and associating with him, he entered and found many people come together'. This resembles the philosophical activity of Crates, who entered people's houses unannounced and was nicknamed 'the door-opener' (D.L. 6.86), and who as a Cynic 'saint' enjoyed a very favourable *Nachleben*. If again there are parallels with the Essenes and Josephus' description of them, Luke is again trumping both Essenes and Josephus. Paul is also represented

---

115  LSJ s.v.
116  References and discussion: Alexander (2002) 230; Mason (2005) 113–15; McGing (2006) 134.
117  E.g., Witherington (1998) 253, 276.
118  The expression is itself a Semitism or (better) Septuagintalism: Bauckham (2006) 114 n. 1.

as 'debating/disputing with' the 'Hellenists' (9.29), in a parallel with Stephen (6.9), συζητέω again having philosophical resonances.

It is after the successful missionary activities, both among Jews and Greeks, of Barnabas and Saul that 'in Antioch the disciples were called "Christians" for the first time' (11.26). This Graecised Latin form suggests a coinage by Romans in Antioch.[119] It is usually thought to be formed on the analogy of such 'party' terms as *Pompeiani, Sullani, Caesariani*, etc., that is, 'adherents of "x"', in a political or socio-political sense. So in the New Testament, Matthew and Mark refer to 'the Herodians' (Mat. 22.16; Mark 3.6; 12.13). Some scholars, surely less plausibly, associate the usage with philosophical terminology such as *Platonici*, 'followers of Plato'.[120] Of course, in a Jewish, or Jewish-Hellene, context, the lines between political, religious, and philosophical may blur. But, whatever the historical origins and implications of the term, it is more important to site it in context. Classical historians and biographers emphasise moments of change, beginnings, first occurrences, and the like, and so Luke the historian here emphasises a crucial moment in the history of the new religious movement: the moment when it first gets the distinctive name which, by Luke's day, at least in Greek and Roman contexts, had become *the* name for Christians (in contrast to 'the Road', still used by Christians themselves and by some Jews). And, given the context of religious missioning by 'disciples' of Jesus Christ and of the 'succession' thus implied, readers may well feel that Christianity is once again being represented as like a philosophical school and with its own distinctive 'philosophical' identity.

We now come appropriately to Paul in Athens (Acts 17.16–34):[121]

> (16) When Paul was awaiting [Silas and Timothy] in Athens, his spirit was provoked when he observed the city to be full of idols. (17) So he dialogued [διελέγετο] in the synagogues with the Jews and the God-fearers and in the *agora* every day with those who chanced to meet him [τοὺς παρατυχόντας]. (18) Some also of the Epicurean and Stoic philosophers encountered him, and some said, 'What does this seed-collector [σπερμολόγος] mean to say?' But others said, 'he seems to be an announcer of strange divinities'—because he told the good news about *Iesous* and *Anastasis*. (19) And taking hold of him, they led him to the Areopagus, saying, 'May we know what this new teaching is, the one that is spoken by you? (20) For you bring some strange things to our ears; so we wish to

---

119 Barrett (2004) I.556; Goodman (2007) 539–40.
120 Dormeyer–Galindo (2003) 181.
121 Enormous bibliography: see, e.g., Fitzmyer (1998) 613–17; Barrett (2004) II.823–4.

know what these things mean'. (21) All the Athenians and the strangers who lived there held that there was no better way of spending time than in saying or hearing some rather new thing. (22) But Paul, standing in the middle of the Areopagus, said: 'Men of Athens, I observe that you are as fearful of divinities as it is possible to be in all respects [κατὰ πάντα ὡς δεισιδαιμονεστέρους]. (23) For as I went along and observed the objects of your worship, I found also an altar on which was inscribed, "To unknown god". What therefore you worship unknowingly, this I announce to you. (24) The god who made the *kosmos* and everything in it, this god, being lord of heaven and earth, does not inhabit temples made by hand, (25) nor is he served by human hands, as needing anything, since he himself gives to all men life and breath and all things. (26) And he made from one every people of humans to inhabit all the face of the earth, having defined set times and the definitions of their habitation, (27) to seek God, if then they might feel after him and find him, and him not being far from each one of us, (28) for "In him we live and move and are", as even some of those who according to you are poet-makers have said, "For we are actually his offspring". (29) Being then God's offspring, we ought not to believe that the godly is like gold or silver or stone, a sculpting of the art and thought of man. (30) Having, then, overlooked the times of ignorance, God now announces that all humans everywhere should change their way of thinking, (31) because he has fixed a day on which he is going to judge the inhabited world in righteousness, in the power of a man to whom he has appointed it, having provided proof to all by raising him up from the dead'. (32) But when they heard of the rising [ἀνάστασιν] of the dead, some jeered, but others said, 'We will hear you again about this'. (33) It was in this way that Paul went out from their midst. (34) But some men joined him and accepted the proof, among whom was Dionysius the Areopagite and a woman Heifer by name and others with them.

One translation point: the common translations 'to the unknown god' and 'to an unknown god' are needlessly prejudicial. Other translation questions do not affect our topic.

Interpretation needs to register that Luke is bringing Jewish and Christian teaching into relationship not only with Greek philosophical material but also with Euripides' *Bacchae* and with Dionysiac religion.[122] The relevance of this to our topic I defer.

I begin by outlining the basic narrative (and other) patterns.

---

122  Moles (2006a).

First, Paul is playing the role of Socrates. As commentators observe, 17.17 διελέγετο, ἐν τῇ ἀγορᾷ, and τοὺς παρατυγχάνοντας evoke Socrates' characteristic philosophical activity, and 18 'he seems to be an announcer of strange deities' echoes the charge made against Socrates, as reported by Xenophon (*Mem.* 1.1.1 'Socrates acts unjustly in not acknowledging the gods that the city acknowledges, but introducing other new divinities') and Plato (*Apol.* 24b–c: 'other divinities, new ones'): so Plato's *Apology* is again an important text in Acts. The precision with which Luke introduces Socratic 'dialectic' into the narrative is noteworthy: διαλέγομαι is used for the first time in 17.2, of Paul's debates in the synagogue at Thessalonica, as it were, proleptically, and then, as it were, pivotally, in 17.17 of Paul both in the synagogue at Athens and in the *agora*.

Another relevant philosophical pattern—no doubt sometimes contaminated by the Socrates story—is that of the (alleged) trials of famous philosophers before the Areopagus.[123]

Paul being an outsider, the episode also falls into the basic narrative pattern where an outsider comes into a city, observes it, and, in some sense, passes judgement on it, whether by conversation, debate, or otherwise.[124] Odysseus is the paradigm, and in this, as in other respects, the figure of Odysseus greatly influenced Greek historiography. In Herodotean historiography especially, Solon's visit to King Croesus of Lydia, itself *Odyssey*-inspired, becomes an important paradigm (Hdt. 1.29–34).[125] In the cases both of Odysseus, as interpreted in the post-Homeric tradition, and of Solon, the outsider figure may have a philosophical character. He may also, to some degree, represent the author (as Solon represents—to a debatable extent—Herodotus). 16, when Paul is provoked by the sight of all those idols, seems to evoke the particular version of the narrative pattern where the outsider visits the big city and is astonished by it. This is a transparent narrative device, because the historical Paul must have known that Athens, of all Gentile cities, would be like this. This version often combines light fun at the outsider's expense with censure of the city, which the sophisticated reader is invited to see with fresh eyes. Thus the stranger re-focalises the city, so that *it* is revealed as strange. Here the light fun at the outsider's expense is absent (except, of course, in the philosophers' misguided response to Paul), but the re-focalised strangeness is an important effect. Contributory elements are the sort of ironic, quizzical portrait of Athens as a self-parody of itself that we find in Luke's near contemporary, Chariton

---

123 Alexander (2002) 230 n. 1; (2005) 64; cf. D.L. 2.101, 116; 7.168–9; cf. also Cicero's efforts with the Areopagus on behalf of Cratippus (Plut. *Cic.* 24.7).
124 Obviously, Dionysus, too, is relevant here: Moles (2006a).
125 Moles (1996b).

(1.11.6–7),[126] and the tradition of satirical representation of philosophers that stretches from Old Comedy to Lucian.[127]

Paul *qua* 'stranger' might seem inconsistent with the Socratic Paul. Yes and no: the accusation against Socrates imputes 'foreign-ness', and 'strangeness' to the court is one of Socrates' poses in the *Apology* (17d), as Luke evidently has spotted.

Paul's progression through the *agora* recalls a typical *periegesis* description.[128]

A further relevant sub-narrative is that of the taking of an altar inscription, seen in wandering through a city, as a starting-point for philosophical or moral reflection (23). There is a good example in Philostratus' *Life of Apollonius*.[129] Norden, indeed, thought that Luke modelled Paul's behaviour on the historical Apollonius, but the historical value of Philostratus' work is highly doubtful, and it is also possible that, as elsewhere, Philostratus' narrative here shows Dionian, or even Christian, influence.[130]

Another relevant sub-narrative is the taking of a statue as a starting-point for philosophical or religious reflection (16, 23), a pattern illustrated in the great *Olympic Oration* of Dio Chrysostom and, again, in Philostratus (*VA* 4.28). Other more specific philosophical paradigms—whether of the visiting outsider or of the philosophical judge—will be discussed below.

There is also a paradigm that unites life and literature. In as much as Paul, *qua* Socratic figure, is a philosophical figure, and in as much as he is also an outsider visiting a great city, some contemporary readers might well think of the visits of great contemporary philosophers or sophists to great cities and of the literary works thus inspired.[131] Paul is taken to the Areopagus, and there makes a speech, on the Christian God, which includes an appeal to Stoic theology, rather as Dio Chrysostom, on his visit to Olbia/Borysthenes, is taken to the temple of Zeus, the sacred site of the council, and makes a Stoic speech about Zeus' divine governance (*Or.* 36), or the same Dio makes a similar Stoic speech at Olympia (*Or.* 12). Another Dionian reference?

A final basic pattern is more specifically Jewish and/or Christian: a proselytising appeal to gentiles/Greeks through their own religious traditions. Paul's essential rhetorical strategy—a preliminary appeal to the Athenians' own religious traditions through evidently well-known tags—follows a recognised

---

126  Johnson (1992) 314; Alexander (2002) 230 n. 1; (2005) 84, 114.
127  Johnson (1992) 319.
128  Johnson (1992) 318–19.
129  *VA* 4.19; Norden (1913) 35–55.
130  Dionian: Bowie (1978) 1668–70; Christian: n. 82 above.
131  Johnson (1999) 251 (citing Dio Chrysostom).

Jewish mode of proselytising.[132] Norden also showed clear parallels between the pattern of Paul's speech and that of later Christian texts.[133] The latter might of course have been influenced by Acts 17, but both may (also) be reflecting the same approach.

Next, some stock questions.

First: could the historical Paul have made the sort of speech that Luke attributes to him? The answer, arguably (there is much argument), is 'yes'.[134] If so, readers already well informed about Paul will find the narrative in this respect plausible.

Second: does 'Areopagus' mean the hill, or the body, or both? 'Areopagus' certainly means the body, because 34 refers to 'Dionysius the Areopagite', and 33 'Paul went out from their midst' ring-structures with 22 'standing in the midst of the Areopagus', but I think 'Areopagus' also means the hill: dramatically, Paul performs on a distinctive location sacred to a major pagan god, rather as at Lystra he comes into contact with the 'priest of [the temple of] Zeus who was in front of the city' (14.13), or at Ephesus the crowd drag Paul's companions into the theatre and Paul himself wishes to go there in order to address the crowd (19.29–30), or as Dio Chrysostom performs at Olympia and Olbia.

Third: is this a trial?[135] This question subdivides into: (a) *was the historical* Paul tried by the Areopagus? and (b) is Luke *representing* the proceedings as a trial? For reasons to emerge, (b) should be taken first. The Socratic parallels, the echo of the charge against Socrates, the Areopagus' judicial associations, and the evocation of the pattern of 'philosopher on trial before the Areopagus' make the proceedings *look* like a trial; 'taking hold' (19) can be used of strong-arming before judicial authorities (cf. 16.19; 18.17; 21.30, 33), and narrative sequencing (19 ~ 16.19 ~18.17) favours this implication; there is some legal language (31, 34: 'proof'); the introduction into Athens of new divinities was as much a crime in the first century as in the fourth century BCE;[136] and the Areopagus was indeed the body competent to give philosophical figures permission to lecture in Athens.[137]

---

132 Especially Aratus, *Phaen.* 1–9, cited in Aristobulus F 4.6 {= Eus. *PE* 13.12.6}.
133 Norden (1913) 3–30; also Gärtner (1955).
134 Cf., e.g., Bruce (1951) 334–5; Witherington (1998) 523, 533–5; Fitzmyer (1998) 602; Johnson (1999) 251; Klauck (2000) 92–5; Barrett (2004) II.825–6.
135 Different views: trial: Barnes (1969); Hemer (1974); not: Haenchen (1971) 527–8; Barrett (2004) II.832–3. Many equivocate.
136 Jos. *Ap.* 2.266–7.
137 Cf. Cicero's actions in the case of Cratippus (above, n. 000).

On the other hand, there is no formal charge: the speculation in 18, 'but others said, "he seems to be an announcer of strange divinities"', does not amount to this, nor does the apparently polite request in 19: 'May we know what this new teaching is, the one that is spoken by you?', and the Athenians are explicitly motivated by obsession with novelty (21). And at the denouement (32–3), Paul just walks out, an outcome consistent with a trial only if Paul's accusers at that point judged him so risible that further proceedings could simply be dropped. This seems unlikely in itself, and takes no account of the 'others' that said: 'We will hear you again about this'. Nor does the latter remark plausibly imply resumption of a trial. Nor is Paul's own speech a defence speech. In particular, although Plato's *Apology* is in the narrative air, Paul does not use the word *apologia* or any of its cognates, whereas, as we shall see, he does so on subsequent, and analogous, occasions. Finally, while 'taking hold' can be used of strong-arm arrest, it can also be used neutrally (9.27; 23.19), and for proper discussion Paul and the philosophers need somewhere quieter than the *agora*.

If, therefore, the choice is between a trial and not a trial, the answer is the latter. Winter, however, followed by Witherington, has argued that the proceedings represent not a trial but an initial hearing (which the Areopagus had the power to call), with 20 to be interpreted as 'we wish to decide legally what these things mean', which γινώσκω can mean.[138] But this reconstruction likewise fails to cope with (*inter alia*) the emphasis on the Athenians' excessive curiosity, Paul's failure to use the word *apologia*, and his walk-out, and the interpretation of 20 is too narrow, neglecting to integrate the sentiment into the general debate about knowledge and ignorance.

A 'historical' reading of Acts 17 may fairly convict Luke of a lack of precision. But a conclusion more sympathetic to Luke's literary creativity is that he is representing the proceedings not as an actual trial, but as trial-*like*. If so, the answer to the question—*was* the *historical* Paul tried by the Areopagus?—is, surely, negative, because Luke is the only source for these proceedings, and it is implausible to suppose that he is minimising their proper legal force. As to Luke's motives in representing the proceedings as trial-*like*, the negative argument that he would not represent an actual trial if it had not actually occurred again raises questions about Luke's historical accuracy and historical scrupulousness or about his general conception of history which are very variously assessed. My own view is that he simply would not be swayed by such concern; the Preface to Luke does not seriously make against this, since the historiographical criteria—notably 'accuracy' and 'order'—are (a) competitive; (b) conventional; and (c) always relative. But it is in any case more important

---

138   Winter (1996); Witherington (1998) 517.

to consider what positive advantages accrue from his representing the proceedings as trial-*like*. These include: again validating Jesus' prophecy of Luke 21.12ff. (though we will later learn that Paul is 'many-lettered' in his own right); integrating the Areopagus episode into the long series of 'trials', both literal and figurative, faced by the apostles in general and by Paul in particular; beginning, in the appropriate context of Athens, the strong analogy between Socrates and Paul which will continue until the end of Acts; and, through this analogy, reinforcing the thought that Paul's mission must end in his death (cf. the use of the *Apology* in relation to Peter at 4.19 and 5.29); and giving the episode generalising, paradigmatic, power—and 'paradigmatic' in several senses. Further advantages will emerge.

The fourth question effectively encompasses the other three: granted that Paul did visit Athens (1 Thess. 3.1f.), is the whole Areopagus episode fact or fiction?[139] Here again huge general questions arise about Luke's conception of history, and, clearly, for some readers, they are intensified by Acts' status as a foundational Christian text. My own view is that Luke is obviously touching the main bases of traditional and contemporary literary representations of Athens; that some fabrication is demonstrable;[140] that the setting is at least highly constructed, and the episode itself is built from standard narrative patterns; that the shifting composition of Paul's audience (Epicurean and Stoic philosophers, the Areopagus *qua* body, in some sense the Athenians in general, and Athenians *qua* both citizens and resident aliens) suggests an 'ideal scene';[141] and that, if the episode is not an actual trial narrative, or even a 'preliminary hearing' narrative, it becomes in an important respect historically implausible. So I include the episode among the more imaginative feats of ancient historiography.[142] Even those, however, who reject outright fabrication should concede considerable fictionalisation, and so, on either view, appreciation of Luke's fictionalising skills should be an element of at least some readers' response. But it must also of course be to some degree a plausible fiction, in that it represents some true things about Paul, Greek philosophers, both Stoic and Epicurean, Athenians, and perhaps gentiles in general. And it is plausible in many respects (Paul could have argued like this; Athens was snobbish and old-fashioned; the resurrection was incomprehensible to most non-Christians, etc.).

---

139  Fact: Barnes (1969); Hemer (1974); fiction: Dibelius (1956) 26–77; Haenchen (1971) 572–3; Nock (1953) 497–8 = (1972) II.821–2.
140  Notably in the case of 'Dionysius the Areopagite and a woman Heifer by name' (17.34): Moles (2006b) 74, 87 n. 91 {above, pp. 560, 572}.
141  Thus Haenchen (1971) 528.
142  Moles (1993) 118–21 {vol. 2, p. 183–6}; (1996b) 266 {vol. 2, p. 254}.

The way lies open for philosophical analysis.

The episode, delimited by precise road directions (17.15; 18.1), comes more or less in the middle of Acts, whose narrative trajectory goes from Jerusalem to Rome. Athens represents a *tertium quid* between Jerusalem and Rome. The Epicureans and Stoics are 'philosophers' in a simple and recognisable sense: Greeks who '*love* wisdom' and debate how it is to be found. But the *term* (18) is *hapax* in Luke and the whole New Testament. In context, therefore, it has force. The philosophical aspect of Luke's own Preface sharpens the question about the value of the 'philosophy' of *these* 'philosophers'. Luke-Acts, itself with philosophical elements, is addressed to *Theophilos*, '*lover* of God'/'*loved* by God'. A central theme of Acts is that one should 'love God' and not 'fight God'. One should be a 'theophile', not a 'theomach'.[143] Later, we learn that '*love* of *human beings*' (*philanthropia*) is intrinsic to the Christian mission.[144] Earlier, Stephen the Hellenist emphasised that Moses, patriarch of the Jews, had been educated in 'the whole wisdom [*sophia*]' of the Egyptians. Hence Acts 17.16–34 is fundamentally concerned with the questions of the status of Greek *philosophy* within the developing Christian mission and of how far the two can be reconciled.

Scholarly analyses polarise: for some, Paul is extremely—even excessively—conciliatory; for others, sharply critical. Accordingly, my analysis divides into positive and negative elements.

Paul is responding to a request: 'lovers of wisdom', the 'philosophers' 'desire to know' (20). Seemingly, no request could be more admirable or philosophical (~ Arist. *Met.* 980a1). Paul's description of his addressees in 22—as 'being as fearful of divinities as it is possible to be in all respects'—reflects the Athenians' traditional reputation for piety, and can be understood as a *captatio benevolentiae*. The difficulty that a *captatio benevolentiae* was forbidden before the Areopagus (Lucian, *Anach.* 19)—if it is a difficulty (need the dramatic Paul and many of Luke's readers know this?)—is palliated by the fact that the proceedings are not a formal trial—as well as by the fact that the description can also be understood as parresiastically critical (below).

Further conciliation of (some of) his audience is offered in 28: 'for "In him we live and move and are", as even some of those who according to you are poet-makers have said, "for we are actually his offspring"'. I have translated ποιητῶν as 'poet-makers', not only because the notion of 'making' is intrinsic to the Classical conception of 'poetry' but also because there is an implicit analogy, soon explicit, between the 'making' of 'poets' and God's 'making' of the world.

---

143  Moles (2006b) 78 {above, p. 564}.
144  P. 908 below.

Since both Stoics and Epicureans often appealed to the great poetry of the past for philosophical support, Paul, while following a recognised Jewish/Christian path of proselytisation, is also playing the Athenian philosophers' own games.

The conciliation here seems very strong. Law-observant Jews could adopt a wide range of attitudes to gentile gods, from outright denial of their existence, to acceptance of their reality as 'demons', to relatively benevolent allusion to 'angels of the nations', and to acceptance that the Jewish god and Zeus/Jupiter were the same. Naturally, 'it depends what you mean by "is"', and Paul does not use the name Zeus. But this provisional identification affords some basis for shared theology.

It is also important to probe Paul's references. Which 'poet-makers'? The Greek καθ' ὑμᾶς 'is a little more than equivalent to a possessive pronoun ... it means ... that you regard as authoritative ... the sense [is], Poets that you ought to be prepared to listen to'.[145] Scholars debate whether the clause 'as even some of those who according to you are poet-makers have said' looks back to the first quotation or forwards to the second quotation, or even bridges both. It must at least look forward to the second quotation. '[F]or we are actually his offspring' is a direct quotation from the *Phaenomena* of the third-century BCE Greek poet Aratus (*Phaen.* 5). Now, although Aratus came from Soli in Cilicia (whence perhaps an additional and rather ironic felicity: Paul of Tarsus is quoting a fellow-Cilician), he studied in Athens and became a disciple of the Stoic philosopher Cleanthes, who also was not an Athenian but had settled in Athens. Further, *Phaenomena* 5 itself echoes Cleanthes' *Hymn to Zeus* (4; SVF 1.537): 'for we are offspring from you'. Thus, although this use of Aratus is attested in Jewish proselytising before Paul, the double evocation of Aratus and Cleanthes is particularly apposite before an Athenian audience, and one which included Stoics, and the categorisation both of the non-Athenian Aratus and of the non-Athenian Cleanthes as 'those who according to you are poet-makers' is elegantly complimentary of Athenian local pride. The nice footwork of the double allusion and the deft categorisation should also appeal to literary sophisticates both among the dramatic audience and among Luke's readers. Additional felicities are that Cleanthes himself had allegedly been tried before the Areopagus (D.L. 7.168–9) and that the longer citation of Aratus in Aristobulus has surely influenced Paul's thinking and wording more broadly: 'Let us begin with God, whom men never leave *unspoken: full of God* are the streets, and all *the Marketplaces of humanity*, and full the sea and the harbours; and *we are all in need of God everywhere*'.[146]

---

145  Barrett (2004) II.848.
146  Dormeyer–Galindo (2003) {268}.

What of the first quotation? Colaclides suggests allusion to Euripides, *Bacchae* 506: 'you do not know what you are living, nor what you are doing, nor who you are' (Dionysus disguised as the stranger to Pentheus)—convincingly.[147] There is a sustained intertextual relationship between Acts and *Bacchae*, with particularly concentrated allusions elsewhere in Acts 17.[148] The contexts are very similar, the wording close. On this reading, 'some of those who according to you are poet-makers' has precise local force, denoting Euripides, most popular of Athenian poets.

But there are other candidates. The traditional suggestion, now unfashionable, is the legendary Cretan holy man, Epimenides.[149] The complicated arguments attest Luke's literary and philosophical skills.

In his commentary on this passage, the Syriac church father Isho'dad ascribes to a panegyric of Minos over his father Zeus the following sentences: 'They fashioned a tomb for you, O holy and high—the Cretans, always liars, evil beasts, lazy bellies. But you are not dead; you are risen and alive for ever, for in you we live and move and are'. Callimachus, *Hymn to Zeus* 7–8, runs: 'The Cretans are always liars; for they fashioned your tomb, O king; but you did not die; for you are for ever'. Titus 1.12 (on the work of one of Paul's disciples in Crete) reads: 'one of them, their own prophet, said: "Cretans are always liars, evil beasts, lazy bellies"'. The line 'the Cretans … bellies' is attributed by Clement (*Strom.* 1.14.59.1–2) to Epimenides, which fits the allusion in Titus. If so, Callimachus also is imitating Epimenides in *Hymn to Zeus* 7, and Callimachus gives some support to Isho'dad's larger contextualisation of the line 'the Cretans … bellies'. As for Titus, while most Pauline scholars reject Pauline authorship, it is some support for an Epimenidean allusion in Acts 17.28 that one of the Pastoral epistles contains an apparently related allusion. The wider Epimenidean tradition also helps. According to Diogenes Laertius 1.110, the Athenians during a plague sent for Epimenides, who brought some sheep *to the Areopagus* and advised their followers to sacrifice them 'to the local god', and in commemoration '*anonymous*' altars were set up. Unless Isho'dad has carelessly introduced the verse from Luke into his longer quotation and unless Diogenes Laertius' testimony about Epimenides is contaminated by Luke's account of Paul in Athens, *neither* of which seems likely, and *both* of which are extremely unlikely, a cluster of factors certifies an Epimenidean allusion.

---

147   Colaclides (1973); Moles (2006b), 73–4 {above, pp. 559–61}.
148   Moles (2006b) 70–4 {above, pp. 557–61}.
149   Essential is Cadbury (1922) v.246–51, reprised in Bruce (1951) 338–9. Epimenides' doubtful historicity is immaterial: there was an Epimenidean 'tradition'.

Some scholars have argued instead for the Stoic philosopher Posidonius.[150] The sentiment 'in him we live and move and are' can certainly be read as Stoic. The emphasis on God's nearness to men is Stoic.[151] And the broader movement of 27–8 '[to seek God, if then they might feel after him and find him,] and him not being far from each one of us, for "In him we live and move and are"' finds an excellent parallel in Dio's *Olympic Oration* (12.28), where he describes 'the most senior and most ancient human beings' as 'not being settled apart by themselves, far from and outside the divine [Russell conjectures 'God'], but growing in the very midst of it, or rather growing together with it and holding on to it [Reiske conjectures 'held round about'] in every way'. In that speech Dio is writing Stoic and specific Posidonian influence is very plausible,[152] and the speech's 'narrative' corresponds to one of the narrative patterns underlying the Areopagus episode.[153] (Hence: another Dionian echo?) Posidonius, of course, was not a 'poet', but Epimenides, Aratus, and Cleanthes (in the *Hymn to Zeus*) were, and in any case 'poet-maker' can also be understood in the broader sense of 'creative writer', which can include prose writers. Thus a Posidonian allusion is very likely, but does not preclude other possibilities.

A nice final point in Luke's multiple allusions here. Some scholars have read the 'some' in 'some of your poet-makers' as a literary convention for a single allusion.[154] Such usage is common (for example, in Plutarch), and an ancient reader could thus read the 'some'. But the better-read would take it as a true and multiple plural.

In all this, Paul is not so much arguing the case for monotheism as assuming it: exploiting the monotheistic potential of much Greek religious thinking and particularly of Stoic theology, a potential which was becoming something of a tendency within contemporary Greek and Roman religion, as recent scholarship has stressed.[155] With this general line of thought his audience, quiescent till Paul's citation of Jesus' resurrection (32), seems not unhappy. Within it, Paul's most audacious move is his initial appeal to the altar bearing the inscription 'to unknown god' (23). Nearly all scholars have followed Jerome (*Ad Titum* 1.12) in supposing that Paul has simply turned a plural inscription ('to unknown gods') into a singular, and it may be so. But van der Horst, followed by Witherington, has produced plausible arguments for supposing that altar inscriptions 'to unknown god' singular did exist. This in itself would not entail

---

150 Balch (1990); Barrett (2004) II.847–8.
151 Cf. e.g. Sen. *Ep.* 41.1; 73.16; and, in the Stoic-influenced Philo, *De praem. et poen.* 84.
152 Russell (1992) 177.
153 {JLM does not develop this idea in what follows.}
154 Dibelius (1956) 50 n. 76; Haenchen (1971) 525.
155 Athanassiadi–Frede (1999).

a monotheistic perspective. But there is also the possibility that 'unknown' was a recognised epithet of the Jewish god, which would help the push towards monotheism.[156] In short, Paul's appeal to 'unknown god' may invoke a genuine type of inscription, though one not yet found anywhere, least of all in Athens.

Some scholars[157] have seen the appeal as connecting also with Academic 'agnosticism' about the existence of the gods.[158] This is surely wrong. The inscription does not raise the question of whether or not this (or any) god exists, rather of how he is to be named and where he is to be found.

As for the claim that God made human beings 'that they should seek [*zētein*] God' (27), 'seek' can be a philosophical term, especially in relation to 'seeking' the divine,[159] and within the overall texture of Acts it is as if philosophical opponents who debate or dispute with one another (*suzētein*) at least unite in 'seeking' after God.

So much for Paul's conciliation of his audience.

But there are also profoundly critical elements in the episode, as Luke's introductory remarks immediately signal (16). Paul is offended that the Athenians are polytheists, that they are such indiscriminate polytheists, and that they are idolaters. The philosophers' desire to know is really nothing more than desire for novelty (21). Paul's initial description of his addressees can also mean 'you dreadfully superstitious lot!'. In the narrative patterns that underlie the episode, the figure of the stranger is often used to show how 'strange' the city is. Although Paul himself comes into Athens as a stranger, Athens itself is a pretty strange place. When he acts as outsider or as external assessor or judge, he seems to be like the Cynic 'scout' (note the repeated use of the word 'observe'—like *inspexit* in Hor. *Epist.* 1.2.19 of the Cynic-Stoic Ulysses),[160] or 'street' philosopher, he is parresiastically rude to his audience, and he castigates their superstitiousness (a standard Cynic target).[161] Moreover, 28 brings the adjective *diogenēs* into the reader's mind. So Paul is also a Diogenes figure—and appropriately so. Cynics despised the hyper-sophistication of Stoics and Epicureans.

In so far as Paul is also a Socrates figure, his philosophical opponents, themselves heirs of Socrates, ignorantly repeat against him the charge made against

---

156    Van der Horst (1989); Witherington (1998) 521–23.
157    E.g., Wright (2008) II.87.
158    Dormeyer–Galindo (2003) {269–70} appeal to *Epicurean* belief in the 'unknowability' of the gods; this is simply wrong: Epicureans 'know' about the gods: it is the beliefs of 'the many' that are faulty (D.L. 10.123).
159    LSJ s.v. I.4.
160    Moles (1985) 35 {above, p. 363}.
161    Kindstrand (1976) 237.

the historical Socrates. Given that Acts 17 certainly contains some name plays, I wonder whether, since Paul already plays Socrates and the Xenophontic as well as the Platonic Socrates, he is also playing Xenophon: 'speaker of strange things': only so regarded because his audience is profoundly confused about the relationship between the strange and the not-strange. For that sort of implicit name identification of one's literary source one might compare the allusion to Ennius in Horace, *Odes* 3.30.1: *aere perennius*. The Athenian philosophers presumably also take 'Jesus' and 'Rising' (*anastasis*) as strange divinities, on the analogy, familiar from eastern religions, of male god and female consort.[162] They must understand the name Jesus as 'healer', and they are interested because they themselves promise psychic 'healing' (the philosopher as *iatros* etc.). Now Acts itself emphatically exploits the etymological association between *Iesous* and *iaomai*, and it re-activates this association in ch. 17—because the earlier narrative introduces a character named Jason, the Greek equivalent of the Jewish-Greek *Iesous*, and a name that actually means 'healer'.[163] But the philosophers do not understand what Jesus' 'healing' consists of. The true healing of Jesus trumps the psychic 'healing' claimed by the philosophers. And on the level of Paul himself, rather than Jesus, the Epimenidean associations of 'in him we live and move and are' also trump the 'healing' claims of the Athenian philosophers, for the point of Epimenides' visit to Athens was to cure plague.[164] Thus Paul is also an Epimenidean 'healing' philosopher.

There is also the sense that Paul is a better literary critic than the Greek philosophers—and of their own greatest literature. Paul 'reads' and interprets Socrates better, he reads Epimenides, Cleanthes, and Aratus better. Outsider as he is, he even 'reads' Athenian inscriptions better. Nor do intricate Stoic and Epicurean studies in language seem to have done them much good. And if one consults 'poet-makers' to see what they 'make' of God, there is also an important sense in which Paul is the true 'poet' here. Or, of course, Luke himself, who 'made' his first *logos* in such a way that theme and treatment formed a unity (Acts 1.1; Luke 1.1–3).

Nor do the Athenian philosophers keep their own rules. Successful philosophising requires full-hearted cooperation. Paul does his bit philosophically, both by dialectic in the forum and by formal speech to the Areopagus—his interlocutors, 'official' Greek philosophers as they are, and self-styled successors of Socrates, do not. That supplies one explanation why Paul's speech ends

---

162 Already Chrysostom, *Hom. in Acta* 38.1; Haenchen (1971) 518; Fitzmyer (1998) 605.
163 9.34, 10.38. {On healing, see above, Ch. 23.}
164 {D.L. 1.110; cf. [Arist.] *Ath. Pol.* 1; Plut. *Sol.* 12.7–9.}

in 32: the Athenian philosophers are not up to it and either jeer or request adjournment.

Thus far the Athenian philosophers in general, but an important question is the role of the Epicureans. For Epicureanism offers far fewer starting-points for a positive response to Christianity than Stoicism. This emerges clearly from Paul's speech. There are one or two things that Epicureans could accept, but not the fundamentals. Epicureans do not believe that gods intervene actively in the world (18, 26–7), that the apparent plurality of gods conceals one true god (22–3), that any god made the *kosmos* and everything in it and has given life to human beings (24–5), that the purpose of human existence is to seek god (27), that god is immanent (28), that humans should repent because a god announces it (30), that there will be a final judgement day (31), or that there is any possibility of resurrection or anything similar (31).

Why, then, does Luke include them? Not, certainly, because historically they just happened to be there. Is it because at this period the phrase 'Epicureans and Stoics' (*vel sim.*) can function as shorthand for 'Greek and Roman philosophers' in general? That explanation does not work: Paul here himself is appropriating other philosophical roles. Or is it because Luke often represents the audiences of apostolic teaching as falling into two groups: one interested, or at least not dismissive, the other hostile (cf. 2.12f.; 14.4; 23.6; 28.24)? Or, Josephus-like, is Luke suggesting a parallel between Epicureans and Sadducees (who reject resurrection) and Stoics and Pharisees (who accept it)?

To progress, it is worth asking who are the 'some' and 'others' of 18. They are subdivisions of the category of 'some of the Epicurean and Stoic philosophers' (the narrative flow is disturbed if the 'some' lie outside the general category of 'philosophers'), and they have different reactions to Paul's dialectic in the *agora*. But are they the same as the 'some' and 'others' of 32, who have different reactions to the formal speech on the Areopagus? It would seem so,[165] because both in 18 and 32 the 'some' are contemptuous of Paul ('this seed-collector';[166] 'some jeered'), while the 'others' have at least a certain interest in pursuing explanations ('he seems to be an announcer of strange deities'; 'we will hear you again about this').

The next question is whether the 'some—others' contrast merely makes a general contrast, within the category of 'some of the Epicurean and Stoic philosophers', between the less and the more theologically responsive to Paul's teaching, or whether that very contrast differentiates Epicureans and Stoics.

---

165   Cf. Haenchen (1971) 517, 526; Klauck (2000) 78.
166   Extensive discussion of the term's implications in Barrett (2004) 11.830; 'intellectual magpie' (Hanson) is a good gloss, but literal translation conveys more.

The latter seems preferable. It suits the word order of 18 and the characterisation both of 18 and of 32 (Epicureans were good at jeering),[167] as well as the speech's predominant theology (above).

Thus in this encounter with Paul, the Epicureans come off distinctively badly. When they ridicule Paul as a 'seed-collector' (18), they immediately shoot themselves in the foot, 'seeds' being basic to Epicurean materialism.[168] Similarly, at the end of Paul's speech in 32, they are the 'jeerers'. The Stoics, however, are different—in 32 they will hear Paul again, because they have some interest in an afterlife or in a re-jigging of the whole physical system. 32 therefore leaves the door open to Stoics. This is important for the later narrative of Acts—but also corresponds to historical fact: early Christians generally were much more sympathetic to Stoicism. The historical Paul himself was;[169] so were the Church fathers generally.[170]

The inclusion of the Epicureans, then, serves several purposes. One simply is to secure as wide a coverage of pagan philosophers as possible (Socrates, Plato, Xenophon, Epimenides, Diogenes and the Cynics, Stoics, and Epicureans). Another is to play out in the field of philosophy patterns of acceptance or rejection of Christianity, and specifically of resurrection, that recur throughout Acts. The effect is to focus on the key problems of the Christian mission in any context. Another is to distinguish between those Greek philosophers with whom Christians *may* be able to do business and those with whom they cannot.

We are now better able to understand the combination in Paul's speech of considerable conciliation and sharp criticism. The answer lies in the adage 'so near and so far'. The theological thinking of *some* of the Greek philosophers is only a hair's breadth from the Christian truth. That is a source of, and for, encouragement. It is also a source of, and for, sharp criticism. Having got so far, why do they not go the whole way? *Other* Greek philosophers are simply beyond the pale.

The next step is to consider how the episode defines the relationship between Greek philosophy in general and Christianity. Obviously, Christianity is not being defined as immediately and overwhelmingly superior. Equally obviously, it is not being defined as just another philosophy.

---

167  Cf., e.g., Lucr. 2.1ff.; Cic. *Fin.* 1.62.
168  {E.g., Epicur. *Ep.* 1.38, 74; 2.89; Lucr. 1.501.}
169  Cf. n. 50 above.
170  Cf. Just. *Apol.* 1.16.4; 2.13.2–6; Clem. Alex. *Strom.* 1.5.28; Tert. *De an.* 20.1; Sorabji (2000); there are a few, strained attempts to build bridges with Epicureanism: e.g., Justin Mart. PG VI.1581; Tert. *De praescript. haer.* 7 (inveighing against the consequences).

In the first instance, it is, as we have seen, in many ways a better philosophy. This implication is reinforced by paradoxes; for example, for the reader it is Paul, the outsider and a Jew, who plays the role of Socrates, Athenian, greatest of Greek philosophers, and the father of almost all Hellenistic philosophy, and, as in Plato and Xenophon, the accused is really the judge of his accusers. But it is not just a better philosophy. When the Epicureans accuse Paul of being a 'seed-collector', they are not merely accusing him of being an intellectual magpie. Plutarch refers to Aristippus picking up only 'seeds and samples' of Socrates' words (*Mor.* 516C) and Philostratus (*VA* 5.20) uses *spermologos* of the peddler of second-rate religious opinions. So the Epicureans are implicitly accusing Paul of being an intellectual magpie in the field of Socrates' religious thinking. The whole passage speaks against that accusation.[171] Moreover, when the Stoics hazard that 'he seems to be the announcer of strange divinities', readers must be struck not only by the obvious Socratic parallel but also by the fact that this is the only case in Acts, in Luke-Acts, and in the whole New Testament where *daimonia* is used neutrally: everywhere else it means 'demons', a term which of course Jews and Christians can use for the gentile gods. This negative aspect is implicit in Paul's ambiguous characterisation of the Athenians as *deisidaimonesterous*. But in this episode the figure of Socrates is being enlisted on the side of monotheism and just below the surface are several Christianising interpretations of Socrates: Socrates as a Christian *avant la lettre* and expeller of 'demons';[172] the beneficent Socratic *daimonion*, a manifestation of 'the god within', as an anticipation of monotheism and a demonstration of God's close personal connection with human beings.[173] The Stoic-like 'for in him we live and move and are' is easily harmonised with such thinking. Thus Seneca (*Ep.* 41.1): 'God is near to you, with you, within you'. Furthermore, the imagery of 'seeds' in the Epicurean accusation against Paul inevitably interacts with the philosophical and theological discourse (Epicurean 'seeds', notions of 'offspring' and 'fatherhood'). The cumulative effect is to raise the question: who here is the real heir of Socrates? And since the solution to the contrasting aspects of Paul's speech lies in the thought 'so near and so far', the answer obviously is: not the Greek philosophers but Paul.

Acts 17, therefore, stages Christianity's claim to be the correct ultimate interpretation of Socratic philosophy, just as it is the correct ultimate interpretation of Jewish theology. This claim is underwritten by two other factors. The first is

---

171  Note also the use of the noun *spermologia* in Dio 32.9 (Dio's attack on Alexandrian Cynics): again, one wonders about Dionian influence.
172  {Cf., e.g., Döring (1979) 143–61.}
173  Alexander (2005) 64.

the parallel between Paul and Epimenides, with Paul propounding the worship of the unknown god as the solution to Athens' contemporary sickness in the same way as Epimenides prescribed the cult of 'unknown gods' as the solution to Athenian plague and discord. Christian 'philosophy' in the name of *Iesous* ('healer'), will heal the 'ills' of Hellenistic philosophy.[174] The second is the implication of 'foundation', generated partly by the Epimenidean parallel (the 'founding' of the cult of 'unknown gods'), partly by the ending of Paul's speech, and partly by echoes of *Bacchae* and Dionysiac myth.

The speech ends with Paul's citation of Jesus' resurrection as proof that he is God's appointed judge of the world at the last day. As throughout Acts, divine justice trumps human justice: here, the justice of the Areopagus. But more, Paul's proclamation of Jesus' resurrection to an Athenian audience and specifically an Areopagite audience implicitly confutes some well-known denials of bodily resurrection in Athenian literature, in ironic silent counterpoint to the explicit citations of 'those who are in your judgement poet-makers'.[175] The most famous comes in Aeschylus' *Eumenides*, the Athenian poetic text that, not coincidentally, commemorates the founding of the Areopagus. At that first trial, Apollo proclaims as self-evidently true (647–51):

> But when the dust draws *up* the blood of a man once dead, there is no resurrection/*upstanding*. For this my father [Zeus] did not make any *healing* charms, but all other things he arranges by his desire, turning them *up* and down without panting in the least.

Here, by contrast, God does have the power to raise men *up* from the dead and in the case of Jesus has provably done so. Thus the healing Jewish god trumps the supreme Greek god; the resurrection future of human beings under the Jewish god trumps the unambiguously final death of human beings under the Olympians; and the Athenian foundation myth about a court premised on the non-resurrection of men is supplanted by the Christian final judgement premised on the resurrection of the dead.

Acts 17 contains several echoes of *Bacchae* and Dionysiac cult.[176] Besides the parallel between 'in whom we live and move and are' (28) and *Bacchae* 506, there is the pagan philosophers' surmise that Paul seems to be 'an announcer of *strange* divinities', not 'new divinities', as in Plato and Xenophon (18).[177]

---

174  I suspect a parallel in Peter's 'healing' of 'Aeneas' (Acts 10.32–4).
175  Witherington (1998) 519 n. 205; Barrett (2004) II.854; Wright (2008) II.92–4.
176  Moles (2006b) 70–4 {above, pp. 557–61}.
177  {Plat. *Apol.* 24c1: ἕτερα ... δαιμόνια καινά; Xen. *Mem.* 1.1: ἕτερα ... καινὰ δαιμόνια εἰσφέρων}.

The sequence ends with the unhistorical citation of '*Dionysios* the Areopagite' as one of Paul's converts. Given this *Bacchae* presence, the 'mocking' by the Epicureans (32) corresponds to the 'mocking' response of Pentheus to Dionysus in *Bacchae* (272). Just, then, as Euripides' *Bacchae* dramatises the introduction of Bacchic cult into Thebes and in effect into Macedonia and Athens, so Acts 17 dramatises Paul's introduction into Athens of Jesus. Thus Paul's speech enacts in Athens and hence within Greek and Roman religion generally a decisive and distinctively Christian 'refoundation'.[178]

There are perhaps four remaining questions about this tremendous speech.

First, whether it is complete and, if not, why and with what implications.[179] For many reasons, the hypothesis that the speech is *historically* incomplete because the *historical* Paul stopped at this point is naïve.

The end of the speech is satisfyingly closural in several respects. Paul's wording, 'having provided proof to all by raising him from the dead', triumphantly ring-structures with (18) 'because he told the good news about *Iesous* and *Anastasis*/'Rising'. His characterisation of Jesus as a 'man' implicitly counters the philosophers' supposition that he is an announcer of new, or strange, divinities (18). Paul implies the superiority of divine justice to human (above) and confutes Athenian poets' denial of resurrection (above). And to the (limited extent) that the philosophical debate is between polytheism and monotheism Paul has done enough.

The speech is also *dramatically* complete in that the philosophers' response to Paul's mention of Jesus' resurrection ends the proceedings. This may indeed dramatise the historical Paul's description of the Gospel as foolishness to the Greeks (1 Cor. 1.23).[180] Paul's philosophical audience fails his philosophical challenges, indeed more: although desirous of knowledge, even novelty-obsessed, the Athenians, philosophers included, cannot begin to comprehend what is certainly a 'new thing': the proven resurrection of Jesus.

Nevertheless, in one fundamental respect the speech is incomplete: it does not give an adequate account of the role of Jesus, the original 'trigger' of the whole episode. It is important to say that Jesus: (a) was a man, not a 'strange divinity'; (b) rose from the dead; and (c) will be God's appointed judge of the world. But it is not enough to say these things, because throughout Acts Jesus is *also* a divine being and he is twice explicitly described by Paul himself as 'the

---

178  Note Luke's acquaintance with the historical Paul's ideas on the subject.
179  Slightly similarly, Sandnes (1993) argues that Paul's speech uses rhetorical *insinuatio* as a 'dialectical' device to provoke (not satisfy) audience curiosity.
180  The passage has often been read as Paul's rueful acknowledgement of failure in Athens: a reading incompatible with the fictionality of that philosophical encounter.

son of God' (in the strongest sense {9.20; 10.32–3}). Acts' theology is implicitly Trinitarian. The divine Jesus is the Son of God/the Holy Spirit/Lord[181] (and it is also sometimes unclear whether Lord designates Jesus or God). The doctrines of the Incarnation and of the Trinity are, of course, difficult both to comprehend and to expound—and hardly best expounded in a narrative history of the acts of the apostles. Nevertheless, in a relatively developed Christian context, they are inescapably there and Acts must to some extent manage them.

There are two other basic theological questions that Acts has to manage:[182] the ambiguous status of Christianity as between Jewish and non-Jewish and between 'old' and 'new'; and (arguably) the relationship between Jesus-religion and Dionysus-religion. These two questions intersect.

For early Christians, both Jewish and gentile, it is important that (a degree of) 'newness' be suggested by the advent of Jesus—otherwise how are they distinctively different from other Jews/Jews? It is, however, also important that this newness remain unclarified: otherwise, Christians risk de-legitimising themselves, whether in 'internal' religious contexts or in 'external' religio-political contexts, since the Romans tolerated other races' 'ancestral religion', but not 'new' religions (as some already regarded Christianity).[183] Hence much Christian emphasis on 're*newal*'. Now, there is a sub-text running practically throughout Acts whereby Jesus is implicitly compared to Dionysus, and this in numerous ways, including 'newness'. The main vehicle of this sustained comparison (which also, of course, involves contrast) is Euripides' *Bacchae*. As we have seen, Acts 17 is one of the contexts where the parallel between Jesus and Dionysus is strongest, although it remains—and must remain—at the level of implication.

On this level, Jesus, like Dionysus, 'son of Zeus' (as 'Dionysus' means),[184] is alike a 'new' or 'stranger' god,[185] the 'son of god', a god who was a man, and a god who returned from the dead (yet another useful association of the Epimenidean allusion).[186] But unlike Dionysus, Jesus' divine claims are true, and, of course, God, too, is in the end the Jewish god, not Zeus. Nevertheless, as with the initial provisional identification of the Jewish god and Zeus, and as with the quotations from Cleanthes, Aratus, Euripides, Epimenides, etc., these suggestive analogues offer Greeks a way in to Christianity. Hence the

---

181  11.16; Luke's christology: 18.9 Jesus as Lord; Marshall (1980) 296; Witherington (1998) 550.
182  Moles (2006b) 83–7 {above, pp. 569–73}.
183  Suet. *Nero* 16.2; Tac. *Ann.* 15.44.3.
184  That is, in ancient thinking: cf. Eur. *Bacch.* 550–1.
185  For Jesus as 'stranger' (to his own), cf., e.g., Luke 24.18; John 1.11.
186  Son of god: Acts 9.20; 10.32–3; Luke 1.35; 3.22; 4.41; etc.; Jesus ~ Dionysus generally: Tueller (1992); Moles (2006b); Seaford (2006) 120–30.

conversion at the end of the sequence of 'Dionysius the Areopagite and a woman Heifer by name': unhistorical, but proleptic of the conversion of the Dionysiacs.

Now this whole episode is marked by emphases upon 'newness' and 'strangeness' and by inversions of various kinds: Paul the outsider is more like Socrates than the Athenian philosophers; the 'strangers' within Athens are just as novelty-obsessed as the native Athenians; the Athenian philosophers, novelty-obsessed, speak quaintly old-fashioned Greek, etc. These mixed-up categories create several effects. First, as we have repeatedly seen, on the human level, it is the outsider Paul who best negotiates them. Second, Athens appears as a mixed-up sort of place. Third, they suggest some of the problematics of Jesus himself. Fourth, they help to make Athens into a sort of quaint mirror-space where the ambiguities and problematics of Christianity can be reflected and reflected upon in a sanitised environment.[187] And fifth, they suggest Jesus' power to transcend boundaries of space, place, and time. Earlier, in connection with the activities of Jason, Christians are accused of '*up*turning the inhabited world' (17.6). On a straightforwardly political level, the charge is unfounded; at a deeper level, Christianity does indeed turn the world *up*side down, because Jesus' '*up*standing' changes everything. The power of the Aeschylean Zeus is again decisively trumped.[188]

From all this it follows that (some of) the Athenian philosophers' surmise that Paul is introducing strange divinities is not as misguided as Paul's 'incomplete' speech suggests. Rather, here too those philosophers approach the truth, but are prevented from true discernment by their scepticism about the resurrection.

The second remaining question is to define more precisely how this speech plays to the different readerships/audiences of non-Christians and Christians. In several ways, non-Christians are simultaneously encouraged and reproved. Zeus is, provisionally, the same god as the Jewish god—but not really. Athens is complimented—but criticised and re-focalised as a rather odd and strange place. That provides encouragement to Christians—Christianity can more than hold its own against the most sophisticated Greek philosophy, indeed, it has become the true heir to the best of that philosophy. But it also has protreptic power for non-Christians, whose confidence in Greek intellectual

---

187  Moles (2006b) 85 {above, p. 570}; the technique recalls—and is perhaps influenced by—'the mirror of Herodotus': Hartog (1988).
188  Luke works a similar 'turn' in Paul's speech before Felix: denying the charge of bringing about the 'rising [ἐπίστασιν] of a mob' (24.12), he hopes for the 'rising [ἀνάστασιν] of both just and unjust' (24.15).

superiority is challenged. The most sophisticated Athenian philosophers are made to look silly and non-Christians are invited to a radical re-ordering of their mental universe. It is true that this critique is partly made from within Greek philosophy—by Paul's assumption of a Cynic role, and by the adoption of, as it were, non-Christian literary techniques, but only partly so. Non-Christians should take note. This is another way in which Christianity 'turns the world upside down'. Christians may take pleasure from this non-Christian discomfiture, yet such pleasure should be tempered by reflection that the philosophers' assumption that Jesus is a new and strange divinity combines with the 'gap' left by the incompleteness of Paul's speech to adumbrate difficult questions about *Christian* theology. The allusions to Dionysus are there to help Christians as well as non-Christians. The speech and the narrative, then, pose a challenge to *Christian* readers which itself may fairly be termed philosophical. Luke-Acts repeatedly deploys the didactic techniques of leaving 'gaps' which readers have to fill in for themselves and of inviting readers to make negative judgements about others that immediately rebound on the judgemental.

The third question is the relationship between Paul's speech and Stephen's. Both concede some value to alien 'wisdom' and benevolently appropriate it. Stephen (like Moses, and, indeed, like Jesus himself) and Paul are themselves 'wise' in that wisdom. But Paul, while leaving the door open to some Greek philosophers, reveals the shallowness of the 'love of wisdom' of Greek 'philosophers' generally. Stephen's speech is more relaxed about the value of Greek wisdom precisely because he is talking about the kind that has been absorbed into Judaism (through the person of Moses) or into Christianity (through himself and his fellow 'Hellenists'). As between Hellenism and Christianity, therefore, the function of Stephen's speech is to define the acceptable limits of 'Hellenism' *within* Christianity. *Outside* Christianity, Greek philosophy seems tolerable only to the extent that it offers a platform for conversion to Christianity, itself a philosophy in the sense that it is the *fulfilment* of Greek philosophy.

With the fourth remaining question, we move to questions about the practice of mission.

The Areopagus speech has often been read as paradigmatic, in the sense of being an example of how Christians should mission to gentiles relatively unfamiliar with the Jewish background.[189] On this reading, the Areopagus speech and Paul's earlier speech at Lystra (14.15–17) fulfil the same basic function, though the Lystra speech is much shorter and much simpler, as befits both its

---

189  E.g., Dibelius (1956) 82, 165; Haenchen (1971) 529–31; Fitzmyer (1998) 601; Witherington (1998) 533.

unsophisticated audience and the apostles' hasty improvisation, whereas the Areopagus speech is much more measured and has to accommodate sophisticates. If one grants: (a) that the Areopagus speech is not a historical document (whether because Luke's speeches are never thus or the episode is fictional), and (b) that Luke-Acts envisages gentiles among its readers, and if one also takes account of the Jewish and Christian parallels for such approaches to gentiles, then, on the level of *reader* reception, this interpretation must be correct. On this level, Acts 17 can even be read as 'meta'- for Luke-Acts as a whole.

It is, however, a separate question whether the Areopagus speech is supposed to be paradigmatic of how—or of *one* of the ways in which—Christian missionaries should operate orally. Some[190] reject this interpretation, on the grounds that (a) such 'open-air' missioning in gentile contexts is very much the minority mode in Acts; (b) there were considerable practical difficulties for such missioning ('public space' was 'public' only to the 'local public', not to outsider preachers or teachers, who needed sanction from the local magistrates, as this narrative itself conveys, and/or the appropriate social status); (c) historically, early Christianity seems to have grown 'in private'; (d) philosophers did not much protrepticise in public; even Cynic public philosophising is more a matter of literary representation than reality.

So I turn to the question of the contexts of Christian missioning in Acts, also, of course, an important topic in its own right, but I consider only those contexts where there is philosophical colouring.

The material shows the apostles operating in a wide range of philosophical contexts both among Jews and gentiles:

a) 'To the end of the earth': 1.8 (Jesus' commission to the apostles); 28.14–31 (Paul in Rome, to the extent that this context fits Jesus' commission).[191]

b) In public/in the open: 2.14–36 (Peter's speech, which has parresiastic elements (2.29), in Jerusalem at Pentecost); 2.27 (public conversions in response to the apostles' 'communistic' way of life); 17.17–34 (Paul's preaching in the Athenian *agora* and on the Areopagus); 18.28 (Apollos' 'public' 'elenchus' of Achaean Jews); 19.30–1 (Paul's wish to address the Ephesians in the theatre—deterred by his disciples and Asiarchs who were friends of his—but obviously a theoretical possibility); 19.33 (the Jewish Alexander's attempted 'apology' in the theatre at Ephesus); 20.20 (Paul's 'public' teaching of the Ephesians [in contrast with 'in houses']);

---

190  Notably Stowers (1984); Alexander (2002) 234–8; (2005) 197.
191  P. 919 below.

22.1 (Paul's 'apology' to the Jewish crowd in Jerusalem); 26.26 (Paul's assertion to Agrippa that he has never preached 'in a corner');[192]

c) Trials, pre-trials, or trial-like contexts: 4.8–20; 5.29–32 (Peter and John's parresiastic and Socratic response to the Sanhedrin); 17.19–34 (Paul's preaching to the Areopagus); 24.10 (Paul's 'apology' before Felix); 25.8, 16 (Paul's 'apology' before Festus); 26.1–26 (Paul's 'apology' before Festus, Agrippa, and Berenice);

d) Synagogues: 9.27 (Paul's parresiastic teaching in Damascus); 13.46–7, 14.3 (Paul and Barnabas' parresiastic preaching in Pisidian Antioch and in Iconium); 18.4 (Paul's 'dialectic' in the Corinthian synagogue); 18.19 (Paul's 'dialectic' in the Ephesian synagogue); 18.26 (Apollos' parresiastic preaching in Ephesus); 19.8 (Paul's parresiastic dialectic in Ephesus);

e) In private houses or other private contexts: 9.28–9 (Paul in Jerusalem); 10.24–5 (Peter and Cornelius); 18.26 (Priscilla and Aquila's 'more accurate' [ἀκριβέστερον] instruction of Apollos); 19.9 (Paul's 'dialectic' in the 'school of Tyrannus'); 20.7–11 (Paul in 'dialectic' with own disciples); 24.25 (Paul's 'dialectic' with Felix); 28.31 (Paul's parresiastic preaching to 'everyone' in a private hired lodging in Rome)

f) performance before rulers (a category derived from (a), (c), and (e)).

How does this material affect the interpretation of the Lystra and Areopagus speeches? Here we must consider the *temporal nature* and *temporal functions* of the Acts narrative. Like many Classical historiographical narratives, it is (I believe) a composite of three things: (1) what happened (more or less); (2) why we are where we are now; and (3) what we should now do. Furthermore, there are occasions when it is not easy to decide which of these three strands predominates. If this general picture is right, then the fact that public mission to gentiles, in some contrast to public mission to Jews and greater contrast to synagogue mission to Jews, is a minority mode does not necessarily deprive the Lystra or Areopagus episodes of paradigmatic power. The emphasis on the mission to the Jews might be due to (1) and (2)—the apostles did first try to convert their fellow-Jews and their general failure explains why they put much greater emphasis on the gentile mission, whether or not they abandoned the Jewish mission entirely—and might say little about (3), which might be covered instead by the Lystra and Areopagus speeches and other items. Nor does there seem to be much difference between the application of 'public' philosophical modes towards Jews and that towards gentiles. The 'status argument' is countered by the emphasis on Peter and John as 'unlettered and private individuals'

---

192  Implications: p. 900 below.

(4.13), who yet can acquire from the Holy Spirit the requisite 'wisdom' for defending Christianity before powerful and sophisticated non-Christians.[193]

Indeed, given (i) that there is a fairly strong Cynic patina in the representation of the apostles (as, in Luke, in the representation of Jesus); (ii) that this Cynic patina is applied both in Jewish and in gentile contexts; (iii) that Cynic public philosophising is certainly just as much a matter of reality as of literary representation[194] and is attributed both to the apostles and to Jesus; (iv) that there is *some* historical evidence for Christian missioning at street level[195] and that such missioning may have been commoner in the enthusiasm of the Apostolic Age; and (v) that some very visible versions of Christianity (ascetics, holy men) seem to have been influenced by Cynicism,[196] it seems perverse to resist the conclusion that the Lystra and Areopagus speeches represent Luke's view of 'good practice' (not the *only* 'good practice') in Christian attempts to convert gentiles. This conclusion does not conflict with the claim that the Areopagus episode is fiction. Some fictions are truer than historical truth.[197]

The rest of the paper concentrates on Paul, whose ever-increasing narrative prominence attracts almost all the remaining philosophical material in Acts—a factor which itself requires explanation.[198]

## III

In Acts 17, Paul is firmly established as a Socratic figure, one of whose many techniques of persuasion in his encounters both with Jews and with Greek philosophers is Socratic 'dialectic'. This becomes one of Paul's stock modes, both in discussion with Jews in synagogues (18.4, 19; 19.8) and with his own disciples (19.9; 20.7, 9). 19.9, where Paul teaches in the 'school of Tyrannus', again confirms the running analogy with a philosophical school.[199]

---

193  P. 867 above.
194  That is to say, (a) though represented in 'literary' sources (Seneca, Dio, Epictetus, Lucian, Cassius Dio, etc.), it is represented as mundane fact; (b) though sometimes represented in a literary way (e.g., by Dio and Epictetus with allusions to Socrates), it attests mundane fact.
195  E.g., Origen, *Contra Celsum* 3.50.
196  Moles (2006a).
197  Moles (1993) 115–21 {vol. 2, pp. 181–6}.
198  For discussion of the philosophically important 18.24ff. see p. 836 above.
199  Philosophical associations: Witherington (1998) 574ff.; Alexander (2002) 235–7; Dormeyer–Galindo (2003) 290.

20.7–11 (Paul's visit to Troas) even looks like a sort of sanitised Christian equivalent of a Socratic symposium:[200]

> On the first day of the sabbath, when we were gathered together to break bread, Paul dialogued with them, being about to depart on the morrow, and he extended his speech until midnight. There were many lights in the upper chamber where we were gathered ... And when he had gone up and broken the bread and tasted of it, he conversed [ὁμιλήσας, a term which can be used philosophically] with them for a long time, until day-break, and so went out.

Any notion that the representation of Paul *Socraticus* is confined to the Athens episode is immediately untenable.

Acts 17 has also re-introduced Plato's *Apology* into the literary texture of Acts. But Luke does not there use the word *apologia* or cognates, because Paul is not defending himself so much as explaining his teaching and because he is not there in danger of death, since he is not formally on trial or even on pre-trial. After Acts 17, however, he is in renewed danger of death, and the theme of Socratic 'apology' repeatedly recurs, up to the end of the book and indeed, as we shall see, beyond (19.33 [of the Jew Alexander at Ephesus]; 22.1; 24.10; 25.8, 16; 26.1, 2, 24).

From Troas (20.7–11), Paul journeys to Miletus, where he summons the Ephesian elders (20.17–38). His speech is a farewell. Of what kind? Most scholars interpret it as a 'farewell before death' speech, a few[201] as a farewell in the more limited and less dramatic sense that Paul plans missionary activity elsewhere (in Rome and then in Spain) and does not anticipate ever returning to Asia. The former interpretation is, surely, correct: the speech has many parallels, both biblical and non-biblical, with 'farewell before death speeches';[202] and it includes clear foreshadowings of his death (24, 25, 29), as indeed his friends interpret them (37–8 < 25).[203] This sense is reinforced by the parallel

---

200 Dormeyer–Galindo (2003) 308.
201 E.g., Witherington (1998) 612–14; Wright (2008) II.132–3.
202 Johnson (1992) 366–7; Dormeyer–Galindo (2003) 314–15.
203 Note also the evocations of Hector and Andromache (MacDonald [2003]) and of *Il.* 1.5 (~ 27). Witherington's argument ([1998] 618–20, 769, 788–93) that the narrative's recurrent emphasis on Paul's innocence conveys that in Rome, finally, he will be acquitted, hence that Acts herein ends 'happily', founders on: (a) the repeated parallels with Socrates and Jesus: equally innocent, equally doomed; (b) Witherington's admission that, even if Paul survived initially, he succumbed to Roman persecution shortly after; (c) Acts' posteriority to the post-70 Luke; (d) the resultant absurdity: readers, 'happy' that Paul was initially acquitted, 'forget' that he succumbed shortly after. It is true, however, and insufficiently

with Luke 21.5–36, Jesus' farewell address to his disciples just before the Last Supper, by the evocations of Socrates and the *Apology* from Acts 17 onwards, and by a developing analogy between Jesus' journey to Jerusalem and Paul's.[204] Luke nicely cues the Socratic parallel when, in making Paul claim full and frank annunciation of the whole of God's will (sc. including inevitable suffering [20, 27]), he twice uses the verb ὑποστέλλω in a way best paralleled in Plato, *Apology* 24a.

Also evocative of the last days of Socrates[205] are the sudden appearance, in a further parallel farewell scene, of local Christians' 'wives and children' (21.5 ~ *Phaedo* 60a, the removal of the weeping Xanthippe, and 116b (cf. 117d), where Socrates bids farewell to his children and the women of his house, and *Crito* 45c–d, 54b, where he refuses to be influenced by responsibility for his children); the climactic weeping of Paul's friends, related within first person plurals (21.13–14 ~ *Phaedo* 117c–e); their 'keeping quiet' on Paul's request (21.14 ~ *Phaedo* 117e; note the verbal parallel); and his acceptance of death, if it is the will of the Lord (21.13–14 ~ *Crito* 43d). The persistent contact with *Phaedo* is unmistakable.

In the dangerous and violent circumstances in Jerusalem—arrest, near-lynching, repeated legal hearings or trials, intensifying parallels with Jesus' last days—the Socratic parallel recurs when Paul characterises his speech to the people as an *apologia* (22.1).[206] This is the first of his several 'apologies'.

Paul's appearances before the Roman governor Felix (24.1–27) require larger consideration. The rhetorician Tertullus, representing the High Priest, accuses Paul briefly, or shortly (*suntomos*): 'For we have found this man a pestilence and an agitator of civil disturbances among all the Jews in the inhabited world and a leader of the sect of the Nazarenes' (5). The trial situation, the *hairesis* reference (14), Paul's 'apology', his 'dialectic' (12), and 'training' (*askēsis*: 16) reactivate the Socratic parallel, in this second of Paul's 'apologies'. Paul reinforces his traditional Judaism with a paradoxical 'admission' (14): 'But I admit to you this: that according to the Road, which they call a sect, that is how I serve the God of our fathers'. As we have seen, Paul's point is that the Christian 'Road', as 'the only way', trumps any possible implication that there can be legitimately different 'choices' (*haireseis*) within traditional Judaism. His use of the term

---

discussed, that Paul's implied knowledge of his forthcoming death creates interesting and important narrative tensions: cf. pp. 920ff. below.
204   E.g. (among many), Maddox (1982) 66–7, 76–80; Alexander (2005) 73–4, 213.
205   Alexander (2005) 67 (with one addition).
206   Dormeyer–Galindo (2003) 334.

presumably has some appeal to Felix, who already 'knows rather accurately about the Road' (evidently through his Jewish wife).

This provides an appropriate context for consideration of the description of Christianity as 'the Road' (without qualification). Within the New Testament this characterisation is exclusively Lukan (9.2; 19.9, 23; 22.4; 24.14, 22, and here). The evidence of Acts seems enough to show that it was a term applied to Christians in the first century, both by themselves and (seemingly) by others (9.2; 24.22).

The term's origins are disputed.[207] The motif of the good and bad roads (vel sim.) is found both in Old and in New Testaments, as well as in the Qumran material. Since the Qumran community, inspired by Isaiah 40.3 ('Prepare the Road of the Lord, make straight the paths of our God'), regarded itself as 'The Road', (1QS 9.16–21; 8.13–16), the Christians may have got the term from there. Readers who knew about Qumran would certainly see a parallel and read it as implying a Christian claim: 'We are the Road, not Qumran' (especially given the latter's fate in the Jewish War). But one should also consider the usage within Acts' general use of 'road imagery', which (as we have already seen)[208] is extensive and detailed, particularly in its relationship to Paul. Thus an angel of the Lord tells Philip 'to go to the south to the road that goes down from Jerusalem to Gaza' (8.26). There he meets the Ethiopian eunuch and instructs him in response to the request (8.31) to 'lead him along the road' (of interpretation); they go along the road and the eunuch is baptised and 'went on his road rejoicing' (8.36–9). Then Saul embarks on his persecution of 'those of the Road', is converted on the road to Damascus (9.2–8, 27), and found by Ananias in Damascus on the appropriately named Straight Street (9.11). After this, Paul himself is on 'the right road', and thus in 24.14 he can fittingly associate himself with 'the Road'. As we have seen, this 'road imagery' goes right back, through Luke, to the philosophical aspect of Luke's Preface and to Luke's own claim to provide the right 'guide' to the Christian road. At 24.14, then, this imagery becomes tantamount to the claim that Luke-Acts is a guide to the very essence of Christianity as associated with Paul.

In the light of all these factors, the juxtaposition in 24.14 of philosophical *hairesis* and 'the Road' encourages a search for a Greek philosophical parallel,[209] which, indeed, lies ready to hand. Of all the great Greek philosophies, the one known as 'the Road', specifically 'the Short-cut Road' (*suntomos*

---

207   Cf., e.g., Pathrapankal (1979); Witherington (1998) 711; Fitzmyer (1998) 423–4; Barrett (2004) I.448.
208   P. 856 above.
209   Cf. Dormeyer–Galindo (2003) 145.

*hodos*, D.L. 6.105), is Cynicism. Luke nicely cues this association. Paul's invocation in 24.14 of 'the [transcendent] Road' is preceded by Tertullus' appeal to Felix to hear Paul's accusers 'briefly' (24.4 *suntomos*). Tertullus' *rhetorical* 'brevity'/'short-cut' is trumped by the Cynicised Christian '*Short*-cut Road'. This 'Cynicisation' of the Christian Road helps to reinforce the logic of Paul's observations by analogy. The Cynic 'short-cut road' does not actually allow the viability of other roads, and in the *ur*-myth, the Choice of Heracles, there is choice in the sense that humans have free will, but no choice in the sense that one road is good and the other bad. The same applies to the Christian version, as in Luke 13.22ff. cited above.[210] Naturally, however, the Christian road trumps the Cynic one.

There may be a further, meta-literary, implication. 24.14 makes Luke-Acts the 'guide' (Luke 1.1) or 'road' (Acts 8.31) to the 'road' of Christianity, book, theme, and way of life constituting an indissoluble unity. Now scholars have often found Acts (and even Luke-Acts) remarkably short for a work of historiography. Perhaps the answer is that this 'brevity' corresponds rather to the philosophical character of Luke-Acts, as the very *epitome* of Christianity. The Greek *suntomos* and *epitomos* are virtual synonyms, and the title of *epitome* (sc. *hodos*) is a philosophical title, first attested in various *epitomes* written by Epicurus, no doubt in appropriation of Cynic 'brevity', and thereafter by Stoics such as Chrysippus.[211] On this suggestion, not only is Christianity itself the 'short-cut Road', but so also is Luke-Acts the text.

It is worth pausing here briefly to reflect on Luke's literary creativity. The description of Christianity as 'the Road' already existed when Luke was writing and it was also used by Paul and seemingly other Jews (e.g., Drusilla) at the time covered by Acts. Luke has taken it and organically integrated it into his overall road imagery (imagery alike philosophical, historiographical, and religious); and he has also given it extra dimensions by comparing it to the Cynic 'Short-cut Road', in such a way as to emphasise both the relative theological simplicity of Christianity and the brevity of his own written work as containing everything necessary for belief in, and practice of, Christianity.

I revert to the narrative (24.24–6):

> After some days Felix arrived with Drusilla, his wife, who was a Jewess, and he sent for Paul and heard him concerning belief in Christ Jesus. (25) But as he dialogued concerning justice and self-control and the judgement to

---

210  P. 861.
211  Epict. *Ad Herod.* 35; *Ad Pyth.* 84–5 (significantly linking *suntomon* and *epitome*); D.L. 7.189 (Chrysippus).

come, Felix became fearful and answered: 'Go away for now, but when I have an opportunity I will call you', (26) at the same time also hoping that money would be given him by Paul. So he sent for him rather often and conversed with him.

This brilliant little sequence brings together Christianity, Greek philosophy, the superiority of divine to human justice, the tyrant figure's bad conscience and persistent venality, yet also his lingering fascination with the intrepid philosopher.[212] The emphasis on Drusilla, on Paul's choice of self-control as one of Felix's philosophical lessons, and on Felix's sudden fear of divine judgement trades on (some) readers' knowledge, whether from Josephus or elsewhere, that Felix had stolen Drusilla from her Jewish husband.[213] Thus one of Felix's implicitly confuted sins is sexual incontinence.

Arraigned before the new governor Festus, Paul makes his third 'apology' (25.8). His use of *adiko* (25.11) in the extended sense of 'to be in the wrong' recalls Xenophon, *Memorabilia* 1.1, while his readiness to accept death, if necessary, recalls the Socrates of Plato's *Apology* (29a; 35a–b) or *Crito* (43d). The subsequent judicial enquiry before Herod Agrippa II, Bernice, and Festus brings Paul into a trial-*like* situation before a king, and evokes Paul's fourth and last explicit Socratic 'apology' in Acts (26.1–29). To this broadly Socratic situation is added the notion of Pharisaism and Christianity as 'philosophical sects' (26.4–5).

This incident represents yet another fulfilment of Jesus' (alleged) prophecy to his disciples at Luke 21.12;[214] it re-enacts Jesus' own (alleged) appearance before Herod Antipas in Luke 23.7–11 (an incident kept in mind by the allusion at Acts 4.27), and his appearances before Pilate (Luke 23.1–25), even to the extent of 'judgements' of innocence (Luke 23.11, 15; Acts 26.32). Doubtless, one should reject Jesus' prophecy as *post eventum* and Jesus' appearance before Antipas as unhistorical,[215] in which case one possibility is that they have been invented on the basis of the present incident, which *ex hypothesi* itself then becomes historical.[216] The proceedings are, indeed, legally plausible, both in themselves and regarding Festus' appeal to Agrippa, and Josephus confirms that Agrippa and Bernice made courtesy visits to Roman governors, especially

---

212   The tone resembles Mark 6.20 (Herod Antipas' ambiguous attitude to the imprisoned Baptist): Haenchen (1971) 661.
213   Cf., e.g., Haenchen (1971) 661; Witherington (1998) 715.
214   Quoted on p. 867 above.
215   Bond (1998) 148–9.
216   Bond (1998) 149.

at the start of tenures.²¹⁷ Still, the whole atmosphere is very 'theatrical' in a rather novelistic manner; Agrippa's 'acquittal' of Paul remains suspicious (unless one also rejects Pilate's judgement of Jesus' innocence, which seems a step too far); and the episode is certainly very constructed. I suspect substantial, even total, fiction.

Paul's speech culminates in an exchange between Paul and Festus and a longer exchange between Paul and Agrippa (26.24–7):

> (24) As he made this *apologia*, Faustus said in a great voice: 'Paul, you're mad. Your many-letteredness [*ta polla grammata*] is turning you to madness'. (25) But Paul said: 'I am not mad, most powerful Festus, but I am speaking words of truth and restraint. The king knows about these things and to him I speak frankly indeed, for I am persuaded that none of these things is escaping his notice. For *this* has not been done in a corner. (27) Do you believe, King Agrippa, in the prophets? I know that you do believe'.

Thus far the Greek is unproblematic. Now (28) come 'perhaps the most disputed [words] ... in Acts':²¹⁸

> [Agrippa] ἐν ὀλίγῳ με πείθεις Χριστιανὸν ποιῆσαι.²¹⁹

Paul replies (29):

> I would pray to God that *kai en oligōi kai en megalōi* not only you but also all who hear me today should become such as I myself am—except for these chains.

The company withdraws and agrees Paul's innocence, Agrippa saying (ominously): 'this fellow could have been set free if he had not invoked Caesar' (26.32).

Interpretation of Paul's reply (29) depends on 28, whose Greek has been variously understood, as have Agrippa's attitude and narrative function. Is he admiring, ironic, or sarcastic? Is he a Jew in the middle between Festus the Gentile and Paul the Christian? Is he a highly Hellenised and Romanised Jew, and representative of Luke's 'ideal audience'? Is he the kingly representative

---

217  Barrett (2004) II.1134.
218  Barrett (2004) II.1169.
219  The reading in A (πειθη) implies 'you believe', but (a) the reading is very minority; (b) the form is inaccurate; (c) the meaning insufficiently represents Paul's urgency.

of a worldly order always potentially dangerous to Christians? Is he, within Luke-Acts, yet another dodgy Herodian? It at any rate seems clear that he is being represented as functionally Jewish.[220]

Ἐν ὀλίγῳ has been taken in five main ways. Four of these take it as modifying Paul's action. Of these four, three understand different nouns: χρόνῳ ('time'), λόγῳ ('speech'), and πόνῳ ('effort'). The fourth takes the phrase as equivalent to ὀλίγου δεῖν = 'almost'. This last is impossible Greek (many, including myself, believe). Ἐν ὀλίγῳ is a common phrase, with nouns such as χώρῳ (place), λόγῳ ('speech', 'argument'), and χρόνῳ ('time') understood.[221] Here the meanings 'time', 'speech', or 'effort' come to the same, as Barrett notes, though, as he also notes, Paul's μεγάλῳ can hardly be used of time,[222] and πόνῳ is in my view a difficult supplement. The fifth interpretation takes ἐν ὀλίγῳ as modifying Agrippa's action: thus Johnson.[223] This seems hard in itself and makes Paul's response nonsensical.

Ποιῆσαι has been taken in two main ways.[224] The first is 'to *play* the Christian' (or, slangily, 'to *make* the Christian'), a usage for which there is only really one Greek parallel, a Septuagint translation of a Hebrew phrase, though appeal can also be made to the Latin usage with *ago* (with the Latinism *Christianon* 'helping').[225] The second takes 'you' as the understood subject of ποιῆσαι and translates: 'you are trying to persuade me that you have made me a Christian'. This is good Greek and, simply as Greek, much better than the alternative. The key parallel is Xenophon, *Memorabilia* 1.2.49, which in itself may be significant, for in this Socratic and attempted conversion context Luke may well be 'thinking Xenophontically', as he has done elsewhere in Acts. Clearly, however, interpretation of the Greek must take account of the demands both of the wider and of the immediate contexts.

---

220 Scholars differ on whether the Herodians, *qua* Idumaeans, should properly be regarded as Jewish. The Idumaeans so regarded themselves but to Jewish aristocrats they were 'half-Jewish': Schürer (1973) 207 n. 12; Jos. *BJ* 4.4.4; *AJ* 14.15.2. These complexities hardly affect Luke-Acts.
221 LSJ s.v. ὀλίγος IV.3.
222 Barrett (2004) II.1170.
223 Johnson (1992) 440: 'A better resolution is to take *en oligoi* in a non-temporal sense ... This enables us to make good sense both of Agrippa's statement (he sees that "in for a dime is in for a dollar", that an agreement to the prophets already brings him into partial agreement with Paul's position, and he does not want to be led down that logical path), and of Paul's punning response'.
224 A third way is to take it as epexegetic or even purposive after 'persuade'.
225 Barrett (2004) II.1170.

Readers are given sufficient reasons for Agrippa's entry into the narrative (25.13).[226] Some will know more—that he was the last of the Herodians and strongly pro-Roman and that he tried to deter the Jewish Revolt, etc. Luke thrice mentions Agrippa and Bernice together (25.13, 23; 26.30), without explaining her identity or role. Clearly, at least some readers are assumed to know that she was Agrippa's sister, who lived with him after the failure of her various marriages, and accompanied him on state visits. Some Roman readers will also know that she became Titus' mistress but was finally rejected by him. Again, some (including any that read Josephus before Luke) will know more: that Bernice reputedly had an incestuous relationship with her brother, that she was a sister of the adulterous Drusilla, mentioned earlier in the narrative and in an analogous context (Acts 24.24–5), and that she otherwise behaved as a devout Jewess. Here her very juxtaposition with Agrippa makes her look like his wife.[227] (Agrippa's actual marital status is unknown.[228])

On the day, Agrippa and Bernice 'come with much appearance [φαντασίαι][229] and come into the auditorium with military tribunes and men who were leaders of the city'. The emphasis on 'appearance', on 'auditorium', and on the status and numbers involved suggests 'a show put on to gratify Agrippa',[230] himself, seemingly, something of an indolent onlooker on life:[231] here a further parallel with Herod Antipas' 'long desire to see' Jesus in Luke 23.8. The novelistic feel of the episode hardly casts Agrippa, *qua* effective judge, in a favourable initial role. When Agrippa gives Paul permission to speak, Paul begins by playing the game, extending his hand like a trained orator, and in a *captatio benevolentiae* complimenting Agrippa on his deep knowledge of Jewish customs and 'enquiries' (ζητημάτων: philosophical term).[232] This Agrippa certainly had, but would some readers sense shocking and all too visible inconsistency with Agrippa's personal life?[233] Such an implication would cohere with the emphasis on the proceedings' showiness and on Agrippa and Bernice's 'great appearance', and Paul would not be insulting Agrippa so much as conveying—in passing—his knowledge of Agrippa's private realities. There would be a neat parallel with

---

226 Schürer (1973) 471–83 surveys Agrippa usefully.
227 Mason (2005) 164.
228 Schürer (1973) 483 n. 48.
229 This rendering of *phantasiai* (often rendered as 'pomp') maintains the literal meaning of the Greek, is acceptably close to English idiom (cf. 'put in/on an appearance'), and suggests the contrast 'appearance–reality', which affects interpretation.
230 Barrett (2004) II.1146.
231 Schürer (1973) 475.
232 LSJ s.v. II.1.
233 Mason (2005) 164.

Paul's philosophical teaching of Felix, with its veiled allusion to his sexual incontinence with Bernice's own sister, and a neat parallel and contrast with the Athenian philosophers' misapprehensions about 'Jesus and Anastasis' (17.18). Paul's characterisation of Pharisaism as 'the most precise sect of our religion', echoing Josephan phraseology,[234] might key the informed reader to Josephus' notice of the reputed Agrippa-Bernice relationship. Several details, then, help to cast Paul in the role of the Socratic philosopher addressing a depraved and easternised king, and parresiastically so (this explicitly at 26).

Paul also requires Agrippa to listen 'long-sufferingly' (26.3).

After Paul's account of his conversion, he again addresses Agrippa directly (19): 'Wherefore, King Agrippa, I was not unpersuaded by the heavenly vision', that heavenly vision, too, contrasting with the 'great appearance' of king and sister. The motif of obedience to the heavenly vision corresponds to Socrates' quest 'in accordance with the god' in Plato's *Apology* (23b).[235] Then (22–3):

> So, having obtained the help (*epikourias*) that comes from God until this very day, I stand bearing witness both to small and great, saying nothing outside what the prophets and Moses said was destined to happen, whether [as can be established by debate] the anointed one/the Christ [*ho Christos*] must suffer, and whether [ditto], being the first from the rising of the dead, he is destined to proclaim light both to the people and to the nations.

Paul makes five points. First, given sufficient 'proof', 'persuasion'/'belief' is the requisite response to Jesus. The encounter between Paul and Agrippa focuses on this issue (26.19, 26, 27 [*bis*], 28), and in this sense Paul's present speech provides the systematic 'proof' that had been short-circuited in his speech to the Athenian philosophers (17.31 ['proof']). Second, as throughout Acts, divine governance trumps human governance: so much for the present hearing and present company. Third, when Paul, whose name means 'little', claims to bear witness 'both to small and great', he is doubtless punning on his own name and (perhaps) on his own (traditionally small) stature. But he is also inverting categories and suggesting that the great of this world are not great.[236] This coheres with the second point. Fourth, the noun *epikouria*, *hapax* in Luke and in the New Testament as a whole, is used of the 'help' of God, and it is difficult, Acts 17 being a parallel scene, not to feel an implicit contrast with Paul's last encounter

---

234 Above, n. 110.
235 Alexander (2005) 63.
236 Harlé (1977–8) 529–33; this, of course, is a general Lukan theme.

with self-styled 'helpers', the *Epicureans* of 17.18 and 17.32, who vainly uphold '*Epicurus*' as the true 'divine' 'helper'.[237] Fifth, Jesus' resurrection presages salvation both for Jews and for Gentiles.

This summing-up provokes Festus (24, quoted above).

As in Acts 17, a Pauline speech that culminates in Jesus' resurrection and its theological consequences is interrupted by audience incredulity, and Luke again seems to be dramatising 1 Cor. 1.23.[238] Like Greeks, Festus cannot accept Jesus' resurrection. When he ascribes this 'madness' to Paul's 'many-letteredness', he is presumably thinking partly of Paul's appeal to the Jewish prophets and Moses, partly of Paul's virtuosic (and, to him, irritating) multiculturalism: Paul has moved between Greek and Aramaic, he has described his experience on the Road to Damascus in terms of Dionysiac conversion, he has quoted from Euripides' *Bacchae*,[239] he has intermixed Greek and Jewish elements. Festus' 'great voice' may also be taken as registering anger at Paul's provocative redefinition of 'greatness'. But readers should also compare and contrast the High Priest's and the Sadducees' perception of Peter and John: 4.13 'observing the *parrēsia* of Peter and John and perceiving that they were unlettered and private individuals'. The point, presumably, is a 'both-and' one:[240] Christianity embraces both the 'unlettered' and the 'many-lettered'. But not just Christianity: Acts itself as a text. Whether or not the historical Paul did or said these things, it is Luke that is making him do them. So Luke here conveys that Acts can be read on a simple level or on a sophisticated one, and that many-letteredness and un-letteredness are equally viable states for Christians. The implication that Acts can be read on a sophisticated level further supports the notion that Luke is targeting non-Christian and non-Jewish readers, as well as Christian and Jewish ones.

Festus' response intensifies the problem of Agrippa's response.

When Paul addresses Agrippa parresiastically (26), the reference of 'these things' and 'none of these things' is both to the circumstances of Jesus' crucifixion and resurrection and to Paul's proclamation of them.[241] Fittingly, therefore, the phrase 'not in a corner' works on several levels. First, Jesus' crucifixion and resurrection and Paul's Christian missioning have all been public events and

---

237  Moles (2006b) 87–8 {above, pp. 571–2}; cf. p. 905 below. Cf. Moles (2011) 157 {above, pp. 651–2}.
238  Above, p. 888.
239  Moles (2006b) 69–71 {above, pp. 556–8}.
240  Moles (2006b) 96 {above, p. 580} with n. 142.
241  Barrett (2004) II.1168–9, citing John Chrys. *Hom.* 52.4.

thus verified.²⁴² So, too, at the start of the speech (26.4–5), Paul claimed that his pre-Christian career was public knowledge among all Jews. This emphasis counters familiar Greek and Roman allegations of Christian 'secrecy'. Second, it makes a contrast between philosophers who operate in private ('in a corner') and those who operate in public.²⁴³ Paul is like a parresiastic 'public' philosopher. Third, the notion of 'philosophy in a corner' particularly evokes the Epicureans²⁴⁴ (already 'in play' because of *epikouria*), here contrasted with the 'public', parresiastically Cynic-like, Paul. Luke neatly cues this latter allusion with the wording '*none* of these things is *escaping* his *notice*', the negative of the basic Epicurean principle of '*escape notice* living'. Herewith another nail in the coffin of Epicureanism. Pace Johnson,²⁴⁵ Paul sees in *Epicurean* philosophy no basis whatsoever for a continuing 'conversation'. Fourthly, however, there is a barb for Agrippa, parallel to Paul's initial emphasis on Agrippa's great knowledge of Jewish customs and enquiries. The whole stress on the openness of Jesus and of philosophical Christianity as opposed to 'secret' Epicureanism again suggests Agrippa's 'secret vice', for Epicureanism is popularly associated with immoral pleasure; in the stem passage of the expression 'in a corner' (Pl. *Gorg.* 485d), the speaker Callicles is sneering at philosophical effeminacy; 'restraint' can hint at Agrippa's gross 'lack of restraint', in just the same as 'self-control' hints at Felix' incontinence; and the very striking emphasis, '*this* was not done in a corner', inevitably raises the question: *what has* been done in a corner?²⁴⁶

As before, however, Paul is not merely insulting Agrippa. Rather, this tacit but extremely personal rebuke stresses his own formidableness and Agrippa's terrible personal shortcomings and thereby heightens the theological challenge.²⁴⁷

This challenge comprises the following elements: (a) Agrippa knows all about Jesus' resurrection and Paul's proclamation of it, and he has just heard

---

242   Dormeyer–Galindo (2003) 366, 368, oddly take 'not in a corner' as having geographical implication: as denial, against the Roman Festus, that Judaea is a 'corner', rather than, as on the Jewish view, the centre, of the world.
243   Malherbe (1989) 147–63; Witherington (1998) 749–50; cf. Plat. *Gorg.* 485d; Epict. 1.29.36, 55–57; 2.12.17, 13.24–6; 3.22.97; Plut. *Mor.* 777B.
244   E.g., Hor. *C.* 2.6.14; Ferri (1993).
245   {Johnson (1992) 319.}
246   Luke 3.19 (John the Baptist's reproof of Herod Antipas and Herodias for the latter's sexual misbehaviour) is thus a further parallel. Drusilla and Bernice contradict the claim that '*Eros* does not figure anywhere in the book [= Acts], even negatively' (Alexander [2005] 157). Note that allusion to Agrippa's alleged incest, if granted, implies the latter's death: Josephus, silent about the matter in *BJ*, alludes to it in *AJ* 20.7.3; Agrippa died c.92/3 (Schürer [1973] 480–3).
247   Mason (2005) 164 ('devastating barbs') exaggerates.

Paul's own account of his conversion by the risen Jesus; (b) he believes in the prophets (described as foretelling Jesus' resurrection); (c) he therefore has no choice but to accept Paul's conclusions. He is obviously pressing Agrippa hard. Equally obviously, the argument admits gaps: (b) needs interrogation, which the repeated 'whether' actually invites. Equally obviously, Paul's circumstances disallow a comprehensive exposition. Agrippa's controversial response is a response to the implied conclusion (c).

A preliminary consideration is Agrippa's use of the term *Christianos*. It is appropriate to a Roman setting,[248] and it picks up on Paul's allusion (26.23) to 'the anointed one/the Christ' (ὁ Χριστός). But is it here pejorative, as being in context a too narrow 'party' term, when set against Paul's contextualisation of Jesus within the whole of Judaism? That is certainly a possible reading, but further progress must depend on interpretation of the larger questions posed by Agrippa's response.

The rendering of ποιῆσαι as 'to play the Christian' might seem appropriate to the general theatricality of the proceedings. There are even contexts where the notion of 'role-playing' is *philosophically* appropriate. The Stoic Panaetius held that one's moral duty might vary according to the different 'roles' or 'parts' one played, and this doctrine had wide impact. There is even a king–philosopher encounter which embodies a similar notion: Bion of Borysthenes' influential treatment of the relationship between himself and king Antigonus Gonatas.[249] But while such sophisticated moral relativism might presumably be congenial to Agrippa, whether as historical or dramatic figure, it could not be congenial to the dramatic Paul,[250] nor could the dramatic Agrippa have supposed it to be so. To 'play the Christian' would be a very strange gloss on Paul's argument. The response that Paul is seeking from Agrippa is not the trivial one of *'playing the Christian'*, but full acceptance of Paul's teaching about Judaism and Jesus' place within it, as proven by Paul's own experience. Another way of putting this, as made explicit in Paul's reply, is that Agrippa (and all the others) should become like Paul himself.

Paul's reply, of course, also implies that Agrippa's response falls short of (c). Now, both in pre-empting Paul's conclusion (instead of interrogating (b)) and in the phrase 'with little', Agrippa is failing Paul's initial request that he should listen '*long*-sufferingly' (26.3). Agrippa's interjection should therefore be taken as meaning: 'with little *are you trying to persuade* me that you have made me a Christian'. Parallels for the conative present are unnecessary, but in fact 28.23

---

248  See p. 871 above.
249  See Moles (1996a) 108 {above, p. 424}.
250  In some contrast to the historical Paul.

(in a clearly parallel scene, where Paul is *trying to persuade* the Jews of Rome) is parallel. The sentence describes what would be entailed if Agrippa accepted Paul's argument. Agrippa is expressing irritation at what he regards as Paul's attempt to 'bounce' him into implied conclusion (c). Consequently, Barrett's objection to this rendering[251] misses the point.

Given the philosophical aspects of Paul's address, particularly the contrast between public, parresiastic philosophising and 'in a corner' philosophising, Agrippa for his part is presumably likening Paul's behaviour to that of the Cynics, who promise a 'short' conversion to the truth. If so, like Paul himself, he also is playing on Paul's name, though negatively rather than positively. For readers or listeners with Latin (and Luke the writer clearly has some), it is also counter-intuitive that a man called Agrippa (= 'having had a very difficult birth')[252] should 'become' a Christian 'by/with little', or in 'short order'. Paul's reply—'whether by little or by great', however, trumps Agrippa's objection, since it reiterates the point that what to Agrippa is 'little' is actually 'great'. To the extent that this is a 'meta-' scene (since the encounter, which includes a first-person version of Paul's conversion, told by Luke himself in third-person narrative, models the reception of Luke-Acts as a whole), the implication again (as in the encounter with Tertullus) is that Luke-Acts is an appropriately 'short Road'.

As for Agrippa's use of the term *Christianon*, all things considered, it should, in context, be regarded as reductive.

A final interpretative point is the explicit moral exemplarity offered by Paul. It is of course important that Agrippa and co. agree Paul's innocence (as Herod Antipas and Pilate had agreed Jesus'). This is part of a larger message. Nevertheless, the episode is negative about Agrippa. He grasps Paul's theological logic but cannot bring himself to accept it and deflects it with a sneer instead of debating it properly. In these respects, he resembles the Epicureans among the Athenian philosophers (as his devotion to gross pleasure is also vulgarly Epicurean). Agrippa's larger functions include those of the corrupt and depraved king, of the Jewish royalty which served Rome but conspicuously lacked moral integrity and which had the opportunity of accepting Christianity but appeared to be rejecting it, and of the Jewish 'temple establishment', which could not accept resurrection. With all these negatives, he can hardly represent Acts' ideal target audience.[253] It remains true that all readers (including sophisticated Jewish ones) can make the choice that Agrippa did

---

251   Barrett (2004) II.1170–1.
252   Maltby (1991) 20.
253   *Pace* Alexander (2005) 201, 205.

not, and that Christianity offers grace and salvation even to the most depraved. Paul himself illustrates this: persecutor and murderer of Christians, he was 'not unpersuaded' by the vision of the risen Jesus. That choice remains for all persecutors. Similarly, Agrippa the incestuous hypocrite could and should be 'persuaded' by the prophets and Paul.

We proceed to the first sea voyage (27.1–28.10), whose narrative, alike realistic and novelistic, is justly admired. Philosophical elements are readily apparent. Paul repeatedly appears as a (rather Herodotean) 'wise warner' figure (to an extent therefore balancing Gamaliel near the beginning of Acts),[254] and, as we shall see, as the very embodiment of the Platonic or Stoic sage. There is a strong recurrent emphasis (otherwise very rare in the New Testament)[255] on *philanthropia*, 'love of human beings': the centurion's 'philanthropia' towards Paul, the barbarians' *philanthropia* towards the whole shipwrecked company; Publius' *philophrosunē* to the same company. This is *philanthropia* in the strongest possible sense of the term, which transcends barriers between Jew and Gentile, between Greeks and barbarians,[256] and between Romans and their subjects. The emphasis and scale are part of the programme of 1.8 but also seem designed to meet accusations that Christians were unfriendly and unsociable. There is some parallel with Josephus' equally apologetic insistence on Jewish *philanthropia*[257] and presumably therefore also some sense of appropriation ('*we* are the "philanthropes", not the Jews').

Moreover, as we have seen, this Christian *philanthropia* is a *phil*-requisite on a par with *theo-philia* and *philo-sophia*.[258] And in this 'wanderer' narrative, Malta appears as a kind of primitive, innocent, state, instinctively responsive to Paul and the very opposite of sophisticated, effete Athens;[259] there is a whiff of Cynic primitivism, as in Dio Chrysostom's *Euboicus*,[260] though Luke's rustics are not as far upon the road of virtue as Dio's; and the philanthropic cosmopolitanism of the best Greek philosophy—Cynicism and Stoicism—is appropriated and transcended by Paul and the ongoing Christian mission. In neatly punning language worthy of Plato, Dio Chrysostom, or the Cynics,[261] Paul

---

254  5.34–9, though Gamaliel *qua* warner corresponds to Tiresias in *Bacchae*: Moles (2006b) 78 {above, p. 564}.
255  Witherington (1998) 760.
256  The focalisation, within a 'we' narrative, of the Maltesers as 'barbarians' (28.2) is thought-provoking from several points of view.
257  {See, e.g., Jos. *c. Ap.* 2.261.}
258  P. 878 above.
259  Good comment in Dormeyer–Galindo (2003) 379, 382.
260  Moles (1995) 177–80 {above, pp. 188–91}.
261  Moles (2005) 122 {above, p. 265}.

suffers nothing 'out of place' (*atopos*) from his snake-bite, and the narrative continues: 'in the parts *around that place* there were lands belonging to the first man of the island' (28.6–7). Luke deftly conveys that, whatever the place, Paul is never 'out of place' and nothing 'out of place' can ever befall him.[262]

That message continues to the end of Acts, which we have now reached (28.30–1):

> He [Paul] remained [in Rome] for a period of two years in a private hired lodging and he received all who came in to him, (31) heralding the kingdom of God and teaching the things concerning the Lord Jesus Christ with all freedom of speech and unhinderedly.

This end has created enormous scholarly debate and attempts have been made to sanitise it (Acts is incomplete/completed before Paul's death; Luke planned a third book; Theophilos does not need to be told the sequel because he already knows it, etc., etc).

I believe that this is a very great end to an ancient text, at least as good as the end of Herodotus or the end of the *Aeneid*, and—in the New Testament context—on an altogether higher literary level from the end of Mark, arresting and relatively sophisticated though the latter is (as well, presumably, as being one of Luke's influences).[263] Despite some excellent treatments,[264] a 'holistic' interpretation remains a scholarly desideratum, but beyond present purposes. I have discussed the end elsewhere from another point of view, which has some relevance here.[265]

As often with classical literature, readings polarise between 'pessimistic'[266] and 'optimistic'. The former rely both upon the immediately preceding scene, where for the third and last time (cf. 13.46–7; 18.6) Paul challenges a Jewish audience with the thought that Jewish unreceptiveness to the Gospel justifies the 'turn' to the Gentiles,[267] and upon the alleged 'flatness' or 'unresolvedness' of the quoted 28.31. My discussion focuses on the latter passage as being more

---

262  Thus Festus' application of the adjective to Paul in a negative sense (25.5) is itself 'out of place'.
263  I accept that the extant Mark is complete.
264  Dupont (1979); Alexander (2005) 207–29; Parsons (1987) 157–9; useful survey in Barclay (1976) 239–43.
265  Moles (2006b) 88–94 {above, pp. 573–8}.
266  Tannehill (1990) 348 ('Acts ends on a tragic, not a triumphant note'); Alexander (2005) 226–7 ('tragic', 'downbeat tragedy').
267  Both Dupont (1979) and Alexander (2005) 211ff. are very illuminating on the relationship of the end to the rest of Luke-Acts as regards the success or failure of the Jesus mission to the Jews.

germane to our topic, but it will controvert the general pessimistic reading and have something to say about Luke-Acts' representation of 'the Jews" reception of Jesus and Christianity.

Doubtless, those who find the ending flat or unresolved could parallel such an effect with the 'aporetic' inconclusiveness characteristic of many Platonic dialogues, but I do not accept this 'finding'.

Since Paul's martyrdom has been repeatedly foreshadowed, a fact which itself confirms the early Christian tradition of that martyrdom, and since Acts was written post-70,[268] ancient readers (especially those in Rome) know that Paul died in Rome in the Neronian persecution of 64.[269] Is this knowledge interpretatively relevant? Many say not, on the grounds that Acts, not being a biography, 'is not about Paul', and that the end is on other grounds triumphantly affirmative. Thus Johnson: 'Absolutely nothing hinges on the success or failure of Paul's defence before Caesar, for Luke's apologetic has not been concerned primarily with Paul's safety ... What Luke was defending he has successfully concluded: God's fidelity to his people and to his own word'.[270]

Such arguments are too simple. Of course, Acts is not a *biography* of Paul; of course the end is not *only* 'about Paul'; of course, if the emphasis of 28.31 is on 'God's fidelity to his people and to his own word', the end is a successful and positive conclusion. But the nature—as we shall see, the multiple nature—of that successful and positive conclusion has to be defined, and if Paul's death—and, specifically, his death in Rome—has been repeatedly foreshadowed in the narrative and speeches, has, indeed, dominated the last third of the narrative, then that untimely death has to be *part* of the interpretation of the end, has, indeed, in seeming paradox, to be part of the successful conclusion. Luke actually cues this: 28.31 puts Paul's fate on a knife-edge: '[Paul] remained [aorist] for a period of two years'. What happened then? Answer: as everybody knows and as the narrative anticipates, Paul will stand before Caesar, as he requested (25.11), and as Jesus and an angel in visions guaranteed (23.11; 27.23–4); he will be unjustly condemned and put to death.

Why does Luke not directly recount this trial and Paul's doubtless heroic death? There *could* be negative reasons. Was Paul finally deserted by his friends?[271] Might a direct account have been politically dangerous, especially

---

268  N. 35 above.
269  *Pace* Witherington (n. 6); nor does the end allow the gap of an initial innocent verdict followed by execution a few years later (below).
270  Johnson (1992) 476, endorsed by Alexander (2005) 206.
271  Barrett (2004) II.1249–50.

when Luke-Acts' readership included Romans in Rome? But the positive reasons far outweigh such imponderables.

Firstly, Luke does not need to give an account of these events. For the attentive reader, they are already sufficiently anticipated.

Secondly, not only are they sufficiently anticipated, but Acts contains, as it were, 'substitute' accounts. No need for a pre-execution farewell speech by Paul after his farewell to the Ephesian Elders, or for a heroic death scene after the narrative of the death of Stephen, the first Christian martyr, martyrdom which echoed Jesus' death and for which Paul was himself partly responsible,[272] and which prefigured his own. Similarly, Luke's prolonged 'road-to-Jerusalem' build-up to Jesus' death is paralleled in Acts, both by Paul's 'journey to Jersualem' (where he nearly finds death) and by his journey to Rome (where he will indeed find death), so that the former in a sense anticipates his actual death.

Thirdly, because of these very anticipations and 'substitutions', there is a level on which the attentive reader does read the end as representing—symbolically, proleptically—Paul's 'last words' before death. So Alexander writes of 'Paul ... in his Roman prison':[273] this is a slip but an intelligent and sensitive one.

Fourthly, and most important, by *not* directly recounting these events and by just stopping, Luke challenges his readers to face a fundamental question, which contains a whole host of sub-questions: what sort of 'end' is this both to Acts and to Luke-Acts, an 'end' in which both Paul and readers 'end' up in Rome and Paul's own 'end' (in the sense of his death) looms, and how does such an 'end' relate to Jesus' commission, given at the *beginning* of Acts (1.8): 'you will be my witnesses in Jerusalem and in all Judaea and Samaria and *to the end of the earth*', especially since hitherto text, Christian actors, and readers have faithfully followed Jesus' geographical trajectory? In short, the end of the narrative proposes a whole series of 'gaps', which the reader has to fill in.

Acts' 'open' ending is also consistent with two of the work's generic strands: its primary generic affiliation to historiography, where among Luke's predecessors Herodotus most famously contrives an 'open' 'geographical' and 'temporal' ending[274] to his 'text-as-journey'; and the philosophical address, necessarily concerned as it is with the move from text to implementation. The Herodotean precedent means that Luke-Acts is ring-structured by (*inter multa alia*) Herodotean historiography—since the Luke Preface imitates Herodotus' 'demonstration of things demonstrated' and begins the Herodotean

---

272  Johnson (1992) 141.
273  Alexander (2005) 66.
274  Moles (1996b); Dewald (1997).

'text-as-journey' motif—and this is the first of many formal felicities of the end.

Since the end ends with, but also, in a sense, *begins* with Paul, I too will begin with him.

Luke-Acts as a whole is ring-structured by Paul: Paul at the end of Acts matches the Luke Preface's 'brought to fulfilment so as to provide assurance'. Paul must be central to the message—or one of the messages—of Luke-Acts, especially for Theophilos, Luke's 'ideal reader'. In teaching 'in a private hired lodging', Paul is obeying necessity (he is still fettered) but he is also acting both like Peter and John *qua* 'private individuals' at 4.13 (another ring structure, confirming Christianity's move away from the synagogue and official Jewish structures) and like a philosopher.[275]

In 'receiving all who came in to him' 'in private', Paul is (yet again) like Jesus: Luke 9.10–11 'and taking them [the apostles] along, he retired in private into a place called Bethsaida. But the crowds got to know and followed him, and having received them he spoke to them concerning the kingdom of God'. There are obvious similarities and differences, the biggest of the latter being Acts' stress on 'all', as embracing Gentiles as well as Jews, a stress naturally enhanced by the fact that Paul is now teaching in Rome. Paul's 'heralding the kingdom of God' echoes not only Jesus' behaviour in Luke 9.11 (and elsewhere) but also the allusion and question at the beginning of Acts—'Lord, will you re-establish the kingdom to Israel at this time?' (another ring-structure between end and beginning) and the allusions at the beginning of Luke (another ring-structure between end and beginning of Luke-Acts).[276] The same is true of his 'teaching' (διδάσκων): Paul is of course also fulfilling the risen Jesus' injunction to his then apostles to 'bear witness' to him. Paul is by now himself also an apostle, in as much as he has seen (the risen) Jesus and has been 'sent out' to bear witness to him.[277] There is a sense, then, in which the scene is both resumptive and summative of *all* the Gospel activity of Luke-Acts.

But Paul, further and particularly, is teaching 'with all frankness'. This is the final example of the apostles' *parrēsia*, final both as the last example and as the greatest: *parrēsia* under Paul's particular circumstances (house arrest, fetters, imminent death) is especially admirable. The combination of *parrēsia* with 'private' status reinforces the parallel with Peter and John and again suggests parallels with Socrates and the Cynics. But how can Paul be said to be teaching 'unhinderedly'? The popular suggestion that 'unhinderedly' glosses

---

275  P. 904 above.
276  See further Alexander (2005) 207–29.
277  {Acts 26.17: ἐγω ἀποστέλλω σε.}

Paul's relative legal freedom under house arrest[278] is irredeemably trivialising and neglects the interpretatively crucial fact that Paul is poetically and proleptically already *in extremis*. No doubt, and importantly, 'the Word of God is not bound', as 2 Timothy 2.9 says, perhaps even glossing this very passage. But Paul *himself* is, explicitly, also free, and this though he can no longer expect the Dionysus-style epiphanies, breaking of bonds, and bursting of prisons from which he and other apostles had benefited in previous episodes (5.17–20; 12.6–10). In this respect at least the age of miracles is gone and the future Christian narrative will be a different one.[279] There is a sense, then, that by this historiographical ending some at least of the most arresting episodes of Acts are now redefined as *muthos*. But this is no cause for lament: *Christian* freedom is no longer to be defined or confined by physical constraints. Thus the end crucially redefines both imprisonment and liberty in Christian spiritual terms: even *in extremis* Christians are free.[280]

The whole situation and several details have already suggested parallels between Paul and Greek philosophers. These can easily be extended. As we have seen, Plato's *Apology* is important at the start of the Acts narrative, in the case of Peter and John; in Acts 17, where Paul is cast as Socrates and where he undergoes a trial-*like* ordeal but does not use the term *apologia* or cognates; and in Acts 22.1, 24.10, and 26.2, where use of the term *apologia* or cognates keeps the Socratic parallel alive. Now, at the end of Acts, Paul is symbolically, proleptically, speaking his last words before his heroic execution after an unjust state process. Readers know that his final 'apology' will be delivered to the unjust king Nero—a last, 'silent' parallel to all his other explicit 'apologies' and a more specific parallel to Paul's 'apology' before the *relatively* amiable King Herod Agrippa II—and that, like Socrates' 'apology', Paul's will fail, as Agrippa himself had foreseen. Thus Socratic 'apology' (in the sense of 'defence' against a capital charge) 'frames' the overall mission narrative (Paul at the end, Peter and John at the start), and segues back into Luke, with Jesus' prophecies, 21.8–19.

The sequence of 'Apologies'—defence speeches written *after* the execution of the philosopher on trial—imitates Plato, Xenophon, and other Socratics.[281]

---

278 {E.g., Witherington (1998) 814.}
279 Slightly similarly—but less optimistically—Alexander (2005) 228–9.
280 This 'answers' Alexander (2005) 207: 'Paul [has] lost the dynamic freedom of movement which so characterizes his missionary voyages'.
281 However, the old suggestion that Acts as a whole is Luke's defence—even his defence speech—of Paul before Nero (hence the end of the narrative before the trial): (a) is dreadfully reductive of a very multi-faceted text; (b) misses the foreshadowings of Paul's death; (c) misses the force of the 'anti-Roman government' elements; and (d) misses the real 'stability'/'assurance' provided by Luke-Acts (below).

More specifically, at the end of Acts, there is a clear situational parallel with the last days of Socrates, as related in four Platonic dialogues, *Euthyphro*, *Apology*, *Crito*, and *Phaedo*, and especially with the last.[282] Both Socrates and Paul are under guard, either already condemned to death (Socrates) or proleptically so (Paul), yet discoursing freely and bravely to a small audience about ultimate truths. The *Phaedo* parallel at this juncture is helped by Luke's extended use of 'before death' *Phaedo* motifs in the scenes surrounding the Farewell to the Ephesian Elders.[283]

Differently from Socrates, however, the doomed Paul is in Rome in the early 60s just before the first Roman persecution of Christians, persecution to be repeated under Domitian.[284] For readers, therefore, especially Roman readers, the end of Acts yet again dramatises the Dionysiac choice: accept the new god and follow Paul's example, or persecute Paul and his fellow-Christians.[285] From persecution readers are deterred by Gamaliel's warning against *theomachy*, by the fate of the various *theomachoi* within the narrative, by their knowledge of Nero's violent and untimely death, by the coded allusion to that death in the account of the death of Herod Agrippa I (12.22),[286] and by fear of a 'guilty' verdict at the Last Judgement. Towards emulation of Paul they are encouraged by the thought that Christian 'freedom' remains viable *in extremis* and by Luke's commemoration of Paul's inspirational example.

Now, as Paul's companion in Rome, Luke himself would have known of Stoic martyrs such as Seneca and Thrasea Paetus, who died shortly after Paul, and those of the second generation such as the younger Helvidius Priscus who fell under Domitian. Given the philosophical, and especially the Socratic, resonances already noted, Roman readers, too, could hardly fail to align Paul's example with that of Stoic martyrs under Nero and under Domitian, especially as some of them famously at the last emulated Socrates.[287] Such 'readings' were indeed made in analogous situations: disapproving as the Stoics Epictetus and Marcus Aurelius and Galen are of Christian martyrs' alleged lack of philosophical principle, they nevertheless see some sort of analogy with philosophical martyrdom.[288] These considerations suggest that Luke is seeking converts

---

282  Alexander (2005) 66 (also making Paul's hymn-singing in the Philippi prison [16.25] ~ *Phaed.* 60d).
283  P. 896 above.
284  Lane Fox (1986) 432–3 is decisive on Domitianic persecution.
285  See the discussion at Moles (2006b) 91 {above, p. 575}.
286  Klauck (2000) 44; note that this coded allusion constitutes another argument against any reprieve for Paul after the two-year period.
287  Witherington (1998) 62–3, 197; Alexander (2005) 66–7.
288  Epict. 4.7.6; M. Aurel. 11.3; Galen in Walzer (1949) 15–16; Alexander (2002) 245–6.

among the kind of Romans who admired the so-called Stoic martyrs. He would not have agreed with Lane Fox's claim that 'martyrdom was quite unlike a philosopher's noble suicide'.[289] Hitherto, this paper has largely talked of 'Greek philosophers', but Luke here skilfully smuggles in Roman ones.

Hence, I suggest, another resonance in Acts' last word *'unhinderedly'*/ἀκωλύτως. The word is emphatic by position, by quantity, by relative rarity, and by being *hapax* in Luke. The thought is generally compatible with Platonist, Cynic, and Stoic notions about the heroism of the wise man ('free [etc.] on the rack [etc.]'). But the word is also *hapax* in Plato, in the *Cratylus* 415d, where we learn that 'the *flow* of the good soul is always *loose* ... [it] flows *unrestrictedly* and *unhinderedly*'. *Hapax* in Plato, *hapax* in Luke, and both in contexts of metaphorical freedom from bondage. In Plato, the word is associated with 'good flow' (*euroia*), a metaphor from water also important to the Stoics, who constructed Odyssean allegories about storms at sea and shipwrecks.[290] But Paul, also, exhibited nothing if not 'good flow' in that allegorical (as well as real, as well as 'literary') encounter with water. Usefully, the word 'unhinderedly' is also used by the Stoics.[291] Luke's implicit evocation of *euroia* could not be better placed.[292]

'Unhinderedly' may also have another aspect. It is used by Josephus of the Jews' 'unhindered' right to practise their ancestral religion, as reaffirmed by Agrippa and Claudius (*AJ* 16.41: ἀκωλύτως τὴν πάτριον εὐσέβειαν διαφυλάττων). From the point of view of Luke's rivalry with Josephus, that 'unhindered' right looks distinctly less 'unhindered' after the Jewish War of 66–73, the destruction of the Temple, and the persistent Flavian denigration of the Jews.[293] By contrast, Christians are 'unhindered', whatever the Romans do to them and *whatever* their external circumstances.

There are important further dimensions to Paul's last state. Readers know that he will be martyred. This martyrdom mirrors Stephen's, in which Paul was complicit (8.1). Non-Christian readers at least will surely think Paul's martyrdom to be in some sense poetically just—and there are things in the text (as also in Paul's own writings) which make this thought reasonable. Paul emphasises his

---

289  Lane Fox (1986) 545.
290  E.g., Hor. *Epist.* 1.16; Sen. *Ep.* 104.27.
291  {E.g., Epict. 3.12.4.}
292  Alexander (2005) 204: 'Luke's interest in Stoic philosophy is minimal', understates. The storm metaphor is also central to Epicurean thought, as in *ataraxia* ('undisturbedness', of the sea), but there is a crucial difference: Paul and the Stoics heroically overcome such 'storms', the Epicureans just avoid them; and the Epicureans anyway have already been totally defeated (p. 885 above).
293  Goodman (2007) 445ff.

own career as a persecutor (e.g. 22.17–21; 26.9–11), and, when God instructs the naturally apprehensive Ananias to baptise Saul, he ends by saying: 'for *I* shall reveal to him all the things that he must suffer for my name'.[294] But Paul will, as it were, come out the other side, thanks to God's forgiveness.[295] Now Acts' final attitude towards the Jews has been much discussed. In the passage directly before 28.30–1, salvation is said to have been sent to the Gentiles (28.29). But then at the very end 'all' must allow 'including Jews'. Might Paul's trajectory, then, suggest a possible trajectory for Jews who had not (up till the appearance of Acts) accepted Jesus? Paul the Jew, who always remains a Jew,[296] moves from persecution of Christians, including Stephen, to acceptance of Jesus, to Christian mission, to Christian martyrdom—the latter an appropriate atonement for his action against Stephen—and to final forgiveness. Jews who reject Jesus and some of whom persecute Christians are appropriately punished (in the destruction of the Temple and subjugation of Judaea),[297] but may still attain final forgiveness if they accept Jesus, while—like Paul—always remaining Jews. To them, the door (Luke 13.22–30) still remains open—just, even after the devastating punishment of the Jewish War.

Paul, of course, also has a future *beyond* martyrdom, because Jesus' resurrection, on which Acts insists, is a harbinger of the general resurrection of human beings at the end of time. In the last third of the narrative, resurrection has become an increasingly strong emphasis, just as it was in the opening chapters. The general resurrection also coincides with the Last Judgement, the final occasion on which divine justice trumps human justice. Compared with that, Paul's forthcoming trial under Nero is a mere bagatelle. Paul's final resurrection also balances the insistence at the start of the Acts narrative on Jesus' future life, first after the resurrection, then after the ascension (1.2–11).

This aspect of Paul's future prospects, too, has to be brought into comparison with Greek and Roman philosophical martyrs and with their literary commemorations. Socrates in Plato's representation of him is an obviously relevant comparator, especially (again) the Socrates of the *Phaedo*. There, however, while Socrates is literally in prison, the body and life itself are also prisons, from which 'those who have lived with outstanding holiness are freed' (114b), as the soul is freed from the body. Acts completely rejects this Platonic

---

294 Acts 9.16. Hence a certain resemblance to John's treatment of Peter, denier of Jesus, Christian martyr, and (joint) 'hero' at the end of the narrative: 13.36–8; 21.15–19.
295 Again *re* Peter, a similar emphasis in Mark: Bauckham (2006) 180.
296 Cf. Paul's words in his final speech at Acts 28.17: οὐδὲν ἐναντίον ποιήσας τῷ λαῷ ἢ τοῖς ἔθεσι τοῖς πατρῴοις.
297 Acts 6.14 (Jewish theological background in Johnson [1992] 109–10), like Matthew 24.2, is particularly pointed post-70.

pessimism about life and the body and looks forward not to the disembodied life of a soul or even to reincarnation but to the resurrection of the body as a psychosomatic unity. The *Phaedo* comparison regarding Paul at the end of Acts and just before the end of his life balances the *Phaedo* comparison regarding Jesus just before the end of his life in Luke,[298] to satisfying formal, moral, and theological effects.

The Stoics are also relevant comparators, partly because of the Stoic resonances of Paul's last hours, partly because we already know from Acts 17 that Stoics have some interest in an afterlife or something similar. Stoicism has various doctrines on what happens to humans after death but even on the most optimistic of these the souls of the virtuous will survive only until the next conflagration. As for Cynics, also relevant in context because there were Cynic martyrs as well as Stoic ones, mainline Cynicism at least has no interest in an afterlife or anything similar. This trumping of Cynicism mirrors that at 1.8, at the start of Acts. Thus in this eschatological respect also Christianity trumps Platonism, Stoicism, and Cynicism.

This 'trumping' is, of course, not merely theoretical, since both under Nero and under Domitian Christians were put to death just for being Christians. Even on the brink of death at the hands of the Roman state at its most brutal Christians have nothing to fear. Despite everything, Paul's future prospects could not be brighter. 'Unhinderedly' (alpha-privative compound; final, thunderously closural word of Luke-Acts) decisively answers and fulfils, of the words in which Christians have been 'orally instructed', the 'unslippability' (alpha-privative compound; last word of the Prologue to Luke—which is also the Prologue to Luke-Acts). For Theophilos and fellow-Christians, *final* 'stability' or 'assurance' is provided not by Acts' emphasis on Christianity's law-abidingness—important as that emphasis is—but by the doctrine of resurrection. The certainty of life after death or of resurrection trumps everything, if, that is, it is accompanied by the assurance of a 'not guilty' verdict at the Last Judgement. Greeks and Romans, we know, were regularly astonished by the fearlessness of the Christian martyrs, who must correctly have interpreted the ending of Acts. One also recalls Galen's view of the philosophical value of the Gospels.[299] This, obviously, is an important message also for potential converts to Christianity.

---

298 {Sterling (2001) 398.}
299 Cf. above, n. 288.

Scholars have often noted how Paul dominates the second half of Acts,[300] how his sufferings, imprisonments, and trials are emphasised, and how his death is emphatically signposted. Why are these things so emphasised? It is not enough to say: 'because they happened to Paul' (even as 'local hero' of the Roman church), or: 'because they replay what happened to Jesus'. Both statements are true but do not satisfactorily explain the emphases. If the purpose of the narratives is merely factual, then the steadily more exclusive focus on Paul badly neglects other important actors in the history of the first Christians. Equally, why repeat the Jesus narrative at such length and with such emphasis? The point, surely, is that these emphases have paradigmatic significance for all Christians. Acts has to cope with a context where Christian 'witness' as prescribed by the risen Jesus himself (1.8) may involve 'witness' as 'martyrdom', when 'going to the end' may mean the 'end' of a violent death. Stephen is the first pivotal figure here as both 'witness' and 'martyr', his end, as we have seen, parallels Jesus' in some detail, and in all these respects he is followed by Paul himself. These factors themselves encourage a dating of Acts to the 90s or later,[301] because, after the Neronian persecution to which Paul, Peter, and other Christians in Rome fell victim, there was no, or very little, persecution until Domitian. This is not to reduce Acts to the level of 'a response to crisis'. Once Christianity moved out from under its Jewish umbrella, conflict with Rome was always inevitable (given various specific 'triggers'), for the Jews had long ago negotiated tolerance of their monotheism on the ground of its being their ancestral religion, and this tolerance essentially remained even as the imperial cult grew apace and even after the disaster of the Jewish War, whereas Christian monotheism, if exposed to scrutiny, necessarily clashed with the imperial cult (which is why there are several pointed references to it in Acts).[302] Thus these very emphases on suffering and death subserve the greater emphasis on the Christian certainty of resurrection, which is both the very essence of Christianity and the complete answer to persecution.

All this helps to explain some of Acts' generic aspects, which scholars have found so frustrating. Of the emphases I have here been discussing, 'philosophical biography' is the obvious vehicle, hence the increasingly 'biographical' character of the second half of the narrative; but hence, too, the implication that Paul's 'biography' is not just about him: it has a far larger paradigmatic significance.

---

300   Taylor (2006) 83: 'From ch. 13 onwards, the Acts of the Apostles become, to all intents and purposes, the Acts of Paul'.
301   *Contra*, Dormeyer–Galindo (2003) 16.
302   E.g., Peter, Herod.

*Paul's* 'end', therefore, will be a splendid one.

But what of the geographical relationship between a *textual end* in Rome and Jesus' commission of witness to *the end of the earth*? Is Rome itself being focalised as the *end* of the earth? This is an available focalisation (Pss. Sol. 8.16), and even, at one level, within Acts, for in the 'catalogue of the nations' enunciated at the Pentecost event (2.8–11) and centred on Jerusalem, Rome represents the West.[303] Moreover, the notion that Christian mission in, or to, *Rome*, as it were, at the very heart of 'the nations', is a great goal, whose realisation is itself a worthwhile end, has been heavily trailed in the text (19.21; 23.11). This play between 'centre' and 'end' is also found in 1 and 2 Maccabees, which is relevant, as we have seen.[304] The notion that Rome is 'the end' (as goal) seems to find wider support in the text. When Paul's party arrives in Rome, it is escorted into the city as if in an *adventus* ceremony,[305] and there is some sense of 'we have come home'.[306] Paradoxical on one level, it is natural on another: Theophilos and Luke being together in Rome, Luke explains how the Pauline mission, including himself, first got there.[307] This sense can be integrated into a larger geographical movement in Luke-Acts.[308] Luke moves from Rome to Bethlehem, to Nazareth, to Capernaum, to Jerusalem; Acts moves (with considerable zigzagging) from Jerusalem to Rome. This larger movement is even replayed within Acts, which ends with Jews and others in Rome (28.17–30), whereas the catalogue of the nations features 'Romans staying there [in Jerusalem], both Jews and proselytes' (2.10–11). This larger circling movement conveys something of the suggestion of Christian 'imperialism' encountered at the start of Acts:[309] in Luke Rome's power seemed to dictate world events; by the end of Acts roles are, despite all outward appearances, reversed, and it is Christianity that is beginning to dictate world events. Christianity again 'turns the world upside down' (17.6).[310]

Now, although this circling movement in Luke-Acts comports important meaning, Rome can be focalised as the *actual* end of the earth only if Jerusalem remains the centre, but the overall movement of Acts is decisively away from Jerusalem as the centre (especially when readers take—as they

---

303 Bauckham (1995); Alexander (2005) 79, 213.
304 P. 861.
305 Alexander (2005) 212.
306 Alexander (2005) 214, 228.
307 The emphasis being on the Pauline Christian mission, mention of already existing Christians in Rome (28.15) does not take the shine off things, *pace* Alexander (2005) 214.
308 Alexander (2005) 218ff.
309 And also in Paul's sea-voyages, especially that of 27.1–44: Alexander (2005) 84–6.
310 Cf. p. 890 above.

must—a post-70 perspective). Furthermore, the notion of Rome as the end says nothing about those lands and peoples outside the city of Rome which are part of the Roman empire and which have not yet been covered by the Christian mission.[311] Still less does it say anything about lands and peoples outside the borders of the Roman empire up to the 'end(s)' of the earth. Both categories feature in the 'catalogue of the nations' in Acts 2, and cannot therefore be air-brushed out of interpretative consideration. Moreover, other New Testament writings, including Mark, one of Luke's main sources, clearly represent the end of the earth (vel sim.) as meaning what it says, even when Jerusalem is the starting-point.[312] From this overall perspective, then, while mission to Rome, often conceived as the centre of the earth and implicitly so in Acts 28.15 (alluding to the Appian Way),[313] *foreshadows* mission to the end of the earth, that divinely-ordered mission remains to be achieved and the omission is felt.

Thus the 'end' of Acts, in the sense of its divinely-ordered goal, lies far beyond the end of the text, which has only got as far as Rome. At which point, the reader again comes in. Acts is a work of philosophical instruction, Paul and other great Christians in the narrative paradigms for Theophilos and all readers to imitate. Luke-Acts is centrally concerned with the 'succession' of Christianity, and Acts with the transmission of Christianity. The reader's role, therefore, is not merely to interpret the end of the text, but to contribute to bringing about that much greater divinely-ordered end, by filling in the gaps between text and life, or, as it were, by helping to write a new narrative. This explains why at the beginning of Acts Luke refers to Luke as his *first logos* (1.1): the *third logos* is what readers 'write',[314] when they, as it were, *enact* Acts. Because Paul and other Christian martyrs since Paul have died, it is up to readers to take up the torch of the ongoing Christian mission, first in Rome itself and then progressively outwards, in a perpetual relay until that mission is indeed taken to the end of the earth. The Luke Preface's 'succession' notion of 'handing on' from the past is here extended to 'handing on' into the future. In this sense, all readers are called upon to be apostles and to *act* and the Acts of the Apostles *qua* text points the way for necessary future 'acts' of future 'apostles'. The move from 'acts' *qua* commemorated acts to reader *enactment* is the whole point of Greek and Roman biography.[315]

---

311  {Cf. the list of peoples to whom the Apostles speak at Pentecost: Acts 2.8–11.}
312  {Mk 13.10: εἰς πάντα τὰ ἔθνη.}
313  Alexander (2005) 214.
314  Moles (2006a) 91 {above, p. 526}.
315  Cf., e.g., Plut. *Per.* 2.2–4; *Alex.* 1.2–3.

What happens when readers take up the challenge? Acts began not only with Jesus' commission of witness to the end of the earth but also with the question of when the kingdom would come, with the repeated narrative of the ascension (a 'vertical' 'road journey') and with the angels' assurance that on the Day of Judgement Jesus would return the same way as he had ascended. Allusions to the day of judgement are distributed prominently through the narrative. Paul's 'last words' at the end of Acts concern the kingdom. As we have seen, the most complex anticipation in Luke of 'the end of the earth' motif *combines* 'end' geography with *final* realisation of the Kingdom in the 'end' time.[316] There, Luke sounds a theme that is more or less explicit in other gospels, in Revelation and in 2 Peter.[317] And at the beginning of Luke, at the beginning of the Jesus narrative proper, the angel Gabriel prophesies to Mary: 'he will be king over the house of Jacob for the aeons and of his kingdom there will not be an end' (1.33). Thus Luke-Acts enacts a movement from a 'beginning', that of Jesus' ministry (Luke 1.2–3; Acts 1.1), to the 'end' time, just as Mark covers the period from the 'beginning' of 'the good news of Jesus Christ' (1.1) to the 'end' time (13.10–13, 24–7), and John the period from the 'beginning' of the creation (1.1) to the Second Coming (21.23).

In short, the final 'end' that the 'end' of Acts anticipates, and to whose implementation all readers can, and should, contribute, brings *everything* together in a trans*cend*ental 'ending': Christian mission to the end of the earth, the 'end' time, the second coming, the general resurrection, and the last judgement. It is to this, and not to Rome, that all roads eventually lead.

Differently from Platonic eschatological myths, the Christian myth (as pre-quelled by Jesus' resurrection) is provably true and will come to pass, and differently from all Greek philosophies except Cynicism, Christianity is absolutely non-elitist, egalitarian, and empowering of all. And the Christian 'end', like the end of Acts which foreshadows it, is utterly deconstruction-proof.[318]

Since the key to interpretation of the end of Acts lies in the perception of parallels and contrasts with the beginning of Acts and with the beginning of Luke, one may well again be seeing the influence of the end of Herodotus, which 'works' in similar (though surely less complicated) ways.[319]

---

316  Above, pp. 859ff.
317  Mark 13.10–13, 24–7; Matthew 24.14; 28.19–20; Rev. 14.6–7; 2 Peter 3.3–9; also, perhaps, embryonically, John 21.22.
318  Of course, the claim, unassailable in Luke's day, that final mission to the end of the earth and the end time will coincide is, for one writing in the early twenty-first century, hardly any longer tenable; but for the admissibility of unfulfilled prophecies in Jewish thinking cf. Dunn (2003a) 480–3.
319  Above, n. 274.

A last question: given all these parallels and contrasts between ends and beginnings, there must be a relationship between Acts' end and all the ends that it envisages, up to, and including, the end of the world, and the Luke Preface's 'things brought to *fulfilment* amongst us' (1.1). What is the relationship? Is the latter statement only provisional, and is it radically redefined by the former? Or is it rather that the end of Acts encourages readers to think through for themselves the full implications of the phrase 'things brought to fulfilment amongst us'? The second alternative is better. The temporal space between the apparently straightforwardly past 'things brought to fulfilment' and the apparently straightforwardly future 'end things' is bridged by the notion of inaugurated eschatology, which is always implicit in Jesus' resurrection (as both constitutive, and anticipatory, of the general resurrection at the end of time).[320]

Indeed, already at the start of the Acts narrative, Luke 'helps' the attentive reader to think about these things. After the coming of the Holy Spirit at Pentecost, giving the apostles the 'power' promised by Jesus, Peter's speech to 'the men of Judaea and all who dwell in Jerusalem' (the first constituency outlined in Jesus' commission to witness to the end of the earth) begins with an appeal to Joel's prophecy about 'the end days' (2.17). The end of Acts, then, is not so hard. It is, nevertheless, far richer than the end of Dio *Or.* 13, magnificent and philosophically profound as that speech is.

∴

What does Luke know about Greek and Roman philosophy? He knows:

a) about the Epimenidean tradition (Epimenides' visit to Athens, his 'healing' function, his institution of altars to 'anonymous gods') and about one of the poems attributed to him;

b) about Socrates (his characteristic behaviour and self-representation, his dialectic and *elenchus*, symposiastic activity, his *daimonion*, his allegiance to god rather than men, his refusal to be diverted from his philosophical mission, his 'strangeness' in an Athenian trial context, his trial, 'apologies' and heroic death); about the Socratic tradition (who claimed to be Socratics; who could be stigmatised as 'seed-collectors'); about several Christian appropriations of Socrates;

c) about Socratic writings such as Plato's *Apology, Gorgias, Phaedo*, and *Cratylus*, and Xenophon's *Apology* and *Memorabilia*;

d) about two of Aristotle's tags;

---

320  Cf. Wright (2008) 1.7–10; 32–3.

e) about the Cynics (their *parrēsia*, public and 'no-doors-barred' philosophising, their 'communism', contempt for sophisticated philosophers, and attacks on superstition; claims to 'witness' and 'cosmopolitanism'; primitivism; their claim to 'the short-cut Road'; their influence upon Jesus, Paul, and the early Christians generally; Diogenes' *Politeia*; Crates' 'door-opening' activity and selling of his property; Dio Chrysostom as Cynic-influenced);

f) about the Stoics (their doctrine of 'moral progress' and use of 'road imagery', combining horizontal and vertical progression; their theology, their appeal to great literature of the past, some of their writings, including Cleanthes' *Hymn to Zeus* and Aratus' *Phainomena*; something of Posidonius; their claim to be heirs of Socrates; their interest in what happens after death or at the end of the universe; their myths; their 'martyrdoms' under Nero and Domitian; Dio Chrysostom as Stoic-influenced)

g) about the Epicureans (their appeal to great literature of the past; their superciliousness; their materialism and disbelief in divine providence or anything beyond death; their punning on Epicurus' name; their popular association with gross pleasure and the private life; their 'corner');

h) about philosophical schools and their processes for establishing legitimate 'successions';

i) among contemporary philosophers, about Dio Chrysostom (his public performances; his theological preaching; the Cynic and Stoic influences upon him; his *Twelfth* and *Thirteenth Orations*, perhaps also his *Seventh*);

j) about the comparison made by Josephus and earlier Jewish writers between Judaism and its various subdivisions to Greek philosophy and its various sects; about the Jewish philosophical representation of Moses' education;

k) about the representation of Christianity as a philosophy and as a philosophical school and Christianity's claim to fulfil and supersede the best of Greek philosophy; about Christian 'philosophical' teaching in private houses; about the characteristic Jewish-Christian 'protreptic tags' to educated Greeks; about the parallels between Paul and Greek philosophers;

l) about inter-school philosophical polemic;

m) about some of the quasi-technical terminology of Greek philosophy ('apology', 'dialectic', 'elenchus', *katēcheo, prokopē, suzēteo, zēteo, homileo, asphaleia, parrēsia, suntomos hodos, epitomē*, 'seed-collector', 'not in a corner')

n) about philosophical literary forms, such as 'apologies', 'symposia', philosophical letters, epitomes, works of moral philosophy, myths, farewell discourses, and some of their characteristic techniques ('protreptic' 'gaps', direct moral exemplarity, 'write-your-own-life' challenges; translation of myth into reality), road imagery (Plato, Stoic, Cynic) and atopic imagery; philosophy within historiography (~ Herodotus, wise warners, etc.).

If this account is broadly right, Luke knows far more about Greek philosophy than usually supposed (more, surely, than most professional Classicists). Naturally, the formula 'Luke knows' is elastic: Luke knows more about Socrates and the Cynics than about the Epicureans. His philosophical knowledge derives partly from Jewish texts that make analogies between Judaism and Greek philosophy (Josephus, Aristobulus) and Jewish/Christian ones that make analogies between Christianity and pagan philosophy (Paul's letters; Q; Mark). It also derives from real life (Paul's partially philosophical activity; observation of Cynic behaviour and of its influence on some Christians; awareness of the widespread representation of Christianity and other Jewish sects as branches of 'philosophy'; knowledge about Stoic martyrs in Rome and about the philosophical activity of such as Dio). That it also derives from Greek philosophical texts is somewhat controversial, some scholars preferring to invoke 'general knowledge', 'story patterns', or the like. But Luke's engagement with the *Septuagint* shows him to be a highly intertextual writer and it is difficult to see why this same intertextuality should not also apply to Classical texts: the apparent verbal and contextual echoes of (e.g.) Plato's *Apology* and *Phaedo* (as of other Classical authors such as Herodotus, Thucydides, Homer and Euripides [*Bacchae*]) are just there and have real interpretative consequences.[321] Of course, 'Luke knows' is again elastic: he evidently knows the *Apology* and *Phaedo* far better than *Cratylus* (as who does not?).

'Luke the man' 'likes' Socrates and the Cynics, has some time for the Stoics and 'dislikes' the Epicureans. 'What Luke knows and likes', however, matters far less than the function(s) of philosophy in Acts and in Luke-Acts as a whole.

The above account already has implications for Luke's projected audience/readership: *some* must be very Hellenised Jews and highly educated Greeks and Romans.[322] Indeed, this inference may be made from the very preface to Luke-Acts, which foregrounds philosophy by various devices, including the use of 'school' terminology, but especially in relation to the 'unslippability' of the Christian Road, and which grafts this philosophical strand on to a Herodotean historiographical conception of text as journey. Luke maintains

---

321   Reluctance to concede Classical allusions seems to me characteristically to reflect 'Christian anxiety': the desire to keep Luke-Acts as a *direct* 'imitation' of the events of its narrative, without allowing any intermediary or contributory role to other literary 'imitations', non-Jewish and non-Christian, of other, 'non-Christian', events.

322   Similarly, from a different perspective, Moles (2006b) 77 {above, p. 563}.

this (partially philosophical) road imagery and represents Jesus himself in (to some extent) philosophical terms (Cynic analogies and influences; symposiastic settings; inter-school polemic; farewell speeches; Socratic analogies; *Phaedo*). In so far as Acts concerns the acts of the original and subsequent apostles, the unified Luke-Acts illustrates the founder-plus-successors pattern of some Hellenistic philosophical biographies. Acts accordingly 'firms up' some latent philosophical aspects of Luke. Within Acts, the first Christians are continually invested with philosophical characteristics (Socratic and Cynic *parrēsia*, Cynic-like 'communism' and sale of property, Cynic-like public performance, status as a philosophical *hairesis*, *ad hoc sophia* in trial situations, Socratic propensity to trial and death, Cratetean 'door-opening' activity, use of private teaching venues, etc.). The analogy between leading Christians and Socrates begins with Peter and John and Stephen but is subject to sustained development in relation to Paul, from his trial-*like* encounter with the Athenian philosophers on the Areopagus, to his use of 'dialectic' and 'apology', to his 'farewell' speech, repeated trials and 'apologies', philosophical deportment during storm, ship-wreck, and exposure to barbarian peoples; and heroic death. That death is also compared to that of 'Stoic martyrs' in Nero's and Domitian's reigns.

These philosophical analogies serve a wide range of functions.

The philosophical road imagery is fundamental to the Christian notion of moral progress in the footsteps of Jesus, to Christian witness, if necessary to the point of martyrdom, and to Christian mission to the end of the earth. It also characterises Luke-Acts as a complete 'Short-Cut Road' to the knowledge and practice of Christianty.

The philosophical associations of Jesus, his disciples, and of later apostles help generally to normalise them in the eyes of Greeks and Romans, to illuminate their characteristic behaviours by philosophical parallels, and to promote some sense of shared values.

The founder-plus-successors philosophical biographical format enables Luke to distinguish legitimate successors of Jesus from illegitimate ones and to incorporate a large element of biography into his overall historiographical project, as appropriate both to Jesus and to the first apostles; the philosophical-biographical element also subserves the ever more insistently paradigmatic quality of the narrative focusing on Paul.

The stronger philosophical analogies (as in Acts 17) serve as Christian protreptic to philosophically minded Greeks and Romans, illustrate how Christians should approach educated Gentiles, stake Christianity's claim to be the true philosophical heir of Socratic, Cynic, and Stoic philosophy, distinguish between Greek philosophies with which conversation is possible and those with which it is not, and demonstrate both to non-Jews and to Christians that Christianity can more than hold its own philosophically and educationally (though 'many-letteredness' is not a *necessary* attribute of Christians).

The sustained analogies between Paul and Socrates emphasise Christianity's claim to fulfil and supersede Socratic philosophy, illuminate Paul's heroic progress from witness to martyrdom by parallels with the life and death of the most famous pagan philosopher of all, whose *Nachleben* was never more flourishing than in the period in which Acts was written,[323] appeal particularly to Greeks and Romans who admired the examples of the Stoic martyrs, emphasise the Christian 'myth''s superior truth value and superior consolatory value to Platonic myths, and reassure Theophilos and all contemporary and later Christians with the absolute guarantee provided by Christian resurrection, a guarantee particularly necessary at times of persecution (as under Nero, Domitian and—even—Trajan), but always potentially necessary, because of the inevitable clash between Christianity and the imperial cult.

To the extent that Luke-Acts extends a benevolent hand towards non-Christians and does so through the medium of philosophy (*inter alia*), as soon as philosophy is embedded in the text, non-Christian and non-Jewish readers may naturally, and not unreasonably, read certain other elements, Jewish-Christian in origin, in philosophical terms, or at the very least find congenial philosophical analogues for them. In the Preface itself, as we have seen, they could read Jesus the Word as equivalent to the *Logos* and would surely register the familiar analogy between Judaism/Christianity and philosophical schools. In both Luke and Acts, Stoics could read the Holy Spirit 'philosophically', *pneuma* being an acceptable Stoic term, and non-Christians in general could read the coming of the Holy Spirit as a process of *entheosis*.[324] Again, those familiar with Plato's *Apology* and related works could read the thrice-recurring 'divine call' narrative of Paul's conversion as an analogue of Socrates' 'conversion' to philosophy on Chaerephon's receipt of the Delphic Oracle,[325] especially in the light of the 'Dionysiac' quality of Paul's conversion, of Luke's nice blurring of *Apology* and *Bacchae* in 17.28 and 34, and of Acts' intertextual engagement with Dio *Or.* 13.[326]

Perhaps particularly intriguing in the present context is the notion of metaphorical 'turning'.

---

323  Cf. more generally Alexander (2005) 67–8, 119.
324  Cf. Edwards (2000).
325  Alexander (2005) 63.
326  Moles (2005) 126 {above, p. 272} n. 140.

The simple verb 'turn' (*strepho*) is used negatively (Acts 7.39, of the Israelites' making the Golden Calf, because 'in their hearts they turned to Egypt'), positively (Acts 7.42, of God's 'turning' the Israelites back to true worship), or neutrally (Acts 13.46, of Paul and Barnabas' 'turning' to the Gentiles because of Jewish rejection of the word of God). The compound 'turn away' (*apostrepho*) is used negatively (Luke 23.14, of the charge that Jesus 'subverted' the people) or positively (Acts 3.26, of Jesus' purpose to 'turn each of you away from your sins'). The compound 'turn to' or 'turn back' (*epistrepho*) is used positively (Luke 1.16, 17). All these usages are variants of 'road imagery', and there are biblical precedents for them and, indeed, some direct biblical allusions.[327] But, obviously, they are also compatible with Classical philosophical road imagery, where there are many parallels for the use of the the simple *strepho* and the compound *epistrepho*, particularly among Platonists.

Not only the Luke Preface but other elements in the narrative give all such 'cross-over' readings encouragement: Acts 17.23 with its initial 'identification' of the Jewish god and Zeus; 28.11, where the sign on the ship that successfully carries Paul to Italy is the Dioscuri, and it almost seems as if the pagan gods are graciously forwarding their own supersession; or 28.6, where the inhabitants of Malta hail Paul as a god and (in contrast to other such incidents in the narrative) are not corrected. In all these cases, the final 'cash-out' meaning of the text is to reject Greek and Roman religion and affirm Christianity, but the initial approach proffers considerable benevolence.

In so far as Acts intertexts with various works of Dio Chrysostom, Luke criticises Cynics for their lack of interest in theology and Stoics for their inability to make the final leap into proper monotheism; proposes, in Paul, a—in some obvious ways—more persuasive and impressive philosophical exemplar than Dio; advances an even more thorough-going programme for the moral reform of Rome and the world; and proclaims a true and all-comprehending eschatological myth.

But Luke also keeps all groups—existing Christians, Jews, and educated Greeks and Romans—on their toes by posing key interpretative questions (in Acts 17 and at the end of Acts) through the device of the 'philosophical gap'.

---

327 Note that many New Testament scholars also regard *metanoia* and *metanoeo* as 'turning' words: e.g., Barrett (2004) 1.154; Wright (2008) 1.42; This is a misconception. While the Septuagint translators used *metanoeo* for a Hebrew word that does embody the notion of 'turning', and while the Latin Fathers rendered *metanoia* by *conversio*, which also embodies that notion, *metanoieo* does not itself include it. The essential idea is of 'change' (*meta*) of 'mind', and that is also a better translation than 'conversion', because it avoids the latter's misleading association of 'turning'. Of course, such a 'change of mind' is conceived of as radical and life-changing.

In so far as Acts is an apologetic history about Judaism covering the period from the immediate aftermath of Jesus' death to (implicitly) the Fall of Jerusalem, the destruction of the Temple, and Christianity's emergence as the 'solution' to Judaism,[328] Luke trumps Josephus' defence and justification of traditional Judaism systematically (Christianity is a major Jewish *hairesis*, indeed more, the Road; Christianity has both subsumed Pharisaism and moved decisively away from the Temple, whose rebuilding Josephus and other law-observant Jews vainly anticipated, etc.); represents the Jewish War and the destruction of the Temple as divine punishment not for civil strife and the profanation of sacred spaces (as in Josephus) but for the rejection of Jesus; and hence propounds a radically different 'solution' for the Jews' contemporary plight.

Apart from the fact that Theophilos (real or imaginary) remained Luke's addressee for the second book, there is no evidence of how Luke-Acts played with its first-generation target readership of educated Greeks and Romans (one of several readerships but the one most resembling present-day Classicists). But speculation is permissible.

They could not have regarded Luke's Greek or his philosophical knowledge as being of the same calibre as those of such contemporary non-Christian competitors as Dio Chrysostom or Plutarch, but they would have recognised that in all possible respects Luke was far superior to Xenophon of Ephesus and measurably more interesting and intelligent than the over-hyped and repetitive Epictetus.

They would have had various responses to Luke's Greek, recognising its serviceable 'professional-man' core, registering something of the stylistic elevation imported by extensive allusions to the Septuagint, and appreciating the periodic 'Classical' writing, notably (for our purposes) in Paul's encounters with the Athenian philosophers and with Agrippa II, his farewell to the Ephesian elders, his first sea voyage, and his last hours.

They would have seen the philosophical packaging (cf. Galen, Papias, and Justin). They would have seen that Luke demonstrates considerable skill in the deployment of his philosophical material: integrating a strongly philosophical strand into a work of historiography (à la Herodotus or Onesicritus), imitating the basic teacher-plus-successors format of (some) Greek philosophical biography, deriving considerable mileage from the philosophical road imagery

---

328  Excellent critique in Alexander (2005) 183–206 of the various understandings of 'apologetic'; the one here corresponds best to Sterling (1992). I think *all* the different understandings have *some* validity; 'in so far as' avoids privileging *this* understanding or even 'apologetic' generically as Acts' dominant concern.

begun in the overall Preface, progressively 'firming up' and 'cashing out' in Acts the philosophical markers set down in Luke, applying an overall Socratic-Cynic patina to the apostles in general, working through the Socratic material in some detail in relation to Paul, inventing some scenes—or elements of scenes (Paul in Athens, the conversion of Dionysius the Areopagite, the hearing before Agrippa II), achieving dense philosophical allusiveness in the Athens episode, creating his effects with great economy (strategic distribution of philosophical references throughout the narrative, use of 'markers', and of *hapax* or infrequent words, skilful placing of key themes or words, 'cueing' devices, deft literary allusions to *Apology*, *Phaedo*, etc.), directing well-aimed swipes at the general breed of over-sophisticated Greek and Roman philosophers, intertexting pointedly with contemporary philosophical luminaries such as Josephus and Dio Chrysostom, and in separate episodes (Athens, the first sea voyage, the farewell speech, the end) writing as well as any of his contemporaries at their best. They would have experienced something of the same pleasure in 'spotting the allusions' and in registering their technical skill when reading Luke as when reading his Greek and Roman contemporaries. They would have appreciated Luke's generic pluralism and flexibility, especially when he increases the biographical element in order to generalise important philosophical and theological themes.

They would also have responded to the attractions of narrative[329]—attractions relatively rare outside historiography, biography, philosophy, rhetoric, and the novel—and of a narrative which, while offering reassuring parallels with narratives with which they were familiar (Jesus ~ Dionysus, Paul ~ Socrates and the Stoic martyrs), yet had some of the charm of novelty and staked a claim to be the greatest story ever told.

By all these factors they should have been very impressed—as should we be. It should have been difficult for them to dismiss this version of Christianity as 'the barbarian', or even 'the simple', philosophy. As with the great Cynics, they would have had the disconcerting experience of encountering a thinker who had sufficient resources of philosophical (and other) *paideia*, yet who held it of little or no ultimate value, and who claimed to 'solve' philosophy in such a way as to render all other philosophy redundant and even, sometimes, rather silly.

As for Luke-Acts' theological purpose, some of them would have accepted that Greek and Roman polytheism offered an uneconomical and chaotic explanation of human relations with the divine; all of them would have been struck by the absoluteness of Christian conviction, even unto death; some of

---

329   Alexander (2005) 69–96, 133–63.

them would have been impressed by it, others repelled;[330] none should have regarded it as under-motivated (Epictetus and Marcus Aurelius should have read Luke-Acts). The majority would have dismissed the resurrection (whether Jesus' or general), as Acts fully acknowledges. Luke could not have downplayed that: it being the very basis of Christianity, of Christian conviction, and of Christian 'unslippability'. At the same time, hankering for an afterlife or something similar can be found among very sophisticated contemporary Greek and Roman philosophers (Cicero, Dio, Plutarch, and Marcus Aurelius, for example); it has been argued that such phenomena as 'Nero redivivus' and novelistic 'apparent deaths' constitute some sort of response to the Jesus *muthos*;[331] and the doctrine of resurrection certainly contributed to the progressive advance of Christianity.

## Bibliography

Adinolfi, M. (1990) 'Il Socrate dell'Apologia platonica e il Pietro di Atti 4–5 di fronte alla libertà religiosa', *Anton* 65: 422–41.

Alexander, L. C. A. (1986) 'Luke's Preface in the Pattern of Greek Preface-Writing', *NovT* 28: 48–74.

Alexander, L. C. A. (1993) *The Preface to Luke's Gospel: Literary Convention and Social Context in Luke 1.1.4 and Acts 1.1* (Cambridge).

Alexander, L. C. A. (1994) 'Paul and the Hellenistic Schools: the Evidence of Galen', in T. Engberg-Pederson, ed., *Paul in his Hellenistic Context* (Philadelphia and Edinburgh) 60–83.

Alexander, L. C. A. (1999) 'Formal Elements and Genre: Which Greco-Roman Prologues Most Closely Parallel the Lukan Prologues?' in D. P. Moessner, ed., *Jesus and the Heritage of Israel: Luke's Narrative Claim upon Israel's Legacy* (Harrisburg, Pa.) 9–26.

Alexander, L. C. A. (2001) '*IPSE DIXIT*: Citation of Authority in Paul and the Jewish and Hellenistic Schools', in Engberg-Pederson (2001) 103–27.

Alexander, L. C. A. (2002) 'Foolishness to the Greeks: Jews and Christians in the Public Life of the Empire', in G. Clark and T. Rajak, edd., *Philosophy and Power in the Graeco-Roman World: Essays in Honour of Miriam Griffin* (Oxford) 229–50.

---

330  There is, after all, much to be said for religious pluralism, as later Themistius eloquently argued. Since the Christian 'end' is coercive on the Dionysus/Jesus principle 'either for me or against me', and Christianity is the 'choice' which everybody is called to make, Acts, like the rest of the New Testament, can reasonably be condemned as anti-Jewish, hence 'anti-Semitic', 'anti-Muslim', illiberal, etc.

331  Wright (2003) 68ff.

Alexander, L. C. A. (2005) *Acts in Its Ancient Literary Context: A Classicist Looks at the Acts of the Apostles* (London and New York).

Athanassiadi P. and M. Frede, edd. (1999) *Pagan Monotheism in Late Antiquity* (Oxford).

Aune, D. E. (2002) 'Luke 1:1–4: Historical or Scientific Prooimion?', in A. Christopherson, B. Longenecker, J. Frey, and C. Claussen, edd., *Paul, Luke, and the Graeco-Roman World: Essays in Honour of Alexander J. M. Wedderburn* (Sheffield) 138–48.

Balch, D. L. (1990) 'The Areopagus Speech: An Appeal to the Stoic Historian Posidonius against Later Stoics and the Epicureans', in D. Balch et al., edd., *Greeks, Romans and Christians* (Minneapolis) 52–79.

Barclay, W. (1976) *The Acts of the Apostles* (Edinburgh).

Barnes, T. D. (1969) 'An Apostle on Trial', *JTS* 20: 407–19.

Barrett, C. K. (2004) *A Critical and Exegetical Commentary on The Acts of the Apostles*, 2 vols. (London and New York).

Bauckham, R. J. (1995a) 'James and the Jerusalem Church', in id. (1995b) 415–80.

Bauckham, R. J., ed. (1995b) *The Book of Acts in its First-Century Setting: Volume 4: Palestinian Setting* (Grand Rapids and Carlisle).

Bauckham, R. J. (2006) *Jesus and the Eyewitnesses: the Gospels as Eyewitness Testimony* (Grand Rapids and Cambridge).

Baur, F. C. (1831) 'Die Christuspartei in der korinthischen Gemeinde, der Gegensatz des petrinischen und paulinischen Christentums in der ältesten Kirche, der Apostel Petrus in Rom', *Tübinger Zeitschrift für Theologie* v:4: 61–206; repr. in id., *Ausgewählte Werke in Einzelausgaben: I: Historisch-kritische Untersuchungen zum neuen Testament*, ed. K. Scholder (Stuttgart, 1963) 1–146.

Billerbeck, M. (1978) *Epiktet: vom Kynismus* (Leiden).

Bond, H. K. (1998) *Pontius Pilate in History and Interpretation* (Cambridge).

Boring, M. E., et al., edd. (1995) *Hellenistic Commentary to the New Testament* (Nashville).

Boring, M. E. (2006) *Mark: a Commentary* (Louisville, Ky.).

Bowie, E. L. (1978) 'Apollonius of Tyana: Tradition and Reality', *ANRW* II.16.2: 1652–99.

Brown, R. E. (1997) *An Introduction to the New Testament* (New York, London, Toronto, Sydney, and Auckland).

Bruce, F. F. (1951) *The Acts of the Apostles: the Greek Text with Introduction and Commentary* (London).

Byrskog, S. (2000) *Story as History—History as Story: The Gospel Tradition in the Context of Ancient Oral History* (Tübingen).

Cadbury, H. (1922) 'Commentary on the Preface of Luke', in F. J. Foakes Jackson and K. Lake, edd., *The Beginnings of Christianity: Part I The Acts of the Apostles*, Volume 2, *Prolegomena II Criticsm* (London) 489–510.

Colaclides, P. (1973) '*Acts* 17, 28a and *Bacchae* 506', *Vigiliae Christianae* 27: 161–4.

de Meeus, X. (1961) 'Composition de Luc XIV et genre symposiaque', *ETL* 37: 847–70.

Dewald, C. J. (1997) 'Wanton Kings, Pickled Heroes, and Gnomic Founding Fathers: Strategies of Meaning at the End of Herodotus' *Histories*', in D. Roberts, D. Fowler, and F. Dunn, edd., *Classical Closure: Reading the End in Greek and Latin Literature* (Princeton) 62–82; repr. in R. Munson, ed., *Herodotus*, 2 vols. (Oxford, 2013) 1.379–401.

Dibelius, M. (1956) *Studies in the Acts of the Apostles* (London and New York).

Döring, K. (1979) *Exemplum Socratis: Studien zur Sokratesnachwirkung in der kynisch-stoischen Popularphilosophie der frühen Kaiserzeit und im frühen Christentum* (Wiesbaden).

Dormeyer, D. and G. Galindo (2003) *Die Apostelgeschichte: ein Kommentar für die Praxis* (Stuttgart).

Downing, F. G. (1988) *Christ and the Cynics: Jesus and other Radical Preachers in First-Century Tradition* (Sheffield).

Dunn, J. D. G. (2003a) *Jesus Remembered: Christianity in the Making*, vol. 1 (Grand Rapids and Cambridge).

Dunn, J. D. G., ed. (2003b) *The Cambridge Companion to St Paul* (Cambridge).

Dupont, J. (1979) 'La conclusion des Actes et son rapport à l'ensemble de l'ouvrage de Luc', in J. Kremer, ed., *Les Acts des Apôtres: Traditions, rédaction, théologie* (Leuven) 359–404.

Edwards, M. (2000) 'Birth, Death, and Divinity in Porphyry's *Life of Plotinus*', in T. Hägg and P. Rousseau, edd., *Greek Biography and Panegyric in Late Antiquity* (Berkeley and Los Angeles) 52–71.

Engberg-Pedersen, T. (2000) *Paul and the Stoics* (Edinburgh).

Engberg-Pedersen, T., ed. (2001) *Paul Beyond the Judaism—Hellenism Divide* (Louisville).

Ferri, R. (1993) *I dispiacieri di un epicureo: uno studio sulla poetica oraziana delle Epistole (con un capitolo su Persio)* (Pisa).

Fitzmyer, J. A. (1998) *The Acts of the Apostles* (New York).

Gärtner, B. (1955) *The Areopagus Speech and Natural Revelation* (Uppsala).

Geiger, J. (1985) *Cornelius Nepos and Ancient Political Biography* (Stuttgart).

Goodman, M. (2007) *Rome and Jerusalem: the Clash of Ancient Civilizations* (London).

Goodspeed, E. J. (1937) *An Introduction to the New Testament* (Chicago).

Green, J. B. (1997) *The Gospel of Luke* (Grand Rapids).

Haenchen, E. (1971) *The Acts of the Apostles* (Oxford and Philadelphia).

Harlé, P. (1977–8) 'Un "private joke" de Paul dans le livre des Actes (xxvi.28–29)', *NTS* 24: 527–33.

Harrison, S. J. (2000) *Apuleius: A Latin Sophist* (Oxford).

Hartog, F. (1988) *The Mirror of Herodotus: the Representation of the Other in the Writing of History* (Berkeley, Los Angeles, and London); trans. by J. Lloyd of Hartog (1980).

Hemer, C. J. (1974) 'Paul at Athens: a Topographical Note', *NTS* 20: 341–2.

Hengel, M. (2000) *The Four Gospels and the One Gospel of Jesus Christ: An Investigation of the Collection and Origin of the Canonical Gospels* (London and Harrisburg, Pa.).

Holtzmann, H. J. (1873) 'Lucas und Josephus', *ZWT* 16: 85–93.

Hultgren, A. J. (2003) 'The Pastorals', in Dunn (2003b) 141–55.

Hunter, A. (2006) *Wisdom Literature* (London).

Johnson, L. T. (1991) *The Gospel of Luke* (Collegeville, Minn.).

Johnson, L. T. (1992) *The Acts of the Apostles* (Collegeville, Minn.).

Johnson, L. T. (1999) *The Writings of the New Testament: An Interpretation*, revised edition (London and Minneapolis).

Kindstrand, J. F. (1976) *Bion of Borysthenes: a Collection of the Fragments with Introduction and Commentary* (Uppsala).

Kirk, G. S., J. E. Raven, and M. Schofield, edd. (1984) *The Presocratic Philosophers*[2] (Cambridge).

Klauck, H.-J. (2000) *Magic and Paganism in Early Christianity: the World of the Acts of the Apostles* (Edinburgh).

Kloppenborg, J. S. (1992) '*Exitus clari uiri*: the Death of Jesus in Luke', *Toronto Journal of Theology* 8: 106–20.

Knox, J. (1942) *Marcion and the New Testament: An Essay in the Early History of the Canon* (Chicago).

König, J. (2006) 'The Cynic and Christian Lives of Lucian's *Peregrinus*', in McGing and Mossman (2006) 227–54.

Krenkel, M. (1894) *Josephus und Lucas: Der schriftstellerische Einfluss des jüdischen Geschichtschreibers auf den christlichen* (Leipzig).

Kurz, W. S. (1985) 'Luke 22:14–38 and Greco-Roman and Biblical Farewell Addresses', *JBL* 104: 289–305.

de Labriolle, P. (1950) *La réaction païenne: étude sur la polémique antichrétienne du I$^{er}$ au VI$^e$ siècle*[11] (Paris).

Lane Fox, R. (1986) *Pagans and Christians* (Hardmondsworth; New York, 1987).

Lane Fox, R. (1991) *The Unauthorized Version: Truth and Fiction in the Bible* (London and New York).

MacDonald, D. R. (2003) *Does the New Testament Imitate Homer? Four Cases from the Acts of the Apostles* (New Haven).

Maddox, R. (1982) *The Purpose of Luke-Acts* (Edinburgh).

Malherbe, A. J. (1989) *Paul and the Popular Philosophers* (Minneapolis).

Maltby, R. (1991) *A Lexicon of Ancient Latin Etymologies* (Leeds).

Marshall, I. H. (1980) *The Acts of the Apostles: An Introduction and Commentary* (Leicester and Grand Rapids).

Mason, S. (1995) 'Chief Priests, Sadducees, Pharisees and Sanhedrin in Acts', in Bauckham (1995b) 115–77.

Mason, S. (2005c) *Josephus and the New Testament*² (Peabody, Mass.).

McGing, B. (2006) 'Philo's Adaptation of the Bible in his *Life of Moses*', in id. and Mossman (2006) 117–140.

McGing, B. and J. Mossman, edd. (2006) *The Limits of Ancient Biography* (Swansea).

Moles, J. L. (1985) 'Cynicism in Horace *Epistles* I', *PLLS* 5: 33–60 [above, Ch. 14].

Moles, J. L. (1993) 'Truth and Untruth in Herodotus and Thucydides', in C. Gill and T. P. Wiseman, edd., *Lies and Fiction in the Ancient World* (Exeter and Austin) 88–121 [vol. 2, Ch. 49].

Moles, J. L. (1995) 'Dio Chrysostom, Greece, and Rome', in D. C. Innes, H. Hine, and C. Pelling, edd., *Ethics and Rhetoric: Classical Essays for Donald Russell on his Seventy-Fifth Birthday* (Oxford) 177–92 [above, Ch. 7].

Moles, J. L. (1996a) 'Cynic Cosmopolitanism', in R. B. Branham and M.-O. Goulet-Cazé, edd., *The Cynics* (Berkeley and Los Angeles) 105–20 [above, Ch. 16].

Moles, J. L. (1996b) 'Herodotus Warns the Athenians', *PLLS* 9: 259–84 [vol. 2, Ch. 52].

Moles, J. L. (1999) 'ΑΝΑΘΗΜΑ ΚΑΙ ΚΤΗΜΑ: the Inscriptional Inheritance of Ancient Historiography', *Histos* 3: 27–69 [vol. 2, Ch. 54].

Moles, J. L. (2000) 'The Cynics', in Rowe and Schofield (2000) 415–34 [above, Ch. 17].

Moles, J. L. (2005) 'The Thirteenth Oration of Dio Chrysostom: Complexity and Simplicity, Rhetoric and Moralism, Literature and Life', *JHS* 125: 112–38 [above, Ch. 10].

Moles, J. L. (2006a) 'Cynic Influence upon First-century Judaism and Early Christianity?', in McGing and Mossman (2006) 89–116 [above, Ch. 20].

Moles, J. L. (2006b) 'Jesus and Dionysus in *The Acts of the Apostles* and Early Christianity' *Hermathena* 180: 65–104 [above, Ch. 21].

Moles, J. L. (2011) 'Jesus the Healer in the Gospels, the Acts of the Apostles, and Early Christianity', *Histos* 5: 117–82 [above, Ch. 23].

Moloney, F. J. (1998) *The Gospel of John* (Collegeville, Mn.).

Morgan, R. (1994) 'Which Was the Fourth Gospel? The Order of the Gospels and the Unity of Scripture', *JSNT* 54: 3–28.

Nock, A. D. (1953) 'Review of Dibelius, *Aufsätze zur Apostelgeschichte*', *Gnomon* 25: 497–506; repr. in id., *Essays on Religion and the Ancient World*, ed. Z. Stewart (Harvard and Oxford, 1972) 821–32.

Norden, E. (1913) *Agnostos Theos: Untersuchungen zur Formen-Geschichte religiöser Rede* (Leipzig).

O'Neill, J. C. (1970) *The Theology of Acts in its Historical Setting*² (London).

Parsons, M. C. (1987) *The Departure of Jesus in Luke-Acts: The Ascension Narratives in Context* (Sheffield).

Pathrapankal, J. (1979) 'Christianity as a "Way" according to the Acts of the Apostles', in Kremer (1979) 533–9.

Pelling, C. B. R. (1980) 'Plutarch's Adaptation of his Source Material', *JHS* 100: 127–40; repr. in id., *Plutarch and History: Eighteen Studies* (London and Swansea, 2002) 91–116.
Ramsay, W. M. (1895) *St. Paul the Traveller and the Roman Citizen* (New York and London).
Robbins, V. K. (1978) 'By Land and By Sea: The We-Passages and Ancient Sea Voyages', in C. H. Talbert, ed., *Perspectives on Luke-Acts* (Macon, Ga. and Edinburgh) 215–42.
Rowe, C. and M. Schofield, edd. (2000) *The Cambridge History of Greek and Roman Political Thought* (Cambridge).
Runia, D. T. (1986) *Philo of Alexandria and the Timaeus of Plato*² (Leiden).
Russell, D. A., ed. (1992) *Dio Chrysostom: Orations VII, XII, XXXVI* (Cambridge).
Rydbeck, L. (1967) *Fachprosa, vermeintliche Volkssprache und Neues Testament: zur Beurteilung der sprachlichen Niveauunterschiede im nachklassischen Griechisch* (Lund).
Ryken, L., J. C. Wilhoit, and T. Longman III, edd. (1998) *Dictionary of Biblical Imagery* (Downers Grove, Ill.).
Sampley, J. P. (2003) *Paul in the Greco-Roman World: A Handbook* (Harrisburg, Pa.).
Sandnes, K. O. (1993) 'Paul and Socrates: The Aim of Paul's Areopagus Speech', *JSNT* 50: 13–26.
Schürer, E. (1973) *The History of the Jewish People in the Age of Jesus Christ (175 BC–AD 135)*, vol. 1, new English version revised by G. Vermes and F. Millar (Edinburgh).
Seaford, R. (2006) *Dionysos* (London and New York).
Shiner, W. T. (1995) *Follow Me! Disciples in Markan Rhetoric* (Atlanta).
Sorabji, R. (2000) *Emotions and Peace of Mind: From Stoic Agitation to Christian Temptation* (Oxford).
Steele, E. S. (1984) 'Luke 11.37–54: A Modified Hellenistic Symposium?', *JBL* 103: 379–94.
Sterling, G. E. (1992) *Historiography and Self-Definition: Josephos, Luke-Acts, and Apologetic Historiography* (Leiden).
Sterling, G. E. (2001) 'Mors Philosophi: the Death of Jesus in Luke', *HTR* 94: 383–402.
Stinton, T. C. W. (1975) '*Hamartia* in Aristotle and Greek Tragedy', *CQ* 25: 221–54; repr. in id., *Collected Papers on Greek Tragedy* (Oxford, 1990) 143–86.
Stowers, S. K. (1984) 'Social Status, Public Speaking, and Private Teaching: the Circumstances of Paul's Preaching Activity', *NT* 26: 59–82.
Stowers, S. K. (2001) 'Does Pauline Christianity Resemble a Hellenistic Philosophy?', in Engberg-Pederson (2001) 89–102.
Streeter, B. L. (1930) *The Four Gospels: A Study of Origins* (London).
Stuckenbruck, L. T. (2003) 'Colossians and Philemon', in Dunn (2003b) 116–132.
Talbert, C. H. (1974) *Literary Patterns, Theological Themes, and the Genre of Luke-Acts* (Missoula).

Tannehill, R. C. (1990) *The Narrative Unity of Luke-Acts: A Literary Interpretation. Volume 2: The Acts of the Apostles* (Minneapolis).

Taylor, J. (2006) 'The Acts of the Apostles as Biography' in McGing–Mossman (2006) 77–88.

Thompson, M. M. (2006) 'The Gospel According to John', in S. C. Barton, ed., *The Cambridge Companion to the Gospels* (Cambridge) 182–200.

Thornton, C.-J. (1991) *Der Zeuge des Zeugen: Lukas als Historiker der Paulusreisen* (Tübingen).

Tobin, T. H. (1992) 'Logos', *ABD* IV.348–56.

Townsend, J. T. (1984) 'The Date of Luke-Acts', in C. H. Talbert, ed., *Luke-Acts: New Perspectives from the Society of Biblical Literature Seminar* (New York) 47–62.

Tueller, M. (1992) 'Literary Representations of the New God: Jesus and Dionysus' (B.A. thesis, Harvard).

Turner, C. H. (1925) 'Marcan Usage: Notes Critical and Exegetical on the Second Gospel V. The Movements of Jesus and His Disciples and the Crowd', *JTS* 26: 225–40.

Tyson, J. (1992) *Images of Judaism in Luke-Acts* (Columbia, S.C.).

van der Horst, P. W. (1989) 'The Altar of the "Unknown God" in Athens (Acts 17:23) and the Cult of "Unknown Gods" in the Hellenistic and Roman Periods', *ANRW* II.18.2: 1426–56.

Wallace, R. and W. Williams (1993) *The Acts of the Apostles: a Companion* (London and New York).

Walzer, R. (1949) *Galen on Christians and Jews* (Oxford).

Williams, G. (1980) *Figures of Thought in Roman Poetry* (New Haven).

Winston, D. (1985) *Logos and Mystical Theology in Philo of Alexandria* (Cincinnati).

Winter, B. W. (1996) 'On Introducing Gods to Athens: An Alternative Reading of Acts 17:18–20', *Tyndale Bulletin* 47: 71–90.

Witherington, B. (1998) *The Acts of the Apostles: a Socio-rhetorical Commentary* (Grand Rapids and Cambridge).

Wright, N. T. (2003) *The Resurrection of the Son of God* (London).

Wright, N. T. (2008) *Acts for Everyone*, 2 vols. (London and Louisville, Ky.).

CHAPTER 29

# What's in a Name? Χριστός/χρηστός and χριστιανοί/χρηστιανοί in the First Century AD

## 1   Introduction: Current Scholarship*

This matter of nomenclature belongs within large and contentious debate about: the cohesiveness of 'the Jesus movement' (or 'movements') and of 'Christianity'; the legitimacy of that latter term; the relationship between 'Christianity' (or 'Christianities') and Judaism (or 'Judaisms'); and Roman 'persecution' of Christianity. Throughout, I try to frame discussion in ways that take account of these debates but are not paralysed by them. Further, paradoxically, my material offers ammunition both to those who wish to generalise about 'Christianity' and to those who seek to demythologise it (who could infer that 'Christianity' was invented on the basis of a whole series of puns). My initial focus is restricted to a matter of language. But it will rapidly become clear that this matter has itself huge implications.

The spelling variations between Χριστός and Χρηστός, their cognate forms, and Latin equivalents have been extensively studied and solid conclusions have been reached,[1] which I briefly summarise, in so far as they affect this paper, highlighting outstanding disagreements.

The eta form of the name is far the commoner pagan usage. It is of course technically incorrect, which can always be noted, by informed pagans[2] as well as by Christians.[3] Nevertheless, Christian acknowledgement of that form, at least from the second century, is considerable and varied.

---

* Versions were given at the Durham New Testament Seminar on 1st December 2008, the Newcastle Classics Seminar on 7th October 2009, and the Manchester Erhardt Seminar on 12th November 2009. I thank: all who commented on those occasions; Professor Tony Woodman and Dr James Wilberding for many conversations; Dr Livia Capponi, Professor Adrian Gratwick, and Mr Jerry Paterson for comments on an early draft; and Dr Todd Lutz for other kindness. All translations are mine.
1  Lipsius (1873); Blass (1895); Fuchs (1950) Angello (1953); Gibson (1978); Karrer (1991), esp. 70–87; *TLL*, Supp. Onomast. II s.v. 'Christus' 409–12; Edwards (1991); Hengel (1995); Levinskaya (1996) 174–82; Van Voorst (2000); Wright (2003) 554–7; Harris (2005); Cappelletti (2006) 69–79; Pachoumi (2007) 59–60; Parsons (2007); Dunn (2009); MacCullough (2009).
2  E.g. Tac., *Ann.* 15.44.2–3 (below, p. 948).
3  Tertull. *Apol.* 3.5; *ad nat.* 1.3; Lact. *Inst. Div.* 1.4.

Church Fathers pun on it, by (among other things) applying to 'Christos' the *adjective* χρηστός. The root meaning of this very common adjective[4] is 'useful' (~ χράομαι), with derived implications such as 'good', 'kind', 'helpful', 'generous', and 'profitable'. It can be applied to the divine, alike by pagans, Jews, and Christians, and in power relations it can be applied both to the holders of power (God/gods, rulers, masters, as 'benevolent', 'merciful', 'generous', etc.) and to those affected by it (subjects and slaves, as 'loyal', 'useful', etc.). It thus fits easily within discussion of reciprocity relationships. It is also often applied to the dead, especially in funerary addresses, including Diaspora Jewish ones.[5] The adjective generated a common name, Χρηστός in Greek, 'Chrestus' in Latin, which is found at all social levels, including among slaves.[6] That, as noun or adjective, it could be applied to slaves sometimes seems to have caused chariness about applying it to the free.[7] In the Greek of our period, eta and iota were pronounced the same—as *ee* (ī)[8]—and could therefore be interchangeable even in writing, which, when taken with other factors (to be discussed), made it easy both for pagans to refer to Χριστός and Χριστιανοί as Χρηστός and Χρηστιανοί and for Church Fathers to pun on Χριστός/χρηστός. It is true that in Latin the case ought to be different, for, though the first syllables of both 'Chrestus'/'Chrestiani' and 'Christus'/'Christiani' are long, they should not sound the same.[9] Nevertheless, the existence of the 'e' forms in Latin has to be explained by analogy with the Greek eta forms, which were clearly sometimes 'felt', and the relevant Latin vowels were presumably sometimes actually pronounced 'Greek-style' as 'ee'.

Some later Christians even themselves adopted the eta forms, especially on inscriptions but also in literary texts. Some Christians used both forms in inscriptions, sometimes even adjacently. Such variation often appears to mean nothing (other than that both spellings were available and common). But Christian adoption of the eta form can sometimes have active force: to dilute Jesus' Jewishness, by subtracting the notion of Messiahship inherent in the original term,[10] or to point positive theological reflections.[11]

The overall picture, then, at least from the mid-second century, is rather mixed.

4    LSJ, s.v.; Moulton (1977) 438.
5    Cf., e.g., Williams (1998) 126; Capponi (2007) 149, 178–88, 189–97.
6    Capponi (2010) 221–3.
7    Braun (1994) 41.
8    {Horrocks (1997) 102ff. for spoken *koinē* in the Roman period.}
9    As Tert. *Apol.* 3.5 notes ('when it is badly pronounced "Chrestianus" by you').
10   Edwards (1991) 233.
11   Pachoumi (2007) 59–60.

Scholars generally seem to regard the first century as different, though from a range of different perspectives. Distinguished scholars of early Christianity such as Rowland, Fredriksen, Humphries, Knight, MacCullough, Brent, and Green evidently see no real problem, in as much as they either simply do not discuss the matter, or accord it no greater significance than variation of orthography or misspelling.[12] For Peter Parsons, while there may be a problem, there is no usable evidence: 'how far early Christians understood the distinction, we cannot say'.[13] For Martin Karrer, the problem is slight: 'die neutestamentlichen Hinweise blieben auch damit schmal'.[14] There is, indeed, a handful of cases in the New Testament where most commentators (especially recent ones) see punning, but it is very small, and at the time of writing there remain many fine scholars who explain the three New Testament cases of manuscript variation between the two forms and the controversial Tacitean and Suetonian notices in simple terms of unproblematic 'confusion' or spelling 'error'.

At the most basic level, there is indeed spelling 'confusion' or 'error', but that is the beginning of the matter, not the end. I shall argue that the name of 'Christ' (however spelled) was *inevitably* and *multiply* contested *from the 30s of the first century onwards*, and I shall tell a story about names, power, defamation, reclamation, pedagogy, and cultural appropriation in the earliest period of Christianity, a period which, on this analysis, will emerge as in essential respects the most formative period of Christianity. This last notion is of course itself highly controversial, but my material will support the claims of Larry Hurtado that Jesus was divinised from the very start of Christianity.[15]

When above I say 'story', I mean something not absolutely provable, something with elements of imaginative reconstruction, or *muthos*. This 'story' is a stitch-work from various materials: a selective account (surely nowadays substantially unproblematic) of some of the many ways in which punning and naming work in the ancient world; a preliminary potted history of the names in question that combines known facts with inferences about how 'things must have been'; the puns on 'Christ' made by the Church Fathers; and a survey of New Testament puns. These materials should have interlocking force. The selective account illustrates the ubiquity and range of the phenomenon and the *possibilities* for our case. The history of the relevant names suggests certain key issues; these seem to be reflected also in the survey. The Patristic punning

---

12   E.g., Rowland (1985); Fredriksen (1988); Humphries (2006); Brent (2009).
13   Parsons (2007) 203.
14   Karrer (1991) 78.
15   Hurtado (1999/2000); (2003a); (2003b); (2005); a more 'yes and no' position in Dunn (2010).

seems to echo punning already present in the New Testament and in pagan writers writing about the first century. Indeed, most of the things I say about the New Testament can be found in one form or another in the Church Fathers, but scholars do not seem to retroject this material or its insights into the first century. The Patristic punning has already been adequately (though far from exhaustively) documented, and excellently discussed, by Blass, as long ago as 1895, and, much more recently, by Karrer in his important 1991 monograph. Nevertheless, I shall here briefly summarise it by way of further adumbration of the possibilities within the New Testament.

## 2 Punning and Naming in the Ancient World[16]

Punning is rife both in the Jewish and Gentile worlds, and both orally and in writing, and at both the most popular and the most sophisticated levels. One of its many forms is appeal to etymology and to different etymologies, including invention of etymologies. Another is substitution of synonyms (which is also part of Jewish pesher technique).[17] Thus in Livy 6.1.10 'quae … ad sacra pertinebant a pontificibus maxime ut religione obstrictos haberent multitudinis animos suppressa', the use of 'obstringere' = 'bind' alludes punningly to the popular derivation of *religio* from *re-ligare*.[18] Another is punning on words that sound identical or very similar but have very different meanings (thus, hearing of Herod's execution of his sons, Augustus quipped, 'it is better to be Herod's pig than his son').[19]

Intellectual interest in punning is found among sophists, rhetoricians, grammarians, and philosophers.[20] One particular focus was double-ness or the play of opposites. The Presocratic philosopher Heraclitus noted that *bios* meant both 'bow' and 'life', the one dealing death to the other (21 B 48 D–K {= D 53 L–M}), the Cynic Diogenes that the high Homeric phrase 'he lashed [the horses] to make them go' also meant 'he lashed an olive' (D.L. 6.55). Licentious Roman youths heard Sallust's portentous 'bellum patrare' ('prosecute a war')

---

16   Huge bibliography, e.g.: Woodhead (1928); Ahl (1985); Maltby (1991); O'Hara (1996); Lateiner (2005); Irwin (2007); Moles (2011).
17   See, e.g., Vermes (2000) 133ff., 230f.
18   Kraus (1994) 92.
19   Macrobius gives it in Latin, though the pun is in Greek: *Sat.* 2.4.11: *melius est Herodis porcum* [ὗς] *esse quam filium* [υἱός].
20   Cf., e.g., Plato's *Cratylus*.

as 'do a pretty boy' (Quint. 8.3.44). Rhetoricians admired the repetition of the same word or term in pointedly different senses.[21]

A phenomenon distinct from punning but allied to it is the intense juxtaposition of similar sounds in order to suggest causal patterns (which I shall call 'sonic associativeness'). Thus at Livy 6.2.9 'imperator terroris intulerat', the 'cluster of similar sounds reinforces the connection between the general and the fear he inspires'.[22]

Names are words: the Greek *onoma* covers both categories; while 'name' does not seem to be generally recognised among the numerous meanings of *logos*,[23] the *verb lego* can certainly mean 'to name',[24] and it is difficult to see why this should not also be a possible implication of *logos*.[25] Hymns place tremendous emphasis on divine names, their powers and implications. Names may have magic power. Ancient names are 'speaking names'. They are religiously, morally, and interpretatively telling: Oedipus, who does not *know where* he is, whose *foot*—indeed, penis—is *swollen*; Pentheus, born for grief; Odysseus—who knows (*oida*), who travels (*hodos*), who hates and is hated (*odussomai*); Achilles—the *barley* man who fills the battle-*fields* with blood. In Roman contexts, such puns may be bilingual: Aeneas who is 'terrible',[26] 'Nero' who is 'fortis',[27] Parthenope who evokes Virgil 'the virgin'.[28] The great pagan gods were often polyonomous: even their individual names often interpreted as polysemous. By contrast, the accusative form [Δία] of the greatest Greek god, Zeus, could be used as a transcendental signifier (διά), signifying 'Zeus' as cause of everything and through and outside time.[29]

Individuals may have two quite different names (Paris/Alexander; Pyrrhus/Neoptolemus). Identity or similarity of name may highlight opposition: Hera hates Heracles. Names may be palindromic: Roma/amor. Names may be linked anagrammatically: Camena/Maecenas.[30] Philosophers made capital out of their names (Aristotle, whose 'telos' was 'the best'; Diogenes, 'son of Zeus'; Epicurus, 'the helper', Horatius, man 'of the hour', etc.).[31]

---

21   {For *distinctio* see Lausberg (1998) §§660–2.}
22   Kraus (1994) 99.
23   *LSJ* s.v.; Moulton (1977) 249.
24   *LSJ* s.v. 16.
25   See p. 971 below.
26   Virg. *Aen.* 12.947 (*terribilis* ~ αἰνός), with du Quesnay ap. Bowie, et al. (1977) 139.
27   {Maltby (1991) 409.}
28   Virg. *Geo.* 4.563 with *Vita Donati* 36; and cf. vol. 2, Ch. 73.
29   Hes. *Theog.* 465 with punning on Δίος and διά: see Moles (2000) 192 {above, p. 210} with n. 17.
30   {Hor. *Epist.* 1.1.1–3 with Oberhelman–Armstrong (1995) 241 n. 42.}
31   Reckford (1997).

Names also have social and political significance. They both confer identity and affect reputation, including *Nachleben*: in Greek and Latin, as in English, the word 'name' means both 'identifier' and 'repute'. Names can be bestowed honorifically (*Augustus* Caesar, Jesus *Christ*), but name-calling is *also* part of philosophical, social, and political invective. It is often crude: Cleisthenes of Sicyon renamed the three tribes that were not his own 'pigmen', 'donkeymen', and 'swinemen' (Hdt. 5.68.1). It could also sometimes be sophisticated: to call Brutus and Cassius 'Pompeiani' was to impute narrow partisanship—even absurd partisanship, since Pompey himself was dead. Proper names themselves can attract scorn: Cicero the chick-pea (Plut. *Cic.* 1.4), Tiberius to the Tiber! (Suet. *Tib.* 75.1). Such name-calling belongs within the general rhetorical strategy of hostile appropriation of one's opponent's language. Similarly, writers may appropriate other writers' names: 'Hesiod' 'out-Homers' Homer; Horace 'out-Enniuses' Ennius; Virgil 'out*fights*' 'Calli*machus*'.[32] Suppression or erasure of names could occur within *damnatio memoriae*.[33] But minority or oppressed groups may revalue a negative name. Diogenes turned 'dog' into a boast. And the verdict of history may rehabilitate: in time, no one criticised the philosophical 'descendants' of Socrates for styling themselves 'Socratici', even though Socrates had been executed by the state as impious and as a corrupter. In time, all Romans called themselves 'Christians' or 'Chrestians', even though 'Christ' had been executed by the Roman state as a political subversive.

## 3    The Names in Question

At some time after his death in 30, some of his followers proclaimed 'Jesus Christ' as Lord. In a Greek-language context—the ever more dominant context of early Christianity[34]—both names had strong implications. 'Jesus' as translation of the Jewish name 'Joshua' denoted 'Yahweh is salvation'; the association is fundamental in the New Testament;[35] Jesus as *Greek* name denoted 'healer';[36] this association too is fundamental in the New Testament, has deep theological import (because Jesus' 'healing' has Messianic and eschatological implication), and produces significant puns.[37] 'Christ' identifies Jesus as the

---

32   {See above, n. 28.}
33   E.g., *Senatus Consultum de Cn. Pisone Patre* 82–3, 99–100; Tac. *Ann.* 3.17.4; Flower (2006) 58–9, 116–17.
34   Johnson (1986) 71ff.
35   See Moles (2011) 127 {above, p. 621} with n. 46.
36   See in general Moles (2011).
37   See Moles (2011) §1.5 {above, pp. 621–5}.

Messiah (ὁ Χριστός = the 'anointed one'). But 'Christ' also serves as a functional, specifying 'surname' (Jesus itself being a very common name).[38] From early on, both Jesus and Χριστός became for Christians *sacra nomina* which underpinned the divinisation of Jesus.[39] Later, 'Jesus Christ' could function as a magic name; even in the first century, it can be a sort of sublimated magic name, in that it overpowers the claims of false magicians.[40]

The name or title of Christ, however, had intrinsic, potential negatives. It may well have been raised at Jesus' trial, since it bore on the question: 'Are you king of the Jews?', a question whose own historicity is supported by the 'titulus' on the cross.[41] Certainly, since he was condemned, the name had negative potential alike among the great majority of Jews, who rejected Jesus' claims (whether of Messiahship or divinity), among Romans, and among Greeks. Indeed, for law-observant Jews, because Jesus was hanged from a tree, the name Christos as applied to him was accursed.[42] Of course, in the view of virtually everyone, crucifixion brought shame on the victim, and for centuries many Christians found Christ's crucifixion a source of shame.[43] From all these aspects, the name 'Christ' had negative *potential*, which, of course, does not mean that such 'potential' was *always* and *everywhere activated*.

Given Jesus' own centrality to the Jesus-movement, it was always possible (if other factors came into play) that the followers of 'Christ' would sometime be named after him. According to the author of Acts[44] (whom there seems no reason to disbelieve on the point), the phenomenon first occurred in Syrian Antioch (Acts 11.26). On our chronology, this would be in the early 40s:[45]

> When [Barnabas] had found [Saul], he brought him to Antioch. And it happened to them to be brought together in the church for a whole year and to teach a large crowd, and it was in Antioch that the disciples first operated under the name (χρηματίσαι) of "Christians".

---

38  Christian denial of this (e.g., by Lact. *Div. Inst.* 4.7.4) comes later.
39  Hurtado (2003a) 625–7.
40  Acts 6.16–18, with Klauck (2000) 69–70.
41  Dunn (2003) 651–4.
42  Deuteronomy 27.26; 21.23; Galatians 3.13.
43  E.g., Hebrews 12.2.
44  For whose traditional identification with Luke, companion of Paul, the arguments are (I believe) extremely strong; but the question hardly matters here (readers may take subsequent 'Lukes' as conventional).
45  For an outline of Pauline chronology see Fitzmyer (1998) 139–41; further on this passage, p. 945 below.

This is a more complicated passage than scholars generally realise,[46] but I here analyse it solely in relation to the immediate question.

As all commentators emphasise, the ending -ιανος is the Greek version of the Latin ending -ianus; Syrian Antioch was a Roman colony; and so the very form points to the name having been created in, or for, a Roman context.

Now, when it is used in connection with 'naming', the verb χρηματίζω in its active form can cover both the 'passive' meaning of 'be called' and the 'middle' meaning of 'call oneself'.[47] Almost all commentators take it for granted that one has to choose between these, and almost all then take the verb in the 'passive' sense, and infer—given the Roman context—that this naming was done by Romans. Thus (on this interpretation) 'Christian' denotes 'follower of Christ' as (in the first instance) viewed from a Roman perspective. Mattingly has ingeniously suggested that an additional impulse for the first Christians being so named by Romans was the performance of the *Augustiani* in c.60.[48] But the suggestion is anyway redundant, and the chronology does not fit the first occurrence of the name in the early 40s.

Todd Klutz has made a different inference: Christians were so called by Jews, not within a Jewish context (the 'Roman' form excludes this, and, among themselves Jews who rejected Jesus avoided using the term 'Christ' of him),[49] but in order to single them out to Romans as followers of an enemy of Rome.[50] This equally ingenious suggestion takes account alike of the term's Roman-ness, of its potentially pejorative aspect, of the immediate context (because in the Acts narrative the Antioch item falls within a context of persecution [11.19ff.: scattered ministries after the persecution in Jerusalem; 12.1ff.: persecution by Herod Agrippa I]), of the single other occurrence of the term in Acts, where it is used by Agrippa II before a Roman governor (below), and of the fact that, throughout this narrative, persecution comes mainly from Jews. But the first three considerations apply equally to the usual answer of 'by the Romans', and the last two considerations have little positive force. Acts also contains both generalised and implicit allusions to Roman persecution. The same is true of Luke, which is relevant, because, as most New Testament scholars agree, Luke-Acts constitutes a two-book unity.[51] This very passage, indeed, could be read as including such an allusion (below). Given the multiplicity of 'drivers' of

---

46   See below.
47   LSJ s.v. III.1.
48   Mattingly (1958) 29–31.
49   Recent survey on this subject by Bird (2007) and Rowe (2007).
50   Klutz (2008).
51   Talbert (1974); Talbert–Stepp (2003).

Acts' very complex narrative, the fact that 11.26 is 'sandwiched' between Jewish persecutions creates no presumption of allusion to Jewish persecution here.

Thus far hypotheses based on the 'passive' understanding of χρηματίζω.

Bickerman, however, has argued that χρηματίζω here means 'called themselves'.[52] The argument rests on the claim that in Luke and elsewhere this 'middle' use is far commoner than the 'passive'. The point then is that in a Gentile/Roman context such as Antioch the early followers of Jesus needed to use a different name from such 'internal' self-designations as 'the saints', 'the brothers', etc. The Latinate form indicates not the source of the coinage, but the context in which it was first deployed. Apparent non-use of the term 'Christian' by Christians before the second century (or thereabouts) indicates not alienation from it but rather their sense of propriety about context, and Christians from the second century internalise the usage because the context then is mainly Gentile.

As regards Bickerman's linguistic claim, it is far from clear that the 'middle' usage is much commoner than the 'passive', or certainly so much commoner as to make the interpretation automatically more plausible in any particular passage. It is true that in the previous chapter Luke uses χρηματίζω in a grammatically passive form (ἐχρηματίσθη, 10.22) and that the two usages should be thematically linked (I shall return to this), but this does not help the case that χρηματίζω should here be understood as 'middle' or 'passive'.

In reality, at least at first reading, 'innocent' readers are hardly required to make a determination between 'middle' and 'passive' meanings of this formally active verb. It is presumably true that informed readers might in this respect 'hear' the verb one way or another according to their pre-existing knowledge of who gave the name, but Luke should in the first instance be understood as making a more general point: that this was the first occurrence of the name. Later analysis will show that a 'passive' nuance is part of the meaning of the passage, but a 'passive' of a rather different kind than 'they were first called Christians by the Romans'.

This means, of course, only that Luke's authority here cannot be invoked on one side or the other of the two interpretations: it does not dispose of the historical problem: who did the naming?

Against Bickerman's hypothesis are the non-occurrence of the name in Paul (which is particularly significant, considering his copious use of the name 'Christ') and the further internal evidence of Acts. When any disciples or apostles take their message to Gentiles, they do not use it. When Paul is talking before the Roman governor Festus and the Jewish Agrippa II, he does

---

52   Bickerman (1949).

not himself use the term, preferring the 'internal' Jewish vocabulary of 'the prophets and Moses' (26.22). It is Agrippa who uses the term and he does so at least partly because of the presence of Romans. The hypothesis is yet further weakened by the facts that both the Roman Tacitus explicitly and the Jewish or Christian writer of 1 Peter implicitly attest the term as coming from non-Christians.[53] Tacitus is writing about 110 but dates the invention of the term to 64 or earlier (which is sufficiently compatible with an Antiochene origin in c.40). The date (and authorship) of 1 Peter is disputed, but these questions hardly affect this particular issue. Against Klutz's idea is also the explicit testimony of the Tacitus passage. All told, the Roman provenance of the term should be accepted.

The passage (Acts 26.28) where Luke has Agrippa II use the name in an exchange with Paul, before the Roman governor Festus, in Palestinian Caesarea, in about 60 (on our chronology) also requires consideration:

ἐν ὀλίγῳ με πείθεις Χριστιανὸν ποιῆσαι.

Barrett comments: 'Agrippa's words to Paul are perhaps the most disputed, as regards their construction and meaning, in Acts'.[54] Correspondingly, scholars have taken the use of the term 'Christian' in context very diversely: as neutral, pejorative, or even approbatory.[55] Construal of the Greek inevitably involves one's reading of the whole Festus–Agrippa–Paul encounter, which raises difficult questions, both historical and interpretative. I follow Fridrichsen, Zerwick, and Turner in construing: 'Are you trying to persuade me that you have made me a Christian with so little?'. I also think that the tone is pejorative, and that this implication satisfies: (a) the natural prejudices of the listening Roman governor; (b) the fact that Paul does not use the term, hence Agrippa's use of it belittles Paul's claims by reducing Jesus to the status of a partisan leader; (c) Agrippa's more general 'belittling' of Paul (whose own name, of course, means 'little').[56]

Difficult as this passage is, the *availability* of the term at this time and in this place is, from the other indications, wholly plausible, and the fact that it is used before a Roman governor is at least consistent with Roman provenance. The negative implications, if accepted, are also consistent with everything we have seen so far.

---

53   On 1 Peter see p. 956 below.
54   Barrett (2004) 1169.
55   Barrett (2004) 1169–71.
56   {See above, Ch. 21, pp. 563ff. with n. 52; ch. 28, p. 907.}

Within Rome itself, the name 'Christian' is first unequivocally attested as having been used in the context of the Great Fire of 64 (below), but Suetonius, *Claud.* 25.4, can hardly be evaded, fiercely debated as it remains:[57]

> Iudaeos impulsore Chresto assidue tumultuantis Roma expulit.
>
> The Jews constantly rioting at the instigation of Chrestus he [Claudius] expelled from Rome.

There are various problems with the Latin: (1) is 'constantly rioting' adjectival in relation to the generality of Jews in Rome, or is it defining of a particular category of Jews in Rome? (2) does 'at the instigation of Chrestus' go with 'constantly rioting' or with the main verb?

The wording seems to make 'Chrestus' both alive and present in Rome at the time. How, then, could 'Chresto' be Jesus? This difficulty does not rule out the interpretation, for the simple reason that all interpretations of the passage encounter difficulties. The difficulty can be explained in various ways: Suetonius may be writing carelessly (always possible), or he may be ignorant of basic facts about Jesus (not impossible but not very likely), or he may not realise that this 'Chrestus' is Jesus, if, say, he is working from a police report; it is often observed that the item belongs within a series of what look like 'police measures', and from a contemporary Roman perspective Christian talk of the risen Jesus might naturally imply 'life' in the normal sense of the term. So Luke makes the Roman governor Festus tell Agrippa and Berenice that the chief priests and elders 'had certain enquiries ... with regard to [Paul] concerning ... a certain Jesus who was dead but whom Paul asserted to live' (Acts 25.19).

Like most scholars who have considered the problem, I think 'Chresto' is Jesus, and for the following reasons: (a) 'Chresto' certainly can represent 'Christo' (the form actually here read by the fifth-century Christian Orosius, 7.6.15); (b) the availability, only shortly afterwards, in Neronian Rome, of the 'e' form of 'Christian' is attested by Tacitus; (c) the form 'Chrestiani' in Tacitus must imply a prior 'Chrestus' (see below); (d) equally, here, a political agitator such as Suetonius represents 'Chrestus' as being would certainly have followers, who would naturally be called 'Chrestiani'; (e) public dissension between Jews and 'Christians' in Rome (as in other places) is attested at the right general period both by Paul and by Acts; (f) the Jews with whom Paul stayed in Corinth and who had fallen under this decree seem already to be Christian (Acts 18.2, 18, 26); (g) 'the Jews in general in Rome' did not 'constantly riot' and

---

57  Very select bibliography: Sordi (1995); Cappelletti (2006) 73–81; Capponi (2010) 217ff.

it is completely implausible to suppose that Claudius would attempt a mass expulsion of Jews from Rome or that Suetonius would so represent him, hence Suetonius is talking about a particular category of Jews who constantly rioted, and logic almost seems to demand explanation of why they did so, hence 'at the instigation of Chrestus'; (h) the interlocking word order also points strongly against taking the latter phrase with the main verb; and (i) in both the local and temporal contexts, it seems highly implausible to hypothesise a 'Chrestus' other than Jesus as the catalyst of such constant inter-Jewish rioting.

Thus, within a decade or so of Jesus' death, (some) Romans at Antioch found (some of) Jesus' followers so recognisably different from Jews that they gave them a separate name which identified them through their continuing and recognisable allegiance to their dead leader. The form of the name (Χριστιανοί/Christianoi) indicates a Roman perception of Jesus' followers as a quasi-political group. This is natural, Jesus having been crucified on a political charge. The Acts passage evokes persecution of Christians. All these general associations are evident also in the Suetonius passage, the only difference being that the latter keeps Christians within a Jewish context. This presumably reflects differences between Antioch and Rome in Christian penetration into the Gentile world, but also allows the inference that in the 40s the Roman authorities in Rome still regarded Christianity as a Jewish phenomenon, as indeed the Roman authorities in Judaea and the East did generally in the 40s and 50s.

It follows that, since most Jews, Romans, and Greeks who knew the circumstances held Jesus to have been justly crucified, his followers would have been associated with shame, disgrace, failure, political subversion, and death. To this list, we may add three further well-known associations: that of 'newness';[58] that of otherness, foreignness, even barbarian-ness (according to Tertullian the very name 'Christian' sounded 'barbarous' and 'foreign' to Greeks and Romans); and that of outrageous and illegal misbehaviour (incest and cannibalism). Again, it is unnecessary—and would clearly be implausible—to claim that such associations were always active. The point is rather that they are available associations which become active under certain stimuli.

The next relevant text is Tacitus' notice (*Ann.* 15.44.2–3) about the Neronian persecution of 64, the great richness of which (as of Acts 11.26) has not in general been sufficiently appreciated:

> Ergo abolendo rumori Nero subdidit reos et quaesitissimis poenis adfecit, quos per flagitia inuisos uulgus Chrestianos appellabat. Auctor nominis

---

58  Cf., e.g., Suet. *Nero* 16.2; Tac. *Ann.* 15.44.3, where the origin is dated as *Tiberio imperitante*.

eius Christus Tiberio imperitante per procuratonem Pontius Pilatum supplicio adfectus est. repressaque in praesens exitiabilis superstitio rursum erumpebat, non modo per Iudaeam, originem eius mali, sed per urbem etiam quo cuncta undique atrocia aut pudenda confluunt celebranturque. igitur primum correpti qui fatebantur, deinde indicio eorum multitudo ingens haud proinde in crimine incendii quam odio humani generis conuicti sunt. et pereuntibus addita ludibria, ut ferarum tergis contecti laniatu canum interirent, aut crucibus adfixi aut flammandi, atque ubi defecisset dies in usum nocturni luminis urerentur. hortos suos ei spectaculo Nero obtulerat et circense ludicrum edebat, habitu aurigae permixtus plebi uel curriculo insistens. Unde quamquam aduersus sontis et nouissima exempla meritos miseratio oriebatur, tamquam non utilitate publica sed in saeuitiam unius absumerentur.

Therefore for the abolition of the rumour [that he himself had started the Great Fire] Nero put up defendants and inflicted the most recherché punishments [of death] on those, hated through their shameful acts, whom the vulgar called 'Chrestiani'. The author of that name Christus was afflicted with the punishment [of death] during the rule of Tiberius through the agency of the procurator Pontius Pilate. And the pernicious superstition, suppressed for the present, was breaking out again, not only through Judaea, the origin of that evil, but also through the city where all atrocious and shameful things from everywhere flow together and become numerous. First of all, then, were arrested those who confessed, then, by their evidence, a huge multitude were convicted not so much on the charge of incendiarism as for hatred of the human race. And mockings were added to them as they died, as that they perished, covered in the hides of wild beasts, through the laceration of dogs, or fixed and to be burned on crosses, or, when day had faded, that they were torched for the use of night lighting. Nero had offered his own gardens for that spectacle and was giving a circus game, mixing with the people in the garb of a charioteer or standing on his chariot. Whence there originated pity, even towards the guilty and those who merited the most extreme exemplary punishments, as though they were despatched not in accordance with public utility but for the savagery of one man.

Most Tacitean scholars nowadays rightly consider the 'Chrestianos' of the Medicean manuscript to be the original and correct reading, which means that the 'Christianos' of the other manuscripts is a misguided 'normalisation' and

Tacitus is 'tacitly' correcting what he regards as a vulgar misnomer.⁵⁹ But how is the name being understood by 'the vulgar'? Since the *-ianus* ending denotes 'follower of "x"', they must be taking the name as deriving from the group's ultimate leader, whom they understand to have been called 'Chrestus' and to have been a quasi-political figure. In this respect, the Tacitus notice seems consistent both with Suetonius, *Claudius* 25.4, and Acts 11.26. One could automatically assume that 'the vulgar' know that this proper name means 'good', but in fact the context proves this. As Hommel notes,⁶⁰ when 'the vulgar' call Nero's victims 'Chrestians', there is an ironic point: those who 'are *hated* through their *shameful acts*' (presumably, the usual alleged cannibalism and incest) are called 'Goodies' ('Chrestiani'). The so-called 'Goodies' are in fact 'baddies'. Thus there is an immediate bilingual play here between 'flagitia' (Latin) and 'Chrestianos' (Latin, but with its Greek adjectival meaning understood). Such 'street' bilingualism is quite at home in Roman popular culture.⁶¹

But there is more. Aristotle (F 592 R) quotes the phrase χρηστὸν ποιεῖν (lit. 'make [someone] good') from a treaty between Sparta and Tegea, and interprets it as a euphemism for 'kill'. This interpretation is accepted by Plutarch (*Quaest. Rom.* 277B–C *Quaest. Graec.* 292B). It is also accepted in Liddell and Scott, s.v. χρηστός. In their Supplement, they cite Hesychius for the sense οἱ καταδεδικασμένοι ('condemned'), and therefore prefer the sense, in the Aristotelian fragment, of 'killable'.⁶² It is true that Felix Jacoby argued that in the treaty the phrase 'make good' meant 'make a citizen', but his arguments were powerfully controverted by Thomas Braun.⁶³ The broad Aristotelian/Plutarchean interpretation should stand. From our point of view, the difference between 'dead' and 'killable' does not much matter. Although the passages cited seem to constitute the sum total of the direct evidence for the usage χρηστὸν ποιεῖν as = 'kill' or 'make killable', the usage was evidently understood by the Spartans and Tegeans concerned, by Aristotle, by Plutarch, his circle, and his readers, and by Hesychius, so it is sufficiently well established. It can indeed be derived from first principles: χρηστός can undoubtedly *refer to* the dead, and ποιεῖν plus

---

59   {See, e.g., Koestermann (1968) 253–4.}
60   Hommel (1951).
61   Horsfall {(2003) 48–74.}.
62   {Hesych. s.v. χρηστοί (736 Hansen–Cunningham); reference is to the Supplement of 1968, edited by E. A. Barber; the later Revised Supplement (1996) does not cite Hesychius, but maintains the possibility that 'good' is a euphemism for 'dead'.}
63   Braun (1994).

predicative adjective (= 'make' [someone] 'something') is completely normal Greek.⁶⁴

Karrer, following the main-text Liddell and Scott interpretation of χρηστός as = 'dead' in the Aristotle fragment, sees in the Tacitus passage a malign Roman folk etymology of 'Chrestiani',⁶⁵ and this brilliant suggestion, which seems to have eluded Tacitean scholarship, is surely right: 'a*ffecit* ... *Chrestianos*' and '*Christus* ... ad*fectus* est' gloss χρηστὸν ποιεῖν = 'kill'. Here again, given also 'suppliciis' (characteristically, and certainly here, of the punishment of death),⁶⁶ one recalls the common application of χρηστός to the dead.

Hence, for the Roman mob, 'Chrestus' and 'Chrestianus' spelled not only 'good' and 'bad' but also 'dead', as in American gangster threats: 'you're dead'. 'Chrestus' had not only been put to death, he was always marked for death, and thoroughly deserved it: a poor look-out for any of his followers who became known as Chrestians, because their own 'shameful acts' merited death. This etymology of 'Christian' and 'Christ' involves an even more complex bilingual pun than 'good'/'bad'.

Suetonius, *Nero* 16.2 now also becomes relevant:

> Affecti suppliciis Christiani, genus hominum superstitionis nouae ac maleficae.

> There were afflicted with punishments [of death] the Christians, a race of men belonging to a new and evil-inflicting superstition.

On the grounds both of Suetonian usage and of later writers' usage, Bradley convincingly argued for 'affecti' as the right reading here instead of 'afflicti'.⁶⁷

But the matter goes beyond style. Suetonius' 'affecti suppliciis Christiani' is very close to Tacitus' 'poenis affecit ... Chrestianos ... Christus ... supplicio adfectus est'. Further, while 'maleficae' may well allude to the specific accusation of witchcraft that was commonly made against Christians,⁶⁸ there is certainly interaction between 'a*ffecti* suppliciis' and 'male*ficae*': the Christians '*do* bad things' and are themselves accordingly '*done* with punishments'. The contrast in Tacitus between the Christians' alleged 'goodness' and their actual 'badness' is surely also latent here. So also (surely) is the malign pun on 'Christians'

---

64 LSJ s.v. ποιέω III.
65 {Karrer (1991) 82.}
66 *OLD* s.v. *supplicium* 3b.
67 Bradley (1972).
68 Bradley (1978) 105.

being 'made good', that is, punished by 'death' for their 'badness'. As for the relationship of this passage to the Tacitean passage on Nero, either Suetonius is directly working from Tacitus, or he provides further evidence for popular bilingual punning on the name 'Christian', or both. The first possibility, likely, I think, but not formally provable, need not entail abandonment of the identification, in *Claudius* 25.4, of 'Chresto' as Jesus (if Suetonius is writing carelessly, or if he does not himself make the identification). Cf. also Orosius 7.7.10 (imitating Suetonius): 'primus Romae *Christianos suppliciis* et *mortibus adfecit*'.

The Tacitus passage, then, shows pagans engaging in complex and polemical bilingual punning on Chrestiani and Chrestus as early as 64. The Suetonius Nero passage reinforces this picture. The Tacitus passage also shows that though some Romans knew of Christianity's Jewish origins, by 64 'Chrestians'/'Christians' in Rome were generally regarded as distinct from Jews.

Further, since Chrestos/Chrestus was a common slave name and Christ and Christians could be associated with political disturbances, there were contexts, as, surely, in these very passages from Tacitus and Suetonius (both *Nero* 16.2 and *Claudius* 25.4), where the names were also regarded as slavish and redolent of Christianity's allegedly low-class origins and continuing low-class recruitment. To this pejorative implication, Christians could have had two responses: they themselves were 'slaves' of Christ on a par with 'slaves of Caesar', in as much as Christ had comparable status to Caesar; but also, and much more radically, 'Christ' as 'slave' or 'servant' subverted worldly hierarchies.

The collocation, in the Tacitus passage, of 'the vulgar' and 'the Goodies', suggests yet another resonance. The adjective 'good' had already been appropriated by aristocrats: the so-called *agathoi* or *boni*. So Christians qua 'Goodies' could also look like pretentious upstarts, the more strikingly for their generally low worldly status.

Almost all of this reflects pagan perspectives, though the Tacitus passage also allows the inference that Roman Christians made a connection between their name and χρηστός in the sense of 'good'—an inference which will be validated in Christian contexts.

Also requiring consideration for this same period is the equally controversial passage from the early fifth century Christian historian, Sulpicius Severus (*Chronica* 2.30.6–8):

> Fertur Titus adhibito consilio prius deliberasse, an templum tanti operis euerteret. Etenim nonnullis uidebatur, aedem sacratam ultra omnia mortalia illustrem non oportere deleri, quae seruata modestiae Romanae testimonium, diruta perennem crudelitatis notam praeberet. At contra alii et Titus ipse euertendum in primis templum censebant, quo plenius

Iudaeorum et Christianorum religio tolleretur: quippe has religiones, licet contrarias sibi, isdem tamen ab auctoribus profectas. Christianos ex Iudaeis extitisse: radice sublata stirpem facile perituram. ita Dei nutu accensis omnium animis templum dirutum.

It is reported that Titus, having summoned a council, first weighed up whether he should overturn a temple of such great work. For it seemed to some that a consecrated building illustrious beyond all mortal things should not be destroyed, whose preservation would provide a testimonial of Roman moderation, whose demolition an everlasting mark of their cruelty. But on the other side others—and Titus himself—stated their opinion that the temple above all should be overturned, in order that the religion of the Jews and Christians should be removed more fully: for these religions, granted that they were opposed to each other, nevertheless had set out from the same authors. The Christians had sprung from the Jews: the root deported, the branch would easily perish. In this way, by the nod of God, the minds of all fired up, the temple was demolished.

As most scholars agree, the arguments for Tacitean provenance (from the lost part of the *Histories*) are very strong,[69] and disagreement nowadays largely focuses on the questions of whether this account is to be preferred to Josephus' (where Titus wants to preserve the Temple);[70] of how close Sulpicius is to Tacitus, both in factual detail and in style; and of the degree of Christianisation of the Tacitean original: Sulpicius' Christian theological 'conclusion' cannot be Tacitean (though there could of course have been a pagan equivalent); most think (rightly, I believe) that Tacitus would have used 'superstitio' rather than 'religio'; and—crucially for us—many doubt the very mention of Christians. Further complications come with Orosius' slightly later account, which, while broadly consonant, proffering the same theological 'conclusion', and (surely) showing direct use of Sulpicius among other sources, omits the mention of the Christians and also differs in details (7.9.4–6):

quod [templum] tamen postquam in potestatem redactum opere atque antiquitate suspexit, diu deliberauit utrum tamquam incitamentum hostium incenderet an in testimonium uictoriae reseruaret. sed Ecclesia Dei iam per totum orbem uberrime germinante, hoc tam quam effetum ac uacuum nullique usui bono commodo arbitrio Dei auferendum

---

69  The connection was first made by Jacob Bernays in 1861.
70  Jos. *BJ* 6.429ff.

fuit. itaque Titus, imperator ab exercitu pronuntiatus, templum in Hierosolymis incendit ac diruit.

which temple, however, after he looked up to it, when it had been reduced into his power, for its work and antiquity, he weighed up for a long time whether he should burn it as a goad of the enemy or preserve for a testimony of victory. But as the Church of God was already most richly germinating through the whole world, the building, exhausted one might say and empty and capable of no good use, should be removed in accordance with the will of God. And so Titus, pronounced imperator by the army, burned the temple in Jerusalem and demolished it.

The question for us is whether the mention, in Sulpicius Severus, of the Christians is post-eventum Christian invention, designed to increase the tally of persecution under the pagan emperors, especially, perhaps, under the brother of one of the great persecutors,[71] or whether it has any historical plausibility in the context of the siege of Jerusalem in 70, and, if so, what implications there are.

Titus and his *consilium* certainly could have had access to good information about Judaism and Christianity, through Jews such as Agrippa II (who was fighting on the Roman side) and Romans such as Cestius. Given Christian origins (and despite some obvious counter-factors), it would not have been unreasonable to connect Christians with the Temple. Some Jerusalem Christians certainly continued to attend the Temple into the 60s. Given Roman knowledge of the role played by Messianic nationalism in the Jewish Revolt and given the availability of information about Christianity, it would also not have been unreasonable to consider the possibility that 'Christians' (as '"Messiah" partisans') were complicit in that revolt. Some of them may indeed have been. Such a possibility might have gained colour from the very recent 'proven' incendiarism of Christians in Rome, the extreme brutality of whose punishment (with all due allowance for Nero's particular contribution) indicates high-level Roman hostility to Christians at this time. That hostility was certainly shared by Tacitus, who, if our item was available to him, would certainly have commemorated it. While scholarly judgements of the quality of the Latin vary, my own view is that the intricacy of the interplay between the various image patterns (surely, appropriately Livy-like)[72] deserves a high appraisal.

---

71   Domitian did persecute Christians: 1 Clemens 1.1 with Barnard (1978) 139–42; and a Domitianic dating remains the mostly likely for *Revelation*: Yarbro Collins (1984) 54–83.
72   Cf. Livy, *praef.* {4–5, 9}; 6.{1.3}.

On the positive side, the mention of the Christians does not actually fit the usual Christian narrative of the destruction of the Temple (arguably, implicit in the Gospels, and certainly, explicit in the Church Fathers)[73]—that it was God's punishment for the Jews' rejection both of Jesus himself and of the subsequent Jesus movement led by Paul, Peter, and others and that Jesus therefore supplanted, or even, in some versions, 'destroyed', the Temple. The mention seems to be part of a different narrative.

What, next, of the analysis of the relationship between Judaism and Christianity? Dunn takes the initial 'the religion[74] [singular] of the Jews and Christians' as one view, the subsequent 'these religions [plural], etc.' as another view, the former being that of those arguing for the destruction of the Temple at the time, the latter being Tacitus' own view.[75] This is clearly wrong, as the accusative and infinitives of the second formulation prove. Rather, there is a process of redefinition. The religion of the Jews and Christians is first presented as singular, but the mention of the two groups allows for a redefinition of that singular religion as two religions, initially on the ground that they are 'opposed to each other'. The relationship between 'one-ness' and 'two-ness' is then explored: they 'had set out from the same authors. The Christians had sprung from the Jews: the root deported, the branch would easily perish'. The explanation thus consists in this 'root and branch' relationship, which has become adversarial but remains fundamental.

This analysis is not negligible. Romans certainly knew that Jews and Christians could be opposed, as illustrated by numerous episodes in the 50s, in a wide range of locations. They must already have known of this in Rome itself (if, among other pieces of evidence, Suetonius, *Claudius* 25.4 glosses 'Christ', and given that in 64 there was no persecution of Jews). And the 'root and branch' relationship was of course fundamental to Christian self-definition. Furthermore, one of the earliest terms for Christians used by Jews was 'Nazareans', which can be understood as 'from Nazareth' or as 'branch people' or, indeed, as both. In short, there is a strong possibility that the passage's organic 'root and branch' imagery embodies an etymological understanding of one of the Christians' best-known names, especially when they were being considered in relation to Judaism, and that this is yet another case of bilingual punning on the phenomenon of 'Christianity'.

---

73  Lampe (1984).
74  That Tacitus (arguably) wrote 'superstitio' and 'superstitiones' does not affect the present argument.
75  Dunn (2009) 58.

Of course, the Romans in general did not intend the destruction of either Judaism or Christianity. But the Flavians sought complete victory over the Jews as over an external enemy and the comprehensive settlement was heavily punitive.[76] Similarly, the characterisation of Christianity as quasi-revolutionary and a consequent Roman desire to 'remove' it fit the general context of the 60s and—still more—the particular stresses of the siege of Jerusalem. In the former context, note Tacitus' wording at *Annales* 15.44.3: 'Nero subdidit reos'. Nothing here requires that the Christians be seen as the ring-leaders of the Jewish revolt: a construction for which there is no (other) evidence.

In short, for our purposes, this passage exhibits: strong elite Roman hostility to Christianity viewed as a quasi-political phenomenon; some knowledge of Christianity and its relationship to Judaism; interest in the meaning of the name of 'Christian'; and sophisticated bilingual punning. I think that the passage, including the mention of the Christians, is authentically Tacitean and that it provides support for some important elements of our analysis so far and for the occurrence of these phenomena at an early date.

Next for consideration is the use of the word 'Christian' in 1 Peter, a letter addressed to Christians in Asia Minor. It is variously dated: from sometime in the 50s (and even as written by Jesus' disciple Peter) to the 80s or 90s, which is the majority modern dating[77] and one which seems to be supported by the relevant passage, precisely on the theme of persecution (4.12–16):

> Beloved, do not make strange at the fiery ordeal which comes among you to test you, (13) but rejoice in so far as you share in the sufferings of Christ, in order that you also may rejoice and be glad in the revelation of his glory. (14) If you are abused in the name of Christ, you are blessed, because the spirit of glory and of God rests upon you. (15) For let none of you suffer as a murderer or a thief or an evil-doer or a meddler. (16) But if as a Christian, let him not be ashamed, but let him glorify God in that name.

Here the name 'Christian' is being used by non-Christians, both as a form of abuse (14) and in contexts of legal persecution (15–16). In these respects the letter is consistent with everything we have seen so far. An important difference is that, though it is non-Christians who use the name 'Christian', when they do so, Christians should accept it as glorifying God. In this sense, the letter marks a half-way house between the first century and the second.

---

76   Recently: Goodman (2007) ch. 12.
77   {Elliott (2000) 134–8.}

So much for the name 'Christian' as used by Romans (in the first century) and by other Gentiles (1 Peter). It was not used—or not at least generally used—by non-Christian Jews, because it might imply their acceptance of Jesus as Messiah: hence other names such as 'the sect of the Nazoraean', etc. If they did use it, it was qualified in some way, by irony or sarcasm, as in Agrippa II's use of the term to Paul (whether historical or *ben trovato*), or by a distancing 'so-called' formula, as in Josephus' allusions to 'Christ' and 'Christians' (if, of course, one accepts their genuineness).[78]

So long as they remained within Judaism, Jesus' followers did not need any distinctively new name and so they called themselves such things as 'the Way', 'the believers', 'the holy ones', 'the disciples', 'the brothers', etc. Nor, as we have seen, did they assume any new name in their dealings with non-Jews. Only in the second century, or possibly slightly earlier, did they begin actively to call themselves 'Christians'. This self-designation is not found in First Clemens in the mid-90s, but occurs in the *Didache* (date disputed but generally now thought to be first century) and Ignatius of Antioch (date: *c*.35–107); whether his place of birth affected his usage is unclear.[79] This change presumably reflects both the futility of disowning a now very well-established name and some version of the 'Parting of the Ways': some Christians now had to admit some sort of more or less decisive separation from (some) Jews. It also, however, attests Christians' recuperation of a name invented by Romans and characteristically negative, a recuperation which might by then risk martyrdom precisely for their being 'Christians'.

Thus both the names Christ and Christian (whether with iota or eta) were on several levels *intrinsically* difficult, and *potentially* even dangerous, for Christians, and this from very early—already in the 30s. These difficulties and dangers increased by stages: once Jewish 'Christians' (so named) had public disputes with fellow-Jews; once Jewish 'Christians' turned increasingly to Gentiles, progressively abandoning the synagogue; once Gentile 'Christians' became involved in disputes with Jews; once 'Christians' became available scapegoats for unscrupulous emperors (Nero, Domitian); once a precedent had been established for legal attacks on 'Christians' *qua* Christians (Domitian, Pliny), whatever the other drawbacks of their name, so that they were persecuted, precisely, *sub nomine Christi*; once Romans and Romanising Jews had hailed Vespasian as that age's Messiah (Jos. *BJ* 6.312–14; Tac. *Hist.* 5.13.2; Suet. *Vesp.* 4.5)—a rival, then, to *Jesus* Christ; and once Romans and others realised

---

[78] Jos. *AJ* 18.63–4.
[79] Ignatius, *Ephes.* 2.4.1: πρέπον οὖν ἐστὶν μὴ μόνον καλεῖσθαι Χριστιανούς, ἀλλὰ καὶ εἶναι; Blass (1895) 469; cf. Van Voorst (2000) 36.

that Christians *qua* Christians could never worship the emperor and no longer enjoyed the Jews' exemption in that regard, having become recognisably distinct from them. Note that one way Christians on trial could save themselves was by cursing the name Christ, just as law-observant Jews had done in relation to Jesus. Again, none of this is to claim that the early 'Christians' faced *systematic persecution*.

Of course, these *potentially* numerous and heavy negatives could be countered by strong positives. The Christian claim that Jesus was the Messiah rested—it seems—on the resurrection. Paradoxically, therefore, the death associations of Chrestos advertised Christianity's central claim. An apparent doubleness can be exploited (provided, of course, that the arguments for the resurrection are sufficiently strong, as to early Christians they were). The death associations of Chrestianoi found concrete expression in Christian martyrdoms; Greek and Roman pagans generally admired heroic deaths; and Christian martyrdoms won the exasperated admiration of some pagans, including philosophers. They could even arouse pity (as in 64). Hence the Gospels and Acts contain various hooks for admirers of philosophical martyrs such as Socrates and some Stoics.[80] The name Chrestos/Chrestus also had a big simple positive, fully recognised by Church Fathers: surely everybody could be persuaded that the good was good, especially since—as already noted—'good' can be a divine epithet in paganism, and the word had a wide range of usefully benevolent associations. Thus when Christians tried to convert pagans devoted to gods often polyonomous and polysemous, the rich polysemous implications of the double name 'Jesus Christ' must have been a positive asset (provided, that is, the negative associations could be erased): far more so than such Jewish names as Yaweh (supposedly unutterable), or the Most High (not restrictedly Jewish), or Adonai (too Jewish). This 'must have' inference can be supported by New Testament passages.

## 4 The Patristic Material[81]

Among Patristic writers the association of 'Christ'/'Christian' with 'good' or 'goodness' is common. Justin Martyr, writing in the mid-second century is one

---

80  See above, Ch. 28.
81  {It is clear from JLM's notes to this section that a final version would have had more examples.}

of many Christian authors to note that the very name constituted grounds for accusation:[82]

> ὅσον γε ἐκ τοῦ κατηγορουμένου ἡμῶν ὀνόματος, χρηστότατοι ὑπάρχομεν.... Χριστιανοὶ γὰρ εἶναι κατηγορούμεθα· τὸ δὲ χρηστὸν μισεῖσθαι οὐ δίκαιον.
>
> since to the extent that it derives from the name we are accused of, we are *chrestotatoi* ... for we are accused of being Christians, but to hate the *chreston* is not just.

Tertullian argues that the pronunciation testified to Christ's goodness:[83]

> Itaque de nominis merito si qui reatus est nominum, si qua accusatio uocabulorum, ego arbitror nullam esse uocabulo aut nomini querellam, nisi cum quid aut barbarum sonat aut infaustum sapit uel inpudicum uel aliter quam enuntiantem deceat aut audientem delectet. haec uocabulorum aut nominum crimina, sicuti uerborum atque sermonum barbarismus est uitium et soloecismus et insulsior figura. Christianum uero nomen, quantum significatio est, de unctione interpretatur. Etiam cum corrupte a uobis Chrestiani pronuntiamur (nam ne nominis quidem ipsius liquido certi estis), sic quoque de suauitate uel bonitate modulatum est.
>
> But when it comes to the merit of a name—if a name faces charges or a word comes under accusation—I reject that a name or a word can give offense, unless of course the word sounds vulgar or implies bad luck or is degrading both for the speaker and the listener. Such words are to be condemned as crude, incorrect, or disgusting. The literal meaning of the word 'Christian', however, is 'an anointing'. Even if you mispronounce the word as 'chrestian'—you are not entirely clear about our name—your pronunciation suggests sweetness and goodness.

Theophilos, on the other hand, puns on the 'Christian' association with 'anointing':[84]

---

82  Just. 1 *Apol.* 4.1, 5.
83  Tert. *ad Nationes* 1.3.8; trans. by Q. Howe.
84  Theoph. *ad Autolycum* 1.12: περὶ δὲ τοῦ σε καταγελᾶν μου, καλοῦντα με χριστιανόν, οὐκ οἶδας ὃ λέγεις. πρῶτον μὲν ὅτι τὸ χριστὸν ἡδύ καὶ εὔχρηστος καὶ ἀκαταγέλαστόν ἐστιν. ποῖον γὰρ πλοῖον δύναται εὔχρηστον εἶναι καὶ σώζεσθαι, ἐὰν μὴ πρῶτον χρισθῇ; ἢ ποῖος πύργος ἢ οἰκία εὔμορφος καὶ εὔχρηστός ἐστιν, ἐπὰν οὐ κέχρισται; τίς δὲ ἄνθρωπος εἰσελθὼν εἰς τόνδε τὸν βίον ἢ ἀθλῶν οὐ

As for your laughing at me and calling me 'Christian' [χριστιανόν], you know not what you are saying. First, because that which is anointed [χριστόν] is sweet and useful [εὔχρηστον], and not subject to ridicule. For what ship can be useful and safe, if it is not first anointed [χρισθῇ, presumably here meaning 'caulked']? Or what tower or house is beautiful and useful when it has not been anointed? And what man, when he enters into this life or is about to wrestle, is not anointed with oil? What work of art, what ornament has beauty unless it is anointed and burnished? The air finally and all that is under heaven is so to say anointed by light and spirit. And do *you* not wish to be anointed with the oil of God? So then it is for the sake of this that we are called Christians: because we are anointed with the oil of God.

Clement of Alexandria argues that the whole life of those who know *christos* is *chrestus*,[85] and that 'those who believe in *Christos* are immediately *chrestoi* and said to be so'.[86]

## 5   The New Testament Material

As we have seen, the general pagan eta usage is based on the fact that iota and eta forms were pronounced the same and, often, written interchangeably. The usual hypothesis is that pagans could make no sense of the iota form, hence, when they heard 'chreestos', they heard it as 'chrestos',[87] which meant things to them (whether as a neutral proper name, a slavish name, a synonym for 'dead' or 'liable to death', a sneer at claimed—but falsified—'goodness', etc).

The general incomprehensibility to pagans of the iota form can certainly be exaggerated. Some pagans, as we have seen, knew that it was the correct form; 'anointing' can be part of certain pagan political, religious, and social practices; some pagans were relatively well-informed about Judaism; Vespasian and his entourage knew about Jewish 'Messiahship', etc., etc. Moreover, the eta form could, as we have seen, have usefully malign implications. Nevertheless, the usual hypothesis must be *broadly* right—as we have seen, there is support for it

---

χρίεται ἐλαίῳ; ποῖον δὲ ἔργον ἢ κόσμιον δύναται εὐμορφίαν ἔχειν, ἐὰν μὴ χρισθῇ καὶ στιλβωθῇ; εἶτα ἀὴρ μὲν καὶ πᾶσα ἡ ὑπ' οὐρανὸν τρόπῳ τινὶ χρίεται φωτὶ καὶ πνεύματι. σὺ δὲ οὐ βούλει χρισθῆναι ἔλαιον θεοῦ; τοιγαροῦν ἡμεῖς τούτου εἵνεκεν καλούμεθα χριστιανοὶ ὅτι χρειόμεθα ἔλαιον θεοῦ.

85   Clem. *Protr.* 12.123: χρηστὸς ὁ σύμπας ἀνθρώπων βίος τῶν Χριστὸν ἐγνωκότων.
86   Clem. *Strom.* 2.4.18: αὐτίκα οἱ εἰς τὸν Χριστὸν πεπιστευκότες χρηστοί τε εἰσὶ καὶ λέγονται.
87   E.g., Blass (1895) 467.

in the Church Fathers. But, much more important for our purposes: if the two forms sounded identical to pagans, they also sounded identical to Christians. Achtemeier is one of very few New Testament scholars to give this any general weight.[88] Add that, as we have seen, puns and name plays are anciently ubiquitous and can articulate power struggles; that the first Christians, committed to the name Christos, had to defend it from various attacks both by pagans and law-observant Jews; that New Testament texts, while written, were 'received' orally/aurally; that even ancient readers generally read aloud; and that in the first century the proportion of Christians who 'thought Greek' constantly increased.

Hence my survey of relevant New Testament puns, arguing that (1) the numerical incidence is far greater than scholarship recognises; (2) the punning has far greater significance than its numerical incidence. The survey is only representative. There are many more examples. Nothing here denies that 'Christ' *also* denotes 'anointed' *and* functions as a surname. In order to bring out the oral/aural effects, I sometimes transliterate the eta forms as 'Chreestos'/'chreestos'.

I work from a series of 'stem' passages, where such punning is accepted, or at least considered in existing scholarship, and 'branch out' to others, according to the different meanings of χρηστός and cognates. Of course, the classification of different 'meanings' is to some extent artificial, because these various 'meanings' are in reality only different aspects of the one meaning, 'useful', and also, as we shall see, there is constant overlap of 'meanings'. So far as I am aware, these 'branch' suggestions are new, but I do not claim to have checked in all relevant New Testament scholarship.

A preliminary difficulty: is this enquiry at once aborted by Jesus' encounter with the rich young man in the Synoptic gospels (Mark 10.17–18; Matt. 19.16–22; Luke 18.18–23), where he rejects the application of the epithet 'good' to himself because it applies to God alone? (The fact that in these contexts the word used for 'good' is ἀγαθός does not dispose of the difficulty.) No: the problematics of this rejection—much debated by ancient and modern commentators—seem containable. One can solve the Christological and consistency difficulties in various ways: a 'historical Jesus' relic amidst the general Chreestianising spin of the Gospels;[89] some version of the Messianic secret; rhetorical reproof of the particular addressee; or developmental Chreestology: even Jesus had to become Christos/Chrestus. The incident may even have the positive narrative function of foregrounding the question of Jesus' Goodness, with a capital 'g'.

---

88   Achtemeier (1990); Elliott (2000) 404.
89   Vermes (2000) 157–280.

Our stem passage for 'Christ' as 'useful' comes from Philemon (8–11, 20), almost unanimously considered genuinely Pauline by modern scholars and dated c.61–3:[90]

> Therefore, though I have much freedom of speech in Chreestos (ἐν Χριστῷ) to enjoin upon you what is requisite, (9) I call upon you rather through love, being such as I am, Paul, an old man and a chained prisoner also for Chreestos Jesus (Χριστοῦ Ἰησοῦ). (10) I call upon you concerning my child, whom I begot in my chains, 'Beneficial' ('Ὀνήσιμον), (11) the one who once was useless (ἄχρηστον) to you, but now is very useful (εὔχρηστον) both to you and to me ... (20) Yes, brother, I would derive some benefit (ὀναίμην) from you in the Lord. Refresh my heart in Chreestos (ἐν Χριστῷ).

In prison and in chains, Paul has converted a slave called 'Onesimos'. This is a common slave name, which means 'Beneficial', and is analogous to the application of Χρηστός as adjective or name to slaves. Pre-conversion, despite his name, he was 'useless'; post-conversion, he is, in religious terms, 'very useful'. In the first instance, there is punning (by virtue of the 'substitution-of-synonyms' technique) between 'beneficial' and 'useless'/'useful'; in the second, between 'useless'/'useful' and *Chreestos*, 'heard' as 'useful' (χρηστός). Several thoughts are created. 'Onesimos'' 'usefulness' as a slave is redefined in terms of his 'usefulness' as a Christian. In so far as 'Onesimos' (slave name) interacts with 'Chreestos' (slave name), one is reminded that Christ could be accused of slavish status but that 'Chreestianity' subverts and inverts worldly hierarchies. Note also Paul's stress on his own resultant 'freedom of speech in Chreestos'. This 'slavish' 'Chreestos' is also 'the Lord', 'Chreestos' also having divine application. Christ here appears as the 'slave king'. And the meaning 'useful' also shades into meanings such as 'merciful' and 'kind'.

The punning here could hardly be more sustained or meaningful. Further, literal paternity is also overridden by 'religious' paternity. Not far away also, therefore, is the notion of the ultimate 'fatherhood' of 'Chreestos'. This is already a passage of enormously wide implication, touching on many of the most important elements of the 'Chreestian' message.

Compare 1 Corinthians 7.20–2, Pauline and datable c.54–5:

> every one should remain in the calling in which he was called. (21) You were called as a slave—let it not concern you. But if you actually can become free, *use* it rather. (22) For he who was called as a slave in the Lord

---

90  Fitzmyer (2000) 9–10.

is a freedman of the Lord, similarly, he who was called as a free man is a slave of *Christ*.

This, though much less elaborate than the *Philemon* passage, is clearly playing with the same sort of slavery inversions.

Note also 1 Corinthians 9.12, where 'useful' and 'good' are combined: 'we have not *used* this right but we tolerate all things in order that we may not put an obstacle to the *good* news of the *Christ*'.

Cf. also Galatians 5.2, universally recognised as genuinely Pauline and dated to the early 50s. 'Look, I, Paul, say to you that, if you receive circumcision, *Chreestos* (Χριστός) will not *help/advantage* (ὠφελήσει) you'. ὠφελήσει is a synonym of 'be useful', and the collocation with *Chreestos* is found elsewhere in the New Testament, as we shall see, as well as in the Church Fathers.[91] As in *Philemon*, 'usefulness' is redefined from one context (Jewish circumcision) to another ('Chreestos').

Next is Colossians 2.8:

> See that there will be no one who makes you his prey by philosophy and *empty* [κενῆς] deceit according to the tradition of human beings, according to the elements of the universe and not according to *Chreestos* (κατὰ Χριστόν).

The passage is a Christianisation of the Socratic attack on physical philosophy as morally useless (Plato, *Apology* 19c); here that attack targets pagan philosophy in general. 'The useful' is a standard criterion of intellectual debate, and sophistry, philosophy, etc. are often criticised as 'useless', here 'empty': there is an implicit contrast between the 'uselessness' of philosophy and the 'usefulness' of Christ. The 'substitution by synonym' technique here extends to *achreeston* as implied negative of *Chreeston*. As in the other two passages, the thought moves from what is wrongly considered 'useful' to what is rightly considered 'useful' in Christian terms. A huge branch of pagan learning is totally dismissed in favour of the authority of Chreestos and the dismissal is effected through the appropriation and maximalisation of an enlightened pagan attitude.

The authenticity of Colossians is disputed. Some scholars, probably a majority, consider it 'school of Paul' rather than genuine Paul.[92] My general thesis is helped by either view. On the former, the passage illustrates the *diffusion* of

---

91 Below, p. 969.
92 Barth–Blanke (1994) 114–26.

Christian play on *Chreestos*; on the latter, it further illustrates the importance of the play for Christianity's 'founding Father'.

We shall see other puns on 'useful'.

Philemon has the notion of 'Christ' as 'kind' in the background. Our stem passage for that notion in the foreground is Ephesians 4.32. The authenticity of Ephesians is hotly disputed, probably a majority of scholars regarding it as 'school of Paul':

> Be kind (χρηστοί) to one another, good-hearted, being gracious to one another, just as God ἐν Χριστῷ gave grace to you.

The notion that Christians should be *chreestoi* to one another is rooted in God's grace as expressed ἐν *Chreestoi*. This also reminds us that Chreestianity is partly about the Chreestification—the being made Chreest-like—of Chresstians. This passage must also be read in the light of the preceding (Ephes. 2.4–10):

> God, being rich in pity, because of his great love with which he loved us (5), even when we were corpses in our fallings by the wayside, made us live together with Christ (by grace you have been saved) (6) and raised us up with him [Christ] and seated us with him in the heavenly places in Christ Jesus (ἐν Χριστῷ Ἰησοῦ), (7) so that he might demonstrate in the coming ages the overflowing riches of his grace in kindness (ἐν χρηστότητι) towards us in Christ Jesus (ἐν Χριστῷ Ἰησοῦ). (8) For by grace you are saved through faith; and this is not from you, but it is the gift of God; (9) not from works, lest anyone should boast. (10) For we are His making, created in Christ Jesus (ἐν Χριστῷ Ἰησοῦ) for good (ἀγαθοῖς) works which God prepared beforehand, that we should walk in them.

ἐν Χρεεστῷ Ἰεεσοῦ sounds like a jingling refrain. The primary pun is on *Chreestos/chreestotees* in the sense of 'benevolence'/'kindness', though there is also a pun on *chreestos*/ἀγαθός. *Chreestos* is a second creator and mediator, instrumental in implementing the *chreestotees* of God. The latter word translates God's 'goodness' in the Septuagint. The punning *Chreestos/chreestos*, therefore, underpins three very large theological ideas: Christ as mediator between God and man; Christ as 'kind' to humans and himself 'loyal' to God (this emphasises the hierarchical chain of reciprocity between God, Jesus, and humans); and *Chreestos* as the incarnation of God's *goodness*. That 'Christos' sounded the same as 'Chrestos', the Septuagint word for God as 'good', is accidental (unless, with the Church Fathers, one here sees divine providence): but the New Testament transforms this happy accident into deep *Chreestology*.

Compare also Titus 3.4–7 (almost universally nowadays regarded as non-Pauline):[93]

> When the goodness (χρηστότης) and loving kindness appeared of our saviour God, (5) not as a result of the deeds which we did in righteousness but in accordance with his pity did he save us through the washing of regeneration and renewal of the Holy Spirit, (6) which he poured out upon us richly through Jesus Christ (Ἰησοῦ Χριστοῦ) our saviour, (7) so that being justified in his grace we might become heirs as regards hope of eternal life.

Beginning and end are ring-structured ('saviour' ~ 'saviour'); clearly, the chreestotees of God our Saviour is manifested in our Saviour Jesus Chreestos. Here chreestotes = 'benevolence'.

Galatians 5.22–4: 'But the fruit of the Spirit is love, joy, peace, long-sufferingness, kindness [χρηστότης], goodness, faithfulness, (23) gentleness, self-control; against such things there is no law. (24) and those who are of Christ Jesus have crucified the flesh with its passions and desires'.

Romans 2.1–16 on the righteous judgement of God starts with allusions to God's 'judgement' (2.2–3, 5); but then asks: 'do you despise the riches of his kindness [χρηστότητος] and forbearance and long-sufferingness, not knowing that the kindness [τὸ χρηστόν] of God leads you to change of mind?' (4–5); the section ends (16) with ring-structure, 'on a day when God will judge the secret things of men according to my good news through the agency of Christ Jesus', with Jesus' 'goodness' both emphasising God's justice and holding out prospect of divine 'kindness'.

Several of the above passages have played with the subsidiary implication *Chreestos/chreestos* in the broad sense of 'good'. For this, our stem passage is 1 Peter 2.1–3. As we have seen, majority modern opinion does not accept the authorship of Peter the disciple:

> So putting away all badness (κακίαν) and all deception and hypocrisies and envies and all ill-speakings, (2) like newborn babes, yearn for the undeceptive spiritual milk, in order that in it you may grow to salvation, (3) if you have tasted that the Lord is good/Christ [χρηστός/Χριστός (massive MSS split)].

---

93    Quinn (1990) 17–21.

There is a broad contrast between 'badness' and 'goodness'. Peter has earlier (1.3) referred to 'our Lord Jesus Christ' and several times (1.1, 2, 3, 7, 11, 13, 19) to Jesus Christ. It is Christ who is instrumental in the change between vice and virtue. At 2.1–3 the MSS split between χρηστός and χριστός. Jesus is the incarnation of Goodness. But also: Peter has just applied the term 'Lord' to God as well (1.25, quoting Isaiah 40.8 with a significant change), and 2.3 itself quotes Psalm 33.9, of God as 'good', so the punning 'the Lord is good' and 'the Lord is Christ' blurs Father and the Son. As in Ephesians 4.32, no epithet could convey better than *chreestos* Jesus' mediating role between God and man or his ambiguous divine identity. Another question—relevant to the interpretation of other passages—is whether 2.3 *also* alludes to the Lord's Supper. It surely does. Again, this is about Chreestians' becoming Chreest-like, the Eucharist's main function.

Cf. also 1 Peter 3.15–16:

> Reverence (the) Christ (τὸν Χριστὸν) as Lord in your hearts, prepared always to make a defence to everyone who calls you to account concerning the hope that is in you, (16) but with gentleness and holy fear, having a good (ἀγαθήν) conscience, so that, while you are ill spoken of, those who are reviling your good (ἀγαθήν) behaviour in Christ (ἐν Χριστῷ) may be completely shamed.

Clearly, especially when taken with the earlier passage, τὸν *Chreeston* and ἀγαθήν and ἀγαθήν and ἐν *Chreestoi* interact (and with elegant chiasmus, be it noted).

Compare also the Pauline 1 Corinthians 15.30–4, datable *c*.54–5:

> Why am I in danger every hour? (31) I die every day, I swear by the pride in you that I have in Christ Jesus (Χριστῷ Ἰησοῦ) our Lord. (32) If, on the human level, I fought with beasts in Ephesus, what is the profit (ὄφελος) for me? If corpses are not raised, 'let us eat and drink, for we die tomorrow'. (33) Do not err: 'bad associations destroy good (χρηστά) characters'. (34) Sober up righteously and do not go wrong. For some have no knowledge of God. I speak to turn you to the right.

Amidst the obscurities of this passage, one thing is clear: the guarantor of *chreesta* characters is *Chreestoi* Ἰησοῦ. There is also a punning connection with *chreestos* as 'useful'/'profitable' (cf. ὄφελος and Philemon 8–11, 20).

Romans 16.18 'for such [those who create dissensions and difficulties] do not serve our Lord *Chreest* [Χριστῷ] but their own belly, and through their [speciously] *good*-talking [χρηστολογίας] and well-speaking [εὐλογίας] they deceive the hearts of the "un-bad" [ἀκάκων]'.

Next, the (probably) non-Pauline Ephesians 4.20–1: 'You did not so learn (the) Christ! (ἐμάθετε τὸν Χριστόν), (21) if indeed you heard about him and were taught in him, as the truth is in Jesus'. The phrase to learn (the) Christ is startling, though glossed in the following 'if'-clause, and the practice was widespread. The noun would be Χριστομαθία, as found in the Church Fathers and modern Greek. But χρηστομαθία, pronounced identically, is used Classically of 'compendious learning of good bits' (e.g., morally improving excerpts from an author), characteristically for philosophical ends.[94] Our writer is implicitly substituting Χριστομαθία for χρηστομαθία, because it is *Chreestos* who is *chreestos*. This play on χρηστομαθία and Χριστομαθία is found in Clement of Alexandria, who presumably recognised it here.[95] In this case, identity of sound makes a crucial distinction. The technique seems philosophical, along the lines suggested by Heraclitus and Diogenes, and its application is rhetorically clever: a philosophical technique is turned against philosophy itself.

The wider implications of this passage are very great. As already noted, writing the *sacra nomina* 'Jesus' and 'Christ' played an important part in *Christian* formation;[96] so also did *recitation* of the name 'Jesus'.[97] So now also, it appears, did vocalisation of the name 'Chreestos'. Thus, as an early Christian, whenever one hears the name Chreestos, one hears the word 'good'; whenever one hears the word 'good', one hears the name 'Chreestos'. Whenever one thinks of 'education' or 'philosophy', which aim for 'the good', one should think only of 'Chreestos'. Whenever one thinks of compendious learning—a great phenomenon of the age[98]—one should think only of the compendious learning of Chreestos—in whom 'all things are summated' or 'headed up' (Eph. 1.10): itself an epitome term. Pagans rightly regarded early Christians generally as Classically uneducated. Early Christianity has no interest in wholesale absorption of Classical learning. But it does have an interest in showing—both to itself and to outsiders—that it surpasses Classical learning. Hence such passages as Acts 17 (Paul before the Athenian philosophers) and the present, which deftly appropriate Classical techniques to deflate Classicism itself. Epitome

---

94  LSJ s.v. χρηστομάθεια II.
95  Note that he puns on *chrestomathia* in the sense of Greek learning as sweetener/appetizer to Christian learning (*Strom.* 1.1.16.1): καὶ ἡ τῆς χρηστομαθίας περιουσία οἷον ἥδυσμά τί ἐστιν ....
96  See above, n. 39.
97  {Hurtado (2003a) 197ff., 389ff.}
98  {See, e.g., Livy's comprehensive history of Rome, the universal histories of Diodorus or Nicolaus of Damascus, or Strabo's compendious *Geography*.}

culture claims that all you need to know is epitomised versions of things. Christians reply that all you need to know is the *epitome* that is *Chreestos*.[99] A particular aspect is the philosophisation of Jesus: to the pagans' question: what is 'the good'? (one translation being, precisely, *to chreeston*), Christians reply: *Chreestos*, goodness instantiated, and superior even to such admittedly fine pagan exemplars of goodness as Socrates or the Cynics. And unlike the finicky Stoics, Chresstians could produce a completely perfect *sapiens*. Thus Luke implicitly compares Jesus and the Stoic *sapiens*, when he says that the boy 'Jesus *advanced* in wisdom' (2.52). Note also that Justin Martyr associates *to chreeston* with *Chreestianoi* and must have made the philosophical move that I have just done.[100]

It's worth reiterating the neatness of the play on Χριστομαθία and χρηστομαθία, with all that flows from it. A pagan reading Ephesians 4.20–1 or hearing the Chreestian answer to the question: what is *to chreeston*? would be both amused and challenged. If early Christians, who reject Classical *paideia*, are to reject it convincingly, they have, as it were, to undermine it from inside: to hollow out its own categories. Here, as elsewhere, one might compare Christian techniques with those of Diogenes and the Cynics: Diogenes completely rejects conventional *paideia* and indeed conventional 'philosophy', but he can only do so convincingly if he shows himself master of that *paideia* and if he can defeat Plato and other 'big-name' philosophers in philosophical repartee. If you're going to do rejectionism, you've got to do it with a certain style and wit.

I would say Chreestos as 'dead' is everywhere implied in the New Testament. But Romans 8.34 is a particularly clear case: 'Is it Jesus Christ [*Chreestos*] [who is to condemn], the one who died, or rather was raised?'. Here both alternatives ('died'/'raised') define 'Chreestos'. Also common in Paul—and possibly pre-Pauline—is the tag 'Chreest *died* for us'. It's extraordinarily concentrated, containing several interlocking levels of meaning. Consider also the doctrine 'the chreest must suffer' (Luke 24.26, etc.). Christians supported this by Isaiah 53 (the man of sorrows, acquainted with grief), which they were the first to read as applying to the Messiah. 'Suffer' refers to Chreest's passion, including his death. So the tag 'the chreest must suffer' includes a *per definitionem* justification. Remember that Christians, like pagan moralists, used memorable tags as a way of learning.

Van Voorst[101] suggests possible punning between χρηστός ~ χάρις/'grace' in Ephesians 4.32 (a passage already considered for *Chreestos* ~ 'kind'):

---

99   {See above, Ch. 28, p. 898.}
100  Above, Ch. 28, p. 856.
101  Van Voorst (2000) 36 n. 47.

> Be kind [χρηστοί] to one another, good-hearted, being gracious [χαριζόμενοι] to one another, just as God in Christ [ἐν Χριστῷ] gave grace [ἐχαρίσατο] to you.

The possibility of a relationship with χάρις is indeed bound to occur to anyone looking for puns on *Chreestos*. Neither difference of quantity (the first syllable of *Chreestos* is long, that of χάρις short) nor accentuation (the accent on the second syllable of *Chreestos*, on the first of χάρις) matters. It is worth noting, with Karrer,[102] that the medieval Fathers, Bernard of Clairvaux, and Aquinas, pun on 'Christus' and 'gratia', the Latin cognate of χάρις—a relic, perhaps, of a tradition going back to the Greek Fathers; that in the Septuagint χάρις is a key attribute of God (so perhaps transferable to Jesus); and that a strong association is made by some of the Greek Church Fathers between Jesus and χάρις, the latter sometimes being used as a title of Jesus.

In the case of Ephesians 4.32, a pun looks persuasive. Being *chreestos* is defined as being 'kind' or 'good'-hearted and then further defined as being 'gracious', in imitation of God's 'grace' as manifested in the person of *Chreestos*.

There are indeed numerous New Testament passages where there look to be sonically insistent relationships between *Chreestos* and χάρις, as part of a systematic 'Christology'.

Ephesians 2.4–10:

> God, being rich in pity, because of his great love with which he loved us (5), even when we were corpses in our fallings by the wayside, made us live together with Christ—by grace [τῷ Χριστῷ—χάριτι] you have been saved—(6) and raised us up with him, and seated us with him in the heavenly places in Christ Jesus [ἐν Χριστῷ Ἰησοῦ], (7) so that he might demonstrate in the coming ages the overflowing riches of his grace [χάριτος] in kindness [ἐν χρηστότητι] towards us in Christ Jesus [ἐν Χριστῷ Ἰησοῦ]. (8) For by grace [χάριτι] you are saved through faith; and this is not from you, but it is the gift of God; (9) not from works, lest anyone should boast. (10) For we are His making, created in Christ Jesus [ἐν Χριστῷ Ἰησοῦ] for good [ἀγαθοῖς] works which God prepared beforehand, that we should walk in them.

So we encounter in close succession Χριστῷ, χάριτι, Χριστῷ, χάριτος, χρηστότητι, Χριστῷ, and χάριτι.

Ephesians 1.5–10:

---

102 {Karrer (1991) 91 n. 13.}

Destining us for the position of sons through Jesus Christ ['Ιησοῦ Χριστοῦ] to him, according to the benevolent thinking of his will, (6) to the praise of the thought of his grace [χάριτος], with which he graced [ἐχαρίτωσεν] us in the beloved. (7) In whom we have redemption through his blood, the release of our fallings by the wayside, according to the riches of his grace [χάριτος], (8) which he lavished on us, (9) making known to us the mystery of his will, according to the benevolent thinking which he set forth in Christ [ἐν τῷ Χριστῷ], (10) for the organisation of the fulfilment of time, to sum up all things in Christ [ἐν τῷ Χριστῷ], the things in the heavenly places and the things on earth.

Christ is the summation of all things; God's χάρις is ἐν τῷ Χριστῷ.
Titus 3.4–7:

When the goodness (χρηστότης) and loving kindness appeared of our saviour God, (5) not as a result of the deeds which we did in righteousness but in accordance with his pity did he save us through the washing of regeneration and renewal of the Holy Spirit, (6) which he poured out upon us richly through Jesus Christ ['Ιησοῦ Χριστοῦ] our saviour, (7) so that being justified in his grace [χάριτι] we might become heirs as regards hope of eternal life.

Luke 6.32–5:

And if you love those that love you, what grace [χάρις] accrues to you? For even sinners love those that love them. (34) And if you lend to those from whom you expect to get, what grace [χάρις] accrues to you? (35) But love your enemies and do good [ἀγαθοποιεῖτε] and lend, expecting nothing back, and your reward will be much, and you will be sons of the Highest, because he himself is good [χρηστός] to the ungracious [ἀχαρίστους] and wicked [πονηρούς].

1 Peter 1.10–11:

Concerning which salvation [sc. the salvation of your souls] the prophets who prophesied concerning the grace [χάριτος] towards you searched out and inquired, (11) inquiring to whom or to what time the spirit of Christ [Χριστοῦ] in them made clear, when witnessing in advance to the sufferings with regard to Christ [Χριστόν] and the subsequent glories.

1 Peter 1.13:

> Wherefore, gird up your minds and in sobriety hope completely upon the grace [χάριν] that is coming to you in the revelation of Jesus Christ [Χριστοῦ].

Galatians 5.1–6:

> Christ [Χριστός] has freed you for freedom. Stand, then, and do not hold yourself under again to a yoke of slavery. (2) Look, I, Paul, say to you that, if you receive circumcision, Christ [Χριστός] will not help/advantage [ὠφελήσει] you. (3) I bear witness again to every man who receives circumcision that he is indebted to keep the whole law. (4) You are severed from Christ [Χριστοῦ], you who justify yourselves in law, you have fallen away from grace [χάριτος]. (5) For *we*, by the Spirit, through belief, await the hope of justice. (6) For in Christ [ἐν τῷ Χριστῷ] Jesus neither circumcision nor uncircumcision has any strength but belief in action through love.

One might also consider the John *Prologue*. John's highly abstract and hymnic prologue about the λόγος culminates, by the device of 'late-naming', in a name (17): Ἰησοῦ Χριστοῦ. 'Late-naming' gives names emphasis and, frequently, explains them in the light of what precedes. Can there be no connection between 17 Χριστοῦ and 14 πλήρης χάριτος and 16 'from his fullness [πληρώματος] we all received grace for grace [χάριν ἀντὶ χάριτος]'? Χριστοῦ (17) is the fulfilment/embodiment of God's χάρις—and looks and sounds like it.

And the Christian Grace. There are many occurrences of this in the New Testament. Typical is Romans 1.6: 'Grace [χάρις] to you and peace from God our father and the Lord Jesus Christ [Χριστοῦ]'. We note that the Grace begins with the word χάρις and ends with the word Χριστοῦ. It is generally agreed that the Grace combines (1) the Greek equivalent of the Jewish 'Shalom' ['peace'] and (2) the Greek form of greeting χαῖρε/χαίρετε ('hail'), with Paul (or his predecessors) substituting the cognate but stronger χάρις for χαῖρε/χαίρετε. The latter form of greeting is often used in letters; so is the former; and the combination had already been made in Hellenistic contexts before Paul or the early Christians. The combination is therefore well suited to the New Testament context of the letters of Paul and other early Christians. But there is a very common Greek epitaph (also found in Jewish contexts) where χαῖρε is combined with address to, or description of, the dead person as χρηστός.[103] That is,

---

103  E.g., Peek (1955) 414 ff.

the Christian Grace also combines standard letter and epitaph formula, and the collocation of sound between *Chreestos* and *charis* is already established in the reader's or listener's consciousness. The general point then is: our 'dead' Chreest 'lives' (in contrast to all other recipients of epitaphs) and is therefore Chreest as Messiah, who illustrates and embodies God's Grace. He can therefore 'address' us directly in a letter.[104] Hence the 'real' writer of the New Testament letters is *Chreestos* and Paul and the others are only exegetes of *Chreestos*' letters.

Chreestos, then, is the dominant sound of the early Christians' sound world. The punning associations will *always* be there, sometimes on the surface (where χρηστός or cognates appear in the immediate vicinity), sometimes just beneath it.

The association also creates so to say implicit interpretative structures. For example, a major theme of Romans is the χρηστότης of God, which calls the Romans to repentance and which they are called to emulate (2.4; 3.12; 11.22). The text also repeatedly emphasises Χριστοῦ Ἰησοῦ (1.1, 4, 6, 8; 2.16; 3.22, 24; 5.1, 11). The connection between the two is one that Paul does not need to—and does not—spell out. The punning association also suggests a *via media* between Hengel's claim that in Paul Χριστός functions (only) as a name or title and Wright's claim that it *always* has active Messianic force.[105] This constant repetition of *Chreestos* (also) functions as a sort of insistent pedagogic background back-beat: *chreestos, chreestos, chreestos*, God is Good all the time, etc.

But I turn rather to polyphonic punning, where the reader or listener is multiply challenged and the challenge focuses the question: do you accept or reject Jesus *Chreestos*? Let us look again at Acts 11.26, which will bring us back to the term *Christianoi*:

> when [Barnabas] had found [Saul], he brought him to Antioch. And it happened to them to be brought together in the church for a whole year and to teach a large crowd, and in Antioch the disciples were first operated as Chrestians/Christians.

There is a technical textual problem. The first hand of Codex Sinaiticus has χρηματίσαι τε πρώτως ἐν Ἀντιοχείᾳ τοὺς μαθητὰς Χρηστιανούς, whereas all other manuscripts and—I think—all modern editors have Χριστιανούς. On one level, the variation between Χριστιανούς and Χρηστιανούς does not matter,

---

104  There are other parallels for this kind of thing in New Testament writings, e.g., the very insistent application to Jesus of the present tense in Mark, with (e.g.) Boring, (2006) 24: 'employing the historical present more than 150 times'.
105  Hengel (1995) 1–7; Wright (2003) 554ff.

because χρηματίσαι is cognate with χρηστός, the adjective behind the proper name Χρηστός. So Luke is connecting the proper name with the notion of 'usefulness', and the eta quality of the name is 'felt', even if Χριστιανούς is read. But it is interesting that the possessor of that first hand saw the connection between proper name and χρηματίσαι, as no modern commentator has done. Is it possible that Luke himself actually wrote Χρηστιανούς, both to make the etymological connection clear and to reflect majority pagan orthography? But Χριστιανούς, pronounced the same, also conveys the etymological connection and Luke is hardly making a Tacitean point about correct spelling and derivation. Χριστιανούς has a further plus: keeping the notion of Messiahship. The majority reading is in fact subtler. We can now analyse the passage.

Χριστιανούς is not Jesus' followers' own term, but Romans', from whose perspective it is disparaging—and that on several levels. The notice is sandwiched between persecutions: one, post-Stephen, in Jerusalem (11.19) and one spear-headed by Herod (12.1–18). The naming of the Χριστιανοί here evokes the Roman persecutions of Jesus' followers under that name. The Romanised Lukas may well therefore imply the specific association between Χρηστιανοί and death. All this looks very ominous. But there are positives. When a group (here represented by a 'large crowd') gets a name, it is a defining moment, and the emphasis on 'first' registers this with appropriate historiographical solemnity. The moment is further emphasised by its being the culmination of a series of narrative episodes.[106] The naming therefore fulfils the characteristic functions of the device of 'late naming'. And within the unity that is Luke-Acts, Jesus' followers are called by a name that directly recalls Jesus himself, thereby emphasising the general 'succession' quality of Acts. Thus Acts goes some way towards positive Christian acceptance of the name Χριστιανοί/Χρηστιανοί. In this it is like 1 Peter, but it goes further than that text in several respects. Importantly, the use of the word χρηματίσαι for 'be called' suppresses any gap between 'name' and 'reality'. The etymological association between χρηματίσαι and χρηστός implies that this name is 'for real': the name is the thing itself. These people really were true followers of Christ, the Useful and Good, in being themselves 'useful' and 'good'. They were also, as it were, *descendants* of the true king, the anointed messiah. They were truly *chreestified*. *This* name is the *best* of all names.

Outsiders, then, might hear Χριστιανούς/Χρηστιανούς as pejorative, but they would be wrong on many different levels. With his habitual brilliant economy Luke deftly sketches almost all the various aspects of the name 'Christian'/'Chrestian'.

---

106  Dunn (2009) 303–6.

Another case is Matthew 27.15–24:

> At the feast the governor was accustomed to release for the crowd one prisoner whom they wanted. (16) And they had at that time a notorious prisoner called Barabbas. (17) So when they had gathered, Pilate said to them: 'Who do you want me to release for you, Barabbas or Jesus who is called Christ [χριστόν]?' (18) For he knew that they had handed him over *because of envy*. (19) When he was sitting on the judgement seat, his wife sent to him, saying: 'Have nothing to do with that *righteous* [δικαίῳ] man; for I have suffered much because of him today in a dream'. (20) But the chief priests and the elders persuaded the crowds to ask for Barabbas but to destroy Jesus. (21) The governor said to them in answer: 'Which of the two do you want me to release for you?' And they said: 'Barabbas'. (22) Pilate says to them: 'what, then, shall I do to Jesus the one who is called Christ [χριστόν]?' They all say: 'let him be crucified'. (23) But he said: 'No: for what *bad* [κακόν] thing has he done?' But they kept shouting even more: 'let him be crucified'. (24) But Pilate, seeing that he was helping [ὠφελεῖ] nothing, but rather a riot was beginning, etc.

Caiaphas has asked Jesus if he is 'the Chreestos/Χριστός (26.63), the son of God', primarily 'the Messiah', though, especially given the collocation with God, readers or listeners must also hear 'the good one'. Pilate redefines *Christos* as 'good' *simplex*: cf. 'because of envy', have 'nothing' to do with 'that *righteous* one', 'what *bad* thing has he done?', 'he's not *kakos*, he's *chreestos*'. He also redefines it as 'the helpful one', hence his attempt to 'help' Jesus and his cessation when he sees that he is 'helping nothing'. But for the Jewish leaders, and then for 'all the people' 'rioting', *chreestos spells* 'death': they interpret it in the same murderous way as the Roman mob of Neronian Rome. Worse, they are baying for the death of 'the good one': they're theicides, justly punished, readers know, by the sack of Jerusalem, the destruction of the Temple, the deaths of well over a million Jews, and the imposition of a punitive tax on all Jews everywhere. It's a brilliant though horrible sequence.

• • •

In Philippians 2.6ff. Paul quotes what looks like an early Christian hymn, in which the name Jesus Chreestos is already 'the name which is above every name'. Almost from the beginning, Christians thought that in that name, especially its second element, and despite its obvious negatives, they had found the transcendental signifier. In practice, they used the name for a wide variety of purposes: to denote Jesus' Messiahship; to distinguish their Jesus from others; to express the paradox that Jesus' messiahship rested on death, but then resurrection; to recast Christos as 'good', 'useful' and 'profitable'; to attract pagans to the new 'good' god; to din in the essences of Christianity; to convey Christian rejection of Classical philosophy and culture in favour of the true *goodness* of *Christ* and to do this by neat subversion of Classical techniques; to appropriate the entire epitome culture by making Christ the epitome of everything; and to plot various aspects of Christ's divine status: as mediator between God and humans; as the incarnation of God's goodness; as, in effect, the good God himself. *Pace* Parsons, we can say with absolute confidence that the New Testament writers and, presumably, their audiences or readerships fully understood the distinction—indeed the many distinctions—between the iota and eta forms; and *pace* Karrer, they exploited the punning potential of the name *Chreestos* extensively, ingeniously, and profoundly.

Some final general points: (1) The early Christians were possessed of immense verbal resourcefulness. (2) It is impossible to divorce that resourcefulness from their conceptions of realities—inevitable, of course, in people who believed that Jesus was God was the Word—or name, because *logos* also means 'name'. (3) Since naming and punning are power plays, our topic touches the New Testament debate over whether Christianity was oppositionalist (a better term than counter-cultural) or accommodationist: the present material is totally totalising.[107] (4) For twenty-first century Chreestians, this very thing raises questions of value. Even if (as I do not believe) the 'Jews' of Matthew's trial scene are just the Jerusalem Jews, the implicit allegedly Chreestian theology—Jewish murderers of the *Chreestos* punished by the Jewish War—is vile, untenable, and historically calamitous. Finally, a particular point for me as a Classicist, these New Testament Chreestians seem to be saying, unequivocally: away with Classical *chreestomathia*.

## Bibliography

Achtemeier, P. J. (1990) '"Omne Verbum Sonat": The New Testament and the Oral Environment of Late Western Antiquity', *Journal of Biblical Literature* 190/1: 3–27.

Ahl, F. M. (1985) *Metaformations: Soundplay and Wordplay in Ovid and Other Classical Poets* (Ithaca).

Angello, S. (1953) *Silloge di iscrizioni paleocristiane della Sicilia* (Rome).

---

107 Moles (2014).

Barnard, L. W. (1978) *Studies in Church History and Patristics* (Thessalonike).
Barrett, C. K. (2004) *A Critical and Exegetical Commentary on The Acts of the Apostles, Volumes I and II* (London and New York).
Barth, M. and H. Blanke (1994) *Colossians*, trans. by A. B. Beck (New York).
Bickerman, E. J. (1949) 'The Name of Christians', *HTR* 42: 109–24.
Bird, M. F. (2007) 'The Unity of Luke-Acts in Recent Discussion', *JSNT* 29: 425–48.
Blass, F. (1895) 'ΧΡΗΣΤΙΑΝΟΙ–ΧΡΙΣΤΙΑΝΟΙ', *Hermes* 30: 465–70.
Boring, M. E. (2006) *Mark: a Commentary* (Louisville and London).
Bowie, A. M., et al. (1977) 'Topics in the *Aeneid*', *LCM* 2: 138–40.
Bradley, K. R. (1972) 'Suetonius, *Nero* 16.2: 'Afflicti Suppliciis Christiani', *CR* 22: 9–10.
Bradley, K. R. (1978) *Suetonius' Life of Nero: An Historical Commentary* (Brussels).
Braun, T. (1994) 'Χρηστοὺς ποιεῖν', *CQ* 44: 40–5.
Brent, A. (2009) *A Political History of Early Christianity* (London).
Cappelletti, S. (2006) *The Jewish Community of Rome From the Second Century B.C. to the Third Century C.E.* (Leiden).
Capponi, L. (2007) *Il tempio di Leontopoli in Egitto: identità politica e religiosa dei Giudei di Onia (c. 150 a.C.–73 d.C.)* (Pisa).
Capponi, L. (2010) '*Impulsore Chresto*: una risposta dai papiri', in S. Bussi and D. Foraboschi, edd., *Roma e l'eredità ellenistica. Atti del convegno internazionale, Milano, Università Statale, 14–16 gennaio 2009* (Studi Ellenistici XXI; Pisa and Rome) 217–26.
Dunn, J. D. G. (2003) *Jesus Remembered: Christianity in the Making*, vol. 1 (Grand Rapids and Cambridge).
Dunn, J. D. G. (2009) *Beginning from Jerusalem: Christianity in the Making*, vol. 2 (Grand Rapids and Cambridge).
Dunn, J. D. G. (2010) *Did the First Christians Worship Jesus?: The New Testament Evidence* (London and Westminster).
Edwards, M. J. (1991) 'ΧΡΗΣΤΟΣ in a Magical Papyrus', *ZPE* 85: 232–6.
Elliott, J. H. (2000) *1 Peter* (New York).
Fitzmyer, J. A. (1998) *The Acts of the Apostles* (New York, etc.).
Fitzmyer, J. A. (2000) *The Letter to Philemon* (New York).
Flower, H. I. (2006) *The Art of Forgetting: Disgrace and Oblivion in Roman Political Culture* (Chapel Hill and London).
Fredriksen, P. (1988) *From Jesus to Christ: the Origins of the New Testament Images of Jesus* (New Haven and London).
Fuchs, H. (1950) 'Tacitus über die Christen', *VC* 4: 65–93.
Gibson, E. (1978) *The 'Christians for Christians' Inscriptions of Phrygia* (Harvard Theological Studies 32; Missoula, Montana).

Goodman, M. (2007) *Rome and Jerusalem: the Clash of Ancient Civilizations* (London and New York).

Harris W. V., ed. (2005) *The Spread of Christianity in the First Four Centuries: Essays in Explanation* (Leiden).

Hengel, M. (1995) 'Jesus, the Messiah of Israel', in id., *Studies in Early Christology* (Edinburgh) 1–72.

Hommel, H. (1951) 'Tacitus und die Christen: Ann. XV 44, 2–5', *Theologia Viatorum* 3: 10–30; repr. in id., *Sebasmata: Studien zur antiken Religionsgeschichte und zum frühen Christentum*, 2 vols (Tübingen, 1984) II.174–99.

Horrocks, G. (1997) *Greek: A History of the Language and its Speakers* (London and New York).

Horsfall, N. (2003) *The Culture of the Roman Plebs* (London).

Humphries, M. (2006) *Early Christianity* (Abingdon and New York).

Hurtado, L. (1999/2000) *At the Origins of Christian Worship: The Context and Character of Earliest Christian Devotion* (Carlisle and Grand Rapids).

Hurtado, L. (2003a) *Lord Jesus Christ: Devotion to Jesus in Earliest Christianity* (Grand Rapids and Cambridge).

Hurtado, L. (2003b) 'Homage to the Historical Jesus and Early Christian Devotion', *Journal for the Study of the Historical Jesus* 1/2: 131–46.

Hurtado, L. (2005) *How on Earth did Jesus Become a God? Historical Questions about Earliest Devotion to Jesus* (Grand Rapids).

Irwin, E. (2007) '"What's in a Name?" and Exploring the Comparable: Onomastics, Ethnography, and *Kratos* in Thrace (5.1–2 and 3–10)', in ead. and E. Greenwood, edd., *Reading Herodotus: A Study of the* Logoi *in Book 5 of Herodotus'* Histories (Cambridge) 41–87.

Johnson, L. T. (1986) *The Writings of the New Testament: An Interpretation* (Philadelphia).

Karrer, M. (1991) *Der Gesalbte: Die Grundlagen des Christustitels* (Göttingen).

Klauck, H.-J. (2000) *Magic and Paganism in Early Christianity: the World of the Acts of the Apostles* (Edinburgh).

Klutz, T. (2008) '*Christianos*: Defining the Self in the Acts of the Apostles', in N. Green and M. Searle-Chatterjee, edd., *Religion, Language and Power* (New York and London) 167–85.

Koestermann, E. (1968) *Cornelius Tacitus, Annalen Band IV: Buch 14–16* (Heidelberg).

Kraus, C. S., ed. (1994) *Livy: Ab Urbe Condita Book VI* (Cambridge).

Lampe, G. W. H. (1984) 'A.D. 70 in Christian Reflection', in E. Bammel and C. F. D. Moule, edd., *Jesus and the Politics of His Day* (Cambridge) 153–71.

Lateiner, D. (2005) 'Signifying Names and Other Ominous Accidental Utterances in Classical Historiography', *GRBS* 45: 35–57.

Lausberg, H. (1998) *Handbook of Literary Rhetoric* (Leiden).

Levinskaya, I. (1996) *The Book of Acts in its First-Century Setting, Volume 5: Diaspora Setting* (Grand Rapids).
Lipsius, R. A. (1873) *Ueber den Ursprung und den ältesten Gebrauch des Christennamens* (Gratulationsschr. Jena).
MacCullough, D. (2009) *A History of Christianity* (London).
Maltby, R. (1991) *A Lexicon of Ancient Latin Etymologies* (Leeds).
Mattingly, H. B. (1958) 'The Origin of the Name *Christiani*', *JTS* 9: 26–37.
Moles, J. L. (2000) 'The Dionian *Charidemus*', in S. Swain, ed., *Dio Chrysostom: Politics, Letters, and Philosophy* (Oxford) 187–210 [above, Ch. 8].
Moles, J. L. (2011) 'Jesus the Healer in the Gospels, the *Acts of the Apostles*, and Early Christianity', *Histos* 5: 117–82 [above, Ch. 23].
Moles, J. L. (2014) 'Accommodation or Opposition? Luke-Acts on Rome', in J. M. Madsen and R. Rees, edd., *Double Vision: Reflections of Roman Rule in Greek and Latin Writing* (Leiden) 79–104 [above, Ch. 25].
Moulton, H. K. (1977) *The Analytical Greek Lexicon Revised* (London; Grand Rapids, 1978).
O'Hara, J. J. *True Names: Vergil and the Alexandrian Tradition of Etymological Wordplay* (Ann Arbor, 1996).
Oberhelman, S. and D. Armstrong (1995) 'Satire as Poetry and the Impossibility of Metathesis in Horace's *Satires*', in D. Obbink, ed., *Philodemus and Poetry* (New York and Oxford) 233–54.
Pachoumi, E. (2007) *The Greek Magical Papyri: Diversity and Unity* (diss., Newcastle).
Parsons, P. (2007) *The City of the Sharp-Nosed Fish: Everyday Life in the Nile Valley* (London).
Peek, W. (1955) *Griechische Vers-Inschriften, Band I: Grab-Epigramme* (Berlin).
Quinn, J. D. (1990) *The Letter to Titus* (New York).
Reckford, K. J. (1997) 'Horatius: the Man and the Hour', *AJPh* 118: 538–612.
Rowe, C. K. (2007) 'Literary Unity and Reception History: Reading Luke-Acts as Luke and Acts', *JSNT* 29: 449–57.
Rowland, C. (1985) *Christian Origins: An Account of the Setting and Character of the most Important Messianic Sect of Judaism* (London 1985).
Sordi, M. (1995) 'L'espulsione degli Ebrei da Roma nel 49 d.c.', in ead., ed., *Coercizione e mobilità umana nel mondo antico* (Milan) 259–77.
Talbert, C. H. (1974) *Literary Patterns, Theological Themes, and the Genre of Luke-Acts* (Missoula).
Talbert, C. H. and P. Stepp (2003) 'Succession in Luke-Acts and in the Lukan Milieu', in C. H. Talbert, ed., *Reading Luke-Acts in Its Mediterranean Milieu* (Leiden) 19–55.
Van Voorst, R. E. (2000) *Jesus outside the New Testament: an Introduction to the Ancient Evidence* (Grand Rapids and Cambridge).

Vermes, G. (2000) *The Changing Faces of Jesus* (London and New York).
Williams, M. H. (1998) *The Jews among the Greeks and Romans: A Diasporan Sourcebook* (London).
Woodhead, W. (1928) *Etymologizing in Greek Literature from Homer to Philo Judaeus* (Toronto).
Wright, N. T. (2003) *The Resurrection of the Son of God* (London).
Yarbro Collins, A. (1984) *Crisis and Catharsis: The Power of the Apocalypse* (Philadelphia).

CHAPTER 30

# Selling Christian Happiness to Pagans: The Case of Luke-Acts

## 1  Preliminaries*

Luke-Acts, as it is generally referred to by New Testament scholars, is a very difficult and a very controversial text, and no one can usefully discuss any particular aspect of it without first spelling out such basic assumptions as are relevant to that aspect. For this paper my basic assumptions, which are widely, although not universally, held, are as follows: the text is a two-book unity;[1] its basic genre is Classical historiography,[2] though like many works of Classical historiography it richly incorporates other genres, including biography;[3] Acts implicitly alludes to Paul the Apostle's trial and death in Rome in 64, the year of the first great Roman persecution of Christianity;[4] and the double work Luke-Acts implicitly alludes to the capture of Jerusalem and the destruction of the Temple in 70.[5]

As to other preliminary matters, I accept the title of Luke-Acts for convenience, though it certainly was not the original title, a point to which I shall return and which is highly germane to our topic.[6] Regardless of the question of the title and following Christian tradition, I am content to call the author Luke, since the question of authorship little affects the present question. On

---

\*  The oral version was delivered at the 13th University of South Africa Classics Colloquium, Pretoria, 25th October, 2012. I thank Professor Philip Bosman for inviting me; all the organisers for the wonderful hospitality which made the whole conference such a fittingly happy time; all those who commented on the paper in discussion; and Dr Stephen Barton for kindly reading a written version, giving valuable bibliographical help, and sending me copies of two of his own papers. I owe my title to an important study by Professor Bosman on a similar question about Cynicism (Bosman (2006)). All translations are my own. Naturally, this is an academic paper, not a sermon: all theology is Luke-focalised. The paper has overlaps with some of my other papers, but the focus and the great bulk of the material are distinctive.

1  Basic statements: Talbert (1974); Tannehill (1986–90).
2  Plümacher (2006); Moles (2011b); Keener (2009) 85–94.
3  Biography: Burridge (1992/2004).
4  See above, Ch. 28, pp. 910ff.
5  See above, Ch. 27, pp. 787ff.
6  See below, p. 991.

dating, I am content with a broad dating of towards the end of the first century (certainly, post-70) or at the very beginning of the second.[7]

The topic I am concerned with has recently been well discussed by two New Testament scholars, Stephen Barton and Joel Green.[8] Although the conclusions of the three of us are congruent in many respects, the New Testament scholars' approach is more theological and more didactic than mine; they do not envisage any pagan audience or readers for the text and therefore (I believe) miss many of its emphases and implications; I draw attention to many other important aspects and subtleties of the text which they do not; and I hope to offer a much more organic and thorough-going account of the role of happiness in Luke's version of Christianity. Without undue captiousness, I shall signal some of these differences in the course of the paper.

## 2    Happiness

Happiness, of course, is as difficult to define as it is to secure. Whether, or to what extent, ancient notions of happiness correspond to modern ones is also a subject of considerable scholarly debate. But one should not become paralysed by such definitional and terminological matters. It is enough to adopt a broad definition of happiness as a state of wellbeing, as measured by various criteria (naturally, themselves debatable), or as felt by its possessor (whether rightly or wrongly), or both; to accept that, in Julia Annas' words, 'The question "In what does happiness consist?" is the most important and central question in ancient ethics';[9] and to note that the topic of happiness is a major concern of many different genres of Classical literature, including historiography (especially, of course, Herodotus'),[10] the genre to which Luke-Acts in the first instance belongs; philosophy, a genre with which Luke-Acts has important affinities;[11] and tragedy, a genre which Luke-Acts sometimes exploits.[12] Furthermore, it is a widespread ancient assumption, particularly among philosophers, that happiness and virtue go together—and one can hardly deny that Luke-Acts is concerned with virtue in some applications of the term, even though Luke does not actually use the Greek word ἀρετή, which is a very rare word in the whole

---

7    See above, Ch. 28, pp. 850ff.
8    Barton (2013); Green (2012). {JLM left the second name out; I have assumed that he meant to refer to Joel Green, but there are other possibilities.}
9    Annas (1993) 46.
10   Hdt. 1.29–33.
11   See above, Ch. 28.
12   Moles (2006b); Lee (2013); Morgan (2014).

of the New Testament.[13] Although this omission is not of great concern to our topic, I shall return to it in due course.[14]

## 3   Difficulties of the Topic

Many readers will find it immediately counter-intuitive to suppose that the work is trying to 'sell' anything that might be described as 'Christian happiness' to pagans.[15] There are four obvious difficulties.

First, the very notion that Luke is trying to 'sell' Christianity may cause discomfort to some readers, modern as well as ancient. In the Classical context, that metaphor goes back to the fifth-century Greek sophists who 'sold' their knowledge literally and who were much criticised by Socrates and Plato and most of their successors for so doing, and the metaphor is just as ambivalent in the modern world.

The second is the question of audience or readership:[16] are there any indications that this includes anyone besides Christians, whether initiands[17] or committed Christians?

The third is that Christianity was in some essential respects a very 'difficult sell' to anyone in the ancient world: while many modern scholars may dispute or problematise the notion of Roman 'persecution', it remains true that Jesus Christ, the 'founder'[18] of Christianity, had been put to death by a Roman governor on a charge of treason; that his followers, 'Christians', were therefore by their very name[19] vulnerable to prosecution; that Christianity was counter-cultural in many significant ways and that this factor aroused general

---

13  1 Peter 2.9; 2 Peter 1.3, 5 (*bis*).
14  Below, pp. 994ff.
15  I pass over the debates about the appropriateness of using the categories of 'Christian' and 'pagan' in relation to the first century; the terms, while rough and in different degrees anachronistic, are pragmatically useful, and 'Christian' is additionally justified by the New Testament evidence, including Luke himself (Acts 11.26; 26.28; 1 Peter 4.16). For recent discussion see Jones (2014) ch. 1.
16  Luke's 'targets' certainly included individual readers; a single reader reading to a 'house group', followed by group discussion, seems to have been a norm of early Christianity, but this factor should not be used (as it sometimes is) to minimise textual subtleties. In the sequel, I refer to 'audience' and 'readership' more or less indifferently.
17  The addressee, Theophilos (Lk 1.3; Acts 1.1), whether he is a real person or a useful construct (a question that need not concern us), is clearly represented as a 'catechumen': Fitzmyer (1981–5) 1.300.
18  The term is of course contentious: I use it because that is the way he seemed to Romans—cf. Tacitus' use of 'auctor' at *Ann.* 15.44.3.
19  {Plin. *Ep.* 10.96.2: *flagitia cohaerentia nomini.*}

and widespread pagan hostility beyond the directly 'political' questions;[20] and that at least after the Neronian persecution many people—both Christian and non-Christian—knew that Christians could suffer death for their religion, precisely as their 'founder' had done.[21]

The fourth is the fact that Luke—in common with all the other New Testament writers—never uses the commonest Greek word for 'happiness', which is εὐδαιμονία, or any of its equally common cognates. The situation therefore is even more extreme than with the word ἀρετή.

These difficulties necessitate a rather elaborate and rather circuitous exposition. To the first, third, and fourth difficulties I shall return at the appropriate junctures.[22] The second difficulty, central as it is to our topic, must be dealt with immediately.

## 4    A Pagan Audience/Readership?

It must be admitted that a large majority of New Testament scholars envisages a solely Christian audience, whether Luke's own hypothetical 'community' of Christians (the usual hypothesis),[23] or (a minority hypothesis) an 'international' Christian audience.[24] There are of course exceptions. Manfred Lang's audacious thought-experiment concludes that Luke's ideal reader is someone like Lucilius, pupil of the great Roman Stoic philosopher Seneca, or Pompeius Paulinus, the dedicatee of Seneca's *de Breuitate Vitae*.[25] My arguments complement his.

I do not at all deny the existence of a Christian audience or audiences. Nevertheless, there seems to be no good reason to *restrict* the text to Christians.[26] The missionary 'programme' of Luke-Acts mandates Jesus' disci-

---

20  Moles (2014).
21  Many modern accounts of early Christian history minimise the basic legal factors; for views similar to my own see Engberg (2007).
22  See next section.
23  All the Gospels claimed as 'community texts': summary in Bauckham (1998) 13–22. Lk 1.1–2 (ἐν ἡμῖν ... ἡμῖν), combined with the address to Theophilos (whether a real person or a constructed figure—a question that need not concern us) and the notorious 'we-passages' (Acts 16.10–17; 20.5–15; 21.1–18; 27.1–28.16), gives some colour to the notion of a Lukan 'community'. See Moles (2013) 111 {above, p. 690}.
24  See the contributions in Bauckham (1998), esp. 44–8.
25  Lang (2008).
26  Similarly, Moles (2013) 101 {above, p. 678}, and Moles (2014); the question of whether Luke finally writes off the Jews in general for rejecting both Jesus and the subsequent Jesus movement is a separate question and one that need not concern us.

ples to convert 'all nations' (Luke 24.47; Acts 26.23). The text provides as it were fair copies of the sorts of things Christians should say to a range of pagans (Roman governors, primitive pagans, Roman client kings, etc.),[27] so pagans of different kinds are definitely being appealed to at least at one remove. It is not then a big step to suggest that they are being appealed to directly. Indeed, the positive prominence of the category of 'the good Roman' is hard to explain unless this is so. This last factor applies even to the work's addressee, 'the most powerful Theophilos', since his status as 'most powerful' (Luke 1.3) and his knowledge of Christianity (Luke 1.4) find parallels in two Roman governors in Acts: Sergius Paulus, who 'was a learned man … and wanted to hear the word of God' (Acts 13.7), and Claudius Lysias, who 'was the chiliarch of the cohort' (21.31), which suggests that he is—or is to be conceived of as being—of similar, and implicitly Roman, status (whatever his immediate ethnicity, actual or constructed).[28]

Another very prominent category in the double work are 'God-fearers', that is, pagan followers of Judaism who had not formally converted to it,[29] so it is natural to suppose that Luke-Acts is also 'targeting' them. Interesting, too, are the numerous suggested analogies between Judaeo-Christian theology and pagan theology: for example, Jesus' mythical birth narrative;[30] the intermittent designation of the Jewish God as the Hypsistos—the monotheistic god common to Jews and pagans;[31] the representation of Paul and Barnabas at Lystra (Acts 14) as almost like pagan deities visiting the outback;[32] Paul's almost assimilation, before the Athenian philosophers and the Areopagus, of the Jewish-Christian god with the unnamed Zeus (Acts 17.23–8); the implicit comparisons between Ἰησός as ἰατρός and various pagan healing gods;[33] the allusion to the Dioscuri as the sign of the ship that carried Paul to Italy (Acts 28.11); the intermittent representations of Jesus and Paul as Hellenistic 'holy man' figures; and the sustained comparison between Jesus and Dionysus.[34] Since these parallels concede a certain limited validity to pagan religious experience and thought, they seem to function as doors through which pagans can pass to the Christian truth.

---

27  See above, ch. 28.
28  {*Chiliarchos* is the Greek term for the Latin *tribunus militum*.}
29  For God-fearers see Fitzmyer (1998) 449–50 (with earlier bibliography).
30  Lk 2.1–20, with Johnson (1991) 49–53.
31  Moles (2011a) 152 {above, p. 646} with n. 126.
32  E.g., Ovid, *Met.* 8.611–720 (the Baucis and Philemon episode).
33  Moles (2011a).
34  Seaford (1997); Moles (2006b).

Consideration must also be given to the Classical elements of Luke-Acts. The mere presence of such elements does not prove appeal to pagans: such elements can promote 'internal' self-validation, as they seem to do in some Jewish writings.[35] But the more numerous and organic they are, the more likely they are to be functioning as 'hooks' to catch pagans, particularly educated ones; in this, Josephus' more or less contemporaneous *Jewish Antiquities*, explicitly addressed to non-Jews (*AJ* 1.5, 9), furnishes a useful possible parallel. I summarise some of these numerous and organic Classical elements below,[36] but one in particular should be considered here.

## 5  Luke-Acts and Philosophy

It is an important consideration that Luke-Acts' philosophical elements are foregrounded in the Preface, as we shall see.[37] Then in the Luke narrative Jesus the teacher has his pupils; his calls to the disciples ('follow me') find their best parallels in Greek philosophical material, not Jewish tradition; he seems almost to be running a 'school' like that of John the Baptist or the Pharisees; he attends the equivalent of symposia at which the equivalents of 'problems' or 'aporiai' are debated; he has Socratic-style exchanges, and he looks in some ways pretty Cynic, as, for example, in his 'mission statements', his denial of family, or his thoroughly un-Jewish indifference to burial.[38] Then, with intensification of effect, in Acts, come the Cynic-like communism of the first Christian community in Jerusalem; Peter, John, and, especially, Paul as Socratic figures;[39] quite sustained use of Plato's *Apology*;[40] much emphasis on philosophical *parrhesia*,[41] the great philosophical debate in Acts 17, the use of διαλέγομαι to describe Paul's teaching mode (17.2, 17; 18.4, 19; 19.8, 9; 20.7, 9; 24.12, 25); after the Athens debate, a whole string of 'apologies' before various audiences, the designation of Christianity as a *hairesis* (Acts 24.5, 14; 28.22), and Paul at the end in Neronian Rome looking like Socrates the night before he died or like a Roman philosophical martyr. And in both books the use of συζητέω of quasi-philosophical 'enquiries'.[42]

---

35  As seen, for example, in the writings of Philo and Josephus.
36  See below, pp. 998ff.
37  See below, pp. 989ff.
38  Moles (2006a) 101 {above, p. 540} with n. 105.
39  See above, ch. 27 §3.3.
40  Alexander (2005) 61–7.
41  Dupertuis (2013).
42  See above, Ch. 28, p. 870.

This material is very extensive, and it has immediate implications. In Luke-Acts Christianity looks—in some ways—very like a philosophy, as its parent Judaism does too, in some Jewish texts, and Luke-Acts as a text bills itself as *inter alia* a work of philosophy.[43] Of course, in the Graeco-Roman world non-philosophers could regard philosophy negatively, as well as positively, but the representation of Christianity as a philosophy helps to familiarise it and normalise it, as least for those pagans not constitutionally hostile to it, while pagans already of philosophical bent might become interested in this 'new' 'Christian philosophy', as some indeed did.

## 6   Christianity as Philosophy

But Christianity does not merely look like a philosophy. The appearance of Paul before the Areopagus[44] is obviously one of the key scenes where within the narrative Christians appeal to pagans. But the scene also has 'external' significances: it provides another 'fair copy' of how Christian readers should behave, this time how they may appeal to philosophical pagans, and it can itself be given metaliterary force, as dramatising the desired effect of Luke-Acts itself on such pagan readers. The scene also considers happiness, since the main ancient 'experts' on happiness, at least in their own estimation, were philosophers. And the scene actually makes the strongest possible philosophical claim (Acts 17.17–18):

> He *dialogued* (διελέγετο) in the synagogue with the Jews and God-fearers and *in the agora* (ἐν τῇ ἀγορᾷ) every day with those *who happened to come by* (πρὸς τοὺς παρατυγχάνοντας). (18) And some also of the Epicurean and Stoic philosophers[45] encountered him, and some said: 'What then would this seed-collector wish to say?' But others said: 'He seems to be an announcer of strange divinities (ξένων δαιμονίων δοκεῖ καταγγελεὺς εἶναι)'.

Here it is Paul who is the Socrates figure, and the 'official' Athenian philosophers, who ought to be Socrates' successors, if their philosophical thinking were any good, ignorantly make against Paul the very same charge[46] which

---

43   Above, Ch. 28.
44   The question of whether this scene is historical or fictional need not concern us (discussion above, Ch. 28, pp. 848ff.): enough that it is thematically important.
45   Note that φιλόσοφος is hapax in Luke-Acts and the New Testament.
46   I sidestep as immaterial the question of whether the philosophers are (represented as) making a *legal* charge against Paul.

non-philosophers had made against Socrates. In this scene, therefore, Luke already stages the claim—explicit in later Christian apologists—that Christianity is the true fulfilment of pagan philosophy. He thus issues a direct challenge to the philosophical pagans—indeed, to any educated pagans—among his audience. No doubt some pagans among his readership would have been familiar with analogous claims among Hellenistic Jewish writers. But in the first or second century this Christian claim has a challenging novelty of appeal which the Jewish one obviously lacks. Luke-Acts thus emerges as a philosophical text, or, more precisely, as a work of historiography which has philosophical elements (a common enough type of historiography in the ancient world: one has only to think of Herodotus, Xenophon, Onesicritus, Posidonius, and Sallust). And paradoxically it is the text's philosophical status that now enables us to explain the first of our initial difficulties: the complete absence from Luke-Acts and the entire New Testament of the specific word εὐδαιμονία, the word so much used by Greek philosophers to denote happiness.

## 7    Philosophy, Happiness, and Εὐδαιμονία

Since pagan philosophy generally promises 'happiness' (whether or not that is a particular philosophy's formal *telos*), then, to the extent that it represents itself as a philosophical text, Luke-Acts must again be committed to providing happiness. But the reason for the absence of the usual word is obvious and is indeed heavily implied in Acts 17, where the text makes its most obvious claim to being a philosophical text and where, as we have seen, the Greek philosophers surmise that Paul is introducing strange δαίμονες (17.18), and Paul addresses his audience as δεισιδαιμονεστέρους (17.22), which they can take as complimentary and which does indeed provide a basis for discussion, but which is also implicitly critical of their enslavement to δαίμονες,[47] which to Christians are either non-existent beings, or if existent, demons, and in both cases idolatrous. Thus early Christians simply cannot use the term εὐδαιμονία (or its cognates), because of its polytheistic implications, though some more relaxed later Christians did.[48] But the easily explained, indeed, pointed, absence in Luke-Acts of the commonest Greek *word* for happiness does not at all dispense Christianity from the need to offer 'happiness' to its pagan readers

---

47   Klauck (2000) 81–2.
48   *Narratio de rebus Persicis*, p. 15.10 Bratke; note also the use of the verb εὐδαιμονέω in the (to some extent Hellenised) Jewish writers Philo (e.g., *Leg. Allegor.* 2.102–3, 218, etc.) and Josephus (e.g., *Ap.* 1.224).

and all its readers, potentially indeed extending to all human kind. No greater demand could be made of any text.

To summarise our general argument so far: a rich combination of factors validate the conclusion that Luke-Acts' ideal readership, then, is everybody who can understand Greek, and it is a suggestive fact that Luke-Acts found pagan Greek readers from the second century onwards.[49] One might even suggest that, since the world obviously includes people who cannot understand Greek, the text must be committed to 'speaking' to them also, even if through the medium of translation, and that one of the points of the Pentecost event, when 'each heard his own language spoken' (Acts 2.6), is to show the 'ideal' comprehensibility of the Lukan version of the Christian message to all nations irrespective of language.

If then, Luke-Acts' ideal audience *includes* pagans in general, to whom it is trying to 'sell' Christian 'happiness', it has to make some initial appeal to them in order to persuade them at least to consider 'buying' 'the product'. It has, in other words, to dangle before pagan readers the prospect of 'pleasure'—that 'pleasure' which is widely recognised in the ancient world as one of the foremost enticements to, and products of, reading (or hearing) works of literature.[50]

## 8  The Pleasure of the Text Itself

By what literary means, then, does Luke-Acts make this initial appeal to its pagan readers? All Lukan scholars acknowledge Luke's abundant possession of basic literary skills—his vivid scene-painting, his story-telling flair, his ability to spin long narrative threads, his mastery of structure, and his creation of narrative tension, skills which are more or less appreciable, in principle, by readers or listeners of any type, including the poor and uneducated. Luke-Acts also contains plenty of obvious material which falls into the ancient categories of 'the charming' and 'the wonderful'. Less well recognised is Luke's mastery of sustained image-patterning, examples of which we shall see in this paper,[51] and of the intermixing of imagery, of which we also shall see examples.[52] As I have already suggested, the text also exhibits great generic richness, complexity, and variety. The Preface is itself a brilliantly written 'invitation' to any sophisticated

---

49   See above, Ch. 28, n. 82.
50   {Already in the *Odyssey* (12.188) the 'two things promised by the Sirens ... are pleasure and knowledge': Verdenius (1983) 48ff., with numerous examples.}
51   Another is 'the road': Baban (2006); Morgan (2013).
52   Pp. 992–3 below.

'Classical' reader.⁵³ In it Luke-Acts bills itself as Classical historiography in the tradition of Herodotus, Thucydides, and others, and Luke contrives some very dense and skilful historiographical allusions, but he tellingly combines 'great' historiography with 'individual-orientated' historiography and biography.⁵⁴ Luke also uses tragedy, especially *Bacchae*, as a major structuring and thematic device in Acts.⁵⁵ From time to time, too, Acts' lively and varied narrative ('the most exciting book in the New Testament')⁵⁶ invites comparisons with the Greek novel, Greek and Roman epic, and even Classical comedy.⁵⁷ He is also capable of extremely dense literary allusion, not only to the Jewish Bible but also to Classical literature: Acts 17 alludes to *Bacchae*, the *Apologies* both of Plato and Xenophon, Cleanthes, Aratus, Posidonius, the *Eumenides*, and perhaps Dio of Prusa;⁵⁸ and the Preface is similarly Classically dense. He is also capable of extremely economical literary allusion.⁵⁹ As to language, generally speaking, Luke writes widely accessible 'Fachprosa' (what might be called 'civil service' Greek);⁶⁰ but he is actually very creative verbally, e.g., in his use of *hapaxes*, of which we shall see some examples in this paper. He is capable too of elevating his style and diction—for instance, in the Preface, in Acts 7 (which boasts optatives, employed by the effete Athenian philosophers and then ironically capped by Paul [17.27]), in the shipwreck narrative (Acts 27.6–44) and the end of Acts (28.30–1)—to levels worthy of his great pagan contemporaries Dio and Plutarch, in which contexts, he is surely implying, in recognisably Socratic or Cynic style: I can do this stuff if I choose to, so do not dare to despise me, but mostly I do not choose to. There is some appeal, then, to Greek and Roman literary models and standards.

Luke's very varied literary skills, then, should appeal to a very wide range of pagan readers and conduce to the 'pleasure' of *any* reader or listener, whether Christian, Jewish, or pagan.

Not only does such literary 'pleasure' help to make an initial appeal to the reader, but the provision of 'pleasure'/'sweetness'/'honey' as a way of 'sweetening' 'the useful'/'the true'/'wormwood', etc. is a recognised didactic device in ancient literature, as was well recognised in Richard Pervo's influential book

---

53  For justification of these controversial claims see Plümacher (2006); Moles (2011b), (2013), and Ch. 27 above.
54  Moles (2013) 120 {above, p. 701}.
55  See above, n. 34.
56  Dunn (1996) ix.
57  Much material in Pervo (1987); Alexander (2005).
58  See above, Ch. 28, *passim*.
59  Above, ch. 27.
60  Alexander (2005) 231–52.

on Acts.[61] And the 'pleasure' derived from literature may itself be a component of a 'happy' life. Thus the literary qualities of Luke-Acts themselves make some contribution to the goal of 'selling Christian happiness to pagans'.

## 9  Readers' Expectations: Questions of Titulature and Genre

After this sketch of some of the literary qualities of the text which themselves conduce to happiness, it is time to examine the text itself in detail. One should of course begin at the beginning—at the start of the text, where ancient writers begin to shape readers' expectations.

The Preface runs (Luke 1.1–4):

> Ἐπειδήπερ πολλοὶ ἐπεχείρησαν ἀνατάξασθαι διήγησιν περὶ τῶν πεπληροφορημένων ἐν ἡμῖν πραγμάτων, (2) καθὼς παρέδοσαν ἡμῖν οἱ ἀπ' ἀρχῆς αὐτόπται καὶ ὑπηρέται γενόμενοι τοῦ λόγου, (3) ἔδοξε κἀμοὶ παρηκολουθηκότι ἄνωθεν πᾶσιν ἀκριβῶς καθεξῆς σοι γράψαι, κράτιστε Θεόφιλε, (4) ἵνα ἐπιγνῷς περὶ ὧν κατηχήθης λόγων τὴν ἀσφάλειαν.[62]

> Since indeed many have set their hand to draw up [ἀνατάξασθαι] a narrative guide [διήγησιν] about the things done which have been persuasively brought to fulfilment [πεπληροφορημένων] amongst us, (2) just as those who became from the beginning eyewitnesses and servants of the word gave them on to us, (3) it seemed good to me also, having closely followed [παρηκολουθηκότι] all of them accurately from the up [ἄνωθεν], to write them down for you in order [καθεξῆς], most powerful Theophilos [κράτιστε Θεόφιλε], (4) so that you may additionally know/experience/recognise [ἐπιγνῷς] the truth/security/safety/unslipperiness [τὴν ἀσφάλειαν] about the words in which you have been orally instructed.

This is an extremely economical and complicated piece of writing but for present purposes, only two elements require consideration. The first is the question whether Luke, the first book of the double work, or Luke-Acts, the double work itself, had a title, and if so, what the title or titles were. The question of titulature is complicated by the facts that (a) even single ancient works can have more than one title and (b) Luke-Acts is a double work.

---

61  Pervo (1987).
62  I have discussed the Preface several times previously from different aspects: above, Chs. 22, 27, and 28. Here I keep the focus rigorously on what is relevant to our topic.

Most scholars think that the traditional Gospel titles ('The Gospel according to so-and-so') are not original;[63] a distinguished minority thinks that they were.[64] This difficult question concerning the traditional title of Luke cannot of course be resolved here, but one can bypass it by noting that the lexicon of 'good news' is insistent and widespread throughout Luke and Acts. Thus in Luke the angel Gabriel tells Zacharias (1.19) 'I was sent to speak to you and tell this good news' (that his wife will bear a son John who will turn many of the sons of Israel to the Lord); an angel tells the frightened shepherds (2.10) 'I announce the good news of great joy ... to all the people' (the birth of the saviour); John's ministry is summed up in the words (3.18) 'he brought good news to the people'; Jesus himself (4.18) invokes the words of the prophet Isaiah (Isa. 61.1–2) 'The spirit of the Lord is upon me, whence he anointed me to bring good news to beggars'; Jesus (4.43) tells the crowds who have witnessed his healings and exorcisms 'I must give the good news of the kingdom of God to the other cities, because it was for this that I was sent'; Jesus (7.22) adduces to the followers of John among the proofs of his status as the coming one the fact that 'beggars are being given good news'; Jesus' mission is summed up as 'proclaiming and announcing the good news of the kingdom of God' (8.1). Εὐαγγέλιον makes people happy.[65]

From this significant volume of material four things emerge: (1) what is in question is 'good news' as both spoken (and enacted) by Jesus (and by God and other representatives of God besides Jesus) and spoken about him (and about God and Jesus' relationship to him); (2) irrespective of title, it is reasonable to classify Luke generically as a 'gospel', or, better, as a gospel *as well as* a work of historiography, in parallel and tension with pagan texts which announce 'good news',[66] and to regard Acts too as having some sort of relationship with this textual genre (as well, of course, with other genres); (3) 'happiness' and related emotions (joy, relief, etc.) are a natural response to 'good news', and this link is indeed explicit in some of the items cited; (4) consequently, irrespective of titular and generic controversies, we now find yet further proof that the production of 'happiness' and of related emotions is intrinsic to the purpose of Luke-Acts.

---

63  Representative arguments: Watson (2013) 413–14, 417–18.
64  Hengel (2000) 48–56; Bauckham (2006) 300–5.
65  Note that Luke 2.10 provides immediate confirmation of the link between 'good news' and 'happiness'.
66  Above, ch. 27, pp. 824–5.

## 10   Truth and Security

The second element which crucially affects readers' expectations is the difficult clause in the Preface where Luke spells out to Theophilos the goal of his work (Luke 1.4): 'so that you may additionally know/experience/recognise the truth/security/safety/unslipperiness about the words in which you have been orally instructed'.

Now New Testament scholars debate whether ἀσφάλειαν here means 'truth' or 'reliability'. If the Preface advertises—as it does—a work of historiography,[67] some truth claim is an appropriate element, and the difference between the renderings 'truth' and 'reliability' hardly matters. But to *restrict* ἀσφάλειαν to the meaning of 'historical truth' is both to downplay the sheer emphasis of the word and its climactic position as the very last word of the Preface and grievously to underestimate the density and virtuosity of Luke's writing within the Preface. Ἀσφάλειαν acquires important additional resonances from the fact that it functions as the 'solution' to several interrelated threads and, as said 'solution', it comes appropriately as the very last word.

First, since, as we have seen, readers readily acquire the notion that this text promises 'happiness' (or related states), it is relevant that ancient notions of happiness generally often begin (and sometimes effectively end) with the absence of negative states. Particularly, in ancient philosophy, 'happiness' is often largely secured by, even sometimes virtually equivalent to, the removal of 'unhappiness' (as caused by pain, fear, superstition, desire, passion, need, etc.), or other negative states, which removal is often expressed by negative compound nouns and adjectives. Here we have a negative compound ἀσφάλειαν, which guarantees 'security from falling'. Second, the words παρέδοσαν and παρηκολουθηκότι suggest 'succession' within a 'school' context, and the suggested 'school' can hardly be anything other than a philosophical one. It is therefore immediately pointed that ἀσφάλεια is a widespread philosophical goal, common, for example, to Platonists, Cynics, Stoics, and Epicureans (even if somewhat variously understood).[68] Third, the words διήγησιν, πεπληροφορημένων and παρηκολουθηκότι create multiple 'road imagery' in which ἀσφάλειαν plays its part: Luke-Acts promises a 'way of life', which is a 'safe road'; Christianity is itself 'the road which saves you from falling'; the 'narrative road instantiates the road of life'.[69] Alert pagan readers should perceive this the more appropriately because Christianity itself described as 'the Way', or

---

67   See Moles (2011b); above, ch. 27, pp. 801ff.
68   Above, ch. 27, p. 809.
69   Detailed analysis in Moles (2013).

as a 'route to happiness'.[70] Fourth, the final purpose clause has parallels in the statements of purpose of historians such as Herodotus, Thucydides, Sallust, and Livy and images both the text and its theme as an inscription or building:[71] Christianity is the building that will not fall (unlike the Jewish Temple or the Roman Empire). Fifth, the words ἐπεχείρησαν and ἀκριβῶς create artistic imagery, so that ἀσφάλειαν is the 'true representation' at the end of this process. And sixth and finally, the words πεπληροφορημένων, ἀκριβῶς, ἐπιγνῷς and ἀσφάλειαν create financial or legal imagery.[72] It is at this point therefore that we can dispose of the first of our initial difficulties for our topic. For the financial or legal imagery of the Preface clearly imply both that Luke's own 'credit' and the 'credit' of the Christianity he is trying to 'sell' are in question *and* that the reader should 'recognise' his 'obligation' to 'buy'. Thus Luke-Acts is indeed billing itself as a 'sell'. Here the obvious pagan parallel, albeit later, is with Lucian's *Sale of Lives* (i.e., different types of philosophical lives), though with the equally obvious differences that Lucian's project is satirical and that Luke is not presenting his reader with a *range* of choices. In Luke's Preface the now rather banal notion of 'the "contract" with the reader' acquires immeasurable import. The financial/legal imagery also feeds into the narrative, because 'belief' is often expressed through financial imagery and because God has a 'contract' or Covenant' with the Jewish people and, now, with pagans.

By these interlinked image chains, then, Luke gives the notion of Christian 'security' tremendous force. Is there any difficulty in connecting these rich associations of 'security' with the relatively straightforward notion of historiographical 'truth'? No, for this text gives the 'truth' about 'the Truth', that 'truth' which provides absolute 'security'.

At this point we may return to the question of titulature. Ancient titles are often derived from key words in prefaces. With all due allowance for multiplicity of titles, the best single title for the double work is in fact Πρὸς Θεόφιλον περὶ ἀσφαλείας Book 1 and 2. The Preface, then, provides yet further proof of the centrality of the provision of happiness to the purpose of Luke-Acts.

It is now time to move into the narrative. That narrative is formally historical, relating the biography of Jesus and the beginnings and early history of Christianity after Jesus' death and resurrection. But it is also didactic: *qua* historiography/biography, it is exemplary, and *qua* philosophy, it is protreptic.[73] So the representations of happiness within the narrative (provided, of course,

---

70  For 'the way', see Morgan (2013); for the Cynic equivalent see Prince (2015) 399–402.
71  Moles (2011b).
72  Above, ch. 27 §§2.16 (artistic), 2.19 (financial).
73  See above, ch. 27 §6.5.

that they are not vicious) represent things to which all readers can and should aspire, and which the text guarantees them if they are willing to choose Christianity.

Because the Preface ends with the notion of the removal of a negative and because ancient happiness involves (to a greater or lesser degree) removal of negatives, we should begin with the constant exhortations 'Do not fear'. These are delivered by angels, themselves initially objects of fear, to Zechariah, father of John the Baptist, whose prayer for a son has been answered (Luke 1.13); to Mary, who has found favour with God and will become the mother of Jesus (1.30); and to the shepherds, for the good news of the birth of the Saviour, Christ the Lord (2.10). They are also delivered by Jesus himself to Simon, because he will henceforth be catching men instead of fish (5.10); to the man who reports the death of Jairus' daughter, because she will be saved if he believes (8.50); to his friends because those who kill the body can do no more, whereas, while it is right to fear the devil who can cast people into hell, they should not fear death, because God will remember them (12.4–7); and to his flock because God the Father will provide for their bodily needs and give them the Kingdom (12.32). Similarly, in Acts God tells Paul through a vision to continue to proclaim Jesus, because he will keep him from harm (18.9), and an angel tells Paul not to be afraid, because God will save all on board the ship bound for Italy and Paul will be able to testify before Caesar (27.24).

But Luke-Acts promises far more than the mere removal of fear or of other negative states or conditions, so I next consider happiness as a positive state of well-being.

It is legitimate to consider the adjective μακάριος and its cognates under this heading, because in pagan texts they can be used of the 'happiness' or 'blessedness' of human beings and sometimes associated with εὐδαιμονία, sometimes distinguished from it.[74] Thus in Luke Elizabeth pronounces Mary μακαρία 'blessed/happy' for believing that what the angel of the Lord spoke to her would be fulfilled (1.45), and Mary herself declares (1.48): 'From now on all generations will call me blessed/happy' (μακαρίουσιν). Similarly, in the list of 'Beatitudes', 'blessed'/'happy' are the poor, the hungry, the weeping, the hated, the excluded, the reviled, and those whose name is cast out as wicked for the sake of the 'Son of man' (6.20–2), because their situation will be reversed at the end of time. The same judgement is made of those who take no offence at Jesus (7.23), of the eyes that see what Jesus' disciples see (10.23), of 'those who hear the word of God and keep it' (11.28). A parable emphatically pronounces

---

74  {Cf., e.g., Plat. *Rep.* 354a μακάριος τε καὶ εὐδαίμων; μακάριος contrasted with εὐδαίμων: Arist. *EN* 1101a7.}

happy/blessed those who 'wakefully' await the end of time (12.37–43). Jesus spells out the link between 'blessedness' in the here and now and eschatological blessedness (14.14): 'And you will be blessed [when you invite the poor, the maimed, the lame and the blind to dinner], because they cannot repay you. For you will be repaid at the resurrection of the just', to which a fellow-guest responds (14.15): 'Blessed is he who shall eat bread in the kingdom of God'. Thus 'happiness' or 'blessedness' is always seen within the perspective of so-called inaugurated eschatology.

A particularly interesting case comes in Acts in Paul's valedictory address to the Ephesian Elders (20.35): 'In all things I have shown you that you must take up the cause of the weak by so toiling, and remember the words of the Lord Jesus, that he himself said: "It is more blessed to give than to receive"'. This articulates the principle that happiness or blessedness comes from continual altruistic activity, specifically from helping the poor.[75]

I next consider the various forms of happiness as experienced rather than as protreptic or consolatory, as we have seen up to this point.

'Joy' may be defined as an extreme form of happiness. It is of some interest to philosophers such as the Epicureans and Stoics, and it is naturally much registered in non-philosophical Greek texts.[76] It is usually understood as being triggered by specific events or experiences or news and as being of short duration.

In Luke 'joy' (χαρά) will mark Zechariah's reaction to John's birth (Luke 1.14) and the shepherds' and all the peoples' to Jesus' birth (2.10). Jesus' Seventy Disciples, victorious over the powers of Satan, return with joy (10.17–24). There is more joy in Heaven over one sinner who repents than over ninety-nine just persons who need no repentance (15.7, 10). In an interesting psychological representation, Jesus' disciples disbelieve in the risen Jesus 'for joy' (24.41), are convinced, and after Jesus' ascension return to Jerusalem 'with great joy' (24.52). In Acts joy marks the reaction of a Samarian city to Philip's preaching and healing (8.8), Rhoda the maid's reaction when she recognises the voice of the freed Peter (12.14), the disciples' reaction to the conversion of Gentiles and their own escape from persecution (13.52), and the brethren's reaction to the conversion of the Gentiles (15.3).

---

75   And it does so in a particularly interesting manner, because this saying of Jesus is otherwise unattested and the best parallel comes in Thucydides 2.97.4: 'They [the Thracian Odrysians] established the opposite custom to that of the Persian kingship ... to take rather than to give'. The Persian kings, it seems, held to the principle that it was better to give than to take. Cf. Plut. *Reg. et Imp. Apophth.* 173D (Artaxerxes I); 181F (Ptolemy I).
76   There is also an extensive Jewish background: Douglas (1996) 193–4; 211–12; Fishbane (1998); Potkay (2007); Barton (2013).

The verb χαίρομαι ('rejoice') is used of people's reaction to the Baptist's birth (Luke 1.14, 58), of followers of Jesus who are hated but whose reward will be great in heaven (6.23), of the feeling the disciples should have, not because the spirits are subject to them, but because their names are written in heaven (10.20), of the whole crowd's reaction to Jesus' glorious deeds (13.17), of the shepherd's finding lost sheep (15.5), of the feeling the brother ought to have at the saving of his Prodigal brother (15.32), of Zacchaeus' joyful reception of Jesus (19.6), and of the disciples' reaction to all the mighty works they have seen (19.37). In Acts, the apostles rejoice in being dishonoured for the name of Jesus Christ (5.41 ~ Luke 6.23); the Ethiopian eunuch rejoices for being on the right road (8.39), that is, for having chosen the 'road' that is Christianity; Barnabas rejoices at the grace of God;[77] the Gentiles rejoice at the word of God (13.48); and the Antiochenes at the Jerusalem Decree (15.31).

There is also 'exultation' (ἀγαλλίασις). Near the start of the Luke narrative (1.14), an angel tells Zechariah that at the birth of John the Baptist 'you will have joy (χαρά) and exultation and many will rejoice at his birth', and the baby John then leaps in his mother's womb in exultation on hearing the voice of the also pregnant Mary (1.44). Mary's spirit exults in God (1.47); and Jesus exults in the Holy Spirit (10.21). Near the start of the Acts narrative, the Believers experience exultation in their communal life in Jerusalem (2.46). Though the word occurs rarely, 'exultation' happens at critical moments in the gradual fulfilment of the divine purpose.

'Gladness' (εὐφραίνω/εὐφροσύνη) characterises the celebrations at the return of the Prodigal Son (Luke 15.23, 24, 29, 32) and David's confidence in the support of the Lord (Acts 2.26).[78]

In Acts 'cheerfulness' (εὐθυμία) centres on Paul: he himself begins his defence before the Roman governor Felix 'cheerfully' (24.10), and he urges 'cheerfulness' upon the sailors during the storm (27.22, 25), with due success (27.36). Such 'cheerfulness' characterises alike the imperturbable philosophical figure and 'the good leader' in times of danger.

These categories easily can be extended. Relevant also both etymologically and thematically are the noun χάρις and the verb χαρίζομαι: in Luke, of God's 'favour' for Mary (1.28, 30) and upon the boy Jesus (2.40); of the 'grace' of Jesus' words in the synagogue at Nazareth (4.22); of the 'favour' of Jesus' healings (7.21); of the 'favour' shown by the creditor in the parable (7.42–3). In Acts, of God's 'grace' upon all the apostles in Jerusalem (4.33); of Stephen's 'grace'

---

77   11.23 ἰδὼν τὴν χάριν τοῦ θεοῦ, ἐχάρη, the pun emphasising the link between grace and joy.
78   *Contra*, of misguided hedonism: Luke 12.19; 16.19; of misguided pride in idolatrous representations: Acts 7.41.

and 'power' in doing great signs among the people (6.8); of Joseph's 'favour' before Pharaoh (7.10); of David's 'favour' in the sight of God (7.46); of the 'grace' (χάρις) of God manifested in mass conversions and Barnabas' 'joy' (ἐχάρη) at this (11.23); of the 'grace' of God (13.43); of the 'grace' of the Lord (14.3) and of God (14.24); the salvific power of the 'grace' of the Lord Jesus (15.11) and of the Lord (15.40); of those who had believed through grace (18.27); of the good news of the grace of God (20.24); of the word of God's 'race' (20.32); of God's 'favour' in granting the lives of all Paul's fellow-sailors (27.24).

Important also within the whole complex is the verb εὐχαριστέω (of human 'thanks' for divine grace/favour): in Luke, of the Samaritan leper healed by Jesus and 'thanking' him (17.16); of Jesus himself 'giving thanks' at the Last Supper (22.17. 19); in Acts, of Paul in the same action as Jesus' (27.35); Paul thanks God on seeing landmarks for Rome (28.15); *contra*, Luke 18.11 (Pharisee thanking God for being unlike other men).

From this material we may draw a number of conclusions:

1. Volume: it is important first to appreciate the sheer volume of Luke's use of the lexicon of happiness, which should surprise readers new to the text (that is, for us, pagan readers or listeners), or even those modern Christians whose consumption of the text is confined to listening to bite-sized chunks on Sundays. William Morrice has described Luke as 'the gospel of joy', and Luke's use of such terminology is far greater than that of any of the other Evangelists. Indeed, of 326 instances of words for joy in the New Testament Luke-Acts contains 24%.[79] Very few pagan readers, of course, would be aware of these considerations, but they would certainly register the fact that Luke-Acts is a far 'happier' text than virtually any corresponding work of pagan historiography or biography—the genres with which Luke-Acts is most nearly aligned. The sheer volume of this material substantiates our earlier claims that the production of happiness and related emotions and states of mind is central to the purpose of Luke-Acts *qua* Gospel, philosophical text, and guarantor of *asphaleia*.

2. The material is reinforced by narrative patterning and architecture. 'Joy' is foregrounded as the essential human response to the birth of Jesus right at the start of Luke-Acts, and Luke is ring-structured by human 'joy' at Jesus' birth, resurrection and ascension. The very last word of Acts, ἀκωλύτως (a four-syllable alpha-privative compound word) rings with ἀσφάλειαν, the very last word of the *Preface* to Luke-Acts.[80] If the text and what it represents (Christianity) is a building that will not fall, then

---

79   Morrice (1985) 91–9.
80   Moles (2013) 114 {above, p. 694}.

3. The lexicon of happiness combines the negative ('don't fear') with positives ('do rejoice', etc.), combining basic reassurance against fear with positive exhortations to happiness.
4. Granted the pointed exclusion of εὐδαιμονία, the lexicon of happiness has a very wide range of components, although there is particular emphasis on 'joy'.
5. Such 'joy' is open to all human beings, whatever their social rank, throughout the world, although there is particular emphasis on the poor and marginalised. We may ask with which particular pagan philosophies Luke sees the greatest prospect of a successful conversation, in that they may afford 'doors' through which pagans may pass to the Christian truth. It so happens that *asphaleia* is a term much used by Epicureans in their quest for political (and other) 'security',[81] Epicureans are named in Acts 17 (17.18), and in the third century Origen knew of 'Epicurean Christians' (*Contra Celsum* 4.75). But Luke writes them off: the 'jeerers' of Acts 17.32 are surely the Epicureans, and they are jeering because of the suggestion of an afterlife. In Acts 26.22 Paul uses the term ἐπικουρία (hapax in Luke and in the New Testament) of 'the help that comes from God'. Thus 'Epicureans', despite their name, are 'helpless at helping'.[82] On the other hand, those who will hear Paul again about the resurrection (17.32) must be the Stoics, who had some interest in the possibilities of an afterlife and to whom the door is kept open in other ways, e.g., by the representation of Paul as like a Neronian Stoic martyr. And in representing Jesus himself and the apostles as in some ways Cynic-like, Luke conveys some Christian respect for Cynic ethics (with some obvious exclusions), an attitude which was to have a long history and affect both Christian behaviour and self-representation (e.g., artistic representations of Jesus as like a Cynic philosopher).[83]
6. Joy is also felt in heaven. Ideally speaking, this joy is reciprocal between man and God: ideally speaking, the *cosmos* is suffused by joy.
7. Joy suffuses the Christian life, whether Christians are responding to divine revelations, living their communal life, celebrating the Eucharist, or helping others by healing them or converting them.

---

81  {Epicur. *Sent.* VII, XIII, XIV;} Schofield (1999) 749–50.
82  Moles (2006b) 87–8 {above, pp. 571–3}.
83  Moles (2006a).

8. Contrary to the norm, this joy lasts individual life-times. Christians are objectively 'happy', but their 'happiness' as experienced takes the form of continuous 'joy'.
9. In particular, 'joy' marks crucial moments in the Christian story.
10. This joy spills across boundaries, so that the salutation χαῖρε, God's and Jesus' *charis*, and human beings' *charis* towards them, are all part of the same thing; and the vehicle of this *chara* and *charis* is Jesus the Christ *qua chreestos*.[84]

The joy and happiness promised readers by acceptance of Christianity are thus immense and thoroughgoing. There remains our third initial difficulty: how can this promise be made when Christians could be, and often were, put to death for their religion? This difficulty cannot be ducked—and Luke makes no attempt to do so. It is true that some attempt is made to dissuade Roman readers from persecution of Christianity. But the problems of Christianity's radical counter-culturalism and of its consequent vulnerability to persecution cannot be evaded. So the question arises: how *concrete* is this contract—or covenant—of joy and happiness and ultimate security between man and God? What is its essential basis? Further, as we have seen, within the overall architecture of Luke-Acts, ἀσφάλειαν at the end of the Preface 'rings' with the very last word of Acts, ἀκωλύτως: the text as a building (a) is absolutely secure and (b) allows absolute freedom, even when, like Paul, you're fettered and—symbolically—near death. Both in philosophical contexts and within the image chains, the operative idea of ἀσφάλεια is its basic meaning, that of security from falling. Christianity will not fall—unlike the Temple, unlike, indeed, the Roman empire; the 'credit system' that is Christianity will not fall—unlike Leeman Brothers; Christians themselves will not fall, because, like Jesus, they will be 'raised up': ἀσφάλεια is guaranteed by ἀνάστασις. This last observation is absolutely elementary—my excuse is that New Testament scholars don't say it—or, apparently, see it. Whether they die naturally or unnaturally through persecution, Christians' inevitable death is trumped by resurrection. Christianity unifies life and death and solves the problem of death. Resurrection is the ultimate guarantee of the Christian contract, or covenant, with god. This point is, I believe, rammed home by various plays on the name 'Christ', though that belongs to another study.[85]

If the acid test of happiness is, call no man happy until he is dead,[86] Christianity has the complete answer.

---

84  See above, ch. 10.
85  Above, ch. 29.
86  Hdt. 1.32.5 (Solon to Croesus).

In all sorts of obvious ways, then, and in the most profound ways, Christian philosophical happiness decisively defeats all versions of pagan philosophical happiness, so it is in pagans' interest to convert to Christianity, even given the ever-present threat of persecution of Christians, extending unto death.

Of course, Christian philosophical happiness bests all versions of pagan happiness, *only if* you 'buy' Christianity itself, which, for Luke, means, as it has to be, buying the truth of Jesus' resurrection, of which Luke-Acts aspires in various obvious ways to being a 'proof text'. That is a matter for theologians, not classicists. These 'proofs' are of course conveyed in a text whose literary qualities have much to offer pagans. That indeed is a matter for literary critics, but literary criticism is no substitute for theology.

## Bibliography

Alexander, L. C. A. (2005) *Acts in Its Ancient Literary Context: A Classicist Looks at the Acts of the Apostles* (London and New York).

Annas, J. (1993) *The Morality of Happiness* (New York and Oxford).

Baban, O. D. (2006) *On the Road Encounters in Luke-Acts: Hellenistic Mimesis and Luke's Theology of the Way* (Milton Keynes).

Barton, S. C. (2013) 'Spirituality and the Emotions in Early Christianity: The Case of Joy', in A. T. Lincoln, G. McConville, and L. K. Petersen, edd., *The Bible and Spirituality: Essays in Reading Scripture Spiritually* (Eugene, Or.) 171–93.

Bauckham, R. J., ed. (1998) *The Gospels for All Christians: Rethinking the Gospel Audiences* (Edinburgh and Grand Rapids).

Bauckham, R. J. (2006) *Jesus and the Eyewitnesses: the Gospels as Eyewitness Testimony* (Grand Rapids and Cambridge).

Bosman, P. (2006) 'Selling Cynicism: the Pragmatics of Diogenes' Comic Performances', *CQ* 56: 93–104.

Burridge, R. A. (1992) *What are the Gospels? A Comparison with Graeco-Roman Biography* (Cambridge; $^2$2004 Grand Rapids).

Douglas, M. (1996) 'The Cosmic Joke', in ead., *Thought Styles: Critical Essays on Good Taste* (London) 193–212.

Dunn, J. D. G. (1996) *The Acts of the Apostles* (Peterborough).

Dupertuis, R. (2013) 'Bold Speech, Opposition and Philosophical Imagery in Acts', in Dupertuis and Penner (2013) 153–68.

Dupertuis, R. and T. Penner, edd. (2013) *Engaging Early Christian History: Reading Acts in the Second Century* (Durham and Bristol, Ct.).

Engberg, J. (2007) Impulsore Chresto: *Opposition to Christianity in the Roman Empire c. 50–250 AD* (Frankfurt am Main).

Fishbane, M. (1998) 'Joy and Jewish Spirituality', in id., *The Exegetical Imagination: On Jewish Thought and Theology* (Cambridge, Mass. and London) 151–72.

Fitzmyer, J. A. (1981–5) *The Gospel According to Luke*, 2 vols. (New York).

Fitzmyer, J. A. (1998) *The Acts of the Apostles* (New York).

Green, J. B. (2012) '"We Had to Celebrate and Rejoice!" Happiness in the Topsy-Turvy World of Luke-Acts', in B. A. Strawn, ed., *The Bible and the Pursuit of Happiness* (New York and Oxford) 169–86.

Hengel, M. (2000) *The Four Gospels and the One Gospel of Jesus Christ: An Investigation of the Collection and Origin of the Canonical Gospels* (London and Harrisburg, Pa.).

Johnson, L. T. (1991) *The Gospel of Luke* (Collegeville, Minn.).

Jones, C. P. (2014) *Between Pagan and Christian* (Cambridge, Mass.).

Keener, C. S. (2009) *The Historical Jesus of the Gospels* (Grand Rapids and Cambridge).

Klauck, H.-J. (2000) *Magic and Paganism in Early Christianity: the World of the Acts of the Apostles* (Edinburgh).

Lang, M. (2008) *Die Kunst des christlichen Lebens: rezeptionsästhetische Studien zum lukanischen Paulusbild* (Leipzig).

Lee, D. (2013) Luke-Acts *and 'Tragic History'* (Tübingen).

Moles, J. L. (2006a) 'Cynic Influence upon First-Century Judaism and Early Christianity?', in B. McGing and J. Mossman, edd., *The Limits of Biography* (London and Swansea) 89–116 [above, Ch. 20].

Moles, J. L. (2006b) 'Jesus and Dionysus in *The Acts of the Apostles* and Early Christianity' *Hermathena* 180: 65–104 [above, Ch. 21].

Moles, J. L. (2011a) 'Jesus the Healer in the Gospels, the Acts of the Apostles, and Early Christianity', *Histos* 5: 117–82 [above, Ch. 23].

Moles, J. L. (2011b) 'Luke's Preface: The Greek Decree, Classical Historiography and Christian Redefinitions', *NTS* 57: 1–22 [above, Ch. 22].

Moles, J. L. (2013) 'Time and Space Travel in Luke-Acts', in Dupertuis and Penner (2013) 101–22 [above, Ch. 24].

Moles, J. L. (2014) 'Accommodation or Opposition? Luke-Acts on Rome', in J. M. Madsen and R. Rees, edd., *Double Vision: Reflections of Roman Rule in Greek and Latin Writing* (Leiden) 79–104 [above, Ch. 25].

Morgan, J. M. (2013) *Encountering Images of Spiritual Transformation: The Thoroughfare Motif Within the Plot of Luke-Acts* (Eugene, Or.).

Morgan, J. M. (2014) 'Review of Lee (2013)', *Histos* 8: xlvii–lii.

Morrice, W. (1985) *Joy in the New Testament* (Grand Rapids).

Pervo, R. I. (1987) *Profit with Delight: the Literary Genre of the Acts of the Apostles* (Philadelphia).

Plümacher, E. (2006) 'Stichwort: Lukas, Historiker', *ZNT* 18: 2–8.
Potkay, A. (2007) *The Story of Joy: From the Bible to Late Romanticism* (Cambridge).
Prince, S. (2015) *Antisthenes of Athens: Texts, Translations, and Commentary* (Ann Arbor).
Schofield, M. (1999) 'Social and Political Thought', in K. Algra, J. Barnes, J. Mansfeld, and M. Schofield, edd., *The Cambridge History of Hellenistic Philosophy* (Cambridge) 739–70.
Seaford, R. (1997) 'Thunder, Lightning and Earthquake in the *Bacchae* and the Acts of the Apostles', in A. B. Lloyd, ed., *What is a God? Studies in the Nature of Greek Divinity* (London) 139–51.
Talbert, C. H. (1974) *Literary Patterns, Theological Themes, and the Genre of Luke-Acts* (Missoula).
Tannehill, R. C. (1986–90) *The Narrative Unity of Luke-Acts: a Literary Interpretation*, 2 vols. (Philadelphia).
Verdenius, W. J. (1983) 'The Principles of Greek Literary Criticism', *Mnemosyne* 36: 14–59.
Watson, F. (2013) *Gospel Writing: A Canonical Perspective* (Grand Rapids and Cambridge).

# Index Locorum

## 1. Greek and Roman Authors

**Achilles Tatius,** *Leucippe et Clitophon*
8.9.3      196 n. 30

**Aelian,** *Variae Historiae*
13.20      410

**Aelius Aristides,** *Orationes*
36.96 Keil      134 n. 68
46.23      272 n. 138
46, p. 404 Dindorf      42
50.100 Keil      42 n. 104

**Aeschylus**
*Agamemnon*
1624      561 n. 27
*Eumenides*
647–51      887
647–8      651 n. 143
650      797 n. 53
651      685 n. 43
*Prometheus Vinctus*
323      561 n. 27

**Ammianus Marcellinus**
31.16.8–9      749
31.6.9      750

**[Anacharsis]**
*Epistle* 5.3      427 n. 27

**Andocides**
6.19      190 n. 13

**Anonymous Tragedian**
Trag. adesp. 374N ~ TrGF 88 F 3      378 n. 71

**Anonymous,** *Narratio de rebus Persicis*
p. 15.10 Bratke      987 n. 48

*Anthologia Palatina*
7.417      347 n. 133, 392 n. 13, 422 n. 4
11.158      347 n. 132
11.218      196 n. 30
11.418      114 n. 15, 115 n. 15
12.101      347 n. 133
16.334      430 n. 55

**Antiphon**
F 44 DK      425 n. 18

**Antisthenes** (Decleva Caizzi ~ Prince)
1 ~ 41A      332 n. 73
14.4 ~ 53.4      332 n. 73
15 ~ 54      69 n. 13
15.2 ~ 54.2      330 n. 63
15.8 ~ 54.8      83 n. 43, 330 n. 63, 332 n. 73
15.10 ~ 54.10      83 n. 43, 332 n. 73
16 ~ 62      69 n. 13
19 ~ 85      358 n. 24
20A ~ 86A      332 n. 73
20B ~ 86B      332 n. 73
27 ~ 96      94 n. 69, 258 n. 46, 299, 335 n. 87, 481–4, 503–8 *passim*
67 ~ 105      335 n. 88, 356 n. 14
72 ~ 134r      357 n. 19
77 ~ 109      332 n. 73, 373 n. 47
106 ~ 69      332 n. 73
107 ~ 13A      332 n. 73
117.22 ~ 82.22      336 n. 94, 338 n. 101
128A ~ 12A      330 n. 63
135A ~ 22A      357 n. 18
185 ~ 169      332 n. 73
186 ~ 167      332 n. 73, 357 n. 17, 338 n. 101
195 ~ 7      357 n. 18

**Apollodorus Seleuciensis**
17 (*SVF* III.261)      398 n. 29, 340 n. 108

**Apollonius Rhodius,** *Argonautica*
1–2      744

**Appian**
*praef.* 15.62      592, 813
*Bellum Ciuile* 5.2      868

## Apuleius
*Apologia*
22     347 n. 133

*Asclepius*
14.1     42 n. 103

*de dogmate Platonis*
2.9.14     42 n. 103

*Florida*
14     370 n. 36
18.18     42 n. 103
22     81 n. 38, 332 n. 73, 429 n. 48

## Aratus, *Phaenomena*
1–9     875 n. 132
1–5     743
5     560, 879

## Aristobulus of Alexandria
F 1     751
F 4.6     875 n. 132
F 506     46 n. 118

## Aristophanes
*Clouds*
965     254 n. 19
967     254 n. 19, 278
985–6     254 n. 19, 278

*Wealth*
1151     425 n. 18

## Aristotle
[*Athenaion Politeia*] 1     883 n. 164

*Ethica Nicomachea*
1101a7     994 n. 74
1101b     120 n. 33
1125a–12     209 n. 16
1155a21     425 n. 18
1155a32ff     373 n. 49
1159b7ff     373 n. 46
1168b1ff.     866
1373b18     425 n. 18

*Metaphysics*
980a1     878

*Poetics*
1451b11     822
1451b16     224 n. 56

*Politics*
1253a26–9     429 n. 45, 445

*Rhetorica*
1385b13     336 n. 94
1386a24     336 n. 94

*Fragmenta*
5     44 n. 109
140     24
592     950
646–7     162

## Arrian
*Anabasis*
1.12.5     592 n. 34, 813 n. 141
7.2     406

*Indica*
1.4–5     578 n. 131
5.12     578 n. 131

## Athenaeus
157b     347 n. 133
159c     398 n. 32, 455
220d     489 n. 16
502c     347 n. 133

## Augustus, *Res Gestae*
praef.     597, 598 with n. 78

## Aurelius Victor, *de Caesaribus*
5.2–5     151 n. 116
5.2–4     151 n. 116
13.6     158 n. 126
13.9     133

## Bion of Borysthenes (Kindstrand)
*Testimonia*
T 8a     463 n. 5
T 8b     463 n. 5
T 15     462 n. 4
T 16     462 n. 4
T 17     462 n. 4
T 18     462 n. 4

*Fragmenta*

| | |
|---|---|
| F 1 | 463 with n. 6 |
| F 1A | 462 n. 4, 476 n. 37 |
| F 2 | 463 |
| F 3 | 364 |
| F 6 | 426 n. 23 |
| F 16 | 296 n. 6, 454 n. 26, 463 |
| F 16A | 125, 375 n. 60, 378 n. 73, 409 nn. 70–1, 423 n. 11, 424 n. 15 |
| F 17 | 423 n. 11, 454 n. 26 |
| F 17.7–9 | 427 n. 29 |
| F 17.7 | 431 n. 61 |
| F 17.8–9 | 427 n. 27 |
| F 23 | 358 n. 25, 377 n. 67 |
| F 68 | 217, 476 n. 38 |
| F 75 | 332 n. 73 |

**Caesar**, *de bello Gallico*

| | |
|---|---|
| 3.53 | 380 n. 77 |

**Callimachus**, *Hymnus in Iouem*

| | |
|---|---|
| 7–8 | 880 |

**Callinus** (*IEG*²)

| | |
|---|---|
| 1.8–9 | 82 n. 41 |

**Calpurnius Siculus**, *Eclogues*

| | |
|---|---|
| 7 | 570 n. 82 |

**Cassius Dio**

| | |
|---|---|
| 47.49.1f. | 378 n. 71 |
| 60.15.3 | 30 n. 41 |
| 62(63).9 | 71 |
| 62.26.2 | 320 n. 13 |
| 62.26.13 | 320 n. 14 |
| 65.8 | 613 n. 2 |
| 65.12.1 | 176 n. 156 |
| 66.12.2 | 30 n. 41 |
| 66.13 | 34 nn. 56–57, 325 n. 37 |
| 66.13.1 | 349 n. 136 |
| 66.13.2 | 232 n. 14 |
| 66.15 | 26 n. 15 |
| 67.4.1 | 121 n. 37 |
| 67.12.1 | 138 n. 83, 297 n. 9 |
| 68.1.3 | 109 n. 12 |
| 68.7.4 | 115 |
| 68.10.2 | 161 n. 138 |
| 68.15.4–6 | 90 n. 61 |
| 68.15.4 | 140 n. 89 |
| 68.16.1 | 133 |
| 68.17.1 | 87 n. 53, 101 n. 90, 113 |
| 68.29–30 | 75 n. 9, 113 |
| 68.3.4 | 114 n. 15, 128 n. 51 |
| 68.6.4 | 100 n. 86 |
| 68.7.3 | 90 n. 61, 95 n. 75, 98 n. 82, 100 n. 86, 109 n. 13, 136 n. 75, 140 n. 89 |
| 68.7.4 | 161 n. 138 |
| 73.23 | 747 n. 53 |

**Catullus**

| | |
|---|---|
| 11.10–12 | 862 n. 88 |

**Cercidas**

| | |
|---|---|
| F 4 Powell = 1 Livrea | 410, 455 |

**Chariton**, *de Chaerea et Callirhoe*

| | |
|---|---|
| 1.11.6–7 | 874 |

**Cicero**

*Academica*

| | |
|---|---|
| 2.8 | 472 |
| 2.27 | 595 n. 61, 808 n. 111 |
| 2.139 | 368 n. 30, 473 |

*Brutus*

| | |
|---|---|
| 331 | 134 n. 66 |

*de Amicitia*

| | |
|---|---|
| 88 | 373 n. 46 |

*Epistulae ad Atticum*

| | |
|---|---|
| 2.9.1 | 385 n. 88 |
| 12.38a.2 | 384 n. 85 |

*Epistulae ad Familiares*

| | |
|---|---|
| 15.16.3 | 24 n. 3 |
| 15.17.3 | 24 n. 3 |

*Epistulae ad Quintum Fratrem*

| | |
|---|---|
| 2.10(9).3 | 333 n. 80 |

*de Finibus*

| | |
|---|---|
| 1.62 | 885 n. 167 |
| 3.48 | 365 n. 16 |
| 3.68 | 348 |

## de Inuentione

| | |
|---|---|
| 1.2 | 124 n. 40 |
| 1.3 | 124 n. 40 |

## de Natura Deorum

| | |
|---|---|
| 1.102 | 366 n. 22 |

## de Officiis

| | |
|---|---|
| 1.9 | 367 n. 27 |
| 1.17 | 375 n. 56 |
| 1.107ff | 375 n. 56, 462 n. 1 |
| 1.110 | 372 nn. 41–2 |
| 1.124ff | 462 n. 1 |
| 1.128 | 347, 349, 375 n. 56, 385 n. 90 |
| 1.148 | 347, 372 n. 44, 375 n. 56 |
| 2.31ff | 375 n. 56 |
| 3.7–10 | 367 n. 27 |
| 3.44 | 79 n. 29 |

## In Pisonem

| | |
|---|---|
| 37 | 210, 366 n. 22 |

## de Republica

| | |
|---|---|
| 6.26 | 79 n. 29 |

## Tusculanae Disputationes

| | |
|---|---|
| 4.7 | 472 |
| 5.92 | 90 n. 58, 440 |
| 5.108 | 392 n. 12, 422 n. 5 |

## Crates

[*Epistulae*]

| | |
|---|---|
| 3 | 429 n. 51 |
| 7.1 | 429 n. 49 |
| 16 | 429 n. 44 |
| 16.1 | 350 n. 143 |
| 19 | 347 n. 133, 381 n. 78 |
| 24 | 99 n. 85, 339 n. 105 |
| 27 | 432 n. 70 |
| 28.3 | 341 n. 115, 357 n. 17 |
| 28.6 | 356 n. 14 |
| 29.1 | 332 n. 73, 350 n. 143 |
| 29.2–5 | 341 n. 115 |
| 29.2 | 99 n. 85, 339 n. 105 |
| 29.4 | 332 n. 73 |
| 32.3 | 339 n. 103, 400 n. 38, 433 n. 74 |
| 33 | 92 n. 65 |
| 34.1 | 363 n. 11 |
| 34.2 | 335 n. 88 |
| 40.5 | 332 n. 73, 335 n. 88 |
| 41 | 432 n. 70 |

*Fragmenta* (Diehl)

| | |
|---|---|
| F 1 | 329 n. 53, 332 n. 73, 373 n. 47, 431 nn. 61 and 63 |
| F 7 | 91 n. 64 |

## Demetrius, *de Elocutione*

| | |
|---|---|
| 259 | 452 |
| 261 | 125 n. 42, 282 n. 191, 326 n. 43 |
| 287–98 | 119 |
| 288 | 122 |
| 291 | 120 n. 33 |
| 292 | 120 with n. 33, 122 |
| 294 | 119, 120 n. 33 |
| 295 | 120 with n. 33, 123 |

## Democritus

| | |
|---|---|
| F 247 D–K | 422 n. 5, 425 n. 18 |

## Demosthenes, *Orationes*

| | |
|---|---|
| 59.21 | 25 |

## Dio Chrysostom

[*Epistles*]

| | |
|---|---|
| 2 (Hercher, p. 259) | 232 n. 13 |
| 5 (Hercher, p. 259) | 40 n. 91 |

| | |
|---|---|
| Κώμης Ἐγκώμιον | 51 nn. 139 and 141 |
| *Oration* 1 | 74, 77, 84, 102, 109, 120–54 *passim*, 165, 203, 211 n. 20, 220, 225, 229, 252 n. 11, 266 n. 117, 271 n. 135, 273, 277, 279, 282, 287 n. 220, 294 n. 3, 298, 301, 304, 308, 309, 311, 414 n. 80, 457 |
| 1.1–10 | 76 |
| 1.1–8 | 84, 97, 113 |
| 1.1–3 | 120 |
| 1.1f. | 121 |
| 1.1 | 213 n. 22, 233 |
| 1.2f. | 121 |

**Dio Chrysostom** (*cont.*)
[*Epistles*] (*cont.*)

| | | | |
|---|---|---|---|
| 1.2 | 132 | 1.37–48 | 159 |
| 1.4f. | 121 | 1.37–47 | 132, 139 |
| 1.4 | 122, 125 with n. 43, 142, 154 | 1.37–41 | 128, 132, 193 |
| | | 1.37 | 130, 132 |
| 1.5 | 122, 123, 129, 132 | 1.42ff | 153 |
| 1.6f. | 123 | 1.42–8 | 134 |
| 1.7 | 32 n. 48, 123 | 1.42–7 | 132 |
| 1.8f | 127, 134, 139, 142 | 1.43–7 | 153 |
| 1.8 | 115, 124, 128, 129, 134, 137, 152, 244, 262 n. 85 | 1.44 | 133, 252 n. 8 |
| | | 1.45 | 128, 133 |
| | | 1.46f | 133 |
| 1.9f | 121, 171 n. 146 | 1.47 | 115 n. 17 |
| 1.9 | 40, 51 nn. 135 and 138, 53, 121, 124, 125, 127, 128, 129, 130, 135, 139, 141, 142, 155, 260 n. 63, 268 n. 122, 281 n. 183, 295, 409, 413 n. 80 | 1.48 | 132 |
| | | 1.49ff. | 273 |
| | | 1.49 | 134, 139, 142, 208 n. 10, 273 n. 143, 286 n. 217 |
| | | 1.50–1 | 135, 260 n. 63 |
| | | 1.50 | 38 n. 75, 51 n. 138, 54, 128, 135, 137, 138, 139, 141, 244, 270 n. 128, 286 n. 218 |
| 1.10 | 41 n. 92, 124 n. 40, 125, 127, 135, 141, 142, 159, | | |
| 1.11–14 | 128 n. 53, 129 | 1.51 | 135 |
| 1.11 | 127, 128 | 1.52ff. | 53 n. 148, 82 with nn. 39 and 42 |
| 1.12f. | 129 | | |
| 1.12 | 115 n. 17, 128, 129 | 1.52–4 | 142 |
| 1.13 | 115 n. 17, 128, 135 | 1.52 | 137 n. 82, 153, 281 n. 183 |
| 1.14 | 77 n. 21, 87, 93, 128 with n. 53, 129 | 1.53 | 142, 262 n. 85, 281 n. 186, 286 n. 217 |
| 1.15–36 | 129 | 1.55 | 51 n. 138, 52 n. 145, 82, 137, 138 n. 82, 139, 271 n. 135, 273 n. 143 |
| 1.15f. | 129 | | |
| 1.15 | 120 n. 33, 129, 130 with n. 56, 131 | | |
| | | 1.56–8 | 270 n. 129 |
| 1.16 | 129, 130 | 1.56 | 46 n. 118, 51 n. 138, 76 n. 17, 82, 95 n. 73, 124, 137, 138 with n. 82, 140, 141, 142, 274 n. 154, 297 |
| 1.17ff. | 129 | | |
| 1.17 | 77 n. 21, 136 | | |
| 1.19 | 136 | | |
| 1.20 | 123, 130, 131, 141 | 1.57 | 40 n. 88, 138 n. 82, 307 |
| 1.21 | 130, 141 | 1.58ff. | 153 |
| 1.22 | 130 | 1.58 | 115, 139 with n. 85, 142, 429 n. 47 |
| 1.23–4 | 32 n. 48 | | |
| 1.25 | 90 n. 61, 130, 131 | 1.59 | 115 n. 17, 123, 128, 140, 297 n. 11, 306 |
| 1.26 | 91 n. 62, 130, 136 | | |
| 1.27 | 130, 131, 132 | 1.60 | 140 |
| 1.28 | 130, 131 | 1.61–3 | 140, 297 n. 10 |
| 1.30–3 | 131 | 1.61 | 40 with nn. 88 and 89, 115, 140, 141, 213 n. 22, 307, 405 n. 54, 678 |
| 1.30–2 | 123, 130, 131 | | |
| 1.33 | 93 n. 67, 131, 141 | | |
| 1.35 | 132 | 1.62ff. | 99 |
| 1.36 | 130, 136, 168 | 1.63 | 140, 306 |

**Dio Chrysostom** (*cont.*)
[*Epistles*] (*cont.*)

| | |
|---|---|
| 1.64–7 | 128 |
| 1.64 | 123, 141 |
| 1.65ff. | 142, 234 n. 26 |
| 1.66ff. | 272 n. 141 |
| 1.66 | 142 |
| 1.67 | 245 |
| 1.69 | 142, 244 |
| 1.70–84 | 490 n. 23 |
| 1.71 | 91 n. 64, 123 |
| 1.73 | 123, 128 |
| 1.74 | 91 n. 64 |
| 1.75 | 175, 262 n. 85, 281 n. 186 |
| 1.79 | 128 n. 53, 266 n. 115 |
| 1.83f. | 128 |
| 1.83 | 130 n. 57 |
| 1.84 | 81 n. 34, 83 n. 43, 123, 153, 332 n. 73 |

*Oration* 2 — 74, 77, 84, 97, 102, 113, 154–64 *passim*, 196 nn. 31 and 32, 203, 225, 229, 240 n. 54, 277 with n. 172, 279, 294 n. 3, 297

| | |
|---|---|
| 2.1f. | 136 n. 75 |
| 2.3 | 171 n. 146 |
| 2.12 | 51 n. 139 |
| 2.18–24 | 41 n. 92 |
| 2.18 | 41 |
| 2.22f | 179 |
| 2.24 | 41 |
| 2.26 | 115, 124 |
| 2.49 | 99 |
| 2.55f. | 125 n. 43 |
| 2.72 | 128 |
| 2.78 | 173 |
| 2.79 | 76, 81 n. 34 |

*Oration* 3 — 74, 77, 105–9, 166–77 *passim*, 203, 229, 255, 277, 279, 294 n. 3, 298, 301, 304

| | |
|---|---|
| 3.1–3 | 76, 262 n. 85 |
| 3.1–2 | 55 |
| 3.1 | 115 n. 17 |
| 3.2f. | 115 |
| 3.2 | 91 n. 62, 105 with n. 3, 106, 159, 177 |
| 3.3–5 | 130 n. 57 |
| 3.3 | 109, 124 n. 40, 163, 277 n. 172 |
| 3.4f | 133 n. 64 |
| 3.5 | 108 |
| 3.7 | 108 |
| 3.8 | 108 |
| 3.10 | 49, n. 126, 133 n. 64 |
| 3.12–25 | 95 n. 73, 111, 130, 140, 275 n. 159 |
| 3.12 | 34 n. 58, 277 n. 170 |
| 3.12ff. | 109 |
| 3.13 | 34 n. 58, 63, 105 n. 3, 132 |
| 3.15 | 39 n. 85 |
| 3.18 | 120 n. 33 |
| 3.25 | 109 n. 12, 130 n. 56 |
| 3.26–7 | 254 n. 28 |
| 3.26 | 109 |
| 3.27 | 39 n. 83, 40 nn. 88 and 90, 55 |
| 3.30–41 | |
| 3.32–41 | 177 |
| 3.34 | 275 n. 155 |
| 3.38 | 87 n. 54, 128 n. 53 |
| 3.41 | 128 n. 53, 266 n. 115 |
| 3.50–4 | 128 |
| 3.50 | 275 n. 155 |
| 3.54 | 142 n. 93 |
| 3.56 | 109 |
| 3.65 | 128 |
| 3.83–4 | 109 |
| 3.88f | 133 n. 64 |
| 3.123ff. | 109 |
| 3.123 | 109 |
| 3.127 | 109 |
| 3.133ff. | 109 with n. 13 |
| 3.134 | 71 |
| 3.135ff. | 81 n. 34, 109 |
| 3.135–8 | 136 n. 75 |

*Oration* 4 — 72, 73–104 *passim*, 76, 106 n. 6, 113, 164–6 *passim*, 203, 220, 225, 229, 255, 259 n. 54, 266 n. 115, 277, 279, 282, 287 n. 220, 294 n. 3, 296, 297, 298 with n. 12, 301, 302, 304, 305, 308, 309, 311 318 n. 4, 333, 457, 491

INDEX LOCORUM

*Oration* 4 (*cont.*)
| | |
|---|---|
| 4.1–3 | 55 n. 151 |
| 4.1 | 84, 85, 89, 115 n. 17, 124, 260 n. 63 |
| 4.3 | 75, 76, 80, 84 with n. 49, 155 n. 124 |
| 4.4–74 | 92–3 n. 65 |
| 4.4–10 | 87, 90 |
| 4.4–5 | 98 n. 79 |
| 4.4 | 77 n. 21, 87, 93, 128 n. 53, 484 |
| 4.5 | 89, 90 |
| 4.6–11 | 260 n. 63 |
| 4.6–10 | 88 |
| 4.6 | 89, 91, 340 n. 111 |
| 4.6–7 | 89 |
| 4.6f. | 364 n. 15 |
| 4.7 | 86, 89, 377 n. 65 |
| 4.8 | 89, 90, 140 n. 89, 298 n. 14, 306, 405 n. 53, 601 n. 102, 807 n. 106 |
| 4.9 | 90 |
| 4.10–12 | 98 n. 79 |
| 4.10 | 89 |
| 4.11 | 484 |
| 4.11–15 | 90 |
| 4.13 | 392 n. 11, 422 n. 4, 427 nn. 27 and 28 |
| 4.14 | 39 n. 82, 40 n. 90, 90, 243 |
| 4.15 | 89, 91, 98 nn. 78 and 79, 159 |
| 4.16–19 | 91 |
| 4.17 | 177 |
| 4.18 | 98 n. 78, 143 n. 98, 379 n. 76 |
| 4.19ff. | 93 |
| 4.19 | 32 n. 48 |
| 4.20 | 93, 98 n. 78 |
| 4.21–3 | 128 |
| 4.23 | 93, 98 n. 78 |
| 4.24 | 93, 334 n. 82 |
| 4.24–5 | 93, 484 |
| 4.25 | 87 n. 54, 128 n. 53, 266 n. 115 |
| 4.26 | 93, 98 n. 78 |
| 4.27 | 128, 194 n. 23, 210 n. 17 |
| 4.27–39 | 95, 140 |
| 4.28 | 39 n. 81, 40 n. 90, 43 |
| 4.29 | 41 n. 93, 80 n. 31, 93, 414 n. 80 |
| 4.29–38 | 484–92 *passim* |
| 4.29–37 | 243, 245 |
| 4.29–35 | 299 |
| 4.29–33 | 481 n. 4, 492 n. 33, 495 |
| 4.29ff | 115, 259, 300, 301, 335 n. 87, 484 |
| 4.30 | 98 n. 79, 212 |
| 4.31 | 94, 128, 489 |
| 4.31f. | 94 n. 71 |
| 4.32 | 39 n. 83, 40 n. 90, 94, 99 |
| 4.33 | 46 n. 118, 92 n. 65, 95, 101, 243, 244 |
| 4.33–8 | 39 nn. 80, 81, 82, and 84, 307 |
| 4.34–5 | 95, 136 n. 75 |
| 4.35 | 40 n. 90, 43, 95 n. 73, 243 |
| 4.36 | 40 n. 90, 98 n. 78, 243 |
| 4.37 | 266 n. 117 |
| 4.38–43 | 128 |
| 4.38 | 40 nn. 88 and 89, 94, 95, 340 n. 111, 363 n. 11 |
| 4.39ff | 486 |
| 4.39f. | 95 |
| 4.39 | 98 n. 78, 366 n. 20 |
| 4.43 | 95 |
| 4.43–72 | 97 |
| 4.44 | 96 |
| 4.46–51 | 97 |
| 4.46–9 | 96 |
| 4.46 | 177 |
| 4.47–9 | 98 |
| 4.47 | 486 |
| 4.49 | 98 n. 78 |
| 4.49–51 | 177 |
| 4.50–1 | 96, 98 |
| 4.51 | 96 |
| 4.52 | 98 n. 78, 100 |
| 4.53 | 484 |
| 4.53–4 | 405 n. 53 |
| 4.55 | 98 n. 78 |
| 4.57 | 339 n. 104 |
| 4.58 | 98 with n. 78 |
| 4.59–60 | 96 |
| 4.59 | 96, 98 |
| 4.60–4 | 99 |
| 4.61ff. | 93 n. 67 |

*Oration* 4 (*cont.*)

| | | | |
|---|---|---|---|
| 4.61–4 | 96 | | nn. 39, 42, and 45, 101, 102, 241 n. 61, 242 n. 68, 340 n. 111, 430 n. 53, 486 |
| 4.61 | 98 n. 78, 266 n. 115 | | |
| 4.62 | 99 | | |
| 4.63–4 | 89 | *Oration* 5 | 76, 241 n. 61 |
| 4.63 | 100 | 5.3 | 134 n. 69 |
| 4.64 | 96, 98 with n. 78 | 5.18 | 76 |
| 4.65–6 | 96 | 5.21 | 146 n. 104 |
| 4.66ff | 486 | 5.23 | 146 n. 104 |
| 4.66–70 | 96 | 5.24 | 30 n. 39, 134 n. 68 |
| 4.66 | 86, 92 n. 65, 99 n. 85, 339 n. 105 | *Oration* 6 | 49, 73, 126 n. 44, 164, 232 n. 15, 266 n. 115, 303–9 *passim*, 333 |
| 4.70 | 96, 99 n. 85, 484 | | |
| 4.71 | 98 n. 78 | | |
| 4.72 | 94, 96 | 6.1ff | 90 n. 58, 260 n. 63 |
| 4.73 | 76, 241 n. 61, 277 n. 170 | 6.1–7 | 539 n. 103 |
| 4.74–139 | 245 | 6.12–13 | 427 n. 29 |
| 4.75–139 | 73, 76, 78, 79, 241 n. 61 | 6.16ff | 326 n. 41 |
| 4.74 | 134 n. 68 | 6.19–20 | 429 n. 40 |
| 4.75ff. | 79 | 6.21 | 39 nn. 77, 78, and 84, 40 n. 90, 307 |
| 4.75–6 | 78 | | |
| 4.75 | 77, 100, 486 | 6.22–5 | 400 n. 38, 433 n. 74 |
| 4.76 | 77 | 6.22f. | 339 n. 103 |
| 4.77–8 | 98 n. 78, 100 | 6.22 | 339 n. 102 |
| 4.77 | 100 | 6.25 | 423 n. 9, 427 n. 29, 429 n. 43, 528 n. 26 |
| 4.78ff. | 100 | | |
| 4.78 | 40 n. 87 | 6.28 | 423 n. 9 |
| 4.79–81 | 26 n. 17, 34 n. 54, 285 n. 209 | 6.30 | 427 n. 29 |
| | | 6.31 | 423 n. 9, 429 n. 44 |
| 4.79–80 | 77 | 6.34 | 34 n. 58 |
| 4.79 | 41, 78 | 6.35–62 | 456 |
| 4.80 | 78 n. 27, 80 n. 31 | 6.39 | 305 |
| 4.83ff. | 80 n. 31 | 6.45 | 305 |
| 4.83–138 | 79 | 6.57 | 305 |
| 4.83–4 | 77 | 6.58 | 34 n. 58 |
| 4.91–132 | 77 | 6.60 | 306, 330 n. 63, 405 n. 53 |
| 4.101 | 100 n. 88 | 6.60–2 | 192 |
| 4.102 | 486 with n. 12 | | |
| 4.103 | 100 n. 88 | *Oration* 7 | 53 n. 148, 77, 180, 187, 188–91 *passim*, 214, 220, 225, 254 n. 18, 276, 277 with n. 170, 282, 287 n. 220, 296, 311 |
| 4.110 | 100 n. 110 | | |
| 4.117–21 | 100 | | |
| 4.124 | 41 n. 92, 101 | | |
| 4.127 | 101 | | |
| 4.132 | 39 nn. 78 and 85, 40 n. 90, 101 | 7.1 | 46 n. 118, 51 n. 138, 186, 266 n. 117 |
| 4.133–8 | 77 | 7.2–3 | 54 |
| 4.139 | 77 n. 22, 78 with n. 27, 79, 80 with n. 31, 81, 82 with | 7.3 | 51 n. 138 |
| | | 7.4 | 51 n. 139 |

INDEX LOCORUM

| | | | |
|---|---|---|---|
| *Oration* 7 (*cont.*) | | 9.1 | 332 n. 73 |
| 7.8–9 | 306 | 9.8 | 54 |
| 7.8 | 38 n. 75, 51 n. 141 | 9.9 | 38 n. 75, 91 n. 64 |
| 7.9 | 51 n. 138, 260 n. 63 | 9.10–11 | 50 |
| 7.22–63 | 570 n. 82 | 9.14ff. | 50 |
| 7.49 | 41 n. 93 | 9.16 | 341 n. 114 |
| 7.65f. | 136 n. 76 | | |
| 7.66 | 34 n. 58, 48, 115 n. 15, 151, 187, 231, 252 n. 6 | *Oration* 10 | |
| | | 10 | 49, 50 n. 133, 51 n. 142, 73, 164, 232 n. 15, 268 n. 121, 296, 303–9 *passim*, 310, 311, 333 |
| 7.81f. | 136 n. 76 | | |
| 7.81 | 46 n. 118, 51 n. 138, 76 n. 17, 260 n. 63, 296 n. 7 | | |
| 7.83–90 | 188 n. 4 | 10.17ff | 274 n. 154 |
| 7.98 | 40 n. 87 | 10.22 | 339 n. 104 |
| 7.102 | 30 n. 39 | 10.23 | 45 n. 113 |
| 7.117 | 38 n. 75, 51 n. 139 | 10.26 | 44 |
| 7.123 | 39 n. 85, 40 n. 88 | 10.27–8 | 429 n. 51 |
| 7.124 | 40 n. 87 | 10.27 | 339 n. 104 |
| 7.127–32 | 46 n. 118 | 10.28 | 335 n. 88 |
| 7.127 | 266 n. 117 | 10.30 | 50, 341 n. 114 |
| 7.133–4 | 239 n. 50 | 10.32 | 39 nn. 81 and 84, 40 n. 90, 307 |
| 7.138 | 202 | | |
| 7.146 | 187 | | |
| | | *Oration* 11 | 285 n. 207 |
| *Oration* 8 | 49, 73, 126 n. 44, 164, 232 n. 15, 302, 303–9 *passim*, 333, | 11.4 | 43 |
| | | 11.6 | 39 nn. 76 and 79, 40 n. 89, 43 with n. 106, 58 n. 71, 277 n. 170 |
| 8.1–2 | 295 n. 4, 301, 302 n. 22 | | |
| 8.1 | 260 n. 63, 261 n. 73 | 11.7 | 43 n. 106 |
| 8.5 | 377 n. 64 | 11.14 | 39 nn. 76, 79, and 82, 43 with n. 106, 58 n. 171 |
| 8.8 | 307 | | |
| 8.9 | 39 nn. 79 and 82, 40 nn. 89 and 90 | 11.22–3 | 45 n. 113 |
| | | 11.37ff. | 53 n. 148 |
| 8.12 | 34 n. 54, 341 n. 114 | 11.37 | 45 n. 113, 137 n. 79, 262 n. 85 |
| 8.15 | 50, 341 n. 114 | | |
| 8.29–35 | 53 n. 148 | 11.137–42 | 492 n. 33 |
| 8.29–33 | 306 | 11.137 | 43 |
| 8.29 | 51 n. 138, 140 n. 87, 141 n. 90 | 11.138 | 43, 64 |
| | | 11.141–2 | 43 |
| 8.30–1 | 38 n. 75 | 11.145 | 58 n. 171 |
| 8.33 | 39 n. 77, 39 n. 78, 40 n. 90, 307, 528 n. 26 | 11.146 | 58 n. 171 |
| | | 11.150 | 45 n. 113 |
| 8.35–6 | 423 n. 8 | *Oration* 12 | 186, 188, 192–5 *passim*, 201, 202, 214, 220, 225, 252 n. 11, 273, 282, 287 n. 219, 298 |
| 8.35 | 146 n. 104 | | |
| 8.36 | 39 n. 80, 40 n. 90, 307 | | |
| *Oration* 9 | 49, 73, 164, 232 n. 15, 303–9 *passim*, 333 | | |
| | | 12.1–13 | 38 n. 75 |

INDEX LOCORUM

*Oration* 12 (*cont.*)
| | |
|---|---|
| 12.1 | 51 n. 136, 187, 273 n. 143 |
| 12.2ff. | 40 n. 90 |
| 12.2–3 | 39 n. 77 |
| 12.2 | 38 n. 75 |
| 12.5–8 | 52 n. 145 |
| 12.5 | 39 n. 77, 39 n. 82, 40 n. 90, 41 n. 93, 56, 58 n. 171 |
| 12.6–8 | 276 n. 167 |
| 12.9 | 41 n. 95, 56, 58 n. 171, 286 n. 218 |
| 12.10ff. | 39 n. 85 |
| 12.10–20 | 271 n. 136 |
| 12.10f. | 40 n. 90 |
| 12.10 | 39 n. 82, 40 n. 88 |
| 12.11 | 39 n. 78 |
| 12.12 | 28 n. 27, 51 n. 141, 124 n. 40, 262 nn. 80 and 85, 282 n. 192 |
| 12.13–16 | 308 |
| 12.13–14 | 55 |
| 12.13 | 39 nn. 76, 82, 85, and 86, 40 nn. 87 and 90 |
| 12.14 | 26 n. 14, 39 n. 77, 40 n. 90, 58 n. 171 |
| 12.15 | 39 n. 82, 40 n. 90, 41 n. 93, 51 nn. 139 and 141, 56, 58 n. 171, 186 |
| 12.16ff. | 273 n. 148 |
| 12.16–21 | 151 n. 117 |
| 12.16–20 | 179, 239 n. 50, 260 n. 63 |
| 12.16 | 46 n. 118, 51 n. 138, 53, 76 n. 17, 263 n. 90, 266 n. 117, 273 n. 143, 864 n. 99 |
| 12.17–20 | 298 n. 14, 306 |
| 12.17 | 40 n. 87 |
| 12.19 | 51 n. 141 |
| 12.21ff | 187 |
| 12.27–8 | 262 n. 85, 282 n. 192 |
| 12.28 | 651 n. 146, 881 |
| 12.36 | 40 n. 88 |
| 12.37 | 40 n. 88 |
| 12.38 | 30 n. 39, 41 n. 95, 46 n. 118 |
| 12.43 | 30 n. 39, 40 n. 87, 46 n. 118 |
| 12.47–8 | 282 n. 192 |
| 12.47 | 187 |
| 12.48 | 41 n. 95 |
| 12.51 | 219 |
| 12.69 | 187 |
| 12.84 | 40 n. 87 |
| 12.85 | 38 n. 75, 51 n. 141, 188 n. 5, 210 n. 17, 239 n. 50, 286 n. 218 |

*Oration* 13   82, 191, 250–87 *passim*, 296, 298, 301, 502–8 *passim*, 575 n. 112, 607 n. 119, 697, 732 n. 104

| | |
|---|---|
| 13.1 | 31 n. 46, 47 n. 121, 232 n. 16, 233 |
| 13.2 | 57 n. 167 |
| 13.3 | 57 n. 167 |
| 13.4 | 54 |
| 13.5 | 57 n. 167 |
| 13.6–8 | 56 n. 166 |
| 13.8 | 57 n. 167 |
| 13.9–10 | 57 |
| 13.9 | 57, 862 n. 89 |
| 13.10ff. | 57 |
| 13.10–11 | 51 n. 138 |
| 13.10 | 38 n. 75, 54, 57 |
| 13.11–12 | 46 n. 118 |
| 13.11 | 38 n. 74, 52, 57 |
| 13.12 | 41 n. 95, 51 n. 136 |
| 13.13 | 34 n. 58, 57 |
| 13.14–37 | 55 |
| 13.14–15 | 46 n. 118, 124 n. 40 |
| 13.15 | 55 |
| 13.22–3 | 41 n. 93 |
| 13.24 | 491 n. 28 |
| 13.30 | 491 |
| 13.34 | 193, 607 n. 119 |
| 13.37 | 491, 495 |

| | |
|---|---|
| *Oration* 14 | 49 |
| *Oration* 15 | 49, 310 |
| *Oration* 16 | 49, 732 n. 104 |

*Oration* 17
| | |
|---|---|
| 17.2 | 56 |
| 17.5 | 56 |

# INDEX LOCORUM

| | | | |
|---|---|---|---|
| *Oration* 18 | 41 n. 92, 47, 186, 277 n. 172, 279 | *Oration* 28 | 31, 36 with n. 65, 205 |
| 18.2 | 48 n. 122 | 28.5–7 | 31 n. 44 |
| 18.2ff. | 44 | | |
| 18.2–3 | 48 n. 122 | *Oration* 29 | 31, 36 with n. 65, 205 |
| 18.7 | 40 n. 88, 48 n. 122 | 29.4–8 | 31 n. 44 |
| 18.12 | 39 n. 76, 56 n. 164 | | |
| 18.14 | 41 n. 93 | *Oration* 30 | 205–26 *passim*, 266 n. 117, 273, 280 n. 179, 282, 287 n. 220 |
| 18.16ff. | 47 n. 122 | | |
| 18.18–19 | 41 | 30.1 | 266 n. 116, 273 n. 143 |
| | | 30.8ff. | 53 n. 148 |
| *Oration* 19 | 54 | 30.10–24 | 50 |
| 19.1 | 260 n. 63 | 30.20 | 50, 51 n. 138, 53 |
| 19.1–2 | 264 | 30.23 | 50 |
| 19.1 | 51 with nn. 138 and 141, 56, 86 n. 52, 126, 150 | 30.25–7 | 50 |
| | | 30.25 | 50, 53, 137 n. 79 |
| 19.3ff. | 44 | 30.28–45 | 50 |
| 19.3 | 25 n. 11 | 30.30 | 529 n. 28 |
| 19.4 | 40 n. 91, 41 n. 93 | 30.35 | 275 n. 160, 277 n. 174 |
| | | 30.45 | 266 n. 116, 270 n. 132 |
| *Oration* 20 | | 30.46 | 273 n. 143 |
| 20.2 | 50 n. 132 | | |
| 20.24 | 49 | *Oration* 31 | 36, 37 |
| | | 31.6 | 41 n. 94 |
| *Oration* 21 | | 31.10 | 40 n. 88 |
| 21.8 | 49 | 31.15 | 49 n. 129 |
| 21.9 | 70 | 31.16 | 48 |
| 21.11 | 40 n. 88 | 31.24 | 57 n. 168 |
| | | 31.62 | 64 |
| *Oration* 22 | 41 n. 93, 50 n. 132 | 31.110 | 36 n. 67 |
| 22.1 | 39 n. 85 | 31.122 | 29, 67, 232 n. 13, 265 n. 108 |
| 22.2 | 41 | 31.125 | 188 n. 5, 239 n. 50, 275 n. 160 |
| 22.5 | 39 n. 85, 44 | | |
| | | 31.161 | 46 n. 118 |
| *Oration* 23 | 49 | 31.162–3 | 36 nn. 68–9 |
| 23.9 | 41 n. 95 | | |
| | | *Oration* 32 | 37, 41 n. 95, 67 |
| *Oration* 24 | | 32.2 | 32 n. 48 |
| 24.3–4 | 41 n. 92 | 32.3 | 83 n. 43, 332 n. 73 |
| | | 32.8 | 41 n. 95, 50 n. 132 |
| *Oration* 25 | 49, 81 with n. 35, 83, 81 n. 36 | 32.9 | 32 n. 48, 41 n. 95, 48, 378, 651 n. 146, 886 n. 171 |
| 25.7 | | | |
| | | 32.10 | 39 with nn. 78, 81, and 85, 40 n. 87, 41 n. 93 |
| *Oration* 26 | | | |
| 26.8 | 50 n. 132 | 32.11 | 38, 39 nn. 78 and 85 |
| | | 32.12–13 | 52 n. 145 |
| *Oration* 27 | | 32.12 | 52, 56, 234 n. 26, 429 n. 47 |
| 27.6 | 40 n. 88 | 32.18–19 | 38 n. 74 |

| | | | |
|---|---|---|---|
| *Oration* 32 (*cont.*) | | 33.41 | 32 n. 48, 68 |
| 32.19 | 41 n. 93 | 33.51 | 68 |
| 32.20 | 41 n. 95, 50 n. 132 | 33.53–4 | 51 n. 135 |
| 32.21–2 | 234 with n. 26 | 33.57 | 32 n. 48 |
| 32.21 | 52 n. 145, 142, 429 n. 47 | | |
| 32.22 | 38 | *Oration* 34 | 38 n. 73, 65, 67, 69 |
| 32.24 | 46 n. 118 | 34.2–3 | 38 n. 74, 41 n. 95 |
| 32.25 | 234 n. 26 | 34.2 | 38 n. 75, 48, 126, 286 n. 218 |
| 32.26 | 32 n. 48 | | |
| 32.29 | 32 n. 48 | 34.3 | 38 n. 75, 41 n. 95 |
| 32.31 | 31 | 34.4–5 | 52 n. 145 |
| 32.33 | 46 n. 118 | 34.4 | 68 |
| 32.35 | 64 | 34.7ff. | 65 |
| 32.35ff. | 65 | 34.7 | 64 |
| 32.35–7 | 32 n. 48 | 34.10–11 | 68 |
| 32.36 | 272 n. 138 | 34.14 | 68 |
| 32.39 | 38, 40 n. 91, 41 n. 93 | 34.29 | 40 n. 87 |
| 32.47 | 32 n. 48 | 34.31 | 41 n. 93 |
| 32.52 | 36 nn. 68–9 | 34.34 | 50 n. 132 |
| 32.60 | 32 n. 48 | 34.39 | 188 n. 5, 239 n. 50, 275 n. 160 |
| 32.63–6 | 53 n. 148 | | |
| 32.67 | 32 n. 48 | 34.45 | 65 |
| 32.68 | 38, 40 n. 87, 41 n. 93 | 34.47 | 68 |
| 32.88 | 32 n. 48 | 34.51 | 188 n. 5, 239 n. 50, 275 n. 160 |
| 32.95–6 | 234 n. 26 | | |
| 32.95 | 32 n. 48 | 34.53 | 30 n. 39 |
| 32.96 | 32 n. 48 | | |
| | | *Oration* 35 | 38 n. 73 |
| *Oration* 33 | 38 n. 73, 63, 66, 67, 68, 69 | 35.1–2 | 40 n. 91 |
| 33.1ff. | 68 | 35.1 | 39 nn. 78 and 85, 41 n. 96 |
| 33.1–5 | 40 n. 87 | 35.2–3 | 51 n. 139 |
| 33.1–3 | 40 n. 91 | 35.2 | 38 n. 74, 40 n. 88, 51 n. 139 |
| 33.2ff. | 39 n. 86, 65 | 35.3 | 38 n. 75 |
| 33.3 | 42 | 35.4 | 38 n. 74 |
| 33.4 | 39 n. 84 | 35.8ff. | 39 n. 86 |
| 33.5 | 40 n. 88 | 35.8–10 | 39 n. 82 |
| 33.8 | 38 n. 74, 41 n. 95, 68 | 35.8 | 39 n. 78 |
| 33.13–16 | 68 | 35.9 | 39 nn. 81 and 84 |
| 33.14–16 | 38 n. 74 | 35.10 | 39 n. 82, 41 n. 96, 43 |
| 33.14–15 | 69 n. 13, 286 n. 218 | 35.11–12 | 38 n. 75 |
| 33.14 | 38 n. 75, 39 nn. 82 and 83, 41 n. 95, 51 n. 139, 68, 69, 126 | 35.15 | 41 n. 93 |
| | | *Oration* 36 | 49, 186, 188, 195–202 *passim*, 214, 225, 254 n. 18, 273, 279, 280 n. 180, 282, 287 n. 220 |
| 33.15 | 38 n. 75, 54, 69, 260 n. 63 | | |
| 33.16 | 41 n. 95 | | |
| 33.17ff. | 65 | | |
| 33.22 | 32 n. 48 | 36.1 | 151 n. 117, 260 n. 63, 271 n. 136 |
| 33.23 | 40 n. 87 | | |
| 33.24 | 32 n. 48 | 36.7 | 210 |

# INDEX LOCORUM

| | | | |
|---|---|---|---|
| *Oration* 36 (*cont.*) | | 43.3 | 56 n. 164 |
| 36.8 | 40 n. 91, 44, 46 | 43.6 | 39 n. 85, 41 n. 93 |
| 36.17 | 51 nn. 136 and 139, 239 n. 51 | 43.8–12 | 55 |
| | | 43.11 | 197 |
| 36.22 | 392 n. 20 | | |
| 36.25 | 52 n. 145 | *Oration* 44 | 108 n. 10 |
| 36.30 | 49 | 44.5 | 28, 231 n. 8 |
| 36.32 | 49 | 44.6 | 44, 51 n. 143, 53, 197 |
| 36.34 | 262 n. 85 | 44.10 | 41, 108 n. 10 |
| 36.39–40 | 53 n. 148 | 44.11 | 108 n. 10 |
| 36.43 | 187, 273 n. 143 | 44.12 | 107, 108 with n. 10, 197, 240 n. 57 |
| 36.58–60 | 262 n. 85 | | |
| | | *Oration* 45 | |
| [*Oration* 37] | 46, 49 n. 129, 205, 225 | 45.1ff. | 34 n. 58 |
| 37.27 | 52 n. 145 | 45.1–2 | 51 n. 141, 232 |
| 37.28 | 26 n. 14, 40 n. 88 | 45.1 | 52 n. 145, 63, 81, 93, 134, 260 n. 63, 266 n. 115 |
| *Oration* 38 | | 45.2–3 | 106–7, 150 n. 112, 151 |
| 38.1 | 39 n. 86 | 45.2 | 51 n. 138, 109, 142, 197, 232 with n. 28 |
| 38.10 | 39 n. 83 | | |
| 38.51 | 52 n. 145 | 45.3 | 105, 106, 115 n. 15, 149, 151, 162 |
| *Oration* 39 | 40 n. 87 | | |
| 39.2ff. | 65 | 45.4 | 114, 138 n. 83, 297 n. 9 |
| 39.3 | 32 n. 48 | 45.10 | 50 n. 133, 263 n. 90 |
| 39.4 | 252 n. 8 | 45.11 | 54 |
| 39.5 | 32 n. 48 | 45.12 | 41 n. 95, 51 n. 138 |
| 39.7 | 51 n. 141 | 45.23 | 270 n. 130 |
| *Oration* 40 | | *Oration* 46 | 47, 52 n. 147 |
| 40.1 | 63 | 46.2 | 47 |
| 40.2 | 51 n. 141, 54, 221, 263 n. 90 | 46.3–4 | 28, 231 n. 8 |
| 40.5 | 108, 162, 197, 240 n. 57 | 46.3 | 28 nn. 28–29 |
| 40.12 | 50 n. 132, 263 n. 90 | 46.7 | 40 n. 91 |
| 40.13–15 | 197 | 46.13 | 47 n. 120 |
| 40.13 | 235 n. 31 | 46.14 | 47 |
| 40.15 | 162 | | |
| 40.35–41 | 49 n. 130, 199 | *Oration* 47 | 46 |
| | | 47.1 | 40 n. 91, 46 |
| *Oration* 41 | | 47.2–3 | 50 n. 132 |
| 41.6 | 28, 231 n. 8, 286 n. 213 | 47.6 | 56 |
| 41.9 | 275 n. 155 | 47.7 | 33 n. 52 |
| 41.12 | 41 n. 94 | 47.8 | 40 n. 91, 46 n. 118, 76 n. 17 |
| | | 47.13 | 162, 240 n. 57 |
| *Oration* 42 | 40 n. 91, 41 n. 95 | 47.16 | 39 n. 76, 40 n. 90, 46 n. 118 |
| 42.2 | 46 n. 118 | | |
| | | 47.22 | 105, 106, 115 n. 15, 149, 151 |
| *Oration* 43 | | 47.23 | 51 n. 141 |
| 43.2 | 46 n. 118 | 47.25 | 38 n. 75, 51 n. 139 |

*Oration* 48
| | |
|---|---|
| 48.5 | 151 n. 117 |
| 48.7 | 32 n. 48 |
| 48.8 | 51 n. 141 |
| 48.9 | 65 |
| 48.14 | 41 n. 95 |
| 48.15 | 30 n. 39 |
| 48.17 | 47 n. 120 |

*Oration* 49  41 n. 95, 50 n. 132, 179, 240 n. 55
| | |
|---|---|
| 49.3 | 50 n. 132 |
| 49.4f. | 177 |
| 49.4 | 149 |
| 49.11–13 | 41 n. 95 |
| 49.11–12 | 38 n. 75 |
| 49.14 | 41 n. 95 |

*Oration* 50
| | |
|---|---|
| 50.2 | 56 n. 164, 221 |
| 50.5–6 | 47 n. 120 |
| 50.8 | 34 n. 58, 41 n. 95, 63 |
| 50.10 | 47 n. 120 |

*Oration* 52  46 n. 115, 277 n. 172
| | |
|---|---|
| 52.1 | 51 n. 141 |
| 52.3 | 51 n. 141 |
| 52.6 | 51 n. 141 |
| 52.9 | 46 n. 118 |
| 52.11 | 44 |

*Oration* 53  178, 240 n. 55
| | |
|---|---|
| 53.9 | 51 n. 138, 178 |
| 53.10 | 178 |
| 53.11 | 174 |

*Oration* 54  33 n. 52, 39 nn. 81 and 85, 178, 240 n. 55
| | |
|---|---|
| 54.1 | 26 n. 14, 40 n. 87 |
| 54.3 | 39 n. 85, 41 n. 93 |

*Oration* 55  45, 178, 240 n. 55
| | |
|---|---|
| 55.1 | 55 |
| 55.7 | 39 nn. 77 and 81, 40 n. 90, 43, 46 n. 118 |
| 55.11 | 134 n. 68 |

*Oration* 56  49, 115 n. 15, 178, 240 n. 55
| | |
|---|---|
| 56.8–16 | 115 n. 15, 149, 158 |
| 56.12 | 39 n. 85, 41 n. 93 |

*Oration* 57  41 n. 92, 178, 240 n. 55, 275 n. 159, 277 n. 170
| | |
|---|---|
| 57.1–12 | 149, 158 |
| 57.8 | 41 n. 92 |
| 57.10f. | 115 n. 15 |
| 57.10 | 111, 119, 151 |
| 57.11 | 73 n. 4, 111, 178, 240, 241 |
| 57.12 | 151, 246 |

*Oration* 58  49 n. 129
| | |
|---|---|
| 58.2 | 39 n. 83, 40 n. 88 |

*Oration* 60  43, 45
| | |
|---|---|
| 60.9 | 41 n. 95 |
| 60.10 | 55 |

*Oration* 62  115 n. 15
| | |
|---|---|
| 62.1 | 178 |
| 62.3 | 49 n. 126, 178 |
| 62.7 | 49 n. 126 |

*Oration* 63
| | |
|---|---|
| 63.3 | 41 n. 93 |

*Oration* 64  46, 205, 225

*Oration* 65  46
| | |
|---|---|
| 65.7 | 30 n. 39 |
| 65.8 | 30 n. 39 |
| 65.10 | 30 n. 39 |
| 65.13 | 30 n. 39 |

*Oration* 66  63, 71, 72
| | |
|---|---|
| 66.2 | 38 n. 75, 70 |
| 66.4 | 70 |
| 66.5 | 70 |
| 66.6 | 34 n. 58, 69, 575 n. 114 |
| 66.12 | 39 nn. 82 and 85 |
| 66.13 | 305 n. 31 |
| 66.25 | 38 n. 75 |

*Oration* 69
| | |
|---|---|
| 69.3 | 41 n. 93 |
| 69.5 | 41 n. 93 |

| | | | |
|---|---|---|---|
| *Oration* 70 | 56 | **Diodorus,** *Bibliotheca Historica* | |
| 70.8 | 38 n. 75, 282 n. 192, 286 n. 218 | 6.6 {6.5 CS} | 572 n. 94 |
| 70.8–10 | 41 n. 95 | **Diogenes of Babylon** | |
| | | F 51 (SVF *III*.220) | 342 n. 119 |
| *Oration* 71 | 44 | | |
| | | **Diogenes Laertius,** *Vitae Philosophorum* | |
| *Oration* 72 | 38 n. 75, 252 n. 11, 276, 277 | 1.110 | 880, 883 n. 164 |
| 72.2 | 51 n. 139, 126, 268 n. 122 | 2.7 | 422 n. 5 |
| 72.11–12 | 262 n. 85 | 2.66–8 | 368 n. 31 |
| 72.11 | 268 n. 122 | 2.66 | 364 n. 15, 375 nn. 59 and 60, 405 n. 51, 409 n. 70 |
| 72.13–16 | 276 n. 167 | | |
| 72.13 | 134 n. 68, 282 n. 191, 284 n. 204 | 2.75 | 368 n. 31, 377 n. 64, 473 |
| | | 2.101 | 873 n. 123 |
| 72.15–16 | 38 n. 75, 51 n. 139, 262 n. 85 | 2.116 | 873 n. 123 |
| | | 3.34 | 812 n. 131 |
| 72.16 | 124 n. 40 | 3.51 | 595, 808 n. 111 |
| | | 4.46 | 462 n. 4 |
| *Oration* 73 | 49 | 4.48 | 358 n. 25, 377 n. 67 |
| | | 5.2 | 367 |
| *Oration* 74 | 45 | 6.2 | 259 n. 53, 261 n. 72, 267, 330 n. 63, 358 n. 24, 377 n. 67, 446, 490 n. 22 |
| *Oration* 75 | 41 n. 94, 45 n. 114, 49 n. 129 | | |
| | | 6.4 | 332 n. 73 |
| | | 6.5 | 431 n. 61 |
| *Oration* 76 | 41 n. 94, 45 n. 114 | 6.6 | 332 n. 73, 338 n. 101, 357 n. 17, 661 n. 178 |
| 76.4 | 41 n. 93 | | |
| | | 6.10–13 | 392 |
| *Orations* 77/8 | 45 | 6.10–11 | 392 |
| 77/8.27 | 39 nn. 77, 82, and 85 | 6.11 | 261 n. 69, 377 n. 67 |
| 77/8.37 | 51 n. 139 | 6.12 | 357 n. 19, 431 n. 61 |
| | | 6.14–15 | 259 n. 53, 490 n. 22 |
| *Oration* 79 | 63, 64, 65, 66, 191, 276, 277 | 6.14 | 357 n. 18, 377 n. 65 |
| 79.1 | 64, 65, 252 n. 8 | 6.15 | 446 |
| 79.4–5 | 188 n. 4 | 6.16 | 431 n. 61 |
| 79.4 | 64, 65 | 6.17–18 | 271 n. 137 |
| 79.5 | 64, 65, 275 n. 155 | 6.17 | 332 n. 73 |
| 79.6 | 65 | 6.18 | 332 n. 73 |
| | | 6.20–1 | 57 n. 168 |
| *Oration* 80 | 63, 64, 65, 66 | 6.20 | 423 n. 9, 426 n. 21, 443 |
| 80.1 | 41 n. 93 | 6.21 | 39 n. 82, 255 n. 30, 443 |
| 80.3 | 65 | 6.22 | 339 n. 102, 445, 454 |
| 80.4 | 65 | 6.23 | 532 n. 59 |
| 80.7 | 65 | 6.24 | 335 n. 88, 356 n. 14, 428 n. 34, 430 n. 52, 456 |
| *de Virtutibus Alexandri* | 126 n. 47 | 6.25–6 | 444 |
| | | 6.26 | 430 n. 55 |

**Diogenes Laertius** (*cont.*)

| | | | |
|---|---|---|---|
| 6.27 | 137 n. 79, 326 n. 39, 356 n. 12, 357 n. 18, 366 n. 20, 446 | 6.67 | 444 |
| | | 6.68 | 261 n. 77 |
| | | 6.69 | 39 n. 82, 326 n. 40, 444 |
| 6.28 | 426 n. 23 | 6.70–3 | 389–402 *passim* |
| 6.29–31 | 443 | 6.70–1 | 329 n. 58, 358 n. 24, 359 n. 27 |
| 6.29 | 91 n. 64, 255 n. 31, 358 n. 22, 423 n. 9, 456 | 6.70 | 259 n. 51, 302, 318 n. 4, 329 n. 57, 335 n. 90, 431 n. 66, 445, 453, 489 n. 14 |
| 6.30f. | 332 n. 73 | | |
| 6.30 | 91 n. 64, 332 n. 73 | 6.71 | 90 n. 58, 357 n. 19, 377 n. 67, 339 nn. 102 and 106, 371 n. 40, 445, 446 with n. 10, 528 n. 26 |
| 6.31 | 136 n. 74 | | |
| 6.32 | 440 | | |
| 6.33 | 357 n. 18 | | |
| 6.34 | 428 n. 30, 456 | 6.72 | 357 n. 19, 389 n. 1, 410, 422, 423 n. 10, 424, 426 n. 24, 427, 428 n. 37, 429 nn. 40 and 46, 436 n. 82, 445, 446, 449 with n. 15, 450, 451, 452, 530 n. 40, 539 nn. 99 and 100, 540, 722 n. 71, 808 n. 111, 866 n. 103 |
| 6.35 | 98 n. 81, 262 n. 78, 283 n. 194, 326 n. 42, 331 n. 67, 356 n. 14 | | |
| 6.36 | 332 n. 73 | | |
| 6.37 | 261 n. 77, 395, 428 n. 37, 429 nn. 46 and 50, 449, 452 | | |
| 6.38 | 254 n. 21, 255 n. 31, 282 n. 191, 283 n. 194, 330 n. 63, 393, 422 with n. 7, 440, 451, 531 n. 50, 539 n. 103 | 6.73 | 260 n. 58, 261 n. 77, 335 nn. 87 and 88, 339 n. 107, 426 n. 23, 428 nn. 30, 31, and 33, 429 n. 50, 430 n. 52, 432 n. 72, 433 n. 73, 453, 492 n. 30, 531 n. 44, 864 n. 99 |
| 6.39 | 426 n. 23 | | |
| 6.40 | 444 | | |
| 6.41 | 331 n. 69, 431 n. 64, 456 | | |
| 6.43 | 332 n. 73, 357 n. 18, 456 | 6.74–5 | 443 |
| 6.44 | 259 n. 51, 339 n. 103, 400 n. 38, 427 n. 29, 429 n. 43, 433 n. 74, 446, 452, 489 n. 14, 528 n. 26 | 6.74 | 81 n. 48, 91 n. 64, 332 n. 73, 412, 429 n. 48, 456 |
| | | 6.75 | 332 n. 73 |
| | | 6.76–7 | 394 n. 20 |
| 6.45 | 405 n. 51 | 6.76 | 408, 428 n. 30, 429 n. 49 |
| 6.49 | 57 n. 168, 255 n. 30 | 6.77 | 94 n. 68, 410, 428 n. 30 |
| 6.50 | 456 | 6.78–97 | 531 n. 47 |
| 6.51 | 354, 429 nn. 44 and 45, 452 | 6.78 | 330 n. 63, 430 n. 55 |
| | | 6.79 | 428 n. 32, 540 n. 105 |
| 6.52 | 354, 356 | 6.83 | 339 n. 104 |
| 6.54 | 358 n. 22, 445 | 6.84 | 366 n. 20 |
| 6.55 | 940 | 6.85 | 397 n. 26, 403, 405 n. 53, 423 n. 9, 427 nn. 26 and 29, 452, 456 |
| 6.56 | 331 n. 69, 432 n. 71 | | |
| 6.57 | 405 | | |
| 6.58 | 405, 444 | 6.86 | 332 n. 73, 356 n. 14, 870 |
| 6.59 | 357 n. 18, 446 | 6.87–8 | 333 n. 77, 403, 455 |
| 6.60 | 331 n. 69, 431 n. 64 | 6.87 | 866 |
| 6.63 | 389, 391, 392, 393, 394, 395, 398, 405 n. 51, 422, 424, 448, 449 n. 15 | 6.89 | 329 n. 56, 398 n. 30, 432 n. 67 |

INDEX LOCORUM 1019

**Diogenes Laertius** (*cont.*)
| | |
|---|---|
| 6.93 | 392 n. 13, 395, 398, 403, 410, 422 n. 4, 423 n. 9, 427 n. 26, 428 n. 39, 446, 451 455, 539 n. 99 |
| 6.96–7 | |
| 6.96 | 357 n. 19, 445 |
| 6.98 | 392 n. 13, 422 n. 4, 427 nn. 27 and 29 |
| 6.99 | 347 n. 133 |
| 6.102 | 332 n. 73, 429 n. 47, 452 |
| 6.103–5 | 392 |
| 6.103–4 | 260 n. 58, 335 n. 87, 366 n. 20, 349 n. 139, 492 n. 30 |
| 6.103 | 322 n. 25, 426 n. 23, 445, 525 n. 10 |
| 6.104 | 90 n. 58, 330 n. 63, 335 n. 87, 346 n. 130, 429 nn. 44 and 45, 445, 452 |
| 6.105 | 328 nn. 49 and 51, 335 n. 89, 357, 373 n. 50, 428 n. 36, 429 n. 45, 431 nn. 60 and 65, 446, 452, 540 with n. 104, 898 |
| 7.2 | 57 n. 168 |
| 7.4 | 336 n. 94 |
| 7.32–4 | 336 n. 95 |
| 7.32–3 | 434 n. 78 |
| 7.121 | 398 n. 29, 340 n. 108, 807 n. 108 |
| 7.128 | 375 n. 56 |
| 7.168–9 | 873 n. 123, 879 |
| 7.168 | 51 n. 135, 217 |
| 7.169 | 51 n. 135, 217 |
| 7.171 | 51 n. 135, 217 |
| 7.182 | 39 n. 82 |
| 7.189 | 898 n. 211 |
| 10.119 | 458 |
| 10.120 | 39 n. 82 |
| 10.123 | 882 n. 158 |

**Diogenes of Oenanda**
| | |
|---|---|
| F 30 Smith | 402 |
| F 56 Smith | 401 n. 42, 402 |

**Dionysius of Halicarnassus**
*Antiquitates Romanae*
| | |
|---|---|
| 1.6.3 | 593 n. 47 |

*de Isocrate*
| | |
|---|---|
| 18.2–4 | 24 |

*de Lysia*
| | |
|---|---|
| 1.5 | 25 n. 12 |
| 3.7 | 25 n. 12 |
| 16.2 | 25 n. 12 |

*de Oratoribus antiquis*
| | |
|---|---|
| praef. 1 | 124 n. 40 |
| [περὶ ἐσχηματισμένων] | |
| II.295ff. U–R | 119 |

**Ennius**, *Annales*
| | |
|---|---|
| 343Sk | 494 |

[**Epicharmus**] 17D  78 n. 27

**Epictetus**
*Dissertationes*
| | |
|---|---|
| 1.1.22–4 | 563 n. 41 |
| 1.1.23 | 86 n. 52 |
| 1.4 | 342 n. 119 |
| 1.9.1 | 392 n. 12, 422 n. 5 |
| 1.9.9 | 371 n. 40 |
| 1.13.3 | 342 n. 119 |
| 1.14.12–14 | 79 n. 29 |
| 1.18 | 342 n. 119 |
| 1.18.17 | 86 n. 52 |
| 1.19.8 | 86 n. 52 |
| 1.24.6–7 | 332 n. 73 |
| 1.24.20 | 210 n. 19 |
| 1.25.22 | 324 n. 33 |
| 1.28.10–11 | 342 n. 119 |
| 1.29.5–8 | 563 n. 41 |
| 1.29.36 | 905 n. 243 |
| 1.29.55–7 | 905 n. 243 |
| 1.29.64–5 | 342 n. 119 |
| 2.7.3 | 79 n. 29 |
| 2.8.11ff. | 79 n. 29 |
| 2.12.17 | 905 n. 243 |
| 2.13.7 | 601 n. 102 |
| 2.13.24–6 | 905 n. 243 |
| 2.16.33 | 79 n. 29 |
| 2.16.37 | 210 n. 19 |
| 2.16.44 | 146 n. 104 |
| 2.18.29 | 572 n. 93 |
| 3.10.5 | 86 n. 52 |
| 3.12.4 | 915 n. 291 |
| 3.22 | 335 n. 92, 342 n. 119, 529 |
| 3.22.2 | 296 n. 8, 429 n. 47, 452 |
| 3.22.17 | 332 n. 73, 336 |

**Epictetus** (*cont.*)
*Dissertationes* (*cont.*)

| | |
|---|---|
| 3.22.18 | 91 n. 64 |
| 3.22.23 | 296 n. 8, 342 n. 119, 429 n. 47, 452 |
| 3.22.24 | 332 n. 73, 336 |
| 3.22.26 | 257 n. 37, 261 |
| 3.22.34 | 347 n. 133 |
| 3.22.45–8 | 392 n. 11, 422 n. 4 |
| 3.22.45–7 | 423 n. 9 |
| 3.22.46 | 430 n. 55 |
| 3.22.50–1 | 430 n. 55 |
| 3.22.53 | 339 n. 104, 429 n. 47, 452 |
| 3.22.57 | 347 n. 133 |
| 3.22.59 | 296 n. 8 |
| 3.22.60 | 90 n. 58 |
| 3.22.62ff. | 336 n. 93, 364 n. 15 |
| 3.22.63 | 347 n. 133 |
| 3.22.67 | 331 n. 71 |
| 3.22.69 | 296 n. 8, 429 n. 47, 452 |
| 3.22.72 | 332 n. 73, 342 n. 119 |
| 3.22.77 | 332 n. 73 |
| 3.22.81 | 399 n. 37 |
| 3.22.84–5 | 397 n. 26, 427 n. 26, 451 |
| 3.22.86 | 430 n. 55 |
| 3.22.88 | 430 n. 55 |
| 3.22.90 | 99 n. 84, 282 n. 191 |
| 3.22.94 | 405 n. 53 |
| 3.22.97 | 905 n. 243 |
| 3.22.97f. | 342 n. 119 |
| 3.22.99 | 93 n. 67 |
| 3.24.13 | 141 n. 90, 146 n. 104 |
| 3.24.64–6 | 392 n. 11, 422 n. 4, 427 n. 28 |
| 3.24.64 | 329 n. 55, 332, 333, 334 n. 82, 432 n. 68, 447 |
| 3.24.65–6 | 423 n. 9 |
| 3.24.66 | 342 n. 119, 427 n. 27 |
| 3.24.79 | 342 n. 119 |
| 3.24.85–6 | 224 n. 59 |
| 3.24.112 | 430 n. 55 |
| 3.26.27 | 86 n. 52 |
| 3.26.31f. | 140 n. 87 |
| 3.26.32 | 146 n. 104 |
| 3.26.33 | 405 n. 54 |
| 4.1.107 | 224 n. 59 |
| 4.1.111 | 224 n. 59 |
| 4.1.151 | 86 n. 52 |
| 4.4.27 | 342 n. 119 |
| 4.4.38 | 81 n. 37 |
| 4.6.2 | 342 n. 119 |
| 4.6.20 | 332 n. 73 |
| 4.7.6 | 914 n. 288 |
| 4.8.30 | 347 n. 133 |
| 4.8.34 | 347 n. 133, 370 n. 36, 430 n. 55 |
| 4.12.19 | 342 n. 119 |

*Encheiridion*

| | |
|---|---|
| 3.11 | 224 n. 59 |
| 9 | 86 n. 52 |
| 15 | 210 n. 19 |

*Fragmenta*

| | |
|---|---|
| F 27 Schweighäuser = 25 Oldfather | 342 n. 119 |

**Epicurus**
*Epistula ad Herodotum*

| | |
|---|---|
| 35 | 898 n. 211 |
| 38 | 885 n. 168 |
| 74 | 885 n. 168 |

*Epistula ad Pythoclem*

| | |
|---|---|
| 84–5 | 898 n. 211 |
| 89 | 885 n. 168 |

*Gnomologium Vaticanum*

| | |
|---|---|
| 88 | 465 n. 15 |

*Κύριαι δόξαι*

| | |
|---|---|
| 21–2 | 374 n. 52 |

*Sententiae*

| | |
|---|---|
| VII | 998 n. 81 |
| XIII | 998 n. 81 |
| XIV | 998 n. 81 |

*Fragmenta*

| | |
|---|---|
| F 29.28.5–6 | 595 n. 60, 808 n. 111 |
| F 29.28.11–12 | 595 n. 60, 808 n. 111 |
| F 29.30.16 | 595 n. 60, 808 n. 111 |
| F 30.31.1 | 595 n. 60, 808 n. 111 |
| F 31.2.4–6 | 595 n. 60, 808 n. 111 |
| F 36.10.3 | 595 n. 60, 808 n. 111 |
| F 69 | 465 n. 15 |
| F 174 | 374 n. 52 |

*Fragmenta (cont.)*

| | |
|---|---|
| F 175 | 374 n. 52 |
| F 450 | 368 n. 30 |
| F 544 | 366 n. 22 |

## Euripides
*Bacchae*

| | |
|---|---|
| 2 | 558 |
| 13–22 | 581 n. 147 |
| 45 | 557 |
| 100 | 558 |
| 216 | 558 |
| 219–20 | 558 |
| 221–2 | 562 n. 34 |
| 247 | 558 |
| 256 | 558 |
| 272 | 558, 560, 888 |
| 318–21 | 566 n. 54 |
| 325 | 557 |
| 447–8 | 557 |
| 467 | 558 |
| 500 | 560 |
| 506 | 558, 649 n. 141, 880, 887 |
| 540–4 | 557 |
| 550–1 | 572 n. 90, 889 n. 184 |
| 576–641 | 554–63 *passim*, 565 |
| 620 | 557, 568 |
| 635–6 | 557 |
| 644–6 | 561 |
| 686–8 | 562 n. 34 |
| 788 | 557 |
| 794–5 | 558 |
| 1255–6 | 557 |

*Hercules Furens*

| | |
|---|---|
| 1197 | 141 n. 90 |

*Iphigeneia Taurensis*

| | |
|---|---|
| 1395f | 561 n. 27 |

*Fragments*

| | |
|---|---|
| F 777 | 425 n. 18 |
| F 902 | 425 n. 18 |
| F 1018 | 78 n. 27 |
| F 1047 | 425 n. 18 |

**Florus**, *Epitome Rerum Romanorum*

| | |
|---|---|
| praef. 7 | 82 n. 42 |
| 2.17.11 | 378 n. 71 |

**Fronto**, *Epistulae* (van den Hout)

| | |
|---|---|
| 133 | 28 |
| 135 | 232 n. 13, 264 n. 105 |
| 198 | 87 n. 53, 101 n. 90, 113 |
| 199f. | 90 n. 60, 132 n. 62 |

## Galen
*de constitutione artis medicae*

| | |
|---|---|
| 1–9 | 796 n. 50 |

*de ordine librorum propriorum*

| | |
|---|---|
| 19.51–2 | 796 n. 50 |

*de animi cuiuslibet peccatorum dignotione et curatione*

| | |
|---|---|
| 3 | 398 n. 29 |

**Aulus Gellius**, *Noctes Atticae*

| | |
|---|---|
| 13.13.2 | 30 n. 41 |

*Gnomologium Vaticanum*

| | |
|---|---|
| 386 | 356 n. 14 |

**Gorgias**, *Helen*

| | |
|---|---|
| 8–14 | 44 |

**Hecataeus of Miletus** (*FGrHist* 1)

| | |
|---|---|
| F 1a | 592, 746, 813 |

## Heraclitus
[*Epistulae*]

| | |
|---|---|
| 4.2 | 432 n. 70 |
| 5.2 | 392 n. 13, 422 n. 4, 423 n. 9 |
| 5.3 | 341 n. 115, 432 n. 70 |
| 7 | 432 n. 70 |
| 7.2 | 341 n. 117 |
| 9.2 | 392 n. 13, 396, 399 n. 37, 400 n. 39, 434, 451 |
| 9.3 | 429 n. 47 |
| 9.4 | 392 n. 13 |
| 9.7 | 392 n. 13 |
| 36.9.2 | 422 n. 4 |
| 36.9.4 | 422 n. 4 |
| 36.9.7 | 422 n. 4 |

*Fragmenta* (Diels–Kranz)

| | |
|---|---|
| B 48 | 940 |
| B 114 | 425 n. 18 |
| B 119 | 78 n. 27 |

**Heraclitus**, *Quaestiones Homericae*
| | |
|---|---|
| 4.1 | 363 n. 11 |
| 79.2 | 366 n. 22 |

**Hermogenes**, *de Inuentione*
| | |
|---|---|
| 204ff. Rabe | 119 |
| 491Spengel | 137 n. 79 |

**Herodotus**
| | |
|---|---|
| *praef.* | 592, 598, 599 n. 82, 602, 604, 684, 746, 793, 797, 799, 802, 813 |
| 1.5.1 | 281 n. 187 |
| 1.5.3–4 | 252, 600 n. 90, 604, 684 n. 39, 685, 732, 798 n. 55 |
| 1.5.3 | 135, 136, 281 n. 187, 602, 604, 683, 692, 796 n. 50, 799, 802 |
| 1.5.4 | 604, 799 |
| 1.29 | 44 n. 109, 53 |
| 1.29ff. | 798 n. 56 |
| 1.29–34 | 873 |
| 1.29–33 | 685, 981 n. 10 |
| 1.29.1–30.2 | 268 n. 121 |
| 1.30.2–33 | 252 |
| 1.30.2 | 125 n. 41 |
| 1.32 | 254 n. 23 |
| 1.32.1 | 254 n. 21 |
| 1.32.2–4 | 254 n. 21 |
| 1.32.5 | 999 n. 86 |
| 1.55 | 254 n. 23 |
| 1.95.1 | 598, 799 |
| 1.105 | 269 n. 127 |
| 1.189 | 269 n. 127 |
| 2.19–33 | 794 n. 42 |
| 2.29.1 | 593 n. 42, 683 n. 32, 799 n. 68 |
| 2.81.2 | 135 n. 70 |
| 2.107 | 269 n. 127 |
| 3.115.2 | 593 n. 42, 683 n. 32, 799 n. 68 |
| 4.16.1 | 593 n. 42, 683 n. 32, 799 n. 68 |
| 4.71.4 | 254 n. 23 |
| 4.76.2 | 268 n. 121 |
| 5.68 | 942 |
| 7.140–1 | 268 n. 121 |
| 7.140 | 273 n. 147 |
| 7.220 | 720 |
| 8.79.4 | 593 n. 42, 683 n. 32, 799 n. 68 |
| 8.80.1 | 593 n. 42, 683 n. 32, 799 n. 68 |

**Hesiod**
*Opera et Dies*
| | |
|---|---|
| 5–7 | 193 |
| 5–8 | 492 n. 33 |
| 405 | 371 n. 38 |

*Theogonia*
| | |
|---|---|
| 1 | 281 n. 187 |
| 23–4 | 742 |
| 36 | 281 n. 187 |
| 39 | 750 |
| 104–15 | 743 |
| 465 | 210 n. 17, 941 n. 29 |

**Hesychius**, *Lexicon*
| | |
|---|---|
| 736 Hansen–Cunningham | 950 n. 62 |

**Homer**
*Ilias*
| | |
|---|---|
| 1.1 | 743 |
| 1.5 | 895 n. 203 |
| 3.65 | 207 |
| 21.50 | 298 n. 14, 306 |
| 23.161–77 | 276 n. 162 |

*Odysseia*
| | |
|---|---|
| 1.1–3 | 363 |
| 1.1 | 743 |
| 1.3 | 135, 136 |
| 1.48–59 | 254 n. 20 |
| 4.244–6 | 69 |
| 12.188 | 988 n. 50 |
| 12.383 | 124 n. 40 |
| 14.122–7 | 268 n. 121 |
| 17.222 | 54, 135 |
| 22.1 | 54, 236, 303 n. 25 |
| 24.249–50 | 194, 239 n. 50 |
| 24.257 | 239 n. 50 |

**Horace**
*Ars Poetica*
| | |
|---|---|
| 309–22 | 474 |
| 333–4 | 462 |
| 476 | 477 n. 41 |

# INDEX LOCORUM

*Carmina*

| | |
|---|---|
| 1.1 | 469, 471 |
| 1.1.2 | 469, 470 |
| 1.1.35 | 470 |
| 1.3.9ff | 469 n. 25 |
| 1.6 | 471 |
| 1.7 | 469, 470, 471 |
| 1.8 | 471 |
| 1.9 | 469 |
| 1.11 | 469 |
| 1.12.1ff. | 187 |
| 1.12.55–6 | 862 n. 88 |
| 1.16.9ff | 469 n. 25 |
| 1.19.20 | 470 n. 27 |
| 1.22 | 469, 470, 471 |
| 1.28.4ff | 469 n. 25 |
| 1.29 | 380 n. 77, 469, 471 |
| 1.31 | 469, 470 |
| 1.31.6 | 469 n. 25 |
| 1.32 | 469, 470 |
| 1.32.13 | 470 |
| 1.32.15 | 470 |
| 1.34 | 469, 470 |
| 1.34.2 | 476 |
| 1.37 | 470 |
| 1.38 | 469 |
| 2.2 | 469, 470, 471 |
| 2.2.13ff | 469 n. 25 |
| 2.3 | 469, 471 |
| 2.3.17–24 | 476 n. 36 |
| 2.7 | 470, 471 |
| 2.7.15f | 476 n. 36 |
| 2.10 | 470, 471 |
| 2.11 | 469, 471 |
| 2.13.25ff. | 470 |
| 2.13.25–8 | 470 |
| 2.14.21ff. | 469 n. 25 |
| 2.15 | 469, 471 |
| 2.16 | 469 |
| 2.16.14 | 905 n. 244 |
| 2.16.32 | 470 n. 27 |
| 2.18 | 469, 471 |
| 2.18.12–14 | 469 n. 24 |
| 3.1 | 469, 470, 471 |
| 3.2 | 469, 470, 471 |
| 3.2.13 | 470 |
| 3.3 | 469, 470, 471 |
| 3.3.9 | 141 n. 90 |
| 3.8 | 469 |
| 3.8.28 | 470 n. 27 |
| 3.16 | 470, 471 |
| 3.16.25–8 | 469 n. 25 |
| 3.16.37–8 | 469 n. 24 |
| 3.21 | 465 n. 16, 470, 471 |
| 3.24 | 469 |
| 3.28 | 470 |
| 3.29 | 469, 470, 471 |
| 3.29.48 | 470 n. 27 |
| 3.29.55–6 | 469 n. 25 |
| 3.30 | 475, 681 |
| 3.30.1 | 750, 805, 883 |
| 4.6.44 | 746 n. 51 |
| 4.12 | 476 |
| 4.12.1 | 745 n. 47 |

*Epistulae*

| | |
|---|---|
| 1.1 | 366, 383 |
| 1.1.1–19 | 471–5 |
| 1.1.1–3 | 941 n. 30 |
| 1.1.2–4 | 476 n. 38 |
| 1.1.4 | 476 n. 36 |
| 1.1.3–4 | 380 n. 77, 476 n. 36 |
| 1.1.3 | 475 |
| 1.1.7–8 | 476 n. 38 |
| 1.1.7 | 474 |
| 1.1.10–11 | 363, 476 n. 36 |
| 1.1.10 | 363 n. 10, 365, 367, 476 nn. 36 and 38 |
| 1.1.11 | 367 |
| 1.1.15 | 364 |
| 1.1.15f. | 476 n. 36 |
| 1.1.16f. | 386 |
| 1.1.16 | 364, 365, 383 |
| 1.1.16–19 | 368, 369 n. 32, 381 |
| 1.1.18 | 365, 368 n. 30 |
| 1.1.27 | 365 |
| 1.1.41f | 368 n. 29, 375 n. 60 |
| 1.1.59f | 370 |
| 1.1.60 | 474 |
| 1.1.76 | 474 n. 31 |
| 1.1.106ff. | 367 |
| 1.1.106–8 | 474 |
| 1.1.107 | 370 |
| 1.1.108 | 362 |
| 1.2 | 126 n. 45, 362–9, 380, 382, 383, 474, 475 |

*Epistulae (cont.)*

| | |
|---|---|
| 1.2.2 | 380 n. 77 |
| 1.2.3–5 | 474 n. 31 |
| 1.2.10 | 370 |
| 1.2.11f. | 382 |
| 1.2.17–31 | 381 |
| 1.2.17–22 | 473 |
| 1.2.17 | 375 n. 60 |
| 1.2.19 | 882 |
| 1.2.21 | 382 |
| 1.2.23–31 | 473 |
| 1.2.70–1 | 474 with n. 33 |
| 1.2.71 | 367, 476 n. 36 |
| 1.3.28–9 | 474 |
| 1.4 | 474 |
| 1.4.10 | 376 n. 63 |
| 1.4.15 | 367 |
| 1.4.15–16 | 210, 366, 368 n. 30, 474 n. 34 |
| 1.5 | 474 |
| 1.6.56 | 381 n. 79 |
| 1.7.1–2 | 474 n. 31 |
| 1.7.45 | 474 n. 34 |
| 1.7.98 | 372 n. 41, 474 n. 33 |
| 1.8 | 380 n. 77 |
| 1.8.2–12 | 474 n. 31 |
| 1.10 | 368 n. 29, 369–75 *passim*, 382, 384, 474 |
| 1.10.3 | 383 |
| 1.10.8 | 383, 386 |
| 1.10.12 | 383 |
| 1.10.25 | 368 n. 30 |
| 1.10.42–3 | 474 n. 33 |
| 1.10.42 | 383 |
| 1.10.45 | 383 |
| 1.10.46 | 366 n. 22 |
| 1.10.49–50 | 474 n. 31 |
| 1.10.50 | 383 |
| 1.11.22ff | 474 n. 34 |
| 1.12 | 371, 380 n. 77, 475 |
| 1.13 | 475 |
| 1.14.12–13 | 474 n. 31 |
| 1.14.15 | 474 n. 31 |
| 1.14.35 | 367 n. 23 |
| 1.14.44 | 474 n. 33 |
| 1.15.24 | 366, 368 n. 30 |
| 1.16 | 369, 474, 915 n. 290 |
| 1.16.15 | 474 n. 34 |
| 1.16.52ff | 386 |
| 1.16.73–9 | 563 n. 41 |
| 1.17 | 362, 365 n. 19, 368 n. 30, 375–82 *passim*, 384, 397 n. 28, 474, 475 |
| 1.17.6–10 | 369, 474 n. 34 |
| 1.17.6 | 367 n. 23 |
| 1.17.9 | 376 n. 63 |
| 1.17.23ff | 369 |
| 1.17.27ff | 369 |
| 1.17.29 | 409 n. 70, 474 n. 33 |
| 1.17.33ff | 383 |
| 1.17.33–42 | 365 n. 18 |
| 1.17.35 | 474 n. 30 |
| 1.17.42 | 378 n. 70 |
| 1.17.58ff. | 385 |
| 1.18 | 362, 365 n. 19, 368 n. 30, 380, 382, 474 |
| 1.18.2–4 | 369 n. 33 |
| 1.18.5–8 | 369, 379 |
| 1.18.6–8 | 475 |
| 1.18.10–14 | 369 n. 33 |
| 1.18.15–20 | 369, 379 |
| 1.18.86f. | 378 n. 70 |
| 1.18.96ff. | 475 |
| 1.18.96 | 474 n. 32 |
| 1.18.100 | 474 n. 32 |
| 1.18.102f. | 369 |
| 1.18.104ff. | 474 n. 34, 475 with n. 35 |
| 1.19 | 475 with n. 35 |
| 1.19.12f. | 385 |
| 1.19.23–5 | 466 n. 20 |
| 1.20 | 475 n. 35, 476 n. 36 |
| 1.20.23 | 376 n. 62, 382, 474 n. 30 |
| 2.1 | 476 |
| 2.1.1ff. | 124 |
| 2.1.111 | 477 n. 42 |
| 2.1.126–31 | 462 |
| 2.2 | 475 |
| 2.2.1–19 | 476 n. 36 |
| 2.2.41–5 | 476 |
| 2.2.47 | 476 n. 36 |
| 2.2.55–7 | 476 n. 36 |
| 2.2.57ff. | 476 |
| 2.2.57–60 | 462 |
| 2.2.59–60 | 476 n. 36 |
| 2.2.60 | 409, 464, 466 n. 20 |
| 2.2.99 | 476 n. 36 |

INDEX LOCORUM

| | | | |
|---|---|---|---|
| *Epistulae* (cont.) | | 17.16 | 468 |
| 2.2.141–2 | 476 n. 36 | 17.24 | 468 |
| 2.2.175–9 | 476 n. 36 | 17.31–2 | 468 |
| 2.2.198 | 476 n. 38 | 17.64 | 468 |
| 2.2.199–200 | 476 n. 36 | | |
| 2.2.203f | 367 n. 24 | *Satirae* | |
| 2.2.204 | 476 n. 36 | 1 | 465 n. 11 |
| 2.2.213–16 | 476 n. 38 | 1.1 | 464, 465, 469, 476, 477 |
| 2.2.214 | 477 n. 41 | 1.1.13–14 | 464 |
| | | 1.1.23–7 | 464 |
| *Epodi* | | 1.1.74–5 | 465 n. 14 |
| 1 | 467, 468, 470 | 1.1.118–21 | 476 n. 38 |
| 2.19 | 467 | 1.1.119–21 | 465 |
| 2.37–8 | 468 | 1.1.119–20 | 477 n. 41 |
| 2.40 | 468 | 1.1.120 | 465 n. 12 |
| 3 | 466 n. 19 | 1.10 | 462 n. 3 |
| 3.4 | 468 | 1.10.4 | 463 |
| 3.17 | 468 | 1.10.81 | 465 |
| 4.4 | 468 | 1.2 | 465 |
| 4.11 | 468 | 1.2.92–3 | 465 |
| 5 | 466 n. 19 | 1.2.111–12 | 465 n. 14 |
| 5.4 | 468 | 1.2.121–2 | 465 |
| 5.14 | 468 | 1.2.134 | 465 n. 12 |
| 5.31 | 468 | 1.3.76–7 | 465 n. 14 |
| 5.83–4 | 468 | 1.3.81 | 30 n. 41 |
| 6 | 466 with n. 21, 468 | 1.3.96ff | 465 n. 12 |
| 8.2 | 468 | 1.3.97–114 | 465 n. 14 |
| 8.7 | 468 | 1.4 | 466 n. 21, 462 n. 3 |
| 8.9 | 468 | 1.4.5 | 464 |
| 9 | 468, 470 | 1.4.8 | 463 |
| 9.19–20 | 468 | 1.4.85 | 465 |
| 9.37–8 | 468 | 1.4.91 | 465 |
| 10.17 | 468 | 1.4.100 | 465 |
| 11 | 468 | 1.4.105ff. | 465 n. 13 |
| 11.25 | 373 n. 46 | 1.4.106 | 464 |
| 12 | 468 | 1.4.132 | 373 n. 46 |
| 13.3–4 | 468 | 1.5.40 | 465 |
| 13.9–10 | 468 | 1.5.44 | 465 n. 14 |
| 13.17–18 | 468 | 1.5.101–3 | 465 n. 14 |
| 14 | 468 | 1.6 | 462 n. 3, 463, 465 n. 13, 468 n. 23 |
| 15 | 468 | | |
| 16.2 | 468, 620 | 1.6.62f. | 376 n. 62 |
| 16.5 | 468 | 1.6.119ff | 465 n. 17 |
| 16.16 | 468 | 1.6.128–31 | 465 n. 14 |
| 16.35 | 468 | 1.8.48 | 465 n. 10 |
| 16.37 | 468 | 2 | 465 n. 11 |
| 16.39 | 468 | 2.1 | 462 n. 3 |
| 17 | 466 n. 19 | 2.1.47ff. | 466 n. 21 |

*Satirae (cont.)*

| | |
|---|---|
| 2.1.48 | 465 n. 10 |
| 2.1.84–5 | 465 |
| 2.2 | 137 n. 79, 462 n. 3, 465 n. 13 |
| 2.2.6 | 462 n. 3 |
| 2.2.14–20 | 465 n. 14 |
| 2.2.25 | 465 n. 14 |
| 2.2.53ff | 465 |
| 2.2.56 | 385 |
| 2.2.132ff | 476 n. 36 |
| 2.3 | 465 n. 12 |
| 2.3.11–12 | 462 n. 3 |
| 2.3.12 | 466 |
| 2.4 | 466 |
| 2.6 | 465 n. 13, 466 |
| 2.6.17 | 473 n. 29 |
| 2.6.93–7 | 465 n. 14 |
| 2.8.95 | 465 n. 10 |

**Iamblichus,** *de Vita Pythagorica*

| | |
|---|---|
| 167–8 | 865 n. 100 |

**Isocrates,** *Antidosis*

| | |
|---|---|
| 251 | 44 n. 109 |

**Julian**
*Caesares*

| | |
|---|---|
| 327b | 159 n. 131 |
| 328b | 115 n. 15 |
| 333a | 75 n. 9, 113 |
| 333b | 161 n. 138 |
| 335d | 113 |
| 336a–c | 669 |

*Contra Galilaeos*

| | |
|---|---|
| 191d–e | 668 |
| 200a–b | 668 |
| 235b–238d | 668 |

*Orationes*

| | |
|---|---|
| 6.181b | 347 n. 133 |
| 6.183b | 339 n. 104 |
| 6.185a | 339 n. 104 |
| 6.187c | 430 n. 55 |
| 6.188aff. | 339 n. 104 |
| 6.188a–b | 57 n. 168 |
| 6.190c–193c | 428 n. 30 |
| 6.195b | 91 n. 64 |
| 6.200b | 81 n. 38, 332 n. 73, 429 n. 48 |
| 6.201b–c | 333 n. 78 |
| 6.201b | 332 n. 73 |
| 6.201c | 332 n. 73, 392 nn. 11 and 13, 399 n. 37, 422 n. 4, 430 n. 55, 436 n. 83 |
| 7.208d | 57 n. 168 |
| 7.211b–d | 57 n. 168 |
| 7.211b–c | 339 n. 104 |
| 7.212c | 179 |
| 7.212d | 56 n. 161 |
| 7.213a | 332 n. 73 |
| 7.238b–d | 57 n. 168 |
| 7.238b–c | 392 n. 11, 422 n. 4 |

**Juvenal**

| | |
|---|---|
| 3.116f | 320 n. 13 |
| 4.145 | 146 |
| 13.121–2 | 349 n. 141 |
| 13.121 | 341 n. 117 |

**Laberius,** *Compitalia*

| | |
|---|---|
| F 3 Ribbeck (~ F22 Panayotakis) | 347 n. 132 |

**Libanius,** *Orationes*

| | |
|---|---|
| 26.6 | 570 n. 82 |
| 27.6 | 570 n. 82 |

**Livy**

| | |
|---|---|
| *praef.* 1 | 592 n. 34, 605, 796, 804, 813 n. 141 |
| *praef.* 4–5 | 954 n. 72 |
| *praef.* 9 | 603, 666 n. 191, 954 n. 72 |
| *praef.* 10 | 598 n. 78, 603, 803, 809 |
| *praef.* 13 | 747 n. 53 |
| 6.1.1–3 | 689 n. 57 |
| 6.1.3 | 954 n. 72 |
| 6.1.10 | 940 |
| 6.29 | 941 |

**Lucian**
*Anacharsis*

| | |
|---|---|
| 19 | 878 |

## INDEX LOCORUM

[*Cynicus*]

| | |
|---|---|
| 7 | 429 n. 43 |
| 11 | 429 n. 43 |
| 12 | 429 n. 44 |
| 13 | 405 n. 54 |
| 15 | 392 n. 13, 422 n. 4, 427 nn. 27 and 29 |
| 18 | 429 n. 43 |

*de Saltatione*

| | |
|---|---|
| 63 | 324 n. 33 |

*Demonax*

| | |
|---|---|
| 3 | 341 n. 115 |
| 7 | 341 n. 115 |
| 9 | 332 n. 73, 414 |
| 10 | 329 n. 54, 415 |
| 11 | 334 n. 82, 414 |
| 18 | 414 |
| 21 | 329 n. 54, 333 n. 79, 432 n. 71 |
| 38 | 414 |
| 40 | 414 |
| 50 | 414 |
| 51 | 414 |
| 63 | 81 n. 38, 332 n. 73, 429 n. 48 |
| 64 | 415 |

*Fugitiui*

| | |
|---|---|
| 13 | 864 n. 99 |
| 17 | 339 n. 103 |

*Quomodo historia conscribenda sit*

| | |
|---|---|
| 40 | 406 n. 58 |

*Imagines*

| | |
|---|---|
| 17 | 90 n. 58 |

*Aduersus Indoctum*

| | |
|---|---|
| 19 | 563 n. 41 |

*Menippus siue necyomantia*

| | |
|---|---|
| 4 | 601 n. 102, 807 n. 106 |

*de Parasito*

| | |
|---|---|
| 10 | 381 n. 78 |

*de Morte Peregrini*

| | |
|---|---|
| 18 | 29, 34 n. 58, 63 |
| 23 | 359 n. 26 |
| 33 | 332 n. 73 |

*Piscator*

| | |
|---|---|
| 45 | 332 n. 73 |

*Vitarum Auctio*

| | |
|---|---|
| 7ff. | 349 n. 140 |
| 8 | 332 n. 73, 392 n. 11, 422 n. 4 |
| 9 | 339 n. 105, 341 n. 117, 423 n. 9 |
| 10–11 | 430 n. 55 |
| 11 | 864 n. 99 |
| 20ff | 349 n. 140 |

**Lucretius**

| | |
|---|---|
| 1.501 | 885 n. 168 |
| 2.1ff | 885 n. 167 |
| 3.938 | 476 n. 38, 477 n. 41, 465 n. 15 |
| 3.959–60 | 465 n. 15 |
| 5.1129f | 499 |

**Lysias**

| | |
|---|---|
| 31.6 | 425 n. 18 |

**Macrobius,** *Saturnalia*

| | |
|---|---|
| 2.4.11 | 940 n. 19 |

**Marcus Aurelius,** *Meditationes*

| | |
|---|---|
| 1.14.1 | 242 n. 66 |
| 2.1 | 342 n. 119 |
| 2.13 | 79 n. 29, 342 n. 119 |
| 2.17 | 79 n. 29 |
| 3.3.2 | 79 n. 29 |
| 3.4 | 342 n. 119 |
| 3.4.3 | 79 n. 29 |
| 3.5.1 | 79 n. 29 |
| 3.6.2 | 79 n. 29 |
| 3.7 | 79 n. 29 |
| 3.11 | 342 n. 119 |
| 3.12 | 79 n. 29 |
| 3.16.2 | 79 n. 29 |
| 4.2 | 342 n. 119 |

**Marcus Aurelius,** *Meditationes (cont.)*

| | |
|---|---|
| 4.49.2 | 358 n. 25 |
| 5.10.2 | 79 n. 29 |
| 5.27 | 79 n. 29 |
| 5.28 | 342 n. 119 |
| 6.27 | 342 n. 119 |
| 6.47 | 342 n. 119 |
| 7.17 | 79 n. 29 |
| 7.22 | 342 n. 119 |
| 7.26 | 342 n. 119 |
| 7.31 | 342 n. 119 |
| 7.36 | 332 n. 73 |
| 7.63 | 342 n. 119 |
| 7.70 | 342 n. 119 |
| 8.8 | 342 n. 119 |
| 8.14 | 342 n. 119 |
| 8.45 | 79 n. 29 |
| 9.11 | 342 n. 119 |
| 9.42 | 342 n. 119 |
| 10.13 | 79 n. 29 |
| 11.3 | 914 n. 288 |
| 11.12.12 | 342 n. 119 |
| 11.18.3 | 342 n. 119 |
| 11.18.9 | 342 n. 119 |
| 12.3 | 79 n. 29 |
| 12.26 | 79 n. 29 |

**Martial**

| | |
|---|---|
| 8.70.7 | 159 n. 133 |
| 9.26.9f. | 159 n. 133 |
| 10.72 | 121 |
| 12.4 | 124 |
| 14.73 | 87 n. 54 |

**Maximus of Tyre,** *Dissertationes*

| | |
|---|---|
| 1.3.2–4 | 363 n. 11 |
| 1.26.310f. | 363 n. 11 |
| 4.3c | 134 n. 68 |
| 15.9c–d | 332 n. 73 |
| 30.3 | 366 n. 22 |
| 36 | 339 n. 103, 427 nn. 27 and 29, 433 n. 74 |
| 36.1 | 335 n. 88, 430 n. 53 |
| 36.4 | 392 n. 13, 422 n. 4 |
| 36.5 | 392 n. 11, 422 n. 4, 423 n. 9 |

**Menander**
*Epitrepontes*

| | |
|---|---|
| 1096 | 83 n. 43 |

[*Monostichoi*]

| | |
|---|---|
| 735 Jaekel | 425 n. 18 |

**Menander Rhetor**

| | |
|---|---|
| 368.3–8 | 119 n. 30 |
| 372.21–5 | 121 |
| 377.1 | 121 n. 38 |
| 377.2–9 | 121 |
| 390.2–4 | 148 |

**Musonius Rufus** (Hense)

| | |
|---|---|
| p. 42.1–2 (F 9) | 392 n. 12, 422 n. 5 |
| p. 44 (F 9) | 265 n. 110 |
| p. 125 (F 39) | 342 n. 119 |

**Cornelius Nepos,** *Vitae*
*praef.*     600 n. 90, 684 n. 39, 798 n. 55

*Pelopidas*

| | |
|---|---|
| 1.1 | 600 n. 90, 684 n. 39, 798 n. 55 |

**Onesicritus** (*FGrHist* 134)

| | |
|---|---|
| T 7 | 406 n. 58 |
| F 17 | 99 n. 85, 298 n. 16, 318 n. 6, 327 n. 47, 332 n. 73, 339 nn. 103 and 105, 405–8, 427 n. 29, 429 nn. 41 and 47, 430 n. 53, 433 n. 74, 452, 528 n. 26, 532 n. 59 |

**Ovid**
*Metamorphoses*

| | |
|---|---|
| 1.414 | 378 n. 70 |
| 8.611–720 | 984 n. 32 |
| 14.159 | 378 n. 70 |

*Tristia*

| | |
|---|---|
| 1.2.85 | 273 n. 147 |
| 2.195 | 273 n. 147 |
| 3.3.3 | 273 n. 147 |

**Panaetius** (van Straaten)

| | |
|---|---|
| F 97 | 372 n. 41 |
| F 114 | 338 n. 99 |

**Papyri**

| | |
|---|---|
| P.Ber. 13044 | 92 n. 65 |

**Papyri** (*cont.*)
P. Genèv. Inv. 271   92 n. 65, 341 n. 112
P. Genèv. Inv. 271, col. ii, 45ff.
                     341 n. 113
P. Genèv. Inv. 271, col. ii, 45–6
                     430 n. 53
P. Genèv. Inv. 271, col. iv, 53ff.
                     99 n. 85
P. Giss. 1.27        600 n. 92, 685 n. 44, 801
                     n. 77

**Philostratus**
*Epistulae*
1–8          30 n. 38
9            37, 30 n. 38
10           30 n. 38
15–18        30 n. 38
20–21        31 n. 43
50–2         30 n. 38
60           30 n. 38
90           30 n. 38

*Vita Apollonii*
1.2          42 n. 97
1.7          42 n. 97
1.13         30 n. 38
1.16         42 n. 97
2.20         42 n. 97
2.26         30 n. 38, 42 n. 97
2.40         42 n. 97
4.19         874 n. 129
4.22         29 n. 35
4.25         32 n. 50, 48 n. 123
4.28         874
4.42         32 n. 50, 324 n. 33
4.46         31 n. 43
5.19         31 n. 43, 32 n. 50, 324 nn.
             33 and 35
5.20         886
5.26         29 n. 35
5.27–40      234
5.27–38      29, 30 n. 38, 31 n. 43, 231 n.
             10, 238
5.27         42 n. 98
5.28         30 n. 38
5.31–32      30 n. 38
5.31         36 n. 64
5.33ff.      30 n. 41
5.33         30 n. 38
5.37–38      30 n. 38
5.37         30 nn. 38 and 39
5.39         30 n. 38
5.40         30 n. 38, 37, 238
5.41         31 n. 43
6.7          30 n. 38
6.9          30 n. 38
6.13         30 n. 38
6.28–33      31 n. 43
6.28         30 n. 38
6.31         32 n. 50
6.33         32 n. 50
6.36         42 n. 99
7.8          233
7.9          30 n. 38
7.10         32 n. 50
7.16         31 n. 43, 42 n. 98, 324 n. 33
7.36         30 n. 38
8.3          30 n. 38
8.7.2        30 n. 38, 31 n. 43
8.7.3        31 n. 43, 42 n. 99
8.7.11       30 n. 38
8.7.12       30 n. 38
8.7.16       30 n. 38
8.10         32 n. 50
8.12         32 n. 50
8.13         32 n. 50
8.26         70
8.21         42 n. 98

*Vitae Sophistarum*
481          230 n. 6
484          27
487          47
507          230 n. 6
487–9        270 n. 128, 271 n. 136
487–8        285 n. 205
488          29, 30 n. 39, 46, 50 with n.
             134, 54, 115 nn. 15 and 16,
             150, 151, 159, 179, 207, 220
             n. 48, 236, 239 n. 50, 242
             n. 65, 246 n. 80, 254 n. 21,
             303 n. 25
490          46
491          46 n. 116, 47
492          27, 46
493          26

## 1030　INDEX LOCORUM

*Vitae Sophistarum* (cont.)
| | |
|---|---|
| 532 | 95 n. 73 |
| 539 | 46 |
| 576 | 46 n. 116 |

**Photius**, *Bibliotheca*
| | |
|---|---|
| 209 | 141 n. 90 |

**Phrynichus**, *Ecloga*
| | |
|---|---|
| 399 Fisher | 599 n. 84 |

**Pindar**, *Pythia*
| | |
|---|---|
| 4.119 | 621 n. 48 |
| 4.270 | 621 n. 48 |
| 6.7 | 805 |
| 6.8 | 681 |

**Plato**
*Alcibiades I*
| | |
|---|---|
| 104c–d | 484 |
| 105a–c | 484 |
| 105d | 484 |
| 106eff | 484 |
| 112b | 486 |
| 118a | 484 |
| 120e9 | 489 |
| 121a–124b | 484 |
| 122a | 199 |
| 121cff. | 486 |
| 122c | 486 with n. 12 |
| 124a–b | 486 |
| 128eff. | 486 |
| 129eff. | 486 |
| 133c | 486 |
| 135a–c | 486 |

*Apologia Socratis*
| | |
|---|---|
| 17d | 874 |
| 20e | 57 |
| 21cff. | 57 |
| 22a | 125 n. 41, 141 n. 90, 268 n. 121, 472 |
| 22b | 57 |
| 23a12 | 430 n. 55 |
| 23b | 903 |
| 24b–c | 558, 873 |
| 24d–25a | 254 n. 27 |
| 28b–29d | 867 |
| 29a | 899 |
| 29d | 254 n. 27, 831 n. 204, 867 |
| 30a–b | 254 n. 27 |
| 31b | 254 n. 27 |
| 35a–b | 899 |
| 36c | 254 n. 27 |
| 36d | 254 n. 27, 283 n. 195 |

[*Axiochus*]
| | |
|---|---|
| 371a | 199 |

*Clitophon*
| | |
|---|---|
| 407a | 255 |
| 407b | 256 |
| 407c–d | 257 |
| 407e | 254 n. 27 |

*Cratylus*
| | |
|---|---|
| 415d | 915 |

*Crito*
| | |
|---|---|
| 43d | 896, 899 |
| 45c–d | 896 |
| 54b | 896 |
| 108c–d | 208 n. 10 |

[*Epistulae*]
| | |
|---|---|
| 2.310d | 93 n. 662.310eff.　85 |
| 7.335a | 135 n. 70 |

*Gorgias*
| | |
|---|---|
| 470e | 167 |
| 485d | 728 n. 90, 905 with n. 243 |
| 493a | 135 |
| 509a | 254 n. 28 |
| 523a | 134 n. 69, 208 n. 10 |

*Leges*
| | |
|---|---|
| 656c | 212 |
| 713c–d | 83, 210 n. 17 |
| 713d | 81 n. 35, 83 |
| 713e | 79 n. 28 |
| 739c | 865 n. 100 |
| 775e | 83 n. 43 |
| 865d | 134 n. 69 |
| 872d | 134 n. 69 |
| 927a | 134 n. 69 |

*Menexenus*
244d–46a     257 n. 43

*Phaedo*
60a     896
60d     914 n. 282
114b     916
116b     896
117c–e     896
117d     896
117e     896

*Phaedrus*
246bff     473
257d     24
275e     211
276e     134 n. 68

*Politicus*
268e     134 n. 68
271d     261 n. 69
299b7     46 n. 118

*Protagoras*
320c     134 n. 68
337c–d     425 n. 18

*Res Publica*
347b     79
354a     994 n. 74
360eff.     78
361b–c     85
361d–e     86
364b     219
367bff.     78
369b     261 n. 69
372eff.     79
373d–e     79
375a     155
376d     134 n. 68
389e     78
390d–e     79
391c     79
399b–c     78
399e     79
401a–402a     78 n. 26
402e     78
420cff.     78
422a     79, 865 n. 100
442c     78
443d     78 n. 26
445cff.     78
449c     865 n. 100
475a–b     79
485e     78, 79
490c     78
491aff.     78
539b     155
540a     81 n. 35
544aff.     78
545aff.     78, 79
548a     78
551aff.     78
555c     78
556b     79
580d–581d     78 n. 26
581a–b     78
581a     78
581c     79
592b     394 n. 20
592b3     451 n. 19
617d–e     79 n. 30
618aff.     78
618a–b     79 n. 30
620d–e     79 n. 30

*Symposium*
182b     257 n. 43
193a     257 n. 43
193a2     217 n. 37
201d     135
202e     207 n. 6
207d     208
209d     211

*Theaetetus*
173e1–174a1     425 n. 18

*Timaeus*
20d     208 n. 10
21a     208 n. 10
90a     79 n. 28

**Pliny the Elder**, *Historia Naturalis*
3.39     272 n. 138
7.19.79–80     432 n. 70

## Pliny the Younger

### Epistulae

| | |
|---|---|
| 1.10.1 | 121 |
| 1.13.1 | 121 |
| 3.18.2f. | 119 |
| 3.18.2 | 120 n. 33 |
| 3.18.5 | 121 |
| 4.22.4–6 | 131 |
| 6.29 | 412 |
| 6.31.9 | 151 n. 116 |
| 6.31.12 | 114 n. 15 |
| 8.16.3–4 | 333 n. 80 |
| 8.22.3 | 342 n. 119 |
| 10.1 | 82 n. 42, 138 n. 83, 297 n. 9 |
| 10.41.1 | 87 n. 53, 102 n. 91, 113 |
| 10.41.5 | 87 n. 53, 102 n. 91, 113 |
| 10.81–2 | 221 |
| 10.96.2 | 726 n. 83, 982 n. 19 |
| 10.102 | 82 n. 42, 138 n. 83, 297 n. 9 |

### Panegyricus

| | |
|---|---|
| 1.3–5 | 134 n. 67 |
| 1.3–6 | 128 |
| 1.5 | 143 |
| 2.2–3 | 678 |
| 2.3 | 130 n. 55, 134 |
| 2.6 | 131 |
| 3.4 | 120 n. 33 |
| 4.1 | 120 n. 33, 131 |
| 4.5 | 130 n. 55 |
| 4.7 | 144, 145 |
| 5.1f. | 128 |
| 5.2–9 | 82 n. 42, 138 n. 83, 297 n. 9 |
| 5.3f. | 143 |
| 6.1–7.3 | 141 n. 92 |
| 6.7 | 114 n. 10 |
| 7.3 | 130 n. 55 |
| 7.5 | 128 |
| 8.1–3 | 128 |
| 8.1 | 143 |
| 8.2 | 114 n. 10 |
| 8.4–6 | 141 n. 92 |
| 9.2f. | 114 n. 10 |
| 10.1 | 141 n. 92 |
| 10.3 | 114 n. 10 |
| 10.4 | 128 |
| 11.3 | 134 |
| 11.4 | 137 n. 80 |
| 12.1–15.5 | 114 n. 10 |
| 12.1 | 137 n. 80 |
| 13.1ff. | 90 n. 59 |
| 13.3 | 130 n. 55 |
| 13.4f | 137 n. 80 |
| 13.5 | 114 n. 13 |
| 14.1 | 114 |
| 14.5 | 140 with n. 86 |
| 15.5 | 130 n. 55 |
| 16.1f. | 114 n. 10 |
| 16.2 | 132 |
| 16.3–19.4 | 114 n. 10 |
| 16.3 | 121 n. 37 |
| 17.1–4 | 150 |
| 18.1 | 137 n. 80 |
| 19.3 | 130 n. 55 |
| 22.1f. | 150 |
| 28.6 | 132 n. 61 |
| 33.1–4 | 132 n. 62 |
| 33.4 | 134 |
| 34f. | 131 |
| 36.2 | 145 |
| 43.3 | 132 n. 61 |
| 45.6 | 132 n. 61 |
| 46.2–4 | 161 |
| 47–9 | 106 n. 6 |
| 47.1–2 | 235 n. 29, 271 n. 134 |
| 47.6 | 130 n. 55 |
| 48.3 | 130 n. 55 |
| 49.1 | 134 |
| 49.2f | 140 n. 89 |
| 49.8 | 128 |
| 50.4 | 161 |
| 51.1–3 | 161 |
| 52.2f | 134 |
| 52.2–4 | 134 n. 67 |
| 54.1 | 121 n. 37 |
| 55.11 | 144 |
| 61.1 | 137 n. 80 |
| 62.9 | 132 n. 61 |
| 65.1–3 | 145 |
| 65.1 | 133 n. 64 |
| 65.2 | 128 |
| 66.4 | 91 n. 62 |
| 67.4–8 | 129 |
| 67.5 | 148 |
| 67.8 | 133 |
| 68.1 | 129, 148 |

INDEX LOCORUM 1033

*Panegyricus (cont.)*

| | |
|---|---|
| 74.1 | 130 |
| 74.4 | 130 |
| 76.1 | 137 n. 80 |
| 77.3 | 145 |
| 77.5 | 130 n. 55 |
| 79.5 | 130 n. 55 |
| 80.3 | 134 n. 67 |
| 80.4f. | 128 |
| 81 | 95 n. 75, 109 n. 13 |
| 81.1–3 | 136 n. 75, 176 n. 158 |
| 81–2 | 109 nn. 12 and 13 |
| 85.7 | 132 n. 61 |
| 86.3 | 130 n. 55 |
| 88.5 | 114 n. 14 |
| 88.8 | 128 |
| 94.5 | 129, 141 n. 91 |

**Plutarch**

*Moralia*

| | |
|---|---|
| 4E | 257 n. 37 |
| 50B | 373 n. 46 |
| 51C | 373 n. 46 |
| 55B | 120 n. 33 |
| 56F | 71 |
| 59B | 120 n. 33 |
| 59D | 373 n. 46 |
| 70C | 332 n. 73 |
| 74C | 332 n. 73 |
| 80A | 42 n. 105 |
| 82A | 332 n. 73 |
| 89B | 332 n. 73, 373 n. 47 |
| 171E | 601 n. 102, 807 n. 106 |
| 172E | 124 |
| 173D | 995 n. 75 |
| 181F | 995 n. 75 |
| 277B–C | 950 |
| 292B | 950 |
| 323C | 25 |
| 326A | 25 |
| 329A–B | 337 n. 95, 400, 433 |
| 329A–D | 392 n. 13, 422 n. 4, 433 n. 75 |
| 329B | 336 |
| 329C | 332 n. 73, 337, 408, 433 |
| 330C | 368 n. 31 |
| 332B | 427 n. 29 |
| 332B–C | 392 n. 11, 422 n. 4 |
| 345E | 740 n. 30 |
| 351A | 42 |
| 385E | 44 |
| 439E | 340 n. 109 |
| 516C | 886 |
| 552F | 354 n. 8 |
| 600F–601A | 392 n. 12, 422 n. 5 |
| 601A | 425 n. 20 |
| 606C | 332 n. 73 |
| 613A | 42 n. 105 |
| 613C | 42 n. 105 |
| 615B | 42 n. 105 |
| 618E | 42 n. 105 |
| 621B | 42 n. 105 |
| 632E | 332 n. 73 |
| 659F | 42 n. 105 |
| 667D | 42 n. 105 |
| 671C–672C | 578 n. 123 |
| 710B | 26 |
| 759D | 398 n. 29 |
| 776C | 42 n. 105 |
| 777B | 905 n. 243 |
| 778B | 42 n. 105 |
| 778C | 366 n. 22 |
| 783C–D | 456 |
| 785A | 42 n. 105 |
| 785F–786A | 38 n. 75 |
| 790F | 42 n. 105 |
| 791A–B | 25 n. 11 |
| 791E | 42 n. 105 |
| 814A–C | 277 n. 175 |
| 1039E | 335 n. 88, 356 n. 14 |
| 1063A | 365 n. 16 |
| 1087B | 366 n. 22 |
| 1093C | 366 n. 22 |

*Lives*

*Alexander*

| | |
|---|---|
| 1.1–2 | 600 n. 90, 684 n. 39, 798 n. 55 |
| 1.2–3 | 920 n. 315 |
| 14.5 | 440 |
| 65.2 | 429 n. 47, 452 |

*Antony*

| | |
|---|---|
| 24 | 578 n. 131 |

*Brutus*

| | |
|---|---|
| 33.5 | 42 n. 105 |
| 33.6 | 354 n. 8 |
| 34.4–7 | 411 |
| 34.5 | 379 n. 76 |
| 34.5–8 | 332 n. 73 |
| 55.2 | 666 n. 191 |

*Caesar*

| | |
|---|---|
| 60.6 | 134 n. 66 |

*Cicero*

| | |
|---|---|
| 1.4 | 942 |
| 24.7 | 873 n. 123 |

*Cato Minor*

| | |
|---|---|
| 67–70 | 55 n. 152 |

*Crassus*

| | |
|---|---|
| 12 | 411 |

*Demosthenes*

| | |
|---|---|
| 9.1 | 42 n. 105 |

*Lycurgus*

| | |
|---|---|
| 31.2 | 428 n. 38 |

*Themistocles*

| | |
|---|---|
| 2.4 | 44 n. 110 |

*Pericles*

| | |
|---|---|
| 2.2–4 | 920 n. 315 |

*Pompey*

| | |
|---|---|
| 23 | 411 |

*Solon*

| | |
|---|---|
| 12.7–9 | 883 n. 164 |

**Polybius**

| | |
|---|---|
| 3.1.5–4.1 | 599, 800 |
| 3.4.13 | 593, 799, 801 |

**Posidonius**

| | |
|---|---|
| F 187 | 79 n. 29 |

**Pseudo-Acro**, *Commentum in Horati Epistulas*

| | |
|---|---|
| 1.49 | 370 n. 35 |

**Quintilian**, *Institutio Oratoria*

| | |
|---|---|
| 1.1.9 | 342 n. 119 |
| 1.9.1–5 | 120 n. 36 |
| 2.8.1–5 | 367 n. 24 |
| 3.8.70 | 119 |
| 8.3.44 | 941 |
| 8.6.20 | 694, 810, 854 |
| 9.2.64–99 | 119 |
| 9.2.64f. | 122 |
| 9.2.64 | 119 |
| 9.2.65 | 119 |
| 9.2.66 | 122 |
| 9.2.75 | 122 |

*Scholia uetera in Iuuenalem*

| | |
|---|---|
| 1.33 | 317 n. 3, 321 n. 20 |

*Scriptores Historiae Augustae*
*Alexander Severus*

| | |
|---|---|
| 65.5 | 131, 151 n. 116 |

*Hadrianus*

| | |
|---|---|
| 2.7 | 161 n. 138 |
| 3.11 | 159 n. 131 |
| 4.5 | 161 n. 138 |
| 4.9 | 75 n. 9, 113 |

**Seneca the Elder**, *Suasoriae*

| | |
|---|---|
| 1.6 | 578 n. 131 |

**Seneca the Younger**
*ad Polybium*

| | |
|---|---|
| 13.1 | 666 n. 191 |
| 14.1 | 666 n. 191 |

*de beata Vita*

| | |
|---|---|
| 18.3 | 329 n. 60 |

*de Beneficiis*

| | |
|---|---|
| 7.8.2 | 329 n. 60, 398 nn. 29 and 31 |
| 7.8.3 | 430 n. 55 |

*de Breuitate Vitae*

| | |
|---|---|
| 14.2 | 350 |

*de Clementia*

| | |
|---|---|
| 1 | 153 |
| 1.19.2f. | 93 n. 67 |

*de Prouidentia*

| | |
|---|---|
| 3.2 | 358 n. 25 |
| 4.3 | 358 n. 25 |
| 4.16 | 358 n. 25 |

*Epistulae Morales*

| | |
|---|---|
| 5.2–6 | 374 n. 51 |
| 5.2–4 | 430 n. 55 |
| 5.2 | 379 n. 76 |
| 5.4 | 371 n. 40 |
| 7.6–8 | 374 n. 51 |
| 7.9 | 430 n. 55 |
| 9.1ff. | 374 n. 52 |
| 18.3 | 374 n. 51 |
| 20.9 | 430 n. 55 |
| 21.1–2 | 857 n. 72 |
| 22.12 | 364 n. 16 |
| 28.4 | 273 n. 147, 862 n. 89 |
| 28.7 | 365 n. 17 |
| 33.2 | 366 n. 22 |
| 41.1 | 881 n. 151, 886 |
| 68.10 | 368 n. 30 |
| 73.16 | 881 n. 151 |
| 85.5 | 329 n. 56 |
| 85.28 | 358 n. 25 |
| 90.16 | 371 n. 40 |
| 94.39 | 120 n. 33 |
| 96.1 | 358 n. 25 |
| 99.5 | 333 n. 80 |
| 104.27 | 915 n. 290 |
| 116.5 | 338 n. 99 |

*de Otio*

| | |
|---|---|
| 6.4–5 | 400 n. 39 |
| Sen Prov 6.6 | 371 n. 40 |
| Sen Tranq 8.5 | 371 n. 40 |
| Sen. Ep. 41.1–2 | 79 n. 29 |

**Silius Italicus,** *Punica*

| | |
|---|---|
| 3.625f | 134 |

**[Socrates]**

| | |
|---|---|
| Ep. 12 (p. 618 Hercher–Simon) | 332 n. 73 |

**Solon** ($IEG^2$)

| | |
|---|---|
| F 13 | 329 n. 53 |

**Sophocles**
*Antigone*

| | |
|---|---|
| 1144 | 572 n. 97 |

*Electra*

| | |
|---|---|
| 233–6 | 254 n. 21 |

**Statius,** *Silvae*

| | |
|---|---|
| 4.3.128ff. | 134 |

**Stobaeus**

| | |
|---|---|
| 2.1.11 | 426 n. 23 |
| 2.103.14–17 | 391, 450 |
| 3.1.55 | 332 n. 73 |
| 3.1.98 | 427 nn. 27 and 29 |
| 3.8.20 | 332 n. 73, 334 n. 83, 373 n. 47 |
| 3.13.43 | 357 n. 17, 338 n. 101 |
| 3.13.44 | 332 n. 73, 373 n. 47, 431 n. 63 |
| 3.17.17 | 368 n. 31 |
| 3.40.2a | 425 n. 18 |
| 3.40.8 | 392 n. 13, 422 n. 4 |
| 3.40.9 | 392 n. 12, 422 n. 5 |
| 4.29.19 | 90 n. 58 |
| 4.192.7–9 | 457 |
| 4.381.20–1 | 401 n. 41 |
| 4.4.28 | 424 n. 13 |

**Strabo,** *Geographica*

| | |
|---|---|
| 15.1.63–5 | 298 n. 16, 405–8 |
| 15.1.63–4 | 429 n. 47, 452 |
| 15.1.64–5 | 318 n. 6, 339 n. 105, 427 n. 29, 429 n. 41 |
| 15.1.64 | 99 n. 85, 327 n. 47, 332 n. 73, 339 n. 103, 400 n. 38, 433 n. 74, 528 n. 26 |
| 15.1.65 | 99 n. 85, 332 n. 73, 337 n. 98, 341 n. 114, 430 n. 53, 434 n. 77 |
| 16.1.65 | 426 n. 23 |

**Suetonius**
*Augustus*

| | |
|---|---|
| 89.3 | 241 n. 62 |

*Claudius*

| | |
|---|---|
| 10.3ff. | 30 n. 41 |
| 25.4 | 616 n. 22, 947, 950, 952, 955 |

*Domitianus*

| | |
|---|---|
| 2.3 | 146 n. 102 |
| 4.4 | 121 n. 37, 161 n. 137 |

## Domitianus (cont.)

| | |
|---|---|
| 5 | 161 n. 135 |
| 10.4 | 116 |
| 12.1 | 161 n. 135 |
| 13 | 632 n. 91 |
| 13.2 | 134 |
| 19 | 176 n. 158 |
| 19.1 | 121 n. 37 |
| 22 | 121 n. 37 |

## Nero

| | |
|---|---|
| 16.2 | 616 n. 22, 889 n. 183, 948 n. 58, 951, 952 |

## Tiberius

| | |
|---|---|
| 75.1 | 942 |

## Titus

| | |
|---|---|
| 9.3 | 146 n. 102 |

## Vespasianus

| | |
|---|---|
| 4.5 | 957 |
| 7.2 | 613 n. 2 |
| 13 | 325 n. 37 |
| 25 | 176 n. 156 |

## Vita Horatii

| | |
|---|---|
| II.486 (Loeb ed.) | 476 n. 39 |
| II.486–8 (Loeb ed.) | 476 n. 40 |

## Tacitus

### Agricola

| | |
|---|---|
| 2.3 | 747 |
| 3.1 | 121, 276 n. 164, 678 |
| 3.2 | 747 |
| 4.3 | 325 n. 38 |
| 39.1 | 121 n. 37 |
| 41.1–3 | 121 n. 37 |
| 42.4 | 325 n. 38 |
| 44.5 | 121, 138 n. 83, 297 n. 9 |
| 45.1 | 146 |

### Annales

| | |
|---|---|
| 1.4.2 | 30 n. 41 |
| 1.9.4 | 666 n. 191 |
| 1.33.3 | 30 n. 41 |
| 2.28.2 | 30 n. 41 |
| 3.17.4 | 942 n. 33 |
| 3.65 | 748 |
| 4.17.3 | 666 n. 191 |
| 4.32.1–2 | 600 n. 90, 684 n. 39, 798 n. 55 |
| 4.34–5 | 749 |
| 14.16.2 | 241 n. 62 |
| 15.44.2–5 | 616 n. 22 |
| 15.44.2–3 | 937 n. 2, 948 |
| 15.44.2 | 615 n. 17, 723 n. 72 |
| 15.44.3 | 889 n. 183, 948 n. 58, 956, 982 n. 18 |
| 15.52.4 | 30 n. 41 |
| 15.62–4 | 55 n. 154, 207 |
| 15.63.3 | 207 |
| 15.67 | 71 |
| 16.21.1 | 320 n. 14 |
| 16.22 | 346 n. 129, 411 n. 75 |
| 16.22.4 | 346 n. 129 |
| 16.23.1f. | 323 n. 29 |
| 16.23.1 | 320 n. 14 |
| 16.30.1–33.2 | 320 n. 14 |
| 16.32.3 | 320 n. 13 |
| 16.34 | 48 n. 123 |
| 16.34–5 | 55 n. 153, 207 |

### Historiae

| | |
|---|---|
| 1.1 | 121, 750 n. 58 |
| 2.91 | 320 n. 16 |
| 3.81 | 159 n. 130, 192 n. 19, 303 n. 26 |
| 4.6ff | 320 n. 17 |
| 4.6 | 320 n. 15 |
| 4.6.1 | 325 n. 38 |
| 4.7 | 129, 176 n. 156, 322 n. 28, 342 n. 120, 613 n. 2 |
| 4.9 | 321 n. 18 |
| 4.10 | 325 n. 38 |
| 4.40.3 | 321, 325 n. 38, 430 n. 55 |
| 5.5.5 | 578 n. 123 |
| 5.13.2 | 957 |

### Fragments

| | |
|---|---|
| Tac F 2 | 616 n. 22 |

## Teles (Hense)

| | |
|---|---|
| 3.21.1–22.7 | 392 n. 13 |
| 5.1–6.1 | 409 n. 70, 424 n. 15 |
| 5.2–6.8 | 375 n. 60 |

**Teles** (Hense) (*cont.*)
| | |
|---|---|
| 6.5–8.5 | 423 n. 11 |
| 7.3 | 431 n. 61 |
| 7.4–6 | 427 n. 29 |
| 7.5–6 | 427 n. 27 |
| 10–11 | 536 n. 82 |
| 10.6ff. | 536 n. 82 |
| 16.4–7 | 375 n. 60 |
| 21.1–22.7 | 422 n. 4 |
| 52.2–5 | 375 n. 60 |
| 55 | 329 n. 56 |

**Themistius**, de Virtute
| | |
|---|---|
| p. 43 Mach | 258, 299, 481–4 |

*Orationes*
| | |
|---|---|
| 139a | 31 with n. 44 |
| 245d | 42 n. 103 |
| 260c | 42 n. 103 |
| 336c | 42 n. 103 |
| 345c | 42 n. 103 |

**Theon**, *Progymnasmata*
| | |
|---|---|
| 35 | 357 n. 18 |

**Thucydides**
| | |
|---|---|
| 1.1.1–23 | 602, 800, 802 |
| 1.1–3 | 684 |
| 1.1.1–2 | 599 n. 82, 797 |
| 1.1.1 | 281 n. 187, 592 with n. 37, 603, 604, 683, 796, 800, 803, 813 |
| 1.1.3 | 685, 688, 689 732, 746, 823 |
| 1.2 | 824 |
| 1.20.1 | 688, 689, 823 |
| 1.21–22 | 592 n. 38, 798 n. 57 |
| 1.21.2 | 689 |
| 1.22 | 254 n. 23, 604, 829 |
| 1.22.1–23.1 | 688 |
| 1.22.1–2 | 593 n. 47, 604, 683, 800 |
| 1.22.2–3 | 823 |
| 1.22.2 | 604, 683, 800 |
| 1.22.3–4 | 604, 683, 800 |
| 1.22.3 | 604, 683, 800, 822 |
| 1.22.4 | 593 n. 45, 600 n. 93, 602, 604, 605, 648 n. 132, 681, 683, 688, 732, 800, 802, 804, 805, 809 |
| 1.70.3 | 254 n. 23 |
| 1.124.2 | 132 n. 60 |
| 2.24.3 | 425 n. 18 |
| 2.47–53 | 794 n. 42 |
| 2.97.4 | 830, 995 n. 75 |
| 5.26 | 254 nn. 23 and 24 |
| 5.26.1 | 592 n. 37, 604, 683, 800 |
| 5.26.4 | 604, 800 |
| 5.26.5 | 604, 683, 800 |

**Timaeus** (*FGrHist* 566)
| | |
|---|---|
| F 13a | 865 n. 100 |

**Valerius Maximus**, *Facta et Dicta Memorabilia*
| | |
|---|---|
| 1.2 ext. 3 | 578 n. 123 |

**Velleius Paterculus**
| | |
|---|---|
| 2.1.1 | 699 |
| 2.55.1 | 699 |
| 2.86.1 | 699 |
| 2.99.4 | 699 |

**Virgil**
*Aeneid*
| | |
|---|---|
| 1.11 | 728 |
| 1.102–12 | 605 n. 113, 728 n. 92 |
| 1.278–9 | 713 |
| 1.279 | 714 |
| 1.287 | 862 n. 88 |
| 1.742–6 | 497 |
| 4.33–61 | 497 n. 49 |
| 6.146–7 | 496 |
| 6.210–11 | 496 |
| 6.836–40 | 501 |
| 6.846 | 496 |
| 6.847ff. | 260, 275 n. 156 |
| 6.847–53 | 480–508 *passim*, 606 n. 118 |
| 6.849–50 | 497 |
| 6.851 | 493 n. 36 |
| 6.888–92 | 499 |
| 7.37–44 | 689 n. 57 |
| 10.63–95 | 497 n. 49 |
| 12.946–7 | 645 |
| 12.947 | 941 n. 26 |

*Georgics*

| | |
|---|---|
| 1.424–37 | 744 |
| 1.425 | 745 |
| 1.429 | 745 |
| 1.430–1 | 745 |
| 1.431 | 745 |
| 1.433 | 745 |
| 3.46 | 750 |
| 4.559–66 | 745, 753 n. 72 |
| 4.563 | 941 n. 28 |

**Vitae Vergilianae Antiquae**

| | |
|---|---|
| Vita Donati 36 | 941 n. 28 |

**Vitruvius,** *de Architectura*

| | |
|---|---|
| *Praef.* 1 | 124 |

**Xenophon**
*Agesilaus*

| | |
|---|---|
| 2.12 | 119 n. 30 |

*Anabasis*

| | |
|---|---|
| 3.1.5–8 | 254 n. 26 |

*Apologia Socratis*

| | |
|---|---|
| 27 | 870 |

*Hellenica*

| | |
|---|---|
| 2.3.56 | 600 n. 90, 684 n. 39, 798 n. 55 |
| 3.1.2 | 740 n. 30 |
| 5.4.51 | 601 n. 98, 682, 796 |
| 7.2.1 | 600 n. 90, 684 n. 39, 798 n. 55 |

*Memorabilia*

| | |
|---|---|
| 1.1 | 899 |
| 1.1.1 | 558, 873 |
| 1.2.49 | 901 |
| 1.5 | 125 |
| 2.1.12–13 | 397 n. 25, 425 n. 20, 451 n. 18 |
| 2.1.13 | 473 |
| 2.1.21 | 489 n. 15, 490 n. 23 |
| 2.1.21–33 | 296 |
| 2.1.21–34 | 473 |
| 2.1.23 | 143 |
| 2.1.29 | 143 |
| 2.2.13 | 472 |
| 4.3.8 | 173 |
| 4.4.5–6 | 254 n. 28 |
| 4.64 | 332 n. 73 |

*Symposium*

| | |
|---|---|
| 1.1 | 600 n. 90, 684 n. 39, 798 n. 55 |
| 1.26 | 210 n. 18 |
| 4.34ff. | 319 n. 8 |
| 4.34–44 | 424 n. 17 |
| 4.37 | 336 n. 94, 338 n. 101 |

**Zonaras,** *Epitome Historiarum*

| | |
|---|---|
| 10.20 | 378 n. 71 |

## II. Jewish and Christian Authors

### (a) Biblical Books

**Genesis**

| | |
|---|---|
| 1.1 | 689, 824 |
| 11.1–9 | 656 |

**Exodus**

| | |
|---|---|
| 15.26 | 623, 645, 661 |
| 17.14 | 751, 752 |
| 24.4 | 751 |
| 28.11 | 751 n. 65 |
| 28.12 | 751 n. 65 |
| 34.27 | 751 |

**Deuteronomy**

| | |
|---|---|
| 27.26 | 943 n. 42 |
| 31.24–6 | 752 |
| 31.9 | 751, 752 |
| 6.13 | 719 |

**Joshua**

| | |
|---|---|
| 8.31–4 | 752 |

**1 Samuel**

| | |
|---|---|
| 25.24 | 620 |
| 26.17–18 | 556 |

**1 Kings**

| | |
|---|---|
| 17.17–24 | 629 |

# INDEX LOCORUM

**2 Kings**
| | |
|---|---|
| 4.34–5 | 629 |

**2 Chronicles**
| | |
|---|---|
| 16.12–13 | 661 |
| 34.14 | 752 |

**Job**
| | |
|---|---|
| 38.14 | 751 n. 65 |
| 41.7 | 751 n. 65 |

**Psalms**
| | |
|---|---|
| 2.8 | 698, 827, 861 |
| 8.15 | 272 n. 140, 697 |
| 8.16 | 919 |
| 22.2 | 629, 637 |
| 33.9 | 966 |
| 87.6 | 597 n. 66 |

**Song of Songs**
| | |
|---|---|
| 1.1 | 751 n. 64 |
| 1.4 | 751 n. 64 |
| 8.6 | 751 n. 65 |
| 8.10–11 | 751 n. 64 |

**Isaiah**
| | |
|---|---|
| 1.1–2 | 752 |
| 6.1–13 | 555, 752 |
| 6.9ff. | 634 |
| 6.10 | 664 |
| 7.14 | 631 |
| 12.1–3 | 751 n. 64 |
| 35.3–5 | 751 n. 64 |
| 40.3–5 | 716 |
| 40.3 | 897 |
| 40.8 | 966 |
| 41.9 | 633 |
| 42.1–4 | 633 |
| 42.6 | 827 |
| 45.23 | 657 |
| 46.13 | 827 |
| 49.6 | 573 n. 101, 698, 827 with n. 193, 861 |
| 49.9 | 827 |
| 53 | 968 |
| 53.4 | 633 |
| 53.5 | 633, 664 |
| 59.26 | 659 |
| 61.1–2 | 991 |

**Jeremiah**
| | |
|---|---|
| 1.4–10 | 555 |
| 22.24 | 751 n. 65 |

**Ezekiel**
| | |
|---|---|
| 1.28–2.1 | 555 |
| 28.12 | 751 n. 65 |

**Daniel**
| | |
|---|---|
| 10.5–11 | 555 |

**Hosea**
| | |
|---|---|
| 1.1–2 | 752 |
| 1.7 | 751 n. 64 |
| 6.6 | 769 |

**Joel**
| | |
|---|---|
| 1.1 | 752 |
| 1.2 | 752 |
| 2.17 | 922 |

**Micah**
| | |
|---|---|
| 7.18 | 751 n. 64 |

**Haggai**
| | |
|---|---|
| 2.23 | 751 n. 65 |

**Malachi**
| | |
|---|---|
| 3.1 | 751 n. 64 |

**Matthew**
| | |
|---|---|
| 1.1–25 | 776 |
| 1.1 | 630, 689, 824 |
| 1.15 | 777 |
| 1.18 | 630 |
| 1.21 | 630, 631, 635, 636, 637, 658, 736, 767 n. 102 |
| 1.23 | 630, 635, 775, 776 |
| 1.25 | 630 |
| 2.17 | 661 |
| 4.8 | 541 |
| 4.18 | 735 n. 3 |
| 4.23 | 631 |
| 4.24 | 631 |
| 5.7 | 769, 770 |
| 5.10–12 | 771 |
| 7.13–14 | 541 |
| 8.2–4 | 631 |
| 8.5–17 | 633 |

**Matthew** (*cont.*)

| | | | |
|---|---|---|---|
| 8.5–13 | 631 | 10.3 | 763, 768 |
| 8.6 | 631, 632, 647 n. 127 | 10.8 | 633, 637 |
| 8.7 | 631, 632, 633 | 10.9–10 | 540 |
| 8.8 | 631, 647 n. 127 | 11.4–5 | 633 |
| 8.9 | 631 | 11.5 | 637 |
| 8.10–12 | 631 | 11.28–30 | 771, 772 |
| 8.10 | 538 n. 96, 631 | 11.29 | 769 |
| 8.13 | 631, 696 | 12.1–8 | 759 n. 77 |
| 8.14–15 | 632 | 12.2 | 770 |
| 8.14 | 632 | 12.7 | 770 |
| 8.15 | 637 | 12.9–13 | 633 |
| 8.16–17 | 633 | 12.15 | 633 |
| 8.16 | 633 | 12.21 | 633, 636 |
| 8.17 | 633, 636 | 12.22 | 634 |
| 8.18 | 633 | 12.24–43 | 634 |
| 8.19–20 | 538 n. 94 | 12.46–50 | 540 |
| 8.21–2 | 540 | 13.13–17 | 634, 638 |
| 8.28–34 | 534 n. 70, 633 | 13.14 | 636 |
| 8.34 | 633 | 13.17 | 636 |
| 9.2 | 633 | 13.47–52 | 773 |
| 9.4 | 633 | 13.52 | 772, 773 |
| 9.5–7 | 637 | 14.13–21 | 636 |
| 9.9–14 | 754–79 *passim* | 14.13 | 636 |
| 9.9–13 | 735 n. 2 | 14.14 | 636 |
| 9.9 | 735, 761 n. 82, 765, 766, 768 | 14.16 | 636 |
| | | 14.29 | 636 |
| 9.10 | 766 | 14.30 | 636 |
| 9.12 | 766 | 14.31 | 636 |
| 9.13 | 759, 766, 767, 769, 770 | 14.34–36 | 636 |
| 9.14–15 | 563 n. 38 | 15.5–6 | 770 n. 113 |
| 9.14 | 766, 767 | 15.21–8 | 636 |
| 9.15–17 | 773 | 15.21 | 636 |
| 9.15 | 773 | 15.22 | 771 |
| 9.18–26 | 633 | 15.25 | 623 n. 59 |
| 9.19 | 633 | 15.28 | 636, 696 |
| 9.21 | 633 | 15.29 | 636 |
| 9.22 | 633 | 15.30 | 636 |
| 9.23 | 633 | 16.14 | 636 |
| 9.25 | 637 | 16.18 | 767 |
| 9.27–31 | 633 | 17.3–12 | 636 |
| 9.27 | 771 | 17.14–20 | 636 |
| 9.32–4 | 633 | 17.15 | 771 |
| 9.35–7 | 633 | 17.16 | 636 |
| 9.35 | 633 | 17.17 | 636 |
| 10.1–15 | 633 | 17.18 | 636 |
| 10.1–4 | 759 | 17.19 | 636 |
| 10.1 | 633 | 18.33 | 771 |
| | | 19.1–2 | 636 |

# INDEX LOCORUM

**Matthew** (*cont.*)

| | |
|---|---|
| 19.7–8 | 752 |
| 19.16–22 | 961 |
| 20.29–34 | 636 |
| 20.30 | 636 |
| 20.30–1 | 771 |
| 20.32 | 636 |
| 20.34 | 636 |
| 21.14 | 636 |
| 22.16 | 871 |
| 24.2 | 916 n. 297 |
| 24.14 | 921 n. 317 |
| 24.32 | 769 |
| 24.32–5 | 771, 773 |
| 26.63 | 974 |
| 27.15–24 | 974 |
| 27.32–50 | 636, 658, 736 |
| 27.40 | 636, 637 |
| 27.42 | 636, 637 |
| 27.47 | 637 |
| 27.49 | 636, 637 |
| 27.57–61 | 776 |
| 27.57–60 | 773 |
| 27.57 | 773 |
| 27.66 | 753 n. 71 |
| 28.6 | 637 |
| 28.16–20 | 775, 776 |
| 28.18–19 | 538 n. 96 |
| 28.18 | 776 |
| 28.19 | 615, 776 |
| 28.19–20 | 921 n. 317 |
| 28.20 | 776 |

**Mark**

| | |
|---|---|
| 1.1 | 615, 626, 689, 737, 814, 824, 858 |
| 1.9 | 626 |
| 1.14 | 626 |
| 1.16–18 | 755 |
| 1.17 | 626 |
| 1.19–20 | 755 |
| 1.21 | 629 n. 82 |
| 1.23 | 626 |
| 1.24 | 626 |
| 1.25 | 626 |
| 1.26 | 626 |
| 1.27 | 626 |
| 1.31 | 629 |
| 1.34 | 626 |
| 1.40 | 626 |
| 1.41 | 626 with n. 72, 629 n. 82 |
| 1.42 | 626 |
| 1.44 | 626, 629 n. 82 |
| 2.3 | 629 n. 82 |
| 2.4 | 629 n. 82 |
| 2.5 | 626, 627, 629 n. 82, 766 |
| 2.8 | 626, 629 n. 82, 766 |
| 2.9 | 627, 629, 766 |
| 2.10 | 629 n. 82 |
| 2.11–12 | 629 |
| 2.12 | 626 |
| 2.14–18 | 754–5, 758 |
| 2.14–17 | 755 |
| 2.14 | 761 n. 82 |
| 2.15–16 | 760 |
| 2.16–17 | 856 |
| 2.17 | 627, 628, 664, 766 |
| 2.18 | 755 |
| 2.18–20 | 563 n. 38 |
| 3.2 | 627 |
| 3.3 | 629 n. 82 |
| 3.4 | 629 n. 82 |
| 3.5 | 629 n. 82 |
| 3.10 | 627 |
| 3.13–19 | 756 |
| 3.16–19 | 819 n. 168, 855 n. 63 |
| 3.16–17 | 762, 765 |
| 3.16 | 871 |
| 3.21 | 540 |
| 3.31–5 | 540 |
| 5.1–20 | 534 n. 70 |
| 5.2 | 627 |
| 5.6 | 627 |
| 5.7 | 627 |
| 5.8 | 627 |
| 5.9 | 627, 629 n. 82 |
| 5.15 | 627 629 n. 82 |
| 5.19 | 629 n. 82 |
| 5.20 | 627 |
| 5.22 | 629 n. 82 |
| 5.22–43 | 627 |
| 5.23 | 627, 628, 629 n. 82 |
| 5.26 | 627 |
| 5.28 | 627, 628 |
| 5.29–30 | 627, 696 |
| 5.34 | 627, 628 |

**Mark** (*cont.*)

| | |
|---|---|
| 5.36 | 627, 629 n. 82 |
| 5.38 | 629 n. 82 |
| 5.39 | 629 n. 82 |
| 5.40 | 629 n. 82 |
| 5.41 | 629 n. 82 |
| 5.41–2 | 627, 629 |
| 6.1–6 | 628 |
| 6.4 | 628 |
| 6.5 | 628 |
| 6.7–13 | 540, 628 |
| 6.15 | 629 |
| 6.20 | 899 n. 212 |
| 6.56 | 628 |
| 7.10 | 752 |
| 7.19 | 628 |
| 7.26 | 536 |
| 7.31–7 | 628 |
| 7.32 | 629 n. 82 |
| 8.5–13 | 639 |
| 8.22–6 | 613 n. 2, 628 |
| 8.22 | 629 n. 82 |
| 8.28 | 629 |
| 9.1 | 698 |
| 9.4–13 | 629 |
| 9.14–29 | 628 |
| 9.19 | 629 n. 82 |
| 9.22 | 623 n. 59 |
| 9.23 | 628 |
| 9.25 | 628 |
| 9.27 | 628, 629 |
| 10.17–18 | 961 |
| 10.25 | 525 |
| 10.46–52 | 628 |
| 10.47 | 628 |
| 10.49 | 628 |
| 10.50 | 628 |
| 10.51 | 628 |
| 10.52 | 628 |
| 12.13 | 871 |
| 12.24 | 752 |
| 13.1–2 | 574 n. 106 |
| 13.10–13 | 921 n. 317 |
| 13.10 | 538 n. 96, 920 n. 312 |
| 13.14 | 615 n. 16 |
| 13.24–7 | 921 n. 317 |
| 15.30–1 | 628 |
| 15.34 | 628, 629 |
| 15.35 | 629 |
| 15.36 | 629, 637 |
| 15.37 | 629 |
| 15.42–6 | 774 |
| 16.1–7 | 629 |
| 16.6 | 629 |
| 16.8 | 695 |

**Luke**

| | |
|---|---|
| 1.1 | 575, 588, 589, 599, 681 n. 20, 699, 700, 789, 816, 823, 839, 898 |
| 1.1–2 | 983 n. 23 |
| 1.1–3 | 619 n. 37, 619 n. 38, 691, 834, 883 |
| 1.1–4 | 587–608 *passim*, 680, 615 n. 15, 686 n. 45, 693, 695, 710, 725, 739 nn. 26 and 27, 741 n. 37, 789–816 *passim*, 990 |
| 1.2 | 641, 648 n. 135, 687, 688, 691, 695, 698, 699, 790, 799, 807, 811, 817, 820, 821, 822 |
| 1.2–3 | 921 |
| 1.3–4 | 788 |
| 1.3 | 564, 593, 615 n. 16, 648 n. 132, 687, 691, 692, 695, 790, 791, 811, 813, 822, 823, 833, 848, 982 n. 17, 984 |
| 1.4 | 600, 687, 695, 700, 729, 789 n. 14, 791, 795, 799, 804, 822, 848, 984, 992 |
| 1.6–7 | 857 |
| 1.7 | 857 |
| 1.13 | 994 |
| 1.14 | 995, 996 |
| 1.15 | 822 n. 179 |
| 1.16 | 927 |
| 1.17 | 822 n. 179, 927 |
| 1.19 | 814 n. 148, 822 n. 180, 991 |
| 1.26–38 | 793, 818 |
| 1.26 | 822 n. 180 |
| 1.28 | 996 |
| 1.30 | 994, 996 |
| 1.31 | 641 |
| 1.32–3 | 827 |
| 1.32 | 572 |

INDEX LOCORUM 1043

| | | | |
|---|---|---|---|
| 1.33 | 596, 698, 713, 727, 817, 862 | 3.19 | 722, 905 n. 246 |
| 1.35 | 572, 822 n. 179, 889 n. 186 | 3.21 | 641 |
| 1.41 | 822 n. 179 | 3.22 | 822 n. 179, 889 n. 186 |
| 1.44 | 996 | 3.23–4.11 | 778 |
| 1.45 | 994 | 3.23 | 641 |
| 1.46–55 | 713 | 4.1–13 | 719 |
| 1.47 | 996 | 4.1–8 | 719 |
| 1.48 | 994 | 4.1 | 641, 822 n. 179 |
| 1.52 | 596, 606, 687, 817 | 4.4 | 641 |
| 1.58 | 996 | 4.5–6 | 541 |
| 1.67 | 822 n. 179 | 4.12 | 641 |
| 2.1ff. | 817 | 4.14 | 641, 822 n. 179 |
| 2.1–40 | 641 | 4.15 | 822 |
| 2.1–20 | 984 n. 30 | 4.16–30 | 641, 642 |
| 2.1–5 | 596, 598, 695 | 4.18 | 641, 699, 814 n. 148, 822 nn. 179 and 180, 991 |
| 2.1–3 | 714 | | |
| 2.1–2 | 817 | 4.21 | 821 |
| 2.1 | 593 | 4.22 | 641, 996 |
| 2.2 | 714 | 4.23 | 641 |
| 2.10 | 814 n. 148, 991 with n. 65, 994, 995 | 4.27 | 641 |
| | | 4.31–41 | 641 |
| 2.11 | 715, 727 | 4.31 | 822 |
| 2.21 | 641 | 4.32 | 866 |
| 2.25 | 822 n. 179 | 4.33 | 641 |
| 2.26 | 822 n. 179 | 4.34 | 641 |
| 2.27 | 641, 822 n. 179 | 4.36 | 641 |
| 2.29 | 819 n. 165 | 4.39 | 642 |
| 2.30–2 | 716 | 4.40 | 641 |
| 2.30 | 820 | 4.41 | 889 n. 186 |
| 2.32 | 827, 861 n. 84 | 4.43 | 699, 814 nn. 147 and 148, 822 n. 180, 991 |
| 2.33 | 697 | | |
| 2.34 | 606 n. 116, 687, 820, 823, 830 | 5.10 | 994 |
| | | 5.12–16 | 641 |
| 2.40 | 996 | 5.12 | 641 |
| 2.41–52 | 641 | 5.13 | 641 |
| 2.43 | 641 | 5.14 | 641 |
| 2.46 | 996 | 5.15 | 641 |
| 2.49 | 820, 856 | 5.17–26 | 641 |
| 2.51 | 857 | 5.17 | 641, 696, 822 |
| 2.52 | 601 n. 99, 641, 687, 820, 856, 968 | 5.19 | 696 |
| | | 5.23–4 | 642 |
| 3.1–2 | 714, 817 | 5.25 | 642 |
| 3.4–6 | 716 | 5.27–33 | 756 |
| 3.13–14 | 716 | 5.27–30 | 717 |
| 3.16 | 822 n. 179 | 5.27 | 820 |
| 3.17 | 718 | 5.30–3 | 819, 856 |
| 3.18 | 814 n. 148, 991 | 5.30 | 717 |
| 3.19–20 | 565 n. 53 | 5.33–8 | 562 |

Luke (*cont.*)

| | | | |
|---|---|---|---|
| 5.39 | 563 n. 38 | 9.1–6 | 642 |
| 6.6 | 822 | 9.1–5 | 856 |
| 6.8 | 820 | 9.2 | 822 n. 180 |
| 6.12–16 | 757 | 9.6 | 814 n. 148 |
| 6.13 | 822 with n. 180 | 9.7–9 | 565 n. 53 |
| 6.18–19 | 641 | 9.9 | 722 |
| 6.18 | 641 | 9.10–11 | 912 |
| 6.19 | 641 | 9.10 | 822 n. 180 |
| 6.20–37 | 719 | 9.11 | 573 n. 103, 642, 912 |
| 6.20–2 | 994 | 9.22 | 720, 820, 822 with n. 181, 857 |
| 6.23 | 996 | 9.23 | 820, 857 |
| 6.27 | 716 | 9.24 | 719 |
| 6.32–5 | 970 | 9.25 | 719 |
| 6.37 | 719 n. 59 | 9.31 | 687, 821, 857 |
| 6.39 | 687, 820, 857 | 9.37–43 | 642 |
| 6.41 | 820 | 9.38 | 623 n. 59 |
| 6.48–9 | 687, 820 | 9.41 | 642 |
| 6.49 | 687, 820 | 9.42 | 642 |
| 7.1–10 | 641 | 9.48 | 699, 822 n. 180 |
| 7.2–10 | 717 | 9.50 | 719 n. 59 |
| 7.3 | 641 | 9.51ff. | 820, 857 |
| 7.4 | 641 | 9.51–19.41 | 601 n. 99 |
| 7.5 | 717 | 9.52 | 822 n. 180 |
| 7.6–8 | 717 | 9.57–61 | 820 |
| 7.6 | 641, 717 | 9.57–8 | 538 n. 94 |
| 7.7 | 641, 696 | 9.59–60 | 540 |
| 7.9 | 641, 696, 717 | 10.1 | 822 n. 180 |
| 7.10 | 641 | 10.3 | 822 n. 180 |
| 7.14 | 642 | 10.4 | 540 |
| 7.21 | 996 | 10.9–11 | 719 n. 61 |
| 7.22 | 642, 814 nn. 147 and 148, 991 | 10.9 | 642 |
| | | 10.12–15 | 718 |
| 7.23 | 994 | 10.16 | 699, 822 n. 180 |
| 7.27 | 822 n. 180 | 10.17–24 | 995 |
| 7.32 | 562, 579 n. 134 | 10.17 | 642 |
| 7.36–50 | 720, 819, 856 | 10.20 | 996 |
| 7.38 | 720 | 10.21 | 822 n. 179, 996 |
| 7.42–3 | 996 | 10.22 | 572 |
| 8.1 | 814 n. 148, 991 | 10.23–4 | 820 |
| 8.3 | 819 n. 164 | 10.23 | 994 |
| 8.8 | 995 | 10.37 | 820 |
| 8.26–39 | 534 n. 70 | 11.1 | 822 |
| 8.43–8 | 641 | 11.13 | 822 n. 179 |
| 8.46–7 | 696 | 11.14–23 | 719 |
| 8.47 | 641 | 11.18–20 | 719 n. 61 |
| 8.50 | 994 | 11.23 | 719 |
| 8.54 | 642 | 11.2–4 | 719 |

# INDEX LOCORUM

| | | | |
|---|---|---|---|
| 11.28 | 994 | 14.27 | 820, 857 |
| 11.29–32 | 718 | 15.3 | 995 |
| 11.31–2 | 827, 861 | 15.5 | 996 |
| 11.37–53 | 819, 856 | 15.7 | 995 |
| 11.49 | 822 n. 180 | 15.10 | 995 |
| 12.4–7 | 994 | 15.23 | 996 |
| 12.10 | 822 n. 179 | 15.24 | 996 |
| 12.11 | 720, 868 | 15.29 | 819 n. 165, 996 |
| 12.12 | 822 n. 179, 867, 870 | 15.32 | 996 |
| 12.14 | 995 | 16.13 | 719, 819 n. 165 |
| 12.19 | 996 n. 78 | 16.16 | 814 n. 148 |
| 12.32 | 994 | 16.19–31 | 722 |
| 12.33 | 866 | 16.19 | 996 n. 78 |
| 12.35–48 | 718 | 17.5 | 822 n. 180 |
| 12.37 | 819 nn. 164 and 165 | 17.7ff. | 819 n. 165 |
| 12.37–43 | 995 | 17.11–19 | 642 |
| 12.43 | 819 n. 165 | 17.13 | 642 |
| 12.49–51 | 720 | 17.14 | 642 |
| 12.50 | 821 | 17.15 | 642 |
| 12.54–6 | 718 | 17.16 | 997 |
| 13.1 | 722 | 17.17 | 642 |
| 13.3 | 718 | 17.19 | 642 |
| 13.5 | 718 | 17.24 | 718 |
| 13.14–15 | 634 | 17.25 | 720, 822 n. 181 |
| 13.14 | 642 | 17.30–7 | 718 |
| 13.17 | 996 | 18.1–8 | 718 |
| 13.22–30 | 827, 861, 916 | 18.9 | 994 |
| 13.23–4 | 541 | 18.11 | 997 |
| 13.24–8 | 718 | 18.14 | 719 |
| 13.29–30 | 698, 718 | 18.18–23 | 961 |
| 13.30 | 719, 827 | 18.31 | 821 |
| 13.31 | 722 | 18.32 | 720 |
| 13.32 | 642, 644, 821 | 18.33 | 820 |
| 13.33–19.44 | 710 | 18.34 | 683 n. 34, 820 |
| 13.34 | 822 n. 180 | 18.35 | 820 |
| 13.52 | 995 | 18.35–43 | 642 |
| 14.1–24 | 819, 856 | 18.37 | 642 |
| 14.1–6 | 642 | 18.38 | 623 n. 59, 642 |
| 14.3 | 642 | 18.40 | 642 |
| 14.4 | 642 | 18.42 | 642 |
| 14.11 | 719 | 19.1–30 | 717 |
| 14.13 | 865 | 19.6 | 996 |
| 14.14 | 606 n. 116, 718, 820, 823, 995 | 19.7 | 717 |
| | | 19.11–27 | 718 |
| 14.15 | 995 | 19.13ff. | 819 n. 165 |
| 14.17ff. | 819 n. 165 | 19.29 | 822 n. 180 |
| 14.17 | 822 n. 180 | 19.32 | 822 n. 180 |
| 14.21 | 865 | 19.37 | 996 |

**Luke** (*cont.*)

| | |
|---|---|
| 19.41ff. | 574 n. 106 |
| 19.42–4 | 720 |
| 19.42 | 820 |
| 19.44 | 687, 720, 820 |
| 20.1 | 814 n. 148 |
| 20.10ff. | 819 n. 165 |
| 20.10 | 822 n. 180 |
| 20.13–16 | 572 |
| 20.17 | 687, 820 |
| 20.25 | 720 |
| 20.27ff. | 823 |
| 20.27 | 606 n. 116, 820 |
| 20.33 | 606 n. 116, 820 |
| 20.35 | 606 n. 116, 820, 995 |
| 20.36 | 606 n. 116, 820 |
| 21.5–36 | 896 |
| 21.5–7 | 720 |
| 21.5 | 687, 820 |
| 21.12ff. | 877 |
| 21.12–17 | 720 |
| 21.12–15 | 867 |
| 21.12 | 899 |
| 21.15 | 870 |
| 21.17 | 723 |
| 21.20–4 | 718, 720 |
| 21.24 | 687, 820 |
| 21.27–36 | 718 |
| 22.1–23.46 | 822 n. 181 |
| 22.2ff. | 721 |
| 22.8 | 822 n. 180 |
| 22.14–38 | 819, 856 |
| 22.14–23 | 721 |
| 22.14 | 822 n. 180 |
| 22.15 | 822 n. 181 |
| 22.16 | 821 |
| 22.17 | 997 |
| 22.19 | 562, 997 |
| 22.25–27 | 721 |
| 22.26–7 | 819 n. 164 |
| 22.29–30 | 572 |
| 22.30 | 718, 719 n. 61 |
| 22.35 | 822 n. 180 |
| 22.37 | 821 |
| 22.42 | 572 |
| 22.47 | 721 |
| 22.49–51 | 721 |
| 22.67–70 | 721 |
| 22.70 | 572 |
| 23.1–25 | 899 |
| 23.1–23 | 714 |
| 23.2–3 | 828 |
| 23.7–12 | 565 n. 53 |
| 23.7–11 | 899 |
| 23.7 | 861 n. 85 |
| 23.8 | 726, 731 n. 102, 902 |
| 23.11 | 714, 899 |
| 23.12 | 861 n. 85 |
| 23.14 | 927 |
| 23.15 | 899 |
| 23.25 | 721 |
| 23.27 | 717 |
| 23.33–43 | 642 |
| 23.34 | 564, 642 |
| 23.35 | 642 |
| 23.36 | 720 |
| 23.37 | 642 |
| 23.38 | 828 |
| 23.39 | 642 |
| 23.46 | 817 |
| 23.47 | 722 |
| 24.1–53 | 817 |
| 24.6–7 | 606 n. 116 |
| 24.7 | 822 |
| 24.10 | 822 n. 180 |
| 24.18 | 889 n. 185 |
| 24.19 | 870 |
| 24.20 | 722 n. 68 |
| 24.26 | 822 n. 181, 968 |
| 24.30 | 562 |
| 24.34 | 606 n. 116 |
| 24.36 | 688, 823 |
| 24.41 | 995 |
| 24.44 | 752, 821 |
| 24.45–8 | 861 |
| 24.46 | 606 n. 116, 822 n. 181 |
| 24.47–8 | 826 |
| 24.47 | 615, 985 |
| 24.49 | 822 n. 180, 826, 832 n. 214 |
| 24.50–3 | 826 |
| 24.52 | 995 |
| 27.24 | 994 |

**John**

| | |
|---|---|
| 1 | 648 |
| 1.1ff. | 824 n. 185 |

**John** (*cont.*)

| | | | |
|---|---|---|---|
| 1.1–18 | 638, 639 | 12.41 | 640 |
| 1.1–17 | 641 n. 116 | 12.44 | 640 |
| 1.11 | 889 n. 185 | 13.1–17.26 | 640 |
| 1.14 | 971 | 13.1–20 | 640 |
| 1.16 | 971 | 13.1 | 640 |
| 1.17 | 638, 752, 971 | 13.7 | 640 |
| 2.1–11 | 578 n. 132 | 13.8 | 640 |
| 3.11 | 753 n. 73 | 13.10 | 640 |
| 3.33 | 753 n. 71 | 13.11 | 640 |
| 4.43–54 | 638 | 13.29 | 538 n. 95 |
| 4.47 | 638 | 14.6 | 542, 682, 686 n. 45 |
| 5.1–18 | 638 | 15.1 | 578 n. 132, 579 |
| 5.6 | 638, 647 n. 127 | 15.26–7 | 833 |
| 5.8 | 638 | 19.17 | 640 |
| 5.9 | 638 | 19.18 | 640 |
| 5.13 | 638 | 19.19 | 640 |
| 5.14 | 638 | 19.20 | 640 |
| 5.15 | 638, 644 | 19.23 | 640 |
| 5.16–18 | 638 | 19.25 | 640 |
| 5.46 | 752 | 19.26 | 640 |
| 7.23 | 752 | 19.28 | 640 |
| 11.1–44 | 639, 640 | 19.30 | 640 |
| 11.4 | 639 | 19.33 | 640 |
| 11.5 | 639 | 19.38 | 640 |
| 11.9 | 639 | 19.40 | 640 |
| 11.12 | 639 | 19.42 | 640 |
| 11.13 | 639 | 20.2 | 640 |
| 11.17 | 639 | 20.12 | 640 |
| 11.20 | 639 | 20.14 | 640 |
| 11.21 | 639 | 20.15 | 640 |
| 11.23 | 639 | 20.16 | 640 |
| 11.25 | 639 | 20.17 | 640 |
| 11.30 | 639 | 20.19 | 640 |
| 11.33 | 639 | 20.21 | 640 |
| 11.35 | 639 | 20.24 | 640 |
| 11.38 | 639 | 20.26 | 640 |
| 11.39 | 639 | 20.28 | 632 n. 91 |
| 11.40 | 639 | 20.29 | 640 |
| 11.41 | 639 | 20.30 | 640 |
| 11.44 | 639 | 20.31 | 640 |
| 12.6 | 538 n. 95 | 21.1 | 640 |
| 12.20–2 | 660 n. 173 | 21.4 | 640 |
| 12.30 | 640 | 21.5 | 640 |
| 12.35 | 640 | 21.7 | 640 |
| 12.36 | 640 | 21.10 | 640 |
| 12.38–40 | 634, 639 | 21.12 | 640 |
| 12.40 | 640 | 21.13 | 640 |
| | | 21.14 | 640 |

**John** (*cont.*)

| | |
|---|---|
| 21.15 | 640 |
| 21.17 | 640 |
| 21.20 | 640, 835 n. 223 |
| 21.21–4 | 839 n. 248 |
| 21.21 | 640 |
| 21.22–3 | 698 |
| 21.22 | 640, 921 n. 317 |
| 21.23 | 640 |
| 21.24–5 | 615 n. 16, 619 n. 38, 661 n. 179 |
| 21.24 | 753, 753 n. 73 |
| 21.25 | 640 |

**Acts**

| | |
|---|---|
| 1.1–2 | 711, 823 |
| 1.1–3 | 688, 698, 821–8 *passim* |
| 1.1–8 | 860 |
| 1.1–11 | 693 |
| 1.1 | 562, 564, 598, 614 with n. 12, 643, 692, 693, 694, 695, 698, 699, 700, 712, 796, 825, 829, 847, 848, 883, 920, 921, 922, 982 n. 17 |
| 1.2–11 | 916 |
| 1.2 | 823, 828 with n. 197 |
| 1.3 | 574 n. 105 577, 688, 689, 693, 719 n. 62, 822, 823, 824, 828, 832 n. 214 |
| 1.4–5 | 832 n. 214 |
| 1.4–8 | 823 |
| 1.4 | 691 n. 58, 711, 859 |
| 1.5 | 562, 828 |
| 1.5.3–4 | 831 |
| 1.6 | 826, 828 |
| 1.6–7 | 693, 698 |
| 1.8 | 538 n. 96, 573 with n. 101, 574, 600, 615, 679, 693, 694, 697, 698, 708, 711, 713, 716, 825, 826–8 *passim*, 829, 831, 832 n. 214, 858 n. 74, 862, 864, 867, 892, 908, 911, 918 |
| 1.9–11 | 823, 826 |
| 1.10–11 | 857 |
| 1.11 | 643, 697 |
| 1.16 | 828 n. 196, 837 |
| 1.21–2 | 833 |
| 1.22 | 606 n. 116, 829, 830, 833 |
| 1.23–6 | 761 n. 81 |
| 1.26 | 828 n. 197 |
| 1.27 | 833 |
| 1.33 | 921 |
| 2.1–12 | 656 |
| 2.4 | 828 n. 196, 867 |
| 2.6 | 988 |
| 2.6–7 | 579 n. 139 |
| 2.8–11 | 919 |
| 2.10–11 | 919 |
| 2.12f | 884 |
| 2.13 | 561, 562 |
| 2.14–36 | 643, 892 |
| 2.15 | 561 |
| 2.17 | 698, 828 n. 196 |
| 2.17–18 | 562 |
| 2.18 | 828 n. 196 |
| 2.20 | 718 |
| 2.21 | 567 n. 62, 643 |
| 2.22–3 | 722 n. 68 |
| 2.22 | 567 n. 68, 643, 644 |
| 2.24 | 577, 643, 830 |
| 2.25ff | 861 n. 85 |
| 2.26 | 996 |
| 2.27 | 892 |
| 2.28 | 682, 828 n. 196 |
| 2.29 | 694, 831 n. 203, 864, 867, 892 |
| 2.31 | 606 n. 116, 830 |
| 2.31–2 | 577, 643 |
| 2.32 | 829, 830 |
| 2.33 | 562, 828 n. 196 |
| 2.36 | 600 n. 92, 685 n. 44, 801 n. 77 |
| 2.37 | 828 n. 197 |
| 2.41 | 567 n. 62 |
| 2.42 | 562, 828 nn. 195, 197 |
| 2.43 | 828 n. 197 |
| 2.44–5 | 538 n. 95, 831, 865, 866 |
| 2.44–6 | 562, 722 |
| 2.47 | 567 n. 62 |
| 3.1–10 | 644 |
| 3.6 | 644 |
| 3.6–7 | 644 |
| 3.11 | 728 n. 91 |
| 3.12–16 | 644 |
| 3.13–15 | 722 n. 68 |

INDEX LOCORUM 1049

**Acts** (*cont.*)
| | |
|---|---|
| 3.15 | 577, 644, 829 |
| 3.17 | 722 n. 68 |
| 3.17–26 | 731 |
| 3.18 | 829, 837 |
| 3.20 | 699 |
| 3.22 | 577, 830 |
| 3.26 | 927 |
| 4.1ff | 561 |
| 4.1–21 | 869 |
| 4.1 | 564 |
| 4.2 | 577, 606 n. 116, 644, 828 n. 195, 830 |
| 4.8–20 | 893 |
| 4.8 | 828 n. 196 |
| 4.9 | 644 |
| 4.10 | 644 |
| 4.11 | 690 |
| 4.12 | 567 n. 62, 644, 664, 719 |
| 4.13 | 580 n. 142, 694, 830, 831 n. 203, 864, 867, 894, 912 |
| 4.14 | 699 n. 90, 867 |
| 4.18 | 572 n. 96, 644, 828 n. 195 |
| 4.19 | 831 n. 204, 866, 877 |
| 4.22 | 572 n. 96, 644 |
| 4.23–31 | 644 |
| 4.25ff | 722 n. 68 |
| 4.25–6 | 698 |
| 4.25 | 828 n. 196 |
| 4.26 | 719 |
| 4.27 | 644, 899 |
| 4.29 | 645, 831 n. 203, 864 |
| 4.30 | 624 n. 67, 645, 696 |
| 4.31 | 828 n. 196, 831 n. 203, 864 |
| 4.32 | 831 |
| 4.32–7 | 538 n. 95, 722, 865, 866 |
| 4.33 | 606 n. 116, 828 n. 197, 830, 996 |
| 4.34–5 | 831 |
| 4.35 | 828 n. 197 |
| 4.36 | 828 n. 197 |
| 4.37 | 828 n. 197 |
| 5.1–11 | 538 n. 95 |
| 5.2 | 828 n. 197 |
| 5.3 | 828 n. 196 |
| 5.5 | 567 n. 61, 719 |
| 5.9 | 828 n. 196 |
| 5.10 | 567 n. 61, 719 |
| 5.12 | 828 n. 197 |
| 5.15 | 645 |
| 5.16 | 645 |
| 5.17–40 | 869 |
| 5.17–20 | 913 |
| 5.17–18 | 868, 869 |
| 5.17 | 595 n. 53, 831 n. 205 |
| 5.18 | 828 n. 197, 868 |
| 5.19 | 557 |
| 5.19–25 | 561, 564 |
| 5.21 | 828 n. 195 |
| 5.23 | 604 n. 110 |
| 5.25 | 828 n. 195 |
| 5.28 | 828 n. 195 |
| 5.29–32 | 893 |
| 5.29 | 828 n. 197, 831 n. 204, 866, 877 |
| 5.30 | 645, 722 n. 68 |
| 5.31 | 645 |
| 5.32 | 828 n. 196, 829 |
| 5.34–9 | 908 n. 254 |
| 5.34 | 828 n. 197 |
| 5.35 | 567 n. 61 |
| 5.36–7 | 851 |
| 5.37 | 597 n. 67 |
| 5.38–9 | 567 n. 61 |
| 5.39 | 557, 561, 566 |
| 5.40 | 828 n. 197 |
| 5.41 | 996 |
| 5.42 | 828 n. 195 |
| 6.1ff | 869 |
| 6.3 | 828 n. 196, 837 |
| 6.5 | 828 n. 196, 837 |
| 6.6 | 828 n. 197 |
| 6.7 | 698 |
| 6.8 | 837, 997 |
| 6.9 | 871 |
| 6.10 | 828 n. 196, 868, 870 |
| 6.11–7.60 | 870 |
| 6.13–14 | 567 n. 65 |
| 6.14 | 690, 916 n. 297 |
| 6.15 | 870 |
| 6.16–18 | 943 n. 40 |
| 7.2–53 | 690 |
| 7.10 | 997 |
| 7.22 | 571, 870 |
| 7.37 | 830 |
| 7.39 | 927 |

**Acts** (*cont.*)

| | | | |
|---|---|---|---|
| 7.41 | 996 n. 78 | 9.27–8 | 831 n. 203 |
| 7.42 | 927 | 9.27 | 679, 828 n. 197, 864, 876, 893, 897 |
| 7.46 | 997 | 9.28–9 | 870, 893 |
| 7.48 | 567 n. 65 | 9.28 | 864 |
| 7.51 | 828 n. 196 | 9.29 | 871 |
| 7.55–6 | 697 | 9.31 | 828 n. 196 |
| 7.55–9 | 655 | 9.34–5 | 731 |
| 7.55 | 828 n. 196, 837, 870 | 9.34 | 624 n. 67, 645, 696, 883 n. 163 |
| 7.58 | 696 | | |
| 7.58–8.1 | 723 | 9.36 | 837 |
| 7.59 | 697 | 9.40–1 | 645 |
| 7.60 | 564 | 9.40 | 645 |
| 8.1–3 | 564 | 9.41 | 830 |
| 8.1 | 696, 828 n. 197, 915 | 10.1–48 | 717 |
| 8.3 | 723 | 10.1–30 | 646 |
| 8.7–8 | 645 | 10.1–16 | 838 n. 237 |
| 8.12 | 719 n. 62 | 10.14–22 | 579 n. 139 |
| 8.14 | 828 n. 197 | 10.14 | 646 |
| 8.15 | 828 n. 196 | 10.19 | 828 n. 196 |
| 8.17 | 828 n. 196 | 10.24–5 | 893 |
| 8.18 | 828 nn. 196–7 | 10.25 | 870 |
| 8.19 | 828 n. 196 | 10.25–6 | 721 |
| 8.24 | 567 n. 61 | 10.27 | 870 |
| 8.26 | 679, 897 | 10.29 | 646 |
| 8.29 | 828 n. 196 | 10.32–3 | 889 with n. 186 |
| 8.30–1 | 601 n. 99, 831 | 10.34 | 716 |
| 8.31 | 679, 682, 897, 898 | 10.36 | 729 n. 95 |
| 8.36–9 | 679, 897 | 10.38 | 572 n. 96, 624 n. 67, 646, 696, 828 n. 196, 883 n. 163 |
| 8.39 | 828 n. 196, 996 | | |
| 9.1–9 | 646 | 10.39 | 722 n. 68 |
| 9.1–2 | 564, 723 | 10.40 | 646 |
| 9.1 | 557, 566, 568 | 10.41–2 | 829 |
| 9.2–8 | 679, 897 | 10.41 | 646 |
| 9.2 | 601 n. 100, 682 with n. 25, 711, 897 | 10.44 | 828 n. 196 |
| | | 10.45 | 828 n. 196 |
| 9.3–9 | 554–63 *passim*, 711, 723 | 10.47 | 828 n. 196 |
| 9.7 | 568 | 11.1 | 828 n. 197 |
| 9.8–18 | 565 | 11.5–10 | 838 n. 237 |
| 9.11 | 679, 897 | 11.9 | 723 |
| 9.13 | 696 | 11.12 | 828 n. 196 |
| 9.16 | 574 n. 105, 655 n. 159, 696, 697, 726 n. 85, 727, 916 n. 294 | 11.15 | 828 n. 196 |
| | | 11.16 | 828 n. 196, 889 n. 181 |
| | | 11.17 | 565 |
| 9.17 | 645, 696, 828 n. 196 | 11.19ff | 944 |
| 9.18 | 645 | 11.19–30 | 597 n. 72 |
| 9.20 | 572 n. 89, 889 with n. 186 | 11.19 | 973 |
| 9.23ff | 565 | 11.23 | 996 n. 77, 997 |

# INDEX LOCORUM

Acts (*cont.*)
| | |
|---|---|
| 11.24 | 828 n. 196, 837 |
| 11.26 | 569 n. 78, 615 n. 17, 647, 648 n. 132, 659, 681, 707, 724, 726, 828 n. 195, 829, 871, 943, 946, 948, 950, 972, 982 n. 15 |
| 11.28 | 828 n. 196 |
| 11.32 | 659 |
| 12.1ff | 566, 944 |
| 12.1–18 | 973 |
| 12.1–10 | 554, 561 |
| 12.1 | 723 |
| 12.2 | 579 nn. 139–40 |
| 12.6–10 | 913 |
| 12.7 | 557 |
| 12.10 | 557 |
| 12.20–3 | 566, 721 |
| 12.22 | 575 n. 114, 914 |
| 12.23 | 567 n. 61, 568, 718 |
| 12.24 | 698 |
| 12.25 | 837 |
| 13 | 565 n. 52 |
| 13.1 | 828 n. 195 |
| 13.2 | 828 n. 196 |
| 13.4 | 828 n. 196 |
| 13.7–12 | 717 |
| 13.7 | 984 |
| 13.9–12 | 567 n. 61 |
| 13.9 | 565 n. 52, 727, 728, 828 n. 196 |
| 13.10–13 | 921 |
| 13.11 | 719 |
| 13.12 | 579 n. 139, 690, 828 n. 195 |
| 13.16–41 | 646 |
| 13.16 | 718 n. 56 |
| 13.17–41 | 690 |
| 13.23 | 567 n. 62, 646 |
| 13.24–7 | 921 |
| 13.25 | 837 |
| 13.26 | 567 n. 62, 718 n. 56 |
| 13.27–9 | 722 n. 68 |
| 13.27 | 837 |
| 13.30 | 646 |
| 13.31 | 829, 830 |
| 13.33 | 572, 646 |
| 13.34 | 646, 830 |
| 13.36–8 | 916 n. 294 |
| 13.37 | 646 |
| 13.43 | 718 n. 56, 997 |
| 13.46–7 | 653, 695, 893, 909 |
| 13.46 | 831 n. 203, 864, 927 |
| 13.47 | 567 n. 62, 573 n. 101, 698, 861 |
| 13.48 | 996 |
| 13.50 | 718 n. 56 |
| 13.52 | 828 n. 196 |
| 14.1–3 | 699 n. 90 |
| 14.3 | 864, 893, 997 |
| 14.4 | 573 n. 101, 828 with n. 197, 884 |
| 14.8ff | 721 |
| 14.8–10 | 646 |
| 14.9 | 646 |
| 14.10 | 646 |
| 14.13 | 875 |
| 14.14 | 573 n. 101, 828 with n. 197 |
| 14.15–17 | 708, 891 |
| 14.21 | 777, 779 |
| 14.24 | 997 |
| 14.26 | 837 |
| 14.32–3 | 568 n. 74 |
| 15.1–29 | 646 |
| 15.2 | 828 n. 197 |
| 15.3 | 568 n. 74, 695 |
| 15.4 | 828 n. 197 |
| 15.5 | 868, 869 |
| 15.6 | 595, 828 n. 197, 831 |
| 15.7 | 595 |
| 15.8 | 828 n. 196 |
| 15.9 | 646, 716 |
| 15.11 | 646, 997 |
| 15.19–20 | 722 |
| 15.19 | 595, 679, 831 |
| 15.22 | 595, 828 n. 197, 831 |
| 15.23 | 828 n. 197 |
| 15.24ff | 795, 831 |
| 15.24–9 | 593, 595, 722 |
| 15.24 | 589 |
| 15.25 | 589, 590, 595, 795 |
| 15.28 | 590, 593, 595, 795, 814 n. 144, 828 n. 196 |
| 15.29 | 828 n. 196 |
| 15.31 | 996 |
| 15.32–3 | 568 n. 74 |
| 15.33 | 828 n. 197 |

| | | | |
|---|---|---|---|
| Acts (*cont.*) | | 17.18–21 | 558, 708, 728 |
| 15.35 | 828 n. 195 | 17.18 | 572 n. 96, 606 n. 116, 624 n. 67, 648, 650, 690, 696, 729, 830, 835, 876, 878, 884, 885, 887, 888, 903, 904, 987, 998 |
| 15.40 | 997 | | |
| 16 | 650, 651 | | |
| 16.4 | 828 n. 197 | | |
| 16.6 | 828 n. 196 | | |
| 16.7 | 828 n. 196 | 17.19–34 | 893 |
| 16.8 | 858 | 17.19 | 730 n. 101, 828 n. 195 |
| 16.9–11 | 858 | 17.20 | 876, 878 |
| 16.10–17 | 690, 832, 849, 983 n. 23 | 17.21 | 876, 882 |
| 16.10 | 691 n. 58 | 17.22–3 | 884 |
| 16.14 | 718 n. 56 | 17.22 | 560, 570, 648, 875, 987 |
| 16.16ff | 578 n. 126 | 17.23–8 | 984 |
| 16.16–40 | 717, 724 | 17.23 | 648, 651, 721, 874, 881, 927 |
| 16.16–18 | 646 | 17.24–31 | 690 |
| 16.16 | 724 | 17.24–5 | 884 |
| 16.19 | 875 | 17.24 | 567 n. 65, 700 |
| 16.23–30 | 555 | 17.26–7 | 884 |
| 16.25 | 657, 914 n. 282 | 17.26 | 700 |
| 16.26 | 557 | 17.27–9 | 558 |
| 16.26–30 | 561 | 17.27–8 | 881 |
| 16.30 | 647, 717 | 17.27 | 651 n. 146, 797 n. 52, 882, 884 |
| 16.30–1 | 567 n. 62 | | |
| 16.31 | 647 | 17.28 | 566, 571, 649, 651, 751, 878, 882, 884, 887, 926 |
| 16.31–4 | 658 | | |
| 16.37 | 727 | 17.30 | 731, 884 |
| 17 | 566 with n. 57, 569, 570, 571, 572, 578, 616, 652 n. 148, 656, 657, 659, 693, 728, 831 | 17.31–2 | 685 n. 43 |
| | | 17.31 | 567 n. 68, 643, 650, 652, 690, 718, 729, 829, 830, 875, 884, 903 |
| 17.1–34 | 647 | 17.32–3 | 876 |
| 17.2 | 873, 985 | 17.32 | 558, 606 n. 116, 649 n. 140, 650, 655, 693, 830, 881, 884, 885, 888, 904, 998 |
| 17.3 | 574 n. 105, 647, 829 | | |
| 17.4 | 718 n. 56 | | |
| 17.5–9 | 572 n. 96 | 17.33 | 875 |
| 17.5 | 647, 696 | 17.34 | 558, 566, 581, 650, 655, 875, 926 |
| 17.6 | 647, 649, 690, 830, 890, 919 | | |
| | | 18.1 | 878 |
| 17.6–7 | 718, 729 | 18.2 | 947 |
| 17.7 | 647, 696 | 18.4 | 893, 894, 985 |
| 17.9 | 647, 696 | 18.6 | 653, 695, 909 |
| 17.15 | 878 | 18.7 | 718 |
| 17.16–34 | 871–2, 878 | 18.9 | 889 n. 181 |
| 17.16 | 570, 648, 721, 873, 874, 882 | 18.11 | 828 n. 195 |
| 17.17–34 | 892 | 18.12–17 | 724 |
| 17.17–18 | 986 | 18.17 | 875 |
| 17.17 | 569, 651, 696, 718 n. 56, 797 n. 52, 873, 883, 985 | 18.18 | 947 |
| | | 18.19 | 893, 894, 985 |

INDEX LOCORUM 1053

Acts (*cont.*)
| | | | |
|---|---|---|---|
| 18.23 | 831 | 20.37–8 | 895 |
| 18.24ff | 836 | 21.1–18 | 690, 832, 849, 983 n. 23 |
| 18.24 | 835, 848 | 21.4 | 574 n. 105, 828 n. 196 |
| 18.25 | 828 nn. 195–6 | 21.5 | 896 |
| 18.26 | 831 n. 203, 864, 893, 947 | 21.8–19 | 913 |
| 18.27 | 997 | 21.11–14 | 574 n. 105 |
| 18.28 | 892 | 21.11 | 828 n. 196 |
| 19.1–41 | 652 | 21.13–14 | 896 |
| 19.2 | 828 n. 196 | 21.14 | 896 |
| 19.6 | 828 n. 196 | 21.15–19 | 916 n. 294 |
| 19.8 | 719 n. 62, 831 n. 203, 864, 893, 894, 985 | 21.20–6 | 728 |
| | | 21.21 | 828 n. 195 |
| | | 21.23 | 921 |
| 19.9 | 601 n. 100, 682 n. 25, 893, 894, 897, 985 | 21.27–33.3 | 725 |
| | | 21.28 | 828 n. 195 |
| 19.13–17 | 652 | 21.30 | 875 |
| 19.13 | 652 | 21.31 | 984 |
| 19.17 | 652 | 21.33 | 875 |
| 19.20 | 698 | 21.34 | 600 n. 92, 685 n. 44, 801 n. 77 |
| 19.21–28.13 | 727 | | |
| 19.21 | 828 n. 196, 919 | 21.38 | 729, 830 |
| 19.23 | 601 n. 100, 682 n. 25, 897 | 22.1 | 708 n. 11, 893, 895, 896, 913 |
| 19.25 | 719 n. 62 | | |
| 19.29–30 | 875 | 22.2 | 852 |
| 19.30–1 | 892 | 22.3 | 856 n. 65 |
| 19.33 | 708 n. 11, 718, 892, 895 | 22.4 | 601 n. 100, 682 n. 25, 897 |
| 19.35 | 718 | 22.4–5 | 723 |
| 19.37 | 725 | 22.6–20 | 724 |
| 19.38–40 | 725 | 22.6–16 | 652, 711 |
| 20.5–15 | 690, 832, 849, 983 n. 23 | 22.6–11 | 554–63 *passim* |
| 20.7–12 | 567 | 22.15 | 574, 699, 829 |
| 20.7–11 | 893, 895 | 22.17–21 | 829, 916 |
| 20.7 | 562 n. 35, 894, 985 | 22.20 | 574, 723, 829 |
| 20.9 | 894, 985 | 22.21 | 573 n. 101, 828 |
| 20.11 | 562 n. 35 | 22.25–8 | 727 |
| 20.17–38 | 574 n. 105, 726 n. 85, 895 | 22.25–9 | 724 |
| 20.18–35 | 697 | 22.30 | 600 n. 92, 685 n. 44, 801 n. 77 |
| 20.20 | 828 n. 195, 892, 896 | | |
| 20.22 | 828 n. 196 | 22.36 | 722 n. 68 |
| 20.23 | 828 n. 196 | 23.3 | 574 n. 105 |
| 20.24–5 | 727 | 23.6 | 606 n. 116, 729, 830, 884 |
| 20.24 | 574, 895, 997 | 23.8–9 | 828 n. 196 |
| 20.25 | 895 | 23.8 | 606 n. 116, 830 |
| 20.27 | 896 | 23.11 | 573 n. 101, 910, 919 |
| 20.28 | 828 n. 196 | 23.19 | 876 |
| 20.29 | 694, 895 | 23.26 | 590 n. 23, 712, 835 n. 224, 848 n. 14 |
| 20.32 | 997 | | |
| 20.35 | 830 | 23.33–24.27 | 725 |

# 1054 INDEX LOCORUM

Acts (*cont.*)

|  |  |
|---|---|
| 24.1–27 | 896 |
| 24.2 | 729 n. 95 |
| 24.3 | 590 n. 23, 712, 835 n. 224, 848 n. 14 |
| 24.4 | 684 n. 40, 898 |
| 24.5 | 595 n. 53, 649 n. 137, 690, 729, 806 n. 101 830, 831 n. 205, 868, 896, 985 |
| 24.10 | 708 n. 11, 893, 895, 913, 996 |
| 24.12 | 649 n. 137, 690, 830, 890 n. 188, 896, 985 |
| 24.14 | 595 n. 53, 601 n. 100, 682 with n. 25, 728, 806 n. 101, 831 n. 205, 868, 869, 896, 897, 898, 985 |
| 24.15 | 606 n. 116, 649 n. 137, 690, 729, 830, 890 n. 188 |
| 24.16 | 896 |
| 24.21 | 606 n. 116, 729, 830 |
| 24.22 | 601 n. 100, 682, 712, 725, 835, 848, 897 |
| 24.23 | 576 |
| 24.24–5 | 902 |
| 24.24–6 | 898 |
| 24.25 | 690, 693, 718, 893, 985 |
| 25.1–26.32 | 725 |
| 25.5 | 909 n. 262 |
| 25.8 | 708 n. 11, 715 n. 48, 893, 895, 899 |
| 25.10–12 | 724 |
| 25.10–11 | 715 n. 48 |
| 25.11 | 899, 910 |
| 25.13 | 902 |
| 25.16 | 708 n. 11, 893, 895 |
| 25.19 | 947 |
| 25.21 | 715 n. 48 |
| 25.22 | 731 n. 102 |
| 25.23 | 726, 902 |
| 25.26 | 600 n. 92, 685 n. 44, 715 n. 48, 801 n. 77 |
| 26.1–29 | 899 |
| 26.1–26 | 893 |
| 26.1 | 708 n. 11, 895 |
| 26.2–29 | 685 n. 40 |
| 26.2 | 708 n. 11, 895, 913 |
| 26.3 | 903, 906 |
| 26.4–5 | 869, 899, 905 |
| 26.5 | 595 n. 53, 831 n. 205, 852, 868 |
| 26.9–11 | 723, 916 |
| 26.12–18 | 554–63 *passim*, 724 |
| 26.12–17 | 711 |
| 26.14 | 558, 565, 566 |
| 26.15 | 691, 833 |
| 26.16–17 | 573 n. 101 |
| 26.16 | 829 |
| 26.17 | 828, 912 n. 277 |
| 26.18 | 719 |
| 26.19 | 903 |
| 26.22 | 565 n. 52, 572, 600 n. 89, 690, 728, 752, 946, 998 |
| 26.22–3 | 903 |
| 26.23 | 573 n. 101, 606 n. 116, 829, 830, 906, 984 |
| 26.24–7 | 900 |
| 26.24 | 565 n. 52, 600 n. 89, 580, 708 n. 11, 895 |
| 26.25 | 590 n. 23, 712, 835 n. 224, 848 n. 14 |
| 26.26 | 600 with n. 87, 690, 728, 836 n. 228, 837, 864, 893, 903, 904 |
| 26.27 | 694, 903 |
| 26.28–9 | 600 n. 89 |
| 26.28 | 569 n. 78, 681, 693, 707, 723 n. 72, 726, 900, 903, 946, 982 n. 15 |
| 26.29 | 598 n. 75, 699, 718, 900 |
| 26.30 | 902 |
| 26.31 | 726 with n. 85 |
| 26.31–2 | 574 n. 105 |
| 26.32 | 726, 899, 900 |
| 27.1–44 | 919 n. 309 |
| 27.1–43 | 718 |
| 27.1–28.16 | 690, 832, 839, 849, 983 n. 23 |
| 27.1–28.10 | 908 |
| 27.1 | 715 |
| 27.6–44 | 989 |
| 27.11 | 716 |
| 27.13–14 | 728 n. 92 |
| 27.14 | 605 n. 113 |
| 27.17 | 605 n. 113 |
| 27.22 | 996 |

**Acts** (*cont.*)

| | |
|---|---|
| 27.23–4 | 910 |
| 27.24 | 574 n. 105, 616 n. 26, 726 n. 85, 997 |
| 27.25 | 996 |
| 27.35 | 562 with n. 35, 997 |
| 27.36 | 996 |
| 28 | 659 |
| 28.2 | 908 n. 256 |
| 28.3 | 696 |
| 28.6–7 | 909 |
| 28.6 | 721 n. 63, 927 |
| 28.7–9 | 652 |
| 28.7 | 718 |
| 28.11 | 572 with n. 95, 927, 984 |
| 28.14–31 | 892 |
| 28.14 | 658, 697, 714 |
| 28.15 | 711, 920, 997 |
| 28.1–6 | 838 n. 237 |
| 28.16 | 566, 597 n. 70, 697 |
| 28.17–30 | 919 |
| 28.17–22 | 653 |
| 28.17–20 | 724 |
| 28.17 | 656, 728, 916 n. 296 |
| 28.19 | 656 |
| 28.21 | 656 |
| 28.22 | 595 n. 53, 806 n. 101, 831 n. 205, 868, 985 |
| 28.23–8 | 653 |
| 28.23 | 655, 694, 696 |
| 28.24 | 655, 656, 884 |
| 28.25 | 656, 828 with n. 196 |
| 28.26–7 | 653, 695 |
| 28.26 | 694 |
| 28.27 | 572 n. 96, 634, 653, 654, 655, 695, 696 |
| 28.28 | 567 n. 62, 653 |
| 28.29 | 916 |
| 28.30 | 614, 655, 656, 695, 699 |
| 28.30–1 | 652, 653, 655, 693, 695, 707, 719 n. 62, 726, 909, 916, 989 |
| 28.31 | 572 n. 96, 573 with n. 103, 576, 655, 693, 695, 714, 719, 828 with n. 195, 831 n. 203, 839, 864, 893, 909, 910, 915 |

**Romans**

| | |
|---|---|
| 1.1 | 810 n. 122, 814 n. 146, 972 |
| 1.4 | 972 |
| 1.6 | 971, 972 |
| 1.8 | 972 |
| 1.9 | 814 n. 146 |
| 1.16 | 814 n. 146 |
| 2.1–16 | 965 |
| 2.2–3 | 965 |
| 2.4–5 | 965 |
| 2.4 | 972 |
| 2.5 | 965 |
| 2.16 | 965, 972 |
| 3.12 | 972 |
| 3.22 | 972 |
| 3.24 | 972 |
| 5.1 | 972 |
| 5.6–21 | 667 |
| 5.6 | 668 |
| 5.11 | 972 |
| 5.15 | 668 |
| 5.17 | 668 |
| 5.21 | 668 |
| 4.11 | 753 n. 71 |
| 4.21 | 694 n. 75, 810 n. 118, 854 n. 53 |
| 8.34 | 968 |
| 10.5 | 752 |
| 10.17 | 648 n. 133 |
| 11.8 | 658 |
| 11.22 | 972 |
| 11.25 | 658 |
| 11.30–2 | 658 |
| 11.25–6 | 696 |
| 14.5 | 694 n. 75, 810 n. 118, 854 n. 53 |
| 15.24 | 697 |
| 16.18 | 966 |

**1 Corinthians**

| | |
|---|---|
| 1.23 | 888, 904 |
| 2.1–5 | 853 |
| 3.18 | 421 n. 2 |
| 4.15 | 814 n. 146 |
| 7.20–2 | 962 |
| 7.21 | 536 n. 82 |
| 7.27 | 536 n. 82 |
| 9.12 | 963 |

## 1 Corinthians (cont.)

| | |
|---|---|
| 9.2 | 753 n. 71 |
| 11.23 | 579 n. 135 |
| 14.22–3 | 561 n. 33 |
| 15.30–4 | 966 |
| 16.15 | 560 n. 26 |

## 2 Corinthians

| | |
|---|---|
| 1.22 | 753 n. 71 |

## Galatians

| | |
|---|---|
| 1.6 | 814 n. 146 |
| 1.14 | 820 n. 175, 856 n. 70 |
| 3.13 | 943 n. 42 |
| 5.1–6 | 971 |
| 5.2 | 963 |
| 5.13 | 695 |
| 5.22–4 | 965 |

## Ephesians

| | |
|---|---|
| 1.5–10 | 969 |
| 1.10 | 685, 967 |
| 1.13 | 753 n. 71, 814 n. 146 |
| 2.4–10 | 964, 969 |
| 4.20–1 | 967, 968 |
| 4.20 | 685 |
| 4.32 | 965, 966, 968, 969 |
| 6.20 | 864 |

## Philippians

| | |
|---|---|
| 1.12–13 | 616. 22 |
| 1.12 | 820 n. 175, 856 n. 70 |
| 1.25 | 820 n. 175, 856 n. 70 |
| 2.6ff. | 974 |
| 2.9–10 | 657, 665 |
| 2.10 | 654 n. 156, 657 |
| 2.11 | 657 |
| 4.22 | 616 n. 25 |
| 24 | 597 n. 70 |

## Colossians

| | |
|---|---|
| 2 | 810 n. 118, 854 n. 53 |
| 2.2 | 694 n. 75 |
| 2.8 | 853, 963 |
| 4.12 | 694 n. 75, 810 n. 118, 854 n. 53 |
| 4.14 | 597 n. 70, 835 n. 223, 849, 850, 618 |

## 1 Thessalonians

| | |
|---|---|
| 1 | 810 n. 118, 854 n. 53 |
| 1.5 | 694 n. 75 |
| 2.2 | 864 |
| 3.1 | 649 n. 140 |
| 3.1f | 877 |
| 4.14 | 667 |

## 1 Timothy

| | |
|---|---|
| 4.15 | 820 n. 175, 856 n. 70 |

## 2 Timothy

| | |
|---|---|
| 2.9 | 576, 753 n. 71, 913 |
| 2.16 | 820 n. 175, 856 n. 70 |
| 3.9 | 820 n. 175, 856 n. 70 |
| 3.13 | 820 n. 175, 856 n. 70 |
| 4.5 | 694 n. 75, 810 n. 118, 854 n. 53 |
| 4.11 | 597 n. 70, 835 n. 223, 839, 849, 850, |
| 4.17 | 694 n. 75, 810 n. 118, 854 n. 53 |
| 19 | 753 |

## Titus

| | |
|---|---|
| 1.12 | 650, 880 |
| 2.1–15 | 668 |
| 2.9 | 668 |
| 2.13 | 668 |
| 3.4–7 | 965, 970 |

## Philemon

| | |
|---|---|
| 8–11 | 962, 966 |
| 20 | 962, 966 |
| 24 | 849 |

## Hebrews

| | |
|---|---|
| 6.11 | 694 n. 75, 810 n. 118, 854 n. 53 |
| 10.22 | 694 n. 75, 810 n. 118, 854 n. 53 |
| 12.2 | 943 n. 43 |

## James

| | |
|---|---|
| 1.25 | 695 |

## 1 Peter

| | |
|---|---|
| 1.1 | 966 |
| 1.2 | 966 |

## 1 Peter (cont.)

| | |
|---|---|
| 1.3 | 966 |
| 1.7 | 966 |
| 1.10–11 | 970 |
| 1.11 | 966 |
| 1.13 | 966, 971 |
| 1.19 | 966 |
| 1.25 | 966 |
| 2.1–3 | 965, 966 |
| 2.3 | 966 |
| 2.9 | 982 n. 13 |
| 2.16 | 695 |
| 3.15–16 | 966 |
| 3.21 | 667 |
| 4.12–16 | 956 |
| 4.16 | 615 n. 17, 723 n. 72, 982 n. 15 |

## 2 Peter

| | |
|---|---|
| 1.3 | 982 n. 13 |
| 1.5 | 982 n. 13 |
| 3.3–9 | 921 n. 317 |

## 1 John

| | |
|---|---|
| 1.1–5 | 753 n. 73 |
| 1.7.5 | 668 |
| 4.14 | 753 n. 73 |

## 3 John

| | |
|---|---|
| 9–10 | 753 n. 73 |
| 12 | 753 n. 73 |

## Revelation

| | |
|---|---|
| 5.1 | 753 n. 71 |
| 6.1 | 753 n. 71 |
| 7.2 | 753 n. 71 |
| 7.3 | 753 n. 71 |
| 8.1 | 753 n. 71 |
| 9.4 | 753 n. 71 |
| 10.4 | 753 n. 71 |
| 14.6–7 | 921 n. 317 |
| 17.6 | 574 n. 108 |
| 20.3 | 753 n. 71 |
| 22.10 | 753 n. 71 |

## (b) Other

**Ambrose**, *Expositio Euangelii secundum Lucan*

| | |
|---|---|
| prol. 4, 1263A | 806 n. 100 |

**Anonymous**, *Joseph and Aseneth*

| | |
|---|---|
| 14.2–8 | 555, 556 |

**Anonymous**, *Opus imperfectum in Matthaeum*

| | |
|---|---|
| 1 (*PG* LVI.634) | 631 |

***Christus Patiens***    579 n. 138

## 1 Clement

| | |
|---|---|
| 1.1 | 954 n. 71 |
| 5.4–5 | 645 n. 123 |
| 5.6–7 | 574 n. 107 |

## Clement of Alexandria

*Paedagogus*

| | |
|---|---|
| 1.2 | 624 n. 63 |

*Protrepticus*

| | |
|---|---|
| 2.19.3 | 579 n. 138 |
| 2.22.4 | 579 n. 138 |
| 12.123 | 960 n. 85 |

*Stromateis*

| | |
|---|---|
| 1.1.16.1 | 967 n. 95 |
| 1.5.28 | 885 n. 170 |
| 1.14.59.1–2 | 880 |
| 2.4.18 | 960 n. 86 |
| 2.20.121 | 452, 456 |
| 3.17 | 624 n. 63 |
| 4.9 | 762 n. 84 |
| 4.26 | 393 |

**Cyril of Alexandria**, *Fragments*

| | |
|---|---|
| F 166 | 635 |

**Epiphanius**, *Aduersus Haereses*

| | |
|---|---|
| 29.4 | 624 n. 62 |

## Eusebius

*Chronica*

| | |
|---|---|
| 101 Karst | 31 n. 45 |

*Demonstratio Euangelica*

| | |
|---|---|
| 4.10 | 624 n. 62 |

*Historia Ecclesiastica*

| | |
|---|---|
| 2.16–17 | 622 |
| 2.22 | 574 n. 107 |

*Historia Ecclesiastica (cont.)*

| | |
|---|---|
| 2.25 | 574 n. 107 |
| 3.4.1 | 691, 811 n. 126 |
| 3.4.6 | 834 |
| 3.4.7 | 597 n. 71 |
| 3.39 | 739 |
| 3.39.14–16 | 834 n. 221 |
| 3.39.16 | 536 n. 77 |
| 5.20.6 | 806 n. 99 |
| 5.20.7 | 681 n. 19 |

*Praeparatio Euangelica*

| | |
|---|---|
| 6.7.10–19 | 318 n. 4 |
| 13.12.6 | 875 n. 132 |
| 15.20.6 | 212 n. 21 |

**Ignatius**
*ad Ephesios*

| | |
|---|---|
| 2.4.1 | 957 n. 79 |
| 7.1–2 | 624 n. 62 |

*ad Philadelphios*

| | |
|---|---|
| 8.2 | 738 n. 18 |

*Didache*

| | |
|---|---|
| 8.1–2 | 738 n. 18 |
| 11.3–4 | 738 n. 18 |
| 15.3 | 738 n. 18 |

**Irenaeus**, *Adversus Haereses*

| | |
|---|---|
| 3.1.1 | 690 n. 58, 832 n. 209, 849 n. 24 |
| 3.14.1–3 | 832 n. 209 |
| 14.1–3 | 690 n. 58, 849 n. 24 |

**Jerome**
*Chronicon*

| | |
|---|---|
| 189 Helm | 37 n. 70, 232 n. 14 |

*Commentarius in Evangelium sec. Matthaeum*

| | |
|---|---|
| 1.9.9 | 763 |

*de Viris Illustribus*

| | |
|---|---|
| 7 | 597 n. 71, 811 n. 126, 834 |

*Epistula ad Titum*

| | |
|---|---|
| 1.12 | 881 |

**John Chrysostom**
*Homiliae*

| | |
|---|---|
| 52.4 | 600 with n. 87, 728 n. 89, 836 n. 228, 837, 904 n. 241 |

| | |
|---|---|
| *in Acta* 38.1 | 883 n. 162 |
| *in Matthaeum* 30.1 | 762 |

**Josephus**
*Antiquitates Iudaicae*

| | |
|---|---|
| 1.2 | 594 n. 51, 808 n. 112 |
| 1.5 | 985 |
| 1.8 | 839 n. 245 |
| 1.9 | 985 |
| 8.45 | 622 |
| 14.15.2 | 901 n. 220 |
| 16.41 | 915 |
| 16.163 | 591 |
| 17.41 | 831 n. 205, 868 nn. 109 and 110 |
| 18.1–5 | 597 n. 67 |
| 18.1.4 | 851 |
| 18.63–4 | 616 n. 22, 866 n. 102, 957 n. 78 |
| 19.162ff. | 30 n. 41 |
| 20.7.3 | 905 n. 246 |
| 20.9.1 | 616 n. 22 |
| 20.200 | 866 n. 102 |

*Bellum Iudaicum*

| | |
|---|---|
| 1.110 | 595 n. 53, 831 n. 205, 868 n. 109 |
| 2.117–18 | 597 n. 67 |
| 2.122 | 865 n. 100 |
| 2.136 | 622 |
| 2.162 | 595 n. 53, 831 n. 205, 868 nn. 109 and 110 |
| 4.4.4 | 901 n. 220 |
| 6.312–14 | 957 |
| 6.429ff. | 953 |

*Contra Apionem*

| | |
|---|---|
| 1.3 | 593 n. 45 |
| 1.8 | 592 n. 38, 798 n. 57 |
| 1.37–43 | 752 |
| 1.55 | 593, 799 |
| 1.224 | 987 n. 48 |

## Contra Apionem (cont.)
| | |
|---|---|
| 2.261 | 908 n. 257 |
| 2.266–7 | 875 n. 136 |

## Vita
| | |
|---|---|
| 189 | 595 n. 53, 831 n. 205, 868 n. 109 |
| 191 | 595 n. 53, 831 n. 205, 868 n. 110 |

## Justin Martyr
### Apologia Prima
| | |
|---|---|
| 4.1 | 959 n. 82 |
| 4.5 | 959 n. 82 |
| 16.4 | 885 n. 170 |
| 21.2 | 579 n. 138 |
| 54.6 | 579 n. 138 |

### Apologia Secunda
| | |
|---|---|
| 6.6 | 624 n. 63 |
| 13.2–6 | 885 n. 170 |

### Dialogi
| | |
|---|---|
| 8.1 | 601 n. 102, 807 n. 106 |
| 69.2 | 579 n. 138 |
| 103.8 | 811 n. 126, 833 n. 218, 834 |

### Fragmenta
| | |
|---|---|
| Migne, *PG* VI.1581 | 885 n. 170 |

## Lactantius, *Institutiones Diuinae*
| | |
|---|---|
| 1.4 | 937 n. 3 |
| 4.7.4 | 943 n. 38 |

## 1 Maccabees
| | |
|---|---|
| | 568 n. 72, 578, 580 |
| 1.1–3 | 581 n. 146 |
| 1.1 | 827 n. 194, 861 |
| 3.9 | 581 n. 146, 827 n. 194, 861 |
| 8.4 | 581 n. 146, 827 n. 194, 861 |

## 2 Maccabees
| | |
|---|---|
| | 568, 578, 580 |
| 2.26 | 685 |
| 2.28 | 685 |
| 3 | 555, 556 |
| 7.19 | 568 |
| 9.9 | 568 |
| 9.12 | 568 |
| 9.17 | 581 n. 146, 827 n. 194, 861 |

## 3 Maccabees
| | |
|---|---|
| | 568, 578, 580 |
| 3.3–7 | 580 n. 144 |

## Origen, *Contra Celsum*
| | |
|---|---|
| 1.9 | 579 n. 138 |
| 1.25 | 624 n. 63 |
| 1.62 | 762 n. 84 |
| 2.34 | 556, 579 n. 138 |
| 3.16 | 579 n. 138 |
| 3.50 | 894 n. 195 |
| 4.10 | 579 n. 138 |
| 4.75 | 998 |
| 8.41f. | 579 n. 138 |
| 8.48 | 579 n. 138 |

### Fragments
| | |
|---|---|
| F 54 in Jo | 624 n. 63 |

### Homiliae in Lucam
| | |
|---|---|
| 1 | 810 n. 119, 854 n. 54 |

### Protrepticus
| | |
|---|---|
| 12 | 579 n. 138 |

## Orosius, *Historia adversus paganos*
| | |
|---|---|
| 7.6.15 | 947 |
| 7.7.10 | 952 |
| 7.9.4–6 | 953 |

## Philo
### de opificio mundi
| | |
|---|---|
| 3 | 389, 448 |

### de praemiis et poenis
| | |
|---|---|
| | 881 n. 151 |

### Legum allegoricae
| | |
|---|---|
| 2.102–3 | 987 n. 48 |
| 2.218 | 987 n. 48 |

### de uita Mosis
| | |
|---|---|
| 1.157 | 389, 448, 614 n. 11 |

## Qumran Texts
| | |
|---|---|
| 1 QS 5.1–3 | 865 n. 100 |
| 1QS 8.13–16 | 897 |
| 1QS 9.16–21 | 897 |

**Qumran Texts** (*cont.*)
| | |
|---|---|
| 4Q521, 2.1 | 622 |
| 4Q521, 2.8 | 622 |
| 4Q521, 2.12 | 622 |
| CD 9.1–15 | 865 n. 100 |

**Sirach**
| | |
|---|---|
| 17.22 | 751 n. 65 |

**Sulpicius Severus,** *Chronica*
| | |
|---|---|
| 2.30.6–8 | 952 |

**Synesius,** *Dion*
| | |
|---|---|
| 36a–38b | 138 n. 84 |
| 36a | 58 n. 172 |
| 36b | 52 |
| 36b–c | 35 n. 61 |
| 37b | 28 |
| 37c | 58 n. 172 |
| 37d | 26 n. 17, 58 n. 172 |
| 38a–b | 27 |
| 38a | 52 n. 147 |
| 38b | 33 |
| 39a | 52 n. 147, 77 n. 23 |
| 41c | 37 n. 72 |

*Epistulae*
| | |
|---|---|
| Ep 154 Hercher | 27 |

**Tatian,** *Oratio ad Graecos*
| | |
|---|---|
| 29 | 579 n. 140 |

**Tertullian**
*de anima*
| | |
|---|---|
| 20.1 | 885 n. 170 |

*ad Nationes*
| | |
|---|---|
| 1.3 | 937 n. 3 |
| 1.3.8 | 959 n. 83 |

*Apologia*
| | |
|---|---|
| 3.5 | 937 n. 3, 938 n. 9 |
| 46.18 | 853 |

*de praescriptionibus haereticorum*
| | |
|---|---|
| 7 | 853, 885 n. 170 |

**Theophilus,** *Ad Autolycum*
| | |
|---|---|
| 1.12 | 959 n. 84 |

*Gospel of Thomas*
| | |
|---|---|
| 13 | 751 n. 62 |

### III. Epigraphical Texts

*Corpus Inscriptionum Graecarum*
| | |
|---|---|
| III.4699 | 81 n. 36 |

*Corpus Inscriptionum Latinum*
| | |
|---|---|
| IV Suppl 3, fasc 4, no 10529 | 353 n. 1 |

*Inscriptiones Graecae ad Res Romanas Pertinentes*
| | |
|---|---|
| IV.1 | 216 n. 33 |

*Inscriptiones Latinae Selectae*
| | |
|---|---|
| 7784 | 115 n. 15 |

*Orientis Graecae Inscriptiones Selectae*
| | |
|---|---|
| 666.3 | 81 n. 36 |

*Rhodes–Osborne, Greek Historical Inscriptions 404–323 BC*
| | |
|---|---|
| 55 | 591 n. 31 |

*Senatus Consultum de Pisone patre*
| | |
|---|---|
| 82–3 | 942 n. 33 |
| 99–100 | 942 n. 33 |

*Sylloge Inscriptionum Graecarum*
| | |
|---|---|
| 834.21 | 115 n. 15 |

Printed in the United States
by Baker & Taylor Publisher Services